Differentiating the Financial Statements

Fundamental Accounting Principles uses a colour scheme to help students differentiate between the four key financial statements.

Income Statement

Vertically Inclined Rock Gym
Income Statement
For Month Ended January 31, 2011

Revenues:		
Teaching revenue	$ 3,800	
Equipment rental revenue	300	
Total revenues		$ 4,100
Operating expenses:		
Rent expense	$ 1,000	
Salaries expense		
Total operating expenses		
Net income		

Statement of Changes in Equity

Vertically Inclined Rock Gym
Statement of Changes in Equity
For Month Ended January 31, 2011

Virgil Klimb, capital, January 1		$ -0-
Add: Investments by owner	$10,000	
Net income	2,400	12,400
Total		$12,400
		600
		$11,800

Vertically Inclined Rock Gym
Balance Sheet
January 31, 2011

Balance Sheet

Assets		**Liabilities**		
Cash	$ 8,400	Accounts payable	$ 200	
Supplies	3,600	Notes payable	6,000	
Equipment	6,000	Total liabilities		$ 6,200
		Equity		
		Virgil Klimb, capital		11,800
Total assets	$18,000	Total liabilities and equity		$18,000

Vertically Inclined Rock Gym
Statement of Cash Flows
For Month Ended January 31, 2011

Statement of Cash Flows

Cash flows from operating activities		
Cash received from clients	$ 4,100	
Cash paid for supplies	(3,400)	
Cash paid for rent	(1,000)	
Cash paid to employee	(700)	
Net cash used by operating activities		$ (1,000)
Cash flows from investing activities		-0-
Cash flows from financing activities		
Investment by owner	$10,000	
Withdrawal by owner	(600)	
Net cash provided by financing activities		9,400
Net increase in cash		$ 8,400
Cash balance, January 1		-0-
Cash balance, January 31		$ 8,400

VOLUME ONE

Fundamental Accounting Principles

Thirteenth Canadian Edition

Kermit D. Larson
University of Texas—Austin

Tilly Jensen
Athabasca University—Alberta, Canada

The McGraw·Hill Companies

Fundamental Accounting Principles
Volume 1
Thirteenth Canadian Edition

ISBN-13: 978-0-07-096828-8
ISBN-10: 0-07-096828-4

3 4 5 6 7 8 9 10 QDB 1 9 8 7 6 5 4 3 2 1

Printed and bound in the United States of America.

Vice-President and Editor-in-Chief: Joanna Cotton
Executive Sponsoring Editor: Rhondda McNabb
Executive Marketing Manager: Joy Armitage Taylor
Developmental Editor: Suzanne Simpson-Millar
Senior Editorial Associate: Christine Lomas
Supervising Editor: Jessica Barnoski
Copy Editor: Laurel Sparrow
Team Lead, Production: Jennifer Hall
Photo/Permissions Research: My Editor, Inc.
Cover Design: Dave Murphy/Valid Design & Layout
Cover Image: © Anton Vengo/SuperStock
Interior Design: Dave Murphy/Valid Design & Layout
Page Layout: Bookman Typesetting Co. Inc.
Printer: Quad/Graphics

Library and Archives Canada Cataloguing in Publication

Larson, Kermit D.
Fundamental accounting principles / Kermit D. Larson, Tilly Jensen. — 13th Canadian ed.

Includes bibliographical references and index.
ISBN 978-0-07-096828-8 (v. 1)

1. Accounting—Textbooks. I. Jensen, Tilly II. Title.

HF5635.L343 2010 657 C2009-906145-7

About the Authors

Kermit D. Larson, University of Texas – Austin

Kermit D. Larson is the Arthur Andersen & Co. Alumni Professor of Accounting Emeritus at the University of Texas at Austin. He served as chairman of the University of Texas, Department of Accounting, and was visiting associate professor at Tulane University. His scholarly articles have been published in a variety of journals, including *The Accounting Review*, *Journal of Accountancy*, and *Abacus*. He is the author of several books, including *Financial Accounting* and *Fundamentals of Financial* and *Managerial Accounting*, both published by Irwin/McGraw-Hill.

Professor Larson is a member of the American Accounting Association, the Texas Society of CPAs, and the American Institute of CPAs. His positions with the AAA have included vice president, southwest regional service president, and chairperson of several committees, including the Committee of Concepts and Standards. He was a member of the committee that planned the first AAA doctoral consortium and served as its director.

Tilly Jensen, Athabasca University – Alberta, Canada

Tilly Jensen graduated from the University of Alberta with a Bachelor of Commerce and later attained the designation of Certified Management Accountant. She worked in private industry for a number of years before making teaching her full-time career. Tilly was an accounting instructor at the Northern Alberta Institute of Technology (NAIT) in Edmonton, Alberta for almost two decades and recently became an Assistant Professor of Accounting at Athabasca University, Canada's open, online university. She obtained her M.Ed. at the University of Sheffield in Britain while travelling abroad and is currently engaged in doctoral studies at the University of Calgary (via distance) focusing on how educational technologies can be used to enhance critical thinking. Tilly spent four years in the Middle East teaching at Dubai Men's College of the Higher Colleges of Technology in the United Arab Emirates. While overseas, she also taught financial accounting to students enrolled in the Chartered Institute of Management Accountants (CIMA) program, a British professional accounting designation. During a sabbatical, Tilly also taught accounting in China to ESL students at Shenyang Ligong University. She authored LIFA—Lyryx Interactive Financial Accounting—a dynamic, leading-edge, Web-based teaching and learning tool produced by Lyryx. Tilly has also authored material for CGA-Canada. In addition to her professional interests, Tilly places a priority on time spent with her family and friends.

Brief Contents

Contents

To the Instructors—Facilitators of Student Success

As instructors, you and I know that the responsibility for student success lies ultimately with the student. Our role is to create an environment that fosters learning: we can present and demonstrate concepts in a variety of ways and then help students apply those concepts to new situations; we can be there (face to face or online) to respond to their questions with questions that help them find the answer; and we can direct students to a variety of tools to enhance their success. To help with our role, we need quality tools to facilitate student success both in and out of the classroom. In response to instructor requests, the Thirteenth Canadian Edition of *Fundamental Accounting Principles* has incorporated changes necessary to conform with International Financial Reporting Standards (IFRS) while maintaining its sound, pedagogical approach by focusing on students and their success. No other significant organizational changes were made. Why? During the transition period, we, as instructors, need the continued support of *Fundamental Accounting Principles,* a resource that offers stability in pedagogy and superior accuracy and clarity, so that we can focus on substantive changes while facilitating successful student learning.

Student Success *Cycle*

Read the material

Do the exercises

Check your answers

Apply your critical thinking skills

To this end, the Thirteenth Canadian Edition still includes the **Student Success** *Cycle*—**Read–Do–Check–Apply**—throughout the textbook. It is denoted by the symbol shown on the left, and reminds students that to achieve success, they must **read** the textbook, **do** the exercises and problems to practise concepts, **check** their work (taking appropriate remedial action), and **apply** knowledge to demonstrate learning in contrast to memorization.

The **Student Success** *Cycle* is reinforced on **McGraw-Hill Connect™ (www.mcgrawhillconnect.ca)**, where a detailed learning guide is provided to help students master introductory accounting concepts. Student success at the post-secondary level is not measured by how much knowledge a student has acquired but rather by how well a student can **use** or **apply** knowledge. . . a concept also known as critical thinking. If students compartmentalize knowledge, they are challenged when they have to engage in activities of application, analysis, synthesis, or evaluation—the higher-level competencies. We can help students develop higher-level skills by introducing them to a model for critical thinking. Instructors typically give students formulas to perform calculations such as depreciation and interest; why not provide them with a formula for thinking as well?!

An outline of a basic model for teaching/learning critical thinking is provided on the inside cover of this textbook. To foster the development of critical thinking proficiency, analysis-type questions are part of many exercises and problems. In addition, Critical Thinking Mini Cases are available to help students practise applying their understanding of accounting.

Education is a journey that continues over a lifetime. *Fundamental Accounting Principles* provides students with a model and tools for both successful learning and critical thinking that can be used not only in accounting but in other disciplines as well.

Many thanks to the contributions of the dedicated accounting instructors from across Canada whose efforts allow for the continuous improvement of the textbook.

Take care,

Tilly Jensen

Tilly Jensen

To the Students—A Guide For Your Success

Your primary goal in this course should be to learn the basics about financial accounting in order to understand and use financial statements and related information effectively in decision making. These skills are essential, whether you are going to be a business owner, a marketing specialist, or a financial planner, or occupy some other business role.

Student success means different things to many different people. For the purpose of this accounting course, we will define a successful student as having two qualities:

1. Active in the learning process, and
2. Able to apply critical thinking skills.

To learn anything, you must acquire knowledge. For example, I can learn about rock climbing by reading a book. But once I finish the book, will I be able to rock climb? It is very unlikely. I will need to practise. After a couple of hours at a rock climbing gym—first staring at all the handholds, then getting some instruction—I might do some more reading, watch a video, and keep on practising. I will continue to apply my growing knowledge of rock climbing, and over time I will begin to improve.

To learn accounting, you would follow the same process. Begin by reading this textbook. Will you understand accounting after simply reading? It is very unlikely. You will need to practise the concepts by doing the exercises and problems. Then, check your work. Are you on track? If not, do some more reading, get some instruction, use another tool to help you learn the material, but above all, be sure you master the material and apply your knowledge before continuing to new concepts.

The process just described—**read** the material, **do** the exercises, **check** your answers, and **apply** your critical thinking skills—can be summarized as: **Read–Do–Check–Apply**, or the **Student Success** *Cycle*. You will see this symbol—the circular icon shown at right—throughout the textbook; it is a reminder to check your progress and to go to **Connect** at www.mcgrawhillconnect.ca for additional study tools.

Student Success *Cycle*

Read the material
Do the exercises
Check your answers
Apply your critical thinking skills

Once you have acquired knowledge in a specific area and mastered it through practice, you are ready for the next step of the learning process: critical thinking, the Mount Everest of learning. Critical thinking involves the higher-level competencies of application, analysis, synthesis, and evaluation. To make business decisions, you need to ***use*** the knowledge acquired in many subject areas (including accounting, economics, statistics, and so on): critical thinking is the application of knowledge across topics and across disciplines. The inside front cover provides a model to help you improve your critical thinking skill development so that once you ***acquire*** knowledge, you are able to ***apply*** it using analysis, synthesis, and/or evaluation.

This textbook was designed to help you learn efficiently and effectively. If you follow the **Student Success** *Cycle* and use it in conjunction with other tools available on the online **Connect**, you will be successful in learning accounting.

Good luck with your studies,

Tilly Jensen

Inside the Chapters

As educators, instructors strive to create an environment that fosters learning and to provide students with the tools they need to succeed. The Thirteenth Canadian Edition continues to meet and surpass the high standards the market expects from *Fundamental Accounting Principles*. We continue to put learning first, with student-centred pedagogy and teaching critical thinking skills throughout the text.

All the pedagogical tools are carefully designed for ease of use and understanding, helping the instructor teach and giving the students what they need to succeed.

Student Success *Cycle*

Read the material

Do the exercises

Check your answers

Apply your critical thinking skills

Pedagogy

Student Success *Cycle*

Student success at the post-secondary level is not measured by how much knowledge a student has acquired, but rather by how well a student can *use* knowledge. The Student Success Cycle, illustrated by a circular icon (shown at left), reinforces decision-making skills by highlighting key steps toward understanding and critically evaluating the information the student has just read. **Read–Do–Check–Apply**—this reinforces active learning (as opposed to passive learning). This tool is integrated throughout the text, including the chapter opening page, Checkpoint questions, Demonstration problems, and end-of-chapter material.

Critical Thinking Challenge

An essential element of critical thinking is the ability to ask questions while reading (or listening or speaking). These exercises are designed to help students develop the skills related to questioning. Suggested answers are posted on **Connect** at www.mcgrawhillconnect.ca.

number of climbers we could accommodate and added to the variety of types of climbing available in the facility.

"My focus is marketing but I have learned that accounting is invaluable ... it's the language that allows me to talk to and understand my accountant, bookkeeper, banker, lawyer, contractors, and customers ... accounting gives you an advantage."

www.verticallyinclined.com

CRITICAL THINKING CHALLENGE

What questions might Jake need the answers to in order to get a loan from a bank? Who else might require accounting information from Jake's business?

IFRS Highlights

While the thirteenth Canadian edition fully integrates IFRS, for quick reference "IFRS Highlights" boxes have also been added to the end of every chapter, summarizing or further discussing International Financial Reporting Standards as they relate to the introductory financial accounting course.

IFRS HIGHLIGHTS 

The suggested titles of the four basic financial statements are: statement of financial position (called balance sheet in this textbook), statement of income, statement of cash flows, and statement of changes in equity; however, other titles may be used (IAS 1, para. 10).

The ordering of the line items and categories is not prescribed (IAS 1, para. 57).

A discussion paper is reviewing a change in format of the statement of income and balance sheet to group line items by whether they are an operating, investing, or financing activity to be consistent with the statement of cash flows (DP October, 2008).

The Conceptual Framework Joint Project may result in changes to the framework which sets out the concepts that underlie the preparation and presentation of financial statements for external users commonly referred to as the generally accepted accounting principles or GAAP.

SOURCE: http://www.fasb.org/project/conceptual_framework.shtml

Real-World Focus

Like previous editions, the Thirteenth Canadian Edition includes strong ties to the real world of accounting, be it through detailed interviews with businesspeople for the chapter-opening vignettes, examples of ethical standards and treatments, or annual reports for end-of-chapter material. This integration with real-world companies helps engage students while they read.

Learning Objectives

Learning Objectives have long been a standard in the Larson textbook. By giving students a head start on what the following material encompasses, the text readies them for the work ahead.

Checkpoint

This series of questions within the chapter reinforces the material presented immediately before it. These questions allow the students to "Do" problem material referencing what they have just learned, and answers at the end of each chapter will then allow them to "Check" their work. Under each set of Checkpoints is a reference to the Quick Study questions, single-topic exercises available at the end of each chapter. Students can go ahead and try them at this point. Solutions to the Checkpoint questions are at the end of the chapter. Quick Study solutions are available on **Connect**.

5. Why is the business entity principle important?
6. Describe the cost principle and explain why it might be considered reliable.
7. A customer pays cash today for a product that is to be delivered to her next month. When should revenue be recognized?

Do Quick Study questions: QS 2-2, QS 2-3, QS 2-4

Did You Know?

Social responsibility continues to be important for students to learn early in their accounting courses. Through the Did You Know? feature, accounting's role in ethics and social responsibility is described by both reporting and assessing its impact. Relating theory to a real-life situation piques interest and reinforces active learning.

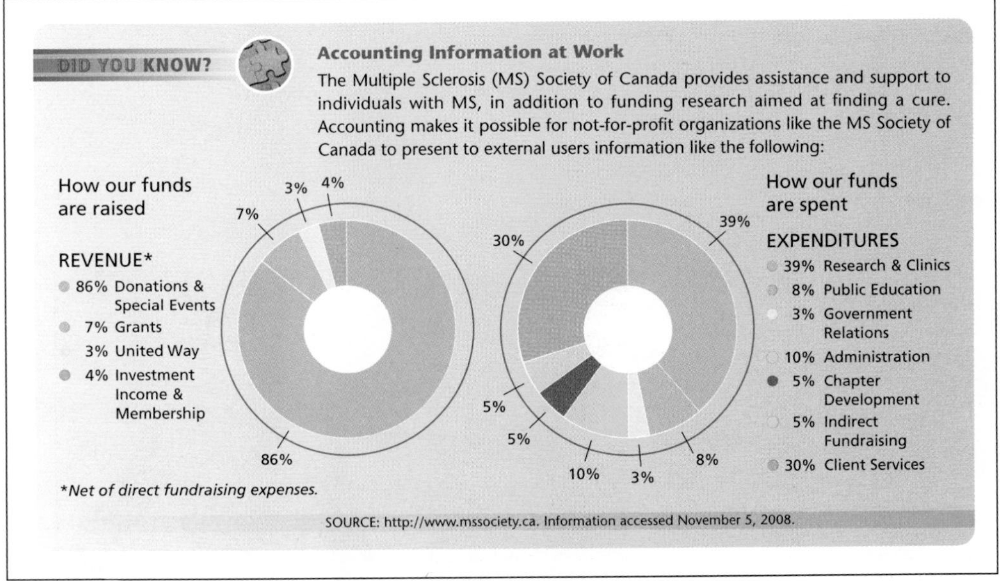

THE LARSON ADVANTAGE

Judgement Call

This feature requires students to make accounting and business decisions by using role-playing to show the interaction of judgement, awareness, and the impact of decisions made. Guidance answers are available at the end of each chapter.

Supplier

You open your own wholesale business, selling home entertainment equipment to small retail outlets. You quickly find that most of your potential customers demand to buy on credit. How can you use the balance sheet in deciding to which customers you wish to extend credit?

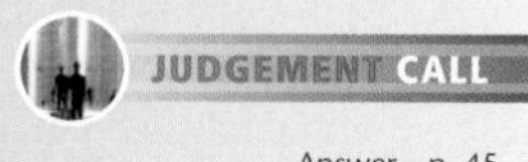

Answer—p. 45

Extend Your Knowledge (EYK)

Supplementary material has been developed to explore some topics in more detail than the textbook can allow. When available, the EYK icon is displayed in the margin, alerting students to visit **Connect** if they choose to delve deeper into the material.

EXTEND YOUR KNOWLEDGE

Understanding Ethics

Ethics are beliefs that differentiate right from wrong. Ethics and laws often coincide, with the result that many unethical actions (such as theft and physical violence) are also illegal. Yet other actions are not against the law but are considered unethical, such as not helping people with certain needs or deliberately withholding critical information from the user.

Annual Reports

Features and assignments that highlight companies such as WestJet (a company that provides services) and Danier (a merchandiser) show accounting in a modern and global context. Because students go directly to the financial statements of real companies, they remain engaged in the active learning process. The audited annual financial statement section of these annual reports are reproduced at the end of both Volumes 1 and 2.

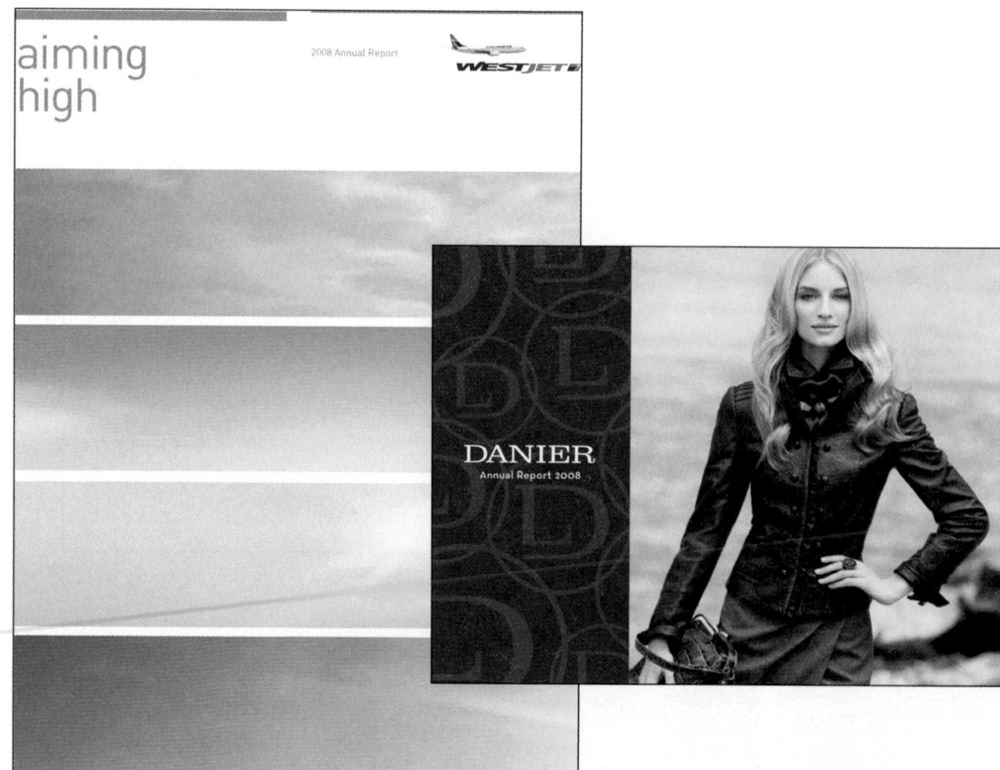

End-of-Chapter Material

Fundamental Accounting Principles sets the standard for quantity and quality of end-of-chapter material.

Summary

LO1 Describe accounting and its goals and uses. Accounting is an information and measurement system that aims to identify, measure, record, and communicate understandable, relevant, reliable, and comparable information about economic activities. It helps us better assess opportunities, products, investments, and social and community responsibilities. The power of accounting is in opening our eyes to new and exciting opportunities. The greatest benefits of understanding accounting often come to those outside of accounting, because an improved understanding of accounting helps us to compete better in today's globally focused and technologically challenging world.

LO2 Describe forms of business organization. Organizations can be classified either as businesses or as

LO3 Identify users and uses of accounting. There are both internal and external users of accounting. Some users and uses of accounting include: (a) management for control, monitoring, and planning; (b) lenders for making decisions regarding loan applications; (c) shareholders for making investment decisions; (d) directors for overseeing management; and (e) employees for judging employment opportunities.

LO4 Explain why ethics and social responsibility are crucial to accounting. The goal of accounting is to provide useful information for decision making. For information to be useful, it must be trusted. This demands ethics and socially responsible behaviour in accounting. Without these, accounting information loses its reliability.

guidance answer to JUDGEMENT CALL 

Entrepreneur
You should probably form your business as a corporation if potential lawsuits are of prime concern. The corporate form of organization would protect your personal property from lawsuits directed at the business, and would place only the corporation's resources at risk. You should also examine the ethical and socially responsible aspects of starting a business where you anticipate injuries to others.

guidance answers to CHECKPOINT 

1. Accounting is an information and measurement system that identifies, measures, records, and communicates understandable, relevant, reliable, and comparable information to people that helps them in making better decisions. It helps people in business to identify and react to investment opportunities, and better assess opportunities, products, investments, and social and community responsibilities.

6. Internal controls are procedures set up to protect assets, ensure that accounting reports are reliable, promote efficiency, and encourage adherence to company policies. Internal controls are crucial if accounting reports are to provide relevant and reliable information.

7. The guidelines for ethical and socially responsible decisions are threefold: (1) identify the ethical and/or social issue; (2) analyze options, considering

Glossary

Accounting An information system that identifies, measures, records, and communicates understandable, relevant, reliable, and comparable information about an organization's economic activities. (p. 2)

Audit A check of an organization's accounting systems and records. (p. 14)

Bookkeeping The part of accounting that involves recording economic transactions, either electronically or manually; also called *recordkeeping*. (p. 3)

Budgeting The process of developing formal plans for future activities, which often serve as a basis for evaluating actual performance. (p. 15)

External users Persons using accounting information who are not directly involved in the running of the organization; examples include shareholders, customers, regulators, and suppliers. (p. 7)

Financial accounting The area of accounting aimed at serving external users. (p. 7)

General accounting The task of recording transactions, processing data, and preparing reports for managers; includes preparing financial statements for disclosure to external users. (p. 15)

Generally accepted accounting principles (GAAP) The rules that indicate acceptable accounting practice. (p. 4)

Summary

Each chapter includes a summary of the chapter by Learning Objective, to reinforce what students have just learned.

Guidance Answers to Judgement Call

These discuss the Judgement Call boxes presented earlier in the chapter, and reinforce the need for decision making and critical thinking skills. This feature fits into the Student Success Cycle by reinforcing the "Apply" step.

Guidance Answers to Checkpoint

The Checkpoint material throughout the chapter allows students to pause and check their progress. This feature reinforces the "Do," "Check," and "Apply" steps of the Student Success Cycle.

Glossary

All terms highlighted in the chapter and their page references are included.

THE LARSON ADVANTAGE

Problem Material

Demonstration Problems

These problems reinforce the chapter material and further bolster the Student Success Cycle.

demonstration problem

After several months of planning, Joane Cardinal started a haircutting business called The Cutlery. The following business activities occurred during its first month, August 2011:

a. On August 1, Cardinal put $16,000 cash into a chequing account in the name of The Cutlery. She also invested $10,000 of equipment that she already owned.

b. On August 2, she paid $2,000 cash for furniture for the shop.

Analysis Component

An analysis component has been added to each Mid- and End-of-Chapter Demonstration Problem, as well as to several Exercises, Problems, and Focus on Financial Statements questions, promoting critical thinking and opportunities for students to practise these skills.

Analysis component:

a. Identify how much of the assets held by The Cutlery are owned by the owner, Joane Cardinal.

b. How much of the total assets are financed by equity? by debt? Explain what it means to 'finance assets by equity' and to 'finance assets by debt.'

Concept Review Questions

These short-answer questions reinforce the chapter content by Learning Objective.

Concept Review Questions

1. Identify four financial statements that a proprietorship presents to its owner and other users.
2. What information is presented in an income statement?
3. What do accountants mean by the term *revenue*?
4. Why does the user of an income statement need to know the time period that it covers?
7. Define (a) assets, (b) liabilities, (c) equity, and (d) net assets.
8. Review Vertically Inclined's financial statements presented in the chapter for the month ended January 31, 2011. Review the balance sheet and determine the business form Virgil Klimb has chosen to organize his business.

Quick Study

These single-topic exercises give the students a quick test of each key element in the chapter and are referenced to Learning Objectives. Answers to these items are available online.

Quick Study

QS 2-1
Financial statements and forms of organization
LO1

SP – Sole proprietorship
P – Partnership
C – Corporation

Identify the type of business organization based on the following independent financial statement findings:

__________ **1.** The equity section of the balance sheet has one capital account.
__________ **2.** The owners receive dividends, a distribution of earnings, in the form of cash.
__________ **3.** There are two capital accounts: Tara Davis, Capital, and Sheila Kelton, Capital.

Exercises

Exercises provide students with an additional opportunity to reinforce basic chapter concepts by Learning Objective. Note: Selected end-of-chapter exercises and problems are marked with an icon. eXcel These can be solved using the Excel templates located on **Connect**.

Exercises

Exercise 2-1
Determining net income
LO1

Check figure:
d. $13,000 net loss

Net income (net loss), owner withdrawals, and owner investment cause equity to change. We also know that revenues less expenses equals net income (loss). Using the following information, calculate net income (loss) for each independent situation.

a. The business earned revenues of $80,000 and had expenses of $65,000.
b. The business showed expenses of $149,000 and revenues of $92,000.
c. The equity at the beginning of the month was $10,000. During the month, the owner made no investments or withdrawals. At the end of the month, equity totalled $86,000.
d. The equity at the beginning of the month was $25,000. During the month, the owner made an investment of $40,000 but made no withdrawals. Equity at the end of the month totalled $52,000.

Problems

Problem 2-1A
Financial statements: analysis of statement of changes in equity
LO1

BT Pool Cleaners began operations on January 1, 2009. The owner invested $10,000 during the first year and was able to withdraw cash of $42,000 after a successful first year.

During the second year of operations, the business reported net income of $175,000, owner withdrawals of $78,000, and no owner investments.

In the third year, BT Pool Cleaners incurred a loss of $5,000. The owner made no withdrawals and no owner investments during this period. At the end of the third year, owner's capital was $120,000.

Check figure:
Net income 2009 = $60,000

Required
Calculate the net income or loss for the first year of operations.

Problems

Problems typically incorporate two or more concepts. As well, there are two groups of Problems: A Problems and Alternate or B Problems. B Problems mirror the A Problems to help improve understanding through repetition.

Ethics Challenge

EC 2-1

Sue Ryskiak is a new entry-level accountant for a mail order company that specializes in supplying skateboards and accessories for the sport. At the end of the fiscal period, Sue is advised by a supervisor to include as revenue for the period any orders that have been charged by phone but not yet completed by shipping the product. Sue is also advised to include as revenue any orders received by mail with cheques enclosed that are also pending fulfillment.

Required
1. Identify relevant accounting principles that Sue should be aware of in view of the supervisor's instructions.
2. What are the ethical factors in this situation?
3. Would you recommend that Sue follow the supervisor's directives?
4. What alternatives might be available to Sue if she decides not to follow the supervisor's directions?

Ethics Challenge

Each chapter includes at least one Ethics Challenge to reinforce critical thinking skills for the students and open up discussion about various ethical topics.

Focus on Financial Statements

FFS 1-1

In the fall of 2005, Andrew Rankin, a former Royal Bank of Canada (RBC) Dominion Securities managing director, was sentenced in Toronto to six months in jail for illegally sharing inside information with a friend, Daniel Duic. Mr. Rankin was charged with leaking corporate secrets regarding Canadian Pacific Ltd., Moffact Communications Inc., Canadian Satellite Communications Inc., Clearnet Communications Inc., Prudential Steel Ltd., Winspear Diamonds Inc., Irwin Toy Ltd., Donohue Inc., Cobequid Life Sciences Inc., and Alliance Forest Products Inc. Mr. Duic made $4.5 million in profits from share trades based on illegal tips regarding these 10 companies and paid a $1.9 million fine.

Required
Financial information about businesses is regularly shared in the newspapers and online with the public. What makes the information sharing that Andrew Rankin engaged in with Daniel Duic illegal?

Focus on Financial Statements

Each chapter includes a technical and analytical question that incorporates into the financial statements all major topics covered up to that point. Additional questions are available online on **Connect**.

Critical Thinking Mini Case

You have worked with XYZ Contractors as the marketing manager for a number of years. Each of your salespeople must submit a monthly report detailing money they spent while conducting business on behalf of XYZ Contractors. Each item on the monthly report must be coded as to the effect on assets, liabilities, and equity. As marketing manager, one of your duties is to review the monthly reports. One salesperson's report for September shows the following:

Date	Description of Transaction	Amount of Transaction	Effect on Assets	Effect on Liabilities	Effect on Equity
Aug. 28	Sold 80 units of product to a customer for cash	$150,000	Increased cash	No effect	Increased revenue
Sept. 10	Purchased new desk for office to be paid in October	$1,500	No effect	Increased accounts payable	Increased office expense
Sept. 2–30	Took clients for lunch and paid cash	$680	Decreased cash		Increased owner investments
Oct. 5	Paid for September cell phone usage	$130	Decreased cash		Increased expenses

Required
Using the elements of critical thinking described on the inside front cover, respond.

Critical Thinking Mini Cases

These cases give students the opportunity to apply critical thinking skills to concepts learned in the chapter, thus further reinforcing the "Apply" step of the Student Success Cycle.

The Accounting Standard

We listened! In addition to obtaining numerous individual reviewer comments, we held focus groups in cities throughout Canada to hear the issues and concerns instructors like you have about the materials you use to teach introductory financial accounting. We were the first textbook to go to these lengths for market research, and we do more every year. We think you'll like what you see.

Throughout the Text

Chapters Overall

- Edited and updated the chapters in general
- Replaced *CICA Handbook* references with IFRS 2009 references
- Included a Critical Thinking Challenge reminder at the end of the chapter which refers the student back to the questions asked at the beginning of the chapter as part of the chapter opening vignette; the answers to these questions are now included both in the solutions manual and on **Connect**
- Included an IFRS Highlights feature at the conclusion of each chapter to identify the impact of IFRS on the chapter
- Incorporated more company examples

End-of-Chapter

- Adjusted the glossary as appropriate
- Renamed the *Questions* to *Concept Review Questions* to better identify the nature of this formative learning tool
- Added new, deleted inappropriate, and updated Quick Study/Exercises/Problems based on reviewer suggestions and IFRS impact
- Based on reviewer suggestion, changed the problem material to better reflect Canada's cultural diversity
- Added Check Figures to the Focus on Financial Statements questions

Chapter 1

- Provided new chapter opening vignette

Chapter 2

- Provided new chapter opening vignette
- Contemporized example company used in the chapter by replacing *Finlay Interiors* with *Vertically Inclined Rock Gym* in an effort to better engage students
- Changed terminology according to IFRS: statement of owner's equity is now statement of changes in equity; cash flow statement is now statement of cash flows
- Updated GAAP: qualitative characteristics of *understandability, relevance, reliability, and comparability* replace *relevance, reliability, consistency, and comparability*; *prudence* replaces *conservatism*, *timeliness* replaces *time period*; *objectivity* is dropped.

Chapter 3

- Contemporized example company used in the chapter by replacing *Finlay Interiors* with *Vertically Inclined Rock Gym*

Chapter 4

- Updated chapter opening vignette to reflect bankruptcy of Nortel, an interesting example for students
- Contemporized example company used in the chapter by replacing *Finlay Interiors* with *Vertically Inclined Rock Gym*
- Changed *amortization* of plant and equipment to *depreciation*
- Combined former Exhibits 4.23 and 4.24 based on reviewer request
- Revised wording in Appendix 4B to improve clarity

Chapter 5

- Contemporized example company used in the chapter by replacing *Finlay Interiors* with *Vertically Inclined Rock Gym*
- Replaced *capital assets* with *property, plant and equipment (PPE)*
- Replaced former work sheet transparencies with comprehensive Exhibit 5.3; an interactive simulation of this exhibit is available on **Connect**

Chapter 6

- Introduced classifying expenses by *function of an expense* vs. *nature of an expense*

Chapter 7

- Provided new chapter opening vignette
- Removed LIFO
- Replaced *lower of cost and market* with *lower of cost and net realizable value*

Chapter 8

- Condensed former *LO5 – Prepare and test the accuracy of subledgers* and combined it as part of *LO3 – Describe the use of controlling accounts and subledgers*
- Removed *Appendix 8B – Journalize and post transactions with sales taxes to special journals*

Chapter 9

- Removed *bank credit card* discussion and combined it with *credit card* section

Chapter 10

- Revised chapter opening vignette
- Combined former *LO4 – Apply the direct write-off method to account for uncollectible accounts receivable* with *LO3 – Estimate uncollectible accounts receivable using approaches based on sales and accounts receivable.*

Chapter 11

- Updated EI, CPP, and income tax to rates effective January 1, 2009
- Updated PST rates

Innovative Technology Supporting Student Success

Fundamental Accounting Principles offers a wealth of resources unmatched in educational publishing.

Connect

McGraw-Hill connect™

(www.mcgrawhillconnect.ca)

For Students:

Developed in partnership with Youthography, a Canadian youth research company, and hundreds of students from across Canada, McGraw-Hill **Connect**™ embraces diverse study behaviours and preferences to maximize active learning and engagement.

With McGraw-Hill **Connect**™, students complete pre- and post-diagnostic assessments that identify knowledge gaps and point them to concepts they need to learn. McGraw-Hill **Connect**™ provides students the option to work through recommended learning exercises and create their own personalized study plan using multiple sources of content, including a searchable e-book, multiple-choice and true/false quizzes, additional chapter-by-chapter exercises and problems, "Help Me Solve It" and "Accounting Cycle Tutorial" interactivities, personal notes, videos, and more. Using the copy, paste, highlight and sticky note features, students collect, organize and customize their study plan content to optimize learning outcomes.

For Instructors:

McGraw-Hill **Connect**™ assessment activities don't stop with students! There is material for instructors to leverage as well, including a personalized teaching plan where instructors can choose from a variety of quizzes to use in class, assign as homework, or add to exams. They can edit existing questions and add new ones; track individual student performance—by question, by assignment, or in relation to the class overall—with detailed grade reports; integrate grade reports easily with Learning Management Systems such as WebCT and Blackboard; and much more. Instructors can also browse or search teaching resources and text-specific supplements and organize them into customizable categories. All the teaching resources are now located in one convenient place.

McGraw-Hill Connect™—helping instructors and students Connect, Learn, Succeed!

Lyryx Interactive Financial Accounting

Lyryx Interactive Financial Accounting (LIFA) is a Web-based assessment tool that has captured the attention of post-secondary schools across the country. By reflecting the classroom environment, LIFA significantly benefits both instructors and students.

Each chapter is broken down into several **Lessons**—condensed versions of the material in the text.

Each Lesson is supported by a self-correcting **Exploration** that allows the students to practise the Lesson's concept. Because these Explorations are algorithmically generated, the students can try them as often as they want and get a different question each time.

Once the students master the Exploration, the instructor can set up a homework assignment, or **Lab**. These Labs are algorithmically generated and automatically graded, so students get instant feedback. Grades are instantly recorded into a Gradebook that the students and the instructor can view. Less of the instructor's time is spent on marking, *and* students get built-in and immediate feedback!

LIFA motivates students in two ways: (1) it is tied to assessment, and (2) Labs can be tried as many times as the students wish, with only the best grade being recorded. Instructors know that if students are doing their accounting homework, they will enjoy success. Recent research has shown that when Labs are tied to assessment, even if they are worth only a small percentage of the total grade for the course, students WILL do their homework—*and more than once!*

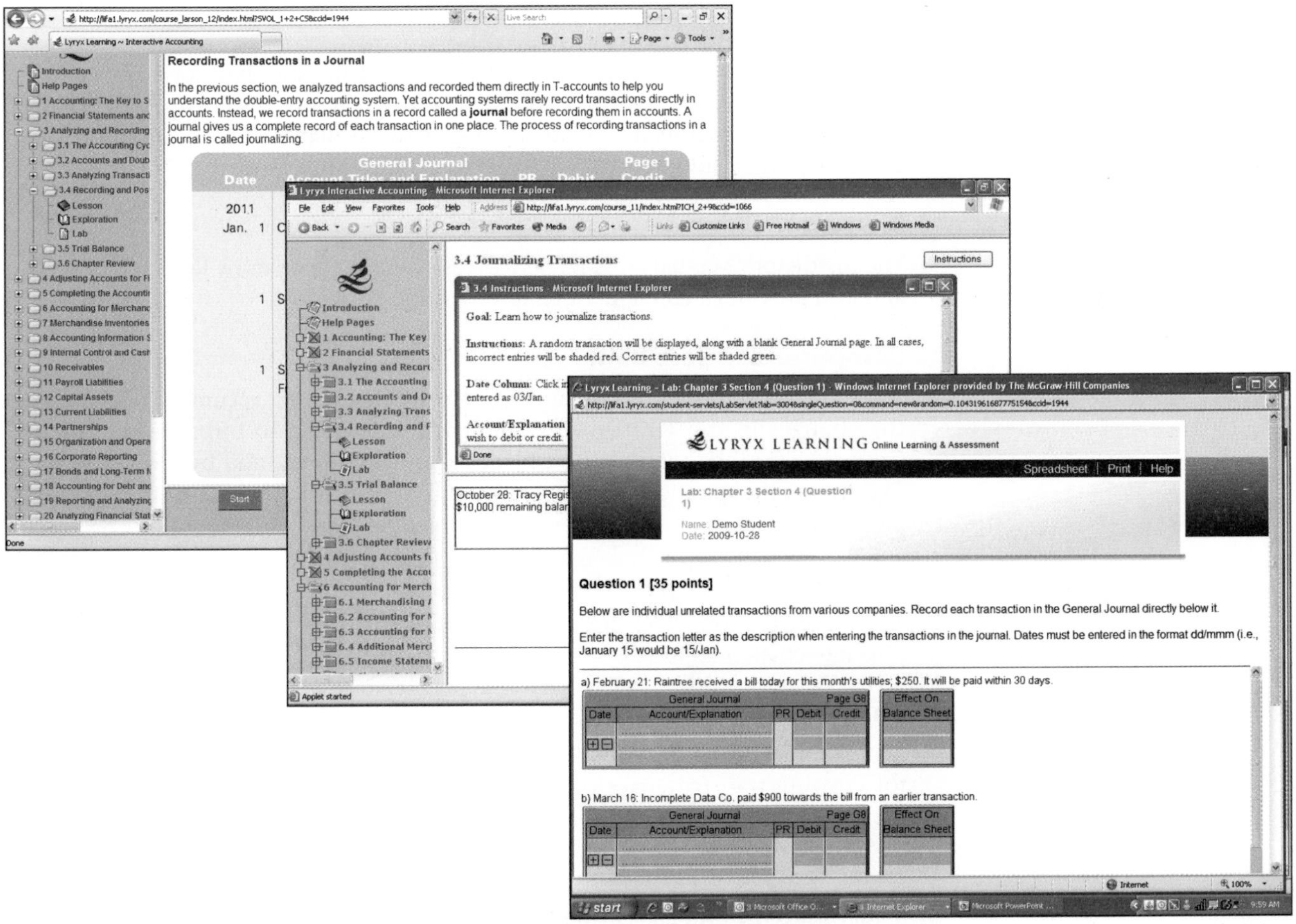

Other Supplements for Students

Working Papers

Available for purchase by students, Working Papers for Volumes 1 and 2 match the end-of-chapter material. They include papers that can be used to solve all of the Quick Study questions, Exercises, and A and B Problem sets.

CourseSmart

CourseSmart brings together thousands of textbooks across hundreds of courses in an eTextbook format providing unique benefits to students and faculty. By purchasing an eTextbook, students can save up to 50 percent off the cost of a print textbook, reduce their impact on the environment, and gain access to powerful Web tools for learning including full text search, notes and highlighting, and e-mail tools for sharing notes between classmates. For faculty, CourseSmart provides instant access to review and compare textbooks and course materials in their discipline area without the time, cost, and environmental impact of mailing print exam copies. For further details contact your *i*Learning Sales Specialist or go to www.coursesmart.com.

Supplements for the Instructor

Instructor supplements are available within **Connect** at www.mcgrawhillconnect.ca.

Solutions Manual

Fundamental Accounting Principles continues to set the standard for accuracy of its problem material. The Solutions Manual has been technically checked for accuracy by multiple instructors during its development. Available in both Microsoft Word and PDF format, solutions for all problem material are included.

Instructor's Manual

The Instructor's Manual cross-references assignment materials by Learning Objective and also provides a convenient chapter outline.

Computerized Test Bank

The test bank has been revised and technically checked for accuracy both to reflect the changes in the Thirteenth Canadian Edition and to improve the quality. Grouped according to Learning Objective, difficulty level, and by level of Bloom's Taxonomy, the questions in the computerized test bank include true/false, multiple choice, matching, short essay, and problem material.

PowerPoint® Presentations

These presentation slides are fully integrated with the text in an effort to better illustrate chapter concepts.

Image Bank

All exhibits and tables displayed in the text are available for your use, whether for creating transparencies or handouts, or customizing your own PowerPoint presentations.

Excel Template Solutions

Solutions to the problems using Excel templates are available.

Support for the Instructor

Service takes on a whole new meaning with McGraw-Hill Ryerson. More than just bringing you the textbook, we have consistently raised the bar in terms of innovation and educational research. These investments in learning and the education community have helped us understand the needs of students and educators across the country, thus allowing us to foster the growth of truly innovative, integrated learning solutions.

Integrated Learning Sales Specialist

Your Integrated Learning Sales Specialist is a McGraw-Hill Ryerson representative who has the experience, product knowledge, training, and support to help you assess and integrate all of the *Fundamental Accounting Principles* supplements, technology, assessment, course management, and services into your course for optimum teaching and learning performance. Whether it is using our test bank software, helping your students improve their grades, or putting your entire course online, your *i*Learning Sales Specialist is there to help you do it. Contact your local *i*Learning Sales Specialist today to learn how to take maximum advantage of McGraw-Hill Ryerson's resources.

*i*Learning Services Program

McGraw-Hill Ryerson offers a unique *i*Services package designed for Canadian faculty. Our mission is to equip providers of higher education with superior tools and resources required for excellence in teaching. For additional information, visit www.mcgrawhill.ca/highereducation/iservices.

McGraw-Hill Ryerson National Teaching and Learning Conference Series

The educational environment has changed tremendously in recent years, and McGraw-Hill Ryerson continues to be committed to helping you acquire the skills you need to succeed in this new milieu. Our innovative Teaching, Technology, and Learning Conference Series brings faculty together from across Canada with 3M Teaching Excellence award winners to share teaching and learning best practices in a collaborative and stimulating environment. Preconference workshops on general topics, such as teaching large classes and technology integration, are also offered. We will also work with you at your own institution to customize workshops that best suit the needs of your school's faculty.

Primis

Through McGraw-Hill Ryerson's custom publishing division, ***Primis***, instructors are able to select cases to accompany *Fundamental Accounting Principles* in a number of ways. Create your own case set, or browse the selection of cases that correspond to the chapter material. Contact your McGraw-Hill Ryerson *i*Learning Sales Specialist for more information.

Developing a Market-Driven Text

The success of this text is the result of an exhaustive process, which has gone beyond the scope of a single edition. Hundreds of instructors and educators across the country have been involved in giving their feedback to help develop the most successful accounting fundamentals text in the country. We owe thanks to all of those who took the time to evaluate this textbook and its supplemental products.

Thirteenth Canadian Edition reviewers

Peter Alpaugh	*George Brown College*
Jerry Aubin	*Algonquin College*
Joan Baines	*Red River College*
Karen Baker	*Loyalist College*
Barry Balanduk	*Red River College*
Warren Beck	*St. Clair College*
Maria Belanger	*Algonquin College*
Mark Binder	*Red River College*
Walt Burton	*Okanagan College*
Andrea Chance	*George Brown College*
Carole Clyne	*Centennial College*
Louise Connors	*Nova Scotia Community College*
Saverio Sonny Costanzo	*Confederation College*
Carolyn Doni	*Cambrian College*
Kim Dyck	*Red River College*
Andrew Dykstra	*Georgian College*
George Fisher	*Douglas College*
David Fleming	*George Brown College*
Jeremy Frape	*Humber College*
Edward Gough	*Centennial College*
Amy Greene	*triOS College*
Susan Haert	*CDI College*
Ken Hartford	*St. Clair College*
Robert Harvey	*Algonquin College*
Robert Stephen Holland	*Nova Scotia Community College*
Paul Hurley	*Durham College*
Don Hutton	*Durham College*
Stephanie Ibach	*Northern Alberta Institute of Technology*
Yvonne Jacobs	*College of North Atlantic*
Hélène L. Labelle	*Canadore College*
Jo-Ann Lamore	*Mohawk College*
Cecile M. Laurin	*Algonquin College*
Darlene Lowe	*Grant MacEwan College*
Doug Mann	*Georgian College*
Bonnie Martel	*Niagara College*
Steve Martin	*Humber College*
Debbie Musil	*Kwantlen University College*
Joe Pidutti	*Durham College*
Doug Ringrose	*Grant MacEwan College*
Janice Robinson	*Durham College*
Joe Rodrigues	*CDI College*
David Scott	*Niagara College*
Don Smith	*Georgian College*
Glen Stanger	*Douglas College*
Rod Tilley	*Mount Saint Vincent University*
Barry Tober	*Niagara College*
Helen Vallee	*Kwantlen University College*
Franc A. Weissenhorn	*Nova Scotia Community College*
Richard Wright	*Fanshawe College*
Brian Yahn	*Northern Alberta Institute of Technology*
Patricia Zima	*Mohawk College*

Twelfth Canadian Edition reviewers

Glenn Arnold	*Northern Alberta Institute of Technology*
Jerry Aubin	*Algonquin College*
Les Barnhouse	*Athabasca University*
Warren Beck	*St. Clair College*
Maria Belanger	*Algonquin College*
Mark Binder	*Red River College*
Dave Bopara	*CDI College*
David Burrell	*Okanagan University College*
Robert A. Coke	*Durham College*
Robert Despatie	*York University—Glendon College*
Randy Dickson	*Red Deer College*
Denise Dodson	*Nova Scotia Community College*
Carolyn Doni	*Cambrian College*
George Fisher	*Simon Fraser/UBC/CGA*
David Fleming	*George Brown College*
Amanda Flint	*Trinity Western University*
Jeremy Frape	*Humber College*
Donna Grace	*Sheridan Institute of Technology and Advanced Learning*
Diana Grant	*Nova Scotia Community College*
Elizabeth Hicks	*Douglas College*
John Holliday	*Northern Alberta Institute of Technology*
Paul Hurley	*Durham College*
Gerri Joosse	*Lethbridge College*
Nadine Lancaster	*British Columbia Institute of Technology*
Doug Leatherdale	*Georgian College*
Cynthia Lone	*Red River College*
Bonnie Martel	*Niagara College*
Debbie Musil	*Kwantlen University College*
Penny Parker	*Fanshawe College*
George Pelzer	*Northern Alberta Institute of Technology*
Guy Penney	*College of the North Atlantic*
Joe Pidutti	*Durham College*
Traven Reed	*Canadore College*
Lou Richards	*Southern Alberta Institute of Technology*
Doug Ringrose	*Grant MacEwan College*
David Sale	*Kwantlen University College*
Gabriela Schneider	*Northern Alberta Institute of Technology*
Donald R. Smith	*Georgian College*
Helen Stavaris	*Dawson College*
Nancy Tait	*Sir Sandford Fleming College*
Denise Terry	*SIAST—Palliser Campus*
Ron Thornbury	*Seneca College*
Rod Tilley	*Mount St. Vincent University*
John Varga	*George Brown College*
Jeannine Wall	*Red River College*
Richard Wright	*Fanshawe College*
Patricia Zima	*Mohawk College*

CHAPTER 1

Accounting: The Key to Success

learning objectives

- **LO1** Describe accounting and its goals and uses.
- **LO2** Describe forms of business organization.
- **LO3** Identify users and uses of accounting.
- **LO4** Explain why ethics and social responsibility are crucial to accounting.
- **LO5** Identify opportunities in accounting and related fields.

Yielding Vertical Results

Vertically Inclined Rock Gym is an indoor climbing facility with more than 7,500 square feet of sculpted cliff walls, ledges, and boulders, a "leap of faith," and more than 4,000 handholds that can challenge the most accomplished climber or provide a unique fitness experience to the novice. Jake Kreutzer, the gym's founder and owner, was a struggling artist and waiter in Vancouver before moving to Victoria where he earned an economics degree. This was followed by short stints at an advertising agency and a sports and fitness magazine as a photographer. After receiving his MBA from the University of Calgary, Jake and his soon-to-be wife, Nancy, moved to Edmonton in 1994. The couple took up rock climbing in the Rockies but because indoor facilities were scarce, they found that climbing wasn't easy to learn or practise. Jake thought that more people would welcome the challenge and excitement of climbing, as he had done, if it was more accessible. From that realization, combined with Jake's desire to own his own business and the addition of several partners, Vertically Inclined was born ... or at least the concept was. Rock climbing gyms were a novel and unproven industry, and the banks were not interested in lending money to a risky startup. So Jake put everything he had into the business and raised the rest of the cash privately. Jake's passion fuelled the persistence needed to navigate around what seemed like endless roadblocks. While establishing the business and creating brand recognition, he was working more than 90 hours per week ... on top of helping his wife care for their newly born twin daughters!

Jake's life is more settled now. He is the sole owner and has a strong management team and reliable staff giving him more time to spend with his family. "Getting to the top of a difficult climb is a lot like succeeding in business. It takes tenacity, perseverance, and an ability to tolerate risk. My accounting and business knowledge helped me understand and learn from the mistakes I inevitably made." Jake chuckles and recounts the story of the licensed lounge and cappuccino bar he opened on the second floor. "The climbers loved it ... but it didn't take long for the numbers to show me that selling 5 beer, 20 cappuccinos, and a few chocolate bars a day didn't cover the additional staffing and product costs ... and it took up most of my time! So, we converted the space to a bouldering wall that increased the number of climbers we could accommodate and added to the variety of types of climbing available in the facility.

"My focus is marketing but I have learned that accounting is invaluable ... it's the language that allows me to talk to and understand my accountant, bookkeeper, banker, lawyer, contractors, and customers ... accounting gives you an advantage."

www.verticallyinclined.com

An essential element of critical thinking is the ability to ask questions while reading (or listening or speaking). This exercise is designed to help students develop the skills related to questioning. Suggested answers are available on Connect at www.mcgrawhillconnect.ca.

CRITICAL THINKING CHALLENGE

What questions might Jake need the answers to in order to get a loan from a bank? Who else might require accounting information from Jake's business?

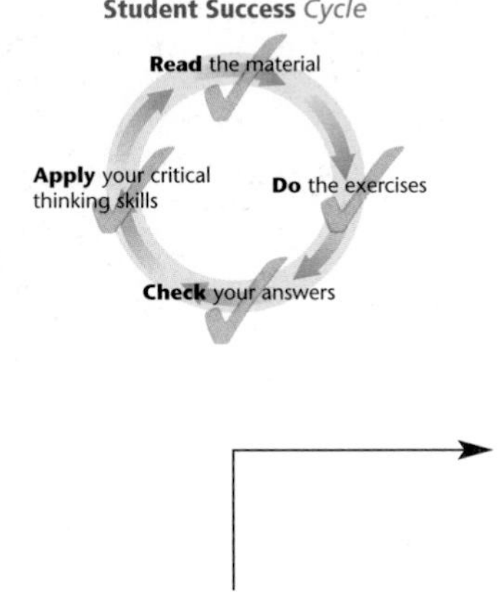

A chapter preview introduces the importance and relevance of the material, and also links these materials to the opening article to motivate you, the reader.

chapter preview

Accounting is at the heart of business: accounting information pulsates throughout an organization, feeding decision makers with details needed to give them an edge over competitors. Decision makers like Jake in the chapter opening story cannot rely on hunches and guesses. Decision makers depend on their knowledge of accounting principles and practices to help them identify and take advantage of opportunities discovered from reviewing large volumes of information. Through your study of this book, you will learn about many of the accounting concepts, procedures, and analyses common to both small and large businesses. This knowledge will provide you with the basics necessary to make better business decisions.

This first chapter serves a dual role. First, it introduces the subject of accounting. It describes accounting, the users and uses of accounting information, the importance of ethics and social responsibility, and opportunities in accounting. This chapter provides a foundation for those students who have little or no understanding of business or the role of accounting in business. Chapter 2 will build on this foundation by focusing on how accounting information is created and communicated.

The second purpose of Chapter 1 is to introduce you to each of the learning features found in most chapters. For example, immediately to the left of the first paragraph above is an explanation of purpose regarding the chapter preview, and two additional features are described in the lower left margin. Some of the features refer to Connect, located on the Web at www.mcgrawhillconnect.ca. Take the time in this chapter to explore and learn the value of these additional resources.

What Is Accounting?

LO1 Describe accounting and its goals and uses.

Each chapter is separated into chunks of information called learning objectives (LO). Each LO tells you what needs to be mastered in that section of reading.

Accounting knowledge is a powerful tool; it is your key to success, according to Jake in the chapter opening story. How does accounting knowledge give you power? What exactly is the focus of accounting? This section answers these fundamental questions.

Power of Accounting

Accounting is an information system that identifies, measures, records, and communicates understandable, relevant, reliable, and comparable information about an organization's economic activities,[1] as shown in Exhibit 1.1. Its objective is to help people make better decisions. It also helps people better assess opportunities, products, investments, and social and community responsibilities. In addition to reporting on the performance of a business, what the business owns, and what it owes, accounting opens our eyes to new and exciting possibilities. Put more simply, accounting involves collecting information, recording it, and then reporting it to various decision makers. In the chapter opening story, for example, Vertically Inclined Rock Gym collected and recorded accounting information so that it could be reported to Jake, the business's owner, to help him make important decisions such as those involved in setting selling prices for various services.

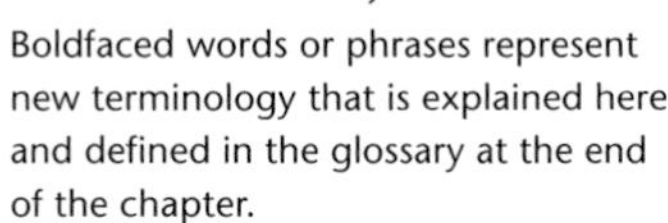

Boldfaced words or phrases represent new terminology that is explained here and defined in the glossary at the end of the chapter.

[1] IFRS 2009, "Framework," para. 24.

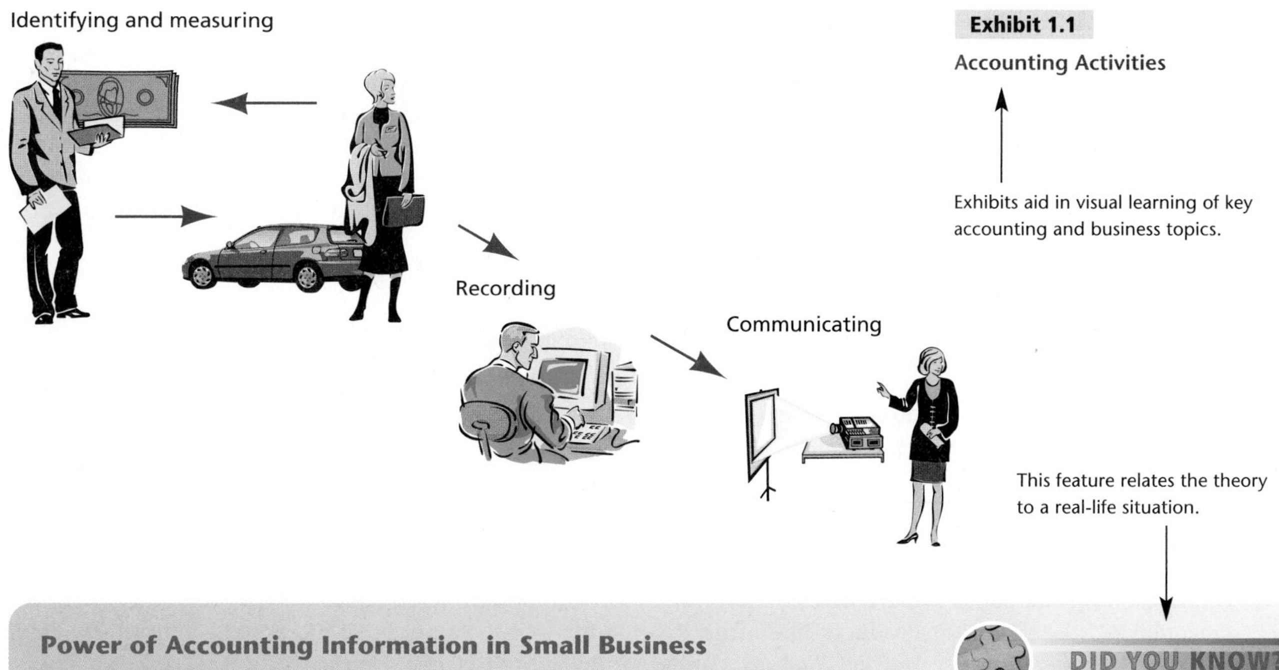

Exhibit 1.1
Accounting Activities

Exhibits aid in visual learning of key accounting and business topics.

This feature relates the theory to a real-life situation.

DID YOU KNOW?

Power of Accounting Information in Small Business

Pete Seerden, owner of ECOF, used to pay thousands of dollars annually in renting warehouse space for his cabinet-making business. "Rent payments were eating into my profits big time. I looked at alternatives and crunched some numbers. I ended up buying my own warehouse. I knew that I was increasing my risk but the upside was that the money I used to pay for rent was now paying for my building. Now, I've expanded my warehouse and am renting a part of it to somebody else."

Pete Seerden is not an accountant but was able to use his knowledge of accounting information to make a successful business decision.

Power of Accounting Information in Big Business

The Toronto-Dominion (TD) Bank teamed up with Starbucks to create an innovative customer experience. The TD Bank became the first major Canadian bank to combine banking with the services of a retailer in one of its branches. In the TD Bank branch at Queen and Bay Streets in downtown Toronto, you can purchase Starbucks products while doing your banking.

This innovative decision was made through an analysis of information from a variety of sources including the accounting information system. By increasing customer exposure for both parties, profits should be positively affected.

Accounting can provide you with important and interesting learning experiences. You will acquire knowledge and skills that will help you in both business and everyday life. For example, you can use accounting knowledge to make better investment decisions or to help you get a loan for a car or a house.

Focus of Accounting

Accounting affects many parts of life. Some examples of common contacts with accounting are through credit approvals, bank accounts, student loan forms, and payroll. These experiences are limited and tend to focus on the *recordkeeping* (or *bookkeeping*) parts of accounting. **Recordkeeping**, or **bookkeeping**, is the recording of financial transactions, either manually or electronically, for the purpose of creating a reliable bank of data. Accounting *involves* the recordkeeping process but *is* much more.

A series of questions in the chapter reinforces the immediately preceding materials. It gives you feedback on your comprehension before you go on to new topics. Answers to these Checkpoint questions are available for you at the end of each chapter.

Accounting also involves designing information systems to provide useful reports to monitor and control an organization's activities. In order to use the reports effectively, decision makers must be able to interpret the information. The skills needed to understand and interpret accounting information come from an insight into each aspect of accounting, including recordkeeping. Because accounting is part of so much that we do in business and our everyday lives, you can enjoy greater opportunities if you understand and are able to use accounting information effectively.

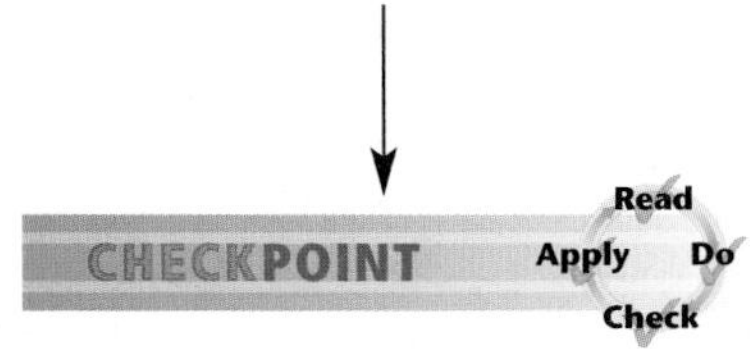

1. What is the major objective of accounting?
2. Distinguish between accounting and recordkeeping.

Answers to the Quick Study (QS) questions are available on Connect.

Do Quick Study questions: QS 1-1, QS 1-2

Forms of Organization

LO2 Describe forms of business organization.

A **business** is one or more individuals selling products or services for profit. Products like athletic apparel (CCM, Bauer, NIKE, Reebok), computers (Dell, Hewlett-Packard, Apple), and clothing (Tilley, Levi's, GAP) are part of our daily lives. Services like information communication (Sympatico, AOL Canada, CompuServe, Microsoft), dining (Tim Hortons, Harvey's, McDonald's, Burger King), and car rental (Tilden, Hertz, Budget) make our lives easier. A business can be as small as an in-home childcare service or as large as Canadian Tire. Nearly 100,000 new businesses are started in Canada each year, with most of them being founded by people who want freedom from ordinary jobs, a new challenge in life, or the advantage of earning extra money.

Most organizations engage in economic activities, such as the business activities of purchasing materials and labour, and selling products and services. They can also involve activities for non-business organizations, more commonly referred to as not-for-profit organizations, such as government, schools, and churches. A common feature in all organizations, both business and non-business, is the power and use of accounting.

Business Organizations

Businesses take one of three forms: sole proprietorship, partnership, or corporation.

Sole Proprietorship

A **sole proprietorship**, or **single proprietorship**, is a business owned by one person. No special legal requirements must be met in order to start this form of business, other than to file for a business licence and register the business name. While it is a separate entity[2] for accounting purposes, it is *not* a separate legal entity from its owner. This means, for example, that a court can order an owner to sell personal belongings to pay a proprietorship's debt. An owner is even responsible for debts that are greater than the resources of the proprietorship; this is known as **unlimited liability**, and is an obvious disadvantage of a sole proprietorship. Because tax authorities do not separate a proprietorship from its owner, the profits of the business are reported and taxed on the owner's personal income tax return. Small retail stores and service businesses often are organized as proprietorships.

[2] The **business entity principle** is one of a group of accounting rules, the **generally accepted accounting principles (GAAP)**, which are discussed in detail in Chapter 2. This principle states that each economic entity or business of the owner must keep accounting records and reports separate from the owner and any other economic entity of the owner.

Partnership

A **partnership**[3] is owned by two or more persons called *partners*. As for a proprietorship, no special legal requirements must be met in order to start a partnership, other than to register the business name and obtain a business licence. To run the business together, the partners need an oral or written agreement that usually indicates how profits and losses are to be shared. A partnership, like a proprietorship, is not legally separate from its owners, therefore each partner's share of profits is reported and taxed on that partner's tax return. Partners are usually subject to *unlimited liability*.

Corporation

A **corporation**[4] is a business that is a separate legal entity chartered (or *incorporated*) under provincial or federal laws. A corporation is responsible for its own acts and its own debts. It can enter into its own contracts, and it can buy, own, and sell property. It can also sue and be sued. Not only does separate legal status give a corporation an unlimited life, but it also entitles the corporation to conduct business with the rights, duties, and responsibilities of a person. As a result, a corporation files a tax return and pays tax on its profits. A corporation acts through its managers, who are its legal agents. Separate legal status also means that the shareholders are not personally liable for corporate acts and debts. Shareholders are legally distinct from the business and their loss is limited to what they invested. This **limited liability** is a key to why corporations can raise resources from shareholders who are not active in managing the business. Ownership, or equity, of all corporations is divided into units called **shares**. Owners of shares are called **shareholders** (the American term for shares is *stock* and for shareholders, *stockholders*). A shareholder can sell or transfer shares to another person without affecting the operations of a corporation. When a corporation issues (or sells) only one class of shares, we call them **common shares**. A corporation that sells its shares to the public is called a **publicly accountable enterprise (PAE)**. The **public sale of shares** refers to the trading of shares in an organized stock market such as the Montreal or Toronto stock exchanges. A **private enterprise (PE)** is a corporation that does not offer its shares for public sale. ACE aviation is an example of a publicly accountable enterprise. Its shares are available on the Toronto Stock Exchange. As of December 31, 2008, ACE Aviation had issued a total of 34,907,000 common shares to the public. This means that ACE Aviation's ownership is divided into 34,907,000 units. A shareholder who owns 349,070 shares of ACE Aviation owns 1%. McCain Foods Limited is a Canadian corporation that is a private enterprise. McCain's shares are held by a small group of individuals and not for sale to the public. Exhibit 1.2 lists some of the characteristics of each business form:

Exhibit 1.2

Characteristics of Business Organizations

	Sole Proprietorship	Partnership	Corporation
Business entity	yes	yes	yes
Legal entity	no	no	yes
Limited liability	no	no	yes
Unlimited life	no	no	yes
Business income is taxed	no	no	yes
One owner allowed	yes	no	yes

Non-Business Organizations

Non-business organizations plan and operate not for profit but rather for other goals such as health, education, religious services, and cultural and social activities.

[3] Partnerships are discussed in greater detail in Chapter 14 in Volume 2 of the textbook.
[4] Corporations are discussed in greater detail in Chapter 15 in Volume 2 of the textbook.

Examples are public schools meeting the needs of citizens, and community care groups meeting the needs of the poor. Non-business organizations do not have an identifiable owner. Still, the demand for accounting information in these organizations is high since they are accountable to their sponsors. These organizations are accountable to taxpayers, donors, lenders, legislators, regulators, and other constituents. Roughly one third of Canadian economic activity is done by government and not-for-profit organizations. Examples of these organizations include hospitals, schools, prisons, churches, the military, public airports, and libraries. In all of these organizations, accounting captures key information about their activities and makes it available to users both internal and external to the organization.

The Judgement Call feature requires you to make accounting and business decisions. It uses role-playing to show the interaction of judgement, the need for business awareness, and the impact of decisions.

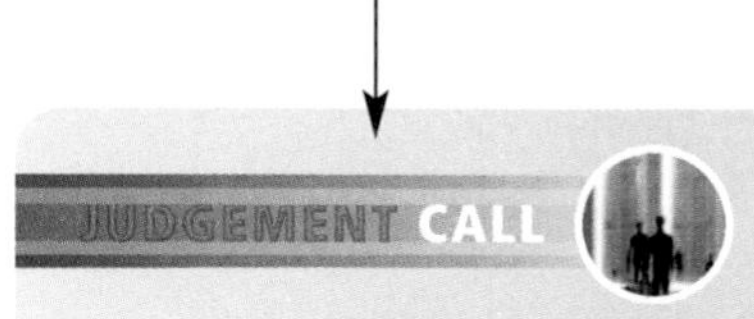

Answer—p. 17

Entrepreneur

You and a friend have developed a new design for mountain bikes that improves speed and performance by a remarkable 25% to 40%. You are planning to form a small business to manufacture and market these bikes. You and your friend are concerned about potential lawsuits from individuals who may become injured because of using the speed feature of the bikes with reckless abandon. What form of organization do you set up?

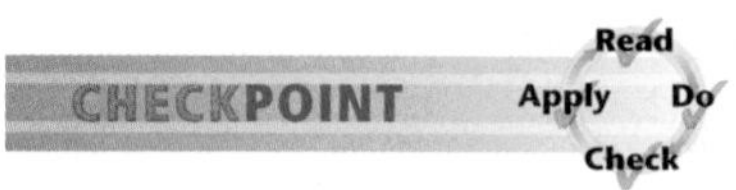

3. What are the three common forms of business organization?

4. Identify examples of non-business organizations.

Do Quick Study question: QS 1-3

All chapters have a Mid-Chapter and End-of-Chapter Demonstration Problem to illustrate and reinforce important topics.

Read Apply Do Check

mid-chapter demonstration problem

For each of the following independent situations, identify which type of business organization is being described (sole proprietorship, partnership, or corporation).

a. ____________ The owners of JenStar can sell or transfer their ownership to another person without affecting the operations of the business.

b. ____________ The 28 owners of InterIsland Tours each have 15,000 shares.

c. ____________ Jan Wallace and Roth Winters are subject to unlimited liability in their business.

d. ____________ Willis Corsairs is responsible for debts that are greater than the resources of his business.

e. ____________ The profits of Perth's Financial Consulting are reported and taxed on the personal tax return of Wyette Perth, the owner.

f. ____________ The six owners of Arcade Unlimited report their respective shares of the business profits on their personal tax returns.

solution

a. Corporation
b. Corporation
c. Partnership
d. Sole proprietorship
e. Sole proprietorship
f. Partnership

Users of Accounting Information

Accounting is a service activity that serves the decision-making needs of *external* and *internal* users.

LO3 | Identify users and uses of accounting.

External Information Users

External users of accounting information are *not* directly involved in running the organization. They include shareholders, lenders, directors, customers, suppliers, regulators, lawyers, brokers, and the press. Each external user has special information needs that depend on the kind of decision to be made. To make a decision, key questions need to be answered; this is often done using information available in accounting reports. Exhibit 1.3 identifies several external users and decisions that require accounting information.

Exhibit 1.3

External Accounting Information Needs

External User Group	Examples of Decisions To Be Made	Questions That Require Accounting Information
Lenders (creditors) lend money or other resources to an organization	To lend money or not	Can current loans be repaid? Can additional loans be repaid? What is the future profit outlook?
Shareholders are the owners of a corporation	To invest or not	What is net income for current and past periods? Do loans seem large or unusual? Do expenses fit the level and type of revenues?
External auditors examine financial statements and provide assurance that they are prepared according to GAAP	To determine the reasonableness of a client's statements	Have all expenses been recorded? Do revenues include only those for the current period?
Employees of an organization, or their union representatives	To determine if wages are fair	Is net income large enough to support a request for increased pay?
Regulators, such as Canada Revenue Agency **(CRA)**	To determine if payroll deductions are calculated properly	Are all employees being paid through the payroll system?
Others		
• Contributors to not-for-profit organizations	To continue financial support of the organization	Are funds being spent in an appropriate manner?
• Suppliers	To determine if goods should be supplied on credit	Is the purchaser able to pay for goods purchased?

External Reporting

Financial accounting is the area of accounting aimed at serving external users. Its primary objective is to provide external reports called *financial statements* to help users analyze an organization's activities. Because external users have limited access to an organization's information, their own success depends on getting external reports that are understandable, relevant, reliable, and comparable. Some governmental and regulatory agencies have the power to get reports in specific forms, but most external users must rely on *general-purpose financial statements*. The term *general-purpose* refers to the broad range of purposes for which external users rely on these statements. *Generally accepted accounting principles (GAAP)* are important in increasing the usefulness of financial statements to users. GAAP are the underlying concepts that make up acceptable accounting practices. GAAP in Canada are undergoing significant changes because of the adoption of **International Financial Reporting Standards (IFRS)**. IFRS are the new "accounting laws" that must be applied by accountants to public companies in Canada starting January 1, 2011, when recording and reporting accounting information. To help highlight the changes to introductory financial accounting because of IFRS, a feature called "IFRS Highlights" will be presented at the end of each chapter. We discuss GAAP and IFRS along with the financial statements in Chapter 2.

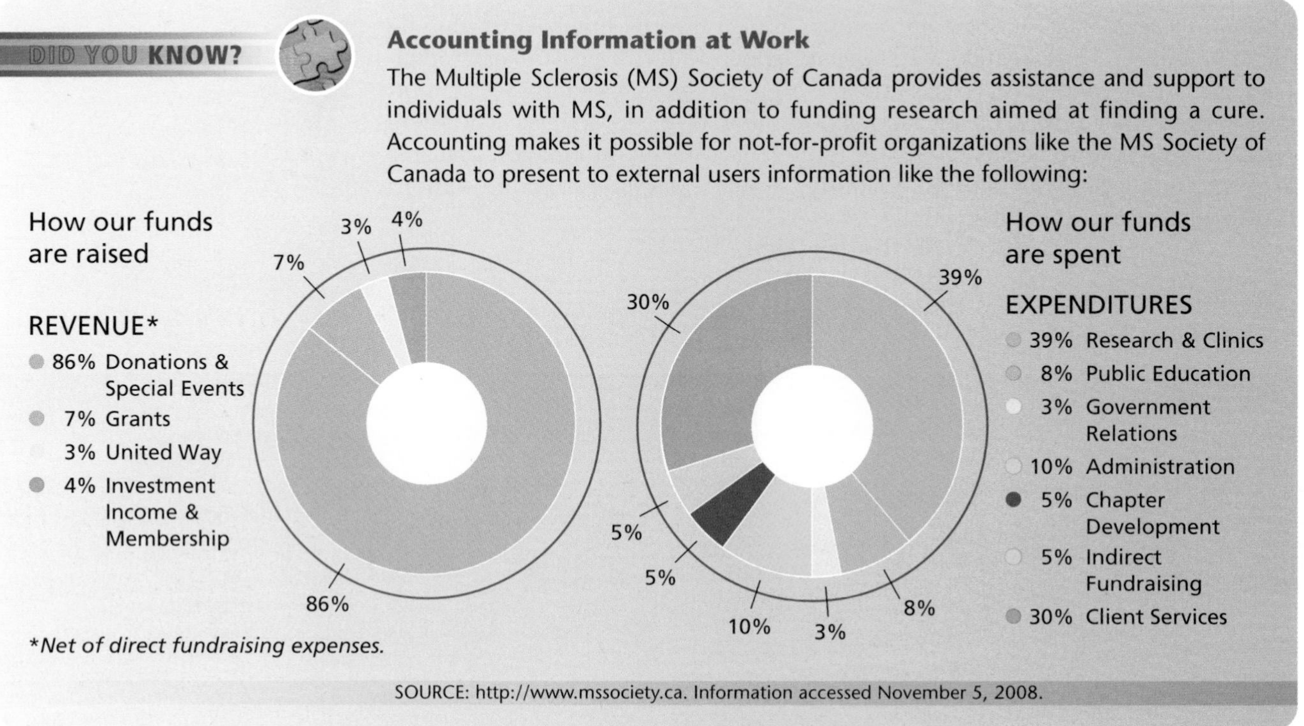

DID YOU KNOW?
Accounting Information at Work
The Multiple Sclerosis (MS) Society of Canada provides assistance and support to individuals with MS, in addition to funding research aimed at finding a cure. Accounting makes it possible for not-for-profit organizations like the MS Society of Canada to present to external users information like the following:
How our funds are raised
REVENUE*
86% Donations & Special Events
7% Grants
3% United Way
4% Investment Income & Membership
3%
4%
7%
86%
*Net of direct fundraising expenses.
How our funds are spent
EXPENDITURES
39% Research & Clinics
8% Public Education
3% Government Relations
10% Administration
5% Chapter Development
5% Indirect Fundraising
30% Client Services
39%
30%
5%
5%
10%
3%
8%
SOURCE: http://www.mssociety.ca. Information accessed November 5, 2008.

Internal Information Users

Internal users of accounting information are those individuals directly involved in managing and operating an organization. The internal role of accounting is to provide information to help internal users improve the efficiency and effectiveness of an organization in delivering products or services.

For example, Kathy Silver, HR Manager Recruitment, Training, and Policy of Shell Canada, says about the role of accounting in the human resources area: "As an HR person, I am often involved in developing proposals for HR initiatives in order to positively affect the company's profitability. In order to get management to support these proposals, I have to be able to clearly demonstrate in financial accounting terms how the proposed HR activities will impact the bottom line and contribute to business success. In today's tough competitive business environment, it is critical that HR professionals have an understanding of financial accounting and are able to speak intelligently about financial issues. Otherwise, they have very little credibility with internal business clients and will have difficulty making a valuable contribution. In addition, HR functions must be managed like any other business and this requires a knowledge of financial accounting; the training department must account for all its expenses and revenues; the payroll department must book all the accounting entries for salaries and tax deductions; the pension and benefits department must be able to book accounting entries for benefits and pensions; the recruitment department must account for recruitment expenses. And all HR departments must manage to a budget and explain variances. HR is not just about people. It is about business and finance and how people can contribute towards business goals. Those who grasp this concept will be much more marketable in the workplace."

Internal Reporting

Managerial accounting is the area of accounting aimed at serving the decision-making needs of internal users. Managerial accounting provides special-purpose reports customized to meet the information needs of internal users. An example of such a report is a listing of credit customers who are late in paying their accounts to Vertically Inclined Rock Gym (refer to the chapter opening story). Another example would be a report showing suppliers owed money by Jake for credit purchases. Internal reports aim to answer such questions as:

- What are the manufacturing expenses per unit of product?
- What is the most profitable mix of goods and/or services?
- What level of revenues is necessary to show net income?
- Which service activities are most profitable?
- Which expenses change with a change in revenues?

This book will help you to learn the skills needed to use accounting information effectively to answer questions like these and those noted in Exhibit 1.4.

Exhibit 1.4

Internal Operating Functions

Internal Function/User Group	Examples of Decisions To Be Made	Questions That Require Accounting Information
Research and Development (R&D)	To engage in a specific R&D project/ product/service	Is there sufficient funding to support this specific R&D? What is the future profit outlook for the result of the R&D?
Purchasing	To determine which supplier to purchase from	Is this supplier a going concern? What payment terms will minimize the cost to the buyer?
Human Resources	To determine wages/salaries to be paid	What effect will a pay increase have on net income? What impact will added payroll benefits have on the balance sheet?
Production	To make or buy	What is the breakeven point? Is a specific product line profitable?
Distribution	To ship via truck or train	Should customers pay for delivery costs?
Marketing	To hire additional sales personnel	How much can be spent on advertising?
Servicing	To provide servicing with in-house resources or subcontract	Do we repair or buy a new machine?

Internal Operating Functions

The responsibilities and duties of internal users extend to every function of an organization. There are at least seven functions common to most organizations, as shown in Exhibit 1.4, and accounting is essential to the smooth operation of each.

Allan Watt, Vice-President Marketing and Communications of the Edmonton Oilers Hockey Club, emphasizes the internal role of accounting: "We don't market anything until we look at the numbers. Business is based on accounting information and if any member of our team is unable to demystify and use the numbers, they can't add value to the process. Accounting numbers dictate absolutely everything that we do in marketing. You can't get past the breakeven point unless you can prepare, read, and stick to a numbers plan. We could win all sorts of marketing awards if we could spend what we wanted, but we can't because it has to make sense in terms of the bottom line. How do you know if it makes sense or not unless you understand accounting?"

To monitor operating functions, managers rely on **internal controls**—procedures set up to protect assets (like cash, equipment, and buildings), ensure that accounting reports are reliable, promote efficiency, and ensure that company policies are followed. For example, certain actions require verification, such as a manager's approval before materials enter production. Internal controls are crucial if accounting reports are to provide relevant and reliable information.

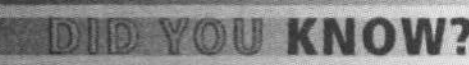

On June 20, 2008, Douglas Beatty, Chief Financial Officer (CFO) of Toronto-based Nortel Networks Corporation, was charged with fraud for misstating the company's financial results in 2002 and 2003. The RCMP said that Beatty is one of the company's three former executives to appear in court over a $3.2 billion accounting fraud that included improperly boosting sales. Nortel was North America's biggest maker of phone gear. This situation occurred because of inadequate internal controls and allegations of unethical behaviour. Nortel applied for bankruptcy protection in January 2009.

SOURCE: *AccountancyAge*, 2009.

Ethics and Social Responsibility

LO4 Explain why ethics and social responsibility are crucial to accounting.

Ethics and ethical behaviour are important to the accounting profession and to those who use accounting information. We are reminded of this when we find stories in the media of cheating, or when we witness wrongful actions by individuals in business. A lack of ethics makes it harder for people to trust one another. If trust is missing, our lives are more difficult, inefficient, and unpleasant. An important goal of accounting is to provide useful information for decision making. For information to be useful, it must be trusted; this demands ethics in accounting. Closely related to ethics is social responsibility. Both are discussed in this section.

Understanding Ethics

EXTEND YOUR KNOWLEDGE

This Extend Your Knowledge icon appears when more information about a topic can be found on the Connect accompanying this text. Go to www.mcgrawhillconnect.ca to find out more. A complete list of Extend Your Knowledge items is located on the back inside cover of the textbook.

Ethics are beliefs that differentiate right from wrong. Ethics and laws often coincide, with the result that many unethical actions (such as theft and physical violence) are also illegal. Yet other actions are not against the law but are considered unethical, such as not helping people with certain needs or deliberately withholding critical information from the user.

Identifying the ethical path is sometimes difficult. The preferred ethical path is to take a course of action that avoids casting doubt on one's decision. For example, as a member of the board for a not-for-profit organization, you are involved in a decision through which your brother's company could win a profitable contract to do work for the organization ... do you participate in the decision or do you remove yourself from the discussion? The ethical answer would be to avoid this conflict of interest by not participating. Accountants have ethical obligations in at least four general areas: they are expected to maintain a high level of professional competence, treat sensitive information as confidential, exercise personal integrity, and be objective in matters of financial disclosure.

Ethics Are Timeless

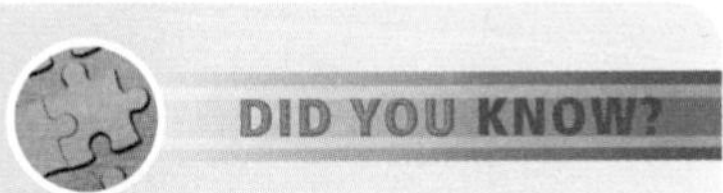

The Rotary 4-Way Test, created by Herbert J. Taylor in 1932, is an internationally renowned guideline for making ethical business choices:

"Of the things we think, say or do:

1. Is it the Truth?
2. Is it Fair to all concerned?
3. Will it build goodwill and better friendships?
4. Will it be beneficial to all concerned?"

SOURCE: www.rotary.org, ® Rotary International. Used with permission.

Organizational Ethics

Organizational ethics are likely learned through management example and leadership. Companies like Shell Canada, The Body Shop, and Royal Bank of Canada work hard to convey the importance of ethics to employees. For example, Shell Canada's code of ethics states that:

> "Shell Canada's reputation and credibility are based upon its total commitment to ethical business practices. To safeguard the Shell reputation, each of us must conduct ourselves in accordance with the highest ethical standards and also be perceived to be acting ethically at all times."
>
> SOURCE: http://shell.ca. Information accessed November 4, 2008.

Ethical practices build trust, which promotes loyalty and long-term relationships with customers, suppliers, employees, and investors. Good ethics add to an organization's reputation and its success. For example, unlike other pet stores, Petcetera, in its attempt to decrease pet abandonment, stopped selling rabbits at Easter because once-sweet Easter bunnies are often left in parks where they rapidly multiply and become a nuisance.

Ethical companies are said to have excellent **corporate governance**, the mechanism by which individuals in a company, in particular the board of directors, are motivated to align their behaviours with the overall corporate good. Since the demise of corporations like Enron and WorldCom, caused by fraudulent accounting activities, corporate governance is in the spotlight. Royal Bank of Canada, with its head office in Montreal, has detailed corporate governance guidelines, an excerpt of which follows:

> "The Bank and its Board of Directors are committed to maintaining high standards of governance in a rapidly changing environment. Our system of corporate governance is subject to continuous review and improvement. The board has proactively adopted governance policies and practices designed to align the interests of the board and management with those of shareholders and to promote the highest standards of ethical behaviour at every level of the organization."

SOURCE: http://www.rbc.com

EXTEND YOUR KNOWLEDGE

CIBC, TD, and RBC: Organizational Ethics?

The ethical behaviour of Canadian banks was put into question when several were named in class-action lawsuits assembled to recover billions of dollars lost by investors because of the collapse of Enron. The lawsuits claim that the banks allegedly helped Enron commit one of the largest accounting frauds in world history. In August 2005, the Canadian Imperial Bank of Commerce (CIBC) announced a U.S.$2.4 billion settlement to extract itself from the class-action lawsuit. The Toronto-Dominion Bank (TD) paid U.S.$130 million to settle claims. TD denied liability or wrongdoing but has raised its reserve set aside to cover related potential liabilities to U.S.$400 million. Canada's largest bank, Royal Bank of Canada (RBC), paid $25 million regarding claims that it aided Enron's accounting fraud but did not admit any wrongdoing.

Accounting Ethics

Ethics are crucial in accounting. Providers of accounting information often face ethical choices as they prepare financial reports. Their choices can affect both the use and the receipt of money, including taxes owed and money shared with owners. Accounting information can affect the price that a buyer pays and the wages paid to workers. It can even affect the success of products, services, and divisions. Misleading information can lead to a wrongful closing of a division, causing workers, customers, and suppliers to be seriously harmed.

Because of the importance of accounting ethics, codes of ethics for accountants are set up and enforced. These codes include those of the Provincial Certified General Accountants' Associations, the Provincial Societies of Management Accountants, and the Provincial Institutes of Chartered Accountants. The codes of all three professional accounting bodies state that accountants have a responsibility to society, they must act in the interest of their client or employer, they must exercise due care and professional judgement and continually upgrade their skills, and they must not be associated with deceptive information. Samples from these codes are presented in Extend Your Knowledge 1-3 on Connect. These codes can be of help when one confronts ethical dilemmas.

EXTEND YOUR KNOWLEDGE

Ethics codes are also useful when one is dealing with confidential information. For example, auditors have access to confidential salaries and an organization's strategies. Organizations can be harmed if auditors pass this information to others. To prevent this, auditors' ethics codes require them to keep information confidential. Internal accountants are also not to use confidential information for personal gain.

DID YOU KNOW?

Livent: An Unethical Example

In October 2002, the RCMP charged Garth Drabinsky and Myron Gottlieb—co-founders of Livent, a once very successful theatre company in Toronto—with 19 counts each of fraud regarding the business's accounting records. The RCMP alleged that Drabinsky and Gottlieb defrauded creditors and private and public investors of about $500 million between December 14, 1989, and June 23, 1998. In March 2009, Drabinsky and Gottlieb were convicted of accounting fraud.

SOURCE: www.nationalpost.com; March 26, 2009.

Ethical Challenge

In our lives, we encounter many situations requiring ethical decisions. We need to remember that accounting must be practised ethically if it is to be useful, and must always ensure that our actions and decisions are ethical.

Social Responsibility

Social responsibility is a concern for the impact of our actions on society as a whole. It requires that an organization identify issues, analyze options, and make socially responsible decisions.

Socially conscious employees, customers, investors, and others see to it that organizations follow claims of social awareness with action, by placing significant pressure on organizations to contribute positively to society. Organizations such as WestJet and Danier Leather take social responsibility seriously. WestJet invests in the community through WestJet Cares, a program that supports ten national charities such as the Boys and Girls Clubs of Canada, Big Brothers Big Sisters Canada, CNIB, Kids Help Phone Canada, KidSport Canada, and Make-A-Wish Canada. Danier Leather sponsors not only Look Good Feel Better, a charity dedicated to helping Canadian women living with cancer, but also the United Way and more than 130 children through the Foster Parents Plan.

5. What is the difference between external and internal users of accounting information?
6. Why are internal controls important?
7. What are the guidelines to use in making ethical and socially responsible decisions?
8. Why are ethics and social responsibility valuable to organizations?
9. Why are ethics crucial to accounting?

Do Quick Study questions: QS 1-4, QS 1-5

Accounting Opportunities

LO5 Identify opportunities in accounting and related fields.

Exhibit 1.5 identifies the countless job opportunities in accounting by classifying accountants according to the kind of work that they perform. In general, accountants work in four broad fields:

- Financial
- Managerial
- Taxation
- Accounting-related

Exhibit 1.5

Opportunities in Practice

Another way to classify accountants is to identify the kinds of organizations in which they work. Most accountants are **private accountants** and work for a single employer, which is often a business. The services of **public accountants** are available to the public, which means that services are provided to many different clients. **Government accountants** work for local, provincial, and federal government agencies. Exhibit 1.6 shows the average annual salaries for various accounting groups.

Exhibit 1.6

Average Annual Salaries for Accounting Positions

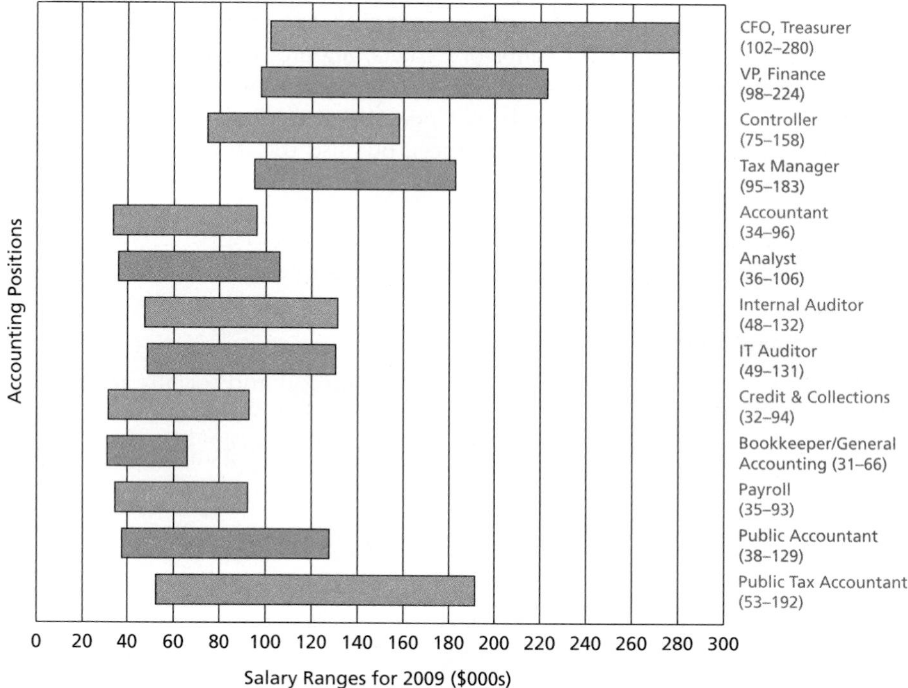

*These values do not include benefits/bonuses.
SOURCE: Extracted from Robert Half 2009 Salary Guide.

Financial Accounting

Financial accounting serves the needs of external users by providing financial statements. Many organizations, both business and non-business, issue their financial statements only after an audit. An **audit** is an independent review and test of an organization's accounting systems and records; it is performed to add credibility to the financial statements.[5] **External auditors** perform the audit function at the request of the board of directors to protect shareholder interests.

Managerial Accounting

Managerial accounting serves the needs of internal users by providing special-purpose reports. These special-purpose reports are the result of general accounting, cost accounting, budgeting, internal auditing, and management consulting.

[5] To achieve this result, audits are performed by independent professionals who are public accountants. Little or no credibility would be added to statements if they were audited by a company's own employees.

General accounting	The task of recording transactions, processing the recorded data, and preparing reports for members of the management team such as the **controller** (the chief accounting officer of an organization).
Cost accounting	The process of accumulating the information that managers need about the various **costs** within the organization.
Budgeting	The process of developing formal plans for an organization's future activities.
Internal auditing	Function performed by auditors employed within the organization for the purpose of evaluating the efficiency and effectiveness of procedures.
Management consulting	Service provided by external accountants where suggestions are offered for improving a company's procedures; suggestions may concern new accounting and internal control systems, new computer systems, budgeting, and employee benefit plans.

Taxation

Income tax raised by federal and provincial governments is based on the income earned by taxpayers. These taxpayers include both individuals and corporate businesses. Sole proprietorships and partnerships are not subject to income tax, but owners of these two non-corporate business forms must pay tax on income earned from these business forms. The amount of tax is based on what the laws define to be income. In the field of **taxation**, tax accountants help taxpayers comply with these laws by preparing their tax returns and providing assistance with tax planning for the future. The government (specifically, Canada Revenue Agency) employs tax accountants for collection and enforcement.

Professional Certification

Many accountants (financial, managerial, tax, and other) have professional accounting status. Accounting is a profession, like law and medicine, because accountants have special abilities and responsibilities. The professional status of an accountant is often indicated by one or more professional certifications. In Canada, there are several accounting organizations that provide the education and training required in order to obtain professional certification. These include the Certified General Accountants' Association, the Society of Management Accountants, and the Institute of Chartered Accountants. Successful completion of one of the prescribed programs leads to the following professional accounting designations: Certified General Accountant **(CGA)**; Certified Management Accountant **(CMA)**; or Chartered Accountant **(CA)**.

Relevant links are included as a source of additional information.

For detailed information regarding professional accounting education programs and journals, refer to the following Web sites: www.cga-canada.org, www.cma-canada.org, and www.cica.ca.

The preceding discussions show how important accounting is for organizations. Regardless of your career goals, you will use accounting information because it is the language of business. The discussion also emphasizes the broad scope and growing number of opportunities available in accounting. This book will help you to take advantage of those opportunities.

10. What is the difference between private and public accountants?

11. What are the four broad fields of accounting?

12. What is the purpose of an audit?

13. Distinguish between managerial and financial accounting.

Do Quick Study question: QS 1-6

After studying the content of each chapter, students are encouraged to return to the Critical Thinking Challenge questions for reflection.

CRITICAL THINKING CHALLENGE

Refer to the Critical Thinking Challenge questions at the beginning of the chapter on page 1. Compare your answers to those suggested on Connect at www.mcgrawhillconnect.ca.

"IFRS Highlights" summarize changes to introductory financial accounting in the chapter because of IFRS.

IFRS are the new "accounting laws" that must be used by accountants in Canada starting January 1, 2011. IFRS are discussed in more detail in Chapter 2 and beyond.

Each chapter includes a summary of the chapter by learning objective.

Summary

LO1 | Describe accounting and its goals and uses. Accounting is an information and measurement system that aims to identify, measure, record, and communicate understandable, relevant, reliable, and comparable information about economic activities. It helps us better assess opportunities, products, investments, and social and community responsibilities. The power of accounting is in opening our eyes to new and exciting opportunities. The greatest benefits of understanding accounting often come to those outside of accounting, because an improved understanding of accounting helps us to compete better in today's globally focused and technologically challenging world.

LO2 | Describe forms of business organization. Organizations can be classified either as businesses or as non-businesses. Businesses are organized for profit, while non-businesses serve us in ways not always measured by profit. Businesses take one of three forms: sole proprietorship, partnership, or corporation. These forms of organization have characteristics that hold important implications for legal liability, taxation, continuity, number of owners, and legal status.

LO3 | Identify users and uses of accounting. There are both internal and external users of accounting. Some users and uses of accounting include: (a) management for control, monitoring, and planning; (b) lenders for making decisions regarding loan applications; (c) shareholders for making investment decisions; (d) directors for overseeing management; and (e) employees for judging employment opportunities.

LO4 | Explain why ethics and social responsibility are crucial to accounting. The goal of accounting is to provide useful information for decision making. For information to be useful, it must be trusted. This demands ethics and socially responsible behaviour in accounting. Without these, accounting information loses its reliability.

LO5 | Identify opportunities in accounting and related fields. Opportunities in accounting and related fields are numerous. They encompass traditional financial and managerial accounting, and taxation, but also include accounting-related fields such as lending, consulting, managing, and planning.

guidance answer to JUDGEMENT CALL

Entrepreneur

You should probably form your business as a corporation if potential lawsuits are of prime concern. The corporate form of organization would protect your personal property from lawsuits directed at the business, and would place only the corporation's resources at risk. You should also examine the ethical and socially responsible aspects of starting a business where you anticipate injuries to others.

guidance answers to CHECKPOINT

Read Apply Do Check

1. Accounting is an information and measurement system that identifies, measures, records, and communicates understandable, relevant, reliable, and comparable information to people that helps them in making better decisions. It helps people in business to identify and react to investment opportunities, and better assess opportunities, products, investments, and social and community responsibilities.
2. Recordkeeping is the recording of financial transactions and events, either manually or electronically. While recordkeeping is essential to data reliability, accounting is this and much more. Accounting includes identifying, measuring, recording, reporting, and analyzing economic events and transactions. It involves interpreting information, and designing information systems to provide useful reports that monitor and control an organization's activities.
3. The three common forms of business organization are sole proprietorships, partnerships, and corporations.
4. Non-business organizations may include public airports, libraries, museums, religious institutions, municipal governments, law enforcement organizations, postal services, colleges, universities, highways, shelters, parks, hospitals, and schools.
5. External users of accounting information are not directly involved in running the organization. Internal users of accounting information are those individuals directly involved in managing and operating an organization.
6. Internal controls are procedures set up to protect assets, ensure that accounting reports are reliable, promote efficiency, and encourage adherence to company policies. Internal controls are crucial if accounting reports are to provide relevant and reliable information.
7. The guidelines for ethical and socially responsible decisions are threefold: (1) identify the ethical and/or social issue; (2) analyze options, considering both good and bad consequences for all individuals affected; and (3) make an ethical/socially responsible decision, choosing the best option after weighing all consequences.
8. Ethics and social responsibility are important for people because, without them, existence is more difficult, inefficient, and unpleasant. They are equally important to organizations, for this same reason. In addition, they often translate into higher profits and a better working environment.
9. Accounting aims to provide useful information for decision making. For information to be useful, it must be trusted. Trustworthiness of information demands ethics in accounting.
10. Private accountants work for a single employer, which is often a business. A public accountant is available to the public, which means that services are provided to many different clients.
11. The four broad fields of accounting are: financial, managerial, taxation, and accounting-related.
12. The purpose of an audit is to add credibility to the financial statements.
13. Managerial accounting is for internal users, while financial accounting is for external users.

demonstration problem

Rupert Jones works in a public accounting firm. The management of ShadowTech Company invites Jones to prepare a bid to review ShadowTech's financial statements. In discussing the review's fee, ShadowTech's management suggests a fee range where the fee amount depends on the reported profit of ShadowTech. The higher its profit, the higher the review fee paid to Jones's firm.

Required

1. Identify the parties potentially affected by this situation.
2. What are the ethical factors in this situation?
3. Would you recommend that Jones accept this review fee arrangement? Why?
4. Describe some of the factors guiding your recommendation.
5. Go to the following Web sites and read the sections noted regarding conflict of interest: http://www.cga-canada.org/en-ca/StandardsLib/ca_ceproc_v2-9.pdf and read Section R202 on pages 9 to 11; http://www.cma-alberta.com/index.cfm/ci_id/8582/la_id/1/document/1/re_id/0 and read Article IV, page 21; http://www.icao.on.ca/Resources/Membershandbook/1011page2635.pdf and read Section 210.

solution

1. Several parties are affected. They most directly include the users of financial statements, such as shareholders, lenders, investors, analysts, suppliers, directors, unions, regulators, and others. They also include the accounting firm (which can be sued if party to misleading statements), and Mr. Jones's business colleagues and family.
2. The value of an outside accountant's report stems from the accountant's independence. If an independent accountant accepts a fee that increases when the client's reported profit increases, the accountant is (or is at least perceived to be) interested in higher profits for the client. This compromises the accountant's independence.
3. To avoid compromising his independence, Jones should not accept this fee arrangement. Further, codes of professional conduct would forbid an accountant from accepting contingent fees that depend on amounts reported in a client's financial statements.
4. Ethical considerations guiding this decision include the potential harm to affected parties by allowing such a fee arrangement to exist. Ethical considerations also guard the profession against unethical actions that could undermine its real and perceived value to society.
5. Type in the Web site URLs and read the noted pages, or go to the respective bodies for your province and search for the Code of Ethics.

The glossary includes terms and phrases explained in the chapter.

Glossary

Accounting An information system that identifies, measures, records, and communicates understandable, relevant, reliable, and comparable information about an organization's economic activities. (p. 2)

Audit A check of an organization's accounting systems and records. (p. 14)

Bookkeeping The part of accounting that involves recording economic transactions, either electronically or manually; also called *recordkeeping*. (p. 3)

Budgeting The process of developing formal plans for future activities, which often serve as a basis for evaluating actual performance. (p. 15)

Business One or more individuals selling products or services for profit. (p. 4)

Business entity principle Every business is accounted for separately from its owner's personal activities. (p. 4)

CA Chartered Accountant; an accountant who has met the examination, education, and experience requirements of the Institute of Chartered Accountants for an individual professionally competent in accounting. (p. 15)

CGA Certified General Accountant; an accountant who has met the examination, education, and experience requirements of the Certified General Accountants' Association for an individual professionally competent in accounting. (p. 15)

CMA Certified Management Accountant; an accountant who has met the examination, education, and experience requirements of the Society of Management Accountants for an individual professionally competent in accounting. (p. 15)

Common shares The name for a corporation's shares when only one class of share capital is issued. (p. 5)

Controller The chief accounting officer of an organization. (p. 15)

Corporate governance The mechanism by which individuals in a company, in particular the board of directors, are motivated to align their behaviours with the overall corporate good. (p. 11)

Corporation A business that is a separate legal entity under provincial or federal laws with owners who are called shareholders. (p. 5)

Cost accounting A managerial accounting activity designed to help managers identify, measure, and control operating costs. (p. 15)

Costs The expenses incurred to earn revenues (or sales). (p. 15)

CRA Canada Revenue Agency; the federal government agency responsible for the collection of tax and enforcement of tax laws. (p. 7)

Ethics Beliefs that differentiate right from wrong. (p. 10)

External auditors/auditing Examine and provide assurance that financial statements are prepared according to generally accepted accounting principles (GAAP). (p. 14)

External users Persons using accounting information who are not directly involved in the running of the organization; examples include shareholders, customers, regulators, and suppliers. (p. 7)

Financial accounting The area of accounting aimed at serving external users. (p. 7)

General accounting The task of recording transactions, processing data, and preparing reports for managers; includes preparing financial statements for disclosure to external users. (p. 15)

Generally accepted accounting principles (GAAP) The rules that indicate acceptable accounting practice. (p. 4)

Government accountants Accountants who work for local, provincial, and federal government agencies. (p. 14)

IFRS See *International Financial Reporting Standards*. (p. 7)

Internal auditors/auditing Employees within organizations who assess whether managers are following established operating procedures and evaluate the efficiency of operating procedures. (p. 15)

Internal controls Procedures set up to protect assets, ensure reliable accounting reports, promote efficiency, and encourage adherence to company policies. (p. 10)

Internal users Persons using accounting information who are directly involved in managing and operating an organization; examples include managers and officers. (p. 8)

International Financial Reporting Standards (IFRS) The standards for financial reporting coming into effect January 2011 in Canada for publicly accountable entities. (p. 7)

Limited liability The owner's liability is limited to the amount of investment in the business. (p. 5)

Management consulting Activity in which suggestions are offered for improving a company's procedures; the suggestions may concern new accounting and internal control systems, new computer systems, budgeting, and employee benefit plans. (p. 15)

Managerial accounting The area of accounting aimed at serving the decision-making needs of internal users. (p. 9)

Partnership A business owned by two or more people that is not organized as a corporation. (p. 5)

Private accountants Accountants who work for a single employer other than the government or a public accounting firm. (p. 14)

Private enterprise (PE) A corporation that does not offer its shares for public sale. (p. 5)

Public accountants Accountants who provide their services to many different clients. (p. 14)

Public sale of shares The trading of shares in an organized stock market. (p. 5)

Publicly accountable enterprise (PAE) A corporation that sells its shares to the public. (p. 5)

Recordkeeping The recording of financial transactions, either manually or electronically; also called *bookkeeping*. (p. 3)

Shareholders The owners of a corporation; also known as stockholders. (p. 5)

Shares Units of ownership in a corporation; also known as stocks. (p. 5)

Single proprietorship A business owned by one individual that is not organized as a corporation; also called a *sole proprietorship*. (p. 4)

Social responsibility A commitment to considering the impact and being accountable for the effects that actions might have on society. (p. 13)

Sole proprietorship A business owned by one person that is not organized as a corporation; also called a *single proprietorship*. (p. 4)

Stock See *shares*. (p. 5)

Stockholders See *shareholders*. (p. 5)

Taxation The field of accounting that includes preparing tax returns and planning future transactions to minimize the amount of tax paid; involves private, public, and government accountants. (p. 15)

Unlimited liability When the debts of a sole proprietorship or partnership are greater than its resources, the owner(s) is (are) financially responsible. (p. 4)

Visit **Connect** at **www.mcgrawhillconnect.ca** for additional study tools, practice quizzes, to search an interactive e-book, and much more.

Short-answer questions reinforce key chapter concepts in order of learning objectives.

Concept Review Questions

1. In the chapter's opening article, what does Jake identify as the key to success in business?
2. Name three real product-based businesses and specify the product that each provides. Name three real service-based businesses and specify the service that each provides.
3. Describe three forms of business organization and their characteristics.
4. Identify the two organizations for which accounting information is available in Appendix I at the end of the book.

5. Identify three types of organizations that can be formed as either profit-oriented businesses, government units, or not-for-profit establishments.
6. What type of accounting information might be useful to those who carry out the marketing activities of a business?
7. Identify four external and internal users and their uses of accounting information.
8. Describe the internal role of accounting for organizations.
9. What is the purpose of accounting in society?
10. What ethical issues might accounting professionals face in dealing with confidential information?
11. Identify four managerial accounting tasks performed by both private and government accountants.
12. Identify two management-consulting services offered by public accounting professionals.
13. What work do tax accounting professionals perform in addition to preparing tax returns?
14. Identify the auditing firm that audited the financial statements of Danier Leather in Appendix I.

Appendix I at the end of the text includes two sets of real-life financial statements to provide you with a frame of reference.

Quick Study questions are single-topic exercises that give the reader a brief test of each key element in the chapter. Answers to the Quick Study (QS) questions are available on Connect.

Quick Study

QS 1-1
Uses of accounting
LO1

You have just graduated from the finance program at a local post-secondary institution. An opportunity to become the marketing manager for a medium-sized florist chain is available to you. You are concerned because you know that accounting plays a major role in the successful execution of this role and accounting was not your best subject. Identify at least two questions or issues for which the marketing manager would require accounting information.

QS 1-2
Accounting vs. recordkeeping
LO1

Each Quick Study, Exercise, and Problem is referenced to a learning objective in the chapter.

Identify whether each of the following functions would be classified as accounting or recordkeeping.

a. Meeting with the mechanical staff to determine new machine requirements for next year.
b. Data entry of sales orders received via the telephone.
c. Analyzing a sales report to determine if the discount policy is effective in getting customers to buy in multiple quantities.
d. Listing cheques received in the mail.

QS 1-3
Business vs. non-business organizations
LO2

Identify whether each of the following represents a business or non-business organization.

Hint: Enhance your research skills and check the Internet to confirm your answers.

a. Highlands United Church
b. Royal Alexandra Hospital
c. Royal Bank of Canada
d. CDI College
e. Loblaw
f. World Vision

QS 1-4
Identifying uses of accounting information
LO3

Identify two possible uses of accounting information.

QS 1-5
Ethics in accounting—applying the Rotary 4-Way Test
LO4

You are a salesperson. At the end of each month, you submit an expense report for reimbursement of personal funds you spent performing business duties such as client luncheons and travel. Last month, you included in your expense report two personal dinners with your spouse. By applying the Rotary 4-Way Test to this situation as identified on page 11 of the textbook, determine whether the behaviour is ethical or not.

QS 1-6
Accounting and accounting-related opportunities
LO5

Identify at least three main areas of accounting for accounting professionals. For each accounting area, identify at least three accounting-related opportunities in practice.

Exercises provide you with an additional opportunity to reinforce basic chapter concepts.

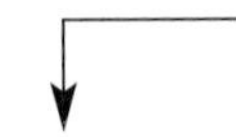

Exercises

Exercise 1-1
Distinguishing business organizations
LO2

This icon indicates that a tutorial showing how to solve the question is available at www.mcgrawhillconnect.ca.

Presented below are descriptions of several different business organizations. Determine whether the situation described refers to a sole proprietorship, partnership, or corporation.

a. Ownership of Cola Corp. is divided into 1,000 shares.
b. Text Tech is owned by Kimberly Fisher, who is personally liable for the debts of the business.
c. Jerry Forrentes and Susan Montgomery own Financial Services, a financial and personal services provider. Neither Forrentes nor Montgomery has personal responsibility for the debts of Financial Services.
d. Nancy Kerr and Frank Levens own Runners, a courier service. Both Kerr and Levens are personally liable for the debts of the business.
e. MRS Consulting Services does not have a separate legal existence apart from the one person who owns it.
f. Biotech Company has one owner and does not pay income taxes.
g. Torby Technologies has two owners and pays its own income taxes.

Exercise 1-2
Users of accounting information
LO3

Identify the users of TLC Daycare's accounting information as internal (I) or external (E).

	I or E
Bank manager	
Owner	
Toy supplier	

	I or E
Parent	
Canada Revenue Agency	
Cleaner contracted by TLC Daycare	

Exercise 1-3
Identifying accounting users and uses
LO3

Identify at least three external users of accounting information and indicate some questions that they might seek to answer through their use of accounting information.

Exercise 1-4
Identifying ethical decisions
LO4

Assume the following role and describe a situation in which ethical considerations play an important part in guiding your action:

a. You are a student in an accounting principles course.
b. You are a manager with responsibility for several employees.
c. You are the inventory manager at a grocery store.
d. You are the human resources manager with responsibility for recruiting and hiring employees.

Exercise 1-5
Applying the Rotary 4-Way Test
LO4

Required
For each situation described below, apply the Rotary 4-Way Test as identified on page 11 of the textbook to determine whether the behaviour is ethical or not.

a. In performing your job, you and a colleague often need to use your company phones to make long distance calls to suppliers. On a number of occasions, you have observed your colleague secretly using his company phone to make personal long distance calls.
b. You and a friend go to the movie theatre and purchase tickets. As you and your friend approach the ticket-taker, you both notice that the three people ahead of you have no tickets. The group and the ticket-taker, who appear to know each other, have a brief conversation and the group is admitted without having purchased tickets.
c. To use the facilities at the local fitness centre, clients can pay a $5 drop-in fee each visit or they can purchase an annual pass for unlimited access. The cashier collects the $5 from drop-in clients and provides them with a cash register receipt only if they ask.

Exercise 1-6
Learning the language of business
LO1,2,3,4

Indicate which description best defines each of the following important terms:

a. Government accountants
b. Internal auditing
c. Canada Revenue Agency
d. Accounting
e. Recordkeeping
f. CGA
g. GAAP
h. Shareholders

____________ **1.** Responsibility of an organization's employees involving examining the organization's recordkeeping processes, assessing whether managers are following established operating procedures, and appraising the efficiency of operating procedures.
____________ **2.** Federal department responsible for collecting federal taxes and enforcing tax law.
____________ **3.** Accounting professionals who provide services to many different clients.
____________ **4.** Accounting professionals employed by federal, provincial, or local branches of government.
____________ **5.** Accounting rules.

Exercise 1-7
Learning the language of business
LO1,3,4,5

Indicate which description best defines each of the following important terms:

a. Audit
b. Recordkeeping
c. Cost accounting
d. GAAP
e. Ethics
f. General accounting
g. Budgeting
h. Taxation

____________ **1.** An accounting specialization that includes planning future transactions to minimize taxes paid.
____________ **2.** A managerial accounting process designed to help managers identify, measure, and control operating costs.
____________ **3.** Principles that determine whether an action is right or wrong.
____________ **4.** An examination of an organization's accounting system and records that adds credibility to financial statements.
____________ **5.** The task of recording transactions, processing recorded data, and preparing reports and financial statements.

Exercise 1-8
Describing accounting responsibilities
LO5

Many accounting professionals work in one of the following three areas:

a. Financial accounting
b. Managerial accounting
c. Taxation accounting

For each of the following responsibilities, identify the area of accounting that most likely involves that responsibility:

_____________ **1.** Auditing financial statements.
_____________ **2.** Planning transactions to minimize taxes paid.
_____________ **3.** Cost accounting.
_____________ **4.** Preparing financial statements.
_____________ **5.** Reviewing financial reports for compliance with provincial securities commissions requirements.
_____________ **6.** Budgeting.
_____________ **7.** Internal auditing.
_____________ **8.** Investigating violations of tax laws.

Problems typically incorporate two or more concepts. There are two groups of problems: A problems and Alternate or B problems. B problems mirror the A problems to help you improve your understanding through repetition.

Problems

Problem 1-1A
Identifying type of business organization
LO2

Complete the chart below by placing a checkmark in the appropriate column.

Characteristic	Type of Business Organization		
	Sole Proprietorship	Partnership	Corporation
Limited liability			
Unlimited liability			
Owners are shareholders			
Owners are partners			
Taxed as a separate legal entity			

Alternate Problems

Problem 1-1B
Identifying type of business organization
LO2

a. Refer to Appendix I at the end of the book. Determine if WestJet Airlines is a sole proprietorship, partnership, or corporation.

b. Refer to Appendix I at the end of the book. Determine if Danier Leather is a sole proprietorship, partnership, or corporation.

DANIER

Ethics Challenge

EC 1-1

Dennis Willaby recently completed his professional accounting program and was hired to work in the accounting office of a large hardware store. A tremendous ice storm struck and caused countless people to be without electricity for extended periods. Dennis's boss instructed him to raise the selling price of the gas-powered generators that people were buying to generate their own electricity until the power could be restored. You have a concern about the ethics and social responsibility issue related to the practice of raising prices during a time of crisis. Comment.

Each chapter will include a technical and analytical question that incorporates into the financial statements all major topics covered up to that point.

Focus on Financial Statements

FFS 1-1

In the fall of 2005, Andrew Rankin, a former Royal Bank of Canada (RBC) Dominion Securities managing director, was sentenced in Toronto to six months in jail for illegally sharing inside information with a friend, Daniel Duic. Mr. Rankin was charged with leaking corporate secrets regarding Canadian Pacific Ltd., Moffact Communications Inc., Canadian Satellite Communications Inc., Clearnet Communications Inc., Prudential Steel Ltd., Winspear Diamonds Inc., Irwin Toy Ltd., Donohue Inc., Cobequid Life Sciences Inc., and Alliance Forest Products Inc. Mr. Duic made $4.5 million in profits from share trades based on illegal tips regarding these 10 companies and paid a $1.9 million fine.

Required

Financial information about businesses is regularly shared in the newspapers and online with the public. What makes the information sharing that Andrew Rankin engaged in with Daniel Duic illegal?

The Mini Cases give students the opportunity to apply critical thinking skills to concepts learned in the chapter.

Critical Thinking Mini Case

For the past five years, XYZ Construction has used about $600 million of materials per year. AU Suppliers has just negotiated a contract with XYZ to supply 70% of its total materials requirements, making XYZ Construction AU Suppliers' largest customer. Because of an economic downturn, XYZ has been having a poor year. This morning, the newspaper reported that XYZ's earnings decreased by 60% this year over last. You just read this newspaper article and, as CEO of AU Suppliers, are thinking about your recent contract with XYZ Construction.

Required

Using the elements of critical thinking described on the inside front cover, respond.

CHAPTER 2

Financial Statements and Accounting Transactions

learning objectives

LO1 Identify and explain the content and reporting aims of financial statements.

LO2 Identify, explain, and apply accounting principles.

LO3 Explain and interpret the accounting equation.

LO4 Analyze business transactions using the accounting equation.

LO5 Prepare financial statements reflecting business transactions.

The Great Cover Up

It's not what you might think! Since 1992, Clement and Laurie LaFrance, the owners of Clement L. Draperies/Budget Blinds Mfg. Ltd., have been covering up—windows and furniture. Employing 12 individuals, they offer customers the latest styles in blinds, window treatments, draperies, upholstery, bedding, and other related products along with interior design consulting. They take great pride in providing customers with reasonably priced, high quality products produced in their Edmonton facility. The husband/wife team work well together—Clement is responsible for staffing and client relations (and fixing sewing machines!) while Laurie monitors the numbers. "She's a magician when it comes to the numbers," says Clement. "Laurie developed and regularly updates a price grid that includes our production costs, materials, and other expenses that we depend on to prepare reliable and competitive estimates for our customers." When asked about the importance of financial statements, Clement says, "You can't operate a business successfully without understanding the numbers; it's impossible." The owners learned early that strong balance sheets are required by financial institutions to justify providing capital for growth and that income statements are a mechanism for tracking performance over time. Although positive cash flow is one of the most important parts of their business, Clement admits that his favourite element on the balance sheet is equity. "Why? Because the bigger the equity, the better our retirement will be!"

www.budgetblindsmfg.ca

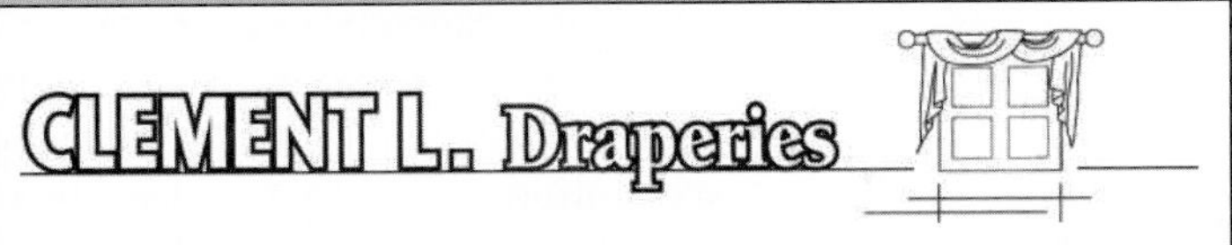

CRITICAL THINKING CHALLENGE

If Clement and Laurie were trying to obtain a bank loan for the business, what kind of financial information might the bank be interested in? Why did Clement say that "positive cash flow is one of the most important parts" of their business? What did Clement mean when he said that "the bigger the equity, the better our retirement will be"?

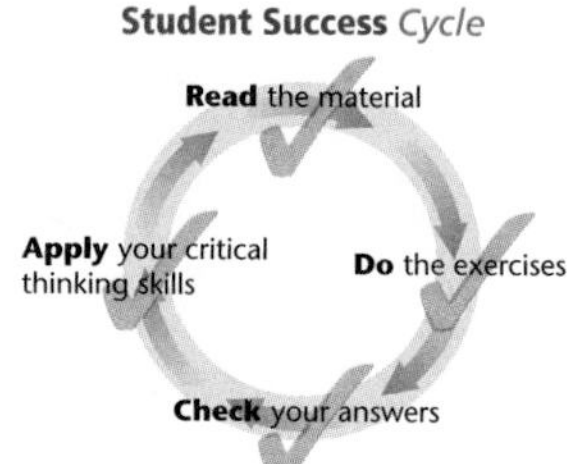

chapter preview

Financial statements report on the financial performance and condition of an organization. They are one of the most important products of accounting and are useful to both internal and external decision makers. Clement and Laurie in the opening article understand that financial statements are the means by which businesspeople communicate. Knowledge of their preparation, organization, and analysis is important.

In this chapter, we describe the kind of information captured and revealed in financial statements. We also discuss the principles and assumptions guiding their preparation under *International Financial Reporting Standards (IFRS)*, which were briefly introduced in Chapter 1. An important part of this chapter is to illustrate how transactions are reflected in financial statements. This chapter devotes special attention to Vertically Inclined Rock Gym, the business featured in the Chapter 1 opening story. Fictitious transactions regarding Vertically Inclined's first month of operations are the focus of our analysis. Vertically Inclined provides indoor rock climbing lessons and related services and was assumed to have been opened on January 1, 2011, by owner Virgil Klimb. (Virgil Klimb is a pseudonym for the actual business owner. ***Virg**il* was derived from the name of the business: **V**ertically **I**nclined **R**ock **G**ym.)

Communicating Through Financial Statements

LO1 Identify and explain the content and reporting aims of financial statements.

We discussed in Chapter 1 how accounting provides useful information that helps internal users P. 8 and external users P. 7 to make better decisions. Many organizations report their accounting information in the form of financial statements, which reveal an organization's financial health and performance in an easy-to-read summary format. They are the primary means of financial communication and are the end result of a process, or cycle, which begins with a business transaction like a sale. These transactions are recorded, classified, sorted, and summarized in order to produce the statements. In this chapter, we follow this process in an informal manner to prepare you for Chapter 3, where we present the formal development of the accounting records that are used by businesses.

Previewing Financial Statements

We will begin our study of the four major financial statements—the income statement, balance sheet, statement of changes in equity, and statement of cash flows—with a brief description of each. How these statements are linked is shown in Exhibit 2.1. Examples of financial statements are illustrated in the following pages using Vertically Inclined Rock Gym.

Exhibit 2.1

Links Between Financial Statements

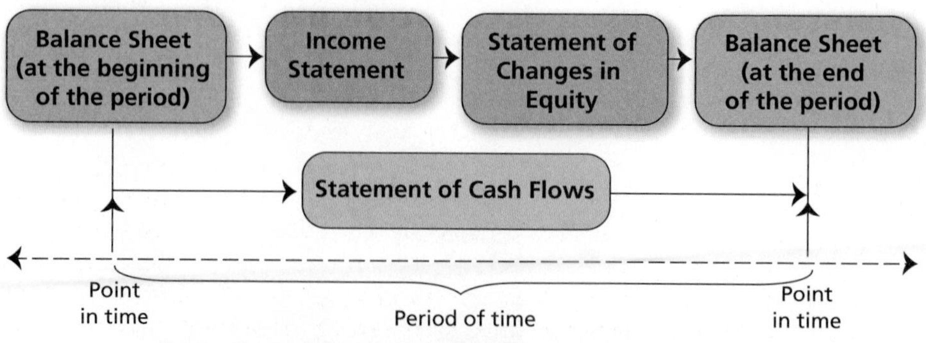

> **NOTE:** Flexibility is permitted by IFRS in the naming of financial statements. For example, the *statement of financial position* is another name for the *balance sheet*. The *statement of profit and loss (P&L), statement of earnings*, and other names are used instead of *income statement*. For consistency, the financial statements will be named as introduced in Exhibit 2.1 throughout this textbook.

A balance sheet reports on an organization's financial position at a *point in time*. The income statement, statement of changes in equity, and statement of cash flows report on performance over a *period of time*.

Selection of a reporting period is up to preparers and users (including regulatory agencies). A one-year, or annual, reporting period is common, as are semiannual, quarterly, and monthly periods. The one-year reporting period is also known as the accounting or **fiscal year**. Businesses whose reporting period follows the **calendar year** begin on January 1 and end on December 31. Many companies choose a fiscal year based on their **natural business year** that ends when sales and inventories are low. For example, Reitman's (Canada) Limited's fiscal year-end is January 31, after the holiday season.

Income Statement

An **income statement** reports *revenues* earned less *expenses* incurred by a business over a period of time.

Revenues are the value of assets exchanged for products and services provided to customers as part of a business's main operations. Assets are economic resources held by a business and include cash, equipment, buildings, and land. Later in the chapter, we will define assets more precisely. The income statement for Vertically Inclined's first month of operations is shown in Exhibit 2.2. It shows that Vertically Inclined earned total revenues of $4,100 during January: $3,800 from teaching revenue plus $300 from equipment rental revenue.

Revenues − Expenses = Net income or Net loss

For example:

$100 Revenues	−	$75 Expenses	=	$25 Net income
		OR		
$300 Revenues	−	$360 Expenses	=	$60 Net loss

Expenses are costs incurred or the using up of assets from generating revenue. The income statement in Exhibit 2.2 shows that Vertically Inclined used up some of its assets in paying for rented space. The $1,000 expense for rental space is reported in the income statement as rent expense. Vertically Inclined also paid for an employee's salary at a cost of $700. This is reported on the income statement as salaries expense. The income statement heading in Exhibit 2.2 identifies the business, the type of statement, and the time period covered. Knowledge of the time period is important for us in judging whether the $2,400 net income earned in January is satisfactory.

A **net income**, or **profit**, means that revenues are more than expenses. A **net loss** means that expenses are more than revenues.

An income statement lists the types and amounts of both revenues and expenses to help users understand and predict company performance. This detailed information is more useful for making decisions than a simple profit or loss number would be.

Statement of Changes in Equity

Equity is equal to total assets minus total liabilities; it represents how much of the assets *belong* to the owner. Equity increases with *owner investments* and net income and decreases with *owner withdrawals* and net loss. **Owner investments** occur when the owner transfers personal assets, such as cash, into the business. Since owner investments do not result from the sale of a product or service, they are ***not*** a revenue and are therefore not reported on the income statement. **Owner withdrawals**, or **withdrawals**, occur when the owner takes cash or other assets from the business. Withdrawals represent a distribution of net income to the owner. Since withdrawals do not help to create revenue, they are ***not*** expenses and therefore are not reported on the income statement.

Exhibit 2.2

Income Statement for Vertically Inclined Rock Gym

Vertically Inclined Rock Gym
Income Statement
For Month Ended January 31, 2011

Revenues:		
Teaching revenue	$ 3,800	
Equipment rental revenue	300	
Total revenues		$ 4,100
Operating expenses:		
Rent expense	$ 1,000	
Salaries expense	700	
Total operating expenses		1,700
Net income		$ 2,400

Exhibit 2.3

Statement of Changes in Equity for Vertically Inclined Rock Gym

Vertically Inclined Rock Gym
Statement of Changes in Equity
For Month Ended January 31, 2011

Virgil Klimb, capital, January 1		$ -0-
Add: Investments by owner	$10,000	
Net income	2,400	12,400
Total		$12,400
Less: Withdrawals by owner		600
Virgil Klimb, capital, January 31		$11,800

Exhibit 2.4

Balance Sheet for Vertically Inclined Rock Gym

Vertically Inclined Rock Gym
Balance Sheet
January 31, 2011

Assets		**Liabilities**		
Cash	$ 8,400	Accounts payable	$ 200	
Supplies	3,600	Notes payable	6,000	
Equipment	6,000	Total liabilities		$ 6,200
		Equity		
		Virgil Klimb, capital		11,800
Total assets	$18,000	Total liabilities and equity		$18,000

Exhibit 2.5

Statement of Cash Flows for Vertically Inclined Rock Gym

The arrows are imaginary but they emphasize the link between statements.

Vertically Inclined Rock Gym
Statement of Cash Flows
For Month Ended January 31, 2011

Cash flows from operating activities		
Cash received from clients	$ 4,100	
Cash paid for supplies	(3,400)	
Cash paid for rent	(1,000)	
Cash paid to employee	(700)	
Net cash used by operating activities		$ (1,000)
Cash flows from investing activities		-0-
Cash flows from financing activities		
Investment by owner	$10,000	
Withdrawal by owner	(600)	
Net cash provided by financing activities		9,400
Net increase in cash		$ 8,400
Cash balance, January 1		-0-
Cash balance, January 31		$ 8,400

The **statement of changes in equity** reports on changes in equity over the reporting period. This statement starts with beginning equity and adjusts it for transactions that (1) increase it (investments by the owner and net income), and (2) decrease it (owner withdrawals and net loss).

The statement of changes in equity for Vertically Inclined's first month of operations is shown in Exhibit 2.3. This statement describes transactions that changed equity during the month. It shows $10,000 of equity created by Virgil Klimb's initial investment. It also shows $2,400 of net income earned during the month. The statement also reports the owner's $600 withdrawal. Vertically Inclined's equity balance at the end of the month is $11,800.

Balance Sheet

The **balance sheet**, or **statement of financial position**, reports the financial position of a business at a point in time, usually at the end of a month or year. It describes financial position by listing the types and dollar amounts of *assets, liabilities,* and *equity*. **Assets** are the properties or economic resources held by a business. A common characteristic of assets is their ability to provide future benefits to the company.[1] A familiar asset is *cash*. Another is **accounts receivable**, an asset created by selling products or services on credit. It reflects amounts owed to a business by its credit customers. These customers, and other individuals and organizations who owe amounts to a business, are called its **debtors**. Other common assets include merchandise held for sale, supplies, equipment, buildings, and land. Discussed in Chapter 5 are other assets having intangible rights, such as those granted by a patent or copyright.

Liabilities are debts or obligations of a business. They are claims of others against the assets of the business. A common characteristic of liabilities is their capacity to reduce future assets or to require future services or products.[2] Typical liabilities include *accounts payable* and *notes payable*. An **account payable** is a liability created by buying products or services on credit. It reflects amounts owed to others. A **note payable** is a liability expressed by a written promise to make a future payment at a specific time. Other common liabilities are salaries and wages owed to employees, and interest payable.

Individuals and organizations who own the right to receive payments from a business are called its **creditors**. One entity's payable is another entity's receivable. If a business fails to pay its obligations, the law gives creditors a right to force sale of its assets to obtain the money to meet their claims. When assets are sold under these conditions, creditors are paid first but only up to the amount of their claims. Any remaining money goes to the owner of the business. Creditors often compare the amounts of liabilities and assets on a balance sheet to help them decide whether to lend money to a business. A loan is less risky if liabilities are small in comparison to assets, because there are more resources than claims on resources. A loan is more risky if liabilities are large compared to assets.

Equity is the owner's claim on the assets of a business. It represents the assets that remain after deducting liabilities,[3] called **net assets**. We explained that net income is the difference between revenues and expenses of a business over a period of time. Net income is also equal to the change in equity due to operating activities over a period of time. In this way, an income statement links balance sheets from the beginning and the end of a reporting period. The causes of changes in equity are highlighted in Exhibit 2.6. Changes in equity are reported in the statement of changes in equity, and give us the ending balance of equity that is reported in the balance sheet.

EXTEND YOUR KNOWLEDGE

2-1

[1] IFRS 2009, IAS 1, para. 15; "Framework," para. 53.
[2] IFRS 2009, IAS 1, para. 15; "Framework," para. 60.
[3] IFRS 2009, IAS 1, para. 15; "Framework," para. 65.

Exhibit 2.6

The Causes of Changes in Equity

Increases in equity are caused by:	**Decreases in equity are caused by:**
• owner investments • revenues	• owner withdrawals • expenses

Exhibit 2.4 shows the balance sheet for Vertically Inclined as of January 31, 2011. The balance sheet heading lists the business name, the statement, and the specific date on which assets and liabilities are identified and measured. The amounts in the balance sheet are measured as of the close of business on that specific date.

The balance sheet for Vertically Inclined shows that it has three different assets at the close of business on January 31, 2011. The assets are cash, supplies, and equipment, for a total dollar amount of $18,000. The balance sheet also shows total liabilities of $6,200. Equity is $11,800. Equity is the difference between assets and liabilities. The statement is named a *balance sheet* because: (1) the total amounts on both sides of the statement are equal; and (2) the reporting of assets, liabilities, and equity is in *balance*.

Statement of Cash Flows

The **statement of cash flows** describes the sources and uses of cash for a reporting period. It also reports the amount of cash at both the beginning and the end of a period. The statement of cash flows is organized by a company's major activities: operating, investing, and financing. Since a company must carefully manage cash if it is to survive and prosper, cash flow information is important.

As an example, the statement of cash flows for Vertically Inclined is shown in Exhibit 2.5 (notice that Vertically Inclined shows both operating and financing activities but it had no investing activities during January). To fully appreciate this financial statement, a solid understanding of some basic accounting concepts is required. Therefore, a detailed discussion has been left to Chapter 19.

Financial Statements and Forms of Organization

Chapter 1 described three different forms of business organization: sole proprietorships P. 4, partnerships P. 5, and corporations P. 5. Exhibit 2.7 summarizes key differences among these three forms of business ownership. While many differences exist, financial statements for these three types of organizations are very similar.

Exhibit 2.7

Financial Statement Differences Based on Type of Business Organization

	Type of Business Organization		
Difference	**Sole Proprietorship**	**Partnership**	**Corporation**
Equity on the balance sheet belongs to:	Sole owner	Partners	Shareholders
Distributions to owners are called:	Withdrawals	Withdrawals	Dividends
When managers are also owners, their salaries are:	Not an expense	Not an expense	An expense

EXTEND YOUR KNOWLEDGE

The emphasis in the early chapters of this book is on sole proprietorships. This allows us to focus on important measurement and reporting issues in accounting without getting caught up in the complexities of additional forms of organization. We do discuss other forms of organization, however, and provide examples when appropriate. Chapters 14, 15, and 16 return to this topic and provide additional detail about the financial statements of partnerships and corporations.

1. What are the four major financial statements?
2. Describe revenues and expenses.
3. Explain assets, liabilities, and equity.
4. What are three differences in financial statements for different forms of organization?

Do Quick Study question: QS 2-1

Generally Accepted Accounting Principles

LO2 | Identify, explain, and apply accounting principles.

The underlying concepts that make up acceptable accounting practices are referred to as **generally accepted accounting principles (GAAP)**. The responsibility for setting accounting principles in Canada has changed because of the adoption of **International Financial Reporting Standards (IFRS)**, as indicated in Chapter 1. Why IFRS instead of Canadian standards? Although professional accountants around the world all follow GAAP, how GAAP are interpreted and applied in the recording and reporting of accounting information differs from country to country. These differences can prevent investors, creditors, and other users of global accounting information from making the most informed decisions possible. To improve the comparability of accounting information, the **International Accounting Standards Board (IASB)** was established to try to achieve global agreement on the use of a common set of accounting standards, namely, IFRS. The long-term goal of the IASB is to have all countries use IFRS. IFRS adopters include the European Union, Australia, China, South Africa, Russia, Hong Kong, Malaysia, Canada, and others. With the signing of the Norwalk Agreement, the United States may soon adopt IFRS. Although IFRS have replaced Canadian accounting standards for publicly accountable enterprises (PAEs), the **Accounting Standards Board (AcSB)**, the body that originally governed accounting standards in Canada, will continue to be active in a new, evolving role, such as developing and maintaining GAAP for private enterprises (PEs).

Accounting principles must be understood in order for us to use and interpret financial statements effectively. A primary purpose of GAAP is to make information in financial statements *understandable, relevant, reliable,* and *comparable.* Information must have **understandability** to be useful to users with reasonable knowledge of accounting as well as business and economic activities. Information that has **relevance** can affect the types of decisions made by users. Information must have **reliability** for decision makers to depend on it. If companies use similar practices, users are able to compare companies and the information possesses **comparability**. GAAP impose limits on the range of accounting practices that companies can use. We describe in this section some of the important accounting principles.

Exhibit 2.8

Building Blocks of GAAP

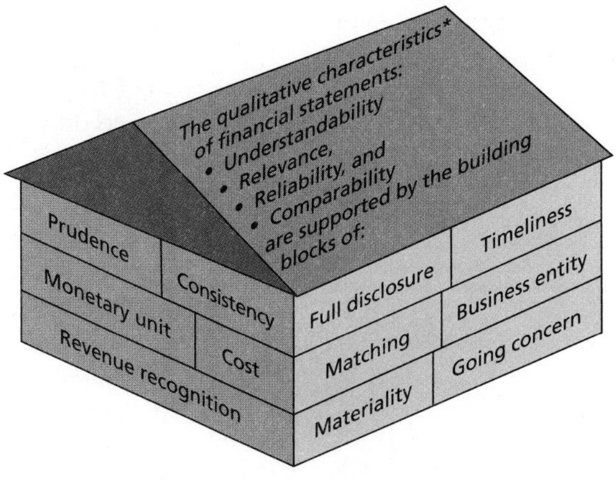

For ease of reference, these principles are also summarized on the inside cover of both Volumes 1 and 2 of the textbook.

*A complete discussion of the IFRS conceptual framework is beyond the scope of a fundamentals textbook and is left for a more advanced course.

Fundamental Building Blocks of Accounting

To use accounting information, we need an understanding of GAAP, the building blocks of accounting, so we emphasize them in the early chapters of this book. As described earlier, IFRS adoption in Canada is causing changes. *Because some of these changes have not yet been confirmed and may impact the underlying concepts related to GAAP, the approach of this textbook will be to focus on the core principles that are most relevant to an introductory textbook.* These are illustrated in Exhibit 2.8. The GAAP described in this chapter include: business entity, cost, going concern, monetary unit, and revenue recognition. General principles described in later chapters (with their relevant chapter in parentheses) include: timeliness (4), matching (4), materiality (7), full disclosure (6), and prudence (7).

Business Entity Principle

Each economic entity or business of the owner must keep accounting records separate from those of the owner and any other economic entity of the owner. Users want information about the performance of a specific entity. If information is mixed between two or more entities, its usefulness decreases.

Example: Looking at Vertically Inclined, Virgil Klimb must not include personal expenses, such as personal clothing and the cost of going to the movies, as expenses of his business.

EXTEND YOUR KNOWLEDGE

Cost Principle

All transactions are recorded based on the actual cash amount received or paid. In the absence of cash, the cash equivalent amount of the exchange is recorded.[4]

Example: If Vertically Inclined purchased used equipment for $5,000 cash, it is recorded in the accounting records at $5,000. It makes no difference if Virgil Klimb thinks that the value of the equipment is $7,000.

Going Concern Principle

Financial statement users assume that the statements reflect a business that is going to continue its operations instead of being closed or sold. Therefore, assets are maintained in the accounting records at cost and not reduced to a liquidation value as if the business were being bought or sold. If a company is to be bought or sold, buyers and sellers are advised to obtain additional information, such as estimated market values, from other sources.[5]

Example: It is assumed from a review of Vertically Inclined's financial statements that the business is continuing its operations, because information to the contrary is not included.

Monetary Unit Principle

Transactions are expressed using units of money as the common denominator. It is assumed that the monetary unit is stable; therefore, a transaction is left as originally recorded and is not later adjusted for changes in currency value or inflation. The greater the changes in currency value and inflation, the more difficult it is to use and interpret financial statements across time.

Example: Assume that in August 2011 Vertically Inclined purchased equipment from a supplier in the United States at a total cost of $1,000 (U.S.), or $1,489 (Cdn) ($1,000/0.6716 exchange rate). If the exchange rate changes several months later to 0.6412, Vertically Inclined does not restate the value of the equipment to $1,560 ($1,000/0.6412 current exchange rate). The equipment remains in the accounting records at $1,489 (Cdn). This is also consistent with the *cost principle.*

Revenue Recognition Principle

Revenue is recorded at the time that it is earned regardless of whether cash or another asset has been exchanged.[6] The amount of revenue to be recorded is measured by the cash plus the cash equivalent value (market value) of any other assets received.

Example: Assume that on April 3, Vertically Inclined performed work for a client in the amount of $600. The client did not pay the $600 until May 15. Revenue is recorded when actually earned on April 3 in the amount of $600, the value of the noncash asset received by Vertically Inclined. Alternatively, if

[4] IFRS 2009, IAS 16, para. 23.
[5] IFRS 2009, IAS 1, para. 25.
[6] IFRS 2009, IAS 18, para. 9–34; "Framework," para. 92–93.

Vertically Inclined received $1,000 on April 15 for work to be done next month, revenue is *not* recorded until the work is actually done in May.

5. Why is the business entity principle important?
6. Describe the cost principle and explain why it might be considered reliable.
7. A customer pays cash today for a product that is to be delivered to her next month. When should revenue be recognized?

Do Quick Study questions: QS 2-2, QS 2-3, QS 2-4

The Accounting Equation

LO3 Explain and interpret the accounting equation.

Notice in Exhibit 2.4 that there are two main sections of the balance sheet: assets on one side and liabilities and equity on the other side. Observe that the total assets of $18,000 equal the total liabilities and equity of $18,000. This equality is known as the *accounting equation*. This equation is based on relationships fundamental to accounting.

When an organization invests in assets, it is the result of an equal amount of financing. This relationship is expressed in the following equation:

Investing = Financing

Since invested amounts are referred to as *assets*, and financing is made up of owner and non-owner financing, we can also express this equality as:

Assets = Non-Owner Financing + Owner Financing

Non-owners are creditors. Creditors and owners hold claims or rights in the assets. Creditors' claims are called *liabilities* and the owner's claim is called *equity*. The equation can be rewritten as shown in Exhibit 2.9.

Exhibit 2.9

The Accounting Equation

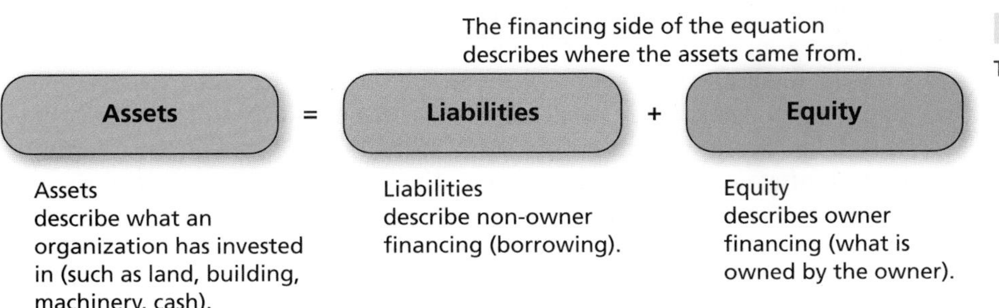

The financing side of the equation describes where the assets came from.
Assets = Liabilities + Equity
$25,000 = $15,000 + $10,000
Borrowing $15,000 from the bank has financed part of your investment.
You, the owner, have financed part of the investment in the car; you own $10,000 of the car; in other words, your equity in the car is $10,000.
Assets describe what an organization has invested in (such as land, building, machinery, cash).
Liabilities describe non-owner financing (borrowing).
Equity describes owner financing (what is owned by the owner).

It is called the **accounting equation** or **balance sheet equation** because of its link to the balance sheet. It describes the relationship between a company's assets, liabilities, and equity. To demonstrate, assume you want to buy a car that costs $25,000. The bank lends you $15,000 and you pay $10,000 out of your personal savings account.

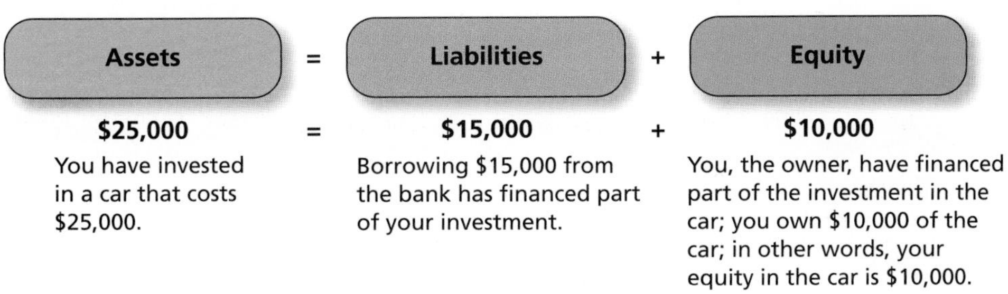

The accounting equation can be changed by moving liabilities to the left side of the equation:

$$\underbrace{\text{Assets} - \text{Liabilities}}_{\textit{Net assets}} = \text{Equity}$$

Assets less liabilities equals *net assets*, another name for equity.

Transactions and the Accounting Equation

LO4 Analyze business transactions using the accounting equation.

To fully reap the benefits of information in financial statements, we need to know how an accounting system captures transactions and reports the data in financial statements. In the next section, we show how to use the accounting equation to keep track of changes in a company's assets, liabilities, and equity in a way that provides useful information.

Transaction Analysis

CAUTION: The illustration of transaction analysis on the following pages is a learning tool to demonstrate the effects of transactions on the accounting equation. How transactions are recorded in the real world is the topic of Chapter 3.

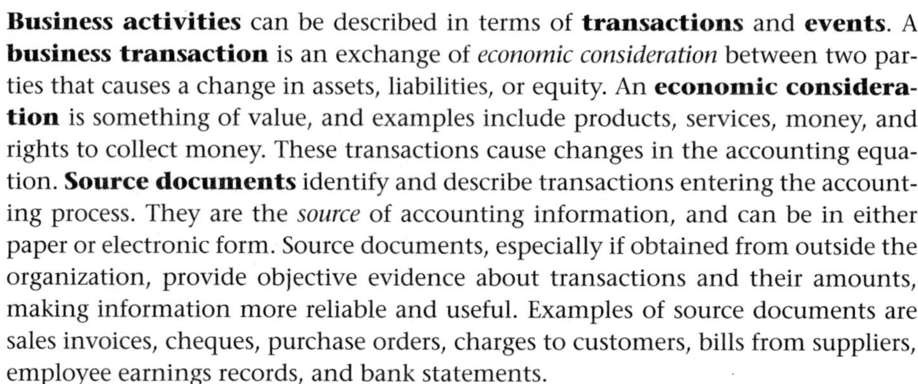

Business activities can be described in terms of **transactions** and **events**. A **business transaction** is an exchange of *economic consideration* between two parties that causes a change in assets, liabilities, or equity. An **economic consideration** is something of value, and examples include products, services, money, and rights to collect money. These transactions cause changes in the accounting equation. **Source documents** identify and describe transactions entering the accounting process. They are the *source* of accounting information, and can be in either paper or electronic form. Source documents, especially if obtained from outside the organization, provide objective evidence about transactions and their amounts, making information more reliable and useful. Examples of source documents are sales invoices, cheques, purchase orders, charges to customers, bills from suppliers, employee earnings records, and bank statements.

EXTEND YOUR KNOWLEDGE

Not all business activities are transactions. **Business events** are activities that do not involve an exchange of economic consideration between two parties and therefore do not affect the accounting equation. Examples include placing an order for supplies, interviewing job applicants, signing a contract, and making a hotel reservation for an out-of-town business trip.

Every transaction leaves the equation in balance. Assets *always* equal the sum of liabilities and equity. We show how this equality is maintained by looking at the assumed activities of Vertically Inclined Rock Gym in its first month of operations.

1. Investment by Owner. On January 1, 2011, Virgil Klimb formed his indoor rock climbing business and set it up as a sole proprietorship. Klimb is the owner and manager of the business. The marketing plan for the business is to focus primarily on providing a safe, high quality, indoor rock climbing facility that offers programs for novice, recreational, and expert climbers. Klimb invests $10,000 cash in the new company, which he deposits in a bank account opened under the name of Vertically Inclined Rock Gym. An exchange has taken place, so this is a transaction. Transactions affect the accounting equation. As shown, this transaction affects both Vertically Inclined's cash (an asset) and equity (called *Virgil Klimb, Capital*), each for $10,000.

	Assets	=	Liabilities	+	Equity	Explanation of Equity Transaction
	Cash	=			Virgil Klimb, Capital	
(1)	+$10,000	=			+$10,000	Investment by Owner

The source of increase in equity is identified as an investment to distinguish it from subsequent transactions affecting equity.

2. Purchase Supplies for Cash. Vertically Inclined uses $2,500 of its cash to purchase supplies. This is a transaction because it involves an exchange of cash, an asset, for another kind of asset, supplies. The transaction produces no expense because no value is lost. The decrease in cash is exactly equal to the increase in supplies. The equation remains in balance.

	Assets		=	Liabilities	+	Equity	Explanation of Equity Transaction
	Cash	**+ Supplies**	=			**Virgil Klimb, Capital**	
Old Bal.	$10,000		=			$10,000	
(2)	−$ 2,500	+$2,500					
New Bal.	$ 7,500 +	$2,500	=			$10,000	
	$10,000		=	$10,000			

3. Purchase Equipment and Supplies on Credit. The owner decides that the business needs equipment and more supplies; these purchases total $7,100. As we see from the accounting equation in (2) above, however, Vertically Inclined has only $7,500 in cash. Concerned that these purchases would use nearly all of Vertically Inclined's cash, Klimb arranges to purchase the items on credit from CanTech Supply Company. This is a transaction because an exchange has occurred: Vertically Inclined has acquired items in exchange for a promise to pay for them later. Supplies cost $1,100, and the equipment costs $6,000. The total liability to CanTech Supply is $7,100. Vertically Inclined will pay for the supplies in 30 days, but has arranged to pay for the equipment by signing a note. The effects of this transaction on the accounting equation are:

	Assets			=	Liabilities		+	Equity	Explanation of Equity Transaction
	Cash	**+ Supplies**	**+ Equipment**	=	**Accounts Payable**	**+ Notes Payable**	+	**Virgil Klimb, Capital**	
Old Bal.	$7,500	$2,500		=				$10,000	
(3)		+$1,100	+$6,000		+$1,100	+$6,000			
New Bal.	$7,500 +	$3,600 +	$6,000	=	$1,100 +	$6,000	+	$10,000	
	$17,100				$17,100				

This purchase increases assets by $7,100, while liabilities (called *accounts payable* and *notes payable*) increase by the same amount. Both of these payables are promises by Vertically Inclined to repay its debt, where the note payable reflects a more formal written agreement. We will discuss these liabilities in detail in later chapters.

4. Services Rendered for Cash. A primary objective of a business is to increase its owner's wealth. This goal is met when a business produces a profit, also called *net income*. Net income is reflected in the accounting equation as an increase in equity. Vertically Inclined earns revenues by teaching climbing in the specially constructed indoor gym, and renting equipment. On January 10, Vertically Inclined provides teaching services to a group of school children in exchange for $2,200 cash. This is a transaction since an exchange has taken place. When revenue is earned in exchange for cash, it affects the accounting equation by increasing cash and equity. Here, cash increases by $2,200 and equity also increases by

$2,200, identified in the far right column as a revenue. These explanations are useful in preparing and understanding a statement of changes in equity and an income statement.

	Assets			=	Liabilities		+	Equity	Explanation of Equity Transaction
	Cash	+ Supplies	+ Equipment	=	Accounts Payable	+ Notes Payable	+	Virgil Klimb, Capital	
Old Bal.	$7,500	+ $3,600	+ $6,000	=	$1,100	+ $6,000	+	$10,000	
(4)	+$2,200							+$ 2,200	Teaching Revenue
New Bal.	$9,700	+ $3,600	+ $6,000	=	$1,100	+ $6,000	+	$12,200	
		$19,300				$19,300			

5. and 6. Payment of Expenses in Cash. On January 10, Vertically Inclined pays its building landlord $1,000 to cover January's rent for space. Since an exchange has taken place, this is a transaction and affects the accounting equation as shown below in line (5). On January 14, Vertically Inclined pays the $700 salary of the business's only employee. This is also a transaction because an exchange has occurred, and it is therefore reflected in the accounting equation in line (6).

	Assets			=	Liabilities		+	Equity	Explanation of Equity Transaction
	Cash	+ Supplies	+ Equipment	=	Accounts Payable	+ Notes Payable	+	Virgil Klimb, Capital	
Old Bal.	$9,700	+ $3,600	+ $6,000	=	$1,100	+ $6,000	+	$12,200	
(5)	−$1,000							−$ 1,000	Rent Expense
Bal.	$8,700	+ $3,600	+ $6,000	=	$1,100	+ $6,000	+	$11,200	
(6)	−$ 700							−$ 700	Salaries Expense
New Bal.	$8,000	+ $3,600	+ $6,000	=	$1,100	+ $6,000	+	$10,500	
		$17,600				$17,600			

Both (5) and (6) produce expenses for Vertically Inclined as noted in the far right column. They use up cash for the purpose of providing services to clients. Unlike the asset purchase in (2), the cash payments in (5) and (6) acquire services. The benefits of these services do *not* last beyond the end of this month. The accounting equation remains in balance, and shows that both transactions reduce cash and Klimb's equity.

7. Service Contract Signed for February and March. On January 14, a customer and Virgil Klimb sign a $65,000 contract that requires Vertically Inclined to teach rock climbing to a group of executives as a team building exercise. Vertically Inclined is expected to perform the services during February and March.

	Assets			=	Liabilities		+	Equity	Explanation of Equity Transaction
	Cash	+ Supplies	+ Equipment	=	Accounts Payable	+ Notes Payable	+	Virgil Klimb, Capital	
Old Bal.	$8,000	+ $3,600	+ $6,000	=	$1,100	+ $6,000	+	$10,500	
(7)									
New Bal.	$8,000	+ $3,600	+ $6,000	=	$1,100	+ $6,000	+	$10,500	
		$17,600				$17,600			

This is a business event and ***not*** a business transaction because there was no economic exchange (nothing has yet been received by Vertically Inclined ***and*** nothing has been provided to the customer as of January 14). Therefore, this has no effect on the accounting equation.

8. Services and Rental Revenues Rendered for Credit. On January 15, Vertically Inclined provided teaching services of $1,600 and rented climbing equipment for $300 to a group of friends; the group's coordinator is billed for $1,900. This is a transaction because an exchange has occurred: Vertically Inclined provided services to a customer and in exchange received an asset, an account receivable, from the customer. The $1,900 increase in assets produces an equal increase in equity. Notice that the increase in equity is identified as two revenue components in the far right column of the accounting equation:

	Assets								=	Liabilities			+	Equity	Explanation of Equity Transaction
	Cash	+	Accounts Receivable	+	Supplies	+	Equipment		=	Accounts Payable	+	Notes Payable	+	Virgil Klimb, Capital	
Old Bal.	$8,000			+	$3,600	+	$6,000		=	$1,100	+	$6,000	+	$10,500	
(8)			+$1,900											+$ 1,600	Teaching Revenue
														+$ 300	Equipment Rental Revenue
New Bal.	$8,000	+	$1,900	+	$3,600	+	$6,000		=	$1,100	+	$6,000	+	$12,400	
			$19,500									$19,500			

9. Receipt of Cash on Account. The amount of $1,900 is received from the client on January 25, ten days after the billing for services in (8). This exchange between Vertically Inclined and the customer represents a transaction and therefore affects the accounting equation. This transaction does not change the total amount of assets and does not affect liabilities or equity. It converts the receivable to cash and *does not* create new revenue. Revenue was recognized when Vertically Inclined provided the services on January 15. Therefore, revenue is *not* recorded on January 25 when the cash is collected. The new balances are:

	Assets								=	Liabilities			+	Equity	Explanation of Equity Transaction
	Cash	+	Accounts Receivable	+	Supplies	+	Equipment		=	Accounts Payable	+	Notes Payable	+	Virgil Klimb, Capital	
Old Bal.	$8,000	+	$1,900	+	$3,600	+	$6,000		=	$1,100	+	$6,000	+	$12,400	
(9)	+$1,900		−$1,900												
New Bal.	$9,900	+	$ -0-	+	$3,600	+	$6,000		=	$1,100	+	$6,000	+	$12,400	
			$19,500									$19,500			

10. Payment of Accounts Payable. Vertically Inclined pays $900 to CanTech Supply on January 25. This is a transaction since an exchange has occurred between Vertically Inclined and CanTech Supply. It therefore affects the accounting equation, as shown on the next page. The $900 payment is for the earlier $1,100 purchase of supplies from CanTech, leaving $200 unpaid. The $6,000 amount due to CanTech for equipment remains unpaid. The accounting equation shows that this transaction decreases Vertically Inclined's cash by $900 and decreases its liability to CanTech Supply by the same amount. As a result, equity does not change. This transaction does not create an expense, even though cash flows out of Vertically Inclined.

	Assets				=	Liabilities	+	Equity	Explanation of Equity Transaction
	Cash	+ Accounts Receivable	+ Supplies	+ Equipment	=	Accounts Payable	+ Notes Payable	+ Virgil Klimb, Capital	
Old Bal.	$9,900	+ $ -0-	+ $3,600	+ $6,000	=	$1,100	+ $6,000	+ $12,400	
(10)	−$ 900					−$ 900			
New Bal.	$9,000	+ $ -0-	+ $3,600	+ $6,000	=	$ 200	+ $6,000	+ $12,400	
	$18,600					$18,600			

11. Withdrawal of Cash by Owner. Klimb withdraws $600 in cash from Vertically Inclined for personal living expenses. An exchange has taken place between the owner and the business, so this is a transaction and affects the accounting equation. Withdrawals are not expenses because they are not part of the company's earnings process. Therefore, withdrawals are not used in calculating net income.

	Assets				=	Liabilities	+	Equity	Explanation of Equity Transaction
	Cash	+ Accounts Receivable	+ Supplies	+ Equipment	=	Accounts Payable	+ Notes Payable	+ Virgil Klimb, Capital	
Old Bal.	$9,000	+ $ -0-	+ $3,600	+ $6,000	=	$ 200	+ $6,000	+ $12,400	
(11)	−$ 600							−$ 600	Withdrawal by Owner
New Bal.	$8,400	+ $ -0-	+ $3,600	+ $6,000	=	$ 200	+ $6,000	+ $11,800	
	$18,000					$18,000			

Summary of Transactions

Summarized in Exhibit 2.10 are the effects of all of Vertically Inclined's January transactions using the accounting equation. Five points should be noted.

1. The accounting equation remains in balance after every transaction.
2. Transactions can be analyzed by their effects on components of the accounting equation. For example, total assets and equity increase by equal amounts in (1), (4), and (8). In (2) and (9), one asset increases while another decreases by an equal amount. For (3), we see equal increases in assets and liabilities. Both assets and equity decrease by equal amounts in (5), (6), and (11). In (10), we see equal decreases in an asset and a liability.
3. Transactions cause assets, liabilities, or equity to change. Notice in Exhibit 2.10 that (1)–(6) and (8)–(11) caused changes to the accounting equation because each transaction involved an exchange; (7) did not involve an exchange and so did not affect the accounting equation.
4. The format of the preceding analysis was used to demonstrate the effects of transactions on the components of the accounting equation; transactions in the real world are not recorded in this manner.
5. The equality of effects in the accounting equation is fundamental to the *double-entry accounting system* that is discussed in the next chapter.

Exhibit 2.10

Summary Analysis of Vertically Inclined's Transactions Using the Accounting Equation

	Assets				=	Liabilities	+	Equity	Explanation of Equity Transaction
	Cash	+ Accounts Receivable	+ Supplies	+ Equipment	=	Accounts Payable	+ Notes Payable	+ Virgil Klimb, Capital	
(1)	$10,000							$10,000	Investment by Owner
(2)	− 2,500		+$ 2,500						
Bal.	$ 7,500		$ 2,500					$10,000	
(3)			+1,100	+6,000		+$1,100	+$6,000		
Bal.	$ 7,500		$ 3,600	$6,000		$1,100	$6,000	$10,000	
(4)	+ 2,200							+ 2,200	Teaching Revenue
Bal.	$ 9,700		$ 3,600	$6,000		$1,100	$6,000	$12,200	
(5)	− 1,000							− 1,000	Rent Expense
Bal.	$ 8,700		$ 3,600	$6,000		$1,100	$6,000	$11,200	
(6)	− 700							− 700	Salaries Expense
Bal.	$ 8,000		$ 3,600	$6,000		$1,100	$6,000	$10,500	
(7)	No entry*								
(8)		+$ 1,900						+ 1,600	Teaching Revenue
								+ 300	Equipment Rental Revenue
Bal.	$ 8,000	$ 1,900	$ 3,600	$6,000		$1,100	$6,000	$12,400	
(9)	+ 1,900	−1,900							
Bal.	$ 9,900	$ -0-	$ 3,600	$6,000		$1,100	$6,000	$12,400	
(10)	− 900					− 900			
Bal.	$ 9,000	$ -0-	$ 3,600	$6,000		$ 200	$6,000	$12,400	
(11)	− 600							− 600	Withdrawal by Owner
Bal.	$ 8,400	+ $ -0-	+ $ 3,600	+ $6,000	=	$ 200	+ $6,000	+ $11,800	
	$18,000					$18,000			

*Note: (7) did not involve an economic transaction between two parties, so it is an event and does not affect the accounting equation.

It is important to recognize that the accounting equation is a representation of the balance sheet. Therefore, we can take the information in Exhibit 2.10 and prepare financial statements for Vertically Inclined. This will be done in the next section.

8. How can a transaction *not* affect liability and equity accounts?
9. Describe a transaction that increases equity and one that decreases it.
10. Identify a transaction that decreases both assets and liabilities.
11. When is the accounting equation in balance, and what does it mean?
12. Explain the difference between a transaction and an event.
13. Identify examples of accounting source documents.
14. Explain the importance of source documents.

Do Quick Study questions: QS 2-5, QS 2-6, QS 2-7, QS 2-8, QS 2-9, QS 2-10

mid-chapter demonstration problem

Part A

Bob Delgado founded a new moving firm as a proprietorship on May 1. The accounting equation showed the following *balances* after each of the company's first five transactions. Analyze the equations and describe each of the five transactions with their amounts.

	Assets									=	Liabilities	+	Equity
Transaction	**Cash**	+	**Accounts Receivable**	+	**Office Supplies**	+	**Truck**	+	**Office Furniture**	=	**Accounts Payable**	+	**Bob Delgado, Capital**
1	$10,000		$ -0-		$ -0-		$45,000		$ -0-		$ -0-		$55,000
2	9,000		-0-		-0-		45,000		1,000		-0-		55,000
3	9,000		-0-		-0-		45,000		6,000		5,000		55,000
4	9,000		3,000		-0-		45,000		6,000		5,000		58,000
5	11,000		1,000		-0-		45,000		6,000		5,000		58,000

Part B

During June, Bob Delgado's second month of operations, transactions occurred, resulting in a $68,000 balance in the column 'Bob Delgado, Capital.' Calculate the net income or loss for June under each of the following independent situations:

1. Bob made no investments or withdrawals during June.
2. Bob invested $15,000 during June and made no withdrawals.
3. Bob withdrew a total of $5,000 during June and made no additional investments.
4. Bob invested $5,000 during June and made withdrawals of $3,000.

Analysis component:

Several activities cause equity to change. Of those activities, which one will help build equity over the long term?

solution

Part A

1. Started the business by investing $10,000 cash and a $45,000 truck.
2. Purchased $1,000 of office furniture by paying cash.
3. Purchased $5,000 of office furniture on account.
4. Billed a customer $3,000 for services performed.
5. Collected $2,000 from a credit customer.

Part B

1.

Assets	=	Liabilities	+	Equity	
$63,000		$5,000		$58,000	Beginning capital on June 1
				+ 0	Plus owner investments during June
				− 0	Less owner withdrawals during June
				+ 10,000	**Plus net income (less net loss) realized during June**
				= $68,000	Equals ending capital on June 30

Calculations: $68,000 − $58,000 = $10,000 net income.

2.

Assets	=	Liabilities	+	Equity	
$63,000		$5,000		$58,000	Beginning capital on June 1
				+ 15,000	Plus owner investments during June
				− 0	Less owner withdrawals during June
				− 5,000	**Plus net income (less net loss) realized during June**
				= $68,000	Equals ending capital on June 30

Calculations: $68,000 − $15,000 − $58,000 = $5,000 net loss.

3.

Assets	=	Liabilities	+	Equity	
$63,000		$5,000		$58,000	Beginning capital on June 1
				+ 0	Plus owner investments during June
				− 5,000	Less owner withdrawals during June
				+ 15,000	**Plus net income (less net loss) realized during June**
				= $68,000	Equals ending capital on June 30

Calculations: $68,000 + $5,000 − $58,000 = $15,000 net income.

4.

Assets	=	Liabilities	+	Equity	
$63,000		$5,000		$58,000	Beginning capital on June 1
				+ 5,000	Plus owner investments during June
				− 3,000	Less owner withdrawals during June
				+ 8,000	**Plus net income (less net loss) realized during June**
				= $68,000	Equals ending capital on June 30

Calculations: $68,000 + $3,000 − $5,000 − $58,000 = $8,000 net income.

Analysis component:

Equity increases because of owner investments and net income (when revenues are greater than expenses) and decreases because of owner withdrawals and net losses (when expenses are greater than revenues). Recurring net income will help build (or grow) equity over the long term.

Financial Statements

LO5 Prepare financial statements reflecting business transactions.

We illustrated financial statements at the beginning of this chapter. These statements are required under GAAP. In this section, we describe how the financial statements shown in Exhibits 2.2 to 2.4 were prepared from the business transactions summarized in Exhibit 2.10. The statement of cash flows, Exhibit 2.5, is left to Chapter 19.

Income Statement

Vertically Inclined's income statement is shown on the right side of Exhibit 2.11. It was prepared using revenue and expense information taken from the equity column in Exhibit 2.10, copied in Exhibit 2.11 on the left side.

Exhibit 2.11

Vertically Inclined's Financial Statements

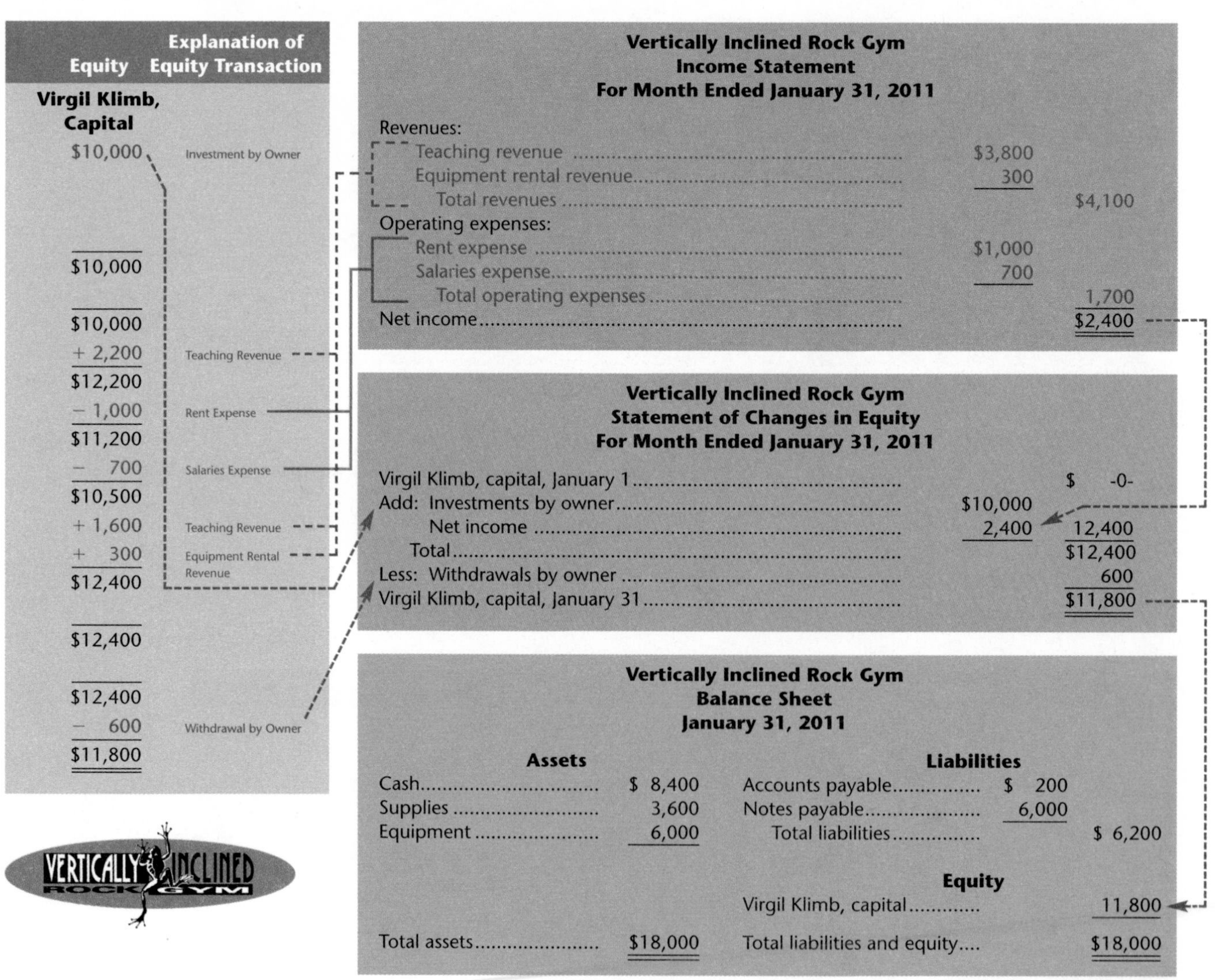

Equity: Virgil Klimb, Capital	Explanation of Equity Transaction
$10,000	Investment by Owner
$10,000	
$10,000	
+ 2,200	Teaching Revenue
$12,200	
− 1,000	Rent Expense
$11,200	
− 700	Salaries Expense
$10,500	
+ 1,600	Teaching Revenue
+ 300	Equipment Rental Revenue
$12,400	
$12,400	
$12,400	
− 600	Withdrawal by Owner
$11,800	

Vertically Inclined Rock Gym
Income Statement
For Month Ended January 31, 2011

Revenues:		
Teaching revenue	$3,800	
Equipment rental revenue	300	
Total revenues		$4,100
Operating expenses:		
Rent expense	$1,000	
Salaries expense	700	
Total operating expenses		1,700
Net income		$2,400

Vertically Inclined Rock Gym
Statement of Changes in Equity
For Month Ended January 31, 2011

Virgil Klimb, capital, January 1		$ -0-
Add: Investments by owner	$10,000	
Net income	2,400	12,400
Total		$12,400
Less: Withdrawals by owner		600
Virgil Klimb, capital, January 31		$11,800

Vertically Inclined Rock Gym
Balance Sheet
January 31, 2011

Assets		**Liabilities**		
Cash	$ 8,400	Accounts payable	$ 200	
Supplies	3,600	Notes payable	6,000	
Equipment	6,000	Total liabilities		$ 6,200
		Equity		
		Virgil Klimb, capital		11,800
Total assets	$18,000	Total liabilities and equity		$18,000

Revenues of $4,100 are reported first and include teaching revenues of $3,800 ($2,200 + $1,600) plus equipment rental revenue of $300. Expenses follow revenues, and can be listed in different ways. For convenience in this chapter, we list larger amounts first. Rent of $1,000 and salaries expenses of $700 result in total operating expenses of $1,700. Net income is reported at the bottom and is the amount earned during January. Owner's investments and withdrawals are *not* part of measuring income; they are shown on the statement of changes in equity.

Statement of Changes in Equity

The second report in Exhibit 2.11 is the statement of changes in equity for Vertically Inclined. Its heading lists the month as January 2011 because this statement describes transactions that happened during that month. The beginning balance of equity is measured as of the start of business on January 1. It is zero because Vertically Inclined did not exist before then. An existing business reports the beginning balance as of the end of the prior reporting period. Vertically Inclined's statement shows that $10,000 of equity is created by Virgil Klimb's initial investment. It also shows the $2,400 of net income earned during the month. This item links the income statement to the statement of changes in equity as shown in Exhibit 2.11. The statement also reports the owner's $600 withdrawal and Vertically Inclined's $11,800 equity balance at the end of the month.

Balance Sheet

The balance sheet in Exhibit 2.11 is the same statement that we described in Exhibit 2.4. Its heading tells us that the statement refers to Vertically Inclined's financial position at the close of business on January 31, 2011. ***Notice that the amounts appearing on the balance sheet came from the column totals summarized in Exhibit 2.10.***

The left side of the balance sheet lists Vertically Inclined's assets: cash, supplies, and equipment. The right side of the balance sheet shows that Vertically Inclined owes $6,200 to creditors, an amount made up of $200 for accounts payable and $6,000 for notes payable. The equity section shows an ending balance of $11,800. Note the link between the ending balance from the statement of changes in equity and the equity balance of the capital account. Also, note that the balance sheet equation, Assets = Liabilities + Equity, is still true ($18,000 = $6,200 + $11,800).

The financial statements for Vertically Inclined can be useful to both internal and external users for making decisions.

Supplier

You open your own wholesale business, selling home entertainment equipment to small retail outlets. You quickly find that most of your potential customers demand to buy on credit. How can you use the balance sheet in deciding to which customers you wish to extend credit?

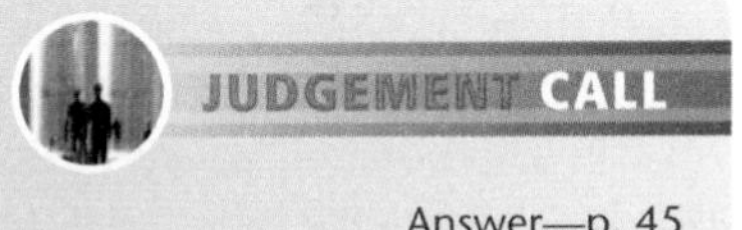

Answer—p. 45

15. Explain the link between an income statement and the statement of changes in equity.

16. Describe the link between a balance sheet and the statement of changes in equity.

Do Quick Study questions: QS 2-11, QS 2-12, QS 2-13, QS 2-14

CRITICAL THINKING CHALLENGE

Refer to the Critical Thinking Challenge questions at the beginning of the chapter on page 25. Compare your answers to those suggested on Connect at www.mcgrawhillconnect.ca.

IFRS HIGHLIGHTS 

The suggested titles of the four basic financial statements are: statement of financial position (called balance sheet in this textbook), statement of income, statement of cash flows, and statement of changes in equity; however, other titles may be used (IAS 1, para. 10).

The ordering of the line items and categories is not prescribed (IAS 1, para. 57).

A discussion paper is reviewing a change in format of the statement of income and balance sheet to group line items by whether they are an operating, investing, or financing activity to be consistent with the statement of cash flows (DP October, 2008).

The Conceptual Framework Joint Project may result in changes to the framework which sets out the concepts that underlie the preparation and presentation of financial statements for external users commonly referred to as the generally accepted accounting principles or GAAP.*

***SOURCE:** http://www.fasb.org/project/conceptual_framework.shtml

Summary

LO1 | Identify and explain the content and reporting aims of financial statements. The major financial statements are: income statement (shows a company's profitability determined as revenues less expenses equals net income or loss), statement of changes in equity (explains how equity changes from the beginning to the end of a period), balance sheet (reports on a company's financial position, including assets, liabilities, and equity), and statement of cash flows (identifying all cash inflows and outflows for the period). The differences in financial statements across forms of business organization are: 1. The equity on the balance sheet belongs to: the sole owner in a sole proprietorship, the partners in a partnership, and the shareholders in a corporation; 2. Distributions of assets to the owner(s) are called withdrawals for both a sole proprietorship and a partnership, and dividends for a corporation; 3. When the owner of a proprietorship or partnership is its manager, no salary expense is reported, while in a corporation, salaries paid to managers who are also shareholders are reported as expenses.

LO2 | Identify, explain, and apply accounting principles. Accounting principles aid in producing understandable, relevant, reliable, and comparable information. The general principles described in this chapter include: business entity, cost, going concern, monetary unit, and revenue recognition. We will discuss others in later chapters. The business entity principle means that a business is accounted for separately from its owners. The cost principle means that financial statements are based on actual costs incurred in business transactions. The going concern principle means that financial statements reflect an assumption that the business continues to operate. The monetary unit principle assumes that transactions can be captured in money terms and that the monetary unit is stable over time. The revenue recognition principle means that revenue is recognized when earned, assets received from selling products and services do not have to be in cash, and revenue recognized is measured by cash received plus the cash equivalent (market) value of other assets received.

LO3 | Explain and interpret the accounting equation. Investing activities are funded by an organization's financing activities. An organization's assets (investments) must equal its financing (from liabilities and from equity). This basic relation gives us the accounting equation: Assets = Liabilities + Equity.

LO4 | Analyze business transactions using the accounting equation. A transaction is an exchange of economic consideration between two parties and affects the accounting equation. The equation is always in balance when business transactions are properly recorded. An economic consideration is something of value; examples include products, services, money, and rights to collect money. Source documents are the source of accounting information. An event does not involve an economic exchange; it has no effect on the accounting equation.

LO5 | Prepare financial statements reflecting business transactions. Using the accounting equation, business transactions can be summarized and organized so that we can readily prepare the financial statements. The balance sheet uses the ending balances in the accounting equation at a point in time. The statement of changes in equity and the income statement use data from the equity account for the period.

guidance answer to JUDGEMENT CALL

Supplier
We can use the balance sheet, or accounting equation, to help us identify risky customers to whom we would not want to extend credit. The accounting equation can be written as: Assets − Liabilities = Equity. A balance sheet provides us with amounts for each of these key components. The lower the equity, the less likely you should be to extend credit. A low equity means that there is little value in the business on which other creditors do not already have claims. Note that any decision to grant credit would normally include an examination of the complete financial statements.

guidance answers to CHECKPOINT

Read Apply Do Check

1. The four major financial statements are: income statement, statement of changes in equity, balance sheet, and statement of cash flows.
2. Revenues are the value of assets received in exchange for products or services provided to customers as part of a business's main operations. Expenses are costs incurred or the using up of assets that results from providing products or services to customers. Expenses also can arise from increases in liabilities.
3. Assets are the properties or economic resources owned by a business. Liabilities are the obligations of a business, representing the claims of others against the assets of a business. Equity is the owner's claim on the assets of the business. It is the assets of a business that remain after deducting liabilities.
4. Three differences in financial statements for different forms of organization are: (i) A proprietorship's equity belongs to one owner. A partnership's equity belongs to the partners. A corporation's equity belongs to the shareholders. (ii) Distributions of cash or other assets to owners of a proprietorship or partnership are called withdrawals. Distributions of cash or other assets to owners of a corporation are called dividends. (iii) When the owner of a sole proprietorship is also its manager, no salary expense is reported on the income statement. The same is true for a partnership. In a corporation, however, salaries paid to all employees, including managers who are shareholders, are reported as expenses.
5. The business entity principle is important to the usefulness of accounting. Users desire information about the performance of a *specific* entity. If information is mixed between two or more entities, its usefulness decreases. It is imperative that the business entity principle be followed.
6. The cost principle determines that financial statements are based on actual costs incurred in business transactions. Information prepared using the cost principle is considered reliable because it can be verified and is not subject to arbitrary manipulation.
7. Revenue should be recognized next month when the product is delivered, according to the revenue recognition principle. This principle states that revenue is recognized when the product has been provided and not necessarily when cash has been received. In this case, the business has received the cash from the customer without providing the product. Therefore, the business has not realized a revenue but instead has incurred a liability; it owes the customer the product.
8. A transaction that involves changing the form of one asset for another asset would *not* affect any liability and equity accounts. (2) offers an example.
9. Performing services for a customer, such as in (4), increases the equity (and assets). Incurring expenses while servicing clients, such as in (5) and (6), decreases the equity (and assets). Other examples include owner investments (1) that increase equity, and owner withdrawals (11) that decrease equity.
10. Payment of a liability with an asset reduces both asset and liability totals. An example is (10), where an account payable is settled by paying cash.
11. The accounting equation is: Assets = Liabilities + Equity. It is in balance when the sum of the assets is equal to the sum of the liabilities and equity accounts. This equation is always in balance, both before and after every transaction. Balance refers to the equality in this equation, which is always maintained.
12. Business transactions are exchanges between two parties and affect the accounting equation. Events do not involve an exchange and therefore do not affect the accounting equation.
13. Examples of source documents are sales invoices, cheques, purchase orders, charges to customers, bills from suppliers, employee earnings records, and bank statements.
14. Source documents serve many purposes, including recordkeeping and internal control. Source documents, especially if obtained from outside the organization, provide evidence about transactions and their

amounts for recording. Evidence is important because it makes information more reliable and useful.

15. An income statement describes a company's revenues and expenses along with the resulting net income or loss. A statement of changes in equity describes changes in equity that *include* net income or loss. Also, both statements report transactions occurring over a period of time.

16. A balance sheet describes a company's financial position (assets, liabilities, and equity) at a point in time. The equity account in the balance sheet is obtained from the statement of changes in equity.

demonstration problem

After several months of planning, Joane Cardinal started a haircutting business called The Cutlery. The following business activities occurred during its first month, August 2011:

a. On August 1, Cardinal put $16,000 cash into a chequing account in the name of The Cutlery. She also invested $10,000 of equipment that she already owned.

b. On August 2, she paid $2,000 cash for furniture for the shop.

c. On August 3, she paid $3,200 cash to rent space in a strip mall for August.

d. On August 4, she equipped the shop by installing the old equipment and some new equipment that she bought on credit for $21,000. This amount is to be repaid in three equal payments at the end of August, September, and October.

e. On August 5, The Cutlery opened for business. Receipts from services provided for cash in the first week and a half of business (ended August 15) were $1,100.

f. On August 15, Cardinal provided haircutting services on account for $750.

g. On August 17, Cardinal received a $750 cheque in the mail for services previously rendered on account.

h. On August 17, Cardinal paid wages of $250 to an assistant for working during the grand opening.

i. On August 18, Cardinal interviewed a job applicant. The applicant was successful in getting the position and will receive $750 per week for part-time work starting in September.

j. Cash receipts from services provided during the second half of August were $1,950.

k. On August 31, Cardinal paid an installment on the account payable created in (d).

l. On August 31, the August hydro bill for $450 was received. It will be paid on September 14.

m. On August 31, Cardinal withdrew $500 cash for her personal use.

Required

1. Arrange the following asset, liability, and equity titles in a table similar to the one in Exhibit 2.10: Cash; Accounts Receivable; Furniture; Store Equipment; Accounts Payable; and Joane Cardinal, Capital. Show the effects of each transaction on the equation. Explain each of the changes in equity.
2. Prepare an income statement for August.
3. Prepare a statement of changes in equity for August.
4. Prepare a balance sheet as of August 31.

Analysis component:

a. Identify how much of the assets held by The Cutlery are owned by the owner, Joane Cardinal.

b. How much of the total assets are financed by equity? by debt? Explain what it means to 'finance assets by equity' and to 'finance assets by debt.'

Planning the Solution

- Set up a table with the appropriate columns, including a final column for describing the transactions that affect equity.
- Identify and analyze each transaction and show its effects as increases or decreases in the appropriate columns. Be sure that the accounting equation remains in balance after each transaction.
- To prepare the income statement, find the revenues and expenses in the Explanation of Equity Transaction column. List those items on the statement, calculate the difference, and label the result as *net income* or *net loss*.
- Use the information in the Explanation of Equity Transaction column to prepare the statement of changes in equity.
- Use the information in the last row of the table to prepare the balance sheet.
- Prepare an answer to each part of the **analysis component** question.

solution

1.

	Assets				= Liabilities	+ Equity	Explanation of Equity Transaction
	Cash +	Accounts Receivable +	Furniture +	Store Equipment	= Accounts Payable +	Joane Cardinal, Capital	
a.	$16,000			$10,000		$26,000	Investment by Owner
b.	− 2,000		+$2,000				
Bal.	$14,000		$2,000	$10,000		$26,000	
c.	− 3,200					− 3,200	Rent Expense
Bal.	$10,800		$2,000	$10,000		$22,800	
d.				+21,000	+$21,000		
Bal.	$10,800		$2,000	$31,000	$21,000	$22,800	
e.	+ 1,100					+ 1,100	Haircutting Services Revenue
Bal.	$11,900		$2,000	$31,000	$21,000	$23,900	
f.		+$750				+ 750	Haircutting Services Revenue
Bal.	$11,900	$750	$2,000	$31,000	$21,000	$24,650	
g.	+ 750	− 750					
Bal.	$12,650	$ -0-	$2,000	$31,000	$21,000	$24,650	
h.	− 250					− 250	Wages Expense
Bal.	$12,400		$2,000	$31,000	$21,000	$24,400	
i.	No entry*						
j.	+ 1,950					+ 1,950	Haircutting Services Revenue
Bal.	$14,350		$2,000	$31,000	$21,000	$26,350	
k.	− 7,000				− 7,000		
Bal.	$ 7,350		$2,000	$31,000	$14,000	$26,350	
l.					+ 450	− 450	Hydro Expense
Bal.	$ 7,350		$2,000	$31,000	$14,450	$25,900	
m.	− 500					− 500	Withdrawal by Owner
Bal.	$ 6,850 +	$ -0- +	$2,000 +	$31,000	= $14,450 +	$25,400	
	= $39,850				= $39,850		

*Note: (i) does not involve an economic exchange between two parties; therefore it does not affect the accounting equation.

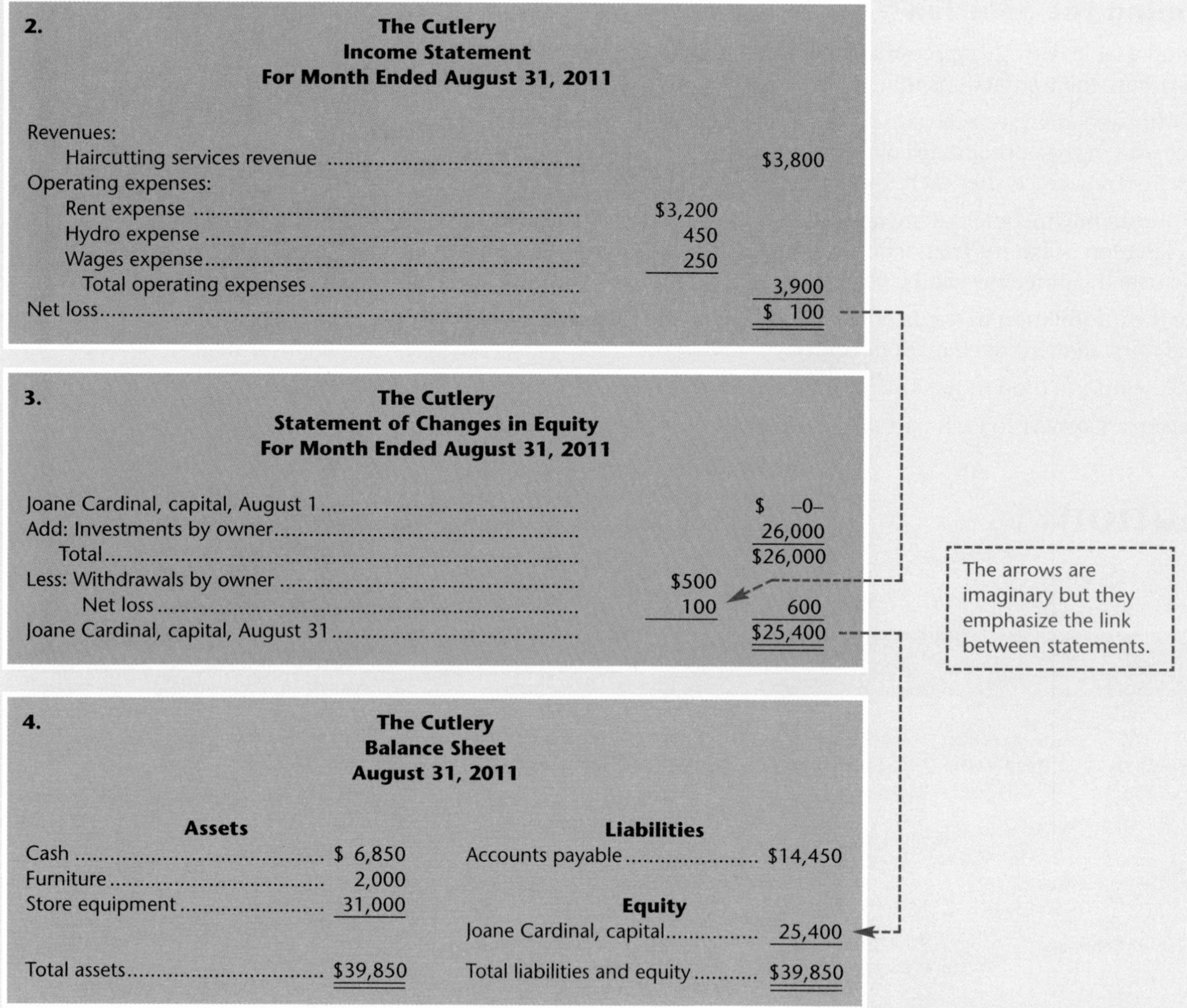

2.

The Cutlery
Income Statement
For Month Ended August 31, 2011

Revenues:		
Haircutting services revenue		$3,800
Operating expenses:		
Rent expense	$3,200	
Hydro expense	450	
Wages expense	250	
Total operating expenses		3,900
Net loss		$ 100

3.

The Cutlery
Statement of Changes in Equity
For Month Ended August 31, 2011

Joane Cardinal, capital, August 1		$ -0-
Add: Investments by owner		26,000
Total		$26,000
Less: Withdrawals by owner	$500	
Net loss	100	600
Joane Cardinal, capital, August 31		$25,400

The arrows are imaginary but they emphasize the link between statements.

4.

The Cutlery
Balance Sheet
August 31, 2011

Assets		**Liabilities**	
Cash	$ 6,850	Accounts payable	$14,450
Furniture	2,000		
Store equipment	31,000	**Equity**	
		Joane Cardinal, capital	25,400
Total assets	$39,850	Total liabilities and equity	$39,850

Analysis component:

a. \$25,400 or 64% (\$25,400/\$39,850 × 100% = 63.74% or 64%) of the total assets are owned by the owner, Joane Cardinal.

b. \$25,400 or 64% (\$25,400/\$39,850 × 100 = 63.74% or 64%) of the total assets are financed by equity. \$14,450 or 36% (\$14,450/\$39,850 × 100% = 36.26% or 36%) of the total assets are financed by debt.

To *finance assets by equity* means that the equity transactions of owner investment, plus net income (or less net loss), and less owner withdrawals resulted in a portion of the assets. In the case of The Cutlery, 64% of the assets at August 31, 2011, resulted from these equity transactions.

To *finance assets by debt* (or liabilities) means that a portion of the assets resulted from borrowings. In the case of The Cutlery, 36% of the assets at August 31, 2011, resulted from, specifically, accounts payable.

Glossary

Accounting equation A description of the relationship between a company's assets, liabilities, and equity; expressed as Assets = Liabilities + Equity; also called the *balance sheet equation.* (p. 33)

Accounting Standards Board (AcSB) Prior to Canada's adoption of IFRS, the AcSB was the authoritative body that set accounting standards for Canada. With IFRS being set by the IASB, the AcSB's new role is evolving. (p. 31)

Account payable A liability created by buying goods or services on credit. (p. 29)

Accounts receivable Assets created by selling products or services on credit. (p. 29)

AcSB See *Accounting Standards Board.* (p. 31)

Assets Properties or economic resources owned by the business; more precisely, resources with an ability to provide future benefits to the business. (p. 29)

Balance sheet A financial statement that reports the financial position of a business at a point in time; lists the types and dollar amounts of assets, liabilities, and equity as of a specific date; also called the *statement of financial position.* (p. 29)

Balance sheet equation Another name for the *accounting equation.* (p. 33)

Business activities All of the transactions and events experienced by a business. (p. 34)

Business entity principle The principle that requires every business to be accounted for separately from its owner or owners; based on the goal of providing relevant information about each business to users. (p. 32)

Business events Activities that do not involve an exchange of economic consideration between two parties and therefore do not affect the accounting equation. (p. 34)

Business transaction An exchange of economic consideration between two parties that causes a change in assets, liabilities, or equity. Examples of economic considerations include products, services, money, and rights to collect money. (p. 34)

Calendar year An accounting year that begins on January 1 and ends on December 31. (p. 27)

Comparability Similarity; ability to be compared with other information. (p. 31)

Cost principle The accounting principle that requires financial statement information to be based on actual costs incurred in business transactions; it requires assets and services to be recorded initially at the cash or cash equivalent amount given in exchange. (p. 32)

Creditors Individuals or organizations entitled to receive payments from a company. (p. 29)

Debtors Individuals or organizations that owe amounts to a business. (p. 29)

Economic consideration Something of value (e.g., products, services, money, and rights to collect money). (p. 34)

Equity The owner's claim on the assets of a business; more precisely, the assets of an entity that remain after deducting its liabilities. Increases with owner investments and net income and decreases with owner withdrawals and net loss, also called *net assets.* (pp. 27, 29)

Expenses Costs incurred or the using up of assets as a result of the major or central operations of a business. (p. 27)

Events See *business events.* (p. 34)

Financial statements The most important products of accounting; include the income statement, statement of changes in equity, balance sheet, and statement of cash flows. (p. 26)

Fiscal year A one-year reporting period. (p. 27)

GAAP See *generally accepted accounting principles.* (p. 31)

Generally accepted accounting principles The underlying concepts adopted by the accounting profession that make up acceptable accounting practices for the preparation of financial statements. (p. 31)

Going concern principle The rule that requires financial statements to reflect the assumption that the business will continue operating instead of being closed or sold, unless evidence shows that it will not continue. (p. 32)

IASB See *International Accounting Standards Board.* (p. 31)

IFRS See *International Financial Reporting Standards.* (p. 31)

Income statement The financial statement that shows, by subtracting expenses from revenues, whether the business earned a profit; it lists the types and amounts of revenues earned and expenses incurred by a business over a period of time. (p. 27)

International Accounting Standards Board (IASB) The body responsible for setting IFRS. (p. 31)

International Financial Reporting Standards (IFRS) The standards for financial reporting coming into effect January 2011 in Canada for publicly accountable entities. (p. 31)

Liabilities The debts or obligations of a business; claims by others that will reduce the future assets of a business or require future services or products. (p. 29)

Monetary unit principle The expression of transactions in money units; examples include units such as the Canadian dollar, American dollar, peso, and pound sterling. (p. 32)

Natural business year A 12-month period that ends when a company's sales activities are at their lowest point. (p. 27)

Net assets Assets minus liabilities; another name for *equity.* (p. 29)

Net income The excess of revenues over expenses for a period; also called *profit.* (p. 27)

Net loss The excess of expenses over revenues for a period. (p. 27)

Note payable A liability expressed by a written promise to make a future payment at a specific time. (p. 29)

Owner investments The transfer of an owner's personal assets to the business. (p. 27)

Owner withdrawals See *withdrawals.* (p. 27)

Profit Another name for *net income*. (p. 27)

Relevance Information must make a difference in the decision-making process. (p. 31)

Reliability The extent to which information is verifiable and neutral; implies a consensus among different measures. (p. 31)

Revenue recognition principle Provides guidance on when revenue should be reflected on the income statement; the rule states that revenue is recorded at the time it is earned regardless of whether cash or another asset has been exchanged. (p. 32)

Revenues The value of assets exchanged for goods or services provided to customers as part of a business's main operations; may occur as inflows of assets or decreases in liabilities. (p. 27)

Source documents Documents that identify and describe transactions entering the accounting process; the source of accounting information, whether in paper or electronic form. (p. 34)

Statement of cash flows A financial statement that describes the sources and uses of cash for a reporting period, i.e., where a company's cash came from (receipts) and where it went during the period (payments); the cash flows are arranged by an organization's major activities: operating, investing, and financing activities. (p. 30)

Statement of changes in equity A financial statement that reports the changes in equity over the reporting period; beginning equity is adjusted for increases such as owner investment or net income and for decreases such as owner withdrawals or a net loss. (p. 29)

Statement of financial position See *balance sheet*. (p. 29)

Transaction See *business transaction*. (p. 34)

Understandability A quality of information that is useful to users with reasonable knowledge of accounting and business and economic activities. (p. 31)

Withdrawals The distributions of cash or other assets from a proprietorship or partnership to its owner or owners. (p. 27)

Visit **Connect** at **www.mcgrawhillconnect.ca** for additional study tools, practice quizzes, to search an interactive e-book, and much more.

Concept Review Questions

1. Identify four financial statements that a proprietorship presents to its owner and other users.
2. What information is presented in an income statement?
3. What do accountants mean by the term *revenue*?
4. Why does the user of an income statement need to know the time period that it covers?
5. What transactions change equity?
6. What information is presented in a balance sheet?
7. Define (a) assets, (b) liabilities, (c) equity, and (d) net assets.
8. Review Vertically Inclined's financial statements presented in the chapter for the month ended January 31, 2011. Review the balance sheet and determine the business form Virgil Klimb has chosen to organize his business.
9. Why is the revenue recognition principle needed? What does it require?

Quick Study

QS 2-1
Financial statements and forms of organization
LO1

SP – Sole proprietorship
P – Partnership
C – Corporation

Identify the type of business organization based on the following independent financial statement findings:

__________ **1.** The equity section of the balance sheet has one capital account.
__________ **2.** The owners receive dividends, a distribution of earnings, in the form of cash.
__________ **3.** There are two capital accounts: Tara Davis, Capital, and Sheila Kelton, Capital.
__________ **4.** The one owner receives distributions of earnings in the form of withdrawals.
__________ **5.** A manager, also the owner of the business, is paid a salary that is recorded as an expense.
__________ **6.** The equity on the balance sheet is held by shareholders.
__________ **7.** The five owners receive distributions of earnings in the form of withdrawals.

QS 2-2
Identifying accounting principles
LO2

Identify which GAAP most directly describes each of the following correct practices:

_______ **a.** Tracy Regis owns two businesses, Second Time Around Clothing and Antique Accents, both of which are sole proprietorships. In having financial statements prepared for the antique store, Regis should be sure that the revenue and expense transactions of Second Time Around are excluded from the statements of Antique Accents.

_______ **b.** In December 2008, Classic Coverings received a customer's order to install carpet and tile in a new house that would not be ready for completion until March 2009. Classic Coverings should record the revenue for the order in March 2009, not in December 2008.

_______ **c.** If $30,000 cash is paid to buy land, the land should be reported on the purchaser's balance sheet at $30,000 although the purchaser was offered $35,000 the following week.

QS 2-3
Identifying accounting principles
LO2

For each of the following, identify which GAAP, if any, has been violated.

_______ **1.** A customer called and made arrangements for Jay's Plumbing to provide $6,000 of services *next month*. Jay, the owner, recorded revenue of $6,000 *this month*. No cash was exchanged.

_______ **2.** Land was purchased for $50,000. The bank appraised it for loan purposes at $68,000. Therefore, the owner of the land recorded it on the balance sheet at $68,000.

_______ **3.** The owner of Dallas Pizza and Don's Deli combines all transactions by keeping only one set of accounting records for both businesses.

_______ **4.** The owner of Pella's Junk Removal has become ill suddenly and is unable to continue the business. Pella's spouse, in need of cash to finance growing personal expenses, took the business's most recent financial statements to the bank and was granted a loan. She did not inform the bank of her husband's inability to work.

_______ **5.** Dale's Consulting Services completed a contract with an organization located overseas. Dale included the revenue on the income statement without converting the foreign currency to Canadian dollars.

QS 2-4
Identifying accounting principles
LO2

For each of the following, identify which GAAP was violated by Delco Consulting. In cases where more than one GAAP applies, name the primary GAAP that was not followed.

_______ **a.** Delco performed work for a client located in China and collected 8,450,000 RMB (Chinese currency), the equivalent of about $1,320,000 Canadian. Delco recorded it as 8,450,000.

_______ **b.** Delco collected $180,000 from a customer on December 20, 2011, for work to be done in February 2012. The $180,000 was recorded as revenue during 2011. Delco's year-end is December 31.

_______ **c.** Delco's December 31, 2011, balance sheet showed total assets of $840,000 and liabilities of $1,120,000. The income statements for the past six years have shown a trend of increasing losses.

_______ **d.** Included in Delco's assets was land and a building purchased for $310,000 and reported on the balance sheet at $470,000.

_______ **e.** Delco's owner, Tom Del, consistently buys personal supplies and charges them to the company.

QS 2-5
Applying the accounting equation
LO3

Determine the missing amount for each of the following equations:

	Assets	=	Liabilities	+	Equity
a.	$ 75,000		$ 40,500		?
b.	$300,000		?		$85,500
c.	?		$187,500		$95,400

QS 2-6
Applying the accounting equation
LO3

Use the accounting equation to determine:

a. The equity in a business that has $374,700 of assets and $252,450 of liabilities.
b. The liabilities of a business having $150,900 of assets and $126,000 of equity.
c. The assets of a business having $37,650 of liabilities and $112,500 of equity.

QS 2-7
Applying the accounting equation
LO3

The balance sheet is a more detailed presentation of the accounting equation. The income statement and statement of changes in equity are linked to the balance sheet (by the accounting equation). Calculate the missing amounts below.

a.

Allin Servicing
Income Statement
For Month Ended April 30, 2011

Revenues	$300
Expenses	?
Net income (loss)	?

Allin Servicing
Statement of Changes in Equity
For Month Ended April 30, 2011

Tim Allin, capital, April 1		$ 50
Add: Investments by owner	$ 30	
Net income	?	?
Total		$255
Less: Withdrawals by owner		?
Tim Allin, capital, April 30		?

Allin Servicing
Balance Sheet
April 30, 2011

Assets		**Liabilities**	
Cash	$ 60	Accounts payable	$ 25
Equipment	?	**Equity**	
		Tim Allin, capital	?
Total assets	$265	Total liabilities and equity	?

b.

Allin Servicing
Income Statement
For Month Ended May 31, 2011

Revenues	?
Expenses	$ 85
Net income (loss)	?

Allin Servicing
Statement of Changes in Equity
For Month Ended May 31, 2011

Tim Allin, capital, May 1		?
Add: Investments by owner	$ 60	
Net income	?	$110
Total		?
Less: Withdrawals by owner		75
Tim Allin, capital, May 31		?

Allin Servicing
Balance Sheet
May 31, 2011

Assets		**Liabilities**	
Cash	$120	Accounts payable	$ 45
Equipment	?	**Equity**	
		Tim Allin, capital	?
Total assets	?	Total liabilities and equity	?

QS 2-8
Applying the accounting equation
LO3

Using the accounting equation provided, calculate:

1. Beginning capital on January 1, 2011, and
2. Ending capital at December 31, 2011.

Assets	=	Liabilities	+	Equity	
$20,000		$15,000		?	Beginning capital on January 1, 2011
				+ 3,000	Plus owner investments during the year
				+ 8,000	Plus net income earned during the year
				− 4,000	Less owner withdrawals during the year
				?	Equals ending capital on December 31, 2011

**Hint: Review Part B of the Mid-Chapter Demonstration Problem before trying this question.*

QS 2-9
Identifying source documents
LO4

Select the items from the following list that are likely to serve as source documents:

a. Income statement
b. Statement of cash flows
c. Telephone bill
d. Invoice from supplier
e. Owner's withdrawals account
f. Balance sheet
g. Bank statement
h. Sales invoice

QS 2-10
Transaction analysis
LO4

For each transaction described, identify which component of the accounting equation increases and/or decreases. The first one is done as an example.

Example: Services were performed for a client on credit.
a. A credit customer paid his account.
b. Supplies were purchased on credit.
c. The balance owing regarding the supplies purchased in part (b) was paid.
d. Last month's telephone bill was received today. It will be paid on the due date, which is 10 days from now.
e. Paid the employees their weekly wage.

Assets	=	Liabilities	+	Equity
Example: *Increase*				*Increases*
a.				
b.				
c.				
d.				
e.				

QS 2-11
Identifying financial statement items
LO1,5

Tim Roadster began Roadster Servicing on April 1, 2011, and showed the following items after the first month of operations. Match each of these items with the financial statement or statements on which it should be presented. Indicate your answer by writing the letter or letters for the correct statement(s) in the blank space next to each item.

a. Income statement **b.** Statement of changes in equity **c.** Balance sheet

	Item	Amount		Item	Amount
____	**1.** Supplies	$10	____	**8.** Utilities expense	$10
____	**2.** Supplies expense	22	____	**9.** Furniture	20
____	**3.** Accounts receivable	25	____	**10.** Fees earned	70
____	**4.** Accounts payable	12	____	**11.** Rent revenue	35
____	**5.** Equipment	40	____	**12.** Salaries expense	45
____	**6.** Tim Roadster's withdrawals in April	35	____	**13.** Tim Roadster's investments in April	60
____	**7.** Notes payable	30	____	**14.** Net income	?

QS 2-12
Calculating financial statement elements
LO1,5

Using the information provided in QS 2-11, calculate each of the following financial statement elements.

1. Total revenues
2. Total operating expenses
3. Net income
4. Total assets
5. Total liabilities
6. Tim Roadster, capital (April 30, 2011)
7. Total liabilities and equity

QS 2-13
Balance sheet
LO1,5

Joan Bennish began Bennish Consulting on May 1, 2011, and reported the items below at May 31, 2011. Match each numbered item with the part of the balance sheet on which it should be presented. If the item does not appear on the balance sheet, choose (d) and identify on which financial statement(s) the item would appear.

a. Asset **c.** Equity
b. Liability **d.** Does not appear on the balance sheet

D	**1.** Net loss	$?	A	**8.** Repair supplies	$ 5
D	**2.** Rent expense	22	B	**9.** Notes payable	25
B	**3.** Rent payable	6	C	**10.** Joan Bennish's withdrawals in May	5
A	**4.** Accounts receivable	14	A	**11.** Truck	15
C	**5.** Joan Bennish's investments in May	30	D	**12.** Consulting fees earned	18
D	**6.** Interest revenue	2	C	**13.** Joan Bennish, capital, May 31, 2011	?
C	**7.** Joan Bennish, capital, May 1, 2011	0	A	**14.** Cash	20

QS 2-14
Calculating financial statement elements
LO1,5

Using the information in QS 2-13, prepare an income statement and statement of changes in equity for the month ended May 31, 2011, and a balance sheet at May 31, 2011.

Exercises

Exercise 2-1
Determining net income
LO1

Check figure:
d. $13,000 net loss

Net income (net loss), owner withdrawals, and owner investment cause equity to change. We also know that revenues less expenses equals net income (loss). Using the following information, calculate net income (loss) for each independent situation.

a. The business earned revenues of $80,000 and had expenses of $65,000.
b. The business showed expenses of $149,000 and revenues of $92,000.
c. The equity at the beginning of the month was $10,000. During the month, the owner made no investments or withdrawals. At the end of the month, equity totalled $86,000.
d. The equity at the beginning of the month was $25,000. During the month, the owner made an investment of $40,000 but made no withdrawals. Equity at the end of the month totalled $52,000.

Exercise 2-2
Missing information
LO1

Check figure:
e. $92,000

Referring to Exhibit 2.3 on page 28, calculate the amount of the missing item in each of the following independent cases:

	a	b	c	d	e
Equity, January 1	$ -0-	$ -0-	$ -0-	$ -0-	$?
Owner's investments during the year	60,000	?	31,500	37,500	150,000
Net income (loss) for the year	15,750	40,500	(4,500)	?	(8,000)
Owner's withdrawals during the year	?	(27,000)	(15,000)	(15,750)	(63,000)
Equity, December 31	51,000	49,500	?	42,750	171,000

Exercise 2-3
Income statement
LO1

Check figure:
Net income = $7,110

This symbol means that an Excel template is available on Connect to help you solve this question.

On November 1, 2011, Jean Dobbs organized a new consulting firm called The Dobbs Group. On November 30, 2011, the company's records showed the following items. Use this information to prepare a November income statement for the business, similar to Exhibit 2.2 on page 28.

Cash	$12,000	Owner's withdrawals	$ 3,360
Accounts receivable	17,000	Consulting fees earned	18,000
Office supplies	2,250	Rent expense	2,550
Automobiles	36,000	Salaries expense	6,000
Office equipment	28,000	Telephone expense	1,680
Accounts payable	7,500	Utilities expenses	660
Owner's investments	84,000		

Exercise 2-4
Statement of changes in equity
LO1

Check figure:
Jean Dobbs, Capital, November 30 = $87,750

Use the facts in Exercise 2-3 to prepare a November statement of changes in equity for The Dobbs Group, similar to Exhibit 2.3 on page 28.

Analysis component:
What activities caused equity to increase during the month of November 2011?

Exercise 2-5
Balance sheet
LO1

Check figure:
Total assets = $95,250

Use the facts in Exercise 2-3 to prepare a November 30 balance sheet for The Dobbs Group, similar to Exhibit 2.4 on page 28.

Analysis component:
Identify how much of the assets held by The Dobbs Group are financed by the owner, Jean Dobbs.

Exercise 2-6
Income statement
LO1

Check figure:
Net loss = $120

On July 1, 2011, Excel Learning Services entered its second month of operations. On July 31, 2011, George Pelzer, the owner, finalized the company's records that showed the following items. Use this information to prepare a July income statement similar to Exhibit 2.2 on page 28.

Accounts payable	$1,400	Owner's investments during July 2011	$1,200
Accounts receivable	2,680	Owner's withdrawals	1,000
Cash	1,600	Supplies	600
Computer equipment	2,200	Textbook rental revenue	300
Furniture	1,800	Tutoring fees earned	4,200
George Pelzer, capital, June 30, 2011*	7,400	Tutors' wages expense	1,540
Office rent expense	2,500	Utilities expense	580

**Hint: The ending capital balance for one period is the beginning capital balance for the next period.*

Exercise 2-7
Statement of changes in equity
LO1

Check figure:
George Pelzer, Capital, July 31 = $7,480

Use the facts in Exercise 2-6 to prepare a July statement of changes in equity for Excel Learning Services, similar to Exhibit 2.3 on page 28.

Analysis component:
Identify those activities that caused equity to decrease during July 2011.

Exercise 2-8
Balance sheet
LO1

Check figure:
Total assets = $8,880

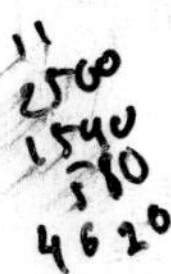

Use the facts in Exercise 2-6 to prepare a July 31 balance sheet for Excel Learning Services, similar to Exhibit 2.4 on page 28.

Analysis component:
Identify how much of the assets held by Excel Learning Services are financed by debt.

Exercise 2-9
Accounting principles
LO2

Match each of these numbered descriptions with the term it best describes. Indicate your answer by writing the letter for the correct principle in the blank space next to each description.

a. Cost principle
b. Business entity principle
c. Revenue recognition principle
d. Going concern principle

_____ **1.** Requires every business to be accounted for separately from its owner or owners.
_____ **2.** Requires financial statement information to be based on costs incurred in transactions.
_____ **3.** Requires financial statements to reflect the assumption that the business will continue operating instead of being closed or sold.
_____ **4.** Requires revenue to be recorded only when the earnings process is complete.

Exercise 2-10
Determining net income
LO1,3

A business had the following amounts of assets and liabilities at the beginning and end of a recent year:

	Assets	Liabilities
Beginning of the year....................	$150,000	$60,000
End of the year	240,000	92,000

Check figure:
b. $100,000 net income

Determine the net income earned or net loss incurred by the business during the year under each of the following unrelated assumptions:

a. The owner made no additional investments in the business and withdrew no assets during the year.
b. The owner made no additional investments in the business during the year but withdrew $3,500 **per month** to pay personal living expenses.
c. The owner withdrew no assets during the year but invested an additional $65,000 cash.
d. The owner withdrew $3,500 **per month** to pay personal living expenses and invested an additional $50,000 cash in the business.

**Hint: Review the Mid-Chapter Demonstration Problem before trying this question.*

Exercise 2-11
Accounting equation
LO3

Check figure:
b. Equity
Aug. 31, 2011 = $16,000

In the following table, the accounting equation is applied to Business A:

	Assets	=	Liabilities	+	Equity
At August 1, 2011	?		$1,000		?
At August 31, 2011	$20,000		?		?

Calculate the missing amounts assuming that:

a. Assets decreased by $5,000 during August, and
b. Liabilities increased by $3,000 during August.

Exercise 2-12
Effects of transactions on the accounting equation
LO2,3,4

Check figure:
Total assets = $3,050

Bridges Consulting provides support to customers in the area of e-commerce. Using the format provided below, show the effects of the activities listed in (a) through (f).

Assets			=	Liabilities	+	Equity
Cash	+ Accounts Receivable	+ Office Supplies	=	Accounts Payable	+	Noel Bridges, Capital

a. Noel Bridges, the owner, invested cash of $2,500 into the business.
b. The owner purchased office supplies on credit; $200.
c. Bridges Consulting did work for a client and received $600 cash.
d. Completed an application form for a $10,000 government grant.
e. The owner paid her assistant's salary; $1,500 cash.
f. Completed work for a customer on credit; $1,250.

Exercise 2-13
Effects of transactions on the accounting equation
LO2,3,4

Check figure:
Total assets = $6,600

DigiCom repairs computers. Using the format provided below, show the effects of the activities listed in (a) through (i).

Assets				=	Liabilities	+	Equity
Cash +	Accounts Receivable +	Parts Supplies +	Equipment	=	Accounts Payable	+	Stacey Crowe, Capital

a. Stacey, owner of DigiCom, invested cash of $7,000 into her business.
b. DigiCom paid $2,500 to cover rent for the current month.
c. DigiCom purchased supplies on credit; $1,200.
d. DigiCom completed work for a client on credit; $3,400.
e. DigiCom purchased a new piece of equipment by paying cash of $950.
f. DigiCom hired a technician, to start next month, who will get paid $5,000 per month.

g. DigiCom paid for the supplies purchased in (c).
h. DigiCom performed work for a client and received cash of $1,400.
i. DigiCom paid the assistant's salary of $2,700.

Exercise 2-14
Analyzing the accounting equation
LO4

Andy Wood began a new consulting firm on January 3. The accounting equation showed the following transactions. Analyze the equation and describe each of the transactions with their amounts. Transaction (a) has been done as an example for you.

	Assets				=	Liabilities +	Equity
Transaction	Cash +	Accounts Receivable	+ Office Supplies +	Office Furniture	=	Accounts Payable +	Andy Wood, Capital
Beginning Balances	-0-	-0-	-0-	-0-		-0-	-0-
a.	+15,000						+15,000
b.	− 500		+500				
c.	− 8,000			+8,000			
d.		+1,000					+ 1,000
e.			+400			+400	
f.	− 250					−250	
g.	+ 750	− 750					
Totals	7,000	250	900	8,000		150	16,000

Description of transaction (a):
a. *The owner invested $15,000 cash into the business.*

Exercise 2-15
Effects of transactions on the accounting equation
LO2,3,4

The following equation shows the effects of transactions on the assets, liabilities, and equity of Pace Design. Describe the transaction that caused each of (a) through (h).

	Assets				=	Liabilities +	Equity
	Cash	+ Accounts Receivable	+ Office Supplies	+ Land	=	Accounts Payable	+ Carol Pace, Capital
a.	−3,000			+3,000			
b.			+400			+400	
c.	−700		+700				
d.		+1,050					+1,050
e.	+1,000						+1,000
f.	−400					−400	
g.	+1,050	−1,050					
h.				+5,000			+5,000

Exercise 2-16
Effects of transactions on the accounting equation
LO2,3,4

Ellen Manson began a professional practice on May 1, 2011, and plans to prepare financial statements at the end of each month. During May, Manson completed these activities:

a. Invested $25,000 cash and equipment that had a $5,000 fair market (cash equivalent) value.
b. Paid $1,300 rent for office space for the month.
c. Purchased $6,000 of additional equipment on credit.
d. Completed work for a client and immediately collected $500 cash.
e. Completed work for a client and sent a bill for $1,000 to be paid within 30 days.
f. Purchased $4,000 of additional equipment for cash.
g. Paid an assistant $1,200 as wages for the month.
h. Collected $250 of the amount owed by the client described in activity (e).
i. Paid for the equipment purchased in activity (c).
j. Withdrew $250 for personal use.

Check figure:
Total assets = $28,750

Required
Create a table like the one in Exhibit 2.10 on page 39, using the following headings for the columns: Cash; Accounts Receivable; Equipment; Accounts Payable; and Ellen Manson, Capital. Then, use additions and subtractions to show the effects of the transactions on the elements of the equation. Show new totals after each transaction. Also, calculate net income or loss for the month of May 2011.

Exercise 2-17

Effects of transactions on the accounting equation
LO2,3,4

Following are six pairs of changes in elements of the accounting equation. Provide an example of a transaction that creates the described effects:

a. Increases an asset and decreases an asset.
b. Decreases an asset and decreases equity.
c. Increases a liability and decreases equity.
d. Increases an asset and increases a liability.
e. Increases an asset and increases equity.
f. Decreases an asset and decreases a liability.

Exercise 2-18

Effects of transactions on the accounting equation
LO2,3,4

Check figure:
Annie Deweerd, Capital = $6,650

Annie Deweerd is a freelance writer who submits articles to various magazines and newspapers. She operates out of a small office where she employs one administrative assistant. The following activities occurred during March 2011, her first month of business:

a. Annie Deweerd invested $2,500 worth of equipment into her business.
b. Submitted a series of articles to *The Globe and Mail* and received $4,000 cash.
c. Purchased supplies on credit; $150.
d. Paid the part-time administrative assistant's salary of $450.
e. Annie Deweerd ordered $3,000 of office equipment from the IKEA catalogue. It is scheduled to arrive in April or May.
f. Paid the rent for the first month; $1,400.
g. Submitted an article to *Report on Business*; will receive $2,000 next month.

Using the format provided below, show the effects of the activities listed in (a) through (g). For each transaction that affects equity, include a brief description beside it (owner investment, owner withdrawal, revenue, expense).

Assets							=	Liabilities	+	Equity	
Cash	+	Accounts Receivable	+	Supplies	+	Equipment	=	Accounts Payable	+	Annie Deweerd, Capital	Explanation of Equity Transaction

Exercise 2-19
Financial statements
LO5

Check figures:
Net income = $4,150;
Total assets = $6,800

Using your answer from Exercise 2-18, prepare an income statement, a statement of changes in equity, and a balance sheet using the formats provided.

Annie Deweerd—Freelance Writing
Income Statement
For Month Ended March 31, 2011

Revenues:		
Freelance writing revenue		
Operating expenses:		
Salaries expense		
Rent expense	____	
Total operating expenses		____
Net income		====

Annie Deweerd—Freelance Writing
Statement of Changes in Equity
For Month Ended March 31, 2011

Annie Deweerd, capital, March 1		
Add: Investments by owner		
Net income	____	
Annie Deweerd, capital, March 31		====

Annie Deweerd—Freelance Writing
Balance Sheet
March 31, 2011

Assets		Liabilities	
Cash		Accounts payable	
Accounts receivable			
Supplies		**Equity**	
Equipment		Annie Deweerd, capital	
Total assets	====	Total liabilities and equity	====

Analysis component:
Identify which assets were financed by:
a. Liabilities **b.** Owner investment **c.** Net income

Also identify the amount(s) for each.

Exercise 2-20
Effects of transactions on the accounting equation
LO2,3,4

excel

Pete Kequahtooway opened a yard care business, Pete's Yard Care, on March 1, 2011. The following activities occurred during his first month of operations:

a. Pete Kequahtooway invested $500 cash and $15,000 of equipment into his business.
b. Purchased various supplies on account; $400.
c. Bought supplies on credit; $600.
d. Pete signed a $4,000 contract to do yard work beginning in May.
e. Did work for a client on account; $550.
f. Performed services for a customer on account; $600.
g. Paid $200 for the supplies purchased in (c).
h. Paid $250 for advertising in the local newspaper.

Check figure:
Cash, March 31, 2011 = $50

Using the format provided below, show the effects of the activities listed in (a) through (h). For each transaction that affects equity, include a brief description beside it (owner investment, owner withdrawal, revenue, expense).

Assets				=	Liabilities	+	Equity	
Cash +	Accounts Receivable +	Supplies +	Equipment	=	Accounts Payable	+	Pete Kequahtooway, Capital	Explanation of Equity Transaction

Exercise 2-21
Financial statements
LO5

Check figure:
Pete Kequahtooway, Capital, March 31, 2011 = $16,400

Using your answer from Exercise 2-20, prepare an income statement, statement of changes in equity, and balance sheet for March 2011.

Analysis component:
Review Pete's income statement. Does the net income of $900 represent $900 of cash? Explain.

Exercise 2-22
Effects of transactions on the accounting equation
LO2,3,4

The June transactions for Otto's Wrecking Service resulted in totals at June 30, 2011, as shown in the following accounting equation format:

Assets				= Liabilities	+ Equity	
Cash +	Accounts Receivable +	Supplies +	Equipment =	Accounts Payable +	Otto Ingles, Capital	Explanation of Equity Transaction
$4,000 +	$1,200 +	$900 +	$7,500 =	$4,000 +	$9,600	

Check figure:
Otto Ingles, Capital, July 31, 2011 = $8,400

During July, the following occurred:

a. Collected $1,000 from a credit customer.
b. Paid $2,000 for equipment purchased on account in June.
c. Did work for a client and collected cash; $700.
d. Paid the part-time worker's wages; $500.
e. Paid the July rent; $1,200.
f. Paid the July utilities; $600.
g. Performed services for a customer on credit; $400.
h. Called a repair person to fix the equipment in August; it will cost $350.

Using the format provided above, show the effects of the activities listed in (a) through (h). For each transaction that affects equity, include a brief description beside it (owner investment, owner withdrawal, revenue, expense).

Exercise 2-23
Financial statements
LO5

Check figures:
Net loss = $1,200;
Total assets = $10,400

Using your answer from Exercise 2-22, prepare an income statement, a statement of changes in equity, and a balance sheet for July 2011.

Analysis component:
Review Otto's balance sheet. How much of the assets are financed by Otto Ingles? How much of the assets are financed by debt?

Problems

Problem 2-1A
Financial statements: analysis of statement of changes in equity
LO1

Check figure:
Net income 2009 = $60,000

BT Pool Cleaners began operations on January 1, 2009. The owner invested $10,000 during the first year and was able to withdraw cash of $42,000 after a successful first year.

During the second year of operations, the business reported net income of $175,000, owner withdrawals of $78,000, and no owner investments.

In the third year, BT Pool Cleaners incurred a loss of $5,000. The owner made no withdrawals and no owner investments during this period. At the end of the third year, owner's capital was $120,000.

Required
Calculate the net income or loss for the first year of operations.

Problem 2-2A

Financial statements

LO1

On August 1, 2010, Bee Clean entered its second year of operations, providing housekeeping services to the elderly and disabled as well as doing small household repairs. On July 31, 2011, Bee Cummins, the owner, finalized the company's records, which showed the following items.

Accounts payable	$14,800	Office equipment	$ 29,200
Accounts receivable	56,000	Prepaid rent	12,000
Cash	11,800	Rent expense	24,000
Furniture	19,000	Repair revenue	6,000
Interest expense	500	Service revenue	142,000
Bee Cummins, capital, July 31, 2010*	79,300	Supplies	2,400
		Supplies expense	11,400
Bee Cummins, withdrawals	34,000	Utilities expense	9,800
Notes payable	20,000	Wages expense	52,000

**Hint: The ending capital balance for one period is the beginning capital balance for the next period. There were no owner investments during the year ended July 31, 2011.*

Required

Prepare an income statement and statement of changes in equity for the year ended July 31, 2011, and balance sheet at July 31, 2011, similar to Exhibits 2.2, 2.3, and 2.4 on page 28.

Check figures:
Net income = $50,300;
Total assets = $130,400

Problem 2-3A

Calculating and interpreting net income and preparing a balance sheet

LO1,3,5

The accounting records of LeClaire Delivery Services show the following assets and liabilities as of the end of 2011 and 2010:

	December 31	
	2011	2010
Cash	$ 9,375	$26,250
Accounts receivable	11,175	14,250
Office supplies	1,650	2,250
Trucks	27,000	27,000
Office equipment	73,500	69,000
Land	22,500	
Building	90,000	
Accounts payable	18,750	3,750
Notes payable	52,500	

During December 2011, the owner, Jess LeClaire, purchased a small office building and moved the business from rented quarters to the new building. The building and the land it occupies cost $112,500. The business paid $60,000 in cash and a note payable was signed for the balance. LeClaire had to invest $17,500 cash in the business to enable it to pay the $60,000. The business earned a net income during 2011, which enabled LeClaire to withdraw $1,500 per month from the business for personal expenses.

Required

1. Prepare balance sheets for the business as of the end of 2010 and the end of 2011.
2. Prepare a calculation to show how much net income was earned by the business during 2011.

Check figures:
1. Total assets 2010 = $138,750;
Total assets 2011 = $235,200

Analysis component:

Assets increased from $138,750 at December 31, 2010, to $235,200 at December 31, 2011. Using numbers wherever possible, explain how these assets were financed.

Problem 2-4A
Missing information
LO3

The following financial statement information is known about five unrelated companies:

	Company A	Company B	Company C	Company D	Company E
December 31, 2010:					
Assets	$90,000	$70,000	$58,000	$160,000	$246,000
Liabilities	47,000	45,000	28,000	76,000	?
December 31, 2011:					
Assets	96,000	82,000	?	250,000	225,000
Liabilities	?	55,000	38,000	128,000	150,000
During 2011:					
Owner investments	10,000	3,000	15,500	?	9,000
Net income	15,000	?	18,000	24,000	36,000
Owner withdrawals	5,000	6,000	7,750	-0-	18,000

Required

1. Answer the following questions about Company A:
   a. What was the equity on December 31, 2010?
   b. What was the equity on December 31, 2011?
   c. What was the amount of liabilities owed on December 31, 2011?
2. Answer the following questions about Company B:
   a. What was the equity on December 31, 2010?
   b. What was the equity on December 31, 2011?
   c. What was the net income for 2011?
3. Calculate the amount of assets owned by Company C on December 31, 2011.
4. Calculate the amount of owner investments in Company D made during 2011.
5. Calculate the amount of liabilities owed by Company E on December 31, 2010.

Problem 2-5A
Analyzing transactions and preparing financial statements
LO2,3,4,5

George Littlechild started a new kitchen and bath design business called Littlechild Enterprises. The following activities occurred during its first month of operations, March 2011:

a. Littlechild invested $160,000 cash and office equipment valued at $60,000 in the business.
b. Purchased a small building for $600,000 to be used as an office. Paid $100,000 in cash and signed a note payable promising to pay the balance over several years.
c. Purchased $8,000 of office supplies for cash.
d. Purchased $72,000 of office equipment on credit.
e. George Littlechild made reservations at a hotel hosting a kitchen and bath design conference in August 2011. He will send a $1,000 deposit on July 1, 2011.
f. Completed a project on credit and billed the client $3,000 for the work.
g. Paid a local newspaper $2,000 for an announcement that the office had opened.
h. Completed a project for a client and collected $4,000 cash.
i. Made a $4,000 payment on the equipment purchased in (d).
j. Received $1,000 from the client described in (f).
k. Paid $7,000 cash for the office secretary's wages.
l. Littlechild withdrew $3,600 cash from the company bank account to pay personal living expenses.

Required

1. Create a table like the one in Exhibit 2.10 on page 39, using the following headings for the columns: Cash; Accounts Receivable; Office Supplies; Office Equipment; Building; Accounts Payable; Notes Payable; and George Littlechild, Capital. Leave space for an Explanation of Equity Transaction column to the right of the Capital column. Identify revenues and expenses by name in the Explanation of Equity Transaction column.
2. Use additions and subtractions to show the transactions' effects on the elements of the equation. Show new totals after each transaction (optional). Also, indicate next to each change in the equity whether it was caused by an investment, a revenue, an expense, or a withdrawal. Determine the final total for each item and verify that the equation is in balance.
3. Prepare an income statement, a statement of changes in equity, and a balance sheet using the formats provided.

Check figures:
2. George Littlechild, Capital, March 31, 2011 = $214,400
3. Net loss = $2,000;
Total assets = $782,400

Littlechild Enterprises
Income Statement
For Month Ended March 31, 2011

Revenues:		
Service revenue		
Operating expenses:		
Wages expense		
Advertising expense		
Total operating expenses		
Net loss		

Littlechild Enterprises
Statement of Changes in Equity
For Month Ended March 31, 2011

George Littlechild, capital, March 1		
Add: Investments by owner		
Total		
Less: Withdrawals by owner		
Net loss		
George Littlechild, capital, March 31		

Littlechild Enterprises
Balance Sheet
March 31, 2011

Assets		Liabilities	
Cash		Accounts payable	
Accounts receivable		Notes payable	
Office supplies		Total liabilities	
Office equipment			
Building		**Equity**	
		George Littlechild, capital	
Total assets		Total liabilities and equity	

Analysis component:
Littlechild Enterprises' assets are financed 73% by debt. What does this mean? As part of your answer, include an explanation of how the 73% was calculated.

Problem 2-6A
Analyzing transactions and preparing financial statements
LO2,3,4,5

Bev Ng started a new business called Keep-Safe that identifies and resolves internal security issues. Operations began on April 1, 2011. The following activities occurred during the month:

Apr.	1	Ng invested $120,000 cash in the business.
	1	Rented a furnished office and paid $6,400 cash for April's rent.
	3	Purchased office supplies for $3,360 cash.
	5	Paid $1,600 cash for the month's cleaning services.
	8	Provided consulting services for a client and immediately collected $9,200 cash.
	12	Provided consulting services for a client on credit, $6,000.
	15	Paid $1,700 cash for an assistant's salary for the first half of the month.
	20	Received payment in full for the services provided on April 12.
	22	Provided consulting services on credit, $5,600.
	23	Purchased additional office supplies on credit, $2,000.
	28	Received full payment for the services provided on April 22.
	29	Paid for the office supplies purchased on April 23.
	30	Purchased $120 of advertising used in April. The payment is due May 15.

Apr.	30	Paid $400 cash for the month's telephone bill.
	30	Paid $960 cash for the month's utilities.
	30	Paid $1,700 cash for an assistant's salary for the second half of the month.
	30	Ng withdrew $2,400 cash from the business for personal use.

Check figures:
3. Net income = $7,920;
Total assets = $125,640

Required

1. Arrange the following asset, liability, and equity titles in an equation like Exhibit 2.10 on page 39: Cash; Accounts Receivable; Office Supplies; Accounts Payable; and Bev Ng, Capital. Include an Explanation of Equity Transaction column.
2. Show the effects of the transactions on the elements of the equation by recording increases and decreases in the appropriate columns. **Do not determine new totals for the items of the equation after each transaction.** Next to each change in equity, state whether it was caused by an investment, a type of revenue, a type of expense, or a withdrawal. Determine the final total for each item and verify that the equation is in balance.
3. Prepare an income statement, a statement of changes in equity, and a balance sheet for April 2011.

Analysis component:
Determine how much of Keep-Safe's total assets at April 30, 2011, were financed by equity. Explain the details of what 'equity financed' means for Keep-Safe for the month ended April 30, 2011.

Problem 2-7A
Analyzing transactions
LO2,3,4

eXcel

Larry Power started a new business in the name of Power Electrical on October 1, 2011. During October, a number of activities occurred and the following totals resulted at October 31, 2011 (shown in accounting equation format):

Assets									=	Liabilities	+	Equity
Cash	+	**Accounts Receivable**	+	**Office Supplies**	+	**Office Equip.**	+	**Electrical Equip.**	=	**Accounts Payable**	+	**Larry Power, Capital**
$80,000	+	$7,000	+	$1,900	+	$28,000	+	$14,000	=	$18,000	+	$112,900

During November, the following occurred:

Nov.	1	Rented office space and paid cash for the month's rent of $5,600.
	3	Purchased electrical equipment for $28,000 from an electrician who was going out of business, by using $21,600 in personal funds and agreeing to pay the balance in 30 days.
	5	Purchased office supplies by paying $1,800 cash.
	6	Completed electrical work and immediately collected $2,000 for doing the work.
	8	Purchased $7,600 of office equipment on credit.
	15	Completed electrical work on credit in the amount of $6,000.
	16	Interviewed and hired a part-time electrician who will be paid $2,400 each month. He will begin work in three weeks.
	18	Purchased $1,000 of office supplies on credit.
	20	Paid for the office equipment purchased on November 8.
	24	Billed a client $1,200 for electrical work; the balance is due in 30 days.
	28	Received $6,000 for the work completed on November 15.
	30	Paid the assistant's salary of $4,400.
	30	Paid the monthly utility bills of $1,400.
	30	Power withdrew $1,400 from the business for personal use.

Check figure:
Cash balance, November 30, 2011 = $65,800

Required
Use additions and subtractions to show the effects of each November activity on the items in the equation. Show new totals after each transaction (optional). Next to each change in equity, state whether the change was caused by an investment, a revenue, an expense, or a withdrawal. Determine the final total for each item and verify that the equation is in balance.

Analysis component:
Revenue is not recorded on November 28. Explain, using your understanding of GAAP.

Problem 2-8A
Preparing financial statements
LO5

Required
Using your answer to Problem 2-7A, prepare an income statement, a statement of changes in equity, and a balance sheet.

Check figures:
Net loss = $2,200;
Total assets = $156,300

Analysis component:
Assets are financed by debt and equity. Net income is a component of equity. Therefore, net income helps to finance assets. Explain how/if net income helped to finance assets for Power Electrical for the month ended November 30, 2011.

Problem 2-9A
Identifying the effects of transactions on the financial statements
LO4,5

Identify how each of the following transactions affects the company's financial statements. For the balance sheet, identify how each transaction affects total assets, total liabilities, and equity. For the income statement, identify how each transaction affects net income. If there is an increase, place a "+" in the column or columns. If there is a decrease, place a "−" in the column or columns. If there is both an increase and a decrease, place a "+/−" in the column or columns. The line for the first transaction is completed as an example.

		Balance Sheet			Income Statement
	Transaction	Total Assets	Total Liabilities	Equity	Net Income
1	Owner invests cash	+		+	
2	Sell services for cash				
3	Acquire services on credit				
4	Pay wages with cash				
5	Owner withdraws cash				
6	Borrow cash with note payable				
7	Sell services on credit				
8	Buy office equipment for cash				
9	Collect receivable from (7)				
10	Buy asset with note payable				

Alternate Problems

Problem 2-1B
Financial statements: analysis of statement of changes in equity
LO1

Dublin Window Cleaners began operations on January 1, 2010. The owner invested $100,000 during the first year and made no withdrawals.

During 2011, the business reported net income of $326,000, owner withdrawals of $104,000, and zero owner investments.

In 2012, Dublin Window Cleaners earned net income of $366,000. The owner withdrew $138,000 during 2012 and made no investments. Owner's capital at December 31, 2012, was $520,000.

Required
Calculate the net income or loss for the year 2010.

Check figure:
2010 Net loss = $30,000

Problem 2-2B

Financial statements

LO1

On January 1, 2011, Fireworks Fantasia entered its third year of operations. On December 31, 2011, Wes Gandalf, the owner, finalized the company's records that showed the following items.

Accounts payable	$ 18,000	Office equipment	$ 24,000
Accounts receivable	14,000	Office supplies	3,000
Advertising expense	9,000	Office supplies expense	3,600
Building	124,000	Rent revenue	66,000
Cash	28,000	Tools	18,000
Fees earned	140,000	Utilities expense	35,600
Fireworks supplies	32,000	Wages expense	92,000
Fireworks supplies expense	82,000	Wes Gandalf, capital,	
Land	112,000	December 31, 2010	375,200
		Wes Gandalf, withdrawals	52,000

**Hint: The ending capital balance for one period is the beginning capital balance for the next period. The owner made investments of $30,000 during the year ended December 31, 2011.*

Check figure:
Wes Gandalf, Capital,
Dec. 31, 2011 = $337,000

Required

Prepare an income statement and statement of changes in equity for the year ended December 31, 2011, and a December 31, 2011, balance sheet, similar to Exhibits 2.2, 2.3, and 2.4 on page 28.

Problem 2-3B

Calculating and interpreting net income and preparing a balance sheet

LO1,3,5

The accounting records of Annand Co. show the following assets and liabilities as of the end of 2011 and 2010:

	December 31	
	2011	2010
Cash	$ 20,000	$ 28,000
Accounts receivable	60,000	50,000
Office supplies	25,000	20,000
Office equipment	120,000	120,000
Machinery	61,000	61,000
Land	130,000	
Building	520,000	
Accounts payable	30,000	10,000
Notes payable	520,000	

During 2011, Dee Annand, the owner, purchased a small office building and moved the business from rented quarters to the new building. The building and the land it occupies cost $650,000. The business paid $130,000 in cash and a note payable was signed for the balance. Annand had to invest an additional $50,000 to enable it to pay the $130,000. The business earned a net income during 2011, which enabled Annand to withdraw $2,000 per month from the business for personal use.

Check figures:
1. Total assets 2010 = $279,000;
Total assets 2011 = $936,000

Required

1. Prepare balance sheets for the business as of the end of 2010 and the end of 2011.
2. Prepare a calculation to show how much net income was earned by the business during 2011.

Analysis component:

Assets increased from $279,000 at December 31, 2010, to $936,000 at December 31, 2011. Using numbers wherever possible, explain how these assets were financed.

Problem 2-4B
Missing information
LO3

The following financial statement information is known about five unrelated companies:

	Company V	Company W	Company X	Company Y	Company Z
December 31, 2010:					
Assets	$45,000	$70,000	$121,500	$82,500	$124,000
Liabilities	30,000	50,000	58,500	61,500	?
December 31, 2011:					
Assets	49,000	90,000	136,500	?	160,000
Liabilities	26,000	?	55,500	72,000	52,000
During 2011:					
Owner investments	6,000	10,000	?	38,100	40,000
Net income	?	30,000	16,500	24,000	32,000
Owner withdrawals	4,500	2,000	-0-	18,000	6,000

Required

1. Answer the following questions about Company V:
   a. What was the equity on December 31, 2010?
   b. What was the equity on December 31, 2011?
   c. What was the net income for 2011?
2. Answer the following questions about Company W:
   a. What was the equity on December 31, 2010?
   b. What was the equity on December 31, 2011?
   c. What was the amount of liabilities owed on December 31, 2011?
3. Calculate the amount of owner investments in Company X made during 2011.
4. Calculate the amount of assets owned by Company Y on December 31, 2011.
5. Calculate the amount of liabilities owed by Company Z on December 31, 2010.

Problem 2-5B
Analyzing transactions and preparing financial statements
LO2,3,4,5

Barb Trent started a new business on January 1, 2011, called Trent Consulting. She develops financial investment plans for young adults. During the business's first year of operations, the following activities occurred:

a. Trent invested $100,000 cash and office equipment valued at $10,000 in the business.
b. Purchased a small building for $240,000 to be used as an office. Paid $20,000 in cash and signed a note payable promising to pay the balance over several years.
c. Purchased $18,000 of office equipment for cash.
d. Purchased $4,000 of office supplies and $6,400 of office equipment on credit.
e. Paid a local newspaper $3,000 for an announcement that the office had opened.
f. Completed a financial plan on credit and billed the client $6,000 for the service.
g. Designed a financial plan for another client and collected a $10,800 cash fee.
h. Trent withdrew $5,500 cash from the company bank account to pay personal expenses.
i. Trent signed a $20,000 contract for the office to be painted in February 2012. A deposit of $6,000 will be paid on January 15, 2012.
j. Received $2,400 from the client described in (f).
k. Paid $1,800 on the equipment purchased in (d).
l. Paid $3,800 cash for the office secretary's wages.

Required

1. Create a table like the one presented in Exhibit 2.10 on page 39, using the following headings for the columns: Cash; Accounts Receivable; Office Supplies; Office Equipment; Building; Accounts Payable; Notes Payable; and Barb Trent, Capital. Leave space for an Explanation of Equity Transaction column to the right of the Capital column. Identify revenues and expenses by name in the Explanation column.
2. Use additions and subtractions to show the effects of the above transactions on the elements of the equation. Show new totals after each transaction (optional). Also, indicate next to each change in the equity whether it was caused by an investment, a revenue, an expense, or a withdrawal. Determine the final total for each item and verify that the equation is in balance.
3. Prepare an income statement, a statement of changes in equity, and a balance sheet for 2011 using the formats provided.

Check figures:
2. Cash balance, December 31, 2011 = $61,100
3. Net income = $10,000; Total assets = $343,100

Trent Consulting
Income Statement
For Year Ended December 31, 2011

Revenues:		
Consulting services revenue		
Operating expenses:		
Wages expense		
Advertising expense	____	
Total operating expenses		____
Net income		====

Trent Consulting
Statement of Changes in Equity
For Year Ended December 31, 2011

Barb Trent, capital, January 1		
Add: Investments by owner		
Net income	____	
Total		
Less: Withdrawals by owner		____
Barb Trent, capital, December 31		====

Trent Consulting
Balance Sheet
December 31, 2011

Assets		**Liabilities**	
Cash		Accounts payable	
Accounts receivable		Notes payable	____
Office supplies		Total liabilities	
Office equipment			
Building		**Equity**	
		Barb Trent, capital	
Total assets	====	Total liabilities and equity	====

Analysis component:
Trent's assets are financed 67% by debt. What does this mean? As part of your answer, include an explanation of how the 67% was calculated.

Problem 2-6B
Analyzing transactions and preparing financial statements
LO2,3,4,5

On June 1, 2011, Kin Pon opened Genstar Maintenance, a new business that provides cleaning and general maintenance services for other businesses. The following activities occurred during the month:

June	1	Pon invested $240,000 cash in the business.
	1	Rented the furnished office of a maintenance company that was going out of business and paid $9,000 cash for the month's rent.
	4	Purchased cleaning supplies for $4,800 cash.
	6	Paid $5,500 cash for advertising the opening of the business.
	8	Completed maintenance services for a customer and immediately collected $1,500 cash.
	14	Completed maintenance services for First Union Centre on credit, $10,600.
	16	Paid $3,800 cash for an assistant's salary for the first half of the month.
	20	Received payment in full for the services completed for First Union Centre on June 14.
	21	Completed maintenance services for Skyway Co. on credit, $7,000.
	22	Purchased additional cleaning supplies on credit, $1,500.
	24	Completed maintenance services for Comfort Motel on credit, $1,650.
	29	Received full payment from Skyway Co. for the work completed on June 21.

June	29	Made a partial payment of $750 for the cleaning supplies purchased on June 22.
	30	Paid $240 cash for the month's telephone bill.
	30	Paid $1,050 cash for the month's utilities.
	30	Paid $3,800 cash for an assistant's salary for the second half of the month.
	30	Pon withdrew $4,000 cash from the business for personal use.

Required

1. Arrange the following asset, liability, and equity titles in an equation like Exhibit 2.10 on page 39: Cash; Accounts Receivable; Cleaning Supplies; Accounts Payable; Kin Pon, Capital. Include an Explanation of Equity Transaction column.
2. Show the effects of the transactions on the elements of the equation by recording increases and decreases in the appropriate columns. **Do not determine new totals for the items of the equation after each transaction.** Next to each change in equity, state whether it was caused by an investment, a type of revenue, a type of expense, or a withdrawal. Determine the final total for each item and verify that the equation is in balance.
3. Prepare an income statement, a statement of changes in equity, and a balance sheet for June 2011.

Check figures:
2. Kin Pon, capital, June 30, 2011 = $233,360
3. Net loss = $2,640; Total assets = $234,110

Analysis component:
Determine how much of Genstar's total assets at June 30, 2011, were financed by equity. Explain the details of what 'equity financed' means for Genstar for the month ended June 30, 2011.

Problem 2-7B
Analyzing transactions
LO2,3,4

Cantu Excavating digs basements for building contractors. It is owned by Robert Cantu and began operations June 1, 2011. The June activities resulted in totals at June 30, 2011, as follows (illustrated in accounting equation format):

Assets									=	Liabilities	+	Equity
Cash	+	Accounts Receivable	+	Office Supplies	+	Office Equip.	+	Excavating Equip.	=	Accounts Payable	+	Robert Cantu, Capital
$12,000	+	$4,600	+	$1,560	+	$9,600	+	$34,000	=	$6,200	+	$55,560

During July, the following occurred:

July	1	Cantu invested $120,000 cash in the business.
	1	Rented office space and paid the month's rent of $1,000.
	1	Purchased excavating equipment for $8,000 by paying $1,600 in cash and agreeing to pay the balance in 30 days.
	6	Purchased office supplies by paying $1,000 cash.
	8	Completed work for a customer and immediately collected $4,400 for doing the work.
	10	Purchased $7,600 of office equipment on credit.
	15	Completed work for a customer on credit in the amount of $4,800.
	17	Purchased $3,840 of office supplies on credit.
	23	Paid for the office equipment purchased on July 10.
	25	Billed a customer $10,000 for completed work; the balance is due in 30 days.
	28	Received $4,800 for the work completed on July 15.
	31	Paid an assistant's salary of $2,520.
	31	Paid the monthly utility bills of $520.
	31	Cantu withdrew $2,400 cash from the business to pay personal expenses.

Required
Use additions and subtractions to show the effects of each July transaction on the items in the equation. Show new totals after each transaction (optional). Next to each change in equity, state whether the change was caused by an investment, a revenue, an expense, or a withdrawal. Determine the final total for each item and verify that the equation is in balance.

Check figure:
Cash balance, July 31 = $124,560

Analysis component:
Identify which GAAP guides your treatment of the July 15 transaction. Explain your answer.

Problem 2-8B
Preparing financial statements
LO5

Check figures:
Net income = $15,160;
Total assets = $204,760

Required
Using your answer to Problem 2-7B, prepare an income statement, a statement of changes in equity, and a balance sheet.

Analysis component:
Assets are financed by debt and equity. Owner investment is a component of equity. Therefore, owner investment helps to finance assets. Explain how/if owner investment helped to finance assets for Cantu Excavating for the month ended July 31, 2011.

Problem 2-9B
Identifying the effects of transactions on the financial statements
LO4,5

You are to identify how each of the following transactions affects the company's financial statements. For the balance sheet, you are to identify how each transaction affects total assets, total liabilities, and equity. For the income statement, you are to identify how each transaction affects net income. If there is an increase, place a "+" in the column or columns. If there is a decrease, place a "−" in the column or columns. If there is both an increase and a decrease, place "+/−" in the column or columns. The line for the first transaction is completed as an example.

		Balance Sheet			Income Statement
	Transaction	**Total Assets**	**Total Liabilities**	**Equity**	**Net Income**
1	Owner invests cash	+		+	
2	Pay wages with cash				
3	Acquire services on credit				
4	Buy store equipment for cash				
5	Borrow cash with note payable				
6	Sell services for cash				
7	Sell services on credit				
8	Pay rent with cash				
9	Owner withdraws cash				
10	Collect receivable from (7)				

Analytical and Review Problem

A & R Problem 2-1

Check figure:
Total assets = $89,775

Jack Tasker opened his Auto Repair Shop in November 2011. The balance sheet at November 30, 2011, prepared by an inexperienced part-time bookkeeper, is shown below.

Required
Prepare a correct balance sheet.

Tasker Auto Repair Shop
Balance Sheet
November 30, 2011

Assets		**Liabilities and Equity**	
Cash	$ 6,300	Parts and supplies	$14,175
Accounts payable	34,650	Accounts receivable	47,250
Equipment	22,050	Mortgage payable	28,350
Jack Tasker, capital	26,775		
Total income	$89,775	Total equities	$89,775

A & R Problem 2-2

Susan Huang began the practice of law October 1, 2011, with an initial investment of $10,500 in cash. She made no withdrawals during the month. After completing the first month of practice, the financial statements were prepared by Ryan Player, the secretary/bookkeeper Ms. Huang had hired. Ms. Huang almost burst out laughing when she saw them. She had completed a course in legal accounting in law school and knew the statements prepared by Mr. Player left much to be desired. Consequently, she asked you to revise the statements. The Player version is presented as follows:

Susan Huang, Lawyer
Balance Sheet
October 31, 2011

Assets		Liabilities and Equity	
Cash	$ 3,780	Susan Huang, capital	$10,500
Furniture	2,100		
Supplies expense	420		
Accounts payable	1,050		
Rent expense	2,100		
Supplies	1,050		
	$10,500		$10,500

Susan Huang, Lawyer
Income Statement
For Month Ended October 31, 2011

Revenues:		
Legal fees	$11,550	
Accounts receivable	2,100	$13,650
Expenses:		
Salaries expense	$ 2,940	
Telephone expense	210	
Law library	8,400	11,550
Profit		$ 2,100

Check figures:
Net income = $5,880;
Total liabilities and equity = $17,430

Required
Prepare the corrected financial statements for Susan Huang.

A & R Problem 2-3

For each of the following activities, identify the effect on each component of the income statement and balance sheet. The first one has been done as an example for you.

1. $14,000 of services were provided to clients on credit today.

	Income Statement		Balance Sheet		
	Revenues	**Expenses**	**Assets**	**Liabilities**	**Equity**
1.	↑ $14,000		↑ $14,000		↑ $14,000

2. $5,000 cash was collected for services performed on credit last month.
3. $25,000 cash was borrowed from the bank.
4. $500 of advertising was done in the local newspaper today on account.
5. $500 was paid regarding the advertising in (4) above.
6. The owner invested an additional $10,000 cash into the business.
7. The owner withdrew $5,000 of cash from the business.
8. The owner took $200 worth of office supplies home for personal use.
9. A new computer was purchased for $2,000 cash.
10. A one-year insurance policy costing $12,000 was purchased today.
11. Purchased $45 of fuel for the van; paid cash.
12. Collected $900 from a client for work performed today.

Ethics Challenge

EC 2-1

Sue Ryskiak is a new entry-level accountant for a mail order company that specializes in supplying skateboards and accessories for the sport. At the end of the fiscal period, Sue is advised by a supervisor to include as revenue for the period any orders that have been charged by phone but not yet completed by shipping the product. Sue is also advised to include as revenue any orders received by mail with cheques enclosed that are also pending fulfillment.

Required

1. Identify relevant accounting principles that Sue should be aware of in view of the supervisor's instructions.
2. What are the ethical factors in this situation?
3. Would you recommend that Sue follow the supervisor's directives?
4. What alternatives might be available to Sue if she decides not to follow the supervisor's directions?

Focus on Financial Statements

FFS 2-1

Glenrose Servicing began operations on June 1, 2011. The transactions for the first two months follow:

2011		
June	1	The owner, Diane Towbell, invested $20,000 cash and office equipment with a value of $6,000.
	5	Glenrose Servicing performed $3,000 of services for a client on account.
	7	Paid rent for June in the amount of $1,500.
	9	Collected $1,000 from the customer of June 5.
	15	Paid $5,000 of mid-month wages to part-time employees.
	17	Provided $2,000 of services to a client and collected the cash immediately.
	29	Received the $300 June utilities bill. It will be paid in July.
	30	Paid $1,500 in wages to part-time employees.
July	5	Did work for a customer on account; $3,500.
	8	Collected $2,000 from credit customers.
	9	Paid $1,500 rent for July.
	12	Purchased $1,800 of additional office equipment on account.
	14	Paid $1,000 of the amount owing regarding July 12.
	15	Paid mid-month wages to part-time staff; $2,500.
	17	Performed services for a customer and immediately collected $4,800.
	25	Paid $300 in utilities for the month of July plus the balance owing from June.
	31	Paid $1,700 in wages to part-time employees.
	31	The owner withdrew cash of $2,000 for personal use.

Check figures:
3. Cash, June 30, 2011 = $15,000;
Total assets, June 30, 2011 = $23,000;
Cash, July 31, 2011 = $12,500;
Total assets, July 31, 2011 = $23,800

Required

1. Create two tables like the one in Exhibit 2.10 on page 39 for each of June and July using the following headings for the columns: Cash; Accounts Receivable; Office Equipment; Accounts Payable; Diane Towbell, Capital; and Explanation of Equity Transaction.
2. Use additions and subtractions to show the effects of the above transactions on the elements of the equation for each of June and July.
3. Prepare an income statement and statement of changes in equity for each of the months ended June 30, and July 31, 2011. Also prepare a balance sheet at June 30, 2011, and July 31, 2011.

Analysis component:

Answer each of the following questions:

1. Assets increased by $800 from June 30, 2011, to July 31, 2011. How was this increase financed?
2. Which financial statement reports on a company's
   a. performance?
   b. financial position?
   Explain what is meant by each of these terms.
3. Explain how Glenrose Servicing's July income statement, statement of changes in equity, and balance sheet are linked.

FFS 2-2

Part A:

1. Refer to page I-26 in Appendix I at the end of the textbook. This page shows the December 31, 2008, balance sheet for WestJet Airlines Ltd., a Canadian airline based in Calgary, Alberta. What types of assets does WestJet have?
2. To what level of significance are the dollar amounts rounded on the financial statements?
3. Prove the accounting equation for WestJet at December 31, 2008.
4. Assume that the personal home of one of the owners of WestJet (a shareholder) is valued at over $2,000,000. Should it be included as an asset on the balance sheet for WestJet? Why or why not?
5. Identify a potential internal user who would be interested in WestJet's statements and explain their interest.

Part B:

DANIER

6. Refer to page I-4 in Appendix I at the end of the textbook. This is the June 28, 2008, balance sheet for Danier Leather Inc., a Canadian specialty clothing designer, manufacturer, and retailer based in Toronto, Ontario. Identify the following for Danier at June 28, 2008:
   - **a.** Total assets
   - **b.** Total net assets (P. 30)
   - **c.** Prove the accounting equation for Danier at June 28, 2008.
7. Notice that the balance sheet provides data for two years. Why do you think information has been presented for both June 28, 2008, and June 30, 2007?
8. Identify a potential external user that would be interested in Danier's statements and explain their interest.

Critical Thinking Mini Case

You have worked with XYZ Contractors as the marketing manager for a number of years. Each of your salespeople must submit a monthly report detailing money they spent while conducting business on behalf of XYZ Contractors. Each item on the monthly report must be coded as to the effect on assets, liabilities, and equity. As marketing manager, one of your duties is to review the monthly reports. One salesperson's report for September shows the following:

Date	Description of Transaction	Amount of Transaction	Effect on Assets	Effect on Liabilities	Effect on Equity
Aug. 28	Sold 80 units of product to a customer for cash	$150,000	Increased cash	No effect	Increased revenue
Sept. 10	Purchased new desk for office to be paid in October	$1,500	No effect	Increased accounts payable	Increased office expense
Sept. 2–30	Took clients for lunch and paid cash	$680	Decreased cash		Increased owner investments
Oct. 5	Paid for September cell phone usage	$130	Decreased cash		Increased expenses

Required

Using the elements of critical thinking described on the inside front cover, respond.

CHAPTER 3

Analyzing and Recording Transactions

learning objectives

- **LO1** Explain the accounting cycle.
- **LO2** Describe an account, its use, and its relationship to the ledger.
- **LO3** Define debits and credits and explain their role in double-entry accounting.
- **LO4** Describe a chart of accounts and its relationship to the ledger.
- **LO5** Analyze the impact of transactions on accounts.
- **LO6** Record transactions in a journal and post entries to a ledger.
- **LO7** Prepare and explain the use of a trial balance.

Rethink Accounting!

Vancouver, BC—Established in 1999, Rethink Advertising's unique approach to marketing has attracted clients that include A&W, A&P, B.C. Automobile Association, Okanagan Springs Brewery, MJB Coffee, and *Maclean's*. The owners—Grais, Shepansky, and Staples—agree that when it comes to accounting, their post-secondary studies provided them with tools that have been critical to their understanding of how to grow the business. Tom Shepansky, a marketing grad, says that "The most important information for us as a small business relates to revenues, cost control, and obviously the impact on our equity. A&W, our first big name account, asked us to provide them with our balance sheet. The CFO was amused by our lack of resources but was willing to give us our first big break. We've come a long way since then but we still grow our company conservatively, out of profits."

Tom Shepansky's advice to business students, especially non-accountants, is to have a solid understanding of accounting. "You need to talk to your accountant about what is going on in the business. You have to be able to ask the tough questions and make the even tougher decisions. How can you do that without a solid understanding of the numbers? Accounting is the foundation of business and allows you to develop a sound and detailed financial plan to be able to grow revenues but, as important, manage expenses. Poor cash flow management has killed more companies than anything else. Take an active interest in all account balances. Learn to respect and value the numbers or they will come back to haunt you."

http://www.rethinkadvertising.com

CRITICAL THINKING CHALLENGE

What does Tom mean when he says, "[We] grow our company conservatively, out of profits"? How else could Tom grow the company? Also, explain Tom's advice: "Take an active interest in all account balances."

chapter preview

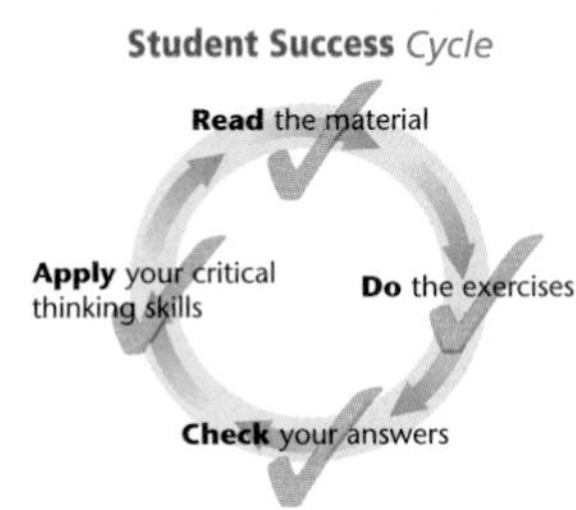

We explained in Chapter 2 how the accounting equation P. 33 helps us understand and analyze transactions and events. Analyzing financial transactions is the first step in the *accounting cycle*. Chapters 3 through 5 continue to explain and demonstrate each of the steps in the accounting cycle. All accounting systems use steps similar to those described here. These procedures are important because they lead to financial statements P. 26. Financial statements—and in particular the information contained in the income statement—are what Rethink in the opening article used to grow the business.

We begin by providing an overview of the accounting cycle. We describe *accounts* and explain their purpose. *Debits* and *credits* are introduced, which enables us to describe the process of recording transactions in a *journal* and *posting* them to a *ledger*. We return to transactions of Vertically Inclined, first introduced in Chapter 1, to illustrate many of these procedures.

The Accounting Cycle

LO1 Explain the accounting cycle.

The **accounting cycle** refers to the steps in preparing financial statements for users. It is called a cycle because the steps are repeated each reporting period. Exhibit 3.1 illustrates the accounting cycle. Chapter 2 introduced transaction analysis, the first step in the accounting cycle. Chapter 3 will focus on the next three steps of the accounting cycle. Step 7, the preparation of financial statements, was introduced in Chapter 2 but is reinforced in Chapters 3 and 4 and is expanded upon in Chapter 5.

Exhibit 3.1
Accounting Cycle

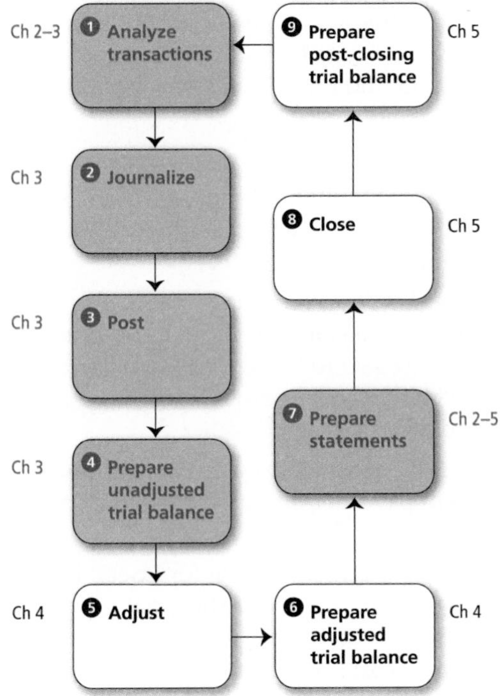

Accounts

LO2 Describe an account, its use, and its relationship to the ledger.

This section explains the importance of an account to accounting and business. We also describe several crucial elements of an accounting system, including ledgers, T-accounts, debits and credits, double-entry accounting, and the chart of accounts.

The Account

An **account** is a detailed record of increases and decreases in a specific asset, liability, or equity item. Information is taken from accounts, analyzed, summarized, and presented in useful reports and financial statements for users. Separate accounts[1] are kept for each type of asset, liability, and equity item. Exhibit 3.2 shows examples of the different types of accounts used by Vertically Inclined.

Exhibit 3.2

Types of Accounts for Vertically Inclined

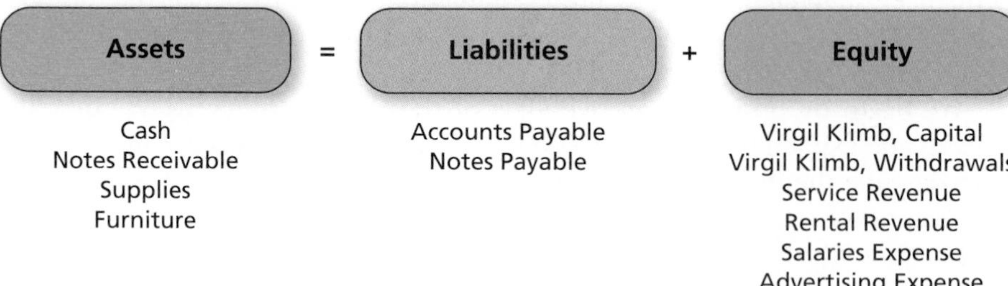

Assets	Liabilities	Equity
Cash	Accounts Payable	Virgil Klimb, Capital
Notes Receivable	Notes Payable	Virgil Klimb, Withdrawals
Supplies		Service Revenue
Furniture		Rental Revenue
		Salaries Expense
		Advertising Expense

A **ledger** is a record containing all accounts used by a business. A ledger is typically in electronic form and is sometimes referred to as the **books**. The term *books* originated when accounting records were maintained manually by recording accounts on separate pages in a special booklet. Books include both the ledger and the *journal*, which is introduced on page 88. Each company will have its own unique set of accounts to suit its type of operation. The remainder of this section introduces accounts that are important to most organizations.

Asset Accounts

Assets are resources controlled by an organization that have future benefits.[2] They have value and are used in the operations of the business to create revenue. For example, Equipment is an asset held by Vertically Inclined for the purpose of creating rental revenue in current and future periods. A separate account is maintained for each asset.

Cash increases and decreases are recorded in a Cash account. Examples are coins, currency, cheques, money orders, and chequing account balances.

Receivables are amounts that the business is expecting to receive in the future. Types of receivables include:

- **Accounts receivable**, which occur when services are performed for or goods are sold to customers in return for promises to pay in the future. These transactions are said to be on credit or *on account*. Accounts receivable are *increased* by services performed or goods sold on credit and *decreased* by customer payments.
- **Notes receivable** (or **promissory notes**), which are unconditional written promises to pay a definite sum of money on demand or on a defined future date(s).

Prepaid Expenses contain payments made for assets that are to be used in the near future. As these assets are used up, the costs of the used assets become expenses. Examples include Office Supplies, Store Supplies, Prepaid Rent, and Prepaid Insurance. A prepaid cost can be initially recorded as an expense *if* it is used up before the end of the period.

Equipment includes assets such as computers, printers, desks, chairs, counters, showcases, and cash registers. These assets are used in the operations of a business for more than one accounting period.

[1] As an example of an account, Exhibit 3.10 shows the Cash account as one of several asset accounts used by Vertically Inclined.

[2] IFRS 2009, "Framework," para. 49(a).

Buildings are assets owned by an organization that can provide space for a store, an office, a warehouse, or a factory. Buildings are assets because they provide benefits.

Land owned by a business is shown as an asset. The cost of land is separated from the cost of buildings located on the land to provide more useful information in financial statements.

Liability Accounts

Liabilities are obligations to transfer assets or provide services to other entities.[3] An organization often has several different liabilities, each of which is represented by a separate account that shows amounts owed to each creditor. The more common liability accounts are described here.

Payables are promises by a business to pay later for an asset or service already received. Types of payables include:

- **Accounts payable**, which occur with the purchase of merchandise, supplies, equipment, or services made by a promise to pay later.
- **Notes payable**, which occur when an organization formally recognizes a promise to pay by signing a promissory note.

Unearned revenues result when customers pay in advance for products or services. Because cash from these transactions is received before revenues are earned, the seller considers them unearned revenues in accordance with the revenue recognition principle. Unearned revenue is a liability because a service or product is *owed* to a customer. It will be earned when the service or product is delivered in the future. Examples of unearned revenue include magazine subscriptions collected in advance by a publisher, sales of gift certificates by stores, airline tickets sold in advance, and rent collected in advance by a landlord.

WestJet Airlines Ltd. reported *advance ticket sales* of $251,354,000 on December 31, 2008.

See Appendix I.

Other Liabilities include wages payable, taxes payable, and interest payable. Each of these is often recorded in a separate liability account. If they are not large in amount, two or more of them may be added and reported as a single amount on the balance sheet.

The liabilities section of WestJet Airlines Ltd.'s balance sheet at December 31, 2008, included accounts payable and accrued liabilities of $249,354,000.

See Appendix I.

Equity Accounts

We described in the previous chapter four types of transactions that affect equity: (1) investments by the owner, (2) withdrawals by the owner, (3) revenues, and (4) expenses. In Chapter 2, we entered all equity transactions in a single column under the owner's name as copied in Exhibit 3.3. When we later prepared the income statement and the statement of changes in equity P. 29, we had to review the items in that column to classify them properly in financial statements.

A preferred approach is to use separate accounts, as illustrated under the Equity heading in Exhibit 3.2.

Exhibit 3.3

Equity Transactions as Analyzed in Chapter 2

Equity	Explanation of Equity Transaction
Virgil Klimb, Capital	
$10,000	Investment by Owner
$10,000	
$10,000	
+ 2,200	Teaching Revenue
$12,200	
− 1,000	Rent Expense
$11,200	
− 700	Salaries Expense
$10,500	
+ 1,600	Teaching Revenue
+ 300	Equipment Rental Revenue
$12,400	
$12,400	
$12,400	
− 600	Withdrawal by Owner
$11,800	

[3] IFRS 2009, "Framework," para. 49(b).

Owner Capital records owner investments. The capital account is identified by including the owner's name. The owner's capital account includes transactions in addition to owner investments, as discussed in the following two paragraphs.

Owner withdrawals are recorded in an account with the name of the owner and the word *Withdrawals*. This account is also sometimes called the owner's *Personal* account or *Drawing* account.

Revenues and expenses incurred for a period is information required by decision makers. Businesses use a variety of accounts to report revenues earned and expenses incurred on income statements. Examples of revenue accounts are Sales, Commissions Earned, Professional Fees Earned, Rent Revenue, Earned Subscription Fees, and Interest Earned. Examples of expense accounts are Advertising Expense, Store Supplies Expense, Office Salaries Expense, Office Supplies Expense, Rent Expense, Utilities Expense, and Insurance Expense.

We can get an idea of the variety of revenues by looking at the chart of accounts in Appendix II. It lists accounts needed to solve some of the exercises and problems in this book.[4]

1. Explain the accounting cycle.
2. Classify the following accounts as either assets, liabilities, or equity: (1) Prepaid Rent, (2) Rent Expense, (3) Unearned Rent, (4) Rent Revenue, (5) Buildings, (6) Owner Capital, (7) Wages Payable, (8) Wages Expense, (9) Office Supplies, and (10) Owner Withdrawals.
3. What is the difference between the accounts Rent Earned, Rent Revenue, and Earned Rent?

Do Quick Study question: QS 3-1

T-Account

A **T-account** is a helpful learning tool that represents an account in the ledger. It shows the effects of individual transactions on specific accounts. The T-account is so named because it looks like the letter T. It is shown in Exhibit 3.4.

Exhibit 3.4

The T-Account

Account Title	
(Left side) *Debit*	(Right side) *Credit*

The format of a T-account includes: (1) the account title on top, (2) a left or debit side, and (3) a right or credit side. Debits and credits are explained in the next section. A T-account provides one side for recording increases in the item and the other side for decreases. As an example, the T-account for Vertically Inclined's Cash account after recording the transactions in Chapter 2 is in Exhibit 3.5.

T-accounts are used throughout this text to help illustrate debits and credits and to solve accounting problems. *This form of account is a learning tool and is typically not used in actual accounting systems. However, many professional accountants often find T-accounts useful for analytical purposes.*

[4] Different companies can use different account titles than those listed in Appendix II. For example, a company might use *Interest Revenue* instead of *Interest Earned*, or *Subscription Fees Revenue* or *Subscription Fees Earned* instead of *Earned Subscription Fees*, or *Rental Expense* instead of *Rent Expense*. It is only important that an account title describes the item it represents. We must use our good judgement when reading financial statements since titles can differ even within the same industry.

Balance of an Account

An **account balance** is the difference between the increases and decreases recorded in an account. To determine the balance, we:

1. Calculate the total increases shown on one side (including the beginning balance)
2. Calculate the total decreases shown on the other side
3. Subtract the sum of the decreases from the sum of the increases, and
4. Calculate the account balance.

The total increases in Vertically Inclined's Cash account are $14,100, the total decreases are $5,700, and the account balance is $8,400. The T-account in Exhibit 3.5 shows how we calculate the $8,400 balance:

Exhibit 3.5

Calculating the Balance of a T-Account

	Cash		
Investment by owner	10,000	2,500	Purchase of supplies
Received from providing consulting services	2,200	1,000	Payment of rent
		700	Payment of salary
Collection of account receivable	1,900	900	Payment of account payable
		600	Withdrawal by owner
Total increases	14,100	5,700	Total decreases
Less decreases	− 5,700		
Balance	8,400		

Debits and Credits

LO3 Define debits and credits and explain their role in double-entry accounting.

The left side of a T-account is always called the **debit** side, often abbreviated Dr. The right side is always called the **credit** side, abbreviated Cr.[5] To enter amounts on the left side of an account is to *debit* the account. To enter amounts on the right side is to *credit* the account. The difference between total debits and total credits for an account is the account balance. When the sum of debits exceeds the sum of credits, the account has a *debit balance*.[6] It has a *credit balance* when the sum of credits exceeds the sum of debits.[7] When the sum of debits equals the sum of credits, the account has a zero balance.

This dual method of recording transactions as debits and credits is an essential feature of *double-entry accounting*, and is the topic of the next section.

[5] These abbreviations are remnants of 18th-century English recordkeeping practices in which the terms *Debitor* and *Creditor* were used instead of *debit* and *credit*. The abbreviations use the first and last letters of these terms where **Dr** resulted from **D**ebito**r**, and **Cr** from **C**redito**r**, just as we still do for *Saint* (St.) and *Doctor* (Dr.).

[6]

	Office Supplies	
	100	60
	300	200
Balance	140	

100 + 300 = 400 total debits; 60 + 200 = 260 total credits; debits are greater than credits, so the 140 balance is a debit (400 − 260).

[7]

Accounts Payable		
350	400	
500	600	
	150	Balance

350 + 500 = 850 total debits; 400 + 600 = 1,000 total credits; credits are greater than debits, so the 150 balance is a credit (1,000 − 850).

Double-Entry Accounting

Debits = Credits

Double-entry accounting means every transaction affects and is recorded in at least two accounts. *The total amount debited must equal the total amount credited* for each transaction. Therefore, the sum of the debits for all entries must equal the sum of the credits for all entries. As well, the sum of debit account balances in the ledger must equal the sum of credit account balances. The only reason that the sum of debit balances would not equal the sum of credit balances is if an error had occurred. Double-entry accounting helps to prevent errors by assuring that debits and credits for each transaction are equal.

The system for recording debits and credits follows from the accounting equation in Exhibit 3.6.

Exhibit 3.6

Accounting Equation

Assets are on the left side of this equation. Liabilities and equity are on the right side. Like any mathematical equation, increases or decreases on one side have equal effects on the other side. For example, the net increase in assets must be accompanied by an identical net increase in the liabilities and equity side. Some transactions affect only one side of the equation. This means that two or more accounts on one side are affected, but their net effect on this one side is zero.

The debit and credit effects for asset, liability, and equity accounts are captured in Exhibit 3.7.

Exhibit 3.7

Debit and Credit Effects for Accounts

CAUTION: We must guard against the error of thinking that the terms debit and credit mean increase or decrease. In an account where a *debit is an increase*, such as an asset, a credit is a decrease. *But* notice that in an account where a debit is a decrease, such as a liability, a *credit is an increase.*

Three important rules for recording transactions in a double-entry accounting system follow from Exhibit 3.7:

1. Increases in assets are debited to asset accounts. Decreases in assets are credited to asset accounts.
2. Increases in liabilities are credited to liability accounts. Decreases in liabilities are debited to liability accounts.
3. Increases in equity are credited to equity accounts. Decreases in equity are debited to equity accounts.

We explained in Chapter 2 how equity increases with owner investments and revenues and decreases with expenses and owner withdrawals. We can therefore expand the accounting equation and debit and credit effects as shown in Exhibit 3.8.

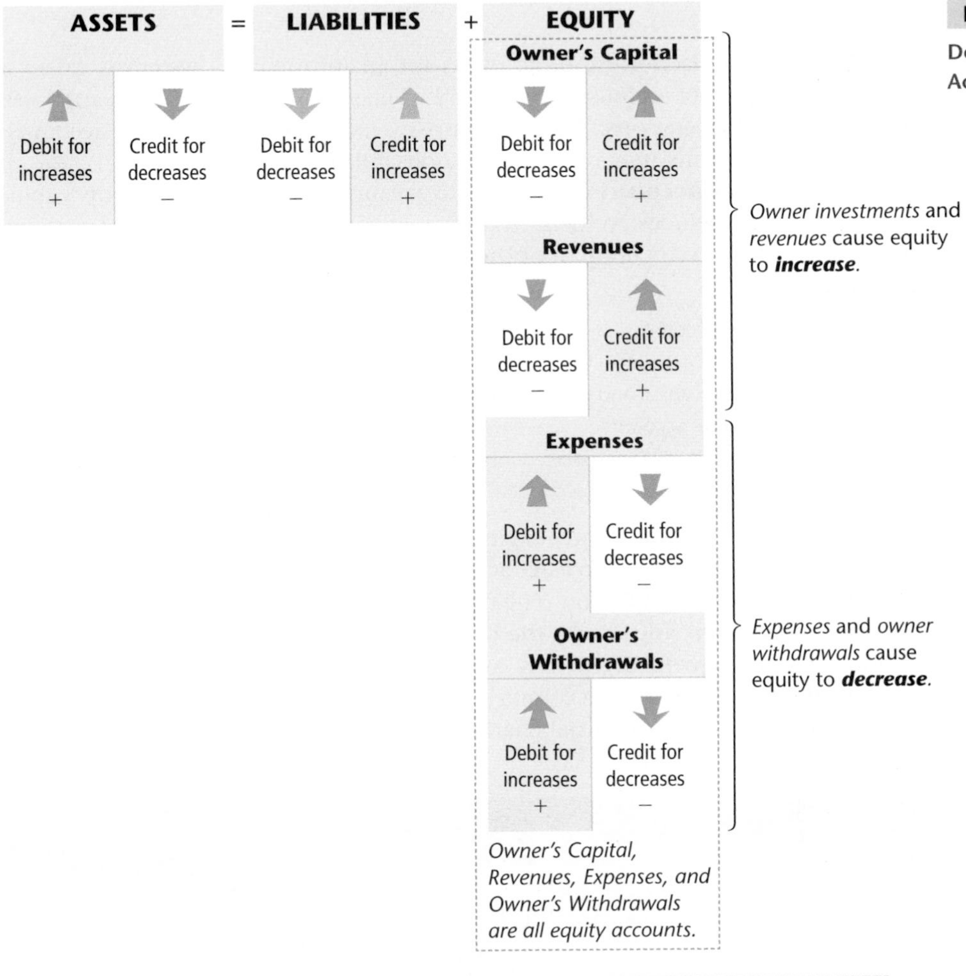

Exhibit 3.8

Debit and Credit Effects for Accounts

The shaded areas in the T-accounts above highlight the *normal balance* of each type of account. The **normal balance** refers to the debit or credit side where *increases* are recorded. For example, the normal balance for an asset account would be a debit because debits cause assets to increase. The normal balance for a revenue account would be a credit because revenues are increased by credits.

Increases in owner's capital or revenues *increase* equity. Increases in owner's withdrawals or expenses *decrease* equity. These important relations are reflected in the following four additional rules:

4. Investments by the owner are credited to owner's capital because they increase equity.
5. Revenues are credited to revenue accounts because they increase equity.
6. Expenses are debited to expense accounts because they decrease equity.
7. Withdrawals made by the owner are debited to owner's withdrawals because they decrease equity.

Our understanding of these diagrams and rules is crucial to analyzing and recording transactions. This also helps us to prepare and analyze financial statements.[8]

[8] We can use good judgement to our advantage in applying double-entry accounting. For example, revenues and expenses normally (but not always) accumulate in business. This means they increase and rarely decrease during an accounting period. Accordingly, we should be alert to decreases in these accounts (debit revenues or credit expenses) to be certain that this is our intent.

Chart of Accounts

LO4 Describe a chart of accounts and its relationship to the ledger.

Recall that the collection of all accounts for an information system is called a *ledger*. The number of accounts needed in the ledger is affected by a company's size and diversity of operations. A small company may have as few as 20 accounts, while a large company may need several thousand.

The **chart of accounts** is a list of all accounts used in the ledger by a company. The chart includes an identification number assigned to each account. The chart of accounts in Appendix II of the text uses the following numbering system for its accounts:

101–199	Asset accounts
201–299	Liability accounts
301–399	Owner capital and withdrawals accounts
401–499	Revenue accounts
501–599[9]	Cost of sales expense accounts
601–699	Operating expense accounts

The numbers provide a three-digit code that is useful in recordkeeping. In this case, the first digit assigned to asset accounts is 1, while the first digit assigned to liability accounts is 2, and so on. The first digit of an account's number also shows whether the account appears on the balance sheet or the income statement. The second and subsequent digits may also relate to the accounts' categories. The numerical basis of a chart of accounts is a fundamental component of a computerized accounting system. A partial chart of accounts for Vertically Inclined follows.

Account Number	Account Name	Account Number	Account Name
101	Cash	301	Virgil Klimb, Capital
106	Accounts Receivable	302	Virgil Klimb, Withdrawals
125	Supplies	403	Teaching Revenue
128	Prepaid Insurance	406	Equipment Rental Revenue
167	Equipment	641	Rent Expense
201	Accounts Payable	622	Salaries Expense
236	Unearned Teaching Revenue	690	Utilities Expense
240	Notes Payable		

4. What is the relationship of an account to the ledger and chart of accounts?
5. What determines the quantity and types of accounts used in the ledger by a company?

Do Quick Study questions: QS 3-2, QS 3-3, QS 3-4, QS 3-5, QS 3-6

[9] Vertically Inclined does not use accounts 501–599. These accounts are used by merchandisers (such as Danier Leather in Appendix I), a topic discussed in Chapter 6.

mid-chapter demonstration problem

Read Apply Do Check

Indicate whether the following transactions increase or decrease the relevant account.

a. A liability account is debited.
b. A revenue account is credited.
c. An asset account is debited.
d. An expense account is credited.
e. Owner's Capital is credited.
f. An asset account is credited.
g. An expense account is debited.
h. A liability account is credited.
i. A revenue account is debited.
j. Owner's Capital is debited.

Analysis component:

Revenues and expenses are both equity accounts. Why is it, then, that increases in revenues are recorded as credits and increases in expenses are recorded as debits?

solution

a. decrease; **b.** increase; **c.** increase; **d.** decrease; **e.** increase; **f.** decrease; **g.** increase; **h.** increase; **i.** decrease; **j.** decrease

Analysis component:

Increases in revenues are recorded as credits because they increase equity; increases in equity are always recorded as credits. Increases in expenses are recorded as debits because they decrease equity; decreases in equity are always recorded as debits.

Analyzing Transactions

LO5 Analyze the impact of transactions on accounts.

We return to the activities of Vertically Inclined to show how debit and credit rules and double-entry accounting are useful in analyzing and processing transactions. We analyze Vertically Inclined's transactions in two steps.

- *Step One* analyzes a transaction and its source document(s).
- *Step Two* applies double-entry accounting to identify the effect of a transaction on account balances.

We should study each transaction thoroughly before proceeding to the next transaction. The first 11 activities are familiar to us from Chapter 2. We expand our analysis of these items and consider four new transactions (numbered 12 through 15) of Vertically Inclined that were omitted earlier.

EXTEND YOUR KNOWLEDGE

1. Investment by owner.

	Cash		101
(1)	10,000		

	Virgil Klimb, Capital		301
		10,000	(1)

Transaction. Virgil Klimb invested $10,000 in Vertically Inclined on January 1, 2011.
Analysis. Assets increase. Equity increases.
Double-entry. Debit the Cash asset account for $10,000. Credit the Virgil Klimb, Capital account in equity for $10,000.

A = L + E[10]
↑ ↑

EXTEND YOUR KNOWLEDGE

[10] The effect of each transaction on the accounting equation is repeated here from Chapter 2 to help you transition to debits and credits.

2. Purchase supplies for cash.

Supplies			125
(2)	2,500		

Cash			101
(1)	10,000	2,500	(2)

Transaction. Vertically Inclined purchases supplies by paying $2,500 cash.
Analysis. Assets increase. Assets decrease. This changes the composition of assets, but does not change the total amount of assets.
Double-entry. Debit the Supplies asset account for $2,500. Credit the Cash asset account for $2,500.

A = L + E
↑↓

3. Purchase equipment and supplies on credit.

Supplies			125
(2)	2,500		
(3)	1,100		

Equipment			167
(3)	6,000		

Accounts Payable			201
		1,100	(3)

Notes Payable			240
		6,000	(3)

Transaction. Vertically Inclined purchases $1,100 of supplies and $6,000 of equipment on credit. Vertically Inclined signs a promissory note for the $6,000 of equipment.
Analysis. Assets increase. Liabilities increase.
Double-entry. Debit two asset accounts: Supplies for $1,100 and Equipment for $6,000. Credit two liability accounts: Accounts Payable for $1,100 and Notes Payable for $6,000.

A = L + E
↑ ↑

4. Services rendered for cash.

Cash			101
(1)	10,000	2,500	(2)
(4)	2,200		

Teaching Revenue			403
		2,200	(4)

Transaction. Vertically Inclined provided teaching services to a group of school children and immediately collected $2,200 cash.
Analysis. Assets increase. Equity increases from Revenue.
Double-entry. Debit the Cash asset account for $2,200. Credit the Teaching Revenue account for $2,200 (this increases equity).

A = L + E
↑ ↑

5. Payment of expense in cash.

Rent Expense			641
(5)	1,000		

Cash			101
(1)	10,000	2,500	(2)
(4)	2,200	1,000	(5)

Transaction. Vertically Inclined pays $1,000 cash for January rent.
Analysis. Assets decrease. Equity decreases from Expense.
Double-entry. Debit the Rent Expense account for $1,000 (this decreases equity). Credit the Cash asset account for $1,000.

A = L + E
↓ ↓

6. Payment of expense in cash.

Salaries Expense			622
(6)	700		

Cash			101
(1)	10,000	2,500	(2)
(4)	2,200	1,000	(5)
		700	(6)

Transaction. Vertically Inclined pays $700 cash for employee's salary for the pay period ending on January 14.
Analysis. Assets decrease. Equity decreases from Expense.
Double-entry. Debit the Salaries Expense account for $700 (this decreases equity). Credit the Cash asset account for $700.

A = L + E
↓ ↓

7. Service contract signed for February and March.

Event. Vertically Inclined signed a contract to teach rock climbing to a group of executives for $5,000 during February and March.

Analysis. There has been no economic exchange between two parties (the services have not been provided and Vertically Inclined did not receive any assets), therefore this has no effect on the accounting equation.

8. Services and rental revenues rendered on credit.

Accounts Receivable			106
(8)	1,900		

Teaching Revenue			403
		2,200	(4)
		1,600	(8)

Equipment Rental Revenue			406
		300	(8)

Transaction. Vertically Inclined provided teaching services of $1,600 and rented climbing equipment for $300 to a customer. The customer is billed $1,900 for the services and Vertically Inclined expects to collect this money in the near future.

Analysis. Assets increase. Equity increases from Revenue.

A = L + E
↑ ↑

Double-entry. Debit the Accounts Receivable asset account for $1,900. Credit two revenue accounts: Teaching Revenue for $1,600 (this increases equity) and Equipment Rental Revenue for $300 (this increases equity).

9. Receipt of cash on account.

Cash			101
(1)	10,000	2,500	(2)
(4)	2,200	1,000	(5)
(9)	1,900	700	(6)

Accounts Receivable			106
(8)	1,900	1,900	(9)

Transaction. On January 25, an amount of $1,900 is received from the client in Transaction 8.

Analysis. Assets increase. Assets decrease. This changes the composition of assets, but does not change the total amount of assets.

A = L + E
↑↓

Double-entry. Debit the Cash asset account for $1,900. Credit the Accounts Receivable asset account for $1,900.

10. Partial payment of accounts payable.

Accounts Payable			201
(10)	900	1,100	(3)

Cash			101
(1)	10,000	2,500	(2)
(4)	2,200	1,000	(5)
(9)	1,900	700	(6)
		900	(10)

Transaction. Vertically Inclined pays CanTech Supply $900 cash toward the account payable of $1,100 owed from the purchase of supplies in Transaction 4.

Analysis. Assets decrease. Liabilities decrease.

A = L + E
↓ ↓

Double-entry. Debit the Accounts Payable liability account for $900. Credit the Cash asset account for $900.

11. Withdrawal of cash by owner.

Virgil Klimb, Withdrawals			302
(11)	600		

Cash			101
(1)	10,000	2,500	(2)
(4)	2,200	1,000	(5)
(9)	1,900	700	(6)
		900	(10)
		600	(11)

Transaction. Virgil Klimb withdraws $600 from Vertically Inclined for personal living expenses.

Analysis. Assets decrease. Equity decreases.

A = L + E
↓ ↓

Double-entry. Debit the Virgil Klimb, Withdrawals account in equity for $600. Credit the Cash asset account for $600.

12. Receipt of cash for future services.

	Cash		101
(1)	10,000	2,500	(2)
(4)	2,200	1,000	(5)
(9)	1,900	700	(6)
(12)	3,000	900	(10)
		600	(11)

	Unearned Teaching Revenue		236
		3,000	(12)

Transaction. Vertically Inclined enters into (signs) a contract with a customer to provide future indoor rock climbing lessons. Vertically Inclined receives $3,000 cash in advance of providing these teaching services.

Analysis. Assets increase. Liabilities increase. Accepting the $3,000 cash obligates Vertically Inclined to perform future services, and is a liability. No revenue is earned until services are provided.

Double-entry. Debit the Cash asset account for $3,000. Credit the Unearned Teaching Revenue liability account for $3,000.

A = L + E
↑ ↑

13. Payment of cash for future insurance coverage.

	Prepaid Insurance		128
(13)	2,400		

	Cash		101
(1)	10,000	2,500	(2)
(4)	2,200	1,000	(5)
(9)	1,900	700	(6)
(12)	3,000	900	(10)
		600	(11)
		2,400	(13)

Transaction. Vertically Inclined pays $2,400 cash (premium) for a two-year insurance policy. Coverage begins on January 1.

Analysis. Assets increase. Assets decrease. This changes the composition of assets from cash to a "right" of insurance coverage. This does not change the total amount of assets. Expense will be incurred as insurance coverage is provided.

Double-entry. Debit the Prepaid Insurance asset account for $2,400. Credit the Cash asset account for $2,400.

A = L + E
↑↓

14. Payment of expense in cash.

	Utilities Expense		690
(14)	230		

	Cash		101
(1)	10,000	2,500	(2)
(4)	2,200	1,000	(5)
(9)	1,900	700	(6)
(12)	3,000	900	(10)
		600	(11)
		2,400	(13)
		230	(14)

Transaction. Vertically Inclined pays $230 cash for January utilities.

Analysis. Assets decrease. Equity decreases from Expense.

Double-entry. Debit the Utilities Expense account for $230 (this decreases equity). Credit the Cash asset account for $230.

A = L + E
↓ ↓

15. Payment of expense in cash.

	Salaries Expense		622
(6)	700		
(15)	700		

	Cash		101
(1)	10,000	2,500	(2)
(4)	2,200	1,000	(5)
(9)	1,900	700	(6)
(12)	3,000	900	(10)
		600	(11)
		2,400	(13)
		230	(14)
		700	(15)

Transaction. Vertically Inclined pays $700 cash for employee's salary for the two-week pay period ending on January 28.

Analysis. Assets decrease. Equity decreases from Expense.

Double-entry. Debit the Salaries Expense account for $700 (this decreases equity). Credit the Cash asset account for $700.

A = L + E
↓ ↓

Accounting Equation Analysis

Exhibit 3.9 shows Vertically Inclined's accounts in the ledger after all 15 transactions are recorded and the balances calculated. For emphasis, the accounts are grouped into three major columns representing the terms in the accounting equation: assets, liabilities, and equity.

Exhibit 3.9

Ledger for Vertically Inclined at January 31, 2011

Assets = Liabilities + Equity

Assets

Cash 101

	Debit	Credit	
(1)	10,000	2,500	(2)
(4)	2,200	1,000	(5)
(9)	1,900	700	(6)
(12)	3,000	900	(10)
		600	(11)
		2,400	(13)
		230	(14)
		700	(15)
Balance	**8,070**		

Accounts Receivable 106

	Debit	Credit	
(8)	1,900	1,900	(9)
Balance	**0**		

Supplies 125

	Debit	Credit	
(2)	2,500		
(3)	1,100		
Balance	**3,600**		

Prepaid Insurance 128

	Debit	Credit	
(13)	2,400		
Balance	**2,400**		

Equipment 167

	Debit	Credit	
(3)	6,000		
Balance	**6,000**		

Liabilities

Accounts Payable 201

	Debit	Credit	
(10)	900	1,100	(3)
		200	Balance

Unearned Teaching Revenue 236

	Debit	Credit	
		3,000	(12)
		3,000	Balance

Notes Payable 240

	Debit	Credit	
		6,000	(3)
		6,000	Balance

Equity

Virgil Klimb, Capital 301

	Debit	Credit	
		10,000	(1)
		10,000	Balance

Virgil Klimb, Withdrawals 302

	Debit	Credit	
(11)	600		
Balance	**600**		

Teaching Revenue 403

	Debit	Credit	
		2,200	(4)
		1,600	(8)
		3,800	Balance

Equipment Rental Revenue 406

	Debit	Credit	
		300	(8)
		300	Balance

Salaries Expense 622

	Debit	Credit	
(6)	700		
(15)	700		
Balance	**1,400**		

Rent Expense 641

	Debit	Credit	
(5)	1,000		
Balance	**1,000**		

Utilities Expense 690

	Debit	Credit	
(14)	230		
Balance	**230**		

Accounts in the white area reflect increases and decreases in equity. Their balances are reported on the income statement or the statement of changes in equity.

TOTALS: **$20,070**[1] = **$9,200**[2] + **$10,870**[3]

[1] $8,070 + $0 + $3,600 + $2,400 + $6,000 = $20,070

[2] $200 + $3,000 + $6,000 = $9,200

[3] $10,000 − $600 + $3,800 + $300 − $1,400 − $1,000 − $230 = $10,870

Exhibit 3.9 highlights several important points. First, as with each transaction, the totals for the three columns show that the accounting equation is in balance:

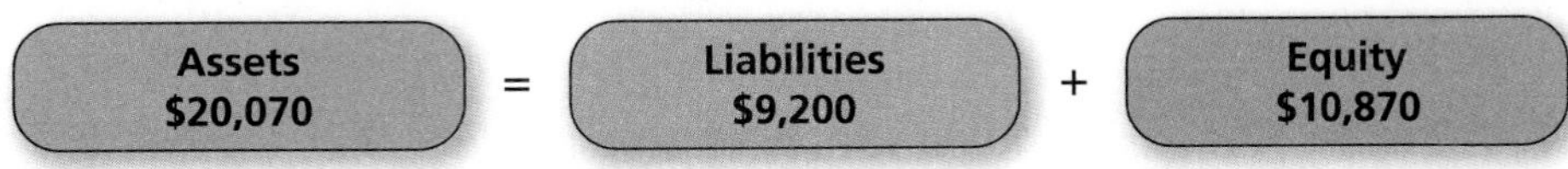

Second, the owner's investment is recorded in the capital account and the withdrawals, revenue, and expense accounts reflect the transactions that change equity. Their ending balances make up the statement of changes in equity. Third, the revenue and expense account balances are summarized and reported in the income statement.

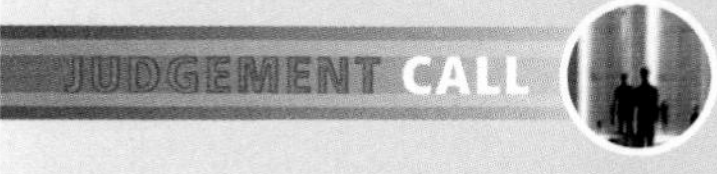

Answer—p. 97

Accounting Clerk

You recently got a job as a part-time accounting clerk to earn extra cash while you attend college. Today, your employer, the owner of the business, made some purchases and instructed you to debit Office Supplies and credit Accounts Payable for the entire amount. He tells you that the invoice is for a few office supplies but mainly for some items that he needed for personal use at home. Explain which GAAP is being violated, and the impact of this error on the financial statements of the business.

6. Does debit always mean increase and credit always mean decrease?
7. What kinds of transactions increase equity? What kinds decrease equity?
8. Why are most accounting systems called *double-entry*?
9. Double-entry accounting requires that (select the best answer):
   a. All transactions that create debits to asset accounts must create credits to liability or equity accounts.
   b. A transaction that requires a debit to a liability account also requires a credit to an asset account.
   c. Every transaction must be recorded with total debits equal to total credits.

Do Quick Study questions: QS 3-7, QS 3-8

Recording and Posting Transactions

LO6 Record transactions in a journal and post entries to a ledger.

In the previous section, we analyzed transactions, *Step One* of the accounting cycle, and recorded their effects directly in T-accounts to help you understand the double-entry accounting system. Yet accounting systems rarely record transactions directly in accounts. Instead, *Step Two* of the accounting cycle requires that we record transactions in a record called a **journal** before recording them in accounts. This is to avoid the potential for error and the difficulty in tracking mistakes. A journal gives us a complete record of each transaction in one place. It also directly links the debits and credits for each transaction. The process of recording transactions in a journal is called **journalizing**.

Step Three of the accounting cycle is to **post**, or transfer, entries from the journal to the ledger. ***Posting occurs after debits and credits for each transaction are entered into a journal***. This process leaves a helpful trail that can be followed in checking for accuracy. This section describes both journalizing and posting of transactions. *Step Four* of the accounting cycle, preparing a *trial balance*, is explained in the next section. Each of these steps in processing transactions is shown in Exhibit 3.10.

Exhibit 3.10

First Four Steps of the Accounting Cycle

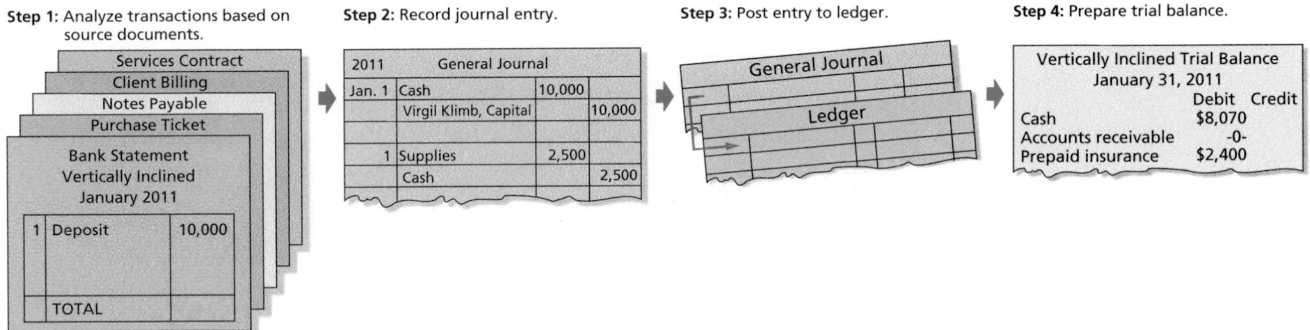

The Journal Entry

The **General Journal** is flexible in that it can be used to record any economic transaction. A General Journal entry includes the following information about each transaction:

1. Date of transaction
2. Titles of affected accounts
3. Dollar amount of each debit and credit
4. Explanation of transaction

Exhibit 3.11 shows how the first three transactions of Vertically Inclined are recorded in a General Journal. A journal is often referred to as the *book of original entry.* Although businesses use computerized systems, this textbook will demonstrate the accounting processes of journalizing and posting using a manual system. Computerized journals and ledgers all operate on the same bases and processes as manual systems.

The third entry in Exhibit 3.11 uses four accounts. There are debits to the two assets purchased, Supplies and Equipment. There are also credits to the two sources of payment, Accounts Payable and Notes Payable. A transaction affecting three or more accounts is called a **compound journal entry**.

Exhibit 3.11

Partial General Journal for Vertically Inclined

General Journal					Page 1
Date		**Account Titles and Explanation**	**PR**	**Debit**	**Credit**
2011					
Jan.	1	Cash		10,000	
		Virgil Klimb, Capital			10,000
		Investment by owner.			
	1	Supplies		2,500	
		Cash			2,500
		Purchased store supplies for cash.			
	1	Supplies		1,100	
		Equipment		6,000	
		Accounts Payable			1,100
		Notes Payable			6,000
		Purchased supplies and equipment on credit.			

Journalizing Transactions

We can identify nine steps in journalizing entries in a General Journal. Review the entries in Exhibit 3.11 when studying these steps.

1. Enter the year on the first line at the top of the first column.
2. Enter the month in Column One on the first line of the journal entry. Later entries for the same month and year on the same page of the journal do not require re-entering the same month and year.
3. Enter the day of the transaction in Column Two on the first line of each entry. Transactions are journalized in date order.
4. Enter the titles of accounts debited. Account titles are taken from the chart of accounts and are aligned with the left margin of the Account Titles and Explanation column.
5. Enter the debit amounts in the Debit column on the same line as the accounts to be debited.
6. Enter the titles of accounts credited. Account titles are taken from the chart of accounts and are indented from the left margin of the Account Titles and Explanation column to distinguish them from debited accounts (an indent of 1 cm is common).
7. Enter the credit amounts in the Credit column on the same line as the accounts to be credited.
8. Enter a brief explanation of the transaction on the line below the entry. This explanation is indented about half as far as the credited account titles to avoid confusing an explanation with accounts. For illustrative purposes, the textbook italicizes explanations so they stand out. This is not normally done.
9. Skip a line after each journal entry for clarity.

A complete journal entry gives us a useful description of the transaction and its effects on the organization.

The **posting reference (PR) column** is left blank when a transaction is initially recorded. Individual account numbers are later entered into the PR column when entries are posted to the ledger.

Computerized systems include error-checking routines that ensure that debits equal credits for each entry. Shortcuts often allow recordkeepers to enter account numbers instead of names, and to enter account names and numbers with pull-down menus.

Balance Column Ledger

T-accounts are a simple and direct learning tool to show how the accounting process works. They allow us to omit less relevant details and concentrate on main ideas. Accounting systems in practice need more structure and use **balance column ledger accounts**. Exhibit 3.12 is an example.

Exhibit 3.12

Cash Account in Balance Column Ledger

		Cash				Account No. 101
Date		Explanation	PR	Debit	Credit	Balance
2011						
Jan.	1		G1	10,000		10,000
	1		G1		2,500	7,500
	10		G1	2,200		9,700

The T-account was derived from the balance column ledger account format and it too has a column for debits and a column for credits. Look at the imaginary T-account superimposed over Exhibit 3.12. The balance column ledger account is different from a T-account because it includes a transaction's date and explanation and has a third column with the balance of the account after each entry is posted. This means that the amount on the last line in this column is the account's current balance. For example, Vertically Inclined's Cash account in Exhibit 3.12 is debited on January 1 for the $10,000 investment by Virgil Klimb. The account then shows a $10,000 debit balance. The account is also credited on January 1 for $2,500, and its new $7,500 balance is shown in the third column. The Cash account is debited for $2,200 on January 10, and its balance increases to a $9,700 debit.

When a balance column ledger is used, the heading of the Balance column does not show whether it is a debit or credit balance. This omission is no problem because every account has a normal balance, as previously highlighted in Exhibit 3.8.

Abnormal Balance

Unusual transactions can sometimes give an abnormal balance to an account. An *abnormal balance* refers to a balance on the side where decreases are recorded. For example, a customer might mistakenly overpay a bill. This gives that customer's account receivable an abnormal credit balance.[11]

Zero Balance

A zero balance for an account is usually shown by writing zeros or a dash in the Balance column. This practice avoids confusion between a zero balance and one omitted in error.

Posting Journal Entries

To ensure that the ledger is up to date, entries are posted as soon as possible. This might be daily, weekly, or monthly. All entries must be posted to the ledger by the end of a reporting period. This is so that account balances are current when financial statements are prepared. Because the ledger is the final destination for individual transactions, it is referred to as the *book of final entry*.

When posting entries to the ledger, the debits in journal entries are copied into ledger accounts as debits, and credits are copied into the ledger as credits. To demonstrate the posting process, Exhibit 3.13 lists six steps to post each debit and credit from a journal entry.

[11] Assume a customer overpaid an account, causing an abnormal balance. To highlight this, brackets can be used as illustrated below or the value could be shown in red.

		Accounts Receivable				Account No. 106
Date		Explanation	PR	Debit	Credit	Balance
2011						
May	1		G1	100		100
	15		G6		125	(25)

Exhibit 3.13

Posting an Entry to the Ledger

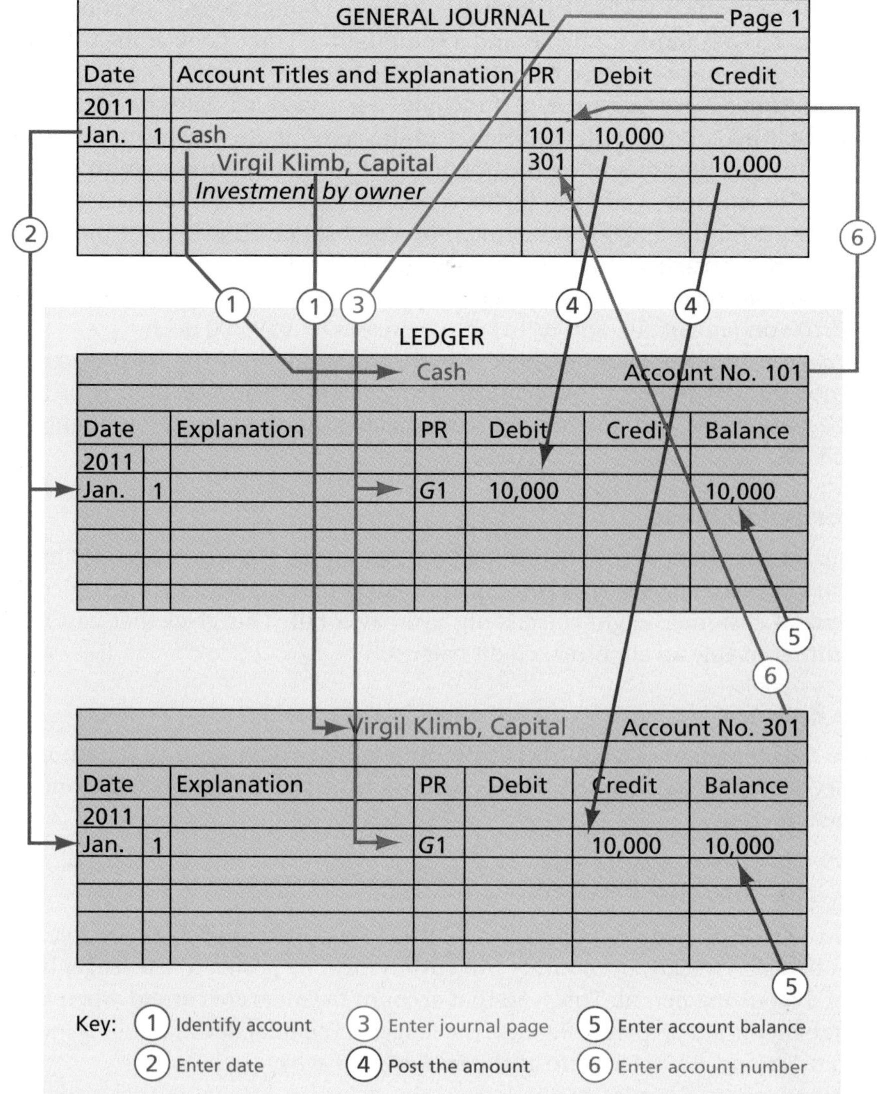

For each journal entry, the usual process is to post debit(s) and then credit(s). The steps in posting are:

1. Identify the ledger account that was debited in the journal entry.
2. Enter the date of the journal entry in this ledger account.
3. Enter the source of the debit in the PR column, both the journal and page. The letter G shows it came from the General Journal.[12]
4. Enter the amount debited from the journal entry into the Debit column of the ledger account.
5. Calculate and enter the account's new balance in the Balance column.
6. Enter the ledger account number in the PR column of the journal entry.

[12] Other journals are identified by their own letters. We discuss other journals later in the book.

Repeat the six steps for credit amounts and Credit columns. Notice that posting does not create new information; posting simply transfers (or copies) information from the General Journal to the appropriate account in the ledger.

Step Six in the posting process for both debit and credit amounts of an entry inserts the account number in the journal's PR column. This creates a cross-reference between the ledger and the journal entry for tracing an amount from one record to another.

Posting in Computerized Systems

Computerized systems require no added effort to post journal entries to the ledger. These systems automatically transfer debit and credit entries from the journal to the ledger database. Journal entries are posted directly to ledger accounts. Many systems have programs that test the reasonableness of a journal entry and the account balance when recorded. For example, a payroll program might alert a preparer to hourly wage rates that are greater than $100.

10. Assume Maria Sanchez, the owner of a new business called RecordLink, invested $15,000 cash and equipment with a market value of $23,000. Assume that RecordLink also took responsibility for an $18,000 note payable issued to finance the purchase of equipment. Prepare the journal entry to record Sanchez's investment.

11. Explain what a compound journal entry is.

12. Why are posting reference numbers entered in the journal when entries are posted to accounts?

Do Quick Study questions: QS 3-9, QS 3-10, QS 3-11

Trial Balance

LO7 Prepare and explain the use of a trial balance.

We know that double-entry accounting records every transaction with equal debits and credits. We also know that an error exists if the sum of debit entries in the ledger does not equal the sum of credit entries. This also means that the sum of debit account balances must equal the sum of credit account balances.

Step Four of the accounting cycle shown in Exhibit 3.1 requires the preparation of a trial balance to check whether debit and credit account balances are equal. A **trial balance** is a list of accounts and their balances at a point in time. Account balances are reported in the debit or credit column of the trial balance. Exhibit 3.14 shows the trial balance for Vertically Inclined after the entries described earlier in the chapter are posted to the ledger.

Another use of the trial balance is as an internal report for preparing financial statements. Preparing statements is easier when we can take account balances from a trial balance instead of searching the ledger. The preparation of financial statements using a trial balance is illustrated in the End-of-Chapter Demonstration Problem. We expand on this process in Chapter 4.

Exhibit 3.14
Trial Balance

Vertically Inclined Rock Gym
Trial Balance
January 31, 2011

Acct. No.	Account	Debit	Credit
101	Cash	$ 8,070	
106	Accounts receivable	-0-	
125	Supplies	3,600	
128	Prepaid insurance	2,400	
167	Equipment	6,000	
201	Accounts payable		$ 200
236	Unearned teaching revenue		3,000
240	Notes payable		6,000
301	Virgil Klimb, capital		10,000
302	Virgil Klimb, withdrawals	600	
403	Teaching revenue		3,800
406	Equipment rental revenue		300
622	Salaries expense	1,400	
641	Rent expense	1,000	
690	Utilities expense	230	
	Totals	$23,300	$23,300

Preparing a Trial Balance

Preparing a trial balance involves five steps:

EXTEND YOUR KNOWLEDGE

1. Identify each account balance from the ledger.
2. List each account and its balance (in the same order as the Chart of Accounts). Debit balances are entered in the Debit column and credit balances in the Credit column.[13]
3. Calculate the total of debit balances.
4. Calculate the total of credit balances.
5. Verify that total debit balances equal total credit balances.

Notice that the total debit balance equals the total credit balance for the trial balance in Exhibit 3.14. If these two totals were not equal, we would know that one or more errors exist. Equality of these two totals does ***not*** guarantee the absence of errors.

Using a Trial Balance

We know that one or more errors exist when a trial balance does not *balance* (when its columns are not equal). When one or more errors exist, they often arise from one of the following steps in the accounting process:

1. Preparing journal entries
2. Posting entries to the ledger
3. Calculating account balances
4. Copying account balances to the trial balance
5. Totalling the trial balance columns

[13] If an account has a zero balance, it can be listed in the trial balance with a zero in the column for its normal balance.

When a trial balance does balance, the accounts are likely free of the kinds of errors that create unequal debits and credits. Yet errors can still exist. One example is when a debit or credit of a correct amount is made to a wrong account. This can occur when either journalizing or posting. The error would produce incorrect balances in two accounts but the trial balance would balance. Another error is to record equal debits and credits of an incorrect amount. This error produces incorrect balances in two accounts but again the debits and credits are equal. We give these examples to show that when a trial balance does balance, it does not prove that all journal entries are recorded and posted correctly.

In a computerized accounting system, the trial balance would ***always*** balance. Accounting software is such that unbalanced entries would not be accepted by the system. However, errors as described in the last paragraph can still exist in a computerized system.

Searching for Errors

When performing accounting manually, if the trial balance does not balance, the error (or errors) must be found and corrected before financial statements are prepared. To search for the error, we check the journalizing, posting, and trial balance preparation process in *reverse order*. Otherwise we would need to look at every transaction until the error was found. The steps involved are:

1. Verify that the trial balance columns are correctly added. If this fails to show the error, then
2. Verify that account balances are accurately copied from the ledger.
3. Determine if a debit or credit balance is mistakenly listed in the trial balance as a credit or debit. Look for this when the difference between total debits and total credits in the trial balance equals twice the amount of the incorrect account balance.
4. Recalculate each account balance. If the error remains, then
5. Verify that each journal entry is properly posted to ledger accounts.
6. Verify that the original journal entry has equal debits and credits.

One frequent error is called a **transposition error**, in which two digits are switched or transposed within a number (e.g., 619 instead of 691). Another type of error, a **slide**,[14] occurs when adding or deleting a zero (or zeros) in a value (e.g., 32 instead of 320). If transposition or a slide is the only error, then the difference between the totals of the trial balance columns will be *evenly divisible by 9*. For example, to find a transposition error:

1. Subtract total debits in the trial balance from total credits.
   Based on the transposition given above, the difference between total debits and credits is $72 ($691 − $619).
2. Divide the difference by 9.
   $72 ÷ 9 = 8
3. The quotient equals the difference between the two transposed numbers.
   8 is the difference between '9' and '1' in both '91' of '691' and '19' of '619.'
4. The number of digits in the quotient tells us the location of the transposition.
   The quotient of 8 is only one digit, so the transposition can be found by checking the first digit from the right in each number.[15]

[14] To find a slide error, follow steps 1 and 2 for a transposition error. The quotient resulting from step 2 identifies the correct value (the incorrect value +/− the correct zeros).

[15] Consider another example where a transposition error involves posting $961 instead of the correct $691. The difference in these numbers is $270, and its quotient is $30 ($270/9). Because the quotient has two digits, it tells us to check the second digits from the right for a transposition of two numbers that have a difference of 3.

Formatting Conventions

Dollar signs are *not* used in journals and ledgers. They *do* appear in financial statements and other reports, including trial balances, to identify the kind of currency being used. This book follows the usual practice of putting a dollar sign beside the first amount in each column of numbers and the first amount appearing after a ruled line that indicates that an addition or subtraction has been performed. The financial statements in Exhibit 2.11 on page 42 demonstrate how dollar signs are used in this book. Different companies use various conventions for dollar signs.

When amounts are entered manually in a formal journal, ledger, or trial balance, commas are not needed to indicate thousands, millions, and so forth. Also, decimal points are not needed to separate dollars and cents. If an amount consists of even dollars without cents, a convenient shortcut uses a dash in the cents column instead of two zeros. However, commas and decimal points are used in financial statements and other reports. An exception is when this detail is not important to users.

WESTJET

It is common for companies to round amounts to the nearest dollar, and to an even higher level for certain accounts. WestJet is typical of many companies in that it rounds its financial statement amounts to the nearest thousand dollars.

CHECKPOINT

13. If a $4,000 debit to Equipment in a journal entry is incorrectly posted to the ledger as a $4,000 credit, and the ledger account has a resulting debit balance of $20,000, what is the effect of this error on the trial balance column totals, assuming no other errors?

14. When are dollar signs typically used in accounting reports?

Do Quick Study questions: QS 3-12, QS 3-13, QS 3-14, QS 3-15

CRITICAL THINKING CHALLENGE

Refer to the Critical Thinking Challenge questions at the beginning of the chapter on page 74. Compare your answers to those suggested on Connect at www.mcgrawhillconnect.ca.

None at the introductory level.

Summary

LO1 | Explain the accounting cycle. The accounting cycle includes the steps in preparing financial statements for users that are repeated each reporting period.

LO2 | Describe an account, its use, and its relationship to the ledger. An account is a detailed record of increases and decreases in a specific asset, liability, or equity item. Information is taken from accounts, analyzed, summarized, and presented in useful reports and financial statements for users.

LO3 | Define debits and credits and explain their role in double-entry accounting. Debit refers to left, and credit refers to right. The following table summarizes debit and credit effects by account type:

	Assets =	Liabilities +	Equity			
			Owner's Capital	Owner's Withdrawals	Revenues	Expenses
Increases	Debits	Credits	Credits	Debits	Credits	Debits
Decreases	Credits	Debits	Debits	Credits	Debits	Credits

Double-entry accounting means that every transaction affects at least two accounts. The total amount debited must equal the total amount credited for each transaction. The system for recording debits and credits follows from the accounting equation. The debit side is the normal balance for assets, owner's withdrawals, and expenses, and the credit side is the normal balance for liabilities, owner's capital, and revenues.

LO4 | Describe a chart of accounts and its relationship to the ledger. A ledger is a record that contains all accounts used by a company. This is what is referred to as *the books*. The chart of accounts is a listing of all accounts and usually includes an identification number that is assigned to each account.

LO5 | Analyze the impact of transactions on accounts. We analyze transactions using the concepts of double-entry accounting. This analysis is performed by determining a transaction's effects on accounts. These effects are recorded in journals and posted to accounts in the ledger.

LO6 | Record transactions in a journal and post entries to a ledger. We record transactions in a journal to give a record of their effects. Each entry in a journal is posted to the accounts in the ledger. This provides information in accounts that is used to produce financial statements. Balance column ledger accounts are widely used and include columns for debits, credits, and the account balance after each entry.

LO7 | Prepare and explain the use of a trial balance. A trial balance is a list of accounts in the ledger showing their debit and credit balances in separate columns. The trial balance is a convenient summary of the ledger's contents and is useful in preparing financial statements. It reveals errors of the kind that produce unequal debit and credit account balances.

guidance answer to JUDGEMENT CALL

Accounting Clerk

The business entity principle is being violated because it requires that the owner's personal expenses be recorded separately from those of his business. By debiting the entire amount to Office Supplies, assets will be overstated on the balance sheet. By crediting Accounts Payable for the whole amount, liabilities will also be overstated. At the end of the accounting period when the amount of supplies used is recorded, Office Supplies Expense will be overstated on the income statement, causing net income to be understated. When net income is too low, equity is also understated.

guidance answers to CHECKPOINT

1. The accounting cycle represents the steps followed each reporting period for the purpose of preparing financial statements.
2. | Assets | Liabilities | Equity |
   |---|---|---|
   | 1, 5, 9 | 3, 7 | 2, 4, 6, 8, 10 |
3. The difference between the three accounts is in the name only; they are variations of a revenue account for rent.
4. An account is a record in the ledger where increases and decreases in a specific asset, liability, or equity

item are recorded and stored. A ledger is a collection of all accounts used by a business. A chart of accounts is a numerical list of the accounts in the ledger. The numbers represent whether the account is an asset, liability, or type of equity.

5. A company's size and diversity affect the number of accounts needed in its ledger. The types of accounts used by a business depend on information that the business needs to both effectively operate and report its activities in financial statements.
6. No. Debit and credit both can mean increase or decrease. The particular meaning depends on the type of account.
7. Equity is increased by revenues and owner's investments in the company. Equity is decreased by expenses and owner's withdrawals.
8. The name *double-entry* is used because all transactions affect and are recorded in at least two accounts. There must be at least one debit in one account and at least one credit in another.
9. c
10. The entry is:

Cash	15,000	
Equipment	23,000	
Notes Payable		18,000
Maria Sanchez, Capital		20,000

11. A compound journal entry is one that affects three or more accounts.
12. Posting reference numbers are entered in the journal when posting to the ledger as a control over the posting process. They provide a cross-reference that allows the bookkeeper or auditor to trace debits and credits from journals to ledgers and vice versa.
13. The effect of this error is to understate the trial balance's debit column total by $8,000.
14. Dollar signs are used in financial statements and other reports to identify the kind of currency being used in the reports. At a minimum, they are placed beside the first and last numbers in each column. Some companies place dollar signs beside any amount that appears after a ruled line to indicate that an addition or subtraction has taken place.

demonstration problem

This Demonstration Problem is based on the same facts as the Demonstration Problem at the end of Chapter 2 except for two additional items: (b) August 1 and (k) August 18. The following activities occurred during the first month of Joane Cardinal's new haircutting business called The Cutlery:

a. On August 1, Cardinal put $16,000 cash into a chequing account in the name of The Cutlery. She also invested $10,000 of equipment that she already owned.

b. On August 1, Cardinal paid $2,400 for six months of insurance effective immediately.

c. On August 2, she paid $2,000 cash for furniture for the shop.

d. On August 3, she paid $3,200 cash to rent space in a strip mall for August.

e. On August 4, she furnished the shop by installing the old equipment and some new equipment that she bought on credit for $21,000. This amount is to be repaid in three equal payments at the end of August, September, and October.

f. On August 5, The Cutlery opened for business. Cash receipts from haircutting services provided in the first week and a half of business (ended August 15) were $1,100.

g. On August 15, Cardinal provided haircutting services on account for $750.

h. On August 17, Cardinal received a $750 cheque in the mail for services previously rendered on account.

i. On August 17, Cardinal paid $250 to an assistant for working during the grand opening.

j. On August 18, Cardinal interviewed a job applicant. The applicant was successful in getting the position and will receive $750 per week for part-time work starting in September.

k. On August 18, a regular customer paid $500 for services to be provided over the next three months.

l. Cash receipts from haircutting services provided during the second half of August were $1,950.

m. On August 31, Cardinal paid an installment on the accounts payable created in (e) above.

n. On August 31, the August hydro bill for $450 was received. It will be paid on September 14.

o. On August 31, she withdrew $500 cash for her personal use.

Required

1. Prepare General Journal entries for the preceding transactions.
2. Open the following accounts: Cash, 101; Accounts Receivable, 106; Prepaid Insurance, 128; Furniture, 161; Store Equipment, 165; Accounts Payable, 201; Unearned Haircutting Services Revenue, 236; Joane Cardinal, Capital, 301; Joane Cardinal, Withdrawals, 302; Haircutting Services Revenue, 403; Wages Expense, 623; Rent Expense, 640; and Hydro Expense, 690.
3. Post the journal entries to the ledger accounts.
4. Prepare a trial balance as of August 31, 2011.
5. Prepare an income statement and a statement of changes in equity for the month ended August 31, 2011, and a balance sheet at August 31, 2011.

Analysis component:

Refer to The Cutlery's August 31, 2011, financial statements. What do each of *equity* and *liabilities* represent?

Planning the Solution

- Analyze each activity to determine if it is a transaction.
- For each transaction, identify the accounts affected and the amount of each effect.
- Use the debit and credit rules to prepare a journal entry for each transaction.
- Post each debit and each credit in the journal entries to the appropriate ledger accounts and cross-reference each amount in the Posting Reference columns in the journal and account.
- Calculate each account balance and list the accounts with their balances on a trial balance.
- Verify that the total debits in the trial balance equal total credits.
- Prepare an income statement, statement of changes in equity, and balance sheet using the information in the trial balance.
- Prepare an answer to each part of the *analysis component* question.

solution

1. General Journal entries:

General Journal				Page G1
Date	**Account Titles and Explanations**	**PR**	**Debit**	**Credit**
2011				
Aug. 1	Cash	101	16,000	
	Store Equipment	165	10,000	
	Joane Cardinal, Capital	301		26,000
	Owner's initial investment.			
1	Prepaid Insurance	128	2,400	
	Cash	101		2,400
	Purchased six months of insurance.			
2	Furniture	161	2,000	
	Cash	101		2,000
	Purchased furniture for cash.			
3	Rent Expense	640	3,200	
	Cash	101		3,200
	Paid rent for August.			
4	Store Equipment	165	21,000	
	Accounts Payable	201		21,000
	Purchased additional equipment on credit.			
15	Cash	101	1,100	
	Haircutting Services Revenue	403		1,100
	Cash receipts from 10 days of operations.			
15	Accounts Receivable	106	750	
	Haircutting Services Revenue	403		750
	To record revenue for services provided on account.			
17	Cash	101	750	
	Accounts Receivable	106		750
	To record cash received as payment on account.			
17	Wages Expense	623	250	
	Cash	101		250
	Paid wages to assistant.			
18	No entry required since there has been no economic exchange.			
18	Cash	101	500	
	Unearned Haircutting Services Revenue	236		500
	To record payment in advance.			
31	Cash	101	1,950	
	Haircutting Services Revenue	403		1,950
	Cash receipts from second half of August.			
31	Accounts Payable	201	7,000	
	Cash	101		7,000
	Paid an installment on accounts payable.			
31	Hydro Expense	690	450	
	Accounts Payable	201		450
	August hydro to be paid by Sept. 14.			
31	Joane Cardinal, Withdrawals	302	500	
	Cash	101		500
	Owner withdrew cash from the business.			

2. & 3. Accounts in the ledger:

Cash					Account No. 101	
Date		**Explanation**	**PR**	**Debit**	**Credit**	**Balance**
2011						
Aug.	1		G1	16,000		16,000
	1		G1		2,400	13,600
	2		G1		2,000	11,600
	3		G1		3,200	8,400
	15		G1	1,100		9,500
	17		G1	750		10,250
	17		G1		250	10,000
	18		G1	500		10,500
	31		G1	1,950		12,450
	31		G1		7,000	5,450
	31		G1		500	4,950

Accounts Receivable					Account No. 106	
Date		**Explanation**	**PR**	**Debit**	**Credit**	**Balance**
2011						
Aug.	15		G1	750		750
	17		G1		750	-0-

Prepaid Insurance					Account No. 128	
Date		**Explanation**	**PR**	**Debit**	**Credit**	**Balance**
2011						
Aug.	1		G1	2,400		2,400

Furniture					Account No. 161	
Date		**Explanation**	**PR**	**Debit**	**Credit**	**Balance**
2011						
Aug.	2		G1	2,000		2,000

Store Equipment					Account No. 165	
Date		**Explanation**	**PR**	**Debit**	**Credit**	**Balance**
2011						
Aug.	1		G1	10,000		10,000
	4		G1	21,000		31,000

Accounts Payable					Account No. 201	
Date		**Explanation**	**PR**	**Debit**	**Credit**	**Balance**
2011						
Aug.	4		G1		21,000	21,000
	31		G1	7,000		14,000
	31		G1		450	14,450

Note: The T-account has been superimposed on each balance column ledger account for illustrative purposes only. It emphasizes that using T-accounts will produce identical balances to the balance column ledger account but in a shortened form. This shortened form is what makes the T-account a convenient tool.

4. & 5.

Unearned Haircutting Services Revenue						Account No. 236
Date		**Explanation**	**PR**	**Debit**	**Credit**	**Balance**
2011						
Aug.	18		G1		500	500

Joane Cardinal, Capital						Account No. 301
Date		**Explanation**	**PR**	**Debit**	**Credit**	**Balance**
2011						
Aug.	1		G1		26,000	26,000

Joane Cardinal, Withdrawals						Account No. 302
Date		**Explanation**	**PR**	**Debit**	**Credit**	**Balance**
2011						
Aug.	31		G1	500		500

Haircutting Services Revenue						Account No. 403
Date		**Explanation**	**PR**	**Debit**	**Credit**	**Balance**
2011						
Aug.	15		G1		1,100	1,100
	15		G1		750	1,850
	31		G1		1,950	3,800

Wages Expense						Account No. 623
Date		**Explanation**	**PR**	**Debit**	**Credit**	**Balance**
2011						
Aug.	17		G1	250		250

Rent Expense						Account No. 640
Date		**Explanation**	**PR**	**Debit**	**Credit**	**Balance**
2011						
Aug.	3		G1	3,200		3,200

Hydro Expense						Account No. 690
Date		**Explanation**	**PR**	**Debit**	**Credit**	**Balance**
2011						
Aug.	31		G1	450		450

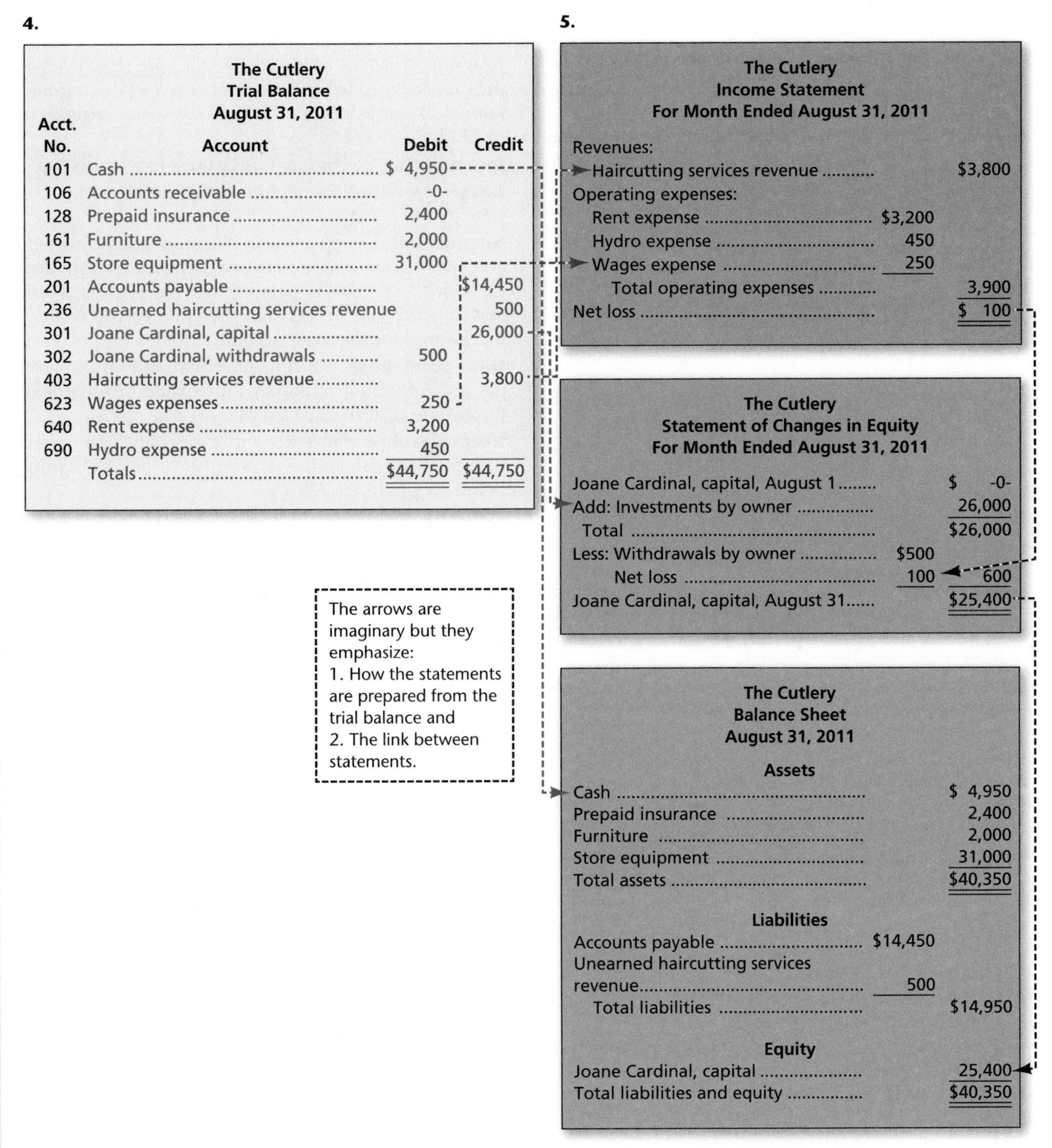

The arrows are imaginary but they emphasize:
1. How the statements are prepared from the trial balance and
2. The link between statements.

4.

The Cutlery
Trial Balance
August 31, 2011

Acct. No.	Account	Debit	Credit
101	Cash	$ 4,950	
106	Accounts receivable	-0-	
128	Prepaid insurance	2,400	
161	Furniture	2,000	
165	Store equipment	31,000	
201	Accounts payable		$14,450
236	Unearned haircutting services revenue		500
301	Joane Cardinal, capital		26,000
302	Joane Cardinal, withdrawals	500	
403	Haircutting services revenue		3,800
623	Wages expenses	250	
640	Rent expense	3,200	
690	Hydro expense	450	
	Totals	$44,750	$44,750

5.

The Cutlery
Income Statement
For Month Ended August 31, 2011

Revenues:		
Haircutting services revenue		$3,800
Operating expenses:		
Rent expense	$3,200	
Hydro expense	450	
Wages expense	250	
Total operating expenses		3,900
Net loss		$ 100

The Cutlery
Statement of Changes in Equity
For Month Ended August 31, 2011

Joane Cardinal, capital, August 1		$ -0-
Add: Investments by owner		26,000
Total		$26,000
Less: Withdrawals by owner	$500	
Net loss	100	600
Joane Cardinal, capital, August 31		$25,400

The Cutlery
Balance Sheet
August 31, 2011

Assets		
Cash		$ 4,950
Prepaid insurance		2,400
Furniture		2,000
Store equipment		31,000
Total assets		$40,350
Liabilities		
Accounts payable	$14,450	
Unearned haircutting services revenue	500	
Total liabilities		$14,950
Equity		
Joane Cardinal, capital		25,400
Total liabilities and equity		$40,350

Analysis component:

Equity represents how much of the total assets are owned (or financed) by the owner of the business. In the case of The Cutlery, the owner, Joane Cardinal, owns $25,400 of the total $40,350 in assets or 63% ($25,400/$40,350 × 100% = 62.949% or 63%). Most of her equity in the business is a result of her $26,000 investment at start-up. The original $26,000 investment was decreased during the month by a $100 net loss and a $500 withdrawal by the owner.

Liabilities represent how much of the total assets have been financed by debt. In the case of The Cutlery, $14,950 or 37% of the total assets are financed by liabilities ($14,950/$40,350 × 100% = 37.051% or 37%).

Glossary

Account A place or location within an accounting system in which the increases and decreases in a specific asset, liability, or equity are recorded and stored. (p. 76)

Account balance The difference between the increases (including the beginning balance) and decreases recorded in an account. (p. 79)

Accounting cycle The steps repeated each reporting period for the purpose of preparing financial statements for users. (p. 75)

Accounts payable Obligations that arise when a promise to pay later is made in connection with purchases of merchandise, supplies, or equipment. (p. 77)

Accounts receivable When services are performed for or goods are sold to customers in return for promises to pay in the future, an *account receivable* is recorded. These transactions are said to be *on credit* or *on account*. Accounts receivable are *increased* by services performed or goods sold on credit and *decreased* by customer payments. (p. 76)

Balance column ledger account An account with debit and credit columns for recording entries and a third column showing the balance of the account after each entry is posted. (p. 90)

Books So named when accounting records were maintained manually by recording accounts on separate pages in a special booklet; the books include both the ledger and the journal. (p. 76)

Chart of accounts A list of all accounts used by a company; includes the identification number assigned to each account. (p. 82)

Compound journal entry A journal entry that affects at least three accounts. (p. 89)

Credit An entry that decreases asset, expense, and owner's withdrawals accounts or increases liability, owner's capital, and revenue accounts; recorded on the right side of a T-account. (p. 79)

Debit An entry that increases asset, expense, and owner's withdrawals accounts or decreases liability, owner's capital, and revenue accounts; recorded on the left side of a T-account. (p. 79)

Double-entry accounting An accounting system where every transaction affects and is recorded in at least two accounts; the sum of the debits for all entries must equal the sum of the credits for all entries. (p. 80)

General Journal The most flexible type of journal; can be used to record any kind of transaction. (p. 89)

Journal A record where transactions are recorded before they are recorded in accounts; amounts are posted from the journal to the ledger; also called the *book of original entry*. (p. 88)

Journalizing Recording transactions in a journal. (p. 88)

Ledger A record containing all accounts used by a business. (p. 76)

Normal balance The debit or credit side on which an account increases. For example, assets increase with debits, therefore the normal balance for an asset is a debit. Revenues increase with credits, therefore a credit is the normal balance for a revenue account. (p. 81)

Note receivable An unconditional written promise to pay a definite sum of money on demand or on a defined future date(s); also called a *promissory note*. (p. 76)

Notes payable Obligations that arise when an organization formally recognizes a promise to pay by signing a promissory note. (p. 77)

Post(ing) Transfer(ring) journal entry information to ledger accounts. (p. 88)

Posting reference (PR) column A column in *journals* where individual account numbers are entered when entries are posted to the ledger. A column in *ledgers* where journal page numbers are entered when entries are posted. (p. 90)

Prepaid Expenses An asset account containing payments made for assets that are not to be used until later. (p. 76)

Promissory note An unconditional written promise to pay a definite sum of money on demand or on a defined future date(s); also called a *note receivable*. (p. 76)

Slide An error that results from adding or deleting a zero (or zeros) in a value. (p. 95)

T-account A simple characterization of an account form used as a helpful tool in showing the effects of transactions on specific accounts. (p. 78)

Transposition error Error due to two digits being switched or transposed within a number. (p. 95)

Trial balance A list of accounts and their balances at a point in time; the total debit balances should equal the total credit balances. (p. 93)

Unearned revenues Liabilities created when customers pay in advance for products or services; created when cash is received before revenues are earned; satisfied by delivering the products or services in the future. (p. 77)

Visit **Connect** at **www.mcgrawhillconnect.ca** for additional study tools, practice quizzes, to search an interactive e-book, and much more.

Concept Review Questions

1. Describe the fundamental steps in the accounting process.
2. What is the difference between a note receivable and an account receivable?
3. Reread the chapter's opening scenario describing Rethink Advertising. Rethink's expenses are about 75% of total revenues. Suggest appropriate account titles for 15 possible expense accounts.

4. Review the Danier Leather balance sheet for fiscal year-end June 28, 2008, in Appendix I. Identify four different asset accounts and four different liability accounts. 
5. If assets are valuable resources and asset accounts have debit balances, why do expense accounts have debit balances?
6. Review the WestJet balance sheet for fiscal year-end December 31, 2008, in Appendix I. Identify three accounts on the balance sheet that would carry debit balances and three accounts on the balance sheet that would carry credit balances.
7. What kinds of transactions can be recorded in a General Journal?
8. Are debits or credits listed first in General Journal entries? Are the debits or the credits indented?
9. Should a transaction be recorded first in a journal or the ledger? Why?
10. Why does the bookkeeper prepare a trial balance?

Quick Study

QS 3-1
Identifying accounts
LO2

Identify the account as an asset, liability, or equity by entering the letter of the account type beside the account name. If the item is an equity account, indicate the type of equity account.

A = Asset
L = Liability
OE = Owner's Capital (Equity)
W = Owner's Withdrawals (Equity)
R = Revenues (Equity)
E = Expenses (Equity)

______ **1.** Buildings
______ **2.** Building Repair Expense
______ **3.** Wages Expense
______ **4.** Wages Payable
______ **5.** Notes Receivable
______ **6.** Notes Payable
______ **7.** Prepaid Advertising
______ **8.** Advertising Expense
______ **9.** Advertising Payable
______ **10.** Unearned Advertising
______ **11.** Advertising Fees Earned
______ **12.** Interest Earned
______ **13.** Interest Expense
______ **14.** Interest Payable
______ **15.** Earned Subscription Fees
______ **16.** Unearned Subscription Fees
______ **17.** Prepaid Subscription Fees
______ **18.** Supplies
______ **19.** Supplies Expense
______ **20.** Rent Revenue
______ **21.** Unearned Rent Revenue
______ **22.** Prepaid Rent
______ **23.** Rent Payable
______ **24.** Service Fees Earned
______ **25.** Jan Sted, Withdrawals
______ **26.** Jan Sted, Capital
______ **27.** Salaries Expense
______ **28.** Salaries Payable
______ **29.** Furniture
______ **30.** Equipment

QS 3-2
Calculating account balances
LO3

Calculate the account balance for each of the following:

Accounts Receivable	
1,000	650
400	920
920	1,500
3,000	

Accounts Payable	
250	250
900	1,800
650	1,400
	650

Service Revenue	
	13,000
	2,500
	810
	3,500

Utilities Expense	
610	
520	
390	
275	

Cash	
3,900	2,400
17,800	3,900
14,500	21,800
340	

Notes Payable	
4,000	50,000
8,000	

QS 3-3
Identifying normal balance as a debit or credit
LO3

Indicate whether the normal balance of each of the following accounts is a debit or a credit:

a. Equipment
b. Land
c. Al Tait, Withdrawals
d. Rent Expense
e. Interest Revenue
f. Prepaid Rent
g. Accounts Receivable
h. Office Supplies
i. Notes Receivable
j. Notes Payable
k. Al Tait, Capital
l. Rent Earned
m. Rent Payable
n. Interest Expense
o. Interest Payable

QS 3-4
Analyzing debit or credit by account
LO3

Identify whether a debit or credit entry would be made to record the indicated change in each of the following accounts:

a. To increase Notes Payable
b. To decrease Accounts Receivable
c. To increase Owner, Capital
d. To decrease Unearned Fees
e. To decrease Prepaid Insurance
f. To decrease Cash
g. To increase Utilities Expense
h. To increase Fees Earned
i. To increase Store Equipment
j. To increase Owner, Withdrawals
k. To decrease Rent Payable
l. To decrease Prepaid Rent
m. To increase Supplies
n. To increase Supplies Expense
o. To decrease Accounts Payable

QS 3-5
Linking credit or debit with normal balance
LO3

Indicate whether a debit or credit is necessary to *decrease* the normal balance of each of the following accounts:

a. Buildings
b. Interest Revenue
c. Bob Norton, Withdrawals
d. Bob Norton, Capital
e. Prepaid Insurance
f. Interest Payable
g. Accounts Receivable
h. Salaries Expense
i. Office Supplies
j. Repair Services Revenue
k. Interest Expense
l. Unearned Revenue
m. Salaries Payable
n. Furniture
o. Interest Receivable

QS 3-6
Developing a chart of accounts
LO4

Using the numbering system on page 82, develop a chart of accounts that assigns an account number to each of the following accounts:

a. Buildings
b. Interest Revenue
c. Bob Norton, Withdrawals
d. Bob Norton, Capital
e. Prepaid Insurance
f. Interest Payable
g. Accounts Receivable
h. Salaries Expense
i. Office Supplies
j. Repair Services Revenue
k. Interest Expense
l. Unearned Revenue
m. Salaries Payable
n. Furniture
o. Interest Receivable

QS 3-7
Recording directly into T-accounts
LO5

1. Record the following transactions directly in the T-accounts provided:
   a. Del Martin invested $15,000 cash into his new business.
   b. Purchased $2,000 of furniture on account.
   c. Purchased $500 of furniture, paying cash.
   d. Did $1,000 of work for a customer; collected cash.
   e. Did $700 of work for a customer on account.
   f. Paid $500 regarding (b).
   g. Collected $300 regarding (e).
   h. Did $400 of work for a client on credit.
2. Calculate the balance in each T-account and prove the accounting equation.

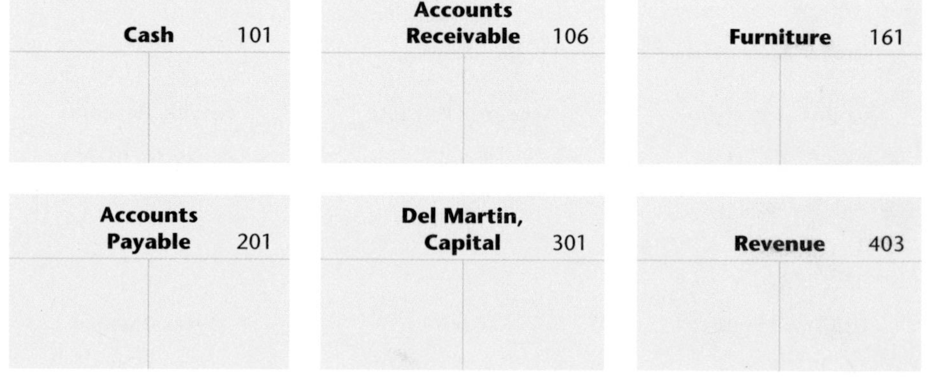

QS 3-8
Recording directly into T-accounts
LO5

Bell Company's records showed the following April 30, 2011, account balances:

Account	Debit	Credit
Cash	Apr 30 15,000	
Accounts Receivable	Apr 30 3,200	
Car		
Accounts Payable		6,000 Apr 30
Unearned Revenue		1,800 Apr 30
Dee Bell, Capital		8,900 Apr 30
Revenue		3,000 Apr 30
Wages Expense	Apr 30 1,500	

1. Using the chart of accounts numbering system on page 82, assign an account number to each account.

2. Record the May 2011 transactions directly in the T-accounts provided:

May		
	2	Dee Bell transferred her personal car valued at $8,000 into the business.
	10	Did $4,000 of work for a customer on account.
	12	Collected $10,000 from a customer for work to be done in July 2011.
	15	Paid wages of $6,000.
	16	Collected $4,000 from the customer of May 10.
	22	Paid half of the outstanding accounts payable.

3. Calculate the May 31, 2011, balance in each T-account and prove the accounting equation.

QS 3-9
Preparing journal entries
LO3, 5, 6

Prepare journal entries for the following transactions that occurred during 2011:

May		
	1	Purchased equipment on account; $500.
	2	Paid for the equipment purchased on May 1.
	3	Purchased supplies for cash; $100.
	4	Paid wages to employees; $2,000.
	5	Performed services for a client and collected cash; $750.
	6	Did work for a customer on credit; $2,500.
	7	Collected the amount owing from the customer of May 6.

QS 3-10
Preparing journal entries
LO3, 5, 6

Prepare journal entries for the following transactions that occurred during January 2011:

January		
	3	Stan Adams opened a landscaping business by investing $60,000 cash and equipment having a $40,000 fair value.
	4	Purchased office supplies on credit for $340.
	6	Received $5,200 for providing landscaping services to a customer.
	15	Paid $200 regarding the office supplies purchase of January 4.
	16	Purchased $700 of office supplies on account.
	30	Paid the balance owing regarding the office supplies purchase of January 4.

QS 3-11
Recording in T-accounts
LO5, 6

a. Set up the following accounts (use the balance column format as illustrated in Exhibit 3.12 on page 90): Cash (101), Office Supplies (124), Equipment (163), Accounts Payable (201), Stan Adams, Capital (301), and Landscaping Services Revenue (403).

b. Post the journal entries from QS 3-10 to the accounts and enter the balance after each posting.

QS 3-12
Preparing a trial balance
LO7

Using the account information shown below, prepare a trial balance at January 31, 2011.

Vahn Landscaping
General Ledger

Cash 101	
5,000	6,000
2,000	4,000
3,000	1,000
8,000	

Equipment 163	
9,000	

Unearned Fees 233	
	2,000

Brea Vahn, Capital 301	
	14,000

Brea Vahn, Withdrawals 302	
1,000	

Fees Earned 401	
	3,000
	8,000

Rent Expense 640	
6,000	

Utilities Expense 690	
4,000	

QS 3-13
Identifying a posting error
LO3, 5, 6, 7

A trial balance has total debits of $21,000 and total credits of $25,500. Which one of the following errors would create this imbalance? Explain.

a. A $4,500 debit to Salaries Expense in a journal entry was incorrectly posted to the ledger as a $4,500 credit, leaving the Salaries Expense account with a $750 debit balance.
b. A $2,250 credit to Teaching Fees Earned in a journal entry was incorrectly posted to the ledger as a $2,250 debit, leaving the Teaching Fees Earned account with a $6,300 credit balance.
c. A $2,250 debit to Rent Expense in a journal entry was incorrectly posted to the ledger as a $2,250 credit, leaving the Rent Expense account with a $3,000 debit balance.

QS 3-14
Identifying a transposition error
LO7

Identify the transposition error in the following trial balance, assuming this is the only error.

SunFlowers
Trial Balance
September 30, 2011

Acct. No.	Account	Debit	Credit
101	Cash	$ 9,800	
165	Equipment	10,350	
201	Accounts payable		$ 750
301	Tracy Rumanko, Capital		3,800
403	Consulting revenue		17,000
640	Rent expense	4,100	
	Totals	$24,250	$21,550

QS 3-15
Identifying a slide error
LO7

Identify the slide error in the following trial balance, assuming this is the only error.

Delwin's Fitness Training
Trial Balance
April 30, 2011

Account	Debit	Credit
Cash	$330	
Supplies	38	
Notes payable		$ 25
Jane Delwin, capital		100
Fees earned		378
Wages expense	360	
Totals	$728	$503

Exercises

Exercise 3-1
Recording the effects of transactions directly in T-accounts
LO3, 5

Check figure:
Total cash = $12,850

Set up the following T-accounts: Cash; Accounts Receivable; Office Supplies; Office Equipment; Accounts Payable; Sandra Moses, Capital; Sandra Moses, Withdrawals; Fees Earned; and Rent Expense. Next, record these transactions of the Northern Lights Company by recording the debit and credit entries directly in the T-accounts. Use the letters beside the transactions to identify the entries. Finally, determine the balance of each account.

a. Sandra Moses invested $25,500 cash in the business.
b. Purchased $750 of office supplies for cash.
c. Purchased $14,100 of office equipment on credit.
d. Received $3,000 cash as fees for services provided to a customer.
e. Paid for the office equipment purchased in transaction (c).
f. Billed a customer $5,400 as fees for services.
g. Paid the monthly rent with $1,050 cash.
h. Collected $2,250 of the account receivable created in transaction (f).
i. Moses withdrew $2,000 cash from the business for personal use.

Exercise 3-2
Recording the effects of transactions directly in T-accounts
LO3, 5

Check figure:
Total cash = $40

Poundmaker Accounting Services began operations on January 1, 2011. Set up the following T-accounts, which show balances at January 31: Cash $700; Accounts Receivable $1,200; Prepaid Insurance $0; Computer Equipment $480; Accounts Payable $60; Notes Payable $0; Neil Poundmaker, Capital $800; Neil Poundmaker, Withdrawals $0; Service Revenue $2,600; Wages Expense $1,080. The activities below occurred during February. Identify the transactions and record them directly in the T-accounts. Use the dates beside the transactions to identify the entries. Also, determine the balance of each account.

Feb.	2	Neil Poundmaker provided services to a customer and collected cash of $2,800.
	10	$7,600 of new computer equipment was purchased for the business by signing a note.
	12	$15,000 of accounting services were performed for a client on account.
	14	Paid the $4,000 annual insurance premium covering the next 12 months.
	18	Billed a client $1,900 for work performed today.
	20	Collected $2,400 from a credit customer.
	21	Poundmaker ordered $1,600 in new accounting software from a local vendor; it will be paid for when it arrives in about two weeks.
	23	Paid the outstanding accounts payable.
	25	Poundmaker withdrew $1,000 cash for personal use.
	26	A part-time employee was paid wages of $800.

Analysis component:
Regarding February 12, which GAAP must be considered in determining the appropriate accounting treatment for this item?

Exercise 3-3
Recording the effects of transactions directly in T-accounts
LO3, 5

Check figure:
Total cash = $2,880

On March 1, 2011, Nels Sigurdsen opened an automotive repair shop called Nels Car Repairs. Set up the following T-accounts that show balances at March 31, 2011: Cash $1,800; Accounts Receivable $4,800; Repair Supplies $1,400; Equipment $7,400; Accounts Payable $500; Nels Sigurdsen, Capital $2,350; Nels Sigurdsen, Withdrawals $500; Repair Revenue $14,000; Rent Expense $950. The activities below occurred during April. Identify the transactions and record them directly in the T-accounts. Use the dates beside the transactions to identify the entries. Also, determine the balance of each account.

Apr.	2	Nels Sigurdsen did some repairs on a car today and immediately collected $780.
	5	Sigurdsen hired a tune-up specialist who will start next month and get paid $3,000 per month.
	9	Repair supplies were purchased on credit; $890.
	10	Paid $400 regarding the supplies purchased on April 9.
	15	Bought a small piece of equipment, paying cash of $300.
	18	Did work for a customer on account; $1,200.
	19	Collected $2,000 regarding a customer's account.
	25	Rented some specialized equipment from Ace Rentals; $250 on account.
	29	Sigurdsen withdrew $1,000 cash for personal use.

Exercise 3-4
Journalizing, posting, preparing a trial balance, and financial statements
LO3, 5, 6, 7

DelaWare incurred the following transactions during July 2011, its first month of operations:

July	1	The owner, Sue Ware, invested $5,000 cash.
	10	Purchased $2,500 worth of equipment on credit.
	12	Performed services for a client and received $10,000 cash.
	14	Paid for expenses; $3,500.
	15	Completed services for a client and sent a bill for $1,500.
	31	The owner withdrew $250 cash for personal use.

Check figures:
4. Total debits = $19,000
5. Total assets = $15,250

Required

1. Create a General Ledger by setting up the following accounts: Cash, 101; Accounts Receivable, 106; Equipment, 150; Accounts Payable, 201; Sue Ware, Capital, 301; Sue Ware, Withdrawals, 302; Revenue, 401; Expenses, 501.
2. Journalize the July transactions in the General Journal.
3. Post the July transactions from your General Journal into your General Ledger accounts.

4. Prepare a trial balance based on the balances in your General Ledger accounts.
5. Prepare an income statement, statement of changes in equity, and balance sheet based on your trial balance.

Analysis component:
Assets are financed by debt and equity transactions, a concept reinforced by the accounting equation: A = L + E. Since accounts receivable are an asset, are they financed by debt and/or equity? Explain.

Exercise 3-5
Chart of accounts
LO4

You have been given the following guide regarding the chart of accounts for Paquette Advisors:

100–199	Assets	400–499	Revenues
200–299	Liabilities	500–599	Expenses
300–399	Equity		

Using the account information from Exercise 3-6, develop a chart of accounts for Paquette Advisors.

Exercise 3-6
Journalizing, posting, preparing a trial balance, and financial statements
LO3, 5, 6, 7

Paquette Advisors showed the following account balances in its General Ledger accounts as at January 31, 2011.

Account	Debit	Credit
Cash	11,500	
Accounts Receivable	6,000	
Office Equipment	12,500	
Accounts Payable		3,000
Unearned Revenue		500
Aaron Paquette, Capital		9,500
Aaron Paquette, Withdrawals	2,000	
Consulting Revenues		37,500
Salaries Expense	10,000	
Rent Expense	7,500	
Utilities Expense	1,000	

During February, the following transactions occurred:

Feb.	1	Performed work for a client and received cash of $8,500.
	5	Paid $2,000 regarding outstanding accounts payable.
	10	Received cash of $2,500 for work to be done in March.
	12	Called FasCo Rentals to book the use of some equipment next month. The $400 rental fee will be paid in full when the equipment is returned.
	17	The owner withdrew cash of $500 for personal use.
	28	Paid salaries of $10,000.

Check figure:
4. Total assets = $28,500

Required
1. Journalize the February transactions in the General Journal.
2. Post the transactions from your General Journal to the General Ledger (T-accounts above).
3. Prepare a trial balance based on the balances in your General Ledger.
4. Prepare the balance sheet as at February 28, 2011.

Analysis component:
Paquette Advisors shows Unearned Revenue on its February 28, 2011, balance sheet. Explain what Unearned Revenue is. As part of your answer, be sure to address why Unearned Revenue is reported as a liability.

Exercise 3-7
Analyzing transactions from T-accounts
LO3, 5

Prepare General Journal entries for each of the seven transactions posted to the following T-accounts. Provide a short description of each transaction. The first description is done as an example.
(a) *The owner invested cash, an automobile, and equipment in the business.*

Cash			
(a)	7,000	3,600	(b)
(e)	2,500	600	(c)
		2,400	(f)
		700	(g)

Office Supplies			
(c)	600		
(d)	200		

Prepaid Insurance			
(b)	3,600		

Equipment			
(a)	5,600		
(d)	9,400		

Automobiles			
(a)	11,000		

Accounts Payable			
(f)	2,400	9,600	(d)

Jerry Steiner, Capital			
		23,600	(a)

Delivery Services Revenue			
		2,500	(e)

Gas and Oil Expense			
(g)	700		

Exercise 3-8
General Journal entries
LO3, 5, 6

TLC Laser Eye Centres showed the following selected activities during the month of April 2011. Journalize the transactions in your General Journal.

April	5	Performed surgery on a customer today and collected $1,500 cash.
	8	Purchased surgical supplies on credit; $3,000.
	15	Paid salaries; $57,000.
	20	Paid for the surgical supplies purchased on April 8.
	21	Contacted a client's lawyer today regarding a complaint about the surgery. The client is planning to sue for $100,000.
	22	Performed six surgeries today, all on credit; $1,500 each.
	29	Collected $3,000 from the credit customers of April 22.
	30	Paid the April utilities bill today; $1,800.

Exercise 3-9
Analyzing and journalizing revenue transactions
LO3, 5, 6

Examine the following transactions and identify those that created revenues for TI Servicing, a sole proprietorship owned by Todd Iver. Prepare General Journal entries to record those transactions and explain why the other transactions did not create revenues.

a. Todd Iver invested $76,500 cash in the business.
b. Provided $2,700 of services on credit.
c. Received $3,150 cash for services provided to a client.
d. Received $18,300 from a client in payment for services to be provided next year.
e. Received $9,000 from a client in partial payment of an account receivable.
f. Borrowed $300,000 from the bank by signing a promissory note.

Exercise 3-10
Analyzing and journalizing expense transactions
LO3, 5, 6

Examine the following transactions and identify those that created expenses for EK Servicing. Prepare General Journal entries to record those transactions and explain why the other transactions did not create expenses.

a. Paid $14,100 cash for office supplies purchased 30 days previously.
b. Paid the $1,125 salary of the receptionist.
c. Paid $45,000 cash for equipment.
d. Paid utility bill with $930 cash.
e. Elijah Kunnuk withdrew $5,000 from the business account for personal use.

Exercise 3-11
Posting from the General Journal to the ledger
LO4, 6

Check figure:
b. Jan. 31, 2011, Cash balance = $3,600

Walker's Inspection Services is in its second month of operations. You have been given the following journal entries regarding its January 2011 transactions.

Required

a. Set up the following accounts (use the balance column format) entering the opening balances brought forward from the end of last month, December 31, 2010: Cash (101) $850; Accounts Receivable (106) $300; Equipment (167) $1,500; Accounts Payable (201) $325; Jay Walker, Capital (301) $2,325; Jay Walker, Withdrawals (302) $300; Fees Earned (401) $1,800; and Salaries Expense (622) $1,500.

b. Post the journal entries to the accounts and enter the balance after each posting.

General Journal — **Page 1**

Date		Account Titles and Explanation	PR	Debit	Credit
2011					
Jan.	1	Cash		3,500	
		Jay Walker, Capital			3,500
		Additional owner investment.			
	12	Accounts Receivable		9,000	
		Fees Earned			9,000
		Performed work for a customer on account.			
	20	Equipment		12,000	
		Accounts Payable			10,000
		Cash			2,000
		Purchased equipment by paying cash and the balance on credit.			
	31	Cash		5,000	
		Accounts Receivable			5,000
		Collected cash from credit customer.			
	31	Salaries Expense		3,000	
		Cash			3,000
		Paid month-end salaries.			
	31	Jay Walker, Withdrawals		750	
		Cash			750
		Jay Walker withdrew cash for personal use.			

Analysis component:
The accounting cycle requires that transactions be journalized in the General Journal and then posted in the General Ledger. This seems to indicate that we are recording the same information in two different places. Why can't we eliminate journalizing or posting?

Exercise 3-12
General Journal entries
LO3, 5, 6

Prepare General Journal entries to record the following August 2011 transactions of a new business called The Pixel Shop.

Aug.	1	Joseph Eetok, the owner, invested $15,000 cash and photography equipment with a fair value of $17,000.
	1	Rented a studio, paying $6,500 for the next three months in advance.
	5	Purchased office supplies for $1,800 cash.
	20	Received $9,200 in photography fees.
	31	Paid $1,100 for August utilities.

Exercise 3-13
Ledger accounts and the trial balance
LO3, 5, 6, 7

Check figure:
Trial balance total debits = $41,200

Set up the following accounts (use the balance column format): Cash (101); Office Supplies (124); Prepaid Rent (131); Photography Equipment (167); Joseph Eetok, Capital (301); Photography Fees Earned (401); and Utilities Expense (690). Then, using your General Journal entries from Exercise 3-12, post to the ledger. Finally, prepare the August 31, 2011, trial balance.

Analysis component:
Joseph Eetok wanted to buy a building for his business and took the August 31, 2011, trial balance to his bank manager. Is the trial balance used for external reporting? Explain.

Exercise 3-14

T-accounts and the trial balance

LO3, 5, 6, 7

Follow the instructions in Exercise 3-13, but instead of using a balance column format for the accounts, use T-accounts.

Exercise 3-15

Preparing financial statements from a trial balance

LO7

Check figures:
Net loss = $5,000;
Total assets = $97,300

Hogan's Consulting showed the following trial balances for its first year just ended December 31, 2011:

Account Title	Debit	Credit
Cash	$ 12,000	
Accounts receivable	8,300	
Prepaid rent	5,000	
Machinery	72,000	
Accounts payable		$ 800
Notes payable		53,500
Lisa Hogan, capital		50,000
Lisa Hogan, withdrawals	2,000	
Consulting fees earned		46,000
Wages expense	37,000	
Rent expense	14,000	
Totals	$150,300	$150,300

Required
Use the information provided to complete an income statement, statement of changes in equity, and balance sheet.

Analysis component:
If Hogan's Consulting continues to experience losses, what alternatives are available to prevent assets from decreasing?

Exercise 3-16

Preparing financial statements from a trial balance

LO7

Check figures:
Net income = $1,090;
Total assets = $2,950

JenCo showed the following trial balance information (in alphabetical order) for its first month just ended March 31, 2011:

Account	Debit	Credit
Accounts payable		$ 260
Accounts receivable	$ 950	
Cash	1,000	
Equipment	700	
Interest expense	10	
Marie Jensen, capital		2,050
Marie Jensen, withdrawals	1,500	
Notes payable		800
Prepaid insurance	300	
Salaries expense	800	
Service revenue		1,900
Unearned service revenue		250
Totals	$5,260	$5,260

Required
Use the information provided to complete an income statement, statement of changes in equity, and balance sheet.

Exercise 3-17
Preparing financial statements from a trial balance

LO7

Check figures:
Net loss = $3,000;
Total assets = $293,000

Nanimahoo Marketing Services has been operating for several years. It showed the following trial balance information (in alphabetical order) for the month just ended March 31, 2011:

Account	Debit	Credit
Accounts payable		$ 46,000
Accounts receivable	$ 14,000	
Building	80,000	
Cash	30,000	
Fees earned		170,000
Dee Nanimahoo, capital*		122,000
Dee Nanimahoo, withdrawals	18,000	
Land	116,000	
Machinery	50,000	
Notes payable		146,000
Office supplies	3,000	
Office supplies expense	7,000	
Wages expense	166,000	
Totals	$484,000	$484,000

*The $122,000 balance includes $10,000 invested by the owner during March.

Required
Using the information provided, prepare an income statement and a statement of changes in equity for the month ended March 31, 2011, and a balance sheet at March 31, 2011.

Exercise 3-18
Effects of posting errors on the trial balance

LO3, 5, 6, 7

Complete the following table by filling in the blanks. For each of the listed posting errors:

1. Enter in column (1) the amount of the difference that the error would create between the two trial balance columns (show a zero if the columns would balance).
2. Identify if there would be a difference between the two columns, and identify in column (2) the trial balance column that would be larger.
3. Identify the account(s) affected in column (3).
4. Identify the amount by which the account(s) is (are) under- or overstated in column (4).
The answer for the first error is provided as an example.

	Description	(1) Difference Between Debit and Credit Columns	(2) Column With the Larger Total	(3) Identify Account(s) Incorrectly Stated	(4) Amount That Account(s) Is (Are) Over- or Understated
a.	*A $2,400 debit to Rent Expense was posted as a $1,590 debit.*	*$810*	*Credit*	*Rent Expense*	*Rent Expense is understated by $810*
b.	A $42,000 debit to Machinery was posted as a debit to Accounts Payable.				
c.	A $4,950 credit to Services Revenue was posted as a $495 credit.				
d.	A $1,440 debit to Store Supplies was not posted at all.				
e.	A $2,250 debit to Prepaid Insurance was posted as a debit to Insurance Expense.				
f.	A $4,050 credit to Cash was posted twice as two credits to the Cash account.				
g.	A $9,900 debit to the owner's withdrawals account was debited to the owner's capital account.				

Exercise 3-19
Analyzing the trial balance
LO3, 5, 6, 7

During March, Bonnie Doan, the owner of Doan Cleaning Services, had trouble keeping her debits and credits equal. The following errors were noted:

a. Bonnie did not post the entry to record $3,500 of services performed on account.
b. In posting a $300 payment on account, Bonnie debited Cash and credited Accounts Payable.
c. In posting a cash payment, Bonnie correctly debited Accounts Payable for $425 but incorrectly credited Cash for $245.
d. In posting a cash receipt of $750, Bonnie debited Cash but forgot to post the credit to Accounts Receivable.
e. In posting the purchase of $1,000 of equipment on credit, Bonnie debited Accounts Payable and credited Equipment.

Required
For each of the errors described, indicate:
1. Whether debits equal credits on the trial balance, and
2. Which account(s) have incorrect balances.

Exercise 3-20
Transposition and slide errors on the trial balance
LO7

Required
Identify the single transposition or slide error in each of the following independent trial balances.

	Case A		Case B		Case C	
Cash	$ 120		$ 3,900		$ 59	
Accounts receivable	260		1,900		46	
Equipment	3,170		12,900		791	
Accounts payable		$ 190		$ 2,350		$ 72
Capital		1,100		16,150		229
Withdrawals	850		7,000		-0-	
Revenue		3,000		9,600		641
Wages expense	610		8,700		10	
Totals	$5,010	$4,290	$34,400	$28,100	$906	$942

Problems

Problem 3-1A
Recording transactions in T-accounts
LO3, 5

Following are business activities completed by Jeff Bridges during the month of November 2011:

a. Invested $40,000 cash and office equipment with a $15,000 fair value in a new sole proprietorship named Bridges Tax Consulting.
b. Purchased land and a small office building. The land was worth $15,000, and the building was worth $85,000. The purchase price was paid with $20,000 cash and a long-term note payable for $80,000.
c. Purchased $1,200 of office supplies on credit.
d. Transferred title of his personal automobile to the business. The automobile had a value of $9,000 and was to be used exclusively in the business.
e. Purchased $3,000 of additional office equipment on credit.
f. Paid $750 wages to an assistant.
g. Provided services to a client and collected $3,000 cash.
h. Paid $400 for the month's utilities.
i. Signed an equipment rental agreement to commence in January. A deposit of $250 must be paid by December 15.
j. Paid the account payable created in transaction (c).
k. Purchased $10,000 of new office equipment by paying $9,300 cash and trading in old equipment with a recorded cost of $700.
l. Completed $2,600 of services for a client. This amount is to be paid within 30 days.
m. Paid $750 wages to an assistant.
n. Received $1,900 payment on the receivable created in transaction (l).
o. Withdrew $3,200 cash from the business for personal use.

Check figure:
2. Cash balance, Nov. 30, 2011 = $9,300

Required

1. Set up the following T-accounts: Cash; Accounts Receivable; Office Supplies; Automobiles; Office Equipment; Building; Land; Accounts Payable; Long-Term Notes Payable; Jeff Bridges, Capital; Jeff Bridges, Withdrawals; Fees Earned; Wages Expense; and Utilities Expense.
2. Record the effects of the transactions by entering debits and credits directly in the T-accounts. Use the transaction letters to identify each debit and credit entry.

Problem 3-2A

Preparing General Journal entries
LO3, 5, 6

Bruce Ibach owns Biotech Fitness Centre, which showed the following selected transactions for the month ended May 31, 2011:

May	1	Purchased new equipment, paying cash of $25,000 and signing a 90-day note payable for the balance of $87,500.
	2	Purchased 12 months of insurance to begin May 2; paid $1,800.
	3	Completed a design for a customer today and received $6,000.
	4	Purchased office supplies on account; $3,750.
	6	Returned to the supplier $500 of defective office supplies purchased on May 4.
	10	Provided services to a client today on account; $11,500.
	15	Paid for the May 4 purchase less the return of May 6.
	20	Received payment from the client of May 10.
	25	Received cash of $600 from a client for work to be done in June.
	31	Paid month-end salaries of $47,000.
	31	Paid the May telephone bill today; $2,250.
	31	Received the May electrical bill today; $900. It will be paid on June 15.

Required

Prepare General Journal entries for each of the above transactions.

Problem 3-3A

Preparing General Journal entries
LO3, 5, 6

Claude Flynne opened a new accounting practice called Flynne, Public Accountant, and completed these activities during March 2011:

Mar.	1	Invested $50,000 in cash and office equipment that had a fair value of $12,000.
	1	Prepaid $3,600 cash for three months' rent for an office.
	3	Made credit purchases of office equipment for $6,000 and office supplies for $1,200.
	5	Completed work for a client and immediately received $1,000 cash.
	9	Completed a $4,000 project for a client, who will pay within 30 days.
	11	Paid the account payable created on March 3.
	15	Paid $3,000 cash for the annual premium on an insurance policy.
	20	Received $3,200 as partial payment for the work completed on March 9.
	22	Placed an order with a supplier for $4,800 of supplies to be delivered April 7. They must be paid for within 15 days of being received.
	23	Completed work for another client for $1,320 on credit.
	27	Flynne withdrew $3,600 cash from the business to pay some personal expenses.
	30	Purchased $400 of additional office supplies on credit.
	31	Paid $350 for the month's utility bill.

Required

Prepare General Journal entries to record the transactions.

Problem 3-4A
Posting, preparing a trial balance
LO4, 6, 7

Check figure:
3. Total Dr = $68,720

Required
Using the General Journal entries prepared in Problem 3-3A, complete the following:
1. Set up the following accounts (use the balance column format): Cash (101); Accounts Receivable (106); Office Supplies (124); Prepaid Insurance (128); Prepaid Rent (131); Office Equipment (163); Accounts Payable (201); Claude Flynne, Capital (301); Claude Flynne, Withdrawals (302); Accounting Fees Earned (401); and Utilities Expense (690).
2. Post the entries to the accounts and enter the balance after each posting.
3. Prepare a trial balance as of the end of the month.

Problem 3-5A
Posting, preparing a trial balance
LO4, 6, 7

Check figure:
3. Total Dr = $68,720

Follow the instructions in Problem 3-4A, but instead of using a balance column format for the accounts in Part 1, use T-accounts.

Problem 3-6A
Preparing and posting General Journal entries; preparing a trial balance
LO3, 4, 5, 6, 7

Jill Wahpoosywan opened a computer consulting business called Techno Wizards and completed the following transactions during May 2011:

May	1	Jill Wahpoosywan invested $200,000 in cash and office equipment that had a fair value of $48,000 in the business.
	1	Prepaid $14,400 cash for three months' rent for an office.
	2	Made credit purchases of office equipment for $24,000 and office supplies for $4,800.
	6	Completed services for a client and immediately received $4,000 cash.
	9	Completed a $16,000 project for a client, who will pay within 30 days.
	10	Paid the account payable created on May 2.
	19	Paid $12,000 cash for the annual premium on an insurance policy.
	22	Received $12,800 as partial payment for the work completed on May 9.
	25	Completed work for another client for $5,280 on credit.
	31	Wahpoosywan withdrew $12,400 cash from the business for personal use.
	31	Purchased $1,600 of additional office supplies on credit.
	31	Paid $1,400 for the month's utility bill.

Check figure:
4. Total Dr = $274,880

Required
1. Prepare General Journal entries to record the transactions. Use page 1 for the journal.
2. Set up the following accounts (use the balance column format): Cash (101); Accounts Receivable (106); Office Supplies (124); Prepaid Insurance (128); Prepaid Rent (131); Office Equipment (163); Accounts Payable (201); Jill Wahpoosywan, Capital (301); Jill Wahpoosywan, Withdrawals (302); Services Revenue (403); and Utilities Expense (690).
3. Post the entries to the accounts and enter the balance after each posting.
4. Prepare a trial balance at May 31, 2011.

Analysis component:
Utilities Expense, Services Revenue, and Jill Wahpoosywan, Withdrawals are equity accounts. Explain why.

Problem 3-7A
Posting, preparing a trial balance
LO3, 4, 5, 6, 7

Check figure:
4. Total Dr = $274,880

Follow the instructions in Problem 3-6A, but instead of using a balance column format for the accounts in Part 2, use T-accounts.

Problem 3-8A
Preparing financial statements from a trial balance
LO7

Techno Wizards
Trial Balance
May 31, 2011

Acct. No.	Account Title	Debit	Credit
101	Cash	$147,800	
106	Accounts receivable	8,480	
124	Office supplies	6,400	
128	Prepaid insurance	12,000	
131	Prepaid rent	14,400	
163	Office equipment	72,000	
201	Accounts payable		$ 1,600
301	Jill Wahpoosywan, capital		248,000
302	Jill Wahpoosywan, withdrawals	12,400	
403	Services revenue		25,280
690	Utilities expense	1,400	
	Totals	$274,880	$274,880

Check figures:
Net income = $23,880;
Total assets = $261,080

Required
Using the trial balance provided above, prepare an income statement and statement of changes in equity for the first month ended May 31, 2011, and a balance sheet at May 31, 2011.

Analysis component:
Prepare two different journal entries, including explanations, that might have created the May 31, 2011, balance in Utilities Expense of $1,400. Use May 31, 2011, as the date for your entries.

Problem 3-9A
Journalizing, posting, preparing a trial balance
LO3, 4, 5, 6, 7

Binbutti Engineering, a sole proprietorship, completed the following transactions during July 2011, the third month of operations:

July	1	Bishr Binbutti, the owner, invested $300,000 cash, office equipment with a value of $12,000, and $90,000 of drafting equipment in the business.
	2	Purchased land for an office. The land was worth $108,000, which was paid with $10,800 cash and a long-term note payable for $97,200.
	3	Purchased a portable building with $150,000 cash and moved it onto the land.
	5	Paid $12,000 cash for the premiums on two one-year insurance policies.
	7	Completed and delivered a set of plans for a client and collected $1,400 cash.
	9	Purchased additional drafting equipment for $45,000. Paid $21,000 cash and signed a long-term note payable for the $24,000 balance.
	10	Completed $4,000 of engineering services for a client. This amount is to be paid within 30 days.
	12	Purchased $4,500 of additional office equipment on credit.
	15	Completed engineering services for $7,000 on credit.
	16	Received a bill for rent on equipment that was used on a completed job. The $13,800 rent must be paid within 30 days.
	17	Collected $400 from the client of July 10.
	19	Paid $12,000 wages to the drafting assistants.
	22	Paid the account payable created on July 12.
	25	Paid $1,350 cash for some repairs to an item of drafting equipment.
	26	Binbutti withdrew $800 cash from the business for personal use.
	30	Paid $12,000 wages to the drafting assistants.
	31	Paid $6,000 cash for advertising in the local newspaper during July.

Required
1. Prepare General Journal entries to record the transactions. Use page 1 for the journal.
2. Set up the following accounts (use the balance column format), entering the balances brought forward from June 30, 2011: Cash (101) $26,000; Accounts Receivable (106) $3,000; Prepaid Insurance (128) $500; Office Equipment (163) $1,700; Drafting Equipment (167) $1,200; Building (173) $42,000; Land (183) $28,000; Accounts Payable (201) $1,740; Long-Term Notes Payable (251) $24,000; Bishr Binbutti, Capital (301) $54,000; Bishr Binbutti, Withdrawals (302) $1,000; Engineering Fees Earned (401) $29,600;

Wages Expense (623) $4,000; Equipment Rental Expense (645) $1,000; Advertising Expense (655) $640; and Repairs Expense (684) $300.
3. Post the entries to the accounts and enter the balance after each posting.
4. Prepare a trial balance at July 31, 2011.

Check figure:
4. Total Dr = $658,740

Problem 3-10A
Posting, preparing a trial balance
LO3, 4, 5, 6, 7

Follow the instructions in Problem 3-9A, but instead of using a balance column format for the accounts in Part 2, use T-accounts.

Check figure:
4. Total Dr = $658,740

Problem 3-11A
Journalizing, posting, preparing a trial balance and financial statements
LO1, 3, 4, 5, 6, 7

Ted Ng began Ng's English School on May 1, 2011. The following activities occurred during July, the third month of operations:

July	1	Purchased supplies on account; $100.
	2	Collected $4,000 for August teaching fees.
	3	Collected $2,000 for July teaching fees.
	4	Paid July rent of $3,000.
	5	Paid $500 for supplies purchased on account last month.
	15	Ng withdrew cash of $500 for personal use.
	20	Paid wages of $1,300.
	31	Purchased a new chair on account; $300.

Required
1. Prepare General Journal entries to record the July transactions.
2. Set up the following T-accounts, entering the balances brought forward from June 30, 2011: Cash (101) $6,000; Supplies (126) $950; Furniture (161) $8,000; Accounts Payable (201) $1,500; Unearned Teaching Revenue (233) $9,800; Ted Ng, Capital (301) $3,000; Ted Ng, Withdrawals (302) $13,000; Teaching Revenue (401) $46,000; Wages Expense (623) $26,350; and Rent Expense (640) $6,000.
3. Post the entries to the accounts; calculate the ending balance in each account.
4. Prepare a trial balance at July 31, 2011.
5. Use the trial balance to prepare an income statement and statement of changes in equity for the three months ended July 31, 2011, as well as a balance sheet at July 31, 2011.

Check figures:
4. Dr = $66,200
5. Net income = $11,350;
Total assets = $16,050

Problem 3-12A
Preparing financial statements from a trial balance
LO7

Binbutti Engineering
Trial Balance
July 31, 2011

Acct. No.	Account Title	Debit	Credit
101	Cash	$ 97,350	
106	Accounts receivable	13,600	
128	Prepaid insurance	12,500	
163	Office equipment	18,200	
167	Drafting equipment	136,200	
173	Building	192,000	
183	Land	136,000	
201	Accounts payable		$ 15,540
251	Long-term notes payable		145,200
301	Bishr Binbutti, capital		456,000
302	Bishr Binbutti, withdrawals	1,800	
401	Engineering fees earned		42,000
623	Wages expense	28,000	
645	Equipment rental expense	14,800	
655	Advertising expense	6,640	
684	Repairs expense	1,650	
	Totals	$658,740	$658,740

Check figures:
Net loss = $9,090;
Total assets = $605,850

Required

Using the trial balance provided above, prepare an income statement and statement of changes in equity for the first three months ended July 31, 2011, and a balance sheet at July 31, 2011.

Analysis component:

Prepare two different journal entries, including explanations, that might have created the July 31, 2011, balance in Engineering Fees Earned of $42,000. Use July 31, 2011, as the date for your entries.

Problem 3-13A
Analyzing trial balance errors
LO3, 5, 6, 7

Wilm Schmidt, the owner of Wilm's Window Washing Services, had difficulty getting the debits to equal credits on the January 31, 2011, trial balance.

Wilm's Window Washing Services Trial Balance January 31, 2011		
	Debit	**Credit**
Cash	$ 11,600	
Accounts receivable	9,240	
Prepaid insurance	2,400	
Equipment	24,000	
Accounts payable		$ 5,400
Wilm Schmidt, capital		45,000
Wilm Schmidt, withdrawals	8,960	
Service revenues		60,400
Salaries expense	32,000	
Insurance expense	5,200	
Maintenance expense	13,000	
Utilities expense	5,200	
Totals	$111,600	$110,800

The following errors were discovered:

a. Wilm did not post a $4,000 purchase of equipment on credit.
b. In posting a $1,400 collection from a credit customer, Wilm debited Accounts Receivable and credited Cash.
c. In posting a cash receipt, Wilm correctly debited Cash for $2,660 but incorrectly credited Accounts Receivable for $6,260.
d. In posting a $4,400 payment on account, Wilm debited Accounts Payable but forgot to post the credit to Cash.
e. In posting the entry for services of $3,600 performed for a customer on credit, Wilm debited Accounts Receivable but credited Maintenance Expense.

Check figure:
Total Dr = $118,400

Required

Prepare a corrected trial balance.

Alternate Problems

Problem 3-1B
Recording transactions in T-accounts
LO3, 5

Peeters Consulting completed these transactions during June 2011:

a. Trevor Peeters, the sole proprietor, invested $46,000 cash and office equipment with a $24,000 fair value in the business.
b. Purchased land and a small office building. The land was worth $268,000 and the building was worth $66,000. The purchase price was paid with $30,000 cash and a long-term note payable for $304,000.
c. Purchased $600 of office supplies on credit.
d. Trevor Peeters transferred title of his personal automobile to the business. The automobile had a value of $7,000 and was to be used exclusively in the business.
e. Purchased $4,600 of additional office equipment on credit.
f. Paid $1,800 salary to an assistant.
g. Provided services to a client and collected $2,700 cash.
h. Paid $1,430 for the month's utilities.
i. Paid the account payable created in transaction (c).

j. Purchased $4,000 of new office equipment by paying $2,400 cash and trading in old equipment with a recorded cost of $1,600.
k. Completed $2,400 of services for a client. This amount is to be paid within 30 days.
l. Paid $1,800 salary to an assistant.
m. Received $1,000 payment on the receivable created in transaction (k).
n. Trevor Peeters withdrew $1,050 cash from the business for personal use.

Required

1. Set up the following T-accounts: Cash; Accounts Receivable; Office Supplies; Automobiles; Office Equipment; Building; Land; Accounts Payable; Long-Term Notes Payable; Trevor Peeters, Capital; Trevor Peeters, Withdrawals; Fees Earned; Salaries Expense; and Utilities Expense.
2. Record the effects of the listed transactions by entering debits and credits directly in the T-accounts. Use the transaction letters to identify each debit and credit entry.

Check figure:
2. Cash balance June 30, 2011 = $10,620

Problem 3-2B
Preparing General Journal entries
LO3, 5, 6

Airdrie Advertising showed the following selected transactions for the month ended March 31, 2011:

Mar.	1	Purchased a new portable building, paying cash of $75,000 and signing a five-year note payable for the balance of $300,000.
	1	Purchased six months of insurance to begin March 1; paid $5,700.
	2	Made a hotel reservation by phone regarding a business meeting to be held on March 28. The full payment of $240 will be required upon arrival at the hotel.
	4	Purchased cleaning supplies on account; $450.
	15	Paid for the March 4 purchase.
	19	Performed advertising work for a client today on account; $35,000.
	20	Collected cash of $8,000 from a customer. The advertising work will be done in April.
	28	Registered at the hotel booked on March 2 and paid the bill. Attended the out-of-town business meeting and returned to the office the next day.
	29	Provided advertising services to the local botanical garden society; collected $5,000.
	30	Paid month-end salaries of $25,600.
	30	Received the March telephone bill today; $1,300. It will be paid April 14.
	30	Collected half of the amount owed by the customer of March 19.

Required

Prepare General Journal entries for each of the above transactions.

Problem 3-3B
Preparing General Journal entries
LO3, 5, 6

Susan Hurley, Public Accountant, completed these activities during September 2011, the first month of operations:

Sept.	1	Began a public accounting practice by investing $16,000 in cash and office equipment having a $4,800 fair value.
	1	Prepaid two months' rent in advance on suitable office space, $4,800.
	2	Purchased on credit office equipment, $4,200, and office supplies, $850.
	4	Completed accounting work for a client and immediately received payment of $1,900 cash.
	8	Completed accounting work on credit for Frontier Bank, $3,600.
	10	Paid for the items purchased on credit on September 2.
	14	Paid the annual $3,300 premium on an insurance policy.
	15	Paid $1,250 to attend an all-day seminar on September 20 regarding ethical accounting practices.
	18	Received payment in full from Frontier Bank for the work completed on September 8.
	20	Attended the seminar paid for on September 15.
	24	Completed accounting work on credit for Travis Realty, $650.
	28	Hurley withdrew $300 cash from the practice to pay personal expenses.
	29	Purchased additional office supplies on credit, $450.
	30	Paid the September utility bills, $730.

Required

Prepare General Journal entries to record the transactions.

Problem 3-4B
Posting, preparing a trial balance
LO4, 6, 7

Check figure:
3. Total Dr = $27,400

Required

Using the General Journal entries prepared in Problem 3-3B, complete the following:

1. Set up the following accounts (use the balance column format): Cash (101); Accounts Receivable (106); Office Supplies (124); Prepaid Insurance (128); Prepaid Rent (131); Office Equipment (163); Accounts Payable (201); Susan Hurley, Capital (301); Susan Hurley, Withdrawals (302); Accounting Fees Earned (401); Professional Development Expense (680); and Utilities Expense (690).
2. Post the entries to the accounts and enter the balance after each posting.
3. Prepare a trial balance as of September 30, 2011.

Problem 3-5B
Posting, preparing a trial balance
LO4, 6, 7

Check figure:
3. Total Dr = $27,400

Follow the instructions in Problem 3-4B, but instead of using a balance column format for the accounts in Part 1, use T-accounts.

Problem 3-6B
Preparing and posting General Journal entries; preparing a trial balance
LO3, 4, 5, 6, 7

Annand Servicing completed these transactions during November 2011:

Nov.	1	Dale Annand, the owner, invested $56,000 cash and office equipment that had a fair value of $32,000 in the business.
	2	Prepaid $18,600 cash for three months' rent for an office.
	4	Made credit purchases of office equipment for $9,000 and office supplies for $1,200.
	8	Completed work for a client and immediately received $5,200 cash.
	12	Completed a $6,800 project for a client, who will pay within 30 days.
	13	Paid the account payable created on November 4.
	19	Paid $10,400 cash as the annual premium on an insurance policy.
	22	Received $1,800 as partial payment for the work completed on November 12.
	24	Completed work for another client for $3,600 on credit.
	28	Annand withdrew $5,300 from the business for personal use.
	29	Purchased $1,700 of additional office supplies on credit.
	30	Paid $9,000 in wages.
	30	Paid $1,650 for the month's utility bill.

Check figure:
4. Total Dr = $105,300

Required

1. Prepare General Journal entries to record the transactions. Use General Journal page 1.
2. Set up the following accounts (use the balance column format): Cash (101); Accounts Receivable (106); Office Supplies (124); Prepaid Insurance (128); Prepaid Rent (131); Office Equipment (163); Accounts Payable (201); Dale Annand, Capital (301); Dale Annand, Withdrawals (302); Service Fees Earned (401); Wages Expense (680); and Utilities Expense (690).
3. Post the entries to the accounts, and enter the balance after each posting.
4. Prepare a trial balance at November 30, 2011.

Analysis component:

Is the November 29 purchase of office supplies recorded as a debit to an asset or an expense account? Explain.

Problem 3-7B
Posting, preparing a trial balance
LO3, 4, 5, 6, 7

Check figure:
4. Trial balance Dr = $105,300

Follow the instructions in Problem 3-6B, but instead of using a balance column format for the accounts in Part 2, use T-accounts.

Problem 3-8B
Preparing financial statements from a trial balance
LO7

Rush Innovations Trial Balance November 30, 2011			
Acct. No.	**Account Title**	**Debit**	**Credit**
101	Cash	$ 23,480	
106	Accounts receivable	7,000	
124	Office supplies	5,800	
128	Prepaid insurance	10,400	
131	Prepaid rent	21,000	
163	Office equipment	68,000	
201	Accounts payable		$ 3,400
301	Jay Rush, capital		146,000
302	Jay Rush, withdrawals	10,600	
401	Service fees earned		15,800
680	Wages expense	16,000	
690	Utilities expense	2,920	
	Totals	$165,200	$165,200

Required
Use the trial balance provided above to prepare an income statement and statement of changes in equity for the first month ended November 30, 2011, and a balance sheet at November 30, 2011.

Check figures:
Net loss = $3,120;
Total assets = $135,680

Analysis component:
Prepare two journal entries, including explanations: one that would have caused Accounts Receivable to increase, and one that would have caused it to decrease. Use November 30, 2011, as the date for your entries.

Problem 3-9B
Journalizing, posting, preparing a trial balance
LO3, 4, 5, 6, 7

At the beginning of June 2011, Wilf Eazy created a hauling company called Eazy-Carry Co. The company had the following transactions during July, its second month of operations:

July	1	Purchased office equipment for $9,000 and a truck for $56,000 by signing a long-term note payable.
	2	Purchased land for an office. The land was worth $124,000, which was paid with $40,800 cash and a long-term note payable for the balance.
	3	Purchased a used portable building with $21,000 cash and moved it onto the land.
	5	Paid $9,600 cash for the premiums on two one-year insurance policies.
	9	Provided services to a client and collected $3,200 cash.
	12	Purchased additional office equipment for $6,500. Paid $700 cash and signed a long-term note payable for the balance.
	15	Completed $3,750 of services for a client. This amount is due within 30 days.
	20	Completed another hauling job for $9,200 on credit.
	21	Received a bill for rent on a specialized hauling truck that was used to complete the job done on July 20. The $1,300 rent must be paid within 30 days.
	22	Collected $5,000 from the client described in the transaction on July 20.
	23	Paid $1,600 wages to an assistant.
	24	Paid the account payable created in the transaction of July 21.
	25	Paid $1,425 cash for some repairs to the truck.
	26	Eazy withdrew $3,875 in cash from the business for personal use.
	27	Paid $1,600 wages to an assistant.
	28	Paid $800 cash for advertising in the local newspaper during July.
	29	Received $1,400 from a client for services to be performed in August.

Check figure:
4. Total Dr = $271,500

Required

1. Prepare General Journal entries to record the transactions. Use page 1 for the journal.
2. Set up the following accounts (use the balance column format), entering the balances brought forward from June 30, 2011: Cash (101) $75,000; Accounts Receivable (106) $950; Prepaid Insurance (128) $275; Trucks (153) $20,800; Office Equipment (163) $1,200; Building (173) $-0-; Land (183) $-0-; Accounts Payable (201) $725; Unearned Fees (233) $-0-; Long-Term Notes Payable (251) $7,000; Wilf Eazy, Capital (301) $83,825; Wilf Eazy, Withdrawals (302) $600; Fees Earned (401) $8,400; Wages Expense (623) $780; Truck Rental Expense (645) $230; Advertising Expense (655) $75; and Repairs Expense (684) $40.
3. Post the entries to the accounts and enter the balance after each posting.
4. Prepare a trial balance as of the end of the month.

Problem 3-10B

Posting, preparing a trial balance
LO3, 4, 5, 6, 7

Check figure:
4. Total Dr = $271,500

Follow the instructions in Problem 3-9B, but instead of using a balance column format for the accounts in Part 2, use T-accounts.

Problem 3-11B

Journalizing, posting, preparing a trial balance and financial statements
LO1, 3, 4, 5, 6, 7

Ike Petrov started a tour company, Tour-Along, on October 1, 2011. The following activities occurred during November, the second month of operations:

Nov.	1	Paid $10,000 regarding purchases made on account during October.
	2	Purchased a $34,000 photocopier, paying $6,000 cash and signing a note payable for the balance.
	3	Purchased office supplies for cash; $800.
	4	Signed a $200,000 contract with RBC to arrange travel for its employees beginning January 1, 2012.
	14	Paid wages of $6,000.
	20	Collected $14,000 for clients travelling in November.
	25	Petrov withdrew $2,000 cash for personal use.
	30	Paid interest on the notes payable; $150.

Check figures:
4. Dr = $137,000
5. Net income = $3,750;
Total assets = $86,750

Required

1. Prepare General Journal entries to record the November transactions.
2. Set up the following T-accounts, entering the balances brought forward from October 31, 2011: Cash (101) $26,000; Office Supplies (124) $900; Office Equipment (163) $36,000; Accounts Payable (201) $43,000; Notes Payable (205) $20,000; Ike Petrov, Capital (301) $8,000; Ike Petrov, Withdrawals (302) $4,000; Travel Revenue (401) $34,000; Wages Expense (623) $38,000; and Interest Expense (633) $100.
3. Post the entries to the accounts; calculate the ending balance in each account.
4. Prepare a trial balance at November 30, 2011.
5. Use the trial balance to prepare an income statement and statement of changes in equity for the two months ended November 30, 2011, as well as a balance sheet at November 30, 2011.

Analysis component:

Part 2 of the *Required* states that the account Ike Petrov, Capital had a balance of $8,000 at October 31, 2011. Explain what this balance represents. *Hint: Prove the accounting equation at October 31, 2011, using the account balance information in part 2 above.*

Problem 3-12B

Preparing financial statements from a trial balance

LO7

Web Search Co. Trial Balance July 31, 2011			
Acct. No.	**Account Title**	**Debit**	**Credit**
101	Cash	$ 36,450	
106	Accounts receivable	18,600	
128	Prepaid insurance	13,750	
163	Office equipment	12,900	
167	Computer equipment	64,600	
173	Building	70,000	
183	Land	60,000	
201	Accounts payable		$ 67,090
233	Unearned fees		2,800
251	Long-term notes payable		58,000
301	Nicole Lundt, capital		120,000
302	Nicole Lundt, withdrawals	8,950	
401	Fees earned		49,100
623	Wages expense	7,960	
645	Computer rental expense	1,100	
655	Advertising expense	1,750	
684	Repairs expense	930	
	Totals	$296,990	$296,990

Required

Using the trial balance provided above, prepare an income statement and a statement of changes in equity for the first two months ended July 31, 2011, and a balance sheet at July 31, 2011.

Check figures:
Net income = $37,360;
Total assets = $276,300

Problem 3-13B

Analyzing trial balance errors

LO3, 5, 6, 7

On January 1, 2011, Bev Horricks started a new business called Dance-A-Lot. Near the end of the year, she hired a new bookkeeper without making a careful reference check. As a result, a number of mistakes have been made in preparing the following trial balance:

Dance-A-Lot Trial Balance December 31, 2011		
	Debit	**Credit**
Cash	$ 5,500	
Accounts receivable		$ 7,900
Office supplies	2,650	
Office equipment	20,500	
Accounts payable		9,465
Bev Horricks, capital	16,745	
Services revenue		22,350
Wages expense		6,000
Rent expense		4,800
Advertising expense		1,250
Totals	$45,395	$52,340

Bev's analysis of the situation has uncovered these errors:

a. The sum of the debits in the Cash account is $37,175 and the sum of the credits is $30,540.

b. A $275 payment from a credit customer was posted to Cash but was not posted to Accounts Receivable.

c. A credit purchase of office supplies for $400 was not posted at all.

d. A transposition error occurred in copying the balance of the Services Revenue account to the trial balance. The correct amount was $23,250.

Other errors were made in placing account balances in the wrong trial balance columns and in taking the totals of the columns.

Check figure:
Total Dr = $49,860

Required

Prepare a corrected trial balance.

Analytical and Review Problems

A & R Problem 3-1

Carlos Young started an engineering firm called Young Engineering. He began operations in March 2011 and completed seven transactions, including his initial investment of $17,000 cash. After these transactions, the ledger included the following accounts with their normal balances:

Cash	$26,660
Office Supplies	660
Prepaid Insurance	3,200
Office Equipment	16,500
Accounts Payable	16,500
Carlos Young, Capital	17,000
Carlos Young, Withdrawals	3,740
Engineering Fees Earned	24,000
Rent Expense	6,740

Required

Preparation component:

Prepare a trial balance for the business.

Analysis component:

Analyze the accounts and balances and prepare narratives that describe each of the seven most likely transactions and their amounts.

A & R Problem 3-2

Nice-n-Fresh Drycleaning showed the following information for its first and second months just ended, March and April of 2011:

Account Title	April 30, 2011	March 31, 2011
Cash	7,000	3,000
Cleaning supplies	3,500	900
Prepaid rent	12,000	16,000
Equipment	76,000	30,000
Accounts payable	700	500
Notes payable	40,000	15,000
Ed Fresh, capital*	?	?

*Ed Fresh made a $10,000 investment during March and had withdrawals of $1,000 in March and $25,100 in April.

Required

Use the information provided to complete a statement of changes in equity and a balance sheet for each of March and April 2011. *NOTE: Prepare the statements on a comparative*[16] *basis similar to the statements for Danier Leather and WestJet in Appendix I at the end of the textbook.*

Analysis component:

a. Liabilities increased by $25,200 from March 31, 2011, to April 30, 2011. Review the balance sheet and identify why liabilities increased.

b. Equity increased by $34,400 during March and by $23,400 during April, yet net income was much higher in April. Explain.

[16] Preparing statements on a *comparative basis* means to have numbers for at least two periods side by side. This kind of presentation provides decision makers with something meaningful against which the current period can be compared.

Ethics Challenge

EC 3-1

You are a cashier at a retail convenience store. When you were hired, the owner explained to you the policy of immediately ringing up each sale. Recently, lunch hour traffic has increased dramatically and the manager asks you to take customers' cash and make change without ringing up sales to avoid delays. The manager says she will add up cash and ring up sales equal to the cash amount after lunch. She says that in this way the register will always be accurate when the owner arrives at 3:00 p.m.

Required

1. Identify the advantages and disadvantages of the manager's suggestion.
2. Identify the ethical dilemma and evaluate at least two courses of action you might consider and why.

Focus on Financial Statements

FFS 3-1

Travis McAllister operates a surveying company. For the first few months of the company's life (through April), the accounting records were maintained by an outside bookkeeping service. According to those records, McAllister's equity balance was $75,000 as of April 30. To save on expenses, McAllister decided to keep the records himself. He managed to record May's transactions properly, but was a bit rusty when the time came to prepare the financial statements. His first versions of the balance sheet and income statement follow. McAllister is bothered that the company apparently operated at a loss during the month, even though he was very busy.

McAllister Surveying
Income Statement
For Month Ended May 31, 2011

Revenue:		
Investments by owner		$ 3,000
Unearned surveying fees		6,000
Total revenues		$ 9,000
Operating expenses:		
Rent expense	$3,100	
Telephone expense	600	
Surveying equipment	5,400	
Advertising expense	3,200	
Utilities expense	300	
Insurance expense	900	
Withdrawals by owner	6,000	
Total operating expenses		19,500
Net income (loss)		$(10,500)

Required

Using the information contained in the original financial statements, prepare revised statements, including a statement of changes in equity, for the month of May.

Analysis component:

The owner, Travis McAllister, made a withdrawal during May. Withdrawals cause equity to decrease. Why would the owner intentionally cause equity to decrease by making a withdrawal?

McAllister Surveying
Balance Sheet
May 31, 2011

Assets		Liabilities	
Cash	$ 3,900	Accounts payable	$ 2,400
Accounts receivable	2,700	Surveying fees earned	18,000
Prepaid insurance	1,800	Short-term notes payable	48,000
Prepaid rent	4,200	Total liabilities	$ 68,400
Office supplies	300		
Buildings	81,000	**Equity**	
Land	36,000	Travis McAllister, capital	64,500
Salaries expense	3,000		
Total assets	$132,900	Total liabilities and equity	$132,900

FFS 3-2

1. Refer to WestJet's income statement on page I-25 in Appendix I at the end of the textbook.
a. Total *Charter and other revenues* for 2008 were $248,205 (thousand).
(i) Prepare two possible journal entries that might have been recorded to create this result.
(ii) What effect do revenues have on the balance sheet?
(iii) What assurances do we have that the revenues appearing on the income statement are for the year 2008? *Hint:* Which GAAP?
b. Total *Interest expense* for 2008 was $76,078 (thousand).
(i) Prepare a possible journal entry that might have recorded the interest expense.
(ii) Do expenses affect the balance sheet? Explain.
2. Refer to WestJet's balance sheet on page I-26 in Appendix I at the end of the textbook. Find the line showing *Advance ticket sales* of $251,354 (thousand).
a. Explain what you think the account *Advance ticket sales* represents.
b. Prepare the journal entry that might have recorded this account balance.

Critical Thinking Mini Case

Prairie Insurance sells life insurance, disability insurance, vehicle insurance, crop insurance, and homeowners' insurance. You are employed by Prairie Insurance and have been promoted to sales division manager for the Western Canadian division. You will be supervising approximately 25 salespeople, along with five administrative assistants at various locations. The salespeople travel extensively and submit expense reports along with sales information monthly. A sample expense report for September shows:

Prairie Insurance—Western Canadian Division Sales Report: John Bishop Month Ended September 30, 2011	
Sales revenue*	$56,000
Expenses**	34,000

*Sales invoices attached
**Receipts attached

The former manager was dismissed because division results have been deteriorating. The consolidated sales report for the past three months shows the following:

Prairie Insurance—Western Canadian Division
Sales Report
Month Ended

	September 30, 2011	August 31, 2011	July 31, 2011
Sales revenue	$680,000	$510,000	$440,000
Expenses	544,000	382,500	321,200
Net income	$136,000	$127,500	$118,800

You learn that the company has one revenue account called Sales Revenue and one expense account called Expenses. You proceed to prepare a brief memo to the company's accountant requesting information that is needed to help you analyze the situation.

Required:
Using the elements of critical thinking described on the inside front cover, respond.

Serial Problem

Echo Systems

(This comprehensive problem starts in this chapter and continues in Chapters 4, 5, and 6. Because of its length, this problem is most easily solved if you use the Working Papers[17] that accompany this text.)

On October 1, 2011, Mary Graham organized a computer service company called Echo Systems. Echo is organized as a sole proprietorship and will provide consulting services, computer system installations, and custom program development. Graham has adopted the calendar year for reporting, and expects to prepare the company's first set of financial statements as of December 31, 2011. The initial chart of accounts for the accounting system includes these items:

[17] If students have not purchased the Working Paper package, the Working Papers for the Serial Problem are available on Connect.

Account Number	Account Name	Account Number	Account Name
101	Cash	301	Mary Graham, Capital
106	Accounts Receivable	302	Mary Graham, Withdrawals
126	Computer Supplies	403	Computer Services Revenue
128	Prepaid Insurance	623	Wages Expense
131	Prepaid Rent	655	Advertising Expense
163	Office Equipment	676	Mileage Expense
167	Computer Equipment	684	Repairs Expense, Computer
201	Accounts Payable	699	Charitable Donations Expense

Part A

Required

1. Set up balance column accounts based on the chart of accounts provided.
2. Prepare journal entries to record each of the following October transactions.
3. Post the October entries.
4. Prepare a trial balance at October 31, 2011.
5. Prepare an income statement and a statement of changes in equity for the month ended October 31, 2011, as well as a balance sheet at October 31, 2011.

Oct.	1	Mary Graham invested $90,000 cash, a $36,000 computer system, and $18,000 of office equipment in the business.
	2	Paid rent in advance of $9,000.
	3	Purchased computer supplies on credit for $2,640 from Abbott Office Products.
	5	Paid $4,320 cash for one year's premium on a property and liability insurance policy.
	6	Billed Capital Leasing $6,600 for installing a new computer.
	8	Paid for the computer supplies purchased from Abbott Office Products.
	10	Hired Carly Smith as a part-time assistant for $200 per day, as needed.
	12	Billed Capital Leasing another $2,400 for computer services rendered.
	15	Received $6,600 from Capital Leasing on its account.
	17	Paid $1,410 to repair computer equipment damaged when moving into the new office.
	20	Paid $3,720 for an advertisement in the local newspaper.
	22	Received $2,400 from Capital Leasing on its account.
	28	Billed Decker Company $6,450 for services.
	31	Paid Carly Smith for seven days' work.
	31	Mary Graham withdrew $7,200 cash from the business for personal use.

Part A
Check figures:
4. Total Dr = $159,450
5. Net income = $8,920; Total assets = $145,720

Part B

Required

6. Prepare journal entries to record each of the following November transactions.
7. Post the November entries.
8. Prepare a trial balance at November 30, 2011.
9. Prepare an income statement and a statement of changes in equity for the two months ended November 30, 2011, as well as a balance sheet at November 30, 2011.

Nov.	1	Reimbursed Mary Graham's business automobile expense for 1,000 kilometres at $1.00 per kilometre.
	2	Received $9,300 cash from Elite Corporation for computer services rendered.
	5	Purchased $1,920 of computer supplies for cash from Abbott Office Products.
	8	Billed Fostek Co. $8,700 for computer services rendered.
	13	Notified by Alamo Engineering Co. that Echo's bid of $7,500 for an upcoming project was accepted.
	18	Received $3,750 from Decker Company against the bill dated October 28.
	22	Donated $1,500 to the United Way in the company's name.
	24	Completed work for Alamo Engineering Co. and sent a bill for $7,500.
	25	Sent another bill to Decker Company for the past due amount of $2,700.
	28	Reimbursed Mary Graham's business automobile expense for 1,200 kilometres at $1.00 per kilometre.
	30	Paid Carly Smith for 14 days' work.
	30	Mary Graham withdrew $3,600 cash from the business for personal use.

Part B
Check figures:
8. Total Dr = $184,950
9. Net income = $27,920; Total assets = $161,120

CHAPTER 4

Adjusting Accounts for Financial Statements

learning objectives

- LO1 | Describe the purpose of adjusting accounts at the end of a period.
- LO2 | Explain how the timeliness, matching, and revenue recognition principles affect the adjusting process.
- LO3 | Explain accrual accounting and cash basis accounting and how accrual accounting adds to the usefulness of financial statements.
- LO4 | Prepare and explain adjusting entries for prepaid expenses, depreciation, unearned revenues, accrued expenses, and accrued revenues.
- LO5 | Explain how accounting adjustments link to financial statements.
- LO6 | Explain and prepare an adjusted trial balance.
- LO7 | Prepare financial statements from an adjusted trial balance.

*APPENDIX 4A

- LO8 | Explain and prepare correcting entries.

*APPENDIX 4B

- LO9 | Identify and explain an alternative in recording prepaids and unearned revenues.

An asterisk (*) identifies appendix material.

Creative Accounting

Brampton, Ontario—The RCMP (Royal Canadian Mounted Police) opened a criminal investigation regarding irregular accounting practices at Nortel Networks Corp., Canada's largest high-tech company and one of the world's leading suppliers of telecommunications equipment. Analysts have speculated that the firings of chief executive Frank Dunn, the CFO, and the controller stem from Nortel making 2002 earnings look artificially worse than they were and 2003 earnings look better. Why? It is assumed that this was done so executives could collect an estimated $20 million in bonuses linked to the company's return to profitability. The company currently provides biweekly performance updates required by the Ontario Securities Commission, auditing Nortel's results going back to 2000. Nortel is facing about $1 billion in class-action lawsuits related to the accounting scandal. In 2009, Nortel filed for bankruptcy protection. The lesson to be learned is that creative accounting was not the type of innovative practice Nortel needed to stay solvent.

http://www.nortel.com

CRITICAL THINKING CHALLENGE

Assuming you were a Nortel executive, how could you inflate 2003 earnings and shrink 2002 earnings? Explain how GAAP were violated by this strategy.

chapter preview

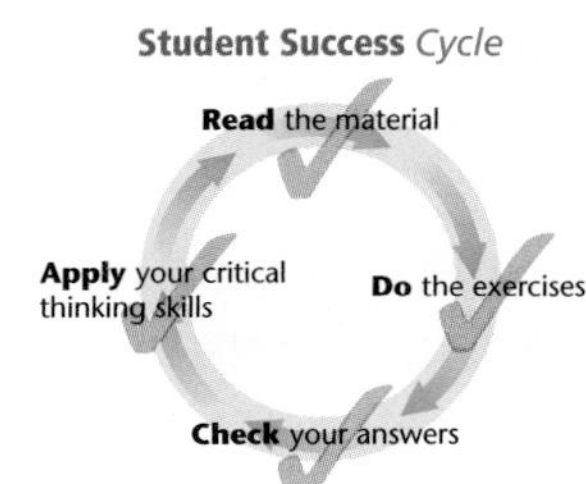

Financial statements P. 26 reflect revenues when earned and expenses when incurred. This is known as *accrual basis accounting*. Accrual basis accounting is achieved by following the steps of the accounting cycle P. 75. We described the first four of these steps in Chapter 3.

An important part of the accounting cycle is the adjustment of account balances. The adjusted account balances are what is reported in financial statements that are prepared according to generally accepted accounting principles P. 31. Adjustment of accounts is necessary so that financial statements at the end of a reporting period reflect the effects of all transactions. This chapter emphasizes Steps Five and Six of the accounting cycle as highlighted in Exhibit 4.1. Preparation of financial statements, Step Seven of the accounting cycle, is reinforced in this chapter, with an emphasis on how *adjusting entries* impact the financial statements. Nortel, in the chapter opener, likely used adjusting entries to play an important role in producing irregular financial statements. To illustrate the adjusting process, we continue with the example of Vertically Inclined used in previous chapters.

Purpose of Adjusting

LO1 Describe the purpose of adjusting accounts at the end of a period.

The usual process during an accounting period is to record *external transactions*. **External transactions** are exchanges between two parties; these were the focus of Chapters 2 and 3. After external transactions are recorded, several accounts in the ledger need adjustment for their balances to appear in financial statements. This need arises because *internal transactions* remain unrecorded. **Internal transactions** represent exchanges within an organization that affect the accounting equation and are the focus of this chapter.

An example is the cost of certain assets that expire or are used up as time passes. The Prepaid Insurance account of Vertically Inclined is one of these. Vertically Inclined's trial balance (Exhibit 4.2) shows Prepaid Insurance with a balance of $2,400. This amount is the premium for two years of insurance protection beginning on January 1, 2011. By January 31, 2011, because one month's coverage is used up, the $2,400 is no longer the correct account balance for Prepaid Insurance. The Prepaid Insurance account balance must be reduced by one month's cost, or $100 ($2,400/24 months). The income statement P. 27 must report this $100 cost as insurance expense for January.

Another example is the $3,600 balance in Supplies. Part of this balance includes the cost of supplies that were used in January. The cost of the supplies used must be reported as an expense in January. The balances of both the Prepaid Insurance and Supplies accounts must be *adjusted* before they are reported on the January 31 balance sheet P. 29.

Another adjustment necessary for Vertically Inclined relates to one month's usage of equipment. The balances of the Unearned Teaching Revenue, Teaching Revenue, and Salaries Expense accounts often also need adjusting before they appear on the statements. We explain *why* this adjusting process is carried out in the next section.

Exhibit 4.1

Steps in the Accounting Cycle Introduced in Chapter 4

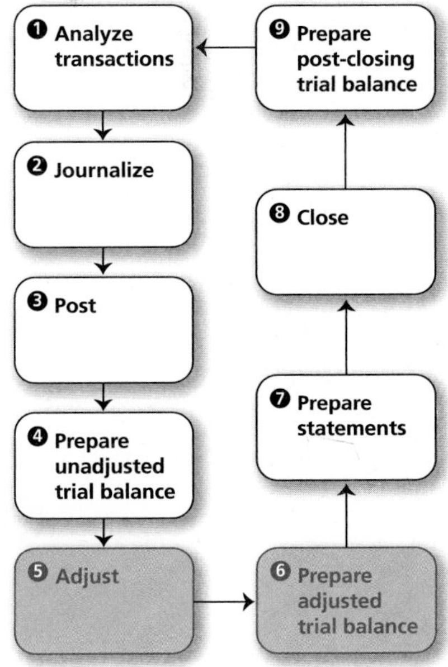

Exhibit 4.2

Trial Balance

Vertically Inclined Rock Gym Trial Balance January 31, 2011		
	Debit	**Credit**
Cash	$ 8,070	
Accounts receivable	-0-	
Prepaid insurance	2,400	
Supplies	3,600	
Equipment	6,000	
Accounts payable		$ 200
Unearned teaching revenue		3,000
Notes payable		6,000
Virgil Klimb, capital		10,000
Virgil Klimb, withdrawals	600	
Teaching revenue		3,800
Equipment rental revenue		300
Rent expense	1,000	
Salaries expense	1,400	
Utilities expense	230	
Totals	$23,300	$23,300

GAAP and the Adjusting Process

LO2 Explain how the timeliness, matching, and revenue recognition principles affect the adjusting process.

The adjusting process is based on three generally accepted accounting principles: the timeliness principle, the revenue recognition principle, and the matching principle. In this section, we explain how GAAP add to the usefulness of financial statements.

The Accounting Period

The adjusting process is often linked to timeliness of information. Information must reach decision makers frequently and promptly, therefore accounting systems need to prepare periodic reports at regular intervals. This results in an accounting process impacted by the *timeliness principle.*[1] The **timeliness principle** assumes that an organization's activities can be divided into specific time periods such as a month, a three-month quarter, or a year, as illustrated in Exhibit 4.3. It requires that statements be presented at least annually.

Exhibit 4.3

Accounting Periods

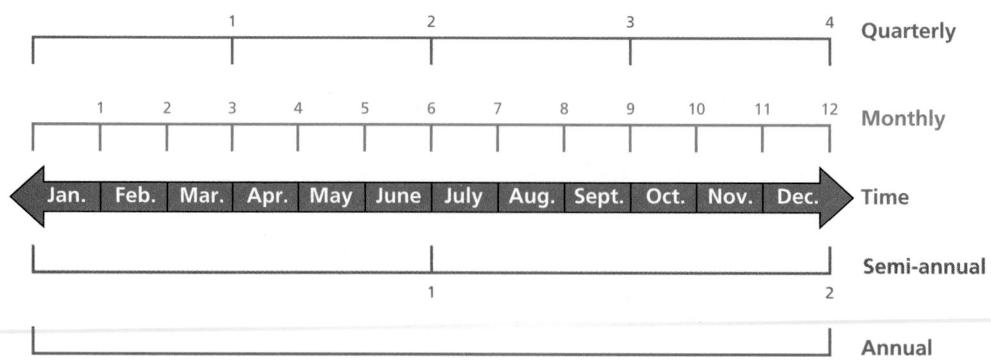

[1] IFRS 2009, IAS 1, para. 36; "Framework," para. 43.

Time periods covered by statements are called **accounting periods** (or **reporting periods**). Reports covering a one-year period are known as *annual financial statements*. Recall that a company can adopt a *fiscal year* P. 27 based on the *calendar year* P. 27 or its *natural business year* P. 27.

Many organizations also prepare **interim financial reports** covering one, three (quarterly), or six (semi-annual) months of activity.

Recognizing Revenues and Expenses

Because of the need for regular reporting of information, activities are often reported on or before their completion so as not to mislead decision makers. These activities are recorded through the adjusting process. Two main generally accepted accounting principles are used in the adjusting process: the *matching principle* and the *revenue recognition principle*. The **matching principle** aims to report or *match* expenses in the same accounting period as the revenues they helped to earn.[2] For example, assume that as part of a $500 teaching services contract Vertically Inclined is to supply a detailed written plan to one of its customers in March. In the process of earning this $500 in revenue, Vertically Inclined will use $150 of office supplies purchased and paid for in February. The $150 of office supplies used in *March* is an expense that will be reported on the *March* income statement even though the supplies were purchased and paid for in February. The $150 of office supplies used in March must be ***matched*** against the $500 of March revenues in accordance with the matching principle. Financial statements will reflect accurate information about the income actually earned during the period only if expenses are properly matched against the revenues they helped to create.

To illustrate *revenue recognition*, we will look at two situations. First, assume that in March, Vertically Inclined provides $500 of teaching services to a client and collects the cash immediately. The $500 of revenue is earned in March and is reported on the March income statement in accordance with the revenue recognition principle. Second, assume that Vertically Inclined collected $1,000 cash in March for work to be done in April. The $1,000 of revenue will be earned in April and will therefore be reported on the April income statement; the $1,000 will *not* be reported as revenue in March because it has not yet been earned. A major goal of the adjusting process is to have revenue *recognized* (reported) in the time period when it is *earned* regardless of when the cash is actually received. This concept is the foundation on which the *accrual basis of accounting* was developed.

Accrual Basis Compared to Cash Basis

LO3 Explain accrual accounting and cash basis accounting and how accrual accounting adds to the usefulness of financial statements.

Accrual basis accounting is founded on the revenue recognition principle, where revenues and expenses are *recognized* or recorded when earned or incurred regardless of when cash is received or paid. The word *accrual* and its root word *accrue* mean *to accumulate* or *to add*. So accrual basis accounting means that revenues and expenses must be *added* or *matched* to the *time period* in which they actually happened; when cash was received or paid is irrelevant to the recording of revenues and expenses. Accrual basis accounting, then, is based on the three GAAP of *revenue recognition, matching*, and *timeliness*.

In contrast, **cash basis accounting** recognizes revenues and expenses when *cash* is received or paid. Cash basis accounting for the income statement, balance sheet, and statement of changes in equity is *not* consistent with generally accepted accounting principles. It is commonly held that accrual basis accounting provides a better indication of business performance than information about current cash receipts and payments. Accrual basis accounting also increases the comparability of financial statements from one period to another. Yet information about cash flows is also useful. This is why companies also include a cash flow statement, discussed in Chapter 19.

Accrual Basis Accounting

Revenues (= when earned)
− Expenses (= when incurred)
Net Income

Cash Basis Accounting

Revenues (= cash receipts)
− Expenses (= cash payments)
Net Income

[2] IFRS 2009, IAS 18, para. 19; "Framework," para. 95.

1. Describe a company's annual reporting period.
2. Why do companies prepare interim financial statements?
3. What accounting principles most directly lead to the adjusting process?
4. Is cash basis accounting consistent with generally accepted accounting principles?

Do Quick Study questions: QS 4-1, QS 4-2

Adjusting Accounts

The process of adjusting accounts is similar to our process of analyzing and recording transactions in Chapter 3. We must analyze each account balance and the transactions that affect it to determine any needed adjustments. An **adjusting entry** is recorded at the ***end*** of the accounting period to bring an asset or liability account balance to its proper amount. This entry also updates the related expense or revenue account and is necessary to prepare the financial statements. Adjustments are journalized in the General Journal and then posted to accounts in the ledger like any other entry. This next section shows the mechanics of adjusting entries and their links to financial statements.

Framework for Adjustments

LO4 Prepare and explain adjusting entries for prepaid expenses, depreciation, unearned revenues, accrued expenses, and accrued revenues.

It is helpful to group adjustments by their timing of cash receipt or payment in comparison to when they are recognized as revenues or expenses. Exhibit 4.4 identifies the five main adjustments, each of which is detailed in the following sections.

Exhibit 4.4

Framework for Adjustments

EXTEND YOUR KNOWLEDGE

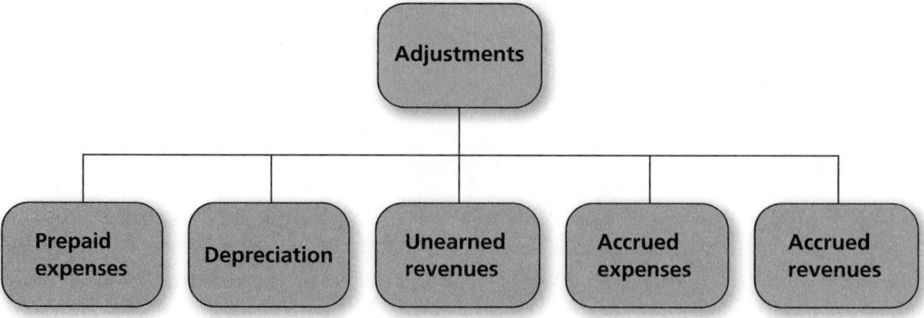

Adjusting Prepaid Expenses

Prepaid expenses[3] refer to items *paid for* in advance of receiving their benefits. Prepaid expenses are assets. As these assets are used, their costs become expenses. Prepaids are common in business. For example, Leon's reported $1,490,000 of prepaid expenses at December 31, 2008, $32,289,000 of prepaids appear on Maple Leaf Foods' December 31, 2008, balance sheet, and Canadian Tire showed $40,200,000 of prepaid expenses on its January 3, 2009, financial statements. Adjusting entries for prepaids involve increasing (debiting) expenses and decreasing (crediting) assets as shown in Exhibit 4.5.

[3] Prepaids are also called *deferrals* because the recognition of the expense or revenue on the income statement is *deferred* to a future accounting period.

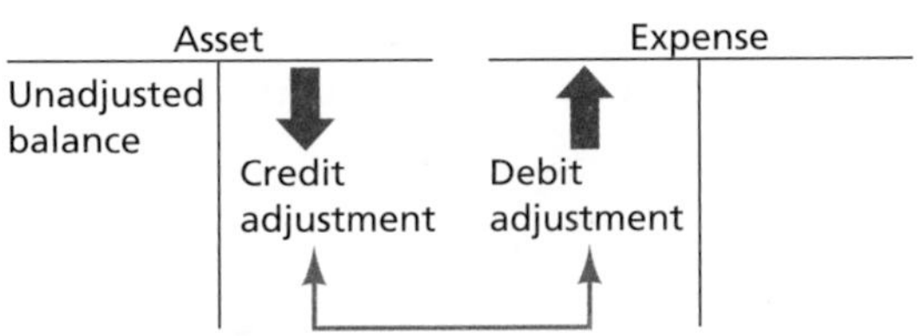

Exhibit 4.5

Adjusting for Prepaid Expenses

The three common prepaid expenses are insurance, supplies, and depreciation.

Prepaid Insurance

We illustrate prepaid insurance using Vertically Inclined's payment of $2,400 for two years of insurance protection beginning on January 1, 2011. The following entry records the purchase of the insurance:

Jan. 1	Prepaid Insurance	2,400	
	Cash		2,400
	To record purchase of insurance for 24 months.		

By January 31, one month's insurance coverage is used, causing a portion of the asset Prepaid Insurance to become an expense. This expense is $100 ($2,400 × 1/24). Our adjusting entry to record this expense and reduce the asset is:

Adjustment (a)

Jan. 31	Insurance Expense	100	
	Prepaid Insurance................................		100
	To record expired insurance.		

Posting this adjusting entry affects the accounts shown in Exhibit 4.6:

Exhibit 4.6

Insurance Accounts After Adjusting for Prepaids

Prepaid Insurance			
Jan. 1	2,400	100	Jan. 31
Balance	2,300		

Insurance Expense		
Jan. 31	100	

After posting, the $100 balance in Insurance Expense and the $2,300 balance in Prepaid Insurance are ready for reporting in the financial statements. If the adjustment is *not* made at January 31, then (a) expenses are understated by $100 and net income is overstated by $100 for the January income statement, and (b) both Prepaid Insurance and equity are overstated by $100 in the January 31 balance sheet.

Supplies

Vertically Inclined purchased $3,600 of supplies in January and used some of them during this month. Daily usage of supplies was not recorded in Vertically Inclined's accounts because this information was not needed. When we report account balances in financial statements only at the end of a month, recordkeeping costs can be reduced by making only one adjusting entry at that time. This entry needs to record the total cost of all supplies used in the month.

The cost of supplies used during January must be recognized as an expense. Vertically Inclined calculates ("takes inventory of") the remaining unused supplies. The cost of the remaining supplies is then deducted from the cost of the purchased supplies to calculate the amount used. Vertically Inclined has $2,550 of supplies remaining out of the $3,600 ($2,500 + $1,100) purchased in January. The $1,050 difference between these two amounts is the cost of the supplies used. This amount is January's Supplies Expense. Our adjusting entry to record this expense and reduce the Supplies asset account is:

Adjustment (b)

Jan.	31	Supplies Expense	1,050	
		Supplies		1,050
		To record supplies used.		

Posting this adjusting entry affects the accounts shown in Exhibit 4.7:

Exhibit 4.7

Supplies Accounts After Adjusting for Prepaids

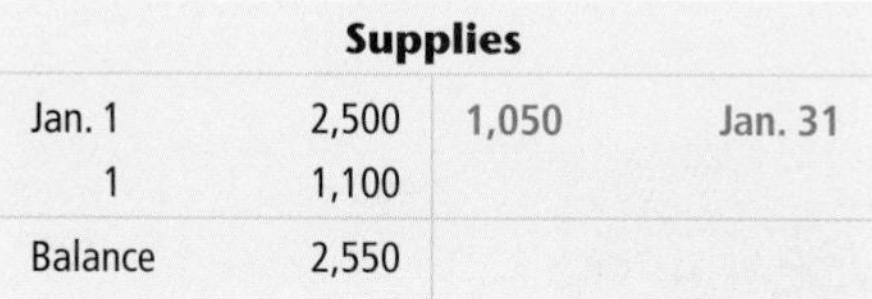

Supplies			
Jan. 1	2,500	1,050	Jan. 31
1	1,100		
Balance	2,550		

Supplies Expense		
Jan. 31	1,050	

The balance of the Supplies account is $2,550 after posting and equals the cost of remaining unused supplies. If the adjustment is *not* made at January 31, then (a) expenses are understated by $1,050 and net income overstated by $1,050 for the January income statement, and (b) both Supplies and equity are overstated by $1,050 in the January 31 balance sheet.

Other Prepaid Expenses

There are other prepaid expenses (including Prepaid Rent), which are accounted for in exactly the same manner as Insurance and Supplies above. We should also note that some prepaid expenses are both paid for and fully used up within a single accounting period. One example is when a company pays monthly rent on the first day of each month. The payment creates a prepaid expense on the first day of each month that fully expires by the end of the month. In these special cases, we can record the cash paid with a debit to the expense account instead of an asset account.

5. If the entry to adjust Prepaid Insurance was not recorded, what effect would this have on each component of the accounting equation?

Do Quick Study question: QS 4-3

Adjusting for Depreciation[4]

Property, plant and equipment (PPE) assets are used to produce and sell products and services, and **intangible assets** (such as patents) convey the right to use a product or process. Both of these asset groups are expected to provide benefits for more than one accounting period. Examples of property, plant and equipment assets are land, buildings, machines, vehicles, and fixtures. Because these assets (except for land) wear out or decline in usefulness as they are used, an expense must be recorded to match the cost of the asset over the time the asset helped earn revenues. **Depreciation** is the process of calculating expense from matching (or allocating) the cost of plant and equipment assets over their expected useful lives. Businesses that have significant dollars invested in plant and equipment can have large amounts of depreciation appearing on the income statement. For example,

[4] Prior to 2011, the term **amortization** was used instead of *depreciation*. In 2011, IFRS will be adopted in Canada and the term *depreciation* is to be used for plant and equipment (IFRS 2009, IAS 16, para. 43). *Amortization* will continue to be used for intangible assets (IFRS 2009, IAS 38, para. 97). *Intangible assets* are introduced in Chapter 5. *Amortization* for intangible assets is discussed in more detail in Chapter 12.

Bombardier Inc. reported buildings and equipment that cost $2,857 million with $555 million of corresponding depreciation in its January 31, 2009, financial statements. On its December 31, 2008, statements, Suncor reported depreciation of $1 billion related to plant and equipment that cost $34 billion.

Vertically Inclined uses equipment in earning revenue. This equipment's cost must be depreciated to match the cost of the equipment over the time that the equipment helps earn revenue. Recall that Vertically Inclined purchased equipment for $6,000 on January 1. Virgil Klimb expects the equipment to have a useful life (benefit period) of two years. Virgil expects to sell the equipment for about $1,200 at the end of two years. This means that the *net cost* expected to expire over the estimated useful life is $4,800 (=$6,000 − $1,200).

Straight-Line Depreciation

Calculated as:

$$= \frac{\text{Cost of asset} - \text{Estimated value at end of estimated useful life}}{\text{Estimated useful life}}$$

$$= \frac{\$6{,}000 - \$1{,}200}{24 \text{ months}}$$

$$= \$200 \text{ per month}$$

There are several methods that we can use to allocate this $4,800 net cost to expense. Vertically Inclined uses *straight-line depreciation.*[5] The **straight-line depreciation method** allocates equal amounts of an asset's net cost over its estimated useful life. When the $4,800 net cost is divided by the asset's useful life of 24 months (2 years × 12 months per year), we get an average monthly cost of $200 ($4,800/24). Our adjusting entry to record monthly depreciation expense is:

Adjustment (c)

Jan.	31	Depreciation Expense, Equipment.................	200	
		Accumulated Depreciation, Equipment		200
		To record monthly depreciation on equipment		

Posting this adjusting entry affects the accounts shown in Exhibit 4.8:

Exhibit 4.8

Accounts After Depreciation Adjustments

Equipment			
Jan. 1	6,000		
Bal.	6,000		

Accumulated Depreciation, Equipment			
		200	Jan. 31

Depreciation Expense, Equipment			
Jan. 31	200		

Accumulated depreciation is recorded in a *contra asset account.* A **contra account** is an account that is linked with another account and has an opposite normal balance to its counterpart. It is reported as a subtraction from the other account's balance. On Vertically Inclined's balance sheet, the balance in the contra asset account, *Accumulated Depreciation, Equipment,* will be subtracted from the Equipment account balance as shown in Exhibit 4.10. The cost of the asset less its accumulated depreciation is the **book value of the asset**. The **market value of an asset** is the amount it can be sold for. Market value is not tied to the book value of an asset.

After posting the adjustment, the *Equipment* account less its *Accumulated Depreciation, Equipment* account equals the January 31 balance sheet amount for this asset. The balance in the Depreciation Expense, Equipment account is the expense reported in the January income statement. If the adjustment is *not* made at January 31, then (a) expenses are understated by $200 and net income is overstated by $200 for the January income statement, and (b) both assets and equity are overstated by $200 in the January 31 balance sheet.

The use of the contra asset account Accumulated Depreciation allows balance sheet readers to know both the cost of assets and the total amount of depreciation charged to expense to date. Notice that the title of the contra account is

[5] We explain the details of *depreciation* methods in Chapter 12 (Volume 2). We briefly describe the straight-line method here to help you understand the adjusting process.

Accumulated Depreciation. This means that the account includes *total* depreciation expense for all prior periods when the assets were being used. Vertically Inclined's Equipment and Accumulated Depreciation, Equipment accounts would appear on March 31, 2011, as shown in Exhibit 4.10, after the three monthly adjusting entries detailed in Exhibit 4.9.

Exhibit 4.9

Accounts After Three Months of Depreciation Adjustments

Equipment		
Jan. 1	6,000	
Total	6,000	

Accumulated Depreciation, Equipment		
	200	Jan. 31
	200	Feb. 28
	200	Mar. 31
	600	Total

Exhibit 4.10

Accumulated Depreciation Contra Account in the Balance Sheet

Assets		
Cash		$
Equipment	**$6,000**	
Less: Accumulated depreciation	**600**	**5,400**
Total assets		$

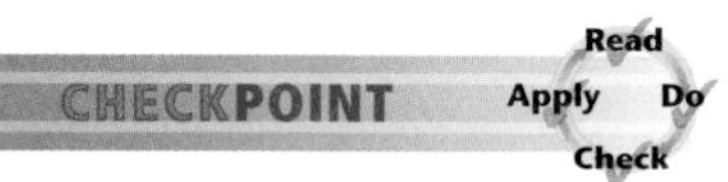

6. If the year-end adjusting entry to record depreciation expense was not recorded, what effect would this have on each component of the accounting equation?
7. Explain what a contra account is.

Do Quick Study question: QS 4-4

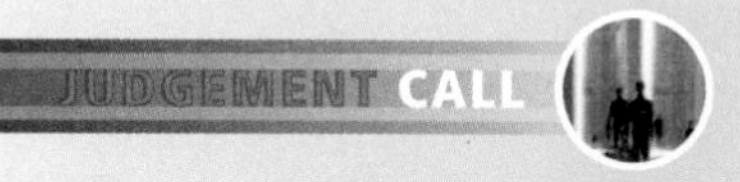

Answer—p. 151

Small Business Owner

You are preparing to make an offer to purchase a small family-run restaurant. The manager gives you a copy of her depreciation schedule for the restaurant's building and equipment. It shows costs of $75,000 and accumulated depreciation of $55,000. This leaves a net total for building and equipment of $20,000. Is this information valuable in deciding on a purchase offer for the restaurant?

Adjusting Unearned Revenues

Unearned revenues refer to cash received in advance of providing products and services. Unearned revenues, also known as *deferred revenues*, are a *liability*. When cash is accepted, an obligation to provide products and services is also accepted. As products and services are provided, the amount of unearned revenues becomes *earned* revenues. Adjusting entries for unearned revenues involve increasing (crediting) revenues and decreasing (debiting) unearned revenues as shown in Exhibit 4.11. These adjustments reflect economic events (including passage of time) that impact unearned revenues.

Exhibit 4.11

Adjusting for Unearned Revenues

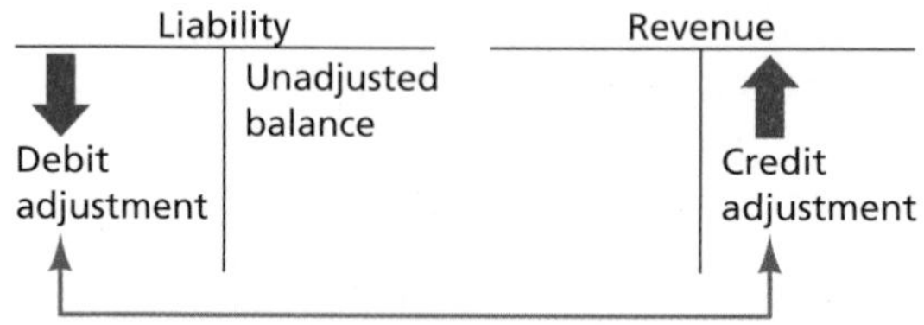

We see an example of unearned revenues in Rogers Communications' 2008 annual report. Rogers reports unearned revenue of $239 million on its balance sheet that includes subscriber deposits and amounts received related to services to be provided in the future. Another example is WestJet, which reports advance (unearned) ticket sales at December 31, 2008, of $251,354,000.

Vertically Inclined also has unearned revenues. On January 26, Vertically Inclined agreed to provide teaching services to a client for a fixed fee of $1,500 per month. On that same day, this client paid the first two months' fees in advance, covering the period from January 27 to March 27. The entry to record the cash received in advance is:

Jan.	26	Cash	3,000	
		Unearned Teaching Revenue		3,000
		Received advance payment for services over the next two months.		

This advance payment increases cash and creates an obligation to provide teaching services over the next two months. As time passes, Vertically Inclined will earn this payment. No external transactions are linked with this earnings process. By January 31, Vertically Inclined provides five days of teaching that amounts to revenue of $250 (=$1,500 × 5/30). The revenue recognition principle requires that $250 of unearned revenue is reported as revenue on the January income statement. The adjusting entry to reduce the liability account and recognize earned revenue is:

Adjustment (d)

Jan.	31	Unearned Teaching Revenue	250	
		Teaching Revenue		250
		To record the earned portion of revenue received in advance calculated as $1,500 × 5/30.		

The accounts look as shown in Exhibit 4.12 after posting the adjusting entry.

Exhibit 4.12

Unearned Revenue and Revenue Accounts After Adjustments

Unearned Teaching Revenue			
Jan. 31	250	3,000	Jan. 26
		2,750	Balance

Teaching Revenue			
		2,200	Jan. 10
		1,600	15
		250	31
		4,050	Total

The adjusting entry transfers $250 out of Unearned Teaching Revenue (a liability account) to a revenue account. If the adjustment is *not* made, then (a) revenue and net income are understated by $250 in the January income statement, and (b) Unearned Teaching Revenue is overstated and equity understated by $250 on the January 31 balance sheet.

8. AltaCo credited Unearned Revenue for $20,000 received on November 3, 2011, for work to be done just prior to Christmas. The work was completed as scheduled. If Unearned Revenue is not adjusted at year-end to reflect the completion of the work, which GAAP will be violated and why?
9. Describe how an unearned revenue arises. Give an example.

Do Quick Study question: QS 4-5

Adjusting Accrued Expenses

Accrued expenses refer to costs incurred in a period that are both unpaid and unrecorded. For example, Loblaw Companies Limited reported $2,823 million of accounts payable and accrued liabilities on its January 3, 2009, balance sheet. Accrued expenses are part of expenses and reported on the income statement. Adjusting entries for recording accrued expenses involve increasing (debiting) expenses and increasing (crediting) liabilities as shown in Exhibit 4.13.

Exhibit 4.13

Adjusting for Accrued Expenses

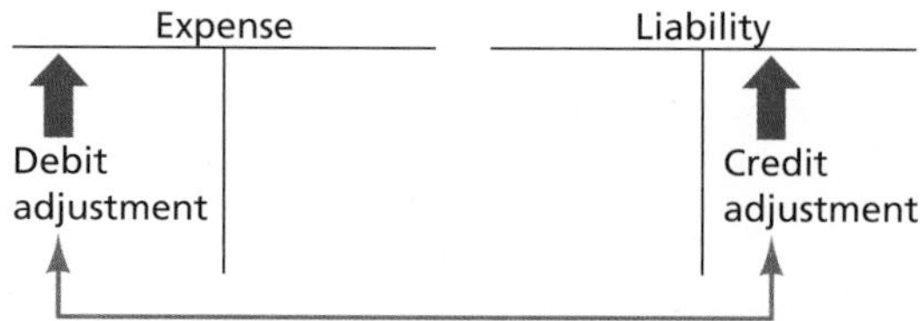

Common examples of accrued expenses are interest, salaries, rent, and taxes. We use interest and salaries to show how to adjust accounts for accrued expenses.

Accrued Interest Expense

It is common for companies to have accrued interest expense on notes payable and certain accounts payable at the end of a period. Interest expense is incurred with the passage of time. Unless interest is paid on the last day of an accounting period, we need to adjust accounts for interest expense incurred but not yet paid.

Interest of $35 has accrued on Vertically Inclined's $6,000, 7%, six-month note payable for the month of January.[6] The journal entry is:

Adjustment (e)

Jan.	31	Interest Expense	35	
		Interest Payable		35
		To record accrued interest.		

After the adjusting entry is posted, the expense and liability accounts appear as shown in Exhibit 4.14.

Exhibit 4.14

Notes Payable and Interest Accounts After Accrual Adjustments

Notes Payable			
		6,000	Jan. 1

Interest Expense			
Jan. 31	35		

Interest Payable			
		35	Jan. 31

This means that $35 of interest expense is reported on the income statement and that $35 interest payable is reported on the balance sheet. Notice that the Notes Payable account is *not* affected by recording interest. If the interest adjustment is not made, then (a) Interest Expense is understated and net income overstated by

[6] Interest on the $6,000, 7%, six-month note payable was calculated using the formula

Interest = Principal of the note × Annual interest rate × Time expressed in years OR $i = Prt$.

Therefore $6,000 × 7% × 1/12 = $35.
Where the term of the note is in days, Interest = Principal × Rate × $\frac{\text{Exact days}}{365}$.
Interest is discussed in greater detail in Chapter 10.

$35 in the January income statement, and (b) Interest Payable is understated and equity overstated by $35 on the January 31 balance sheet.

The $6,000 principal and total interest of $210 ($6,000 × 7% × 6/12 = $210) will be paid six months from January 1, the date the note was issued.[7]

Accrued Salaries Expense

Vertically Inclined's only employee earns $70 per day or $350 for a five-day workweek beginning on Monday and ending on Friday. This employee gets paid every two weeks on Friday. On the 14th and the 28th of January, the wages are paid, recorded in the journal, and posted to the ledger. The *unadjusted* Salaries Expense and Cash paid for salaries appear as shown in Exhibit 4.15.

Exhibit 4.15

Salary and Cash Accounts Before Adjusting

Cash			
		700	Jan. 14
		700	28

Salaries Expense			
Jan. 14	700		
28	700		

The calendar in Exhibit 4.16 shows one working day after the January 28 payday (January 31). This means that the employee earns one day's salary by the close of business on Monday, January 31. While this salary expense is incurred, it is not yet paid or recorded by the company. The period-end adjusting entry to account for accrued salaries is:

Adjustment (f)

Jan.	31	Salaries Expense	70	
		Salaries Payable		70
		To record one day's accrued salary; 1 × $70.		

Exhibit 4.16

Salary Accrual Period and Paydays

JANUARY 2011						
Sun	Mon	Tue	Wed	Thu	Fri	Sat
						1
2	3	4	5	6	7	8
9	10	11	12	13	14	15
16	17	18	19	20	21	22
23	24	25	26	27	28	29
30	31					

FEBRUARY 2011						
Sun	Mon	Tue	Wed	Thu	Fri	Sat
		1	2	3	4	5
6	7	8	9	10	11	12
13	14	15	16	17	18	19
20	21	22	23	24	25	26
27	28					

Salary expense incurred Payday Payday

[7] When the note payable and accrued interest are paid on July 1, six months after the date of issue on January 1, the entry would be (assuming interest expense of $35 per month has accrued):

July	1	Notes Payable	6,000	
		Interest Payable...	210	
		Cash		6,210
		To record payment of note payable and accrued interest.		

After the adjusting entry is posted, the expense and liability accounts appear as shown in Exhibit 4.17.

Exhibit 4.17

Salary Accounts After Accrual Adjustments

Salaries Expense		
Jan. 14	700	
28	700	
31	70	
Total	1,470	

Salaries Payable		
	70	Jan. 31

EXTEND YOUR KNOWLEDGE

This means that $1,470 of salaries expense is reported on the income statement and that $70 in salaries payable (liability) is reported in the balance sheet. If the adjustment is *not* made, then (a) Salaries Expense is understated and net income overstated by $70 in the January income statement, and (b) Salaries Payable is understated and equity overstated by $70 on the January 31 balance sheet.

The accrued salaries are paid on the first payday of the next bi-weekly period, which occurs on Friday, February 11. The entry includes the added salaries expense for the nine days worked in February:

Feb. 11	Salaries Payable	70	
	Salaries Expense	630	
	Cash		700
	Paid two weeks' salary including one day accrued in January (1 day at $70; 9 days at $70 = $630).		

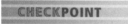

CHECKPOINT

10. In error, the May utility bill for $6,900 was not included in the May 31 adjusting entries. What effect would this error have on the components of the accounting equation?

11. What is an accrued expense? Give an example.

12. Music-Mart records $1,000 of accrued salaries on December 31. Five days later on January 5 (the next payday), salaries of $7,000 are paid. What is the January 5 entry?

Do Quick Study question: QS 4-6

Adjusting Accrued Revenues

When products and services are delivered, we expect to receive payment for them. **Accrued revenues** refer to revenues earned in a period that are both unrecorded and not yet received in cash (or other assets). Accrued revenues are part of revenues and must be reported on the income statement. The adjusting entries increase (debit) assets and increase (credit) revenues as shown in Exhibit 4.18.

Exhibit 4.18

Adjusting for Accrued Revenues

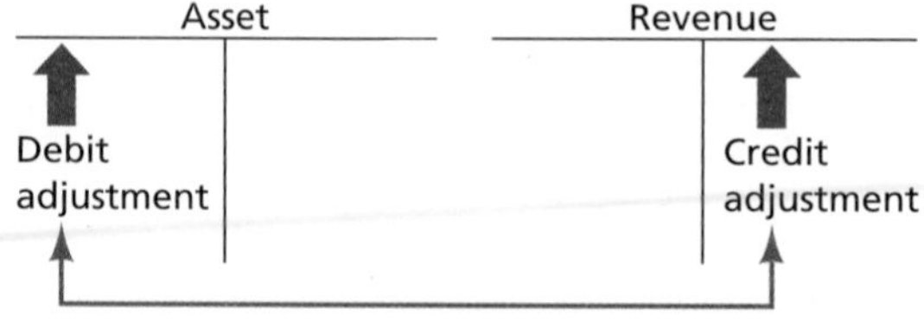

Common examples of accrued revenues are fees for services and products, interest revenue, and rent revenue. We use service fees and interest revenue to show how to adjust accounts for accrued revenues.

Accrued Services Revenue

Accrued revenues are earned but unrecorded because either the customer has not paid for them or the seller has not yet billed the customer. Vertically Inclined provides us with an example of an accrued revenue. In the second week of January, Vertically Inclined agrees to provide teaching services to a client for a fixed fee of \$2,700 per month from January 11 to February 10, or 30 days of service. The client agrees to pay \$2,700 cash to Vertically Inclined on February 10, 2011, when the service period is complete.

At January 31, 2011, 20 days of services are already provided to the client. Since the contracted services are not yet entirely provided, the client is not yet billed nor has Vertically Inclined recorded the services already provided. Vertically Inclined has earned \$1,800 (=\$2,700 × 20/30). The *revenue recognition principle* requires that we report the \$1,800 on the January income statement because it is earned in January. The balance sheet also must report that this client owes Vertically Inclined \$1,800. The year-end adjusting entry to account for accrued teaching services revenue is:

Adjustment (g)

Date		Account	Debit	Credit
Jan.	31	Accounts Receivable	1,800	
		Teaching Revenue		1,800
		To record 20 days' accrued revenue.		

After the adjusting entry is posted, the affected accounts look as shown in Exhibit 4.19.

Exhibit 4.19

Receivable and Revenue Accounts After Accrual Adjustments

Accounts Receivable			
Jan. 15	1,900	1,900	Jan. 25
31	1,800		
Balance	1,800		

Teaching Revenue		
	2,200	Jan. 10
	1,600	15
	250	31
	1,800	31
	5,850	Total

Accounts receivable are reported on the balance sheet at \$1,800, and \$5,850 of revenues are reported on the income statement. If the adjustment is *not* made, then (a) both Teaching Revenue and net income are understated by \$1,800 in the January income statement, and (b) both Accounts Receivable and equity are understated by \$1,800 on the January 31 balance sheet.

When the first month's fee is received on February 10, Vertically Inclined makes the following entry to remove the accrued asset (accounts receivable) and recognize the added 10 days of revenue earned in February:

Date		Account	Debit	Credit
Feb.	10	Cash	2,700	
		Accounts Receivable		1,800
		Teaching Revenue		900
		Received cash for accrued asset and earned teaching revenue; \$900 = \$2,700 × 10/30.		

Accrued Interest Revenue

In addition to the accrued interest expense we described earlier, interest can yield an accrued revenue when a company is owed money (or other assets) by a debtor. If a company is holding notes or accounts receivable that produce interest revenue, we must adjust the accounts to record any earned and yet uncollected interest revenue. The adjusting entry is recorded as a debit to Interest Receivable (asset) and a credit to Interest Revenue (equity).

13. An adjusting entry to record $6,000 of accrued interest revenue was omitted due to an oversight. What effect would this error have on the components of the accounting equation?

Do Quick Study questions: QS 4-7, QS 4-8

Adjustments and Financial Statements

LO5 Explain how accounting adjustments link to financial statements.

Exhibit 4.20 lists the five major types of transactions requiring adjustment. Adjusting entries are necessary for each. Understanding this exhibit is important to understanding the adjusting process and its link to financial statements. Remember that each adjusting entry affects both income statement accounts and balance sheet accounts.

Exhibit 4.20

Summary of Adjustments and Financial Statement Links

Type	Before Adjusting: Balance Sheet Account	Before Adjusting: Income Statement Account	Adjusting Entry			
Prepaid Expense	Asset & equity overstated	Expense understated	Dr Expense.............. Cr Asset	XX	XX	where XX = how much of the prepaid was used during the period
Depreciation	Asset & equity overstated	Expense understated	Dr Expense.............. Cr Contra Asset.....	XX	XX	where XX = how much of the asset's cost was matched as an expense to the period
Unearned Revenues	Liability overstated; equity understated	Revenue understated	Dr Liability............... Cr Revenue	XX	XX	where XX = how much of the liability was earned during the period
Accrued Expenses	Liability understated; equity overstated	Expense understated	Dr Expense.............. Cr Liability	XX	XX	where XX = the amount of the unpaid and unrecorded expense for the period
Accrued Revenues	Asset & equity understated	Revenue understated	Dr Asset................... Cr Revenue	XX	XX	where XX = the amount of the uncollected and unrecorded revenue for the period

Note that adjusting entries related to the framework in Exhibit 4.20 never affect cash.[8] A common error made by students learning to prepare adjusting entries is either to debit or to credit cash. In the case of prepaids and unearned revenues, cash has already been correctly recorded; it is the prepaids and unearned revenues account balances that need to be *fixed* or adjusted. In the case of accrued revenues and expenses, cash will be received or paid in the future and is not to be accounted for until that time; it is the revenue or expense account balance that needs to be fixed or adjusted. Depreciation is a non-cash transaction and therefore does not affect cash.

Exhibit 4.21 summarizes the adjusting entries of Vertically Inclined on January 31. The posting of adjusting entries to individual ledger accounts was shown when we described the transactions above and is not repeated here. Adjusting entries are often set apart from other journal entries with the caption Adjusting Entries, as shown in Exhibit 4.21.

[8] Adjusting entries related to bank reconciliations affect cash but these adjustments are excluded from the framework in Exhibit 4.20 and will be discussed in Chapter 9.

Exhibit 4.21

Journalizing Adjusting Entries of Vertically Inclined

GENERAL JOURNAL				Page 2
Date	**Account Titles and Explanations**	**PR**	**Debit**	**Credit**
2011	**Adjusting Entries**			
Jan. 31	Insurance Expense		100	
	Prepaid Insurance			100
	To record expired insurance; $2,400/24.			
31	Supplies Expense		1,050	
	Supplies			1,050
	To record supplies used; $3,600 − $2,550.			
31	Depreciation Expense, Equipment		200	
	Accumulated Depreciation, Equipment			200
	To record monthly depreciation on equipment; $6,000 − $1,200 = $4,800/24.			
31	Unearned Teaching Revenue		250	
	Teaching Revenue			250
	To record earned revenue received in advance; $1,500 × 5/30.			
31	Interest Expense		35	
	Interest Payable			35
	To record one month of accrued interest.			
31	Salaries Expense		70	
	Salaries Payable			70
	To record one day's accrued salary; 1 × $70.			
31	Accounts Receivable		1,800	
	Teaching Revenue			1,800
	To record 20 days of accrued revenue; $2,700 × 20/30.			

14. Explain how adjusting entries are linked to the components of the accounting equation.

Do Quick Study questions: QS 4-9, QS 4-10

mid-chapter demonstration problem

The owner of a lawn service company prepares ***annual*** financial statements.

Part A

Prepare the appropriate adjusting entries for July 31, 2011, based on the following information available at the end of July.

a. The annual insurance amounting to $1,200 went into effect on May 1, 2011. The Prepaid Insurance account was debited and Cash credited on the same date.

b. The lawn service company's lawn tractor was purchased for $3,200 in 2009. The value of the lawn tractor at the end of its estimated four-year useful life was determined to be $800. This information was made available to record depreciation for the year ended July 31, 2011.

c. On April 1, 2011, a customer paid for a six-month lawn service plan to begin June 1, 2011. The journal entry credited the Unearned Service Fees account when the $3,000 payment was received. The monthly fee is $500.

d. The last weekly salary of $1,400 was paid to employees on Friday, July 27. Employees are paid based on a five-day workweek. Salaries for July 30 and 31 have accrued.

e. Service fees of $1,800 were earned by July 31 but not recorded.

Part B

Refer to (d) above. Prepare the entry to pay the salaries on Friday, August 3.

Analysis component:

Refer to the chapter opening vignette. Nortel understated its 2002 earnings. Omitting which of the adjustments in Part A would accomplish this?

solution

Part A

a.	July 31	Insurance Expense	300	
		Prepaid Insurance		300
		To record insurance for May, June, and July; calculated as: $1,200/12 = $100 × 3 = $300.		

b.	31	Depreciation Expense, Lawn Tractor	600	
		Accumulated Depreciation, Lawn Tractor		600
		Annual depreciation, calculated as $3,200 − $800 = $2,400/4 years = $600/year.		

c.	31	Unearned Service Fees	1,000	
		Service Fees Earned		1,000
		To record service fees earned for June and July; calculated as $500 × 2 = $1,000.		

d.	31	Salaries Expense	560	
		Salaries Payable		560
		To record salaries for the last two days of July, calculated as $1,400/5 = $280/day × 2 days = $560.		

e.	31	Accounts Receivable	1,800	
		Service Fees Earned		1,800
		To record accrued service revenue for July.		

Part B

Aug. 3	Salaries Payable	560	
	Salaries Expense	840	
	Cash		1,400
	To record payment of weekly salaries; where salaries expense is calculated as $1,400/5 = $280/day × 3 days = $840.		

Analysis component:

Omitting adjustments (c) and (e) would cause revenues to be understated; hence, earnings or net income would also be understated.

Adjusted Trial Balance

LO6 | Explain and prepare an adjusted trial balance.

An **unadjusted trial balance** is a listing of accounts and balances prepared *before* adjustments are recorded. An **adjusted trial balance** is a list of accounts and balances prepared *after* adjusting entries are recorded and posted to the ledger. Exhibit 4.22 shows the unadjusted and adjusted trial balances for Vertically Inclined at January 31, 2011. Notice several new accounts arising from the adjusting entries. The listing of accounts is also slightly changed to match the order listed in the Chart of Accounts in Appendix II at the end of the book.

Exhibit 4.22

Unadjusted and Adjusted Trial Balance for Vertically Inclined

Vertically Inclined Rock Gym
Trial Balances
January 31, 2011

	Unadjusted Trial Balance		Adjustments		Adjusted Trial Balance	
	Dr.	Cr.	Dr.	Cr.	Dr.	Cr.
Cash	$ 8,070				$ 8,070	
Accounts receivable			(g) $1,800		1,800	
Supplies	3,600			(b) $1,050	2,550	
Prepaid insurance	2,400			(a) 100	2,300	
Equipment	6,000				6,000	
Accumulated depreciation, equipment				(c) 200		$ 200
Accounts payable		$ 200				200
Interest payable				(e) 35		35
Salaries payable				(f) 70		70
Unearned teaching revenue		3,000	(d) 250			2,750
Notes payable		6,000				6,000
Virgil Klimb, capital		10,000				10,000
Virgil Klimb, withdrawals	600				600	
Teaching revenue		3,800		(d) 250 (g) 1,800		5,850
Equipment rental revenue		300				300
Depreciation expense, equipment			(c) 200		200	
Salaries expense	1,400		(f) 70		1,470	
Interest expense			(e) 35		35	
Insurance expense			(a) 100		100	
Rent expense	1,000				1,000	
Supplies expense			(b) 1,050		1,050	
Utilities expense	230				230	
Totals	$23,300	$23,300	$3,505	$3,505	$25,405	$25,405

Preparing Financial Statements

LO7 | Prepare financial statements from an adjusted trial balance.

We can prepare financial statements directly from information in the *adjusted* trial balance. An adjusted trial balance includes all balances appearing in financial statements. We know that a trial balance summarizes information in the ledger by listing accounts and their balances. This summary is easier to work from than the entire ledger when preparing financial statements.

Exhibit 4.23 shows how Vertically Inclined's revenue and expense balances are transferred from the adjusted trial balance to (1) the income statement, and (2) the statement of changes in equity. Note how we use the net income and withdrawals account to prepare the statement of changes in equity.

Exhibit 4.23

Preparing the Income Statement, Statement of Changes in Equity, and Balance Sheet From the Adjusted Trial Balance

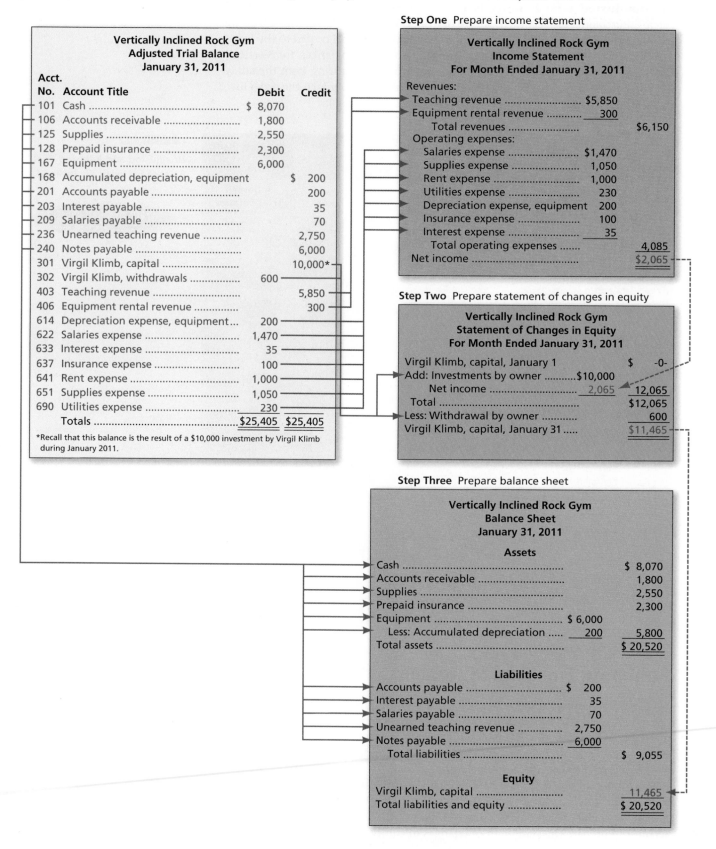

Vertically Inclined Rock Gym
Adjusted Trial Balance
January 31, 2011

Acct. No.	Account Title	Debit	Credit
101	Cash	$ 8,070	
106	Accounts receivable	1,800	
125	Supplies	2,550	
128	Prepaid insurance	2,300	
167	Equipment	6,000	
168	Accumulated depreciation, equipment		$ 200
201	Accounts payable		200
203	Interest payable		35
209	Salaries payable		70
236	Unearned teaching revenue		2,750
240	Notes payable		6,000
301	Virgil Klimb, capital		10,000*
302	Virgil Klimb, withdrawals	600	
403	Teaching revenue		5,850
406	Equipment rental revenue		300
614	Depreciation expense, equipment	200	
622	Salaries expense	1,470	
633	Interest expense	35	
637	Insurance expense	100	
641	Rent expense	1,000	
651	Supplies expense	1,050	
690	Utilities expense	230	
	Totals	$25,405	$25,405

*Recall that this balance is the result of a $10,000 investment by Virgil Klimb during January 2011.

Step One Prepare income statement

Vertically Inclined Rock Gym
Income Statement
For Month Ended January 31, 2011

Revenues:		
Teaching revenue	$5,850	
Equipment rental revenue	300	
Total revenues		$6,150
Operating expenses:		
Salaries expense	$1,470	
Supplies expense	1,050	
Rent expense	1,000	
Utilities expense	230	
Depreciation expense, equipment	200	
Insurance expense	100	
Interest expense	35	
Total operating expenses		4,085
Net income		$2,065

Step Two Prepare statement of changes in equity

Vertically Inclined Rock Gym
Statement of Changes in Equity
For Month Ended January 31, 2011

Virgil Klimb, capital, January 1		$ -0-
Add: Investments by owner	$10,000	
Net income	2,065	12,065
Total		$12,065
Less: Withdrawal by owner		600
Virgil Klimb, capital, January 31		$11,465

Step Three Prepare balance sheet

Vertically Inclined Rock Gym
Balance Sheet
January 31, 2011

Assets		
Cash		$ 8,070
Accounts receivable		1,800
Supplies		2,550
Prepaid insurance		2,300
Equipment	$ 6,000	
Less: Accumulated depreciation	200	5,800
Total assets		$ 20,520
Liabilities		
Accounts payable	$ 200	
Interest payable	35	
Salaries payable	70	
Unearned teaching revenue	2,750	
Notes payable	6,000	
Total liabilities		$ 9,055
Equity		
Virgil Klimb, capital		11,465
Total liabilities and equity		$ 20,520

Exhibit 4.23 also shows how Vertically Inclined's asset and liability balances on the adjusted trial balance are transferred to the balance sheet. The ending equity is determined on the statement of changes in equity and transferred to the balance sheet. There are different formats for the balance sheet. The **account form balance sheet**, used in previous chapters, lists assets on the left and liabilities and equity on the right side of the balance sheet. Its name comes from its link to the accounting equation, *Assets* = *Liabilities* + *Equity*. The balance sheet in Exhibit 2.11 (on P. 42) is in account form. The **report form balance sheet** lists items vertically, as shown in Exhibit 4.23. Both forms are widely used and are considered equally helpful to users. For consistency, we will use the report form in the preparation of financial statements from this point forward.

We usually prepare financial statements in the order shown: income statement, statement of changes in equity, and balance sheet. This order makes sense since the balance sheet uses information from the statement of changes in equity, which in turn uses information from the income statement.

15. Jordan Air Company has the following information in its unadjusted and adjusted trial balances:

	Unadjusted		Adjusted	
	Debit	Credit	Debit	Credit
Prepaid insurance	$6,200		$5,900	
Salaries payable		$ -0-		$1,400

What are the adjusting entries that Jordan Air likely recorded?

16. What types of accounts are taken from the adjusted trial balance to prepare an income statement?

17. In preparing financial statements from an adjusted trial balance, what statement is usually prepared first? second? third? Explain why.

Do Quick Study question: QS 4-11

Answer—p. 151

Financial Officer

You are the financial officer for a retail outlet company. At the calendar year-end when you are reviewing adjusting entries to record accruals, you are called into the president's office. The president asks about accrued expenses and instructs you not to record these expenses until next year because they will not be paid until January or later. The president also asks how much the current year's revenues increased because of the recent purchase order from a new customer. You state that there is no effect on sales until next year because the purchase order says merchandise is to be delivered after January 15 and that is when your company plans to make delivery. The president points out that the order is already received, and your company is ready to make delivery, and tells you to record this sale in the current year. Your company would report a net income instead of a net loss if you carried out the president's orders for adjusting accruals. What do you do?

CRITICAL THINKING CHALLENGE

Refer to the Critical Thinking Challenge questions at the beginning of the chapter on page 130. Compare your answers to those suggested on Connect at www.mcgrawhillconnect.ca.

IFRS HIGHLIGHTS 

The IFRS Framework, para. 43, refers to the "timeliness" principle; this term will replace the "time period" principle (timeliness is reinforced in IFRS 2009, IAS 1, para. 36), under "Frequency of Reporting."

The term *amortization* is replaced with *depreciation* for tangible assets; *amortization* will continue to be used for intangible assets (IFRS 2009, IAS 38, para. 97); intangibles are discussed in more detail in Chapter 12.

Summary

LO1 Describe the purpose of adjusting accounts at the end of a period. After external transactions are recorded, several accounts need adjusting for their balances to be correct because internal transactions remain unrecorded. The purpose of adjusting accounts at the end of a period is to recognize unrecorded revenues and expenses.

LO2 Explain how the timeliness, matching, and revenue recognition principles affect the adjusting process. The value of information is often linked to its timeliness, so accounting systems prepare periodic reports at regular intervals such as a month, a three-month quarter, or at minimum, once a year. Adjustments are made so that revenues and expenses are recognized as they occur and matched to the proper period.

LO3 Explain accrual accounting and cash basis accounting and how accrual accounting adds to the usefulness of financial statements. Accrual accounting recognizes revenue when earned and expenses when incurred, not necessarily when cash inflows and outflows occur. Cash basis accounting recognizes revenues when cash is received and expenses when cash is paid; it is not in accordance with GAAP.

LO4 Prepare and explain adjusting entries for prepaid expenses, depreciation, unearned revenues, accrued expenses, and accrued revenues. Prepaid expenses, an asset, refer to items paid for in advance of receiving their benefits. As this asset is used, its cost becomes an expense.

Dr. Expense	xx	
Cr. Prepaid		xx
To adjust prepaid for amount used.		

Depreciation is the expense created by spreading the cost of plant and equipment assets over the periods these assets are used. Accumulated Depreciation, a contra asset account, is credited to track the total amount of the plant and equipment asset used.

Dr. Depreciation Expense	xx	
Cr. Accumulated Depreciation		xx
To adjust for depreciation.		

Unearned revenues, a liability, refer to cash received in advance of providing products and services. As products and services are provided, the amount of unearned revenues becomes earned revenues.

Dr. Unearned Revenue	xx	
Cr. Revenue		xx
To adjust for unearned revenue that is earned.		

Accrued expenses are costs incurred in a period that are unpaid and unrecorded.

Dr. Expense	xx	
Cr. Liability		xx
To adjust for unrecorded and unpaid expenses.		

Accrued revenues are revenues earned in a period that are unrecorded and not yet collected.

Dr. Receivable	xx	
Cr. Revenue		xx
To adjust for unrecorded revenues not yet collected.		

LO5 Explain how accounting adjustments link to financial statements. Accounting adjustments bring an asset or liability account balance to its correct amount and update related expense or revenue accounts. Every adjusting entry affects one or more income statement *and* balance sheet accounts. An adjusting entry never affects cash. Adjustments are necessary for transactions that extend over more than one period. Exhibit 4.20 summarizes financial statement links by type of adjustment.

LO6 Explain and prepare an adjusted trial balance. An adjusted trial balance is a list of accounts and balances prepared after adjusting entries are recorded and posted to the ledger. Financial statements are often prepared from the adjusted trial balance.

LO7 Prepare financial statements from an adjusted trial balance. We can prepare financial statements directly from the adjusted trial balance that includes all account balances. Revenue and expense balances are transferred to the income statement and statement of changes in equity. Asset, liability, and equity balances are transferred to the balance sheet. We usually prepare statements in the following order: income statement, statement of changes in equity, and balance sheet.

guidance answers to JUDGEMENT CALL

Small Business Owner

We know that depreciation is a process of cost allocation, not asset valuation. Knowing the depreciation schedule of the restaurant is not especially useful in your estimation of what the restaurant's building and equipment are currently worth. Your assessment of the age, quality, and usefulness of the building and equipment is much more important. Also, you would use the current market values of similar assets in estimating the value of this restaurant's building and equipment.

Financial Officer

It appears that you must make a choice either to follow the president's orders or not to follow them. The requirements of acceptable practice are clear. Omitting adjustments and early recognition of revenue can mislead users of financial statements (including managers, owners, and lenders). One action is to request a second meeting with the president where you explain that accruing expenses and recognizing revenue when earned are required practices. You should also mention the ethical implications of not complying with accepted practice. Point out that the president's orders involve intentional falsification of the statements. If the president persists, you might discuss the situation with legal counsel and any auditors involved. Your ethical action might cost you this job. But the potential pitfalls of falsifying statements, damaging your reputation, losing your personal integrity, and other costs are too great.

guidance answers to CHECKPOINT

Read Apply Do Check

1. An annual reporting (or accounting) period covers one year and refers to the preparation of annual financial statements. The annual reporting period can follow the calendar year or a fiscal year. The fiscal year can follow the business's natural business year.
2. Interim (less than one year) financial statements are prepared to provide decision makers with information frequently and promptly.
3. The revenue recognition principle, the timeliness principle, and the matching principle lead most directly to the adjusting process.
4. No. Cash basis accounting is not consistent with generally accepted accounting principles.
5. If Prepaid Insurance is not adjusted, assets and equity will be overstated.
6. If the adjusting entry to record depreciation was not recorded, assets and equity would be overstated.
7. A contra account is an account that is subtracted from the balance of a related account. Use of a contra account often provides more complete information than simply reporting a net amount.
8. The revenue recognition principle will be violated because revenues earned have not been recognized. The matching principle will also be violated because revenues earned will not be assigned to the correct accounting period—the period in which the expenses related to the revenues were incurred.
9. An unearned revenue arises when cash is (or other assets are) received from a customer before the services and products are delivered to the customer. Magazine subscription receipts in advance are one example.
10. The omission of the \$6,900 interest expense accrual will cause liabilities to be understated by \$6,900 and equity to be overstated by \$6,900.
11. An accrued expense refers to costs incurred in a period that are both unpaid and unrecorded prior to adjusting entries. One example is salaries earned by employees but not yet paid at the end of a period.
12. The January 5 entry to settle the accrued salaries and pay for added salaries is:

Jan. 5	Salaries Payable..........................	1,000	
	Salaries Expense..........................	6,000	
	Cash..................................		7,000
	Paid salary including accrual from December.		

13. The omission of an adjusting entry to record \$6,000 of accrued interest would cause assets and equity to be understated by \$6,000 each.
14. The various adjusting entries are linked to the accounting equation as follows: (a) adjustment of prepaids and the recording of depreciation cause assets and equity to decrease; (b) adjustment of unearned amounts causes liabilities to decrease and equity to increase; (c) accrual of revenues causes assets and equity to increase; and (d) accrual of expenses causes liabilities to increase and equity to decrease.

15. The probable adjusting entries of Jordan Air are:

Insurance Expense	300	
Prepaid Insurance		300
To record insurance expired.		

Salaries Expense	1,400	
Salaries Payable		1,400
To record accrued salaries.		

16. Revenue accounts and expense accounts.

17. The income statement is usually prepared first, followed by the statement of changes in equity because net income (loss) from the income statement flows into the statement of changes in equity. The balance sheet is then prepared since the ending capital balance from the statement of changes in equity flows into the equity section of the balance sheet.

demonstration problem

The following information continues with The Cutlery, featured in the Chapter 3 Demonstration Problem. After the first month of business, The Cutlery's August 31, 2011, unadjusted trial balance appeared as follows:

The Cutlery
Trial Balance
August 31, 2011

Account	Debit	Credit
Cash	$ 4,950	
Accounts receivable	-0-	
Prepaid insurance	2,400	
Furniture	2,000	
Store equipment	31,000	
Accounts payable		$14,450
Unearned haircutting services revenue		500
Joane Cardinal, capital		26,000
Joane Cardinal, withdrawals	500	
Haircutting services revenue		3,800
Wages expense	250	
Rent expense	3,200	
Hydro expense	450	
Totals	$44,750	$44,750

The following additional information is available for the *month* just ended:

a. Depreciation of $100 per month will be taken on the furniture.

b. It is estimated that the store equipment will have a $1,000 value at the end of its estimated five-year (or 60-month) useful life. Joane Cardinal will record a full month of depreciation for August.

c. It was determined that the balance in unearned haircutting services revenue at August 31 should be $420.

d. The prepaid insurance represents six months of insurance beginning August 1.

e. On August 31, The Cutlery provided $130 of services to a client who will pay in September.

f. On August 31, Joane Cardinal received the business's August cell phone bill totalling $50. It will be paid in September.

Required

1. Prepare the adjusting entries needed on August 31, 2011, to record the previously unrecorded items.
2. Prepare T-accounts for accounts affected by the adjusting entries. Post the adjusting entries to the T-accounts.
3. Prepare an adjusted trial balance.
4. Prepare an income statement, a statement of changes in equity, and a balance sheet.

Analysis component:

Calculate the net effect of the adjusting entries on the balance sheet. Is net income positively or negatively affected by these adjusting entries overall? Could the opposite effect be achieved? If so, how?

Planning the Solution

- Analyze the information for each situation to determine which accounts need to be updated with an adjustment.
- Calculate the dollar amount of each adjustment and prepare the necessary journal entries.
- Show the amount entered by each adjustment in the designated accounts and determine the adjusted balance.
- Determine each entry's effect on net income for the year and on total assets, total liabilities, and equity at the end of the year.
- Using the adjusted balances, prepare an adjusted trial balance.
- Using the adjusted trial balance, prepare the income statement, statement of changes in equity, and balance sheet.
- Analyze the adjusting entries and calculate the effect on each component of the accounting equation.

solution

1. Adjusting journal entries.

	Date	Account	Debit	Credit
a.	Aug. 31	Depreciation Expense, Furniture	100	
		Accumulated Depreciation, Furniture		100
		To record depreciation expense for the month of August for the furniture.		
b.	31	Depreciation Expense, Store Equipment	500	
		Accumulated Depreciation, Store Equipment		500
		To record depreciation expense for the month; (\$31,000 − \$1,000)/60 months = \$500/month.		
c.	31	Unearned Haircutting Services Revenue	80	
		Haircutting Services Revenue		80
		To recognize haircutting services revenue earned; \$500 − \$420 = \$80.		
d.	31	Insurance Expense	400	
		Prepaid Insurance		400
		To adjust for the expired portion of prepaid insurance; \$2,400/6 months = \$400/month.		

e.	31	Accounts Receivable	130	
		Haircutting Services Revenue		130
		To record revenue earned.		

f.	31	Phone Expense	50	
		Accounts Payable		50
		To record August cell phone bill.		

2.

Accounts Receivable

	Debit	Credit	
(e)	130		

Prepaid Insurance

	Debit	Credit	
Balance	2,400	400	(d)
Balance	2,000		

Accumulated Depreciation, Furniture

	Debit	Credit	
		100	(a)

Accumulated Depreciation, Store Equipment

	Debit	Credit	
		500	(b)

Accounts Payable

	Debit	Credit	
		14,450	Balance
		50	(f)
		14,500	Balance

Unearned Haircutting Services Revenue

	Debit	Credit	
(c)	80	500	Balance
		420	Balance

Haircutting Services Revenue

	Debit	Credit	
		3,800	Balance
		80	(c)
		130	(e)
		4,010	Balance

Depreciation Expense, Furniture

	Debit	Credit	
(a)	100		

Depreciation Expense, Store Equipment

	Debit	Credit	
(b)	500		

Insurance Expense

	Debit	Credit	
(d)	400		

Phone Expense

	Debit	Credit	
(f)	50		

3.

The Cutlery
Adjusted Trial Balance
August 31, 2011

Account	Debit	Credit
Cash	$ 4,950	
Accounts receivable	130	
Prepaid insurance	2,000	
Furniture	2,000	
Accumulated depreciation, furniture		$ 100
Store equipment	31,000	
Accumulated depreciation, store equipment		500
Accounts payable		14,500
Unearned haircutting services revenue		420
Joane Cardinal, capital		26,000
Joane Cardinal, withdrawals	500	
Haircutting services revenue		4,010
Depreciation expense, furniture	100	
Depreciation expense, store equipment	500	
Wages expense	250	
Insurance expense	400	
Rent expense	3,200	
Hydro expense	450	
Phone expense	50	
Totals	$45,530	$45,530

4.

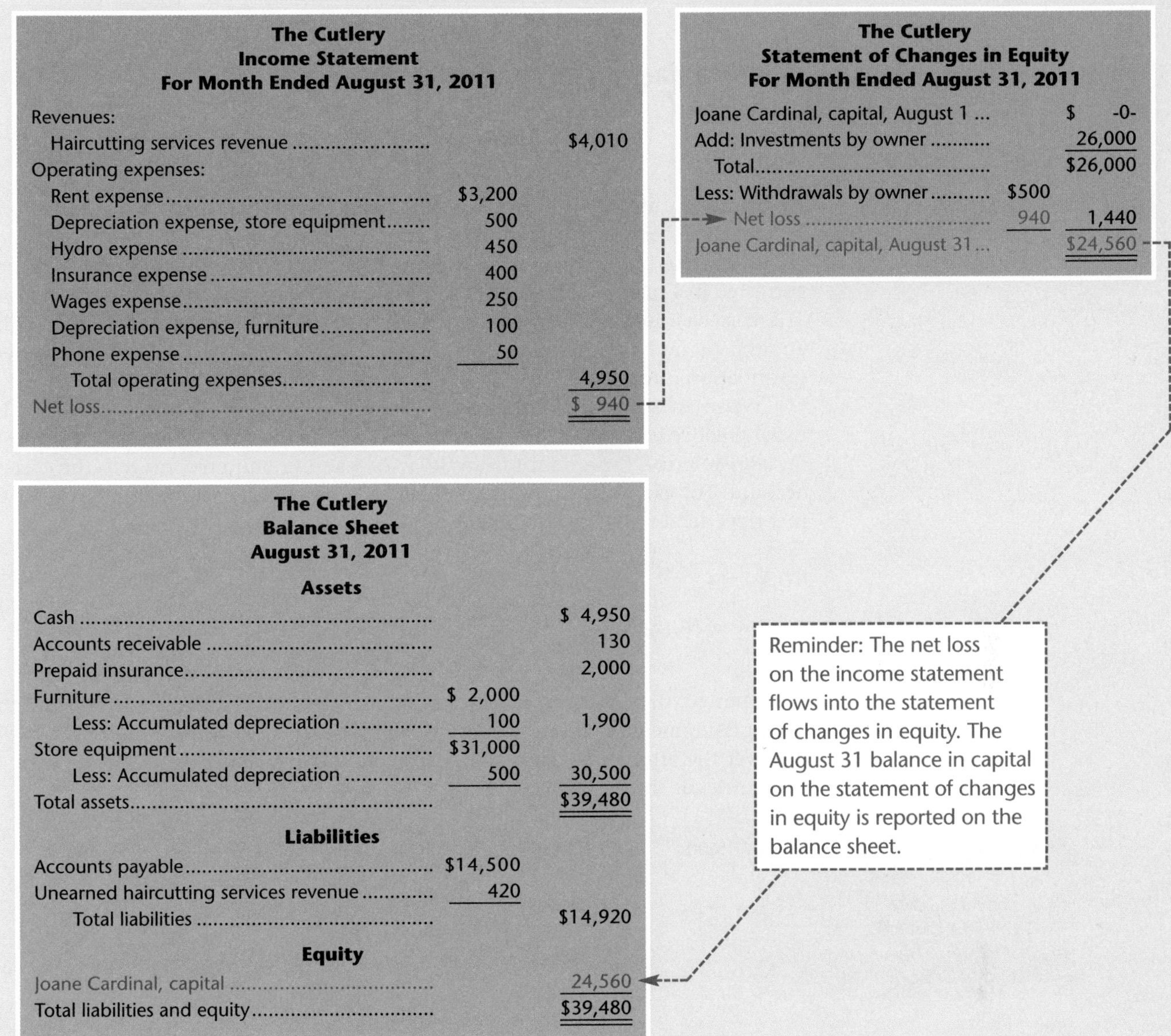

The Cutlery
Income Statement
For Month Ended August 31, 2011

Revenues:		
Haircutting services revenue		$4,010
Operating expenses:		
Rent expense	$3,200	
Depreciation expense, store equipment	500	
Hydro expense	450	
Insurance expense	400	
Wages expense	250	
Depreciation expense, furniture	100	
Phone expense	50	
Total operating expenses		4,950
Net loss		$ 940

The Cutlery
Statement of Changes in Equity
For Month Ended August 31, 2011

Joane Cardinal, capital, August 1		$ -0-
Add: Investments by owner		26,000
Total		$26,000
Less: Withdrawals by owner	$500	
Net loss	940	1,440
Joane Cardinal, capital, August 31		$24,560

The Cutlery
Balance Sheet
August 31, 2011

Assets		
Cash		$ 4,950
Accounts receivable		130
Prepaid insurance		2,000
Furniture	$ 2,000	
Less: Accumulated depreciation	100	1,900
Store equipment	$31,000	
Less: Accumulated depreciation	500	30,500
Total assets		$39,480
Liabilities		
Accounts payable	$14,500	
Unearned haircutting services revenue	420	
Total liabilities		$14,920
Equity		
Joane Cardinal, capital		24,560
Total liabilities and equity		$39,480

Reminder: The net loss on the income statement flows into the statement of changes in equity. The August 31 balance in capital on the statement of changes in equity is reported on the balance sheet.

Analysis component:

The net effect of the adjustments on assets, liabilities, and equity is detailed below.

Entry	a.	b.	c.	d.	e.	f.	Net effect
Assets	$100 ↓	$500 ↓	No effect	$400 ↓	$130 ↑	No effect	$870 ↓
Liabilities	No effect	No effect	$80 ↓	No effect	No effect	$50 ↑	$30 ↓
Equity	$100 ↓	$500 ↓	$80 ↑	$400 ↓	$130 ↑	$50 ↓	$840 ↓

Equity decreased by $840 as a result of the adjusting entries. All of the adjustments that affected equity were income statement items (revenues or expenses), therefore net income was negatively affected by the adjusting entries (a net decrease in income of $840).

The opposite effect could have been achieved if accrued revenues (Dr Receivables and Cr Revenues) plus the adjustment of unearned amounts (Dr Unearned Revenues and Cr Revenues) were greater than the adjustment of prepaids (Dr Expense and Cr Prepaid) plus depreciation (Dr Depreciation Expense and Cr Accumulated Depreciation) and accrued expenses (Dr Expense and Cr Payable).

APPENDIX 4A

Correcting Errors

LO8 Explain and prepare correcting entries.

Correcting entries, as the term implies, account for the correction of errors, and are not to be confused with adjusting entries.

If an error in a journal entry is discovered before the error is posted, it can be corrected in a manual system by drawing a line through the incorrect information. The correct information is written above it to create a record of change for the auditor. Many computerized systems allow the operator to replace the incorrect information directly.

When an error in a journal entry is *not* discovered until after it is posted, the usual practice is to correct the error by creating *another* journal entry.[9] This *correcting entry* removes the amount from the wrong account and records it to the correct account. For example, suppose we recorded a purchase of office supplies with an incorrect debit to Office Equipment as follows:

Oct. 14	Office Equipment	1,600	
	Cash		1,600
	To record the purchase of office supplies.		

Once posted, the Office Supplies account balance is understated by $1,600 and the Office Equipment account balance is overstated by the same amount. When we discover the error three days later, a correcting entry is made using either one or two entries as shown below:

17	Office Supplies	1,600	
	Office Equipment		1,600
	To correct the entry of October 14 that incorrectly debited Office Equipment instead of Office Supplies.		

OR

17	Cash	1,600	
	Office Equipment		1,600
	To reverse the incorrect entry.		
17	Office Supplies	1,600	
	Cash		1,600
	To journalize the purchase of office supplies correctly.		

In the approach to the left, the credit removes the error and the debit correctly records supplies. Alternatively, the two entries on the right could be used: the first entry reverses the incorrect entry *entirely*, and the second entry records the transaction as it should have been. Both methods achieve the same final results.

Computerized systems often use similar correcting entries. The exact procedure depends on the system used and management policy. Yet nearly all systems include controls to show when and where a correction is made.

18. On March 14, Accounts Receivable was debited for $4,100 and Service Revenue was credited for $4,100. At the end of the month, it was discovered that the March 14 entry should have been credited to Rent Revenue. What correcting entry is required?

Do Quick Study questions: *QS 4-12, *QS 4-13

[9] For tracking purposes, correcting entries must be referenced to the incorrect entry and any calculations are to be documented.

APPENDIX 4B

An Alternative in Recording Prepaids and Unearned Revenues

This section explains an alternative in recording prepaid expenses and unearned revenues.

LO[9] Identify and explain an alternative in recording prepaids and unearned revenues.

Recording Prepaid Expenses in Expense Accounts

We explained that prepaid expenses are assets when they are purchased and are recorded with debits to asset accounts. Adjusting entries transfer the used amounts to expense accounts at the end of an accounting period.

There is an acceptable alternative practice of recording *all* prepaid expenses with debits to expense accounts. If any prepaids remain unused at the end of an accounting period, then adjusting entries transfer the unused portions from expense accounts to asset accounts. The financial statements are identical under either procedure, but the adjusting entries are different.

To illustrate, let's look at Vertically Inclined's cash payment for 24 months of insurance coverage beginning on January 1. Vertically Inclined recorded that payment with a debit to an asset account, but alternatively it could have been recorded as a debit to an expense account. Exhibit 4B.1 shows the two approaches.

Exhibit 4B.1
Initial Entry for Prepaid Expenses for Two Approaches

		Payment Recorded as Asset		Payment Recorded as Expense	
Jan. 1	Prepaid Insurance	2,400			
	Cash		2,400		
1	Insurance Expense			2,400	
	Cash				2,400

On January 31, insurance protection for one month is used up. This means $100 ($2,400/24) is the expense for January. Exhibit 4B.2 shows that the adjusting entry depends on how the original payment is recorded:

Exhibit 4B.2
Adjusting Entry for Prepaid Expenses for Two Approaches

		Payment Recorded as Asset		Payment Recorded as Expense	
Jan. 31	Insurance Expense	100			
	Prepaid Insurance		100		
31	Prepaid Insurance			2,300	
	Insurance Expense				2,300

When these entries are posted, we can see in Exhibit 4B.3 that these two approaches give identical adjusted account balances at January 31.

Exhibit 4B.3

Account Balances Under Two Approaches for Recording Prepaid Expenses

Payment Recorded as Asset

Prepaid Insurance			
Jan. 1	2,400	100	Jan. 31
Balance	2,300		

Insurance Expense			
Jan. 31	100		

Payment Recorded as Expense

Prepaid Insurance			
Jan. 31	2,300		

Insurance Expense			
Jan. 1	2,400	2,300	Jan. 31
Balance	100		

Recording Unearned Revenues in Revenue Accounts

Unearned revenues are liabilities requiring delivery of products and services and are recorded as credits to liability accounts when cash and other assets are received. Adjusting entries at the end of an accounting period transfer to revenue accounts the earned portion of unearned revenues.

An acceptable alternative is to record *all* unearned revenues with credits to revenue accounts. If any revenues are unearned at the end of an accounting period, then adjusting entries transfer the unearned portions from revenue accounts to unearned revenue accounts. While the adjusting entries are different for these two approaches, the financial statements are identical.

To illustrate, let's look at Vertically Inclined's January 26 receipt of $3,000 for teaching services covering the period January 27 to March 27. Vertically Inclined recorded this transaction with a credit to a liability account. The alternative, shown in Exhibit 4B.4, is to record it with a credit to a revenue account as follows:

Exhibit 4B.4

Initial Entry for Unearned Revenues for Two Approaches

		Receipt Recorded as Liability		Receipt Recorded as Revenue	
Jan. 26	Cash	3,000			
	Unearned Teaching Revenue		3,000		
26	Cash			3,000	
	Teaching Revenue				3,000

By the end of the accounting period (January 31), Vertically Inclined earns $250 of this revenue. This means that $250 of the liability is satisfied. Depending on how the initial receipt is recorded, Exhibit 4B.5 shows the the adjusting entry:

Exhibit 4B.5

Adjusting Entry for Unearned Revenues for Two Approaches

		Receipt Recorded as Liability		Receipt Recorded as Revenue	
Jan. 31	Unearned Teaching Revenue	250			
	Teaching Revenue		250		
31	Teaching Revenue			2,750	
	Unearned Teaching Revenue				2,750

After adjusting entries are posted, the two approaches give identical adjusted account balances at January 31 as shown in Exhibit 4B.6.

Exhibit 4B.6

Account Balances Under Two Approaches for Recording Unearned Revenues

Receipt Recorded as Liability

Unearned Teaching Revenue			
Jan. 31	250	3,000	Jan. 26
		2,750	Balance

Teaching Revenue			
		250	Jan. 31

Receipt Recorded as Revenue

Unearned Teaching Revenue			
		2,750	Jan. 31

Teaching Revenue			
Jan. 31	2,750	3,000	Jan. 26
		250	Balance

19. Miller Company records cash receipts of unearned revenues and cash payments of prepaid expenses in balance sheet accounts. Bud Company records these items in income statement accounts. Explain any difference in the financial statements of these two companies from their different ways of recording prepaids.

Do Quick Study question: *QS 4-14

Summary of Appendix 4A and Appendix 4B

LO8 | Explain and prepare correcting entries. A correcting entry is required when an error in a journal entry is not discovered until after it has been posted. The correcting entry can be done in one of two ways: the incorrect portion of the entry can be corrected, or the entire incorrect entry can be reversed and the correct entry recorded; both methods accomplish the same result.

LO9 | Identify and explain an alternative in recording prepaids and unearned revenues. It is acceptable to charge all prepaid expenses to expense accounts when they are purchased. When this is done, adjusting entries must transfer any unexpired amounts from expense accounts to asset accounts. It is also acceptable to credit all unearned revenues to revenue accounts when cash is received. In this case the adjusting entries must transfer any unearned amounts from revenue accounts to unearned revenue accounts.

18. The correcting entry can be done in one of two ways:

31	Service Revenue	4,100	
	Rent Revenue		4,100
	To correct the March 14 entry.		

OR

31	Service Revenue	4,100	
	Accounts Receivable		4,100
	To reverse the incorrect March 14 entry.		
31	Accounts Receivable	4,100	
	Rent Revenue		4,100
	To enter the correct entry for March 14.		

19. When adjusting entries are correctly prepared, the financial statements of these companies will be identical under both approaches.

Glossary

Account form balance sheet A balance sheet that lists assets on the left and liabilities and equity on the right side of the balance sheet. (p. 149)

Accounting period Time frame covered by financial statements and other reports; also called *reporting periods.* (p. 133)

Accrual basis accounting The approach to preparing financial statements that uses the adjusting process to recognize revenues when earned and expenses when incurred, not when cash is paid or received; the basis for generally accepted accounting principles. (p. 133)

Accrued expenses Costs incurred in a period that are both unpaid and unrecorded; adjusting entries for recording accrued expenses involve increasing (debiting) expenses and increasing (crediting) liabilities. (p. 140)

Accrued revenues Revenues earned in a period that are both unrecorded and not yet received in cash (or other assets); adjusting entries for recording accrued revenues involve increasing (debiting) assets and increasing (crediting) revenues. (p. 142)

Adjusted trial balance A listing of accounts and balances prepared after adjustments are recorded and posted to the ledger. (p. 147)

Adjusting entry A journal entry at the end of an accounting period to bring an asset or liability account balance to its proper amount while also updating the related expense or revenue account. (p. 134)

Amortization The expense created by allocating the cost of intangible assets to the periods in which they are used; represents the expense of using these assets. (p. 136)

Book value of an asset The cost of the asset less its accumulated depreciation. (p. 137)

Cash basis accounting Revenues are recognized when cash is received, and expenses are recorded when cash is paid. (p. 133)

Contra account An account linked with another account and having an opposite normal balance; reported as a subtraction from the other account's balance so that more complete information than simply the net amount is provided. (p. 137)

Correcting entries Accounting entries made in order to correct errors. (p. 156)

Depreciation The expense created by allocating the cost of plant and equipment to the periods in which they are used; represents the expense of using the assets. (p. 136)

External transactions Exchanges between the entity and some other person or organization. (p. 131)

Intangible assets Long-lived assets that have no physical substance but convey a right to use a product or process. (p. 136)

Interim financial reports Financial reports covering less than one year; usually based on one-, three- or six-month periods. (p. 133)

Internal transactions Exchanges within an organization that can also affect the accounting equation. (p. 131)

Market value of an asset Amount an asset can be sold for. Market value is not tied to the book value of an asset. (p. 137)

Matching principle The broad principle that requires expenses to be reported in the same period as the revenues that were earned as a result of the expenses. (p. 133)

Prepaid expenses Items that are paid for in advance of receiving their benefits. These are assets. (p. 134)

Property, plant and equipment (PPE) Tangible long-lived assets used to produce goods or services. (p. 136)

Report form balance sheet A balance sheet that lists items vertically with assets above the liabilities and equity. (p. 149)

Reporting period See *accounting period.* (p. 133)

Straight-line depreciation method Allocates equal amounts of an asset's cost to depreciation expense during its useful life. (p. 137)

Timeliness principle A broad principle that assumes that an organization's activities can be divided into specific time periods such as months, quarters, or years. (p. 132)

Unadjusted trial balance A listing of accounts and balances prepared before adjustments are recorded and posted to the ledger. (p. 147)

Unearned revenues Liabilities created when customers pay in advance for products or services; created when cash is received before revenues are earned; satisfied by delivering the products or services in the future. (p. 138)

Visit **Connect** at **www.mcgrawhillconnect.ca**
for additional study tools, practice quizzes,
to search an interactive e-book, and much more.

Concept Review Questions

1. What type of business is most likely to select a fiscal year that corresponds to the natural business year instead of the calendar year?
2. What is the difference between the cash basis and accrual basis of accounting?
3. Why is the accrual basis of accounting preferred over the cash basis?
4. Where is a prepaid expense reported in the financial statements?
5. What kinds of assets require adjusting entries to record depreciation?

6. What contra account is used when recording and reporting the effects of depreciation? Why is it used?
7. Where is an unearned revenue reported in the financial statements?
8. What is an accrued revenue? Give an example.
9. Review the consolidated balance sheet of Danier Leather in Appendix I. Identify an asset account that requires adjustment before annual financial statements can be prepared. What would be the effect on the income statement if this asset account were not adjusted?

DANIER

10. Review the income statement of WestJet in Appendix I. How much depreciation was recorded in the adjusting entry for depreciation at the end of 2008?

WESTJET

*11. If a company initially records prepaid expenses with debits to expense accounts, what type of account is debited in the adjusting entries for prepaid expenses?

Quick Study

QS 4-1
GAAP and adjusting entries
LO2

For each of the following, identify the primary GAAP that has been violated and explain why.

1. Delta Company prepared its first set of financial statements for the three years ended July 31, 2011.
2. Warren Consulting purchased $9,800 of supplies on September 30, 2011, and debited Office Supplies Expense. Warren's year-end is September 30.
3. On May 3, 2011, Mindy Car Wash collected $3,000 in advance from a new limousine company to begin operating June 1, 2011. Mindy credited a revenue account for the $3,000.
4. On November 15, 2011, TelsCo rented equipment for $1,500. TelsCo is not recording the transaction until it pays (payment is required 15 days from the rental date).

QS 4-2
Accrual and cash accounting
LO3

In its first year of operations, Harris Co. earned $39,000 in revenues and received $33,000 cash from customers. The company incurred expenses of $22,500, but had not paid for $2,250 of them at year-end. In addition, Harris prepaid $3,750 for expenses that would be incurred the next year. Calculate the first year's net income under the cash basis and calculate the first year's net income under the accrual basis.

QS 4-3
Preparing adjusting entries—prepaid expense
LO4

Fargo's Detective Agency purchased a two-year insurance policy on April 1, 2011, paying cash of $7,680. Its year-end is December 31.

a. Record the journal entry on April 1, 2011.
b. Record the adjusting entry on December 31, 2011.
c. Record the adjusting entry on December 31, 2012.
d. How much of the insurance policy purchased on April 1, 2011, was actually used during the year 2013?

QS 4-4
Preparing adjusting entries—depreciation expense
LO4

Softrock Minerals purchased a vehicle on March 1, 2011, for cash of $32,000. It will be used by the president for business purposes for four years and then sold for about $8,000. Softrock's year-end is December 31. Record the entry on March 1, 2011, and the adjusting entry required at the year-ends of 2011 and 2012.

QS 4-5
Preparing adjusting entries—unearned revenue
LO4

On November 1, 2011, Fastfoot Industries collected $12,000 from a customer for services to be provided in the future. On December 31, 2011, Fastfoot's year-end, it was determined that $3,000 of this amount remained unearned. Prepare the entries for November 1 and December 31.

QS 4-6
Preparing adjusting entries—accrued expenses
LO4

On December 31, 2011, Allied Consulting received the telephone bill for December usage of $1,840. It must be paid by January 14, 2012. Record the adjusting entry on December 31, 2011, and the entry to record the payment on January 14, 2012.

QS 4-7
Preparing adjusting entries—accrued revenues
LO4

TigrSoft recorded unbilled and uncollected revenues of $17,000 on March 31, 2011. On April 16, $12,000 of these were collected. Prepare the entries for March 31 and April 16.

An asterisk (*) identifies assignment material based on Appendix 4A or Appendix 4B.

QS 4-8
Preparing adjusting entries
LO4

Stark Company records prepayments of expenses in asset accounts and receipts of unearned revenues in liability accounts. Using the list of accounts provided, identify the debit and credit entry required for each of the annual adjustments described in (a) through (e). The first one is done as an example.

1. Cash
2. Prepaid Advertising
3. Advertising Payable
4. Advertising Expense
5. Accounts Receivable
6. Equipment Expense
7. Depreciation Expense
8. Accumulated Depreciation—Equipment
9. Equipment
10. Services Revenue Earned
11. Unearned Services Revenue

	Debits	Credits
Example: Accrual of uncollected and unrecorded services earned.	*5*	*10*
a. Accrual of unpaid and unrecorded advertising that was used by Stark Company.	_____	_____
b. Adjustment of Unearned Services Revenue to recognize earned revenue.	_____	_____
c. Recorded revenue for work completed this accounting period; the cash will be received in the next period.	_____	_____
d. The cost of Equipment was matched to the time periods benefited.	_____	_____
e. Adjustment of Prepaid Advertising to recognize the portion used.	_____	_____

QS 4-9
Recording and analyzing adjusting entries
LO4, 5

Adjusting entries affect one balance sheet account and one income statement account. For the entries listed below, identify the account to be debited and the account to be credited. Indicate which of the two accounts is the income statement account and which is the balance sheet account.

a. Entry to record annual depreciation expense.
b. Entry to show wages earned by employees but not yet paid.
c. Entry to show revenue earned that was previously received as cash in advance.
d. Entry to show expiration of prepaid insurance.
e. Entry to show revenue earned but not yet billed.

QS 4-10
Linking adjustments to financial statements
LO5

For each type of adjustment in (a) through (e), indicate the effect on net income (overstated or understated) if the adjustment is not recorded.

	If adjustment is not recorded:			
Type of Adjustment	**Net income will be overstated, understated, or no effect**	**Assets will be overstated, understated, or no effect**	**Liabilities will be overstated, understated, or no effect**	**Equity will be overstated, understated, or no effect**
a. Prepaid Expenses				
b. Depreciation				
c. Unearned Revenues				
d. Accrued Expenses				
e. Accrued Revenues				

QS 4-11
Interpreting adjusting entries
LO4, 6

The following information has been taken from Shank Company's unadjusted and adjusted trial balances at October 31, 2011.

	Unadjusted		Adjusted	
	Debit	**Credit**	**Debit**	**Credit**
Prepaid insurance	$3,100		$2,350	
Interest payable		$ -0-		$ 750
Insurance expense	-0-		750	
Interest expense	-0-		750	

Given this trial balance information, prepare the adjusting journal entries.

***QS 4-12**
Correcting entries
LO8

The following entry was recorded on November 14.

Nov.	14	Salaries Expense	14,800	
		Cash		14,800
		To record supplies expense.		

At month-end, it was discovered that *Supplies Expense* should have been debited on November 14 instead of *Salaries Expense*. Prepare the correcting entry required on November 30.

***QS 4-13**
Correcting entries
LO8

The following entry was recorded on January 10.

Jan.	10	Office Furniture	25,000	
		Accounts Payable		25,000
		To record purchase of computer equipment by borrowing from the bank.		

At month-end, it was discovered that on January 10, computer equipment was purchased for $25,000 by borrowing from the bank. Prepare the correcting entry required on January 31.

***QS 4-14**
Recording prepaids and unearned amounts as expenses and revenues
LO9

Foster Company initially records prepaid and unearned items in income statement accounts. Given Foster Company's practices, what is the appropriate adjusting entry for each of the following at November 30, 2011, the end of the company's first accounting period?

a. There are unpaid salaries of $3,000.
b. Unused office supplies of $800 were counted at year-end. There was no beginning balance in office supplies.
c. Earned but unbilled consulting fees of $2,300 were discovered.
d. It was determined that there were unearned fees of $4,200.

Exercises

Exercise 4-1
Identifying adjusting entries
LO4

For each entry (1) to (12) below, enter the letter of the explanation that describes it in the blank space to the left. You can use some letters more than once.

a. To record depreciation expense.
b. To record an accrued expense.
c. To record the use of a prepaid expense.
d. To record accrued revenue.
e. To record the earning of previously unearned revenue.
f. Not an adjusting entry.

___ 1.	Depreciation Expense	3,000	
	Accumulated Depreciation		3,000
___ 2.	Unearned Professional Fees	2,000	
	Professional Fees Earned		2,000
___ 3.	Rent Expense	1,000	
	Prepaid Rent		1,000
___ 4.	Interest Expense	4,000	
	Interest Payable		4,000
___ 5.	Prepaid Rent	3,500	
	Cash		3,500
___ 6.	Salaries Expense	5,000	
	Salaries Payable		5,000
___ 7.	Insurance Expense	6,000	
	Prepaid Insurance		6,000
___ 8.	Salaries Payable	1,500	
	Cash		1,500
___ 9.	Cash	6,500	
	Unearned Professional Fees		6,500
___ 10.	Cash	9,000	
	Interest Receivable		9,000
___ 11.	Interest Receivable	7,000	
	Interest Earned		7,000
___ 12.	Cash	8,000	
	Accounts Receivable		8,000

An asterisk (*) identifies assignment material based on Appendix 4A or Appendix 4B.

Exercise 4-2
Adjusting entries
LO4

Prepare adjusting journal entries for the year ended December 31, 2011, for each of the independent situations in (a) to (f). Assume that prepaid expenses are initially recorded in asset accounts. Assume that fees collected in advance of work are initially recorded as liabilities.

a. Depreciation on the company's equipment for 2011 was estimated to be $32,000.
b. The Prepaid Insurance account had a $14,000 debit balance at December 31, 2011, before adjusting for the costs of any expired coverage. An analysis of the company's insurance policies showed $2,080 of unexpired insurance remaining.
c. The Office Supplies account had a $600 debit balance on January 1, 2011; $5,360 of office supplies were purchased during the year; and the December 31, 2011, count showed that $708 of supplies are on hand.
d. Two-thirds of the work for a $30,000 fee received in advance has now been performed.
e. The Prepaid Insurance account had an $11,200 debit balance at December 31, 2011, before adjusting for the costs of any expired coverage. An analysis of the company's insurance policies showed that $9,200 of coverage had expired.
f. Wages of $8,000 have been earned by workers but not paid as of December 31, 2011.
g. Record the January 6, 2012, payment of $20,000 in wages, inclusive of the $8,000 December 31, 2011, accrual in (f) above.

Exercise 4-3
Adjusting entries
LO4

Enviro Waste's year-end is December 31. The information in (a) to (e) is available at year-end for the preparation of adjusting entries:

a. Of the $18,500 balance in Unearned Revenue, $2,500 remains unearned.
b. The annual building depreciation is $10,500.
c. The Spare Parts Inventory account shows an unadjusted balance of $450. A physical count reveals a balance on hand of $100.
d. Unbilled and uncollected services provided to customers totalled $3,550.
e. The utility bill for the month of December was received but is unpaid; $1,300.

Required

Prepare the required adjusting entries at December 31, 2011, for (a) to (e) and the subsequent cash entries required for (f) and (g).

f. The accrued revenues of $3,550 recorded in (d) were collected on January 4, 2012.
g. The $1,300 utility bill accrued in (e) was paid on January 14, 2012.

Exercise 4-4
Adjusting entries
LO4

Monague Company prepares monthly financial statements. The information in (a) to (e) is available for the preparation of adjusting entries for the month ended September 30, 2011:

a. Of the $18,000 balance in Unearned Revenue, $12,000 has been earned.
b. Furniture costing $7,200 was purchased last year. It will be used for four years and donated to charity after that time.
c. The Office Supplies account shows an unadjusted balance of $6,000. A physical count reveals that $5,000 has been used.
d. Services provided to customers today (month-end) but unbilled total $28,000.
e. Rent of $7,000 for the month of September is unpaid and unrecorded.

Required

Prepare the required adjusting entries at September 30, 2011, for (a) to (e) and the subsequent entries required for (f) and (g).

f. The $28,000 of service revenue accrued in (d) was collected on October 3, 2011.
g. The $7,000 of rent accrued in (e) was paid on October 4, 2011.

Exercise 4-5
Unearned and accrued revenues
LO4

Landmark Properties owns and operates an apartment building and prepares annual financial statements based on a March 31 fiscal year-end.

a. The tenants of one of the apartments paid five months' rent in advance on November 1, 2010. The monthly rental is $1,500 per month. The journal entry credited the Unearned Rent account when the payment was received. No other entry had been recorded prior to March 31, 2011. Give the adjusting journal entry that should be recorded on March 31, 2011.
b. On January 1, 2011, the tenants of another apartment moved in and paid the first month's rent. The $1,350 payment was recorded with a credit to the Rent Earned account. However, the tenants have not paid the rent for February or March. They have agreed to pay it as soon as possible. Give the adjusting journal entry that should be recorded on March 31, 2011.
c. On April 22, 2011, the tenants described in (b) paid $4,050 rent for February, March, and April. Give the journal entry to record the cash collection.

Exercise 4-6
Identifying adjusting entries
LO4

Selected information in T-account format is presented below. Journalize the most likely adjustments that caused the balances to change.

a. Accounts Receivable	
Unadjusted Bal. 12,000 Dec. 31/11	
Adjusted Bal. 14,000 Dec. 31/11	

b. Prepaid Rent	
Unadjusted Bal. 28,000 Dec. 31/11	
Adjusted Bal. 20,000 Dec. 31/11	

c. Accumulated Depreciation, Machinery	
	4,800 Unadjusted Bal. Dec. 31/11
	5,200 Adjusted Bal. Dec. 31/11

d. Unearned Fees	
	3,400 Unadjusted Bal. Dec. 31/11
	600 Adjusted Bal. Dec. 31/11

e. Salaries Expense	
Unadjusted Bal. 70,000 Dec. 31/11	
Adjusted Bal. 75,000 Dec. 31/11	

Exercise 4-7
Missing data in supplies expense calculations
LO4, 5

Determine the missing amounts in each of these four independent situations:

	a	b	c	d
Supplies on hand, January 1	$ 300	$1,600	$1,360	?
Supplies purchased during the year	2,100	5,400	?	$6,000
Supplies on hand, December 31	750	?	1,840	800
Supplies expense for the year	?	1,300	9,600	6,575

Exercise 4-8
Adjusting and subsequent cash entries for accrued expenses
LO4

Delcor Management has five part-time employees, each of whom earns $200 per day. They are normally paid on Fridays for work completed on Monday through Friday of the same week. They were all paid in full on Friday, December 28, 2012. The next week, all five of the employees worked only four days because New Year's Day was an unpaid holiday. Show the adjusting entry that would be recorded on Monday, December 31, 2012, Delcor's year-end, and the journal entry that would be made to record paying the employees' wages on Friday, January 4, 2013.

Exercise 4-9
Adjustments and subsequent cash entries for accrued expenses
LO4

The following three situations require adjusting journal entries to prepare financial statements as of April 30, 2011. For each situation, present the adjusting entry and the entry that would be made to record the payment of the accrued liability during May 2011.

a. The company has a $780,000 note payable that requires 0.8% interest to be paid each month on the 20th of the month. The interest was last paid on April 20 and the next payment is due on May 20.

b. The total weekly salaries expense for all employees is $9,000. This amount is paid at the end of the day on Friday of each week with five working days. April 30 falls on a Tuesday this year, which means that the employees had worked two days since the last payday. The next payday is May 3.

c. On April 1, the company retained a lawyer at a flat monthly fee of $2,500. This amount is payable on the 12th of the following month.

Exercise 4-10
Identifying the effects of adjusting entries
LO4, 5

Following are two income statements for Javelin Company for the month ended December 31, 2011. The left column was prepared before any adjusting entries were recorded and the right column includes the effects of adjusting entries. The company records cash receipts and disbursements related to unearned and prepaid items in balance sheet accounts. Analyze the statements and prepare the adjusting entries that must have been recorded. (Note: Of the $12,000 increase in *Fees earned*, 30% represents additional fees earned but not billed. The other 70% was earned by performing services that the customers had paid for in advance.)

Javelin Company
Income Statements
For Month Ended December 31, 2011

	Before Adjustments	Adjustments	After Adjustments
Revenues:			
Fees earned	$ 48,000		$ 60,000
Commissions earned	85,000		85,000
Total revenues	$133,000		$145,000
Operating expenses:			
Depreciation expense, computers	$ -0-		$ 3,000
Depreciation expense, office furniture	-0-		3,500
Salaries expense	25,000		29,900
Insurance expense	-0-		2,600
Rent expense	9,000		9,000
Office supplies expense	-0-		960
Advertising expense	6,000		6,000
Utilities expense	2,500		2,640
Total operating expenses	$ 42,500		$ 57,600
Net income	$ 90,500		$ 87,400

Analysis component:
Identify and explain which GAAP requires that adjusting entries be recorded. By how much would revenues, expenses, and net income be overstated/understated if adjustments were *not* recorded at December 31, 2011, for Javelin Company?

Exercise 4-11
Adjusting entries
LO4, 6

Check figure:
Adjusted trial balance, debits = $65,000

Nuna Music
Trial Balances
February 28, 2011

	Unadjusted Trial Balance		Adjustments		Adjusted Trial Balance	
	Dr.	**Cr.**	**Dr.**	**Cr.**	**Dr.**	**Cr.**
Cash	$ 5,000					
Accounts receivable	4,500					
Prepaid insurance	700					
Equipment	12,000					
Accumulated depreciation, equipment		$ 6,000				
Accounts payable		1,200				
Abraham Nuna, capital		9,000				
Abraham Nuna, withdrawals	3,000					
Revenues		45,000				
Depreciation expense, equipment	-0-					
Salaries expense	29,000					
Insurance expense	7,000					
Totals	$61,200	$61,200				

Additional information:

a. Annual depreciation of the equipment; $2,400.
b. $250 of the Prepaid Insurance balance has expired.
c. Unbilled and unrecorded revenues at year-end totalled $1,400.

Required

Referring to Exhibit 4.22, use the information provided to complete the columns.

Exercise 4-12
Preparing financial statements
LO7

Check figure:
Total assets = $14,950

Using the completed adjusted trial balance columns from Exercise 4-11, prepare an income statement, a statement of changes in equity, and a balance sheet for the year ended February 28, 2011. Assume that the owner made no investments during the year.

Analysis component:

Which GAAP requires the preparation of financial statements?

***Exercise 4-13**
Journalizing correcting entries
LO8

For each of the following incorrect entries, journalize the appropriate correcting entry(ies).

a. The purchase of office supplies on credit for $1,800 was recorded as:

Office Supplies	1,800	
Cash		1,800

b. A credit customer paid her account in full: $4,500. This was recorded as:

Cash	4,500	
Revenue		4,500

c. The owner withdrew cash of $1,500. This was recorded as:

Salaries Expense	1,500	
Cash		1,500

d. Work was performed for a customer today and cash of $750 was received. This was recorded as:

Cash	750	
Accounts Receivable		750

Analysis component:

If the error in (b) is not corrected, what is the effect on the income statement and balance sheet?

***Exercise 4-14**
Entering adjustments for prepaid items recorded in expense and revenue accounts
LO9

Classic Customs began operations on December 1, 2011. In setting up the bookkeeping procedures, the company decided to debit expense accounts when the company prepays its expenses and to credit revenue accounts when customers pay for services in advance. Prepare journal entries for items (a) through (c) and adjusting entries as of December 31, 2011, for items (d) through (f):

a. Supplies were purchased on December 1 for $6,000.
b. The company prepaid insurance premiums of $2,880 on December 2.
c. On December 15, the company received an advance payment of $24,000 from one customer for remodelling work.
d. By counting the supplies on December 31, Classic Customs determined that $3,840 was on hand.
e. An analysis of the insurance policies in effect on December 31 showed that $480 of insurance coverage had expired.
f. As of December 31, it was determined that $7,200 of the amount received in advance on December 15 had been earned.

An asterisk (*) identifies assignment material based on Appendix 4A or Appendix 4B.

*Exercise 4-15

Alternative procedures for revenues received in advance

LO9

Pavillion Company experienced the following events and transactions during July:

July	1	Received $2,000 in advance of performing work for Andrew Renking.
	6	Received $8,400 in advance of performing work for Matt Swarbuck.
	12	Completed the job for Andrew Renking.
	18	Received $7,500 in advance of performing work for Drew Sayer.
	27	Completed the job for Matt Swarbuck.
	31	The job for Drew Sayer has not been started.

a. Give journal entries (including any adjusting entry as of the end of the month) to record these items using the procedure of initially crediting the Unearned Fees account when a payment is received from a customer in advance of performing services.

b. Give journal entries (including any adjusting entry as of the end of the month) to record these items using the procedure of initially crediting the Fees Earned account when a payment is received from a customer in advance of performing services.

c. Under each method, determine the amount of earned fees that should be reported on the income statement for July and the amount of unearned fees that should appear on the balance sheet as of July 31.

Problems

Problem 4-1A

Preparing adjusting entries—prepaid expenses

LO4

Impala Window Washing Services prepares adjustments monthly and shows the following selected accounts on its December 31, 2011, unadjusted trial balance:

Account	Debit	Credit
Prepaid insurance	$ 6,000	
Prepaid office rent	72,000	
Prepaid subscriptions	900	
Prepaid equipment rental	28,000	

Required

Prepare the required monthly adjusting entries at December 31, 2011, based on the following additional information:

a. The remaining balance in Prepaid Insurance was for a six-month insurance policy purchased for $12,000 and in effect on September 1, 2011.

b. $6,000 of the balance in Prepaid Office Rent had not been used as at December 31, 2011.

c. $240 of the balance in Prepaid Subscriptions had been used as at December 31, 2011.

d. The company paid $36,000 on April 1, 2011, to rent equipment for a three-year period beginning April 1, 2011.

Analysis component:

If the above adjustments were not recorded, identify the types of accounts that would be affected and if they would be over- or understated.

Problem 4-2A

Preparing adjusting entries—depreciation expense

LO4

Details regarding Leroux Steel's purchases of plant and equipment items during 2011 follow:

Date of Purchase	Plant and Equipment Item	Cost	Estimated Useful Life	Estimated Sales Value at End of Estimated Useful Life
a. Jan. 1	Machine A	$28,000	5 years	$ -0-
b. Apr. 1	Machine B	56,000	4 years	8,000
c. Nov. 1	Machine C	8,400	2 years	1,200

Required

Prepare the annual adjusting entry at December 31, 2011, Leroux's year-end, for each plant and equipment item.

Analysis component:

What is the purpose of recording depreciation? If depreciation is not recorded, how would the income statement be affected?

An asterisk (*) identifies assignment material based on Appendix 4A or Appendix 4B.

Problem 4-3A
Preparing adjusting entries—unearned revenues
LO4

Outdoor's Best pre-sells yard maintenance packages for the gardening season. During October, the company collects cash from clients for Christmas trees to be delivered in December. Snow removal services are also provided. Outdoor's Best prepares adjusting entries monthly. The following selected accounts appear on the November 30, 2011, unadjusted trial balance:

Account	Debit	Credit
Unearned lawn services		$72,800
Unearned garden services...............		20,500
Unearned snow removal services		9,000
Unearned Christmas tree sales		43,500

Required
Prepare the monthly adjusting journal entries at November 30, 2011, using the following additional information.

a. $66,000 of the Unearned Lawn Services account represents payments received from customers for the 2012 season. The remainder represents fall lawn services actually performed during November 2011.
b. $19,500 of the Unearned Garden Services account had been earned by November 30, 2011.
c. $8,750 of the Unearned Snow Removal Services account remained unearned at November 30, 2011.
d. Outdoor's arranges with its customers to deliver trees from December 5 to December 20. As a result, the Unearned Christmas Tree Sales account will be earned in total by December 20.

Analysis component:
If the Unearned Lawn Services of $72,800 had been recorded as a revenue when received instead of as a liability, what would the effect have been on the November 30, 2011, financial statements assuming no adjustment was made on November 30, 2011?

Problem 4-4A
Preparing adjusting and subsequent cash entries—accrued expenses
LO4

Mannix Resources prepares adjusting entries monthly. In reviewing the accounts on March 31, Mannix Resources discovered the following:

a. Interest of $2,250 had accrued on the note payable as at March 31. It is to be paid on April 2.
b. Unpaid and unrecorded salaries at March 31 totalled $19,600. The $19,600 plus salaries of $29,400 for the first three days of April were paid on April 3.
c. The March telephone bill for $960 is unpaid and unrecorded at March 31. It is to be paid on April 15.
d. Mannix normally pays rent in three-month installments. At March 31, rent of $5,000 per month had not been paid for February, March, or April. Rent of $5,000 was correctly accrued at the end of February. The balance owing plus rent for May, June, and July was paid on April 26.
e. Mannix pays commissions to the technicians at the rate of 4% of services performed. During March, total services performed were $960,000. Commissions are unrecorded and unpaid at March 31. Commissions are paid on the 15th of the following month.

Required
Using the information provided above, prepare the monthly adjusting journal entries at March 31 along with the appropriate subsequent cash entries.

Problem 4-5A
Preparing adjusting and subsequent cash entries—accrued revenues
LO4

In reviewing the accounts on March 31 for the year just ended, DigiTech discovered the following:

a. DigiTech owns the building that it occupies. Part of the building is rented to E-Quip Company for $3,200 per month. E-Quip had not paid the March rent as at March 31. On April 3, DigiTech collected the rent accrued on March 31.
b. Services performed but unrecorded at March 31 totalled $10,800. This amount was collected on April 7.
c. Interest for the month of March had accrued on a note receivable in the amount of $700. The interest accrued on March 31 was collected on April 1.
d. On February 1, DigiTech signed a $24,000 six-month contract to perform services for a client. DigiTech has been providing the services but as of March 31 no cash had been received. On April 2, DigiTech collected the revenue accrued on March 31.

Required
Using the information provided above, prepare the annual adjusting journal entries at March 31 along with the appropriate subsequent cash entries.

Problem 4-6A
Adjusting entries; adjusted trial balance
LO4, 6

PacRim Careers provides training to individuals who pay tuition directly to the business. The business also offers extension training to groups in off-site locations. Additional information available at the December 31, 2011, year-end follows:

a. An analysis of the company's policies shows that $6,000 of insurance coverage has expired.
b. An inventory shows that teaching supplies costing $5,200 are on hand at the end of the year.
c. The estimated annual depreciation on the equipment is $24,000.
d. The estimated annual depreciation on the professional library is $12,000.
e. The school offers off-campus services for specific employers. On November 1, the company agreed to do a special six-month course for a client. The contract calls for a monthly fee of $4,400, and the client paid the first five months' fees in advance. When the cash was received, the Unearned Extension Fees account was credited.
f. On October 15, the school agreed to teach a four-month class for an individual for $6,000 tuition per month payable at the end of the class. The services to date have been provided as agreed, but no payment has been received.
g. The school's two employees are paid weekly. As of the end of the year, two days' wages have accrued at the rate of $200 per day for each employee.
h. The balance in the Prepaid Rent account represents the rent for December.

PacRim Careers
Trial Balances
December 31, 2011

	Unadjusted Trial Balance		Adjustments		Adjusted Trial Balance	
Account	**Debit**	**Credit**	**Debit**	**Credit**	**Debit**	**Credit**
Cash	$ 52,000					
Accounts receivable	-0-					
Teaching supplies	20,000					
Prepaid insurance	30,000					
Prepaid rent	4,000					
Professional library	60,000					
Accumulated depreciation, professional library		$ 18,000				
Equipment	140,000					
Accumulated depreciation, equipment		32,000				
Accounts payable		72,000				
Salaries payable		-0-				
Unearned extension fees		22,000				
Karoo Ashevak, capital		127,200				
Karoo Ashevak, withdrawals	80,000					
Tuition fees earned		204,000				
Extension fees earned		76,000				
Depreciation expense, equipment	-0-					
Depreciation expense, professional library	-0-					
Salaries expense	96,000					
Insurance expense	-0-					
Rent expense	44,000					
Teaching supplies expense	-0-					
Advertising expense	14,000					
Utilities expense	11,200					
Totals	$551,200	$551,200				

Check figure:
2. Adjusted Trial Balance debits = $603,000

Required

1. Prepare the necessary annual adjusting journal entries at December 31, 2011, based on (a) to (h) above.

Analysis component:

2. Refer to the format presented in Exhibit 4.22 and complete the adjusted trial balance using the information in (a) through (h) above.
3. If the adjustments were *not* recorded, calculate the over- or understatement of income.
4. Is it ethical to ignore adjusting entries?

Problem 4-7A
Adjusting entries
LO4

Wedona Energy Consultants prepares adjusting entries monthly. Based on an analysis of the unadjusted trial balance at January 31, 2011, the following information was available for the preparation of the January 31, 2011, month-end adjusting entries:

a. Equipment purchased on November 1 of this accounting period for $36,000 is estimated to have a useful life of three years. After three years of use, it is expected that the equipment will be scrapped due to technological obsolescence.
b. Of the $9,000 balance in Unearned Consulting Fees, $3,000 had been earned.
c. The Prepaid Rent account showed a balance of $22,500. This was paid on January 1 of this accounting period and represents six months of rent commencing on the same date.
d. Accrued wages at January 31 totalled $9,000.
e. One month of interest had accrued at the rate of 7% per year on a $42,000 note payable.
f. Unrecorded and uncollected consulting fees at month-end were $4,750.
g. A $1,350 insurance policy was purchased on April 1 of the current accounting period and debited to the Prepaid Insurance account. Coverage began April 1 for 18 months.
h. The monthly depreciation on the office furniture was $450.
i. Repair revenues accrued at month-end totalled $2,050.
j. The Store Supplies account had a balance of $800 at the beginning of January. During January, $1,500 of supplies were purchased and debited to the Store Supplies account. At month-end, a count of the supplies revealed a balance of $150.

Required
Prepare adjusting journal entries for the month ended January 31, 2011, based on the above.

Problem 4-8A
Adjusting and subsequent cash journal entries
LO4

The following information concerns the adjusting entries to be recorded on November 30, 2011, for RaiLink's year just ended.

a. The Office Supplies account started the year with a $6,000 balance. During 2011, the company purchased supplies at a cost of $24,800, which was added to the Office Supplies account. The inventory of supplies on hand at November 30 had a cost of $5,280.
b. An analysis of the company's insurance policies provided these facts:

Policy	Date of Purchase	Years of Coverage	Total Cost
1	March 1, 2010	2	$31,680
2	March 1, 2011	3	26,136
3	July 1, 2011	1	5,400

The total premium for each policy was paid in full at the purchase date, and the Prepaid Insurance account was debited for the full cost. *Appropriate adjusting entries have been made to November 30, 2010.*

c. The company has 15 employees who earn a total of $4,200 in salaries for every working day. They are paid each Monday for their work in the five-day workweek ending on the preceding Friday. November 30, 2011, falls on a Wednesday, and all 15 employees worked the first three days of the week. They will be paid salaries for five full days on Monday, December 5, 2011.
d. The company purchased a building on July 1, 2011. The building cost $1,710,000 and is expected to have a $90,000 residual value at the end of its predicted 30-year life.
e. Because the company is not large enough to occupy the entire building, it arranged to rent some space to a tenant at $4,800 per month, starting on October 1, 2011. The rent was paid on time on October 1, and the amount received was credited to the Rent Earned account. However, the tenant has not paid the November rent. The company has worked out an agreement with the tenant, who has promised to pay both November's and December's rent in full on December 15.
f. On October 1, the company also rented space to another tenant for $4,350 per month. The tenant paid five months' rent in advance on that date. The payment was recorded with a credit to the Unearned Rent account.

Required
1. Use the information to prepare the annual adjusting entries as of November 30, 2011.
2. Prepare journal entries to record the subsequent cash transactions in December 2011 described in parts (c) and (e).

Problem 4-9A
Adjusting entries
LO4

Rainmaker Environmental Consultants is just finishing its second year of operations. The company's unadjusted trial balance at October 31, 2011, follows:

Rainmaker Environmental Consultants
Unadjusted Trial Balance
October 31, 2011

Acct. No.	Account	Debit	Credit
101	Cash	$ 28,000	
106	Accounts receivable	56,000	
109	Interest receivable	-0-	
111	Notes receivable	30,000	
126	Supplies	4,600	
128	Prepaid insurance	9,350	
131	Prepaid rent	21,000	
161	Office furniture	61,440	
162	Accumulated depreciation, office furniture		$ 20,480
201	Accounts payable		35,000
210	Wages payable		-0-
233	Unearned consulting fees		13,160
301	Jeff Moore, capital		60,000
302	Jeff Moore, withdrawals	16,450	
401	Consulting fees earned		314,600
409	Interest revenue		1,400
601	Depreciation expense, office furniture	-0-	
622	Wages expense	147,000	
637	Insurance expense	-0-	
640	Rent expense	64,000	
650	Supplies expense	6,800	
	Totals	$444,640	$444,640

Rainmaker prepares adjustments each October 31. The following additional information is available on October 31, 2011.

a. It was determined that $12,000 of the unearned consulting fees had not yet been earned.
b. It was discovered that $6,000 of the balance in the Consulting Fees Earned account was for services to be performed in November.
c. The balance in the Prepaid Rent account represents three months of rent beginning September 1, 2011.
d. Accrued wages at October 31 totalled $6,800.
e. The office furniture was purchased on March 1, 2010, and has an estimated useful life of two years. After two years of use, it is expected that the furniture will be worthless.
f. Accrued consulting fees at year-end totalled $4,200.
g. Interest of $200 had accrued on the note receivable for the month of October.
h. The balance in the Prepaid Insurance account represents the remaining balance of a two-year policy purchased on April 1, 2010.
i. A count of the supplies on October 31 revealed a balance remaining of $900.

Required
Prepare the annual adjusting journal entries for October 31, 2011, based on the above.

Problem 4-10A
Posting, adjusted trial balance, and preparing financial statements
LO6, 7

Check figures:
3. Adjusted trial balance, debits = $486,560
4. Net income = $35,940

Required
Using the information in Problem 4-9A, complete the following:

1. Set up balance column accounts for Rainmaker Environmental Consultants and enter the balances listed in the unadjusted trial balance.
2. Post the adjusting entries prepared in Problem 4-9A to the accounts.
3. Prepare an adjusted trial balance.
4. Use the adjusted trial balance to prepare an income statement, a statement of changes in equity, and a balance sheet. Assume that the owner, Jeff Moore, made no owner investments during the year.

Analysis component:
Assume that total revenues and expenses reported for the year ended October 31, 2010, were $189,000 and $157,600, respectively. Compare the business's financial performance for the years ended October 31, 2010 and 2011.

Note
For Part 1, your instructor may ask you to set up T-accounts instead of balance column accounts. The solution is available in both formats.

Problem 4-11A
Adjusting entries
LO4

Arrow Hospitality prepares adjustments monthly and showed the following at September 30, 2011:

Arrow Hospitality Trial Balances September 30, 2011						
	Unadjusted Trial Balance		Adjustments		Adjusted Trial Balance	
Account	**Debit**	**Credit**	**Debit**	**Credit**	**Debit**	**Credit**
Cash	$ 6,000					
Accounts receivable	11,200					
Repair supplies	2,200					
Prepaid rent	14,000					
Office furniture	26,000					
Accounts payable		$ 8,000				
Notes payable		21,600				
Eli Arrow, capital		67,758				
Eli Arrow, withdrawals	5,000					
Hospitality revenues		128,000				
Salaries expense	144,000					
Wages expense	16,958					
Totals	$225,358	$225,358				

Additional information available for the month ended September 30, 2011:

a. Interest of $162 had accrued on the notes payable for the month of September.
b. The office furniture was acquired on September 1, 2011, and has an estimated four-year life. The furniture will be sold for about $2,000 at the end of its four-year life.
c. A count of the Repair Supplies revealed a balance on hand of $700.
d. A review of the Prepaid Rent account showed that $10,000 had been used during September.
e. Accrued wages of $2,800 had not been recorded at month-end.
f. The September Internet bill for $100 had been received and must be paid by October 14.
g. Accrued revenues of $6,200 were not recorded at September 30.

Required
Prepare adjusting entries for the month ended September 30, 2011 for each of (a) through (g) above.

Problem 4-12A
Preparation of financial statements
LO6, 7

Check figures:
1. Adjustments columns = $21,262; Adjusted trial balance columns = $235,120
2. Net loss = $41,820

Required
1. Using the format presented in Problem 4-11A, complete the adjusted trial balance by including the adjusting entries prepared in Problem 4-11A.
2. Prepare an income statement, a statement of changes in equity and a balance sheet based on the adjusted trial balance completed in Part 1. Assume that the owner, Eli Arrow, made an investment during September of $3,600.

Analysis component:
Assume that total assets reported at August 31, 2011, were $76,900. Determine what total liabilities and equity were on that date and comment on the change in the financial position from August to September.

Problem 4-13A

Preparing financial statements from the adjusted trial balance

LO7

This adjusted trial balance is for GalaVu Entertainment as of its December 31, 2011, year-end:

	Debit	Credit
Accounts receivable	$ 22,000	
Accounts payable		$ 44,000
Accumulated depreciation, automobiles		21,000
Accumulated depreciation, equipment		5,000
Advertising expense	25,000	
Automobiles	80,000	
Cash	11,000	
Depreciation expense, automobiles	9,000	
Depreciation expense, equipment	5,000	
Equipment	65,000	
Fees earned		160,000
Interest earned		8,000
Interest expense	12,000	
Interest payable		6,000
Interest receivable	5,000	
John Conroe, capital		123,900
John Conroe, withdrawals	19,000	
Land	35,000	
Long-term notes payable		115,000
Notes receivable (due in 90 days)	80,000	
Office supplies	4,000	
Office supplies expense	13,000	
Repairs expense, automobiles	8,400	
Salaries expense	90,000	
Salaries payable		5,500
Unearned fees		11,000
Wages expense	16,000	
Totals	$499,400	$499,400

Check figures:
a. Net loss = $10,400
c. Total assets = $276,000

Required

Use the information in the trial balance to prepare:

a. The income statement for the year ended December 31, 2011.

b. The statement of changes in equity for the year ended December 31, 2011, assuming that the owner made additional investments of $50,000 during the year.

c. The balance sheet as of December 31, 2011.

Analysis component:

The owner, John Conroe, is very pleased with the change in the business's financial position. Specifically, he noted that his equity increased. "My banker told me that as long as equity is increasing, my business is doing great." Comment.

Problem 4-14A

Journalizing, posting, adjusted trial balance, adjusting entries, financial statements

LO4, 5, 6, 7

On August 1, 2011, Delanie Tugut began a tour company in the Northwest Territories called Tugut Arctic Tours. The following occurred during the first month of operations:

Aug.	1	Purchased office furniture on account; $5,200.
	1	Delanie Tugut invested $7,000 cash into her new business.
	2	Collected $3,900 in advance for a three-week guided caribou hunt beginning the last week of August.
	3	Paid $6,000 for six months' rent for office space effective August 1.
	4	Received $3,000 for a four-day northern lights viewing tour just completed.
	7	Paid $1,500 for hotel expenses regarding the August 4 tour.
	15	Delanie withdrew cash of $500 for personal use.
	22	Met with a Japanese tour guide to discuss a $150,000 tour contract.
	31	Paid wages of $1,300.

Required

1. Prepare General Journal entries to record the August transactions.
2. Set up the following T-accounts: Cash (101); Prepaid Rent (131); Office Furniture (161); Accumulated Depreciation, Office Furniture (162); Accounts Payable (201); Unearned Revenue (233); Delanie Tugut, Capital (301); Delanie Tugut, Withdrawals (302); Revenue (401); Depreciation Expense, Office Furniture (602); Wages Expense (623); Rent Expense (640); Telephone Expense (688); and Hotel Expenses (696).

3. Post the entries to the accounts; calculate the ending balance in each account.
4. Prepare an unadjusted trial balance at August 31, 2011.
5. Use the following information to prepare and post adjusting entries on August 31:
   a. The office furniture has an estimated life of four years and a $208 residual value.
   b. Two-thirds of the August 2 advance has been earned.
   c. One month of the Prepaid Rent has been used.
   d. The August telephone bill was not received as of August 31 but amounted to $320.
6. Prepare an adjusted trial balance.
7. Prepare an income statement, a statement of changes in equity, and a balance sheet.

Check figures:
3. Cash balance, Aug. 31, 2011 = $4,600
4. Dr = $19,100
6. Dr = $19,524
7. Net income = $1,376

Analysis component:
When a company shows revenue on its income statement, does this mean that cash equal to revenues was received during the period in which the revenues were reported?

*Problem 4-15A

Correcting entries

LO8

The accountant for Karma Counselling Services found several errors in reviewing the unadjusted trial balance on September 30. You are to prepare correcting entries based on the following information:

a. The Counselling Fees Earned account included an entry debiting cash for $7,000 that should have been debited to Accounts Receivable.
b. Utilities Expense was debited $1,680 that should have been recorded as Telephone Expense.
c. The *Office* Supplies account shows a credit of $2,800 regarding the use of *Cleaning* Supplies.
d. A transaction involving $19,600 of service revenue performed on account was incorrectly recorded as a debit to Accounts Payable and a credit to Unearned Service Revenue.
e. Equipment was incorrectly debited for $1,200 with a corresponding credit to Accounts Payable regarding supplies that were sold to a neighbouring store on credit.

Required
Journalize the correcting entries required on September 30.

Analysis component:
The error in (b) shows that an incorrect expense account was debited. Since the net effect on the financial statements is nil after recording the correction, is it necessary to prepare a correcting entry for this type of error?

*Problem 4-16A

Recording prepaid expenses and unearned revenues

LO9

Willis Consulting follows the approach of recording prepaid expenses as expenses and unearned revenues as revenues. Willis's unadjusted trial balance for the year ended March 31, 2011, follows.

Willis Consulting
Trial Balances
March 31, 2011

	Unadjusted Trial Balance		Adjustments		Adjusted Trial Balance	
Account	**Debit**	**Credit**	**Debit**	**Credit**	**Debit**	**Credit**
Cash	$ 20,000					
Accounts receivable	49,700					
Prepaid rent	-0-					
Prepaid insurance	-0-					
Accounts payable		$ 2,500				
Unearned consulting fees		-0-				
Bruce Willis, capital		15,600				
Consulting fees earned		82,000				
Rent expense	28,000					
Insurance expense	2,400					
Totals	$100,100	$100,100				

Additional information:
a. A review of the Consulting Fees Earned account showed that $5,600 of the balance has not yet been earned.
b. The balance in the Rent Expense account was paid on January 15, 2011, and represents seven months of rent beginning February 1, 2011.
c. It was determined that $1,900 of the balance in the Insurance Expense account was used by March 31, 2011.

Required
Refer to Exhibit 4.22 and use the information provided to complete the columns above.

Check figure:
Adjusted trial balance, debits = $100,100

An asterisk (*) identifies assignment material based on Appendix 4A or Appendix 4B.

*Problem 4-17A

Recording prepaid expenses and unearned revenues

LO4, 9

The following events occurred for a company during the last two months of its fiscal year ended December 31, 2011:

Nov.	1	Paid $3,000 for future newspaper advertising.
	1	Paid $4,320 for insurance through October 31 of the following year.
	30	Received $6,600 for future services to be provided to a customer.
Dec.	1	Paid $5,400 for the services of a consultant, to be received over the next three months.
	15	Received $15,300 for future services to be provided to a customer.
	31	Of the advertising paid for on November 1, $1,800 worth had not yet been published by the newspaper.
	31	Part of the insurance paid for on November 1 had expired.
	31	Services worth $2,400 had not yet been provided to the customer who paid on November 30.
	31	One-third of the consulting services paid for on December 1 had been received.
	31	The company had performed $6,000 of the services that the customer had paid for on December 15.

Required

1. Prepare the November and December entries for the above activities under the approach that records prepaid expenses as assets and records unearned revenues as liabilities. Also, prepare adjusting entries at the end of the year.

2. Prepare the November and December entries under the approach that records prepaid expenses as expenses and records unearned revenues as revenues. Also, prepare adjusting entries at the end of the year.

Analysis component:

Explain why the alternative sets of entries in requirements 1 and 2 do not result in different financial statement amounts.

Alternate Problems

Problem 4-1B

Preparing adjusting entries—prepaid expenses

LO4

Domino's Cleaning Services is gathering information for its year-end, April 30, 2011. Selected accounts on the April 30, 2011, unadjusted trial balance are reproduced below:

Account	Debit	Credit
Prepaid equipment rental	$18,000	
Prepaid warehouse rental	15,600	
Prepaid insurance	7,200	
Cleaning supplies	2,900	

Required

Prepare the required annual adjusting entries at April 30, 2011, based on the following additional information:

a. The balance in the Prepaid Equipment Rental account is for 18 months of equipment rental that began December 1, 2010.

b. $6,000 of the balance in the Prepaid Warehouse Rental account had been used as of April 30, 2011.

c. The balance in the Prepaid Insurance account represents six months of insurance effective February 1, 2011.

d. A count of the cleaning supplies revealed that $2,400 had been used.

Analysis component:

Which GAAP require the recording of adjusting entries and why?

An asterisk (*) identifies assignment material based on Appendix 4A or Appendix 4B.

Problem 4-2B

Preparing adjusting entries—depreciation expense

LO4

Zebra Consulting prepares adjusting entries and financial statements monthly. Details regarding Zebra Consulting's plant and equipment items follow:

Date of Purchase	Plant and Equipment Item	Cost	Estimated Useful Life	Estimated Sales Value at End of Estimated Useful Life
a. Dec. 1, 2010	Furniture	$ 61,200	3 years	$ -0-
b. Mar. 1, 2011	Equipment	420,000	10 years	24,000
c. Nov. 1, 2011	Building	615,200	15 years	140,000

Required

Prepare the monthly adjusting entry to record depreciation for each plant and equipment item at November 30, 2011.

Analysis component:

What is the purpose of recording depreciation? If depreciation is not recorded, how would each of the components of the accounting equation be affected?

Problem 4-3B

Preparing adjusting entries—unearned revenues

LO4

Blackfeather Tours sells scuba diving and kayaking excursions, along with a number of unique sightseeing packages. The company requires a 50% payment from the customer at the time of booking. The following selected accounts appear on Blackfeather's January 31, 2011, year-end unadjusted trial balance:

Account	Debit	Credit
Unearned heli-tour revenue		$ 52,000
Unearned tour package revenue		960,000
Unearned scuba diving revenue......		266,000
Unearned kayaking tour revenue		128,000

Required

Prepare the annual adjusting journal entries at January 31, 2011, using the following additional information:

a. Blackfeather Tours has custom helicopter packages in which groups are flown in and out of island retreats. The balance in this unearned account is for a group scheduled for early March 2011.

b. $794,000 of the Unearned Tour Package Revenue account had been earned by January 31, 2011.

c. $72,000 of the Unearned Scuba Diving Revenue account remained unearned at January 31, 2011.

d. $16,700 of the Unearned Kayaking Tour Revenue account represents payments received from customers for February and March 2011. The balance in the account is for tours provided in January 2011.

Analysis component:

Using your understanding of GAAP, explain how and why unearned revenues are adjusted at the end of the accounting period.

Problem 4-4B
Preparing adjusting and subsequent cash entries—accrued expenses
LO4

In reviewing the accounts on September 30, 2011, for the year just ended, Geek Designers discovered the following:

a. Interest of $7,600 had accrued on the bank loan as at September 30. It is to be paid on October 2.

b. Accrued wages at September 30 totalled $54,000. On October 4, the first biweekly payday of October, $90,000 was paid to employees representing the six days accrued on September 30 plus the first four working days in October.

c. The September cell phone bill for $360 was unpaid and unrecorded at September 30. It will be paid on October 5.

d. On September 30, $780 of cable charges were accrued regarding the past two months of usage that were not recorded or paid. This amount was paid on October 2.

e. $3,900 of property taxes covering September were accrued on September 30. This amount was paid on October 15.

Required
Using the information provided above, prepare the annual adjusting journal entries at September 30 along with the appropriate subsequent cash entries.

Problem 4-5B
Preparing adjusting and subsequent cash entries—accrued revenues
LO4

WonderWeb prepares adjusting entries monthly. In reviewing the accounts on March 31, 2011, WonderWeb discovered the following:

a. Interest of $1,300 had accrued on the note receivable as of March 31. The accrual, representing 25 days in March plus an additional five days in April, was collected on April 5.

b. Accrued consulting fees totalling $10,800 were not recorded on March 31. This amount was collected on April 6.

c. Web design work totalling $13,600 was completed on March 31 but not recorded. This amount was collected on April 13.

d. WonderWeb rents the basement of its building to a student. The student has not paid the March rent of $700 as at March 31. On April 27, the March rent plus the rent for April was collected.

Required
Using the information provided above, prepare the March 31 month-end adjusting journal entries along with the appropriate subsequent cash entries.

Problem 4-6B
Adjusting entries; adjusted trial balance
LO4, 6

excel

Fawcett Institute provides one-on-one training to individuals who pay tuition directly to the business and also offers extension training to groups in off-site locations. Fawcett prepares adjusting entries monthly.

Additional information available on December 31, 2011:

a. An analysis of the company's policies shows that $12,800 of insurance coverage has expired.
b. An inventory shows that teaching supplies costing $5,000 are on hand at the end of the month.
c. The estimated monthly depreciation on the equipment is $800.
d. The estimated monthly depreciation on the professional library is $400.
e. The school offers off-campus services for specific operators. On December 1, the company agreed to do a special four-month course for a client. The contract calls for a $9,200 monthly fee, and the client paid the first two months' fees in advance. When the cash was received, the Unearned Extension Fees account was credited.
f. On December 15, the school agreed to teach a four-month class to an individual for $4,400 tuition per month payable at the end of the class. The services have been provided as agreed, and no payment has been received.
g. The school's only employee is paid weekly. As of the end of the month, wages of $1,080 have accrued.
h. The balance in the Prepaid Rent account represents the rent for December, January, February, and March.

Fawcett Institute
Trial Balance
December 31, 2011

	Unadjusted Trial Balance		Adjustments		Adjusted Trial Balance	
Account	**Debit**	**Credit**	**Debit**	**Credit**	**Debit**	**Credit**
Cash	$100,000					
Accounts receivable	-0-					
Teaching supplies	120,000					
Prepaid insurance	36,000					
Prepaid rent	5,200					
Professional library	20,000					
Accumulated depreciation, professional library		$ 3,000				
Equipment	60,000					
Accumulated depreciation, equipment		32,000				
Accounts payable		24,400				
Salaries payable		-0-				
Unearned extension fees		55,200				
Jay Fawcett, capital		137,000				
Jay Fawcett, withdrawals	40,000					
Tuition fees earned		210,000				
Extension fees earned		124,000				
Depreciation expense, equipment	-0-					
Depreciation expense, professional library	-0-					
Salaries expense	143,600					
Insurance expense	-0-					
Rent expense	-0-					
Teaching supplies expense	-0-					
Advertising expense	36,000					
Utilities expense	24,800					
Totals	$585,600	$585,600				

Required

1. Prepare the necessary December 31, 2011, month-end adjusting journal entries based on (a) through (h) above.

Check figure:
2. Adjusted Trial Balance, debits = $590,080

Analysis component:

2. Refer to the format presented in Exhibit 4.22 and prepare an adjusted trial balance using the information in (a) through (h) above.
3. If the adjustments were *not* recorded, calculate the over- or understatement of income.
4. Is it ethical to ignore adjusting entries?

Problem 4-7B
Adjusting entries
LO4

Kazz Industries' year-end is May 31. Based on an analysis of the unadjusted trial balance at May 31, 2011, the following information was available:

a. Machinery costing $42,000 was acquired on September 1 of this accounting period. It is estimated to have a useful life of six years. The machinery will have no value at the end of its six-year life.
b. It was determined that $6,000 of completed work was included in the $16,000 Unearned Revenue account balance at year-end.
c. The Prepaid Insurance account showed a balance of $180,000. This was paid and takes effect on March 1 of this accounting period and represents a two-year policy.
d. Accrued salaries at year-end were $10,000.
e. $5,040 of interest had accrued on the $144,000 note payable.
f. Accrued revenues at year-end totalled $3,400.
g. $24,000 worth of advertising was prepaid on January 1 of the current accounting period and debited to the Prepaid Advertising account. This covered four months of advertising beginning on the same date.
h. The annual depreciation on the office equipment was $3,600.
i. Interest revenue accrued at year-end totalled $700.
j. The Office Supplies account had a balance of $4,000 at the beginning of the accounting period. During the year, $10,000 of supplies were purchased and debited to the Office Supplies account. At year-end, a count of the supplies revealed that $11,000 had been used.

Required
Prepare adjusting journal entries for the year ended May 31, 2011, based on the above.

Problem 4-8B
Identifying adjusting and subsequent cash journal entries
LO4

Valor Ventures prepares adjusting entries monthly. The following information concerns the adjusting entries that need to be recorded on October 31, 2011, for the month just ended.

a. The Office Supplies account had a $1,000 balance on October 1. During October, the company purchased supplies at a cost of $7,300, which was added to the Office Supplies account. The inventory of supplies on hand at October 31 had a cost of $1,400.
b. An analysis of the company's insurance policies provided these facts:

Policy	Date of Purchase	Years of Coverage	Total Cost
1	April 1, 2010	2	$6,000
2	April 1, 2011	3	7,200
3	August 1, 2011	1	1,320

The total premium for each policy was paid in full at the purchase date, and the Prepaid Insurance account was debited for the full cost. *Appropriate adjusting entries have been made to September 30, 2011.*

c. The company has 10 employees who earn a total of $1,600 for every working day. They are paid each Monday for their work in the five-day workweek ending on the preceding Friday. October 31, 2011, falls on a Monday, and all 10 employees worked the first day of the week. They will be paid salaries for five full days on Monday, November 7, 2011.
d. The company purchased a building on August 1, 2009. The building cost $310,000, and is expected to have a $40,000 residual value at the end of its predicted 25-year life.
e. Because the company is not large enough to occupy the entire building, it arranged to rent some space to a tenant at $1,200 per month, starting on September 1, 2011. The rent was paid on time on September 1, and the amount received was credited to the Rent Earned account. However, the tenant has not paid the October rent. The company has worked out an agreement with the tenant, who has promised to pay both October's and November's rent in full on November 15.
f. On October 1, the company also rented space to another tenant for $1,050 per month. The tenant paid five months' rent in advance on that date. The payment was recorded with a credit to the Unearned Rent account.

Required
1. Use the information to prepare the October 31, 2011, month-end adjusting entries.
2. Prepare journal entries to record the subsequent cash transactions described in items (c) and (e).

Problem 4-9B
Adjusting journal entries
LO4

Ben Hallmark, the owner of Hallmark Surveying Services, has been in business for two years. The unadjusted trial balance at December 31, regarding the month just ended, follows:

Hallmark Surveying Services
Unadjusted Trial Balance
December 31, 2011

Acct. No.	Account	Debit	Credit
101	Cash	$ 5,600	
106	Accounts receivable	7,910	
126	Supplies	640	
128	Prepaid advertising	5,600	
131	Prepaid rent	27,000	
167	Surveying equipment	58,000	
168	Accumulated depreciation, surveying equipment		$ 7,348
201	Accounts payable		3,800
203	Interest payable		-0-
210	Wages payable		-0-
233	Unearned surveying fees		4,800
251	Notes payable		36,000
301	Ben Hallmark, capital		28,652
302	Ben Hallmark, withdrawals	4,300	
401	Surveying fees earned		134,098
601	Depreciation expense, surveying equipment	-0-	
622	Salaries expense	38,000	
623	Wages expense	39,726	
633	Interest expense	-0-	
637	Insurance expense	6,000	
640	Rent expense	-0-	
650	Supplies expense	2,958	
655	Advertising expense	-0-	
671	Gas and oil expense	6,564	
684	Repairs expense	12,400	
690	Utilities expense	-0-	
	Totals	$214,698	$214,698

The following additional information is available on December 31, 2011:

a. Depreciation on the equipment for the month was $334.
b. $4,000 of the balance in Unearned Surveying Fees is unearned at December 31.
c. The balance in Prepaid Rent is for six months of rent beginning December 1.
d. Accrued wages at month-end were $10,000.
e. December's interest in the amount of $210 had accrued on the notes payable.
f. Accrued surveying fees at month-end totalled $1,580.
g. The balance in Prepaid Advertising covers four months of advertising beginning December 15.
h. A count of the supplies on December 31 showed $300 had been used.
i. The December electricity bill for $1,080 was received on December 31. It is unrecorded and unpaid.

Required
Prepare adjusting journal entries for the month ended December 31, 2011, based on the above.

Analysis component:
Explain the differences between *Accumulated Depreciation* and *Depreciation Expense.*

Problem 4-10B

Posting, adjusted trial balance, and preparing financial statements

LO6, 7

Check figures:

3. Adjusted trial balance, debits = $227,902
4. Net income = $13,706

Required

Using the information in Problem 4-9B, complete the following:

1. Set up balance column accounts for Hallmark Surveying Services and enter the balances listed in the unadjusted trial balance.
2. Post the adjusting entries prepared in Problem 4-9B to the balance column accounts.
3. Prepare an adjusted trial balance.
4. Use the adjusted trial balance to prepare an income statement, a statement of changes in equity, and a balance sheet. Assume that the owner, Ben Hallmark, made owner investments of $4,000 during the month.

Analysis component:

At December 31, 2011, how much of the business's assets are financed by the owner? by debt? Assuming total assets at the end of the previous month totalled $84,200, did equity financing increase or decrease during December? Generally speaking, is this a favourable or unfavourable change?

Note

For Part 1, your instructor may ask you to set up T-accounts instead of balance column accounts. The solution is available in both formats.

Problem 4-11B

Adjusting entries

LO4

B52 Skate Training prepares adjustments annually and showed the following on its June 30, 2011, year-end:

B52 Skate Training
Unadjusted Trial Balance
June 30, 2011

	Unadjusted Trial Balance		Adjustments		Adjusted Trial Balance	
Account	**Debit**	**Credit**	**Debit**	**Credit**	**Debit**	**Credit**
Cash	$ 112,000					
Accounts receivable	28,000					
Repair supplies	2,800					
Prepaid arena rental	182,000					
Skate equipment	428,000					
Accumulated depreciation, skate equipment		$ 164,000				
Accounts payable		5,400				
Unearned training fees		19,600				
Notes payable		160,000				
Ben Gibson, capital		451,400				
Ben Gibson, withdrawals	72,000					
Training fees earned		550,000				
Salaries expense	350,000					
Arena rental expense	168,000					
Other expenses	7,600					
Totals	$1,350,400	$1,350,400				

Additional information available at year-end:

a. The Prepaid Arena Rental of $182,000 was paid on February 1, 2011. It represents seven months of rent on the arena.
b. A count of the Repair Supplies at year-end revealed that $1,900 had been used.
c. Annual depreciation of the skate equipment was $82,000.
d. A review of the Unearned Training Fees account at year-end showed that included in the balance was $12,600 that had not yet been earned.
e. Accrued salaries of $58,000 had not been recorded at year-end.
f. Interest of $1,800 had accrued regarding the Notes Payable.
g. On June 5, 2011, cash of $92,000 was received for 2011/2012 training sessions (lessons begin in October). This amount is included in the Training Fees Earned balance.

Required

Prepare the annual adjusting entries on June 30, 2011, for each of (a) through (g) above.

Required

1. Using the format presented in Problem 4-11B, complete the adjusted trial balance by including the adjusting entries prepared in Problem 4-11B.
2. Prepare an income statement, a statement of changes in equity, and a balance sheet based on the adjusted trial balance completed in Part 1. Assume that the owner, Ben Gibson, made an investment during the year of $20,000.

Analysis component:

Assume that total liabilities reported at June 30, 2010, were $90,000. Determine what equity and total assets were on that date and comment on the change in the financial position from 2010 to 2011.

Problem 4-12B

Preparing financial statement

LO6, 7

Check figures:

1. Adjustments columns = $372,700; Adjusted trial balance columns = $1,492,200
2. Net loss = $334,300

Problem 4-13B

Preparing financial statements from the adjusted trial balance

LO7

This adjusted trial balance is for Mad Catz Courier as of its December 31, 2011, month-end:

	Debit	Credit
Accounts payable		$ 62,000
Accounts receivable	$ 55,000	
Accumulated depreciation, equipment		95,000
Accumulated depreciation, trucks		24,000
Advertising expense	13,200	
Cash	24,000	
Delivery fees earned		290,000
Depreciation expense, equipment	23,000	
Depreciation expense, trucks	12,000	
Equipment	130,000	
Interest earned		12,000
Interest expense	12,500	
Interest payable		11,000
Interest receivable	3,000	
Land	45,000	
Long-term notes payable		95,000
Madison Catz, capital		57,500
Madison Catz, withdrawals	20,000	
Notes receivable (due in 90 days)	100,000	
Office supplies	6,000	
Office supplies expense	16,500	
Repairs expense	17,300	
Salaries expense	32,000	
Salaries payable		15,000
Trucks	62,000	
Unearned delivery fees		55,000
Wages expense	145,000	
Totals	$716,500	$716,500

Required

Use the information in the trial balance to prepare:

1. The income statement for the month ended December 31, 2011.
2. The statement of changes in equity for the month ended December 31, 2011, assuming the owner invested $10,000 during December.
3. The balance sheet as of December 31, 2011.

Check figures:

1. Net income = $30,500
3. Total assets = $306,000

Problem 4-14B

Journalizing, posting, adjusted trial balance, adjusting entries, financial statements

LO4, 5, 6, 7

On July 1, 2011, Melanie Thornhill began her third month of operating an electronics repair shop called MT Repairs out of her dad's garage. The following occurred during the third month of operations:

July	1	Collected $3,600 as a deposit for work to be done at the local college in the fall.
	1	Melanie Thornhill withdrew $4,000 cash for personal expenses.
	2	Paid $2,200 for repair supplies purchased on account last month.
	3	Did work for a client and immediately collected $1,400.
	4	Performed services for a customer and collected $3,600.
	7	Hired a new technician to start next week on a casual basis at $400 per day.
	15	Melanie withdrew cash of $1,000 for personal use.
	22	Purchased repair supplies for cash; $1,600.
	31	Paid wages of $2,800.

Required

1. Prepare General Journal entries to record the July transactions.
2. Set up the following T-accounts with June 30 adjusted balances: Cash (101), $6,400; Repair Supplies (131), $3,000; Tools (161), $16,800; Accumulated Depreciation, Tools (162), $560; Accounts Payable (201), $3,200; Unearned Revenue (233), $700; Melanie Thornhill, Capital (301) $?; Melanie Thornhill, Withdrawals (302), $0; Revenue (401), $25,800; Depreciation Expense, Tools (602), $560; Wages Expense (623), $1,960; Rent Expense (640), $8,000; and Repair Supplies Expense (696), $2,700.
3. Post the entries to the accounts; calculate the ending balance in each account.
4. Prepare an unadjusted trial balance at July 31, 2011.
5. Use the following information to prepare and post adjusting entries for the month of July:
   a. The tools have an estimated life of five years with no residual value.
   b. One-quarter of the repair supplies balance remained on hand at July 31.
   c. Accrued the July rent expense of $4,000; it will be paid in August.
   d. $3,800 of the unearned revenues remained unearned as at July 31.
6. Prepare an adjusted trial balance.
7. Prepare an income statement and a statement of changes in equity for the three months ended July 31, 2011, and a July 31, 2011, balance sheet.

Check figures:
3. Cash balance, July 31, 2011 = $3,400
4. Dr = $45,820
6. Dr = $50,100
7. Net income = $7,550

Analysis component:
When a company shows expenses on its income statement, does this mean that cash equal to the expenses was paid during the period in which the expenses were reported?

*Problem 4-15B

Correcting entries

LO8

As the accountant for Jasper's Telemarketing Services, you discovered the following errors in the May 31 unadjusted trial balance that require correction:

a. Advertising Expense was debited and Accounts Receivable was credited on May 17 for $24,000 of repairs paid for by Jasper's.
b. On May 18, Computer Equipment was debited and Accounts Payable was credited, each for $16,000 regarding the purchase of office furniture in exchange for a promissory note.
c. On May 28, Cash was debited and Telemarketing Fees Earned was credited for $20,000 cash received in advance from a client.
d. The Telephone Expense account included $3,600 of delivery expense.
e. The Telemarketing Fees Earned account was credited for $900 of interest revenue.

Required

Journalize the correcting entries required on May 31.

Analysis component:
The error in (e) shows that an incorrect revenue account was credited. Since the net effect on the financial statements is nil after recording the correction, is it necessary to prepare a correcting entry for this type of error?

An asterisk (*) identifies assignment material based on Appendix 4A or Appendix 4B.

***Problem 4-16B**
Recording prepaid expenses and unearned revenues
LO9

Rainbow Janitorial Services follows the approach of recording prepaid expenses as expenses and unearned revenues as revenues. Rainbow's unadjusted trial balance for the year ended October 31, 2011, follows.

Rainbow Janitorial Services
Trial Balances
October 31, 2011

Account	Unadjusted Trial Balance		Adjustments		Adjusted Trial Balance	
	Debit	Credit	Debit	Credit	Debit	Credit
Cash	$ 14,500					
Accounts receivable	9,000					
Prepaid advertising	-0-					
Cleaning supplies	-0-					
Equipment	31,000					
Accumulated depreciation, equipment		$ 1,500				
Unearned window washing fees		-0-				
Unearned office cleaning fees		-0-				
William Nahanee, capital		9,150				
Window washing fees earned		38,000				
Office cleaning fees earned		69,000				
Advertising expense	3,650					
Salaries expense	48,500					
Depreciation expense, equipment	-0-					
Cleaning supplies expense	11,000					
Totals	$117,650	$117,650				

Additional information:

a. On October 31, a physical count revealed cleaning supplies on hand of $1,550.
b. Annual depreciation on the equipment is $1,500.
c. It was determined that $4,250 of the balance in Office Cleaning Fees Earned had not yet been earned as of October 31.
d. A review of the Window Washing Fees Earned account showed that only $35,500 had been earned as of October 31.
e. $2,500 of the total recorded in the Advertising Expense account had not yet been used.

Required
Refer to Exhibit 4.22 and use the information provided to complete the columns above.

Check figure:
Adjusted trial balance, debits = $119,150

***Problem 4-17B**
Recording prepaid expenses and unearned revenues
LO4, 9

The following occurred for a company during the last two months of its fiscal year ended May 31, 2011:

Apr.	1	Paid $6,900 for future consulting services.
	1	Paid $5,400 for insurance through March 31 of the following year.
	30	Received $15,000 for future services to be provided to a customer.
May	1	Paid $6,900 for future newspaper advertising.
	23	Received $18,900 for future services to be provided to a customer.
	31	Of the consulting services paid for on April 1, $3,000 worth had been received.
	31	Part of the insurance paid for on April 1 had expired.
	31	Services worth $7,200 had not yet been provided to the customer who paid on April 30.
	31	Of the advertising paid for on May 1, $2,100 worth had not been published yet.
	31	The company had performed $9,000 of the services that the customer had paid for on May 23.

Required

1. Prepare entries for April and May under the approach that records prepaid expenses and unearned revenues in balance sheet accounts. Also, prepare adjusting entries at the end of the year.
2. Prepare entries for April and May under the approach that records prepaid expenses and unearned revenues in income statement accounts. Also, prepare adjusting entries at the end of the year.

Analysis component:
Explain why the alternative sets of entries in requirements 1 and 2 do not result in different financial statement amounts.

An asterisk (*) identifies assignment material based on Appendix 4A or Appendix 4B.

Analytical and Review Problem

A & R Problem 4-1

The Salaries Payable account of James Bay Company Limited appears below:

Salaries Payable			
		22,520	Bal. Jan. 1, 2011
Entries during 2011	398,120	388,400	Entries during 2011

The company records the salary expense and related liability at the end of each week and pays the employees on the last Friday of the month.

Required

Calculate:

1. What was the salary expense for 2011?
2. How much was paid to employees in 2011 for work done in 2010?
3. How much was paid to employees in 2011 for work done in 2011?
4. How much will be paid to employees in 2012 for work done in 2011?

Ethics Challenge

EC 4-1

Jackie Houston is a new accountant for Seitzer Company. She is learning on the job from Bob Welch, who has already worked several years for Seitzer. Jackie and Bob are preparing the year-end adjusting entries. Jackie has calculated that depreciation expense for the fiscal year should be recorded as:

Depreciation Expense, Equipment.................	123,546	
Accum. Dep., Equipment.....................		123,546

Bob is rechecking the numbers and says that he agrees with her computation. However, he says that the credit entry should be made directly to the Equipment account. He argues that while accumulated depreciation is taught in the classroom, "It is easier to ignore the contra account and just credit the Equipment account directly for the annual depreciation. Besides, the balance sheet shows the same amount for total assets under both methods."

Required

1. How should depreciation be recorded? Do you support Jackie or Bob?
2. Evaluate the strengths and weaknesses of Bob's reasons for preferring his method.
3. Indicate whether the situation faced by Jackie is an ethical problem.

Focus on Financial Statements

FFS 4-1

eXcel

You have been given the following information for RPE Consulting for the year ended July 31, 2011.

RPE Consulting
Trial Balances
July 31, 2011

	Unadjusted Trial Balance		Adjustments		Adjusted Trial Balance	
Account	**Debit**	**Credit**	**Debit**	**Credit**	**Debit**	**Credit**
Accounts payable		$ 9,300				$ 10,200
Accounts receivable	$ 12,000				$ 22,460	
Accum. dep., office equipment		12,000				18,000
Advertising expense	13,800				14,700	
Cash	27,000				27,000	
Consulting fees earned		156,000				168,160
Depreciation expense, office equipment	-0-				6,000	
Insurance expense	-0-				2,440	
Interest expense	1,400				2,200	
Interest payable		-0-				800
Notes payable		44,000				44,000
Office equipment	92,000				92,000	
Office supplies	18,000				3,000	
Office supplies expense	-0-				15,000	
Prepaid insurance	7,320				4,880	
Ray Edds, capital		28,420				28,420
Ray Edds, withdrawals	10,000				10,000	
Rent expense	13,200				13,200	
Salaries expense	71,000				77,600	
Salaries payable		-0-				6,600
Unearned consulting fees		16,000				14,300
Totals	$265,720	$265,720			$290,480	$290,480

Required

1. Prepare the company's income statement, statement of changes in equity, and balance sheet. Assume that the owner, Ray Edds, invested $20,000 during the year ended July 31, 2011.

Analysis component:

2. Analyze the unadjusted and adjusted trial balances and identify the adjustments that must have been made by inserting them in the two middle columns. Label each entry with a letter.
3. If the adjustments had not been recorded, identify the net overstatement/understatement of each component of the accounting equation.

FFS 4-2

Part 1

Refer to WestJet's income statement on page I-25 in Appendix I at the end of the textbook.

a. Prepare two possible adjusting entries that would have caused 2008 *Guest revenues* to increase.
b. Prepare two possible adjusting entries that would have caused 2008 *Aircraft leasing expenses* to increase.

Part 2

Refer to WestJet's balance sheet on page I-26 in Appendix I at the end of the textbook.

c. Prepare the possible adjusting entry that would have caused the December 31, 2008, balance in *Prepaid expenses and deposits* to decrease.
d. Prepare a possible adjusting entry that would have caused the December 31, 2008, balance in *Accounts payable and accrued liabilities* to increase.

Critical Thinking Mini Case

It's a week before Scotiabank's October 31, 2011, year-end. You are the personnel director and are reviewing some financial information regarding the March 1, 2009, purchase of office furniture for the western region offices totalling $700,000 ($300,000 was paid in cash and the balance was financed over four years at 4% annual interest with annual principal payments of $100,000). The useful life of the furniture was estimated to be five years with a projected resale value at that time of $20,000. Insurance was purchased on the furniture at a cost of $8,000 annually, payable each March 1. You leave the office for the day wondering what needs to be considered regarding these items in preparation for year-end.

Required

Using the elements of critical thinking described on the inside front cover, respond.

Serial Problem

Echo Systems

(This comprehensive problem was introduced in Chapter 3 and continues in Chapters 5 and 6. If the Chapter 3 segment has not been completed, the assignment can begin at this point. You need to use the facts presented on PP. 128–129 in Chapter 3. Because of its length, this problem is most easily solved if you use the Working Papers[10] that accompany this book.)

After the success of its first two months, Mary Graham has decided to continue operating Echo Systems. (The transactions that occurred in these months are described in Chapter 3.) Before proceeding in December, Graham adds these new accounts to the chart of accounts for the ledger:

Account	No.
Accumulated Depreciation, Office Equipment	164
Accumulated Depreciation, Computer Equipment	168
Wages Payable	210
Unearned Computer Services Revenue	236
Depreciation Expense, Office Equipment	612
Depreciation Expense, Computer Equipment	613
Insurance Expense	637
Rent Expense	640
Computer Supplies Expense	652

Required

1. Prepare journal entries to record each of the following transactions for Echo Systems. Post the entries to the accounts in the ledger.

Dec.	3	Paid $2,100 to the Lakeshore Mall for the company's share of mall advertising costs.
	3	Paid $1,200 to repair the company's computer.
	4	Received $7,500 from Alamo Engineering Co. for the receivable from the prior month.
	10	Paid Carly Smith for six days' work at the rate of $200 per day.
	14	Notified by Alamo Engineering Co. that Echo's bid of $12,000 on a proposed project was accepted. Alamo paid an advance of $3,000.
	17	Purchased $2,310 of computer supplies on credit from Abbott Office Products.
	18	Sent a reminder to Fostek Co. to pay the fee for services originally recorded on November 8.
	20	Completed a project for Elite Corporation and received $11,250 cash.
	24–28	Took the week off for the holidays.
	31	Received $5,700 from Fostek Co. on its receivable.
	31	Reimbursed Mary Graham's business automobile expenses of 600 kilometres at $1.00 per kilometre.
	31	Mary Graham withdrew $3,600 cash from the business.

2. Prepare adjusting entries to record the following additional information collected on December 31, 2011. Post the entries to the accounts in the ledger.
   a. The December 31 inventory of computer supplies was $1,440.
   b. Three months have passed since the annual insurance premium was paid.
   c. As of the end of the year, Carly Smith has not been paid for four days of work at the rate of $200 per day.
   d. The computer is expected to have a four-year life with no residual value.
   e. The office equipment is expected to have a three-year life with no residual value.
   f. Prepaid rent for three of the four months has expired.
3. Prepare an adjusted trial balance as of December 31, 2011.
4. Prepare an income statement and statement of changes in equity for the three months ended December 31, 2011.
5. Prepare a balance sheet as of December 31, 2011.

[10] If students have not purchased the Working Papers package, the Working Papers for the Serial Problem are available on Connect.

CHAPTER 5

Completing the Accounting Cycle and Classifying Accounts

learning objectives

- **LO1** Describe and prepare a work sheet and explain its usefulness.
- **LO2** Describe the closing process and explain why temporary accounts are closed each period.
- **LO3** Prepare closing entries.
- **LO4** Explain and prepare a post-closing trial balance.
- **LO5** Complete the steps in the accounting cycle.
- **LO6** Explain and prepare a classified balance sheet.

*APPENDIX 5A

- **LO7** Prepare reversing entries and explain their purpose.

*APPENDIX 5B

- **LO8** Calculate the current ratio and describe what it reveals about a company's financial condition.

The Sweet Taste of Success

Sharon Beasley began selling Mrs. Beasley's Cookies to a small list of customers: hospitals, universities, and schools. Initially, she baked the cookies in space rented from a local bakery. To finance her own facility, she needed a long-term bank loan. The bank needed to analyze her financial statements, in particular, the classified balance sheet. By reviewing current assets and current liabilities, the bank would be better able to determine if Mrs. Beasley's Cookies could make the loan payments. Based on a solid balance sheet and knowing Sharon's customers were dependable for payment, the bank granted the loan. Today, the business is financing growth by reinvesting profits.

Sharon's biggest financial challenge was the cost of distribution. She concluded that to gain efficiencies she had to take advantage of someone else's distribution chain. She accomplished this by adding 70 Sobeys stores and 70 Co-op Atlantic stores to her customer list. Sobeys and Co-op each distribute to individual stores from their own central warehouses, and this significant increase in Mrs. Beasley's business required only two additional deliveries: one to Sobeys' warehouse and another to Co-op's warehouse. To meet this new customer demand, Mrs. Beasley's increased its property, plant and equipment assets by adding warehouse space instead of delivery vehicles.

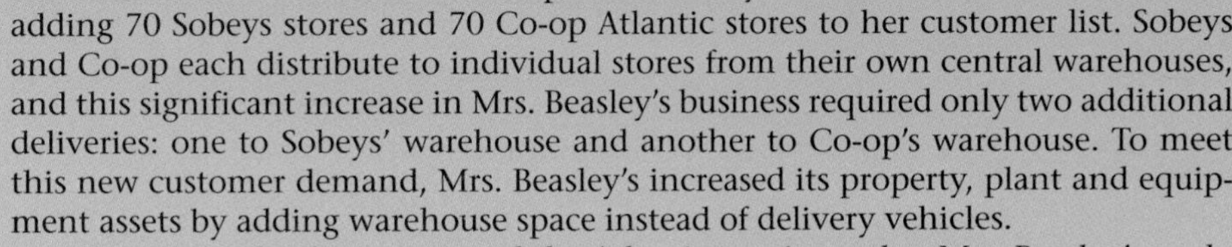

Sharon Beasley has convinced the Atlantic provinces that Mrs. Beasley's cookies are as good as homemade. Her next goal is to double the business by expanding westward. We wish her sweet success!

CRITICAL THINKING CHALLENGE

In what ways did the purchase of a bakery affect the financial statements differently than Mrs. Beasley's original rental of a bakery? If your job was to review bank loan applications for a bank, what financial statement information would you examine (and why) regarding Mrs. Beasley's loan application to purchase additional warehouse space? What does it mean to "finance growth by reinvesting profits"?

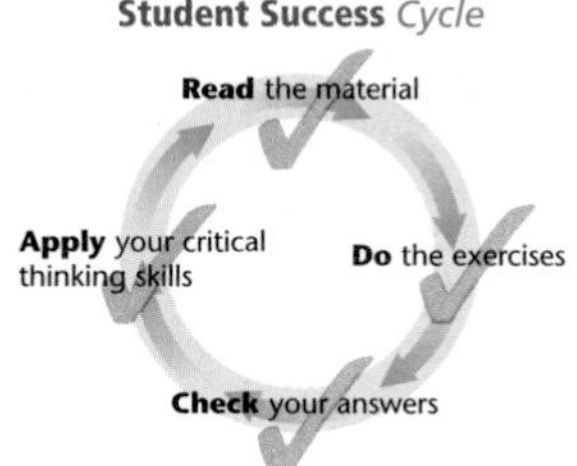

chapter preview

Many of the important steps in the accounting cycle leading to financial statements are explained in earlier chapters. We described how transactions are analyzed, journalized, and posted. We also described important adjusting entries that are often necessary to properly reflect revenues when earned and expenses when incurred.

This chapter begins with the introduction of the work sheet, an optional tool useful in preparing financial statements. Chapter 5 also describes the final steps in the accounting cycle (Exhibit 5.1), Steps 8 and 9, involving the closing process that prepares revenue, expense, and withdrawals accounts for the next reporting period and updates the owner's capital account. We also explain how accounts are classified on a balance sheet P. 29 to give more useful information to decision makers. These tools for managing data are the kind Sharon Beasley refers to in the opening article; such tools improve decision making.

Work Sheet as a Tool

LO1 Describe and prepare a work sheet and explain its usefulness.

When organizing the information presented in formal reports to internal P. 8 and external users P. 7, accountants prepare numerous analyses and informal documents. These informal documents, called **working papers**, are important tools for accountants. The **work sheet** is an *optional* working paper that can simplify the accountant's efforts in preparing financial statements. It is not distributed to decision makers. The work sheet is prepared before making adjusting entries at the end of a reporting period. It gathers information about the accounts, the needed adjustments, and the financial statements. When it is finished, the work sheet contains information that is recorded in the journal and then presented in the statements.

Exhibit 5.1

Steps in the Accounting Cycle Introduced in Chapter 5

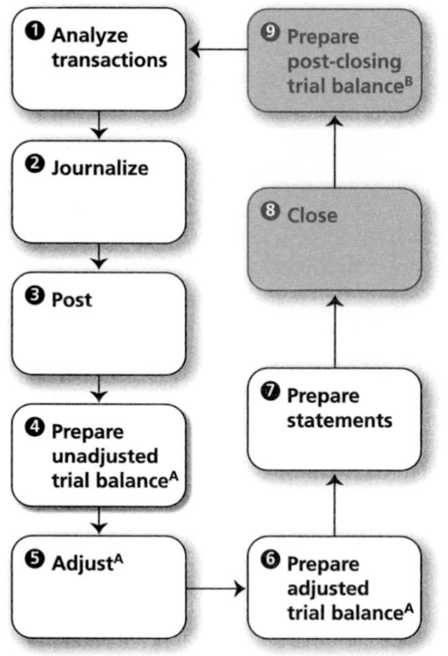

[A] Steps 4, 5, and 6 can be done on a *work sheet*.
[B] *Reversing entries* are optional and, if prepared, are done between Steps 9 and 1. Reversing entries are covered in Appendix 5A.

Benefits of a Work Sheet

When a business has only a few accounts and adjustments, preparing a work sheet is unnecessary. Computerized accounting systems prepare financial statements without the need for a work sheet. Yet there are several potential benefits to using a manual or electronic work sheet:

1. It is useful in preparing interim (monthly or quarterly) financial statements when journalizing and posting of adjusting entries are postponed until the year-end.
2. It captures the entire accounting process, linking economic transactions to their effects in financial statements.
3. Auditors of financial statements often use a work sheet for planning and organizing the audit. It can also be used to reflect any additional adjustments necessary as a result of the audit.
4. It helps preparers to avoid errors when working with a lot of information in accounting systems involving many accounts and adjustments.

Using a Work Sheet

Exhibit 5.2 on page 191 shows a blank work sheet. Notice that it has five sets of double columns for the:

1. Unadjusted trial balance.
2. Adjustments.
3. Adjusted trial balance.
4. Income statement.
5. Balance sheet and statement of changes in equity.

EXTEND YOUR KNOWLEDGE

Exhibit 5.2

Preparing the Work Sheet at the End of the Accounting Period

Vertically Inclined Rock Gym
Work Sheet
For Month Ended January 31, 2011

The heading should identify the entity, the document, and the time period.

Account	Unadjusted Trial Balance		Adjustments		Adjusted Trial Balance		Income Statement		Balance Sheet & Statement of Changes in Equity	
	Dr	Cr	Dr	Cr	Dr	Cr	Dr	Cr	Dr	Cr

The work sheet can be prepared manually or with a computer spreadsheet program.

The work sheet collects and summarizes the information used to prepare adjusting entries, financial statements, and closing entries.

The purpose of double columns is to accommodate both debits and credits. Because the statement of changes in equity includes only a few items, they are simply listed with the balance sheet items.

The work sheet can be completed by following five steps.

Enter Unadjusted Trial Balance

To begin the work sheet, we list the number and title of each account from the ledger along with the account's unadjusted debit or credit balance as shown in Exhibit 5.3.[1] We use the information of Vertically Inclined Rock Gym to describe and interpret the work sheet.

Enter Adjustments

Step 2 begins with the entry of adjustments in the adjustment columns. The adjustments shown in Exhibit 5.3 are the same as those discussed in Chapter 4. They are as follows:

a. Expiration of $100 of prepaid insurance.
b. Used $1,050 of supplies.
c. Depreciation on equipment of $200.
d. Earned $250 of revenue received in advance.
e. Accrued interest of $35 on the note payable.
f. Accrued $70 of salaries owed to an employee.
g. Accrued $1,800 of revenue owed by a customer.

To help you correctly match the debit and credit of each adjusting entry, notice that an identifying letter is used for each adjustment. In entering adjustments, we sometimes find additional accounts that need to be inserted on the work sheet. Additional accounts are inserted below the initial list. ***After entering adjustments on a work sheet, we still must enter adjusting entries in the journal and post them to the ledger.***

Prepare Adjusted Trial Balance

The adjusted trial balance is prepared by combining the adjustments with the unadjusted balances for each account. As an example, in Exhibit 5.3, the Supplies account has a $3,600 debit balance in the Unadjusted Trial Balance columns. This $3,600 debit is combined with the $1,050 credit in the Adjustments columns to give Supplies a $2,550 debit in the Adjusted Trial Balance columns. The totals of the Adjusted Trial Balance columns confirm the equality of debits and credits.

Extend Adjusted Trial Balance Amounts to Financial Statement Columns

This step involves sorting adjusted amounts to their proper financial statement columns. Expense items go to the Income Statement Debit column, and revenues to the Income Statement Credit column. Assets and withdrawals go to the Balance Sheet and Statement of Changes in Equity Debit column. Liabilities and owner's capital go to the Balance Sheet and Statement of Changes in Equity Credit column. Recall that accumulated depreciation P. 136 is a contra asset account P. 137, so it also goes to the Balance Sheet and Statement of Changes in Equity Credit column as shown in Exhibit 5.3. Each statement column is totalled. Notice in Exhibit 5.3 that the debits do not equal the credits (explained in Step Five).

[1] In practice, accounts with a zero balance that are likely to require an adjusting entry would also be listed.

Exhibit 5.3

Work Sheet

NOTE: The steps for completing a work sheet are colour coded to follow the description on pages 192 to 195.

Vertically Inclined Rock Gym
Work Sheet
For Month Ended January 31, 2011

Account	Unadjusted Trial Balance		Adjustments		Adjusted Trial Balance		Income Statement		Balance Sheet & Statement of Changes in Equity	
	Dr	Cr	Dr	Cr	Dr	Cr	Dr	Cr	Dr	Cr
101 Cash	8,070				8,070				8,070	
125 Supplies	3,600			b) 1,050	2,550				2,550	
128 Prepaid insurance	2,400			a) 100	2,300				2,300	
167 Equipment	6,000				6,000				6,000	
168 Accumulated depreciation, equipment				c) 200		200				200
201 Accounts payable		200				200				200
236 Unearned teaching revenue		3,000	d) 250			2,750				2,750
240 Notes payable		6,000				6,000				6,000
301 Virgil Klimb, capital		10,000				10,000				10,000
302 Virgil Klimb, withdrawals	600				600				600	
403 Teaching revenue		3,800		d) 250 g) 1,800		5,850		5,850		
406 Equipment rental revenue		300				300		300		
622 Salaries expense	1,400		f) 70		1,470		1,470			
641 Rent expense	1,000				1,000		1,000			
690 Utilities expense	230				230		230			
Totals	23,300	23,300								
637 Insurance expense			a) 100		100		100			
651 Supplies expense			b) 1,050		1,050		1,050			
614 Depreciation expense, equipment			c) 200		200		200			
209 Salaries payable				f) 70		70				70
633 Interest expense			e) 35		35		35			
203 Interest payable				e) 35		35				35
106 Accounts receivable			g) 1,800		1,800				1,800	
Totals			3,505	3,505	25,405	25,405	4,085	6,150	21,320	19,255
Net income							2,065			2,065
Totals							6,150	6,150	21,320	21,320

(1) When entering the unadjusted trial balances, include all accounts that have balances or that are expected to have balances after adjustments.

(2) Adjustments may create the need for additional accounts. Add new accounts to the existing list as required.

These two columns must show equal totals.

Enter the drafts of the adjusting entries and find the total debits and credits.

These two columns must show equal totals.

(3) Sum the unadjusted trial balance accounts with the adjustments, and enter them in the adjusted trial balance.

These two columns must show equal totals.

Extend revenues and expenses from the adjusted trial balance columns to these columns.

The totals are not equal because the debit and the credit balances in the revenue and expense accounts are not equal.

(4) Extend assets, liabilities, and the owner's capital and withdrawals from the adjusted trial balance columns to these columns.

The totals are not equal because the net income component of equity is missing.

Add two new lines for the net income (or loss) and the totals.

(5)

Enter the net income amount as the difference between the debits and the credits in the Income Statement columns.

Also enter the net income amount in the credit column to include in equity the change caused by net income.

Enter Net Income (or Loss) and Balance the Financial Statement Columns

The difference between the debit and credit totals of the Income Statement columns is net income or net loss. If the Credit total exceeds the Debit total, there is a net income. If the Debit total exceeds the Credit total, there is a net loss. In Exhibit 5.3, Vertically Inclined's work sheet shows the Credit total to exceed the Debit total, resulting in net income of $2,065. The difference is added to the *Income Statement* and *Balance Sheet & Statement of Changes in Equity* columns for balancing. In the case of Vertically Inclined where a net income of $2,065 has been calculated, the $2,065 is listed as a *debit* in the Income Statement columns. It is also listed in the Balance Sheet & Statement of Changes in Equity columns, but as a *credit*. The new totals are entered for both sets of columns, showing that the Income Statement columns and Balance Sheet & Statement of Changes in Equity columns now balance. If they do not balance, an error has occurred in the completion of the work sheet.[2] The term *Net income* (or *Net loss*) is listed in the Account column to label the $2,065.

Adding net income to the last Credit column implies that it is to be added to owner's capital. If a loss occurs, it is listed in the last Debit column, implying that it is to be subtracted from owner's capital.

Prepare Financial Statements From Work Sheet Information

A work sheet is not a substitute for financial statements. The completed work sheet is used to prepare the financial statements. The Income Statement columns are used to prepare the income statement. The statement of changes in equity and balance sheet are prepared using the information in the Balance Sheet & Statement of Changes in Equity columns. While the ending balance of owner's capital does not appear in the last two columns as a single amount, it is calculated as the owner's capital account balance plus net income (or minus net loss) minus the withdrawals account balance. The opening capital balance for the period would be determined by subtracting any owner investments made during the period from the owner's capital account balance, as shown in the last credit column on the work sheet. Exhibit 5.4 shows the statements for Vertically Inclined as prepared from the work sheet.[3]

Work sheets are also useful in analyzing the effects of proposed or *what-if* transactions. This is done by entering their adjusted financial statement amounts in the first two columns and arranging them in the form of financial statements. Proposed transactions are entered in the second two columns. Extended amounts in the last columns show the effects of these proposed transactions on financial statements. These final columns are called **pro forma statements** because they show the statements *as if* the proposed transactions had occurred.

1. Where do we get the amounts entered in the Unadjusted Trial Balance columns of a work sheet?
2. What are the advantages of using a work sheet to prepare adjusting entries?
3. What are the benefits of a work sheet?

Do Quick Study questions: QS 5-1, QS 5-2, QS 5-3, QS 5-4

[2] If the columns balance, an error(s) could still be present. For example, the columns would still balance if Accounts Payable were listed as a credit, but in the Income Statement columns. Net income would be incorrect, but the columns would still balance.

[3] Notice that the $21,320 balance of the last two columns in the work sheet in Exhibit 5.3 does not agree with the balance of $20,520 on the balance sheet; there is a difference of $800 (= $21,320 − $20,520). *This is not an error!* Notice that accumulated depreciation of $200 is subtracted on the balance sheet to arrive at total assets; it is *added* in the last Credit column on the work sheet. Also, withdrawals of $600 are *subtracted* on the statement of changes in equity to arrive at ending capital; on the work sheet, they are *added* in the last Debit column. These two items account for the difference of $800 (= $200 + $600).

Exhibit 5.4

Step 6—Prepare Financial Statements From Work Sheet Information

Vertically Inclined Rock Gym
Income Statement
For Month Ended January 31, 2011

Revenues:		
Teaching revenue	$5,850	
Equipment rental revenue	300	
Total revenues		$6,150
Operating expenses:		
Salaries expense	$1,470	
Supplies expense	1,050	
Rent expense	1,000	
Utilities expense	230	
Depreciation expense, equipment	200	
Insurance expense	100	
Interest expense	35	
Total operating expenses		4,085
Net income		$2,065

Vertically Inclined Rock Gym
Statement of Changes in Equity
For Month Ended January 31, 2011

Virgil Klimb, capital, January 1		$ -0-
Add: Investments by owner	$10,000	
Net income	2,065	12,065
Total		$12,065
Less: Withdrawals by owner		600
Virgil Klimb, capital, January 31		$11,465

Vertically Inclined Rock Gym
Balance Sheet
January 31, 2011

Assets		
Cash		$ 8,070
Accounts receivable		1,800
Supplies		2,550
Prepaid insurance		2,300
Equipment	$ 6,000	
Less: Accumulated depreciation	200	5,800
Total assets		$20,520
Liabilities		
Accounts payable	$ 200	
Interest payable	35	
Salaries payable	70	
Unearned teaching revenue	2,750	
Notes payable	6,000	
Total liabilities		$ 9,055
Equity		
Virgil Klimb, capital		11,465
Total liabilities and equity		$20,520

Closing Process

LO2 Describe the closing process and explain why temporary accounts are closed each period.

The **closing process** is an important step of the accounting cycle that is performed at the end of an accounting period after financial statements are prepared. It prepares accounts for recording the transactions of the next period.

An income statement aims to report revenues earned and expenses incurred during one accounting period. We know that the net income (or loss) from the income statement is shown on the statement of changes in equity, along with withdrawals, to show the change caused to the owner's capital account during one period. Because revenues, expenses, and withdrawals are a part of equity, their balances need to be transferred to the owner's capital account at the end of the period. This transfer of account balances is accomplished by using closing entries.

Therefore, closing entries are a necessary step because we want the:

EXTEND YOUR KNOWLEDGE

1. Revenue, expense, and withdrawals accounts to begin with zero balances to measure the results from the period just ending.
2. Owner's capital account to reflect:
   a. Increases from net income (or decreases from net losses), and
   b. Decreases from withdrawals

   from the period just ending.

In the closing process, we must:

1. Identify accounts for closing,
2. Record and post the closing entries, and
3. Prepare the post-closing trial balance.

Identify Accounts for Closing—Temporary and Permanent Accounts

Temporary (or nominal) accounts accumulate data related to one accounting period. They include all income statement accounts, withdrawals accounts, and the *Income Summary*. They are temporary because the accounts are opened at the beginning of a period, used to record transactions for that period, and then closed at the end of the period by transferring their balances to the owner's capital account. They are *temporary* because the accounts describe transactions or changes that have occurred rather than the financial position that exists at the end of the period. ***Only temporary accounts are closed.***

Permanent (or real) accounts report on transactions related to one or more future accounting periods. They carry their ending balances into the next period, and include all balance sheet accounts. ***Asset, liability, and owner's capital accounts are not closed*** as long as a company continues to own the assets, owe the liabilities, and have equity. They are permanent because they describe the existing financial position.

Temporary Accounts	Permanent Accounts
Revenues	Assets
Expenses	Liabilities
Withdrawals	Owner's Capital
Income Summary	

Recording and Posting Closing Entries

LO3 | Prepare closing entries.

Recording and posting **closing entries** transfers the end-of-period balances in the revenue, expense, and withdrawals to the permanent owner's capital account.

To close revenue and expense accounts, we transfer their balances first to an account called *Income Summary*. **Income Summary** is a temporary account that contains a credit for the sum of all revenues and a debit for the sum of all expenses. Its balance equals net income or net loss, and is transferred to the owner's capital account. Next, we transfer the withdrawals account balance to the owner's capital account. After these closing entries are posted, the revenue, expense, Income Summary, and withdrawals accounts have zero balances. These accounts are then said to be closed or cleared. The four-step closing process is illustrated in Exhibit 5.5.

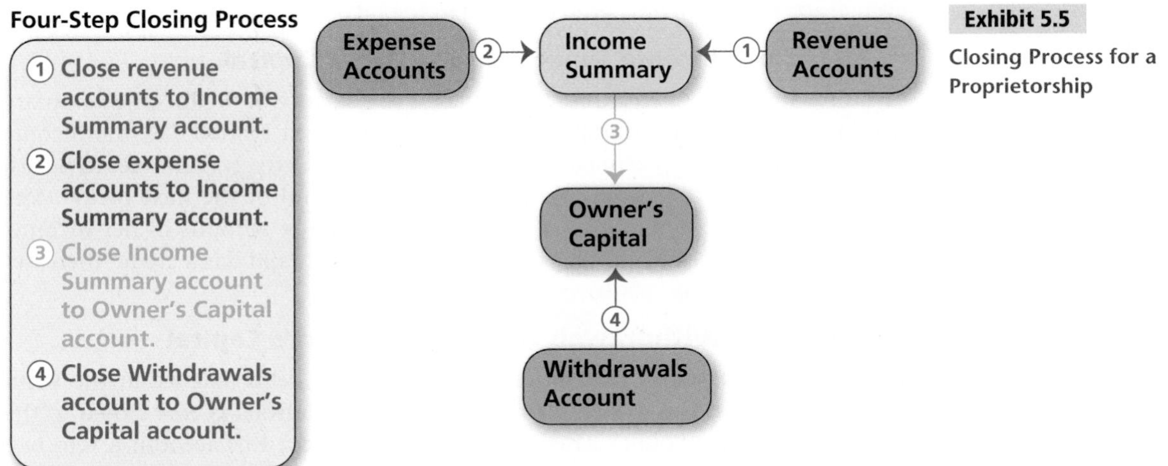
Four-Step Closing Process
① Close revenue accounts to Income Summary account.
② Close expense accounts to Income Summary account.
③ Close Income Summary account to Owner's Capital account.
④ Close Withdrawals account to Owner's Capital account.
Expense Accounts
Income Summary
Revenue Accounts
Owner's Capital
Withdrawals Account

Exhibit 5.5
Closing Process for a Proprietorship

Vertically Inclined's adjusted trial balance on January 31, 2011, is shown in Exhibit 5.6. Exhibit 5.7 shows the four closing entries necessary to close Vertically Inclined's revenue, expense, Income Summary, and withdrawals accounts. We explain each of these four entries.

Entry 1: Close Credit Balances in Revenue Accounts to Income Summary

The first closing entry in Exhibit 5.7 transfers credit balances in revenue accounts to the Income Summary account. We get accounts with credit balances to zero by debiting them as shown in Exhibit 5.8. This prepares each account to record new revenues for the next period. The Income Summary account is created and used only for the closing process. The $6,150 total credit balance in Income Summary equals the total revenues for the year.

Entry 2: Close Debit Balances in Expense Accounts to Income Summary

The second closing entry in Exhibit 5.7 transfers debit balances in expense accounts to the Income Summary account. We get the debit balances in the expense accounts to zero by crediting them as shown in Exhibit 5.8. This prepares each account for expense entries for the next period. The entry makes the balance of Income Summary equal to January's net income of $2,065. All debit and credit balances related to expense and revenue accounts have now been collected in the Income Summary account.

Entry 3: Close Income Summary to Owner's Capital

The third closing entry in Exhibit 5.7 transfers the balance of the Income Summary account to the owner's capital account. As illustrated in Exhibit 5.8, the Income Summary account has a zero balance after posting this entry. It continues to have a zero balance until the closing process occurs at the end of the next period. The owner's capital account has now been increased by the amount of net income. Since we know that the normal balance P. 81 of owner's capital is a credit, increases to owner's capital from net income are credits.

Entry 4: Close Withdrawals Account to Owner's Capital

The fourth closing entry in Exhibit 5.7 transfers any debit balance in the withdrawals account to the owner's capital account (withdrawals ***is not*** closed to the Income Summary account). This entry gives the withdrawals account a zero balance, and the account is ready to accumulate next period's payments to the owner. As illustrated in Exhibit 5.8, this entry reduces the Virgil Klimb, Capital account balance to $11,465, the amount reported on the balance sheet.

Exhibit 5.6

Adjusted Trial Balance

Vertically Inclined Rock Gym
Adjusted Trial Balance
January 31, 2011

	Debit	Credit
Cash	$ 8,070	
Accounts receivable	1,800	
Supplies	2,550	
Prepaid insurance	2,300	
Equipment	6,000	
Accumulated depreciation, equipment		$ 200
Accounts payable		200
Interest payable		35
Notes payable		6,000
Salaries payable		70
Unearned teaching revenue		2,750
Virgil Klimb, capital		10,000
Virgil Klimb, withdrawals	600	
Teaching revenue		5,850
Equipment rental revenue		300
Depreciation expense, equipment	200	
Salaries expense	1,470	
Interest expense	35	
Insurance expense	100	
Rent expense	1,000	
Supplies expense	1,050	
Utilities expense	230	
Totals	$25,405	$25,405

Exhibit 5.7

Closing Entries for Vertically Inclined

Entry 1:	**Close revenue accounts**		
Jan. 31	Teaching Revenue	5,850	
	Equipment Rental Revenue	300	
	Income Summary		6,150
	To close the revenue accounts.		
Entry 2:	**Close expense accounts**		
31	Income Summary	4,085	
	Depreciation Expense, Equipment		200
	Salaries Expense		1,470
	Interest Expense		35
	Insurance Expense		100
	Rent Expense		1,000
	Supplies Expense		1,050
	Utilities Expense		230
	To close expense accounts.		
Entry 3:	**Close Income Summary to owner's capital**		
31	Income Summary	2,065	
	Virgil Klimb, Capital		2,065
	To close the Income Summary account.		
Entry 4:	**Close withdrawals account to owner's capital**		
31	Virgil Klimb, Capital	600	
	Virgil Klimb, Withdrawals		600
	To close the withdrawals account.		

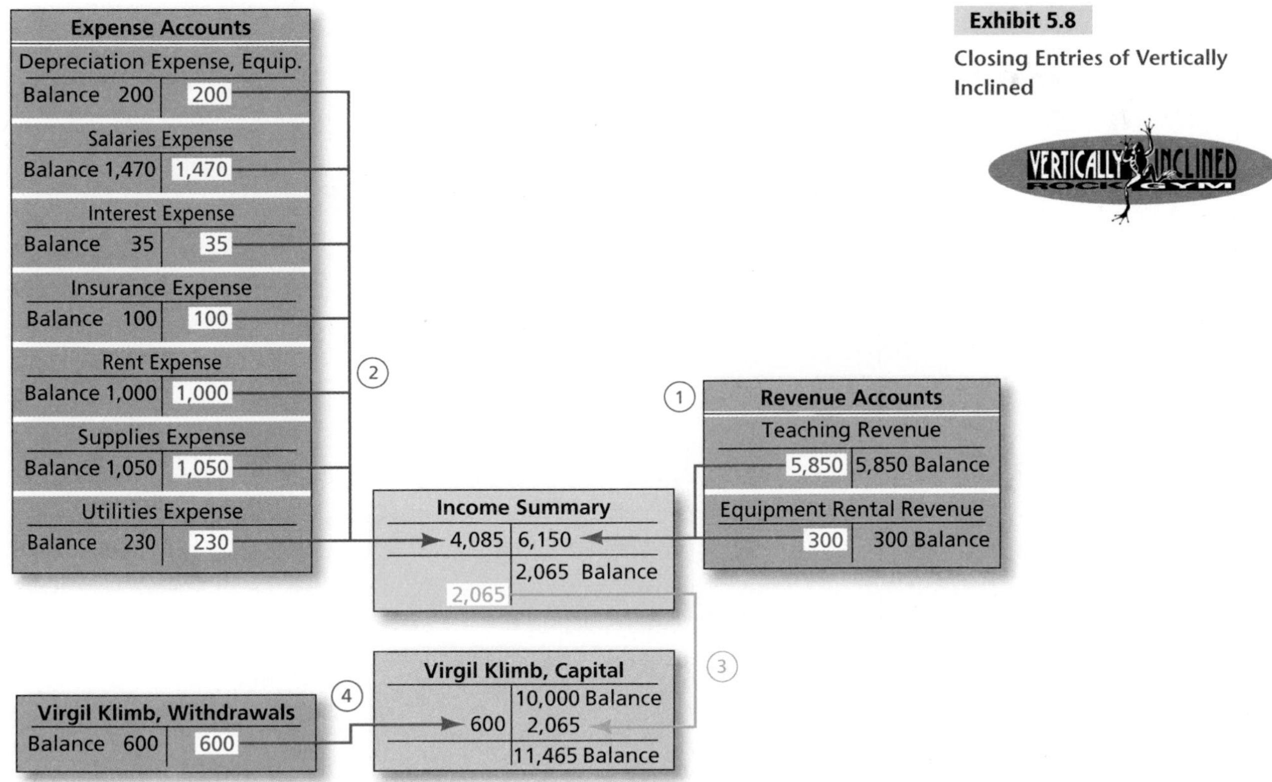

Exhibit 5.8

Closing Entries of Vertically Inclined

Sources of Closing Entry Information

We can identify the accounts that need to be closed and the amounts in the closing entries by looking to individual revenue, expense, and withdrawals accounts in the ledger.[4] If we prepare an adjusted trial balance after the adjusting process, the information for closing entries is available on the trial balance as illustrated in Exhibit 5.6.

Exhibit 5.9 highlights the posting of closing entries of Exhibit 5.7 in the ledger accounts for Vertically Inclined. Notice that all of the temporary accounts (revenues, expenses, and withdrawals) have a zero balance. The closing process transferred the balances of the temporary accounts to the Virgil Klimb, Capital account. The capital account balance of $11,465 includes owner investment of $10,000 and net income of $2,065, less withdrawals of $600.

Exhibit 5.9

Ledger After the Closing Process for Vertically Inclined

Ledger

Asset Accounts

Cash			101
Jan. 1	10,000	2,500	Jan. 1
10	2,200	2,400	1
25	1,900	1,000	10
26	3,000	700	14
		900	25
		600	26
		230	26
		700	28
Bal.	8,070		

Accounts Receivable			106
Jan. 15	1,900	1,900	Jan. 25
31	1,800		
Bal.	1,800		

Supplies			125
Jan. 1	2,500	1,050	Jan. 31
1	1,100		
Bal.	2,550		

Prepaid Insurance			128
Jan. 1	2,400	100	Jan. 31
Bal.	2,300		

Equipment			167
Jan. 1	6,000		
Bal.	6,000		

Accumulated Depreciation, Equipment			168
		200	Jan. 31
		200	Bal.

Liability and Equity Accounts

Accounts Payable			201
Jan. 25	900	1,100	Jan. 1
		200	Bal.

Interest Payable			203
		35	Jan. 31
		35	Bal.

Salaries Payable			209
		70	Jan. 31
		70	Bal.

Unearned Teaching Revenue			236
Jan. 31	250	3,000	Jan. 26
		2,750	Bal.

Notes Payable			240
		6,000	Jan. 1
		6,000	Bal.

Virgil Klimb, Capital			301
Jan. 31	600	10,000	Jan. 1
		2,065	31
		11,465	Bal.

Virgil Klimb, Withdrawals			302
Jan. 26	600	600	Jan. 31
Bal.	-0-		

[4] When accounting software is in use, closing entries are done automatically.

Exhibit 5.9 (continued)

Ledger After the Closing Process for Vertically Inclined

Revenues and Expense Accounts (including Income Summary)

Teaching Revenue			403
Jan. 31	5,850	2,200	Jan. 10
		1,600	15
		250	31
		1,800	31
		-0-	Bal.

Equipment Rental Revenue			406
Jan. 31	300	300	Jan. 15
		-0-	Bal.

Depreciation Expense, Equipment			614
Jan. 31	200	200	Jan. 31
Bal.	-0-		

Salaries Expense			622
Jan. 14	700	1,470	Jan. 31
28	700		
31	70		
Bal.	-0-		

Interest Expense			633
Jan. 31	35	35	Jan. 31
Bal.	-0-		

Insurance Expense			637
Jan. 31	100	100	Jan. 31
Bal.	-0-		

Rent Expense			641
Jan. 10	1,000	1,000	Jan. 31
Bal.	-0-		

Supplies Expense			651
Jan. 31	1,050	1,050	Jan. 31
Bal.	-0-		

Utilities Expense			690
Jan. 26	230	230	Jan. 31
Bal.	-0-		

Income Summary			901
Jan. 31	4,085	6,150	Jan. 31
31	2,065	2,065	Bal.
		-0-	Bal.

4. What are the four major closing entries?
5. Why are revenue and expense accounts called temporary? Are there other temporary accounts?

Do Quick Study questions: QS 5-5, QS 5-6, QS 5-7

Preparing a Post-Closing Trial Balance

LO4 Explain and prepare a post-closing trial balance.

A **post-closing trial balance** is a list of permanent accounts and their balances from the ledger after all closing entries are journalized and posted. It is a list of balances for accounts not closed. These accounts are a company's assets, liabilities, and equity at the end of a period. They are identical to those in the balance sheet. The aim of a post-closing trial balance is to verify that (1) total debits equal total credits for permanent accounts, and (2) all temporary accounts have zero balances.

Vertically Inclined's post-closing trial balance is shown in Exhibit 5.10 and is the last step in the accounting process. The post-closing trial balance in Exhibit 5.10 was created by listing the account balances found in Exhibit 5.9. Like the trial balance, the post-closing trial balance does not prove that all transactions are recorded or that the ledger is correct.

Exhibit 5.10

Post-Closing Trial Balance

Vertically Inclined Rock Gym
Post-Closing Trial Balance
January 31, 2011

	Debit	Credit
Cash	$ 8,070	
Accounts receivable	1,800	
Supplies	2,550	
Prepaid insurance	2,300	
Equipment	6,000	
Accumulated depreciation, equipment		$ 200
Accounts payable		200
Interest payable		35
Salaries payable		70
Unearned teaching revenue		2,750
Notes payable		6,000
Virgil Klimb, capital		11,465
Totals	$20,720	$20,720

Closing Entries After Period-End Date

We are not usually able to make closing entries on the last day of each period. This is because information about certain transactions that require *adjusting* is not always available until several days or even weeks later. Because some adjusting entries are recorded later, closing entries are recorded later, but both are dated as of the last day of the period. Financial statements therefore reflect what is known on the date they are prepared instead of what was known as of the last day of the period.

One example is a company that receives a utility bill on February 14 for costs incurred for the month of January. When the bill is received, the company records the expense and the payable as of January 31. The January income statement then reflects expenses incurred in January and the January 31 balance sheet includes the payable, even though the amounts are not actually known on January 31.

6. What accounts are listed on the post-closing trial balance?

Do Quick Study question: QS 5-8

Completing the Accounting Cycle

LO5 Complete the steps in the accounting cycle.

We have now completed the steps in the accounting cycle which have been the focus in this and the previous chapters. Let's now briefly summarize these steps in Exhibit 5.11 to emphasize their importance in providing users with information for decision making.

1. Analyze transactions	Analyze transactions in preparation for journalizing.
2. Journalize	Record debits and credits with explanations in a journal.
3. Post	Transfer debits and credits from journal entries to the ledger accounts.
4. Unadjusted trial balance[A]	Summarize ledger accounts and amounts.
5. Adjust[A]	Record adjustments to bring account balances up to date; journalize and post adjusting entries to the accounts.
6. Adjusted trial balance[A]	Summarize adjusted ledger accounts and amounts.
7. Prepare statements	Use adjusted trial balance to prepare: income statement, statement of changes in equity, balance sheet, and statement of cash flows (details of preparing the statement of cash flows are in Chapter 19).
8. Close	Journalize and post entries to close temporary accounts (revenue, expense, and withdrawals) and update the owner's capital account.
9. Post-closing trial balance[B]	Test clerical accuracy of adjusting and closing steps.

[A] Steps 4, 5, and 6 can be done on a work sheet.
[B] *Reversing entries* are optional and, if prepared, are done between Steps 9 and 1. Reversing entries are covered in Appendix 5A.

Exhibit 5.11

Summary of Steps in the Accounting Cycle

EXTEND YOUR KNOWLEDGE

Read Apply Do Check CHECKPOINT

7. What steps in the accounting cycle are optional?

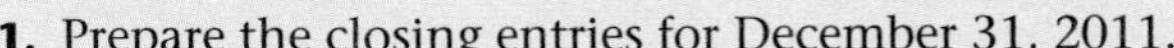

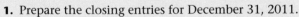

The closing process just demonstrated using account information for Vertically Inclined was a case where revenues were greater than expenses, thus creating net income. The closing process is applied in an identical manner when a net loss occurs, as illustrated in the following Mid-Chapter Demonstration Problem.

mid-chapter demonstration problem

Read Apply Do Check

Using the account information in the following adjusted trial balance for Booster's Towing Service:

1. Prepare the closing entries for December 31, 2011.
2. Post the closing entries.
3. Prepare the post-closing trial balance at December 31, 2011.

Analysis component:

Rather than closing temporary accounts, it would be more efficient to record all transactions affecting temporary accounts (revenues, expenses, and owner withdrawals) directly into capital. Explain why this would be problematic.

Booster's Towing Service
Adjusted Trial Balance
December 31, 2011

	Debit	Credit
Cash	$ 7,000	
Accounts receivable	3,000	
Tow truck	31,000	
Accumulated depreciation, tow truck		$27,000
Salaries payable		700
Terry Booster, capital		17,200
Terry Booster, withdrawals	2,300	
Towing revenue		38,000
Salaries expense	30,000	
Depreciation expense, tow truck	5,000	
Utilities expense	4,600	
Totals	$82,900	$82,900

Planning the solution:

1. Journalize the four closing entries.
2. Post the closing entries.
3. Prepare the post-closing trial balance.
4. Prepare a response to the analysis question.

solution

Part 1

Entry 1:	**Close the revenue account:**		
Dec. 31	Towing Revenue	38,000	
	Income Summary		38,000
	To close the revenue account.		

Entry 2:	**Close the expense accounts:**		
31	Income Summary	39,600	
	Salaries Expense		30,000
	Depreciation Expense, Tow Truck		5,000
	Utilities Expense		4,600
	To close the expense accounts.		

Entry 3:	**Close Income Summary to owner's capital:**		
31	Terry Booster, Capital	1,600	
	Income Summary		1,600
	To close the net loss in the Income Summary account to capital.		

Entry 4:	**Close withdrawals account to owner's capital:**		
31	Terry Booster, Capital	2,300	
	Terry Booster, Withdrawals		2,300
	To close the withdrawals account.		

Part 2

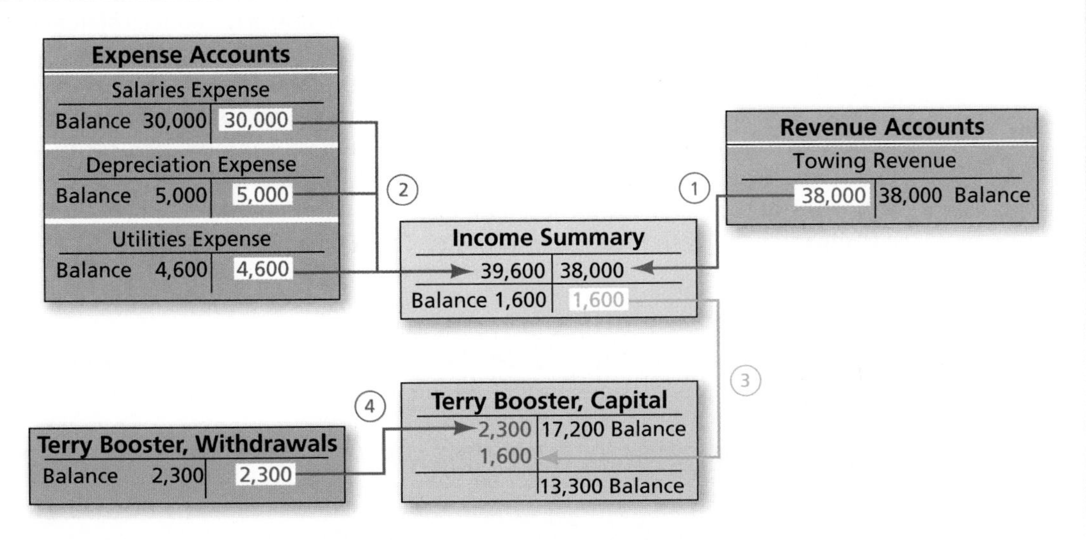

Part 3

Booster's Towing Service Post-Closing Trial Balance December 31, 2011		
	Debit	**Credit**
Cash	$ 7,000	
Accounts receivable	3,000	
Tow truck	31,000	
Accumulated depreciation, tow truck		$27,000
Salaries payable		700
Terry Booster, capital		13,300
Totals	$41,000	$41,000

Analysis component:

It might be more efficient to record all transactions affecting temporary accounts directly in capital, but the result would be that the information needed by decision makers regarding the business's performance would be *hidden* within the capital account balance. The purpose of using temporary accounts is to have revenues and expenses appear on the income statement to detail the business's performance for the period. The resulting net income or loss is then combined with owner withdrawals and owner investments as part of capital to show the business's equity position at a specific point in time.

Classified Balance Sheet

LO6 Explain and prepare a classified balance sheet.

Our discussion to this point has been limited to unclassified financial statements. An **unclassified balance sheet** is one in which items are broadly grouped into assets, liabilities, and equity. One example is Vertically Inclined's balance sheet in Exhibit 5.4. A **classified balance sheet** organizes assets and liabilities into important subgroups to provide users with more useful information for making decisions. One example is information to differentiate liabilities that are due shortly from those not due for several years. Information in this case helps us assess a company's ability to meet liabilities when they come due.

EXTEND YOUR KNOWLEDGE

Classification Scheme

There is no required layout for a classified balance sheet.[5] Yet a classified balance sheet often contains common groupings, including those shown in Exhibit 5.12:

Exhibit 5.12

Sections of a Classified Balance Sheet

Assets	Liabilities and Equity
Current Assets	Current Liabilities
Long-Term Investments*	Long-Term Liabilities
Property, Plant and Equipment*	Equity
Intangible Assets*	
*Noncurrent assets	

One of the more important classifications is the separation between current and noncurrent items for both assets and liabilities. Current items are those that are expected to come due within the longer of one year or the company's normal *operating cycle*. An **operating cycle** is the average length of time between (1) paying employees who perform services and receiving cash from customers (for a service company) or (2) paying for merchandise and receiving cash from customers (for a company that sells goods).[6]

Exhibit 5.13 shows the steps of an operating cycle for both service and merchandising companies.

Exhibit 5.13

Operating Cycles for a Service Company and a Merchandising Company

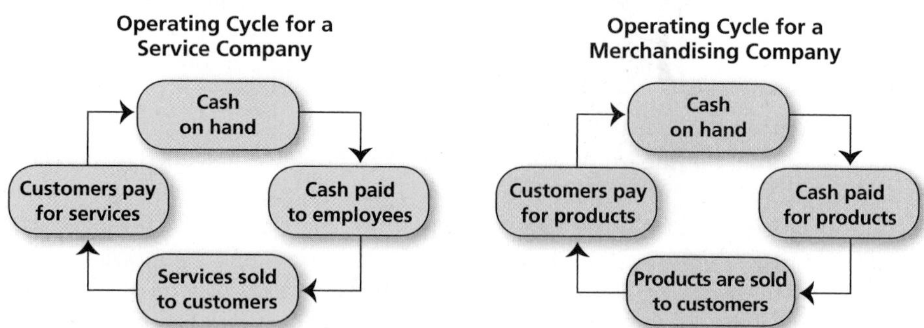

Most operating cycles are less than one year. This means that most companies use a one-year period in deciding which assets and liabilities are current. Yet there are companies with an operating cycle that is longer than one year. One example is a company that routinely allows customers to take more than one year to pay for purchases. Another example is a producer of beverages and other products that require aging for several years. These companies use their operating cycle in deciding which balance sheet items are current.[7]

[5] IFRS 2009, IAS 1, para. 57.
[6] IFRS 2009, IAS 1, para. 68.
[7] In these uncommon situations, companies provide supplemental information about their current assets and liabilities to allow users to compare them with other companies.

A balance sheet lists current assets before long-term assets, and current liabilities before long-term liabilities. This highlights assets that are most easily converted to cash, and liabilities that are shortly coming due. Items in the current group are usually listed in the order of how quickly they could be converted to or paid in cash.

Classification Example

The balance sheet for Music Components is shown in Exhibit 5.14. It shows the most commonly used groupings. Its assets are classified into (1) current assets, (2) long-term investments, (3) property, plant and equipment, and (4) intangible assets. Its liabilities are classified as either current or long-term. Not all companies use the same categories of assets and liabilities on their balance sheets. TransCanada PipeLines Limited's December 31, 2008, balance sheet lists four asset classes: current assets; property, plant and equipment; goodwill; and other assets.

Exhibit 5.14

A Classified Balance Sheet

Music Components
Balance Sheet[8]
January 31, 2011

Assets			
Current assets:			
Cash		$ 6,500	
Short-term investments		2,100	
Accounts receivable		4,400	
Merchandise inventory		29,000	
Prepaid expenses		2,400	
Total current assets			$ 44,400
Long-term investments:			
Notes receivable, due March 31, 2013		$ 18,000	
Land not currently used in operations		48,000	
Total investments			66,000
Property, plant and equipment:			
Land		$ 73,200	
Buildings	$170,000		
Less: Accumulated depreciation	45,000	125,000	
Store equipment	$ 33,200		
Less: Accumulated depreciation	8,000	25,200	
Total property, plant and equipment			223,400
Intangible assets:			
Trademark			10,000
Total assets			$343,800
Liabilities			
Current liabilities:			
Accounts payable	$ 15,300		
Wages payable	3,200		
Notes payable	3,000		
Current portion of long-term liabilities	7,500		
Total current liabilities		$ 29,000	
Long-term liabilities:			
Notes payable (less current portion)		150,000	
Total liabilities			$179,000
Equity			
Donald Bowie, capital			164,800
Total liabilities and equity			$343,800

[8] The classified balance sheet is labelled *"Balance Sheet"*; it is not labelled *"Classified Balance Sheet,"* a common error made by students.

Classification Groups

Current Assets

Current assets are cash and other resources that are expected to be sold, collected, or used within the longer of one year or the company's operating cycle.[9] Examples are cash, short-term investments, accounts receivable, notes receivable, goods for sale to customers (called *merchandise inventory* or *inventory*), and prepaid expenses. As of December 31, 2008, Maple Leaf Foods' current assets were reported as shown in Exhibit 5.15.

Exhibit 5.15

Current Assets Section

Maple Leaf Foods	
Current assets (in thousands)	
Cash	$ 28,222
Accounts receivable	202,285
Inventories	351,064
Prepaid expenses and other assets	52,030
Total current assets	$633,601

A company's prepaid expenses are usually small compared to other assets, and are often combined and shown as a single item. It is likely that prepaid expenses in Exhibits 5.14 and 5.15 include such items as prepaid insurance, prepaid rent, office supplies, and store supplies. Prepaid expenses are usually listed last because they will not be converted to cash.

Long-Term Investments

Long-term investments are held for more than one year or the operating cycle. Notes receivable and investments in shares and bonds are in many cases long-term assets. Note that the *short-term* investments in Exhibit 5.14 are current assets and not shown as long-term investments. We explain the differences between short- and long-term investments later in this book. Long-term investments also often include land that is not being used in operations.

Property, Plant and Equipment (PPE)

Property, plant and equipment (PPE) are tangible assets used for more than one accounting period to produce or sell products and services.[10] Examples of PPE are equipment, vehicles, buildings, and land. Land held for future expansion is generally a long-term investment and not a PPE asset since it is not used to produce or sell products and services. The order of listing PPE assets within this category varies.

Intangible Assets

Intangible assets are long-term resources used to produce or sell products and services; they lack physical form.[11] Examples are patents, trademarks, copyrights, and franchises. Their value comes from the privileges or rights granted to or held by the owner. Barrick Gold Corporation lists intangible assets at December 31, 2008, as shown in Exhibit 5.16.

Exhibit 5.16

Intangible Assets Section

Barrick Gold Corporation (in millions)	
Intangible assets	$75

[9] IFRS 2009, IAS 1, para. 66.
[10] IFRS 2009, IAS 16, para. 6–7.
[11] IFRS 2009, IAS 38, para. 8–12. Intangible assets are subject to *amortization* in a way similar to how plant and equipment are depreciated. *Amortization* is discussed in Chapter 12.

Current Liabilities

Current liabilities are obligations due to be paid or settled within the longer of one year or the operating cycle. They are usually settled by paying out current assets. Current liabilities include accounts payable, notes payable, wages payable, taxes payable, interest payable, and unearned revenues. Any portion of a long-term liability due to be paid within the longer of one year or the operating cycle is a current liability. Exhibit 5.14 shows how the current portion of long-term liabilities is usually reported. Unearned revenues are current liabilities when they will be settled by delivering products or services within the longer of the year or the operating cycle. While practice varies, current liabilities are often reported in the order of those to be settled first.

Long-Term Liabilities

Long-term liabilities are obligations due beyond the longer of one year or the operating cycle. Notes payable, mortgages payable, bonds payable, and lease obligations are often long-term liabilities. If a portion of a long-term liability is to be paid within the period immediately following the balance sheet date, it must be separated and shown as a current liability on the balance sheet. For example, assume the Long-Term Notes Payable account at December 31, 2011, shows a balance of $150,000. We know that $25,000 of this amount will be paid during 2012. On the December 31, 2011, balance sheet, the $25,000 current portion is disclosed as a current liability and the balance of $125,000 ($150,000 − $25,000) is listed as a long-term liability as follows:

EXTEND YOUR KNOWLEDGE

Liabilities	
Current liabilities:	
Current portion of long-term notes payable	$ 25,000
Long-term liabilities:	
Long-term notes payable (less current portion)	125,000

Equity

Equity is the owner's claim on the assets of a company. In a sole proprietorship, it is reported in the equity section with an owner's capital account. The equity sections of a partnership and corporation are discussed in detail in later chapters.

Read Apply Do Check CHECKPOINT

8. Identify which of the following assets are classified as (1) current assets, (2) property, plant and equipment, or (3) intangible assets: (a) land used in operations; (b) office supplies; (c) receivables from customers due in 10 months; (d) insurance protection for the next nine months; (e) trucks used to provide services to customers; (f) trademarks used in advertising the company's services.
9. Name two examples of assets classified as long-term investments on the balance sheet.
10. Explain an operating cycle for a service company, and identify its importance to the classified balance sheet.

Do Quick Study questions: QS 5-10, QS 5-11, QS 5-12

CRITICAL THINKING CHALLENGE

Refer to the Critical Thinking Challenge questions at the beginning of the chapter on page 189. Compare your answers to those suggested on Connect at www.mcgrawhillconnect.ca.

IFRS HIGHLIGHTS 

Regarding classified balance sheets, IAS 1, para. 57, does not prescribe the order or format in which an entity presents items, therefore a great deal of flexibility is permitted. This means that users of financial statements need to be prepared to see a variety of presentation formats.

IFRS do not use the term *capital assets*. IFRS use the terms *property, plant and equipment* and *intangible assets* to describe the tangible and intangible long-lived assets used in the operations of a business to generate revenue. *Goodwill*, although closely related to intangible assets, is required by IFRS to be identified separately. Goodwill is discussed in more detail in Chapter 12.

Summary

LO1 | Describe and prepare a work sheet and explain its usefulness. A work sheet is optional and can be a useful tool when preparing and analyzing financial statements. It is helpful at the end of a period for preparing adjusting entries, an adjusted trial balance, and financial statements. A work sheet often contains five pairs of columns for an unadjusted trial balance, the adjustments, an adjusted trial balance, an income statement, and the balance sheet and statement of changes in equity.

LO2 | Describe the closing process and explain why temporary accounts are closed each period. The closing process is the final step of the accounting cycle; it closes temporary accounts at the end of each accounting period: (1) to update the owner's capital account for revenue, expense, and withdrawals transactions recorded for the period; and (2) to prepare revenue, expense, and withdrawals accounts for the next reporting period by giving them zero balances.

LO3 | Prepare closing entries. Closing entries involve four steps: (1) close credit balances in revenue accounts to Income Summary, (2) close debit balances in expense accounts to Income Summary, (3) close Income Summary to owner's capital, and (4) close the withdrawals account to owner's capital.

LO4 | Explain and prepare a post-closing trial balance. A post-closing trial balance is a list of permanent accounts and their balances after all closing entries are journalized and posted. Permanent accounts are asset, liability, and equity accounts. The purpose of a post-closing trial balance is to verify that (1) total debits equal total credits for permanent accounts and (2) all temporary accounts have zero balances.

LO5 | Complete the steps in the accounting cycle. The accounting cycle consists of nine steps: (1) analyze transactions, (2) journalize, (3) post, (4) prepare unadjusted trial balance, (5) adjust, (6) prepare adjusted trial balance, (7) prepare statements, (8) close, and (9) prepare post-closing trial balance. If a work sheet is prepared, it covers Steps 4 to 6. Reversing entries are an optional step that is done between Steps 9 and 1.

LO6 | Explain and prepare a classified balance sheet. Classified balance sheets usually report four groups of assets: current assets; long-term investments; property, plant and equipment; and intangible assets. Also, they include at least two groups of liabilities: current and long-term. The equity section on the balance sheet for a proprietorship reports the capital account balance.

guidance answers to CHECKPOINT

1. Amounts in the Unadjusted Trial Balance columns are taken from account balances in the ledger.
2. A work sheet offers the advantage of listing on one page all of the necessary information to make adjusting entries.
3. A work sheet can help in: (a) preparing interim financial statements, (b) linking transactions and events to their effects in financial statements, (c) showing adjustments for audit purposes, (d) avoiding errors, and (e) showing effects of proposed or "what-if" transactions.
4. The four major closing entries consist of closing: (1) credit balances in revenue accounts to Income Summary, (2) debit balances in expense accounts to Income Summary, (3) Income Summary to owner's capital, and (4) withdrawals account to owner's capital.
5. Revenue and expense accounts are called temporary because they are opened and closed every reporting period. The Income Summary and owner's withdrawals accounts are also temporary accounts.

6. Permanent accounts are listed on the post-closing trial balance. These accounts are the asset, liability, and equity accounts.
7. Making reversing entries is an optional step in the accounting cycle. Also, a work sheet is an optional tool for completing Steps 4 to 6.
8. Current assets: *b, c, d*. Property, plant and equipment: *a, e*. Intangible assets: *f*.
9. Notes receivable, land not currently used in business operations.
10. An operating cycle for a service company is the average time between (1) paying employees who do the services and (2) receiving cash from customers. Knowing the operating cycle allows current versus long-term assets and liabilities to be disclosed appropriately on the balance sheet.

demonstration problem

The partial adjusted trial balance for Westside Appliance Repair shows the following account balances as at December 31, 2011.

			Debit	Credit
______	101	Cash	$ 15,000	
______	106	Accounts receivable	22,665	
______	124	Spare parts supplies	5,800	
______	128	Prepaid insurance	8,700	
______	141	Notes receivable[A]	36,900	
______	163	Office equipment	12,510	
______	164	Accumulated depreciation, office equipment		$ 2,825
______	173	Building	129,000	
______	174	Accumulated depreciation, building		33,000
______	183	Land	55,000	
______	191	Patent	11,500	
______	193	Franchise	26,000	
______	201	Accounts payable		16,500
______	209	Salaries payable		26,300
______	230	Unearned fees		7,600
______	251	Long-term notes payable[B]		142,000
______	301	Brian Westside, capital[C]		104,000
______	302	Brian Westside, withdrawals	72,000	

[A]The note receivable is due to be collected May 1, 2013.
[B]$22,000 of the December 31, 2011, balance in notes payable will be paid during 2012.
[C]Brian Westside, the owner, invested $5,000 during the accounting period.

Required

Using the information provided above for Westside Appliance Repair,

1. Prepare a classified balance sheet at December 31, 2011. For simplicity, Westside Appliance lists accounts on the balance sheet in account order.
2. Prepare a statement of changes in equity for the year ended December 31, 2011.

Analysis component:

Refer to the chapter opening vignette. Sharon Beasley financed growth by reinvesting profits. Is Brian Westside, the owner of Westside Appliance Repair, following a similar practice? Explain.

Planning the Solution

1. Prepare a classified balance sheet by first listing all of the classification headings under each of assets and liabilities. Then, sort the accounts by listing them under the appropriate heading. *Hint: Place an 'X' in the column provided to the left of the account number column on the adjusted trial balance as you transfer*

account information from the adjusted trial balance to the balance sheet. This process will help you determine whether all of the appropriate accounts have been transferred to the balance sheet.

2. Prepare a statement of changes in equity. *Hint: Revenue and expense information has not been provided from which to calculate net income or net loss. However, you will be able to determine what the net income or loss was by taking into consideration the balance sheet prepared in Step 1 and the other elements of equity that have been provided.*

3. Review the information and prepare an answer to the analysis component question.

solution

1. Prepare a classified balance sheet.

Westside Appliance Repair
Balance Sheet
December 31, 2011

Assets			
Current assets:			
Cash		$ 15,000	
Accounts receivable		22,665	
Spare parts supplies		5,800	
Prepaid insurance		8,700	
Total current assets			$ 52,165
Long-term investments:			
Notes receivable			36,900
Property, plant and equipment:			
Land		$ 55,000	
Building	$129,000		
Less: Accumulated depreciation	33,000	96,000	
Office equipment	$ 12,510		
Less: Accumulated depreciation	2,825	9,685	
Total property, plant and equipment			160,685
Intangible assets:			
Patent		$ 11,500	
Franchise		26,000	
Total intangible assets			37,500
Total assets			$287,250
Liabilities			
Current liabilities:			
Accounts payable	$ 16,500		
Salaries payable	26,300		
Unearned fees	7,600		
Current portion of long-term notes payable	22,000		
Total current liabilities		$ 72,400	
Long-term liabilities:			
Long-term notes payable (less current portion)		120,000	
Total liabilities			$192,400
Equity			
Brian Westside, capital			94,850
Total liabilities and equity			$287,250

2. Prepare a statement of changes in equity.

Westside Appliance Repair
Statement of Changes in Equity
For Year Ended December 31, 2011

Brian Westside, capital December 31, 2010		$ 99,000[1]
Add: Net income	$62,850[3]	
Investment by owner	5,000	67,850[4]
Total		$166,850[2]
Less: Withdrawals by owner		72,000
Brian Westside, capital, December 31, 2011		$ 94,850

[1]Adjusted capital balance on December 31, 2011 = $104,000; $104,000 – $5,000 owner investment during 2011 = $99,000 capital balance on December 31, 2010.
[2]$94,850 post-closing balance per December 31, 2011, balance sheet + $72,000 owner withdrawals = $166,850
[3]$166,850 – $5,000 – $99,000 = $62,850
[4]$62,850 + $5,000 = $67,850

3. Brian Westside is not reinvesting profits. This is evident from the amount of his withdrawals, $72,000, which represents 115% of net income ($72,000/$62,850 × 100% = 115%). Reinvesting profits means that as net income causes equity to increase, assets are retained by the business for the purpose of growth rather than being withdrawn, which depletes assets.

APPENDIX 5A

Reversing Entries

Reversing Entries

LO7 Prepare reversing entries and explain their purpose.

Reversing entries are optional entries used to simplify recordkeeping. They are prepared on the first day of the new accounting period. Reversing entries are prepared for those adjusting entries that created accrued assets and liabilities (such as interest receivable and salaries payable).

Exhibit 5A.1 shows how reversing entries work for Vertically Inclined. The top of the exhibit shows the adjusting entry recorded by Vertically Inclined on January 31, 2011, for earned but unpaid salary. The entry recorded one day's salary to increase January's total salary expense to $1,470. The entry also recognized a liability of $70. The expense is reported on January's income statement and the expense account is closed. As a result, the ledger on February 1, 2011, reflects a $70 liability and a zero balance in the Salaries Expense account. At this point, February 1, the choice is made to use reversing entries or not.

Accounting *Without* Reversing Entries

The path down the left side of Exhibit 5A.1 is described in Chapter 4. That is, when the next payday occurs on February 11, we record payment with a compound entry that debits both the expense and liability accounts. Posting that entry creates a $630 balance in the expense account and reduces the liability account balance to zero because the debt has been settled.

The disadvantage of this approach is the complex entry required on February 11. Paying the accrued liability means that this entry differs from the routine entries made on all other paydays. To construct the proper entry on February 11, we must recall the effect of the adjusting entry. Reversing entries overcome this disadvantage.

Accounting *With* Reversing Entries

The right side of Exhibit 5A.1 shows how a reversing entry on February 1 overcomes the disadvantage of the complex February 11 entry. The reversing entry is the exact opposite of the adjusting entry recorded on January 31. The Salaries Payable liability is debited for $70, meaning that this account now has a zero balance after the entry is posted. Technically, the Salaries Payable account now understates the liability, but this is not a problem since financial statements are not prepared before the liability is settled on February 11. The credit to the Salaries Expense account is unusual because it gives the account an *abnormal credit balance.*

Because of the reversing entry, the February 11 entry to record payment is simple. This entry debits the Salaries Expense account for the full $700 paid. It is the same as all other entries made to record 10 days' salary for the employee.

Exhibit 5A.1

Reversing Entries for Accrued Expenses

Accrue salaries expense on January 31, 2011:

Salaries Expense 70
    Salaries Payable 70

Salaries Expense

Jan. 12	700		
26	700		
31	70		

Salaries Payable

		70	Jan. 31

No reversing entry recorded on February 1, 2011:

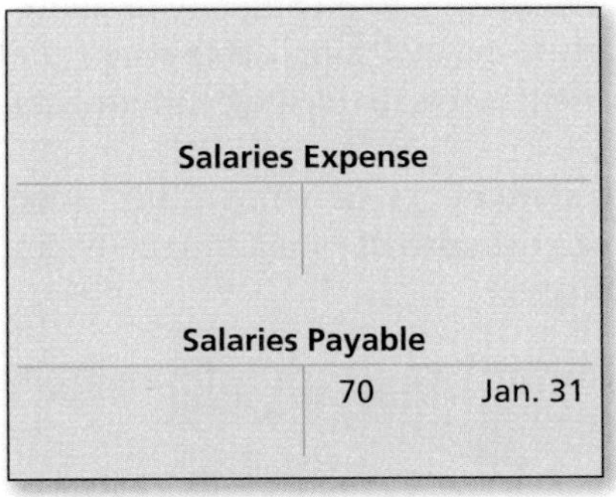

Salaries Expense

Salaries Payable

		70	Jan. 31

Reversing entry recorded on February 1, 2011:

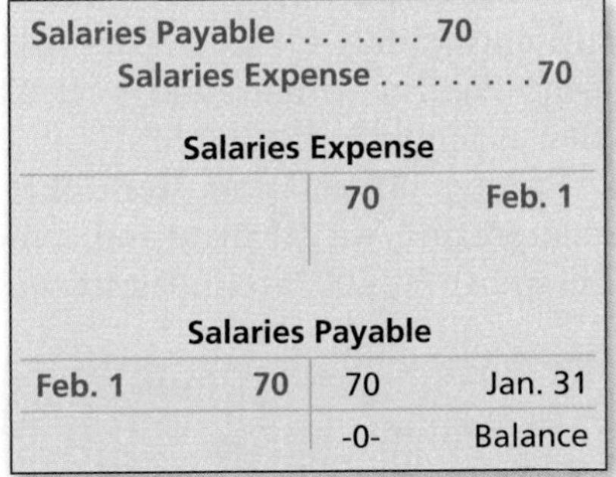

Salaries Payable 70
    Salaries Expense 70

Salaries Expense

		70	Feb. 1

Salaries Payable

Feb. 1	70	70	Jan. 31
		-0-	Balance

Pay the accrued and current salaries on February 11, the first payday in February 2011:

Salaries Expense 630
Salaries Payable 70
    Cash 700

Salaries Expense

Feb. 11	630		

Salaries Payable

Feb. 11	70	70	Jan. 31
		-0-	Balance

Salaries Expense 700
    Cash 700

Salaries Expense

Feb. 11	700	70	Feb. 1
Balance	630		

Salaries Payable

Feb. 11	70	70	Jan. 31
		-0-	Balance

After the payment entry is posted, the expense and liability accounts have exactly the same balances whether reversing occurs or not.

CHECKPOINT

11. How are financial statements affected by a decision to make reversing entries?

Do Quick Study question: *QS 5-13

APPENDIX 5B

Using the Information

Current Ratio

LO8 Calculate the current ratio and describe what it reveals about a company's financial condition.

Exhibit 5B.1

Current Ratio

$$\text{Current ratio} = \frac{\text{Current assets}}{\text{Current liabilities}}$$

Financial statements are important tools for helping decision makers to determine a company's ability to pay its debts in the near future.

The **current ratio** is one important measure used to evaluate a company's ability to pay its short-term obligations. The *ability to pay* day-to-day obligations (current liabilities) with existing *liquid assets* is commonly referred to as **liquidity**. **Liquid assets** are those that can easily be converted to cash or used to pay for services or obligations. Cash is the most liquid asset. The current ratio helps us to make decisions like whether or not to lend money to a company or allow a customer to buy on credit, or how to use cash to pay existing debts when they come due. The current ratio is calculated as current assets divided by current liabilities, as shown in Exhibit 5B.1.

Using information from the financial statements of High Liner Foods Incorporated, we calculate and compare its current ratios at January 3, 2009, and December 29, 2007 (rounded to two decimal places):

January 3, 2009	December 29, 2007
$\frac{\$221,128,000}{\$116,443,000} = 1.90$	$\frac{\$191,675,000}{\$113,388,000} = 1.69$

High Liner's current ratio at January 3, 2009, can also be expressed as 1.90:1, meaning that there are $1.90 of current assets available to cover each $1.00 of current debt. This tells us that High Liner is in a good position to pay its day-to-day obligations and improved from December 29, 2007, to January 3, 2009. Although it varies between industries, generally speaking, an acceptable (favourable) current ratio falls between 1.5 and 2.0. When the current ratio is less than this, a company would likely face challenges in covering current liabilities with current assets. A current ratio greater than 2:1 may signal that an excess of current assets exists. Excessive current assets represent an inefficient use of assets.

12. If a company misclassifies a portion of liabilities as long-term when they are short-term, how does this affect its current ratio?

Do Quick Study question: *QS 5-14

Summary of Appendix 5A and Appendix 5B

LO7 Prepare reversing entries and explain their purpose. Reversing entries are an optional step. They are applied to accrued assets and liabilities. The purpose of reversing entries is to simplify subsequent journal entries. Financial statements are unaffected by the choice to use reversing entries or not.

LO8 Calculate the current ratio and describe what it reveals about a company's financial condition. A company's current ratio is defined as current assets divided by current liabilities. We use it to evaluate a company's ability to pay its current liabilities out of current assets.

guidance answers to CHECKPOINT

11. Financial statements are unchanged by the choice of using reversing entries or not.

12. Since the current ratio is defined as current assets divided by current liabilities, then ignoring a portion of current liabilities (1) decreases the reported amount of current liabilities and (2) increases the current ratio because current assets are now divided by a smaller number.

Glossary

Classified balance sheet A balance sheet that presents the assets and liabilities in relevant subgroups. (p. 206)

Closing entries Journal entries recorded at the end of each accounting period that transfer the end-of-period balances in revenue, expense, and withdrawals accounts to the permanent owner's capital account in order to prepare for the upcoming period and update the owner's capital account for the period just finished. (p. 197)

Closing process A step at the end of the accounting period that prepares accounts for recording the transactions of the next period. (p. 196)

Current assets Cash or other assets that are expected to be sold, collected, or used within the longer of one year or the company's operating cycle. (p. 208)

Current liabilities Obligations due to be paid or settled within the longer of one year or the operating cycle. (p. 209)

Current ratio A ratio that is used to evaluate a company's ability to pay its short-term obligations, calculated by dividing current assets by current liabilities. (p. 216)

Equity The owner's claim on the assets of a company. (p. 209)

Income Summary A temporary account used only in the closing process to which the balances of revenue and expense accounts are transferred; its balance equals net income or net loss and is transferred to the owner's capital account. (p. 197)

Intangible assets Long-lived assets that lack physical form and are used to produce or sell products or services. (p. 208)

Liquid assets Assets that can easily be converted to cash or used to pay for services or obligations; cash is the most liquid asset. (p. 216)

Liquidity The ability to pay day-to-day obligations (current liabilities) with existing liquid assets. (p. 216)

Long-term investments Assets not used in day-to-day operating activities that are held for more than one year or the operating cycle, such as a long-term note receivable. (p. 208)

Long-term liabilities Obligations that are not due to be paid within the longer of one year or the operating cycle. (p. 209)

Nominal accounts See *temporary accounts*. (p. 196)

Operating cycle For a business, the average time between paying cash for employee salaries or merchandise and receiving cash from customers. (p. 206)

Permanent accounts Accounts that are used to report on activities related to one or more future accounting periods; their balances are carried into the next period, and include all balance sheet accounts; permanent account balances are not closed as long as the company continues to own the assets, owe the liabilities, and have equity; also called *real accounts*. (p. 196)

Post-closing trial balance A list of permanent accounts and their balances from the ledger after all closing entries are journalized and posted; a list of balances for all accounts not closed. (p. 201)

PPE See *property, plant and equipment*. (p. 208)

Pro forma statements Statements that show the effects of the proposed transactions as if the transactions had already occurred. (p. 194)

Property, plant and equipment (PPE) Long-lived tangible assets used to produce or sell products and services; abbreviated *PPE*. (p. 208)

Real accounts See *permanent accounts*. (p. 196)

Reversing entries Optional entries recorded at the beginning of a new period that prepare the accounts for simplified journal entries subsequent to accrual adjusting entries. (p. 214)

Temporary accounts Accounts that are used to describe revenues, expenses, and owner's withdrawals for one accounting period; they are closed at the end of the reporting period; also called *nominal accounts*. (p. 196)

Unclassified balance sheet A balance sheet that broadly groups the assets, liabilities, and equity. (p. 206)

Working papers Internal documents that are used to assist the preparers in doing the analyses and organizing the information for reports to be presented to internal and external decision makers. (p. 190)

Work sheet A 10-column spreadsheet used to draft a company's unadjusted trial balance, adjusting entries, adjusted trial balance, and financial statements; an optional step in the accounting process. (p. 190)

Visit **Connect** at **www.mcgrawhillconnect.ca** for additional study tools, practice quizzes, to search an interactive e-book, and much more.

Concept Review Questions

1. What tasks are performed with the work sheet?
2. Why are the debit and credit entries in the Adjustments columns of the work sheet identified with letters?
3. What two purposes are accomplished by recording closing entries?
4. What are the four closing entries?
5. What accounts are affected by closing entries? What accounts are not affected?
6. Describe the similarities and differences between adjusting and closing entries.
7. What is the purpose of the Income Summary account?
8. Explain whether an error has occurred if a post-closing trial balance includes a Depreciation Expense, Building account.
9. Refer to Danier's income statement in Appendix I at the end of the book. What journal entry was recorded as of June 28, 2008, to close the Interest Expense account? DANIER
10. What is a company's operating cycle?
11. How is an unearned revenue classified on the balance sheet?
12. What classes of assets and liabilities are shown on a typical classified balance sheet?
13. What are the characteristics of property, plant and equipment?
14. Refer to the December 31, 2008, balance sheet for WestJet in Appendix I at the end of the book. What amount of WestJet's long-term debt is coming due before December 31, 2009? WESTJET

*15. How do reversing entries simplify a company's bookkeeping efforts?

*16. If a company had accrued unpaid salaries expense of $500 at the end of a fiscal year, what reversing entry could be made? When would it be made?

Quick Study

QS 5-1
Applying a work sheet
LO1

In preparing a work sheet, indicate the financial statement debit column to which a normal balance of each of the following accounts should be extended. Use *IS* for the Income Statement Debit column and *BS* for the Balance Sheet or Statement of Changes in Equity Debit column.

1. Equipment
2. Owner, withdrawals
3. Insurance expense
4. Prepaid insurance
5. Accounts receivable
6. Depreciation expense, equipment

QS 5-2
Completing a work sheet
LO1

Enter the following unadjusted trial balance and adjustment information onto a work sheet. Complete the work sheet.

	Unadjusted Trial Balance		Adjustments	
Account	**Dr.**	**Cr.**	**Dr.**	**Cr.**
Cash	15			
Accounts receivable	22			
Supplies	25			8
Ed Wolt, capital		40		
Ed Wolt, withdrawals	12			
Fees earned		48		
Supplies expense	14		8	
Totals	88	88	8	8

An asterisk (*) identifies assignment material based on Appendix 5A or Appendix 5B.

QS 5-3
Work sheet information
LO1

The following information is from the work sheet for Pursley Company as of December 31, 2011. Using this information, determine the amount that should be reported for Alice Pursley, Capital on the December 31, 2011, balance sheet.

	Income Statement		Balance Sheet and Statement of Changes in Equity	
	Debit	Credit	Debit	Credit
Cash			7,000	
Alice Pursley, capital				50,000
Alice Pursley, withdrawals			32,000	
Totals	125,000	184,000		

QS 5-4
Interpreting a work sheet
LO1

The following information is from the work sheet for Hascal Company as of December 31, 2011. Using this information, determine the amount for Sam Hascal, Capital that should be reported on the December 31, 2011, balance sheet.

	Income Statement		Balance Sheet and Statement of Changes in Equity	
	Debit	Credit	Debit	Credit
Cash			4,500	
Sam Hascal, capital				165,000
Sam Hascal, withdrawals			32,000	
Totals	115,000	74,000		

QS 5-5
Effects of closing entries
LO2,3

Jontil Co. began the current period with a $14,000 balance in the Peter Jontil, Capital account. At the end of the period, the company's adjusted account balances include the following temporary accounts with normal balances:

Service fee earned	$35,000	Interest earned	$3,500
Salaries expense	19,000	Peter Jontil, withdrawals	6,000
Depreciation expense	4,000	Utilities expense	2,300

a. After closing the revenue and expense accounts, what will be the balance of the Income Summary account?
b. After all of the closing entries are journalized and posted, what will be the balance of the Peter Jontil, Capital account?

QS 5-6
Closing entries
LO3

Jaspur Rentals showed the following adjusted account balances on April 30, 2011. Prepare and post the closing entries.

Assets	
250	

Liabilities	
	30

Capital	
	200

Withdrawals	
20	

Revenue	
	100

Expenses	
60	

Income Summary	

QS 5-7
Closing entries
LO3

Warden Repairs showed the following adjusted account balances on October 31, 2011. Prepare and post the closing entries.

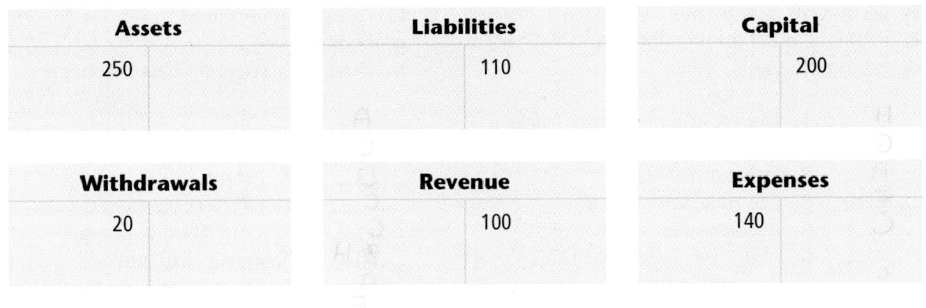

Assets	
250	

Liabilities	
	110

Capital	
	200

Withdrawals	
20	

Revenue	
	100

Expenses	
140	

Income Summary	

QS 5-8
Post-closing trial balance
LO4

SilverStar Automotive showed the following account balances at October 31, 2011, after posting the closing entries. Prepare the post-closing trial balance.

Cash		
Bal.	40	

Accounts Receivable		
Bal.	20	

Unearned Revenue		
	10	Bal.

Capital		
5	40	
	15	
	50	Bal.

Withdrawals		
	5	5
Bal.	-0-	

Revenues		
23	23	
	-0-	Bal.

Expenses		
	8	8
Bal.	-0-	

QS 5-9
Explaining the accounting cycle
LO5

List the following steps of the accounting cycle in the proper order:

a. Preparing the unadjusted trial balance.
b. Preparing the post-closing trial balance.
c. Journalizing and posting adjusting entries.
d. Journalizing and posting closing entries.
e. Preparing the financial statements.
f. Journalizing transactions.
g. Posting the transaction entries.
h. Completing the work sheet.

QS 5-10
Classifying balance sheet items
LO6

The following are categories on a classified balance sheet:

a. Current assets
b. Long-term investments
c. Property, plant and equipment
d. Intangible assets
e. Current liabilities
f. Long-term liabilities

For each of the following items, select the letter that identifies the balance sheet category in which the item should appear.

c **1.** Store equipment
e **2.** Wages payable
a **3.** Cash
f **4.** Notes payable (due in three years)
b **5.** Land not currently used in business operations
a **6.** Accounts receivable
d **7.** Trademarks

QS 5-11
Balance sheet classifications
LO6

In the blank space beside each numbered balance sheet item, enter the letter of its balance sheet classification. If the item should not appear on the balance sheet, enter an *h* in the blank.

a. Current assets
b. Long-term investments
c. Property, plant and equipment
d. Intangible assets
e. Current liabilities
f. Long-term liabilities
g. Equity
h. Does not appear on balance sheet

____ **1.** Depreciation expense, trucks
____ **2.** Lee Hale, capital
____ **3.** Interest receivable
____ **4.** Lee Hale, withdrawals
____ **5.** Automobiles
____ **6.** Notes payable (due in three years)
____ **7.** Accounts payable
____ **8.** Prepaid insurance
____ **9.** Land not currently used in business operations
____ **10.** Unearned services revenue
____ **11.** Accumulated depreciation, trucks
____ **12.** Cash
____ **13.** Building
____ **14.** Patent
____ **15.** Office equipment
____ **16.** Land (used in operations)
____ **17.** Repairs expense
____ **18.** Prepaid property taxes
____ **19.** Notes payable (due in two months)
____ **20.** Notes receivable (due in two years)

QS 5-12
Classifying liabilities
LO6

Use the following March 31, 2011, year-end adjusted balances to prepare Jardine Servicing's liabilities section on its March 31, 2011, classified balance sheet.

Accounts payable	$ 14,000
Unearned fees	26,000
Notes payable, due February 1, 2012	45,000
Mortgage payable*	115,000

*$56,000 of this amount will be paid by March 31, 2012.

***QS 5-13**
Reversing entries
LO7

On December 31, 2011, Ace Management Co. prepared an adjusting entry to accrue $9,800 of earned but unrecorded rent revenue. On January 20, 2012, Ace received rent payments in the amount of $15,500. Assuming Ace uses reversing entries, prepare the 2012 entries pertaining to the rent transactions.

***QS 5-14**
Calculating current ratio
LO8

Calculate Tucker Company's current ratio, given the following information about its assets and liabilities (round to two decimal places) and compare it to the industry average current ratio of 2.2.

Accounts receivable	$15,000	Long-term notes payable*	$20,000
Accounts payable	10,000	Office supplies	1,800
Buildings	42,000	Prepaid insurance	2,500
Cash	6,000	Unearned services revenue	4,000

*Due in three years.

An asterisk (*) identifies assignment material based on Appendix 5A or Appendix 5B.

Exercises

Exercise 5-1
Extending adjusted account balances on a work sheet
LO1

These accounts are from the Adjusted Trial Balance columns in a company's 10-column work sheet. In the blank space beside each account, write the letter of the appropriate financial statement column to which a normal account balance should be extended.

a. Debit column for the income statement.
b. Credit column for the income statement.
c. Debit column for the balance sheet and statement of changes in equity.
d. Credit column for the balance sheet and statement of changes in equity.

_______ **1.** Roberta Jefferson, withdrawals
_______ **2.** Interest earned
_______ **3.** Accumulated depreciation, machinery
_______ **4.** Service fees revenue
_______ **5.** Accounts receivable
_______ **6.** Rent expense
_______ **7.** Depreciation expense, machinery
_______ **8.** Accounts payable
_______ **9.** Cash
_______ **10.** Office supplies
_______ **11.** Roberta Jefferson, capital
_______ **12.** Wages payable
_______ **13.** Machinery
_______ **14.** Insurance expense
_______ **15.** Interest expense
_______ **16.** Interest receivable

Exercise 5-2
Extending accounts in the work sheet
LO1

Check figure:
Net income = $15,150

The Adjusted Trial Balance columns of a 10-column work sheet for Webber Co. follow. Complete the work sheet by extending the account balances into the appropriate financial statement columns and by entering the amount of net income or loss for the reporting period.

		Debit	Credit
101	Cash	$ 3,000	
106	Accounts receivable	13,100	
153	Trucks	41,000	
154	Accumulated depreciation, trucks		$ 16,500
193	Franchise	15,000	
201	Accounts payable		7,000
209	Salaries payable		1,600
233	Unearned fees		1,300
301	Bo Webber, capital		37,750
302	Bo Webber, withdrawals	7,200	
401	Plumbing fees earned		49,000
611	Depreciation expense, trucks	5,500	
622	Salaries expense	18,500	
640	Rent expense	6,000	
677	Miscellaneous expense	3,850	
	Totals	$113,150	$113,150

Exercise 5-3
Preparing a work sheet
LO1

The December 31, 2011, unadjusted trial balance for Musical Sensations after its second year of operations follows:

Account	Debit	Credit
Cash	$ 14,000	
Accounts receivable	26,000	
Office supplies	950	
Musical equipment	212,000	
Accumulated depreciation, musical equipment		$ 16,200
Accounts payable		3,350
Unearned performance revenue		12,400
Jim Daley, capital		272,000
Jim Daley, withdrawals	52,000	
Performance revenue		119,000
Salaries expense	76,000	
Travelling expense	42,000	
Totals	$422,950	$422,950

Check figure:
3. Adjusted trial balance columns = $452,950

Required
1. Enter the unadjusted trial balance onto a work sheet.
2. Using the following additional information, enter the adjustments into the work sheet:
   a. A review of the Unearned Performance Revenue account revealed a balance remaining of $1,800.
   b. Annual depreciation on the musical equipment is $16,200.
   c. Accrued salaries at December 31 totalled $13,800.
   d. It was determined that $430 of the balance in the Office Supplies account had been used.
3. Complete the work sheet.
4. Calculate the balance in the capital account as it would appear on the December 31, 2011, balance sheet.

Exercise 5-4
Work sheet interpretation and closing entries
LO1, 3

Below are excerpts from the work sheets of two businesses as at March 31, 2011. Those rows that calculate totals are at the bottom of the last two sets of columns.

Required
Do the following for each business:
1. Identify the net income or net loss for the year ended March 31, 2011.
2. Prepare the entry to close the Income Summary account to capital.
3. Calculate the post-closing balance in capital at March 31, 2011.

a.

Income Statement		Balance Sheet and Statement of Changes in Equity	
Debit	Credit	Debit	Credit
263,700	300,500	357,300	320,500
36,800			36,800
300,500	300,500	357,300	357,300

*The adjusted balances in withdrawals and capital were $17,000 and $63,000, respectively.

b.

Income Statement		Balance Sheet and Statement of Changes in Equity	
Debit	Credit	Debit	Credit
540,000	480,000	945,000	1,005,000
	60,000	60,000	
540,000	540,000	1,005,000	1,005,000

*The adjusted balances in withdrawals and capital were $0 and $114,000, respectively.

Exercise 5-5
Completing the income statement columns and preparing closing entries
LO1, 3

These partially completed Income Statement columns from a 10-column work sheet are for the Winston Sail'em Boat Rental Company for the year ended December 31, 2011. Use the information to determine the amount that should be entered on the net income line of the work sheet. In addition, prepare closing entries for the company. The owner's name is Carl Winston, and the preclosing balance of the withdrawals account is $18,000.

	Debit	Credit
Rent earned		99,000
Salaries expense	35,300	
Insurance expense	4,400	
Dock rental expense	12,000	
Boat supplies expense	6,220	
Depreciation expense, boats	21,500	
Totals		
Net income		
Totals		

Exercise 5-6
Preparing closing entries and the post-closing trial balance
LO2, 3, 4

Check figure:
Post-closing trial balance columns = $51,600

The adjusted trial balance at April 30, 2011, for Block Plumbing Co. follows. Prepare the four closing entries and the post-closing trial balance.

		Debit	Credit
101	Cash	$ 4,100	
106	Accounts receivable	12,000	
153	Trucks	20,500	
154	Accumulated depreciation, trucks		$ 8,250
193	Franchise	15,000	
201	Accounts payable		7,000
209	Salaries payable		1,600
233	Unearned fees		1,300
301	Frank Block, capital		32,250
302	Frank Block, withdrawals	7,200	
401	Plumbing fees earned		39,500
611	Depreciation expense, trucks	5,500	
622	Salaries expense	15,750	
640	Rent expense	6,000	
677	Advertising expense	3,850	
901	Income summary		
	Totals	$89,900	$89,900

Exercise 5-7
Closing entries
LO2, 3

Following is the adjusted trial balance, with accounts in alphabetical order, for KRG Television as at January 31, 2011:

	Debit	Credit
Accounts receivable	$ 13,000	
Accumulated depreciation, equipment		$ 12,000
Cash	9,000	
Depreciation expense, equipment	2,000	
Equipment	22,000	
Interest revenue		450
Kate Goldberg, capital		19,950
Kate Goldberg, withdrawals	4,000	
Rent expense	7,400	
Salaries expense	56,000	
Subscription revenues		62,000
Unearned subscription revenue		19,000
Totals	$113,400	$113,400

Required
Prepare the closing entries.

Exercise 5-8
Closing entries
LO2, 3

The following adjusted trial balance contains the accounts and balances of Weller Co. as of December 31, 2011, the end of its fiscal year:

No.	Title	Debit	Credit
101	Cash	$ 36,000	
126	Supplies	24,000	
128	Prepaid insurance	4,000	
167	Equipment	46,000	
168	Accumulated depreciation, equipment		$ 13,000
301	Jo Weller, capital		110,400
302	Jo Weller, withdrawals	12,000	
404	Services revenue		72,000
612	Depreciation expense, equipment	4,000	
622	Salaries expense	42,000	
637	Insurance expense	3,000	
640	Rent expense	22,000	
652	Supplies expense	2,400	
	Totals	$195,400	$195,400

Required
Prepare the closing entries for the company.

Exercise 5-9
Closing entries
LO2, 3

Following is the adjusted trial balance, with accounts in alphabetical order, for eSOFT as at September 30, 2011:

	Debit	Credit
Accounts payable		$ 4,500
Accumulated depreciation, office equipment		10,500
Cash	$ 24,500	
Consulting fees earned		68,000
Depreciation expense, office equipment	3,500	
Office equipment	31,500	
Prepaid rent	14,000	
Sandra Sloley, capital		23,000
Sandra Sloley, withdrawals	19,000	
Unearned consulting fees		1,750
Rent expense	1,750	
Wages expense	13,500	
Totals	$107,750	$107,750

Required
Prepare the closing entries.

Exercise 5-10
Preparing and posting closing entries
LO2, 3

Check figure:
Post-closing balance, Marcy Jones, Capital = $41,900

Set up the following T-accounts for Jones's Consulting with the balances provided. Prepare closing entries at December 31, 2011, and post them to the accounts.

Assets			
Dec. 31	80,000		

Liabilities			
		38,100	Dec. 31

Marcy Jones, Capital			
		41,000	Dec. 31

Rent Expense			
Dec. 31	8,600		

Marcy Jones, Withdrawals			
Dec. 31	24,000		

Salaries Expense			
Dec. 31	20,000		

Income Summary			

Insurance Expense			
Dec. 31	3,500		

Services Revenue			
		73,000	Dec. 31

Depreciation Expense			
Dec. 31	16,000		

Exercise 5-11
Post-closing trial balance
LO4

Required
Using your answer from Exercise 5-10, prepare a post-closing trial balance.

Exercise 5-12
Post-closing trial balance
LO2, 3, 4

Bill's Roofing Services showed the following post-closing trial balance after the posting of the closing entries on June 30, 2011:

	Debit	Credit
Cash	$ 42,000	
Accounts receivable	13,000	
Equipment	36,000	
Accumulated depreciation, equipment		$ 12,000
Trucks	138,000	
Accumulated depreciation, trucks		66,000
Accounts payable		5,800
Bill Duggan, capital		216,200
Bill Duggan, withdrawals	72,000	
Interest revenue		1,150
Other expenses	150	
Totals	$301,150	$301,150

Required
1. Identify the error(s) in the post-closing trial balance.
2. What entry is required to correct the error?
3. Calculate the correct balance at June 30, 2011, for Bill Duggan, Capital.

Exercise 5-13
Post-closing trial balance
LO2, 3, 4

The March 31, 2011, adjusted trial balance for Whimsly Refrigeration Repairs is shown below with accounts in alphabetical order.

		Debit	Credit
_____	Accounts payable		$ 11,000
_____	Accounts receivable	$ 59,000	
_____	Accumulated depreciation, equipment		9,000
_____	Accumulated depreciation, truck		21,000
_____	Cash	29,000	
_____	Depreciation expense	3,800	
_____	Equipment	13,000	
_____	Franchise	17,800	
_____	Gas and oil expense	7,500	
_____	Interest expense	4,500	
_____	Interest payable		750
_____	Land not currently used in business operations	52,000	
_____	Long-term notes payable[1]		35,000
_____	Notes payable, due February 1, 2012		7,000
_____	Notes receivable[2]	6,000	
_____	Patent	7,000	
_____	Prepaid rent	14,000	
_____	Rent expense	39,000	
_____	Repair revenue		247,000
_____	Repair supplies	17,000	
_____	Repair supplies expense	14,000	
_____	Sid Whimsly, capital		24,050
_____	Sid Whimsly, withdrawals	49,000	
_____	Truck	26,000	
_____	Unearned repair revenue		3,800
	Totals	$358,600	$358,600

[1]$5,000 of the long-term note payable is due during the year ended March 31, 2012.
[2]$2,000 of the notes receivable will be collected by March 31, 2012.

Check figure:
b. = $153,250

Required

Preparation component:

a. Place an 'X' in the space provided beside each *account balance* that would *not* appear on the post-closing trial balance.
b. Calculate the post-closing balance in the owner's capital.

Analysis component:

Explain why the account balances identified in part (a) would not appear on the post-closing trial balance.

Exercise 5-14
Classified balance sheet
LO6

Check figure:
i. = $210,800

Using the information in Exercise 5-13, calculate each of the following:

a. Current assets
b. Property, plant and equipment
c. Intangible assets
d. Long-term investments
e. Total assets
f. Current liabilities
g. Long-term liabilities
h. Total liabilities
i. Total liabilities and equity

Exercise 5-15
Classified balance sheet
LO6

A partial alphabetized list of adjusted account balances for Dover Pacific Tours as at November 30, 2011, is shown on the next page (all accounts have normal balances). Pat Dover, the owner, uses the following account classification system:

101–149	Current assets	190–199	Long-term investments
150–169	Property, plant and equipment	201–249	Current liabilities
170–189	Intangible assets	250–299	Long-term liabilities

Acct. No.	Account Title	Adjusted Account Balance
201	Accounts payable	$11,000
106	Accounts receivable	13,000
155	Accumulated depreciation, office furniture	3,600
153	Accumulated depreciation, vehicles	17,000
101	Cash	5,000
172	Copyright	1,000
240	Notes payable	4,000
270	Notes payable[1]	20,500
195	Notes receivable[2]	20,500
154	Office furniture	6,500
110	Prepaid insurance	700
112	Prepaid rent	9,000
205	Salaries payable	900
118	Supplies	2,250
206	Unearned touring revenue	23,000
152	Vehicles	64,000

[1]$10,000 of this note payable is to be paid by November 30, 2012.
[2]$7,500 of the notes receivable is to be collected by November 30, 2012.

Required
Prepare a classified balance sheet.

Check figure:
Total assets = $101,350

Exercise 5-16
Preparing a classified balance sheet
LO6

Check figure:
Total assets = $235,500

Use the following adjusted trial balance of Hanson Trucking Company to prepare a classified balance sheet as of December 31, 2011.

Account Title	Debit	Credit
Cash	$ 7,000	
Accounts receivable	16,500	
Office supplies	2,000	
Trucks	170,000	
Accumulated depreciation, trucks		$ 35,000
Land	75,000	
Accounts payable		11,000
Interest payable		3,000
Long-term notes payable (due in 4 years)		52,000
Stanley Hanson, capital		161,000
Stanley Hanson, withdrawals	19,000	
Trucking fees earned		128,000
Depreciation expense, trucks	22,500	
Salaries expense	60,000	
Office supplies expense	7,000	
Repairs expense, trucks	11,000	
Total	$390,000	$390,000

Exercise 5-17

Comprehensive accounting cycle

LO2, 3, 4, 5, 6

After five years of operations, Svenson's Tutoring Clinic showed the following post-closing balances at December 31, 2011.

Cash		Accounts Receivable		Prepaid Rent		Office Equipment	
2,000		5,000		3,000		20,000	

Accumulated Depreciation, Office Equipment		Unearned Fees		Leda Svenson, Capital		Leda Svenson, Withdrawals	
	10,000		2,900		17,100	-0-	

Tutoring Fees Earned		Rent Expense		Depreciation Expense		Advertising Expense	
	-0-	-0-		-0-		-0-	

Check figures:
c. Total debits = $38,000
e. Total debits = $40,000
f. Net income = $3,400;
Total assets = $18,000
h. Total debits = $30,000

Required

Analysis component:

a. Explain why Leda Svenson, Withdrawals, Tutoring Fees Earned, Rent Expense, Depreciation Expense, and Advertising Expense have zero balances.

Preparation component:

b. Journalize and post the following transactions that occurred during 2012.
Jan 15 Provided $8,000 of tutoring services on account.
Feb. 20 Paid $2,000 for advertising that appeared in today's newspaper.
Jul. 7 Collected $9,000 from credit customers.
Dec. 10 The owner withdrew $3,000 cash for personal use.

c. Prepare an unadjusted trial balance as at December 31, 2012.

d. Journalize and post the adjusting entries on December 31, 2012, based on the following additional information:
– Annual depreciation on the office equipment is $2,000.
– $2,400 of the balance in unearned fees has been earned.
– The entire balance in prepaid rent has expired.

e. Prepare an adjusted trial balance at December 31, 2012.

f. Prepare an income statement, statement of changes in equity, and classified balance sheet.

g. Journalize and post the closing entries.

h. Prepare a post-closing trial balance.

*Exercise 5-18

Reversing entries

LO7

Breaker Corporation records prepaid assets and unearned revenues in balance sheet accounts. The following information was used to prepare adjusting entries for Breaker Corporation as of August 31, 2011, the end of the company's fiscal year:

a. The company has earned $5,000 of unrecorded service fees.

b. The expired portion of prepaid insurance is $2,700.

c. The earned portion of the Unearned Fees account balance is $1,900.

d. Depreciation expense for the office equipment is $2,300.

e. Employees have earned but have not been paid salaries of $2,400.

Required

Prepare the appropriate reversing entries that would simplify the bookkeeping effort for recording subsequent cash transactions related to these adjustments.

An asterisk (*) identifies assignment material based on Appendix 5A or Appendix 5B.

***Exercise 5-19**
Reversing entries
LO7

The following conditions existed for Maxit Co. on October 31, 2011, the end of its fiscal year:

a. Maxit rents a building for $3,200 per month. By a prearrangement, the company delayed paying October's rent until November 5. On this date, the company paid the rent for both October and November.

b. Maxit rents space in a building it owns to a tenant for $750 per month. By prearrangement, the tenant delayed paying the October rent until November 8. On this date, the tenant paid the rent for both October and November.

Required

1. Prepare the adjusting entries that Maxit should record for these situations as of October 31.
2. Assuming that Maxit does not use reversing entries, prepare journal entries to record Maxit's payment of rent on November 5 and the collection of rent on November 8 from Maxit's tenant.
3. Assuming that Maxit does use reversing entries, prepare those entries and the journal entries to record Maxit's payment of rent on November 5 and the collection of rent on November 8 from Maxit's tenant.

***Exercise 5-20**
Calculating the current ratio
LO8

Calculate (to two decimal places) the current ratio in each of the following cases and indicate whether it is *Favourable* (F) or *Unfavourable* (U) (assuming that the current ratio for the industry is an average of 1.1):

	Case 1	Case 2	Case 3	Case 4
Current Assets	$78,000	$104,000	$44,000	$84,500
Current Liabilities	31,000	75,000	48,000	80,600

Problems

Problem 5-1A
Completing a work sheet
LO1

The March 31, 2011, unadjusted trial balance for Nanimahoo Rentals after its first year of operations is shown below:

		Unadjusted Trial Balance	
No.	**Account**	**Debit**	**Credit**
101	Cash	$ 17,000	
110	Rent receivable	60,000	
124	Office supplies	6,800	
141	Notes receivable, due 2014	143,000	
161	Furniture	46,000	
173	Building	625,000	
183	Land	110,000	
191	Patent	3,000	
201	Accounts payable		$ 5,800
252	Long-term note payable		375,000
301	Joan Nanimahoo, capital		499,525
302	Joan Nanimahoo, withdrawals	28,000	
406	Rent earned		406,200
620	Office salaries expense	124,000	
633	Interest expense	20,625	
655	Advertising expense	28,000	
673	Janitorial expense	41,000	
690	Utilities expense	34,100	
	Totals	$1,286,525	$1,286,525

An asterisk (*) identifies assignment material based on Appendix 5A or Appendix 5B.

Required

1. Enter the unadjusted trial balance onto a work sheet.
2. Using the following additional information, enter the adjustments into the work sheet (the Chart of Accounts at the back of the textbook may be useful when additional accounts are required):
   a. It was determined that the balance in the Rent Receivable account at March 31 should be $68,000.
   b. A count of the office supplies showed $6,100 of the balance had been used.
   c. Annual depreciation on the building is $25,000 and $3,500 on the furniture.
   d. The five part-time office staff members each get paid $1,050 bi-weekly. The last bi-weekly pay period ended Friday, March 24. At March 31, five days' salary had accrued.
   e. A review of the balance in Advertising Expense showed that $400 was for advertisements to appear in the April issue of *Canadian Business* magazine.
   f. Accrued utilities at March 31 totalled $2,620.
   g. March interest of $1,875 on the long-term note payable is unrecorded and unpaid as of March 31.
3. Complete the work sheet.

Check figure:
3. Adjusted trial balance columns = $1,330,145

Problem 5-2A
Completing a work sheet
LO1

eXcel

The June 30, 2011, unadjusted trial balance for Trenton Consulting after its first year of operations follows:

Account	Debit	Credit
Cash	3,440	
Accounts receivable	2,990	
Prepaid rent	6,600	
Equipment	6,400	
Accounts payable		1,440
Toni Trenton, capital		26,650
Toni Trenton, withdrawals	800	
Consulting fees earned		30,200
Wages expense	28,120	
Insurance expense	1,620	
Rent expense	8,320	
Totals	58,290	58,290

Check figure:
3. Adjusted trial balance columns = $65,150

Required

1. Enter the unadjusted trial balance onto a work sheet.
2. Using the following additional information, enter the adjustments onto the work sheet:
   a. Annual depreciation on the equipment is $2,540.
   b. The balance in the Prepaid Rent account is for six months of rent commencing March 1, 2011.
   c. Unpaid and unrecorded wages at June 30 totalled $2,500.
   d. Accrued revenues at June 30 totalled $1,820.
3. Complete the work sheet.
4. Calculate the balance in the capital account as it would appear on the June 30, 2011, balance sheet.

Analysis component:
What effect does a net loss have on the accounting equation?

Problem 5-3A
Work sheet, journal entries, and financial statements
LO1, 6

This unadjusted trial balance is for Challenger Construction at the end of its fiscal year, September 30, 2011. The beginning balance of the owner's capital account was $25,320 and the owner invested another $30,000 cash in the company during the year.

No.	Account	Debit	Credit
101	Cash	$ 36,000	
126	Supplies	18,800	
128	Prepaid insurance	12,400	
149	Land not currently used in operations	50,000	
167	Equipment	106,000	
168	Accumulated depreciation, equipment		$ 40,500
191	Copyright	6,000	
201	Accounts payable		9,600
203	Interest payable		-0-
210	Wages payable		-0-
251	Long-term notes payable		50,000
301	Chris Challenger, capital		55,320
302	Chris Challenger, withdrawals	72,000	
401	Construction fees earned		280,000
612	Depreciation expense, equipment	-0-	
623	Wages expense	82,000	
633	Interest expense	3,000	
637	Insurance expense	-0-	
640	Rent expense	26,400	
652	Supplies expense	-0-	
683	Business taxes expense	10,000	
684	Repairs expense	5,020	
690	Utilities expense	7,800	
	Totals	$435,420	$435,420

Required

1. Prepare a 10-column work sheet for fiscal 2011, starting with the unadjusted trial balance and including these additional facts:
   a. The inventory of supplies at the end of the year had a cost of $5,000.
   b. The cost of expired insurance for the year is $8,000.
   c. Annual depreciation of the equipment is $18,000.
   d. The September utilities expense was not included in the trial balance because the bill arrived after it was prepared. Its $800 amount needs to be recorded.
   e. The company's employees have earned $3,000 of accrued wages.
   f. The interest expense of $500 for September has not yet been paid or recorded.
2. Use the work sheet to prepare the adjusting and closing entries.
3. Prepare an income statement, a statement of changes in equity, and a classified balance sheet. $16,000 of the long-term note payable is to be paid by September 30, 2012.

Check figures:
1. Adjusted trial balance columns = $457,720
3. Net income = $101,680; Total assets = $148,900

Analysis component:

Analyze the following potential errors and describe how each would affect the 10-column work sheet. Explain whether the error is likely to be discovered in completing the work sheet and, if not, the effect of the error on the financial statements.

a. The adjustment to record used supplies was credited to Supplies for $5,000 and debited the same amount to Supplies Expense.
b. When completing the adjusted trial balance in the work sheet, the $36,000 cash balance was incorrectly entered in the Credit column.

Problem 5-4A
Closing entries
LO2, 3, 4

MY Autobody's adjusted trial balance on December 31, 2011, appears in the work sheet as follows:

No.	Account	Debit	Credit
101	Cash	$ 26,000	
124	Shop supplies	2,400	
128	Prepaid insurance	3,900	
167	Equipment	96,000	
168	Accumulated depreciation, equipment		$ 8,000
201	Accounts payable		24,000
210	Wages payable		1,000
301	Mike Yang, capital		136,400
302	Mike Yang, withdrawals	30,000	
401	Repair fees earned		155,500
612	Depreciation expense, equipment	8,000	
623	Wages expense	107,000	
637	Insurance expense	1,400	
640	Rent expense	41,600	
650	Office supplies expense	5,200	
690	Utilities expense	3,400	
	Totals	$324,900	$324,900

Check figure:
2. Post-closing trial balance = $128,300

Required
1. Prepare closing entries.
2. Prepare the post-closing trial balance at December 31, 2011.

Problem 5-5A
Financial statements
LO6

Check figures:
Net loss = $11,100;
Total assets = $120,300

Using the information from Problem 5-4A, prepare an income statement and a statement of changes in equity for the year ended December 31, 2011, and a classified balance sheet at December 31, 2011. There were no investments by the owner during the year.

Analysis component:
MY Autobody experienced a loss during 2011. If you were one of the business's creditors, should this loss cause you to be concerned about being paid in 2012?

Problem 5-6A
Closing entries
LO2, 3

The adjusted trial balance for Lloyd Construction as of December 31, 2011, follows:

No.	Account	Debit	Credit
101	Cash	$ 8,000	
104	Short-term investments	44,000	
126	Supplies	14,200	
149	Notes receivable	42,000	
167	Equipment	78,000	
168	Accumulated depreciation, equipment		$ 40,000
173	Building	260,000	
174	Accumulated depreciation, building		150,000
183	Land	90,000	
193	Franchise	28,000	
201	Accounts payable		31,000
203	Interest payable		3,000
233	Unearned professional fees		13,000
251	Long-term notes payable		132,000
301	Sig Lloyd, capital		143,800
302	Sig Lloyd, withdrawals	24,000	
401	Professional fees earned		192,000
406	Rent earned		26,000
606	Depreciation expense, building	20,000	
612	Depreciation expense, equipment	8,000	
623	Wages expense	64,000	
633	Interest expense	8,200	
637	Insurance expense	18,000	
652	Supplies expense	12,800	
688	Telephone expense	4,400	
690	Utilities expense	7,200	
	Totals	$730,800	$730,800

An analysis of other information reveals that Lloyd Construction is required to make a $50,000 payment on the long-term notes payable during 2012. The notes receivable are due May 1, 2013. Also, Sig Lloyd invested $100,000 cash early in 2011.

Required
Prepare the closing entries made at the end of the year.

Problem 5-7A
Financial statements
LO6

Using the adjusted trial balance in Problem 5-6A, prepare the income statement and statement of changes in equity for the year ended December 31, 2011, and the classified balance sheet at December 31, 2011.

Check figures:
Net income = $75,400;
Total assets = $374,200

Analysis component:
Why must liabilities be separated on the balance sheet between *current* and *long-term*? What effect would it have had on Lloyd's balance sheet if the long-term note was not separated?

Problem 5-8A
Closing entries
LO2, 3

The March 31, 2011, adjusted trial balance for Brenner Climbing Adventures has been alphabetized as follows:

No.	Account	Debit	Credit
201	Accounts payable		$ 1,200
103	Accounts receivable	$ 3,350	
168	Accumulated depreciation, equipment		7,000
300	Becky Brenner, capital		34,700
301	Becky Brenner, withdrawals	23,500	
101	Cash	7,500	
194	Copyright	6,000	
606	Depreciation expense, equipment	1,050	
167	Equipment	20,500	
633	Insurance expense	1,950	
623	Interest expense	330	
141	Notes receivable, due January 1, 2014	10,000	
233	Long-term notes payable		5,500
610	Rent expense	7,500	
402	Revenues		61,350
126	Supplies	270	
637	Supplies expense	1,800	
652	Telephone expense	2,100	
203	Unearned revenues		11,000
688	Utilities expense	900	
612	Wages expense	34,000	
	Totals	$120,750	$120,750

Required
Journalize the closing entries.

Problem 5-9A
Financial statements
LO6

Check figures:
Net income = $11,720;
Total assets = $40,620

Using the information in Problem 5-8A, prepare an income statement and a statement of changes in equity for the year ended March 31, 2011, and a classified balance sheet at March 31, 2011. The owner made an additional investment during the year of $2,500. A $3,000 payment on the long-term notes payable will be made during the year ended March 31, 2012.

Analysis component:
Why might Brenner Climbing Adventures be tempted to report the notes receivable as a current asset on the March 31, 2011, balance sheet?

Problem 5-10A
Analyzing closing entries
LO2, 3, 4

The following closing entries were prepared for Apex Architectural Designs regarding its year just ended June 30, 2011:

2011				
June	30	Design Fees Earned	124,000	
		Income Summary		124,000
		To close the revenue account.		
	30	Income Summary	73,020	
		Depreciation Expense, Office Equipment		1,750
		Depreciation Expense, Office Furniture		950
		Insurance Expense		600
		Interest Expense		720
		Supplies Expense		2,150
		Telephone Expense		1,600
		Utilities Expense		750
		Salaries Expense		64,500
		To close expense accounts.		

June	30	Income Summary	50,980	
		Noel Apex, Capital		50,980
		To close Income Summary to capital.		
	30	Noel Apex, Capital	35,000	
		Noel Apex, Withdrawals		35,000
		To close withdrawals to capital.		

Required

1. Prepare an income statement based on the information provided.
2. Calculate the post-closing balance in the capital account at June 30, 2011, given that the adjusted balance on June 30, 2010, was $86,000.

Check figure:
1. Net income = $50,980

Problem 5-11A
Preparing financial statements
LO6

The adjusted trial balance for Impressions Dance School has been provided for the year ended September 30, 2011. The new bookkeeper alphabetized the accounts.

Account	Debit	Credit
Accounts payable		$ 27,320
Accounts receivable	$ 6,580	
Accumulated depreciation, automobiles		39,360
Accumulated depreciation, building		144,000
Alisha Bjorn, capital		168,960
Alisha Bjorn, withdrawals	10,000	
Automobiles	65,600	
Building	240,000	
Cash	10,120	
Copyright	4,360	
Depreciation expense, automobiles	6,560	
Depreciation expense, building	29,600	
Fees earned		154,680
Gas, oil, and repairs expense	29,600	
Land	28,000	
Land for future expansion	50,000	
Notes payable*		90,000
Patents	8,600	
Rent earned		18,000
Salaries expense	174,000	
Store supplies	2,800	
Unearned fees		23,500
Totals	$665,820	$665,820

*The notes payable plus interest are due in 18 months.

Required

Prepare an income statement and a statement of changes in equity for the year ended September 30, 2011, plus a September 30, 2011, classified balance sheet. The owner made no investments during the year.

Check figures:
Net loss = $67,080;
Total assets = $232,700

Analysis component:

Alisha wants to buy a new car for the business. As her bank manager, what do you advise?

Problem 5-12A ✓ H.W

Preparing a classified balance sheet
LO6

An alphabetical list of the adjusted trial balance accounts for North Country Rentals after its first year of operations ending March 31, 2011, is shown below:

Account	Adjusted Account Balance*
Accounts payable	$ 8,420
Accumulated depreciation, building	25,000
Accumulated depreciation, furniture	3,500
Advertising expense	27,600
Building	625,000
Cash	17,000
Depreciation expense, building	25,000
Depreciation expense, furniture	3,500
Furniture	46,000
Interest expense	22,500
Interest payable	1,875
Janitorial expense	41,000
Land	110,000
Long-term notes payable	375,000
Notes receivable, due 2014	143,000
Office salaries expense	126,625
Office supplies	700
Office supplies expense	6,100
Patent	3,000
Prepaid advertising	400
Rent earned	414,200
Rent receivable	68,000
Salaries payable	2,625
Utilities expense	36,720
Wyett North, capital	499,525
Wyett North, withdrawals	28,000

*Assume all accounts have a normal balance.

Check figure:
2. Total assets = $984,600

Required

1. Calculate the capital balance as it would appear on the March 31, 2011, balance sheet.
2. Prepare a classified balance sheet. Assume that $75,000 of the Long-Term Notes Payable will be paid during the year ended March 31, 2012. Also, $40,000 of the notes receivable will be collected by March 31, 2012.

Analysis component:
North Country shows an adjusted balance in the *Long-Term Notes Payable* account of $375,000 at March 31, 2011. Review the balance sheet just prepared and make a reasonable assumption about what the $375,000 was most logically used for by North Country. Explain whether or not this is generally considered a good use of borrowed funds and why.

Problem 5-13A

Performing the steps in the accounting cycle
LO2, 3, 4, 5, 6

On June 1, 2011, Sam Near created a new travel agency called Tours-For-Less. These activities occurred during the company's first month:

June	1	Near created the new company by investing $40,000 cash, $5,000 of furniture, and computer equipment worth $60,000.
	2	The company rented furnished office space by paying $3,200 rent for the first month.
	3	The company purchased $2,400 of office supplies for cash.
	10	The company paid $7,200 for the premium on a one-year insurance policy.
	14	The owner's assistant was paid $3,600 for two weeks' salary.
	24	The company collected $13,600 of commissions from airlines on tickets obtained for customers.
	28	The assistant was paid another $3,600 for two weeks' salary.
	29	The company paid the month's $3,500 phone bill.
	30	The company repaired its computer for $700 on account.
	30	The owner withdrew $2,850 cash from the business for personal use.

The company's chart of accounts included these accounts:

101	Cash	302	Sam Near, Withdrawals
106	Accounts Receivable	405	Commissions Earned
124	Office Supplies	610	Depreciation Expense, Furniture
128	Prepaid Insurance	612	Depreciation Expense, Computer Equipment
160	Furniture		
161	Accumulated Depreciation, Furniture	622	Salaries Expense
167	Computer Equipment	637	Insurance Expense
168	Accumulated Depreciation, Computer Equipment	640	Rent Expense
		650	Office Supplies Expense
201	Accounts Payable	684	Repairs Expense
209	Salaries Payable	688	Telephone Expense
301	Sam Near, Capital	901	Income Summary

Required

1. Set up each of the listed accounts. *Note: Your instructor will tell you to use either the balance column format or T-accounts.*

2. Prepare journal entries to record the transactions for June and post them to the accounts.

3. Use the following information to journalize and post the adjustments for the month:

a. Two-thirds of one month's insurance coverage was consumed.

b. There were $1,600 of office supplies on hand at the end of the month.

c. Depreciation on the computer equipment was estimated to be $1,650 and $400 on the furniture.

d. The assistant had earned $320 of unpaid and unrecorded salary.

e. The company had earned $3,500 of commissions that had not yet been billed.

4. Prepare an income statement, a statement of changes in equity, and a classified balance sheet.

5. Prepare journal entries to close the temporary accounts and post them to the accounts.

6. Prepare a post-closing trial balance.

Check figures:
4. Net loss = $1,070;
Total assets = $102,100;
6. Post-closing trial balance = $104,150

***Problem 5-14A**
Adjusting, reversing, and subsequent cash entries
LO7

The unadjusted trial balance for Lewis Fitness Centre as of December 31, 2011, follows:

Account	Debit	Credit
Cash	$ 22,000	
Accounts receivable	-0-	
Supplies	9,000	
Equipment	300,000	
Accumulated depreciation, equipment		$ 30,000
Interest payable		-0-
Salaries payable		-0-
Unearned membership fees		48,000
Notes payable		100,000
Bev Lewis, capital		116,500
Bev Lewis, withdrawals	60,000	
Membership fees earned		180,000
Depreciation expense, equipment	-0-	
Salaries expense	76,000	
Interest expense	7,500	
Supplies expense	-0-	
Totals	$474,500	$474,500

An asterisk (*) identifies assignment material based on Appendix 5A or Appendix 5B.

Information necessary to prepare adjusting entries is as follows:

- **a.** As of December 31, employees have earned $1,600 of unpaid and unrecorded wages. The next payday is January 4, and the total wages to be paid will be $2,400.
- **b.** The cost of supplies on hand at December 31 is $3,600.
- **c.** The note payable requires an interest payment to be made every three months. The amount of unrecorded accrued interest at December 31 is $2,500, and the next payment is due on January 15. This payment will be $3,000.
- **d.** An analysis of the unearned membership fees shows that $32,000 remains unearned at December 31.
- **e.** In addition to the membership fees included in the revenue account, the company has earned another $24,000 in fees that will be collected on January 21. The company is also expected to collect $14,000 on the same day for new fees earned during January.
- **f.** Depreciation expense for the year is $30,000.

Required

1. Prepare adjusting journal entries.
2. Prepare journal entries to reverse the effects of the adjusting entries that involve accruals.
3. Prepare journal entries to record the cash payments and collections that are described for January.

Alternate Problems

Problem 5-1B

Completing a work sheet

LO1

eXcel

The July 31, 2011, unadjusted trial balance for Daimler Tours after its first month of operations is shown below:

No.	Account	Debit	Credit
101	Cash	$ 8,900	
106	Accounts receivable	21,250	
111	Notes receivable, due February 2012	14,000	
128	Prepaid insurance	10,500	
161	Furniture	6,750	
201	Accounts payable		$ 6,925
230	Unearned tour revenue		14,000
301	Jan Rider, capital		60,975
302	Jan Rider, withdrawals	-0-	
403	Tour revenue		15,500
623	Wages expense	36,000	
	Totals	$97,400	$97,400

Check figure:
3. Adjusted trial balance columns = $110,504

Required

1. Enter the unadjusted trial balance onto a work sheet.
2. Using the following additional information, enter the adjustments into the work sheet (the Chart of Accounts at the back of the textbook may be useful when additional accounts are required):
   - **a.** Interest of $200 had accrued on the note receivable by month-end.
   - **b.** The July utility bill for $325 was received in the mail on July 31. It is unpaid and unrecorded.
   - **c.** Depreciation on the furniture for the month of July is $175.
   - **d.** The balance in Prepaid Insurance is from a six-month policy that went into effect on July 1, 2011.
   - **e.** The company has four employees, each of whom gets paid $315 every Friday for a five-day workweek. July 31 falls on a Tuesday, therefore two days of accrued wages need to be recorded.
   - **f.** At July 31, it was determined that $4,900 of the balance in Unearned Tour Revenue was not yet earned.
   - **g.** Daimler Tours signed a contract with a school effective July 9 for four weeks. From Monday through Friday each week, Daimler Tours will be taking a total of 40 children camping. The charge is $17.50 per day per child. The school will pay Daimler Tours at the end of the four-week period, on Friday, August 3. No entries have been recorded to date regarding this contract.
3. Complete the work sheet.

Problem 5-2B

Completing a work sheet—net income

LO1

The December 31, 2011, unadjusted trial balance for Tucker Photographers after the first month of operations is shown below:

Account	Debit	Credit
Cash	$28,000	
Accounts receivable	6,200	
Prepaid equipment rental	3,860	
Automobile	52,000	
Accumulated depreciation, automobile		$ -0-
Accounts payable		1,920
Unearned fees		5,740
Jim Tucker, capital		78,800
Jim Tucker, withdrawals	1,400	
Fees earned		8,400
Depreciation expense, automobile	-0-	
Equipment rental expense	3,400	
Totals	$94,860	$94,860

Required

1. Enter the unadjusted trial balance onto a work sheet.
2. Using the following additional information, enter the adjustments into the work sheet.
   a. It was determined that $2,480 of the balance in the Prepaid Equipment Rental account had been used during December.
   b. Depreciation on the automobile for the month of December was $550.
   c. Accrued utilities expense of $1,960 was unrecorded at December 31.
   d. $500 of the Unearned Fees account had been earned by December 31.
3. Complete the work sheet.
4. Calculate the balance in the capital account as it would appear on the December 31, 2011, balance sheet.

Check figure:
3. Adjusted trial balance columns = $97,370

Analysis component:
What effect does a net income have on the balance sheet?

Problem 5-3B

Work sheet, journal entries, financial statements

LO1, 6

Presented below is the unadjusted trial balance of Webster Demolition Company as of June 30, 2011, the end of its fiscal year. The beginning balance of the owner's capital account was $18,450 and the owner invested another $15,000 cash in the company during the year.

		Debit	Credit
101	Cash	$ 4,500	
126	Supplies	9,000	
128	Prepaid insurance	7,300	
167	Equipment	70,000	
168	Accumulated depreciation, equipment		$ 5,000
201	Accounts payable		8,000
203	Interest payable		-0-
210	Wages payable		-0-
251	Long-term notes payable		45,000
301	Rusty Webster, capital		33,450
302	Rusty Webster, withdrawals	2,000	
401	Demolition fees earned		68,500
612	Depreciation expense, equipment	-0-	
623	Wages expense	25,700	
633	Interest expense	1,100	
637	Insurance expense	-0-	
640	Rent expense	24,400	
652	Supplies expense	-0-	
683	Business tax expense	4,200	
684	Repairs expense	3,350	
690	Utilities expense	8,400	
	Totals	$159,950	$159,950

Check figures:
1. Adjusted trial balance columns = $170,500
3. Net loss = $19,900; Total assets = $66,100

Required

Preparation component:

1. Prepare a 10-column work sheet for 2011, starting with the unadjusted trial balance and including these additional facts:
   a. The inventory of supplies at the end of the year had a cost of $4,050.
   b. The cost of expired insurance for the year is $5,750.
   c. Annual depreciation on the equipment is $9,000.
   d. The June utilities expense of $350 was not included in the trial balance because the bill arrived after it was prepared. The $350 amount owed needs to be recorded.
   e. The company's employees have earned $1,100 of accrued wages.
   f. Interest of $100 for June has not yet been paid or recorded. In addition, the company is required to make a $2,000 payment on the note on August 30, 2011.
2. Use the work sheet to journalize the adjusting and closing entries.
3. Prepare an income statement, a statement of changes in equity, and a classified balance sheet.

Analysis component:

Analyze the following independent errors and describe how each would affect the 10-column work sheet. Explain whether the error is likely to be discovered in completing the work sheet and, if not, the effect of the error on the financial statements.

a. The adjustment for consumption of the insurance coverage credited the Prepaid Insurance account for $1,550 and debited the same amount to the Insurance Expense account.
b. When completing the adjusted trial balance in the work sheet, the $3,350 Repairs Expense account balance was extended to the Debit column for the balance sheet.

Problem 5-4B
Closing entries
LO2, 3, 4

Dillan's Tailoring Services' adjusted trial balance on December 31, 2011, appears as follows:

No.	Account	Debit	Credit
101	Cash	$ 26,900	
125	Store supplies	8,280	
128	Prepaid insurance	4,400	
167	Equipment	66,000	
168	Accumulated depreciation, equipment		$ 18,000
201	Accounts payable		42,000
210	Wages payable		6,400
301	Vy Dillan, capital		23,300
302	Vy Dillan, withdrawals	32,000	
401	Sewing fees earned		124,000
612	Depreciation expense, equipment	6,000	
623	Wages expense	56,800	
637	Insurance expense	2,200	
640	Rent expense	4,800	
651	Store supplies expense	2,600	
690	Utilities expense	3,720	
	Totals	$213,700	$213,700

Check figure:
2. Post-closing trial balance = $105,580

Required

1. Prepare closing entries.
2. Prepare a post-closing trial balance.

Problem 5-5B
Financial statements
LO6

Check figures:
Net income = $47,880; Total assets = $87,580

Using the information from Problem 5-4B, prepare an income statement and a statement of changes in equity for the year ended December 31, 2011, and a classified balance sheet at December 31, 2011. The owner made no investments during the year.

Analysis component:

Dillan's Tailoring Services experienced a net income during 2011. If you were one of the business's creditors, would you conclude that because of this net income Dillan's Tailoring will pay its obligations in 2012?

Problem 5-6B
Closing entries
LO2, 3

The adjusted trial balance for Warren's Photo Studio as of December 31, 2011, follows:

No.	Account	Debit	Credit
101	Cash	$ 12,800	
104	Short-term investments	20,400	
126	Supplies	7,200	
149	Notes receivable, due May 1, 2013	70,000	
167	Equipment	36,000	
168	Accumulated depreciation, equipment		$ 6,000
173	Building	120,000	
174	Accumulated depreciation, building		58,000
183	Land	57,000	
193	Franchise	16,000	
201	Accounts payable		5,000
203	Unearned professional fees		1,300
233	Long-term notes payable		64,000
251	Warren Jones, capital		174,632
301	Warren Jones, withdrawals	12,000	
302	Photography fees earned		94,000
401	Interest earned		1,000
605	Depreciation expense, building	4,000	
606	Depreciation expense, equipment	3,000	
612	Wages expense	34,000	
623	Interest expense	2,400	
633	Insurance expense	2,850	
637	Supplies expense	1,800	
652	Telephone expense	842	
688	Utilities expense	3,640	
	Totals	$403,932	$403,932

An analysis of other information reveals that Warren's Photo Studio is required to make a $52,800 payment on the long-term notes payable during 2012. Also, Warren Jones invested $40,000 cash early in the year.

Required
Prepare the closing entries made at the end of the year.

Problem 5-7B
Financial statements
LO6

Using the adjusted trial balance in Problem 5-6B, prepare the income statement, statement of changes in equity, and classified balance sheet.

Analysis component:
Why must liabilities be separated on the balance sheet between *current* and *long-term*? What effect would it have had on Warren's balance sheet if the long-term notes were not separated?

Check figures:
Net income = $42,468;
Total assets = $275,400

Problem 5-8B
Closing entries
LO2, 3

The December 31, 2011, adjusted trial balance for Eagle Consulting Services has been alphabetized as follows:

No.	Account	Debit	Credit
201	Accounts payable		$ 600
168	Accumulated depreciation, equipment		8,500
184	Accumulated depreciation, office furniture		3,450
101	Cash	$ 1,750	
302	Consulting fees earned		48,500
194	Copyright	3,500	
251	Dan Eagle, capital		30,680
301	Dan Eagle, withdrawals	4,000	
406	Depreciation expense, equipment	1,000	
606	Depreciation expense, office furniture	700	
167	Equipment	16,000	
633	Insurance expense	600	
401	Interest earned		1,150
623	Interest expense	360	
233	Long-term notes payable		4,000
145	Notes receivable	5,000	
183	Office furniture	5,100	
104	Short-term investments	7,000	
126	Supplies	750	
637	Supplies expense	2,150	
652	Telephone expense	470	
203	Unearned consulting fees		375
688	Utilities expense	10,875	
612	Wages expense	38,000	
	Totals	$97,255	$97,255

Required
Prepare the closing entries.

Problem 5-9B
Financial statements
LO6

Check figures:
Net loss = $4,505;
Total assets = $27,150

Using the information in Problem 5-8B, prepare an income statement and a statement of changes in equity for the year ended December 31, 2011, and a classified balance sheet at December 31, 2011. The owner made no additional investments during the year. A $2,500 payment on the long-term notes payable will be made during 2012. Also, $1,500 of the notes receivable will be collected by December 31, 2012.

Analysis component:
Eagle Consulting's equity decreased by $8,505 during 2011. What effect does a decrease in equity have on the other major components of the balance sheet?

Problem 5-10B
Analyzing closing entries
LO2, 3, 4

The following closing entries were prepared for Greenway Gardening Services regarding the year ended October 31, 2011:

		2011		
Oct.	31	Service Revenue	148,000	
		Income Summary		148,000
		To close the revenue account.		
	31	Income Summary	178,260	
		Depreciation Expense, Gardening Equipment		9,600
		Depreciation Expense, Vehicles		10,600
		Insurance Expense		7,200
		Interest Expense		1,360
		Supplies Expense		24,800
		Telephone Expense		1,700
		Utilities Expense		1,800
		Fuel Expense		9,200
		Wages Expense		112,000
		To close expense accounts.		

Oct.	31	Grant Greenway, Capital Income Summary *To close the Income Summary to capital.*	30,260	30,260
	31	Grant Greenway, Capital Grant Greenway, Withdrawals *To close withdrawals to capital.*	10,000	10,000

Required

1. Prepare an income statement based on the information provided.
2. Calculate the post-closing balance in the capital account at October 31, 2011, given that the adjusted balance on October 31, 2010, was $76,000.

Check figure:
1. Total operating expenses = $178,260

Problem 5-11B

Preparing financial statements
LO6

Check figures:
Net income = $50,600;
Total assets = $181,120

Required

Using the adjusted trial balance below, for FairQuest Drill Servicing for the year ended August 31, 2011, prepare an income statement, statement of changes in equity, and classified balance sheet. The owner made a $50,000 investment into the business during the year.

No.	Account	Debit	Credit
101	Cash	$ 10,000	
106	Accounts receivable	36,000	
109	Interest receivable	280	
124	Office supplies	1,700	
141	Long-term investment in Nova shares	58,000	
161	Furniture	106,000	
162	Accumulated depreciation, furniture		$ 43,500
193	Franchise	12,640	
201	Accounts payable		29,900
205	Notes payable, due in 7 months		3,200
230	Unearned servicing revenue		5,000
251	Long-term notes payable*		28,000
301	Jade Fairquest, capital		98,420
302	Jade Fairquest, withdrawals	34,000	
403	Drill servicing revenue		212,000
409	Interest earned		2,600
601	Depreciation expense, furniture	2,060	
623	Wages expense	142,000	
637	Insurance expense	16,680	
688	Telephone expense	2,800	
690	Utilities expense	460	
	Totals	$422,620	$422,620

*An $18,000 payment will be made on the long-term notes payable during the year ended August 31, 2012.

Analysis component:
Why might FairQuest Drill Servicing be tempted to report the investment in Nova shares as a current asset on the August 31, 2011, balance sheet?

Problem 5-12B
Preparing a classified balance sheet
LO6

An alphabetical list of the adjusted trial balance accounts at July 31, 2011, for Delta Tours after its first month of operations is shown below:

Account	Adjusted Account Balance*
Accounts payable	$ 29,000
Accounts receivable	132,600
Accumulated depreciation, furniture	700
Cash	35,600
Depreciation expense, furniture	700
Furniture	27,000
Insurance expense	5,250
Interest receivable	800
Interest revenue	800
Jan Delta, capital	243,900
Jan Delta, withdrawals	-0-
Notes receivable (due in 6 months)	56,000
Prepaid insurance	36,750
Tour revenue	146,000
Unearned tour revenue	19,600
Utility expense	1,300
Wages expense	146,016
Wages payable	2,016

*Assume all accounts have a normal balance.

Check figure:
2. Total assets = $288,050

Required

1. Calculate the capital balance as it would appear on the July 31, 2011, balance sheet.
2. Prepare a classified balance sheet.

Problem 5-13B
Performing the steps in the accounting cycle
LO2, 3, 4, 5, 6

On July 1, 2011, Amy Young created a new self-storage business called Young Co. These events occurred during the company's first month:

July	1	Young invested $40,000 cash and land and buildings worth $320,000 and $240,000, respectively.
	2	Rented equipment by paying $3,600 rent for the first month.
	5	Purchased $4,600 of office supplies for cash.
	10	Paid $10,800 for the premium on a one-year insurance policy effective today.
	14	Paid an employee $1,800 for two weeks' salary.
	24	Collected $17,600 of storage fees from customers.
	28	Paid another $1,800 for two weeks' salary.
	29	Paid the month's $600 phone bill.
	30	Repaired leaking roof for $1,700 on account.
	31	Young withdrew $3,200 cash from the business for personal use.

The company's chart of accounts included these accounts:

101	Cash	201	Accounts Payable	637	Insurance Expense
106	Accounts Receivable	209	Salaries Payable	640	Equipment Rental Expense
124	Office Supplies	301	Amy Young, Capital	650	Office Supplies Expense
128	Prepaid Insurance	302	Amy Young, Withdrawals	684	Repairs Expense
170	Land	401	Storage Fees Earned	688	Telephone Expense
173	Buildings	606	Depreciation Expense, Buildings	901	Income Summary
174	Accumulated Depreciation, Buildings	622	Salaries Expense		

Required

1. Set up each of the listed accounts. *Note: Your instructor will tell you to use either the balance column format or T-accounts.*
2. Prepare journal entries to record the transactions for July and post them to the accounts. Record prepaid and unearned items in balance sheet accounts.

3. Use the following information to journalize and post the adjustments for the month:
   a. Two-thirds of one month's insurance coverage was consumed.
   b. There was $3,100 of office supplies on hand at the end of the month.
   c. Depreciation on the buildings was estimated to be $2,400 per month.
   d. The employee had earned $360 of unpaid and unrecorded salary.
   e. The company had earned $1,900 of storage fees that had not yet been billed.
4. Prepare an income statement, a statement of changes in equity, and a classified balance sheet.
5. Prepare journal entries to close the temporary accounts and post them to the accounts.
6. Prepare a post-closing trial balance.

Check figures:
4. Net income = $5,140; Total assets = $604,000
6. Post-closing trial balance = $606,400

***Problem 5-14B**
Adjusting, reversing, and subsequent cash entries
LO7

IBS Company's unadjusted trial balance on December 31, 2011, the end of its annual accounting period, is as follows:

Account	Debit	Credit
Cash	$ 73,725	
Note receivable	37,500	
Office supplies	4,200	
Land	45,000	
Unearned service fees		$ 18,000
Note payable		90,000
Jean Boat, capital		37,500
Jean Boat, withdrawals	60,000	
Service fees earned		267,000
Interest revenue		2,550
Rent revenue		12,375
Salaries expense	193,500	
Insurance expense	4,950	
Interest expense	8,550	
Totals	$427,425	$427,425

Information necessary to prepare adjusting entries is as follows:

a. Employees, who are paid $7,500 every two weeks, have earned $5,250 since the last payment. The next payment of $7,500 will be on January 4.
b. IBS rents office space to a tenant who has paid only $450 of the $1,125 rent for December. On January 12, the tenant will pay the remainder along with the rent for January.
c. An inventory of office supplies discloses $675 of unused supplies.
d. Premiums for insurance against injuries to employees are paid monthly. The $450 premium for December will be paid January 12.
e. IBS owes $90,000 on a note payable that requires quarterly payments of accrued interest. The quarterly payments of $2,700 each are made on the 15th of January, April, July, and October.
f. An analysis of IBS's service contracts with customers shows that $6,300 of the amount customers have prepaid remains unearned.
g. IBS has a $37,500 note receivable on which interest of $175 has accrued. On January 22, the note and the total accrued interest of $575 will be repaid to IBS.
h. IBS has earned but unrecorded revenue for $8,250 for services provided to a customer who will pay for the work on January 24. At that time, the customer will also pay $3,100 for services IBS will perform in early January.

Required

1. Prepare adjusting journal entries.
2. Prepare reversing entries.
3. Prepare journal entries to record the January 2012 cash receipts and cash payments identified in the above information.

An asterisk (*) identifies assignment material based on Appendix 5A or Appendix 5B.

Analytical and Review Problems

A & R Problem 5-1

The owner of Dynamo Stores has come to you for assistance because his bookkeeper has just moved to another city. The following is the only information his bookkeeper left him.

1. Balance sheets as of December 31, 2011 and 2012.

	2012	2011
Assets	$168,000	$210,000
Liabilities	$ 42,000	$ 63,000
Capital	126,000	147,000
	$168,000	$210,000

2. The owner withdrew $105,000 in 2012 for his personal use.

3. The business incurred total expenses of $168,000 for 2012, of which $126,000 was for wages and $42,000 was for advertising.

Required

1. Calculate the net income and total revenue for 2012.

2. Prepare closing entries for 2012.

A & R Problem 5-2

The partially completed work sheet for the current fiscal year of Sandy's Delivery Service appears below:

Sandy's Delivery Service
Work Sheet
For the Year Ended December 31, 2011

	Unadjusted Trial Balance		Adjustments		Adjusted Trial Balance		Income Statement		Balance Sheet & Statement of Changes in Equity	
Account	**Debit**	**Credit**	**Debit**	**Credit**	**Debit**	**Credit**	**Debit**	**Credit**	**Debit**	**Credit**
Cash	10,650									
Accounts receivable	7,000				9,000					
Supplies	4,200								1,600	
Prepaid insurance	2,400									
Prepaid rent	1,800									
Delivery trucks	40,000				40,000					
Accounts payable		3,130				3,130				
Unearned delivery fees		4,500								2,000
Sandra Berlasty, capital		50,000								
Sandra Berlasty, withdrawals	3,000									
Delivery service revenue		18,500								
Advertising expense	600									
Gas and oil expense	680									
Salaries expense	5,600									
Utilities expense	200									
Totals	76,130	76,130								
Insurance expense					800					
Rent expense					900					
Supplies expense										
Dep. expense, delivery trucks										
Accumulated dep., delivery trucks										2,000
Salaries payable										400
Net Income										

Required

1. Complete the work sheet.

2. Journalize the adjusting and closing entries (omit narratives).

Ethics Challenge

EC 5-1

On January 20, 2011, Jennifer Nelson, the staff accountant for Newby Enterprises, is feeling pressure to complete the preparation of the annual financial statements. The president of the company has said he needs up-to-date financial statements to share with several bankers on January 21 at a dinner meeting that has been called to discuss the possibility of Newby obtaining loan financing for a special building project. Jennifer knows that she won't be able to gather all the needed information in the next 24 hours to prepare the entire set of adjusting entries that must be posted before the financial statements will accurately portray the company's performance and financial position for the fiscal period just ended December 31, 2010. Jennifer ultimately decides to estimate several expense accruals at the last minute. When deciding on estimates for the expenses Jennifer uses low estimates as she doesn't want to make the financial statements look worse than they possibly are in reality. Jennifer finishes the financial statements before the deadline and gives them to the president without mentioning that several accounts could only be estimated as to their balance on December 31, 2010.

Required

1. List several courses of action that Jennifer could have taken instead of the one on which she ultimately decided.
2. If you had been in Jennifer's situation, what would you have done? Briefly justify your response.

Focus on Financial Statements

FFS 5-1

Sarda Electrical Servicing began operations two years ago. Its adjusted account balances at December 31, 2011, are listed alphabetically below. The owner, Nymeth Sarda, made a $20,000 investment early in the year just ended December 31, 2011.

Check figures:
1. Net income = $70,575; Total assets = $95,850
3. Post-closing trial balance = $121,350

Required

1. Prepare an income statement, statement of changes in equity, and classified balance sheet based on the information provided.
2. Prepare the closing entries.
3. Prepare the post-closing trial balance.

Account	Account Balance*
Accounts payable	$ 21,000
Accounts receivable	10,500
Accumulated depreciation, tools	4,500
Accumulated depreciation, truck	21,000
Cash	5,000
Copyright	5,100
Depreciation expense, tools	2,250
Depreciation expense, truck	3,600
Electrical fees earned	126,600
Electrical supplies	19,000
Insurance expense	1,275
Interest expense	900
Notes receivable**	12,000
Nymeth Sarda, capital	27,825
Nymeth Sarda, withdrawals	61,500
Notes payable, due August 31, 2013	27,000
Notes payable, due June 1, 2012	2,550
Prepaid insurance	1,050
Prepaid rent	7,200
Rent expense	21,000
Salaries expense	27,000
Salaries payable	3,150
Tools	21,000
Truck	40,500
Unearned electrical fees	5,250

*Assume all account balances are normal.
**$2,000 of the note is due September 15, 2012.

Analysis component:
Refer to the chapter opening vignette. Sharon Beasley financed growth by reinvesting profits. Is Nymeth Sarda, the owner of Sarda Electrical Servicing, following a similar practice? Explain.

FFS 5-2

ClubLink Corporation, headquartered in King City, Ontario, is Canada's largest owner, operator, and developer of golf courses and resorts. An excerpt from its comparative balance sheet at December 31, 2008, shows the following assets and liabilities, in alphabetical order:

(thousands of dollars)	**2008**	**2007**
Accounts payable and accrued liabilities	$ 12,725	$ 14,934
Accounts receivable	2,044	2,366
Cash	12,798	1,004
Current portion of long-term debt	28,342	12,820
Current portion of mortgages and loans receivable	8,473	763
Inventories and prepaid expenses	3,920	3,724
Intangible assets	4,032	4,296
Long-term liabilities, less current portion	281,128	282,348
Mortgages and loans receivable, less current portion	6,388	6,306
Other current assets	3,230	3,230
Other current liabilities	4,189	5,413
Other long-term assets	726	726
Other long-term liabilities	77,716	73,134
Prepaid annual dues and deposits*	5,733	5,021
Property, plant and equipment assets	534,611	540,744

*These are dues and deposits collected in advance from ClubLink's golf club and resort members.

Required

Part 1

a. Calculate total current assets at December 31, 2008, and December 31, 2007.
b. Calculate total current liabilities at December 31, 2008, and December 31, 2007.

***Part 2**

c. Calculate the current ratio for December 31, 2008 and December 31, 2007 (round to two decimal places).
d. Was the change in the ratio favourable or unfavourable?

Critical Thinking Mini Case

The owner of Delton Property Rentals, Teal Delton, has requested an emergency meeting with you, a representative from the bank. "Our accountant has been on leave for the past several months and her replacement has resigned suddenly. I'm told we can't pay our employees this month and your bank won't lend us any money. I don't understand. We have lots of assets that can be used to pay expenses, as you can see from our balance sheet."

Delton Property Rentals
Balance Sheet
March 31

	2011	**2010**
Assets	$2,850,000	$750,000
Liabilities	2,780,000	240,000
Equity	70,000	510,000

An asterisk (*) identifies assignment material based on Appendix 5A or Appendix 5B.

You explain to Mr. Delton that you will need to obtain some additional information. He faxes you the following:

Delton Property Rentals Post-Closing Trial Balance March 31		
	2011	**2010**
Accounts payable	$ 340,000	$ 7,000
Accounts receivable	75,000	215,000
Accumulated depreciation, buildings	165,000	150,000
Accumulated depreciation, equipment	35,000	30,000
Buildings	2,112,000	430,000
Cash	15,000	40,000
Equipment	45,000	45,000
Land	675,000	150,000
Notes payable*	2,440,000	204,000
Notes receivable, due Nov. 30, 2015	120,000	-0-
Supplies	8,000	50,000
Teal Delton, capital**	70,000	510,000
Unearned fees	-0-	29,000

*$200,000 principal is due annually each February 1.
**No withdrawals were made during 2010 or 2011.

Required
Using the elements of critical thinking described on the inside front cover, comment.

Serial Problem

Echo Systems

(The first two segments of this comprehensive problem were in Chapters 3 and 4, and the final segment is presented in Chapter 6. If the Chapter 3 and 4 segments have not been completed, the assignment can begin at this point. It is recommended that you use the Working Papers[12] that accompany this book because they reflect the account balances that resulted from posting the entries required in Chapters 3 and 4.)

The transactions of Echo Systems for October through December 2011 have been recorded in the problem segments in Chapters 3 and 4, as well as the year-end adjusting entries. Prior to closing the revenue and expense accounts for 2011, the accounting system is modified to include the Income Summary account, which is given the number 901.

Required
1. Record and post the appropriate closing entries.
2. Prepare a post-closing trial balance.

Check figure:
2. Total credits in post-closing trial balance = $155,720

[12] If students have not purchased the Working Papers package, the Working Papers for the serial problem are available on Connect.

CHAPTER 6

Accounting for Merchandising Activities

learning objectives

- **LO1** Describe merchandising and identify and explain the important income statement and balance sheet components for a merchandising company.
- **LO2** Describe both perpetual and periodic inventory systems.
- **LO3** Analyze and record transactions for merchandise purchases and sales using a perpetual system.
- **LO4** Prepare adjustments for a merchandising company.
- **LO5** Define, prepare, and use merchandising income statements.
- **LO6** Prepare closing entries for a merchandising company.

*APPENDIX 6A

- **LO7** Record and compare merchandising transactions using both periodic and perpetual inventory systems.

*APPENDIX 6B

- **LO8** Explain and record Provincial Sales Tax (PST) and Goods and Services Tax (GST).

In the Black!

Toronto-based Danier Leather Inc. designs and manufactures high-quality leather and suede clothing and accessories that it sells in its 98 retail outlets as well as online.

According to Bryan Tatoff, a Chartered Accountant and the Senior Vice-President, CFO, and Secretary of Danier Leather Inc., "Our business is all about satisfying customers' needs, which means having the right merchandise at the right gross profit." Danier has a perpetual inventory management system to track merchandise inventory. Bryan Tatoff noted that "Danier recently upgraded the merchandising system to provide even more detail than we had before. It not only tracks inventory by stock keeping unit (SKU), it allows us to report on merchandise by attribute, such as the type of collar, belt or no belt, or zipper or button. Danier's perpetual merchandising system provides us with information on what is selling, why it is selling, and what we need more of. It also helps us know where every unit is in the chain so if a customer comes into our Victoria store and the store doesn't have the correct size, we can get it from another store."

Danier experiences less fashion risk than other clothing retailers because 80% of merchandise sold is black. "The challenge," says Bryan, "is financial flexibility; we have to make money on buying as well as selling. We have to take advantage of and buy as much superior leather [as possible] when the price is right. When we negotiate bulk purchases, the balance sheet is impacted in terms of assets (inventory) along with liabilities yet one of our goals is to be as debt-free as possible."

An important part of Danier's philosophy is to exercise social responsibility through its involvement with the United Way and by sponsoring more than 100 children under the Foster Parents Plan. By being both financially astute and socially responsible, Danier Leather continues to hold its own in a highly volatile industry.

www.danier.ca

CRITICAL THINKING CHALLENGE

Why would Danier Leather choose a perpetual inventory system over periodic? Is the periodic inventory system acceptable under GAAP? Bryan Tatoff says that one of the company's goals "is to be as debt-free as possible." Why? Why would Danier upgrade the merchandising system to report on merchandise attributes?

chapter preview

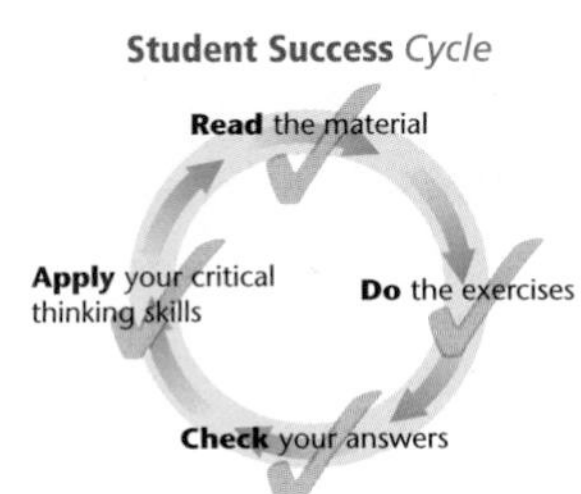

Our emphasis in previous chapters was on the accounting and reporting activities of companies providing services. Chapter 6 emphasizes merchandising, a major part of modern business. Consumers expect a wealth of products, discount prices, inventory on demand, and high quality. This chapter introduces us to the business and accounting practices used by companies engaged in merchandising activities. These companies buy products and then resell them to customers. We show how financial statements capture merchandising transactions. The new financial statement elements created by merchandising transactions are explained. We also analyze and record merchandise purchases and sales of these companies. Adjusting entries and the closing process for merchandising companies are explained. An understanding of these important topics is what Bryan Tatoff of Danier Leather in the opening article considers necessary to ensure continued success.

Merchandising Activities

LO1 Describe merchandising and identify and explain the important income statement and balance sheet components for a merchandising company.

A merchandising company's activities are different from those of a service company. A **merchandiser** earns net income by buying and selling merchandise. **Merchandise** consists of products, also called *goods*, that a company acquires for the purpose of reselling them to customers. The cost of these goods is an expense called **cost of goods sold (COGS)**.[1]

Merchandisers are often identified as either *wholesalers* or *retailers*. A **wholesaler** is a company that buys products from manufacturers or other wholesalers and sells them to retailers or other wholesalers. Wholesalers include companies such as Tricana, Western Family Foods, and Westfair Foods. A **retailer** is an *intermediary* that buys products from manufacturers or wholesalers and sells them to consumers. Examples of retailers include Danier Leather, Loblaw, Zellers, Canadian Tire, and The Gap. Some retailers, such as Bell Canada, often sell both products and services.

Reporting Financial Performance

Net income to a merchandiser results when revenue from selling merchandise exceeds both the cost of merchandise sold to customers and the cost of other operating expenses for the period (see Exhibit 6.1). The usual accounting term for revenues from selling merchandise is *sales*. **Net sales** refers to the result of subtracting *sales discounts*[2] and *sales returns and allowances*[2] from total or gross sales. The term used for the cost of buying and preparing the merchandise is an expense called *cost of goods sold*.[3] A merchandiser's other expenses are often called *operating expenses*.

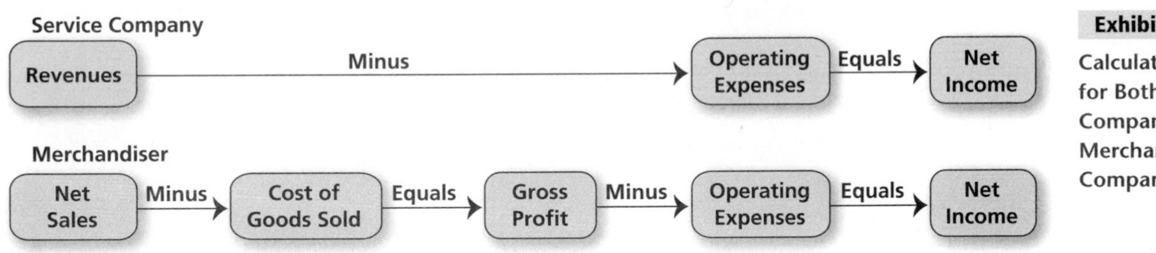

Exhibit 6.1
Calculating Income for Both a Service Company and a Merchandising Company

[1] *Cost of goods sold* is also commonly called **cost of sales**.
[2] *Sales discounts* and *sales returns and allowances* are discussed in more detail later in this chapter.
[3] When preparing the income statement using the "function of expense" method per IFRS 2009, IAS 1, para. 103, cost of goods sold must be shown separately from other expenses.

Exhibit 6.2

Summarized Income Statement Information for a Merchandiser

Z-Mart Summarized Income Statement Information For Year Ended December 31, 2011	
Net sales	$314,700
Cost of goods sold	230,400
Gross profit from sales	$ 84,300
Total operating expenses and other revenues and expenses	68,960
Net income	$ 15,340

The summarized income statement information for Z-Mart in Exhibit 6.2 shows us how net sales, gross profit, and income are related. This statement shows that Z-Mart sold products to customers for $314,700. Z-Mart acquired these goods at a cost of $230,400. This yields an $84,300 gross profit. **Gross profit**, also called **gross margin**, equals net sales less cost of goods sold. Changes in gross profit often greatly impact a merchandiser's operations since gross profit must cover all other expenses and yield a return for the owner. Z-Mart, for instance, used gross profit to cover $68,960 of operating and other revenues and expenses. This left $15,340 in net income for the year 2011.

Reporting Financial Position

A merchandising company's balance sheet includes an item not on the balance sheet of a service company. This item is a current asset called *merchandise inventory*. **Merchandise inventory**, or **inventory**, refers to products a company owns for the purpose of selling to customers. Exhibit 6.3 shows the classified balance sheet P. 206 for Z-Mart, highlighting merchandise inventory of $21,000. The cost of this asset includes the cost incurred to buy the goods, ship them to the store, and otherwise make them ready for sale. Although companies usually hold inventories of

Exhibit 6.3

Classified Balance Sheet for a Merchandiser

Z-Mart Balance Sheet December 31, 2011			
Assets			
Current assets:			
Cash		$ 8,200	
Accounts receivable		11,200	
Merchandise inventory		**21,000**	
Prepaid expenses		1,100	
Total current assets			$41,500
Plant and equipment:			
Office equipment	$ 4,200		
Less: Accumulated depreciation	1,400	$ 2,800	
Store equipment	$30,000		
Less: Accumulated depreciation	6,000	24,000	
Total plant and equipment			26,800
Total assets			$68,300
Liabilities			
Current liabilities:			
Accounts payable		$ 16,000	
Salaries payable		800	
Total liabilities			$16,800
Equity			
Kent Marty, capital			51,500
Total liabilities and equity			$68,300

other items such as supplies, *most companies simply refer to merchandise inventory as inventory*. We will use both terms in reference to merchandise inventory.

Operating Cycle

A merchandising company's operating cycle[4] begins with the purchase of merchandise and ends with the collection of cash from the sale of merchandise.

Exhibit 6.4 graphically shows an operating cycle for a merchandiser with (1) cash sales and (2) credit sales. Credit sales delay the receipt of cash until the account receivable is paid by the customer. Companies try to shorten their operating cycles to increase income. Assets tied up in the form of merchandise inventory or receivables are not productive assets. Merchandise inventory is not productive (earning income) until it is sold. Receivables need to be collected so that the resulting cash can be used to earn income. The length of an operating cycle differs across the types of businesses. Department stores such as Sears commonly have operating cycles of three to five months, but operating cycles for grocery merchants such as Loblaw and Safeway usually range from one to two months.

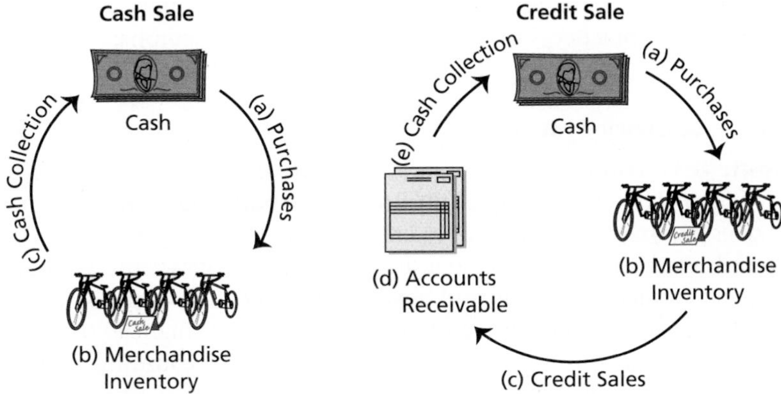

Exhibit 6.4
Operating Cycle of a Merchandiser

Inventory Systems

Exhibit 6.5 shows that a company's merchandise available for sale is a combination of what it begins with (beginning inventory) and what it purchases (net cost of purchases). The merchandise available is either sold (cost of goods sold) or kept for future sales (ending inventory).

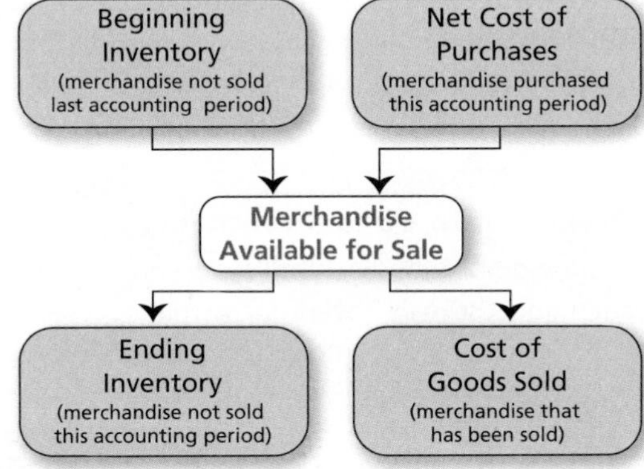

Exhibit 6.5
Merchandising Cost Flow

Two inventory accounting systems are used to collect information about cost of goods sold and cost of inventory on hand: *perpetual* and *periodic*. Both inventory systems are generally accepted, therefore, companies have a choice. We introduce these systems in this section.

[4] IFRS 2009, IAS 1, para. 68.

Perpetual Inventory System

LO2 Describe both perpetual and periodic inventory systems.

Merchandise Inventory (MI)			
Beginning MI	10	LESS	
PLUS		COGS	COGS
Purchases	50	55 --->	55
EQUALS			
Ending MI	5		

Under a perpetual system, the MI account is updated continually for purchases and goods sold. The balance in MI and COGS is always up to date.

A **perpetual inventory system** gives a continuous record of the amount of inventory on hand. A perpetual system accumulates the net cost of merchandise purchases in the inventory account and transfers the cost of each sale from the inventory account to the Cost of Goods Sold account (COGS) when an item is sold, as shown in the illustration to the left. With a perpetual system, we can find out the cost of merchandise on hand at any time by looking at the balance of the inventory account. We can also find out the cost of goods sold to date during a period by looking at the balance in the Cost of Goods Sold account.

Before advancements in computing technology, a perpetual system was often limited to businesses making a small number of daily sales, such as automobile dealers and major appliance stores. Because there were relatively few transactions, a perpetual system was feasible. Today, with widespread use of computing technology, the use of a perpetual system has dramatically grown to include merchandisers with high-volume sales as well, such as Wal-Mart, Canadian Tire, Superstore, Staples, Leon's, and London Drugs. The number of companies that use a perpetual system continues to increase.

Because perpetual inventory systems give users more timely information and are widely used in practice, our discussion in this chapter emphasizes a perpetual system.

Periodic Inventory System

Merchandise Inventory (MI)		
Beginning MI	10	

PLUS

Purchases		
Purchases	50	

LESS

Ending MI (per a physical count)

5

EQUALS

COGS

55

Under a periodic system, the MI account is updated when a physical count is performed. COGS is *calculated* once ending MI is known.

A **periodic inventory system** requires updating the inventory account only at the *end of a period* to reflect the quantity and cost of both goods on hand and goods sold. It does not require continual updating of the inventory account. The company records the cost of new merchandise in a temporary expense account called *Purchases*. When merchandise is sold, revenue is recorded but the cost of the merchandise sold is *not* recorded as a cost at this time. When financial statements are prepared, the company takes a *physical count of inventory* by counting the quantities of merchandise on hand. Cost of merchandise on hand is determined by relating the quantities on hand to records showing each item's original cost. This cost of merchandise on hand is used to compute cost of goods sold as shown to the left. The inventory account is then adjusted to reflect the amount computed from the physical count of inventory.

Periodic systems were historically used by companies such as hardware, drug, and department stores that sold large quantities of low-value items. Before computers and scanners, it was not feasible for accounting systems to track such small items as nails, pencils, toothpaste, paper clips, and socks through inventory and into customers' hands. *We analyze and record merchandising transactions using both periodic and perpetual inventory systems in Appendix 6A.*

DID YOU KNOW?

From Periodic to Perpetual to Virtual Inventory Systems

"Traditional models . . . are going away," according to Keyur Patel, a KPMG partner. Web businesses are changing the way inventory is managed and accounted for. Rather than risk having too little or too much in inventory along with all of the related costs, e-businesses are turning to the manufacturers to package and ship products direct to consumers. The result is that these merchants maintain zero inventory. Instead, they take customer orders and transmit that information directly to the respective manufacturer, who fulfills the distribution obligation to the customer. Therefore, for these merchants, discussion of an inventory costing system has become redundant.

Source: www.planetit.com

1. Describe a company's cost of goods sold.
2. What is gross profit for a merchandising company?
3. Explain why use of the perpetual inventory system has grown dramatically.

Do Quick Study questions: QS 6-1, QS 6-2, QS 6-3, QS 6-4

Accounting for Merchandise Transactions—Perpetual Inventory System

LO3 Analyze and record transactions for merchandise purchases and sales using a perpetual system.

Recording merchandise transactions involves issues regarding the purchase and sale of merchandise inventory. In this first section, we will examine purchase transactions and associated items. Then, in the next section, transactions related to sales will be examined.

Accounting for Merchandise Purchases—Perpetual Inventory System

With a perpetual inventory system, the cost of merchandise bought for resale is recorded in the Merchandise Inventory account. Z-Mart records a $1,200 credit purchase of merchandise on November 2 with this entry:

Nov.	2	Merchandise Inventory	1,200	
		Accounts Payable		1,200
		Purchased merchandise on credit.		

Note that neither GST (Goods and Services Tax) nor PST (Provincial Sales Tax) has been considered in this transaction. The accounting for GST and PST is deferred to Appendix 6B. Although GST and PST affect merchandising transactions, they are specifically a tax issue. To include discussion of GST and PST at this point would complicate merchandising transactions for the introductory student.

The invoice for this merchandise is shown in Exhibit 6.6. The buyer usually receives the original, while the seller keeps a copy. This single source document

Exhibit 6.6

Invoice

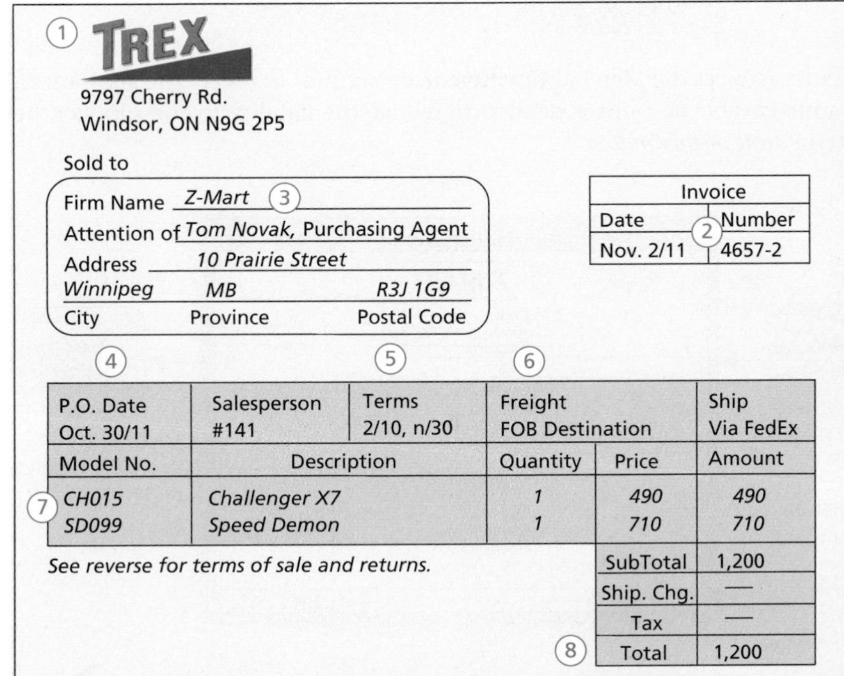

(1) TREX
9797 Cherry Rd.
Windsor, ON N9G 2P5

Sold to
Firm Name *Z-Mart* (3)
Attention of *Tom Novak*, Purchasing Agent
Address *10 Prairie Street*
Winnipeg (City) *MB* (Province) *R3J 1G9* (Postal Code)

Invoice	
Date	(2) Number
Nov. 2/11	4657-2

(4) (5) (6)

P.O. Date Oct. 30/11	Salesperson #141	Terms 2/10, n/30	Freight FOB Destination		Ship Via FedEx
Model No.	Description		Quantity	Price	Amount
(7) *CH015*	*Challenger X7*		*1*	*490*	*490*
SD099	*Speed Demon*		*1*	*710*	*710*
See reverse for terms of sale and returns.				SubTotal	1,200
				Ship. Chg.	—
				Tax	—
			(8)	Total	1,200

(1) Seller
(2) Invoice date
(3) Purchaser
(4) Order date
(5) Credit terms
(6) Freight terms
(7) Goods
(8) Total invoice amount

serves as the purchase invoice of Z-Mart (buyer) and the sales invoice for Trex (seller). The amount recorded for merchandise inventory includes its purchase cost, shipping fees, taxes, and any other costs necessary to make it ready for sale.

To calculate the total cost of merchandise purchases, we must adjust the invoice cost for:

(1) Any returns and allowances for unsatisfactory items received from a supplier;

(2) Any discounts given to a purchaser by a supplier for early payment; and

(3) Any required freight costs paid by a purchaser.

This section explains these items in more detail.

Purchase Returns and Allowances

Purchase returns are merchandise received by a purchaser but returned to the supplier. Reasons for returns vary. Perhaps the merchandise received was the wrong colour or size. A *purchase allowance* is a reduction in the cost of defective merchandise received by a purchaser from a supplier. Purchasers will often keep defective merchandise that is still marketable if the supplier grants an acceptable allowance. For example, assume that the merchandise received by the purchaser was furniture scratched during shipment. The purchaser may repair the furniture if the supplier provides an allowance.

The purchaser usually informs the supplier in writing of any returns and allowances. This is done with a letter or a **debit memorandum**, a form issued by the purchaser to inform the supplier of a debit made to the supplier's account, including the reason for a return or allowance. The purchaser sends the debit memorandum to the supplier and also keeps a copy.

To illustrate how a buyer accounts for an allowance, we assume that the Speed Demon mountain bike purchased by Z-Mart on November 2 was discovered to be defective when received on November 5. Exhibit 6.7 shows the debit memorandum prepared by Z-Mart requesting an allowance from Trex. The November 5 entry by Z-Mart for the purchase allowance is:

Date	Account	Debit	Credit
Nov. 5	Accounts Payable	300	
	Merchandise Inventory		300
	Purchase allowance re debit memo dated November 5.		

The entry reduces the Merchandise Inventory account to reflect the allowance. The Accounts Payable account is debited to reduce the liability to the supplier, hence the term *debit memorandum*.

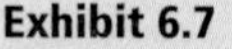
Exhibit 6.7

Debit Memorandum: Z-Mart proposes $300 allowance from Trex

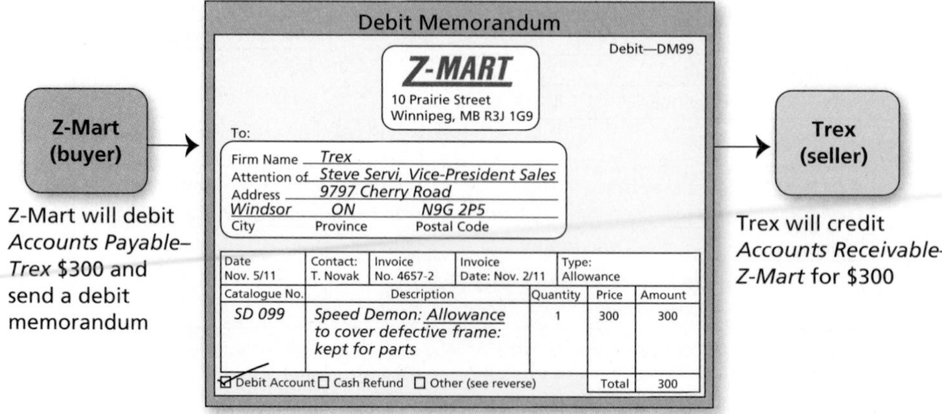

Z-Mart (buyer)
Z-Mart will debit *Accounts Payable–Trex* $300 and send a debit memorandum
Trex (seller)
Trex will credit *Accounts Receivable–Z-Mart* for $300

Debit Memorandum

Debit—DM99

Z-MART
10 Prairie Street
Winnipeg, MB R3J 1G9

To:
Firm Name: Trex
Attention of: Steve Servi, Vice-President Sales
Address: 9797 Cherry Road
City: Windsor Province: ON Postal Code: N9G 2P5

Date	Contact:	Invoice	Invoice	Type:
Nov. 5/11	T. Novak	No. 4657-2	Date: Nov. 2/11	Allowance

Catalogue No.	Description	Quantity	Price	Amount
SD 099	Speed Demon: Allowance to cover defective frame: kept for parts	1	300	300
☑ Debit Account ☐ Cash Refund ☐ Other (see reverse)			Total	300

If this had been a return, then the recorded cost[5] of the defective merchandise would be entered. If there is a refund of cash, then the Cash account is debited for $300 instead of Accounts Payable as follows:

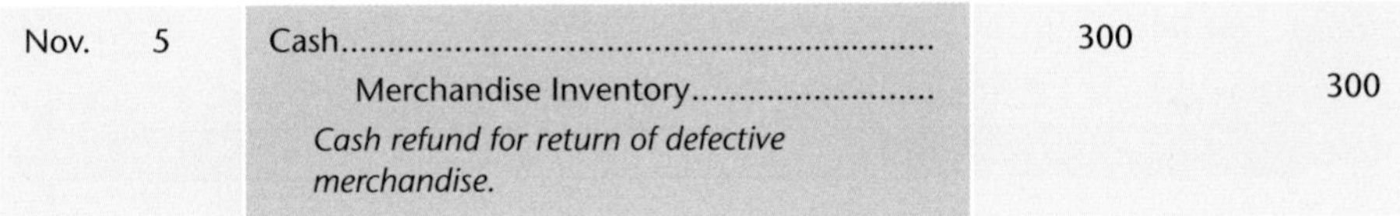

Nov. 5	Cash	300	
	Merchandise Inventory		300
	Cash refund for return of defective merchandise.		

Trade Discounts

When a manufacturer or wholesaler prepares a catalogue of items that it has for sale, each item is usually given a **list price**, also called a **catalogue price**. Often the intended selling price equals list price minus a given percentage called a **trade discount**. The amount of trade discount usually depends on the quantities purchased and on whether a buyer is a wholesaler, retailer, or final consumer. For example, a wholesaler buying 50,000 pens might be granted a 35% trade discount, while a retailer purchasing 500 pens might be granted a 5% trade discount.

Trade discounts are commonly used by manufacturers and wholesalers to change selling prices without republishing their catalogues. When a seller wants to change selling prices, it can notify its customers merely by sending them a new table of trade discounts that they can apply to catalogue prices.

Because a list price is not intended to reflect the actual selling price of merchandise, a buyer records the net amount of list price minus trade discount rather than accounting separately for the discount. For example, on November 2, Z-Mart purchased inventory that was listed at $2,000 in the catalogue. Since Z-Mart receives a 40% trade discount, the company records the transaction at $1,200 [= $2,000 − (40% × $2,000)].

Purchase Discounts

The purchase of goods on credit requires a clear statement of the *credit terms* to avoid misunderstanding. **Credit terms** are a listing of the amounts and timing of payments between a buyer and seller. In some industries, purchasers expect terms requiring full or "net" payment within 10 days after the end of a month in which purchases occur. These credit terms are entered on sales invoices or tickets as "n/10 EOM." The **EOM** refers to "end of month." In some other industries, invoices are often due and payable 30 calendar days after the invoice date. These credit terms are entered as "n/30," meaning "net amount due in 30 days." The 30-day period is called the **credit period**. Credit terms may include a **cash discount**. A buyer views a cash discount as a **purchase discount**. If cash discounts for early payment exist, they are described in the credit terms on an invoice. Referring to Exhibit 6.6, notice that Z-Mart's November 2 credit purchase was on terms of 2/10, n/30. These credit terms mean there is a 30-day credit period before full payment is due. The seller allows Z-Mart to deduct 2% of the invoice amount from the payment if it is paid within 10 days of the invoice date. Sellers do this to encourage early payment. The 10 days are the **discount period**, the period in which the reduced payment can be made. Exhibit 6.8 explains these credit terms.

[5] Recorded cost is the cost reported in a Merchandise Inventory account minus any discounts.

Exhibit 6.8

Credit Terms Illustration—2/10, n/30

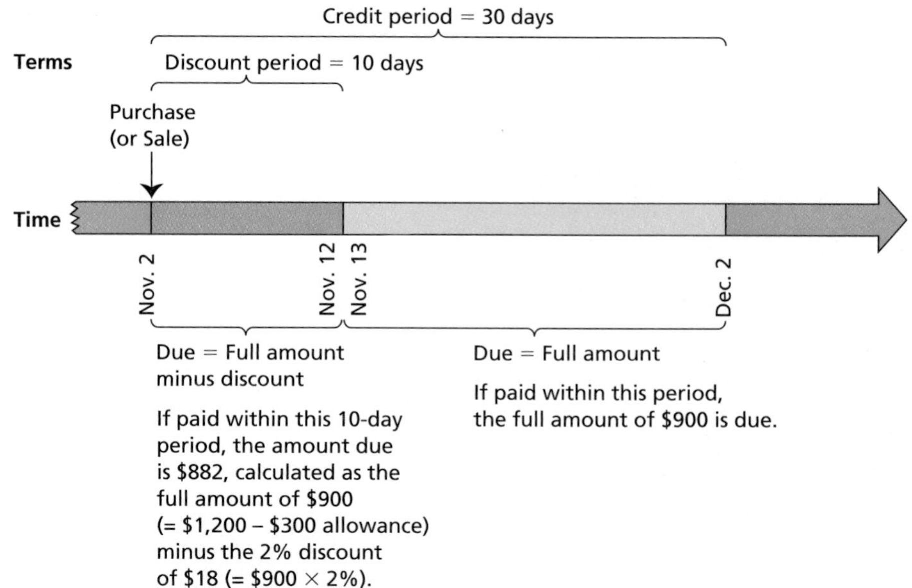

When Z-Mart takes advantage of the discount and pays the amount due on November 12, the entry to record payment is:

Nov. 12	Accounts Payable	900	
	Merchandise Inventory		18
	Cash		882
	Paid for the purchase of November 2 less the allowance of November 5 and the discount; $1,200 − $300 = $900; 2% × $900 = $18; $900 − $18 = $882.		

Notice that this entry shows that when goods are returned within the discount period, a buyer will take the discount only on the remaining balance of the invoice.

Z-Mart's Merchandise Inventory account now reflects the net cost of merchandise purchased. Its Accounts Payable account also shows the debt to be satisfied.

Merchandise Inventory			
Nov. 2	1,200	300	Nov. 5
		18	Nov. 12
Balance	882		

Accounts Payable			
Nov. 5	300	1,200	Nov. 2
Nov. 12	900		
		-0-	Balance

Managing Discounts

A buyer's failure to pay within a discount period is often quite expensive. If Z-Mart does not pay within the 10-day discount period, it delays the payment by 20 more days. This delay costs Z-Mart an added 2%. Most buyers try to take advantage of purchase discounts. For Z-Mart's terms of 2/10, n/30, missing the 2% discount for an additional 20 days is equal to an annual interest rate of 36.5%, calculated as (365 days ÷ 20 days × 2%).

Most companies set up a system to pay invoices with favourable discounts within the discount period. Careful cash management means that no invoice is paid until the last day of a discount period. Computerized systems achieve this goal by using a code that identifies the last date in the discount period. When that date occurs, the system automatically identifies accounts to be paid.[6]

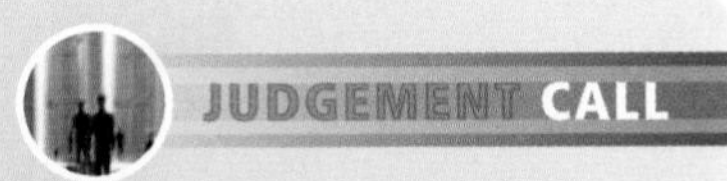

Accounts Payable Manager

You are the new accounts payable manager for a merchandising company that purchases its merchandise on credit. You are trained for your new job by the outgoing employee. You are to oversee payment of payables to maintain the company's credit standing with suppliers and to take advantage of favourable cash discounts. The outgoing employee explains that the computer system is programmed to prepare cheques for amounts net of favourable cash discounts, and cheques are dated the last day of the discount period. You are told that cheques are not mailed until five days later, however. "It's simple," this employee explains. "Our company gets free use of cash for an extra five days, and our department looks better. When a supplier complains, we blame the computer system and the mail room." Your first invoice arrives with a 10-day discount period for a $10,000 purchase. This transaction occurs on April 9 with credit terms of 2/10, n/30. Do you mail the $9,800 cheque on April 19 or April 24?

Answer—p. 278

Transfer of Ownership

The point where ownership of merchandise inventory transfers from the buyer to the seller must be identified on the invoice because it determines who pays transportation costs and other incidental costs of transit such as insurance. The party responsible for paying shipping costs is also responsible for insuring the merchandise during transport. The point of transfer is called the **FOB** point, where FOB stands for *free on board.*

Exhibit 6.9 identifies two alternative points of transfer. *FOB shipping point,* also called *FOB factory,* means the buyer accepts ownership at the seller's place of business. The buyer is then responsible for paying shipping costs and bears the risk of

Exhibit 6.9

Identifying Transfer of Ownership

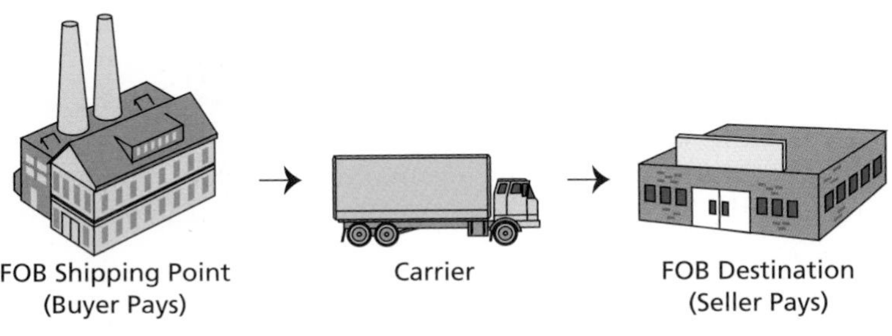

	Ownership transfers when goods:	Transportation costs paid by:
FOB Shipping Point	Leave the seller's warehouse	Buyer
FOB Destination	Arrive at buyer's warehouse	Seller

[6] Companies that automatically take advantage of favourable discounts use the *net method* to record merchandise purchases as opposed to using the gross invoice amount when debiting Merchandise Inventory and crediting Accounts Payable (as illustrated in the textbook on page 257; known as the *gross method*). Under the net method, both Merchandise Inventory and Accounts Payable are debited/credited for the gross purchase amount *less* the discount. If payment is not made within the discount period, the payment would debit Accounts Payable for the net amount originally recorded, debit *Discounts Lost* for the amount of the lost discount, and credit Cash for the gross amount of the invoice. The gross method more strictly adheres to the revenue recognition principle P. 32 than the net method, hence its inclusion in the textbook.

damage or loss when goods are in transit. The goods are part of the buyer's inventory when they are in transit since ownership has transferred to the buyer.

FOB destination means ownership of the goods transfers to the buyer at the buyer's place of business. The seller is responsible for paying shipping charges and bears the risk of damage or loss in transit. The seller does not record revenue from this sale until the goods arrive at the destination because this transaction is not complete before that point.

There are situations when the party not responsible for shipping costs pays the carrier. In these cases, the party paying these costs either bills the party responsible or, more commonly, adjusts its account payable or receivable with the other party.

Transportation Costs

Shipping costs on purchases are called **transportation-in** or **freight-in** costs. Z-Mart's $1,200 purchase on November 2 is on terms of FOB destination. This means that Z-Mart is not responsible for paying transportation costs.

A different situation arises when a company is responsible for paying transportation costs. The cost principle P. 32 requires these transportation costs to be included as part of the cost of merchandise inventory. This means that a separate entry is necessary when they are not listed on the invoice. For example, Z-Mart's entry to record a $75 freight charge to an independent carrier for merchandise purchased FOB shipping point is:

Date		Account	Debit	Credit
Nov.	24	Merchandise Inventory..................................	75	
		Cash		75
		Paid freight charges on purchased merchandise.		

The costs of shipping goods to customers are different from transportation-in costs. **Transportation-out** or **freight-out** costs regarding the shipping of goods to customers are debited to the Delivery Expense account when the seller is responsible for these costs, and are reported as a selling expense in the income statement.

Recording Purchases Information

We have explained how purchase returns and allowances, purchase discounts, and transportation-in are included in calculating the total cost of merchandise inventory. Z-Mart's 2011 net cost of merchandise purchases is summarized in Exhibit 6.10.

Exhibit 6.10

Net Cost of Merchandise Purchases Calculation—Perpetual

Net Cost of Purchases during 2011 = $232,400

Merchandise Inventory			
Dec. 31, 2010, balance	19,000		
Reflects entries to record **purchases of merchandise** during 2011	235,800	4,200	Reflects entries to record **purchase discounts** ....during 2011
Reflects **transportation-in** costs incurred during 2011	2,300	1,500	Reflects entries to record **purchase returns and** ....**allowances** during 2011

4. Refer to Exhibit 6.6 on page 257. When the merchandise inventory is shipped by Trex to Z-Mart, identify when ownership transfers.
5. How long are the credit and discount periods when credit terms are 2/10, n/60?
6. Identify items subtracted from the list amount when calculating purchase price: (a) freight-in, (b) trade discount, (c) purchase discount, (d) purchase return and/or allowance.

Do Quick Study questions: QS 6-5, QS 6-6, QS 6-7

Accounting for Merchandise Sales—Perpetual Inventory System

Merchandising companies also must account for sales, sales discounts, sales returns and allowances, and cost of goods sold. A merchandising company such as Z-Mart reports these items in an income statement, as shown in Exhibit 6.11.

Exhibit 6.11

Gross Profit Section of Income Statement

Z-Mart Calculation of Gross Profit For Year Ended December 31, 2011		
Sales		$321,000
Less: Sales discounts	$4,300	
Sales returns and allowances	2,000	6,300
Net sales		$314,700
Cost of goods sold		230,400
Gross profit from sales		$ 84,300

This section explains how information in this calculation is derived from transactions involving sales, sales discounts, and sales returns and allowances.

Sales Transactions

Accounting for a sales transaction for a seller of merchandise involves capturing information about two related parts:

1. Revenue received in the form of an asset from a customer, and
2. Recognizing the cost of merchandise sold to a customer.

As an example, Z-Mart sold $2,400 of merchandise on credit on November 3. The revenue part of this transaction is recorded as:

Nov. 3	Accounts Receivable	2,400	
	Sales		2,400
	Sold merchandise on credit.		

This entry reflects an increase in Z-Mart's assets in the form of an account receivable. It also shows the revenue from the credit sale. If the sale is for cash, the debit is to Cash instead of Accounts Receivable.

The expense or cost of the merchandise sold by Z-Mart on November 3 is $1,600. We explain in Chapter 7 how the cost of this merchandise is calculated.

The entry to record the cost part of this sales transaction (under a perpetual inventory system) is:

Nov. 3	Cost of Goods Sold	1,600	
	Merchandise Inventory		1,600
	To record the cost of Nov. 3 sale and reduce inventory.		

This entry records the cost of the merchandise sold as an expense and reduces the Merchandise Inventory account to reflect the remaining balance of inventory on hand.

Sales Discounts

When sellers offer credit terms that include a cash discount, the cash discount is referred to as a **sales discount**. Sales discounts can encourage prompt payments, improve cash flow, and also reduce future efforts and costs of billing customers.

A seller does not know whether a customer will pay within the discount period and take advantage of a cash discount at the time of a credit sale, so a sales discount is usually not recorded until a customer pays within the discount period. As an example, Z-Mart completed a credit sale for $1,000 on November 12, subject to terms of 2/10, n/60 (the cost of the inventory sold was $600). The entry to record this sale is:

Nov. 12	Accounts Receivable	1,000	
	Sales		1,000
	Sold merchandise under terms of 2/10, n/60.		
12	Cost of Goods Sold	600	
	Merchandise Inventory		600
	To record the cost of the Nov. 12 sale and reduce inventory.		

This entry records the receivable and the revenue as if the full amount will be paid by the customer.

The customer has two options. One option is to wait 60 days until January 11 and pay the full $1,000. In this case, Z-Mart records the payment as:

Jan. 11	Cash	1,000	
	Accounts Receivable		1,000
	Received payment for November 12 sale.		

The customer's second option is to pay $980 within a 10-day period that runs through November 22. If the customer pays on or before November 22, Z-Mart records the payment as:

Nov. 22	Cash	980	
	Sales Discounts	20	
	Accounts Receivable		1,000
	Received payment for November 12 sale less the discount; $1,000 × 2% = $20.		

Sales discounts are recorded in a *contra revenue* account called Sales Discounts. This is so management can monitor sales discounts to assess their effectiveness and cost. The Sales Discounts account is deducted from the Sales account when calculating a company's net sales (refer to Exhibit 6.11). While information about sales discounts is useful internally, it is seldom reported on income statements distributed to external users P. 7.

Sales Returns and Allowances

Sales returns refer to merchandise that customers return to the seller after a sale. Customers return merchandise for a variety of reasons, such as having received an incorrect item or one of poor quality. Many companies allow customers to return merchandise for a full refund. *Sales allowances* refer to reductions in the selling price of merchandise sold to customers. This can occur with damaged merchandise that a customer is willing to purchase if the selling price is decreased. **Sales returns and allowances** involve dissatisfied customers and the possibility of lost future sales. To monitor these problems managers need detailed information, so many accounting systems record returns and allowances in a separate contra revenue account.

Recall Z-Mart's sale of merchandise on November 3. As already recorded, the merchandise is sold for $2,400 and cost $1,600, but what if the customer returns part of the merchandise on November 6, when returned items sell for $800 and cost $600? The revenue part of this transaction must reflect the decrease in sales from the customer's return:

Nov.	6	Sales Returns and Allowances	800	
		Accounts Receivable		800
		Customer returned merchandise.		

Z-Mart can record this return with a debit to the Sales account instead of Sales Returns and Allowances. This method provides the same net sales, but does not provide information needed by managers to monitor returns and allowances. By using the Sales Returns and Allowances contra account, this information is available. Published income statements usually omit this detail and show only net sales.

If the merchandise returned to Z-Mart is not defective and can be resold to another customer, then Z-Mart returns these goods to its inventory. The entry necessary to restore the cost of these goods to the Merchandise Inventory account is:

Nov.	6	Merchandise Inventory	600	
		Cost of Goods Sold		600
		Returned goods to inventory.		

If the merchandise returned is defective, however, the seller may discard the returned items. In this case, the cost of returned merchandise is not restored to the Merchandise Inventory account. Instead, most companies leave the cost of defective merchandise in the Cost of Goods Sold account.[7]

Another possibility is that $800 of the merchandise sold by Z-Mart on November 3 is defective but the customer decides to keep it because Z-Mart grants the customer a price reduction of $500. The only entry that Z-Mart must make in this case is one to reflect the decrease in revenue:

Nov.	6	Sales Returns and Allowances	500	
		Accounts Receivable		500
		To record sales allowance.		

[7] When managers want to monitor the cost of defective merchandise, a better method is to remove the cost from Cost of Goods Sold and charge it to a *Loss From Defective Merchandise* account.

As shown in Exhibit 6.12, the seller prepares a **credit memorandum** to confirm a customer's return or allowance. A credit memorandum informs a customer of a credit to his or her account receivable, hence the term *credit memorandum*.

Exhibit 6.12

Credit Memorandum

Case: Z-Mart (seller) accepts $800 of returned merchandise from Bricks (buyer)

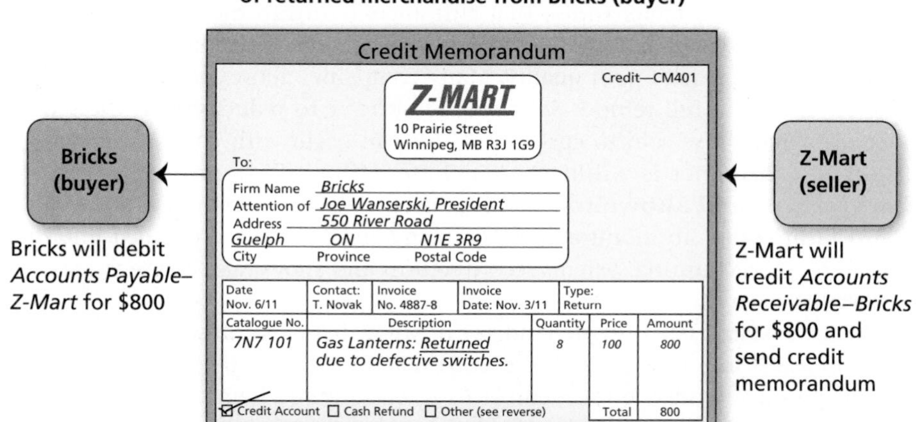
Bricks (buyer)
Bricks will debit *Accounts Payable–Z-Mart* for $800
Z-Mart (seller)
Z-Mart will credit *Accounts Receivable–Bricks* for $800 and send credit memorandum

Credit Memorandum

Credit—CM401

Z-MART
10 Prairie Street
Winnipeg, MB R3J 1G9

To:
Firm Name *Bricks*
Attention of *Joe Wanserski, President*
Address *550 River Road*
Guelph *ON* *N1E 3R9*
City Province Postal Code

Date	Contact:	Invoice	Invoice	Type:		
Nov. 6/11	T. Novak	No. 4887-8	Date: Nov. 3/11	Return		
Catalogue No.	Description			Quantity	Price	Amount
7N7 101	*Gas Lanterns: Returned due to defective switches.*			*8*	*100*	*800*
☑ Credit Account ☐ Cash Refund ☐ Other (see reverse)					Total	800

The information in a credit memorandum is similar to that of a debit memorandum. The following table summarizes what debit and credit memoranda (memos) are and why they arise:

Debit Memo	Credit Memo
What is a debit memo? • A document prepared by the purchaser to "debit" or reduce the purchaser's account payable	What is a credit memo? • A document prepared by the seller to "credit" or reduce the customer's account receivable
Why is a debit memo issued? • To reduce the purchaser's account payable because of: 1. Return of unsatisfactory goods 2. Allowance 3. Error	Why is a credit memo issued? • To reduce the seller's account receivable because of: 1. Return of unsatisfactory goods 2. Allowance 3. Error

CHECKPOINT
Read
Apply
Do
Check

7. Why are sales discounts and sales returns and allowances recorded in contra revenue accounts instead of directly in the Sales account?
8. Under what conditions are two entries necessary to record a sales return?
9. When merchandise is sold on credit and the seller notifies the buyer of a price reduction, does the seller send a credit memorandum or a debit memorandum?

Do Quick Study questions: QS 6-8, QS 6-9, QS 6-10, QS 6-11

mid-chapter demonstration problem

Beta Company, a retail store, had the following transactions in March:

March	2	Purchased merchandise from Alfa Company under the following terms: $1,800 invoice price, 2/15, n/60, FOB factory. (The cost of the merchandise to Alfa Company was $990.)
	3	Paid CanPar Shipping $125 for shipping charges on the purchase of March 2.
	4	Returned to Alfa Company unacceptable merchandise that had an invoice price of $300 (and a cost to Alfa of $165). Alfa returned the merchandise to inventory.
	17	Sent a cheque to Alfa Company for the March 2 purchase, net of the discount and the returned merchandise.

Required

Assuming both Beta and Alfa use a perpetual inventory system:

a. Present the journal entries Beta Company should record for these transactions.

b. Present the journal entries Alfa Company should record for these transactions.

Analysis component:

Who should be insuring the merchandise during shipping: Beta or Alfa? Explain.

solution

a.

	Beta Company (the buyer)		
March 2	Merchandise Inventory	1,800	
	Accounts Payable—Alfa Company		1,800
	Purchased merchandise on credit.		
3	Merchandise Inventory	125	
	Cash		125
	Paid shipping charges on purchased merchandise.		
4	Accounts Payable—Alfa Company	300	
	Merchandise Inventory		300
	Returned unacceptable merchandise.		
17	Accounts Payable—Alfa Company	1,500	
	Merchandise Inventory		30
	Cash		1,470
	Paid balance within the discount period and took a 2% discount.		

b.

Alfa Company (the seller)		
Accounts Receivable—Beta Company	1,800	
Sales		1,800
Sold merchandise under terms 2/15, n/60.		
Cost of Goods Sold	990	
Merchandise Inventory		990
Recorded cost of sales.		
No entry		
Sales Returns and Allowances	300	
Accounts Receivable—Beta Company		300
Customer returned merchandise.		
Merchandise Inventory	165	
Cost of Goods Sold		165
Merchandise returned to inventory.		
Cash	1,470	
Sales Discounts	30	
Accounts Receivable—Beta Company		1,500
Received payment for March 2 sale less the return and discount.		

Analysis component:

Beta should be insuring the merchandise during shipping because the terms, FOB factory, transfer ownership to Beta the moment the merchandise leaves Alfa.

Additional Merchandising Issues—Perpetual Inventory System

This section identifies and explains how merchandising activities affect other accounting processes. We address preparing adjusting entries, and relations between important accounts.

Adjusting Entries

LO4 Prepare adjustments for a merchandising company.

Most adjusting entries are the same for merchandising companies and service companies and involve prepaid expenses, unearned revenues, depreciation, accrued expenses, and accrued revenues.

A merchandising company using a perpetual inventory system needs one additional adjustment to update the Merchandise Inventory account for any losses of merchandise. Merchandising companies can lose merchandise in several ways, including theft and deterioration, referred to as **shrinkage**.

While a perpetual inventory system tracks all goods as they move into and out of the company, a perpetual system is unable to measure shrinkage directly. Yet we can calculate shrinkage by comparing the recorded quantities of inventory with a physical count, usually performed at least once annually to verify the Merchandise Inventory account. Most companies record any necessary adjustment due to shrinkage by charging it to Cost of Goods Sold, assuming that shrinkage is not abnormally large.

As an example, Z-Mart's Merchandise Inventory account at the end of 2011 had an unadjusted balance of $21,250, but a physical count of inventory revealed only $21,000 of inventory on hand. The adjusting entry to record this $250 shrinkage is:

Dec. 31	Cost of Goods Sold	250	
	Merchandise Inventory		250
	To adjust for $250 shrinkage disclosed by physical count of inventory.		

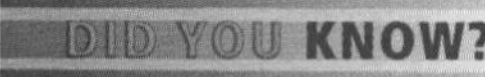

A study by GPI Atlantic reports that businesses have to build the cost of security systems, guards, shoplifting, and employee theft—all related to shrinkage—into their product pricing. The average Nova Scotian household, according to the study, pays $800 more per year because of shrinkage.

Source: eda.gov.ns.ca/press

10. When a merchandising company uses a perpetual inventory system, why is it often necessary to adjust the Merchandise Inventory balance with an adjusting entry?

Do Quick Study question: QS 6-12

Summary of Merchandising Cost Flows

The Merchandise Inventory account balance at the end of one period is the amount of beginning inventory in the next period.

To summarize the effects of merchandising transactions on the Merchandise Inventory and Cost of Goods Sold accounts, Z-Mart's merchandising activities during 2011 are illustrated in Exhibit 6.13. Most amounts in these T-accounts are summary representations of several entries during the year 2011. Notice that the Cost of Goods Sold balance of $230,400 is the amount reported in the income statement information in Exhibit 6.2. The Merchandise Inventory balance of $21,000 is the amount reported as a current asset on the balance sheet in Exhibit 6.3. These amounts also appear on Z-Mart's adjusted trial balance in Exhibits 6.14 and 6.20.

Exhibit 6.13

Summary of Z-Mart's Merchandising Activities for 2011 Reflected in T-accounts

	Merchandise Inventory			
	Dec. 31, 2010, balance	19,000		
Net cost of purchases	Reflects entries to record **purchases of merchandise** during 2011	235,800	4,200	Reflects entries to record **purchase discounts** during 2011
Net cost of purchases	Reflects **transportation-in** costs incurred during 2011	2,300	1,500	Reflects entries to record **purchase returns and allowances** during 2011
	Reflects entries to record **merchandise returned by customers** and restored to inventory during 2011	1,400	231,550	Reflects **cost of sales** transactions during 2011
	Dec. 31, 2011, unadjusted balance	21,250	250	Dec. 31, 2011, adjustment for **shrinkage**
	Dec. 31, 2011, adjusted balance	21,000		

	Cost of Goods Sold			
Cost of goods sold transferred from inventory account.	Reflects entries to record the **cost of sales** for 2011	231,550	1,400	Reflects entries to record **merchandise returned** by customers and restored to inventory during 2011
	Dec. 31, 2011, unadjusted balance	230,150		
	Dec. 31, 2011, adjustment for **shrinkage**	250		
	Dec. 31, 2011 adjusted balance	230,400		

Income Statement Formats—Perpetual Inventory System

LO5 Define, prepare, and use merchandising income statements.

Companies have flexibility as to what format can be used for the presentation of financial statements. As a result, there will be many different formats in practice. However, there are minimum classification requirements regarding how expenses are to be shown on the income statement. The first part of this section looks at formulating a draft income statement through the preparation of a work sheet. The second part of this section describes the classification requirements for expenses and illustrates three presentation formats using Z-Mart's data.

A Work Sheet for a Merchandising Company

Exhibit 6.14 presents a work sheet that could be prepared in the process of developing Z-Mart's 2011 financial statements.

Exhibit 6.14

Work Sheet (Perpetual) for Z-Mart for Year Ended December 31, 2011

		Unadjusted Trial Balance		Adjustments		Adjusted Trial Balance		Income Statement		Balance Sheet & Statement of Changes in Equity	
No.	Account	Debit	Credit	Debit	Credit	Debit	Credit	Debit	Credit	Debit	Credit
101	Cash	8,200				8,200				8,200	
106	Accounts receivable	11,200				11,200				11,200	
119	**Merchandise inventory**	**21,250**			**(g) 250**	**21,000**				**21,000**	
124	Office supplies	2,350			(c) 1,800	550				550	
125	Store supplies	1,450			(b) 1,200	250				250	
128	Prepaid insurance	900			(a) 600	300				300	
163	Office equipment	4,200				4,200				4,200	
164	Accum. dep., office equipment		700		(e) 700		1,400				1,400
165	Store equipment	30,000				30,000				30,000	
166	Accum. dep., store equipment		3,000		(d) 3,000		6,000				6,000
201	Accounts payable		16,000				16,000				16,000
209	Salaries payable				(f) 800		800				800
301	Kent Marty, capital		40,160				40,160				40,160
302	Kent Marty, withdrawals	4,000				4,000				4,000	
406	Rent revenue		2,800				2,800		2,800		
413	**Sales**		**321,000**				**321,000**		**321,000**		
414	**Sales returns and allowances**	**2,000**				**2,000**		**2,000**			
415	**Sales discounts**	**4,300**				**4,300**		**4,300**			
502	**Cost of goods sold**	**230,150**		**(g) 250**		**230,400**		**230,400**			
612	Dep. expense, store equipment			(d) 3,000		3,000		3,000			
613	Dep. expense, office equipment			(e) 700		700		700			
620	Office salaries expense	25,000		(f) 300		25,300		25,300			
621	Sales salaries expense	18,000		(f) 500		18,500		18,500			
633	Interest expense	360				360		360			
637	Insurance expense			(a) 600		600		600			
641	Rent expense, office space	900				900		900			
642	Rent expense, selling space	8,100				8,100		8,100			
650	Office supplies expense			(c) 1,800		1,800		1,800			
651	Store supplies expense			(b) 1,200		1,200		1,200			
655	Advertising expense	11,300				11,300		11,300			
	Totals	383,660	383,660	8,350	8,350	388,160	388,160	308,460	323,800	79,700	64,360
	Net income							15,340			15,340
	Totals							323,800	323,800	79,700	79,700

The adjustments in the work sheet reflect the following:

a. Expiration of $600 of prepaid insurance.
b. Use of $1,200 of store supplies.
c. Use of $1,800 of office supplies.
d. Depreciation of the store equipment for $3,000.
e. Depreciation of the office equipment for $700.
f. Accrual of $300 of unpaid office salaries and $500 of unpaid store salaries.
g. Physical count of merchandise inventory revealed $21,000 on hand.

The financial statement columns in Exhibit 6.14 are used to develop the company's financial statements.

Expense Classification Requirements

Expenses are to be shown on an income statement based on either their *nature* or their *function*.[8] In previous chapters, expenses were listed on the income statement based on their *nature*. The **nature of an expense** is determined by its basic characteristics or what it is. For example, when expenses are identified on the income statement as depreciation, rent, property tax, and salaries, the nature of each expense is being identified. The **function of an expense** describes the grouping of expenses based on their purpose or what they relate to. For example, an income statement that shows cost of goods sold, *selling expenses*, and *general and administrative expenses* has grouped expenses by their function. When expenses are grouped by function, additional information must be *disclosed* to show the nature of expenses within each group.[9] The **full disclosure principle** is the generally accepted accounting principle that requires financial statements to report all relevant information about the operations and financial position of the entity. Information that is relevant but not included in the body of the statements is provided in **notes to financial statements** such as those for WestJet in Appendix I of the text.

Multiple-Step Income Statement

There are two general types of multiple-step income statements: the *multiple-step* format and the *classified, multiple-step* format. Both formats can be used in either a perpetual or periodic inventory system.

Classified, Multiple-Step Format (for internal reporting)

Exhibit 6.15 shows a **classified, multiple-step income statement** for Z-Mart. This format is useful for internal reporting because of the detail it includes, such as the calculation of net sales. The difference between net sales and cost of goods sold is Z-Mart's gross profit.

Exhibit 6.15 shows operating expenses, a broad function or category. Operating expenses are divided into two additional functions: *selling expenses* and *general and administrative expenses*. **Selling expenses** include the expenses of promoting sales through displaying and advertising merchandise, making sales, and delivering goods to customers. In Exhibit 6.15, the selling expenses are disclosed within the body of the statement by providing detailed information on the nature of expenses, including sales salaries, advertising, rent expense allocated to selling, depreciation on the store equipment, and store supplies. **General and administrative expenses** support the overall operations of a company and include

[8] IFRS 2009, IAS 1, para. 99–105.
[9] IFRS 2009, IAS 1, para. 104. Although students at the introductory level should understand the concept of disclosure, the actual preparation of notes is left to a more advanced accounting course.

expenses related to accounting, human resource management, and financial management. In Exhibit 6.15, the general and administrative expenses section provides detail on the nature of these expenses by including office salaries, office supplies, rent expense allocated to the general and administrative category, depreciation on the office equipment, and insurance expense.

Notice that an expense may be divided between categories when it contributes to more than one activity. For example, Exhibit 6.15 shows that Z-Mart allocates rent expense of $9,000 for its store building between two categories: $8,100 is a selling expense, while $900 is listed as a general and administrative expense based on relative rental values.[10]

Revenues and expenses that are ***not*** part of normal operating activities are reported under the functional heading *Other revenues and expenses* of the income statement. Z-Mart's main operating activity is merchandising, therefore rent revenue—not a merchandising activity—is added under *Other revenues and expenses.* Another example, interest expense, arises because of a financing (or borrowing) activity and not because of Z-Mart's merchandising (or operating) activities. It is subtracted under *Other revenues and expenses* as highlighted in Exhibit 6.15. Other examples of *Other revenues and expenses* include dividend income and gains and losses on the sale of property, plant and equipment assets.

Exhibit 6.15

Classified, Multiple-Step Income Statement—Perpetual Inventory System

Z-Mart
Income Statement
For Year Ended December 31, 2011

Sales			$321,000
Less: Sales discounts		$ 4,300	
Sales returns and allowances		2,000	6,300
Net sales			$314,700
Cost of goods sold			230,400
Gross profit from sales			$ 84,300
Operating expenses:			
Selling expenses:			
Sales salaries expense	$18,500		
Advertising expense	11,300		
Rent expense, selling space	8,100		
Depreciation expense, store equipment	3,000		
Store supplies expense	1,200		
Total selling expenses		$42,100	
General and administrative expenses:			
Office salaries expense	$25,300		
Office supplies expense	1,800		
Rent expense, office space	900		
Depreciation expense, office equipment	700		
Insurance expense	600		
Total general and administrative expenses		29,300	
Total operating expenses			71,400
Income from operations			$ 12,900
Other revenues and expenses:			
Rent revenue		$ 2,800	
Interest expense		360	2,440
Net income			$ 15,340

Rent revenue is added

Interest expense is subtracted

to get total *Other revenues and expenses.*

[10] These expenses can be recorded in a single ledger account or in two separate accounts. If they are recorded in one account, we allocate its balance between the two expenses when preparing statements.

Multiple-Step Format (for external reporting)

Exhibit 6.16 shows a multiple-step income statement format that can be used in external reports. In comparison to Exhibit 6.15, a multiple-step statement leaves out the detailed calculation of net sales. The functional categories of *selling expenses* and *general and administrative expenses* are not included on a multiple-step income statement; operating expenses are listed by nature only on a multiple-step income statement.

Exhibit 6.16

Multiple-Step Income Statement—Perpetual Inventory System

Z-Mart **Income Statement** **For Year Ended December 31, 2011**		
Net sales		$314,700
Cost of goods sold		230,400
Gross profit from sales		$ 84,300
Operating expenses:		
Salaries expense	$43,800	
Advertising expense	11,300	
Rent expense	9,000	
Depreciation expense	3,700	
Supplies expense	3,000	
Insurance expense	600	
Total operating expenses		71,400
Income from operations		$ 12,900
Other revenues and expenses:		
Rent revenue	$ 2,800	
Interest expense	360	2,440
Net income		$ 15,340

Single-Step Income Statement

A **single-step income statement** is another format for external reporting. It shows items based on their function only and is shown in Exhibit 6.17 for Z-Mart. This simple format includes cost of goods sold as an operating expense and shows only one subtotal for total expenses. Because operating expenses are highly summarized on a single-step income statement, additional information regarding the nature of expenses included in each function must be disclosed in the notes to the financial statements.

Exhibit 6.17

Single-Step Income Statement—Perpetual Inventory System

Z-Mart **Income Statement** **For Year Ended December 31, 2011**		
Revenues:		
Net sales	$314,700	
Rent revenue	2,800	
Total revenues		$317,500
Expenses:		
Cost of goods sold	$230,400	
Selling expenses	42,100	
General and administrative expense	29,300	
Interest expense	360	
Total expenses		302,160
Net income		$ 15,340

Companies can use formats that combine features of both the single- and multiple-step statements for external reporting. As long as income statement items are shown sensibly and minimum requirements are satisfied, management can choose the presentation format.

Gross Profit Ratio

Gross profit, also called gross margin, is the relation between sales and cost of goods sold. A merchandising company needs sufficient gross profit to cover operating expenses or it will likely fail. To help us focus on gross profit, users often calculate a gross profit ratio. The **gross profit ratio**, or **gross margin ratio**, is defined as shown in Exhibit 6.18.

Exhibit 6.18

Gross Profit Ratio

$$\text{Gross profit ratio} = \frac{\text{Gross profit from sales}}{\text{Net sales}} \times 100\%$$

Exhibit 6.19 shows the gross profit ratios of Z-Mart for the years 2009, 2010, and 2011.

Exhibit 6.19

Z-Mart's Gross Profit Ratio

	2011	2010	2009
Units sold	214,000	160,000	100,000
Gross profit from sales	$84,300	$69,440	$46,400
Net sales	$314,700	$248,000	$160,000
Gross profit ratio	26.8%	28.0%	29.0%

This ratio represents the gross profit in each dollar of sales. For example, Exhibit 6.19 shows that Z-Mart's gross profit ratio in 2009 was 29.0%. This means that each $1 of sales yielded 29¢ in gross profit to cover all other expenses. Exhibit 6.19 shows that Z-Mart's gross profit ratio decreased from 2009 to 2011, reflecting an unfavourable trend. How is this possible given that net sales and gross profit in dollars are both increasing? If net sales are increasing but at a slower rate than the increase in cost of goods sold, gross profit on sales will grow but at a decreasing rate.[11] Success for companies such as Z-Mart depends on a gross profit that adequately covers operating expenses.

CHECKPOINT 

11. What income statement format shows detailed calculations for net sales? What format gives no subtotals except total expenses?
12. K-One Merchandising shows gross profit ratios of 39%, 39.5%, and 41% for 2009, 2010, and 2011 respectively. Assuming that all other factors have remained constant, does this reflect a favourable (good) or unfavourable (bad) trend?

Do Quick Study questions: QS 6-13, QS 6-14

[11] A more detailed analysis of the information in Exhibit 6.19 shows that net sales are increasing but at a slower rate than the increases in cost of goods sold. This has caused gross profit to shrink as a percentage of sales (an unfavourable trend). This conclusion is supported by the following:

	2011	% Change	2010	% Change	2009
Units sold	214,000	33.8	160,000	60.0	100,000
Net sales	$314,700	26.9	$248,000	55.0	$160,000
COGS	230,400	29.0	178,560	57.2	113,600
Gross profit from sales	$ 84,300	21.4	$ 69,440	49.7	$ 46,400
Gross profit ratio	26.8%	−4.3	28.0%	−3.4	29.0%

Closing Entries for a Merchandising Company—Perpetual Inventory System

LO6 Prepare closing entries for a merchandising company.

When using a perpetual system, closing entries are similar for merchandising companies and service companies. Both use an adjusted trial balance to prepare closing entries. The one difference is that we must close the additional temporary accounts related to merchandising activities.

These accounts are bolded in the adjusted trial balance in Exhibit 6.20 and include: Sales, Sales Discounts, Sales Returns and Allowances, and Cost of Goods Sold. The closing process for a merchandiser is identical to that described in Chapter 5 for a service company. The closing entries for Z-Mart are shown in Exhibit 6.21. Notice that the temporary accounts unique to a merchandiser are highlighted for you in these closing entries.

Exhibit 6.20

Adjusted Trial Balance

Z-Mart
Adjusted Trial Balance
December 31, 2011

	Debit	Credit
Cash	$ 8,200	
Accounts receivable	11,200	
Merchandise inventory	21,000	
Office supplies	550	
Store supplies	250	
Prepaid insurance	300	
Office equipment	4,200	
Accumulated depreciation, office equipment		$ 1,400
Store equipment	30,000	
Accumulated depreciation, store equipment		6,000
Accounts payable		16,000
Salaries payable		800
Kent Marty, capital		40,160
Kent Marty, withdrawals	4,000	
Rent revenue		2,800
Sales		**321,000**
Sales returns and allowances	**2,000**	
Sales discounts	**4,300**	
Cost of goods sold	**230,400**	
Depreciation expense, store equipment	3,000	
Depreciation expense, office equipment	700	
Office salaries expense	25,300	
Sales salaries expense	18,500	
Interest expense	360	
Insurance expense	600	
Rent expense, office space	900	
Rent expense, selling space	8,100	
Office supplies expense	1,800	
Store supplies expense	1,200	
Advertising expense	11,300	
Totals	$388,160	$388,160

The temporary accounts unique to a merchandiser are highlighted here and in the closing entries shown in Exhibit 6.21.

Exhibit 6.21

Closing Entries for Z-Mart

Entry 1: Close Credit Balances in Temporary Accounts to Income Summary.
Z-Mart has two temporary accounts with credit balances and they are closed with the entry:

Dec.	31	Rent Revenue	2,800	
		Sales	**321,000**	
		Income Summary		323,800
		To close temporary accounts having credit balances.		

Posting this entry to the ledger gives a zero balance to the Rent Revenue and Sales accounts and opens the Income Summary account.

Entry 2: Close Debit Balances in Temporary Accounts to Income Summary.
Temporary accounts having debit balances include Cost of Goods Sold, Sales Discounts, and Sales Returns and Allowances. This second entry yields the amount of net income as the balance in the Income Summary account. Z-Mart's second closing entry is:

As contra revenue accounts, these are income statement accounts and must be closed.

Dec.	31	Income Summary	308,460	
		Sales Discounts		**4,300**
		Sales Returns and Allowances		**2,000**
		Cost of Goods Sold		**230,400**
		Depreciation Expense, Store Equipment		3,000
		Depreciation Expense, Office Equipment		700
		Office Salaries Expense		25,300
		Sales Salaries Expense		18,500
		Interest Expense		360
		Insurance Expense		600
		Rent Expense, Office Space		900
		Rent Expense, Selling Space		8,100
		Office Supplies Expense		1,800
		Store Supplies Expense		1,200
		Advertising Expense		11,300
		To close temporary accounts having debit balances.		

Entry 3: Close Income Summary to Owner's Capital.
The third closing entry is the same for a merchandising company and a service company. It closes the Income Summary account and updates the owner's capital account for income or loss. Z-Mart's third closing entry is:

Dec.	31	Income Summary	15,340	
		Kent Marty, Capital		15,340
		To close the income summary account.		

Notice that the $15,340 amount in the entry is net income reported on the income statement in Exhibits 6.15 to 6.17.

Entry 4: Close Withdrawals Account to Owner's Capital.
The fourth closing entry for a merchandising company is the same as the fourth closing entry for a service company. It closes the withdrawals account and reduces the owner's capital account balance to the amount shown on the balance sheet. The fourth closing entry for Z-Mart is:

Dec.	31	Kent Marty, Capital	4,000	
		Kent Marty, Withdrawals		4,000
		To close the withdrawals account.		

When this entry is posted, all temporary accounts are closed and ready to record events for the year 2012. The owner's capital account is also updated and reflects transactions of 2011.

13. What temporary accounts do you expect to find in a merchandising business but not in a service business?
14. Describe the closing entries normally made by a merchandising company.

Do Quick Study question: QS 6-15

CRITICAL THINKING CHALLENGE

Refer to the Critical Thinking Challenge questions at the beginning of the chapter on page 252. Compare your answers to those suggested on Connect at www.mcgrawhillconnect.ca.

IFRS HIGHLIGHTS

Expenses on income statements are to be presented either by function or by nature. If they are presented by function, additional disclosure must be made that includes depreciation and amortization expense and employee benefits expense (IAS 1, para. 99–105). (Amortization expense is discussed in Chapter 12.)

Summary

LO1 | Describe merchandising and identify and explain the important income statement and balance sheet components for a merchandising company. Operations of merchandising companies involve buying products and reselling them. A merchandiser's costs on an income statement include an amount for cost of goods sold. Gross profit, or gross margin, equals net sales minus cost of goods sold. The current asset section of the balance sheet includes merchandise inventory, which refers to the products a merchandiser sells and has on hand at the balance sheet date.

LO2 | Describe both perpetual and periodic inventory systems. A perpetual inventory system continuously tracks the cost of goods on hand and the cost of goods sold. A periodic system accumulates the cost of goods *purchased* during the period and does not compute the amount of inventory on hand or the cost of goods sold until the end of a period.

LO3 | Analyze and record transactions for merchandise purchases and sales using a perpetual system. For a perpetual inventory system, purchases net of trade discounts are added (debited) to the Merchandise Inventory account. Purchase discounts and purchase returns and allowances are subtracted from (credited to) Merchandise Inventory, and transportation-in costs are added (debited) to Merchandise Inventory. A merchandiser records sales at list price less any trade discounts. The cost of items sold is transferred from Merchandise Inventory to Cost of Goods Sold. Refunds or credits given to customers for unsatisfactory merchandise are recorded (debited) in Sales Returns and Allowances, a contra account to Sales. If merchandise is returned and restored to inventory, the cost of this merchandise is removed from Cost of Goods Sold and transferred back to Merchandise Inventory. When cash discounts from the sales price are offered and customers pay within the discount period, the seller records (debits) discounts in Sales Discounts, a contra account to Sales. Debit and credit memoranda are documents sent between buyers and sellers to communicate that the sender is either debiting or crediting an account of the recipient.

LO4 | Prepare adjustments for a merchandising company. With a perpetual inventory system, it is often necessary to make an adjustment for inventory shrinkage. This is calculated by comparing a physical count of inventory with the Merchandise Inventory account balance. Shrinkage is normally charged to Cost of Goods Sold.

LO5 | Define, prepare, and use merchandising income statements. Multiple-step income statements show items by both function and nature. Classified multiple-step income statements are usually limited to internal use and show the calculation of net sales, and report expenses by function—such as selling and general and administrative—supported by a list of expenses by nature. The format of income statements published for external parties is flexible and includes the multiple-step or single-step format. The single-step format shows expenses by function with supporting note disclosure about the nature of the expenses. The gross profit ratio is calculated as gross profit divided by net sales. It is an indicator of a company's profitability before deducting operating expenses. A gross profit ratio must be large enough to cover operating expenses and give an adequate net income.

LO6 Prepare closing entries for a merchandising company. Temporary accounts of merchandising companies include Sales, Sales Discounts, Sales Returns and Allowances, and Cost of Goods Sold. Each is closed to Income Summary.

guidance answer to JUDGEMENT CALL

Accounts Payable Manager

Your decision is whether to comply with prior policy or create new policy not to abuse discounts offered by suppliers. Your first step should be to meet with your superior to find out if the automatic late payment policy is the actual policy and, if so, its rationale. It is possible that the prior employee was reprimanded because of this behaviour. If it is the policy to pay late, then you must apply your own sense of right and wrong.

One point of view is that the late payment policy is unethical. A deliberate plan to make late payments means that the company lies when it pretends to make purchases within the credit terms. There is the potential that your company could lose its ability to get future credit.

Another view is that the late payment policy is acceptable. There may exist markets in which attempts to take discounts through late payments are accepted as a continued phase of price negotiation. Also, your company's suppliers can respond by billing your company for the discounts not accepted because of late payments. This is a dubious viewpoint, especially given the old employee's proposal to cover up late payments as computer or mail problems, and given that some suppliers have previously complained.

guidance answers to CHECKPOINT

1. Cost of goods sold is the cost of merchandise sold to customers during a period.
2. Gross profit is the difference between net sales and cost of goods sold.
3. Widespread use of computing and related technology has dramatically increased use of the perpetual inventory system in practice.
4. The invoice indicates that the shipping terms are FOB destination, which means that Trex maintains ownership until the merchandise inventory reaches Z-Mart. Trex must therefore bear the freight costs and is responsible for insuring the merchandise inventory during transport.
5. Under credit terms of 2/10, n/60, the credit period is 60 days and the discount period is 10 days.
6. *b*
7. Recording sales discounts and sales returns and allowances separately from sales gives useful information to managers for internal monitoring and decision making.
8. When a customer returns merchandise and the seller restores the merchandise to inventory, two entries are necessary. One entry records the decrease in revenue and credits the customer's account. The second entry debits inventory and reduces cost of goods sold.
9. There will be a credit memorandum showing the *credit* to the seller's account receivable.
10. Merchandise Inventory balance may need adjusting to reflect shrinkage.
11. Classified, multiple-step income statement. Single-step income statement.
12. All other factors remaining constant, this reflects a favourable trend because K-One is showing an increase in gross profit per $1 of net sales over time (from 39¢ of gross profit per $1 of net sales in 2009 to 41¢ of gross profit per $1 of net sales in 2011). This indicates that K-One is generating more gross profit to cover operating expenses, which appears to be favourable.
13. Sales, Sales Discounts, Sales Returns and Allowances, and Cost of Goods Sold.
14. Four closing entries (the same for merchandising and service companies): (1) close credit balances in temporary accounts to income summary, (2) close debit balances in temporary accounts to income summary, (3) close income summary to owner's capital, and (4) close withdrawals account to owner's capital.

demonstration problem

Use the following adjusted trial balance and additional information to complete the requirements:

Ingersoll Antiques Adjusted Trial Balance December 31, 2011		
Cash	$ 19,300	
Merchandise inventory	50,000	
Store supplies	1,000	
Equipment	44,600	
Accumulated depreciation, equipment		$ 16,500
Accounts payable		8,000
Salaries payable		1,000
Dee Rizzo, capital		69,000
Dee Rizzo, withdrawals	8,000	
Interest revenue		300
Sales		325,000
Sales discounts	6,000	
Sales returns and allowances	5,000	
Cost of goods sold	148,000	
Depreciation expense, store equipment	4,000	
Depreciation expense, office equipment	1,500	
Sales salaries expense	28,000	
Office salaries expense	32,000	
Insurance expense	12,000	
Rent expense (70% is store, 30% is office)	24,000	
Store supplies expense	6,000	
Advertising expense	30,400	
Totals	$419,800	$419,800

Ingersoll Antiques showed the following additional information regarding merchandising activities for 2011:

Invoice cost of merchandise purchases	$140,000
Purchase discounts	3,500
Purchase returns and allowances	2,600
Transportation-in	4,000

Required

1. Use the additional information to calculate the total cost of merchandise purchases.
2. Prepare a 2011 classified, multiple-step income statement for internal use similar to Exhibit 6.15.
3. Present a single-step income statement for 2011 similar to the one in Exhibit 6.17.
4. Prepare closing entries.

Analysis component:

Calculate the gross profit ratio for Ingersoll and for Danier Leather (refer to Appendix I at the back of the textbook). Round calculations to two decimal places. Can you compare the gross profit ratios for these two companies? Explain.

Planning the Solution

- Calculate the total cost of merchandise purchases.
- Calculate net sales. Subtract cost of goods sold from net sales to get gross profit. Then, classify the operating expenses as selling expenses and general and administrative expenses.
- To prepare the single-step income statement, begin with the net sales and interest earned. Then, subtract the cost of goods sold and operating expenses.
- The first closing entry debits all temporary accounts with credit balances and opens the Income Summary account. The second closing entry credits all temporary accounts with debit balances. The third entry closes the Income Summary account to the owner's capital account, and the fourth closing entry closes the withdrawals account to the capital account.
- Prepare an answer to the analysis component.

solution

1.

Invoice cost of merchandise purchases	$140,000
Less: Purchase discounts	3,500
Purchase returns and allowances	2,600
Add: Transportation-in	4,000
Total cost of merchandise purchases	$137,900

2. Classified, multiple-step income statement

Ingersoll Antiques
Income Statement
For Year Ended December 31, 2011

Sales			$325,000
Less: Sales discounts		$ 6,000	
Sales returns and allowances		5,000	11,000
Net sales			$314,000
Cost of goods sold			148,000
Gross profit from sales			$166,000
Operating expenses:			
Selling expenses:			
Advertising expense	$30,400		
Sales salaries expense	28,000		
Rent expense, selling space	16,800		
Store supplies expense	6,000		
Depreciation expense, store equipment	4,000		
Total selling expenses		$85,200	
General and administrative expenses:			
Office salaries expense	$32,000		
Insurance expense	12,000		
Rent expense, office space	7,200		
Depreciation expense, office equipment	1,500		
Total general and administrative expenses		52,700	
Total operating expenses			137,900
Income from operations			$ 28,100
Other revenues and expenses:			
Interest revenue			300
Net income			$ 28,400

3. Single-step income statement

Ingersoll Antiques Income Statement For Year Ended December 31, 2011		
Revenues:		
Net sales		$314,000
Interest revenue		300
Total revenues		$314,300
Expenses:		
Cost of goods sold	$148,000	
Selling expenses	85,200	
General and administrative expense	52,700	
Total expenses		285,900
Net income		$ 28,400

4.

Date		Account	Debit	Credit
Dec.	31	Sales	325,000	
		Interest Revenue	300	
		Income Summary		325,300
		To close temporary accounts with credit balances to Income Summary.		
	31	Income Summary	296,900	
		Sales Discounts		6,000
		Sales Returns and Allowances		5,000
		Cost of Goods Sold		148,000
		Depreciation Expense, Store Equipment		4,000
		Depreciation Expense, Office Equipment		1,500
		Sales Salaries Expense		28,000
		Office Salaries Expense		32,000
		Insurance Expense		12,000
		Rent Expense		24,000
		Store Supplies Expense		6,000
		Advertising Expense		30,400
		To close temporary accounts with debit balances to Income Summary.		
	31	Income Summary	28,400	
		Dee Rizzo, Capital		28,400
		To close the income summary account to capital.		
	31	Dee Rizzo, Capital	8,000	
		Dee Rizzo, Withdrawals		8,000
		To close the withdrawals account to capital.		

Analysis component:

The gross profit ratio for Ingersoll is 52.87% ($166,000/$314,000 × 100%) and 46.58% ($76,185,000/$163,550,000 × 100%) for Danier's year ended June 28, 2008. You cannot compare the gross profit ratios for these two companies because they are in different industries: antiques vs. clothing.

APPENDIX 6A

Periodic and Perpetual Inventory Systems Compared

Accounting Comparisons

LO7 Record and compare merchandising transactions using both periodic and perpetual inventory systems.

Recall that under a perpetual system, the Merchandise Inventory account is updated after each purchase and each sale. The Cost of Goods Sold account is also updated after each sale so that during the period the account balance reflects the period's total cost of goods sold to date. At the end of the period, a physical count of the merchandise inventory is performed to adjust Merchandise Inventory and Cost of Goods Sold.

Under a periodic inventory system, the Merchandise Inventory account is updated only once each accounting period. This update occurs at the *end* of the period based on a physical count of the merchandise inventory. During the next period, the Merchandise Inventory balance remains unchanged. It reflects the beginning inventory balance until it is updated again at the end of the period. In a periodic inventory system, cost of goods sold is *not* recorded as each sale occurs. Instead, the total cost of goods sold during the period is calculated at the end of the period.

Recording Merchandise Transactions

Under a perpetual system, each purchase, purchase return and allowance, purchase discount, and transportation-in transaction is recorded in the Merchandise Inventory account. Under a periodic system, a separate temporary account is set up for each of these items. At the end of a period, each of these temporary accounts is closed and the Merchandise Inventory account is updated. To illustrate the differences, we use parallel columns to show journal entries for the most common transactions using both periodic and perpetual inventory systems (we drop explanations for simplicity).

Purchases

Z-Mart purchases merchandise for $1,200 on credit with terms of 2/10, n/30, and records this purchase as:

Periodic		
Purchases	1,200	
Accounts Payable		1,200

Perpetual		
Merchandise Inventory	1,200	
Accounts Payable		1,200

The periodic system debits all merchandise purchases to an expense account called *Purchases*.

Purchase Returns and Allowances

Z-Mart returns merchandise purchased on November 2 because of defects. If the recorded cost[12] of the defective merchandise is $300, Z-Mart records the return with this entry:

Periodic		
Accounts Payable	300	
Purchase Returns and Allowances..................................		300

Perpetual		
Accounts Payable	300	
Merchandise Inventory		300

This entry is the same if Z-Mart is granted a price reduction (allowance) instead of returning the merchandise. In the periodic system, the entry credits a contra expense account called **Purchase Returns and Allowances** that accumulates the cost of all returns and allowances transactions during a period. Because Purchase Returns and Allowances is a contra expense account related to the Purchases account, it is subtracted from Purchases when determining net purchases as shown in Exhibit 6A.1.

Purchase Discount

When Z-Mart pays the supplier for the previous purchase within the discount period, the required payment is $882 (= $1,200 − $300 = $900 × 98% = $882) and is recorded as:

Periodic		
Accounts Payable	900	
Purchase Discounts		18
Cash		882

Perpetual		
Accounts Payable	900	
Merchandise Inventory		18
Cash		882

The periodic system credits a contra expense account called *Purchase Discounts* that accumulates discounts taken on purchase transactions during the period. Purchase Discounts, like Purchase Returns and Allowances, is subtracted from the Purchases account balance as shown in Exhibit 6A.1. If payment is delayed until after the discount period expires, the entry under both the periodic and perpetual methods is to debit Accounts Payable and credit Cash for $900 each.

Transportation-In

Z-Mart paid a $75 freight charge to haul merchandise to its store. In the periodic system, this cost is charged to an expense account known as *Transportation-In*. Transportation-in is included as part of the $232,400 total cost of merchandise purchased as shown in Exhibit 6A.1.

Periodic		
Transportation-In..............................	75	
Cash		75

Perpetual		
Merchandise Inventory......................	75	
Cash		75

[12] Recorded cost is the cost recorded in the account after any discounts.

Exhibit 6A.1

Calculation of Net Purchases and Cost of Goods Purchased Under a Periodic Inventory System

Purchases		$235,800
Less: Purchase discounts	$4,200	
Purchase returns and allowances	1,500	5,700
Net purchases		$230,100
Add: Transportation-in		2,300
Cost of goods purchased		$232,400

Sales

Z-Mart sold $2,400 of merchandise on credit and Z-Mart's cost of this merchandise is $1,600:

Periodic		
Accounts Receivable	2,400	
Sales		2,400

Perpetual		
Accounts Receivable	2,400	
Sales		2,400
Cost of Goods Sold	1,600	
Merchandise Inventory		1,600

Under the periodic system, the cost of goods sold is *not* recorded at the time of sale. We later show how the periodic system calculates total cost of goods sold at the end of a period.

Sales Returns

A customer returns part of the merchandise from the previous transaction, where returned items sell for $800 and cost $600. Z-Mart restores the merchandise to inventory and records the return as:

Periodic		
Sales Returns and Allowances	800	
Accounts Receivable		800

Perpetual		
Sales Returns and Allowances	800	
Accounts Receivable		800
Merchandise Inventory	600	
Cost of Goods Sold		600

The periodic system records only the revenue reduction.

Z-Mart's unadjusted trial balances at the end of 2011 under each system are shown in Exhibit 6A.2. Notice that the differences between the unadjusted trial balances have been highlighted.

Exhibit 6A.2

Comparison of Unadjusted Trial Balances—Periodic and Perpetual

Z-Mart Unadjusted Trial Balance December 31, 2011 Periodic		
Cash	$ 8,200	
Accounts receivable	11,200	
Merchandise inventory	**19,000**	
Office supplies	2,350	
Store supplies	1,450	
Prepaid insurance	900	
Office equipment	4,200	
Accumulated depreciation, office equipment		$ 700
Store equipment	30,000	
Accumulated depreciation, store equipment		3,000
Accounts payable		16,000
Kent Marty, capital		40,160
Kent Marty, withdrawals	4,000	
Rent revenue		2,800
Sales		321,000
Sales discounts	4,300	
Sales returns and allowances	2,000	
Purchases	**235,800**	
Purchase discounts		**4,200**
Purchase returns and allowances		**1,500**
Transportation-in	**2,300**	
Office salaries expense	25,000	
Sales salaries expense	18,000	
Interest expense	360	
Rent expense, office space	900	
Rent expense, selling space	8,100	
Advertising expense	11,300	
Totals	$389,360	$389,360

Z-Mart Unadjusted Trial Balance December 31, 2011 Perpetual		
Cash	$ 8,200	
Accounts receivable	11,200	
Merchandise inventory	**21,250**	
Office supplies	2,350	
Store supplies	1,450	
Prepaid insurance	900	
Office equipment	4,200	
Accumulated depreciation, office equipment		$ 700
Store equipment	30,000	
Accumulated depreciation, store equipment		3,000
Accounts payable		16,000
Kent Marty, capital		40,160
Kent Marty, withdrawals	4,000	
Rent revenue		2,800
Sales		321,000
Sales discounts	4,300	
Sales returns and allowances	2,000	
Cost of goods sold	**230,150**	
Office salaries expense	25,000	
Sales salaries expense	18,000	
Interest expense	360	
Rent expense, office space	900	
Rent expense, selling space	8,100	
Advertising expense	11,300	
Totals	$383,660	$383,660

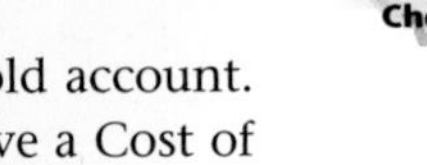

CHECKPOINT

15. Identify those accounts included on the periodic unadjusted trial balance that are not on the perpetual unadjusted trial balance.

16. The perpetual unadjusted trial balance has a Cost of Goods Sold account. Explain why the periodic unadjusted trial balance does not have a Cost of Goods Sold account.

Do Quick Study questions: *QS 6-16, *QS 6-17

mid-appendix demonstration problem

This is the same as the Mid-Chapter Demonstration Problem on page 267, except that now you will assume a *periodic inventory system*.

Beta Company, a retail store, had the following transactions in March:

March	2	Purchased merchandise from Alfa Company under the following terms: $1,800 invoice price, 2/15, n/60, FOB factory. (The cost of the merchandise to Alfa Company was $990.)
	3	Paid CanPar Shipping $125 for shipping charges on the purchase of March 2.
	4	Returned to Alfa Company unacceptable merchandise that had an invoice price of $300 (and a cost to Alfa of $165). Alfa returned the merchandise to inventory.
	17	Sent a cheque to Alfa Company for the March 2 purchase, net of the discount and the returned merchandise.

Required

Assuming both Beta and Alfa use a periodic inventory system:

a. Present the journal entries Beta Company should record for these transactions.

b. Present the journal entries Alfa Company should record for these transactions.

solution

a.

	Beta Company (the buyer)		
March 2	Purchases	1,800	
	Accounts Payable—Alfa Company		1,800
	Purchased merchandise on credit.		
3	Transportation-In	125	
	Cash		125
	Paid shipping charges on purchased merchandise.		
4	Accounts Payable—Alfa Company	300	
	Purchase Returns and Allowances		300
	Returned unacceptable merchandise.		
17	Accounts Payable—Alfa Company	1,500	
	Purchase Discounts		30
	Cash		1,470
	Paid balance within the discount period and took a 2% discount.		

b.

Alfa Company (the seller)		
Accounts Receivable—Beta Company	1,800	
Sales		1,800
Sold merchandise under terms 2/15, n/60.		
No entry		
Sales Returns and Allowances	300	
Accounts Receivable—Beta Company		300
Customer returned merchandise.		
Cash	1,470	
Sales Discounts	30	
Accounts Receivable—Beta Company		1,500
Received payment for March 2 sale less the return and discount.		

Adjusting Entries

The adjusting entries recorded under a periodic and a perpetual inventory system are identical except for the treatment of merchandise inventory. Under a perpetual inventory system, recall that the adjusting entry shown below was recorded to reflect shrinkage of $250 (the difference between the $21,250 unadjusted balance in Merchandise Inventory shown in Exhibit 6A.2 and the $21,000 physical count). Under a periodic inventory system, there is no corresponding adjustment to update the $19,000 unadjusted balance in Merchandise Inventory shown in Exhibit 6A.2. Instead, we use closing entries to update the Merchandise Inventory account. We show the closing entry approach to update Merchandise Inventory in the next section.

Periodic	Perpetual		
No entry	Cost of Goods Sold	250	
	Merchandise Inventory		250

A Work Sheet and an Income Statement for a Merchandising Company—Periodic Inventory

Exhibit 6A.3 presents a version of the work sheet that the accountant for Z-Mart could prepare in the process of developing its financial statements. Note the differences (bolded) from the work sheet on page 270 in Exhibit 6.14.

In particular, the unadjusted trial balance includes the beginning inventory balance of $19,000. The beginning inventory balance is entered in the Debit column for the income statement. The ending inventory balance of $21,000 is entered in the Credit column of the income statement ***and*** the Debit column of the balance sheet. This step allows the calculation of cost of goods sold to be included in net income while the correct ending inventory balance is included on the balance sheet. Recall that cost of goods sold is calculated as:

Beginning merchandise inventory	$ 19,000
Plus: Net cost of purchases	232,400
Less: Ending merchandise inventory	21,000
Equals: Cost of goods sold	$230,400

The adjustments in the work sheet reflect the following:

a. Expiration of $600 of prepaid insurance.

b. Use of $1,200 of store supplies.

c. Use of $1,800 of office supplies.

d. Depreciation of the store equipment for $3,000.

e. Depreciation of the office equipment for $700.

f. Accrual of $300 of unpaid office salaries and $500 of unpaid store salaries.

Once the adjusted amounts are extended into the financial statement columns, the accountant uses the information to develop the company's financial statements.

Exhibit 6A.3

Work Sheet for Z-Mart for the Year Ended December 31, 2011

		Unadjusted Trial Balance		Adjustments		Adjusted Trial Balance		Income Statement		Balance Sheet & Statement of Changes in Equity	
No.	Account	Debit	Credit	Debit	Credit	Debit	Credit	Debit	Credit	Debit	Credit
101	Cash	8,200				8,200				8,200	
106	Accounts receivable	11,200				11,200				11,200	
119	**Merchandise inventory**	**19,000**				**19,000**		**19,000**	**21,000**	**21,000**	
124	Office supplies	2,350			(c) 1,800	550				550	
125	Store supplies	1,450			(b) 1,200	250				250	
128	Prepaid insurance	900			(a) 600	300				300	
163	Office equipment	4,200				4,200				4,200	
164	Accum. dep., office equipment		700		(e) 700		1,400				1,400
165	Store equipment	30,000				30,000				30,000	
166	Accum. dep., store equipment		3,000		(d) 3,000		6,000				6,000
201	Accounts payable		16,000				16,000				16,000
209	Salaries payable				(f) 800		800				800
301	Kent Marty, capital		40,160				40,160				40,160
302	Kent Marty, withdrawals	4,000				4,000				4,000	
406	Rent revenue		2,800				2,800		2,800		
413	Sales		321,000				321,000		321,000		
414	Sales returns and allowances	2,000				2,000		2,000			
415	Sales discounts	4,300				4,300		4,300			
505	**Purchases**	**235,800**				**235,800**		**235,800**			
506	**Purchase returns and allowances**		**1,500**				**1,500**		**1,500**		
507	**Purchase discounts**		**4,200**				**4,200**		**4,200**		
508	**Transportation-in**	**2,300**				**2,300**		**2,300**			
612	Dep. expense, store equipment			(d) 3,000		3,000		3,000			
613	Dep. expense, office equipment			(e) 700		700		700			
620	Office salaries expense	25,000		(f) 300		25,300		25,300			
621	Sales salaries expense	18,000		(f) 500		18,500		18,500			
633	Interest expense	360				360		360			
637	Insurance expense			(a) 600		600		600			
641	Rent expense, office space	900				900		900			
642	Rent expense, selling space	8,100				8,100		8,100			
650	Office supplies expense			(c) 1,800		1,800		1,800			
651	Store supplies expense			(b) 1,200		1,200		1,200			
655	Advertising expense	11,300				11,300		11,300			
	Totals	389,360	389,360	8,100	8,100	393,860	393,860	335,160	350,500	79,700	64,360
	Net Income							15,340			15,340
	Totals							350,500	350,500	79,700	79,700

Note: Notice that ***both beginning and ending inventory appear in the income statement*** columns of the work sheet. This is because both amounts are part of the cost of goods sold calculation in a periodic inventory system (Beginning MI = Net cost of purchases − Ending MI = COGS). Be alert to the fact that ***ending inventory appears on the balance sheet*** since that is the actual balance on hand at December 31, 2011.

The classified, multiple-step income statement under a periodic inventory system is shown in Exhibit 6A.4.

Exhibit 6A.4

Classified, Multiple-Step Income Statement—Periodic

Z-Mart
Income Statement
For Year Ended December 31, 2011

Sales				$321,000
Less: Sales discounts			$ 4,300	
Sales returns and allowances			2,000	6,300
Net sales				$314,700
Cost of goods sold				
Merchandise inventory, Dec. 31, 2010			$ 19,000	
Purchases		$235,800		
Less: Purchase returns and allowances	$1,500			
Purchase discounts	4,200	5,700		
Net purchases		$230,100		
Add: Transportation-in		2,300		
Cost of goods purchased			232,400	
Goods available for sale			$251,400	
Less: Merchandise inventory, Dec. 31, 2011			21,000	
Cost of goods sold				230,400
Gross profit from sales				$ 84,300
Operating expenses:				
Selling expenses:				
Sales salaries expense		$ 18,500		
Advertising expense		11,300		
Rent expense, selling space		8,100		
Depreciation expense, store equipment		3,000		
Store supplies expense		1,200		
Total selling expenses			$ 42,100	
General and administrative expenses				
Office salaries expense		$ 25,300		
Office supplies expense		1,800		
Rent expense, office space		900		
Depreciation expense, office equipment		700		
Insurance expense		600		
Total general and administrative expense			29,300	
Total operating expenses				71,400
Income from operations				$ 12,900
Other revenues and expenses:				
Rent revenue			$ 2,800	
Interest expense			360	2,440
Net income				$ 15,340

Closing Entries

The closing entries under a periodic system are the same as for a perpetual system except for the differences highlighted in Exhibit 6A.5. In a periodic system, notice that the temporary accounts for Purchases, Purchase Discounts, Purchase Returns and Allowances, and Transportation-In must be closed. Because the transactions reflected by these accounts are included in the Cost of Goods Sold account under a perpetual inventory system, the closing entries under a perpetual system involve fewer accounts.

Exhibit 6A.5

Comparison of Closing Entries—Periodic and Perpetual

Periodic — Closing Entries

Account	Debit	Credit
(1)		
Rent Revenue	2,800	
Sales	321,000	
Merchandise Inventory†	**21,000**	
Purchase Discounts	**4,200**	
Purchase Returns and Allowances	**1,500**	
Income Summary		350,500
(2)		
Income Summary	335,160	
Sales Discounts		4,300
Sales Returns and Allowances		2,000
Merchandise Inventory‡		**19,000**
Purchases		**235,800**
Transportation-In		**2,300**
Depreciation Expense, Store Equipment		3,000
Depreciation Expense, Office Equipment		700
Office Salaries Expense		25,300
Sales Salaries Expense		18,500
Interest Expense		360
Insurance Expense		600
Rent Expense, Office Space		900
Rent Expense, Selling Space		8,100
Office Supplies Expense		1,800
Store Supplies Expense		1,200
Advertising Expense		11,300
(3)		
Income Summary	15,340	
Kent Marty, Capital		15,340
(4)		
Kent Marty, Capital	4,000	
Kent Marty, Withdrawals		4,000

Perpetual — Closing Entries

Account	Debit	Credit
(1)		
Rent Revenue	2,800	
Sales	321,000	
Income Summary		323,800
(2)		
Income Summary	308,460	
Sales Discounts		4,300
Sales Returns and Allowances		2,000
Cost of Goods Sold		**230,400**
Depreciation Expense, Store Equipment		3,000
Depreciation Expense, Office Equipment		700
Office Salaries Expense		25,300
Sales Salaries Expense		18,500
Interest Expense		360
Insurance Expense		600
Rent Expense, Office Space		900
Rent Expense, Selling Space		8,100
Office Supplies Expense		1,800
Store Supplies Expense		1,200
Advertising Expense		11,300
(3)		
Income Summary	15,340	
Kent Marty, Capital		15,340
(4)		
Kent Marty, Capital	4,000	
Kent Marty, Withdrawals		4,000

†This is the *ending* merchandise inventory balance being **added** to the account.
‡This is the *beginning* merchandise inventory balance being **subtracted** from the account.

The closing entries under a periodic system also involve the Merchandise Inventory account. The $19,000 unadjusted balance in the Merchandise Inventory account shown in Exhibit 6A.2 is beginning inventory. Therefore, the Merchandise Inventory account needs to be updated to reflect the ending merchandise inventory actually on hand of $21,000. Different approaches can be used to update the balance in Merchandise Inventory. We will update Merchandise Inventory using the closing entry approach. The closing entry approach removes the beginning inventory amount (by crediting Merchandise Inventory) and replaces it with the correct ending inventory value (by debiting Merchandise Inventory). These entries are highlighted in Exhibit 6A.5.

By updating Merchandise Inventory and closing Purchases, Purchase Discounts, Purchase Returns and Allowances, and Transportation-In, the periodic system transfers the cost of goods sold amount to Income Summary. Review the periodic side of Exhibit 6A.5 and notice that the boldface items affect Income Summary, as shown in Exhibit 6A.6:

Exhibit 6A.6

Merchandising Cost Flows Across Periods

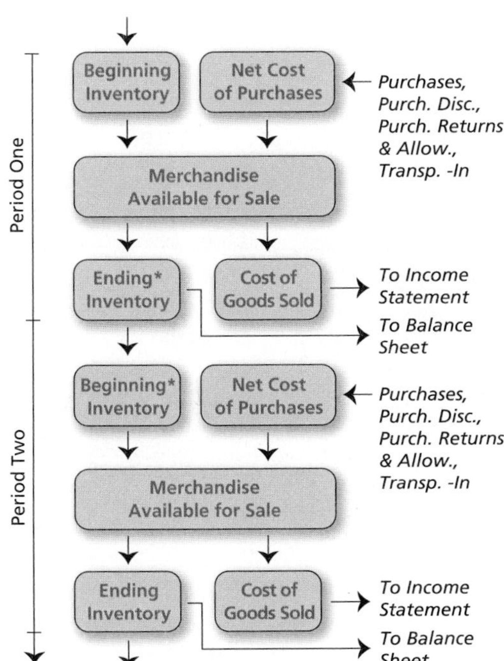

*One period's ending inventory is the next period's beginning inventory.

Credited to Income Summary in the first closing entry:	
Merchandise Inventory (ending balance)	$ 21,000
Purchase Discounts	4,200
Purchase Returns and Allowances	1,500
Debited to Income Summary in the second closing entry:	
Merchandise Inventory (beginning balance)	(19,000)
Purchases	(235,800)
Transportation-in	(2,300)
Net effect on Income Summary	$(230,400)

This $230,400 effect on Income Summary is the cost of goods sold amount. This figure is confirmed as follows:

Beginning inventory		$ 19,000
Purchases	$235,800	
Less: Purchase discounts	4,200	
Less: Purchase returns and allowances	1,500	
Add: Transportation-in	2,300	
Net cost of goods purchased		232,400
Cost of goods available for sale		$251,400
Less: Ending inventory		21,000
Cost of goods sold		$230,400

The periodic system transfers cost of goods sold to the Income Summary account but does not use a Cost of Goods Sold account. Exhibit 6A.6 shows the relation between inventory, purchases, and cost of goods sold across periods.

The periodic system does not measure shrinkage. Instead it calculates cost of goods available for sale, subtracts the cost of ending inventory, and defines the difference as cost of goods sold, which includes shrinkage.

17. Why does the Merchandise Inventory account on the periodic unadjusted trial balance differ from the Merchandise Inventory balance on the perpetual unadjusted trial balance?
18. What account is used in a perpetual inventory system but not in a periodic system?
19. Which of the following accounts are temporary accounts? (a) Merchandise Inventory, (b) Purchases, (c) Transportation-In
20. How is cost of goods sold calculated under a periodic inventory accounting system?

Do Quick Study questions: *QS 6-18, *QS 6-19, *QS 6-20

demonstration problem

This is the same as the Demonstration Problem on page 279 except that now you will assume a *periodic inventory system.*

Use the following adjusted trial balance and additional information to complete the requirements:

Ingersoll Antiques Adjusted Trial Balance December 31, 2011		
Cash	$ 19,300	
Merchandise inventory	60,100	
Store supplies	1,000	
Equipment	44,600	
Accumulated depreciation, equipment		$ 16,500
Accounts payable		8,000
Salaries payable		1,000
Dee Rizzo, capital		69,000
Dee Rizzo, withdrawals	8,000	
Interest revenue		300
Sales		325,000
Sales discounts	6,000	
Sales returns and allowances	5,000	
Purchases	140,000	
Purchase discounts		3,500
Purchase returns and allowances		2,600
Transportation-in	4,000	
Depreciation expense, store equipment	4,000	
Depreciation expense, office equipment	1,500	
Sales salaries expense	28,000	
Office salaries expense	32,000	
Insurance expense	12,000	
Rent expense (70% is store, 30% is office)	24,000	
Store supplies expense	6,000	
Advertising expense	30,400	
Totals	$425,900	$425,900

Ingersoll Antiques performed a physical inventory count on December 31, 2011, that revealed a balance of merchandise inventory on hand of $50,000.

Required

1. Prepare a 2011 classified, multiple-step income statement for internal use.
2. Prepare closing entries.

Planning the Solution

- Calculate net sales. Calculate cost of goods sold and subtract it from net sales to get gross profit. Then classify the operating expenses as selling expenses and general and administrative expenses.
- The first closing entry debits all temporary accounts with credit balances along with the ending merchandise inventory balance and opens the Income Summary account. The second closing entry credits all temporary accounts with debit balances as well as the beginning merchandise inventory balance. The third entry closes the Income Summary account to the owner's capital account, and the fourth closing entry closes the withdrawals account to the capital account.

solution

1. Classified, multiple-step income statement

Ingersoll Antiques
Income Statement
For Year Ended December 31, 2011

Sales				$325,000
Less: Sales discounts			$ 6,000	
Sales returns and allowances			5,000	11,000
Net sales				$314,000
Cost of goods sold:				
Merchandise inventory, December 31, 2010			60,100	
Purchases		$140,000		
Less: Purchase returns and allowances	$2,600			
Purchase discounts	3,500	6,100		
Net purchases		$133,900		
Add: Transportation-in		4,000		
Cost of goods purchased:			137,900	
Goods available for sale			$198,000	
Less: Merchandise inventory, December 31, 2011			50,000	
Cost of goods sold				148,000
Gross profit from sales				$166,000
Operating expenses:				
Selling expenses:				
Advertising expense		$ 30,400		
Sales salaries expense		28,000		
Rent expense, selling space[1]		16,800		
Store supplies expense		6,000		
Depreciation expense, store equipment		4,000		
Total selling expenses			$ 85,200	
General and administrative expenses:				
Office salaries expense		$ 32,000		
Insurance expense		12,000		
Rent expense, selling space[2]		7,200		
Depreciation expense, office equipment		1,500		
Total general and administrative expenses			52,700	
Total operating expenses				137,900
Income from operations				$ 28,100
Other revenues and expenses:				
Interest revenue				300
Net income				$ 28,400

[1]Calculated as: $24,000 × 70% = $16,800
[2]Calculated as: $24,000 × 30% = $7,200

2. Closing entries

Date		Account	Debit	Credit
Dec.	31	Sales	325,000	
		Interest Revenue	300	
		Purchase Returns and Allowances	2,600	
		Purchase Discounts	3,500	
		Merchandise Inventory	50,000	
		Income Summary		381,400
		To close temporary accounts with credit balances and update merchandise inventory to reflect the December 31 balance on hand.		
	31	Income Summary	353,000	
		Merchandise Inventory		60,100
		Sales Discounts		6,000
		Sales Returns and Allowances		5,000
		Purchases		140,000
		Transportation-In		4,000
		Depreciation Expense, Store Equipment		4,000
		Depreciation Expense, Office Equipment		1,500
		Sales Salaries Expense		28,000
		Office Salaries Expense		32,000
		Insurance Expense		12,000
		Rent Expense		24,000
		Store Supplies Expense		6,000
		Advertising Expense		30,400
		To close temporary accounts with debit balances and remove beginning merchandise inventory.		
	31	Income Summary	28,400	
		Dee Rizzo, Capital		28,400
		To close the income summary account.		
	31	Dee Rizzo, Capital	8,000	
		Dee Rizzo, Withdrawals		8,000
		To close the withdrawals account.		

APPENDIX 6B

Sales Tax

LO8 Explain and record Provincial Sales Tax (PST) and Goods and Services Tax (GST).

This section looks at the additional issue of recording sales tax. Most provinces and the federal government require retailers to collect sales tax from customers and to send these taxes periodically to the appropriate agency.

Provincial Sales Tax

Provincial Sales Tax (PST) is a tax applied on sales to the final consumers of products and/or services. All provinces except Alberta (and the territories) require retailers to collect PST from their customers and to remit this tax periodically to the appropriate provincial authority. It should be noted that not all sales are subject to PST.[13] PST collected is credited to a separate account, as shown in the following example where JC Sales sells merchandise on January 5 costing $600 for $900 on account (assuming PST of 5%).

As well as being collected, PST may be *paid* on items purchased for use or on long-term assets acquired. In these cases, the PST paid is part of the expense or asset cost associated with the purchase.

Goods and Services Tax

The **Goods and Services Tax (GST)** is a 5%[14] tax on almost all goods and services provided in Canada. It is a federal tax on the consumer. However, unlike the PST, businesses pay GST up front but generally receive a full credit or refund for all GST paid. Ultimately only the final consumer pays this tax. This is because businesses collect GST on sales, but since they receive full credit for GST paid on their purchases, they only remit the difference to the appropriate federal authority. The **Harmonized Sales Tax (HST)** is a combined GST and PST rate applied to taxable supplies. At the time of writing, New Brunswick, Nova Scotia, and Newfoundland and Labrador apply HST of 13%. Ontario will apply HST of 13% as of July 1, 2010, and on the same date British Columbia will apply HST of 12%.

PST and GST are accounted for under both perpetual and periodic inventory systems. To illustrate, assume JC Sales, a merchandiser located in Manitoba, purchases $600 of merchandise inventory on January 3 with terms n/10. These items are then sold for $900 on January 5 with terms of n/15. JC Sales records these transactions as follows:[15]

Jan.	3	Merchandise Inventory	600	
		GST Receivable[16]	30	
		Accounts Payable		630
		To record the purchase of merchandise on account; $600 × 5% = $30 GST.		

[13] A detailed discussion of the liabilities created by PST and GST is found in Chapter 13.
[14] Effective January 1, 2008.
[15] Assume that all amounts here and in related end-of-chapter materials are before PST and GST.
[16] Some businesses will debit GST Payable instead of GST Receivable because they use only one account for GST. In such a case, when the account has a credit balance, cash must be paid to the Receiver General for Canada. When the account has a debit balance, a refund is applied for.

Jan.	5	Accounts Receivable	1,008	
		Sales		900
		PST Payable		63
		GST Payable		45
		To record the sale of merchandise on account; \$900 × 7% = \$63 PST; \$900 × 5% = \$45 GST; \$900 + \$63 + \$45 = \$1,008.		
	5	Cost of Goods Sold	600	
		Merchandise Inventory		600
		To record the cost of sales.		

PST and GST are calculated as a percentage of the selling price, except in Quebec and PEI, where GST is initially calculated as a percentage of the selling price and PST is calculated as a percentage of the total of the selling price plus the GST. It should also be noted that while GST is a 5% federal tax, and thus is uniform in all of the provinces, PST is a provincial tax and differs in percentage from province to province. The detailed rates for each province are provided in Exhibit 6B.1.

To continue the example, assume the January 3 purchase is paid on January 13 and the sale of January 5 is collected on January 20. Assuming no other purchases and sales during the month, the January sales taxes are paid to the appropriate government bodies on February 28. The entries to record these transactions are:

Jan.	13	Accounts Payable	630	
		Cash		630
		To record payment of January 3 purchase.		
	20	Cash	1,008	
		Accounts Receivable		1,008
		To record collection of January 5 sale.		
Feb.	28	PST Payable	63	
		Cash		63
		To record payment of PST to provincial government authority.		
	28	GST Payable	45	
		Cash		15
		GST Receivable		30
		To record payment of GST to Receiver General for Canada.		

EXTEND YOUR KNOWLEDGE

6-1

Examples demonstrating PST/GST for each region in Canada can be found online in Extend Your Knowledge 6-1, along with reinforcement exercises.

Exhibit 6B.1

Sales Tax Rates

	PST Rate	GST Rate	HST Rate*
Alberta	-0-	5%	—
Manitoba	7%	5%	—
Northwest Territories	-0-	5%	—
Nunavut	-0-	5%	—
Prince Edward Island**	10%	5%	—
Quebec**	7.5%	5%	—
Saskatchewan	5%	5%	—
Yukon	-0-	5%	—
British Columbia***	—	—	12%
New Brunswick	—	—	13%
Nova Scotia	—	—	13%
Newfoundland and Labrador	—	—	13%
Ontario***	—	—	13%

*A Harmonized Sales Tax (HST) is applied in place of PST and GST. HST is the combination of the PST with the GST for a total sales tax. For New Brunswick, Nova Scotia, Newfoundland and Labrador, and Ontario, the PST of 8% is combined with the GST of 5% for HST of 13%. British Columbia combines its PST of 7% with the GST of 5% for HST of 12%.
**In Quebec and Prince Edward Island, PST = PST% × (Sales price + GST).
***Effective July 1, 2010.

21. What is the difference between PST, GST, and HST?

Do Quick Study questions: *QS 6-21, *QS 6-22, *QS 6-23, *QS 6-24

Summary of Appendix 6A and Appendix 6B

LO7 | Record and compare merchandising transactions using both periodic and perpetual inventory systems. Transactions involving the sale and purchase of merchandise are recorded and analyzed under both inventory systems. Adjusting and closing entries for both inventory systems are also illustrated and explained.

LO8 | Explain and record Provincial Sales Tax (PST) and Goods and Services Tax (GST). PST is a tax applied on sales to final consumers that varies in percent between provinces. GST is a 5% tax collected on most sales but full credit is received for GST paid by a GST registrant (business). Harmonized Sales Tax (HST) is a combined GST and PST rate applied to taxable supplies.

guidance answers to CHECKPOINT

15. The beginning Merchandise Inventory balance of $19,000 is included on the periodic unadjusted trial balance and not the perpetual along with Purchases, Purchase Discounts, Purchase Returns and Allowances, and Transportation-In.

16. Cost of Goods Sold is calculated under the periodic system using the account balances of Merchandise Inventory (beginning inventory balance), Purchases, Purchase Discounts, Purchase Returns and Allowances, Transportation-In, and subtracting the ending inventory amount determined through a physical count.

17. The Merchandise Inventory account on the periodic unadjusted trial balance represents the balance at the beginning of the period. The Merchandise Inventory account on the perpetual unadjusted trial balance has been adjusted regularly during the accounting period for all transactions affecting inventory, such as purchases, returns, discounts, transportation-in, and cost of sales, and therefore represents the balance at the end of the period.

18. Cost of Goods Sold.

19. (b) Purchases and (c) Transportation-In.

20. Under a periodic inventory system, the cost of goods sold is determined at the end of an accounting period by adding the net cost of goods purchased to the beginning inventory and subtracting the ending inventory.

21. PST is Provincial Sales Tax and varies across Canada. GST is the Goods and Services Tax of 5% that is constant across Canada. HST is Harmonized Sales Tax that is a combination of the Provincial Sales Tax applicable in the jurisdictions and the 5% Goods and Services Tax.

Glossary

Cash discount A reduction in the price of merchandise that is granted by a seller to a purchaser in exchange for the purchaser paying within a specified period of time called the *discount period.* (p. 259)

Catalogue price See *list price.* (p. 259)

Classified, multiple-step income statement An income statement format that shows intermediate totals between sales and net income and detailed computations of net sales and cost of goods sold. (p. 271)

Cost of goods sold (COGS) The cost of merchandise sold to customers during a period; also commonly referred to as *cost of sales.* (p. 253)

Cost of sales See *cost of goods sold.* (p. 253)

Credit memorandum A notification that the sender has entered a credit in the recipient's account maintained by the sender. (p. 266)

Credit period The time period that can pass before a customer's payment is due. (p. 259)

Credit terms The description of the amounts and timing of payments that a buyer agrees to make in the future. (p. 259)

Debit memorandum A notification that the sender has entered a debit in the recipient's account maintained by the sender. (p. 258)

Discount period The time period in which a cash discount is available and a reduced payment can be made by the buyer. (p. 259)

EOM The abbreviation for *end of month,* used to describe credit terms for some transactions. (p. 259)

FOB The abbreviation for *free on board,* the designated point at which ownership of goods passes to the buyer; *FOB shipping point* (or factory) means that the buyer pays the shipping costs and accepts ownership of the goods at the seller's place of business; *FOB destination* means that the seller pays the shipping costs and the ownership of the goods transfers to the buyer at the buyer's place of business. (p. 261)

Freight-in See *transportation-in.* (p. 262)

Freight-out See *transportation-out.* (p. 262)

Full disclosure principle The generally accepted accounting principle that requires financial statements to report all relevant information about the operations and financial position of the entity; disclosure of items not contained in the body of financial statements is often accomplished by providing notes to financial statements such as those for WestJet in Appendix I of the text. (p. 271)

Function of an expense A method of classifying or grouping expenses based on their purpose or what the expenses relate to, such as cost of goods sold, selling expenses, and general and administrative expenses; this method must also provide additional information to show the nature of expenses within each group. (p. 271)

General and administrative expenses Expenses that support the overall operations of a business and include the expenses of such activities as providing accounting services, human resource management, and financial management. (p. 271)

Goods and Services Tax (GST) A federal tax on almost all goods and services provided in Canada. (p. 295)

Gross margin The difference between net sales and the cost of goods sold; also called *gross profit.* (p. 254)

Gross margin ratio See *gross profit ratio.* (p. 274)

Gross profit The difference between net sales and the cost of goods sold; also called *gross margin.* (p. 254)

Gross profit ratio Gross profit from sales (net sales minus cost of goods sold) divided by net sales; also called *gross margin ratio.* (p. 274)

Harmonized Sales Tax (HST) A combined GST and PST rate applied to taxable supplies. (p. 295)

Inventory See *merchandise inventory.* (p. 254)

List price The catalogue price of an item before any trade discount is deducted. (p. 259)

Merchandise Products, also called *goods,* that a company acquires for the purpose of reselling them to customers. (p. 253)

Merchandise inventory Products that a company owns for the purpose of selling them to customers. Also called *inventory.* (p. 254)

Merchandiser Earns net income by buying and selling merchandise. (p. 253)

Nature of an expense A method of classifying an expense based on its basic characteristics or what it is. For example, when expenses are identified on the income statement as depreciation, rent, property tax, and salaries, the nature of the expense is being identified. (p. 271)

Net sales Calculated as gross sales less sales discounts and sales returns and allowances. (p. 253)

Notes to financial statements An integral part of financial statements that provides relevant information about the operations and financial position of the entity in addition to that contained in the financial statements; providing notes complies with the full disclosure principle; for an example, see the notes for WestJet in Appendix I of the text. (p. 271)

Periodic inventory system A method of accounting that records the cost of inventory purchased but does not track the quantity on hand or sold to customers; the records are updated at the end of each period to reflect the results of physical counts of the items on hand. (p. 256)

Perpetual inventory system A method of accounting that maintains continuous records of the cost of inventory on hand and the cost of goods sold. (p. 256)

Provincial Sales Tax (PST) A tax applied on sales to the final consumers of products and/or services. (p. 295)

Purchase discount A term used by a purchaser to describe a cash discount granted to the purchaser for paying within the discount period. (p. 259)

Purchase Returns and Allowances A contra expense account used when a periodic inventory system is in place in which purchase returns and/or purchase allowances are recorded. (p. 283)

Retailer An intermediary that buys products from manufacturers or wholesalers and sells them to consumers. (p. 253)

Sales discount A term used by a seller to describe a cash discount granted to customers for paying within the discount period. (p. 264)

Sales returns and allowances A contra revenue account in which sales returns and/or sales allowances are recorded. (p. 265)

Selling expenses The expenses of promoting sales by displaying and advertising the merchandise, making sales, and delivering goods to customers. (p. 271)

Shrinkage Inventory losses that occur as a result of theft or deterioration. (p. 268)

Single-step income statement An income statement format that includes cost of goods sold as an operating expense and shows only one subtotal for total expenses. (p. 273)

Trade discount A reduction below a list or catalogue price that may vary in amount for wholesalers, retailers, and final consumers. (p. 259)

Transportation-in The cost to the purchaser to transport merchandise purchased to the purchaser; transportation-in is part of Cost of Goods Sold. (p. 262)

Transportation-out The cost to the seller to transport merchandise sold to the customer; transportation-out is a selling expense. (p. 262)

Wholesaler A company that buys products from manufacturers or other wholesalers and sells them to retailers or other wholesalers. (p. 253)

Visit **Connect** at **www.mcgrawhillconnect.ca** for additional study tools, practice quizzes, to search an interactive e-book, and much more.

Concept Review Questions

1. Refer to the income statement for WestJet in Appendix I. Is WestJet a merchandiser?
2. Refer to the income statement for Danier in Appendix I. Is a detailed calculation of the cost of goods sold presented?
3. In comparing the accounts of a merchandising company with those of a service company, what additional accounts would the merchandising company be likely to use, assuming it employs a perpetual inventory system?
4. What items appear in the financial statements of merchandising companies but not in the statements of service companies?
5. Explain how a business can earn a gross profit on its sales and still have a net loss.
6. Distinguish between cash discounts and trade discounts. Is the amount of a trade discount on purchased merchandise recorded in the accounts?
7. Why would a company's manager be concerned about the quantity of its purchase returns if its suppliers allow unlimited returns?
8. Danier needs to be skillful in negotiating purchase contracts with suppliers. What shipping terms should Danier negotiate to minimize its freight-in costs?
9. Does the sender of a debit memorandum record a debit or a credit in the account of the recipient? Which does the recipient record?
10. What is the difference between a sales discount and a purchase discount?
11. Why would a company offer a cash discount?
12. Briefly explain why a company's manager would want the accounting system to record a customer's return of unsatisfactory goods in the Sales Returns and Allowances account instead of the Sales account. In addition, explain whether the information would be useful for external decision makers.
13. How does a company that uses a perpetual inventory system determine the amount of inventory shrinkage?
14. What is the difference between single-step and multiple-step income statement formats?

Quick Study

QS 6-1
Components of income for a merchandiser
LO1

Referring to the format presented in Exhibit 6.2, calculate gross profit and the net income or net loss for each of the following.

	A	B	C	D	E
Net sales	$14,000	$102,000	$68,000	$540,000	$398,000
Cost of goods sold	8,000	64,000	31,000	320,000	215,000
Operating expenses	9,000	31,000	22,000	261,000	106,000

QS 6-2
Contrasting periodic and perpetual systems
LO2

For each description below, identify the inventory system as either periodic or perpetual.

a. Requires a physical count of inventory to determine the amount of inventory to report on the balance sheet.
b. Records the cost of goods sold each time a sales transaction occurs.
c. Provides more timely information to managers.
d. Was traditionally used by companies such as drug and department stores that sold large quantities of low-valued items.
e. Requires an adjusting entry to record inventory shrinkage.

QS 6-3
Perpetual and periodic inventory systems
LO2

For each situation given, calculate cost of goods sold and identify if the information provided reflects a perpetual or periodic inventory system.

a.

Merchandise Inventory		
Beginning Inventory	150	?
Purchases	340	
Ending Inventory	60	

Cost of Goods Sold	
?	

b.

Merchandise Inventory*		
Beginning Inventory	150	

Purchases	
340	

*A physical inventory count at year-end showed a balance on hand of $60.

QS 6-4
Perpetual and periodic inventory systems
LO2

For each situation given, calculate cost of goods sold and identify if the information provided reflects a perpetual or periodic inventory system.

a. Merchandise Inventory shows a balance at January 1, 2011, of $170, the Purchases account has a balance of $700 at December 31, 2011, and a physical count of merchandise inventory on the same date reveals a balance of $120 on hand.
b. Merchandise Inventory shows a $200 balance at January 1, 2011, purchases during the period of $1,000, and a balance of $75 at December 31, 2011, after the adjustment for shrinkage.

QS 6-5
Merchandise purchase transactions—perpetual
LO3

Journalize each of the following transactions assuming a perpetual inventory system.

May	1	Purchased $1,200 of merchandise inventory; terms 1/10, n/30.
	14	Paid for the May 1 purchase.
	15	Purchased $3,000 of merchandise inventory; terms 2/15, n/30.
	30	Paid for the May 15 purchase, less the applicable discount.

QS 6-6
Merchandise purchase: allowance—perpetual
LO3

Journalize each of the following transactions assuming a perpetual inventory system.

Aug.	2	Purchased $14,000 of merchandise inventory; terms 1/5, n/15.
	4	Received a credit memorandum from the supplier confirming a $1,500 allowance regarding the August 2 purchase.
	17	Paid for the August 2 purchase, less the allowance.

QS 6-7
Merchandise purchase: trade discount, return—perpetual
LO3

Prepare journal entries to record each of the following transactions of a merchandising company. Show any supporting calculations. Assume a perpetual inventory system.

Mar.	5	Purchased 500 units of product with a list price of $5 per unit. The purchaser was granted a trade discount of 20% and the terms of the sale were 2/10, n/60.
	7	Returned 50 defective units from the March 5 purchase and received full credit.
	15	Paid the amount due resulting from the March 5 purchase, less the return on March 7 and applicable discount.

QS 6-8
Sale of merchandise transactions—perpetual
LO3

Journalize each of the following transactions assuming a perpetual inventory system.

Sept.	1	Sold merchandise to JenAir for $6,000 (cost of sales $4,200); terms 2/10, n/30.
	14	Collected the amount owing regarding the September 1 sale to JenAir.
	15	Sold merchandise costing $1,500 to Dennis Leval for $1,800; terms 2/10, n/30.
	25	Collected the amount owing from the September 15 sale to Dennis Leval, less the applicable discount.

QS 6-9
Sale of merchandise: allowance—perpetual
LO3

Journalize each of the following transactions assuming a perpetual inventory system.

Oct.	15	Sold merchandise to Leslie Garth for $900 (cost of sales $600); terms 1/5, n/20.
	16	Issued a $100 credit memorandum to Leslie Garth regarding an allowance on the October 15 sale.
	25	Collected the amount owing regarding the October 15 sale to Leslie Garth, less the allowance granted on October 16.

QS 6-10
Sale of merchandise: return—perpetual
LO3

Prepare journal entries to record each of the following transactions of a merchandising company. Show any supporting calculations. Assume a perpetual inventory system.

Apr.	1	Sold merchandise for $2,000, granting the customer terms of 2/10, EOM. The cost of the merchandise was $1,400.
	4	The customer in the April 1 sale returned merchandise and received credit for $500. The merchandise, which had cost $350, was returned to inventory.
	11	Received payment for the amount due resulting from the April 1 sale, less the return and applicable discount, on April 4.

QS 6-11
Profitability
LO1, 3, 5

Using a format similar to Exhibit 6.11, calculate net sales, gross profit from sales, and the gross profit ratio (round to two decimal places).

	a	b	c	d
Sales	$130,000	$512,000	$35,700	$245,700
Sales discounts	4,200	16,500	400	3,500
Sales returns and allowances	17,000	5,000	5,000	700
Cost of goods sold	76,600	326,700	21,300	125,900

QS 6-12
Shrinkage
LO4

Beamer Company's unadjusted ledger on July 31, the end of the fiscal year, includes the following accounts, which have normal balances (assume a perpetual inventory system):

Merchandise inventory	$ 34,800
Joy Beamer, capital	115,300
Joy Beamer, withdrawals	4,000
Sales	157,200
Sales discounts	1,700
Sales returns and allowances	3,500
Cost of goods sold	102,000
Depreciation expense	7,300
Salaries expense	29,500
Miscellaneous expenses	2,000

A physical count of the inventory discloses that the cost of the merchandise on hand is $32,900. Prepare the entry to record this information and calculate gross profit.

QS 6-13
Classified multi-step vs. single-step income statements
LO5

Use the following adjusted trial balance information for JetCo's December 31, 2011, year-end to prepare (a) a classified multi-step income statement, and (b) a single-step income statement.

Account	Debit	Credit
Advertising expense	$ 6	
Assets	120	
Cost of goods sold	60	
Interest revenue		$ 5
Liabilities		90
Lisa Jet, capital		31
Lisa Jet, withdrawals	8	
Office salaries expense	10	
Office supplies expense	3	
Sales		100
Sales discounts	4	
Sales salaries expense	15	

QS 6-14
Gross profit ratio
LO5

Willaby Company had net sales of $248,000 and cost of goods sold of $114,080. Calculate and interpret the gross profit ratio, assuming the gross profit ratio for the industry is an average of 53%.

QS 6-15
Closing entries
LO6

Use the following adjusted trial balance information to prepare closing entries for TI Company at December 31, 2011.

Account	Debit	Credit
Accounts payable		$ 6
Accumulated depreciation, building		8
Advertising expense	$ 7	
Depreciation expense	2	
Building	50	
Cash	5	
Cost of goods sold	25	
Merchandise inventory	10	
Sales		70
Sales discounts	3	
Sales returns and allowances	4	
Tony Ingram, capital		23
Tony Ingram, withdrawals	1	

***QS 6-16**
Merchandise purchase transactions—periodic
LO7

Using the information in QS 6-5 through QS 6-7, prepare journal entries to record each of the transactions of the merchandising companies assuming a periodic inventory system.

***QS 6-17**
Sale of merchandise transactions—periodic
LO7

Using the information in QS 6-8 through QS 6-10, prepare journal entries to record each of the transactions of the merchandising companies assuming a periodic inventory system.

An asterisk (*) identifies assignment material based on Appendix 6A or Appendix 6B.

***QS 6-18**
Cost of goods sold—periodic
LO7

Using the following information, calculate cost of goods sold for the year ended December 31, 2011.

Merchandise inventory (January 1, 2011)	$ 40,000
Kay Bondar, capital	102,000
Kay Bondar, withdrawals	65,000
Sales	450,000
Sales returns and allowances	27,000
Purchases	180,000
Purchase discounts	1,400
Transportation-in	14,000
Merchandise inventory (December 31, 2011)	22,000
Salaries expense	120,000
Depreciation expense	31,000

***QS 6-19**
Closing entries—periodic
LO7

Using the information in *QS 6-18, prepare the closing entries.

***QS 6-20**
Profitability—periodic
LO5, 7

Calculate net sales, cost of goods sold, gross profit, and the gross profit ratio (round to two decimal places) in each of the following situations.

	a	b	c	d
Sales	$130,000	$512,000	$35,700	$245,700
Sales discounts	4,200	16,500	400	3,500
Merchandise inventory, Jan. 1, 2011	8,000	21,000	1,500	4,300
Purchases	120,000	350,000	29,000	131,000
Purchase returns and allowances	4,000	14,000	750	3,100
Merchandise inventory, Dec. 1, 2011	7,500	22,000	900	4,100

***QS 6-21**
Sales tax on purchases—perpetual
LO3, 8

On March 1, Dolomite Sales purchased $5,000 of merchandise on account. Record the entry on March 1 including 5% GST. Assume a perpetual inventory system.

***QS 6-22**
Sales tax on sales—perpetual
LO3, 8

On March 17, Dolomite Sales sold merchandise on credit for $5,800 (cost of sales $5,000). Assuming 7% PST and 5% GST, record the entries on March 17. Assume a perpetual inventory system.

***QS 6-23**
Sales tax on purchases—periodic
LO7, 8

On March 1, Dolomite Sales purchased $5,000 of merchandise on account. Record the entry on March 1 including 5% GST. Assume a periodic inventory system.

***QS 6-24**
Sales tax on sales—periodic
LO7, 8

On March 17, Dolomite Sales sold merchandise on credit for $5,800 (cost of sales $5,000). Assuming 7% PST and 5% GST, record the entry on March 17. Assume a periodic inventory system.

An asterisk (*) identifies assignment material based on Appendix 6A or Appendix 6B.

Exercises

Exercise 6-1
Calculating income statement components
LO1

Referring to Exhibit 6.2, calculate the missing amounts.

	a	b	c	d	e
Sales	$240,000	$140,000	$75,000	$?	$?
Cost of goods sold	?	?	42,000	268,000	46,000
Gross profit from sales	114,000	?	?	?	39,000
Operating expenses	95,000	82,000	?	146,000	?
Net income (loss)	?	(28,000)	(8,000)	48,000	(14,000)

Exercise 6-2
Recording journal entries for merchandise purchase transactions—perpetual
LO3

Journalize each of the following transactions assuming a perpetual inventory system.

Feb.	1	Purchased $7,000 of merchandise inventory; terms 1/10, n/30.
	5	$2,400 of merchandise inventory was purchased for cash.
	6	Purchased $10,000 of merchandise inventory; terms 2/15, n/45.
	9	Purchased $900 of office supplies; terms n/15.
	10	Contacted a major supplier to place an order for $200,000 of merchandise in exchange for a 30% trade discount to be shipped on April 1 FOB destination.
	11	Paid for the merchandise purchased on February 1.
	24	Paid for the office supplies purchased on February 9.
Mar.	23	Paid for the February 6 purchase.

Exercise 6-3
Recording journal entries for merchandise purchase transactions—perpetual
LO3

Prepare journal entries for March 2011 to record the following transactions for a retail store. Assume a perpetual inventory system.

Mar.	2	Purchased merchandise from Blanton Company under the following terms: $3,600 invoice price, 2/15, n/60, FOB factory.
	3	Paid $200 for shipping charges on the purchase of March 2.
	4	Returned to Blanton Company unacceptable merchandise that had an invoice price of $600.
	17	Sent a cheque to Blanton Company for the March 2 purchase, net of the returned merchandise and applicable discount.
	18	Purchased merchandise from Fleming Corp. under the following terms: $7,500 invoice price, 2/10, n/30, FOB destination.
	21	After brief negotiations, received from Fleming Corp. a $2,100 allowance on the purchase of March 18.
	28	Sent a cheque to Fleming Corp. paying for the March 18 purchase, net of the discount and the allowance.

Exercise 6-4
Recording journal entries for merchandise sales transactions—perpetual
LO3

Journalize each of the following transactions assuming a perpetual inventory system.

Jan.	5	Sold merchandise to a customer for $4,000; terms 1/10, n/30 (cost of sales $3,200).
	7	Made a cash sale of $3,600 of merchandise to a customer today (cost of sales $3,000).
	8	Sold merchandise for $9,600; terms 1/10, n/30 (cost of sales $8,200).
	15	Collected the amount owing from the credit customer of January 5.
Feb.	4	The customer of January 8 paid the balance owing.

Exercise 6-5
Recording journal entries for merchandise sales transactions—perpetual
LO3

Journalize each of the following transactions assuming a perpetual inventory system.

Feb.	1	Sold merchandise with a cost of $2,000 for $2,400; terms 2/10, n/30, FOB destination.
	2	Paid $150 to ship the merchandise sold on February 1.
	3	The customer of February 1 returned half of the amount purchased because it was the incorrect product; it was returned to inventory.
	4	Sold merchandise to a customer for $3,800 (cost of sales $3,100); terms 2/10, n/30, FOB destination.
	11	Collected the amount owing from the customer of February 1.
	23	Sold merchandise to a customer for cash of $1,200 (cost of sales $950).
	28	The customer of February 4 paid the amount owing.

Exercise 6-6
Analyzing and recording merchandise transactions—perpetual
LO3

On March 1, 2011, Sundown Company purchased merchandise for resale from Raintree with an invoice price of $11,000 and credit terms of 3/10, n/60. The merchandise had cost Raintree $7,500. Sundown paid on March 11. Assume that both the buyer and seller use perpetual inventory systems.

Required

a. Prepare the entries that the purchaser should record for the purchase and payment.

b. Prepare the entries that the seller should record for the sale and collection.

Analysis component:

Assume that the buyer borrowed enough cash to pay the balance on the last day of the discount period at an annual interest rate of 8% and paid it back on the last day of the credit period. Calculate how much the buyer saved by following this strategy. *Use a 365-day year and round all calculations to the nearest whole cent.*

Exercise 6-7
Analyzing and recording merchandise transactions—perpetual
LO3

On May 11, 2011, Wilson Purchasing purchased $30,000 of merchandise from Hostel Sales; terms 3/10, n/90, FOB Hostel Sales. The cost of the goods to Hostel was $20,000. Wilson paid $335 to Express Shipping Service for the delivery charges on the merchandise on May 11. On May 12, Wilson returned $1,200 of goods to Hostel Sales, which restored them to inventory. The returned goods had cost Hostel $800. On May 20, Wilson mailed a cheque to Hostel for the amount owed on that date. Hostel received and recorded the cheque on May 21.

Required

a. Present the journal entries that Wilson Purchasing should record for these transactions. Assume that Wilson uses a perpetual inventory system.

b. Present the journal entries that Hostel Sales should record for these transactions. Assume that Hostel uses a perpetual inventory system.

Analysis component:

Assume that the buyer, Wilson Purchasing, borrowed enough cash to pay the balance on the last day of the discount period at an annual interest rate of 5% and paid it back on the last day of the credit period. Calculate how much the buyer saved by following this strategy. *Use a 365-day year and round all calculations to the nearest whole cent.*

Exercise 6-8
Merchandising terms
LO1, 2, 3

Insert the letter for each term in the blank space beside the definition that it most closely matches:

a. Cash discount
b. Credit period
c. Discount period
d. FOB destination
e. FOB shipping point
f. Gross profit
g. Merchandise inventory
h. Purchase discount
i. Sales discount
j. Trade discount

_______ **1.** An agreement that ownership of goods is transferred at the buyer's place of business.
_______ **2.** The time period in which a cash discount is available.
_______ **3.** The difference between net sales and the cost of goods sold.
_______ **4.** A reduction in a receivable or payable that is granted if it is paid within the discount period.
_______ **5.** A purchaser's description of a cash discount received from a supplier of goods.
_______ **6.** An agreement that ownership of goods is transferred at the seller's place of business.
_______ **7.** A reduction below a list or catalogue price that is negotiated in setting the selling price of goods.
_______ **8.** A seller's description of a cash discount granted to customers in return for early payment.
_______ **9.** The time period that can pass before a customer's payment is due.
_______ **10.** The goods that a company owns and expects to sell to its customers.

Exercise 6-9
Effects of merchandising activities on the accounts—perpetual
LO3, 4

The following amounts summarize Transeer Company's merchandising activities during 2011. Set up T-accounts for Merchandise Inventory and Cost of Goods Sold (see Exhibit 6.13). Then record the activities directly in the accounts and calculate the account balances.

Cost of merchandise sold to customers in sales transactions	$186,000
Merchandise inventory balance, Dec. 31, 2010	37,000
Invoice cost of merchandise purchases	190,500
Shrinkage determined on Dec. 31, 2011	32,000
Cost of transportation-in	1,900
Cost of merchandise returned by customers and restored to inventory	2,200
Purchase discounts received	1,600
Purchase returns and allowances received	4,100

Analysis component:
You are the inventory manager and have reviewed these numbers. Comment on the shrinkage.

Exercise 6-10
Calculating expenses and cost of goods sold—perpetual
LO1, 3, 5

Westlawn Company discloses the following for the year ended May 31, 2011:

Sales	$500,000
Sales discounts	17,000
Sales returns	3,000
Gross profit from sales	124,000
Net loss	28,000

Required
Calculate (a) net sales, (b) total operating expenses, (c) cost of goods sold, and (d) gross profit ratio (round to two decimal places).

Analysis component:
Refer to your answer in part (d). Westlawn experienced a gross profit ratio for the year ended May 31, 2010, of 23%. Is the change in the ratio favourable or unfavourable?

Exercise 6-11
Calculating income statement components
LO1, 5

Referring to Exhibit 6.15, calculate the missing amounts (round to two decimal places).

	Company A		Company B	
	2011	2010	2011	2010
Sales	$256,000	$160,000	$?	$50,000
Sales discounts	2,560	?	1,100	500
Sales returns and allowances	?	16,000	5,500	?
Net sales	?	142,400	?	47,000
Cost of goods sold	153,600	?	55,000	?
Gross profit from sales	48,640	?	48,400	22,000
Selling expenses	17,920	16,000	24,200	?
Administrative expenses	25,600	?	29,700	11,000
Total operating expenses	?	40,000	?	?
Net income (loss)	?	14,400	?	2,000
Gross profit ratio	?	?	?	?

Analysis component:
Company A and Company B are in similar industries. Comment on their comparative performances.

***Exercise 6-12**
Calculating cost of goods sold
LO2, 3, 7

Refer to Exhibit 6A.4 and determine each of the missing numbers in the following situations:

	a	b	c
Purchases	$90,000	$160,000	$122,000
Purchase discounts	4,000	?	2,600
Purchase returns and allowances	3,000	6,000	4,400
Transportation-in	?	14,000	16,000
Beginning inventory	7,000	?	36,000
Cost of goods purchased	89,400	158,000	?
Ending inventory	4,400	30,000	?
Cost of goods sold	?	166,400	136,520

***Exercise 6-13**
Calculating expenses and income
LO1, 2, 3, 5, 7

Referring to Exhibit 6A.4, fill in the following blanks. Identify any losses by putting the amount in brackets.

	Company A		Company B	
	2011	2010	2011	2010
Sales	$120,000	$180,000	$90,000	$?
Cost of goods sold:				
Merchandise inventory (beginning)	18,700	22,300	9,875	9,000
Net cost of merchandise purchases	72,000	?	?	26,100
Merchandise inventory (ending)	?	(18,700)	(8,920)	(9,875)
Cost of goods sold	74,300	108,000	?	?
Gross profit from sales	?	?	39,545	19,775
Operating expenses	36,000	54,000	27,000	?
Net income (loss)	9,700	18,000	?	6,275
Gross profit ratio	?	?	?	?

Analysis component:
Company A and Company B are in similar industries. Comment on their gross profit ratios.

An asterisk (*) identifies assignment material based on Appendix 6A or Appendix 6B.

***Exercise 6-14**
Components of cost of goods sold
LO1, 2, 3, 5, 7

Referring to Exhibit 6A.4, use the data provided to determine each of the missing numbers in the following situations:

	a	b	c
Invoice cost of merchandise purchases	$45,000	$20,000	$15,250
Purchase discounts	2,000	?	325
Purchase returns and allowances	1,500	750	550
Cost of transportation-in	?	1,750	2,000
Merchandise inventory (beginning of period)	3,500	?	4,500
Net cost of merchandise purchases	44,700	19,750	?
Merchandise inventory (end of period)	2,200	3,750	?
Cost of goods sold	?	20,800	17,065

Exercise 6-15
Preparing an income statement and closing entries—perpetual
LO5, 6

Check figure:
a. Net income = $6,565

The following account information, in alphabetical order, was taken from the work sheet of Compu-Soft for the month ended November 30, 2011.

Required

a. Prepare a multiple-step income statement for the month ended November 30, 2011.
b. Prepare closing entries.
c. Calculate the post-closing balance in the capital account at November 30, 2011.

		Adjusted Trial Balance	
	Account	Debit	Credit
201	Accounts payable		$ 600
106	Accounts receivable	$ 850	
166	Accumulated depreciation, store equipment		4,550
101	Cash	1,800	
502	Cost of goods sold	14,800	
612	Depreciation expense, store equipment	120	
301	Peter Delta, capital		1,635
302	Peter Delta, withdrawals	3,500	
406	Rent revenue		850
413	Sales		27,700
415	Sales discounts	45	
414	Sales returns and allowances	720	
165	Store equipment	7,200	
690	Utilities expense	2,100	
623	Wages expense	4,200	
	Totals	$35,335	$35,335

Analysis component:
Assume that for the month ended October 31, 2011, net sales were $32,000, cost of goods sold was $19,200, and income from operations was $8,000. Calculate and compare the company's gross profit ratios for October and November.

An asterisk (*) identifies assignment material based on Appendix 6A or Appendix 6B.

Exercise 6-16
Adjusting and closing entries, preparing a work sheet and income statement—perpetual
LO5, 6

The following list of accounts is taken from the December 31, 2011, unadjusted trial balance of Perdu Sales, a business that is owned by Eldon Perdu.

	Debit	Credit
Cash	$ 26,000	
Merchandise inventory	2,000	
Prepaid selling expense	8,000	
Store equipment	40,000	
Accumulated depreciation, store equipment		$ 9,000
Accounts payable		14,840
Salaries payable		-0-
Eldon Perdu, capital		45,600
Eldon Perdu, withdrawals	3,600	
Sales		858,000
Sales returns and allowances	33,000	
Sales discounts	8,000	
Cost of goods sold	424,840	
Sales salaries expense	94,000	
Utilities expense, store	28,000	
Other selling expenses	70,000	
Other administrative expenses	190,000	

Additional information:
Accrued sales salaries amount to $3,200. Prepaid selling expenses of $1,500 have expired. Depreciation for the period is $2,500.

Required
Assuming a perpetual inventory system:
a. Prepare a work sheet.
b. Prepare a classified multiple-step income statement for the year ended December 31, 2011.
c. Journalize the closing entries.

Check figures:
a. Balance sheet columns = $78,100
b. Net income = $2,960

Analysis component:
Assume that for the year ended December 31, 2010, net sales were $600,000; operating expenses were $344,000; and there was a net loss of $14,000. Calculate and compare the company's gross profit ratios for 2010 and 2011.

Exercise 6-17
Preparing reports from closing entries—perpetual
LO5, 6

The following closing entries for Sabba Co. were made on January 31, 2011, the end of its annual accounting period:

			Debit	Credit
Jan.	31	Sales	531,000	
		Income Summary		531,000
		To close temporary accounts with credit balances.		
	31	Income Summary	548,750	
		Cost of Goods Sold		301,000
		Sales Returns and Allowances		14,000
		Sales Discounts		7,000
		Selling Expenses		117,000
		General and Administrative Expenses		109,000
		Interest Expense		750
		To close temporary accounts with debit balances.		

Required
Use the information in the closing entries to prepare:
a. A calculation of net sales.
b. A single-step income statement for the year.

Check figure:
b. Net loss = $17,750

***Exercise 6-18**
Journal entries to contrast the periodic and perpetual systems
LO3, 7

Journalize the following merchandising transactions for Scout Systems assuming; (a) a periodic system, and (b) a perpetual system.

Nov.	1	Scout Systems purchases merchandise for $2,800 on credit with terms of 2/10, n/30.
	5	Scout Systems pays for the previous purchase.
	7	Scout Systems receives payment for returned defective merchandise of $200 that was purchased on November 1.
	10	Scout Systems pays $160 to transport merchandise to its store.
	13	Scout Systems sells merchandise for $3,000 on account. The cost of the merchandise was $1,500.
	16	A customer returns merchandise from the November 13 transaction. The returned item sold for $400 and cost $200. The item will be returned to inventory.

***Exercise 6-19**
Recording journal entries for merchandise purchase transactions—periodic
LO7

Using the information in Exercise 6-2, prepare journal entries to record the transactions assuming a periodic inventory system.

***Exercise 6-20**
Recording journal entries for merchandise purchase transactions—periodic
LO7

Using the information in Exercise 6-3, prepare journal entries to record the March transactions assuming a periodic inventory system.

***Exercise 6-21**
Recording journal entries for merchandise sales transactions—periodic
LO7

Using the information in Exercise 6-4, prepare journal entries to record the transactions assuming a periodic inventory system.

***Exercise 6-22**
Recording journal entries for merchandise sales transactions—periodic
LO7

Using the information in Exercise 6-5, prepare journal entries to record the transactions assuming a periodic inventory system.

***Exercise 6-23**
Analyzing and recording merchandise transactions and discounts—periodic
LO7

Using the information in Exercise 6-6, and assuming instead a periodic inventory system:

a. Prepare the entries that the purchaser should record for the purchase and payment.
b. Prepare the entries that the seller should record for the sale and collection.

***Exercise 6-24**
Analyzing and recording merchandise transactions and returns—periodic
LO7

Using the information in Exercise 6-7:

a. Present the journal entries that Wilson Purchasing should record for these transactions assuming a periodic inventory system.
b. Present the journal entries that Hostel Sales should record for these transactions assuming a periodic inventory system.

An asterisk (*) identifies assignment material based on Appendix 6A or Appendix 6B.

*Exercise 6-25

Calculating expenses and cost of goods sold—periodic
LO5, 7

Friar Company discloses the following information for the year ended October 31, 2011:

Sales	$340,000
Sales discounts	5,500
Sales returns	14,000
Merchandise inventory (beginning of period)	30,000
Invoice cost of merchandise purchases	175,000
Purchase discounts	3,600
Purchase returns and allowances	6,000
Cost of transportation-in	11,000
Gross profit from sales	145,000
Net income	65,000

Required
Calculate (a) total operating expenses, (b) cost of goods sold, (c) merchandise inventory (end of period), and (d) gross profit ratio (round to two decimal places).

Check figure:
c. $30,900

Analysis component:
Assuming that the gross profit ratio for the year ended October 31, 2010, was 47%, compare Friar Company's performance from 2010 to 2011.

*Exercise 6-26

Preparing a work sheet—periodic
LO7

eXcel

The following unadjusted trial balance relates to Dewer's Stop 'n Shop at the end of its fiscal year, December 31, 2011.

No.	Title	Debit	Credit
101	Cash	$ 7,400	
106	Accounts receivable	3,600	
119	Merchandise inventory	2,400	
125	Store supplies	1,200	
201	Accounts payable		$ 280
209	Salaries payable		
301	Mi Dewer, capital		11,570
302	Mi Dewer, withdrawals	750	
413	Sales		12,000
414	Sales returns and allowances	290	
505	Purchases	6,400	
506	Purchases discounts		250
507	Transportation-in	160	
622	Salaries expense	1,400	
640	Rent expense	500	
651	Store supplies expense		
	Totals	$24,100	$24,100

Required
Use the preceding information and the following additional facts to complete a work sheet for the company.

a. The ending inventory of store supplies was $900.
b. Accrued salaries at the end of the year were $120.
c. The ending merchandise inventory was $2,720.

Check figure:
Income statement columns = $14,970

An asterisk (*) identifies assignment material based on Appendix 6A or Appendix 6B.

*Exercise 6-27
Preparing reports from closing entries—periodic
LO7

The following closing entries for Fox Fixtures Co. were made on March 31, 2011, the end of its annual accounting period:

1.	Interest Revenue	1,200	
	Merchandise Inventory	11,000	
	Sales	445,000	
	Purchase Returns and Allowances	22,000	
	Purchase Discounts	11,400	
	Income Summary		490,600
	To close temporary accounts with credit balances and record the ending inventory.		
2.	Income Summary	453,300	
	Merchandise Inventory		15,000
	Sales Returns and Allowances		25,000
	Sales Discounts		16,000
	Purchases		286,000
	Transportation-In		8,800
	Selling Expenses		69,000
	General and Administrative Expenses		33,500
	To close temporary accounts with debit balances and to remove the beginning inventory balance.		

Check figure:
d. Net income = $37,300

Required
Use the information in the closing entries to prepare:
a. A calculation of net sales.
b. A calculation of cost of goods purchased.
c. A calculation of cost of goods sold.
d. A multiple-step income statement for the year.

*Exercise 6-28
Preparing an income statement and closing entries—periodic
LO7

The following adjusted account information, in alphabetical order, was taken from the work sheet of John's Electronics for the month ended April 30, 2011. A physical count on April 30, 2011, revealed a merchandise inventory balance actually on hand of $2,460.

	Account	Debit	Credit
201	Accounts payable		$ 2,118
154	Accumulated depreciation, trucks		14,200
101	Cash	$ 4,600	
611	Depreciation expense, delivery trucks	640	
633	Interest expense	130	
301	John Yu, capital		30,300
302	John Yu, withdrawals	9,200	
119	Merchandise inventory	6,200	
507	Purchase discounts		28
506	Purchase returns and allowances		110
505	Purchases	16,676	
413	Sales		33,700
414	Sales returns and allowances	1,740	
688	Telephone expense, office	150	
689	Telephone expense, store	340	
508	Transportation-in	380	
153	Trucks	29,600	
623	Wages expense, office	2,800	
624	Wages expense, selling	8,000	
	Totals	$80,456	$80,456

Check figure:
c. Net loss = $758

Required
a. Calculate net sales.
b. Calculate cost of goods sold.
c. Prepare a classified multiple-step income statement for the month ended April 30, 2011.
d. Prepare closing entries.
e. Calculate the post-closing balance in the capital account at April 30, 2011.

An asterisk (*) identifies assignment material based on Appendix 6A or Appendix 6B.

***Exercise 6-29**
Sales taxes—perpetual
LO3, 8

Journalize each of the following transactions assuming a perpetual inventory system and PST at 8% along with 5% GST.

June	1	Purchased $2,000 of merchandise; terms 1/10, n/30.
	5	Sold $1,000 of merchandise for $1,400; terms n/15.

***Exercise 6-30**
Sales taxes—periodic
LO7, 8

Journalize each of the transactions in *Exercise 6-29 assuming a periodic inventory system and PST at 8% along with 5% GST.

Problems

Problem 6-1A
Journal entries for merchandising activities—perpetual
LO3

Part 1
Prepare General Journal entries to record the following perpetual system merchandising transactions of Belton Company. *Use a separate account for each receivable and payable; for example, record the sale on June 1 in Accounts Receivable—Avery & Wiest.*

June	1	Sold merchandise to Avery & Wiest for $7,000; terms 2/5, n/15, FOB destination (cost of sales $6,250).
	2	Purchased $3,500 of merchandise from Angolac Suppliers; terms 1/10, n/20, FOB shipping point.
	4	Purchased merchandise inventory from Bastille Sales for $14,500; terms 1/15, n/45, FOB Bastille Sales.
	5	Sold merchandise to Gelgar for $11,000; terms 2/5, n/15, FOB destination (cost of sales $9,000).
	6	Collected the amount owing from Avery & Wiest regarding the June 1 sale.
	12	Paid Angolac Suppliers for the June 2 purchase.
	20	Collected the amount owing from Gelgar regarding the June 5 sale.
	30	Paid Bastille Sales for the June 4 purchase.

Part 2
Based on the information provided above, calculate: (a) net sales, (b) cost of goods sold, and (c) gross profit for the month ended June 30, 2011.

Check figure:
2c. $2,610

Problem 6-2A
Journal entries for merchandising activities—perpetual
LO3

Prepare General Journal entries to record the following perpetual system merchandising transactions of Belton Company. *Use a separate account for each receivable and payable; example, record the purchase July 1 in Accounts Payable—Jones Company.* Do the analysis component on p. 314.

July	1	Purchased merchandise from Jones Company for $12,000 under credit terms of 1/15, n/30, FOB factory.
	2	Sold merchandise to Terra Co. for $1,600 under credit terms of 2/10, n/60, FOB shipping point. The merchandise had cost $1,000.
	3	Paid $200 for freight charges on the purchase of July 1.
	8	Sold merchandise that cost $2,400 for $3,200 cash.
	9	Purchased merchandise from Keene Co. for $4,600 under credit terms of 2/15, n/60, FOB destination.
	12	Received a $400 credit memorandum acknowledging the return of merchandise purchased on July 9.
	12	Received the balance due from Terra Co. for the credit sale dated July 2.
	13	Purchased office supplies from EastCo on credit, $960, n/30.
	16	Paid the balance due to Jones Company.
	19	Sold merchandise that cost $1,800 to Urban Co. for $2,500 under credit terms of 2/15, n/60, FOB shipping point.
	21	Issued a $300 credit memorandum to Urban Co. for an allowance on goods sold on July 19.
	22	Received a debit memorandum from Urban Co. for an error that overstated the total invoice by $100.
	29	Paid Keene Co. the balance due.
	30	Received the balance due from Urban Co. for the credit sale dated July 19.
	31	Sold merchandise that cost $6,400 to Terra Co. for $10,000 under credit terms of 2/10, n/60, FOB shipping point.

An asterisk (*) identifies assignment material based on Appendix 6A or Appendix 6B.

Analysis component:

As the senior purchaser for Belton Company, you are concerned that the purchase discounts you have negotiated are not being taken advantage of by the accounts payable department. Calculate the cost of the lost discount regarding the July 9 purchase and explain to accounts payable when to take advantage of discounts (assume a 6% interest rate; round calculations to four decimal places).

Problem 6-3A

Journal entries for merchandising activities—perpetual

LO3

Prepare General Journal entries to record the following perpetual system merchandising transactions of Hanifin Company. *Use a separate account for each receivable and payable; for example, record the purchase on August 1 in Accounts Payable—Dickson Company.*

Aug.	1	Purchased merchandise from Dickson Company for $3,000 under credit terms of 1/10, n/30, FOB destination.
	4	At Dickson's request, paid $50 for freight charges on the August 1 purchase, reducing the amount owed to Dickson.
	5	Sold merchandise to Griften Corp. for $2,100 under credit terms of 2/10, n/60, FOB destination. The merchandise had cost $1,500.
	8	Purchased merchandise from Kendall Corporation for $2,650 under credit terms of 1/10, n/45, FOB shipping point.
	9	Paid $60 shipping charges related to the August 5 sale to Griften Corp.
	10	Griften returned merchandise from the August 5 sale that had cost $250 and been sold for $350. The merchandise was restored to inventory.
	12	After negotiations with Kendall Corporation concerning problems with the merchandise purchased on August 8, received a credit memorandum from Kendall granting a price reduction of $400.
	15	Received balance due from Griften Corp. for the August 5 sale.
	17	Purchased office equipment from WestCo on credit, $600, n/45.
	18	Paid the amount due Kendall Corporation for the August 8 purchase.
	19	Sold merchandise to Farley for $1,800 under credit terms of 1/10, n/30, FOB shipping point. The merchandise had cost $1,250.
	22	Farley requested a price reduction on the August 19 sale because the merchandise did not meet specifications. Sent Farley a credit memorandum for $300 to resolve the issue.
	29	Received Farley's payment of the amount due from the August 19 purchase.
	30	Paid Dickson Company the amount due from the August 1 purchase.

Problem 6-4A

Work sheet and income statement—perpetual

LO5

Information from the unadjusted trial balance of Jumbo's on December 31, 2011, the end of the annual accounting period, is as follows:

	Debit	Credit
Cash	$ 10,275	
Accounts receivable	22,665	
Merchandise inventory	54,365	
Store supplies	2,415	
Office supplies	775	
Prepaid insurance	3,255	
Equipment	74,490	
Accumulated depreciation, equipment		$ 13,655
Accounts payable		8,000
Salaries payable		-0-
Sally Fowler, capital		166,015
Sally Fowler, withdrawals	15,000	
Interest revenue		310
Sales		502,140
Sales returns and allowances	5,070	
Cost of goods sold	381,160	
Salaries expense	91,550	
Rent expense	29,100	
Supplies expense	-0-	
Depreciation expense, equipment	-0-	
Insurance expense	-0-	
Totals	$690,120	$690,120

Required

1. Copy the unadjusted trial balance on a work sheet form and complete the work sheet using the information that follows:
   a. A review of the store supplies on December 31, 2011, revealed a balance on hand of $415; a similar examination of the office supplies showed that $700 had been used.
   b. The balance in the Prepaid Insurance account was reviewed and it was determined that $455 was unused at December 31, 2011.
   c. The records show that the equipment was estimated to have a total estimated useful life of 10 years with a resale value at the end of its life of $14,490.
   d. Accrued salaries payable, $655.
   e. A count of the merchandise inventory revealed a balance on hand December 31, 2011, of $53,800.
2. Prepare a multiple-step income statement showing the expenses in detail.

Check figures:
1. Income statement columns = $519,600
2. Net loss = $17,150

Analysis component:
Explain why *Interest Revenue* is shown under *Other revenues and expenses* on the multiple-step income statement.

Problem 6-5A
Income statement calculations and formats—perpetual
LO5

The following amounts appeared on Davison Company's adjusted trial balance as of October 31, 2011, the end of its fiscal year:

	Debit	Credit
Merchandise inventory	$ 62,000	
Other assets	256,800	
Liabilities		$ 70,000
Brenda Davison, capital		234,180
Brenda Davison, withdrawals	32,000	
Interest revenue		1,120
Sales		424,000
Sales discounts	6,500	
Sales returns and allowances	28,000	
Cost of goods sold	165,200	
Sales salaries expense	58,000	
Rent expense, selling space	20,000	
Store supplies expense	5,000	
Advertising expense	36,000	
Office salaries expense	53,000	
Rent expense, office space	5,200	
Office supplies expense	1,600	
Totals	$729,300	$729,300

Required

1. Prepare a classified, multiple-step income statement for internal use (see Exhibit 6.15) that lists the company's net sales, cost of goods sold, and gross profit, as well as the components and amounts of selling expenses and general and administrative expenses.
2. Present a condensed single-step income statement (see Exhibit 6.17) that lists these costs: cost of goods sold, selling expenses, and general and administrative expenses.

Check figure:
1. Income from operations = $45,500

Problem 6-6A
Closing entries—perpetual
LO6

Use the data for Davison Company in Problem 6-5A to prepare compound closing entries for the company as of October 31.

Problem 6-7A

Income statements—perpetual

LO5

On December 31, 2011, the end of Plymouth Electronics' annual accounting period, the financial statement columns of its work sheet appeared as follows:

	Income Statement		Balance Sheet and Statement of Changes in Equity	
	Debit	**Credit**	**Debit**	**Credit**
Merchandise inventory			66,545	
Other assets			487,785	
Celine Plymouth, capital				200,000
Liabilities				312,370
Celine Plymouth, withdrawals			50,000	
Interest earned		720		
Sales		963,000		
Sales returns and allowances	5,715			
Sales discounts	14,580			
Cost of goods sold	652,025			
Sales salaries expense	80,080			
Rent expense, selling space	33,000			
Store supplies expense	1,620			
Depreciation expense, store equipment	8,910			
Office salaries expense	65,945			
Rent expense, office space	3,000			
Office supplies expense	735			
Insurance expense	3,390			
Depreciation expense, office equipment	2,760			
Totals	871,760	963,720	604,330	512,370
Net income	91,960			91,960
Totals	963,720	963,720	604,330	604,330

Check figure:
1. Income from operations = $91,240

Required

1. Prepare a 2011 classified, multiple-step income statement for Plymouth Electronics, like Exhibit 6.15.
2. Prepare a single-step income statement, like Exhibit 6.17.

Analysis component:

The gross profit ratio for Plymouth Electronics' year ended December 31, 2010, was 32%. Calculate this ratio for the year ended December 31, 2011, and compare it to the prior year, commenting on whether the change was favourable or unfavourable.

Problem 6-8A

Closing entries—perpetual

LO6

Using the information in Problem 6-7A, prepare compound closing entries for Plymouth Electronics.

Problem 6-9A
Income statements—perpetual
LO5

The following adjusted trial balance for Bell Servicing was prepared at the end of the fiscal year, December 31, 2011:

		Debit	Credit
101	Cash	$ 8,000	
119	Merchandise inventory	16,200	
125	Supplies	10,000	
128	Prepaid insurance	4,000	
165	Store equipment	36,400	
166	Accumulated depreciation, store equipment		$ 5,000
167	Office equipment	50,000	
168	Accumulated depreciation, office equipment		7,000
201	Accounts payable		16,000
301	Jonah Bell, capital		70,400
302	Jonah Bell, withdrawals	7,000	
413	Sales		180,000
415	Sales discounts	2,000	
505	Cost of goods sold	74,800	
612	Depreciation expense, store equipment	1,400	
613	Depreciation expense, office equipment	1,800	
622	Sales salaries expense	20,000	
623	Office salaries expense	12,000	
637	Insurance expense, store	2,000	
638	Insurance expense, office	1,600	
640	Rent expense, office space	3,000	
641	Rent expense, selling space	7,000	
651	Office supplies expense	1,200	
652	Store supplies expense	2,400	
655	Advertising expense	17,600	
	Totals	$278,400	$278,400

Required

1. Prepare a classified multiple-step income statement that would be used by the business's owner (like Exhibit 6.15).
2. Prepare a multiple-step income statement that would be used by external users (like Exhibit 6.16).
3. Prepare a single-step income statement that would be provided to decision makers outside the company (like Exhibit 6.17).

Check figures:
1. Operating expenses = $70,000; Net income = $33,200

Analysis component:
If you were a decision maker external to Bell Servicing, which income statement format would you prefer and why, if you had a choice? Which income statement format(s) could you expect as an external user? Why?

***Problem 6-10A**
Journal entries for merchandising activities—periodic
LO7

Using the information provided in Part 1 of Problem 6-1A, journalize each of the transactions assuming a periodic inventory system.

An asterisk (*) identifies assignment material based on Appendix 6A or Appendix 6B.

***Problem 6-11A**
Journal entries for merchandising transactions—periodic
LO7

Prepare General Journal entries to record the following periodic system merchandising transactions for Schafer Merchandising. *Use a separate account for each receivable and payable:*

Oct.	1	Purchased merchandise from Zeon Company on credit, terms 2/10, n/30, $14,400.
	2	Sold merchandise for cash, $1,500.
	7	Purchased merchandise on credit from Billings Co., terms 2/10, n/30, $10,500, FOB the seller's factory.
	7	Paid $450 cash for freight charges on the merchandise shipment of the previous transaction.
	8	Purchased delivery equipment from Finlay Supplies on credit, $24,000.
	12	Sold merchandise on credit to Comry Holdings, terms 2/15, 1/30, n/60, $6,000.
	13	Received a $1,500 credit memorandum for merchandise purchased on October 7 and returned for credit.
	13	Purchased office supplies on credit from Staples, $480, n/30.
	15	Sold merchandise on credit to Tom Willis, terms 2/10, 1/30, n/60, $4,200.
	15	Paid for the merchandise purchased on October 7.
	16	Received a credit memorandum for unsatisfactory office supplies purchased on October 13 and returned, $120.
	19	Issued a $420 credit memorandum to the customer who purchased merchandise on October 15 and returned a portion for credit.
	25	Received payment for the merchandise sold on October 15.
	29	The customer of October 12 paid for the purchase of that date.
	31	Paid for the merchandise purchased on October 1.

***Problem 6-12A**
Income statement calculations and formats—periodic
LO7

The following amounts appeared on the Mendelstein Company's adjusted trial balance as of October 31, 2011, the end of its fiscal year:

	Debit	Credit
Merchandise inventory	$ 12,500	
Other assets	70,000	
Liabilities		$ 18,500
Joe Mendelstein, capital		78,675
Joe Mendelstein, withdrawals	8,500	
Interest revenue		150
Sales		85,000
Sales returns and allowances	7,500	
Sales discounts	1,125	
Purchases	45,000	
Purchases returns and allowances		2,150
Purchases discounts		900
Transportation-in	1,550	
Sales salaries expense	14,000	
Rent expense, selling space	5,000	
Store supplies expense	1,500	
Advertising expense	9,000	
Office salaries expense	8,000	
Rent expense, office space	1,250	
Office supplies expense	450	
Totals	$185,375	$185,375

A physical count shows that the cost of the ending inventory is $13,500.

Check figures:
3. $42,500
4. Loss from operations = $5,325; Net loss = $5,175

Required

1. Calculate the company's net sales for the year.
2. Calculate the company's cost of goods purchased for the year.
3. Calculate the company's cost of goods sold for the year.
4. Present a multiple-step income statement that lists the company's net sales, cost of goods sold, and gross profit from sales.
5. Present a condensed single-step income statement that lists these expenses: cost of goods sold, selling expenses, and general and administrative expenses.

An asterisk (*) identifies assignment material based on Appendix 6A or Appendix 6B.

*Problem 6-13A

Closing entries—periodic
LO7

Use the data for the Mendelstein Company in *Problem 6-12A to prepare compound closing entries for the company as of October 31.

*Problem 6-14A

Work sheet and closing entries—periodic
LO7

Information from the December 31, 2011, year-end, unadjusted trial balance of Woodstock Store is as follows:

	Debit	Credit
Cash	$ 7,305	
Merchandise inventory	47,000	
Store supplies	1,715	
Office supplies	645	
Prepaid insurance	3,960	
Store equipment	57,615	
Accumulated depreciation, store equipment		$ 8,750
Office equipment	14,400	
Accumulated depreciation, office equipment		9,000
Accounts payable		4,000
Zen Woodstock, capital		89,080
Zen Woodstock, withdrawals	31,500	
Rental revenue		680
Sales		478,850
Sales returns and allowances	2,915	
Sales discounts	5,190	
Purchases	331,315	
Purchase returns and allowances		1,845
Purchase discounts		4,725
Transportation-in	2,810	
Sales salaries expense	34,710	
Rent expense, selling space	24,000	
Advertising expense	1,220	
Store supplies expense	-0-	
Depreciation expense, store equipment	-0-	
Office salaries expense	27,630	
Rent expense, office space	3,000	
Office supplies expense	-0-	
Insurance expense	-0-	
Depreciation expense, office equipment	-0-	
Totals	$596,930	$596,930

Required

1. Copy the unadjusted trial balance on a work sheet form and complete the work sheet using the following information:

a. The balance on January 1, 2011, in the Store Supplies account was $840. During the year, $875 of store supplies were purchased and debited to the Store Supplies account. A physical count on December 31, 2011, shows an ending balance of $385.

b. The balance on January 1, 2011, in the Office Supplies account was $50. Office supplies of $595 were bought in 2011 and added to the Office Supplies account. An examination of the office supplies at year-end revealed that $465 had been used.

c. The balance in the Prepaid Insurance account represents a policy purchased on September 1, 2011; it was valid for 18 months from that date.

d. The store equipment was originally estimated to have a useful life of 15 years and a residual value of $5,115.

e. When the office equipment was purchased, it was estimated that it would last four years and have no residual value.

f. Ending merchandise inventory, $48,980.

2. Journalize closing entries for the store. Use page 10 for your journal.

3. Open a balance column Merchandise Inventory account (110) and enter a December 31, 2010, balance of $47,000. Then post those portions of the closing entries that affect the account.

Check figure:
1. Balance sheet columns = $163,445

An asterisk (*) identifies assignment material based on Appendix 6A or Appendix 6B.

***Problem 6-15A**
Classified, multi-step income statement—periodic
LO7

Using the information in *Problem 6-14A, prepare a classified multi-step income statement, like Exhibit 6A.4.

***Problem 6-16A**
Sales taxes—perpetual
LO3, 8

Journalize each of the following transactions assuming a perpetual inventory system and PST at 8% along with 5% GST. *Note: Any available cash discount is taken only on the sale price before taxes.*

Aug.	1	Purchased $1,000 of merchandise for cash.
	2	Purchased $3,400 of merchandise; terms 2/10, n/30.
	5	Sold merchandise costing $1,800 for $2,600; terms 1/10, n/30.
	12	Paid for the merchandise purchased on August 2.
	15	Collected the amount owing from the customer of August 5.
	17	Purchased $6,000 of merchandise; terms n/15.
	19	Recorded $7,000 of cash sales (cost of sales $5,800).

***Problem 6-17A**
Sales taxes—periodic
LO7, 8

Journalize each of the transactions in *Problem 6-16A assuming a periodic inventory system and PST at 7% along with 5% GST.

Alternate Problems

Problem 6-1B
Journal entries for merchandising activities—perpetual
LO3

Part 1
Prepare General Journal entries to record the following perpetual system merchandising transactions of Lyryx Company. *Use a separate account for each receivable and payable; for example, record the sale on March 6 in Accounts Receivable—Tessier & Welsh.*

Mar.	5	Purchased $50,000 of merchandise from Delton Suppliers paying cash.
	6	Sold merchandise for $32,000 to Tessier & Welsh; terms 2/10, n/30, FOB destination (cost of sales $25,600).
	7	Purchased merchandise from Janz Company for $64,000; terms 1/10, n/45, FOB shipping point.
	8	Paid $150 shipping costs regarding the purchase of March 7.
	9	Sold merchandise for $56,000 to Parker Company; terms 2/10, n/30, FOB destination (cost of sales $46,000).
	10	Purchased $14,000 of merchandise from Delton Suppliers; terms 2/10, n/45, FOB destination.
	16	Collected the balance owing from Tessier & Welsh regarding the March 6 sale.
	17	Paid for the March 7 purchase from Janz Company.
	30	Paid for the March 10 purchase from Delton Suppliers.
	31	Collected the balance owing from Parker Company regarding the sale of March 9.

Check figure:
2c. = $15,760

Part 2
Based on the information provided above, calculate: (a) net sales, (b) cost of goods sold, and (c) gross profit for the month ended March 31, 2011.

An asterisk (*) identifies assignment material based on Appendix 6A or Appendix 6B.

Problem 6-2B

Journal entries for merchandising activities—perpetual

LO3

Prepare General Journal entries to record the following perpetual system merchandising transactions of Lyryx Company. *Use a separate account for each receivable and payable; for example, record the purchase on May 2 in Accounts Payable—Mobley Co.*

May	2	Purchased merchandise from Mobley Co. for $18,000 under credit terms of 1/15, n/30, FOB factory.
	4	Sold merchandise to Cornerstone Co. for $2,400 under credit terms of 2/10, n/60, FOB shipping point. The merchandise had cost $1,500.
	4	Paid $300 for freight charges on the purchase of May 2.
	9	Sold merchandise that cost $3,600 for $4,800 cash.
	10	Purchased merchandise from Richter Co. for $6,900 under credit terms of 2/15, n/60, FOB destination.
	12	Received a $600 credit memorandum acknowledging the return of merchandise purchased on May 10.
	14	Received the balance due from Cornerstone Co. for the credit sale dated May 4.
	15	Sold for cash a piece of office equipment at its original cost, $1,000.
	17	Paid the balance due to Mobley Co.
	18	Purchased $1,640 of cleaning supplies from A & Z Suppliers; terms n/15.
	20	Sold merchandise that cost $2,700 to Harrill Co. for $3,750 under credit terms of 2/15, n/60, FOB shipping point.
	22	Issued a $600 credit memorandum to Harrill Co. for an allowance on goods sold on May 20.
	23	Received a debit memorandum from Harrill Co. for an error that overstated the total invoice by $150.
	25	Paid Richter Co. the balance due.
	31	Received the balance due from Harrill Co. for the credit sale dated May 20.
	31	Sold merchandise that cost $9,600 to Cornerstone Co. for $15,000 under credit terms of 2/10, n/60, FOB shipping point.

Analysis component:

You are working in Lyryx's accounts payable department and have been instructed to pay the Richter account on the last day of the discount period even though the money will have to be borrowed at 6% interest. Why would the company borrow to pay within the discount period? Show your calculations (round to two decimal places).

Problem 6-3B
Journal entries for merchandising activities—perpetual
LO3

Prepare General Journal entries to record the following perpetual system merchandising transactions of Goodfish Lake Company. *Use a separate account for each receivable and payable; for example, record the purchase on July 3 in Accounts Payable—CMP Corp.*

July	3	Purchased merchandise from CMP Corp. for $30,000 under credit terms of 1/10, n/30, FOB destination.
	4	At CMP's request, paid $500 for freight charges on the July 3 purchase, reducing the amount owed to CMP.
	7	Sold merchandise to Harbison Co. for $21,000 under credit terms of 2/10, n/60, FOB destination. The merchandise had cost $15,000.
	10	Purchased merchandise from Cimarron Corporation for $26,500 under credit terms of 1/10, n/45, FOB shipping point.
	11	Paid $600 shipping charges related to the July 7 sale to Harbison Co.
	12	Harbison returned merchandise from the July 7 sale that had cost $2,500 and been sold for $3,500. The merchandise was restored to inventory.
	14	After negotiations with Cimarron Corporation concerning problems with the merchandise purchased on July 10, received a credit memorandum from Cimarron granting a price reduction of $4,100.
	17	Received balance due from Harbison Co. for the July 7 sale.
	18	Sold for cash a piece of vacant land for its original cost of $30,000.
	19	Purchased a used van for the business, $36,000; paid cash of $10,000 and borrowed the balance from the bank.
	20	Paid the amount due Cimarron Corporation for the July 10 purchase.
	21	Sold merchandise to Hess for $18,000 under credit terms of 1/10, n/30, FOB shipping point. The merchandise had cost $12,500.
	24	Hess requested a price reduction on the July 21 sale because the merchandise did not meet specifications. Sent Hess a credit memorandum for $3,000 to resolve the issue.
	31	Received Hess's payment of the amount due from the July 21 purchase.
	31	Paid CMP Corp. the amount due from the July 3 purchase.

Analysis component:
Regarding the July 24 transaction, what alternative is there to granting a credit memorandum? Be sure to identify and explain an advantage and disadvantage of the alternative.

Problem 6-4B
Adjusting entries and income statements—perpetual
LO5

The following information is from the unadjusted trial balance for Journey's End Company prepared at October 31, 2011, the end of the fiscal year:

	Debit	Credit
Cash	$ 12,800	
Merchandise inventory	46,000	
Store supplies	18,900	
Prepaid insurance	9,500	
Store equipment	167,600	
Accumulated depreciation, store equipment		$ 60,000
Accounts payable		32,000
Dallas End, capital		160,800
Dallas End, withdrawals	12,000	
Sales		396,000
Sales discounts	4,000	
Sales returns and allowances	8,000	
Cost of goods sold	149,600	
Depreciation expense, store equipment	-0-	
Salaries expense	124,000	
Interest expense	800	
Insurance expense	-0-	
Rent expense	56,000	
Store supplies expense	-0-	
Advertising expense	39,600	
Totals	$648,800	$648,800

Rent and salaries expense are equally divided between the selling and administrative functions. Journey's End Company uses a perpetual inventory system.

Required

1. Copy the unadjusted trial balance on a work sheet form and complete the work sheet using the following information:
   a. Store supplies on hand at year-end amount to $6,600.
   b. The balance in the Prepaid Insurance account represents 19 months of insurance that was in effect starting November 1, 2010.
   c. The store equipment was purchased several years ago, when it was estimated to have a 20-year useful life and a resale value at the end of its life of $47,600.
   d. A physical count of the ending merchandise inventory shows $44,400 of goods on hand.
2. Prepare a multiple-step income statement (see Exhibit 6.16).

Check figures:
1. Income statement columns = $407,900
2. Net loss = $11,900

Analysis component:
Explain why *Interest Expense* is shown under *Other revenues and expenses* on the multiple-step income statement.

Problem 6-5B
Income statement calculations and formats—perpetual
LO5

The following amounts appeared on Excel Company's adjusted trial balance as of May 31, 2011, the end of its fiscal year:

	Debit	Credit
Merchandise inventory	$ 93,000	
Other assets	385,200	
Liabilities		$ 105,000
Reena Excel, capital		352,950
Reena Excel, withdrawals	48,000	
Sales		636,000
Sales discounts	9,750	
Sales returns and allowances	42,000	
Cost of goods sold	247,800	
Sales salaries expense	87,000	
Rent expense, selling space	30,000	
Store supplies expense	7,500	
Advertising expense	54,000	
Office salaries expense	79,500	
Rent expense, office space	7,800	
Office supplies expense	2,400	
Totals	$1,093,950	$1,093,950

Required

1. Present a classified multiple-step income statement for internal users (see Exhibit 6.15) that lists the company's net sales, cost of goods sold, and gross profit, as well as the components and amounts of selling expenses and general and administrative expenses.
2. Present a condensed single-step income statement (see Exhibit 6.17) that lists these costs: cost of goods sold, selling expenses, and general and administrative expenses.

Check figure:
1. Net income = $68,250

Problem 6-6B
Closing entries—perpetual
LO6

Use the data for Excel Company in Problem 6-5B to prepare compound closing entries for the company as of May 31.

Problem 6-7B
Income statements—perpetual
LO5

On December 31, 2011, the end of Ucore Sales' annual accounting period, the financial statement columns of its work sheet appeared as follows in alphabetical order:

	Income Statement		Balance Sheet and Statement of Changes in Equity	
	Debit	**Credit**	**Debit**	**Credit**
Cost of goods sold	129,964			
Depreciation expense, office equipment	690			
Depreciation expense, store equipment	3,204			
Insurance expense	1,240			
Liabilities				84,000
Lyle Ucore, capital				46,547
Lyle Ucore, withdrawals			20,500	
Merchandise inventory			3,400	
Other assets			104,000	
Rent expense (80% sales)	9,950			
Salaries expense (70% sales)	42,710			
Sales		189,258		
Sales discounts	278			
Sales returns and allowances	1,469			
Supplies expense (35% sales)	2,400			
Totals	191,905	189,258	127,900	130,547
Net loss		2,647	2,647	
Totals	191,905	191,905	130,547	130,547

Check figure:
1. Total operating expenses = $60,194

Required

1. Prepare a classified, multiple-step income statement for Ucore Sales, like Exhibit 6.15.
2. Prepare a single-step income statement, like Exhibit 6.17.

Analysis component:

The gross profit ratio for Ucore Sales' year ended December 31, 2010, was 28%. Calculate this ratio for the year ended December 31, 2011, and compare it to the prior year, commenting on whether the change was favourable or unfavourable (round to two decimal places).

Problem 6-8B
Closing entries—perpetual
LO6

Using the information in Problem 6-7B, prepare compound closing entries for Ucore Sales.

Problem 6-9B
Income statements—perpetual
LO5

The following adjusted trial balance information was taken from the end of the July 31, 2011, fiscal year for Brilliant Sales:

		Debit	Credit
101	Cash	$ 2,100	
119	Merchandise inventory	5,750	
125	Supplies	2,400	
128	Prepaid insurance	1,150	
165	Store equipment	10,000	
166	Accumulated depreciation, store equipment		$ 7,500
167	Office equipment	10,950	
168	Accumulated depreciation, office equipment		7,500
201	Accounts payable		6,400
301	Ty Brilliant, capital		22,600
302	Ty Brilliant, withdrawals	600	
413	Sales		39,250
415	Sales discounts	500	
505	Cost of goods sold	23,700	
612	Depreciation expense, store equipment	500	
613	Depreciation expense, office equipment	1,250	
622	Sales salaries expense	9,000	
623	Office salaries expense	2,500	
637	Insurance expense, store	375	
638	Insurance expense, office	125	
640	Rent expense, office space	2,500	
641	Rent expense, selling space	3,500	
651	Office supplies expense	600	
652	Store supplies expense	800	
655	Advertising expense	4,950	
	Totals	$83,250	$83,250

Brilliant Sales uses a perpetual inventory system.

Required

1. Prepare a classified multiple-step income statement for use by internal users (like Exhibit 6.15).
2. Prepare a multiple-step income statement for external users (like Exhibit 6.16).
3. Prepare a single-step income statement (like Exhibit 6.17).

Check figures:
1. Operating expenses = $26,100
2. Net loss = $11,050

*Problem 6-10B
Journal entries for merchandising activities—periodic
LO7

Using the information provided in Part 1 of Problem 6-1B, journalize each of the transactions assuming a periodic inventory system.

An asterisk (*) identifies assignment material based on Appendix 6A or Appendix 6B.

***Problem 6-11B**
Journal entries for merchandising transactions—periodic
LO7

Prepare General Journal entries to record the following periodic system transactions of Inter-Cap Merchandising. *Use a separate account for each receivable and payable.*

March	1	Purchased merchandise on credit from Zender Holdings, terms 1/10, n/15, $40,000.
	2	Sold merchandise for cash, $3,600.
	7	Purchased merchandise on credit from Red River Co., terms 2/10, n/30, $32,000, FOB the seller's factory.
	8	Incurred freight charges for $700 on credit to Dan's Shipping regarding the merchandise shipment of the previous transaction.
	12	Sold merchandise on credit to Bev Dole, terms 2/10, n/45, $18,000.
	13	Received a $1,000 credit memorandum for merchandise purchased on March 7 and returned for credit.
	14	Purchased furniture for the office on credit from Wilson Supplies, $3,200.
	15	Sold merchandise on credit to Ted Smith, terms 2/10, n/45, $34,000.
	16	Paid for the merchandise purchased on March 7.
	17	Issued a credit memorandum to the customer of March 15 granting an allowance of $2,000 due to damage during shipment.
	19	The supplier issued a credit memorandum for $1,500 regarding unsatisfactory furniture purchased on March 14 and returned.
	24	Received payment for the merchandise sold on March 15.
	27	The customer of March 12 paid for the purchase of that date.
	31	Paid for the merchandise purchased on March 1.

***Problem 6-12B**
Income statement calculations and formats—periodic
LO7

The following amounts appeared on the Mullen Company's adjusted trial balance in alphabetical order as of November 30, 2011, the end of its fiscal year:

	Debit	Credit
Advertising expense	$ 3,000	
Interest expense	350	
Liabilities		$ 31,000
Merchandise inventory	25,000	
Mitsy Mullen, capital		133,500
Mitsy Mullen, withdrawals	10,000	
Other assets	144,650	
Purchase discounts		1,150
Purchase returns and allowances		4,050
Purchases	120,000	
Rent expense (75% selling)	36,000	
Salaries expense (60% selling)	60,000	
Sales		270,000
Sales discounts	2,350	
Sales returns and allowances	28,500	
Supplies expense (80% selling)	5,000	
Transportation-in	4,850	
Totals	$439,700	$439,700

A physical count shows that the cost of the ending inventory is $16,000.

Required
1. Calculate the company's net sales for the year.
2. Calculate the company's cost of goods purchased for the year.

An asterisk (*) identifies assignment material based on Appendix 6A or Appendix 6B.

3. Calculate the company's cost of goods sold for the year.
4. Present a multiple-step income statement (like Exhibit 6.16) that lists the company's net sales, cost of goods sold, and gross profit, as well as the components and amounts of selling expenses and general and administrative expenses.
5. Present a single-step income statement (like Exhibit 6.17) that lists these expenses: cost of goods sold, selling expenses, general and administrative expenses, and interest expense.

Check figures:
3. $128,650
4. Income from operations = $6,500

*Problem 6-13B
Closing entries—periodic
LO7

Use the data for the Mullen Company in *Problem 6-12B to prepare compound closing entries for the company as of November 30, 2011.

*Problem 6-14B
Work sheet and closing entries—periodic
LO7

excel

Information from the March 31, 2011, year-end, unadjusted trial balance of The Online Store is as follows:

	Debit	Credit
Cash	$ 7,000	
Merchandise inventory	48,000	
Supplies	600	
Prepaid rent	7,000	
Store equipment	60,000	
Accumulated depreciation, store equipment		$ 14,000
Office equipment	23,000	
Accumulated depreciation, office equipment		6,500
Accounts payable		16,000
Lucy Baker, capital		134,600
Lucy Baker, withdrawals	34,000	
Sales		499,000
Sales returns and allowances	11,500	
Sales discounts	6,000	
Purchases	346,000	
Purchase returns and allowances		2,850
Purchase discounts		7,150
Transportation-in	16,000	
Salaries expense (60% selling, 40% office)	60,000	
Rent expense (80% selling space; 20% office space)	45,500	
Advertising expense	7,000	
Supplies expense (30% selling supplies; 70% office supplies)	8,500	
Depreciation expense, store equipment	-0-	
Depreciation expense, office equipment	-0-	
Totals	$680,100	$680,100

Required
1. Copy the unadjusted trial balance on a work sheet form and complete the work sheet using the following information:
   a. Supplies inventory at year-end, $450.
   b. The balance in the Prepaid Rent account represents a seven-month contract effective November 1, 2010.
   c. Depreciation on the store equipment, $1,600.
   d. The useful life and trade-in value of the office equipment were originally estimated to be seven years and $250, respectively.
   e. Ending merchandise inventory, $9,000.
2. Journalize closing entries for the store. Use page 14 for your journal.
3. Open a balance column Merchandise Inventory account (110) and enter the March 31, 2010, balance of $48,000. Then post those portions of the closing entries that affect the account.

Check figure:
1. Balance sheet columns = $175,950

An asterisk (*) identifies assignment material based on Appendix 6A or Appendix 6B.

***Problem 6-15B**
Classified, multi-step income statement—periodic
LO7

Using the information in *Problem 6-14B, prepare a classified multi-step income statement (like Exhibit 6A.4).

***Problem 6-16B**
Sales taxes—perpetual
LO3, 8

Journalize each of the following transactions assuming a perpetual inventory system and PST at 8% along with 5% GST. *Note: Any available cash discount is taken only on the sale price before taxes.*

Sept.	2	Recorded $7,000 of cash sales (cost of sales $5,800).
	3	Purchased $8,000 of merchandise inventory for cash.
	7	Purchased $5,000 of merchandise; terms 1/10, n/45.
	8	Sold merchandise costing $13,200 for $15,000; terms 2/10, n/30.
	17	Paid for the merchandise purchased on September 7.
	18	Collected the amount owing from the customer of September 8.

***Problem 6-17B**
Sales taxes—periodic
LO7, 8

Journalize each of the transactions in *Problem 6-16B assuming a periodic inventory system and PST at 8% along with 5% GST.

Analytical and Review Problem

A & R Problem 6-1—perpetual

The following income statement was prepared by an office clerk hired for July. As the accounting supervisor, you recognize that it is incorrect and prepare a corrected multi-step income statement.

Demo Sales
Income Statement
For Month Ended July 31, 2011

Sales		$562,140
Accounts receivable		37,000
Unearned sales		18,000
Net sales		$617,140
Operating expenses:		
Accumulated depreciation, equipment	$ 30,000	
Advertising expense	14,000	
Cost of goods sold	394,000	
Depreciation expense, equipment	3,000	
Insurance expense	2,500	
Interest expense	1,700	
Interest payable	250	
Jen Conway, withdrawals	14,000	
Office supplies	9,000	
Prepaid insurance	14,000	
Prepaid rent	25,000	
Rent expense	5,000	
Salaries payable	175,000	
Sales discounts	2,800	690,250
Net loss		$ 73,110

EXTEND YOUR KNOWLEDGE

An asterisk (*) identifies assignment material based on Appendix 6A or Appendix 6B.

Ethics Challenge

EC 6-1

Claire Phelps is a popular high school student who attends approximately four dances a year at her high school. Each dance requires a new dress and accessories that necessitate a financial outlay of $100 to $200 per event. Claire's parents inform her that she is "on her own" with respect to financing the dresses. After incurring a major hit to her savings for the first dance in her second year, Claire developed a different approach. She buys the dress on credit the week before the dance, wears it to the dance, and returns the dress the next week to the store for a full refund on her charge card.

Required

1. Comment on the ethics exhibited by Claire and possible consequences of her actions.
2. How does the store account for the dresses that Claire returns?

Focus on Financial Statements

FFS 6-1

Colombia Textiles began operations several years ago. Its post-closing trial balance at December 31, 2011, is shown below (with accounts listed in alphabetical order):

Account	Account Balance[1] ($000s)
Accounts payable	17
Accounts receivable	106
Accumulated depreciation, office furniture	38
Accumulated depreciation, store fixtures	61
Brandy Colombia, capital[2]	308
Cash	48
Franchise	62
Merchandise inventory	236
Notes payable[3]	225
Notes receivable[4]	14
Office furniture	52
Office supplies	5
Prepaid rent	32
Store fixtures	106
Unearned sales	12

[1]Assume all accounts have a normal balance.
[2]The owner, Brandy Colombia, made no investments during 2011.
[3]$180,000 of the note is due after December 31, 2012.
[4]$3,000 of the notes receivable will be collected during 2012.

Additional information: The following closing entries were recorded on December 31, 2011, for the year just ended.

2011			
Dec. 31	Sales	640	
	Interest Earned	2	
	Income Summary		642
	To close temporary credit balance accounts to the Income Summary account.		
31	Income Summary	796	
	Depreciation Expense, Office Furniture		13
	Depreciation Expense, Store Fixtures		6
	Cost of Goods Sold		459
	Delivery Expense		21
	Interest Expense		4
	Office Salaries Expense		63
	Office Supplies Expense		17
	Rent Expense, Office		21
	Rent Expense, Sales		46
	Sales Discounts		7
	Sales Returns and Allowances		19
	Sales Salaries Expense		120
	To close temporary debit balance accounts to the Income Summary account.		
31	Brandy Colombia, Capital	154	
	Income Summary		154
	To close the Income Summary account to Capital.		
31	Brandy Colombia, Capital	78	
	Brandy Colombia, Withdrawals		78
	To close Withdrawals to Capital.		

Check figures:
Net loss = $154;
Total current assets = $430;
Total assets = $562;
Total current liabilities = $74

Required
Using the information provided, prepare a single-step income statement, statement of changes in equity, and classified balance sheet.

Analysis component:
Refer to Danier Leather's June 28, 2008, balance sheet in Appendix I at the back of the textbook. Compare Danier's liabilities to those of Colombia Textiles. Ignoring the balance sheet dates, which company has the stronger balance sheet? *(A balance sheet is considered to be stronger the fewer liabilities it has as a percentage of total assets.)*

FFS 6-2

Required

Answer the following questions.

a. Based on a review of the income statement for Danier on page I-3 in Appendix I at the end of the textbook, determine if Danier sells products or services. Explain your answer.

b. Based on a review of WestJet's income statement on page I-25 in Appendix I at the end of the textbook, determine if WestJet sells products or services. Explain your answer.

c. The income statement for Danier shows a gross profit of $76,185 (thousand) for the year ended June 28, 2008. Explain what this gross profit represents.

d. Did Danier have sufficient gross profit to cover operating expenses for the year ended June 28, 2008?

e. Is the income statement format used by Danier a classified multi-step, a multi-step, or a single-step? (Compare the income statement for Danier to those in Exhibits 6.15, 6.16, and 6.17 on pages 272 and 273 of the textbook.)

f. Refer to the balance sheets for Danier and WestJet on pages I-4 and I-26, respectively, in Appendix I at the end of the textbook. Both balance sheets include *Inventory*. Explain how *Inventory* is unique for each of these companies.

Critical Thinking Mini Case

You have just graduated with a business diploma in management and have been hired as the inventory manager for a local sporting goods store. Your first task is to review and assess the following information:

	2011	2010
Cost of merchandise sold to customers in sales transactions	$480,000	$320,000
Merchandise inventory balance, beginning of year	?	84,000
Invoice cost of merchandise purchases	510,000	240,000
Shrinkage determined at end of year	2,500	14,000
Cost of transportation-in	25,500	12,000
Cost of merchandise returned by customers and restored to inventory	115,000	22,400
Purchase discounts received	5,100	2,400
Purchase returns and allowances received	2,550	1,200

Required:

Using the elements of critical thinking described on the inside front cover, comment.

Serial Problem

Echo Systems—perpetual or *periodic

Note: Solutions are available for both perpetual and *periodic.

(The first three segments of this comprehensive problem were presented in Chapters 3, 4, and 5. If those segments have not been completed, the assignment can begin at this point. However, you should use the Working Papers[17] that accompany this text because they reflect the account balances that resulted from posting the entries required in Chapters 3, 4, and 5.)

Earlier segments of this problem have described how Mary Graham created Echo Systems on October 1, 2011. The company has been successful, and its list of customers has started to grow. To accommodate the growth, the accounting system is ready to be modified to set up separate accounts for each customer. The following list of customers includes the account number used for each account and any balance as of the end of 2011. Graham decided to add a fourth digit with a decimal point to the 106 account number that had been used for the single Accounts Receivable account. This modification allows the existing chart of accounts to continue being used. The list also shows the balances that two customers owed as of December 31, 2011:

Customer Account	No.	Dec. 31 Balance
Alamo Engineering Co.	106.1	-0-
Buckman Services	106.2	-0-
Capital Leasing	106.3	-0-
Decker Co.	106.4	$2,700
Elite Corporation	106.5	-0-
Fostek Co.	106.6	$3,000
Grandview Co.	106.7	-0-
Hacienda, Inc.	106.8	-0-
Images, Inc.	106.9	-0-

In response to frequent requests from customers, Graham has decided to begin selling computer software. The company will extend credit terms of 1/10, n/30 to customers who purchase merchandise. No cash discount will be available on consulting fees. The following additional accounts were added to the General Ledger to allow the system to account for the company's new merchandising activities:

Account (Periodic)	No.
Merchandise Inventory	119
Sales	413
Sales Discounts	414
Sales Returns and Allowances	415
Purchases	505
Purchase Returns and Allowances	506
Purchase Discounts	507
Transportation-In	508

OR

Account (Perpetual)	No.
Merchandise Inventory	119
Sales	413
Sales Discounts	414
Sales Returns and Allowances	415
Cost of Goods Sold	502

Because the accounting system does not use reversing entries, all revenue and expense accounts have zero balances as of January 1, 2012.

[17] If students have not purchased the Working Papers package, the Working Papers for the Serial Problem are available on Connect.

Required

1. Prepare journal entries to record each of the following transactions for Echo Systems, assuming either a perpetual system or a periodic system.

	2012	
Jan.	4	Paid Carly Smith for five days at the rate of $200 per day, including one day in addition to the four unpaid days from the prior year.
	5	Mary Graham invested an additional $48,000 cash in the business.
	7	Purchased $11,200 of merchandise from Shephard Corp. with terms of 1/10, n/30, FOB shipping point.
	9	Received $3,000 from Fostek Co. as final payment on its account.
	11	Completed five-day project for Alamo Engineering Co. and billed them $9,000, which is the total price of $12,000 less the advance payment of $3,000.
	13	Sold merchandise with a retail value of $8,400 and a cost of $6,720 to Elite Corporation with terms of 1/10, n/30, FOB shipping point.
	15	Paid $1,400 for freight charges on the merchandise purchased on January 7.
	16	Received $6,000 cash from Grandview Co. for computer services.
	17	Paid Shephard Corp. for the purchase on January 7.
	20	Elite Corporation returned $800 of defective merchandise from its purchase on January 13. The returned merchandise, which had a cost of $640, was scrapped.
	22	Received the balance due from Elite Corporation.
	24	Returned defective merchandise to Shephard Corp. and accepted credit against future purchases. Its cost, net of the discount, was $792.
	26	Purchased $16,000 of merchandise from Shephard Corp. with terms of 1/10, n/30, FOB destination.
	26	Sold merchandise with a cost of $9,280 for $11,600 on credit to Hacienda, Inc.
	29	Received a $792 credit memo from Shephard Corp. concerning the merchandise returned on January 24.
	31	Paid Carly Smith for 10 days' work at $200 per day.
Feb.	1	Paid $6,750 to the Lakeshore Mall for another three months' rent in advance.
	3	Paid Shephard Corp. for the balance due.
	5	Paid $1,600 to the local newspaper for advertising.
	11	Received the balance due from Alamo Engineering Co. for fees billed on January 11.
	15	Mary Graham withdrew $9,600 cash for personal use.
	23	Sold merchandise with a cost of $5,120 for $6,400 on credit to Grandview Co.; terms 1/10, n/30.
	26	Paid Carly Smith for eight days' work at $200 per day.
	27	Reimbursed Mary Graham's business automobile expenses for 600 kilometres at $1.00 per kilometre.
Mar.	8	Purchased $4,800 of computer supplies from Abbott Office Products on credit.
	9	Received the balance due from Grandview Co. for merchandise sold on February 23.
	11	Repaired the company's computer paying cash of $1,720.
	16	Received $8,520 cash from Images, Inc. for computing services.
	19	Paid the full amount due to Abbott Office Products, including amounts created on December 17 and March 8.
	24	Billed Capital Leasing for $11,800 of computing services.
	25	Sold merchandise with a cost of $2,004 for $3,600 on credit to Buckman Services.
	30	Sold merchandise with a cost of $2,200 for $4,440 on credit to Decker Company.
	31	Reimbursed Mary Graham's business automobile expenses for 400 kilometres at $1.00 per kilometre.

2. Post the journal entries to the accounts in the company's General Ledger. (Use asset, liability, and equity accounts that start with balances as of December 31, 2011.)

Check figures:
4. Net income = $23,198
6. Total current assets = $162,358;
Total assets = $208,858

3. Prepare a partial work sheet consisting of the first six columns showing the unadjusted trial balance, the March 31 adjustments described in (a) through (g) below, and the adjusted trial balance. *Do not prepare closing entries and do not journalize the adjusting entries or post them to the ledger.*
   a. The March 31 computer supplies on hand is $4,230.
   b. Three more months have passed since the company purchased the annual insurance policy at the cost of $4,320.
   c. Carly Smith has not been paid for seven days of work.
   d. Three months have passed since any prepaid rent cost has been transferred to expense. The monthly rent is $2,250.
   e. Depreciation on the computer for January through March is $2,250.
   f. Depreciation on the office equipment for January through March is $1,500.
   g. The March 31 inventory of merchandise is $1,960.

4. Prepare an interim single-step income statement for the three months ended March 31, 2012. List all expenses without differentiating between selling expenses and general and administrative expenses.

5. Prepare an interim statement of changes in equity for the three months ended March 31, 2012.

6. Prepare an interim classified balance sheet as of March 31, 2012.

CHAPTER 7

Merchandise Inventory and Cost of Sales

learning objectives

LO1 | Identify the components and costs included in merchandise inventory.

LO2 | Calculate cost of goods sold and merchandise inventory using specific identification, moving weighted average, and FIFO—perpetual.

LO3 | Analyze the effects of the costing methods on financial reporting.

LO4 | Calculate the lower of cost and net realizable value of inventory.

LO5 | Analyze the effects of inventory errors on current and future financial statements—perpetual.

LO6 | Apply both the gross profit and retail inventory methods to estimate inventory.

*APPENDIX 7A

LO7 | Calculate cost of goods sold and merchandise inventory using FIFO—periodic, weighted average, and specific identification.

LO8 | Analyze the effects of inventory errors on current and future financial statements—periodic.

*APPENDIX 7B

LO9 | Assess inventory management using both merchandise turnover and days' sales in inventory.

The Inventory Challenge

Inventory management is a priority for merchandisers given today's economic downturn, especially for a business as highly competitive as Rona's. With its head office in Boucherville, Quebec, Rona offers services and products to consumers of housing and home improvement products. It operates a network of stores under banners such as Totem, Chester Dawe, Botanix, Noble Trade, Dick's Lumber, and Curtis Lumber. To help meet consumer demand as efficiently as possible, Rona has nine distribution centres across Canada with a total of 197,976 square metres of indoor space and 143,071 square metres of outdoor lumberyard—that's a combined total of about 42 football fields to handle all the inventory! For the year ended December 28, 2008, those distribution centres moved more than $3.57 billion of inventory that retailed for $4.89 billion. Rona's December 28, 2008, balance sheet shows inventory of $763 million representing 72% of total current assets on the same date. To cost its 90,000 products efficiently and effectively, Rona has implemented a state of the art, real-time inventory management system that incorporates the weighted average method. To optimize inventory processes and decisions, Rona's goals for 2009 included refining its inventory demand planning; reducing inventory levels and improving inventory turnover to reduce inventory holding costs; reviewing the distribution alternatives regarding Chinese imports; and investigating cost saving strategies regarding transportation services and routes and warehousing. Rona sees the economic downturn as an opportunity to get creative and offer consumers more for less.

www.rona.ca

CRITICAL THINKING CHALLENGE

Would Rona have a merchandise turnover similar to Danier Leather's? Explain why or why not. What does "inventory demand planning" refer to? What would the effect of cost saving strategies be on the weighted average cost of inventory?

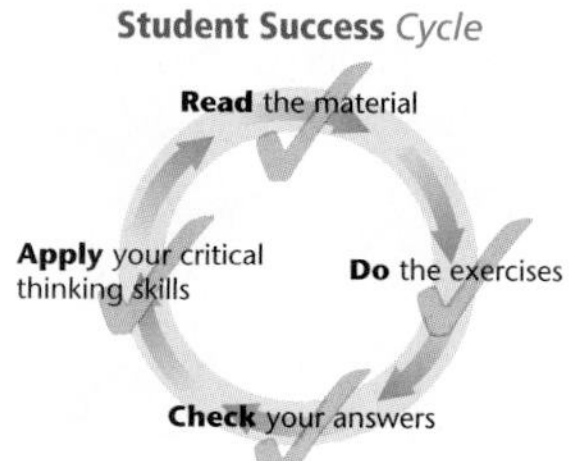

chapter preview

Activities of merchandising companies involve the purchase and resale of products. We explained accounting for merchandisers in the last chapter and explained how perpetual and periodic inventory systems P. 256 account for merchandise inventory. In this chapter, we extend our study and analysis of inventory by identifying the items that make up inventory and how they are evaluated. We also explain methods used to assign costs to merchandise inventory and to cost of goods sold. These methods include those that differ from historical cost. The principles and methods we describe are used in department stores, grocery stores, and many other merchandising companies that purchase products for resale. These principles and methods affect reported amounts of income, assets, and equity. Understanding these fundamental concepts of inventory accounting increases our ability to analyze and interpret financial statements. As is the case for Rona in the opening article, an understanding of these topics also helps in managing inventory.

Accounting for inventory affects both the balance sheet and income statement. A major goal in accounting for inventory is matching P. 133 relevant costs against revenues. This is important in order to calculate income properly.[1] We use the matching principle when accounting for inventory to decide how much of the cost of the goods available for sale is deducted from sales and how much is carried forward as inventory and matched against future sales. Management must make this decision and several others when accounting for inventory. These decisions include selecting the:

- Items included and their costs
- Costing method (specific identification, moving weighted average, or FIFO)
- Inventory system (perpetual or periodic)
- Use of net realizable value or other estimates.

These selections affect the reported amounts for inventory, cost of goods sold, gross profit P. 254, income, current assets, and other accounts. This chapter discusses all of these important issues and their reporting effects.

Inventory Items and Costs

Items in Merchandise Inventory

LO1 Identify the components and costs included in merchandise inventory.

Merchandise inventory includes all goods owned by a company and held for sale. This rule holds regardless of where goods are located at the time inventory is counted. Most inventory items are no problem when applying this rule, but certain items require special attention. These include goods in transit, goods on consignment, and goods damaged or obsolete.

Goods in Transit

Do we include in a purchaser's inventory the goods in transit from a supplier? Our answer depends on whether the rights and risks of ownership have passed from the supplier to the purchaser: whether the goods are FOB shipping point P. 261 or FOB destination P. 261. If ownership has passed to the purchaser, they are included in the purchaser's inventory.

[1] IFRS 2009, IAS 2, par. 1.

Goods on Consignment

Goods on consignment are goods shipped by their owner, called the **consignor**, to another party called the **consignee**. A consignee is to sell goods for the owner without ever having legal title to the goods. Consigned goods are owned by the consignor and are reported in the consignor's inventory.

Goods Damaged or Obsolete

Damaged goods and obsolete (or deteriorated) goods are not counted in inventory if they are unsaleable. If these goods are saleable at a reduced price, they are included in inventory at a conservative estimate of their *net realizable value.* **Net realizable value (NRV)** is sales price minus the cost of making the sale. The period when damage or obsolescence (or deterioration) occurs is the period where the loss is reported.

Costs of Merchandise Inventory

Costs included in merchandise inventory are those expenditures necessary, directly or indirectly, in bringing an item to a saleable condition and location.[2] This means the cost of an inventory item includes its invoice price minus any discount, plus any added or incidental costs necessary to put it in a place and condition for sale. Added or incidental costs can include import duties, transportation-in, storage, insurance, and costs incurred in an aging process (for example, aging of wine and cheese).

Accounting principles imply that incidental costs are assigned to every unit purchased. This is so that all inventory costs are properly matched against revenue in the period when inventory is sold. The **materiality principle** or the **cost-to-benefit constraint** states that an amount may not be ignored if its effect on the financial statements is important to their users. The *materiality principle* is used by some companies not to assign incidental costs of acquiring merchandise to inventory. These companies argue either that incidental costs are immaterial or that the effort in assigning these costs to inventory outweighs the benefits. Such companies price inventory using invoice prices only. When this is done, the incidental costs are allocated to cost of goods sold in the period when they are incurred.

Physical Count of Merchandise Inventory

To help determine the value of inventory included on financial statements, units on hand need to be confirmed through a **physical count** (also known as **taking an inventory**). This often occurs at the end of the fiscal year P. 27 or when inventory amounts are low. The physical count is used to adjust the Merchandise Inventory account balance to the actual inventory on hand. In a perpetual inventory system, this is done by debiting Cost of Goods Sold and crediting Merchandise Inventory if the physical count is less than the unadjusted balance in the Merchandise Inventory account. If the count is more than the unadjusted balance, the entry is the opposite. Differences occur because of events including theft, loss, damage, and errors. This means that nearly all companies take a physical count of inventory at least once each year regardless of whether a perpetual or periodic inventory system is in place.

When performing a physical count of inventory, *internal controls* should be followed to minimize errors. **Internal controls**, discussed in more detail in Chapter 9, are the policies and procedures used to protect assets, ensure reliable

[2] IFRS 2009, IAS 2, par. 10–22.

Exhibit 7.1

Inventory Ticket

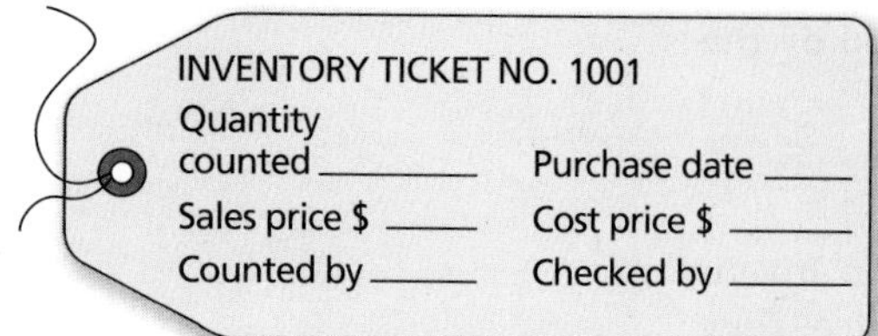

accounting, promote efficient operations, and urge adherence to company policies. An example of an internal control technique is the use of prenumbered inventory tickets, one for each product on hand, to reduce the risk of items being counted more than once or omitted. We show a typical inventory ticket in Exhibit 7.1. By multiplying the number of units counted for each product by its unit cost, we get the dollar amount for each product in inventory. The sum total of all products is the dollar amount reported for inventory on the balance sheet.

In lieu of inventory tickets, the merchandise inventory items of many businesses are labelled with UPC (Universal Product Code) bar codes. The UPC bar codes are not only used for the pricing and costing of sales, but can also be used to make physical counts easier.

If you look at any grocery product, you will find a UPC bar code printed on the package. Universal Product Codes were created in 1973 to assist in the checkout and inventory process of grocery stores, and UPC bar codes have since spread to nearly every item in the retail world. The Uniform Code Council (UCC) is responsible for issuing the manufacturer's portion of the code. The manufacturer's UPC coordinator assigns the next digits as the item number. The retailer can then assign a price to each individual UPC code along with costing information. In this way, inventory and sales records can be updated instantly when the bar code is scanned.

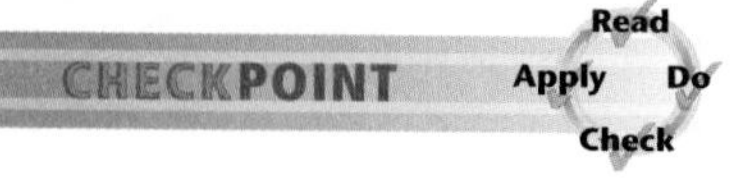

1. If General Electric sells goods to The Bay with terms FOB General Electric's factory, does General Electric or The Bay report these goods in its inventory when they are in transit?
2. An art gallery purchases a painting for $11,400. Additional costs in obtaining and offering the artwork for sale include $130 for transportation-in, $150 for import duties, $100 for insurance during shipment, $180 for advertising, $400 for framing, and $800 for sales salaries. For calculating inventory cost, what is assigned to the painting?

Do Quick Study questions: QS 7-1, QS 7-2, QS 7-3, QS 7-4

Assigning Costs to Inventory

LO2 Calculate cost of goods sold and merchandise inventory using specific identification, moving weighted average, and FIFO—perpetual.

One of the most important decisions in accounting for inventory is determining the per unit costs assigned to inventory items. When all units are purchased at the same unit cost, this process is simple, but when identical items are purchased at different costs, a question arises as to what amounts are recorded in cost of goods sold when sales occur and what amounts remain in inventory. When using a perpetual inventory system, we must record cost of goods sold and reductions in inventory as sales occur. A periodic inventory system determines cost of goods sold and inventory amounts at the end of a period. How we assign these costs to inventory and cost of goods sold affects the reported amounts for both systems, as shown in Exhibit 7A.5 on page 364.

Three methods are often used in assigning costs to inventory and cost of goods sold:

- First-in, first-out (FIFO)
- Moving weighted average
- Specific identification

Each method assumes a particular pattern for how costs flow through inventory. All three methods are accepted under GAAP P. 4 and are described in this section.[3] The last-in, first-out (LIFO) method is another way to assign costs to inventory and is popular in the United States, but it is not permitted under GAAP or the Canadian *Income Tax Act*.[4]

If a business has inventory items that are ordinarily interchangeable, either the FIFO or moving weighted average method may be used. A business is required to use the specific identification method for inventory items that are not ordinarily interchangeable. Examples of inventory that would be costed using specific identification might include custom furniture where each piece produced is different or cars at an automobile dealership, each with a unique serial number and unique options. Loblaw Companies Limited chose to use FIFO as per its 2008 annual report. Canadian Tire and Maple Leaf Foods Inc. also use FIFO. Some companies use different methods for different types of inventory. Perlite Canada Inc. uses FIFO for one type of inventory and moving weighted average for another, while Bombardier Inc. uses three methods: specific identification, moving weighted average, and FIFO depending on the inventory item.

We use information from Trekking, a sporting goods store, to describe the three methods. Among its many products, Trekking carries one type of mountain bike. Its mountain bike ("unit") inventory at the beginning of August 2011 and its purchases during August are shown in Exhibit 7.2.

Exhibit 7.2

Cost of Goods Available for Sale

		Units		Cost Per Unit		Total Cost
Aug. 1	Beginning inventory	10	@	$ 91	=	$ 910
3	Purchased	15	@	$106	=	$1,590
17	Purchased	20	@	$115	=	$2,300
Total goods available for sale		45 Units available for sale				$4,800 Total cost of goods that were available for sale

Trekking had two sales of mountain bikes to two different biking clubs in August, as shown in Exhibit 7.3. Trekking ends August with 11 bikes in inventory (45 units available for sale less 34 units sold).

Exhibit 7.3

Retail Sales of Goods

		Units		Selling Price Per Unit		Total Sales
Aug. 14	Sales	20	@	$133	=	$2,660
28	Sales	14	@	$150	=	$2,100
		34 Units				$4,760

[3] Physical flow of goods depends on the type of product and the way it is used. Perishable goods such as fresh fruit demand that a business attempt to sell them in a first-in, first-out pattern. Other products such as canned food can often be sold in a random pattern.

[4] IFRS 2009, IAS 2, par. 23–25.

In this section, we will determine how much of the cost of goods available for sale is to be assigned to cost of goods sold and to ending merchandise inventory using the three different cost flow assumptions.

We explained in the last chapter how use of a perpetual inventory system is increasing dramatically due to advances in information and computing technology. Widespread use of electronic scanners and product bar codes further encourages its use. Accordingly, we discuss the assignment of costs to cost of goods sold and merchandise inventory in a perpetual system. The assignment of costs to inventory using a periodic system is discussed in Appendix 7A.

First-In, First-Out

The **first-in, first-out (FIFO)** method of assigning cost to inventory and the goods sold assumes that inventory items are sold in the order acquired. When sales occur, costs of the earliest units purchased are charged to cost of goods sold. This leaves the costs from the most recent purchases in inventory. Use of FIFO for Trekking means the costs of mountain bikes are assigned to inventory and goods sold as shown in Exhibit 7.4.

Exhibit 7.4

FIFO Calculations—Perpetual

Date	Purchases			Sales (at cost)			Inventory Balance		
	Units	Unit Cost	Total Cost	Units	Unit Cost	Cost of Goods Sold	Units	Unit Cost	Total Cost
Aug. 1	Beginning inventory 10 @	$ 91	= $ 910				10 @	$ 91	= $ 910
3	15 @	$106	= $1,590				10 @ 15 @	$ 91 $106	= $ 910 = $1,590
14				10 @ 10 @	$ 91 $106	= $ 910 = $1,060	5 @	$106	= $ 530
17	20 @	$115	= $2,300				5 @ 20 @	$106 $115	= $ 530 = $2,300
28				5 @ 9 @	$106 $115	= $ 530 = $1,035	11 @	$115	= $1,265
Totals	45		$4,800	34		$3,535	11		$1,265

Cost of goods available for sale = Cost of goods sold + Ending inventory

① Under FIFO, units are assumed to be sold in the order acquired; therefore, of the 20 units sold on August 14, the first 10 units come from beginning inventory.

② The remaining 10 units sold on August 14 come from the next purchase, August 3.

③ All of the units from beginning inventory have been sold but 5 units remain from the August 3 purchase.

Trekking's cost of goods sold on the income statement is $3,535 (= $910 + $1,060 + $530 + $1,035) and its ending inventory reported on the balance sheet is $1,265.

Moving Weighted Average

The **moving weighted average** inventory costing method (**weighted average** when a periodic inventory system is in place) requires calculating the average cost per unit of merchandise inventory at the time of each purchase. The average is calculated by dividing the cost of goods available for sale by the units on hand. Using the moving weighted average method for Trekking means the costs of mountain bikes are assigned to inventory and goods sold as shown in Exhibit 7.5.

Exhibit 7.5

Moving Weighted Average Calculations—Perpetual

Date	Purchases Units	Purchases Unit Cost	Purchases Total Cost	Sales (at cost) Units	Sales (at cost) Unit Cost	Sales (at cost) Cost of Goods Sold	Inventory Balance (b) Units	Inventory Balance (a)÷(b) Average Cost/Unit	Inventory Balance (a) Total Cost
Aug. 1	Beginning inventory 10 @	$ 91	= $ 910				10	$ 91	$ 910
3	15 @	$106	= $1,590				25	$100	$2,500
14				20 @	$100	= $2,000	5	$100	$ 500
17	20 @	$115	= $2,300				25	$112	$2,800
28				14 @	$112	= $1,568	11	$112	$1,232
Totals	**45**		**$4,800**	**34**		**$3,568**	**11**		**$1,232**

Cost of goods available for sale = Cost of goods sold + Ending inventory

Inventory Balance Calculations		
10		$ 910
+ 15	@ $106	+ $1,590
25 ÷		$2,500
25		$2,500
− 20	@ $100	− $2,000
5		$ 500
5		$ 500
+ 20	@ $115 =	+ $2,300
25		$2,800
25		$2,800
− 14	@ $112 =	− $1,568
11		$1,232

① August 1 beginning inventory in units and dollars.

② August 1 beginning inventory is added to the purchase of August 3 to determine the total cost of the units in inventory on August 3.

③ The total cost of all units is divided by the total number of units to get the average cost per unit of $100 on August 3.

④ The most current average cost is assigned as the cost per unit sold.

Trekking's cost of goods sold reported on the income statement is $3,568 (= $2,000 + $1,568) and its ending inventory reported on the balance sheet is $1,232. The moving weighted average perpetual system often raises a rounding problem in the calculations because the currency figures are limited to two decimal places. The typical solution is to adjust or "plug" the inventory figure after calculating the cost of goods sold amount at the moving weighted average cost.

Specific Identification

When each item sold and remaining in inventory can be directly identified with a specific purchase and its invoice, we can use **specific identification** to assign costs. Trekking's internal documents reveal that on August 14, 20 units were sold; specifically, these were 8 units from beginning inventory and 12 units from the August 3 purchase. On August 28, 14 units were sold; specifically, these were 2 units from beginning inventory and 12 units from the August 17 purchase. Specific identification assigns costs to the goods sold and to ending inventory based on specific items identified, as shown in Exhibit 7.6.

Exhibit 7.6

Specific Identification Calculations—Perpetual

Date	Purchases			Sales (at cost)			Inventory Balance		
	Units	Unit Cost	Total Cost	Units	Unit Cost	Cost of Goods Sold	Units	Unit Cost	Total Cost
Aug. 1	Beginning inventory 10 @	$ 91	= $ 910				10 @	$ 91	= $ 910
3	15 @	$106	= $1,590				10 @ ① 15 @ ③	$ 91 $106	= $ 910 = $1,590
14				8 @ 12 @	$ 91 $106	= $ 728 = $1,272	2 @ ② 3 @ ④	$ 91 $106	= $ 182 = $ 318
17	20 @	$115	= $2,300				2 @ 3 @ 20 @	$ 91 $106 $115	= $ 182 = $ 318 = $2,300
28				2 @ 12 @	$ 91 $115	= $ 182 = $1,380	3 @ 8 @	$106 $115	= $ 318 = $ 920
Totals	45		$4,800	34		$3,562	11		$1,238

Cost of goods available for sale = Cost of goods sold + Ending inventory

① Of the 10 units from beginning inventory, 8 were specifically identified as being sold.

② Of the 10 units from beginning inventory, 2 remain in ending inventory.

③ Of the 15 units purchased on August 3, 12 were specifically identified as being sold.

④ Of the 15 units purchased on August 3, 3 remain in ending inventory.

When using specific identification, Trekking's cost of goods sold reported on the income statement is $3,562 (= $728 + $1,272 + $182 + $1,380) and its ending inventory reported on the balance sheet is $1,238.

The specific identification method works best when each item of inventory is unique or different, as in an antique store, an art gallery, or a custom furniture manufacturer. For example, a car dealership would use specific identification because each car has a unique serial number, known as the vehicle identification number (VIN). In all cases where specific identification is used, each inventory item needs to be identified separately.

When inventory items are similar (such as bags of sugar, pallets of concrete blocks, or loaves of bread), specific units being purchased and sold cannot be easily traced; large quantities are often purchased at different times, possibly with different costs. When the cost is greater than the benefit of tracking the sale of individual units that are similar, one of the other methods may be better conceptually and more efficient to use.

Notice in Exhibit 7.7 that the total units and cost of the goods available for sale are the same regardless of the method used. What is different is the dollar amount assigned to the ending inventory and the cost of goods sold.

Exhibit 7.7

Comparison of Inventory Methods

	FIFO		Moving Weighted Average		Specific Identification	
	Units	$	Units	$	Units	$
Cost of Goods Sold (or Cost of Sales)	34	$3,535	34	$3,568	34	$3,562
Ending Inventory	11	1,265	11	1,232	11	1,238
Goods Available for Sale	45	$4,800	45	$4,800	45	$4,800

Inventory Costing and Technology

A perpetual inventory system can be kept in either electronic or manual form. A manual form is often too costly for businesses, especially those with many purchases and sales or many units in inventory. Advances in information and computing technology have greatly reduced the cost of an electronic perpetual inventory system, and many companies are now asking whether they can afford not to have one. This is because timely access to information is being used strategically by companies to gain a competitive advantage. Scanned sales data, for instance, can reveal crucial information on buying patterns, and can also help companies target promotional and advertising activities. These and other applications have greatly increased the use of the perpetual system. Maintaining inventory records is discussed in Chapter 8 beginning on page 396.

3. What accounting principle most governs allocations of cost of goods available for sale between ending inventory and cost of goods sold?

Do Quick Study questions: QS 7-5, QS 7-6, QS 7-7, QS 7-8

mid-chapter demonstration problem

Tale Company uses a perpetual inventory system and had the following beginning inventory and purchases during January 2011:

Date			Item X				
			Units		Unit Cost		Total Cost
Jan.	1	Inventory..............................	300	@	$14	=	$ 4,200
	16	Purchase..............................	200	@	15	=	3,000
	20	Purchase..............................	300	@	16	=	4,800
		Total units and cost of goods available for sale.........	800				$12,000

Sales of units were as follows (all on credit):

Jan.	15	200 units at $30
	28	460 units at $35
Total units sold		660

Additional data for use in applying the specific identification method:

The specific units sold were:

Jan.	15	200 units from the January 1 units on hand
	28	75 units from the January 1 units on hand 150 units from the January 16 purchase, and 235 units from the January 20 purchase

Required

1. Calculate the ending inventory and the cost of goods sold under a perpetual inventory system by applying each of the three different methods of inventory costing:

a. FIFO

b. Moving weighted average

c. Specific identification

2. Using your calculations from Part 1, record the purchase on January 16 and the sale on January 28 for each of:

a. FIFO

b. Moving weighted average

c. Specific identification

Analysis component:

A new supplier has approached Tale Company, offering the merchandise inventory to Tale at $11 per unit. What should Tale consider when deciding whether or not to change to the new supplier?

Planning the Solution

- Prepare a perpetual FIFO schedule showing the composition of beginning inventory and how the composition of inventory changes after each purchase of inventory and after each sale.
- Make a schedule of purchases and sales, recalculating the average cost of inventory after each purchase to arrive at the moving weighted average cost of ending inventory. Add up the average costs associated with each sale to determine the cost of goods sold using the moving weighted average method.
- Prepare a schedule showing the calculation of the cost of goods sold and ending inventory using the specific identification method. Use the information provided to determine the cost of the specific units sold and which specific units remain in inventory.
- Journalize the purchase on January 16 and the sale on January 28 by taking the relevant information from the schedules prepared in Part 1 for each method.
- Prepare an answer to the analysis question.

solution

1a. FIFO Perpetual

Date	Purchases			Sales (at cost)			Inventory Balance		
	Units	Unit Cost	Total Cost	Units	Unit Cost	Cost of Goods Sold	Units	Unit Cost	Total Cost
Jan. 1	Beginning inventory 300 @	$14 =	$4,200	①			300 @	$14 =	$4,200
15				200 @	$14 =	$2,800	② 100 @	$14 =	$1,400
16	200 @	$15 =	$3,000				100 @ 200 @	$14 = $15 =	$1,400 $3,000
20	300 @	$16 =	$4,800	③			100 @ 200 @ 300 @	$14 = $15 = $16 =	$1,400 $3,000 $4,800
28				100 @ 200 @ 160 @	$14 = $15 = $16 =	$1,400 $3,000 $2,560	④ 140 @	$16 =	$2,240
Totals	800		$12,000	660		$9,760	140		$2,240

Cost of goods available for sale = Cost of goods sold + Ending inventory

① Under FIFO, units are assumed to be sold in the order acquired; therefore the 200 units sold on January 15 come from beginning inventory.
② The 100 units remaining in inventory after the January 15 sale are from beginning inventory.
③ The 460 units sold on January 28 are assumed to be the 100 units from beginning inventory, plus the 200 units purchased on January 16, plus 160 units from the January 20 purchase.
④ All of the units remaining in inventory after the January 28 sale are from the January 20 purchase.

1b. Moving Weighted Average Perpetual

Date	Purchases			Sales (at cost)			Inventory Balance		
						Cost of	(b)	(a) ÷ (b)	(a)
		Unit	Total		Unit	Goods		Average	Total
Total	Units	Cost	Cost	Units	Cost	Sold	Units	Cost/Unit	Cost
Jan. 1	Beginning inventory 300 @	$14	= $4,200				300 @	$14.00	= $4,200.00
15				200 @	$14.00	= $2,800.00	100 @	$14.00	= $1,400.00
16	200 @	$15	= $3,000				300 @	$14.67	= $4,400.00
20	300 @	$16	= $4,800				600 @	$15.33	= $9,200.00
28				460 @	$15.33	= $7,051.80	140 @	$15.34*	= $2,148.20
Totals	800		$12,000	660		$9,851.80	140		2,148.20

Cost of goods available for sale = Cost of goods sold + Ending inventory

Inventory Balance Calculations

Date	Units		Unit Cost		Amount
Jan. 1					
15	300				$ 4,200.00
	− 200	@	$14.00	=	− $ 2,800.00
	100				$ 1,400.00
16	100				$ 1,400.00
	+ 200	@	$15.00	=	+ $ 3,000.00
	300				$ 4,400.00
20	300				$ 4,400.00
	+ 300	@	$16.00	=	+ $ 4,800.00
	600				$ 9,200.00
28	600				$ 9,200.00
	− 460	@	$15.33	=	− $ 7,051.80
	140				$ 2,148.20

*Cost/unit changed due to rounding

① The most current average cost per unit is assigned to the units sold.

② The beginning balance less the units sold equals the remaining inventory.

③ The total cost remaining in inventory divided by the total units remaining equals the average unit cost. Notice that the average unit cost does not change because of a sale.

1c. Specific Identification

Date	Purchases			Sales (at cost)			Inventory Balance		
		Unit	Total		Unit	Cost of Goods		Unit	Total
	Units	Cost	Cost	Units	Cost	Sold	Units	Cost	Cost
Jan. 1	Beginning inventory 300 @	$14	= $4,200				300 @	$14	= $4,200
15				200 @	$14	= $2,800	100 @	$14	= $1,400
16	200 @	$15	= $3,000				100 @	$14	= $1,400
							200 @	$15	= $3,000
20	300 @	$16	= $4,800				100 @	$14	= $1,400
							200 @	$15	= $3,000
							300 @	$16	= $4,800
28				75 @	$14	= $1,050	25 @	$14	= $ 350
				150 @	$15	= $2,250	50 @	$15	= $ 750
				235 @	$16	= $3,760	65 @	$16	= $1,040
Totals	800		$12,000	660		$9,860	140		$2,140

Cost of goods available for sale = Cost of goods sold + Ending inventory

① 200 of the beginning inventory units were specifically identified as being sold on January 15. Therefore, the 100 units remaining on January 15 are identified as units from beginning inventory.

② The units sold on January 28 are specifically identified. The units sold determines exactly which units are remaining.

2.

			a. FIFO		b. Moving Weighted Average		c. Specific Identification	
2011								
Jan.	16	Merchandise Inventory	3,000		3,000		3,000	
		Accounts Payable		3,000		3,000		3,000
		To record purchase of merchandise on credit.						
	28	Accounts Receivable	16,100		16,100		16,100	
		Sales		16,100		16,100		16,100
		To record credit sales; 460 units × $35 = $16,100.						
	28	Cost of Goods Sold	6,960		7,052*		7,060	
		Merchandise Inventory		6,960		7,052*		7,060
		To record the sale of merchandise.						

*Rounded to nearest whole dollar for simplicity

Analysis component:

Tale should consider the following (as well as other possibilities):

- The quality of the merchandise inventory offered by the new supplier
- Whether the new supplier can meet Tale's merchandise inventory quantity needs
- Whether the new supplier will deliver merchandise when required (dependable)
- The payment/delivery terms
- What kind of service the new supplier provides (customer support)
- Whether the new supplier can provide references (from satisfied customers; reputation)
- The duration of the $11 per unit offer and potential price increases

Financial Reporting and Inventory

This section reviews the financial reporting issues related to inventory, including inventory disclosure, consistency, and prudence. As well, we look at the effects of inventory errors.

LO3 Analyze the effects of the costing methods on financial reporting.

Financial Reporting

In our analysis of financial statements, it is important to know and understand inventory costing methods because the method used can have a material impact on the income statement and balance sheet, as illustrated in Exhibit 7.8. For this reason, the inventory costing method used must be *disclosed* P. 271 in the notes to the financial statements.

Exhibit 7.8

Income Statement and Balance Sheet Effects of Inventory Costing Methods

Trekking Company
Income Statement—Mountain Bikes
For Month Ended August 31, 2011

	FIFO	**Moving Weighted Average**	**Specific Identification**
Sales	$4,760	$4,760	$4,760
Cost of goods sold*	3,535	3,568	3,562
Gross profit from sales	$1,225	$1,192	$1,198
Operating expenses	374	374	374
Income from operations	$ 851	$ 818	$ 824

*From Exhibit 7.7

Partial Balance Sheet

Assets			
Current assets:			
Merchandise inventory*	$1,265	$1,232	$1,238

*From Exhibit 7.7

When purchase prices do not change, the choice of an inventory costing method is unimportant. All methods assign the same cost amounts when prices remain constant. When purchase prices are rising or falling, however, the methods are likely to assign different cost amounts.

Because Trekking's purchase prices rose in August, FIFO assigned the least amount to cost of goods sold. This led to the highest gross profit and the highest income. This result will always occur in times of rising prices because the most recent and therefore most costly units are in ending inventory, leaving the least expensive units in cost of goods sold.[5]

Because inventory costing methods can materially affect amounts on financial statements, a manager would want to use the method that gave the most favourable results. For example, if management bonus plans were based on net income, managers might pick the method that gave them the highest bonus each period. If managers were allowed to change methods each period, it would be more difficult for users of financial statements to compare a company's financial statements from one period to the next. If income increased, for instance, a user would need to decide whether it resulted from successful operations or from the accounting method change. The *consistency principle* is used to avoid this problem.

The **consistency principle** requires a company to use the same accounting methods period after period so that the financial statements are comparable across periods.[6] The consistency principle applies to all accounting methods.

The consistency principle *does not* require a company to use one method exclusively. It can use different methods to value different categories of inventory. As mentioned earlier, Bombardier Inc. uses three methods (specific identification, weighted average, and FIFO) to assign costs to various types of inventory. Also, the consistency principle does not mean that a company can never change from one accounting method to another. Instead, it means a company must argue that the method to which it is changing will improve its financial reporting. Under this circumstance, a change is acceptable; yet, when such a change is made, the full disclosure principle requires that the notes to the statements report the type of change, its justification, and its effect on net income.[7]

[5] The moving weighted average amount can be higher or lower than the FIFO amount depending on whether prices steadily increase or decrease.

[6] IFRS 2009, IAS 1, par. 45.

[7] IFRS 2009, IAS 8, par. 14–18 and 28–31.

Inventory Manager

You are the inventory manager for a merchandiser. Your compensation includes a bonus plan based on the amount of gross profit reported in the financial statements. Your superior comes to you and asks your opinion about changing the inventory costing method from moving weighted average to FIFO. Since costs have been rising and are expected to continue to rise, your superior predicts the company will be more attractive to investors because of the reported higher income using FIFO. You realize this proposed change will likely increase your bonus as well. What do you recommend?

Answer—p. 358

Exhibit 7.9 summarizes advantages and disadvantages for the cost flow assumptions discussed.

Exhibit 7.9

Advantages and Disadvantages of Cost Flow Assumptions

	FIFO	Moving Weighted Average	Specific Identification
Advantages:	Most current values are on the balance sheet as ending inventory	Smooths out purchase price changes	Exactly matches costs and revenues
Disadvantages:	Cost of goods sold does not reflect current costs, so does not accurately match expenses to revenue	Averaging does not accurately match expenses to revenues	Relatively more costly to implement and maintain

4. Give examples of types of businesses that might use specific identification despite the disadvantage indicated in Exhibit 7.9. Explain why these businesses might choose to use specific identification.
5. When costs and prices are rising, what effect does moving weighted average have on a balance sheet compared to FIFO?

Do Quick Study question: QS 7-9

Lower of Cost and Net Realizable Value (LCNRV)

LO4 Calculate the lower of cost and net realizable value of inventory.

The cost of inventory is not necessarily the amount always reported on a balance sheet. The *prudence principle* requires that inventory be reported at net realizable value (NRV) when NRV is lower than cost.[8] Merchandise inventory is then said to be reported on the balance sheet at the **lower of cost and net realizable value (LCNRV)**. The **prudence principle** requires a degree of caution when exercising judgement so that assets and income are not overstated and liabilities and expenses are not understated.[9] Why? If, for example, the December 31, 2011, inventory of a music store included eight-track tapes that cost the merchandiser a total of $100,000 but had an NRV on that date of $500, which value is *most realistic*—cost or NRV? Because we know that eight-track tapes are essentially obsolete, inventory should be written down and reported at the NRV of $500 to ensure that assets and income are not overstated. If the NRV of the inventory were to recover after the

[8] IFRS 2009, IAS 2, par. 28.
[9] IFRS 2009, "Framework," par. 37.

balance sheet date, the inventory write-down would be reversed. The reversal is limited to the amount of the write-down to ensure that inventory is always reported at the lower of cost and NRV. The concept of inventory write-downs and reversals will be demonstrated in the next section.

Calculating the Lower of Cost and Net Realizable Value (LCNRV)

The decline in merchandise inventory from cost to NRV is recorded in an adjusting entry at the end of the period. LCNRV is applied in one of two ways:

(1) Usually item by item, or

(2) To groups of similar or related items.[10]

We show in Exhibit 7.10 how LCNRV is applied to the ending inventory of Jumbo, a sports retailer.

Exhibit 7.10

LCNRV Calculations

Inventory Items	No. of Units	Cost/ Unit	Total Cost	NRV/ Unit	Total NRV	LCNRV applied to: Items	LCNRV applied to: Groups
Bicycles:							
Roadster	25	$ 750	$ 18,750	$ 790	$19,750	$ 18,750	
Sprint	60	1,100	66,000	1,100	66,000	66,000	
Group subtotal			$ 84,750		$88,750		$ 84,750
Motorized Quads:							
A1 Series	21	$1,800	$ 37,800	$1,300	$27,300	$ 27,300	
Trax-4	29	2,200	63,800	2,250	65,250	63,800	
Group subtotal			$101,600		$92,550		$ 92,550
Totals			$186,350			$175,850	$177,300

Using the information in Exhibit 7.10 to demonstrate the application of LCNRV on an item-by-item basis, we see that total LCNRV is $175,850. Therefore, $175,850 must be reported on the balance sheet. To achieve this, inventory needs to be reduced by $10,500, which is the difference between the total cost of $186,350 and total LCNRV of $175,850. The entry is:

Cost of Goods Sold	10,500	
Merchandise Inventory		10,500
To write inventory down to LCNRV; $186,350 − $175,850 = $10,500.		

After posting this entry, merchandise inventory would appear on the balance sheet as:

Current assets:	
Cash	$ x,xxx
Accounts receivable	x,xxx
Merchandise inventory, at LCNRV	**175,850**

[10] IFRS 2009, IAS 2, par. 29.

Assume that the A1 Series quads in Exhibit 7.10 are still on hand at the end of the next accounting period. There is evidence that their NRV has increased to $1,450 per unit. The original write-down can be reversed (but is limited to the amount of the original write-down).[11] The entry is:

Merchandise Inventory.................................	3,150	
Cost of Goods Sold		3,150
To reverse the inventory write-down; $1,450 − $1,300 = $150; $150 × 21 units = $3,150.		

Either of the two applications of LCNRV—to items or to groups—is acceptable in practice. Danier Leather reports that its inventories are valued at the lower of cost and NRV.

DANIER

To demonstrate the application of LCNRV to groups, refer to the information in Exhibit 7.10. The entry to write inventory down to LCNRV applied to groups is:

Cost of Goods Sold	9,050	
Merchandise Inventory.........................		9,050
To write inventory down to LCNRV; $186,350 − $177,300 = $9,050.		

6. Refer to the information in Exhibit 7.10. Assume that LCNRV was applied to inventory on an item-by-item basis. In the next accounting period, the NRV of the A1 Series increased to $1,900 per unit because the factory burned down, causing a shortage in the marketplace. Jumbo had four of the previously written down A1 Series left in ending inventory a year after the original write-down. What entry, if any, is required in applying LCNRV to the remaining four units?
7. A company's ending inventory includes the following items:

Product	Units on Hand	Unit Cost	NRV Per Unit
A	20	$ 6	$ 5
B	40	9	8
C	10	12	15

Using LCNRV applied separately to individual items, calculate the reported amount for inventory.

Do Quick Study question: QS 7-10

Errors in Reporting Inventory

LO5 Analyze the effects of inventory errors on current and future financial statements—perpetual.

Companies must take care in calculating and taking a physical count of inventory. If inventory is reported in error, it causes misstatements of cost of goods sold, gross profit, net income, current assets, and equity. It also means misstatements will exist in the next period's statements. This is because ending inventory of one period is the beginning inventory of the next. An error carried forward causes misstatements of the next period's cost of goods sold, gross profit, and net income. Since the inventory amount often is large, misstatements can reduce the usefulness of financial statements.

[11] IFRS 2009, IAS 2, par. 33.

Income Statement Effects

The income statement effects of an inventory error are evident when looking at the components of cost of goods sold in each of the alternative presentations in Exhibit 7.11.

Exhibit 7.11

Cost of Goods Sold Components—Periodic

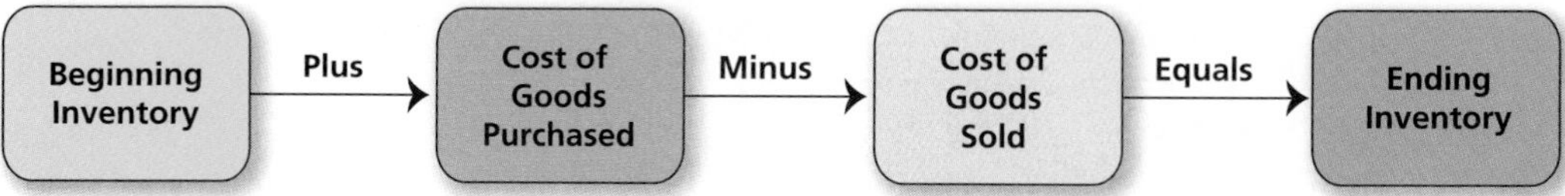

or, stated another way:

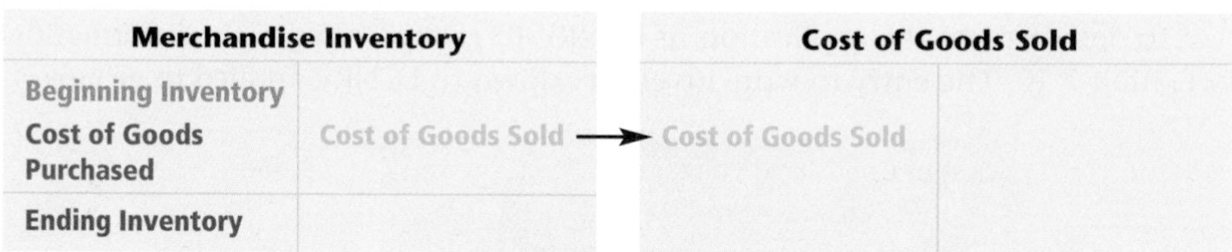

The effect of an inventory error on cost of goods sold is determined by calculating the inventory correctly and comparing the result to the result of the calculation when using the incorrect amount, as in Exhibit 7.12.

Exhibit 7.12

Effects of $2,000 Overstatement in Ending Inventory for 2011 on Three Periods' Income Statement Information—Perpetual

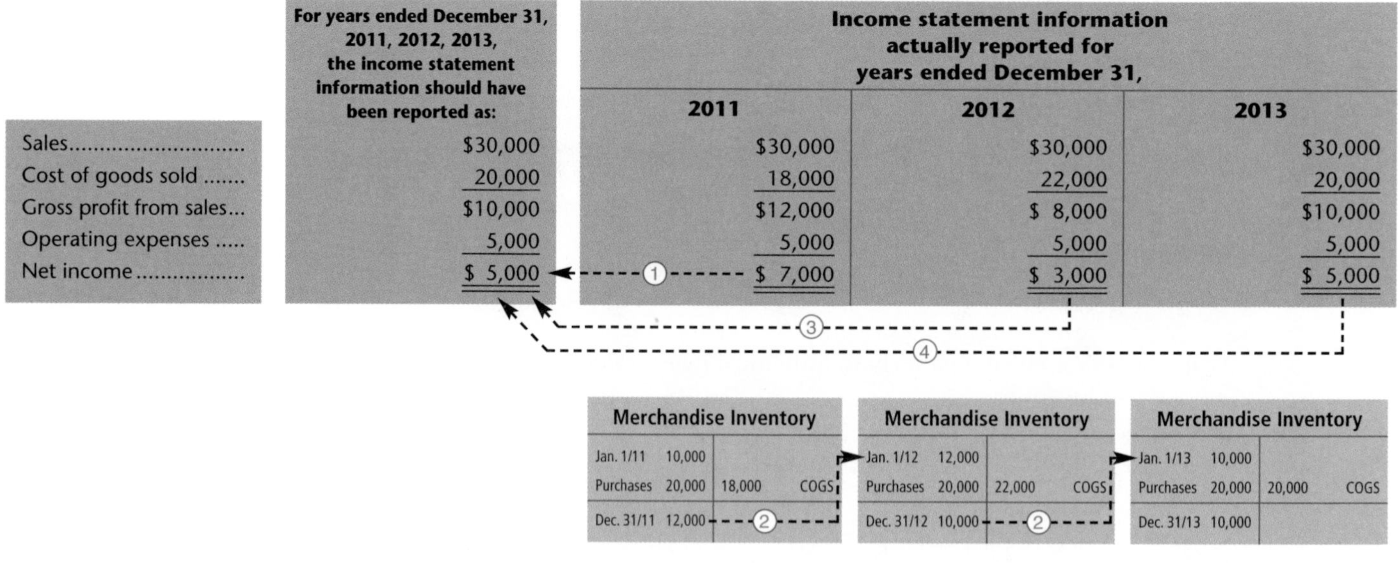

	For years ended December 31, 2011, 2012, 2013, the income statement information should have been reported as:	Income statement information actually reported for years ended December 31, 2011	2012	2013
Sales	$30,000	$30,000	$30,000	$30,000
Cost of goods sold	20,000	18,000	22,000	20,000
Gross profit from sales	$10,000	$12,000	$ 8,000	$10,000
Operating expenses	5,000	5,000	5,000	5,000
Net income	$ 5,000	$ 7,000	$ 3,000	$ 5,000

Merchandise Inventory			
Jan. 1/11	10,000		
Purchases	20,000	18,000	COGS
Dec. 31/11	12,000		

Merchandise Inventory			
Jan. 1/12	12,000		
Purchases	20,000	22,000	COGS
Dec. 31/12	10,000		

Merchandise Inventory			
Jan. 1/13	10,000		
Purchases	20,000	20,000	COGS
Dec. 31/13	10,000		

① 2011 net income and gross profit are overstated (too high) and cost of goods sold is understated (too low) when ending inventory is overstated (too high).
② Ending inventory for one period becomes the beginning inventory for the next period, carrying forward any errors that existed.
③ 2012 net income and gross profit are understated (too low) and cost of goods sold is overstated (too high) when beginning inventory is overstated (too high). Notice that the error has reversed itself in 2012, the second year.
④ An inventory error in the year 2011 does not affect 2013.

Exhibit 7.12 assumes that $2,000 of merchandise sold but awaiting delivery was incorrectly included in ending inventory on December 31, 2011. This ending inventory error carries over to the next period as a beginning inventory error yielding a reverse effect. We can see that overstating ending inventory will understate cost of goods sold. An understatement of cost of goods sold yields an overstatement of net income. We can do the same analysis with understating ending inventory and for an error in beginning inventory. Exhibit 7.13 shows the effects of inventory errors on the current period's income statement amounts.

Exhibit 7.13

Effect of Inventory Errors on This Period's Income Statement

Inventory Error	Cost of Goods Sold	Net Income
Understate ending inventory	Overstated	Understated
Understate beginning inventory	Understated	Overstated
Overstate ending inventory	Understated	Overstated
Overstate beginning inventory	Overstated	Understated

Notice that inventory errors yield opposite effects in cost of goods sold and net income.

Because an inventory error causes an offsetting error in the next period, it is sometimes said to be *self-correcting*. Do not think, however, that this makes inventory errors less serious. Managers, lenders, owners, and other users make important decisions on changes in net income and cost of goods sold. Imagine how a lender's decision would be affected by each of the graphs presented in Exhibit 7.14. Inventory errors must be avoided.

Exhibit 7.14

Graphing the Effects of Inventory Errors on Net Income

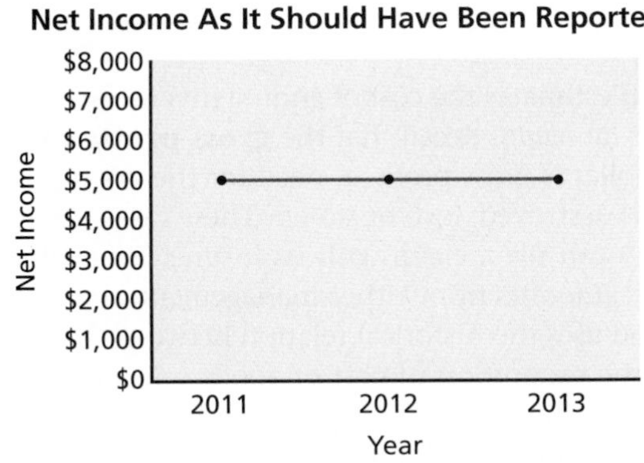

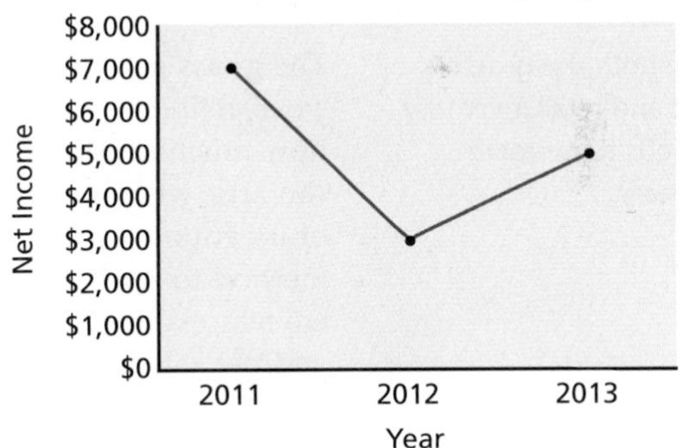

Balance Sheet Effects

Balance sheet effects of an inventory error are made evident by looking at the components of the accounting equation in Exhibit 7.15.

Exhibit 7.15

Accounting Equation

Assets = Liabilities + Equity

We can see, for example, that understating ending inventory will understate both current and total assets. An understatement of ending inventory also yields an understatement in equity because of the understatement of net income. We can do the same analysis with overstating ending inventory. Exhibit 7.16 shows the effects of inventory errors on the current period's balance sheet amounts.

Exhibit 7.16

Effects of Inventory Errors on This Period's Balance Sheet

Inventory Error	Assets	Equity
Understate ending inventory	Understated	Understated
Overstate ending inventory	Overstated	Overstated

Errors in beginning inventory do not yield misstatements in the balance sheet, but they do affect the income statement.

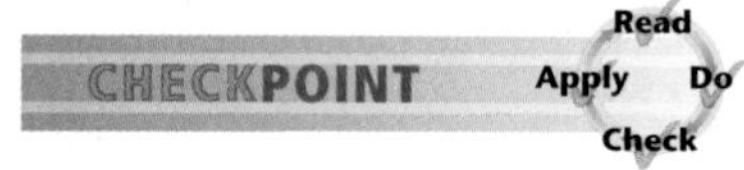

8. During 2012, a company discovered that the merchandise inventory reported on the 2011 balance sheet was overstated by $10,000. Did this error cause cost of goods sold to be overstated or understated in 2011? in 2012? By how much?

Do Quick Study question: QS 7-11

Estimating Inventory

This section describes methods to estimate inventory. Knowledge of these methods is important for preparers and users in understanding and analyzing financial information.

Gross Profit Method

LO6 Apply both the gross profit and retail inventory methods to estimate inventory.

The **gross profit method** estimates the cost of ending inventory by applying the *gross profit ratio* to net sales (at *retail*). Recall that the **gross profit ratio** measures how much of each sales dollar is gross profit. A need for the gross profit estimate can arise when inventory is destroyed, lost, or stolen. These cases need an estimate of inventory so a company can file a claim with its insurer. Users also apply this method to see if inventory amounts from either management or a physical count are reasonable. This method uses the historical relation between cost of goods sold and net sales to estimate the proportion of cost of goods sold making up current sales. This cost of goods sold estimate is then subtracted from cost of goods available for sale to give us an estimate of ending inventory at cost.

To illustrate, assume the following in March of 2011 when the company's inventory is destroyed by fire:

Sales	$31,500
Sales returns	1,500
Inventory, January 1, 2011	12,000
Net cost of goods purchased	20,500
Gross profit ratio	30%

To estimate the inventory loss, we first need to recognize that each dollar of net sales is made up of gross profit and cost of goods sold. If this company's gross profit ratio is 30% as given, then 30% of each net sales dollar is gross profit and 70% is cost of goods sold. We show in Exhibit 7.17 how this 70% is used to estimate lost inventory.

Exhibit 7.17

Calculating Inventory Using the Gross Profit Method

Step 1:

Sales	$31,500
Less: Sales returns	1,500
Net sales	$30,000
Less: COGS*	**21,000**
Gross profit from sales	30% or $9,000

Step 2:

Inventory, January 1, 2011	$ 12,000
Add: Net cost of goods purchased	20,500
Less: COGS	**21,000**
Estimated March inventory	**$11,500**

*If gross profit equals 30% of net sales or $9,000 (30% × $30,000), then COGS must equal 70% of net sales or $21,000 (70% × $30,000).

In Step 1 we use income statement relationships to calculate the dollar value of the estimated cost of goods sold. In Step 2 we use our understanding of the cost of goods sold components as described earlier in Exhibit 7.11 to determine the estimated March inventory.

Retail Inventory Method

Many companies prepare financial statements on a quarterly or monthly basis. The cost of goods sold information needed to prepare these interim financial reports is readily available if a perpetual inventory system is used. A periodic system, however, requires a physical inventory to determine cost of goods sold. To avoid the time-consuming and expensive process of taking a physical inventory each month or quarter, some companies use the **retail inventory method** to estimate cost of goods sold and ending inventory. Some companies even use the retail inventory method to prepare the annual statements since it is acceptable for income tax purposes. Reitman's (Canada) Limited, for instance, reports in its 2008 annual report that:

> Merchandise inventories are accounted for by the retail method.

All companies should take a physical inventory at least once each year to identify any errors or shortages.

Calculating the Retail Inventory Estimate

When the retail inventory method is used to estimate inventory, we need to know the amount of inventory a company had at the beginning of the period in both *cost* and *retail* amounts. The **retail** amount of inventory refers to its dollar amount measured using selling prices of inventory items. We also need the net amount of goods purchased (minus returns, allowances, and discounts) during the period, both at cost and at retail. The amount of net sales at retail is also needed.

A three-step process is used to estimate ending inventory after we calculate the amount of goods available for sale during the period both at cost and at retail. This process is shown in Exhibit 7.18.

Exhibit 7.18

Inventory Estimation Using Retail Inventory Method

The reasoning behind the retail inventory method is that if we can get a good estimate of the cost to retail ratio, then we can multiply ending inventory at retail by this ratio to estimate ending inventory at cost. We show in Exhibit 7.19 how these steps are applied to estimate ending inventory.

Exhibit 7.19

Calculating Ending Inventory Using the Retail Inventory Method

		At Cost	At Retail
	Goods available for sale:		
	Beginning inventory	$20,500	$ 34,500
	Cost of goods purchased	39,500	65,500
	Goods available for sale	$60,000	$100,000
Step 1:	Less: Net sales at retail		70,000
	Ending inventory at retail		$ 30,000
Step 2:	Cost to retail ratio: ($60,000 ÷ $100,000)		× 60%
Step 3:	Estimated ending inventory at cost		$ 18,000

Estimating Physical Inventory at Cost

Items for sale by retailers usually carry price tags listing selling prices. When a retailer takes a physical inventory, it commonly totals inventory using selling prices of items on hand. It then reduces the dollar total of this inventory to a cost basis by applying the cost to retail ratio. This is done because selling prices are readily available and using the cost to retail ratio eliminates the need to look up invoice prices of items on hand.

Let's assume that the company in Exhibit 7.19 estimates its inventory by the retail method and takes a physical inventory using selling prices. If the retail value of this physical inventory is $29,600, then we can calculate the cost of this inventory by applying its cost to retail ratio as follows: $29,600 × 60% = $17,760. The $17,760 cost figure for ending physical inventory is an acceptable number for annual financial statements. It is also acceptable to CRA for tax reporting.

Estimating Inventory Shortage at Cost

The inventory estimate in Exhibit 7.19 is an estimate of the amount of goods on hand (at cost). Since it is calculated by deducting sales from goods available for sale (at retail), it does not reveal any shrinkage due to breakage, loss, or theft. However, we can estimate the amount of shrinkage by comparing the inventory calculated in Exhibit 7.19 with the amount from taking a physical inventory. In Exhibit 7.19, for example, we estimated ending inventory at retail as $30,000, but a physical inventory revealed only $29,600 of inventory on hand (at retail). The company has an inventory shortage (at retail) of $400, calculated as $30,000 − $29,600. The inventory shortage (at cost) is $240, calculated as $400 × 60%.

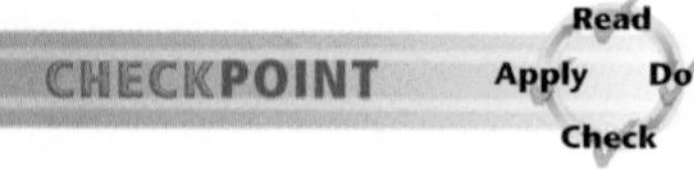

9. The following data pertain to a company's inventory during 2011:

	Cost	Retail
Beginning inventory	$324,000	$530,000
Cost of goods purchased	195,000	335,000
Net sales		320,000

Using the retail method, estimate the cost of ending inventory.

Do Quick Study questions: QS 7-12, QS 7-13, QS 7-14, QS 7-15

CRITICAL THINKING CHALLENGE

Refer to the Critical Thinking Challenge questions at the beginning of the chapter on page 335. Compare your answers to those suggested on Connect at www.mcgrawhillconnect.ca.

IFRS HIGHLIGHTS

Cost of inventories shall be assigned using first-in, first-out (FIFO), weighted average cost, or specific identification (IFRS 2009, IAS 2, para. 23–25); last-in, first-out (LIFO) is not permitted under IFRS.

Inventories will be presented on the balance sheet at the lower of cost and net realizable value on an item-by-item basis or, in some circumstances, it may be appropriate to group similar or related items (IFRS 2009, IAS 2, para. 28–29).

Summary

LO1 | Identify the components and costs included in merchandise inventory. Merchandise inventory comprises goods owned by a company and held for resale. Goods in transit are reported in inventory of the company that holds ownership rights. Goods out on consignment are reported in inventory of the consignor. Goods damaged or obsolete are reported in inventory at a conservative estimate of their net realizable value, calculated as sales price minus the selling costs. Costs of merchandise inventory include expenditures necessary, directly or indirectly, in bringing an item to a saleable condition and location (in other words, the invoice price minus any discount, plus any added or incidental costs necessary to put it in a place and condition for sale).

LO2 | Calculate cost of goods sold and merchandise inventory using specific identification, moving weighted average, and FIFO—perpetual. Costs are assigned to the cost of goods sold account each time that a sale occurs in a perpetual system. Specific identification assigns cost by referring to the actual cost of the unit sold. Moving weighted average assigns a weighted average cost per unit calculated by taking the current balance in the merchandise inventory account and dividing it by the total items available for sale to determine the weighted average cost per unit. FIFO assigns cost assuming units purchased earliest are the first units sold.

LO3 | Analyze the effects of the costing methods on financial reporting. When purchase prices are rising or falling, the inventory methods are likely to assign different cost amounts. Specific identification exactly matches costs and revenues. Moving weighted average smooths out price changes. FIFO assigns an amount to inventory closely approximating current replacement cost. The method(s) used must be disclosed in the notes to the financial statements and be consistent from period to period.

LO4 | Calculate the lower of cost and net realizable value of inventory. Inventory is reported at **net realizable value (NRV)** when NRV is lower than cost. This is called the lower of cost and net realizable value (LCNRV) of inventory. LCNRV can be applied by item or by categories of similar or related items.

LO5 | Analyze the effects of inventory errors on current and future financial statements—perpetual. An error in the amount of ending inventory affects assets (inventory), net income (cost of goods sold), and equity of that period. Since ending inventory is next period's beginning inventory, an error in ending inventory affects next period's cost of goods sold and net income. The financial statement effects of errors in one period are offset (reversed) in the next.

LO6 | Apply both the gross profit and retail inventory methods to estimate inventory. The gross profit method involves two calculations: (1) net sales at retail multiplied by the gross profit ratio gives estimated cost of goods sold; and (2) goods available at cost minus estimated cost of goods sold gives estimated ending inventory at cost. The retail inventory method involves three calculations: (1) goods available at retail minus net sales at retail gives ending inventory at retail; (2) goods available at cost divided by goods available at retail gives the cost to retail ratio; and (3) ending inventory at retail is multiplied by the cost to retail ratio to give estimated ending inventory at cost.

guidance answer to JUDGEMENT CALL

Inventory Manager

Your recommendation is a difficult one. Increased profits may attract investors but they will also increase your bonus. The question becomes one of motivation. That is, would the change really be better for the investors, or would the change take place only because your bonus would increase? This presents the classic conflict of interests. Another problem is that profits can be manipulated by changing accounting methods, and if this is the motivation the profession would frown on the change.

guidance answers to CHECKPOINT

1. The Bay.
2. Total cost is \$12,180, calculated as:

   \$11,400 + \$130 + \$150 + \$100 + \$400.
3. The matching principle.
4. Businesses that sell unique, high dollar value merchandise in relatively low volume levels might choose specific identification. Car dealerships are a good example because each car received as merchandise inventory is unique in terms of both features and identification number. Using specific identification allows the business to accurately tag each item coming in and going out.
5. Moving weighted average gives a lower inventory figure on the balance sheet as compared to FIFO. FIFO's inventory amount will approximate current replacement costs. Moving weighted average costs increase but more slowly because of the effect of averaging.
6. Because these units are the same ones that were originally written down, a reversal is appropriate and would be recorded as:

Merchandise Inventory	2,000	
Cost of Goods Sold..........................		2,000
\$1,800 − \$1,300 = \$500/unit original write-down; \$500 × 4 = \$2,000 maximum reversal		

7. The reported inventory amount is \$540, calculated as (20 × \$5) + (40 × \$8) + (10 × \$12).
8. Cost of goods sold is understated by \$10,000 in 2011 and overstated by \$10,000 in 2012.
9. The estimated ending inventory (at cost) is \$327,000 and is calculated as:

   Step 1: (\$530,000 + \$335,000) − \$320,000 = \$545,000

   Step 2: $\frac{\$324{,}000 + \$195{,}000}{\$530{,}000 + \$335{,}000} = 60\%$

   Step 3: \$545,000 × 60% = \$327,000

demonstration problem

Part 1

Lipke Sales prepared the following schedule comparing the total cost and NRV of its December 31, 2011, ending inventory:

	Total Cost	Total NRV	LCNRV applied to: Products	Group*
Product A	$ 29,000	$ 28,000		
Product B	46,000	36,000		
Product C	17,000	17,000		
Product D	31,000	30,000		
Product E	3,000	7,000		
Totals	$126,000	$118,000		

*Assume that all products are similar.

Required

a. Calculate the merchandise inventory value that should appear on Lipke Sales' December 31, 2011, balance sheet. Apply LCNRV to each product and to inventory as a group by completing the schedule provided.

b. Based on your calculations in part (a), prepare the appropriate adjusting entry at year-end assuming LCNRV is applied to inventory as a group.

Analysis component:

Assuming the adjustment in part (b) is not recorded, identify the over- or understatement of net income, assets, and equity.

Part 2

Coe Company had $435,000 of sales during each of three consecutive years, and it purchased merchandise costing $300,000 during each of the years. It also maintained a $105,000 inventory from the beginning to the end of the three-year period. However, $15,000 of merchandise inventory purchased FOB shipping point on December 31, 2011, was accidentally excluded from the December 31, 2011, inventory. This error caused the company's ending 2011 inventory to appear on the statements at $90,000 rather than at the correct $105,000.

Required

1. Calculate the actual amount of the company's gross profit in each of the years.
2. Prepare a comparative income statement like Exhibit 7.12 to show the effect of this error on the company's cost of goods sold and gross profit in 2011, 2012, and 2013.

solution

Part 1

a.

	Total Cost	Total NRV	LCNRV applied to: Products	Group*
Product A	$ 29,000	$ 28,000	**$ 28,000**	
Product B	46,000	36,000	**36,000**	
Product C	17,000	17,000	**17,000**	
Product D	31,000	30,000	**30,000**	
Product E	3,000	7,000	**3,000**	
Totals	$126,000	$118,000	**$114,000**	**$118,000**

*Assume that all products are similar.

b.

2011 Dec. 31	Cost of Goods Sold	8,000	
	Merchandise Inventory		8,000
	To write inventory down to LCNRV.		

Analysis component:

If the adjusting entry in part (b) is not recorded, net income would be overstated, assets would be overstated, and equity would also be overstated, each by $8,000.

Part 2

1. $435,000 – ($105,000 + $300,000 – $105,000) = $135,000

2.

	For years ended December 31, 2011, 2012, 2013, the income statement information should have been reported as:	Income statement information actually reported for years ended December 31, 2011	2012	2013
Sales	$435,000	$435,000	$435,000	$435,000
Cost of goods sold	300,000	315,000	285,000	300,000
Gross profit from sales	$135,000	$120,000	$150,000	$135,000

Merchandise Inventory (2011)		
Jan. 1/11 105,000		
Purchases 300,000	315,000	COGS
Dec. 31/11 90,000		

Merchandise Inventory (2012)		
Jan. 1/12 90,000		
Purchases 300,000	285,000	COGS
Dec. 31/12 105,000		

Merchandise Inventory (2013)		
Jan. 1/13 105,000		
Purchases 300,000	300,000	COGS
Dec. 31/13 105,000		

APPENDIX 7A

Assigning Costs to Inventory and Inventory Errors–Periodic System

LO7 | Calculate cost of goods sold and merchandise inventory using FIFO—periodic, weighted average, and specific identification.

The aim of the periodic system is the same as the perpetual system: to assign costs to the inventory and the goods sold. The same three methods are used in assigning costs: first-in, first-out; weighted average; and specific identification. We use information from Trekking to describe how we assign costs using these three methods with a periodic system. Data for sales and purchases are reported in the chapter in Exhibits 7.2 and 7.3 and are not repeated here.

First-In, First-Out

The first-in, first-out (FIFO) method of assigning cost to inventory and goods sold using the periodic system is shown in Exhibit 7A.1.

Exhibit 7A.1

FIFO Calculations—Periodic

Total cost of 45 units available for sale	$4,800
Less: **Ending inventory** priced using FIFO:	
11 units from August 17 purchase at $115 each	1,265
Cost of goods sold	**$3,535**

Trekking's ending inventory reported on the balance sheet is $1,265 and its cost of goods sold reported on the income statement is $3,535. The assignment of costs to cost of goods sold and inventory using FIFO is the same for both the perpetual and periodic systems, as summarized in Exhibit 7A.4. This will always occur because the most recent purchases are in ending inventory under both systems.

Weighted Average

The **weighted average** inventory costing method involves three important steps, as illustrated in Exhibits 7A.2 and 7A.3. First, we multiply the per unit cost for beginning inventory and each particular purchase by their corresponding number of units. Second, we add these amounts and divide by the total number of units available for sale to find the *weighted average cost per unit.*

Exhibit 7A.2

Weighted Average Cost Per Unit—Periodic

Step 1:

Aug.	1	Beginning inventory	10 units	@	$ 91	=	$ 910	
	3	Purchased	15 units	@	106	=	1,590	
	17	Purchased	20 units	@	115	=	2,300	
			45 units available for sale				**$4,800**	Total cost of goods available for sale

Step 2: $4,800/45 = **$106.67** weighted average cost per unit

The third step is to use the weighted average cost per unit to assign costs to inventory and to units sold:

Exhibit 7A.3

Weighted Average Calculations—Periodic

Step 3:

Total cost of 45 units available for sale	$4,800
Less: **Ending inventory** priced on a weighted average cost basis:	
11 units at $106.67 each	1,173*
Cost of goods sold (= 34 units × $106.67)	**$3,627***

*Rounded to nearest whole dollar.

The assignment of costs to cost of goods sold and inventory using weighted average usually gives different results depending on whether a perpetual or periodic system is used, as shown in Exhibit 7A.4. This is because weighted average under a perpetual system recalculates the per unit cost at the time of each purchase. Under the periodic system, the per unit cost is only calculated at the end of a period.

Specific Identification

The amounts of cost assigned to inventory and cost of goods sold are the same under the perpetual and periodic systems as detailed in Exhibit 7A.4. This is because specific identification precisely defines which units are in inventory and which are sold.

Exhibit 7A.4 compares the inventory methods for both the periodic and perpetual systems.

Exhibit 7A.4

Comparison of Inventory Methods—Periodic and Perpetual

	FIFO		Weighted Average		Specific Identification	
	Perpetual	Periodic	Perpetual	Periodic*	Perpetual	Periodic
COGS	$3,535	$3,535	$3,568	$3,627	$3,562	$3,562
Ending Inventory	1,265	1,265	1,232	1,173	1,238	1,238
Cost of Goods Available for Sale	$4,800	$4,800	$4,800	$4,800	$4,800	$4,800

*Rounded to the nearest whole dollar for simplicity

Exhibit 7A.4 shows that the figures for specific identification and FIFO are identical under periodic and perpetual systems. However, the figures for weighted average will differ between the perpetual and periodic systems.

10. A company uses a periodic inventory system and reports the following beginning inventory and purchases (and ends the period with 30 units on hand):

	Units	Cost Per Unit
Beginning Inventory	100	$10
Purchases #1	40	12
#2	20	14

a. Calculate ending inventory using FIFO.

b. Calculate cost of goods sold using weighted average.

Do Quick Study question: *QS 7-16

Errors in Reporting Inventory

LO8 Analyze the effects of inventory errors on current and future financial statements—periodic.

On pages 351 to 354, inventory errors were described. Exhibits 7.11 and 7.12 were based on a perpetual inventory system. Those exhibits are reflected below under the assumption of a periodic inventory system.

Income Statement Effects of Inventory Errors

The income statement effects of an inventory error are evident when looking at the components of cost of goods sold in Exhibit 7A.5.

Exhibit 7A.5

Cost of Goods Sold Components—Periodic

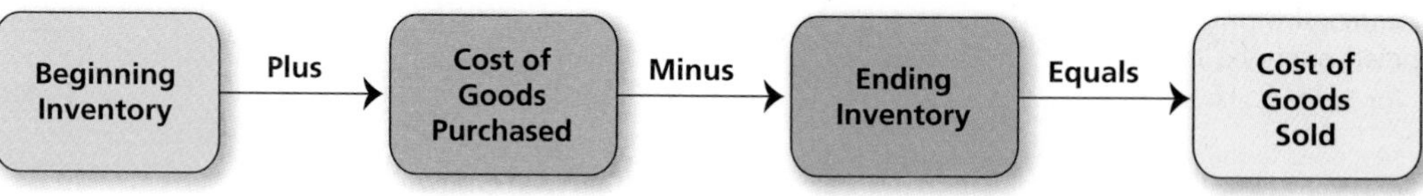

The effect of an inventory error on cost of goods sold is determined by calculating the inventory correctly and comparing it to the result of the calculation when using the incorrect amount, as in Exhibit 7A.6.

Exhibit 7A.6 assumes that $2,000 of merchandise sold but awaiting delivery was incorrectly included in ending inventory on December 31, 2011.

Exhibit 7A.6

Effects of $2,000 Overstatement in Ending Inventory for 2011 on Three Periods' Income Statement Information—Periodic

	For years ended December 31, 2011, 2012, 2013, the income statement information should have been reported as:		Income statement information actually reported for years ended December 31, 2011		2012		2013	
Sales		$30,000		$30,000		$30,000		$30,000
Cost of goods sold:								
Beginning inventory	$10,000		$10,000		$12,000		$10,000	
Add: Purchases	20,000		20,000		20,000		20,000	
Less: Ending inventory	10,000		12,000		10,000		10,000	
Cost of goods sold		20,000		18,000		22,000		20,000
Gross profit		$10,000		$12,000		$ 8,000		$10,000
Operating expenses		5,000		5,000		5,000		5,000
Net income		$ 5,000		$ 7,000		$ 3,000		$ 5,000

(1) 2011 net income and gross profit are overstated (too high) and cost of goods sold is understated (too low) when ending inventory is overstated (too high).

(2) Ending inventory for one period becomes the beginning inventory for the next period, carrying forward any errors that existed.

(3) 2012 net income and gross profit are understated (too low) and cost of goods sold is overstated (too high) when beginning inventory is overstated (too high). Notice that the error has reversed itself in 2012, the second year.

(4) An inventory error in the year 2011 does not affect 2013.

demonstration problem

Tale Company uses a periodic inventory system and had the following beginning inventory and purchases during January 2011:

		Units		Cost Per Unit		Total Cost
Jan. 1	Beginning inventory	300	@	$ 14	=	$ 4,200
16	Purchased	200	@	15	=	3,000
20	Purchased	300	@	16	=	4,800
Total goods available for sale		800				$12,000

Sales of units were as follows:

Jan. 15	200	units at $30
28	460	units at $35
Total units sold	660	

Additional data for use in applying the specific identification method:

The specific units sold were:

Jan. 15	200 units from the January 1 units on hand
28	75 units from the January 1 units on hand
	150 units from the January 16 purchase, and
	235 units from the January 20 purchase

Required

Using the preceding information, calculate the ending inventory and the cost of goods sold under a periodic inventory system by applying each of the three different methods of inventory costing:

a. FIFO

b. Weighted average, and

c. Specific identification

Planning the Solution

- Prepare a periodic FIFO schedule similar to Exhibit 7A.1 (recall that although the calculations differ, the results are the same under each of the periodic and perpetual systems for FIFO).
- Prepare a periodic weighted average schedule similar to Exhibits 7A.2 and 7A.3.
- Prepare a specific identification schedule similar to Exhibit 7.6 (recall that specific identification is calculated in the same manner under each of the perpetual and periodic systems for specific identification).

solution

a. FIFO

Cost of goods available for sale	$12,000
Less: Ending inventory of 140 units:	
140 @ $16 =	2,240
Equals: Cost of goods sold	$ 9,760

b. Weighted Average

Cost of goods available for sale	$12,000
Less: Ending inventory of 140 units:	
140 × $15 avg. cost/unit*	2,100
Equals: Cost of goods sold	$ 9,900

*$12,000 ÷ 800 units = $15/unit avg. cost

c. Specific Identification

Cost of goods available for sale		$12,000
Less: Ending inventory of 140 units:		
25 @ $14 =	$ 350	
50 @ $15 =	750	
65 @ $16 =	1,040	2,140
Equals: Cost of goods sold		$ 9,860

APPENDIX 7B

Using the Information

Merchandise Turnover and Days' Sales in Inventory

This section describes how we use information about inventory to assess a company's short-term liquidity P. 217 and its management of inventory. Two measures useful for these assessments are defined and explained in this section.

LO[9] Assess inventory management using both merchandise turnover and days' sales in inventory.

Merchandise Turnover

A company's ability to pay its short-term obligations depends, in part, on how quickly it sells its merchandise inventory. The **merchandise turnover**, also called **inventory turnover**, is one ratio used to help analyze short-term liquidity. It is also used to assess whether management is doing a good job of controlling the amount of inventory on hand. The merchandise turnover is defined as shown in Exhibit 7B.1.

Exhibit 7B.1

Merchandise Turnover

$$\text{Merchandise turnover} = \frac{\text{Cost of goods sold}}{\text{Average merchandise inventory}}$$

Average merchandise inventory is usually calculated by adding beginning and ending inventory amounts and dividing the total by 2. If a company's sales vary within the year, it is often better to take an average of inventory amounts at the end of each quarter or month.

The merchandise turnover ratio tells us how many *times* a company turns its inventory over during a period. For example, Exhibit 7B.2 shows the merchandise turnover for Loblaw Companies Limited in comparison to Danier Leather for its year ended June 28, 2008.

As Exhibit 7B.2 illustrates, Loblaw's turnover ratio suggests that the amount of inventory on hand is low and that it is sold more quickly than that of Danier Leather. However, Loblaw sells foodstuffs, and is a different type of business than Danier Leather. Loblaw is part of an industry where it is critical to move merchandise quickly because of the perishable nature of foodstuffs. Danier Leather is in a different industry where merchandise turnovers of 3.12 times per year are typical. Ratio comparisons such as the preceding must be based on companies that are similar in order to be meaningful. There is no simple rule with merchandise turnover, except to say that a high ratio is preferable provided inventory is adequate to meet demand.

Exhibit 7B.2

Merchandise Turnovers Compared for Loblaw Companies Limited and Danier Leather

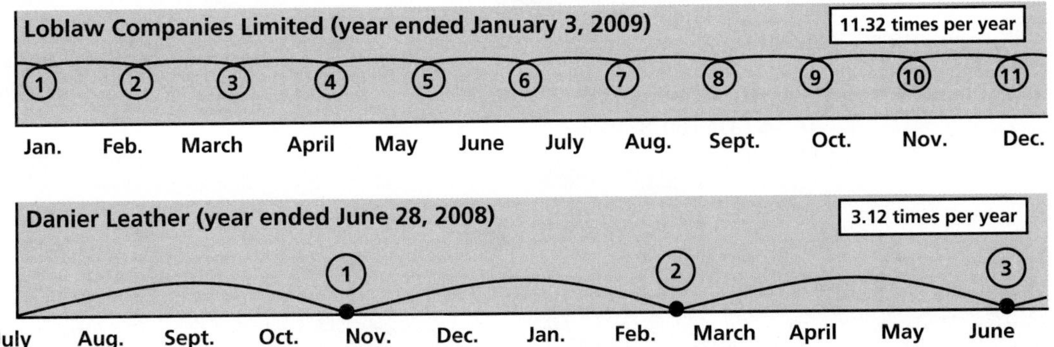

Days' Sales in Inventory

To better interpret merchandise turnover, many users want a measure to determine if inventory levels can meet sales demand. **Days' sales in inventory** is a ratio that estimates how many days it will take to convert inventory on hand into accounts receivable or cash. Days' sales in inventory is calculated as shown in Exhibit 7B.3.

Exhibit 7B.3

Days' Sales in Inventory

$$\text{Days' sales in inventory} = \frac{\text{Ending inventory}}{\text{Cost of goods sold}} \times 365$$

Notice the different focuses of days' sales in inventory and merchandise turnover. Days' sales in inventory focuses on ending inventory, whereas merchandise turnover focuses on average inventory.

11. Company A and Company B sell similar merchandise. Company A has a merchandise turnover of 4.8, while this same ratio is 5.2 for Company B. Which company is more efficient at selling its inventory?

Do Quick Study questions: *QS 7-17, *QS 7-18

Summary of Appendix 7A and Appendix 7B

LO7 | Calculate cost of goods sold and merchandise inventory using FIFO—periodic, weighted average, and specific identification. Periodic systems allocate the cost of goods available for sale between cost of goods sold and ending inventory *at the end of a period.* Specific identification and FIFO give identical results whether the periodic or perpetual system is used. Weighted average cost calculates cost per unit by taking the total cost of both beginning inventory and net purchases and dividing by the total number of units available. It then multiplies cost per unit by the number of units sold to give cost of goods sold.

LO8 | Analyze the effects of inventory errors on current and future financial statements—periodic. An error in the amount of ending inventory affects assets (inventory), net income (cost of goods sold), and equity of that period. Since ending inventory is next period's beginning inventory, an error in ending inventory affects next period's cost of goods sold and net income. The financial statement effects of errors in one period are offset (reversed) in the next.

LO9 | Assess inventory management using both merchandise turnover and days' sales in inventory. We prefer a high merchandise turnover provided inventory is not out of stock and customers are not being turned away. We use days' sales in inventory to assess the likelihood of inventory being out of stock. Together, these ratios help us assess inventory management and evaluate a company's short-term liquidity.

10. a. Ending inventory = (20 × \$14) + (10 × \$12) = \$400

b. Cost of goods sold = [(100 × \$10) + (40 × \$12) + (20 × \$14)]/160 × 30
= \$11 × 30
= \$330

11. Company B is more efficient at selling its inventory because it has higher merchandise turnover.

Glossary

Consignee One who receives and holds goods owned by another party for the purpose of selling the goods for the owner. (p. 337)

Consignor An owner of goods who ships them to another party who will then sell the goods for the owner. (p. 337)

Consistency principle The accounting requirement that a company use the same accounting methods period after period so that the financial statements of succeeding periods will be comparable. (p. 348)

Cost-to-benefit constraint See *materiality principle.* (p. 337)

Days' sales in inventory An estimate of how many days it will take to convert the inventory on hand into accounts receivable or cash; calculated by dividing the ending inventory by cost of goods sold and multiplying the result by 365. (p. 368)

First-in, first-out inventory pricing (FIFO) The pricing of an inventory under the assumption that inventory items are sold in the order acquired; the first items received were the first items sold. (p. 340)

Gross profit method A procedure for estimating an ending inventory in which the past gross profit rate is used to estimate cost of goods sold, which is then subtracted from the cost of goods available for sale to determine the estimated ending inventory. (p. 354)

Gross profit ratio Measures how much of net sales is gross profit; calculated as gross profit divided by net sales; also known as the *gross margin ratio.* (p. 354)

Internal controls The policies and procedures used to protect assets, ensure reliable accounting, promote efficient operations, and urge adherence to company policies. (p. 337)

Inventory turnover See *merchandise turnover.* (p. 367)

Lower of cost and net realizable value (LCNRV) The required method of reporting merchandise inventory in the balance sheet where net realizable value is reported when net realizable value is lower than cost. (p. 349)

Materiality principle This GAAP states that an amount may be ignored if its effect on the financial statements is not important to their users. (p. 337)

Merchandise turnover The number of times a company's average inventory was sold during an accounting period, calculated by dividing cost of goods sold by the average merchandise inventory balance; also called *inventory turnover.* (p. 367)

Moving weighted average A perpetual inventory pricing system in which the unit cost in inventory is recalculated at the time of each purchase by dividing the total cost of goods available for sale at that point in time by the corresponding total units available for sale. The most current moving weighted average cost per unit is multiplied by the units sold to determine cost of goods sold. (p. 341)

Net realizable value (NRV) The expected sales price of an item minus the cost of making the sale. (p. 337)

Physical count To count merchandise inventory for the purpose of reconciling goods actually on hand to the inventory control account in the General Ledger; also called *taking an inventory.* (p. 337)

Prudence principle The accounting principle that says caution is to be exercised when there is uncertainty, so assets and income are not overstated and liabilities and expenses are not understated. (p. 349)

Retail The selling price of merchandise inventory. (p. 355)

Retail inventory method A method for estimating an ending inventory cost based on the ratio of the amount of goods for sale at cost to the amount of goods for sale at marked selling prices. (p. 355)

Specific identification The pricing of an inventory where the purchase invoice of each item in the ending inventory is identified and used to determine the cost assigned to the inventory. (p. 342)

Taking an inventory See *physical count.* (p. 337)

Weighted average (periodic) A periodic inventory pricing system in which the total cost of goods available for sale is divided by the total units available for sale. The resulting weighted average unit cost is multiplied by the units in ending inventory and then by the units that were sold. (p. 362)

Weighted average (perpetual) See *moving weighted average.* (p. 341)

Concept Review Questions

1. Why are incidental costs often ignored in pricing an inventory? Under what accounting principle is this permitted?
2. Give the meanings of the following when applied to inventory: (a) FIFO, and (b) cost.
3. If prices are falling, will the moving weighted average or the FIFO method of inventory valuation result in the lower cost of goods sold?
4. Where is merchandise inventory disclosed in the financial statements?
5. May a company change its inventory pricing method each accounting period?
6. Does the accounting principle of consistency disallow any changes from one accounting method to another?
7. What effect does the full disclosure principle have if a company changes from one acceptable accounting method to another?
8. What guidance for accountants is provided by the prudence principle?
9. What is the usual meaning of NRV as it is used in determining the LCNRV for merchandise inventory?
10. What is meant when it is said that inventory errors correct themselves?
11. If inventory errors correct themselves, why be concerned when such errors are made?
12. Refer to WestJet's financial statements in Appendix I. On December 31, 2008, what percentage of WestJet's assets was represented by what would be WestJet's inventory? Is this merchandise inventory?

WEST JET

13. Refer to Danier's financial statements in Appendix I. Is it possible to determine a cost of goods sold figure for Danier? What is the cost of goods sold figure for Danier?

DANIER

Quick Study

QS 7-1
Inventory ownership
LO1

1. At year-end Carefree Company has shipped, FOB destination, $500 of merchandise that is still in transit to Stark Company. Which company should include the $500 as part of inventory at year-end?
2. Carefree Company has shipped goods to Stark and has an arrangement that Stark will sell the goods for Carefree. Identify the consignor and the consignee. Which company should include any unsold goods as part of inventory?

QS 7-2
Inventory ownership
LO1

Crafts and More, a distributor of handmade gifts, operates out of owner Scott Arlen's home. At the end of the accounting period, Arlen tells us he has 1,500 units of products in his basement, 30 of which were damaged by water leaks and cannot be sold. He also has another 250 units in his van, ready to deliver to fill a customer order, terms FOB destination, and another 70 units out on consignment to a friend who owns a stationery store. How many units should be included in the end-of-period inventory?

QS 7-3
Inventory costs
LO1

A car dealer acquires a used car for $3,000. Additional costs in obtaining and offering the car for sale include $150 for transportation-in, $200 for import duties, $50 for insurance during shipment, $25 for advertising, and $250 for sales staff salaries. For calculating inventory, what cost is assigned to the used car acquired?

QS 7-4
Inventory costs
LO1

Rigby & Son, antique dealers, purchased the contents of an estate for a bulk bid price of $37,500. The terms of the purchase were FOB shipping point, and the cost of transporting the goods to Rigby & Son's warehouse was $1,200. Rigby & Son insured the shipment at a cost of $150. Prior to placing the goods in the store, they cleaned and refurbished some merchandise at a cost of $490 for labour and parts. Determine the cost of the inventory acquired in the purchase of the estate's contents.

QS 7-5
Calculating cost of goods available for sale
LO2

A company has beginning inventory of 10 units at $50. Every week for four weeks an additional 10 units are purchased at respective costs of $51, $52, $55, and $60. 38 units were sold for $72 each. Calculate the total cost of goods that were available for sale and the total units that were available for sale.

QS 7-6
Inventory costing methods—perpetual
LO2

A company had the following beginning inventory and purchases during January for a particular item. On January 28, 345 units were sold. What is the cost of the 140 units that remain in the ending inventory, assuming:
a. FIFO
b. Moving weighted average?
Round numbers to the nearest cent. Assume a perpetual inventory system.

	Units	Unit Cost	Total Cost
Beginning inventory on January 1	310	$3.00	$ 930.00
Purchase on January 9	75	3.20	240.00
Purchase on January 25	100	3.35	335.00
Total available for sale	485		$1,505.00

QS 7-7
Specific identification inventory method
LO2

Refer to the information in QS 7-6. Recall that 345 units were sold on January 28. The units specifically sold were:

- 250 units from beginning inventory
- 50 units from the January 9 purchase
- 45 units from the purchase on January 25.

Calculate cost of goods sold and the cost of ending inventory.

QS 7-8
Inventory costing methods—perpetual
LO2

Bishr Company uses the moving weighted average method for inventory costing. You are to complete the following inventory sheet regarding Product XJ23789 (round calculations to two decimal places):

		Purchases/Transportation-In/ (Purchase Returns/Discounts)			Cost of Goods Sold/ (Returns to Inventory)			Balance in Inventory		
Date		Units	Cost/Unit	Total $	Units	Cost/Unit	Total $	Units	Avg Cost/Unit	Total $
Jan.	1		Brought Forward					10	$15.00	$150.00
	3				6					
	7	25	$18.50	$462.50						
	8			50.00						
	17			(46.25)						
	18				14					

Note: January 8 reflects transportation costs regarding the January 7 purchase. The $46.25 on January 17 represents the discount taken regarding payment of the January 7 purchase within the discount period.

QS 7-9
Contrasting inventory costing methods
LO3

Identify the inventory costing method most closely related to each of the following statements, assuming a period when the cost per unit is increasing:
a. Current cost of inventory not reflected on income statement.
b. Results in a balance sheet inventory closest to replacement costs.
c. Is best when each unit of product has unique features that affect cost.

QS 7-10
Applying LCNRV to inventories
LO4

Thrifty Trading Co. has the following products in its ending inventory at December 31, 2011:

		Per Unit	
Product	Quantity	Cost	NRV
Aprons	9	$6.00	$5.50
Bottles	12	3.50	4.25
Candles	25	8.00	7.00

a. Calculate LCNRV for the inventory as a whole, if applicable.
b. Calculate LCNRV applied separately to each product.
c. Prepare the appropriate adjusting entry, if any, assuming your calculations in (b).

QS 7-11
Inventory errors
LO5, 8

The Weston Company performed a physical inventory count at the end of 2011. It was later determined that certain units were counted twice. Explain how this error affects the following:

a. 2011 cost of goods sold
b. 2011 gross profit
c. 2011 net income
d. 2012 net income
e. The combined two-year income
f. Income in years after 2012.

QS 7-12
Estimating inventories—gross profit method
LO6

The inventory of Bell Department Store was destroyed by a fire on September 10, 2011. The following 2011 data were found in the accounting records:

Jan. 1 inventory	$180,000
Jan. 1–Sept. 10 purchases (net)	$342,000
Jan. 1–Sept. 10 sales	$675,000
2011 estimated gross profit rate	42%

Estimate the cost of the inventory destroyed in the fire using the gross profit method.

QS 7-13
Estimating inventories—gross profit method
LO6

During the past two months, management of Wallace Lake Computing Supplies was closely watching inventory levels due to suspected shrinkage caused by unknown factors. The physical count on July 31, the end of the current month, shows $48,000 of merchandise actually on hand. The accounting records for prior periods indicate that gross profit should be 30% of the $565,000 net sales for July. Inventory at June 30 was actually $65,000 and July purchases were $385,500. Calculate the estimated:

a. Ending inventory
b. Shrinkage.

QS 7-14
Estimating ending inventory—retail method
LO6

Best Stereo Centre showed the following selected information on August 31, 2011:

	Cost	Retail
Cost of goods available for sale	$67,600	$104,000
Net sales		82,000

Using the retail method, estimate the cost of the ending inventory.

QS 7-15
Estimating ending inventory—retail method
LO6

Complete the following schedule by using the retail method to estimate ending inventory for September and October.

	September		October	
	Cost	Retail	Cost	Retail
Beginning inventory	$ 74,950	$112,000		
Cost of goods purchased	395,000	611,000	461,590	674,000
Goods available for sale				
Less: Net sales at retail		614,000		700,000
Ending inventory at retail				
Cost to retail ratio				
Estimated ending inventory				

***QS 7-16**
Inventory costing methods—periodic
LO7

Refer to the information in QS 7-6. Determine the cost of the 140 units that remain in ending inventory, assuming:
a. FIFO
b. Weighted average.
Round numbers to the nearest cent and use a periodic inventory system.

***QS 7-17**
Merchandise turnover
LO9

Huff Company and Mesa Company are similar firms that operate within the same industry. The following information is available.

	Huff			Mesa		
	2011	2010	2009	2011	2010	2009
Merchandise turnover............	23.2	20.9	16.1	13.5	12.0	11.6

Required
Based on the information provided, which company is managing inventory more efficiently? Explain.

***QS 7-18**
Merchandise turnover and days' sales in inventory
LO9

Mixon Company showed the following selected information for the years ended December 31, 2011, 2010, and 2009:

	2011	2010	2009
Cost of goods sold	$410,225	$344,500	$312,600
Merchandise inventory (December 31)	56,195	82,500	111,500

For the years ended 2011 and 2010, calculate:
a. Days' sales in inventory
b. Merchandise turnover.
Indicate if the change in the ratio from 2010 to 2011 is generally considered to be favourable (good) or unfavourable (not good). Round calculations to two decimal places.

Exercises

Exercise 7-1
Alternative cost flow assumptions—perpetual
LO2

eXcel

Parfour made purchases of a particular product in the current year as follows:

Jan. 1	Beginning inventory	100 units	@	$10.00	=	$ 1,000
Mar. 14	Purchased	250 units	@	$15.00	=	3,750
July 30	Purchased	400 units	@	$20.00	=	8,000
Units available for sale		750 units				
Cost of goods available for sale						$12,750

Parfour made sales on the following dates at a selling price of $40 per unit:

Jan. 10	90 units
Mar. 15	140 units
Oct. 5	300 units
Total	530 units

Required
The business uses a perpetual inventory system. Determine the costs that should be assigned to the ending inventory and to goods sold under:
a. FIFO
b. Moving weighted average (round to the nearest whole cent)
Also calculate the gross profit under each method.

Check figures:
COGS
a. $8,350.00
b. $8,613.40

An asterisk (*) identifies assignment material based on Appendix 7A or Appendix 7B.

Exercise 7-2
Specific identification cost flow assumption
LO2

Check figures:
COGS = $8,650;
Gross profit = $12,550

Refer to the data in Exercise 7-1. Assume that Parfour uses the specific identification method to cost inventory. The 530 units were specifically sold as follows:

Jan. 10:	90	units from beginning inventory
Mar. 15:	10	units from beginning inventory, and
	130	units from the March 14 purchase
Oct. 5:	60	units from the March 14 purchase, and
	240	units from the July 30 purchase

Calculate cost of goods sold and the gross profit.

Exercise 7-3
Alternative cost flow assumptions—perpetual inventory system
LO2

Check figures:
3. COGS
a. $4,245.00
b. $4,092.75

Trout Company uses a perpetual inventory system and made purchases and sales of a particular product in 2011 as follows:

Jan. 1	Beginning inventory	120 units	@	$6.00	=	$ 720
Jan. 10	Sold	70 units	@	$15.00	=	1,050
Mar. 7	Purchased	250 units	@	$5.60	=	1,400
Mar. 15	Sold	125 units	@	$15.00	=	1,875
July 28	Purchased	500 units	@	$5.00	=	2,500
Oct. 3	Purchased	450 units	@	$4.60	=	2,070
Oct. 5	Sold	600 units	@	$15.00	=	9,000

Required

1. Calculate the total goods available for sale (in units and cost).
2. Calculate the number of units sold and units remaining in ending inventory.
3. Determine the share of the cost of goods available for sale calculated in Part 1 that should be assigned to ending inventory and to goods sold under:
   a. FIFO
   b. Moving weighted average

Exercise 7-4
Specific identification cost flow assumption
LO2

Check figure:
COGS = $4,018

Use the information in Exercise 7-3. Assume that Trout Company specifically sold the following units:

Jan. 10:	70	units from beginning inventory
Mar. 15:	25	units from beginning inventory, and
	100	units from the March 7 purchase
Oct. 5:	320	units from the July 28 purchase, and
	280	units from the October 3 purchase

Calculate cost to be assigned to ending inventory and cost of goods sold.

Exercise 7-5
Income statement effects of alternative cost flow assumptions
LO3

Use the data in Exercises 7-3 and 7-4 to construct comparative income statements for Trout Company (year-end December 31, 2011), similar to those shown in Exhibit 7.8 in the chapter. Assume that operating expenses are $1,250.

1. Which method results in the highest net income?
2. If costs were rising instead of falling, which method would result in the highest net income?

Exercise 7-6
Moving weighted average cost flow assumption—perpetual
LO2, 3

Telamark Company uses the moving weighted average method for inventory costing. The following incomplete inventory sheet regarding Product W506 is available for the month of March 2011:

Date		Purchases/Transportation-In/ (Purchase Returns/Discounts)			Cost of Goods Sold/ (Returns to Inventory)			Balance in Inventory		
		Units	Cost/Unit	Total $	Units	Cost/Unit	Total $	Units	AvgCost/Unit	Total $
Mar.	1		Brought Forward					50	$95.00	$4,750.00
	2	25	$97.00							
	3				12					
	4				(2)					
	7				48					
	17	15	92.00							
	28				25					

Note: March 4 reflects a return made by a customer of incorrect items shipped on March 3; these items were returned to inventory.

Required
Complete the inventory sheet. Round all calculations to two decimal places.

Analysis component:
The gross profit realized on the sale of Product W506 during February 2011 was 32.16%. The selling price was $148 during both February and March. Calculate the gross profit ratio for Product W506 for March 2011 and determine whether the change is favourable or unfavourable from February. Identify the most probable cause of the change.

Exercise 7-7
Lower of cost and net realizable value
LO4

Showtime Company's ending inventory at December 31, 2011, includes the following items:

Product	Units on Hand	Unit Cost	Net Realizable Value Per Unit
BB	22	$100	$108
FM	15	156	144
MB	36	190	182
SL	40	72	87

Calculate LCNRV for the inventory:
a. As a whole (assuming the items are similar), and
b. Applied separately to each product.
c. Prepare the appropriate adjusting entry, if required, based on your calculations in (b).

Check figures:
a. $14,260
b. $13,792

Exercise 7-8
Analysis of inventory errors
LO5, 8

Assume that The John Henry Company had $900,000 of sales during each of three consecutive years, and it purchased merchandise costing $500,000 during each of the years. It also maintained a $200,000 inventory from the beginning to the end of the three-year period. However, it made an error at the end of the first year, 2011, that caused its ending 2011 inventory to appear on its statements at $180,000 rather than the correct $200,000.

Required
1. Calculate the actual amount of the company's gross profit in each of the years.
2. Prepare a comparative income statement like Exhibit 7.12 (or Exhibit 7A.6) to show the effect of this error on the company's cost of goods sold and gross profit in 2011, 2012, and 2013.

Exercise 7-9
Estimating ending inventory—gross profit method
LO6

On January 1, The Parts Store had a $450,000 inventory at cost. During the first quarter of the year, it purchased $1,590,000 of merchandise, returned $23,100, and paid freight charges on purchased merchandise totalling $37,600. During the past several years, the store's gross profit on sales has averaged 30%. Under the assumption the store had $2,000,000 of sales during the first quarter of the year, use the gross profit method to estimate its inventory at the end of the first quarter.

Exercise 7-10
Estimating ending inventory—retail method
LO6

Check figure:
$35,970.84

During 2011, Harmony Co. sold $260,000 of merchandise at marked retail prices. At the end of 2011, the following information was available from its records:

	At Cost	At Retail
Beginning inventory	$ 63,800	$128,400
Net purchases	115,620	196,800

Use the retail method to estimate Harmony's 2011 ending inventory at cost. Round all calculations to two decimal places.

Exercise 7-11
Reducing physical inventory to cost—retail method
LO6

Assume that in addition to estimating its ending inventory by the retail method, Harmony Co. of Exercise 7-10 also took a physical inventory at the marked selling prices of the inventory items at the end of 2011. Assume further that the total of this physical inventory at marked selling prices was $54,600.

a. Determine the amount of this inventory at cost.

b. Determine Harmony's 2011 inventory shrinkage from breakage, theft, or other causes at retail and at cost.

Round all calculations to two decimal places.

*Exercise 7-12
Alternative cost flow assumptions—periodic
LO7

Paddington Gifts made purchases of a particular product in the current year as follows:

Date						
Jan. 1	Beginning inventory	120 units	@	$6.00	=	$ 720
Mar. 7	Purchased	250 units	@	$5.60	=	1,400
July 28	Purchased	500 units	@	$5.00	=	2,500
Oct. 3	Purchased	450 units	@	$4.40	=	1,980
	Totals	1,320 units				$6,600

Check figure:
a. COGS = $6,380

Required

The business uses a periodic inventory system. Ending inventory consists of 50 units. Calculate the costs to be assigned to the ending inventory and to goods sold under:

a. FIFO

b. A weighted average cost basis

Which method provides the lower net income and why?

*Exercise 7-13
Alternative cost flow assumptions—periodic
LO7

Jasper & Williams made purchases of a particular product in the current year as follows:

Date						
Jan. 1	Beginning inventory	120 units	@	$2.00	=	$ 240
Mar. 7	Purchased	250 units	@	$2.30	=	575
July 28	Purchased	500 units	@	$2.50	=	1,250
Oct. 3	Purchased	50 units	@	$2.86	=	143
	Totals	920 units				$2,208

Check figure:
b. Ending inventory = $360

Required

Ending inventory consists of 150 units. Assuming a periodic system, determine the costs to be assigned to cost of goods sold and ending inventory under:

a. FIFO

b. Weighted average cost basis.

Which method provides the lower net income, and why?

*Exercise 7-14
Specific identification cost flow assumption—periodic
LO7

Use the information in *Exercise 7-13. Assume that the specific identification method is used to assign costs to cost of goods sold ending inventory. The units in ending inventory were specifically identified as follows:

- 80 units from beginning inventory
- 22 units from the March 7 purchase, and
- 48 units from the July 28 purchase.

An asterisk (*) identifies assignment material based on Appendix 7A or Appendix 7B.

Required
Determine the cost to be assigned to ending inventory and cost of goods sold.

Check figure:
COGS = $1,877.40

***Exercise 7-15**
Merchandise turnover and days' sales in inventory
LO9

From the following information for Russo Merchandising Co., calculate merchandise turnover for 2012 and 2011 and days' sales in inventory at December 31, 2012 and 2011. Round answers to one decimal place.

	2012	2011	2010
Cost of goods sold	$643,825	$426,650	$391,300
Merchandise inventory (December 31)	96,400	86,750	91,500

Comment on Russo's efficiency in using its assets to support increasing sales from 2011 to 2012.

Problems

Problem 7-1A
Alternative cost flows—perpetual
LO2

The Stilton Company has the following inventory and credit purchases during the fiscal year ended December 31, 2011.

Beginning	500 units	@	$90/unit
Feb. 10	250 units	@	$84/unit
Aug. 21	130 units	@	$100/unit

Stilton Company has two credit sales during the period. The units have a selling price of $150.00 per unit.

Sales	
Mar. 15..	330 units
Sept. 10...	235 units

Stilton Company uses a perpetual inventory system.

Required
1. Calculate the dollar value of cost of goods sold and ending inventory using:
   a. FIFO
   b. Moving weighted average. Round to two decimal places.
2. Calculate the dollar value of cost of goods sold and ending inventory using specific identification, assuming the sales were specifically identified as follows:

Mar. 15:	170	units from beginning inventory, and
	160	units from the February 10 purchase
Sept. 10:	165	units from beginning inventory, and
	20	units from the February 10 purchase, and
	50	units from the August 21 purchase

3. Using information from your answers in Parts 1 and 2, journalize the credit purchase on February 10 and the credit sale on September 10 for each of:
   a. FIFO
   b. Moving weighted average
   c. Specific identification.

Check figures:
1. Ending inventory
   a. $28,540.00
   b. $28,612.60
2. Ending inventory = $28,730.00

An asterisk (*) identifies assignment material based on Appendix 7A or Appendix 7B.

***Problem 7-2A**
Alternative cost flows—periodic
LO7

Check figures:
Cost of goods sold
a. $50,460.00
b. $50,722.45

Use the data from Problem 7-1A and do Part 1, assuming Stilton Company uses a periodic inventory costing system. Round calculations to two decimal places.

Problem 7-3A
Gross profit comparisons and cost flow assumptions—perpetual
LO2, 3

The Gale Company has the following inventory and purchases during the fiscal year ended December 31, 2011.

Beginning inventory	300 units	@	$80/unit
Feb. 10 purchased	200 units	@	$84/unit
Feb. 20 sold	350 units	@	$160/unit
Mar. 13 purchased	300 units	@	$78/unit
Sept. 5 purchased	250 units	@	$64/unit
Oct. 10 sold	500 units	@	$160/unit

Gale Company employs a perpetual inventory system.

Check figures:
1. Ending inventory
   a. $12,800.00
   b. $14,755.00

Required
1. Calculate the dollar value of ending inventory and cost of goods sold using:
   a. FIFO
   b. Moving weighted average. Round all unit costs to two decimal places.
2. Using your calculations from Part 1, complete the following schedule:

	FIFO	Moving Weighted Average
Sales		
Cost of goods sold		
Gross profit		

Analysis component:
How would the gross profits calculated in Part 2 above change if Gale Company had been experiencing increasing prices in the acquisition of additional inventory?

***Problem 7-4A**
Alternative cost flows—periodic
LO7

Check figures:
1. Cost of goods sold
   a. $67,400
   b. $64,924

Use the data from Problem 7-3A and do Part 1 assuming Gale Company uses a periodic inventory costing system.

Problem 7-5A
Income statement comparisons and cost flow assumptions—perpetual
LO2, 3

During 2011, Fresh Express Company sold 2,500 units of its product on September 20 and 3,000 units on December 22, all at a price of $90 per unit. Incurring operating expenses of $12 per unit sold, it began the year with and made successive purchases of the product as follows:

January 1 beginning inventory	600 units	@	$36 per unit
Purchases:			
February 20	1,500 units	@	$38 per unit
May 16	700 units	@	$40 per unit
December 11	3,300 units	@	$44 per unit
Total	6,100 units		

An asterisk (*) identifies assignment material based on Appendix 7A or Appendix 7B.

Required
Prepare a comparative income statement for the company, showing in adjacent columns the net incomes earned from the sale of the product, assuming the company uses a perpetual inventory system and prices its ending inventory on the basis of:
a. FIFO
b. Moving weighted average cost. Round all unit costs to two decimal places.

Check figure:
a. Net income, FIFO = $203,600

Analysis component:
If the manager of Fresh Express Company earns a bonus based on a percentage of gross profit, which method of inventory costing will she prefer?

*Problem 7-6A
Income statement comparisons and cost flow assumptions—periodic
LO7

Check figure:
Net income weighted average = $201,968

Use the data from Problem 7-5A and do the question assuming Fresh Express Company uses a periodic inventory costing system.

Problem 7-7A
Analysis of inventory errors
LO5, 8

Shockley Co. reported the following amounts in its financial statements:

	Financial Statements for Year Ended December 31		
	2011	2012	2013
(a) Cost of goods sold	$ 715,000	$ 847,000	$ 770,000
(b) Net income	220,000	275,000	231,000
(c) Total current assets	1,155,000	1,265,000	1,100,000
(d) Equity	1,287,000	1,430,000	1,232,000

In making the physical counts of inventory, the following errors were made:
- Inventory on December 31, 2011: understated $66,000
- Inventory on December 31, 2012: overstated $30,000

Required
For each of the preceding financial statement items—(a), (b), (c), and (d)—prepare a schedule similar to the following and show the adjustments that would have been necessary to correct the reported amounts.

	2011	2012	2013
Cost of goods sold:			
Reported	______	______	______
Adjustments: Dec. 31/11 error	______	______	______
Dec. 31/12 error	______	______	______
Corrected	______	______	______

Analysis component:
What is the error in the aggregate net income for the three-year period that resulted from the inventory errors? Explain why this result occurs. Also explain why the understatement of inventory by $66,000 at the end of 2011 resulted in an understatement of equity by the same amount that year.

An asterisk (*) identifies assignment material based on Appendix 7A or Appendix 7B.

Problem 7-8A
Analysis of inventory errors
LO5, 8

While performing a detailed review of its financial records, Doors Unlimited noted the following ending inventory errors:

2011	2012	2013
Understated $55,000	Overstated $16,000	No errors

	2011	2012	2013
Ending inventory as reported	$ 345,000	$ 420,000	$ 392,000
Cost of goods sold as reported	1,300,000	1,750,000	2,100,000
Net income as reported	340,000	516,000	652,000

Required

Calculate the corrected ending inventory and cost of goods sold amounts for each year by completing the following schedule:

	2011	2012	2013
Corrected ending inventory			
Corrected cost of goods sold			
Corrected net income			

Problem 7-9A
Lower of cost and net realizable value
LO4

The following information pertains to the physical inventory of Electronics Unlimited taken at December 31:

		Per Unit	
Product	**Units on Hand**	**Cost**	**NRV**
Audio equipment:			
Receivers	335	$180	$196
CD players	250	222	200
Cassette decks	316	172	190
Turntables	194	104	82
Video equipment:			
Televisions	470	300	250
VCRs	281	186	168
Video cameras	202	620	644
Car audio equipment:			
Cassette radios	175	140	168
CD radios	160	194	210

Check figures:
1a. $540,664
1b. $526,048

Required

1. Calculate the LCNRV:
   a. For the inventory by major group
   b. For the inventory, applied separately to each product.
2. Prepare the appropriate entry, if any, for (a) and (b).

Problem 7-10A
Estimating ending inventory—gross profit method
LO6

The Navarre Company had a fire on February 10, 2011, that destroyed a major portion of its inventory. The salvaged accounting records contained the following information:

Sales, January 1 to February 10	$ 701,200
Net merchandise purchased Jan. 1 to Feb. 10	364,800
Additional information was determined from the 2010 annual report:	
Income statement:	
Sales	$6,400,450
Cost of goods sold	3,521,150
Balance sheet:	
Merchandise inventory	588,200
Navarre was able to salvage inventory with a cost of $212,400.	

Required
Determine the amount of inventory lost by Navarre as a result of the fire. Navarre has a December 31 year-end. *Round the gross profit ratio to the nearest whole percentage point.*

Check figure: $354,940

Problem 7-11A
Gross profit method
LO6

Alanood Company wants to prepare interim financial statements for the first quarter of 2011 but would like to avoid making a physical count of inventory. During the last five years, the company's gross profit rate has averaged 36%. The following information for the year's first quarter is available from its records:

January 1 beginning inventory	$150,130
Purchases	472,600
Purchase returns	6,525
Transportation-in	3,450
Sales	595,575
Sales returns	4,725

Required
Use the gross profit method to prepare an estimate of the company's March 31 inventory.

Check figure: $241,511

Problem 7-12A
Retail inventory method
LO6

The records of Earthly Goods provided the following information for the year ended December 31, 2011.

	At Cost	At Retail
January 1 beginning inventory	$ 942,700	$ 1,854,300
Purchases	6,657,660	12,797,400
Purchase returns	105,600	238,700
Sales		10,991,400
Sales returns		89,200

Required
1. Prepare an estimate of the company's year-end inventory by the retail method. Round all calculations to two decimal places.
2. Under the assumption the company took a year-end physical inventory at marked selling prices that totalled $3,351,600, prepare a schedule showing the store's loss from theft or other causes at cost and at retail.

Check figure: 2. Loss at cost = $82,784

Problem 7-13A
Retail inventory method
LO6

Petcetera had a robbery on the weekend in which a large amount of inventory was taken. The loss is totally covered by insurance. A physical inventory count determined that the cost of the remaining merchandise is $117,000. The following additional information is available:

	At Cost	At Retail
Beginning merchandise inventory	$ 150,000	$ 187,500
Purchase returns and allowances	30,000	40,000
Purchases	2,550,000	3,462,500
Transportation-in	37,500	
Sales		3,285,000
Sales returns and allowances		36,000

Check figure:
2. $153,750

Required

1. Prepare an estimate of ending merchandise inventory using the retail method.
2. Calculate the cost of the stolen inventory.

***Problem 7-14A**
Alternative cost flows—periodic
LO7

Synergy Company began 2011 with 20,000 units of Product X in its inventory that cost $7.50 per unit, and it made successive purchases of the product as follows:

Mar. 7	28,000 units	@	$9.00 each
May 25	30,000 units	@	$11.00 each
Aug. 1	20,000 units	@	$12.00 each
Nov. 10	33,000 units	@	$13.50 each

The company uses a periodic inventory system. On December 31, 2011, a physical count disclosed that 35,000 units of Product X remained in inventory.

Check figures:
2. Cost of goods sold
a. $948,000
b. $1,038,800

Required

1. Prepare a calculation showing the number and total cost of the units available for sale during 2011.
2. Prepare calculations showing the amounts that should be assigned to the 2011 ending inventory and to cost of goods sold, assuming:
a. FIFO
b. Weighted average cost basis (round the average cost per unit to two decimal places).

Alternate Problems

Problem 7-1B
Alternative cost flows—perpetual
LO2

eXcel

The Obama Company has the following inventory purchases during the fiscal year ended December 31, 2011.

Beginning	600 units	@	$110/unit
Feb. 13	200 units	@	$114/unit
Aug. 5	345 units	@	$118/unit

Obama Company has two sales during the period. The units have a selling price of $180 per unit.

Sales	
Feb. 15	300 units
Aug. 10	335 units

Obama Company uses a perpetual inventory system.

An asterisk (*) identifies assignment material based on Appendix 7A or Appendix 7B.

Required

1. Calculate the dollar value of cost of goods sold and ending inventory using
   a. FIFO
   b. Moving weighted average method (round the average cost per unit to two decimal places).
2. Calculate the dollar value of cost of goods sold and ending inventory using specific identification assuming the sales were specifically identified as follows:

Feb. 15:	175	units from beginning inventory
	125	units from the February 13 purchase
Aug. 10:	15	units from beginning inventory
	320	units from the August 5 purchase

3. Using information from your answers in Parts 1 and 2, journalize the credit sale on February 15, and the credit purchase on August 5 for each of:
   a. FIFO
   b. Moving weighted average
   c. Specific identification

Check figures:
1. Ending inventory
   a. $59,520.00
   b. $58,066.90
2. Ending inventory = $56,600.00

*Problem 7-2B

Alternative cost flows—periodic

LO7

Use the data from Problem 7-1B and do Part 1, assuming Obama Company uses a periodic inventory costing system. Round calculations to two decimal places.

Check figures:
Cost of goods sold
a. $69,990.00
b. $71,823.90

Problem 7-3B

Gross profit comparisons and cost flow assumptions—perpetual

LO2, 3

eXcel

The Manson Company has the following sales, inventory, and purchases during the fiscal year ended December 31, 2011.

Beginning inventory	200 units	@	$30/unit
Feb. 20 sold	150 units	@	$40/unit
Apr. 30 purchased	320 units	@	$29/unit
Oct. 5 purchased	250 units	@	$25/unit
Oct. 10 sold	500 units	@	$40/unit

Manson Company employs a perpetual inventory system.

Required

1. Calculate the dollar value of ending inventory and cost of goods sold using:
   a. FIFO
   b. Moving weighted average method. Round all unit costs to two decimal places.
2. Using your calculations from Part 1, complete the following schedule:

	FIFO	Moving Weighted Average
Sales		
Cost of goods sold		
Gross profit		

Check figures:
1. Ending inventory
   a. $3,000
   b. $3,295

Analysis component:
How would the gross profits calculated in Part 2 above change if Manson Company had been experiencing increasing prices in the purchase of additional inventory?

An asterisk (*) identifies assignment material based on Appendix 7A or Appendix 7B.

*Problem 7-4B

Alternative cost flows—periodic

LO7

Check figures:
Cost of goods sold
a. $18,530.00
b. $18,174.80

Use the data from Problem 7-3B and do Part 1 assuming Manson Company uses a periodic inventory costing system. Round calculations to two decimal places.

Problem 7-5B

Income statement comparisons and cost flow assumptions—perpetual

LO2, 3

eXcel

During 2011, the Blizzard Company sold 1,200 units of its product on May 20 and 1,300 units on October 25, all at a price of $49 per unit. Incurring operating expenses of $7 per unit in selling the units, it began the year with, and made successive purchases of, units of the product as follows:

January 1 Beginning inventory	740 units costing $29 per unit		
Purchases:			
April 2	700 units	@	$28 per unit
June 14	600 units	@	$27 per unit
Aug. 29	500 units	@	$26 per unit
Total	2,540 units		

Check figure:
a. Net income, FIFO = $35,780

Required

Prepare a comparative income statement for the company for 2011, showing in adjacent columns the net incomes earned from the sale of the product, assuming the company uses a perpetual inventory system and prices its ending inventory on the basis of:

a. FIFO
b. Moving weighted average cost. Round unit costs to two decimal places.

Analysis component:

If the Blizzard Company's manager earns a bonus based on a percentage of gross profit, which method of inventory costing will she prefer?

*Problem 7-6B

Income statement comparisons and cost flow assumptions—periodic

LO7

Check figure:
Net income, weighted average = $35,846.40

Use the data from Problem 7-5B and do the question assuming Blizzard Company uses a periodic inventory costing system.

Problem 7-7B

Analysis of inventory errors

LO5, 8

Fireplace Company reported the following amounts in its financial statements:

	Financial Statements For Year Ended December 31		
	2011	2012	2013
(a) Cost of goods sold	$102,600	$106,400	$ 98,015
(b) Net income	87,400	105,635	91,955
(c) Total current assets	133,000	138,250	131,475
(d) Equity	152,000	158,000	168,000

In making the physical counts of inventory, the following errors were made:

- Inventory on December 31, 2011: overstated $8,500
- Inventory on December 31, 2012: understated $12,500

An asterisk (*) identifies assignment material based on Appendix 7A or Appendix 7B.

Required

For each of the preceding financial statement items—(a), (b), (c), and (d)—prepare a schedule similar to the following and show the adjustments that would have been necessary to correct the reported amounts.

	2011	2012	2013
Cost of goods sold:			
Reported	______	______	______
Adjustments: Dec. 31/11 error	______	______	______
Dec. 31/12 error	______	______	______
Corrected	______	______	______

Analysis component:

What is the error in the aggregate net income for the three-year period that resulted from the inventory errors?

Problem 7-8B

Analysis of inventory errors

LO5, 8

	Incorrect Income Statement Information For Years Ended December 31				Corrected Income Statement Information For Years Ended December 31			
	2011	%	2012	%	2011	%	2012	%
Sales	$675,000	100	$845,000	100				
Cost of goods sold	405,000	60	422,500	50				
Gross profit	$270,000	40	$422,500	50				

In comparing income statement information for the years ended December 31, 2011 and 2012, the owner noticed an increase in the gross profit. He was puzzled because he knew that inventory costs were increasing.

A detailed review of the records showed the following:

a. Goods with a cost of $37,500 were on consignment at another location. Through an error, they were not included in the inventory of December 31, 2011.

b. $16,000 of merchandise inventory purchased on December 25, 2012, was shipped *FOB Shipping Point* and received on January 6, 2013. It was not included in inventory on December 31, 2012, in error.

c. While performing the physical inventory count on December 31, 2012, a calculation error was discovered that caused inventory on hand to be overstated by $24,500.

Required

1. Using the information provided, complete the schedule showing the corrected income statement information (round percentages to the nearest whole number).
2. Does the new gross profit information reflect the owner's knowledge of increasing inventory costs?

Problem 7-9B
Lower of cost and net realizable value
LO4

The following information pertains to the physical inventory of Geo Furniture Company taken at December 31:

Product	Units on Hand	Per Unit Cost	Per Unit NRV
Office furniture:			
Desks	436	$261	$305
Credenzas	295	227	256
Chairs	587	49	43
Bookshelves	321	93	82
Filing cabinets:			
Two-drawer	214	81	70
Four-drawer	398	135	122
Lateral	175	104	118
Office equipment:			
Fax machines	430	168	200
Copiers	545	317	288
Typewriters	352	125	117

Check figures:
1a. $607,707
1b. $584,444

Required

1. Calculate the LCNRV for the:
   a. Inventory by major category
   b. Inventory, applied separately to each product.
2. Prepare the appropriate entry, if any, for (a) and (b).

Problem 7-10B
Estimating ending inventory—gross profit method
LO6

The Zeon Company had a flood on July 5, 2011, that destroyed all of its inventory. The salvaged accounting records contained the following information:

Sales, January 1 to July 5	$ 737,650
Net merchandise purchased Jan. 1 to July 5	414,900
Additional information was determined from the 2010 annual report:	
Income statement:	
Sales	$2,122,550
Cost of goods sold	1,337,175
Balance sheet:	
Merchandise inventory	131,200
Zeon was unable to salvage any usable inventory after the water subsided.	

Check figure:
$81,380.50

Required

Determine the amount of inventory lost by Zeon as a result of the flood. Zeon has a December 31 year-end. Round the gross profit ratio to the nearest whole percentage point.

Problem 7-11B
Gross profit method
LO6

Belle Equipment Co. wants to prepare interim financial statements for the first quarter of 2011. The company uses a periodic inventory system but would like to avoid making a physical count of inventory. During the last five years, the company's gross profit rate has averaged 30%. The following information for the year's first quarter is available from its records:

January 1 beginning inventory	$ 376,440
Purchases	1,066,050
Purchase returns	19,185
Transportation-in	32,950
Sales	1,855,125
Sales returns	37,100

Check figure:
$183,637.50

Required

Use the gross profit method to prepare an estimate of the company's March 31, 2011, inventory.

Problem 7-12B
Retail inventory method
LO6

The records of The Wilke Co. provided the following information for the year ended December 31, 2011:

	At Cost	At Retail
January 1 beginning inventory	$ 81,670	$114,610
Purchases	502,990	767,060
Purchase returns	10,740	15,330
Sales		786,120
Sales returns		4,480

Check figure:
2. Loss at cost = $4,074.37

Required

1. Prepare an estimate of the company's year-end inventory by the retail method. Round all calculations to two decimal places.
2. Under the assumption the company took a year-end physical inventory at marked selling prices that totalled $78,550, prepare a schedule showing the store's loss from theft or other causes at cost and at retail.

Problem 7-13B
Retail inventory method
LO6

Poundmaker Company just had a fire in its warehouse that destroyed all of its merchandise inventory. The insurance company covers 80% of the loss. The following information is available regarding the year ended March 31, 2011:

	At Cost	At Retail
Beginning merchandise inventory	$ 150,000	$ 250,000
Purchases	2,100,000	3,500,000
Purchase returns and allowances	250,000	400,000
Transportation-in	10,000	
Sales		2,715,000
Sales returns and allowances		35,000

Check figure:
Loss = $80,400

Required

Prepare an estimate of the company's loss using the retail method.

*Problem 7-14B
Alternative cost flows—periodic
LO7

Bonaire Co. began 2011 with 6,300 units of Product B in its inventory that cost $70 each, and it made successive purchases of the product as follows:

Jan. 4	10,500 units	@	$66 each
May 18	13,000 units	@	$64 each
July 9	12,000 units	@	$58 each
Nov. 21	15,500 units	@	$52 each

The company uses a periodic inventory system. On December 31, 2011, a physical count disclosed that 16,500 units of Product B remained in inventory.

Check figures:
2. COGS
a. $2,604,000
b. $2,469,420

Required

1. Prepare a calculation showing the number and total cost of the units available for sale during the year.
2. Prepare calculations showing the amounts that should be assigned to the ending inventory and to cost of goods sold assuming:
   a. FIFO
   b. Weighted average cost basis (round the average unit cost to two decimal places).

An asterisk (*) identifies assignment material based on Appendix 7A or Appendix 7B.

Analytical and Review Problem

A & R Problem 7-1

The records of Thomas Company as of December 31, 2011, show the following:

	Net Purchases	Net Income	Accounts Payable	Inventory
Balance per company's books	$329,000	$22,100	$29,200	$20,500
(a)				
(b)				
(c)				
(d)				
(e)				
Correct balances				

The accountant of Thomas Company discovers in the first week of January 2012 that the following errors were made by his staff.

a. Goods costing $4,500 were in transit (FOB shipping point) and were not included in the ending inventory. The invoice had been received and the purchase recorded.

b. Damaged goods (cost $4,100) that were being held for return to the supplier were included in inventory. The goods had been recorded as a purchase and the entry for the return of these goods had also been made.

c. Inventory items costing $3,900 were incorrectly excluded from the final inventory. These goods had not been recorded as a purchase and had not been paid for by the company.

d. Goods that were shipped FOB destination had not yet arrived and were not included in inventory. However, the invoice had arrived on December 30, 2011, and the purchase for $2,700 was recorded.

e. Goods that cost $2,400 were segregated and not included in inventory because a customer expressed an intention to buy the goods. The sale of the goods for $4,200 had been recorded in December 2011.

Required

Using the format provided above, show the correct amount for net purchases, net income, accounts payable, and inventory for Thomas Company as at December 31, 2011.

Ethics Challenge

EC 7-1

Diversion Inc. is a retail sports store carrying primarily women's golf apparel and equipment. The store is at the end of its second year of operations and, as new businesses often do, is struggling a bit to be profitable. The cost of inventory items has increased just in the short time the store has been in business. In the first year of operations the store accounted for inventory costs using the moving weighted average method. A loan agreement the store has with Dollar Bank, its prime source of financing, requires that the store maintain a certain gross profit and current ratio. The store's owner, Cindy Foor, is looking over Diversion's annual financial statements after year-end inventory has been taken. The numbers are not very favourable and the only way the store can meet the required financial ratios agreed upon with the bank is to change from the moving weighted average to the FIFO method of inventory. Cindy originally decided upon moving weighted average for inventory costing because she felt that moving weighted average yielded a better matching of costs to revenues. Cindy recalculates the ending inventory using FIFO and submits her income statement and balance sheet to the loan officer at the bank for the required bank review of the loan. As Cindy mails the financial statements to the bank, she thankfully reflects on the latitude she has as manager in choosing an inventory costing method.

Required

1. Why does Diversion's use of FIFO improve the gross profit and current ratio?
Note: See page 354 to review the gross profit ratio and page 217 to review the current ratio.

2. Is the action by Diversion's owner ethical?

Focus on Financial Statements

The owner of Fardan Stereo Sales showed the following adjusted trial balance at December 31, 2011: **FFS 7-1**

Account	Account Balance*
Cash	16,000
Accounts receivable	27,000
Merchandise inventory	?
Prepaid rent	36,000
Store fixtures	117,000
Accumulated depreciation, store fixtures	82,000
Trademark	3,000
Accounts payable	18,000
Unearned sales revenue	4,000
Notes payable, due in 2014	22,000
Mikel Fardan, capital	57,000
Mikel Fardan, withdrawals	44,000
Sales	449,000
Sales discounts	6,000
Cost of goods sold	?
Delivery expense	5,000
Rent expense	92,000
Salaries expense	109,000
Interest expense	2,000
Depreciation expense	8,000

*Assume normal account balances.

The owner, Mikel Fardan, is analyzing the effect of the various merchandise inventory costing methods on his financial statements and has prepared the following schedule:

	FIFO	Moving Weighted Average
Merchandise inventory, December 31, 2010	11,000	11,000
Purchases	156,000	156,000
Merchandise inventory, December 31, 2011	?	?
Cost of goods sold	148,000	143,000

Required

1. Calculate the merchandise inventory values at December 31, 2011, under each inventory costing method shown in the schedule above.

2. Prepare a single-step income statement (showing one line each for net sales, cost of goods sold, operating expenses, and interest expense) for the year ended December 31, 2011, along with a balance sheet at December 31, 2011, assuming:

a. FIFO

b. Moving weighted average.

Check figures:
2a. Net income = $79,000
2b. Net income = $84,000

Analysis component:

3. Does the schedule above reflect rising costs for merchandise inventory or falling costs? Explain how you know.

4. Based on your results in Part 2, which method should the owner use if he wants to:

a. Maximize net income?

b. Maximize assets?

FFS 7-2

Required

Answer the following questions.

a. Refer to the balance sheets for Danier and WestJet on pages I-4 and I-26, respectively, in Appendix I at the end of the textbook. Both balance sheets include *Inventory*. Explain how *Inventory* is unique for each of these companies.

b. What method does Danier use to value its inventory? (Refer to the notes to Danier's financial statements on pages I-7 to I-21 of Appendix I at the end of the textbook.)

c. *Inventory* is classified on Danier's balance sheet as what type of asset?

d. Did the balance in inventory for Danier increase or decrease from June 30, 2007, to June 28, 2008?

Critical Thinking Mini Case

The former CEO of Benton Beverages retired and you have been hired in her place. In reviewing the selected financial data shown below, you are puzzled given that industry information clearly shows that the cost of beverages has been on the rise. As you walk about the warehouse area for the first time, you observe that, as pallets of beverages are being moved to the loading dock, empty areas appear behind various rows. You question the forklift driver, who says that the CEO told him always to leave alternating empty rows when stacking pallets. You climb a ladder to get a better view of the inventory layout, gasp, climb down, and determine that an emergency report to the board of directors is required.

	Years Ended December 31,							
	2011		2010		2009		2008	
Sales	$900,000	100%	$750,000	100%	$690,000	100%	$640,000	100%
Cost of goods sold...	459,000	51%	390,000	52%	372,600	54%	352,000	55%

Merchandise Inventory		Merchandise Inventory		Merchandise Inventory		Merchandise Inventory	
85,000[1]		73,000[1]		63,000[1]		45,000[1]	
345,000[2]	396,000[3]	306,000[2]	342,000[3]	312,600[2]	337,600[3]	330,000[2]	332,000[3]
63,000[4]		48,000[4]		35,000[4]		20,000[4]	
97,000[5]		85,000[5]		73,000[5]		63,000[5]	

1. Beginning inventory
2. Purchases during the period
3. Cost of goods sold
4. Year-end adjusting entry
5. Ending inventory

Required

Incorporating the elements of critical thinking on the inside front cover, comment.

CHAPTER 8

Accounting Information Systems

learning objectives

LO1 Explain the relationship of the accounting information system (AIS) to the management information system (MIS) and identify the components of an AIS.

LO2 Explain the goals and uses of special journals.

LO3 Describe the use of controlling accounts and subledgers.

LO4 Journalize and post transactions using special journals.

*APPENDIX 8A

LO5 Journalize and post transactions using special journals in a periodic inventory system.

What's the Score?

After receiving his administrative management diploma, Greg Timko was excited about getting his first job at Canadian Tire as a product relations officer. He had to hit the ground running, and immediately realized that he had a lot to learn. "I hit the wall on my first day. I remember having to deal with the harsh reality that I should have paid better attention in accounting class; I was so unprepared for some important aspects of my new job. The first situation I had to deal with was a floor manager asking how many units of a particular product were in stock and what the credit status of the customer making the request was. I would never have guessed that I would be accessing the company's accounting information system on a regular basis. Back then, I thought that only accountants did that kind of thing."

Greg found that, in order to deal with issues, he would need to search the accounting database for things like product costs, product arrival dates, quantities on hand and in which store they were located, historical sales data to predict seasonal trends and resulting ordering requirements, and customer returns to analyze product quality and assess suppliers. "I still work for Canadian Tire but now I'm a purchasing agent, which means that I'm constantly reviewing purchases, payments, and sales information. It took a real job to convince me that, regardless of what position you hold in the business world, you are going to be retrieving and analyzing information from the accounting information system. To do that, you need to understand journals and especially subledgers."

CRITICAL THINKING CHALLENGE

Where in the accounting information system would Greg have looked to find how many units of a particular product were on hand? What about to find out the balance in a customer's account? What role do you think a purchasing agent for Canadian Tire might play?

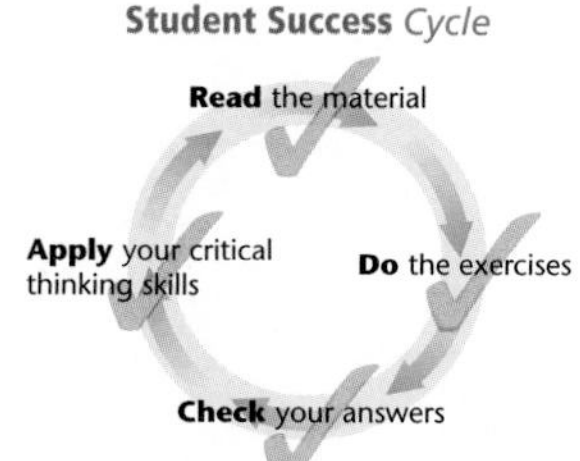

chapter preview

An organization collects and processes a wide range of information. The accounting information system is part of a larger system, the management information system. Accounting information systems must be efficient and effective in meeting the demands of the increasing complexity and volume of financial transactions. In this chapter, we take a brief look at where the accounting information system is positioned in the organization's total information system and how it is structured. We learn about fundamental standards guiding information systems, and we study components of these systems. We also explain procedures that use special journals and subsidiary ledgers to make accounting information systems more efficient. Our understanding of where the details of accounting reports come from makes us better decision makers when using financial information, and it improves our ability to analyze and interpret financial statements. Like Greg Timko says in the opening article, knowledge of these topics helps in running a company successfully.

Information Systems

Management Information Systems

LO1 Explain the relationship of the accounting information system (AIS) to the management information system (MIS) and identify the components of an AIS.

A **management information system (MIS)** is designed to collect and process data within an organization for the purpose of providing users with information. Within the MIS are subsystems: sales and marketing, production, finance, human resources, and accounting. These subsystems and their relationship to the MIS[1] and external and internal users PP. 7/8 are shown in Exhibit 8.1. The arrows illustrate the exchange of information. Notice that each subsystem is both a user and a provider of information.

Exhibit 8.1

Accounting Information System in Relation to Other Information Systems

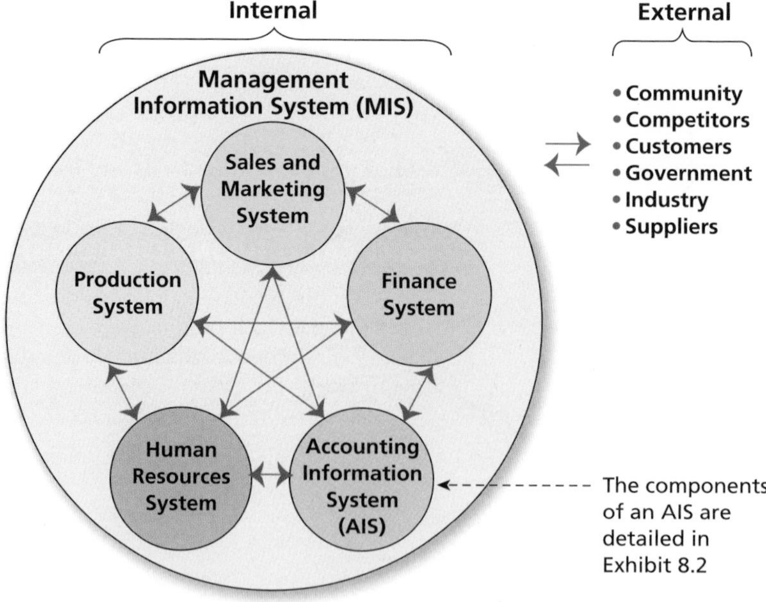

[1] There is discussion as to whether the accounting information system is a subsystem of the MIS or whether the two systems simply overlap. That discussion is beyond the scope of this textbook. Therefore, for the sake of brevity, the position taken here will be that the accounting information system is a subsystem of the MIS.

Accounting Information Systems

An **accounting information system (AIS)** is a group of components that collect and process raw *financial* data into timely, accurate, relevant, and cost-effective information to meet the purposes of internal and external users. The primary components within an AIS are Accounts Payable, Accounts Receivable, and Payroll. Specialty components, such as Property, Plant and Equipment Assets, are often added dependent on the needs of the business. Exhibit 8.2 illustrates these components within the AIS.

Exhibit 8.2

Components of an AIS

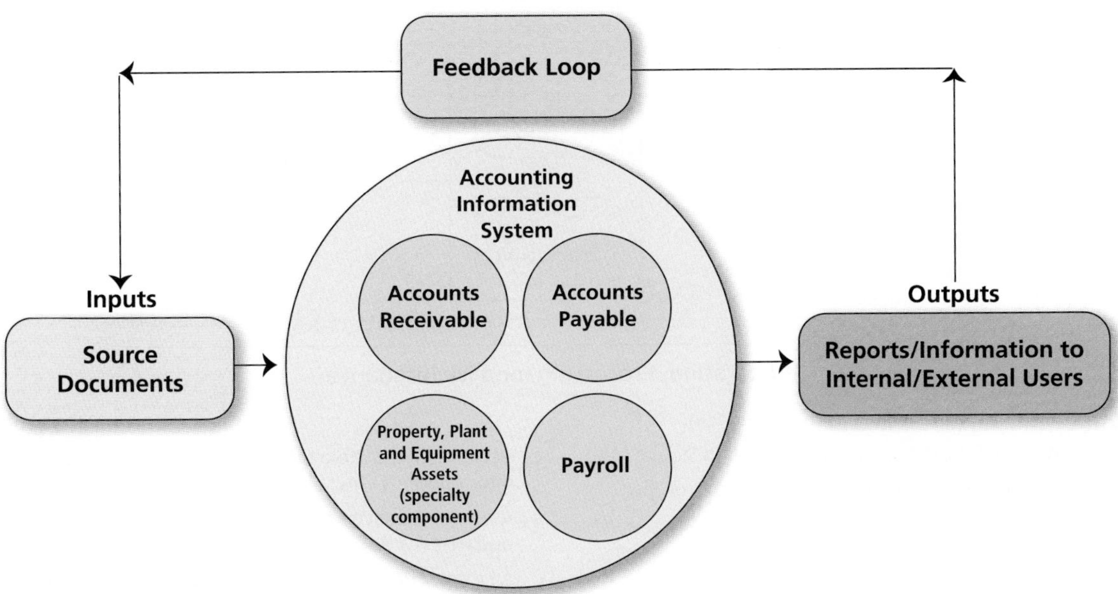

Other components of an AIS include people, data (inputs), software (accounting programs), hardware (computers), and reports (outputs).

Structure of an AIS

How the AIS is structured depends on the requirements of the users. A bank will have different needs than a restaurant or a steel manufacturer; however, the basic structure is similar for any AIS.

The journals and the accounts in the General Ledger form the foundation of the process that produces user reports. The General Ledger system represents the primary database. Because the journal is the book of original entry, it serves as a check to the entries posted in the General Ledger accounts. The accounting components used for operating and financial controls are developed based on the journal and General Ledger systems. For example, the component used for accounts receivable control is related to sales and cash receipts.

Exhibit 8.3 shows the basic structural relationships. The sale of inventory (1) decreases inventory (requiring purchases to replenish stock), and (2) when on credit, creates accounts receivable and initiates the billing process. Accounts receivable are collected (cash receipts) and inventory purchases on account need to be paid (payment of accounts payable). These transactions, plus payroll activity, are posted into the General Ledger.

Exhibit 8.3

Accounting Information System Processing Cycle

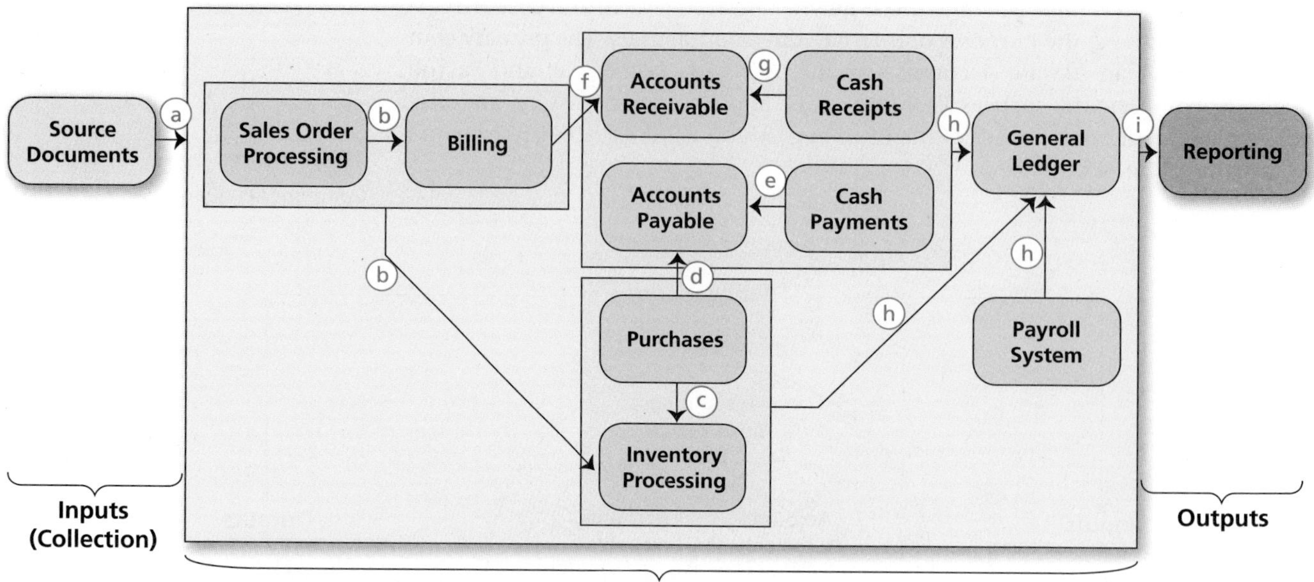

Explanation (not necessarily performed in this sequence):

(a) Source documents enter the Accounting Information System (AIS)

(b) Sales information is used to update records for both billing (Dr Accounts Receivable) and merchandise inventory (Cr Merchandise Inventory)

(c) Purchases are made based on sales information to maintain appropriate levels (Dr Merchandise Inventory)

(d) Purchases information is used to update Accounts Payable (Cr Accounts Payable)

(e) Purchases are paid when due and Accounts Payable is updated (Dr Accounts Payable)

(f) Accounts Receivable records are updated based on sales information (Dr Accounts Receivable)

(g) As cash is received from customers, Accounts Receivable is updated (Cr Accounts Receivable)

(h) All transactions are posted into the General Ledger, including payroll transactions

(i) The AIS generates financial statements at the end of the accounting period in addition to special purpose reports created as needed

Source documents P. 34 provide the basic information processed by an accounting system. Examples are bank statements, cheques received for deposit, invoices from suppliers, billings to customers, and employee earnings records, to name a few. Source documents are often paper-based, but they are increasingly taking electronic form, such as those created by consumers using debit cards in lieu of cash to pay for goods purchased.

Computer hardware is the physical equipment in a computerized system. **Computer software** is the programs that direct the operations of computer hardware. QuickBooks® and Simply Accounting® are examples of accounting software used for small to medium-sized businesses. **Enterprise-application software** (such as SAP® and Oracle®) is an integrated program that manages a company's vital operations from order-taking to manufacturing to accounting, and is commonly used by companies around the world.

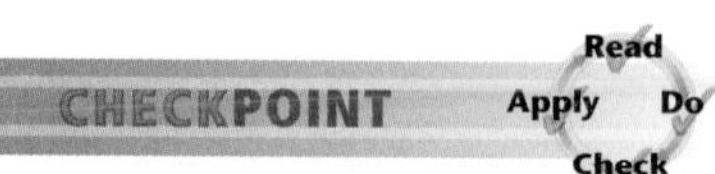

1. Explain the difference between an MIS and an AIS.
2. Name the four basic components of an AIS.

Do Quick Study questions: QS 8-1, QS 8-2

Public Accountant

You are a public accountant consulting with a client. This client's business has grown to the point where the accounting system must be updated to handle both the volume of transactions and management's information needs. Your client requests your advice in purchasing new software for the accounting system. You have been offered a 10% commission by a software company for each purchase of its system by one of your clients. Do you think your evaluation of software alternatives is affected by this commission arrangement? Do you think this commission arrangement is appropriate? Do you tell your client about the commission arrangement before making a recommendation?

Answer—p. 409

Special Journals in Accounting

LO2 | Explain the goals and uses of special journals.

This section focuses on the underlying operations of accounting systems: *special journals* and *subsidiary ledgers* (commonly referred to as *subledgers*). These operations are set up to be efficient in processing transactions and are done almost exclusively using technology. ***The manual approach described in this section has the advantage of clearly illustrating how accounting information moves through a computerized environment. If we do not understand how the information enters and is processed through a computerized system, how can we fully understand the information it creates?***

This section uses selected transactions of Outdoors Unlimited to illustrate special journals and subledgers. Since Outdoors Unlimited uses a *perpetual inventory* system P. 256, the special journals are set up using this system. The special journals in a *periodic* inventory system P. 256 are shown in Appendix 8A.

Basics of Special Journals—Perpetual Inventory System

A General Journal is an all-purpose journal where we can record any transaction. A **special journal** is used in recording and posting transactions of similar type. Most transactions of a merchandiser, for instance, fall into four groups: sales on credit, purchases on credit, cash receipts, and cash disbursements. Exhibit 8.4 shows the special journals for these groups. This section assumes the use of these special journals along with the General Journal.

Sales Journal	Cash Receipts Journal	Purchases Journal	Cash Disbursements Journal	General Journal
For recording credit sales	For recording cash receipts	For recording credit purchases	For recording cash payments	For transactions not in special journals

Exhibit 8.4

Using Special Journals With a General Journal

The General Journal continues to be used for transactions not covered by special journals and for adjusting, closing, and correcting entries.

Subledgers

LO3 | Describe the use of controlling accounts and subledgers.

Accounting information systems must provide several detailed listings of amounts. One of the most important listings is the amounts due from customers, called *accounts receivable*, and amounts owed to creditors, called *accounts payable*. The Accounts Receivable account in the General Ledger (also known as Accounts Receivable Control) shows the total accounts receivable but it is difficult to get information regarding a particular customer. To collect this information we often create a separate ledger called a *subledger* (*subsidiary ledger*).

A **subledger** (or **subsidiary ledger**) is a listing of individual accounts with a common characteristic. Using subledgers removes unnecessary details from the General Ledger. Two common subledgers are:

- **Accounts Receivable Subledger** for storing transaction data with individual customers.
- **Accounts Payable Subledger** for storing transaction data with individual creditors.

Accounts Receivable Subledger

When we recorded credit sales in prior transaction analysis, we debited Accounts Receivable. Yet when a company has more than one credit customer, the accounts receivable records must show how much *each* customer purchased, paid, and still owes. This information is collected by keeping a separate account receivable for each customer in a subledger called the Accounts Receivable Subledger.

The General Ledger continues to keep a single Accounts Receivable account, called the **controlling account** because it is a summary of the *Accounts Receivable Subledger*. Like a General Ledger, a subledger can exist in electronic or paper form. Customer accounts in a subledger are kept separate from the Accounts Receivable account in the General Ledger.

Exhibit 8.5 shows the relation between the Accounts Receivable controlling account and its related accounts in the subledger. After all items are posted, the Accounts Receivable controlling account must equal the sum of balances in the customers' accounts in the Accounts Receivable Subledger.

Exhibit 8.5

Accounts Receivable Controlling Account and Subledger

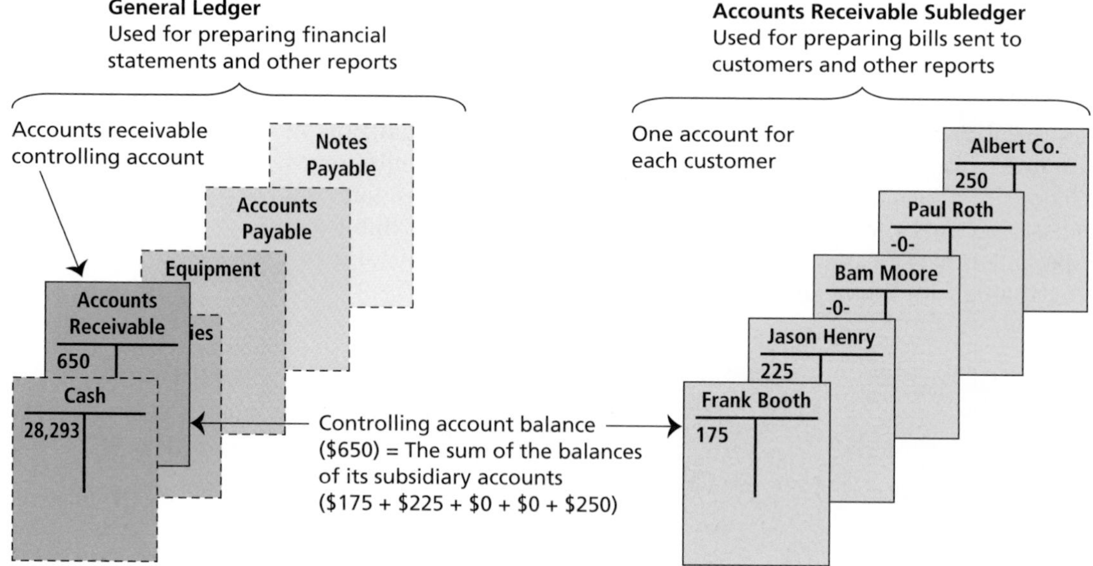

Accounts Payable Subledger

There are other controlling accounts and subledgers. We know, for example, that many companies buy on credit from several suppliers. This means a company must keep a separate account for each creditor by keeping an Accounts Payable controlling account in the General Ledger and a separate account for each creditor in an Accounts Payable Subledger.

Inventory Subledger

Merchandisers often have more than one type of item in inventory. Canadian Tire, for example, stocks thousands of different items from teapots to tents to tires. To manage such extensive stocks of inventory, companies using a perpetual inventory system record transactions affecting each type of inventory in a separate record. This group of individual inventory records makes up the *Inventory Subledger*. By keeping inventory information in separate records, detailed information about quantity, for example, is readily available. Exhibit 8.6 illustrates a typical Inventory Subledger record. This subledger is based on a FIFO P. 340 cost flow assumption.

Exhibit 8.6

Inventory Subledger Record

Item: Leather Sports Bags — Location code: W18C2

Catalogue No.: LSB-117 — Units: Maximum 25 Minimum 5

Date	PR	Purchases Units	Purchases Unit Cost	Purchases Total Cost	Sales (at cost) Units	Sales (at cost) Unit Cost	Sales (at cost) Total Cost	Balance Total Units	Balance Unit Cost	Balance Total Cost
2011 Aug. 1								10	$100	$1,000
12	S2				4	$100	$400	6	100	600
								6	100	
18	P3	20	$110	$2,200				20	110	2,800
30	S2				6	100	600			
					2	110	220	18	110	1,980
Totals		20		$2,200	12		$1,220			

Reitmans (Canada) Limited showed inventory on its January 31, 2009, balance sheet of $64 million. The $64 million is the balance in the Inventory account in the General Ledger and represents the total of the hundreds of individual inventory records in the Inventory Subledger. The total in the General Ledger is known as the controlling account. The balance of the Inventory controlling account must agree with the sum of the balances of the inventory records in the Inventory Subledger.

Other Subledgers

Subledgers are also common for several other accounts. A company with many items of equipment, for example, might keep only one Equipment account in its General Ledger. But this company's Equipment account would control a subledger in which each item of equipment is recorded in a separate account. Similar treatment is common with investments and other large accounts needing separate detailed records.

The Toronto-Dominion Bank (TD), one of the largest banks in Canada, reports in note 30 of its 2008 annual report (and shown in Exhibit 8.7) detailed sales informa-

Exhibit 8.7

Toronto-Dominion Bank's Results by Geography

(millions of Canadian dollars)	Total revenue	Income before provision for income taxes, non-controlling interests, net of tax and equity in net income of associated company	Net income	Total assets
2008				
Canada	$10,770	$3,186	$2,486	$352,418
United States	2,925	216	487	154,418
Other international	974	702	860	56,378
Total	$14,669	$4,104	$3,833	$563,214
2007				
Canada	$10,619	$2,992	$2,314	$275,931
United States	2,370	648	710	79,951
Other international	1,292	1,021	973	66,242
Total	$14,281	$4,661	$3,997	$422,124
2006				
Canada	$ 9,721	$2,423	$1,802	$255,317
United States	2,564	2,538	2,182	83,059
Other international	907	566	619	54,538
Total	$13,192	$5,527	$4,603	$392,914

tion by geographic area, which includes Canada, the United States, and Other International. Yet TD's accounting system most certainly keeps more detailed sales records than reflected in its annual report. TD, for instance, sells hundreds of different products and is likely able to analyze the sales performance of each one of them. This detail can be captured by many different General Ledger sales accounts. But it is likely captured by using supplementary records that function like subledgers. The concept of a subledger can be applied in many different ways to ensure that our accounting system captures sufficient details to support analyses that decision makers need.

3. When special journals are used, where are all cash payments by cheque recorded?

Do Quick Study questions: QS 8-3, QS 8-4, QS 8-5, QS 8-6

mid-chapter demonstration problem

Indicate in which journal each of the following transactions should be recorded. Also, assuming three subledgers are maintained—Accounts Receivable, Accounts Payable, and Merchandise Inventory—identify which subledger(s) if any would be affected by each transaction.

a. Purchase of office supplies for cash.
b. Sale of merchandise on account.
c. Entry to record depreciation expense for the period.
d. Purchase of merchandise on account.
e. Sale of old equipment for cash.
f. Collection of the amount of the sale in (b).

solution

a. Cash Disbursements Journal; no subledger
b. Sales Journal; both the Accounts Receivable and Merchandise Inventory Subledgers
c. General Journal; no subledger
d. Purchases Journal; both the Accounts Payable and Merchandise Inventory Subledgers
e. Cash Receipts Journal; no subledger
f. Cash Receipts Journal; Accounts Receivable Subledger

LO4 Journalize and post transactions using special journals.

The next sections demonstrate the four common special journals: Sales, Cash Receipts, Purchases, and Cash Disbursements. While all of the transactions take place during the month of February, you will note that some of the General Ledger accounts have opening balances as of January 31. These balances are included for demonstration purposes only and to provide some continuity, where necessary. For simplicity, it has been assumed that the Accounts Receivable and Accounts Payable balances are zero at the beginning of February.

Sales Journal

A **Sales Journal** is used to record sales of merchandise on credit. Sales of merchandise for cash are not recorded in a Sales Journal, but instead are recorded in a

Cash Receipts Journal. Sales of nonmerchandise assets on credit are recorded in the General Journal.

Journalizing

Credit sale transactions are recorded with information about each sale entered separately in a Sales Journal. This information is often taken from a copy of the sales ticket or invoice prepared at the time of sale. The top of Exhibit 8.8 shows a Sales Journal from a sporting goods merchandiser, Outdoors Unlimited. The Sales Journal in this exhibit is called a **columnar journal** because it has more than one column for recording the date, customer's name, invoice number, amount of each credit sale, and cost of the merchandise sold.[2]

Exhibit 8.8

Sales Journal With Posting

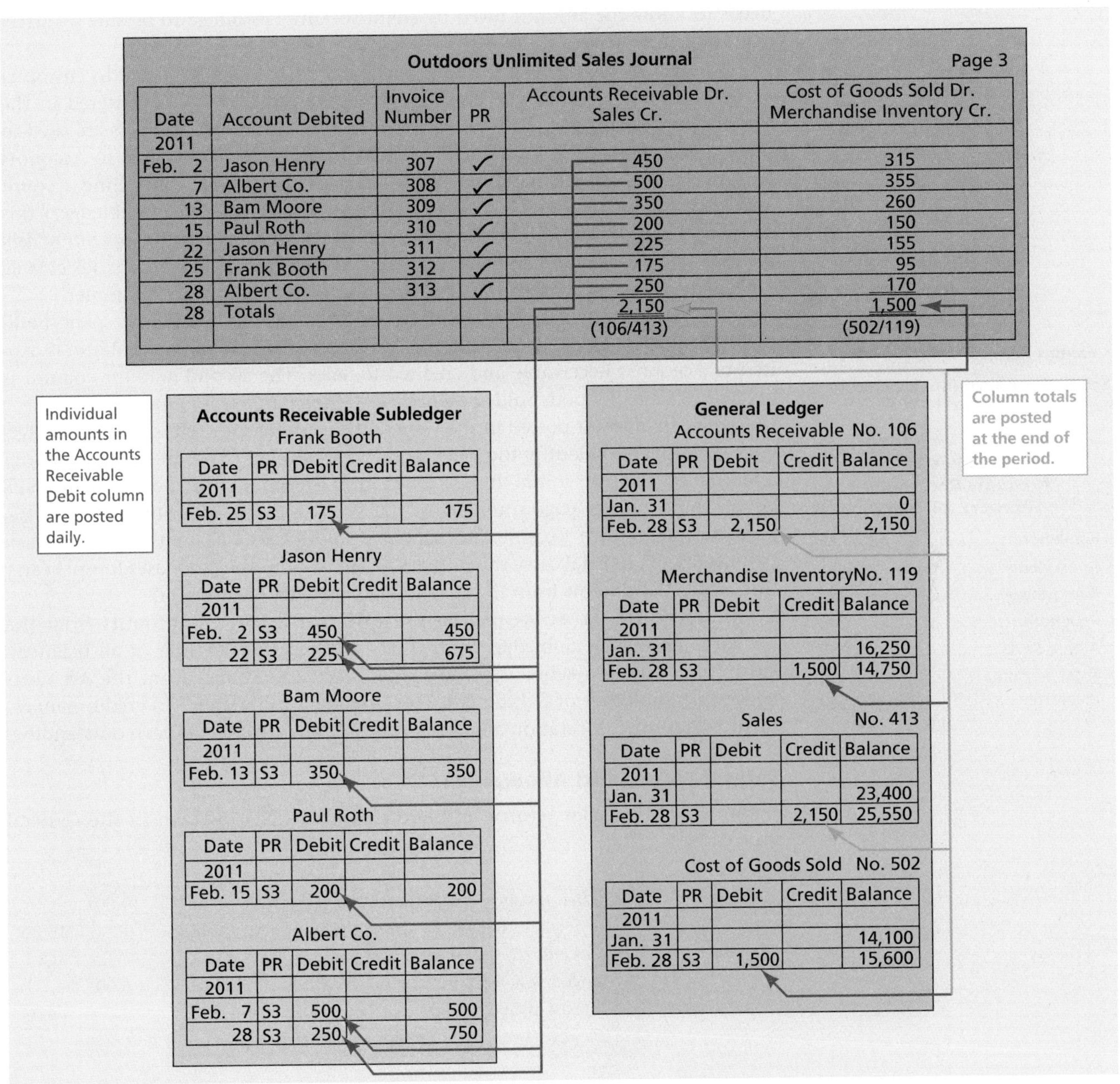

Outdoors Unlimited Sales Journal — Page 3

Date	Account Debited	Invoice Number	PR	Accounts Receivable Dr. Sales Cr.	Cost of Goods Sold Dr. Merchandise Inventory Cr.
2011					
Feb. 2	Jason Henry	307	✓	450	315
7	Albert Co.	308	✓	500	355
13	Bam Moore	309	✓	350	260
15	Paul Roth	310	✓	200	150
22	Jason Henry	311	✓	225	155
25	Frank Booth	312	✓	175	95
28	Albert Co.	313	✓	250	170
28	Totals			2,150	1,500
				(106/413)	(502/119)

Accounts Receivable Subledger

Frank Booth

Date	PR	Debit	Credit	Balance
2011				
Feb. 25	S3	175		175

Jason Henry

Date	PR	Debit	Credit	Balance
2011				
Feb. 2	S3	450		450
22	S3	225		675

Bam Moore

Date	PR	Debit	Credit	Balance
2011				
Feb. 13	S3	350		350

Paul Roth

Date	PR	Debit	Credit	Balance
2011				
Feb. 15	S3	200		200

Albert Co.

Date	PR	Debit	Credit	Balance
2011				
Feb. 7	S3	500		500
28	S3	250		750

General Ledger

Accounts Receivable No. 106

Date	PR	Debit	Credit	Balance
2011				
Jan. 31				0
Feb. 28	S3	2,150		2,150

Merchandise InventoryNo. 119

Date	PR	Debit	Credit	Balance
2011				
Jan. 31				16,250
Feb. 28	S3		1,500	14,750

Sales No. 413

Date	PR	Debit	Credit	Balance
2011				
Jan. 31				23,400
Feb. 28	S3		2,150	25,550

Cost of Goods Sold No. 502

Date	PR	Debit	Credit	Balance
2011				
Jan. 31				14,100
Feb. 28	S3	1,500		15,600

[2] We do not record explanations in any of our special journals for brevity purposes.

Each transaction results in a debit to Accounts Receivable and a credit to Sales, and a debit to Cost of Goods Sold and a credit to Merchandise Inventory. We only need two columns for these four accounts. More columns can be added to include information about taxes, returns, departments, and other details of transactions described later in this section. The Posting Reference (PR) column is *not* used until posting is completed.

Posting

A Sales Journal is posted as shown by following the arrows in Exhibit 8.8. Individual transactions in the Sales Journal are typically posted each day to customer accounts in the Accounts Receivable Subledger to keep customer accounts up to date. This is important for the person granting credit to customers, who needs to know the amount owed by credit-seeking customers to be sure a correct decision can be made.

When sales recorded in the Sales Journal are individually posted to customer accounts in the Accounts Receivable Subledger, check marks are entered in the Sales Journal's Posting Reference column. Customer account numbers are used in place of check marks if available. Note that when debits (or credits) to Accounts Receivable are posted twice (once to the Accounts Receivable controlling account and once to the customer's account in the Accounts Receivable Subledger) this does not violate the accounting equation of debits equal credits. *The equality of debits and credits is always maintained in the General Ledger.* The Accounts Receivable Subledger is a duplicate record with detailed information for each customer.

The Sales Journal's *amount* columns are totalled at the end of the period and posted to the General Ledger accounts. The total of the first amount column is debited to Accounts Receivable and credited to Sales. The second amount column is debited to Cost of Goods Sold and credited to Merchandise Inventory.

For each amount posted in the General Ledger and subledgers, a posting reference is included to identify the journal and page number of the source. We identify a journal by using an initial. Items posted from the Sales Journal carry the initial *S* before their journal page numbers in the Posting Reference columns. Likewise, items from the Cash Receipts Journal carry the initials *CR*, items from the Cash Disbursements Journal carry the initials *CD*, items from the Purchases Journal carry the initial *P*, and items from the General Journal carry the initial *G*.

A **schedule of accounts receivable** is a listing of accounts from the Accounts Receivable Subledger with their balances and the sum of all balances. Exhibit 8.9 shows a schedule of accounts receivable drawn from the Accounts Receivable Subledger of Exhibit 8.8. The schedule can be useful in credit management by adding information about the time each receivable has been outstanding.

Exhibit 8.9

Schedule of Accounts Receivable

Outdoors Unlimited
Schedule of Accounts Receivable
February 28, 2011

Frank Booth	$ 175
Jason Henry	675
Bam Moore	350
Paul Roth	200
Albert Co.	750
Total accounts receivable	$2,150

Sales Returns and Allowances

A company with sales returns and allowances can record them in the General Journal as:

Mar.	7	Sales Returns and Allowances	414	10.00	
		Accounts Receivable—Robert Moore	106/✓		10.00
		Customer returned merchandise.			
	7	Merchandise Inventory	119	6.00	
		Cost of Goods Sold	502		6.00
		The merchandise was returned to inventory.			

The debit in this entry is posted to the Sales Returns and Allowances account. The credit is posted both to the Accounts Receivable controlling account and to the customer's account in the subledger (posted daily). We also include the account number and the check mark, 106/✓, in the PR column on the credit line. This means both the Accounts Receivable controlling account in the General Ledger and the Robert Moore account in the Accounts Receivable Subledger are credited for $10.00. Both are credited because the balance of the controlling account in the General Ledger does not equal the sum of the customer account balances in the subledger unless *both* are credited.

4. How do debits and credits remain equal when credit sales to customers are posted twice (once to the Accounts Receivable controlling account and once to the customer's account in the subledger)?
5. How do we identify the journal from which an amount in a ledger account was posted?

Do Quick Study question: QS 8-7

Cash Receipts Journal

A **Cash Receipts Journal** records *all* receipts of cash. A Cash Receipts Journal must be a columnar journal because different accounts are credited when cash is received from different sources.

Journalizing

Cash receipts usually fall into one of three groups: (1) cash from credit customers in payment of their accounts, (2) cash from cash sales, and (3) cash from other sources. The Cash Receipts Journal in Exhibit 8.10 has a special column for credits when cash is received from one or more of these three sources.

Cash From Credit Customers

To record cash received in payment of a customer's account, the customer's name is first entered in the Cash Receipts Journal's Accounts Credited column. Then the amounts debited to Cash and Sales Discounts, if any, are entered in their respective journal columns, and the amount credited to the customer's account is entered in the Accounts Receivable Credit column. Note that the Accounts Receivable Credit column contains only credits to customer accounts.

To post, individual amounts are posted daily to subledger accounts. Column totals are posted at the end of the period to General Ledger accounts.

Cash Sales

When cash sales are collected and totalled at the end of a day, the daily total is recorded in the Cash Receipts Journal with a debit to Cash and a credit to Sales.[3] At the same time, the cost of sales is accumulated and recorded as a debit to Cost of Goods Sold and a credit to Merchandise Inventory. Cash sales are journalized weekly in Exhibit 8.10 for brevity. By using a separate Sales Credit column, we can post the total cash sales for a month as a single amount, the column total.

[3] Remember that in practice under a perpetual system these cash sales are recorded at the point of sale. To do that here would make this journal extremely lengthy since Outdoors Unlimited is a retailer with many cash sales every day.

Exhibit 8.10

Cash Receipts Journal With Posting

Outdoors Unlimited Cash Receipts Journal

Page 2

Date	Accounts Credited	PR	Explanation	Cash Dr.	Sales Discount Dr.	Accounts Receivable Cr.	Sales Cr.	Other Accounts Cr.	Cost of Goods Sold Dr. Merchandise Inventory Cr.
2011									
Feb. 7	Sales		Cash sales	4,450			4,450		3,150
12	Jason Henry	✓	Invoice, Feb. 2	441	9	450			
14	Sales		Cash sales	3,925			3,925		2,950
17	Albert Co.	✓	Invoice, Feb. 7	490	10	500			
20	Notes Payable	245	Note to bank	750				750	
21	Sales		Cash sales	4,700			4,700		3,400
22	Interest Revenue	409	Bank account	250				250	
23	Bam Moore	✓	Invoice, Feb. 13	343	7	350			
25	Paul Roth	✓	Invoice, Feb. 15	196	4	200			
28	Sales		Cash sales	4,225			4,225		3,050
28	Totals			19,770	30	1,500	17,300	1,000	12,550
				(101)	(415)	(106)	(413)	(X)	(502/119)

Accounts Receivable Subledger

Frank Booth

Date	PR	Debit	Credit	Balance
2011				
Feb. 25	S3	175		175

Jason Henry

Date	PR	Debit	Credit	Balance
2011				
Feb. 2	S3	450		450
12	CR2		450	-0-
22	S3	225		225

Bam Moore

Date	PR	Debit	Credit	Balance
2011				
Feb. 13	S3	350		350
23	CR2		350	-0-

Paul Roth

Date	PR	Debit	Credit	Balance
2011				
Feb. 15	S3	200		200
25	CR2		200	-0-

Albert Co.

Date	PR	Debit	Credit	Balance
2011				
Feb. 7	S3	500		500
17	CR2		500	-0-
28	S3	250		250

Individual amounts in the Accounts Receivable Credit and Other Accounts Credit columns are posted daily.

General Ledger

Cash No. 101

Date	PR	Debit	Credit	Balance
2011				
Jan. 31				9,450
Feb. 28	CR2	19,770		29,220

Accounts Receivable No. 106

Date	PR	Debit	Credit	Balance
2011				
Jan. 31				-0-
Feb. 28	S3	2,150		2,150
28	CR2		1,500	650

Merchandise Inventory No. 119

Date	PR	Debit	Credit	Balance
2011				
Jan. 31				16,250
Feb. 28	S3		1,500	14,750
28	CR2		12,550	2,200

Notes Payable No. 245

Date	PR	Debit	Credit	Balance
2011				
Jan. 31				-0-
Feb. 20	CR2		750	750

Sales No. 413

Date	PR	Debit	Credit	Balance
2011				
Jan. 31				23,400
Feb. 28	S3		2,150	25,550
28	CR2		17,300	42,850

Sales Discounts No. 415

Date	PR	Debit	Credit	Balance
2011				
Jan. 31				35
Feb. 28	CR2	30		65

Interest Revenue No. 409

Date	PR	Debit	Credit	Balance
2011				
Jan. 31				260
Feb. 22	CR2		250	510

Cost of Goods Sold No. 502

Date	PR	Debit	Credit	Balance
2011				
Jan. 31				14,100
Feb. 28	S3	1,500		15,600
28	CR2	12,550		28,150

Column totals except for Other Accounts columns are posted at the end of the period.

The total of the Cost of Goods Sold and Merchandise Inventory amount column is posted to *both* of their General Ledger accounts at the end of the period.

Cash From Other Sources

Other sources of cash include borrowing money from a bank, interest on account, or selling unneeded assets. The Other Accounts Credit column is for receipts that do not occur often enough to warrant a separate column. This means items entered in this column are posted to a variety of General Ledger accounts. These individual items are posted. Therefore, the total in this column is not posted. The Cash Receipts Journal's PR column is used only for postings from the Other Accounts and Accounts Receivable columns. The account numbers in the PR column refer to items that are posted to General Ledger accounts.

Posting

At the end of a period, the amounts in the Cash, Sales Discounts, Accounts Receivable, Sales, Cost of Goods Sold, and Merchandise Inventory columns of the Cash Receipts Journal are posted as column totals. The transactions recorded in all journals must result in equal debits and credits to General Ledger accounts. To be sure that total debits and credits in a columnar journal are equal, we often *crossfoot* column totals before posting them. To **foot** a column of numbers is to add it. To **crossfoot** we add the debit column totals and the credit column totals and compare the two sums for equality. Footing and crossfooting of the numbers in Exhibit 8.11 are as follows:

Exhibit 8.11

Footing and Crossfooting Journal Amounts

Debit Columns		Credit Columns	
Cash Debit	$19,770	Accounts Receivable Credit	$ 1,500
Cost of Goods Sold Debit	12,550	Sales Credit	17,300
Sales Discounts Debit	30	Other Accounts Credit	1,000
		Inventory Credit	12,550
Total	$32,350	Total	$32,350

After crossfooting the journal to confirm that debits equal credits, we post the totals of all but the Other Accounts column as indicated by their column headings. Because items in the Other Accounts column are posted individually, this column total is not posted. We place an 'X' below the Other Accounts column to indicate that this *column total* is not posted. The account numbers of the accounts where the remaining column totals are posted are in parentheses below each column.

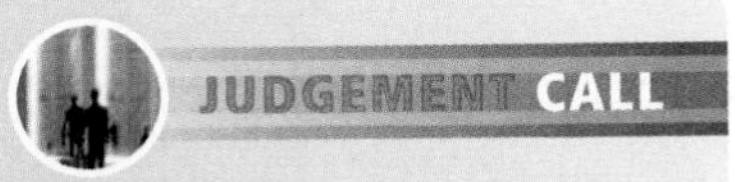

Retailer

You are a retailer in computer equipment and supplies. You want to know how promptly customers are paying their bills. This information can help you in deciding whether to extend credit and in planning your own cash payments. Where might you look for this information?

Answer—p. 409

Purchases Journal

A **Purchases Journal** is used to record *all* purchases on credit. Purchases for cash are recorded in the Cash Disbursements Journal.

Journalizing

A Purchases Journal with one column for dollar amounts can be used to record purchases of merchandise on credit. But a Purchases Journal usually is more useful if it is a multicolumn journal in which all credit purchases, not only merchandise, are recorded. Exhibit 8.12 shows a multicolumn Purchases Journal.

Exhibit 8.12

Purchases Journal With Posting

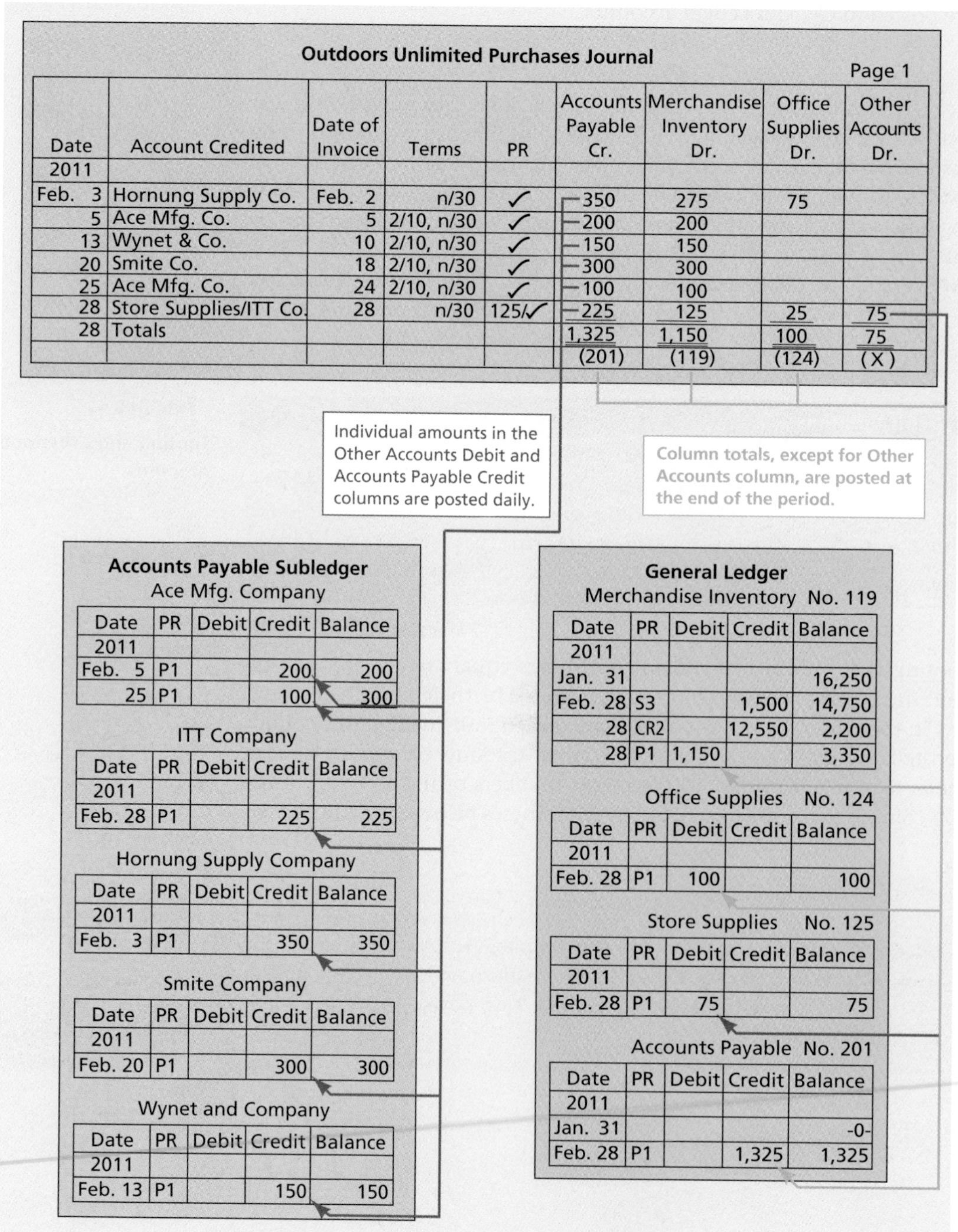

Outdoors Unlimited Purchases Journal Page 1

Date	Account Credited	Date of Invoice	Terms	PR	Accounts Payable Cr.	Merchandise Inventory Dr.	Office Supplies Dr.	Other Accounts Dr.
2011								
Feb. 3	Hornung Supply Co.	Feb. 2	n/30	✓	350	275	75	
5	Ace Mfg. Co.	5	2/10, n/30	✓	200	200		
13	Wynet & Co.	10	2/10, n/30	✓	150	150		
20	Smite Co.	18	2/10, n/30	✓	300	300		
25	Ace Mfg. Co.	24	2/10, n/30	✓	100	100		
28	Store Supplies/ITT Co.	28	n/30	125/✓	225	125	25	75
28	Totals				1,325	1,150	100	75
					(201)	(119)	(124)	(X)

Accounts Payable Subledger

Ace Mfg. Company

Date	PR	Debit	Credit	Balance
2011				
Feb. 5	P1		200	200
25	P1		100	300

ITT Company

Date	PR	Debit	Credit	Balance
2011				
Feb. 28	P1		225	225

Hornung Supply Company

Date	PR	Debit	Credit	Balance
2011				
Feb. 3	P1		350	350

Smite Company

Date	PR	Debit	Credit	Balance
2011				
Feb. 20	P1		300	300

Wynet and Company

Date	PR	Debit	Credit	Balance
2011				
Feb. 13	P1		150	150

General Ledger

Merchandise Inventory No. 119

Date	PR	Debit	Credit	Balance
2011				
Jan. 31				16,250
Feb. 28	S3		1,500	14,750
28	CR2		12,550	2,200
28	P1	1,150		3,350

Office Supplies No. 124

Date	PR	Debit	Credit	Balance
2011				
Feb. 28	P1	100		100

Store Supplies No. 125

Date	PR	Debit	Credit	Balance
2011				
Feb. 28	P1	75		75

Accounts Payable No. 201

Date	PR	Debit	Credit	Balance
2011				
Jan. 31				-0-
Feb. 28	P1		1,325	1,325

Purchase invoices or other source documents are used in recording transactions in the Purchases Journal. Journalizing is similar to the Sales Journal. We use the invoice date and terms to calculate the date when payment for each purchase is due. The Merchandise Inventory Debit column is used for recording merchandise purchases. When a purchase involves an amount recorded in the Other Accounts Debit column, we use the Account column to identify the General Ledger account debited. Outdoors Unlimited also includes a separate column for credit purchases of office supplies. A separate column such as this is useful whenever several transactions involve debits to a specific account. Each company uses its own judgement in deciding on the number of separate columns necessary. The Other Accounts Debit column allows the Purchases Journal to be used for all purchase transactions involving credits to Accounts Payable. The Accounts Payable Credit column is used to record the amounts credited to each creditor's account.

Posting

The amounts in the Accounts Payable Credit column are posted daily to individual creditor accounts in the Accounts Payable Subledger. Individual amounts in the Other Accounts Debit column are posted to their General Ledger accounts. All column totals except the Other Accounts Debit column are posted to their General Ledger accounts. The balance in the Accounts Payable controlling account must equal the sum of the account balances in the Accounts Payable Subledger after posting.

Cash Disbursements Journal

A **Cash Disbursements Journal**, also called a *Cash Payments Journal*, is used to record *all* payments of cash. It is a multicolumn journal because cash payments are made for several different purposes.

Journalizing

A Cash Disbursements Journal is similar to a Cash Receipts Journal except that it has repetitive cash payments instead of receipts. Exhibit 8.13 shows the Cash Disbursements Journal for Outdoors Unlimited. We see repetitive credits to the Cash column of this journal. We also commonly see credits to Merchandise Inventory for purchases discounts and debits to the Accounts Payable account. Many companies purchase merchandise on credit and, therefore, a Merchandise Inventory Debit column is not often needed. Instead, the occasional cash purchase is recorded in the Other Accounts Debit column and Cash Credit column as shown for the February 5 transaction of Exhibit 8.13.

The Cash Disbursements Journal has a column titled Cheque Number (Ch. No.). For control over cash disbursements, all payments except for very small amounts are made by cheque.[4] Cheques should be prenumbered and entered in the journal in numerical order with each cheque's number in the column headed Ch. No. This makes it possible to scan the numbers in the column for omitted cheques. When a Cash Disbursements Journal has a column for cheque numbers, it is sometimes called a **Cheque Register**.

Consistent with the treatment of purchase discounts and transportation-in in Chapter 6 under a perpetual system, Exhibit 8.13 posts these directly to the Merchandise Inventory account.

[4] We describe a system for controlling small cash payments in Chapter 9.

Exhibit 8.13

Cash Disbursements Journal With Posting

Outdoors Unlimited Cash Disbursements Journal

Page 2

Date	Ch. No.	Payee	Account Debited	PR	Cash Cr.	Merchandise Inventory Cr.	Other Accounts Dr.	Accounts Payable Dr.
2011								
Feb. 3	105	L & N Railroad	Inventory re transp-in	119	15		15	
5	106	East Sales Co.	Inventory	119	25		25	
13	107	Ace Mfg. Co.	Ace Mfg. Co.	✓	196	4		200
20	108	Jerry Hale	Salaries Expense	622	250		250	
25	109	Wynet & Co.	Wynet & Co.	✓	147	3		150
28	110	Smite Co.	Smite Co.	✓	294	6		300
28		Totals			927	13	290	650
					(101)	(119)	(X)	(201)

Column totals, except for Other Accounts column, are posted at the end of the period.

Individual amounts in the Other Accounts column and Accounts Payable column are posted daily.

General Ledger

Cash No. 101

Date	PR	Debit	Credit	Balance
2011				
Jan. 31	CR2			9,450
Feb. 28	CR2	19,770		29,220
28	CD2		927	28,293

Merchandise Inventory No. 119

Date	PR	Debit	Credit	Balance
2011				
Jan. 28				16,250
Feb. 3	CD2	15		16,265
5	CD2	25		16,290
28	S3		1,500	14,790
28	CR2		12,550	2,240
28	P1	1,150		3,390
28	CD2		13	3,377

Accounts Payable No. 201

Date	PR	Debit	Credit	Balance
2011				
Jan. 31				-0-
Feb. 28	P1		1,325	1,325
28	CD2	650		675

Salaries Expense No. 622

Date	PR	Debit	Credit	Balance
2011				
Feb. 20	CD2	250		250

Accounts Payable Subledger

Ace Mfg. Company

Date	PR	Debit	Credit	Balance
2011				
Feb. 5	P1		200	200
13	CD2	200		-0-
25	P1		100	100

ITT Company

Date	PR	Debit	Credit	Balance
2011				
Feb. 28	P1		225	225

Hornung Supply Company

Date	PR	Debit	Credit	Balance
2011				
Feb. 3	P1		350	350

Smite Company

Date	PR	Debit	Credit	Balance
2011				
Feb. 20	P1		300	300
28	CD2	300		-0-

Wynet & Company

Date	PR	Debit	Credit	Balance
2011				
Feb. 13	P1		150	150
25	CD2	150		-0-

Posting

Individual amounts in the Accounts Payable Debit column are posted daily to the specific creditors' accounts in the Accounts Payable Subledger. Individual amounts in the Other Accounts Debit column of a Cash Disbursements Journal are posted to their General Ledger accounts. We also crossfoot column totals and post the Accounts Payable Debit column total to the Accounts Payable controlling account. The Merchandise Inventory Credit column total is posted to the Merchandise Inventory account and the Cash Credit column total is posted to the Cash account.

Exhibit 8.14 shows a schedule of accounts payable drawn from the Accounts Payable Subledger of Exhibit 8.13. A **schedule of accounts payable** is a listing of accounts from the Accounts Payable Subledger with their balances and the sum of all balances. This schedule is useful in the management of payables by adding additional information such as when the accounts are due.

Exhibit 8.14

Schedule of Accounts Payable

Outdoors Unlimited
Schedule of Accounts Payable
February 28, 2011

Ace Mfg. Company	$100
ITT Company	225
Hornung Supply Company	350
Total accounts payable	$675

Controller

You are a controller for a merchandising company. You want to analyze your company's cash payments to suppliers, including an analysis of purchases discounts. Where might you look for this information?

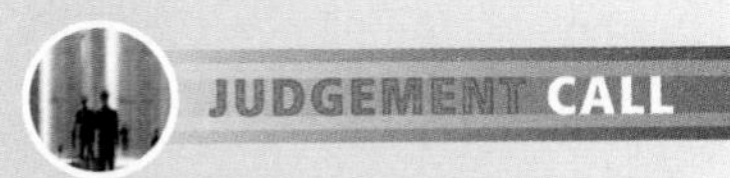

Answer—p. 409

General Journal Transactions

When special journals are used, we still need a General Journal for adjusting, closing, and correcting entries, and for special transactions not recorded in special journals. These special transactions include purchases returns and allowances, purchases of plant assets by issuing a note payable, sales returns, and receiving a note receivable from a customer.

The process to follow when using special journals is based on the first four steps of the accounting cycle: analyze, record, post, and prepare an unadjusted trial balance. The last section described this process in detail. A summary of the steps to follow when working with special journals is to:

1. Analyze
2. Record transactions in the appropriate journal
3. Post
   - Post to the subledger account, if any is affected
   - Post individual amounts in the Other Accounts column to the General Ledger
   - Foot and crossfoot the journals
   - Post column totals from the journals to the General Ledger (except Other Accounts)
4. Prepare a trial balance
   - Agree the total of the accounts in each subledger to the respective controlling account on the trial balance

6. What is the normal recording and posting procedure when using special journals and controlling accounts with subledgers?
7. Why does a company need a General Journal when using special journals for sales, purchases, cash receipts, and cash disbursements?

Do Quick Study questions: QS 8-8, QS 8-9, QS 8-10

CRITICAL THINKING CHALLENGE

Refer to the Critical Thinking Challenge questions at the beginning of the chapter on page 391. Compare your answers to those suggested on Connect at www.mcgrawhillconnect.ca.

IFRS HIGHLIGHTS

IFRS have not caused changes, at the introductory level, to concepts covered in this chapter.

Summary

LO1 | Explain the relationship of the accounting information system (AIS) to the management information system (MIS) and identify the components of an AIS. The MIS includes the subsystems of Finance, Sales and Marketing, Human Resources, Production, and Accounting. Information systems collect and process data based on inputs for the purpose of generating useful information for both internal and external users. An AIS collects financial data and processes it through the relevant component: Accounts Payable, Accounts Receivable, Payroll, or a specialty component such as Property, Plant and Equipment Assets. Source documents have evolved from paper-based to technology-based. General purpose accounting software is available for small to medium-sized businesses, whereas large businesses purchase enterprise-application software programs that can be customized to fit their specific needs.

LO2 | Explain the goals and uses of special journals. Special journals are used for recording and posting transactions of similar type, with each meant to cover one kind of transaction. Four of the most common special journals are the Sales Journal, Cash Receipts Journal, Purchases Journal, and Cash Disbursements Journal.

LO3 | Describe the use of controlling accounts and subledgers. A General Ledger keeps controlling accounts such as Accounts Receivable or Accounts Payable, but details on individual accounts making up the controlling account are kept in a subledger (such as an Accounts Receivable Subledger).

LO4 | Journalize and post transactions using special journals. Special journals are devoted to similar kinds of transactions. Transactions are journalized on one line of a special journal, with columns devoted to specific accounts, dates, names, posting references, explanations, and other necessary information. Posting is threefold: (1) individual amounts in a column that is posted in total to a controlling account at the end of a period (month) are posted regularly (daily) to its account in the subledger, (2) total amounts for all columns except the Other Accounts column are posted at the end of a period (month) to their column's account title, and (3) individual amounts in the Other Accounts column are posted to their General Ledger accounts.

guidance answers to JUDGEMENT CALL

Public Accountant

As a professional accountant, you are guided by the Professional Codes of Conduct described in Chapter 1, page 13. You should recognize the main issue: whether commissions have an actual or perceived impact on the integrity and objectivity of your advice. The code says that you should not accept a commission if you perform either an audit or a review of the client's financial statements or if you review prospective financial information for the client. The code also precludes a commission if you compile the client's statements, unless the compilation report discloses a lack of independence. Even in situations where a commission is allowed, the code requires you to tell the client of your commission arrangement. These suggested actions seem appropriate even if you are not bound by the code. Also, you need to seriously examine the merits of agreeing to a commission arrangement when you are in a position to exploit it.

Retailer

The Accounts Receivable Subledger has much of the information you need. It lists detailed information for each customer's account, including the amounts, dates for transactions, and dates of payments. It can be reorganized into an "aging schedule" to show how long customers wait in paying their bills. We describe an aging schedule in Chapter 10.

Controller

Much of the information you need is in the Accounts Payable Subledger. It contains information for each supplier, the amounts due, and when payments are made. This subledger, along with information on credit terms, should enable you to conduct your analyses.

guidance answers to CHECKPOINT

Read Apply Do Check

1. An AIS is part of the MIS and collects and processes financial data for communication to users. The MIS collects and processes data from sales and marketing, finance, production, human resources, and accounting and provides information to these in turn and also to external users.
2. The four basic components of an AIS are Accounts Payable, Accounts Receivable, Payroll, and specialty components such as Property, Plant and Equipment Assets.
3. All cash payments by cheque are recorded in the Cash Disbursements Journal.
4. The equality of debits and credits is kept within the General Ledger. The subledger keeps the customer's individual account and is used only for supplementary information.
5. An initial and page number of the journal from which the amount was posted is entered in the Posting Reference column of the ledger account next to the amount.
6. The normal recording and posting procedures are threefold. First, transactions are entered in a special journal column if applicable. Second, individual amounts are posted to the subledger accounts. Third, column totals are posted to General Ledger accounts.
7. The General Journal is still needed for adjusting, closing and correcting entries, and for special transactions such as sales returns, purchases returns, plant asset purchases, and sales on credit of assets other than merchandise inventory.

demonstration problem

The Pepper Company completed these transactions during March 2011:

Mar.	1	Merchandise inventory on hand was $28,400.
	1	Adrian Pepper, Capital has an opening balance of $28,400.
	4	Sold merchandise on credit to Jennifer Nelson, invoice #954, $16,800. Cost, $10,100. (Terms of all credit sales are 2/10, n/30.)
	6	Purchased office supplies on credit from Mack Company, $1,220. Invoice dated March 3, terms n/30.
	6	Sold merchandise on credit to Dennie Hoskins, invoice #955, $10,200. Cost, $6,200.
	11	Received merchandise and an invoice dated March 11, terms 2/10, n/30, from Defore Industries, $52,600.
	12	Borrowed $26,000 by giving Commerce Bank a long-term promissory note payable.
	14	Received payment from Jennifer Nelson for the March 4 sale.
	16	Received a credit memorandum from Defore Industries for unsatisfactory merchandise received on March 11 and returned for credit, $200.
	16	Received payment from Dennie Hoskins for the March 6 sale.
	18	Purchased store equipment on credit from Schmidt Supply, invoice dated March 15, terms n/30, $22,850.
	20	Sold merchandise on credit to Marjorie Allen, invoice #956, $5,600. Cost, $3,400.
	21	Sent Defore Industries cheque #516 in payment of its March 11 invoice less returns.
	22	Received merchandise and an invoice dated March 18, terms 2/10, n/30, from the Welch Company, $41,625.
	26	Issued a credit memorandum to Marjorie Allen for defective merchandise sold on March 22 and returned for credit, $600. The merchandise was scrapped and not returned to inventory.
	31	Issued cheque #517, payable to Payroll, in payment of sales salaries for the month, $15,900. For simplicity, we assume one cheque.
	31	Cash sales for the month were $134,680. (Normally, cash sales are recorded daily; however, they are recorded only once in this problem to reduce the repetitive entries.) Cost, $80,800.
	31	Foot and crossfoot the journals and make the month-end postings.

Required

1. Open the following General Ledger accounts: Cash (101), Accounts Receivable (106), Merchandise Inventory (119), Office Supplies (124), Store Equipment (165), Accounts Payable (201), Long-Term Notes Payable (251), Adrian Pepper, Capital (301), Sales (413), Sales Returns and Allowances (414), Sales Discounts (415), Cost of Goods Sold (502), and Sales Salaries Expense (621).
2. Open the following Accounts Receivable Subledger accounts: Marjorie Allen, Dennie Hoskins, and Jennifer Nelson.
3. Open the following Accounts Payable Subledger accounts: Defore Industries, Mack Company, Schmidt Supply, and Welch Company.

4. Enter the transactions in a Purchases Journal, a Sales Journal, a Cash Receipts Journal, a Cash Disbursements Journal, and a General Journal similar to the ones illustrated in the chapter. Post at the end of the month.
5. Prepare a trial balance and prepare schedules of accounts receivable and payable.

Planning the Solution

- Set up the required General Ledger and subledger accounts and the five required journals as illustrated in the chapter.
- First read and analyze each transaction and decide in which special journal (or General Journal) the transaction would be recorded.
- Now record each transaction in the proper journal, posting to the subledgers as appropriate. Also, post transactions affecting the *Other Accounts* column to the corresponding ledger account.
- Once you have recorded all the transactions, total the journal columns.
- Now post column totals from each journal to the appropriate ledger accounts.
- After you have completed posting, prepare a trial balance to prove the equality of the debit and credit balances in your General Ledger.
- Finally, prepare schedules of accounts receivable and accounts payable.

solution

Sales Journal **Page 2**

Date	Account Debited	Invoice No.	PR	Accounts Receivable Dr. Sales Cr.	Cost of Goods Sold/Dr. Merchandise Inventory/Cr.
2011					
Mar. 4	Jennifer Nelson	954	✓	16,800	10,100
6	Dennie Hoskins	955	✓	10,200	6,200
20	Marjorie Allen	956	✓	5,600	3,400
31	Totals			32,600	19,700
				(106/413)	(502/119)

Cash Receipts Journal — Page 3

Date	Account Credited	Explanation	PR	Cash Dr.	Sales Discount Dr.	Accounts Receivable Cr.	Sales Cr.	Other Accounts Cr.	Cost of Goods Sold/Dr Merchandise Inventory/Cr.
2011									
Mar. 12	L.T. Notes Payable	Note to bank	251	26,000				26,000	
14	Jennifer Nelson	Invoice, Mar. 4	✓	16,464	336	16,800			
16	Dennie Hoskins	Invoice, Mar. 6	✓	9,996	204	10,200			
31	Sales	Cash sales		134,680			134,680		80,800
31	Totals			187,140	540	27,000	134,680	26,000	80,800
				(101)	(415)	(106)	(413)	(X)	(502/119)

Purchases Journal — Page 3

Date	Account Credited	Date of Invoice	Terms	PR	Accounts Payable Cr.	Merchandise Inventory Dr.	Office Supplies Dr.	Other Accounts Dr.
2011								
Mar. 6	Office Supplies/Mack Co.	Mar. 3	n/30	✓	1,220		1,220	
11	Defore Industries	Mar. 11	2/10, n/30	✓	52,600	52,600		
18	Store Equipment/Schmidt Supp.	Mar. 15	n/30	165/✓	22,850			22,850
22	Welch Company	Mar. 18	2/10, n/30	✓	41,625	41,625		
31	Totals				118,295	94,225	1,220	22,850
					(201)	(119)	(124)	(X)

Cash Disbursements Journal — Page 4

Date	Ch. No.	Payee	Account Debited	PR	Cash Cr.	Merchandise Inventory Cr.	Other Accounts Dr.	Accounts Payable Dr.
2011								
Mar. 21	516	Defore Industries	Defore Industries	✓	51,352	1,048		52,400
31	517	Payroll	Sales Salaries Expense	621	15,900		15,900	
31		Totals			67,252	1,048	15,900	52,400
					(101)	(119)	(X)	(201)

General Journal — Page 2

Date		Account	PR	Debit	Credit
Mar.	16	Accounts Payable—Defore Industries	201/✓	200	
		Merchandise Inventory	119		200
		Credit memo regarding merchandise returned.			
	26	Sales Returns and Allowances	414	600	
		Accounts Receivable—Marjorie Allen	106/✓		600
		Issued credit memo regarding merchandise returned and scrapped.			

Accounts Receivable Subledger

Marjorie Allen

Date	PR	Debit	Credit	Balance
2011 Mar. 20	S2	5,600		5,600
26	G2		600	5,000

Dennie Hoskins

Date	PR	Debit	Credit	Balance
2011 Mar. 6	S2	10,200		10,200
16	CR3		10,200	-0-

Jennifer Nelson

Date	PR	Debit	Credit	Balance
2011 Mar. 4	S2	16,800		16,800
14	CR3		16,800	-0-

Accounts Payable Subledger

Defore Industries

Date	PR	Debit	Credit	Balance
2011 Mar. 11	P3		52,600	52,600
16	G2	200		52,400
21	CD4	52,400		-0-

Mack Company

Date	PR	Debit	Credit	Balance
2011 Mar. 6	P3		1,220	1,220

Schmidt Supply

Date	PR	Debit	Credit	Balance
2011 Mar. 18	P3		22,850	22,850

Welch Company

Date	PR	Debit	Credit	Balance
2011 Mar. 22	P3		41,625	41,625

General Ledger

Cash Acct. No. 101

Date	Explanation	PR	Debit	Credit	Balance
2011 Mar. 31		CR3	187,140		187,140
31		CD4		67,252	119,888

Accounts Receivable 106

Date	Explanation	PR	Debit	Credit	Balance
2011 Mar. 26		G2		600	(600)
31		S2	32,600		32,000
31		CR3		27,000	5,000

Merchandise Inventory 119

Date	Explanation	PR	Debit	Credit	Balance
2011 Mar. 1	Opening Balance				28,400
16		G2		200	28,200
31		S2		19,700	8,500
31		CR3		80,800	(72,300)
31		P3	94,225		21,925
31		CD4		1,048	20,877

Office Supplies 124

Date	Explanation	PR	Debit	Credit	Balance
2011 Mar. 31		P3	1,220		1,220

Store Equipment 165

Date	Explanation	PR	Debit	Credit	Balance
2011 Mar. 18		P3	22,850		22,850

Accounts Payable 201

Date	Explanation	PR	Debit	Credit	Balance
2011 Mar. 16		G2	200		(200)
31		P3		118,295	118,095
31		CD4	52,400		65,695

Long-Term Notes Payable Acct. No. 251

Date	Explanation	PR	Debit	Credit	Balance
2011 Mar. 12		CR3		26,000	26,000

Adrian Pepper, Capital 301

Date	Explanation	PR	Debit	Credit	Balance
2011 Mar. 1	Opening Balance				28,400

Sales 413

Date	Explanation	PR	Debit	Credit	Balance
2011 Mar. 31		S2		32,600	32,600
31		CR3		134,680	167,280

Sales Returns and Allowances 414

Date	Explanation	PR	Debit	Credit	Balance
2011 Mar. 26		G2	600		600

Sales Discounts 415

Date	Explanation	PR	Debit	Credit	Balance
2011 Mar. 31		CR3	540		540

Cost of Goods Sold 502

Date	Explanation	PR	Debit	Credit	Balance
2011 Mar. 31		S2	19,700		19,700
31		CR3	80,800		100,500

Sales Salaries Expense 621

Date	Explanation	PR	Debit	Credit	Balance
2011 Mar. 31		CD4	15,900		15,900

Pepper Company
Trial Balance
March 31, 2011

Acct.	Title	Debit	Credit
101	Cash	$119,888	
106	Accounts receivable	5,000	
119	Merchandise inventory	20,877	
124	Office supplies	1,220	
165	Store equipment	22,850	
201	Accounts payable		$ 65,695
251	Long-term notes payable		26,000
301	Adrian Pepper, capital		28,400
413	Sales		167,280
414	Sales returns and allowances	600	
415	Sales discounts	540	
502	Cost of goods sold	100,500	
621	Sales salaries expense	15,900	
	Totals	$287,375	$287,375

Pepper Company
Schedule of Accounts Receivable
March 31, 2011

Marjorie Allen	$5,000
Total accounts receivable	$5,000

Pepper Company
Schedule of Accounts Payable
March 31, 2011

Mack Company	$ 1,220
Schmidt Supply	22,850
Welch Company	41,625
Total accounts payable	$65,695

Notice how the totals for both the Schedule of Accounts Receivable and Schedule of Accounts Payable agree to the respective controlling account balances in the trial balance.

APPENDIX 8A

Special Journals Under a Periodic System

This appendix shows the special journals under a periodic inventory system. The Sales Journal and the Cash Receipts Journal each require one less column. The Purchases Journal replaces the *Merchandise Inventory Dr.* column with a *Purchases Dr.* column in a periodic system. The Cash Disbursements Journal replaces the *Inventory Cr.* column with a *Purchases Discounts Cr.* column in a periodic system. These changes are illustrated below.

LO5 Journalize and post transactions using special journals in a periodic inventory system.

Sales Journal

The Sales Journal for Outdoors Unlimited using the periodic inventory system is shown in Exhibit 8A.1. The difference in the Sales Journal between the perpetual and periodic system is the deletion of the cost of goods sold and merchandise inventory amounts for each sale. The periodic system does not record the increase in cost of goods sold and decrease in inventory at the time of sale.

Exhibit 8A.1

Sales Journal—Periodic System

Outdoors Unlimited Sales Journal Page 3

Date	Account Debited	Invoice Number	PR	Accounts Receivable Dr. Sales Cr.
2011				
Feb. 2	Jason Henry	307	✓	450
7	Albert Co.	308	✓	500
13	Bam Moore	309	✓	350
15	Paul Roth	310	✓	200
22	Jason Henry	311	✓	225
25	Frank Booth	312	✓	175
28	Albert Co.	313	✓	250
28	Total			2,150
				(106/413)

Posting from journals to General Ledger accounts and subledgers in a periodic system is identical to the posting process in a perpetual system.

EXTEND YOUR KNOWLEDGE

Cash Receipts Journal

The Cash Receipts Journal under the periodic system is shown in Exhibit 8A.2. Note the deletion of the column on the far right side to record debits to Cost of Goods Sold and credits to Merchandise Inventory for the cost of merchandise sold.

Consistent with the Cash Receipts Journal shown under the perpetual system in the chapter, we only show the weekly cash sale entries.

Exhibit 8A.2

Cash Receipts Journal—Periodic System

Outdoors Unlimited Cash Receipts Journal

Page 2

Date	Accounts Credited	PR	Explanation	Cash Dr.	Sales Discount Dr.	Accounts Receivable Cr.	Sales Cr.	Other Accounts Cr.
2011								
Feb. 7	Sales		Cash sales	4,450			4,450	
12	Jason Henry	✓	Invoice, Feb. 2	441	9	450		
14	Sales		Cash sales	3,925			3,925	
17	Albert Co.	✓	Invoice, Feb. 7	490	10	500		
20	Notes Payable	245	Note to bank	750				750
21	Sales		Cash sales	4,700			4,700	
22	Interest Revenue	409	Bank account	250				250
23	Bam Moore	✓	Invoice, Feb. 13	343	7	350		
25	Paul Roth	✓	Invoice, Feb.15	196	4	200		
28	Sales		Cash sales	4,225			4,225	
28	Totals			19,770	30	1,500	17,300	1,000
				(101)	(415)	(106)	(413)	(X)

Purchases Journal

The Purchases Journal under the periodic system is shown in Exhibit 8A.3. This journal in a perpetual system includes the Merchandise Inventory column where the periodic system has the Purchases column. All else is identical under the two systems.

Exhibit 8A.3

Purchases Journal—Periodic System

Outdoors Unlimited Purchases Journal

Page 1

Date	Account Credited	Date of Invoice	Terms	PR	Accounts Payable Cr.	Purchases Dr.	Office Supplies Dr.	Other Accounts Dr.
2011								
Feb. 3	Hornung Supply Co.	Feb. 2	n/30	✓	350	275	75	
5	Ace Mfg. Co.	5	2/10, n/30	✓	200	200		
13	Wynet & Co.	10	2/10, n/30	✓	150	150		
20	Smite Co.	18	2/10, n/30	✓	300	300		
25	Ace Mfg. Co.	24	2/10, n/30	✓	100	100		
28	Store Supplies/ITT Co.	28	n/30	125/✓	225	125	25	75
28	Totals				1,325	1,150	100	(75)
					(201)	(505)	(124)	(X)

Cash Disbursements Journal

The Cash Disbursements Journal in a periodic system is shown in Exhibit 8A.4. This journal includes the Purchases Discounts column where the perpetual system had the Merchandise Inventory column. All else is identical under the two systems. When a company has several cash purchases of inventory, it often adds a new column for Purchases Debit entries.

Exhibit 8A.4

Cash Disbursements Journal—Periodic System

Outdoors Unlimited Cash Disbursements Journal

Page 2

Date	Ch. No.	Payee	Account Debited	PR	Cash Cr.	Purchases Discounts Cr.	Other Accounts Dr.	Accounts Payable Dr.
2011								
Feb. 3	105	L & N Railroad	Transportation-In	508	15		15	
5	106	East Sales Co.	Purchases	505	25		25	
13	107	Ace Mfg. Co.	Ace Mfg. Co.	✓	196	4		200
20	108	Jerry Hale	Salaries Expense	622	250		250	
25	109	Wynet & Co.	Wynet & Co.	✓	147	3		150
28	110	Smite Co.	Smite Co.	✓	294	6		300
28		Totals			927	13	290	650
					(101)	(507)	(X)	(201)

Summary of Appendix 8A

LO5 | Journalize and post transactions using special journals in a periodic inventory system. Transactions are journalized and posted using special journals in a periodic system. The methods are similar to those in a perpetual system. The primary difference is that cost of goods sold and inventory do not need adjusting at the time of each sale. This normally results in the deletion of one or more columns in each special journal devoted to these accounts.

Glossary

Accounting information system (AIS) The people, records, methods, and equipment that collect and process data from transactions, organize them in useful forms, and communicate results to decision makers. (p. 393)

Accounts Payable Subledger A subsidiary ledger listing individual credit supplier accounts. (p. 396)

Accounts Receivable Subledger A subsidiary ledger listing individual credit customer accounts. (p. 396)

Cash Disbursements Journal The special journal that is used to record all payments of cash; also called *Cash Payments Journal*. (p. 405)

Cash Receipts Journal The special journal that is used to record all receipts of cash. (p. 401)

Cheque Register Another name for a Cash Disbursements Journal when the journal has a column for cheque numbers. (p. 405)

Columnar journal A journal with more than one column. (p. 399)

Computer hardware The physical equipment in a computerized accounting information system. (p. 394)

Computer software The programs that direct the operations of computer hardware. (p. 394)

Controlling account A General Ledger account, the balance of which (after posting) equals the sum of the balances of the accounts in a related subsidiary ledger. (p. 396)

Crossfoot To add debit and credit column totals and compare the sums for equality. (p. 403)

Enterprise-application software Programs that manage a company's vital operations, which range from order-taking programs to manufacturing to accounting. (p. 394)

Foot To add a column of numbers. (p. 403)

Management information system (MIS) Designed to collect and process data within an organization for the purpose of providing users with information. (p. 392)

Purchases Journal A journal that is used to record all purchases on credit. (p. 404)

Sales Journal A journal used to record sales of merchandise on credit. (p. 398)

Schedule of accounts payable A list of the balances of all the accounts in the Accounts Payable Subledger that is summed to show the total amount of accounts payable outstanding. (p. 407)

Schedule of accounts receivable A list of the balances of all the accounts in the Accounts Receivable Subledger that is summed to show the total amount of accounts receivable outstanding. (p. 400)

Special journal Any journal that is used for recording and posting transactions of a similar type. (p. 395)

Subledger See *subsidiary ledger*. (p. 396)

Subsidiary ledger A listing of individual accounts with a common characteristic. (p. 396)

Visit **Connect** at **www.mcgrawhillconnect.ca** for additional study tools, practice quizzes, to search an interactive e-book, and much more.

Concept Review Questions

1. Refer to the chapter opening story. Identify all of the special journals and subledgers that Greg Timko is now likely using for Canadian Tire.
2. When special journals are used, separate special journals normally record each of four different types of transactions. What are these four types of transactions?
3. Why should sales to and receipts of cash from credit customers be recorded and posted daily?
4. Both credits to customer accounts and credits to miscellaneous accounts are individually posted from a Cash Receipts Journal similar to the one in Exhibit 8.10. Why not put both kinds of credits in the same column?
5. When a General Journal entry is used to record a returned credit sale, the credit of the entry must be posted twice. Does this cause the trial balance to be out of balance? Why or why not?
6. What notations are entered into the Posting Reference column of a ledger account?

Quick Study

Note 1: *End-of-chapter items do not include consideration of GST/PST unless stated otherwise.*

Note 2: *When setting up General Ledger accounts, recall that a Chart of Accounts is provided at the end of the textbook, in Appendix II, to assist you in numbering your accounts.*

QS 8-1
AIS and source documents
LO1

Refer to Exhibit 8-2. Identify which component of the AIS would process each of the following source documents:

	Accounts Payable (AP) Accounts Receivable (AR) Payroll (P)
1. Time cards from employees	________
2. Sales invoice; terms 2/10, n/30	________
3. Deposit slip regarding cash collections from credit customers	________
4. Cheque written to pay account with supplier	________

QS 8-2
Inputs and outputs of AIS
LO1

Refer to Exhibit 8-3. Identify each of the following as an *input to* or an *output from* an AIS:

	Input (I) or Output (O)
1. Bank statement	________
2. Sales invoice issued to customer	________
3. Schedule of accounts payable	________
4. Income statement	________
5. Purchase order issued to supplier	________
6. Schedule detailing property, plant and equipment	________
7. Report detailing employee absences/minutes late	________
8. Memorandum issued by supplier regarding defective merchandise	________

QS 8-3
Special journal identification
LO2

Trenton Iron Works uses a Sales Journal, a Purchases Journal, a Cash Receipts Journal, a Cash Disbursements Journal, and a General Journal. Trenton recently completed the following transactions. List the transaction letters and, next to each letter, give the name of the journal in which the transaction should be recorded.

a. Sold merchandise on credit.
b. Purchased shop supplies on credit.
c. Paid an employee's salary.
d. Paid a creditor.
e. Purchased merchandise on credit.
f. Borrowed money from the bank.
g. Sold merchandise for cash.

QS 8-4
Entries belonging to the General Journal—perpetual
LO2

The Nostalgic Book Shop uses a Sales Journal, a Purchases Journal, a Cash Receipts Journal, a Cash Disbursements Journal, and a General Journal. The following transactions occurred during the month of November. Journalize the November transactions that should be recorded in the General Journal, assuming a perpetual inventory system.

Nov.	2	Purchased merchandise on credit for $2,900 from the Ringdol Co., terms 2/10, n/30.
	12	The owner, Jesse Cooke, contributed an automobile worth $15,000 to the business.
	16	Sold merchandise on credit to R. Wyder for $1,100, terms n/30; cost, $700.
	19	R. Wyder returned $150 (cost, $95) of merchandise originally purchased on November 16. The merchandise was returned to inventory.
	28	Returned $170 of defective merchandise to the Ringdol Co. from the November 2 purchase.

QS 8-5
Accounts Receivable Subledger
LO3

Identify the effect caused by each of the following transactions on the Accounts Receivable Subledger:

	Debit (DR), Credit (CR), or No Effect (NE)
1. Sale of merchandise on credit.	______
2. Purchase of merchandise on credit.	______
3. Closing of revenue accounts at year-end.	______
4. Receipt of cash from credit customer.	______
5. Payment to supplier.	______
6. Credit memo issued to customer regarding defective merchandise returned.	______
7. Accrued wages payable at month-end.	______

QS 8-6
Accounts Payable Subledger
LO3

Identify the effect caused by each of the following transactions on the Accounts Payable Subledger:

	Debit (DR), Credit (CR), or No Effect (NE)
1. Purchase of merchandise on credit.	______
2. Sale of merchandise on credit.	______
3. Purchase of office supplies on credit.	______
4. Receipt of cash from credit customer.	______
5. Payment to supplier.	______
6. Memorandum issued by supplier regarding defective merchandise returned.	______
7. Closing of Income Summary to Capital at year-end.	______

QS 8-7
Sales Journal—perpetual
LO4

On a sheet of notebook paper, draw a Sales Journal like the one that appears in Exhibit 8.8 and journalize the following March 2011 sales transactions for Suttleton Company.

Mar.	3	Sold $3,000 of merchandise to Tim Edson (cost $2,040); terms 2/15, n/30; invoice #1103.
	10	$10,800 of merchandise was sold to Willis Company (cost $7,344); terms 2/15, n/30; invoice #1104.
	11	Ellton Kingston purchased $7,400 of merchandise (cost $5,032); terms 2/15, n/30; invoice #1105.

QS 8-8
Cash Receipts Journal—perpetual
LO4

On a sheet of notebook paper, draw a Cash Receipts Journal like the one in Exhibit 8.10 and journalize the following March 2011 cash receipts transactions for Suttleton Company.

Mar.	18	Collected the amount owing regarding the $3,000 of merchandise sold to Tim Edson on March 3; terms 2/15, n/30; invoice #1103.
	30	Willis Company paid for the $10,800 of merchandise purchased on March 10; terms 2/15, n/30; invoice #1104.
	31	Sold $6,200 of merchandise to ABC Company for cash (cost $4,216).

QS 8-9
Purchases Journal—perpetual
LO4

On a sheet of notebook paper, draw a Purchases Journal like the one that appears in Exhibit 8.12 and journalize the following March 2011 transactions for Suttleton Company.

Mar.	2	Purchased $4,800 of merchandise from Tex Company; terms 3/10, n/20.
	12	$14,000 of merchandise was purchased from Littleton; terms 2/15, n/30.
	13	Worsley Company sold Suttleton $9,400 of office furniture; terms 2/15, n/45.

QS 8-10
Cash Disbursements Journal—perpetual
LO4

On a sheet of notebook paper, draw a Cash Disbursements Journal like the one that appears in Exhibit 8.13 and journalize the following March 2011 payments for Suttleton Company (assume the first cheque is #101).

Mar.	14	Paid for the $4,800 March 2 purchase from Tex Company; terms 3/10, n/20.
	27	Paid for the $14,000 purchase of merchandise from Littleton on March 12; terms 2/15, n/30.
	31	Paid Thorn Real Estate Management for the March rent; $6,500.

Exercises

Exercise 8-1
Sales Journal—perpetual
LO4

Spindle Company uses a Sales Journal, a Purchases Journal, a Cash Receipts Journal, a Cash Disbursements Journal, and a General Journal. The following transactions occurred during the month of February 2011:

Feb.	2	Sold merchandise to S. Mayer for $450 cash, invoice #5703. Cost, $200.
	5	Purchased merchandise on credit from Camp Corp., $2,300.
	7	Sold merchandise to J. Eason for $1,150, terms 2/10, n/30, invoice #5704. Cost, $700.
	8	Borrowed $8,000 by giving a note to the bank.
	12	Sold merchandise to P. Lathan for $320, terms n/30, invoice #5705. Cost, $170.
	16	Received $1,127 from J. Eason to pay for the purchase of February 7.
	19	Sold used store equipment to Whiten, Inc., for $900 cash.
	25	Sold merchandise to S. Summers for $550, terms n/30, invoice #5706. Cost, $300.

Required

On a sheet of notebook paper, draw a Sales Journal like the one that appears in Exhibit 8.8. Journalize the February transactions that should be recorded in the Sales Journal.

***Exercise 8-2**
Sales Journal—periodic
LO5

Using the information in Exercise 8-1, complete the requirements assuming a periodic inventory system.

Exercise 8-3
Cash Receipts Journal—perpetual
LO4

StickUps Company uses a Sales Journal, a Purchases Journal, a Cash Receipts Journal, a Cash Disbursements Journal, and a General Journal. The following transactions occurred during the month of September 2011:

Sept.	3	Purchased merchandise on credit for $6,200 from Pacer Co.
	7	Sold merchandise on credit to J. Namal for $1,800, subject to a 2% sales discount if paid by the end of the month. Cost, $1,000.
	9	Borrowed $5,500 by giving a note to the bank.
	13	The owner, Dale Trent, invested an additional $7,000 cash into the business.
	18	Sold merchandise to B. Baird for $460 cash. Cost, $280.
	22	Paid Pacer Co. $6,200 for the merchandise purchased on September 3.
	27	Received $1,764 from J. Namal in payment of the September 7 purchase.
	30	Paid salaries of $3,200.

An asterisk (*) identifies assignment material based on Appendix 8A.

Required

On a sheet of notebook paper, draw a multicolumn Cash Receipts Journal like the one that appears in Exhibit 8.10. Journalize the September transactions that should be recorded in the Cash Receipts Journal.

*Exercise 8-4

Cash Receipts Journal—periodic

LO5

Using the information in Exercise 8-3, complete the requirements assuming a periodic inventory system.

Exercise 8-5

Purchases Journal—perpetual

LO4

Chem Company uses a Sales Journal, a Purchases Journal, a Cash Receipts Journal, a Cash Disbursements Journal, and a General Journal. The following transactions occurred during the month of July 2011:

July	1	Purchased merchandise on credit for $8,100 from Angler, Inc., terms n/30.
	8	Sold merchandise on credit to B. Harren for $1,500, subject to a $30 sales discount if paid by the end of the month. Cost, $820.
	10	The owner of Chem Corp., Pat Johnson, invested $2,000 cash.
	14	Purchased store supplies from Steck Company on credit for $240, terms 2/10, n/30.
	17	Purchased merchandise inventory on credit from Marten Company for $2,600, terms n/30.
	24	Sold merchandise to W. Winger for $630 cash. Cost, $350.
	28	Purchased merchandise inventory from Hadley's for $9,000 cash.
	29	Paid Angler, Inc., $8,100 for the merchandise purchased on July 1.

Required

On a sheet of notebook paper, draw a multicolumn Purchases Journal like the one that appears in Exhibit 8.12. Journalize the July transactions that should be recorded in the Purchases Journal.

*Exercise 8-6

Purchases Journal—periodic

LO5

Using the information in Exercise 8-5, complete the requirements assuming a periodic inventory system.

Exercise 8-7

Cash Disbursements Journal—perpetual

LO4

Xion Supply uses a Sales Journal, a Purchases Journal, a Cash Receipts Journal, a Cash Disbursements Journal, and a General Journal. The following transactions occurred during the month of March 2011:

Mar.	3	Purchased merchandise for $5,500 on credit from Pace, Inc., terms 2/10, n/30.
	9	Issued cheque #210 to Narlin Corp. to buy store supplies for $900.
	12	Sold merchandise on credit to K. Camp for $1,340, terms n/30. Cost, $800.
	17	Issued cheque #211 for $3,000 to repay a note payable to City Bank.
	20	Purchased merchandise for $7,000 on credit from LeBaron, terms 2/10, n/30.
	29	Issued cheque #212 to LeBaron to pay the amount due for the purchase of March 20, less the discount.
	31	Paid salary of $3,400 to E. Brandon by issuing cheque #213.
	31	Issued cheque #214 to Pace, Inc., to pay the amount due for the purchase of March 3.

Required

On a sheet of notebook paper, draw a multicolumn Cash Disbursements Journal like the one that appears in Exhibit 8.13. Journalize the March transactions that should be recorded in the Cash Disbursements Journal.

An asterisk (*) identifies assignment material based on Appendix 8A.

***Exercise 8-8**
Cash Disbursements Journal—periodic
LO5

Using the information in Exercise 8-7, complete the requirements assuming a periodic inventory system.

Exercise 8-9
Special journal transactions—perpetual
LO4

On May 11, 2011, Wilson Purchasing purchased $30,000 of merchandise from Hostel Sales; terms 3/10, n/90, FOB Hostel Sales. The cost of the goods to Hostel was $20,000. Wilson issued cheque #84 in the amount of $335 to pay Express Shipping Service for the delivery charges on the merchandise on May 11. On May 12, Wilson returned $1,200 of goods to Hostel Sales, which restored them to inventory. The returned goods had cost Hostel $800. On May 20, Wilson mailed cheque #85 to Hostel for the amount owed on that date. Hostel received and recorded the cheque on May 21.

Required

1. Record the transactions for Wilson Purchasing in a Purchases Journal, Cash Disbursements Journal, and General Journal as appropriate.
2. Record the transactions for Hostel Sales in a Sales Journal, Cash Receipts Journal, and General Journal as appropriate. Assume invoice #1601 for the May 11 sale.

***Exercise 8-10**
Special journal transactions—periodic
LO5

Using the information in Exercise 8-9, complete the requirements assuming a periodic inventory system.

Required

1. Record the transactions for Wilson Purchasing in a Purchases Journal, Cash Disbursements Journal, and General Journal as appropriate.
2. Record the transactions for Hostel Sales in a Sales Journal, Cash Receipts Journal, and General Journal as appropriate.

Exercise 8-11
Special journal transactions—perpetual
LO4

Simon Pharmacy uses the following journals: Sales Journal, Purchases Journal, Cash Receipts Journal, Cash Disbursements Journal, and General Journal. On June 5, Simon purchased merchandise priced at $24,000, subject to credit terms of 2/10, n/30. On June 14, the pharmacy paid the net amount due. However, in journalizing the payment, the bookkeeper debited Accounts Payable for $24,000 and failed to record the cash discount. Cash was credited for the actual amount paid. In what journals would the transactions of June 5 and June 14 have been recorded? What procedure is likely to discover the error in journalizing the June 14 transaction?

Exercise 8-12
Errors related to the Purchases Journal—perpetual
LO4

A company that records credit purchases in a Purchases Journal and records purchase returns in its General Journal made the following errors. List each error by letter and, opposite each letter, tell when the error should be discovered:

a. Made an addition error in determining the balance of a creditor's account.
b. Made an addition error in totalling the Office Supplies column of the Purchases Journal.
c. Posted a purchase return to the Accounts Payable account and to the creditor's account but did not post to the Merchandise Inventory account.
d. Posted a purchase return to the Merchandise Inventory account and to the Accounts Payable account but did not post to the creditor's account.
e. Correctly recorded a $4,000 purchase in the Purchases Journal but posted it to the creditor's account as a $400 purchase.

An asterisk (*) identifies assignment material based on Appendix 8A.

Exercise 8-13
Posting to subledger accounts—perpetual
LO4

At the end of May 2011, the Sales Journal of Value-Mart Goods appeared as follows:

Sales Journal **Page 4**

Date	Account Debited	Invoice Number	PR	A/R Dr. Sales Cr.	Cost of Goods Sold Dr. Merchandise Inventory Cr.
2011					
May 6	Brad Smithers	190		5,760.00	3,200.00
10	Dan Holland	191		3,880.00	2,200.00
17	Sanders Farrell	192		1,700.00	1,000.00
25	Dan Holland	193		680.00	260.00
31	Totals			12,020.00	6,660.00

Value-Mart had also recorded the return of merchandise with the following General Journal entry:

May 20	Sales Returns and Allowances	500	
	Accounts Receivable—Sanders Farrell		500
	Merchandise Inventory	260	
	Cost of Goods Sold		260
	Customer returned merchandise.		

Required

1. On a sheet of notebook paper, open an Accounts Receivable Subledger that has a T-account for each customer listed in the Sales Journal. Post to the customer accounts the entries in the Sales Journal and any portion of the General Journal entry that affects a customer's account.
2. Open a General Ledger that has T-accounts for Accounts Receivable, Sales, and Sales Returns and Allowances. Post the Sales Journal and any portion of the General Journal entry that affects these accounts. Calculate the ending balance for each account.
3. Prepare a schedule of the accounts in the Accounts Receivable Subledger and add their balances to show that the total equals the balance in the Accounts Receivable controlling account.

***Exercise 8-14**
Posting from special journals and subledgers to T-accounts—periodic system
LO5

Following are the condensed journals of Wilson Bakery Supplies. The journal column headings are incomplete in that they do not indicate whether the columns are debit or credit columns. Assume a periodic inventory system.

Sales Journal

Account	Amount
Jack Hertz	7,400
Trudy Stone	16,800
Dave Waylon	2,000
Total	26,200

Purchases Journal

Account	Amount
Grass Corp.	10,800
Sulter, Inc.	9,000
McGrew Company	3,400
Total	23,200

Sales Returns and Allowances	600	
Accounts Receivable—Jack Hertz		600
Customer returned merchandise.		
Accounts Payable—Grass Corp.	1,500	
Purchase Returns and Allowances		1,500
Returned merchandise.		

An asterisk (*) identifies assignment material based on Appendix 8A.

Cash Receipts Journal

Account	Other Accounts	Accounts Receivable	Sales	Sales Discounts	Cash
Jack Hertz		6,800		136	6,664
Sales			4,500		4,500
Notes Payable	9,000				9,000
Sales			1,250		1,250
Trudy Stone		16,800		336	16,464
Store Equipment	1,000				1,000
Totals	10,000	23,600	5,750	472	38,878

Cash Disbursements Journal

Account	Other Accounts	Accounts Payable	Purchase Discounts	Cash
Prepaid Insurance	1,700			1,700
Sulter, Inc.		9,000	270	8,730
Grass Corp.		9,300	186	9,114
Store Equipment	3,500			3,500
Totals	5,200	18,300	456	23,044

Required

1. Prepare T-accounts on notebook paper for the following General Ledger and subledger accounts. Separate the accounts of each ledger group as follows:

General Ledger Accounts

- Cash
- Accounts Receivable
- Prepaid Insurance
- Store Equipment
- Accounts Payable
- Notes Payable
- Sales
- Sales Discounts
- Sales Returns and Allowances
- Purchases
- Purchase Discounts
- Purchase Returns and Allowances

Accounts Receivable Subledger Accounts

- Jack Hertz
- Trudy Stone
- Dave Waylon

Accounts Payable Subledger Accounts

- Grass Corp.
- McGrew Company
- Sulter, Inc.

2. Without referring to any of the illustrations in the chapter that show complete column headings for the journals, post the journals to the proper T-accounts. Ignore dates.

Problems

Problem 8-1A

Special journals and subledgers—perpetual

LO2, 3, 4

Moore Corporation is a major distributor of office supplies. *All sales are on terms 1/10, n/15.* During March, the following selected transactions occurred. For each transaction, identify into which special journal it should be journalized. Also indicate which subledger(s) is (are) affected. Use the list of codes to label your answers. Moore Corporation uses a perpetual inventory system.

Special Journals	
Sales	S
Purchases	P
Cash Receipts	CR
Cash Disbursements	CD
General Journal	G

Subledgers	
Accounts Receivable	AR
Accounts Payable	AP
Merchandise Inventory	MI
No Effect	NE

Date		Transaction	Special Journal	Subledger(s)
Mar.	1	Sold merchandise on credit.		
	2	Defective merchandise sold on March 1 was returned by the customer. It was scrapped.		
	3	Purchased office equipment on credit terms n/30.		
	5	Received payment regarding the March 1 sale.		
	10	Received a credit memorandum from the supplier regarding defective equipment purchased on March 3.		
	14	Sold merchandise for cash.		
	16	Purchased merchandise inventory on credit; terms 1/5, n/30.		
	17	Paid the balance owing on the March 3 transaction.		
	18	Purchased merchandise inventory for cash.		
	21	Paid for the merchandise purchased on March 16.		
	22	Sold old equipment for cash.		
	30	Paid salaries for the month of March.		
	30	Accrued utilities for the month of March.		
	30	Closed the credit balance in the Income Summary to Capital.		

Problem 8-2A
Special journals—perpetual
LO4

Janish Supplies completed the transactions listed below during April 2011. *All sales are on terms 2/10, n/30.*

April	2	Sold merchandise to Tim Bennett for $35,000 on credit; invoice #306 (cost $22,750).
	3	Cash sales for the day totalled $15,000; invoices #307 to #310 (cost $9,750).
	4	Purchased $48,000 of merchandise from Wallace Brothers; terms 1/10, n/30.
	5	Sold merchandise to Brian Kennedy for $42,000 on credit; invoice #311 (cost $27,300).
	6	Returned $4,200 of defective merchandise purchased on April 4.
	9	Purchased $230 of office supplies; cheque #620.
	11	Purchased $56,000 of merchandise from McKinley & Sons; terms n/30.
	12	Received payment from Tim Bennett regarding the sale of April 2.
	13	Paid for the merchandise purchased on April 4; cheque #621.
	16	Sold merchandise to Wynne Walsh for $14,000 on credit; invoice #312 (cost $9,100).
	19	Issued a credit memo regarding a $3,000 allowance granted to Wynne Walsh to cover defective merchandise sold on April 16.
	20	Received payment from Brian Kennedy for the sale of April 5.
	23	Purchased $3,800 of equipment from Zardon Company; terms 1/15, n/30.
	24	Sold merchandise to Brian Kennedy for $18,000 on credit; invoice #313 (cost $11,700).
	26	Paid for the purchase of April 11; cheque #622.
	27	Received payment from Wynne Walsh regarding the sale of April 16.
	30	Paid April salaries; $36,000; cheque #623. For simplicity, we assume one cheque.

Required

1. Prepare a Sales Journal, Cash Receipts Journal, Purchases Journal, Cash Disbursements Journal, and General Journal like the ones illustrated in this chapter.
2. Journalize the April transactions into the appropriate journal *(do not post to the subledgers or the General Ledger).*

Problem 8-3A
Special journals, subledgers—perpetual
LO4

Newton Company completed these transactions during April 2011. *The terms of all credit sales are 2/10, n/30.*

Apr.	2	Purchased merchandise on credit from Baskin Company, invoice dated April 2, terms 2/10, n/60, $13,300.
	3	Sold merchandise on credit to Linda Hobart, invoice #760, $3,000. Cost, $1,800.
	3	Purchased office supplies on credit from Eau Claire Inc., $1,380. Invoice dated April 2, terms n/10 EOM.
	4	Issued cheque #587 to *The Record* for advertising expense, $999.
	5	Sold merchandise on credit to Paul Abrams, invoice #761, $8,000. Cost, $4,500.
	6	Received an $85 credit memorandum from Eau Claire Inc. for office supplies received on April 3 and returned for credit.
	9	Purchased store equipment on credit from Frank's Supply, invoice dated April 9, terms n/10 EOM, $11,125.
	11	Sold merchandise on credit to Kelly Schaefer, invoice #762, $9,500. Cost, $5,000.
	12	Issued cheque #588 to Baskin Company in payment of its April 2 invoice.
	13	Received payment from Linda Hobart for the April 3 sale.
	13	Sold merchandise on credit to Linda Hobart, invoice #763, $4,100. Cost, $2,400.
	14	Received payment from Paul Abrams for the April 5 sale.
	16	Issued cheque #589, payable to Payroll, in payment of the sales salaries for the first half of the month, $9,750. For simplicity, we assume one cheque.
	16	Cash sales for the first half of the month were $50,840. Cost, $28,000. *Cash sales are usually recorded daily from the cash register readings. However, they are recorded only once in this problem to reduce the repetitive transactions.*

Required

1. Set up Accounts Receivable Subledger accounts for Paul Abrams, Linda Hobart, and Kelly Schaefer.
2. Set up Accounts Payable Subledger accounts for Frank's Supply, Baskin Company, Sprocket Company, and Eau Claire Inc.
3. Journalize the transactions of Newton Company into the appropriate special journal, posting to the subledgers where required. Use page 3 for all journals.

Problem 8-4A

Special journals, subledgers, schedules of accounts receivable and accounts payable, and trial balance—perpetual

LO4

This is a continuation of Problem 8-3A. You must complete Problem 8-3A before attempting this problem. Additional transactions for April follow:

Apr.	17	Purchased merchandise on credit from Sprocket Company, invoice dated April 16, terms 2/10, n/30, $12,750.
	18	Borrowed $50,000 from First Bank by giving a long-term note payable.
	20	Received payment from Kelly Schaefer for the April 11 sale.
	20	Purchased store supplies on credit from Frank's Supply, invoice dated April 19, terms n/10 EOM, $730.
	23	Received a $400 credit memorandum from Sprocket Company for defective merchandise received on April 17 and returned.
	23	Received payment from Linda Hobart for the April 13 sale.
	25	Purchased merchandise on credit from Baskin Company, invoice dated April 24, terms 2/10, n/60, $10,375.
	26	Issued cheque #590 to Sprocket Company in payment of its April 16 invoice.
	27	Sold merchandise on credit to Paul Abrams, invoice #764, $3,070. Cost, $1,600.
	27	Sold merchandise on credit to Kelly Schaefer, invoice #765, $5,700. Cost, $3,000.
	30	Issued cheque #591, payable to Payroll, in payment of the sales salaries for the last half of the month, $9,750. For simplicity, we assume one cheque.
	30	Cash sales for the last half of the month were $70,975. Cost, $37,000.

Check figure:
5. Trial balance = $490,710

Required

1. Set up the following General Ledger accounts: Cash (101); Accounts Receivable (106); Merchandise Inventory (119); Office Supplies (124); Store Supplies (125); Store Equipment (165); Accounts Payable (201); Long-Term Notes Payable (251); Jeff Newton, Capital (301); Sales (413); Sales Discounts (415); Cost of Goods Sold (502); Sales Salaries Expense (621); and Advertising Expense (655). Enter the March 31 balances of $167,000 for Cash; $95,000 for Merchandise Inventory; $95,000 for Jeff Newton, Capital; and $167,000 for Long-Term Notes Payable.
2. Continuing from Problem 8-3A, journalize the remaining April transactions for Newton Company into the appropriate special journal, posting to the subledgers as required.
3. Post the items that should be posted as individual amounts from the journals.
4. Foot and crossfoot the journals and make the month-end postings.
5. Prepare a trial balance of the General Ledger and prepare schedules of accounts receivable and accounts payable.

Analysis component:

Assume that the sum of the account balances on the schedule of accounts receivable does not equal the balance of the controlling amount in the General Ledger. Describe the steps you would go through to discover the error(s).

Problem 8-5A

Special journals, subledgers, schedules of accounts receivable and accounts payable, and trial balance—perpetual
LO4

(If the Working Papers that accompany this textbook are not being used, the forms needed to complete this problem are available on Connect.)

It is October 16, 2011, and you have just taken over the accounting work of Saskan Enterprises, whose annual accounting period ends each October 31. The company's previous accountant journalized its transactions through October 15 and posted all items that required posting as individual amounts, as an examination of the journals and ledgers in the Working Papers will show.

The company completed these transactions beginning on October 16, 2011:

Oct.	16	Sold merchandise on credit to Vickie Foresman, invoice #916, $7,700. Cost, $3,900. *Terms of all credit sales are 2/10, n/30.*
	17	Received a $1,040 credit memorandum from Shore Company for merchandise received on October 15 and returned for credit.
	17	Purchased office supplies on credit from Brown Supply Company, $615. Invoice dated October 16, terms n/10 EOM.
	18	Received a $40 credit memorandum from Brown Supply Company for office supplies received on October 17 and returned for credit.
	20	Issued a credit memorandum to Amy Ihrig for defective merchandise sold on October 15 and returned for credit, $500. The returned merchandise was scrapped.
	21	Purchased store equipment on credit from Brown Supply Company, invoice dated October 21, terms n/10 EOM, $6,700.
	22	Received payment from Vickie Foresman for the October 12 sale.
	23	Issued cheque #623 to Sunshine Company in payment of its October 15 invoice.
	24	Sold merchandise on credit to Bill Grigsby, invoice #917, $1,200. Cost, $700.
	24	Issued cheque #624 to Shore Company in payment of its October 15 invoice.
	25	Received payment from Amy Ihrig for the October 15 sale.
	26	Received merchandise and an invoice dated October 25, terms 2/10, n/60, from Sunshine Company, $8,100.
	29	Sold a neighbouring merchant five boxes of file folders (office supplies) for cash at cost, $50.
	30	Ken Shaw, the owner of Saskan Enterprises, used cheque #625 to withdraw $2,500 cash from the business for personal use.
	31	Issued cheque #626 to Jamie Green, the company's only sales employee, in payment of her salary for the last half of October, $2,020.
	31	Issued cheque #627 to Countywide Electric Company in payment of the October electric bill, $710.
	31	Cash sales for the last half of the month were $29,600. Cost, $16,300. *Cash sales are usually recorded daily but are recorded only twice in this problem to reduce the repetitive transactions.*

Required

1. Record the transactions in the journals provided.
2. Post to the customer and creditor accounts and also post any amounts that should be posted as individual amounts to the General Ledger accounts. (Normally, these amounts are posted daily, but they are posted only once by you in this problem because they are few in number.)
3. Foot and crossfoot the journals and make the month-end postings.
4. Prepare an October 31 trial balance and prepare schedules of accounts receivable and accounts payable.

Check figure:
4. Trial balance = $219,408

Problem 8-6A

Inventory Subledger—perpetual
LO4

The Turner Company sells a product called TurnUp for $25 each and uses a perpetual inventory system to account for its merchandise. The beginning balance of TurnUps and transactions during January 2011 were as follows:

Jan.	1	Balance: 25 units costing $8 each.
	3	Purchased from Curtis & Sons 50 units costing $9 each.
	7	Sold to G. Little 20 units, invoice #103.
	19	Sold to B. Moore 15 units, invoice #104.
	20	Purchased from Norton Industries 30 units costing $11 each.
	24	Sold to C. Woudstra 15 units, invoice #105.
	29	Sold to D. Isla 32 units, invoice #106.

Required

Journalize the January transactions in the Sales and Purchases Journal. Use page 1 for each journal. *Assume all sales and purchases are on credit; terms n/30.* Under the assumption that the company keeps its records on a FIFO basis, you will need to enter the beginning balances and post each transaction on an inventory subledger record like the one illustrated in Exhibit 8.6 in order to determine cost of goods sold for each sale.

***Problem 8-7A**
Special journals, subledgers—periodic
LO5

Using the information in Problem 8-3A, complete the requirements assuming a periodic inventory system.

***Problem 8-8A**
Special journals, subledgers, schedules of accounts receivable and accounts payable, and trial balance—periodic
LO5

Check figure:
5. Trial balance = $491,623

*You must complete *Problem 8-7A before attempting this problem.* Using the information in Problem 8-4A, complete the following requirements assuming a periodic inventory system:

1. Set up the following General Ledger accounts: Cash (101); Accounts Receivable (106); Merchandise Inventory (119); Office Supplies (124); Store Supplies (125); Store Equipment (165); Accounts Payable (201); Long-Term Notes Payable (251); Jeff Newton, Capital (301); Sales (413); Sales Discounts (415); Purchases (505); Purchase Discounts (506); Purchase Returns and Allowances (507); Sales Salaries Expense (621); and Advertising Expense (655). Enter the March 31 balances of $167,000 for Cash; $95,000 for Merchandise Inventory; $95,000 for Jeff Newton, Capital; and $167,000 for Long-Term Notes Payable.
2. Continuing from *Problem 8-7A, journalize the remaining April transactions for Newton Company into the appropriate special journals, posting to the subledgers where required.
3. Post the items that should be posted as individual amounts from the journals.
4. Foot and crossfoot the journals and make the month-end postings.
5. Prepare a trial balance of the General Ledger and prepare schedules of accounts receivable and accounts payable.

Alternate Problems

Problem 8-1B
Special journals and subledgers—perpetual
LO2, 3

Lavender Gifts and Novelties uses a perpetual inventory system. *All sales are on terms of 2/15, n/30.* During May, the following selected transactions occurred. Identify into which special journal each transaction should be journalized. Also indicate which subledger(s) is (are) affected. Use the list of codes to label your answers. Assume a perpetual inventory system.

Special Journals	
Sales	S
Purchases	P
Cash Receipts	CR
Cash Disbursements	CD
General Journal	G

Subledgers	
Accounts Receivable	AR
Accounts Payable	AP
Merchandise Inventory	MI
No Effect	NE

Date	Transaction	Special Journal	Subledger(s)
May 1	The owner invested an automobile into the business.		
2	Sold merchandise and received cash.		
3	Purchased merchandise inventory on credit; terms 1/5, n/30.		
4	Sold merchandise on credit.		
5	The customer of May 4 returned defective merchandise; the merchandise was scrapped.		
6	Regarding the May 3 purchase, received a credit memorandum from the supplier granting an allowance.		
15	Paid mid-month salaries.		
17	Purchased office supplies on credit; terms n/30.		
19	Paid for the balance owing on the May 3 purchase.		
22	Received payment on the May 4 sale.		
25	Borrowed money from the bank.		
29	Purchased merchandise inventory; paid cash.		
30	Accrued interest revenue.		
30	Closed all revenue accounts to the Income Summary account.		

An asterisk (*) identifies assignment material based on Appendix 8A.

Problem 8-2B
Special journals—perpetual
LO4

Fraser Antiques completed the transactions listed below during June 2011. *All sales are on terms 2/10, n/30.*

June	1	Purchased equipment costing $22,500 from Exeter Equipment; terms n/30.
	4	Purchased a collection of antiques for $42,500 from Whitby Co.; terms 1/5, n/15.
	5	Sold a group of antiques to Martha Stohart for $51,000 on credit; invoice #347 (cost $25,500).
	6	Sold an antique to Carol Larson for $4,100 on credit; invoice #348 (cost $2,850).
	7	Received an allowance of $2,400 regarding the June 4 purchase due to damages that occurred during delivery.
	8	Purchased office supplies of $900 from Suppliers Unlimited; terms 2/10, n/30.
	11	Paid for the purchase of June 4; cheque #101.
	12	Received payment from Carol Larson regarding the sale of June 6.
	14	Paid mid-month salaries of $7,500; cheque #102.
	18	Sold an antique to Lars Wilson for $3,000 on credit; invoice #349 (cost $2,450).
	24	Received payment regarding the sale of June 5.
	25	Sold a group of antiques to Nathan Blythe for $12,000 on credit; invoice #350 (cost $7,250).
	26	Nathan Blythe returned one of the antiques purchased on June 25 for $1,400 because it was not suited to his home (cost $1,100). The item was returned to inventory.
	27	Received payment on the sale of June 18.
	28	Paid for the purchase of June 1; cheque #103.
	29	Paid month-end salaries of $7,500; cheque #104.

Required

1. Prepare a General Journal, Sales Journal, Purchases Journal, Cash Receipts Journal, and Cash Disbursements Journal like the ones illustrated in this chapter.
2. Journalize the June transactions into the appropriate journal. *Do not post to the subledgers or General Ledger.*

Problem 8-3B
Special journals, subledgers—perpetual
LO4

Duncan Industries completed these transactions during July 2011. *The terms of all credit sales are 2/10, n/30.*

July	1	Purchased merchandise on credit from Beech Company, invoice dated June 30, terms 2/10, n/30, $12,600.
	3	Issued cheque #300 to *The Weekly Journal* for advertising expense, $1,150.
	5	Sold merchandise on credit to Karen Harden, invoice #918, $36,800. Cost, $20,400.
	6	Sold merchandise on credit to Paul Kane, invoice #919, $15,000. Cost, $8,200.
	7	Purchased store supplies on credit from Blackwater Inc., $2,100. Invoice dated July 7, terms n/10 EOM.
	8	Received a $300 credit memorandum from Blackwater Inc. for store supplies received on July 7 and returned for credit.
	9	Purchased store equipment on credit from Poppe's Supply, invoice dated July 8, terms n/10 EOM, $75,420.
	10	Issued cheque #301 to Beech Company in payment of its June 30 invoice.
	13	Sold merchandise on credit to Kelly Grody, invoice #920, $16,700. Cost, $9,200.
	14	Sold merchandise on credit to Karen Harden, invoice #921, $8,200. Cost, $4,600.
	15	Received payment from Karen Harden for the July 5 sale.
	15	Issued cheque #302, payable to Payroll, in payment of the sales salaries for the first half of the month, $61,240. For simplicity, we assume one cheque.
	15	Cash sales for the first half of the month were $242,740. Cost, $133,400. *Cash sales are usually recorded daily from the cash register readings. However, they are recorded only once in this problem to reduce the repetitive transactions.*

Required

1. Set up Accounts Receivable Subledger accounts for Kelly Grody, Karen Harden, and Paul Kane.
2. Set up Accounts Payable Subledger accounts for Beech Company, Blackwater Inc., Poppe's Supply, and Sprague Company.
3. Journalize the transactions of Duncan Industries into the appropriate special journal, posting to the subledgers where required. Use page 3 for all journals.

Problem 8-4B

Special journals, subledgers, schedules of accounts receivable and accounts payable, and trial balance—perpetual

LO4

This is a continuation of Problem 8-3B. You must complete Problem 8-3B before attempting this problem. Additional transactions for July follow:

July	16	Received payment from Paul Kane for the July 6 sale.
	17	Purchased merchandise on credit from Sprague Company, invoice dated July 17, terms 2/10, n/30, $16,400.
	20	Purchased office supplies on credit from Poppe's Supply, $1,500. Invoice dated July 19, terms n/10 EOM.
	21	Borrowed $40,000 from College Bank by giving a long-term note payable.
	23	Received payment from Kelly Grody for the July 13 sale.
	24	Received payment from Karen Harden for the July 14 sale.
	24	Received a $4,800 credit memorandum from Sprague Company for defective merchandise received on July 17 and returned.
	26	Purchased merchandise on credit from Beech Company, invoice dated July 26, terms 2/10, n/30, $19,540.
	27	Issued cheque #303 to Sprague Company in payment of its July 17 invoice.
	29	Sold merchandise on credit to Paul Kane, invoice #922, $56,180. Cost, $31,000.
	30	Sold merchandise on credit to Kelly Grody, invoice #923, $31,500. Cost, $17,400.
	31	Issued cheque #304, payable to Payroll, in payment of the sales salaries for the last half of the month, $61,240. For simplicity, we assume one cheque.
	31	Cash sales for the last half of the month were $158,040. Cost, $87,000.

Check figure:
5. Trial balance = $1,227,420

Required

1. Set up the following General Ledger accounts: Cash (101); Accounts Receivable (106); Merchandise Inventory (119); Office Supplies (124); Store Supplies (125); Store Equipment (165); Accounts Payable (201); Long-Term Notes Payable (251); Gene Duncan, Capital (301); Sales (413); Sales Discounts (415); Cost of Goods Sold (502); Sales Salaries Expense (621); and Advertising Expense (655). Enter the June 30 balances of $190,000 for Cash; $334,000 for Merchandise Inventory; $190,000 for Gene Duncan, Capital; and $334,000 for Long-Term Notes Payable.
2. Continuing from Problem 8-3B, journalize the remaining July transactions for Duncan Industries into the appropriate special journal, posting to the subledgers as required.
3. Post the items that should be posted as individual amounts from the journals.
4. Foot and crossfoot the journals and make the month-end postings.
5. Prepare a trial balance of the General Ledger and prepare schedules of accounts receivable and accounts payable.

Analysis component:

Assume that the sum of the account balances on the schedule of accounts payable does not equal the balance of the controlling account in the General Ledger. Describe the steps you would go through to discover the error(s).

Problem 8-5B

Special journals, subledgers, schedules of accounts receivable and accounts payable, and trial balance—perpetual

LO4

(If the Working Papers that accompany this textbook are not being used, the forms needed to complete this problem are available on Connect.)

It is October 16, 2011, and you have just taken over the accounting work of China Moon Products, whose annual accounting period ends October 31. The company's previous accountant journalized its transactions through October 15 and posted all items that required posting as individual amounts, as an examination of the journals and ledgers in the Working Papers will show.

The company completed these transactions beginning on October 16, 2011. *Terms of all credit sales are 2/10, n/30.*

Oct.	16	Purchased office supplies on credit from Green Supply Company, $1,530. Invoice dated October 16, terms n/10 EOM.
	16	Sold merchandise on credit to Heather Flatt, invoice #916, $8,580. Cost, $4,920.
	18	Issued a credit memorandum to Amy Izon for defective merchandise sold on October 15 and returned for credit, $400. The returned merchandise was scrapped.
	19	Received a $1,280 credit memorandum from Walters Company for merchandise received on October 15 and returned for credit.
	20	Received a $286 credit memorandum from Green Supply Company for office supplies received on October 16 and returned for credit.
	20	Purchased store equipment on credit from Green Supply Company, invoice dated October 19, terms n/10 EOM, $14,950.
	21	Sold merchandise on credit to Jan Wildman, invoice #917, $11,040. Cost, $6,000.
	22	Received payment from Heather Flatt for the October 12 sale.
	25	Received payment from Amy Izon for the October 15 sale.
	25	Issued cheque #623 to Walters Company in payment of its October 15 invoice.
	25	Issued cheque #624 to Sunshine Company in payment of its October 15 invoice.
	28	Received merchandise with an invoice dated October 28, terms 2/10, n/60, from Sunshine Company, $12,060.
	28	Sold a neighbouring merchant a carton of calculator tape (store supplies) for cash at cost, $116.
	29	Marlee Levin, the owner of China Moon Products, used cheque #625 to withdraw $8,000 cash from the business for personal use.
	30	Issued cheque #626 to Midwest Electric Company in payment of the October electric bill, $1,980.
	30	Issued cheque #627 to Jamie Ford, the company's only sales employee, in payment of her salary for the last half of October, $5,240.
	31	Cash sales for the last half of the month were $132,256. Cost, $72,800. *Cash sales are usually recorded daily but are recorded only twice in this problem to reduce the repetitive transactions.*

Check figure:
4. Trial balance = $511,196

Required

1. Record the transactions in the journals provided.
2. Post to the customer and creditor accounts and also post any amounts that should be posted as individual amounts to the General Ledger accounts. *Normally, these amounts are posted daily, but they are posted only once by you in this problem because they are few in number.*
3. Foot and crossfoot the journals and make the month-end postings.
4. Prepare an October 31 trial balance and prepare schedules of accounts receivable and payable.

Problem 8-6B
Inventory Subledger—perpetual
LO4

The Digit-All Company sells a product called ReCord for $15 each and uses a perpetual inventory system to account for its merchandise. The beginning balance of ReCords and transactions during July 2011 were as follows:

July	1	Balance: 30 units costing $6 each.
	4	Purchased from Tulsco Supply 45 units costing $5 each.
	9	Sold to W. Tilden 10 units, invoice #213.
	15	Sold to J. Samuelson 25 units, invoice #214.
	18	Purchased from Gentry Holdings 30 units costing $4.50 each.
	22	Sold to V. Nels 20 units, invoice #215.
	30	Sold to M. Bains 27 units, invoice #216.

Check figure:
Total COGS for July = $424.74

Required

Journalize the July transactions in the Sales Journal and Purchases Journal. Use page 1 for each journal. *Assume all sales and purchases are on credit; terms n/30.* Under the assumption that the company keeps its records on a weighted average basis, you will need to enter the beginning balances and post each transaction on an Inventory Subledger record like the one illustrated in Exhibit 8.6 in order to determine cost of goods sold.

***Problem 8-7B**
Special journals, subledgers—periodic
LO5

Using the information in Problem 8-3B, complete the requirements assuming a periodic inventory system.

***Problem 8-8B**
Special journals, subledgers, schedules of accounts receivable and accounts payable, and trial balance—periodic
LO5

Check figure:
5. Trial balance = $1,232,704

*You must complete *Problem 8-7B before attempting this problem.* Using the information in Problem 8-4B, complete the following requirements assuming a periodic inventory system:

1. Set up the following General Ledger accounts: Cash (101); Accounts Receivable (106); Merchandise Inventory (119); Office Supplies (124); Store Supplies (125); Store Equipment (165); Accounts Payable (201); Long-Term Notes Payable (251); Gene Duncan, Capital (301); Sales (413); Sales Discounts (415); Purchases (505); Purchase Discounts (506); Purchase Returns and Allowances (507); Sales Salaries Expense (621); and Advertising Expense (655). Enter the June 30 balances of $190,000 for Cash; $334,000 for Merchandise Inventory; $190,000 for Gene Duncan, Capital; and $334,000 for Long-Term Notes Payable.
2. Continuing from *Problem 8-7B, journalize the remaining July transactions for Duncan Industries into the appropriate special journal, posting to the subledgers as required.
3. Post the items that should be posted as individual amounts from the journals.
4. Foot and crossfoot the journals and make the month-end postings.
5. Prepare a trial balance of the General Ledger and prepare schedules of accounts receivable and accounts payable.

An asterisk (*) identifies assignment material based on Appendix 8A.

Analytical and Review Problem—Perpetual

A & R Problem 8-1

The Williams Company sells a product called Mix-Right for $15 each and uses a perpetual inventory system to account for its merchandise. The beginning balance of Mix-Rights and transactions during October 2011 were as follows:

Oct.	1	Balance: 85 units costing $5 each.
	3	Purchased 100 units from Arnold Brothers costing $7.50 each.
	4	Returned 20 of the units purchased on October 3.
	9	Sold 75 units to Kitchen Club, invoice #210.
	15	Purchased 200 units from Arnold Brothers costing $7.75 each.
	18	Sold 150 units to Thorhild Co-op, invoice #211.
	19	Paid for the October 3 purchase; cheque #101.
	23	Paid for the October 15 purchase, cheque #102.
	24	Sold 50 units to Boyle Grocery, invoice #212.
	31	Purchased 75 units from Arnold Brothers costing $8.00 each.

Required
Journalize the October transactions in the Sales, Purchases, and Cash Disbursements Journals. Use page 1 for all your journals. *Assume all sales and purchases are on credit; terms 2/10, n/30.* Under the assumption that the company keeps its records on a weighted average basis, you will need to enter the beginning balances and post each transaction on an Inventory Subledger record like the one illustrated below in order to determine cost of goods sold. Posting to other subledgers is not required.

(If the Working Papers that accompany this textbook are not available, the forms needed to complete this problem are available on Connect.)

Date	PR	Purchases (Returns, Allowances and Discounts)			Sales (At Cost)			Inventory Balance		
		Units	Cost	Total Cost	Units	Cost	Total Cost	(b) Total Units	(a) ÷ (b) Average Cost/Unit	(a) Total Cost

Ethics Challenge

EC 8-1

John Harris is a public accountant and a sole practitioner. He has been practising as an auditor for 10 years. Recently a longstanding audit client asked John to design and implement an integrated computerized accounting information system. The fees associated with this additional engagement with the client are very attractive. However, John wonders if he can remain objective in his evaluation of the client's accounting system and records on subsequent annual audits if he puts himself in the position of auditing a system he was responsible for installing. John knows that the professional auditing standards require him to remain independent in fact and appearance of all of his auditing clients.

Required

1. What do you think auditing standards mean when they require independence in fact? in appearance?
2. Why is it important that auditors remain independent of their clients?
3. Do you think John can accept this engagement and remain independent? Justify your response.

Focus on Financial Statements

FFS 8-1

Mango Designs began selling its custom furniture on June 1, 2011. At the end of the month, the special journals showed the following results:
Other information

- Interest of $200 had accrued on the note payable as of June 30, 2011
- $13,400 of the office supplies had been used by June 30, 2011
- Depreciation on the store equipment was $500 for June

Sales Journal **Page 3**

Date	Account Debited	Invoice Number	PR	A/R Dr. Sales. Cr.	Cost of Goods Sold Dr. Merchandise Inventory Cr.
2011					
June 5	Leslie Haverly	381	✓	8,300	6,200
6	Tomlinson Architects	382	✓	17,900	13,800
13	Dentures Galore	383	✓	38,400	27,150
14	Leslie Haverly	384	✓	2,900	2,400
27	Nelson Consulting	385	✓	22,700	18,500

Cash Receipts Journal **Page 3**

Date	Account Credited	Explanation	PR	Cash Debit	Sales Discount Debit	Accts. Rec. Credit	Sales Credit	Other Accts. Credit	Cost of Goods Sold Dr. Merchandise Inventory Cr.
2011									
June 1	Tom Mandalay	Owner Invmt.	301	75,000				75,000	
10	Notes Payable	L.T. loan	251	50,000				50,000	
15	Leslie Haverly	Sale of June 5	✓	8,134	166	8,300			
20	Cash sales	Cash sales		121,370			121,370		66,700
29	Tomlinson	Sale of June 6	✓	17,900		17,900			

Purchases Journal **Page 3**

Date	Account Credited	Date of Invoice	Terms	PR	Accounts Payable Credit	Merchandise Inventory Debit	Office Supplies Debit	Other Accts. Debit
2011								
June 2	Tenor Company	June 2	2/10, n/60	✓	75,000	75,000		
7	Indago Manufacturers	June 7	n/10 EOM	✓	18,000		18,000	
17	Penray Suppliers	June 17	1/10 EOM	✓	98,000	98,000		
18	Ego/Store Equipment	June 18	n/30	165/✓	32,000			32,000

Cash Disbursements Journal **Page 3**

Date	Ch. No.	Payee	Account Debited	PR	Cash Credit	Merchandise Inventory Credit	Other Accts. Debit	Accts. Payable Debit
2011								
June 3	100	The Daily Gazette	Advertising Expense	655	600		600	
10	101	Tenor Company	Tenor Company	✓	73,500	1,500		75,000
30	102	Payroll	Sales Salaries Expense	621	42,000		42,000	

Required
Using the information provided, prepare a single-step income statement, statement of changes in equity, and classified balance sheet. (*Hint: You may find it useful to use T-accounts.*)

Check figures:
Net income = $19,954;
Total assets = $293,154

Analysis component:
Does Mango Designs use a perpetual or periodic inventory system? Explain how you know.

FFS 8-2

Chapter 8 discusses the Accounts Payable Subledger, Accounts Receivable Subledger, and Inventory Subledger. It also briefly introduces other subledgers such as the Property, Plant and Equipment Asset Subledger.

Required
Review Danier's financial statements in Appendix I at the end of the textbook. Which subledgers might Danier be using and why? Be sure to explain briefly what kind of information these subledgers might include that would be useful to decision makers.

Critical Thinking Mini Case

Northern Outposts Mining Company has 17 mines in various locations throughout Northern Quebec, Nunavut, and the Yukon. You have just been hired as the assistant office manager in the head office, which is located in Whitehorse. Because of your computer expertise, one of your duties will be to generate special purpose reports from the accounting information system. The director of operations has asked you to prepare a report for an afternoon meeting that details all of the property, plant and equipment for each of the 17 mines. You are confident that this should be an easy task but, upon reviewing the accounting records, you discover that all of the information regarding the assets is maintained in only one location, a General Ledger account called Mining Assets!

Required
Using the elements of critical thinking described on the inside front cover, comment.

Comprehensive Problem 8.1—Perpetual

Alpine Company
LO4

Assume it is Monday, May 1, 2011, the first business day of the month, and you have just been hired as the accountant for Alpine Company, which operates with monthly accounting periods. All of the company's accounting work has been completed through the end of April and its ledgers show April 30 balances. Alpine uses a perpetual system to account for inventory. *The terms of all credit sales are 2/10, n/30.* During your first month on the job, you record the following transactions on page 2 of each journal.

Note: If the Working Papers that accompany this textbook are not being used, the forms needed to complete this problem are available on Connect.

Required

Check figures:
3. Net income = $33,128;
Total assets = $387,272

1. Enter the transactions in the appropriate journals and post when instructed to do so.
2. Prepare a trial balance in the Trial Balance columns of the provided work sheet form and complete the work sheet using the following information.
   a. Expired insurance, $553.
   b. Ending store supplies inventory, $2,632.
   c. Ending office supplies inventory, $504.
   d. Estimated depreciation of store equipment, $567.
   e. Estimated depreciation of office equipment, $329.
   f. Ending merchandise inventory, $191,000.
3. Prepare a May classified, multiple-step income statement P. 271, a May statement of changes in equity P. 29, and a May 31 classified balance sheet P. 207.
4. Prepare and post adjusting and closing entries (omit explanations).
5. Prepare a post-closing trial balance P. 202. Also prepare a list of the Accounts Receivable Subledger accounts and a list of the Accounts Payable Subledger accounts.

May	1	Issued cheque #3410 to S&M Management Co. in payment of the May rent, $3,710. *Use two lines to record the transaction. Charge 80% of the rent to Rent Expense, Selling Space, and the balance to Rent Expense, Office Space.*
	2	Sold merchandise on credit to Essex Company, invoice #8785, $6,100. Cost $3,660.
	2	Issued a $175 credit memorandum to Nabors, Inc., for defective merchandise sold on April 28 and discarded when returned to inventory (cost $105) for credit. The total selling price was $4,725.
	3	Received a $798 credit memorandum from Parkay Products for merchandise received on April 29 and returned for credit.
	4	Purchased on credit from Thompson Supply Co.: merchandise, $37,072; store supplies, $574; and office supplies, $83. Invoice dated May 4, terms n/10 EOM.
	5	Received payment from Nabors, Inc. from the sale of April 28.
	8	Issued cheque #3411 to Parkay Products to pay for the $7,098 of merchandise received on April 29 (terms 2/10, n/30).
	9	Sold store supplies to the merchant next door at cost for cash, $350.
	10	Purchased office equipment on credit from Thompson Supply Co., invoice dated May 10, terms n/10 EOM, $4,074.
	11	Received payment from Essex Company for the May 2 sale.
	11	Received merchandise and an invoice dated May 10, terms 2/10, n/30, from Gale, Inc., $8,800.
	12	Received an $854 credit memorandum from Thompson Supply Co. for defective office equipment received on May 10 and returned for credit.
	15	Issued cheque #3412, payable to Payroll, in payment of sales salaries, $5,320, and office salaries, $3,150. For simplicity, we assume one cheque.
	15	Cash sales for the first half of the month, $59,220. Cost $35,532. *Such sales are normally recorded daily. They are recorded only twice in this problem to reduce the repetitive entries.*
	16	Sold merchandise on credit to Essex Company, invoice #8786, $3,990. Cost $2,394.
	17	Received merchandise and an invoice dated May 14, terms 2/10, n/60, from Chandler Corp., $13,650.
	19	Issued cheque #3413 to Gale, Inc. in payment of its May 10 invoice.
	22	Sold merchandise to Oscar Services, invoice #8787, $6,850, terms 2/10, n/60. Cost $4,110.
	23	Issued cheque #3414 to Chandler Corp. in payment of its May 14 invoice.
	24	Purchased on credit from Thompson Supply Co.: merchandise, $8,120; store supplies, $630; and office supplies, $280. Invoice dated May 24, terms n/10 EOM.
	25	Received merchandise and an invoice dated May 23, terms 2/10, n/30, from Parkay Products, $3,080.
	26	Sold merchandise on credit to Deaver Corp., invoice #8788, $14,210. Cost $8,526.
	26	Issued cheque #3415 to Trinity Power in payment of the April electric bill, $1,283.
	29	The owner, Clint Barry, withdrew $7,000 from the business for personal use, using cheque #3416.
	30	Received payment from Oscar Services for the May 22 sale.
	30	Issued cheque #3417, payable to Payroll, in payment of sales salaries, $5,320, and office salaries, $3,150. For simplicity, we assume one cheque.
	31	Cash sales for the last half of the month were $66,052. Cost $39,630.
	31	*Post to the customer and creditor accounts. Also, post individual items that are not included in column totals at the end of the month to the General Ledger accounts. Normally, such items are posted daily, but you are asked to post them only once in this problem because they are few in number.*
	31	*Foot and crossfoot the journals and make the month-end postings.*

*Comprehensive Problem 8.2—Periodic

Alpine Company

LO5

Check figures:
3. Net income = $33,128;
Total assets = $387,272

Required

Using information from Comprehensive Problem 8.1, complete the requirements assuming a periodic inventory system.

Note: If the Working Papers that accompany this textbook are not being used, the forms needed to complete this problem are available on Connect.

An asterisk (*) identifies assignment material based on Appendix 8A.

CHAPTER 9

Internal Control and Cash

learning objectives

LO1 Define, explain the purpose, and identify the principles of internal control.

LO2 Define cash and explain how it is reported.

LO3 Apply internal control to cash.

LO4 Explain and record petty cash fund transactions.

LO5 Explain and identify banking activities and the control features they provide.

LO6 Prepare a bank reconciliation and journalize any resulting adjustment(s).

*APPENDIX 9A

LO7 Calculate the acid-test ratio and explain its use as an indicator of a company's liquidity.

High Cost of Poor Controls

Shirley Hannah applied for a job as the bookkeeper for Leduc's Alberta Legacy Development Society. Little did her employers know that, several years earlier, Hannah had defrauded a Sherwood Park housing co-op out of $57,000; she was the co-op's bookkeeper at the time. Also, as president of a chapter of Job's Daughters, Hannah stole $17,020. The Alberta Legacy Development Society hired her without doing a reference check with her past employers. Over the next several months, Hannah embezzled a total of $16,883.66 from her new employer while the bank sent all statements to her home so she could present fictitious financial reports during the society's meetings. Her wrongdoing went undetected because Hannah was responsible for both writing cheques and preparing the bank reconciliation. The situation didn't come to light until an official from the bank called the society's president to tell him that its account was $12,000 overdrawn. To assess the damage, the society had to get all the bank statements reprinted and spend a lot of time and money reconstructing the financial data. The lesson is to ensure that your organization has a sound system of controls, including management review on a regular basis.

CRITICAL THINKING CHALLENGE

The article states that Shirley Hannah was responsible for both writing cheques and preparing the bank reconciliation. Explain how this would have prevented her employer from uncovering her fraudulent activities.

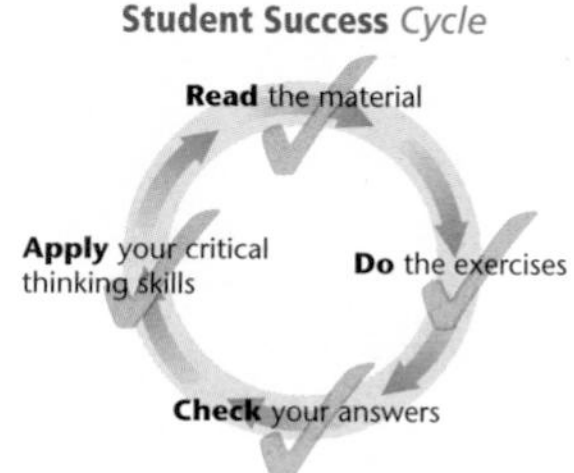

chapter preview

We are all aware of reports and experiences involving theft and fraud. These activities affect us and produce various actions, including locking doors, chaining bikes, reviewing sales receipts, and acquiring alarm systems. A business also takes action to safeguard, control, and manage what it owns. Experience tells us small companies are most vulnerable, usually due to weak internal controls. It is management's responsibility to set up policies and procedures to safeguard a company's assets, especially cash. To do so, management and employees must understand and apply principles of internal control. This chapter introduces these principles to help us learn about the importance of internal control policies and procedures. We focus special attention on cash, because cash is easily transferable and is often at high risk of loss. Controls for cash are explained, including petty cash funds and reconciling bank accounts. Our understanding of these controls and procedures makes us more secure in carrying out business activities and in assessing those activities of companies. As was emphasized in the opening article, internal controls are crucial for the successful operation of an organization.

Internal Control

This section introduces internal control and its fundamental principles. We also discuss the impact of computing technology on internal control and the limitations of control procedures.

Purpose of Internal Control

LO1 Define, explain the purpose, and identify the principles of internal control.

Managers of small businesses often control the entire operation. They participate in all activities from hiring and managing employees to signing all cheques. These managers know from personal contact and observation whether the business is actually receiving the assets and services being paid for. The larger the operation, the more managers must delegate responsibilities and rely on formal procedures rather than personal contact in controlling and knowing all operations of the business.

These managers place a high priority on internal control systems to monitor and control operations. This is because these systems can prevent avoidable losses, help managers plan operations, and monitor company and human performance. An **internal control system** is all policies and procedures used to:

- Protect assets,
- Ensure reliable accounting,
- Promote efficient operations, and
- Encourage adherence to company policies.

Principles of Internal Control

Internal control policies and procedures depend on the nature and size of the business. The fundamental **principles of internal control** are:

1. **Ensure transactions and activities are authorized.**

   Establish responsibilities for each task clearly and for one person. Approvals must be made by authorized individuals. When two salesclerks share access to the same cash register, for instance, neither clerk can prove or disprove any alleged shortage. Instead, a company can use a register with separate cash drawers for each clerk.

2. Maintain records.

Maintain adequate records to help protect assets by ensuring that employees use prescribed procedures. When detailed records of manufacturing equipment and tools are kept, for instance, lost or stolen items are readily noticed. Similarly, the use of a chart of accounts encourages the correct recording of transactions that improves the accuracy of reports.

Preprinted forms and internal business papers are also designed and properly used in a good internal control system. For example, when sales slips are prenumbered and accounted for, a salesperson is not able to pocket cash by making a sale and destroying the sales slip. Computerized point-of-sale systems achieve the same control results.

3. Insure assets and bond key employees.

Insure assets and *bond* key employees to reduce risk of loss from casualty and theft. To **bond** an employee is to purchase an insurance policy, or a bond, against losses from theft by that employee. Bonding reduces the risk of loss suffered from theft in addition to discouraging theft by the bonded employee.

4. Separate recordkeeping and custody of assets.

Recordkeeping should be separated from the custody of assets so a person who controls or has access to an asset is not responsible for the maintenance of that asset's accounting records. The risk of theft or waste is reduced since the person with control over the asset knows that records are kept by another person. The recordkeeper does not have access to the asset and has no reason to falsify records. In situations where recordkeeping is separate from the custody of assets, *collusion* is necessary to hide theft from the records. **Collusion** is not likely because it means two or more people must agree to commit a fraud.

5. Establish a separation of duties.

A **separation of duties** involves dividing responsibility for related transactions between two or more individuals or departments. This is not a call for duplication of work but instead ensures that the work of one acts as a check on the other. An example is requiring two signatures on cheques to verify that disbursements comply with policies and procedures. Other examples of transactions improved by dividing responsibility are issuing purchase orders and receiving merchandise. Having an independent person check incoming goods for quality and quantity encourages more care and attention to detail than when they are checked by the person who placed the order.

6. Apply technological controls.

Cash registers with a locked-in tape or electronic file make a record of each cash sale. A time clock registers the exact time an employee arrives at and departs from the job. Passwords limit access to sensitive information. Mechanical change and currency counters can quickly and accurately count amounts. Personal identification scanners can limit access to only those individuals who are authorized. All of these and other technological controls are effective parts of many internal control systems.

7. Perform internal and external audits.

Perform regular and independent reviews to ensure that internal control procedures are followed. No internal control system is entirely effective, for various reasons such as changes in personnel and time pressures. Reviews are preferably done by internal auditors who are employees not directly involved in operations and who report directly to senior management. Their independent perspective encourages an evaluation of the efficiency as well as the effectiveness of the internal control system.

Many companies also pay for audits by independent external auditors who are professional accountants. These external auditors test the company's financial records and then give an opinion as to whether the company's financial statements are presented fairly in accordance with generally accepted accounting principles. In the process of their evaluation, they often identify internal controls that need improvement.

Technology and Internal Control

The fundamental principles of internal control are relevant no matter what the technological state of the accounting system. This includes all systems from the purely manual to those that are fully automated with only electronic documentation. This section describes some technological impacts to which we must be alert.

Reduced Processing Errors

Provided the software and data entries are correct, the risk of mechanical and mathematical errors is nearly eliminated because of technology. Yet mistakes happen and one must be alert to that possibility. The decreasing human involvement in later data processing can cause data entry errors to go undiscovered. Similarly, errors in software can produce consistent erroneous processing of transactions.

More Extensive Testing

Auditors and others need to test not only samples of data from the electronic accounting system but also the controls over the system itself. The results of the review of the controls over the accounting system will affect the scope of the samples of data tested.

Limited Evidence of Processing

Because many data processing steps are increasingly done by computer, fewer "hard copy" items of documentary evidence are available for review. Yet technologically advanced systems can store additional evidence. They can, for instance, record information such as who made the entries, the date and time, and the source of their entry. Technology can also be designed to require use of passwords or other identification before access to the system is granted. This means that internal control depends more on the design and operation of the information system and less on analysis of the documents left behind by the system.

Crucial Separation of Duties

Technological advances in accounting information systems are so efficient that they often require fewer employees. This reduction in workforce carries a risk that separation of crucial responsibilities is lost. Companies that use advanced technology also need employees with special skills to operate programs and equipment. The duties of these employees must be controlled and monitored to minimize risk of error and fraud. Better control is maintained if, for instance, the person designing and programming the system does not serve as the operator. Also the control over programs and files related to cash receipts and disbursements must be separated. Cheque-writing activities should not be controlled by a computer operator in order to avoid risk of fraud. Yet achieving acceptable separation of duties can be especially difficult in small companies with few employees.

Limitations of Internal Control

All internal control policies and procedures have limitations. Probably the most serious source of these limitations is the human element that we can categorize as either (1) human error, or (2) human fraud.

Human error is a factor whenever internal control policies and procedures are carried out by people. *Human error* can occur from negligence, fatigue, misjudgement, or confusion. *Human fraud* involves intent by people to defeat internal controls for personal gain. This human element highlights the importance of establishing an *internal control environment* that conveys management's attitude and commitment to internal control.

Another important limitation of internal control is the *cost–benefit standard*. This means the costs of internal controls must not exceed their benefits. Analysis of costs and benefits must consider all factors, including the impact on morale. Most companies, for instance, have a legal right to read employees' e-mail. Yet companies seldom exercise that right unless confronted with evidence of potential harm to the company. The same holds for drug testing, phone tapping, and hidden cameras. The bottom line is that no internal control system is perfect and that managers must establish internal control policies and procedures with a net benefit to the company.

The preceding discussion is an introduction to internal controls. The study of *auditing* takes a detailed look at internal controls.

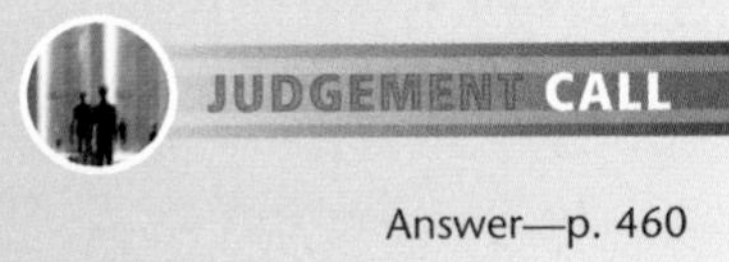

Answer—p. 460

Campaign Manager

You are leading a campaign to influence the government to improve the health care system. Your funding is limited and you try hiring people who are committed to your cause and will work for less. A systems analyst recently volunteered her services and put together a Web strategy to attract supporters. She also strongly encouraged you to force all employees to take at least one week of vacation per year. Why does she feel so strongly about a "forced vacation" policy?

1. Fundamental principles of internal control state that (choose the correct statement):
   a. Responsibility for a series of related transactions (such as placing orders for, receiving, and paying for merchandise) should be assigned to one person.
   b. Responsibility for specific tasks should be shared by two or more employees so that one serves as a check on the other.
   c. Employees who handle cash and negotiable assets are bonded.
2. What are some impacts of computing technology on internal control?

Do Quick Study question: QS 9-1

Cash

LO2 Define cash and explain how it is reported.

Cash is an important asset for every company and must be managed. Companies also need to carefully control access to cash by employees and others who are inclined to take it for personal use. Good accounting systems support both goals by managing how much cash is on hand and controlling who has access to it.

Cash Defined

Cash includes currency, coins, and amounts on deposit in bank accounts, chequing accounts, and some savings accounts.[1] Cash also includes items that are acceptable for deposit in these accounts, such as customers' cheques, cashier's cheques, certified cheques, money orders, and deposits made through electronic funds transfer (EFT).

EXTEND YOUR KNOWLEDGE 9-1

Many companies invest idle cash in assets called *cash equivalents* or short-term investments to increase earnings. Because cash equivalents are similar to cash, many companies combine them with cash as a single item on the balance sheet. WestJet Airlines Ltd., for instance, reports the following on its December 31, 2008, balance sheet:

Cash and cash equivalents.............$820,214 (thousand)

Liquidity

Cash is the usual means of payment when paying for other assets, services, or liabilities. **Liquidity** refers to how easily an asset can be converted into another asset or used in paying for services or obligations. Cash and similar assets are called **liquid assets** because they are converted easily into other assets or used in paying for services or liabilities. A company must own some liquid assets, for example, so that bills are paid on time and purchases are made for cash when necessary.

Control of Cash

LO3 Apply internal control to cash.

It is important that we apply principles of good internal control to cash. Cash is the most liquid of all assets and is easily hidden and moved. A good system of internal control for cash provides adequate procedures for protecting both cash receipts and cash disbursements. These procedures should meet three basic guidelines:

1. Separate handling of cash from recordkeeping of cash.
2. Deposit cash receipts promptly (daily) in a bank.
3. Make cash disbursements by cheque.

The first guideline aims to minimize errors and fraud by a division of duties. When duties are separated, it requires two or more people to collude for cash to be stolen and the theft to be concealed in the accounting records. The second guideline aims to use immediate (daily) deposits of all cash receipts to produce a timely independent test of the accuracy of the count of cash received. It also reduces cash theft or loss, and it reduces the risk of an employee personally using the money before depositing it. The third guideline aims to use payments by cheque to develop a bank record of cash disbursements. This guideline also reduces the risk of cash theft. Often, two signatures are required to ensure that legitimate invoices are being paid.

One exception to the third guideline is to allow small disbursements of currency and coins from a petty cash fund. We describe a petty cash fund later in this section. Another important point is that the deposit of cash receipts and the use of cheques for cash disbursements allow a company to use bank records as a separate external record of cash transactions. We explain how to use bank records to confirm the accuracy of a company's own records later in this section.

Control of Cash Receipts

Internal control of cash receipts ensures that all cash received is properly recorded and deposited. Cash receipts arise from many transactions, including cash sales, collections of customers' accounts, receipts of interest and rent, bank loans, sale of

[1] IFRS 2009, IAS 7, para. 6.

assets, and owners' investments. This section explains internal control over two important types of cash receipts: over-the-counter and mail.

Over-the-Counter Cash Receipts

For purposes of internal control, over-the-counter cash sales should be recorded on a cash register at the time of each sale for internal control. To help ensure that correct amounts are entered, each register should be positioned so customers can read the amounts entered. The design of each cash register should provide a permanent, locked-in record of each transaction. Many software programs accept cash register transactions and enter them in accounting records. Less technology-dependent registers simply print a record of each transaction on a paper tape or electronic file locked inside the register.

Custody over cash should be separate from its recordkeeping; therefore the clerk who has access to cash in the register should not have access to its locked-in record. At the end of the clerk's work period, the clerk should count the cash in the register, record the amount, and turn over the cash and a record of its amount to an employee in the cashier's office. The employee in the cashier's office, like the clerk, has access to the cash and should not have access to accounting records (or the register tape or file). A third employee compares the record of total register transactions (or the register tape or file) with the cash receipts reported by the cashier's office. This record (or register tape or file) is the basis for a journal entry recording over-the-counter cash sales. Note that the third employee has access to the records for cash but not to the actual cash. The clerk and the employee from the cashier's office have access to cash but not to the accounting records. This means the accuracy of cash records and amounts is automatically checked. None of them can make a mistake or divert cash without the difference being revealed.

Cash Over and Short

Sometimes errors in making change are discovered when there is a difference between the cash in a cash register and the record of the amount of cash sales. This difference is reported in the **Cash Over and Short account**. This income statement account, shown under general and administrative expenses, records the income effects of cash overages and cash shortages from errors in making change and missing petty cash receipts. The journal entries to record cash over and short are illustrated later in this chapter.

Cash Receipts by Mail

Control of cash receipts[2] that arrive through the mail starts with the person who opens the mail. In a large business, two people are assigned the task and are present when opening the mail. The person opening the mail makes a list of money received. This list should contain a record of each sender's name, the amount, and an explanation for what purpose the money is sent. Copies of the list are sent with the money to the cashier, and to the accounting area. The cashier deposits the money in the bank, and the recordkeeper records amounts received in the accounting records. In a small business, the owner should assume responsibility for cash.

Control of Cash Disbursements

Control of cash disbursements is especially important for companies. Most large thefts occur from payments of fictitious invoices. The key to controlling cash disbursements is to require that all expenditures be made by cheque, with two signatures if possible when not signed by the owner. The only exception is for small payments from petty cash. Another key is that when the authority to sign cheques is assigned to a person other than the owner, that person must not have access to

[2] Cash receipts by mail are normally in the form of cheques. Cheques are equivalent to cash and would therefore be recorded as cash.

the accounting records. This separation of duties helps prevent an employee from hiding fraudulent disbursements in the accounting records.

The manager of a small business often signs cheques and knows from personal contact that the items being paid for are actually received. This arrangement is impossible in large businesses. Instead, internal control procedures must be substituted for personal contact. These controls are achieved through a *voucher system*. Briefly, the voucher system of control requires that a number of procedures be performed and documents collected to support the validity of each disbursement. These procedures are designed to assure the cheque signer that the obligations recorded were properly incurred and should be paid.

EXTEND YOUR KNOWLEDGE 9-2

The exact procedures used to achieve control over cash vary across companies. They depend on such factors as company size, number of employees, volume of cash transactions, and sources of cash. We must therefore view the procedures described in this section as illustrative of those in practice today.

3. Good internal control procedures for cash receipts imply that (choose one):
   a. All cash disbursements, other than those for very small amounts, are made by cheque.
   b. An accounting employee should count cash received from sales and promptly deposit receipts.
   c. Cash receipts by mail should be opened by an accounting employee who is responsible for recording and depositing receipts.

Do Quick Study questions: QS 9-2, QS 9-3

Petty Cash System of Control

LO4 Explain and record petty cash fund transactions.

A basic principle for controlling cash disbursements is that all payments are made by cheque. An exception to this rule is made for petty cash disbursements. Petty cash disbursements are the *small amount* payments required in most companies for items such as postage, courier fees, repairs, and supplies. To avoid writing cheques for small amounts, a company usually sets up a petty cash fund and uses the money in this fund to make small payments.

Operating a Petty Cash Fund

Establishing a petty cash fund requires estimating the total amount of small payments likely to be made during a short period such as a week or month. A cheque is then drawn by the company cashier's office for an amount slightly in excess of this estimate. To illustrate, assume Z-Mart established a petty cash fund on November 1, 2011, in the amount of $75. A $75 cheque was drawn, cashed, and its proceeds turned over to Jim Gibbs, an office employee designated as the *petty cashier* or *petty cash custodian*. The **petty cashier** is responsible for safekeeping of the cash, for making payments from this fund, and for keeping accurate records. The entry to record the set-up of this petty cash fund is:

Nov.	1	Petty Cash..	75	
		Cash		75
		To establish a petty cash fund.		

This entry transfers $75 from the regular Cash account to the Petty Cash account. After the petty cash fund is established, the ***Petty Cash account is not debited or credited again unless the size of the total fund is changed.***

The petty cashier should keep petty cash in a locked box in a safe place. As each disbursement is made, the person receiving payment signs a *petty cash receipt* or *petty cash ticket* as illustrated in Exhibit 9.1.

Exhibit 9.1

Petty Cash Receipt

Petty Cash Receipt Z-Mart			No. 6
For	Delivery charges	Date	Nov.18/2011
Charge to	Delivery expense	Amount	$5.00
Approved by	*Jim Gibbs*	Received by	*Dick Fitch*

The petty cash receipt is then placed in the petty cash box with the remaining money. When the cash is nearly gone, the fund should be reimbursed. When it is time to reimburse the petty cash fund, the petty cashier should sort the receipts by type and prepare a summary as shown in Exhibit 9.2.

Exhibit 9.2

Petty Cash Payments Report

Z-Mart **Petty Cash Payments Report**			
Receipts:			
Office maintenance			
Nov. 2 Washing windows	$10.00		
17 Washing windows	10.00		
27 Computer repairs	26.50	$46.50	
Transportation-in			
Nov. 5 Delivery of merchandise purchased	$ 6.75		
20 Delivery of merchandise purchased	8.30	15.05	
Delivery expense			
Nov. 28 Customer's package delivered		5.00	
Office supplies			
Nov. 15 Purchased office supplies		4.75	
Total receipts			$71.30
Fund total		$75.00	
Less: Cash remaining		2.20	
Equals: Cash required to replenish petty cash			$72.80
Cash over/(short)			($ 1.50)

This summary and all petty cash receipts are presented to the company's cashier. The company's cashier stamps all receipts paid so they cannot be reused, files them for recordkeeping, records the reimbursement, and gives the petty cashier a cheque for a sum *equal to the fund size less the cash remaining*. In our example, Jim Gibbs had only $2.20 cash remaining in the fund at the end of November. Therefore, the reimbursement cheque is for $72.80 (= $75.00 − $2.20). Notice that Exhibit 9.2 shows total receipts for $71.30. The difference between the total receipts and the reimbursement cheque represents a cash shortage of $1.50 (= $71.30 − $72.80) due to an error. The reimbursement cheque is recorded as follows:

To replenish petty cash:

Cash required to replenish petty cash = Fund size − Cash remaining

To calculate cash over/(short):

Cash over/(short) = Total of petty cash receipts − Cash required to replenish petty cash

Nov. 27	Office Maintenance Expenses	46.50	
	Merchandise Inventory	15.05	
	Delivery Expense	5.00	
	Office Supplies Expense	4.75	
	Cash Over and Short	1.50	
	Cash		72.80
	To reimburse petty cash.		

In the case of an overage in the petty cash fund, a credit to Cash Over and Short is recorded in the reimbursing entry.

When the reimbursement cheque is cashed and the money returned to the cash box, the total money in the box is restored to its original amount of $75.00 (= $72.80 + $2.20). The fund is now ready to begin a new cycle of operations.

Increasing or Decreasing Petty Cash Fund

A decision to increase or decrease a petty cash fund is often made when the fund is being reimbursed. To illustrate, let us assume that Z-Mart decides to increase the petty cash fund by $25, from $75 to $100, on November 27 when it reimburses the fund. This is recorded as follows:

Nov.	27	Petty Cash	25.00	
		Office Maintenance Expenses	46.50	
		Merchandise Inventory	15.05	
		Delivery Expense	5.00	
		Office Supplies Expense	4.75	
		Cash Over and Short	1.50	
		Cash		97.80
		To reimburse petty cash and increase it by $25.00.		

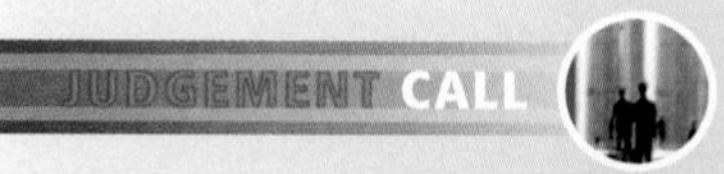

Answer—p. 460

Internal Auditor

You just graduated and have been hired as an internal audit trainee for a company. As part of your training, your supervisor has instructed you to make surprise counts of three $200 petty cash funds. You arrive at the office of one of the petty cashiers while she is on the telephone. You explain the purpose of your visit, and the petty cashier asks politely that you come back after lunch so that she can finish the business she's conducting by long distance. You agree and return after lunch. The petty cashier opens the petty cash box and shows you nine new $20 bills with consecutive serial numbers plus receipts totalling $20. Do you take further action or comment on these events in your report to your supervisor?

4. Why are some cash payments made from a petty cash fund?
5. Why should a petty cash fund be reimbursed at the end of an accounting period?
6. What are three results of reimbursing the petty cash fund?

Do Quick Study questions: QS 9-4, QS 9-5, QS 9-6

mid-chapter demonstration problem

Castillo Company established a $250 petty cash fund on February 10. On February 28, the fund had $180.14 remaining in cash and receipts for these expenditures: postage, $10.51; office supplies, $50.00; and repair expenses, $10.50. Prepare:

a. The February 10 entry to establish the fund,

b. The February 28 entry to record the fund transactions and replenish it, and

c. Independent of (b), the February 28 entry to record the fund transactions and reduce the fund to $100.

Analysis component:

Assume that there was no receipt for the $50.00 of office supplies. Should this amount be reimbursed? Explain why or why not.

Planning the Solution

- Total petty cash receipts.
- Calculate cash required to replenish petty cash.
- Calculate cash over/(short), if any.
- Prepare journal entries as required.
- Prepare an answer to the analysis question.

solution

a.	Feb. 10	Petty Cash Fund	250.00	
		Cash		250.00
		To establish petty cash fund.		
b.	28	Postage Expense	10.51	
		Office Supplies Expense	50.00	
		Repair Expense	10.50	
		Cash		69.86[1]
		Cash Over and Short		1.15[2]
		To reimburse petty cash fund.		

Calculations:

[1]Total of petty cash receipts = $10.51 + $50.00 + $10.50 = $71.01

Cash required to replenish petty cash = Fund size − Cash remaining
= $250 − $180.14
= $69.86

[2]Cash over/(short) = Receipt totals − Cash required
= $71.01 − $69.86
= $1.15

c.	28	Cash	80.14[3]	
		Postage Expense	10.51	
		Office Supplies Expense	50.00	
		Repair Expense	10.50	
		Petty Cash		150.00
		Cash Over and Short		1.15
		To reimburse petty cash fund and decrease it to $100.		

Calculation:

[3]Cash required to replenish petty cash = New fund size − Cash remaining
= $100.00 − $180.14
= −$80.14 (therefore, instead of a credit to Cash, debit Cash)

Analysis component:

The $50.00 should not be reimbursed without a receipt for two reasons. First, it is a basic internal control measure to ensure that only valid expenditures are reimbursed. If receipts were not required, individuals could request reimbursement for fictitious expenditures. Second, GAAP require that transactions be recorded based on verifiable evidence (which is related to internal controls).

Banking Activities as Controls

LO5 Explain and identify banking activities and the control features they provide.

Banks are used by most companies for many different services. One of their most important services is helping companies control cash and cash transactions. Banks safeguard cash, provide detailed and independent records of cash transactions, and are a source of cash financing. This section describes services and documents provided by banking activities that increase managers' control over cash.

Basic Bank Services

This first section explains basic bank services. We include the bank account, bank deposits, and cheques. Each of these services contributes to the control or safeguarding of cash.

Bank Account

EXTEND YOUR KNOWLEDGE 9-3

A bank account is a record set up by a bank for a customer, permitting this customer to deposit money for safeguarding and cheque withdrawals. To control access to a bank account, all persons authorized to use a bank account must sign a signature card. A **signature card** includes the signature of each person authorized to sign cheques from the account. Bank employees use signature cards to verify signatures on cheques. This lowers the risk of loss from forgery for both banks and customers. Many companies have more than one bank account for various reasons such as serving local needs and for special transactions.

Bank Deposit

Each bank deposit is supported by a *deposit slip*. A **deposit slip** lists the items such as currency, coins, and cheques deposited along with each of their dollar amounts. The bank gives the customer a copy of the deposit slip or a deposit receipt as proof of the deposit. Exhibit 9.3 shows a deposit slip.

Exhibit 9.3
Deposit Slip

Front

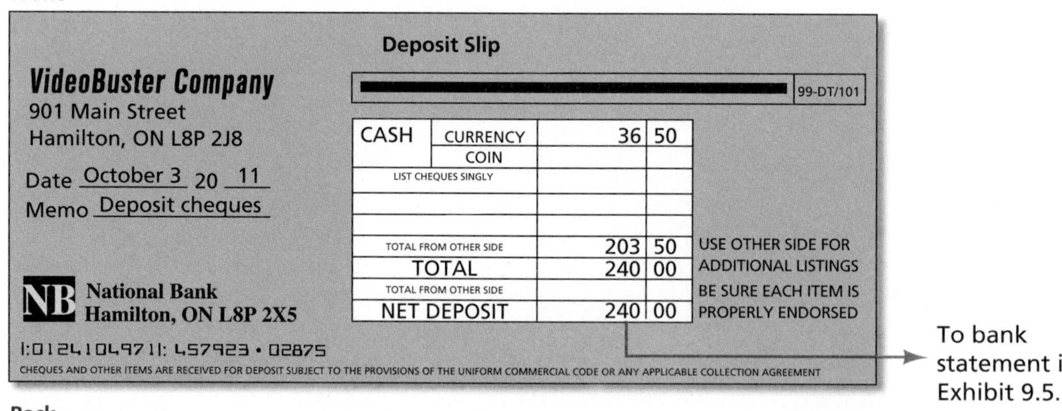

Deposit Slip

VideoBuster Company
901 Main Street
Hamilton, ON L8P 2J8

Date October 3 20 11
Memo Deposit cheques

99-DT/101

CASH	CURRENCY	36	50
	COIN		
LIST CHEQUES SINGLY			
TOTAL FROM OTHER SIDE		203	50
TOTAL		240	00
TOTAL FROM OTHER SIDE			
NET DEPOSIT		240	00

USE OTHER SIDE FOR ADDITIONAL LISTINGS
BE SURE EACH ITEM IS PROPERLY ENDORSED

NB National Bank
Hamilton, ON L8P 2X5

I:01241049711: 457923 • 02875

CHEQUES AND OTHER ITEMS ARE RECEIVED FOR DEPOSIT SUBJECT TO THE PROVISIONS OF THE UNIFORM COMMERCIAL CODE OR ANY APPLICABLE COLLECTION AGREEMENT

To bank statement in Exhibit 9.5.

Back

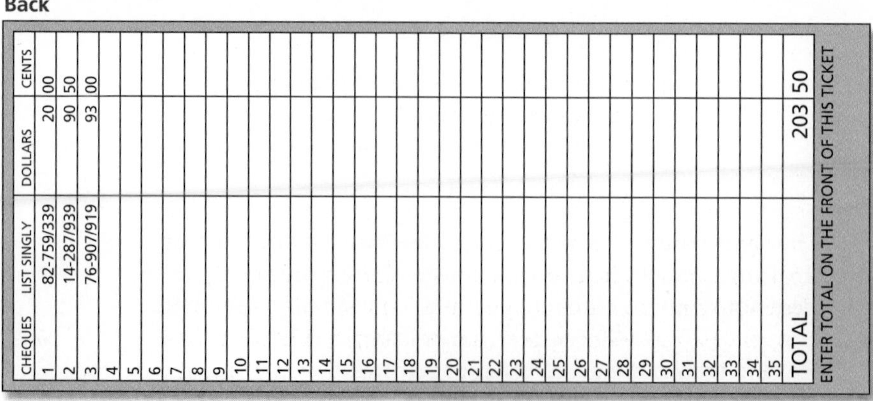

CHEQUES	LIST SINGLY	DOLLARS	CENTS
1	82-759/339	20	00
2	14-287/939	90	50
3	76-907/919	93	00
4			
5			
6			
7			
8			
9			
10			
11			
12			
13			
14			
15			
16			
17			
18			
19			
20			
21			
22			
23			
24			
25			
26			
27			
28			
29			
30			
31			
32			
33			
34			
35			
TOTAL		203	50

ENTER TOTAL ON THE FRONT OF THIS TICKET

Bank Cheque

To withdraw money from an account, a customer uses a *cheque*. A **cheque** is a document signed by the depositor instructing the bank to pay a specified amount of money to a designated recipient. A cheque involves three parties: a *maker* who signs the cheque, a *payee* who is the recipient, and a *bank* on which the cheque is drawn. The bank provides a depositor with cheques that are serially numbered and imprinted with the name and address of both the depositor and the bank. Both cheques and deposit slips are imprinted with identification codes in magnetic ink for computer processing. Exhibit 9.4 shows a cheque. This cheque is accompanied by an optional *remittance advice* giving an explanation for the payment. When a remittance advice is unavailable, the memo line is often used for a brief explanation.

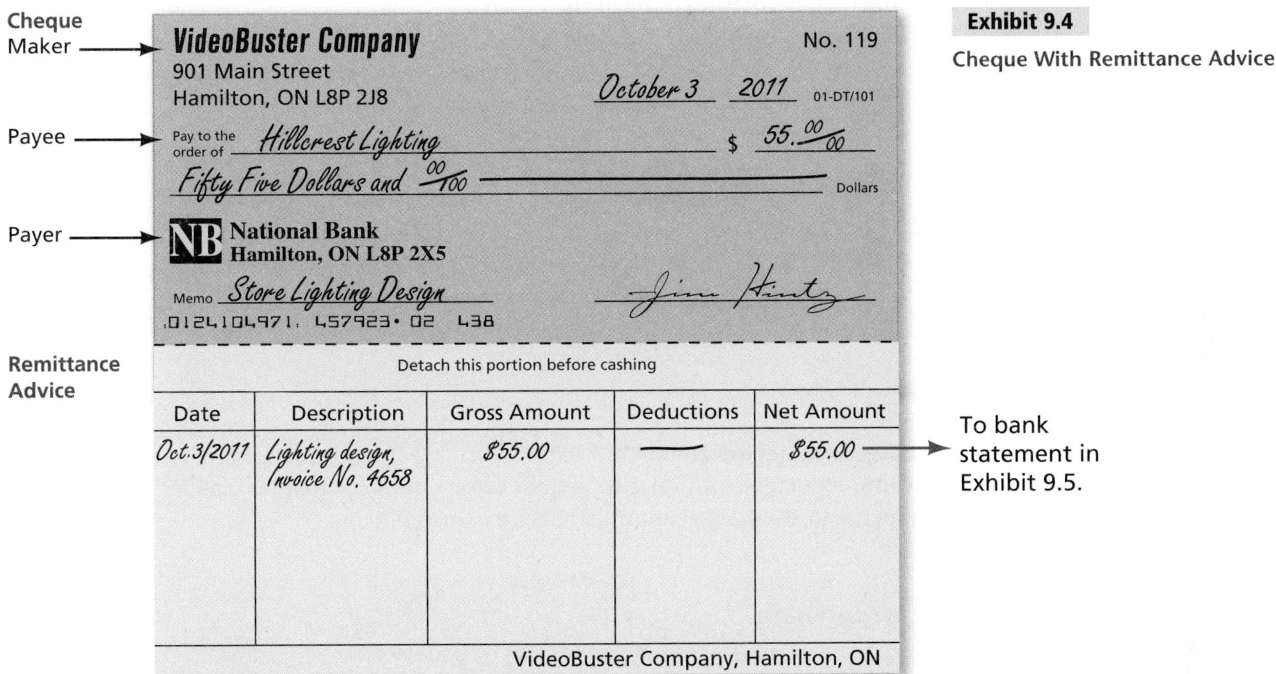

VideoBuster Company
901 Main Street
Hamilton, ON L8P 2J8

No. 119

October 3 2011 01-DT/101

Pay to the order of Hillcrest Lighting $ 55.00/00

Fifty Five Dollars and 00/100 Dollars

NB National Bank
Hamilton, ON L8P 2X5

Memo Store Lighting Design

Jim Hintz

.0124104971. 457923• 02 438

Detach this portion before cashing

Date	Description	Gross Amount	Deductions	Net Amount
Oct.3/2011	Lighting design, Invoice No. 4658	$55.00	—	$55.00

VideoBuster Company, Hamilton, ON

Exhibit 9.4
Cheque With Remittance Advice

Electronic Funds Transfer

Electronic funds transfer (EFT) is the use of electronic communication to transfer cash from one party to another. No paper documents are necessary. Banks simply transfer cash from one account to another with a journal entry. Companies are increasingly using EFT because of its convenience and low cost. It can cost, for instance, up to a dollar to process a cheque through the banking system, whereas the EFT cost is near zero. We see items such as payroll, rent, utilities, insurance, and interest payments being handled by EFT. Technology has decreased the necessity for cheques for some businesses but for others, cheques are still required. For example, Alberta Blue Cross issues more than 110,000 cheques per month, but this number is declining as more payments are being made by direct deposit. The bank statement lists cash withdrawals by EFT with cheques and other deductions. Cash receipts by EFT are listed with deposits and other additions. A bank statement is sometimes a depositor's only notice of an EFT.

Credit Card Transactions

Many companies allow customers to use credit cards such as Visa or MasterCard or American Express to charge purchases. The customer has the convenience of using the credit card instead of using cash or cheques. The retailer enjoys the benefits of being paid by the credit card company. The payment to the retailer normally occurs faster than if the retailer had to collect credit sales personally and the risk of credit customers who do not pay is transferred to the credit card company. The credit card company issues the customer a monthly statement detailing the customer's transactions. The customer pays the credit card company monthly based on the credit terms on the statement.

The seller pays a fee for the services provided by the credit card company. The fee covers the credit card company's costs, which include credit checks on credit card customers, collecting cash, reimbursing retailers, and, of course, a profit margin. Therefore, when the fee is deducted, the cash received by the retailer is less than 100% of the sales value of the transaction. The fee charged by the credit card company can be calculated as a percent of sales or it may vary depending on the volume of sales. For simplicity, we will assume in this textbook that the credit card fee is based on a percent of the sales value.

When a credit card is used, the retailer receives cash, net of the credit card fee, immediately upon deposit of the credit card sales receipt at the bank or when the credit card is processed electronically at the point of sale. For instance, if TechCom has $100 of credit card sales with a 4% fee and cash is received immediately, the entry is (assume cost of sales is $40):

Aug.	15	Cash	96	
		Credit Card Expense	4	
		Sales		100
		To record credit card sales less a 4% credit card expense.		
	15	Cost of Goods Sold	40	
		Merchandise Inventory		40
		To record cost of sales.		

Some firms report credit card expense in the income statement as a type of discount deducted from sales to get net sales. Other companies classify it as a selling expense or even as an administrative expense.

Answer—p. 461

Entrepreneur

You are the owner of a small retail store. You are considering allowing customers to purchase merchandise using credit cards. Until now, your store only accepted cash and cheques. What forms of analysis do you use to make this decision?

Debit Card Transactions

The use of **debit cards** is common and popular with consumers. Payment for a purchase is electronically transferred from the customer's bank account to the vendor's bank account immediately at the point of sale. The customer authorizes the transaction by entering the Personal Identification Number (PIN). Normally, the bank charges the retailer a fee for this service. The entries are identical to a credit card sale. For example, assume a customer purchases a $100 service on October 1 and pays using a debit card. If the bank charges the retailer $0.40 per debit card transaction, the entry is:

Oct.	1	Cash	99.60	
		Debit Card Expense	0.40	
		Service Revenue		100.00
		To record a debit card transaction.		

7. What is a benefit to the retailer of accepting credit and debit cards?

Do Quick Study questions: QS 9-7, QS 9-8

Bank Statement

At least once a month, the bank sends the depositor a bank statement showing the activity in the accounts during the month, or a company can access its banking activity online at any time. Different banks use a variety of formats for their bank statements. Yet all of them include the following items of information:

1. Beginning-of-month balance of the depositor's account.
2. Cheques and other debits decreasing the account during the month.
3. Deposits and other credits increasing the account during the month.
4. End-of-month balance of the depositor's account.

This information reflects the bank's records. Exhibit 9.5 shows a bank statement.

(A) Summarizes changes in the account.
(B) Lists paid cheques in date order along with other debits (or decreases).
(C) Lists deposits and credits (increases) to the account.
(D) Shows the daily account balances.

Exhibit 9.5

Bank Statement

Member CDIC

NB National Bank
Hamilton, ON L8P 2X5

Bank Statement

VideoBuster Company
901 Main Street
Hamilton, ON L8P 2J8

October 31, 2011
Statement Date

494 504 2
Account Number

(A)

Previous Balance	Total Cheques and Debits	Total Deposits and Credits	Current Balance
1,609.58	723.00	1,163.42	2,050.00

(B) Cheques and Debits			(C) Deposits and Credits		(D) Daily Balance	
Date	No.	Amount	Date	Amount	Date	Amount
					OCT01	1,609.58
OCT03	119	55.00	OCT03	240.00	OCT03	1,794.58
OCT09	123	25.00	OCT09	180.00	OCT09	1,949.58
OCT15	127	50.00	OCT15	100.00	OCT15	1,999.58
OCT16		23.00 DM	OCT16	150.00	OCT16	2,126.58
OCT17	122	70.00	OCT17	485.00 CM	OCT17	2,541.58
OCT18	120	200.00			OCT18	2,341.58
OCT19	125	15.00			OCT19	2,326.58
OCT20		20.00 NSF			OCT20	2,306.58
		10.00 DM			OCT20	2,296.58
OCT26	121	120.00			OCT26	2,176.58
OCT29	128	135.00			OCT29	2,041.58
			OCT31	8.42 IN	OCT31	2,050.00

Symbols: CM–Credit Memo DM–Debit Memo EC–Error Correction IN–Interest Earned NSF–Non-sufficient Funds OD–Overdraft SC–Service Charge

< Reconcile the account immediately. >

From deposit slip in Exhibit 9.3.

Originally deposited as part of Oct. 3 deposit (see deposit slip in Exhibit 9.3).

From cheque with remittance advice in Exhibit 9.4.

Notice that 'Deposits' are called credits and 'Cheques' are called debits on the bank statement. This is because the bank statement reports information from the bank's point of view—*that a depositor's account is a liability on the bank's records since the money belongs to the depositor and not the bank.* When a depositor, Smith, puts money into the bank, the bank debits cash and ***credits*** the bank's liability account to Smith. Hence, ***credit memos*** show the bank's increasing liability to Smith. When Smith withdraws money from the bank, the bank records it as a credit to cash and *debits* the bank's liability account for Smith. Therefore, *debit memos* reflect decreases in the bank's liability to Smith.[3]

[3] Recall that a bank records transactions in an identical manner to any other business. For example, on October 3 the bank cashed a cheque written by VideoBuster. This was recorded by the bank as:

VideoBuster Customer Account (a liability to the bank)	55	
Cash (an asset to the bank)		55

Notice on the bank statement in Exhibit 9.5 that this cheque is reported to VideoBuster as a 'debit' because the bank has decreased its liability to VideoBuster. As a second example, on October 3 VideoBuster deposited $240 into its bank account; this was recorded by the bank as:

Cash	240	
VideoBuster Customer Account (a liability to the bank)		240

The bank statement reports this deposit to VideoBuster as a 'credit' because the bank's liability to VideoBuster has increased.

Enclosed with a bank statement are the depositor's cancelled cheques and any debit or credit memoranda affecting the account. **Cancelled cheques** are cheques the bank has paid and deducted from the customer's account during the month. Other deductions also often appear on a bank statement and include: (1) service charges and fees assessed by the bank, (2) customers' cheques deposited that are uncollectible, (3) corrections of previous errors, (4) withdrawals through automated teller machines (ATMs)[4], and (5) periodic payments arranged in advance by a depositor such as insurance and lease payments. Except for service charges, the bank notifies the depositor of each deduction with a debit memorandum when the bank reduces the balance. A copy of each debit memorandum is usually sent with the monthly statement.

While deposits increase a depositor's bank balance, there are other transactions that increase the depositor's account. Examples are amounts the bank collects on behalf of the depositor and corrections of previous errors. Credit memoranda notify the depositor of all increases recorded by the bank. A copy of each credit memorandum is often sent with the bank statement. Another item added to the bank balance is interest earned by the depositor. Many chequing accounts pay the depositor interest based on the average cash balance maintained in the account. The bank computes the amount of interest earned and credits it to the depositor's account each month. In Exhibit 9.5, for instance, the bank credits $8.42 of interest to the account of VideoBuster. We describe the methods used to calculate interest in the next chapter.

Bank Reconciliation

LO6 Prepare a bank reconciliation and journalize any resulting adjustment(s).

When a company deposits all receipts intact and when all payments except petty cash payments are by cheque, the bank statement serves as a device for proving the accuracy of the depositor's cash records. We test the accuracy by preparing a *bank reconciliation*. A **bank reconciliation** is a form of internal control over cash that explains the difference between the balance of a chequing account according to the depositor's records and the balance reported on the bank statement.

Purpose of Bank Reconciliation

The balance of a chequing account reported on the bank statement is rarely equal to the balance in the depositor's accounting records. This is usually due to information that one party has that the other does not. We must therefore prove the accuracy of both the depositor's records and those of the bank. This means we must *reconcile* the two balances and explain or account for the differences in these two balances.

Among the factors causing the bank statement balance to differ from the depositor's book balance are:

1. *Unrecorded deposits* (also known as *deposits in transit* or *outstanding deposits*). These are deposits made and recorded by the depositor but not recorded on the bank statement. For example, companies often make deposits at the end of a business day, after the bank is closed. A deposit in the bank's night depository on the last day of the month is not recorded by the bank until the next business day and does not appear on the bank statement for that month. Also, deposits mailed to the bank near the end of a month may be in transit and unrecorded when the statement is prepared.
2. *Outstanding cheques*. These are cheques written (or drawn) by the depositor, deducted on the depositor's records, and sent to the payees. But they have not yet reached the bank for payment and deduction at the time of the bank statement.
3. *Additions for collections and for interest*. Banks sometimes act as collection agents for their depositors by collecting notes and other items. Banks can also receive electronic funds transfers to the depositor's account. When a bank collects an item, it adds it to the depositor's account, less any service fee. It also sends a credit

[4] Because of a desire to make all disbursements by cheque, most business chequing accounts do not allow ATM withdrawals.

memorandum to notify the depositor of the transaction. When the memorandum is received, it should be recorded by the depositor. Yet these sometimes remain unrecorded until the time of the bank reconciliation.

Many bank accounts earn interest on the average cash balance in the account during the month. If an account earns interest, the bank statement includes a credit for the amount earned during the past month. Notification of earned interest is provided by the bank statement.

4. *Deductions for uncollectible items and for services*. A company sometimes deposits a customer's cheque that is uncollectible. This usually is because the balance in the customer's account is not large enough to cover the cheque. This cheque is called a *non-sufficient funds (NSF)* cheque. The bank initially credited the depositor's account for the amount of the deposited cheque. When the bank learns that the cheque is uncollectible, it debits (reduces) the depositor's account for the amount of that cheque. The bank may also charge the depositor a fee for processing an uncollectible cheque and notify the depositor of the deduction by sending a debit memorandum. While each deduction should be recorded by the depositor when a debit memorandum is received, an entry is sometimes not made until the bank reconciliation is prepared.

   Other possible bank charges to a depositor's account reported on a bank statement include the printing of new cheques and a service charge for maintaining the account. Notification of these charges is *not* provided until the statement is mailed.

5. *Errors*. Both banks and depositors can make errors. For example, a bank error might include a cheque written by *VideoBlaster* Company mistakenly charged against the account of *VideoBuster* Company or a deposit made by *VideoBuster* Company accidentally posted to the account of *Videon* Company. A depositor error might involve a cheque actually written for $102 but recorded in error in the Cash Disbursements Journal as $120. These kinds of errors might not be discovered until the depositor prepares a bank reconciliation.

Steps in Reconciling a Bank Balance

The employee who prepares the bank reconciliation should not be responsible for cash receipts, processing cheques, or maintaining cash records. This employee needs to gather information from the bank statement and from other records. A reconciliation requires this person to:

- Compare deposits on the bank statement with deposits in the accounting records (Cash Receipts Journal and last month's bank reconciliation). Identify any discrepancies and determine which is correct. List any errors or unrecorded deposits.
- Compare cancelled cheques on the bank statement with actual cheques returned with the statement. For each cheque, make sure the correct amount is deducted by the bank and the returned cheque is properly charged to the account. List any discrepancies or errors.
- Compare cancelled cheques on the bank statement with cheques recorded in the books (Cash Disbursements Journal). List any outstanding cheques. Also, while companies with good internal controls would rarely write a cheque without recording it, we should inspect and list any cancelled cheques that are unrecorded in the books.
- Identify any outstanding cheques listed on the previous month's bank reconciliation that are not included in the cancelled cheques on this month's bank statement. List these cheques that remain outstanding at the end of the current month. Send the list to the cashier's office for follow-up with the payees to see if the cheques were actually received.
- Inspect all additions (credits) on the bank statement and determine whether each is recorded in the books. These items include collections by the bank, correction of previous bank statement errors, and interest earned by the depositor. List any unrecorded items.
- Inspect all deductions (debits) to the account on the bank statement and determine whether each is recorded in the books. These include bank charges for newly printed cheques, NSF cheques, and monthly service charges. List items not yet recorded.

When this information is gathered, the employee can complete the reconciliation.

Illustrating a Bank Reconciliation

We illustrate a bank reconciliation by preparing one for VideoBuster as of October 31. We use the guidelines listed above and follow nine specific steps. Follow each step to the corresponding Exhibits 9.5 to 9.8 to see where the information comes from and how it is shown on the bank reconciliation in Exhibit 9.9.

(1) Identify the bank balance of the cash account at October 31 (balance per bank).
- *Bank balance shown on the bank statement is $2,050 (from Exhibit 9.5).*

(2) Identify and list any unrecorded deposits[5] and any bank errors.[5] Add them to the bank balance on the bank reconciliation.
- *A $145 deposit was placed in the bank's night depository on October 31 and is not recorded on the bank statement (from Exhibit 9.6).*

(3) Identify and list any outstanding cheques[5] and any bank errors.[5] Deduct them from the bank balance on the bank reconciliation.
- *A comparison of cancelled cheques with the company's books showed two cheques outstanding: #124 for $150 and #126 for $200 (from Exhibit 9.7).*

(4) Calculate the *adjusted bank balance,* also called *corrected* or *reconciled* balance.
- *See Exhibit 9.9.*

(5) Identify the company's balance of the cash account (book balance).
- *Cash balance shown in the accounting records is $1,404.58 (from Exhibit 9.8).*

(6) Identify and list any unrecorded credit memoranda from the bank, such as interest earned and errors.[5] Add them to the book balance on the bank reconciliation.

(a) *Enclosed with the bank statement is a credit memorandum showing that the bank collected a note receivable for the company on October 17. The note's proceeds of $500 (minus a $15 collection fee) were credited to the company's account. This credit memorandum is not yet recorded by the company (from Exhibit 9.5).*

(b) *The bank statement shows a credit of $8.42 for interest earned on the average cash balance in the account. There was no prior notification of this item and it is not yet recorded on the company's books (from Exhibit 9.5).*

Exhibit 9.5

Bank Statement (repeated from earlier page for ease of reference)

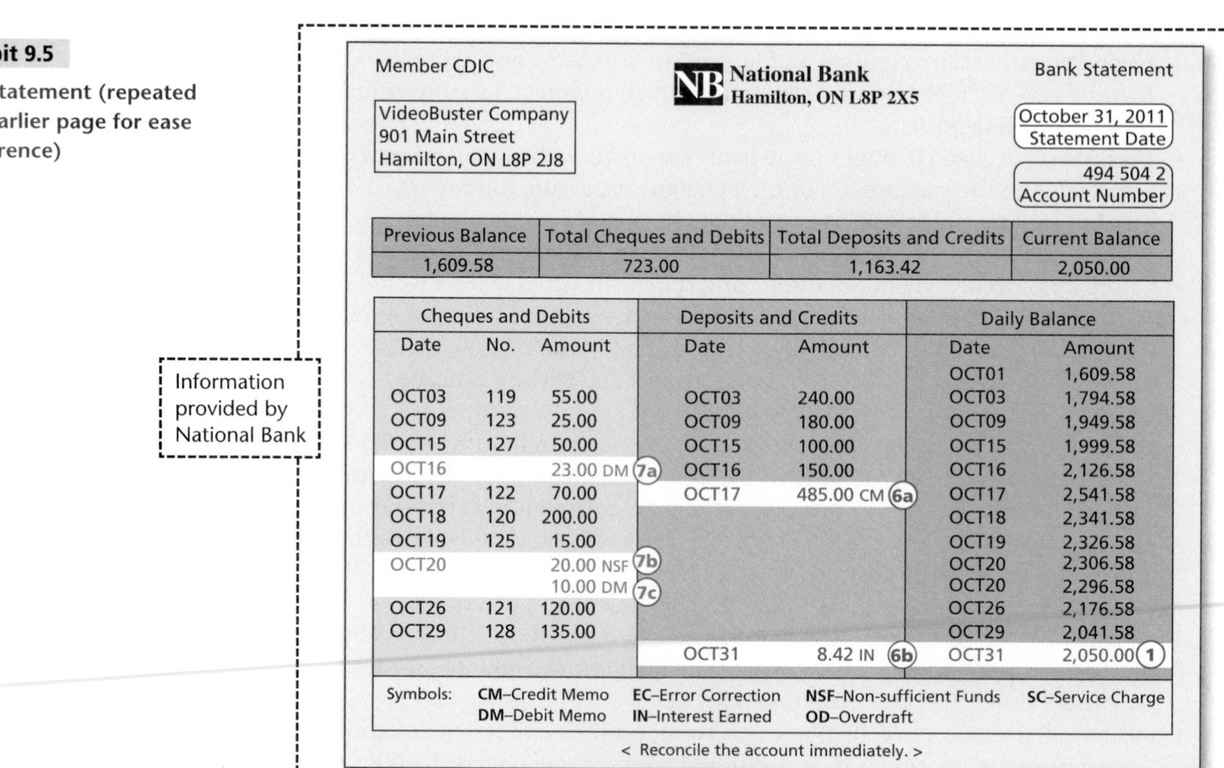

Information provided by National Bank

Member CDIC

NB National Bank
Hamilton, ON L8P 2X5

Bank Statement

VideoBuster Company
901 Main Street
Hamilton, ON L8P 2J8

October 31, 2011
Statement Date

494 504 2
Account Number

Previous Balance	Total Cheques and Debits	Total Deposits and Credits	Current Balance
1,609.58	723.00	1,163.42	2,050.00

Cheques and Debits			Deposits and Credits		Daily Balance	
Date	No.	Amount	Date	Amount	Date	Amount
					OCT01	1,609.58
OCT03	119	55.00	OCT03	240.00	OCT03	1,794.58
OCT09	123	25.00	OCT09	180.00	OCT09	1,949.58
OCT15	127	50.00	OCT15	100.00	OCT15	1,999.58
OCT16		23.00 DM (7a)	OCT16	150.00	OCT16	2,126.58
OCT17	122	70.00	OCT17	485.00 CM (6a)	OCT17	2,541.58
OCT18	120	200.00			OCT18	2,341.58
OCT19	125	15.00			OCT19	2,326.58
OCT20		20.00 NSF (7b)			OCT20	2,306.58
		10.00 DM (7c)			OCT20	2,296.58
OCT26	121	120.00			OCT26	2,176.58
OCT29	128	135.00			OCT29	2,041.58
			OCT31	8.42 IN (6b)	OCT31	2,050.00 (1)

Symbols: CM–Credit Memo, DM–Debit Memo, EC–Error Correction, IN–Interest Earned, NSF–Non-sufficient Funds, OD–Overdraft, SC–Service Charge

< Reconcile the account immediately. >

[5] For simplicity, this example includes no errors and assumes that there were no outstanding cheques or deposits on last month's bank reconciliation. The End-of-Chapter Demonstration Problem beginning on page 461 illustrates these additional complexities.

⑦ Identify and list any unrecorded debit memoranda from the bank, such as service charges and errors.[5] Deduct them from the book balance on the bank reconciliation.

– *Debits on the bank statement that are not recorded on the books include:* ⓐ *a $23 charge for cheques printed by the bank, and* ⓑ *an NSF cheque for $20 plus* ⓒ *a related $10 processing fee. The NSF cheque is from a customer, Frank Heflin, and was originally included as part of the October 3 deposit (from Exhibit 9.5).*

⑧ Calculate the *adjusted book balance*, also called the *corrected* or *reconciled* balance.

– *See Exhibit 9.9.*

⑨ Verify that the two adjusted balances from Steps 4 and 8 are equal. If so, they are reconciled. If not, check for mathematical accuracy and missing data.

– *See Exhibit 9.9.*

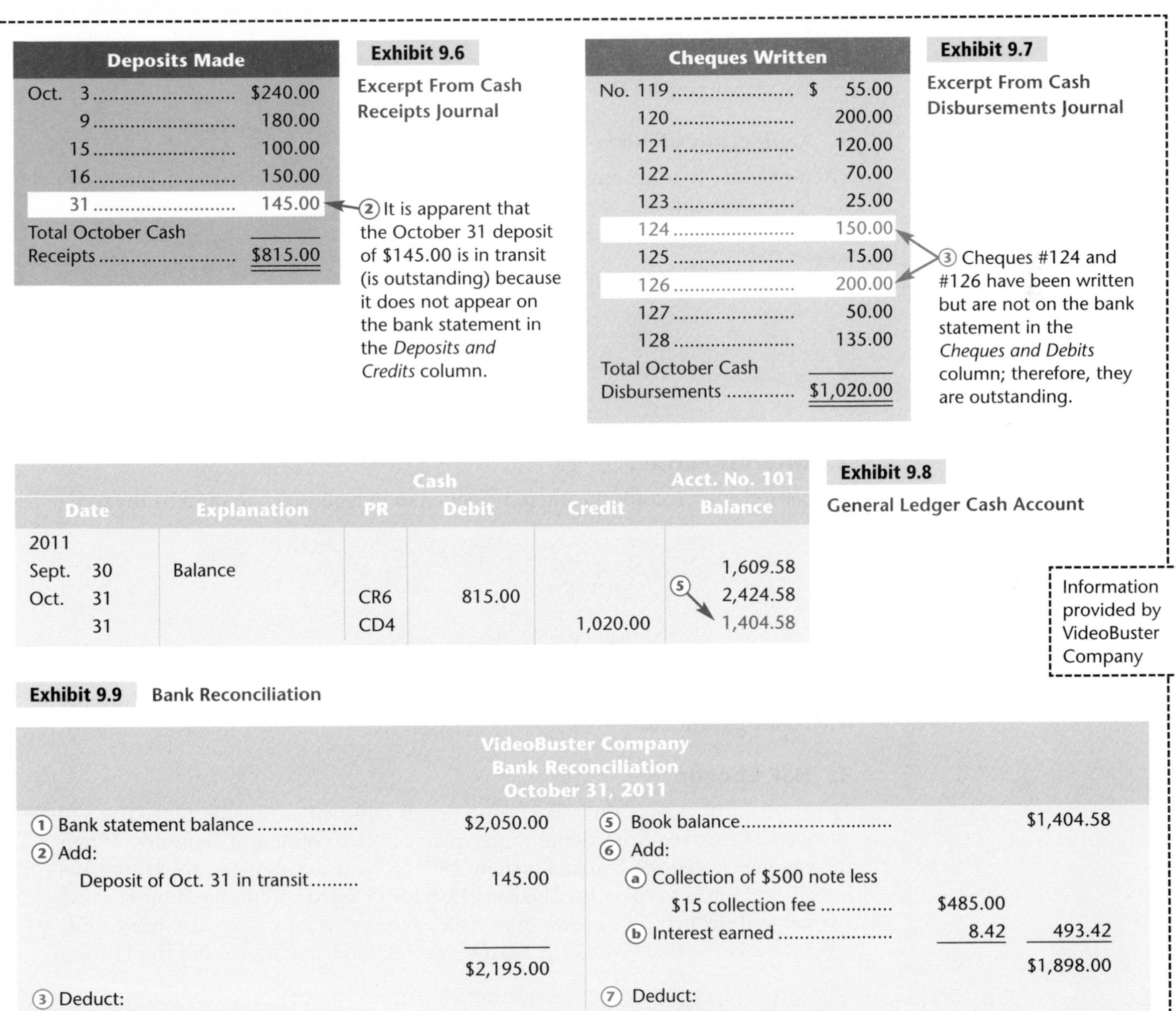

Exhibit 9.6 Excerpt From Cash Receipts Journal

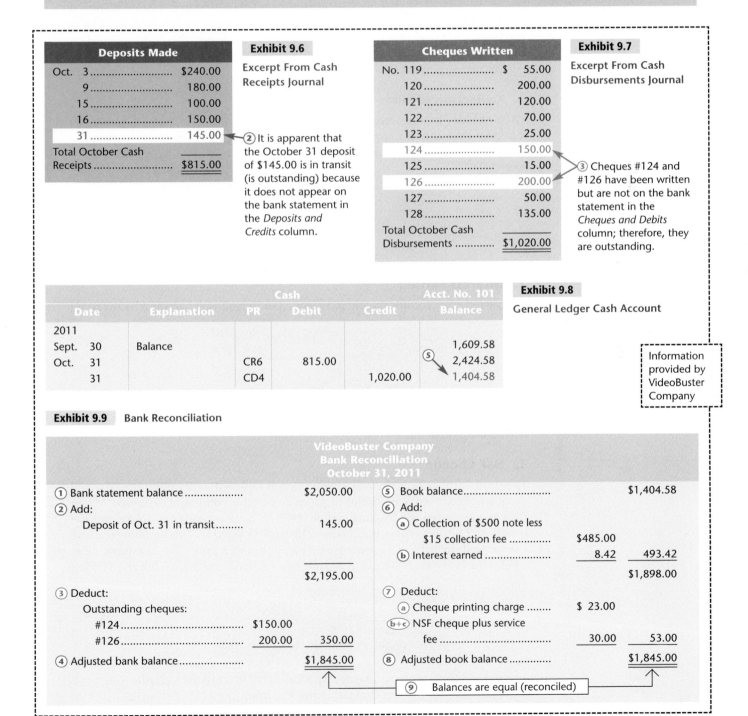

Deposits Made	
Oct. 3	$240.00
9	180.00
15	100.00
16	150.00
31	145.00
Total October Cash Receipts	$815.00

② It is apparent that the October 31 deposit of $145.00 is in transit (is outstanding) because it does not appear on the bank statement in the *Deposits and Credits* column.

Exhibit 9.7 Excerpt From Cash Disbursements Journal

Cheques Written	
No. 119	$ 55.00
120	200.00
121	120.00
122	70.00
123	25.00
124	150.00
125	15.00
126	200.00
127	50.00
128	135.00
Total October Cash Disbursements	$1,020.00

③ Cheques #124 and #126 have been written but are not on the bank statement in the *Cheques and Debits* column; therefore, they are outstanding.

Exhibit 9.8 General Ledger Cash Account

Cash					Acct. No. 101
Date	Explanation	PR	Debit	Credit	Balance
2011					
Sept. 30	Balance				1,609.58
Oct. 31		CR6	815.00		2,424.58
31		CD4		1,020.00	⑤ 1,404.58

Information provided by VideoBuster Company

Exhibit 9.9 Bank Reconciliation

VideoBuster Company
Bank Reconciliation
October 31, 2011

① Bank statement balance		$2,050.00	⑤ Book balance		$1,404.58
② Add:			⑥ Add:		
Deposit of Oct. 31 in transit		145.00	ⓐ Collection of $500 note less $15 collection fee	$485.00	
			ⓑ Interest earned	8.42	493.42
		$2,195.00			$1,898.00
③ Deduct:			⑦ Deduct:		
Outstanding cheques:			ⓐ Cheque printing charge	$ 23.00	
#124	$150.00		ⓑ+ⓒ NSF cheque plus service fee	30.00	53.00
#126	200.00	350.00			
④ Adjusted bank balance		$1,845.00	⑧ Adjusted book balance		$1,845.00

⑨ Balances are equal (reconciled)

When the reconciliation is complete, the employee sends a copy to the accounting department to record any needed journal entries. For instance, entries are needed to record any unrecorded debit and credit memoranda and any company mistakes. The entries resulting from VideoBuster's bank reconciliation are illustrated in the next section. Another copy goes to the cashier's office. This is especially important if the bank has made an error that needs correction.

Recording Adjusting Entries From the Bank Reconciliation

A bank reconciliation helps locate errors by either the bank or the depositor. It also identifies unrecorded items that need recording on the company's books. In VideoBuster's reconciliation, for instance, the adjusted balance of $1,845.00 is the correct balance as of October 31. But the company's accounting records show a $1,404.58 balance. We must prepare journal entries to adjust the book balance to the correct balance. It is important to remember that only the items reconciling the book balance side require adjustment. This means that the following four entries are required for VideoBuster:

1. Collection of Note

The first entry is to record the net proceeds of VideoBuster's note receivable collected by the bank, the expense of having the bank perform that service, and the reduction in the Notes Receivable account:

Oct.	31	Cash	485.00	
		Collection Expense	15.00	
		Notes Receivable		500.00
		To record collection fee and proceeds of a note collected by the bank.		

2. Interest Earned

The second entry records the interest credited to VideoBuster's account by the bank:

	31	Cash	8.42	
		Interest Revenue		8.42
		To record interest earned on the average Cash balance in the chequing account.		

Interest earned is a revenue, and the entry recognizes both the revenue and the related increase in Cash.

3. NSF Cheque

The third entry records the NSF cheque that is returned as uncollectible. The $20 cheque was received from Heflin in payment of his account and deposited. When the cheque cleared the banking system, Heflin's bank account was found to have insufficient funds to cover the cheque. The bank charged $10 for handling the NSF cheque and deducted $30 total from VideoBuster's account. The company must reverse the entry made when the cheque was received and also record the $10 fee:

	31	Accounts Receivable—Frank Heflin	30.00	
		Cash		30.00
		To charge Frank Heflin's account for his NSF cheque and the bank's fee.		

This entry reflects business practice by adding the NSF $10 fee to Heflin's account. The company will try to collect the entire $30 from Heflin.

4. Cheque Printing

The fourth entry debits Office Supplies Expense for the printing of cheques:

31	Office Supplies Expense.................................	23.00	
	Cash		23.00
	Cheque printing charge.		

After these four entries are recorded, the balance of Cash is increased to the correct amount of $1,845 (= $1,404.58 + $485 + $8.42 − $30 − $23).

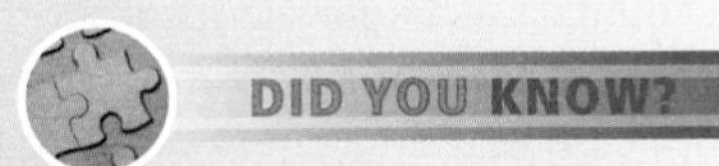

The Financial Transactions and Reports Analysis Centre of Canada, or FINTRAC, is Canada's financial intelligence unit created to collect, analyze, and disclose financial information and intelligence on suspected money laundering and terrorist financing activities. Banks, among others identified in the Proceeds of Crime (Money Laundering) and Terrorist Financing Act and Regulations, are required to report certain transactions to FINTRAC. When there are reasonable grounds to suspect that the information is relevant to threats to the security of Canada, FINTRAC will disclose that information to the Canadian Security and Intelligence Service (CSIS).

Source: http://www.fintrac.gc.ca/

Read Apply Do Check CHECKPOINT

8. What is a bank statement?
9. What is the meaning of the phrase *to reconcile a bank balance*?
10. Why do we reconcile the bank statement balance of cash and the depositor's book balance of cash?
11. List items affecting the bank side of a reconciliation and indicate if the items are added or subtracted.
12. List items affecting the book side of a reconciliation and indicate if the items are added or subtracted.

Do Quick Study questions: QS 9-9, QS 9-10

CRITICAL THINKING CHALLENGE

Refer to the Critical Thinking Challenge questions at the beginning of the chapter on page 439. Compare your answers to those suggested on Connect at www.mcgrawhillconnect.ca.

IFRS HIGHLIGHTS

IFRS have not caused changes, at the introductory level, to concepts covered in this chapter.

Summary

LO1 | Define, explain the purpose, and identify the principles of internal control. An internal control system consists of the policies and procedures that managers use to protect assets, ensure reliable accounting, promote efficient operations, and encourage adherence to company policies. It is a key part of systems design, analysis, and performance. It can prevent avoidable losses and help managers both plan operations and monitor company and human performance.

Principles of good internal control include establishing responsibilities, maintaining adequate records, insuring assets and bonding employees, separating recordkeeping from custody of assets, dividing responsibilities for related transactions, applying technological controls, and performing regular independent reviews.

LO2 | Define cash and explain how it is reported. Cash includes currency and coins, and amounts on deposit in bank, chequing, and some savings accounts. It also includes items that are acceptable for deposit in these accounts. Cash equivalents or short-term investments are similar to cash, therefore most companies combine them with cash as a single item on the balance sheet. Cash and cash equivalents are liquid assets because they are converted easily into other assets or used in paying for services or liabilities.

LO3 | Apply internal control to cash. Internal control of cash receipts ensures that all cash received is properly recorded and deposited. Cash receipts arise from cash sales, collections of customers' accounts, receipts of interest and rent, bank loans, sale of assets, and owner investments. Good internal control for cash receipts by mail includes at least two people being assigned to open the mail and prepare a list with each sender's name, amount of money received, and explanation.

LO4 | Explain and record petty cash fund transactions. To avoid writing cheques for small amounts, a company sets up one or more petty cash funds to pay for items such as postage, courier fees, repairs, and supplies. A petty cashier is responsible for safekeeping of the cash, for making payments from this fund, and for keeping receipts and records. A Petty Cash account is debited when the fund is established or increased in size. The cashier presents all paid receipts to the company's cashier for reimbursement to restore petty cash to its full amount. Petty cash disbursements are recorded whenever the fund is replenished with debits to expense accounts reflecting receipts and a credit to cash.

LO5 | Explain and identify banking activities and the control features they provide. Banks offer several services—such as the bank account, the bank deposit, and chequing—that promote the control or safeguarding of cash. A bank account is set up by a bank and permits a customer to deposit money for safeguarding and cheque withdrawals. A bank deposit is money added to the account with a deposit slip as proof. A cheque is a document signed by the depositor instructing the bank to pay a specified amount of money to a designated recipient. Sales resulting from debit card and credit card transactions are usually deposited into the bank account immediately, less a fee. Electronic funds transfer (EFT) uses electronic communication to transfer cash from one party to another, and it decreases certain risks. Companies increasingly use it because of its convenience and low cost.

LO6 | Prepare a bank reconciliation and journalize any resulting adjustment(s). A bank reconciliation is prepared to prove the accuracy of the depositor's and the bank's records. In completing a reconciliation, the bank statement balance is adjusted for such items as outstanding cheques and unrecorded deposits made on or before the bank statement date but not reflected on the statement. The depositor's cash account balance also often requires adjustment. These adjustments include items such as service charges, bank collections for the depositor, and interest earned on the account balance.

guidance answers to JUDGEMENT CALL

Campaign Manager

A forced vacation policy is part of a system of good internal controls. When employees are forced to take vacations, their ability to hide any fraudulent behaviour decreases. This is because someone must take on the responsibilities of the person on vacation, and the replacement employee potentially can uncover fraudulent behaviour or records. A forced vacation policy is especially important for employees in more sensitive positions of handling money or other easily transferable assets.

Internal Auditor

You inform your supervisor, who emphasizes that the purpose of the surprise visit was defeated because you allowed another employee to interfere with and influence your actions; this was a valuable first lesson! Your problem is now whether to accept the situation or to dig further to see if the petty cashier is abusing petty cash. Since you were asked to postpone your count and the fund consists of new $20 bills, you have legitimate concerns about whether money is being borrowed for personal use. You should conduct a further investigation. One result might show that the most recent reimbursement of the fund was for $180 (= 9 × $20) or more. In that case, this reimbursement can leave the fund with sequentially numbered $20 bills. But if the most recent reimbursement was for less than $180, the presence of nine sequentially numbered $20 bills suggests that the $180 of new $20 bills was obtained from a bank as replacement for bills that had been removed. Neither situation shows that the cashier is stealing money. Yet the second case indicates that the cashier "borrowed" the cash and later replaced it after the auditor showed up. In writing your report, you must not conclude that the cashier is unethical unless evidence along with your knowledge of company policies supports it. Your report must present facts according to the evidence.

Entrepreneur

Your analysis of allowing credit card sales should estimate the benefits against the costs. The primary benefit is the potential to increase sales by attracting customers who prefer the convenience of credit cards. The primary cost is the fee charged by the credit card company for providing this service to your store. Your analysis should therefore estimate the expected increase in sales dollars from allowing credit card sales and then subtract (1) the normal costs and expenses, and (2) the credit card fees associated with this expected increase in sales dollars. If your analysis shows an increase in profit from allowing credit card sales, your store should probably allow them.

guidance answers to CHECKPOINT

1. c
2. Technology reduces processing errors, allows more extensive testing of records, limits the amount of hard evidence of processing steps, and highlights the importance of maintaining separation of duties.
3. a
4. If all cash payments are made by cheque, numerous cheques for small amounts must be written. Because this practice is expensive and time consuming, a petty cash fund is established to make small cash payments.
5. If the petty cash fund is not reimbursed at the end of an accounting period, the transactions in petty cash are not yet recorded in the accounts and the petty cash asset is overstated. But these amounts are rarely large enough to affect users' decisions based on financial statements.
6. First, when the petty cash fund is reimbursed, the petty cash transactions are recorded in their proper accounts. Second, reimbursement also gives money that allows the fund to continue being used. Third, reimbursement identifies any cash shortage or overage in the fund.
7. The retailer receives payment faster than if it had to collect credit sales, and the risk of uncollectible customer accounts is transferred to the credit card company and bank.
8. A bank statement is a report prepared by the bank describing the activities in a depositor's account.
9. To reconcile a bank balance means to explain the difference between the cash balance in the depositor's accounting records and the balance on the bank statement.
10. The purpose of the bank reconciliation is to determine if any errors have been made by the bank or by the depositor and to determine if the bank has completed any transactions affecting the depositor's account that the depositor has not recorded. It is also an internal control mechanism to ensure that the company's cash system is operating properly.
11. Outstanding cheques—subtracted
    Unrecorded deposits—added
12. Bank service charges—subtracted
    Debit memos—subtracted
    NSF cheques—subtracted
    Interest earned—added
    Credit memos—added

demonstration problem

Required

Consider the following information and prepare a bank reconciliation, along with any resulting journal entries, for TJ Company at April 30, 2011.

Analysis component:

Assume that you are the owner of TJ Company and have just read the newspaper article discussed in this chapter's opening story. As a result, you have decided to review the bank reconciliation prepared for April 30. You notice that cheque #808 for $850 is not included with the cancelled cheques that are returned by the bank with the bank statement. Your office is small and is managed by one employee, Brent Wicker. When questioned, Brent cannot locate the missing cheque. What do you do, if anything? Explain.

The bank reconciliation prepared by TJ Company on March 31, 2011, follows:

TJ Company Bank Reconciliation March 31, 2011				
Bank statement balance		$7,670	Book balance	$8,590
Add:				
Deposit of March 31 in transit		1,100		
		$8,770		
Deduct:				
Outstanding cheques:				
#797:	$ 60			
#804:	120	180		
Adjusted bank balance		$8,590	Adjusted book balance	$8,590

The following bank statement is available for April:

Bank Statement To: TJ Company					April 30, 2011 Bank of Nova Scotia
Cheques/Charges/Debits			**Deposits/Credits**		**Balance**
					7,670
#811	04/03	834	04/03	1,100	7,936
#807	04/07	375	04/07	810	8,371
#810	04/13	208	04/13	690	8,853
NSF	04/18	450	04/18	680	9,083
#808	04/23	850	04/23	355	8,588
#797	04/27	60	04/27	750	9,278
#814	04/30	550	04/30	620	9,348
#813	04/30	372	INT	47	9,023
#809	04/30	124			8,899
SC	04/30	32	04/30		8,867
NSF = Not Sufficient Funds		SC = Service Charge		INT = Interest	

A list of deposits made and cheques written during April, taken from the Cash Receipts Journal and Cash Disbursements Journal, is shown below:

Deposits Made	
April 7	$ 810
13	690
18	680
23	355
27	750
30	620
30	770
Total April Cash Receipts	$4,675

Cheques Written	
No. 807	$ 375
808	850
809	124
810	208
811	348
812	207
813	372
814	550
815	405
816	602
Total April Cash Disbursements	$4,041

General Ledger Cash Account:

Cash					Acct. No. 101
Date	**Explanation**	**PR**	**Debit**	**Credit**	**Balance**
2011					
March 31	Balance				8,590
April 30		CR12	4,675		13,265
30		CD14		4,041	9,224

In reviewing cheques returned by the bank, the bookkeeper discovered that cheque #811, for delivery expense, was recorded in the Cash Disbursements Journal incorrectly as $348. The NSF cheque for $450 was that of customer A. Hussain, deposited in April.

Planning the Solution

- Set up a schedule like Exhibit 9.9 with a bank side and a book side for the reconciliation.
- Follow the nine steps used in the chapter to prepare the bank reconciliation.
- For every reconciling item on the book side, prepare an entry, if required.
- Prepare an answer to the analysis question.

solution

TJ Company
Bank Reconciliation
April 30, 2011

Bank statement balance		$8,867	Book balance		$9,224
Add:			Add:		
Deposit of April 30 in transit		770	Interest revenue		47
		$9,637			$9,271
Deduct:			Deduct:		
Outstanding cheques:			Error (cheque #811 for delivery exp)	$486	
#804:	$120		NSF cheque	450	
#812:	207		Service charge	32	968
#815:	405				
#816:	602	1,334			
Adjusted bank balance		$8,303	Adjusted book balance		$8,303

Required Entries

April	30	Cash	47	
		Interest Revenue		47
		To record interest earned.		
	30	Delivery Expense	486	
		Cash		486
		To correct accounting error on cheque #811.		
	30	Accounts Receivable—A. Hussain	450	
		Cash		450
		To reinstate customer account due to NSF cheque.		
	30	Bank Service Charges Expense	32	
		Cash		32
		To record bank service charges.		

Analysis component:

There are several things that need to be done. A review of prior months' bank reconciliations needs to be conducted to determine if this is an anomaly or a recurring event. The journal entry regarding cheque #808 needs to be reviewed to determine the payee. The payee, if identifiable, needs to be contacted to verify the purchase. If this cannot be done, the bank needs to be contacted to determine if its records are able to verify the payee on the cheque. Hopefully, Brent made an honest mistake and misplaced the cheque. However, in the future, the owner of TJ Company should review each bank reconciliation and ensure that the cheques being paid are scrutinized to ensure they are for business-related payments.

APPENDIX 9A

Using the Information

Acid-Test Ratio

LO7 Calculate the acid-test ratio and explain its use as an indicator of a company's liquidity.

We learned in Chapter 6 that merchandise inventory often makes up a large portion of current assets for merchandising companies. We know that merchandise inventory must be sold and any resulting accounts receivable need to be collected before cash is available. This often means that a large part of current assets is not readily available for paying liabilities because it is in the form of merchandise inventory.

We explained in Chapter 5 how the current ratio, calculated as total current assets divided by total current liabilities, is useful in assessing a company's ability to pay current liabilities. Because some current assets, specifically merchandise inventories and prepaids, are not readily available as a source of payment for current liabilities, we look to a measure other than the current ratio to obtain a stricter measure of a company's ability to cover current liabilities: the *acid-test ratio.*

The *acid-test ratio* differs from the current ratio by excluding current assets that are *less liquid,* such as inventory and prepaids. The **acid-test ratio**, also called the **quick ratio**, is defined as shown in Exhibit 9A.1.

Exhibit 9A.1
Acid-Test Ratio

$$\text{Acid-test ratio} = \frac{\text{Quick assets*}}{\text{Current liabilities}}$$

Quick assets** ***are cash, short-term investments, and receivables.

Exhibit 9A.2 shows both the acid-test and current ratios of WestJet.

Exhibit 9A.2
Current and Acid-Test Ratios Compared

	At December 31,				
	2008	2007	2006	2005	2004
Current Ratio	1.25	1.22	0.98	0.85	0.64
Acid-Test Ratio	1.13	1.13	0.84	0.71	0.53

The acid-test ratio is interpreted in a similar manner as the current ratio. In Exhibit 9A.2, WestJet's current ratio at December 31, 2008, shows $1.25 of current assets available to cover each $1.00 of current liability as it comes due. As a stricter measure, the acid-test ratio tells us WestJet had $1.13 of quick assets to cover each $1.00 of current obligations at December 31, 2008. An acid-test ratio equal to or greater than 1 is generally considered favourable (good). Both WestJet's current and acid-test ratios are greater than 1 in only two of the five years shown in Exhibit 9A.2, which indicates that, in the past, it may have had difficulty in covering obligations as they came due. The current and acid-test ratios for both 2008 and 2007 are greater than 1, indicating an improvement in WestJet's ability to pay short-term debt.

CHECKPOINT

13. ABC Company had acid-test ratios of 1.4 and 1.6 for 2011 and 2010, respectively. Is the change in the ratio favourable or unfavourable?

Do Quick Study question: *QS 9-11

Summary of Appendix 9A

LO7 Calculate the acid-test ratio and explain its use as an indicator of a company's liquidity. The acid-test ratio is calculated as quick assets (cash, short-term investments, and receivables) divided by current liabilities. It is an indicator of a company's ability to pay its current liabilities with its existing quick assets. A ratio equal to or greater than 1 is often considered adequate.

13. Unfavourable.

Glossary

Acid-test ratio A ratio used to assess a company's ability to cover its current debts with existing assets calculated as quick assets (cash, short-term investments, and receivables) divided by current liabilities; also called *quick ratio*. (p. 464)

Bank reconciliation An analysis that explains the difference between the balance of a chequing account shown in the depositor's records and the balance reported on the bank statement. (p. 454)

Bond An insurance policy purchased by a company to protect against losses from theft by that employee. (p. 441)

Cancelled cheques Cheques that the bank has paid and deducted from the customer's account during the month. (p. 454)

Cash Includes currency, coins, and amounts on deposit in bank chequing or savings accounts. (p. 444)

Cash Over and Short account An income statement account used to record cash shortages and cash overages arising from omitted petty cash receipts and from errors in making change. (p. 445)

Cheque A document signed by the depositor instructing the bank to pay a specified amount of money to a designated recipient. (p. 451)

Collusion An act in which two or more people agree to commit a fraud. (p. 441)

Debit card Card used at point of sale to transfer payment for a purchase immediately from the customer's to the vendor's bank account. (p. 452)

Deposit slip Bank document that lists the items such as currency, coins, and cheques deposited along with each of their dollar amounts. (p. 450)

Electronic funds transfer The use of electronic communication to transfer cash from one party to another. (p. 451)

Internal control system All the policies and procedures managers use to protect assets, ensure reliable accounting, promote efficient operations, and urge adherence to company policies. (p. 440)

Liquid asset An asset such as cash that is easily converted into other types of assets or used to buy services or to pay liabilities. (p. 444)

Liquidity A characteristic of an asset that refers to how easily the asset can be converted into cash or another type of asset or used in paying for services or obligations. (p. 444)

Petty cashier Employee responsible for safekeeping of the cash, making payments from this fund, and keeping accurate records. (p. 446)

Principles of internal control Fundamental principles of internal control that apply to all companies requiring management to ensure transactions and activities are authorized, maintain records, insure assets, separate recordkeeping and custody of assets, establish a separation of duties, apply technological controls, and perform internal and external audits. (p. 440)

Quick assets Those current assets that are most liquid, specifically cash, short-term investments, and receivables. (p. 464)

Quick ratio See *acid-test ratio*. (p. 464)

Separation of duties An internal control principle requiring the division of responsibility for related transactions between two or more individuals or departments. (p. 441)

Signature card Bank document that includes the signature of each person authorized to sign cheques from the account. (p. 450)

Visit **Connect** at **www.mcgrawhillconnect.ca** for additional study tools, practice quizzes, to search an interactive e-book, and much more.

Concept Review Questions

1. Which of the following assets is most liquid and which is least liquid: merchandise inventory, building, accounts receivable, cash?
2. List the seven broad principles of internal control.
3. Why should the person who keeps the record of an asset not be responsible for custody of the asset?
4. Internal control procedures are important in every business, but at what stage in the development of a business do they become critical?
5. Why should responsibility for a sequence of related transactions be divided among different departments or individuals?
6. Why should all receipts be deposited intact on the day of receipt?
7. When merchandise is purchased for a large store, why are department managers not permitted to deal directly with suppliers?
8. What is a petty cash receipt? Who signs a petty cash receipt?
9. Refer to Danier's balance sheet in Appendix I. What is its cash balance as at June 28, 2008?

DANIER

10. WestJet Airlines showed cash and cash equivalents on December 31, 2008, of $820,214,000. What percentage is this of total assets?

Quick Study

QS 9-1
Internal control objectives
LO1

You are currently part of a university work experience program. Your job placement is at the municipal transit centre. Your supervisor is responsible for the recording and distribution of monthly transit passes to authorized vendors throughout the city. The vendors pay $50 per bus pass and sell them for $55. Your work experience job is to prepare a monthly reconciliation of the transit passes including the quantity sold, the number actually distributed, the unsold passes, and the cash proceeds. You are unable to reconcile the past two months. The bus passes are sequentially numbered and, in checking the sequence, you notice that numbers 9750 to 9820, 11012 to 11750, and 22000 to 22440 cannot be accounted for. You bring this to the attention of the supervisor, who tells you that reconciliations are never done; the job was created by her superior "to give you something to do" so you are told not to worry about it.

a. What is the main objective of internal control and how is it accomplished?
b. Why should recordkeeping for assets be separated from custody over the assets?
c. Do you report your findings?

QS 9-2
Reporting cash and other current assets
LO2

Prepare the current asset section based on the following alphabetized post-closing trial balance information at March 31, 2011, for Whiteagle Company:

Account	Debits	Credits
Accounts payable		$ 7,000
Accounts receivable	$ 4,500	
Accumulated depreciation		9,900
Cash	15,000	
Isaac Whiteagle, capital		25,800
Notes payable, due 2017		14,000
Petty cash	600	
Prepaid rent	3,200	
Property, plant and equipment	38,000	
Unearned revenue		4,600

QS 9-3
Internal controls for cash
LO3

The treasurer of a local not-for-profit organization was found guilty today of defrauding the organization of thousands of dollars. Among the individual's many responsibilities were the recording of cash deposits, the writing of cheques, and the preparation of the bank reconciliation. A member of the organization suspected wrongdoing when the treasurer reported total cash collections of $2,800 regarding the sale of nonsequentially numbered raffle tickets; the member submitted $1,600 to the treasurer and knew that other members had collectively sold in excess of $3,000. The police were consulted and an investigation revealed that not only had the treasurer pocketed an undisclosed amount of cash over a two-year period but he had also made cash withdrawals from the bank and destroyed the debit memos when returned with the bank statement.

a. What three basic guidelines regarding a good system of internal control for cash were not observed?
b. What corrective action should the organization take in the future?

QS 9-4
Petty cash
LO4

The petty cash fund of the Wee Ones Agency was established on May 1, 2011, at $75. At the end of the month, the fund contained $12.74 and had the following receipts: film rentals, $19.40; refreshments for meetings, $22.81 (both expenditures to be classified as Entertainment Expense); postage, $6.95; and printing, $13.10.

1. Prepare the journal entry to record the establishment of the fund.
2. Prepare a summary of the petty cash receipts similar to Exhibit 9.2 and then record the reimbursement on May 31.
3. Explain when the Petty Cash account would be credited in a journal entry.

QS 9-5
Petty cash
LO4

WilsonArt set up a petty cash fund of $200 on March 1, 2011. On March 17, the petty cash box contained $19 and the following receipts: $75 for printing, $48 for taxi fare, and $55 for delivery expense. Record the reimbursement of the fund on March 17.

QS 9-6
Petty cash
LO4

Canmore Consulting established a $100 petty cash fund on September 1, 2011. On September 23, the petty cash box contained $7 and receipts for the following expenses: $32 for entertainment expense (lunch with a client), $45 for computer repair, and $18 for delivery expense. Record the reimbursement of the fund on September 23.

QS 9-7
Credit card transactions
LO5

Journalize the following transactions (assume a perpetual inventory system):

February 1	Recorded $75,000 of sales (cost $62,000) to customers using MasterCard. MasterCard charges the retailer 2.5% for credit card transactions.
February 10	Sold merchandise to customers who paid $28,000 in cash (cost $23,000).

QS 9-8
Debit card transactions
LO5

Journalize the following transactions (assume a perpetual inventory system):

Oct.	1	Recorded sales of $14,000 (cost $8,000) to customers using debit cards. Assume the bank charges 0.25% for all debit card transactions.
	7	Sold merchandise to customers who paid $3,500 in cash (cost $2,800).

QS 9-9
Bank reconciliation
LO6

1. Identify whether each of the following items affects the bank or book side of the reconciliation and indicate if the amount represents an addition or a subtraction:
   a. Deposits in transit.
   b. Interest on average monthly balance.
   c. Credit memos.
   d. Bank service charges.
   e. Outstanding cheques.
   f. Debit memos.
   g. NSF cheques.
2. Which of the previous items require a journal entry?

QS 9-10
Bank reconciliation
LO6

Bolton Company's October 31, 2011, bank statement showed a cash balance of $15,400, while the company's General Ledger Cash account for the same date showed a balance of $13,150. A bank deposit of October 31 for $1,200 does not appear on the bank statement. Cheques #150 for $980 and #169 for $2,515, both written in October, had not cleared the bank during October. Bank service charges for the month were $45. Prepare a bank reconciliation at October 31, 2011, and prepare the necessary entries.

***QS 9-11**
Acid-test ratio
LO7

Your company has a policy of granting credit only to customers whose acid-test ratio is greater than or equal to 1. Based on this policy, determine if the following companies would be granted credit (round to two decimal places). Why or why not?

	Company A	Company B
Cash	$1,200	$1,200
Accounts receivable	2,700	2,700
Inventory	5,000	5,000
Prepaid expenses	600	600
Accounts payable	3,100	4,750
Other current liabilities	250	950

Exercises

Exercise 9-1
Analyzing internal control
LO1

Lombard Company is a young business that has grown rapidly. The company's bookkeeper, who was hired two years ago, left town suddenly after the company's manager discovered that a great deal of money had disappeared over the past 18 months. An audit disclosed that the bookkeeper had written and signed several cheques made payable to the bookkeeper's brother and then recorded the cheques as salaries expense. The brother, who cashed the cheques but had never worked for the company, left town with the bookkeeper. As a result, the company incurred an uninsured loss of $84,000.

Evaluate Lombard Company's internal control system and indicate which principles of internal control appear to have been ignored in this situation.

An asterisk (*) identifies assignment material based on Appendix 9A.

Exercise 9-2
Internal control objectives
LO1

As a member of the city's internal audit team, you have been instructed to observe the procedures regarding the collection of coins from the municipally owned parking meters. You accompany the civic employee on the collection route. The employee uses a key to open the locked coin compartment of the meter and empties its contents into a canvas bag that closes with a drawstring. When the bag is full, the employee closes it, and places it in the vehicle, which is parked along the route. At the end of the day, the civic employee delivers the bags to two individuals in a municipal office who are jointly responsible for counting the contents. Write a brief report regarding your observations and any concerns that you might have.

Exercise 9-3
Recommending internal control procedures
LO1

What internal control procedures would you recommend in each of the following situations?

a. A concession company has one employee who sells T-shirts and sunglasses at the beach. Each day, the employee is given enough shirts and sunglasses to last through the day and enough cash to make change. The money is kept in a box at the stand.

b. An antique store has one employee who is given cash and sent to garage sales each weekend. The employee pays cash for merchandise to be resold at the antique store.

Exercise 9-4
Internal control over cash receipts
LO3

Some of Fannin Co.'s cash receipts from customers are sent to the company in the mail. Fannin's bookkeeper opens the letters and deposits the cash received each day. What internal control problem do you see in this arrangement? What changes would you recommend?

Exercise 9-5
Petty cash fund
LO4

Eanes Co. established a $200 petty cash fund on January 1, 2011. One week later, on January 8, the fund contained $27.50 in cash and receipts for these expenditures: postage, $64.00; transportation-in, $19.00; store supplies, $36.50; and a withdrawal of $53.00 by Jim Eanes, the owner. Eanes uses the perpetual method to account for merchandise inventory.

a. Prepare the journal entry to establish the fund on January 1.

b. Prepare a summary of the petty cash receipts similar to Exhibit 9.2 and record the entry to reimburse the fund on January 8.

Analysis component:
If the January 8 entry to reimburse the fund were not recorded and financial statements were prepared for the month of January, would net income be over- or understated?

Exercise 9-6
Petty cash fund
LO4

Mc Graw Hill connect™

Brady Company established a $400 petty cash fund on September 9, 2011. On September 30, the fund had $146.40 in cash and receipts for these expenditures: transportation-in, $32.45; office supplies, $113.55; and repairs expense, $87.60. Brady uses the perpetual method to account for merchandise inventory. The petty cashier could not account for the $20.00 shortage in the fund.

a. Prepare the September 9 entry to establish the fund.

b. Prepare a summary of the petty cash receipts similar to Exhibit 9.2 and record the entry on September 30 to reimburse the fund and reduce it to $300.

Analysis component:
You are the senior marketing manager and are reviewing the unadjusted account balances for your division. You notice the $20 cash shortage recorded on September 30 regarding petty cash. The current petty cash custodian has been in place for three months. What should be done, if anything? Explain.

Exercise 9-7
Petty cash fund
LO4

Conway Designs established a $300 petty cash fund on October 1, 2011. Prepare the entry to replenish the fund at the end of each of the following months of activity:

a. The petty cash box contained $45 on October 31 along with receipts for $120 for cleaning, $79 for postage, and $60 for delivery expense.

b. On November 30, the petty cash box contained only two receipts, for a $75 computer repair and a $156 entertainment expense. The petty cash custodian counted cash remaining of $67.

c. The petty cash box contained $18 on December 31 plus receipts for $80 for gas expense, $140 for office supplies, and $62 for entertainment expense. In addition to replenishing the fund, it was increased by $100.

Exercise 9-8
Credit card and debit card transactions
LO5

Journalize the following transactions for European Nutrition Consultants:

Oct.	1	Sold services for $105,000 to customers using debit cards. Assume the bank charges 0.5% for all debit card transactions.
	7	Sold services to customers for $37,000 cash.
	8	Recorded Visa credit card sales totalling $61,000. Visa applies fees of 2%.
	10	Sold $84,000 of services to Edson Community Health Clinic, terms 2/15, n/30.
	25	Collected the amount owing regarding the October 10 sale.

Exercise 9-9
Credit card and debit card transactions
LO5

On January 15, LenCon sold merchandise to customers for cash of $56,000 (cost $36,400). Merchandise costing $12,000 was sold to customers for $15,800 on January 17; terms 2/10, n/30. Sales totalling $114,000 (cost $74,100) were recorded on January 20 to customers using MasterCard, a credit card that charges a 2% fee. On January 25, sales of $72,000 (cost $46,800) were made to debit card customers. The bank charges LenCon a flat fee of 0.5% on all debit card transactions.

Required
Prepare journal entries for each of the transactions described (assume a perpetual inventory system).

Analysis component:
Identify the advantages and disadvantages of each type of sale: cash sale, credit sale, credit card sale, or debit card sale. Explain why LenCon would likely accept all these types of sales.

Exercise 9-10
Preparation of bank reconciliation
LO6

The bank reconciliation prepared by Pelzer Holdings on June 30, 2011, appeared as follows:

Pelzer Holdings
Bank Reconciliation
June 30, 2011

Bank statement balance	$8,000	Book balance	$7,480
Add:			
Deposit of June 30 in transit	680		
	$8,680		
Deduct:			
Outstanding cheque #14	1,200		
Adjusted bank balance	$7,480	Adjusted book balance	$7,480

The Cash account in the General Ledger appeared as follows on July 31:

Cash						Acct. No. 101
Date		**Explanation**	**PR**	**Debit**	**Credit**	**Balance**
2011						
June	30	Balance				7,480
July	31		CR3	5,700		13,180
	31		CD6		3,440	9,740

A list of deposits made and cheques written during July, taken from the Cash Receipts Journal and Cash Disbursements Journal, is shown below:

Deposits Made	
July 8	$ 770
11	1,328
24	3,030
31	572
Total July Cash Receipts	$5,700

Cheques Written	
No. 52	$1,840
53	1,320
54	280
Total July Cash Disbursements	$3,440

The following bank statement is available for July:

Bank Statement					
To: Pelzer Holdings					July 31, 2011 Bank of Montreal
Cheques/Charges			Deposits/Credits		Balance
					8,000
NSF	07/02	240	07/02	680	8,440
#53	07/08	1,320	07/08	770	7,890
#96	07/11	560	07/11	1,328	8,658
			07/24	3,030	11,688
#52	07/31	1,840	07/31		9,848
NSF = Not Sufficient Funds		SC = Service Charge	PMT = Principal Payment		INT = Interest

In reviewing cheques returned by the bank, the bookkeeper noted that cheque #96 written by Peltza Holdings in the amount of $560 was charged against Pelzer's account in error by the bank. The NSF cheque was regarding a customer account, Jim Anderson.

Required

1. Prepare a bank reconciliation at July 31.

2. Prepare the necessary journal entries to bring the General Ledger Cash account into agreement with the adjusted balance on the bank reconciliation.

Check figure:
1. Adjusted book balance = $9,500

Analysis component:
If the journal entries in Part 2 are not recorded, what financial statement elements (net income, assets, liabilities, and equity) would be over- or understated?

Exercise 9-11
Bank reconciliation
LO6

Medline Service Co. deposits all receipts intact on the day received and makes all payments by cheque. On July 31, 2011, after all posting was completed, its Cash account showed an $11,352 debit balance. However, Medline's July 31 bank statement showed only $10,332 on deposit in the bank on that day along with the following information.

a. Outstanding cheques, $1,713.

b. Included with the July cancelled cheques returned by the bank was an $18 debit memorandum for bank services.

c. Cheque #919, returned with the cancelled cheques, was correctly drawn for $489 in payment of the utility bill and was paid by the bank on July 15. However, it had been recorded with a debit to Utilities Expense and a credit to Cash as though it were for $498.

d. The July 31 cash receipts, $2,724, were placed in the bank's night depository after banking hours on that date and were unrecorded by the bank at the time the July bank statement was prepared.

Required

a. Prepare a bank reconciliation for Medline at July 31.

b. Give the journal entries that Medline Service Co. should make as a result of having prepared the bank reconciliation in part (a).

Check figure:
Adjusted book balance = $11,343

Analysis component:
Identify whether net income, assets, liabilities, and equity would be over- or understated if the journal entires in part (b) were not recorded.

Exercise 9-12
Bank reconciling items and required entries
LO6

Set up a table with the following headings for a bank reconciliation as of September 30:

Bank Balance		Book Balance			Not Shown on the Reconcil-iation
Add	Deduct	Add	Deduct	Must Adjust	

For each item that follows, place an X in the appropriate columns to indicate whether the item should be added to or deducted from the book or bank balance, or whether it should not appear on the reconciliation. If the book balance is to be adjusted, place a Dr. or Cr. in the Must Adjust column to indicate whether the Cash balance should be debited or credited.

1. Interest earned on the account.
2. Deposit made on September 30 after the bank was closed.
3. Cheques outstanding on August 31 that cleared the bank in September.
4. NSF cheque from customer returned on September 15 but not recorded by the company.
5. Cheques written and mailed to payees on September 30.
6. Deposit made on September 5 that was processed on September 8.
7. Bank service charge.
8. Cheques written and mailed to payees on October 5.
9. Cheques written by another depositor but charged against the company's account.
10. Principal and interest on a note receivable collected by the bank but not recorded by the company.
11. Special charge for collection of note in Item 10 on company's behalf.
12. Cheque written against the account and cleared by the bank; not recorded by the bookkeeper.

*Exercise 9-13
Acid-test ratio
LO7

Calculate the acid-test ratio in each of the following cases:

	Case X	Case Y	Case Z
Cash	$ 800	$ 910	$1,100
Short-term investments	-0-	-0-	500
Receivables	-0-	990	800
Inventory	2,000	1,000	4,000
Prepaid expenses	1,200	600	900
Total current assets	$4,000	$3,500	$7,300
Current liabilities	$2,200	$1,100	$3,650

Required

Which case is in the best position to meet short-term obligations most easily? Explain your choice. *Round calculations to two decimal places.*

An asterisk (*) identifies assignment material based on Appendix 9A.

Problems

Problem 9-1A
Principles of internal control
LO1

For the following five scenarios, identify the principle of internal control that is violated. Next, make a recommendation as to what the business should do to ensure adherence to principles of internal control.

1. At Stratford Iron Company, Jill and Joan alternate lunch hours. Normally Jill is the petty cash custodian, but if someone needs petty cash when Jill is at lunch, Joan fills in as custodian.
2. Nadine McDonald does all the posting of patient charges and payments at the Northampton Medical Clinic. Every night, Nadine backs up the computerized accounting system to a tape and stores the tape in a locked file at her desk.
3. Jack Mawben prides himself on hiring quality workers who require little supervision. As office manager, Jack gives his employees full discretion over their tasks and has seen no reason to perform independent reviews of their work for years.
4. Bill Clark's manager has told him to "reduce overhead" no matter what! Bill decides to raise the deductible on the plant's property insurance from $5,000 to $10,000. This cuts the property insurance premium in half. In a related move, he decides that bonding of the plant's employees is really a waste of money since the company has not experienced any losses due to employee theft. Bill saves the entire amount of the bonding insurance premium by dropping the bonding insurance.
5. Catherine Young records all incoming customer cash receipts for her employer and also posts the customer payments to their accounts.

Problem 9-2A
Establishing, reimbursing, and increasing the petty cash fund
LO4

Palladium Art Gallery completed the following petty cash transactions during February 2011:

Feb.	2	Prepared a $350 cheque, cashed it, and gave the proceeds and the petty cash box to Nick Reed, the petty cashier.
	5	Purchased paper for the copier, $10.13.
	9	Paid $22.50 COD charges on merchandise purchased for resale. *Assume Palladium uses the perpetual method to account for merchandise inventory.*
	12	Paid $9.95 postage to express mail a contract to a client.
	14	Reimbursed Gina Barton, the manager of the business, $100.00 for business auto expenses.
	20	Purchased stationery, $77.76.
	23	Paid a courier $18.00 to deliver merchandise sold to a customer.
	25	Paid $15.10 COD charges on merchandise purchased for resale.
	28	Paid $64.00 for stamps.
	28	Reed sorted the petty cash receipts by accounts affected and exchanged them for a cheque to reimburse the fund for expenditures. However, there was only $29.23 in cash in the fund. In addition, the size of the petty cash fund was increased to $400.

Required

1. Prepare a journal entry to record establishing the petty cash fund.
2. Prepare a summary of petty cash payments, similar to Exhibit 9.2, that has these categories: delivery expense, auto expense, postage expense, merchandise inventory, and office supplies. Sort the payments into the appropriate categories and total the expenditures in each category.
3. Prepare the journal entry to record the reimbursement and the increase of the fund.

Analysis component:

One of your responsibilities as an employee with Palladium Art Gallery is to handle the petty cash fund. You are concerned about the auto expense claims made regularly by Gina Barton, the manager who hired you: Gina tells you how much the expenditures were and you give her the cash out of petty cash. Gina has never given you receipts to substantiate her claims. The owner of the gallery is visiting and asks you how things are going. What should you do, if anything? Explain.

Problem 9-3A

Petty cash fund reimbursement and analysis of errors

LO4

El Gatto Co. has only a General Journal in its accounting system and uses it to record all transactions. However, the company recently set up a petty cash fund to facilitate payments of small items. The following petty cash transactions were noted by the petty cashier as occurring during April 2011:

Apr. 1 Received a company cheque for $250 to establish the petty cash fund.

15 Received a company cheque to replenish the fund for the following expenditures made since April 1 and to increase the fund to $450.

a. Paid $78 for janitorial service.
b. Purchased office supplies for $63.68.
c. Purchased postage stamps for $43.50.
d. Paid $57.15 to *The County Crier* for an advertisement in the newspaper.
e. Discovered that $11.15 remained in the petty cash box.

30 The petty cashier noted that $333.39 remained in the fund and decided that the April 15 increase in the fund was too large. Therefore, a company cheque was issued to replenish the fund for the following expenditures made since April 15 and to reduce the fund to $400.

f. Purchased office supplies for $48.36.
g. Reimbursed office manager for business auto, $28.50.
h. Paid $39.75 courier charges to deliver merchandise to a customer.

Required

Prepare journal entries to record the establishment of the fund on April 1 and its replenishments on April 15 and April 30.

Analysis component:

Explain how the company's financial statements would be affected if the petty cash fund were not replenished and no entry were made on April 30. (*Hint: The amount of office supplies that appears on a balance sheet is determined by a physical count of the supplies on hand.*)

Problem 9-4A

Preparation of bank reconciliation and recording adjustments

LO6

The bank reconciliation prepared by Dartmouth Company on May 31, 2011, appeared as follows:

Dartmouth Company
Bank Reconciliation
May 31, 2011

Bank statement balance		$12,304.75	Book balance		$12,568.32
Add:					
Deposit of April 30 in transit		3,073.47			
		$15,378.22			
Deduct:			Deduct:		
Outstanding cheques:			NSF cheque plus service		
#876	$ 185.30		charge	$356.75	
#882:	3,000.00	3,185.30	Bank service charge	18.65	375.40
Adjusted bank balance		$12,192.92	Adjusted book balance		$12,192.92

The Cash account in the General Ledger appeared as follows on June 30 (Dartmouth uses only a General Journal to record transactions):

Cash						Acct. No. 101
Date		**Explanation**	**PR**	**Debit**	**Credit**	**Balance**
2011						
May	31	Balance				12,192.92
June	1	Cheque #883	GJ16		2,250.00	9,942.92
	1	Cheque #884	GJ16		848.90	9,094.02
	3	Cheque #885	GJ16		1,152.30	7,941.72
	4	Cheque #886	GJ16		1,138.40	6,803.32
	9	Deposit	GJ16	2,385.70		9,189.02
	12	Cheque #887	GJ16		2,113.78	7,075.24
	12	Cheque #888	GJ16		1,186.30	5,888.94
	12	Cheque #889	GJ16		1,238.95	4,649.99
	18	Deposit	GJ16	2,462.95		7,112.94
	20	Cheque #890	GJ16		1,146.40	5,966.54
	21	Cheque #891	GJ16		974.20	4,992.34
	24	Cheque #892	GJ16		1,106.70	3,885.64
	26	Cheque #893	GJ16		1,164.80	2,720.84
	29	Deposit	GJ16	2,220.85		4,941.69

The following bank statement is available for June:

Bank Statement					
To: Dartmouth Company					**June 30, 2011 Bank of Montreal**
Cheques/Charges			**Deposits/Credits**		**Balance**
			05/31		12,304.75
#884	06/01	848.90	06/01	3,073.47	14,529.32
#883	06/04	2,250.00			12,279.32
#876	06/09	185.30	06/09	2,385.70	14,479.72
#889	06/12	1,238.95			13,240.77
#882	06/14	3,000.00			10,240.77
#887	06/18	1,113.78	06/18	2,462.95	11,589.94
#885	06/20	1,152.30			10,437.64
#891	06/21	874.20			9,563.44
#886	06/29	1,138.40			8,425.04
SC	06/30	45.70	06/30		8,379.34
NSF = Not Sufficient Funds		SC = Service Charge	PMT = Principal Payment		INT = Interest

Required

a. Prepare a bank reconciliation at June 30, 2011. Assume that any errors made were by the bookkeeper (cheque #887 was for office supplies; cheque #891 was for utilities expense).

b. Prepare the necessary entries resulting from the bank reconciliation.

Check figure:
Adjusted book balance = $5,995.99

Analysis component:
You have been employed with Dartmouth Company since June 1, 2011, and part of your job is writing and recording cheques as well as preparing the bank reconciliation. To your surprise, the person you replaced brought in the June bank statement as it had been mailed to her home. While preparing the June bank reconciliation, you notice that cheque #882 for $3,000 cleared the bank in June but is not among the cancelled cheques. What should you do? Explain.

Problem 9-5A
Preparation of bank reconciliation and recording adjustments
LO6

The bank reconciliation prepared by Holliday Adventures on March 31, 2011, appeared as follows:

Holliday Adventures Bank Reconciliation March 31, 2011				
Bank statement balance		$34,100	Book balance	$31,500
Add:				
Deposit of March 31 in transit		5,000		
		$39,100		
Deduct:				
Outstanding cheques:				
#79	$5,200			
#84:	2,400	7,600		
Adjusted bank balance		$31,500	Adjusted book balance	$31,500

The Cash account in the General Ledger appeared as follows on April 30:

Cash					Acct. No. 101
Date	**Explanation**	**PR**	**Debit**	**Credit**	**Balance**
2011					
March 31	Balance				31,500.00
April 30		CR11	23,320.00		54,820.00
30		CD14		11,904.00	42,916.00

A list of deposits made and cheques written during April, taken from the Cash Receipts Journal and Cash Disbursements Journal, is shown below:

Deposits Made	
April 7	$ 8,000
13	1,120
18	6,400
23	400
27	3,600
30	3,800
Total April Cash Receipts	$23,320

Cheques Written	
No. 91	$ 800
92	1,120
93	1,896
94	3,100
95	170
96	640
97	480
98	640
99	258
100	2,800
Total April Cash Disbursements	$11,904

The following bank statement is available for April:

Bank Statement					
To: Holliday Adventures					April 30, 2011 Bank of Montreal
Cheques/Charges			Deposits/Credits		Balance
					34,100
#93	04/02	1,698	04/03	5,000	37,402
#92	04/07	1,120	04/07	8,000	44,282
#84	04/13	2,400	04/13	1,120	43,002
NSF	04/18	824	04/18	6,400	48,578
#95	04/23	170	04/23	400	48,808
#99	04/27	258	04/27	3,600	52,150
#98	04/30	640	04/30	3,800	55,310
#97	04/30	480	04/30	INT 94	54,924
#94	04/30	3,100			51,824
PMT	04/30	4,200			47,624
INT	04/30	640			46,984
SC	04/30	80			46,904
NSF = Not Sufficient Funds		SC = Service Charge	PMT = Principal Payment		INT = Interest

In reviewing cheques returned by the bank, the bookkeeper discovered that cheque #93, for delivery expense, was recorded in the Cash Disbursements Journal incorrectly as $1,896. The NSF cheque for $824 was that of customer Jon Smith, deposited in April.

Required

a. Prepare a bank reconciliation at April 30.

b. Prepare the necessary journal entries to bring the General Ledger Cash account into agreement with the adjusted balance on the bank reconciliation.

Check figure:
a. Adjusted book balance = $37,464

Problem 9-6A
Preparation of bank reconciliation and recording adjustments
LO6

The following information was available to reconcile Deweerd Company's book balance of Cash with its bank statement balance as of October 31, 2011:

a. After all posting was completed on October 31, the company's Cash account had a $52,796 debit balance, but its bank statement showed a $56,040 balance.

b. Cheques #3031 for $2,760 and #3040 for $1,104 were outstanding on the September 30 bank reconciliation. Cheque #3040 was returned with the October cancelled cheques, but cheque #3031 was not. It was also found that cheque #3065 for $672 and cheque #3069 for $4,296, both written in October, were not among the cancelled cheques returned with the statement.

c. In comparing the cancelled cheques returned by the bank with the entries in the accounting records, it was found that cheque #3056 for the October rent was correctly written for $2,500 but was erroneously entered in the accounting records as $2,050.

d. A credit memorandum enclosed with the bank statement indicated that the bank had collected an $18,000 non-interest–bearing note for Deweerd, deducted a $90 collection fee, and credited the remainder to the account. This transaction was not recorded by Deweerd before receiving the statement.

e. A debit memorandum for $1,610 listed a $1,590 NSF cheque plus a $20 NSF charge. The cheque had been received from a customer, Jefferson Tyler. Deweerd had not recorded this bounced cheque before receiving the statement.

f. Also enclosed with the statement was a $30 debit memorandum for bank services. It had not been recorded because no previous notification had been received.

g. The October 31 cash receipts, $20,304, were placed in the bank's night depository after banking hours on that date and this amount did not appear on the bank statement.

Required

1. Prepare a bank reconciliation for the company as of October 31, 2011.

2. Prepare the General Journal entries necessary to bring the company's book balance of cash into agreement with the reconciled balance.

Check figure:
1. Adjusted book balance = $68,616

Analysis component:

Assume that an October 31, 2011, bank reconciliation for the company has already been prepared and some of the items were treated incorrectly in preparing the reconciliation. For each of the following errors, explain the effect of the error on: (1) the final balance that was calculated by adjusting the bank statement balance, and (2) the final balance that was calculated by adjusting the Cash account balance.

a. The company's Cash account balance of $52,796 was listed on the reconciliation as $52,697.

b. The bank's collection of an $18,000 note less the $90 collection fee was added to the bank statement balance.

Problem 9-7A

Preparation of bank reconciliation and recording adjustments

LO6

Morgan Company reconciled its bank and book statement balances of Cash on August 31 and showed two cheques outstanding at that time, #5888 for $2,076.10 and #5893 for $968.50. The following information was available for the September 30, 2011, reconciliation:

From the September 30, 2011, bank statement

BALANCE OF PREVIOUS STATEMENT ON AUG. 31/11	33,601.50
6 DEPOSITS AND OTHER CREDITS TOTALLING	22,365.70
9 CHEQUES AND OTHER DEBITS TOTALLING...................	19,240.10
CURRENT BALANCE AS OF SEPT. 30/11	36,727.10

Chequing Account Transactions

Date	Amount	Transaction Description	Date	Amount	Transaction Description
Sept. 05	2,207.50	+Deposit	Sept. 25	4,703.40	+Deposit
12	4,453.80	+Deposit	30	45.00	+Interest
17	1,176.50	−NSF cheque	30	2,770.00	+Credit memo
21	8,186.00	+Deposit			

Date	Cheque No.	Amount	Date	Cheque No.	Amount
Sept. 03	5904	4,160.00	Sept. 22	5888	2,076.10
07	5901	3,648.50	24	5909	3,615.30
08	5905	1,874.00	28	5907	427.70
10	5903	798.20	29	5902	1,463.80

From Morgan Company's accounting records:

Cash					Acct. No. 101
Date	**Explanation**	**PR**	**Debit**	**Credit**	**Balance**
2011					
Aug. 31	Balance				30,556.90
Sept. 30		CR12	22,716.20		53,273.10
30		CD23		18,198.10	35,075.00

Deposits Made	
Sept. 5	$ 2,207.50
12	4,453.80
21	8,186.00
25	4,703.40
30	3,165.50
Total Sept. Cash Receipts	$22,716.20

Cheques Written	
No. 5901	$ 3,648.50
5902	1,463.80
5903	798.20
5904	4,100.00
5905	1,874.00
5906	1,718.60
5907	427.70
5908	552.00
5909	3,615.30
Total Sept. Cash Disbursements	$18,198.10

Cheque #5904 was correctly written for $4,160 to pay for computer equipment; however, the bookkeeper misread the amount and entered it in the accounting records with a debit to Computer Equipment and a credit to Cash as though it were for $4,100.

The NSF cheque was originally received from a customer, Delia Hahn, in payment of her account. Its return was not recorded when the bank first notified the company. The credit memorandum resulted from the collection of a $2,800 note for Morgan Company by the bank. The bank had deducted a $30 collection fee. The collection has not been recorded.

Required

1. Prepare a September 30 bank reconciliation for the company.
2. Prepare the General Journal entries needed to adjust the book balance of cash to the reconciled balance.

Check figure:
1. Adjusted book balance, $36,653.50

Analysis component:

The preceding bank statement discloses three places where the cancelled cheques returned with the bank statement are not numbered sequentially. In other words, some of the prenumbered cheques in the sequence are missing. Several possible situations would explain why the cancelled cheques returned with a bank statement might not be numbered sequentially. Describe three possible explanations.

Problem 9-8A
Preparation of a bank reconciliation and recording adjustments
LO6

Ozzie Mining, owned by Walt Ozzie, showed the following bank reconciliation at March 31:

Ozzie Mining Bank Reconciliation March 31, 2011				
Bank statement balance		$11,200	Book balance	$11,600
Add:				
Deposit of March 31 in transit		10,000		
		$21,200		
Deduct:				
Outstanding cheques:				
#14	$3,200			
#22	6,400	9,600		
Adjusted bank balance		$11,600	Adjusted book balance	$11,600

Cash							Acct. No. 101
Date			Explanation	PR	Debit	Credit	Balance
2011							
Mar.	31		Balance				11,600
Apr.	30			CR17	62,700		74,300
	30			CD13		24,180	50,120

A list of deposits made and cheques written during April, taken from the Cash Receipts Journal and Cash Disbursements Journal, is shown below:

Deposits Made		
April	7	$12,000
	13	2,800
	18	4,000
	23	15,000
	27	2,900
	30	26,000
Total April Cash Receipts		$62,700

Cheques Written		
No.	23	$ 3,600
	24	1,500
	25	2,000
	26	460
	27	1,300
	28	10,400
	29	2,400
	30	200
	31	1,640
	32	680
Total April Cash Disbursements		$24,180

The following bank statement is available for April:

Bank Statement					
To: Ozzie Mining					April 30, 2011 Bank of Canada
Cheques/Charges			Deposits/Credits		Balance
					11,200
#31	04/03	1,640	04/03	10,000	19,560
#28	04/07	16,400	04/07	12,000	15,160
#26	04/13	460	04/13	2,800	17,500
NSF	04/18	8,000	04/18	4,000	13,500
#24	04/23	1,500	04/23	15,000	27,000
#23	04/27	3,600	04/27	2,900	26,300
#29	04/30	2,400	04/30	50,000	73,900
PMT	04/30	20,000			53,900
INT	04/30	1,000			52,900
SC	04/30	240			52,660
NSF = Not Sufficient Funds		SC = Service Charge	PMT = Payment of Principal on the Loan		INT = Interest on Bank Loan

In reviewing cheques returned by the bank, the bookkeeper discovered that cheque #28, for delivery expense, was recorded in the Cash Disbursements Journal correctly as $10,400. The NSF cheque for $8,000 was that of customer Don James, deposited in March.

On the bank statement, there is a deposit of $50,000 dated April 30. It is an investment made by the owner into the business (the bank transferred the funds electronically from the owner's personal account to his business account, which is why it was not recorded in the Cash Receipts Journal).

Required

a. Prepare a bank reconciliation for Ozzie Mining at April 30.

b. Prepare the necessary journal entries to bring the General Ledger Cash account into agreement with the adjusted balance on the bank reconciliation.

Check figure:
a. Adjusted book balance = $70,880

Problem 9-9A

Preparation of a bank reconciliation and recording adjustments

LO6

Presented below is information related to Red Sea Company. The balance according to the books at October 31, 2011, was $83,695.70; cash receipts recorded during November were $347,047.82; and cash disbursements recorded for November were $332,387.08. The balance according to the bank statement on November 30, 2011, was $112,548.40.

The following cheques were outstanding at November 30:

Cheque	Amount
#1224	3,270.58
#1230	4,936.60
#1232	7,250.30
#1233	964.34

Included with the November bank statement and not recorded by the company were a bank debit memo for $54.80 covering bank charges for the month, a debit memo for $744.26 for a customer's cheque (Trevor Clerk) returned and marked NSF, and a credit memo for $2,400 representing interest collected by the bank for Red Sea Company. Cash on hand at November 30, which has been recorded and is awaiting deposit, amounted to $3,830.80.

Required

a. Prepare a bank reconciliation at November 30, 2011.

b. Prepare any journal entries required to adjust the Cash account at November 30.

Check figure:
a. Adjusted book balance = $99,957.38

Problem 9-10A

Preparation of a bank reconciliation and recording adjustments

LO6

The following is information for Dundee Realty:

a. Balance per the bank statement dated October 31, 2011, is $48,260.

b. Balance of the Cash account on the company books as of October 31, 2011, is $38,535.

c. $5,500 of customer deposits were outstanding as of September 30; this amount had been deposited to Dundee's account in October.

d. Cheques written in October that had not cleared the bank as of October 31 were:
#2033, $3,200
#2099, $ 850
#2300, $1,800
#2345, $5,400.

e. The bank charged Dundee's account for a $1,700 cheque of the E-Zone Networks; the cheque was found among the cancelled cheques returned with the bank statement.

f. Bank service charges for October amount to $220.

g. A customer's cheque (Teresa Krant) for $15,800 had been deposited in the bank correctly but was recorded in the accounting records as $18,500.

h. Among the cancelled cheques is one for $890 given in payment of an account payable to Decker Company; the bookkeeper had recorded the cheque incorrectly at $980 in the company records.

i. The bank had collected a $5,000 note plus interest of $350. A fee of $45 was charged for this service.

j. A bank deposit of October 31 for $2,300 does not appear on the bank statement.

Check figure:
1. Adjusted book balance = $41,010

Required

1. Prepare a bank reconciliation statement as of October 31, 2011.
2. Prepare the necessary entries to make the Cash account agree with the bank reconciliation adjusted Cash balance as of October 31.

Analysis component:

Identify the effects on the income statement and balance sheet if the entries in Part 2 were not recorded.

Alternate Problems

Problem 9-1B

Principles of internal control

LO1

For the following five scenarios, identify the principle of internal control that is violated. Next, recommend what the business should do to ensure adherence to principles of internal control.

1. Tamerick Company is a fairly small organization but has segregated the duties of cash receipts and cash disbursements. However, the employee responsible for cash disbursements also reconciles the bank account monthly.
2. Stan Spencer is the most computer literate employee in his company. His boss has recently asked him to put password protection on all the office computers. Stan's main job at the company is to process payroll. Stan has put a password in place that now only allows his boss access to the file where pay rates are changed and personnel are added or deleted from the company payroll.
3. Starlight Theatre has a computerized order-taking system for its tickets. The system is active all week and backed up every Friday night.
4. Trek There Company has two employees handling acquisitions of inventory. One employee places purchase orders and pays vendors. The second employee receives the merchandise.
5. The owner of Holiday Helper uses a cheque protector to perforate cheques, making it difficult for anyone to alter the amount of the cheque. The cheque protector sits on the owner's desk in an office that houses company cheques and is often unlocked.

Problem 9-2B
Establishing, reimbursing, and increasing the petty cash fund
LO4

Dack & Blecker completed the following petty cash transactions during July 2011:

July	5	Prepared a $1,000 cheque, cashed it, and turned the proceeds and the petty cash box over to Jackie Boone, the petty cashier.
	6	Paid $229 COD charges on merchandise purchased for resale. *Dack & Blecker Company uses the perpetual inventory method to account for merchandise inventory.*
	11	Paid $17.50 delivery charges on merchandise sold to a customer.
	12	Purchased file folders, $24.26.
	14	Reimbursed Collin Dodge, the manager of the business, $19.30 for office supplies purchased.
	18	Purchased paper for printer, $45.08.
	27	Paid $94.20 COD charges on merchandise purchased for resale.
	28	Purchased stamps, $32.
	30	Reimbursed Collin Dodge $317.60 for business car expenses.
	31	Jackie Boone sorted the petty cash receipts by accounts affected and exchanged them for a cheque to reimburse the fund for expenditures. However, there was $121.06 in cash in the fund. In addition, the size of the petty cash fund was increased to $1,100.

Required

1. Prepare a General Journal entry to record establishing the petty cash fund.
2. Prepare a summary of petty cash payments similar to Exhibit 9.2 that has these categories: delivery expense, auto expense, postage expense, merchandise inventory, and office supplies.
3. Prepare the General Journal entry to record the reimbursement and the increase of the fund.

Analysis component:

You supervise Jackie Boone, the petty cashier, and while reviewing the accounts you notice that the Cash Over/Short Expense account has a balance for the seven months ended July 31, 2011, of $700. Given the size of the petty cash account, does this balance appear to be unusual? Explain and identify any concerns that you might have.

Problem 9-3B
Petty cash fund; reimbursement and analysis of errors
LO4

The accounting system used by Sharp Company requires that all entries be journalized in a General Journal. To facilitate payments for small items, Sharp established a petty cash fund. The following transactions involving the petty cash fund occurred during February 2011.

Feb.	3	A company cheque for $300 was prepared and made payable to the petty cashier to establish the petty cash fund.
	14	A company cheque was prepared to replenish the fund for the following expenditures made since February 3 and to increase the fund to $350. a. Purchased office supplies, $32.58. b. Paid $35.20 COD charges on merchandise purchased for resale. Sharp uses the perpetual method to account for merchandise inventory. c. Paid $73.14 to Data Services for minor repairs to a computer. d. Paid $29.64 for postage expenses. e. Discovered that only $124.56 remained in the petty cash box.
	28	The petty cashier noted that $97.62 remained in the fund, and decided that the February 14 increase in the fund was not large enough. A company cheque was prepared to replenish the fund for the following expenditures made since February 14, and to increase it to $500. f. Paid $80 to *The Smart Saver* for an advertisement in a monthly newsletter. g. Paid $56.38 for office supplies. h. Paid $116 to Best Movers for delivery of merchandise to a customer.

Required

Prepare General Journal entries to record the establishment of the fund on February 3 and its replenishment on February 14 and February 28.

Analysis component:

Explain how the company's financial statements would be affected if the petty cash fund is not replenished and no entry is made on February 28. (*Hint: The amount of Office Supplies that appears on a balance sheet is determined by a physical count of the supplies on hand.*)

Problem 9-4B
Preparing a bank reconciliation and recording adjustments
LO6

Jeff Auburn, the controller of the Cistern Company, provided the following information:

Cistern Company Bank Reconciliation October 31, 2011					
Bank statement balance		$19,687.60	Book balance		$20,109.38
Add:					
Deposit of Oct. 31 in transit		3,593.00			
		$23,280.60			
Deduct:			Deduct:		
Outstanding cheques:			NSF cheque plus		
#537	$1,896.48		service charge	$570.80	
#542	1,875.44	3,771.92	Bank service charges	29.90	600.70
Adjusted bank balance		$19,508.68	Adjusted book balance		$19,508.68

The Cash account in the General Ledger appeared as follows on November 30 (Cistern Company uses only a General Journal to record transactions):

Cash						Acct. No. 101
Date		Explanation	PR	Debit	Credit	Balance
2011						
Oct.	31	Balance				19,508.68
Nov.	1	Cheque #543	GJ5		3,600.00	15,908.68
	1	Cheque #544	GJ5		1,358.24	14,550.44
	1	Cheque #545	GJ5		1,843.68	12,706.76
	1	Cheque #546	GJ5		1,821.44	10,885.32
	1	Cheque #547	GJ5		1,782.04	9,103.28
	1	Cheque #548	GJ6		1,898.08	7,205.20
	1	Cheque #549	GJ6		1,982.32	5,222.88
	9	Deposit	GJ6	3,817.12		9,040.00
	9	Cheque #550	GJ6		1,834.24	7,205.76
	9	Cheque #551	GJ6		1,398.72	5,807.04
	18	Deposit	GJ6	3,940.72		9,747.76
	20	Cheque #552	GJ6		1,770.72	7,977.04
	27	Cheque #553	GJ6		1,863.68	6,113.36
	29	Deposit	GJ6	3,553.16		9,666.52

The following bank statement is available for November 2011:

Bank Statement					
To: Cistern Company			November 30, 2011 Bank of Canada		
Cheques/Charges			Deposits/Credits		Balance
			10/31		19,687.60
#549	11/01	1,982.32	11/01	3,593.00	21,298.28
#543	11/02	3,600.00			17,698.28
#537	11/07	1,896.48			15,801.80
#551	11/09	1,398.72	11/09	3,817.12	18,220.20
#542	11/12	1,875.44			16,344.76
#544	11/14	1,358.24			14,986.52
#547	11/18	1,782.04	11/18	3,940.72	17,145.20
#545	11/20	1,843.68			15,301.52
#546	11/29	1,821.44			13,480.08
SC	11/30	73.00	11/30		13,407.08
NSF = Not Sufficient Funds		SC = Service Charge	PMT = Principal Payment		INT = Interest

Required

a. Prepare a bank reconciliation for Cistern Company for the month of November 2011.

b. Prepare the necessary entries resulting from the bank reconciliation.

Check figure:
Adjusted book balance = $9,593.52

Analysis component:

You have been employed with Cistern Company since November 1, 2011, and part of your job is writing and recording cheques as well as preparing the bank reconciliation. In reviewing the cheques returned by the bank, you notice that the payee on cheque #543 is the employee you recently replaced. You investigate further and find that the journal entry recording cheque #543 debited Office Supplies Expense. What should you do? Explain.

Problem 9-5B
Preparing a bank reconciliation and recording adjustments
LO6

The bank reconciliation prepared by Westburn Apartments on May 31, 2011, is shown below:

Westburn Apartments Bank Reconciliation May 31, 2011				
Bank statement balance		$ 2,060	Book balance	$8,740
Add:				
Deposit of May 31 in transit		9,600		
		$11,660		
Deduct:				
Outstanding cheques:				
#103	$1,880			
#120	1,040	2,920		
Adjusted bank balance		$ 8,740	Adjusted book balance	$8,740

The Cash account in the General Ledger appeared as follows on June 30:

Cash						Acct. No. 101
Date		**Explanation**	**PR**	**Debit**	**Credit**	**Balance**
2011						
May	31	Balance				8,740
June	30		CR21	90,080		98,820
	30		CD16		35,220	63,600

A list of deposits made and cheques written during June, taken from the Cash Receipts Journal and Cash Disbursements Journal, is shown below:

Deposits Made	
June 5	$ 3,400
10	1,780
15	2,200
20	2,700
27	60,000
30	5,800
30	14,200
Total June Cash Receipts	$90,080

Cheques Written	
No. 127	$ 3,400
128	9,340
129	1,900
130	2,400
131	450
132	2,350
133	3,000
134	3,280
135	1,300
136	7,800
Total June Cash Disbursements	$35,220

The following bank statement is available:

Bank Statement					
To: Westburn Apartments				June 30, 2011 Bank of Nova Scotia	
Cheques/Charges			Deposits/Credits		Balance
					2,060
#133	06/02	3,000	06/02	9,600	8,660
#136	06/05	7,800	06/05	3,400	4,260
#129	06/10	1,900	06/10	1,780	4,140
#130	06/15	2,400	06/15	2,200	3,940
#103	06/20	1,880	06/20	2,700	4,760
#134	06/27	3,280	06/27	60,000	61,480
#128	06/30	9,340	06/30	8,500	60,640
SC	06/30	400			60,240
NSF = Not Sufficient Funds		SC = Service Charge	PMT = Principal Payment		INT = Interest

In reviewing deposits recorded by the bank, the bookkeeper discovered that the deposit from customer Darla Smith dated June 30, recorded in the Cash Receipts Journal incorrectly as $5,800, was recorded by the bank correctly as $8,500.

Required

a. Prepare a bank reconciliation at June 30.

b. Prepare the necessary journal entries to bring the General Ledger Cash account into agreement with the adjusted balance on the bank reconciliation.

Check figure:
a. Adjusted book balance = $65,900

Problem 9-6B

Preparing a bank reconciliation and recording adjustments

LO6

The following information was available to reconcile Fargo Co.'s book cash balance with its bank statement balance as of December 31, 2011:

a. The December 31 Cash balance according to the accounting records was $15,871.85, and the bank statement balance for that date was $22,545.90.

b. Cheque #1273 for $542.10 and cheque #1282 for $195, both written and entered in the accounting records in December, were not among the cancelled cheques returned. Two cheques, #1231 for $1,144.50 and #1242 for $185.25, were outstanding on November 30 when the bank and book statement balances were last reconciled. Cheque #1231 was returned with the December cancelled cheques, but cheque #1242 was not.

c. When the December cheques were compared with entries in the accounting records, it was found that cheque #1267 had been correctly written for $1,217.50 to pay for office supplies, but was erroneously entered in the accounting records as though it were written for $2,117.50.

d. Two debit memoranda were included with the returned cheques and were unrecorded at the time of the reconciliation. One of the debit memoranda was for $396.75 and dealt with an NSF cheque for $366 that had been received from a customer, Tork Industries, in payment of its account. It also assessed a $30.75 fee for processing. The second debit memorandum covered cheque printing and was for $50. These transactions had not been recorded by Fargo before receiving the statement.

e. A credit memorandum indicated that the bank had collected a $10,000 note receivable for the company, deducted a $20 collection fee, and credited the balance to the company's account. This transaction was not recorded by Fargo before receiving the statement.

f. The December 31 cash receipts, $4,681.55, had been placed in the bank's night depository after banking hours on that date and did not appear on the bank statement.

Required

1. Prepare a bank reconciliation for the company as of December 31.

2. Prepare the General Journal entries necessary to bring the company's book balance of Cash into conformity with the reconciled balance.

Check figure:
1. Adjusted book balance = $26,305.10

Analysis component:

Explain the nature of the messages conveyed by a bank to one of its depositors when the bank sends a debit memo and a credit memo to the depositor.

Problem 9-7B
Preparing a bank reconciliation and recording adjustments
LO6

Papier Systems reconciled its book balance of cash with its bank statement balance on April 30 and showed two cheques outstanding at that time, #1771 for $390.50 and #1780 for $662.95. The following information is available for the May 31, 2011, reconciliation:

From the May 31, 2011, bank statement:

BALANCE OF PREVIOUS STATEMENT ON APR. 30/11	$ 9,145.35
5 DEPOSITS AND OTHER CREDITS TOTALLING................	8,208.40
9 CHEQUES AND OTHER DEBITS TOTALLING	6,449.45
CURRENT BALANCE AS OF THIS STATEMENT....................	10,904.30

Chequing Account Transactions

Date	Amount	Transaction Description	Date	Amount	Transaction Description
May 04	1,219.00	+Deposit	May 25	3,600.00	+Credit memo
14	1,449.00	+Deposit	26	1,039.50	+Deposit
18	215.90	−NSF cheque	31	6.00	−Service charge
22	900.90	+Deposit			

Date	Cheque No.	Amount	Date	Cheque No.	Amount
May 01	1784	724.80	May 26	1785	78.60
02	1783	97.65	28	1771	390.50
15	1787	4,016.25	29	1788	277.00
16	1782	642.75			

From Papier Systems' accounting records:

Cash					Acct. No. 101
Date	**Explanation**	**PR**	**Debit**	**Credit**	**Balance**
2011					
Apr. 30	Balance				8,091.90
May 31		CR7	5,871.55		13,963.45
31		CD8		6,263.35	7,700.10

Deposits Made	
May 4	$1,219.00
14	1,449.00
22	900.90
26	1,039.50
31	1,263.15
Total May Cash Receipts........	$5,871.55

Cheques Written	
No. 1782............................	$ 642.75
1783............................	97.65
1784............................	724.80
1785............................	78.60
1786............................	176.55
1787............................	4,016.25
1788............................	207.00
1789............................	319.75
Total May Cash Disbursements......................	$6,263.35

Cheque #1788 was correctly written for $277 to pay for May utilities; however, the bookkeeper misread the amount and entered it in the accounting records with a debit to Utilities Expense and a credit to Cash as though it were for $207. The bank paid and deducted the correct amount.

The NSF cheque was originally received from a customer, Gertie Mayer, in payment of her account. Its return was unrecorded. The credit memorandum resulted from a $3,650 note that the bank had collected for the company. The bank had deducted a $50 collection fee and deposited the remainder in the company's account. The collection has not been recorded.

Required

1. Prepare a bank reconciliation for Papier Systems.
2. Prepare the General Journal entries needed to adjust the book balance of Cash to the reconciled balance.

Check figure:
1. Adjusted book balance = $11,008.20

Analysis component:

The preceding bank statement discloses two places where the cancelled cheques returned with the bank statement are not numbered sequentially. In other words, some of the prenumbered cheques in the sequence are missing. Several possible situations would explain why the cancelled cheques returned with a bank statement might not be numbered sequentially. Describe three possible reasons why this might occur.

Problem 9-8B

Preparing a bank reconciliation and recording adjustments

LO6

Springhills Co. reconciled its bank statement balances of Cash on October 31 and showed two cheques outstanding at that time, #1388 for $3,194 and #1393 for $1,490. The following information was available for the November 30, 2011, reconciliation:

From the November 30 bank statement:

BALANCE OF PREVIOUS STATEMENT ON OCT. 31/11	54,836
5 DEPOSITS AND OTHER CREDITS TOTALLING	34,352
9 CHEQUES AND OTHER DEBITS TOTALLING	32,684
CURRENT BALANCE AS OF NOVEMBER 30/11	56,504

Chequing Account Transactions

Date	Amount	Transaction Description	Date	Amount	Transaction Description
Nov. 05	3,396	+Deposit	Nov. 25	7,236	+Deposit
12	6,852	+Deposit	30	34	+Interest
17	1,810	−NSF cheque	30	4,240	+Credit memorandum
21	12,594	+Deposit			

Date	Cheque No.	Amount	Date	Cheque No.	Amount
Nov. 03	1402	2,252	Nov. 17	1409	5,562
04	1403	1,228	20	1405	2,884
08	1388	3,194	27	1407	658
12	1401	8,726	29	1404	6,370

From Springhills Co.'s accounting records:

Cash					Acct. No. 101
Date	**Explanation**	**PR**	**Debit**	**Credit**	**Balance**
2011					
Oct. 31	Balance				50,152
Nov. 30		CR12	34,948		85,100
30		CD23		28,474	56,626

Deposits Made

Nov. 5	$ 3,396
12	6,852
21	12,594
25	7,236
30	4,870
Total November Cash Receipts	$34,948

Cheques Written

No. 1401	$ 8,726
1402	2,252
1403	1,228
1404	3,670
1405	2,884
1406	2,644
1407	658
1408	850
1409	5,562
Total November Cash Disbursements	$28,474

Cheque #1404 was correctly written for $6,370 to pay for computer equipment: however, the bookkeeper misread the amount and entered it in the accounting records with a debit to Computer Equipment and a credit to Cash as though it were for $3,670.

The NSF cheque was originally received from a customer, Jerry Skyles, in payment of his account. Its return was not recorded when the bank first notified the company. The credit memorandum resulted from the collection of a $4,300 note for Springhills by the bank. The bank had deducted a $60 collection fee. The collection has not been recorded.

Check figure:
1. Adjusted book balance = $56,390

Required

1. Prepare a November 30 bank reconciliation for the company.
2. Prepare the General Journal entries needed to adjust the book balance of Cash to the reconciled balance.

Problem 9-9B

Preparing a bank reconciliation and recording adjustments

LO6

The following information was available to reconcile Dubai Company's book balance of Cash with its bank statement balance as of February 28, 2011.

a. The bank statement at February 28 indicated a balance of $19,200. The General Ledger account for Cash showed a balance at February 28 of $25,984.

b. Of the cheques issued in February, the following were still outstanding:

Cheque	Amount
#202	$3,200
#205	220
#213	70
#240	400

c. Two cheques, #136 for $240 and #200 for $660, were outstanding on Jan. 31 when the bank and book balances were last reconciled. Cheque #136 was returned with the February cancelled cheques but cheque #200 was not.

d. Included with the February bank statement was an NSF cheque for $870 that had been received from a customer, Mrs. Tahani Ahmad, in payment of her account.

e. Cheque #219 was correctly written for $812 in payment for office supplies but was erroneously entered as $821 in the Cash Payments Journal.

f. A debit memorandum for $120 was enclosed with the bank statement. This charge was for printing the chequebook for Dubai Company.

g. Included with the bank statement was a $100 credit memorandum for interest earned on the bank account in February.

h. The February 28 cash receipts amounting to $12,600 had been placed in the bank's night depository after banking hours on that date and did not appear among the deposits on the February bank statement.

i. Included with the bank statement was a credit memorandum, which indicated that the bank had collected a $2,167 note receivable for the company, deducted a $20 collection fee, and credited the balance to the company's account.

Check figure:
1. Adjusted book balance = $27,250

Required

1. Prepare a bank reconciliation for the Dubai Company as of February 28, 2011.
2. Prepare the entries needed to adjust the book balance of Cash to the reconciled balance.

Problem 9-10B

Preparing a bank reconciliation and recording adjustments

LO6

The following is information for the Timbits Cafe:

a. Balance per the bank statement dated December 31, 2011, is $50,860.

b. Balance of Cash account on the company books as of December 31, 2011, is $22,080.

c. A cheque from customer Della Armstrong for $1,680 that had been deposited in the bank was erroneously recorded by the bookkeeper as $6,180.

d. A cheque made out by Neon Company for $4,200 deposited on December 21 is returned by the bank marked NSF; no entry has been made on the company records to reflect the returned cheque.

e. Among the cancelled cheques is one for $345 given in payment of an account payable to CT Financial; the bookkeeper had incorrectly recorded the cheque at $435 in the company records.

f. Bank service charges for December amount to $100.

g. The bank erroneously charged the Timbits Cafe account for a $20,000 cheque of HRD Company; the cheque was found among the cancelled cheques returned with the bank statement.

h. The bank had collected a $30,000 note plus accrued interest amounting to $150; $30,150 was credited to the Timbits Cafe's account; a collection fee of $20 was debited to the Timbits Cafe's account.
i. The bank deposit of December 31 for $3,140 does not appear on the bank statement.
j. Outstanding cheques as of December 31: #197, $8,000; #199, $22,500.

Required

1. Prepare a bank reconciliation as of December 31, 2011.
2. Prepare the necessary entries to make the Cash account agree with the bank reconciliation adjusted Cash balance as of December 31.

Check figure:
1. Adjusted book balance = $43,500

Analysis component:
Identify the effects on the income statement and balance sheet if the adjustments in Part 2 were not recorded.

Analytical and Review Problems

A & R Problem 9-1

You are a college student and have just been hired to work part-time in the accounting department of Candy's Cleaning Services. The person you are replacing had difficulty preparing the bank reconciliation for April 30, which is shown below.

Candy's Cleaning Services Bank Reconciliation April 30, 2011					
Bank balance		$33,452	Book balance		$28,934
			Add:		
Deduct:			Interest	$47	
NSF, customer Bonne	$ 412		Error Chq #93	99	146
					$29,080
Outstanding cheques:			Deduct:		
#879	2,600		Service Charge		40
#100	1,400	4,412	Adjusted book balance		$29,040
Adjusted bank balance		$29,040			

In comparing the bank reconciliation to the Cash account in the General Ledger, you notice a problem. You investigate further and come up with some additional information as follows:

a. The Cash account in the General Ledger showed the following:

Cash						Acct. No. 101
Date		Explanation	PR	Debit	Credit	Balance
2011						
March	31	Balance				28,934
April	30		CR16	56,000		84,934
	30		CD21		63,883	21,051

b. The error in cheque #93, for Utilities Expense, resulted from the bank incorrectly debiting our account for $99; the correct amount entered in the accounting records is $199.
c. The bank statement showed interest expense of $47; there was no other interest.
d. The bank debited our account for cheque #879 written by Candy's Hair Salon.
e. Cheque #86 for $14,000 listed as outstanding on last month's bank reconciliation was not returned with the April 30 bank statement.

Required

1. Prepare a corrected bank reconciliation for April 30, 2011.
2. Record the journal entries resulting from the corrected bank reconciliation.

Check figure:
1. Adjusted book balance = $20,552

A & R Problem 9-2

Your assistant prepared the following bank reconciliation statement. It appears that the statement is unacceptable and the task of preparing a proper reconciliation falls upon you.

Brandon Company Bank Reconciliation May 31, 2011		
Balance per books May 31		$ 9,500
Add:		
Note collected	$1,000	
Interest on note	60	
Deposit in transit	2,455	3,515
		$13,015
Deduct:		
Bank charges	$ 10	
NSF cheque, Rhonda Teal	500	
Outstanding cheques	1,800	
Error in cheque #78 issued for $762 and recorded in the books as $726 (Accounts Payable–Delta Co.)	36	2,346
Indicated bank balance		$10,669
Balance per bank statement		9,359
Discrepancy		$ 1,310

Check figure:
1. Adjusted book balance = $10,014

Required
1. Prepare a proper bank reconciliation showing the true Cash balance.
2. Prepare the necessary journal entries.

A & R Problem 9-3

Wanda White acquired a sports equipment distribution business with a staff of six salespeople and two clerks. Because of the trust that Wanda had in her employees—after all, they were all her friends and just like members of the family—she believed that an honour system in regard to the operation of the petty cash fund was adequate. Consequently, Wanda placed $300 in a coffee jar, which, for convenience, was kept in a cupboard in the common room. All employees had access to the petty cash fund and withdrew amounts as required. No vouchers were required for withdrawals. As required, additional funds were placed in the coffee jar and the amount of the replenishment was charged to "miscellaneous selling expense."

Required
1. From the internal control point of view, discuss the weaknesses of the petty cash fund operation and suggest steps necessary for improvement.
2. Does the petty cash fund operation as described above violate any of the generally accepted accounting principles? If yes, which, and how are the principles violated?

Ethics Challenge

EC 9-1

Marge Page, Dot Night, and Colleen Walker work for a dentist, Dr. Linda Thomen, who is in a private practice. Dr. Thomen is fairly knowledgeable about sound office management practices and has segregated the cash receipt duties as follows. Marge opens the mail and prepares a triplicate list of money received. She sends one copy of the list to Dot, the cashier, who deposits the receipts daily in the bank. Colleen, the recordkeeper, also receives a copy of the list and posts payments to patients' accounts. About once a month the office clerks decide to have an expensive lunch compliments of Dr. Thomen. Dot endorses a patient's cheque in Dr. Thomen's name and cashes it at the bank. Marge destroys the remittance advice accompanying the cheque. Colleen posts the payment to the customer's account as a miscellaneous credit. The clerks justify their actions given their relatively low pay and knowing that Dr. Thomen will likely never miss the payment.

Required
1. Who would be the best person in Dr. Thomen's office to reconcile the bank statement?
2. Would a bank reconciliation detect the office fraud scheme?
3. What are some ways of uncovering this type of scheme?
4. Suggest additional internal controls that Dr. Thomen might want to implement.

Focus on Financial Statements

FFS 9-1

Ellis Worton, the owner of Worton Consulting, showed the following unadjusted account balances at December 31, 2011, the business's year-end (accounts have been listed in alphabetical order):

Account	Account Balance*
Accounts payable	$ 18,000
Accounts receivable	27,000
Accumulated depreciation, store fixtures	82,000
Cash	15,500
Cost of goods sold	298,000
Delivery expense	5,000
Ellis Worton, capital	127,500
Ellis Worton, withdrawals	44,000
Interest expense	2,000
Notes payable (principal of $27,000 to be paid in 2012)	42,000
Petty cash	500
Prepaid rent	10,250
Rent expense	92,000
Salaries expense	109,000
Salaries payable	4,000
Sales	449,000
Sales returns and allowances	6,000
Store fixtures	113,250

*Assume normal account balances.

Other information:

1. There were two reconciling items on the bank reconciliation: an outstanding cheque in the amount of $450 and an NSF cheque for $1,500.
2. A review of the Prepaid Rent account showed that the unexpired portion was $7,000.
3. Annual depreciation on the store fixtures is $8,200.

Required

Prepare the December 31, 2011, classified balance sheet.

Analysis component:

a. Calculate Worton Consulting's current ratio and acid-test ratio at December 31, 2011. Compare and comment. Round calculations to two decimal places.

b. Recalculate the current ratio and acid-test ratio assuming the current portion of the note payable was reported as part of the long-term liabilities. Compare your results to part (a) and comment. Round calculations to two decimal places.

Check figures:
Current assets = $50,000;
Total assets = $73,050

FFS 9-2

Refer to WestJet's December 31, 2008, balance sheet on page I-26 in Appendix I at the end of the textbook.

Required

Answer the following questions.

1. WestJet shows *cash and cash equivalents* on its December 31, 2008, balance sheet. Explain the meaning of *cash* and *cash equivalents.*
2. How much *cash and cash equivalents* did WestJet have on December 31, 2008?
3. By how much did WestJet's cash and cash equivalents increase or decrease from December 31, 2007, to December 31, 2008?

Analysis component:

Is it possible for there to be excessive *cash and cash equivalents*? Explain.

Critical Thinking Mini Case

You are the newly elected vice-president of campus life for the business students' association at your institution. The first big event of the year is a party that has three live bands playing from 5:00 p.m. to midnight; tickets are $20 (cash only). A number of people are helping you sell tickets during the two weeks prior to the event. At the end of each day, you collect the cash from each seller and reconcile it against the tickets sold (the tickets are sequentially numbered). You place your records and the cash in a locked filing cabinet in your office, which is always locked. In less than two weeks, all of the tickets are sold. After collecting the cash from the ticket sellers on the day of the sellout, you're feeling terrific about the success of the sales campaign you organized for the event and go to your office, unlock the door, and immediately notice that the filing cabinet has been tampered with . . . all of the money is gone . . . over $35,000!!

Required

Using the elements of critical thinking described on the inside front cover, comment.

CHAPTER 10

Receivables

learning objectives

LO1 | Describe accounts receivable and how they occur and are recorded.

LO2 | Apply the allowance method to account for uncollectible accounts receivable.

LO3 | Estimate uncollectible accounts receivable using approaches based on sales and accounts receivable.

LO4 | Describe and record a short-term note receivable and calculate its maturity date and interest.

*APPENDIX 10A

LO5 | Explain how receivables can be converted to cash before maturity.

*APPENDIX 10B

LO6 | Calculate accounts receivable turnover and days' sales uncollected to analyze liquidity.

Two Companies, Different Receivables Experiences

Sun-Rype Products Ltd., with its head office in Kelowna, British Columbia, is a manufacturer and marketer of juice-based beverages and fruit snacks. It reported net sales of $125,368,000 for the year ended December 31, 2008. Accounts receivable at December 31, 2008, totalled $11,830,000; no uncollectible accounts were noted, implying that this figure must be immaterial.

With its head office in Toronto, the Canadian Imperial Bank of Commerce (CIBC) is one of Canada's largest banks. Its primary source of revenue is from interest, and during the year ended October 31, 2008, the bank reported $14,163,000,000 of interest earned. The CIBC's October 31, 2008, balance sheet shows credit card receivables of $10,829,000,000 along with estimated uncollectible accounts of $1,446,000,000—yes, almost $1.5 billion!

Both companies have receivables, yet Sun-Rype and CIBC have different experiences in terms of uncollectible accounts. Why? Because of what each company is selling and to whom. The credit managers for both organizations require a solid understanding of collection risk in their specific industry; they must develop policies and procedures to maximize the effective and efficient collection of receivables while minimizing bad debts, which, in the banking industry, can have a huge total dollar value.

CRITICAL THINKING CHALLENGE

How are Sun-Rype's customers different from CIBC's? Why would CIBC experience a higher rate of uncollectible accounts than Sun-Rype does?

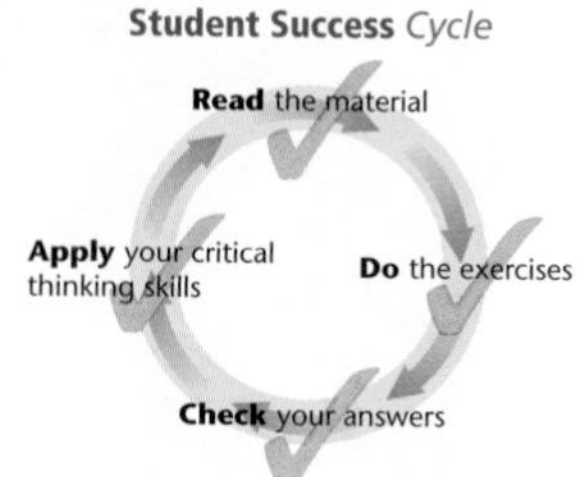

chapter preview

This chapter focuses on accounts receivable and short-term notes receivable. We describe each of these assets, their use in practice, and how they are accounted for and reported in financial statements. This knowledge helps us use accounting information to make better decisions, and can also help in predicting bad debts.

Accounts Receivable

A *receivable* refers to an amount due from another party. The two most common receivables are accounts receivable and notes receivable. Other receivables include interest receivable, rent receivable, tax refund receivable, and amounts due from other parties such as officers and employees.

Accounts receivable are amounts due from customers for credit sales. They are also referred to as **trade receivables** because they result from customers with whom we *trade*. This section begins by describing how accounts receivable arise and their various sources. These sources include sales when customers use the seller's credit cards, and when a company gives credit directly to customers. When a company extends credit directly to customers, it must (1) maintain a separate account receivable for each customer and (2) account for bad debts from credit sales.

Recognizing Accounts Receivable

LO1 Describe accounts receivable and how they occur and are recorded.

Accounts receivable arise from credit sales to customers. The amount of credit sales over cash sales has increased in recent years, reflecting several factors including an efficient banking system and a sound economy. Exhibit 10.1 shows the dollar amounts of accounts receivable and their percent of total assets for five companies.

Exhibit 10.1

Accounts Receivable for Selected Companies

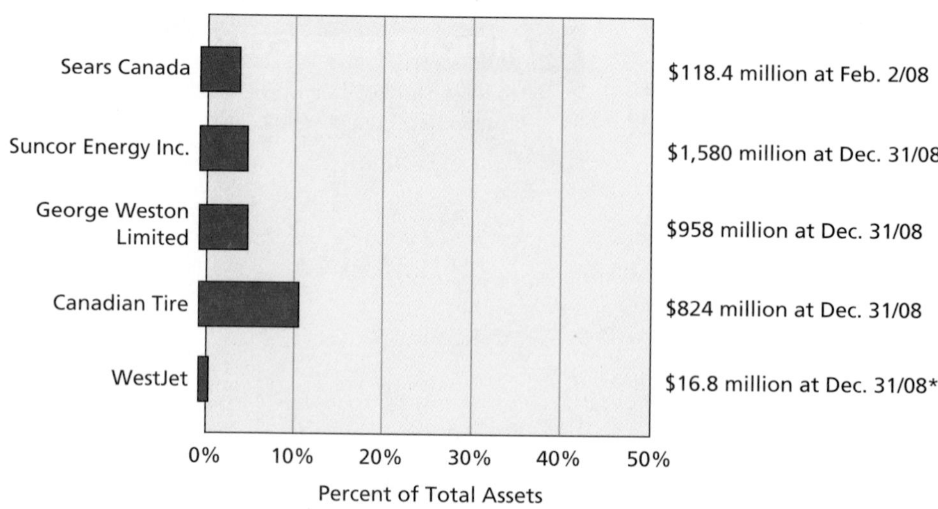

*NOTE: This is 0.51% (less than 1%).

Sales on Credit

To review how accounts receivable from credit sales are recognized, we will record two transactions in the accounting records for TechCom, a small electronics wholesaler. TechCom's *Accounts Receivable controlling account* in the General Ledger and *Accounts Receivable Subledger* prior to recording these transactions are illustrated in Exhibit 10.2.

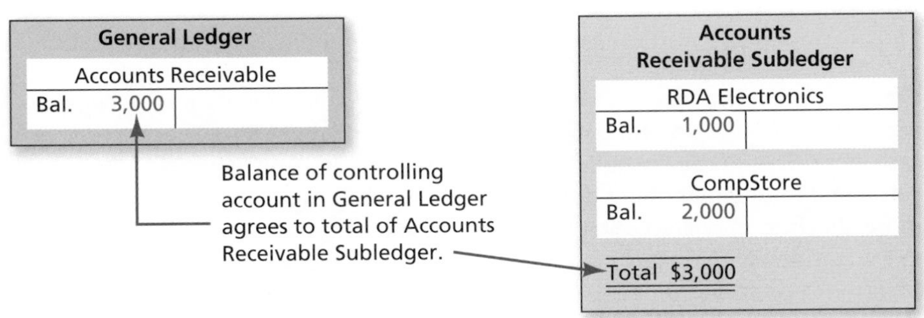

Exhibit 10.2

Accounts Receivable Controlling Account and the Accounts Receivable Subledger

The first transaction to be recorded on July 15 is a credit sale of $950 to CompStore (cost of sales to TechCom is $630 assuming a perpetual inventory system). The second is a collection of $720 from RDA Electronics from prior credit sales. Both transactions are reflected in Exhibit 10.3. Note that these transactions would typically be recorded in the appropriate Sales and Cash Receipts Journals. We use the General Journal format here for simplicity.

July	15	Accounts Receivable—CompStore	950	
		Sales		950
		To record credit sales.		
	15	Cost of Goods Sold	630	
		Merchandise Inventory		630
		To record cost of sales.		
	15	Cash	720	
		Accounts Receivable—RDA Electronics		720
		To record collection of credit sales.		

Exhibit 10.3

Accounts Receivable Transactions

Exhibit 10.4 shows the Accounts Receivable controlling account and the Accounts Receivable Subledger after posting these two transactions.

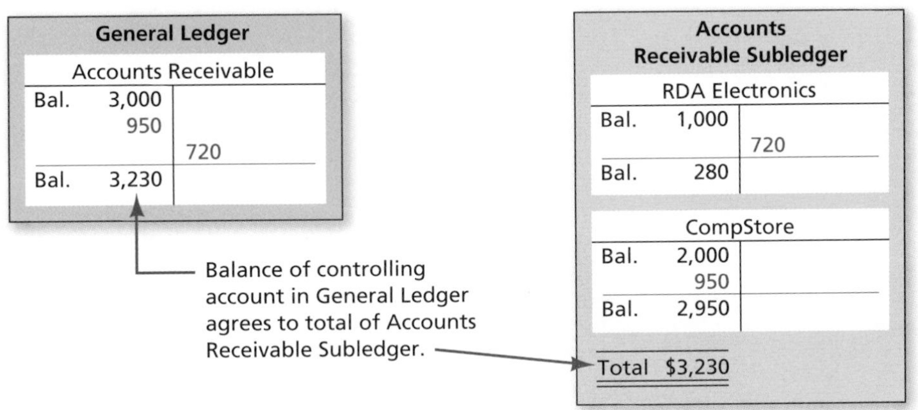

Exhibit 10.4

Accounts Receivable Controlling Account and the Accounts Receivable Subledger

Like many companies, TechCom grants credit directly to qualified customers. Many large retailers such as Canadian Tire maintain their own credit card. This allows them to grant credit to approved customers and to earn interest on any balance not paid within a specified period of time, as well as to avoid the fee charged by credit card companies. The entries in this case are the same as those above except for the possibility of added interest revenue. If a customer owes interest on the bill, then we debit Accounts Receivable and credit Interest Revenue for this amount.

DID YOU KNOW?

Credit management involves establishing policies and procedures around approving credit customers, resolving invoice issues, collecting receivables, and controlling cash flow. The Credit Institute of Canada was created on June 11, 1928, by Parliament for the purpose of developing credit management expertise in Canada. Its mission is to provide credit management resources, education, and certification to its members and it offers the CCP (Certified Credit Professional) program which leads to the professional designation FCI (Fellow Credit Institute).

www.creditedu.org

1. Where on the balance sheet are accounts receivable reported?

Do Quick Study question: QS 10-1

Valuing Accounts Receivable

When a company grants credit to its customers, there are usually a few customers who do not pay what they promised. The accounts of these customers are **uncollectible accounts**, commonly called **bad debts**. The total amount of uncollectible accounts is an expense of selling on credit. Why do companies sell on credit if it is likely some accounts will prove uncollectible? Companies believe granting credit will increase revenues and profits to offset bad debts. They are willing to incur bad debt losses if the net effect is to increase sales and profits.

Two methods are used by companies to account for uncollectible accounts: (1) allowance method, and (2) direct write-off method. Exhibit 10.5 summarizes these methods.

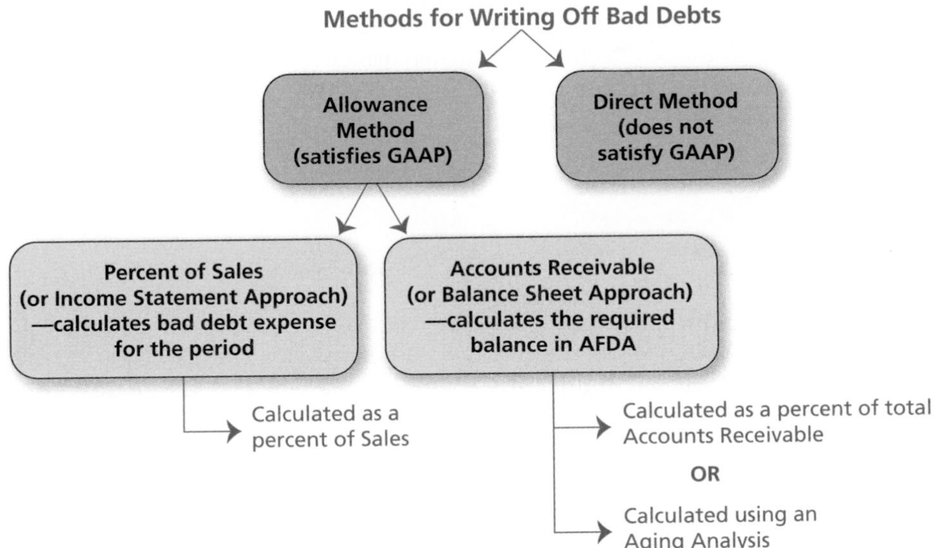

Exhibit 10.5

Methods for Writing Off Bad Debts

Allowance Method

LO2 | Apply the allowance method to account for uncollectible accounts receivable.

The matching principle P. 133 requires that expenses be reported in the same accounting period as the sales they helped produce. This means that if extending credit to customers helped produce sales, any bad debt expense linked to those sales should be matched and reported in the same period as the sales. The **allowance method of accounting for bad debts** satisfies the matching principle by matching the expected loss from uncollectible accounts receivable against the sales they helped produce in that period. How? Since the seller is unable to identify in advance which of the credit sales will become uncollectible, an estimate based on past experience and the experience of similar companies must be used. This means that at the end of each period, the total bad debts expected to result from that period's sales are estimated. An allowance is then recorded for this expected loss. As well as matching, the allowance method satisfies the requirement of the prudence principle. To avoid overstatement, the allowance reduces accounts receivable on the balance sheet to an amount that is expected to be collected. Overstating assets could cause users of the information to make inappropriate business decisions.

Recording Estimated Bad Debt Expense

The allowance method estimates bad debt expense at the end of each accounting period and records it with an adjusting entry P. 134. TechCom, for instance, had credit sales of approximately $300,000 during its first year of operations. At the end of the first year, $20,000 of credit sales remained uncollected. Based on the experience of similar businesses, TechCom estimated bad debt expense to be $1,500. This estimated expense is recorded with the following adjusting entry at the end of the accounting period:

Dec. 31	Bad Debt Expense	1,500	
	Allowance for Doubtful Accounts		1,500
	To record estimated bad debts.		

The debit in this entry means the estimated bad debt expense of $1,500 from selling on credit is matched on the income statement with the $300,000 sales it helped produce. The credit in this entry is to a contra asset P. 137 called **Allowance for Doubtful Accounts**. A contra account is used because at the time of the adjusting entry, we do not know which customers will not pay. Because specific uncollectible accounts are not identifiable at the time of the adjusting entry, they cannot be removed from the Accounts Receivable Subledger. Because the customer accounts are left in the subledger, the controlling account for Accounts Receivable cannot be reduced. Instead, the Allowance for Doubtful Accounts account *must* be credited.

Bad Debts and Related Accounts in Financial Statements

Recall that TechCom has $20,000 of outstanding accounts receivable at the end of its first year of operations. After the bad debt adjusting entry is posted, TechCom's Accounts Receivable, Allowance for Doubtful Accounts, and Bad Debt Expense have balances as shown in Exhibit 10.6.

Exhibit 10.6

General Ledger Balances After Bad Debts Adjustment

Accounts Receivable and *Allowance for Doubtful Accounts* are BOTH balance sheet accounts shown under current assets.

Accounts Receivable		
Dec. 31	20,000	

Allowance for Doubtful Accounts		
	1,500	Dec. 31

Bad Debt Expense is an income statement account and is normally listed as a selling expense.

Bad Debt Expense		
Dec. 31	1,500	

Although $20,000 is legally owed to TechCom by its credit customers, $18,500 (= $20,000 − $1,500) is the **realizable value**, or the estimated amount to be realized in cash collections from customers.

On the balance sheet, the Allowance for Doubtful Accounts is subtracted from Accounts Receivable to show the realizable value. This information is often reported as shown in Exhibit 10.7.

Exhibit 10.7

Balance Sheet Presentation of Allowance for Doubtful Accounts

Current assets:		
Accounts receivable	$20,000	
Less: Allowance for doubtful accounts	1,500	18,500

Often the contra account to Accounts Receivable is not reported separately. This alternative presentation is shown in Exhibit 10.8.

Current assets:	
Accounts receivable (net of $1,500 estimated uncollectible accounts)	$18,500

Exhibit 10.8

Alternative Presentation of Allowance for Doubtful Accounts

Writing Off a Bad Debt

When specific accounts receivable are identified as uncollectible, they must be removed from accounts receivable. This is done by writing them off against the Allowance for Doubtful Accounts. For instance, after spending a year trying to collect from Jack Kent, TechCom finally decides that his $520 account is uncollectible and makes the following entry to write it off:

Jan. 23	Allowance for Doubtful Accounts	520	
	Accounts Receivable—Jack Kent		520
	To write off an uncollectible account.		

After this entry is posted, the General Ledger accounts appear as shown in Exhibit 10.9.

Accounts Receivable

Dec. 31	20,000		
		520	Jan. 23
Balance	19,480		

Allowance for Doubtful Accounts

		1,500	Dec. 31
Jan. 23	520		
		980	Balance

Exhibit 10.9

General Ledger Balances After Posting Write-Off

Note that the expense account is not debited, because bad debt expense is previously estimated and recorded with an adjusting entry at the end of the period in which the sale occurred. While the write-off removes the amount of the account receivable from the ledgers, it does not affect the estimated realizable value of TechCom's net accounts receivable as shown in Exhibit 10.10.

	Before Write-Off (Dec. 31)	After Write-Off (Jan. 23)
Accounts receivable	$20,000	$19,480
Less: Allowance for doubtful accounts......................	1,500	980
Estimated realizable accounts receivable	$18,500	$18,500

Exhibit 10.10

Realizable Value Before and After Write-Off

Neither total assets nor net income is affected by the write-off of a specific account. But both total assets and net income are affected by recognizing the year's bad debt expense in the adjusting entry.

Recovery of a Bad Debt

When a customer fails to pay and the account is written off, his or her credit standing is jeopardized. The customer sometimes chooses to pay all or part of the amount owed after the account is written off as uncollectible. This payment helps restore credit standing. When a recovery of a bad debt occurs, it is recorded in the customer's subsidiary account where this information is retained for use in future credit evaluation.

If on March 11 Jack Kent pays in full his account that TechCom previously wrote off, the entries to record this bad debt recovery are:

Mar.	11	Accounts Receivable—Jack Kent	520	
		Allowance for Doubtful Accounts		520
		To reinstate the account of Jack Kent previously written off.		
	11	Cash..	520	
		Accounts Receivable—Jack Kent		520
		In full payment of account.		

Jack Kent paid the entire amount previously written off, but in some cases a customer may pay only a portion of the amount owed. A question then arises of whether the entire balance of the account is returned to accounts receivable or just the amount paid. The answer is a matter of judgement. If we believe this customer will later pay in full, the entire amount owed is returned to accounts receivable. But only the amount paid is returned if we expect no further collection.

To summarize, the transactions discussed in this chapter[1] that cause changes in Accounts Receivable and Allowance for Doubtful Accounts are illustrated using T-accounts in Exhibit 10.11.

Exhibit 10.11

Summary of Accounts Receivable and Allowance for Doubtful Accounts Transactions

Accounts Receivable		Allowance for Doubtful Accounts	
(a) Sales on credit	(b) Collections received from credit customers		
	(c) Write-off of accounts receivable identified as uncollectible	(c) Write-off of accounts receivable identified as uncollectible	
(d) Recovery (reinstatement of accounts previously written off)	(e) Recovery (collection of reinstated accounts)		(d) Recovery (reinstatement of accounts previously written off)
			(f) Adjusting entry to estimate uncollectible accounts

[1] Remember that Sales Returns and Allowances also cause Accounts Receivable to decrease.

Read Apply Do Check CHECKPOINT

2. Why does the matching principle require that bad debt expenses be estimated?
3. What term describes the balance sheet valuation of accounts receivable less the allowance for doubtful accounts?
4. Why is estimated bad debt expense credited to a contra account rather than to the Accounts Receivable controlling account?
5. Record entries for the following transactions:

January 10, 2011	The $300 account of customer Cool Jam is determined to be uncollectible.
April 12, 2011	Cool Jam pays in full its account that was deemed uncollectible on January 10, 2011.

Do Quick Study questions: QS 10-2, QS 10-3

Estimating Bad Debt Expense

LO3 Estimate uncollectible accounts receivable using approaches based on sales and accounts receivable.

There are two general approaches for estimating bad debt expense. These were introduced briefly in Exhibit 10.5.

Percent of Sales Approach

The **percent of sales approach** (or **income statement approach**) uses income statement relations to estimate bad debts. It is based on the idea that a percentage of a company's credit sales for the period are uncollectible.[2] To demonstrate, assume MusicLand has credit sales of $400,000 in 2011. Based on experience, MusicLand estimates 0.6% of credit sales to be uncollectible. Using this prediction, MusicLand expects $2,400 of bad debt expense from 2011's sales ($400,000 × 0.006 = $2,400). The adjusting entry to record this estimated expense is:

Dec.	31	Bad Debt Expense	2,400	
		Allowance for Doubtful Accounts		2,400
		To record estimated bad debts.		

For demonstration purposes, assume that the Allowance for Doubtful Accounts (AFDA) had an unadjusted credit balance of $200 on December 31. Bad Debt Expense and Allowance for Doubtful Accounts would appear as in Exhibit 10.12 *after* the December 31 adjustment.

Exhibit 10.12

Accounts Receivable and Allowance for Doubtful Accounts Balances After the December 31 Adjustment

Bad Debt Expense			Allowance for Doubtful Accounts	
			200	Unadjusted Balance Dec. 31
Dec. 31 Adjustment	**2,400**		**2,400**	**Dec. 31 Adjustment**
Adjusted Balance Dec. 31	2,400		2,600	Adjusted Balance Dec. 31

[2] Note that the focus is on credit sales. Cash sales do not produce bad debts, and they are generally not used in this estimation. But if cash sales are relatively small compared to credit sales, there is no major impact of including them.

Note that the unadjusted balance of AFDA could be a zero balance, a credit balance, or a debit balance depending on the circumstances. If MusicLand were in its first period of operations, the AFDA would have a zero beginning balance. In the next accounting periods, if write-offs are *greater* than what had been estimated, a *debit* unadjusted balance will result. If *fewer* write-offs occur than what was estimated, as in Exhibit 10.12, a *credit* unadjusted balance will result. If the estimate for bad debts is too high or too low, the percentage used to estimate bad debts can be adjusted in future periods.

Accounts Receivable Approach

The **accounts receivable approach**, also known as the **balance sheet approach**, uses balance sheet relations (Accounts Receivable and the Allowance for Doubtful Accounts) to estimate bad debts. It is based on the idea that some portion of the end-of-period accounts receivable balance is not collectible. The objective for the bad debt adjusting entry is to make the Allowance for Doubtful Accounts balance equal to the portion of outstanding accounts receivable estimated to be uncollectible. To obtain this required balance for the Allowance for Doubtful Accounts account, we compare its balance before the adjustment with the required balance. The difference between the two is debited to Bad Debt Expense and credited to Allowance for Doubtful Accounts. Estimating this required balance for the allowance account is done in one of two ways:

1. By using a simple percent estimate of uncollectibles from the total outstanding accounts receivable, or
2. By aging accounts receivable.

1. *Percent of Accounts Receivable*

Estimating the required balance in the Allowance for Doubtful Accounts by calculating the **percent of accounts receivable** assumes that a percent of a company's outstanding receivables is uncollectible. This estimated percent is based on past experience and the experience of similar companies, and is also affected by recent economic conditions and difficulties faced by customers. The total dollar amount of all outstanding receivables is multiplied by an estimated percent to get the estimated dollar amount of uncollectible accounts. This is the amount to be reported in the balance sheet as the balance for Allowance for Doubtful Accounts. To accomplish this, we prepare the adjusting entry in the amount necessary to give us the required balance in Allowance for Doubtful Accounts.

Assume RGO, an office furniture supplier, has $50,000 of outstanding accounts receivable on December 31. Past experience suggests that 5% of outstanding receivables are uncollectible.

Therefore, we want the Allowance for Doubtful Accounts to show a $2,500 credit balance (5% of $50,000). Assume that the unadjusted balance in the Allowance for Doubtful Accounts at December 31 is currently a $500 credit.

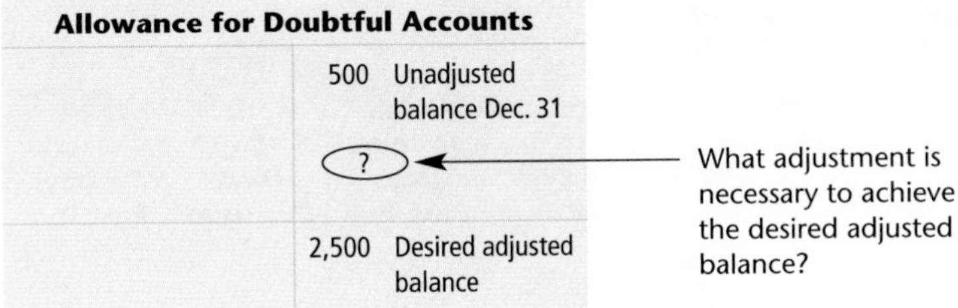

The adjusting entry to give the required $2,500 balance is:

Dec. 31	Bad Debt Expense	2,000	
	Allowance for Doubtful Accounts		2,000
	To record estimated bad debts.		

After this entry is posted, the allowance has a $2,500 credit balance as shown in Exhibit 10.13.

Exhibit 10.13

Allowance for Doubtful Accounts After Bad Debt Adjusting Entry

Allowance for Doubtful Accounts		
	500	Unadjusted balance Dec. 31
	2,000	From Dec. 31 adjusting entry
	2,500	Adjusted balance Dec. 31

Accounts receivable would then be reported as follows on RGO's balance sheet:

Current assets:		
Accounts receivable	$50,000	
Less: Allowance for doubtful accounts	2,500	$47,500
or		
Current assets:		
Accounts receivable (net of $2,500 estimated uncollectible accounts)....		$47,500

2. *Aging of Accounts Receivable*

Normally, the older the account receivable the more likely that it will become uncollectible. An **aging of accounts receivable**, or **aging analysis**, estimates uncollectible accounts by grouping accounts receivable according to how much time has passed since they were created. Groupings depend on the judgement of management but are often based on 30-day periods. Estimated rates of uncollectibility are applied to each class and totalled to get the required balance of the Allowance for Doubtful Accounts. This calculation is illustrated in Exhibit 10.14 for DeCor, an interior design company whose total outstanding accounts receivable at December 31 were $49,900.

Exhibit 10.14

Aging of Accounts Receivable

Notice the percent of uncollectibility increases with the age of the accounts to reflect the increasing risk of noncollection.

DeCor Schedule of Accounts Receivable by Age December 31, 2011						
Customer's Name	**Total**	**Not Yet Due**	**1 to 30 Days Past Due**	**31 to 60 Days Past Due**	**61 to 90 Days Past Due**	**Over 90 Days Past Due**
Charles Abbot	$ 450	$ 450				
Frank Allen	710			$ 710		
George Arden...........	500	300	$ 200			
Paul Baum................	740				$ 100	$ 640
ZZ Services..............	1,000	810	190			
Totals	$49,900	$37,000	$6,500	$3,500	$1,900	$1,000
Percent Uncollectible		× 2%	× 5%	× 10%	× 25%	× 40%
Estimated Uncollectible Accounts	**$2,290**	$ 740	$ 325	$ 350	$ 475	$ 400

The total in the first column tells us the adjusted balance in DeCor's Allowance for Doubtful Accounts should be $2,290 (= $740 + $325 + $350 + $475 + $400). Because DeCor's allowance account as shown below has an unadjusted ***debit balance*** of $200, the required adjustment to the Allowance for Doubtful Accounts needs to be calculated as follows:

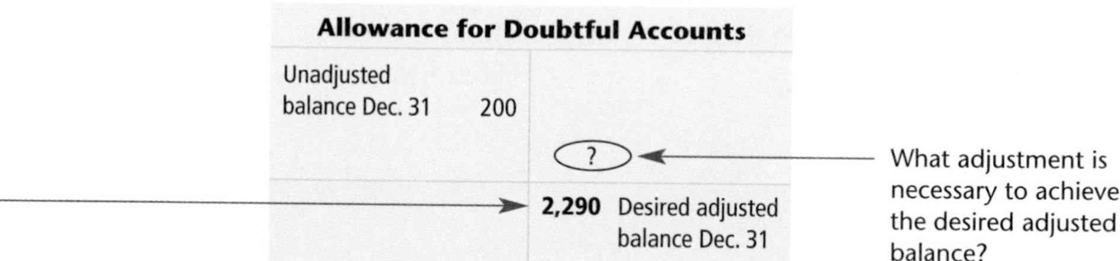

DeCor records the following adjusting entry:

Dec. 31	Bad Debt Expense	2,490	
	Allowance for Doubtful Accounts		2,490
	To record estimated bad debts; $2,290 + $200 = $2,490.		

On the balance sheet, DeCor's accounts receivable would be reported as follows:

Current assets:		
Accounts receivable	$49,900	
Less: Allowance for doubtful accounts	2,290	$47,610

or

Current assets:	
Accounts receivable (net of $2,290 estimated uncollectible accounts).....	$47,610

Exhibit 10.15 summarizes the principles guiding the estimation approaches and their focus of analysis.

Exhibit 10.15

Approaches to Estimate Bad Debts

Income Statement Approach	Balance Sheet Approach	
Income Statement Focus	**Balance Sheet Focus**	**Balance Sheet Focus**
Percent of Sales	Percent of Receivables	Aging of Receivables
Emphasis on Matching	Emphasis on Realizable Value	Emphasis on Realizable Value
Sales ⟷ Bad Debt Expense	Accounts Receivable (total) ⟷ Allowance for Doubtful Accounts	Accounts Receivable (individual) ⟷ Allowance for Doubtful Accounts

Using an aging of receivables is the most reliable of the three calculations because it is based on a more detailed examination of specific accounts. In many cases, the aging analysis is supplemented with information about specific customers, allowing management to decide whether those accounts should be classified as uncollectible. This information is often supplied by the sales and credit department managers.

6. SnoBoard Company's end-of-period Dec. 31, 2011, balance in the Allowance for Doubtful Accounts is a credit of $440. It estimates from an aging of accounts receivable that $6,142 is uncollectible. Prepare SnoBoard's year-end adjusting entry for bad debts.

Do Quick Study questions: QS 10-4, QS 10-5, QS 10-6, QS 10-7

Direct Write-Off Method

An alternative to the allowance method of accounting for bad debts is the *direct write-off method.* The **direct write-off method** records the loss from an uncollectible account receivable at the time it is determined to be uncollectible. No attempt is made to estimate uncollectible accounts or bad debt expense. For example, if TechCom determines on January 23 that it cannot collect $520 owed by an individual named Jack Kent, this loss is recognized using the direct write-off method in the following entry:

Jan.	23	Bad Debt Expense	520	
		Accounts Receivable—Jack Kent		520
		To write off uncollectible accounts under the direct write-off method.		

The allowance method satisfies the generally accepted accounting principles of prudence and matching; the direct write-off method does not.

1. Prudence demands that caution be exercised to prevent the overstatement of assets and net income. Overstated assets and/or net income could result in bad lending or investing decisions. The allowance method, in recognizing that less than 100% of the accounts receivable will be collected (Accounts Receivable less Allowance for Doubtful Accounts), reduces the risk of overstating receivables. Under the direct write-off method, Accounts Receivable are reported on the balance sheet at 100%, which is more than what will typically be collected.
2. Matching requires that expenses be reported in the period in which the revenue was recorded. Often, an uncollectible account receivable is not discovered until the next accounting period. The allowance method attempts to match the expense of uncollectible accounts to the period in which the revenue was recorded by recording an estimate at the end of the period. The direct write-off method does *not* achieve matching since the expense is recorded when an account is identified as uncollectible, which is normally *not* in the period in which the revenue was recorded.

Although the direct write-off method is not in accordance with prudence and matching, *a business may choose to use it* instead of the allowance method. This would occur when uncollectible accounts are not material. The materiality principle states that an amount can be ignored if its effect on the financial statements is unimportant to users. The materiality principle permits the matching principle to be ignored when bad debt expenses are very small in relation to a company's other financial statement items. So the direct write-off method would be used when bad debt expense is unimportant for decisions made by users of the company's financial statements.

7. The direct write-off method is recorded by debiting Bad Debt Expense and crediting the Allowance for Doubtful Accounts.
   a. True
   b. False

Do Quick Study question: QS 10-8

Answer—p. 515

Labour Union Chief

You are representing your employee union in contract negotiations with management. One week prior to contract discussions, management released financial statements showing zero growth in earnings. This is far below the 10% growth predicted earlier. In your review of the financial statements, you find the company increased its "allowance for uncollectible accounts" from 1.5% to 4.5% of accounts receivable. Apart from this change, earnings would show a 9% growth. Does this information affect your negotiations?

mid-chapter demonstration problem

Delcor Industries, a distributor of electrical supplies, had outstanding accounts receivable on December 31, 2011, of $450,000 aged as follows:

Delcor Industries
Schedule of Accounts Receivable by Age
December 31, 2011

Customer's Name	Total	Not Yet Due	1 to 30 Days Past Due	31 to 60 Days Past Due	61 to 90 Days Past Due	Over 90 Days Past Due
Alton Group	$ 90,000		$ 90,000			
Filby's Electrical Service.....................	48,000			$22,000	$26,000	
GDP Servicing	162,000	$120,000	42,000			
Parker's Electrical	80,000	80,000				
Trenton Construction..	15,000					$15,000
Xeon Developments..	55,000	30,000	25,000			
Totals.......................	$450,000	$230,000	$157,000	$22,000	$26,000	$15,000
Percent uncollectible............		× 1%	× 4%	× 8%	× 25%	× 60%
Estimated uncollectible accounts..................						

During the year 2011, the company had sales of $3,720,000, of which $38,000 were cash sales. The Allowance for Doubtful Accounts had an unadjusted debit balance on December 31, 2011, of $3,050.

Required

Prepare the adjusting entry to estimate uncollectible accounts on December 31, 2011, under each of the following independent assumptions, and show the resulting balance sheet presentation for accounts receivable:

a. Bad debts are estimated to be 0.6% of credit sales.

b. Bad debts are estimated to be 4% of outstanding accounts receivable.

c. Bad debts are based on an aging analysis (part of the required information is provided in the schedule above).

Analysis component:

d. If Delcor did not record the adjusting entry to estimate uncollectible accounts receivable, what effect would this have on current assets, equity, and net income?

e. Assume Delcor's competitors report uncollectible accounts receivable of 1% of outstanding receivables. How does Delcor's experience compare?

solution

a. 0.6% × ($3,720,000 − $38,000 = $3,682,000 credit sales) = $22,092

2011				
Dec.	31	Bad Debt Expense	22,092	
		Allowance for Doubtful Accounts		22,092
		To record estimated bad debts.		

Current assets:		
Accounts receivable	$450,000	
Less: Allowance for doubtful accounts........................	19,042*	$430,958
or		
Current assets:		
Accounts receivable (net of $19,042* estimated uncollectible accounts)....		$430,958

**$22,092 credit adjustment − $3,050 debit balance = $19,042.*

b. The required balance in the Allowance for Doubtful Accounts is $18,000 (= 4% × $450,000)

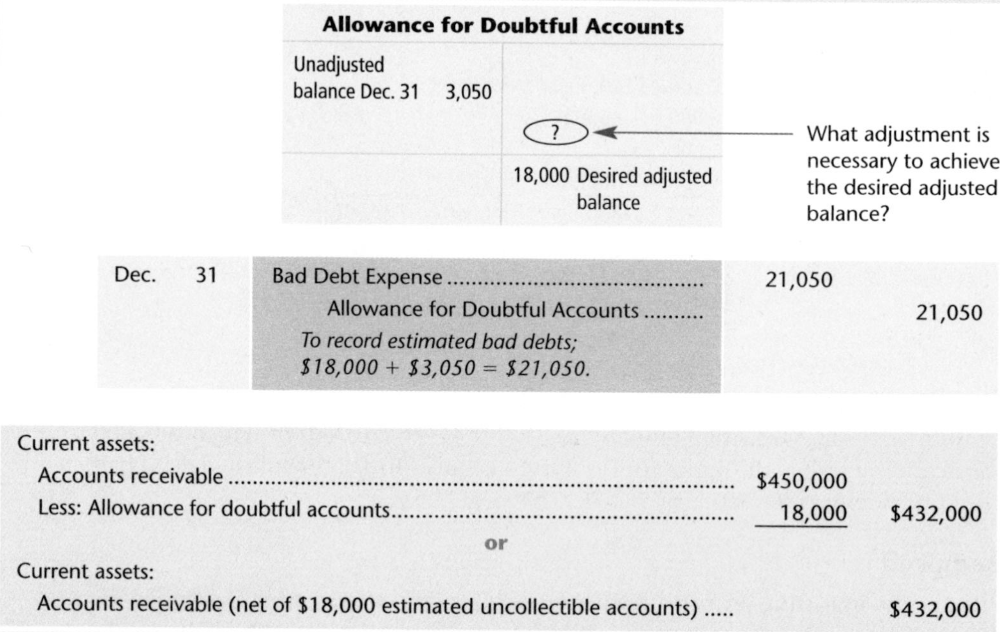

Dec.	31	Bad Debt Expense	21,050	
		Allowance for Doubtful Accounts		21,050
		To record estimated bad debts; $18,000 + $3,050 = $21,050.		

Current assets:		
Accounts receivable	$450,000	
Less: Allowance for doubtful accounts........................	18,000	$432,000
or		
Current assets:		
Accounts receivable (net of $18,000 estimated uncollectible accounts)		$432,000

c. First, calculate total estimated uncollectible accounts by completing the bottom of the aging schedule as follows:

Totals....................	$450,000	$230,000	$157,000	$22,000	$26,000	$15,000
Percent uncollectible		× 1%	× 4%	× 8%	× 25%	× 60%
Estimated uncollectible accounts	$ 25,840	$ 2,300	$ 6,280	$ 1,760	$ 6,500	$ 9,000

Allowance for Doubtful Accounts	
Unadjusted balance Dec. 31 3,050	
	? ← What adjustment is necessary to achieve the desired adjusted balance?
	25,840 Desired adjusted balance Dec. 31

Second, determine what adjustment is necessary to achieve the desired balance of $25,840 in the Allowance for Doubtful Accounts as follows:

Dec.	31	Bad Debt Expense	28,890	
		Allowance for Doubtful Accounts		28,890
		To record estimated bad debts; $25,840 + $3,050.		

Current assets:		
Accounts receivable	$450,000	
Less: Allowance for doubtful accounts	25,840	$424,160
or		
Current assets:		
Accounts receivable (net of $25,840 estimated uncollectible accounts)		$424,160

Analysis component:

d. If Delcor did not record the adjusting entry to estimate uncollectible accounts receivable, current assets would be overstated, equity would be overstated, and net income would be overstated.

e. Delcor's competitors are experiencing a lower rate of uncollectible accounts receivable which, on the surface, appears to be favourable. However, additional information is required. Perhaps Delcor has an aggressive credit policy, granting credit to a wider range of customers, which increases revenues but at the same time increases the risk of uncollectibility but overall increases net income. It may also be that Delcor's experience is the result of weak credit policies that grant credit to riskier customers (regarding collectibility).

Short-Term Notes Receivable

LO4 Describe and record a short-term note receivable and calculate its maturity date and interest.

A **promissory note**, as illustrated in Exhibit 10.16, is a written promise to pay a specified amount of money either on demand or at a definite future date. A **short-term note receivable** (or **note receivable**) is a promissory note that becomes due within the next 12 months or within the business's operating cycle if greater than 12 months.

Exhibit 10.16

Terminology Related to a Promissory Note

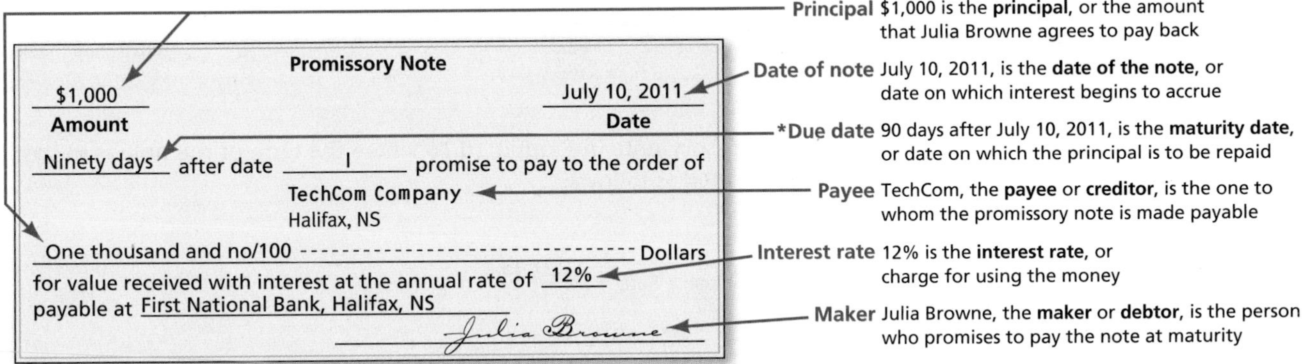

Promissory Note
$1,000
Amount
July 10, 2011
Date
Ninety days after date I promise to pay to the order of
TechCom Company
Halifax, NS
One thousand and no/100 Dollars
for value received with interest at the annual rate of 12%
payable at First National Bank, Halifax, NS
Julia Browne
Principal $1,000 is the principal, or the amount that Julia Browne agrees to pay back
Date of note July 10, 2011, is the date of the note, or date on which interest begins to accrue
*Due date 90 days after July 10, 2011, is the maturity date, or date on which the principal is to be repaid
Payee TechCom, the payee or creditor, is the one to whom the promissory note is made payable
Interest rate 12% is the interest rate, or charge for using the money
Maker Julia Browne, the maker or debtor, is the person who promises to pay the note at maturity

* Note: The **due date** of a note is also referred to as the **maturity date**. The **period** of this note is 90 days, the time from the *date of the note* to its *maturity date* or *due date*.

Calculations for Notes

We need to know two calculations related to notes:

1. How to determine the maturity date, and
2. How to calculate interest.

Maturity Date

A note dated on July 10 with a specified maturity date of July 15 is a five-day note (calculated as July 15 − July 10 = 5 days). A 10-day note dated July 10 would have a maturity date of July 20 (calculated as July 10 + 10 days = July 20). The promissory note dated July 10 in Exhibit 10.16 is a 90-day note and the maturity date is calculated as shown in Exhibit 10.17.

Exhibit 10.17

Maturity Date Calculation

Days in July	31
Minus date of note	10
Days remaining in July	21
Add days in August	31
Add days in September	30
Days to equal 90 days or **Maturity Date, October 8**	8
Period of the note in days	90

The period of a note is sometimes expressed in months or years. When months are used, the note matures and is payable in the month of its maturity on the *same day of the month* as its original date. A three-month note dated July 10, for instance, is payable on October 10. The same analysis applies when years are used.

Interest Calculation

Interest is an annual rate unless otherwise stated. The formula for calculating interest is shown in Exhibit 10.18.

Exhibit 10.18

Formula for Calculating Interest

$$\text{Interest} = \text{Principal of the note} \times \text{Annual interest rate} \times \text{Time expressed in years} \quad \textbf{or} \quad i = Prt$$

Interest on a $1,000, 12%, six-month note is calculated as:

$$\$1{,}000 \times 12\% \times \frac{6}{12} = \underline{\underline{\$60}}$$

Using the promissory note in Exhibit 10.16 where the term of the note is in days, interest is calculated as follows:

$$\text{Interest} = \text{Principal} \times \text{Rate} \times \frac{\text{Exact days}}{365}$$

or

$$\$1{,}000 \times 12\% \times \frac{90}{365} = \underline{\underline{\$29.59}}$$

Unless otherwise instructed, you are to solve problems using the specific number of days and a 365-day year. Interest calculations should be rounded to the nearest whole cent.

Receipt of a Note

To illustrate recording the receipt of a note, we use the $1,000, 90-day, 12% promissory note in Exhibit 10.16. Assume that TechCom receives this note at the time of a product sale to Julia Browne (cost of sales $630). This transaction is recorded as (assuming a perpetual inventory system):

Date		Account	Debit	Credit
July	10	Notes Receivable	1,000	
		Sales		1,000
		Sold merchandise in exchange for a 90-day, 12% note.		
	10	Cost of Goods Sold	630	
		Merchandise Inventory		630
		To record cost of sales.		

A note receivable can also arise when a company accepts a note from an overdue customer as a way of granting a time extension on a past-due account receivable. When this occurs, a company may collect part of the past-due balance in cash. This partial payment forces a concession from the customer, reduces the customer's debt (and the seller's risk), and produces a note for a smaller amount. TechCom, for instance, agreed to accept $1,000 in cash and a $3,000, 60-day, 12% note from Jo Cook to settle her $4,000 past-due account. TechCom made the following entry to record receipt of this cash and note:

Date		Account	Debit	Credit
Dec.	16	Cash	1,000	
		Notes Receivable	3,000	
		Accounts Receivable—Jo Cook		4,000
		Received cash and note in settlement of account.		

End-of-Period Interest Adjustment

When notes receivable are outstanding at the end of an accounting period, accrued interest is calculated and recorded. This recognizes both the interest revenue when it is earned and the added asset (interest receivable) owned by the note's holder. When TechCom's accounting period ends on December 31, $14.79 of interest accrues on the note dated December 16 ($3,000 × 12% × 15/365). The following adjusting entry records this revenue:

Date		Account	Debit	Credit
Dec.	31	Interest Receivable	14.79	
		Interest Revenue		14.79
		To record accrued interest.		

This adjusting entry means that interest revenue appears on the income statement of the period when it is earned. It also means that interest receivable appears on the balance sheet as a current asset.

Honouring a Note

When the note dated December 16 is paid on the maturity date of February 14, the maker of the note, Jo Cook, is **honouring** the note. TechCom's entry to record the cash receipt is:

Feb.	14	Cash	3,059.18	
		Interest Revenue		44.39
		Interest Receivable		14.79
		Notes Receivable		3,000.00
		Received payment of a note and its interest.		

Total interest earned on this note is \$59.18 (= \$3,000 × 12% × 60/365). On February 14, Interest Receivable is credited for \$14.79 to record the collection of the interest accrued on December 31. The interest revenue in this period is \$44.39 (= \$59.18 total interest less \$14.79 interest accrued on December 31) and reflects TechCom's revenue from holding the note from January 1 to February 14.

Dishonouring a Note

Sometimes the maker of a note does not pay the note at maturity; this is known as **dishonouring** the note. The act of dishonouring does not relieve the maker of the obligation to pay. The payee should use every legitimate means to collect. Assume Julia Browne did not pay the note dated July 10 when it matured on October 8. TechCom removes the amount of the note from the Notes Receivable account and charges it back to an account receivable from its maker as follows:

Oct.	8	Accounts Receivable—Julia Browne	1,029.59	
		Interest Revenue		29.59
		Notes Receivable		1,000.00
		To charge the account of Julia Browne for a dishonoured note including interest; \$1,000 × 12% × 90/365.		

Charging a dishonoured note back to the account of its maker serves two purposes. First, it removes the amount of the note from the Notes Receivable account, leaving in the account only notes that have not matured, and records the dishonoured note in the maker's account. Second, and most important, if the maker of the dishonoured note applies for credit in the future, his or her account will show all past dealings, including the dishonoured note. Restoring the account also reminds the company to continue collection efforts for both principal and interest. If the restored account receivable is later identified as being uncollectible, it is written off as follows:

Oct.	31	Allowance for Doubtful Accounts	1,029.59	
		Accounts Receivable—Julia Browne		1,029.59
		To write off an uncollectible account.		

8. Wiley purchases \$7,000 of merchandise from Stamford Company on December 16, 2011. Stamford accepts Wiley's \$7,000, 90-day, 12% note as payment. Stamford's annual accounting period ends on December 31 and it doesn't make reversing entries. Prepare entries for Stamford Company on December 16, 2011, and December 31, 2011.

9. Using the information in Checkpoint 8, prepare Stamford's March 16, 2012, entry if Wiley dishonours the note.

Do Quick Study questions: QS 10-9, QS 10-10, QS 10-11

CRITICAL THINKING CHALLENGE

Refer to the Critical Thinking Challenge questions at the beginning of the chapter on page 495. Compare your answers to those suggested on Connect at www.mcgrawhillconnect.ca.

IFRS HIGHLIGHTS

Trade and other receivables are financial assets (IAS 32, para. 11(c)) shown on the balance sheet (IAS 1, para. 54(h)). IFRS have not caused changes, at the introductory level, to concepts covered in this chapter.

Summary

LO1 | Describe accounts receivable and how they occur and are recorded. Accounts receivable are amounts due from customers for credit sales. The subledger lists the amounts owed by individual customers. Credit sales arise from at least two sources: (1) sales on credit and (2) non-bank credit card sales. Sales on credit refers to a company granting credit directly to customers. Non-bank credit card sales involve use of a third party issuing a credit card.

LO2 | Apply the allowance method to account for uncollectible accounts receivable. Under the allowance method, bad debt expense is estimated at the end of the accounting period by debiting Bad Debt Expense and crediting the Allowance for Doubtful Accounts. When accounts are later identified as being uncollectible, they are written off by debiting the Allowance for Doubtful Accounts and crediting Accounts Receivable.

LO3 | Estimate uncollectible accounts receivable using approaches based on sales and accounts receivable. Uncollectibles are estimated by focusing on either (a) the income statement relation between bad debt expense and credit sales or (b) the balance sheet relation between accounts receivable and the Allowance for Doubtful Accounts. The first approach emphasizes the matching principle for the income statement. The second approach can include either a simple percent relation with accounts receivable or the aging of accounts receivable and emphasizes realizable value of accounts receivable for the balance sheet. Although not acceptable according to GAAP, the direct write-off method debits Bad Debt Expense and credits Accounts Receivable when accounts are determined to be uncollectible. It is used when the amount of bad debt expense is immaterial.

LO4 | Describe and record a short-term note receivable and calculate its maturity date and interest. A short-term note receivable is a written promise to pay a specified amount of money either on demand or at a definite future date, normally within the next 12 months or the business's operating cycle if greater than one year. The maturity date of a note is the day the note (principal and interest) must be repaid. Interest rates are typically stated in annual terms. When a note's time to maturity is more or less than one year, the amount of interest on a note is calculated by expressing time as a fraction of one year and multiplying the note's principal by this fraction and the annual interest rate. It is recorded at its principal amount by debiting the Notes Receivable account and credited to the asset or service provided in return for the note. Interest earned is recorded for the time period it is held in the accounting period reported on. When a note is honoured, the payee debits the money received and credits both Notes Receivable and Interest Revenue. Dishonoured notes are credited to Notes Receivable and Interest Revenue and debited to Accounts Receivable.

guidance answer to JUDGEMENT CALL

Labour Union Chief

Yes, this information is likely to affect your negotiations. The obvious question is why the company increased the allowance to such a large extent. This major increase in allowance means a substantial increase in bad debt expense *and* a decrease in earnings. Also, this change coming immediately prior to labour contract discussions raises concerns since it reduces the union's bargaining power for increased compensation. You want to ask management for supporting documentation justifying this increase. Also, you want data for two or three prior years, and similar data from competitors. These data should give you some sense of whether the change in the allowance for uncollectibles is justified or not.

guidance answers to CHECKPOINT

1. Accounts receivable are typically due within the current accounting period so would be reported on the balance sheet as a current asset.
2. Bad debt expense must be estimated to match it with the sales that gave rise to the accounts receivable. This requires that companies estimate bad debts before they learn which accounts are uncollectible.
3. Realizable value.
4. The estimated amount of bad debt expense cannot be credited to the Accounts Receivable account because the specific customer accounts that will prove uncollectible cannot be identified and removed from the Accounts Receivable Subledger. If the controlling account were credited directly, its balance would not equal the sum of the subsidiary account balances.
5.

2011			
Jan. 10	Allowance for Doubtful Accounts	300	
	Accounts Receivable—Cool Jam....		300
	To record write-off of uncollectible account.		
Apr. 12	Accounts Receivable—Cool Jam	300	
	Allowance for Doubtful Accounts...		300
	To reinstate account previously written off.		
12	Cash	300	
	Accounts Receivable—Cool Jam....		300
	To record collection.		

6.

2011			
Dec. 31	Bad Debt Expense	5,702	
	Allowance for Doubtful Accounts...		5,702
	To record estimated bad debts; \$6,142 − \$440.		

7. False. The direct write-off method is recorded by debiting Bad Debt Expense and crediting Accounts Receivable.
8.

2011			
Dec. 16	Notes Receivable	7,000.00	
	Sales.................................		7,000.00
	To record 90-day, 12% note.		
31	Interest Receivable	34.52	
	Interest Revenue		34.52
	To record accrued interest; \$7,000 × 12% × 15/365.		

9.

2012			
Mar. 16	Accounts Receivable—Wiley....	7,207.12	
	Interest Revenue		172.60
	Interest Receivable............		34.52
	Notes Receivable		7000.00
	To record dishonouring of a bad note; \$7,000 × 12% × 90/365 = \$207.12.		

demonstration problem

Garden Company had a number of transactions involving receivables during the year 2011. Each of them follows.

Required

Prepare journal entries to record these independent transactions on the books of Garden Company. Garden Company's year-end is December 31.

a. On November 15, 2011, Garden Company agreed to accept \$500 in cash and a \$2,000, 90-day, 8% note from Argo Company to settle its \$2,500 past-due account. Determine the maturity date and record the entry on November 15, on December 31, and on the date of maturity.

b. Garden Company held an \$1,800, 6%, 45-day note of Altamira Industries. At maturity, December 15, Altamira dishonoured the note. Record the dishonouring of the Note Receivable.

c. Elko Purchasing Consultants estimates bad debts to be 3.5% of net credit sales. During 2011, total sales were $6,200,000, of which 35% were for cash. Sales returns and allowances for the year were $128,000, all related to credit sales. Accounts receivable in the amount of $130,000 were identified as uncollectible and written off during 2011. Calculate the adjusted balance in the allowance for doubtful accounts at December 31, 2011, assuming a credit balance on January 1, 2011, of $160,000.

Analysis component:

In (b) the note receivable was dishonoured. How should this be classified on the balance sheet?

Planning the Solution

- Examine each item to determine which accounts are affected and perform the required calculations.
- Prepare required journal entries.
- Prepare an answer to the analysis question.

solution

a.

Days in November	30
Minus date of note	15
Days remaining in November	15
Add days in December	31
	46
Add days in January	31
Days to equal 90 days or **Maturity date, February 13**	13
Period of the note in days	90

Date		Account	Debit	Credit
2011				
Nov.	15	Cash	500.00	
		Notes Receivable	2,000.00	
		Accounts Receivable—Argo Company		2,500.00
		Received cash and note in settlement of account.		
Dec.	31	Interest Receivable	20.16	
		Interest Revenue		20.16
		To record accrued interest; $2,000 × 46/365 × 8% = $20.16.		
2012				
Feb.	13	Cash	2,039.45	
		Interest Receivable		20.16
		Interest Revenue		19.29
		Notes Receivable		2,000.00
		Collected note with interest; $2,000 × 90/365 × 8% = $39.45.		

b.

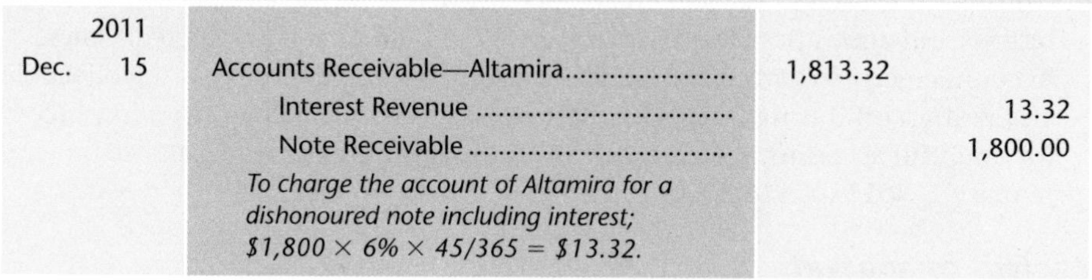

2011			
Dec. 15	Accounts Receivable—Altamira	1,813.32	
	Interest Revenue		13.32
	Note Receivable		1,800.00
	To charge the account of Altamira for a dishonoured note including interest; $1,800 × 6% × 45/365 = $13.32.		

c.

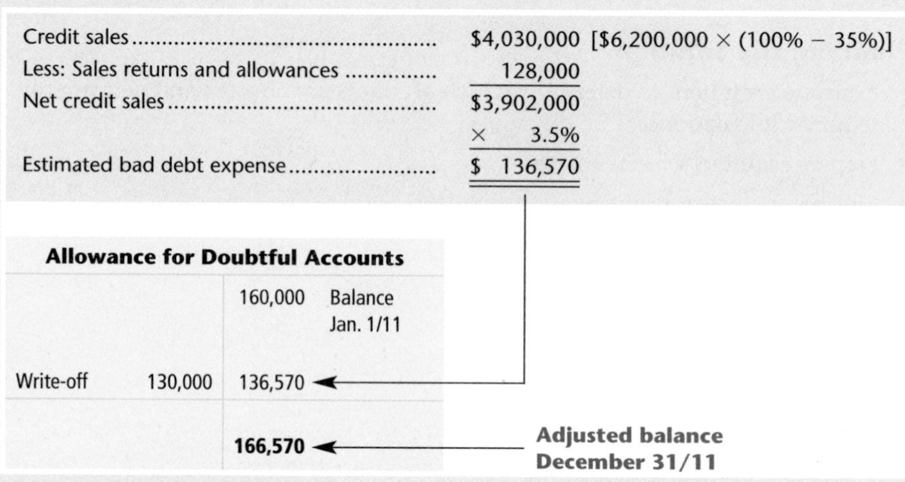

Credit sales	$4,030,000	[$6,200,000 × (100% − 35%)]
Less: Sales returns and allowances	128,000	
Net credit sales	$3,902,000	
	× 3.5%	
Estimated bad debt expense	$ 136,570	

Allowance for Doubtful Accounts

		160,000	Balance Jan. 1/11
Write-off	130,000	136,570	
		166,570	**Adjusted balance December 31/11**

Analysis component:

The dishonoured note receivable in (b) is technically recorded as a current asset on December 15. However, given the high risk of uncollectibility of this receivable, the Allowance for Doubtful Accounts should be adjusted appropriately or the account should be written off or some other appropriate course of action should be taken to ensure that accounts receivable are not overstated at year-end because of this note.

APPENDIX 10A

Converting Receivables to Cash Before Maturity

LO5 | Explain how receivables can be converted to cash before maturity.

Sometimes companies convert receivables to cash before they are due. Reasons for this include the need for cash or a desire not to be involved in collection activities. Converting receivables is usually done either (1) by selling them or (2) by using them as security for a loan. A recent survey showed that about 20% of large companies obtain cash from either the sale of receivables or the pledging of receivables as security. In some industries, such as textiles and furniture, this is common practice. Recently, this practice has spread to other industries, especially the apparel industry. Also, many small companies use sales of receivables as an immediate source of cash. This is especially the case for those selling to companies and government agencies that often delay payment.

Selling Accounts Receivable

A company can sell its accounts receivable to a finance company or bank. The buyer, called a **factor**, charges the seller a *factoring fee* and then collects the receivables as they come due. By incurring a factoring fee, the seller receives cash earlier and passes the risk of bad debts to the factor. The seller also avoids costs of billing and accounting for the receivables.

If TechCom, for instance, sells $20,000 of its accounts receivable and is charged a 2% factoring fee, it records this sale as:

Date		Account	Debit	Credit
Aug.	15	Cash	19,600	
		Factoring Fee Expense	400	
		Accounts Receivable		20,000
		Sold accounts receivable for cash, less a 2% factoring fee.		

Pledging Accounts Receivable as Loan Security

A company can also raise cash by borrowing money and then *pledging* its accounts receivable as security for the loan. Pledging receivables does not transfer the risk of bad debts to the lender. The borrower retains ownership of the receivables. But if the borrower defaults on the loan, the lender has a right to be paid from cash receipts as the accounts receivable are collected. When TechCom borrowed $35,000 and pledged its receivables as security, it recorded this transaction as:

Date		Account	Debit	Credit
Aug.	20	Cash	35,000	
		Notes Payable		35,000
		Borrowed money with the note secured by pledging accounts receivable.		

Because pledged receivables are committed as security for a specific loan, the borrower's financial statements should disclose the pledging of accounts receivable. TechCom, for instance, includes the following note with its financial statements regarding its pledged receivables: "Accounts receivable in the amount of $40,000 are pledged as security for a $35,000 note payable to First National Bank."

Discounting Notes Receivable

Notes receivable can be converted to cash before they mature. Companies who may need cash sooner to meet their obligations can discount (or sell) notes receivable at a financial institution or bank. TechCom, for instance, discounted a $3,000, 90-day, 10% note receivable at First National Bank. TechCom held the note for 50 of the 90 days before discounting it. The bank applied a 12% rate in discounting the note. TechCom received proceeds of $3,033.55 from the bank calculated as:

Principal of Note	$3,000.00
+ Interest from Note ($3,000 × 10% × 90/365)	73.97
= Maturity Value	$3,073.97
− Bank Discount ($3,073.97 × 12% × 40/365)	40.42
= Proceeds	$3,033.55

TechCom recorded the discounting of this note as:

Aug.	25	Cash	3,033.55	
		Interest Revenue		33.55
		Notes Receivable		3,000.00
		Discounted a note receivable.		

Computer programs are used in practice to calculate bank proceeds easily. Notes receivable are discounted without recourse or with recourse. When a note is discounted *without recourse*, the bank assumes the risk of a bad debt loss and the original payee does not have a *contingent liability*. A **contingent liability**[3] is a potential obligation dependent on an uncertain future event arising out of a past transaction. A note discounted without recourse is like an outright sale of an asset. If a note is discounted *with recourse* and the original maker of the note fails to pay the bank when it matures, the original payee of the note must pay for it. This means a company discounting a note with recourse has a contingent liability until the bank is paid. A company should disclose contingent liabilities in notes to its financial statements. TechCom included the following note: "The Company is contingently liable for a $3,000 note receivable discounted with recourse."

Full Disclosure

The disclosure of contingent liabilities in notes is consistent with the full disclosure principle P. 271. Contingent liabilities are discussed in more detail in Chapter 13.

10. A company needs cash and has substantial accounts receivable. What alternatives are available for getting cash from its accounts receivable prior to receiving payments from credit customers?

Do Quick Study questions: *QS 10-12, *QS 10-13

[3] IFRS 2009, IAS 37, para. 10.

APPENDIX 10B

Using the Information

Accounts Receivable Turnover and Days' Sales Uncollected

LO6 Calculate accounts receivable turnover and days' sales uncollected to analyze liquidity.

For a company selling on credit, we want to assess both the *quality* and *liquidity* of its accounts receivable. Quality of receivables refers to the likelihood of collection without loss. Experience shows that the longer receivables are outstanding beyond their due date, the lower the likelihood of collection. Liquidity of receivables refers to the speed or efficiency of collection. Therefore, tools to help monitor receivables are critical to their timely collection.

Accounts Receivable Turnover

The **accounts receivable turnover** is a measure of both the quality and liquidity of accounts receivable. It indicates how often, on average, receivables are received and collected during the period. Accounts receivable turnover also helps us evaluate how well management is doing in granting credit to customers in a desire to increase sales revenues. A high turnover in comparison with competitors suggests that management should consider using more liberal credit terms to increase sales. A low turnover suggests management should consider more strict credit terms and more aggressive collection efforts to avoid having its resources tied up in accounts receivable.

The formula for this ratio is shown in Exhibit 10B.1.

Exhibit 10B.1

Accounts Receivable Turnover Formula

$$\text{Accounts receivable turnover} = \frac{\text{Net sales}}{\text{Average accounts receivable}}$$

Although the numerator of this ratio is more precise if credit sales are used, total net sales is usually used by external users because information about credit sales is typically not reported. The denominator includes accounts receivable and all short-term receivables (including notes receivable) from customers. Average accounts receivable is calculated by adding the balances at the beginning and end of the period and dividing the sum by 2. Some users prefer using gross accounts receivable, before subtracting the allowance for doubtful accounts, but many balance sheets report only the net amount of accounts receivable.

Days' Sales Uncollected

We use the number of **days' sales uncollected** (also known as **days' sales in receivables**) to assess the liquidity of receivables by estimating how much time is likely to pass before we receive cash from credit sales equal to the *current amount* of accounts receivable.[4] The formula for this ratio is shown in Exhibit 10B.2.

Exhibit 10B.2

Days' Sales Uncollected Formula

$$\text{Days' sales uncollected} = \frac{\text{Accounts receivable}}{\text{Net sales}} \times 365$$

Days' sales uncollected is more meaningful if we know the company's credit terms. A rough guideline is that days' sales uncollected should not exceed one and one-third times the days in its: (1) credit period, if discounts are not offered; (2) discount period, if discounts are offered.

Analysis

To perform an analysis using the receivable ratios, we select data from the annual reports of two Canadian food manufacturers, High Liner Foods Incorporated for its years ended January 3, 2009, and December 29, 2007, and Maple Leaf Foods Inc. for its years ended December 31, 2008, and December 31, 2007, as shown in Exhibit 10B.3.

Exhibit 10B.3

Comparison of Accounts Receivable Turnover and Days' Sales Uncollected for High Liner Foods Incorporated and Maple Leaf Foods Inc.

		($ thousands)	
		January 3, 2009	**December 29, 2007**
High Liner Foods Inc.	Accounts receivable	$ 63,873	$ 68,662
	Net sales	615,993	275,391
		December 31, 2008	**December 31, 2007**
Maple Leaf Foods Inc.	Accounts receivable	139,144	202,285
	Net sales	5,242,602	5,209,640

Results for January 3, 2009, and December 31, 2008, respectively:

	Accounts Receivable Turnover	Days' Sales Uncollected
High Liner Foods Inc.	$\frac{\$615,993}{(\$63,873 + \$68,662)/2} = 9.30$ times	$\frac{\$63,873}{\$615,993} \times 365 = 37.85$ days
Maple Leaf Foods Inc.	$\frac{\$5,242,602}{(\$139,144 + \$202,285)/2} = 30.71$ times	$\frac{\$139,144}{\$5,242,602} \times 365 = 9.69$ days

Maple Leaf Foods' accounts receivable turnover of 30.71 times tells us that in 2008 it collected receivables more than three times as fast as High Liner Foods. The days' sales uncollected ratio indicates that High Liner Foods will take 37.85 days to collect the January 3, 2009, balance in accounts receivable as compared to Maple Leaf's 9.69 days to collect its receivables balance on December 31, 2008. Although both companies are in a similar industry, their credit management appears to be significantly different based on a review of the receivables ratios.

[4] When days' sales uncollected is calculated using *average* accounts receivable, the result tells us how many days, *on average*, it takes to collect receivables. The formula in Exhibit 10B.2 tells us how many days it will take to collect the current receivables balance.

11. WebCor reported an accounts receivable turnover at March 31, 2011, of 11. The industry average is 10 for the same date. At March 31, 2010, WebCor reported an accounts receivable turnover of 13. Did WebCor improve regarding its collection of receivables?

Do Quick Study question: *QS 10-14

Summary of Appendix 10A and Appendix 10B

LO5 Explain how receivables can be converted to cash before maturity. There are three usual means to convert receivables to cash before maturity. First, a company can sell accounts receivable to a factor, who charges a factoring fee. Second, a company can borrow money by signing a note payable that is secured by pledging the accounts receivable. Third, notes receivable can be discounted at a bank, with or without recourse. The full disclosure principle requires companies to disclose the amount of receivables pledged and the contingent liability for notes discounted with recourse.

LO6 Calculate accounts receivable turnover and days' sales uncollected to analyze liquidity. Accounts receivable turnover and days' sales uncollected are measures of both the quality and liquidity of accounts receivable. The accounts receivable turnover indicates how often, on average, receivables are received and collected during the period and is calculated as sales divided by average accounts receivable for the period. Days' sales uncollected is calculated as (Accounts receivable ÷ Net sales) × 365 and is used to estimate how much time is likely to pass before cash receipts from net sales are received equal to the average amount of accounts receivable. Both ratios are compared to those for other companies in the same industry, and with prior years' estimates.

guidance answers to CHECKPOINT

10. Alternatives are:

1. Selling their accounts receivable to a factor,
2. Pledging accounts receivable as loan security, and
3. Discounting notes receivable at a bank with or without recourse.

11. At March 31, 2011, WebCor collected its receivables faster than what was reported for the industry average. However, in comparison to its performance in the previous year, WebCor's efficiency in its collection of receivables decreased.

Glossary

Accounts receivable Amounts due from customers for credit sales. Also referred to as *trade receivables*. (p. 496)

Accounts receivable approach A method of estimating bad debts using balance sheet relations. Also known as the *balance sheet approach*. (p. 504)

Accounts receivable turnover A measure of both the quality and liquidity of accounts receivable; it indicates how often, on average, receivables are received and collected during the period; calculated by dividing credit sales (or net sales) by the average accounts receivable balance. (p. 521)

Aging analysis See *aging of accounts receivable*. (p. 505)

Aging of accounts receivable A process of classifying accounts receivable in terms of how long they have been outstanding for the purpose of estimating the amount of uncollectible accounts. (p. 505)

Allowance for Doubtful Accounts A contra asset account with a balance equal to the estimated amount of accounts receivable that will be uncollectible; also called the *Allowance for Uncollectible Accounts*. (p. 500)

Allowance method of accounting for bad debts An accounting procedure that (1) estimates and reports bad debt expense from credit sales during the period of the sales, and (2) reports accounts receivable as the amount of cash proceeds that are expected from their collection (their estimated realizable value). (p. 499)

Bad debts The accounts of customers who do not pay what they have promised to pay; the amount is an expense of selling on credit; also called *uncollectible accounts*. (p. 498)

Balance sheet approach See *accounts receivable approach*. (p. 504)

Contingent liability A potential liability that depends on a future event arising out of a past transaction. (p. 520)

Creditor See *payee*. (p. 511)

Date of a note The date on which interest begins to accrue. (p. 511)

Days' sales uncollected A measure of the liquidity of receivables calculated by taking the balance of receivables and dividing by the credit (or net) sales over the year just completed, and then multiplying by 365 (the number of days in a year); also called *days' sales in receivables*. (p. 522)

Days' sales in receivables See *days' sales uncollected*. (p. 522)

Debtor See *maker of a note*. (p. 511)

Direct write-off method A method of accounting for bad debts that is not generally accepted that records the loss from an uncollectible account receivable at the time it is determined to be uncollectible; no attempt is made to estimate uncollectible accounts or bad debt expense. (p. 507)

Dishonouring a note receivable When a note's maker is unable or refuses to pay at maturity. (p. 514)

Due date of a note See *maturity date*. (p. 511)

Factor The buyer of accounts receivable. (p. 519)

Honouring a note receivable When the maker of the note pays the note in full at maturity. (p. 514)

Income statement approach See *percent of sales approach*. (p. 503)

Interest rate The charge for using (not paying) money until a later date. (p. 511)

Maker of a note One who signs a note and promises to pay it at maturity. (p. 511)

Maturity date of a note The date on which a note and any interest are due and payable. (p. 511)

Note receivable See *short-term note receivable*. (p. 511)

Payee of a note The one to whom a promissory note is made payable. (p. 511)

Percent of accounts receivable approach An approach to estimating bad debts that assumes a percent of outstanding receivables is uncollectible. (p. 504)

Percent of sales approach Uses income statement relations to estimate bad debts. Also known as the *income statement approach*. (p. 503)

Period of a note The time from the date of the note to its maturity date or due date. (p. 511)

Principal of a note The amount that the signer of a promissory note agrees to pay back when it matures, not including the interest. (p. 511)

Promissory note A written promise to pay a specified amount of money either on demand or at a definite future date. (p. 511)

Realizable value The expected proceeds from converting assets into cash. (p. 500)

Short-term note receivable A promissory note that becomes due within the next 12 months or within the business's operating cycle if greater than 12 months. (p. 511)

Trade receivables See *accounts receivable*. (p. 496)

Uncollectible accounts See *bad debts*. (p. 498)

Visit **Connect** at **www.mcgrawhillconnect.ca** for additional study tools, practice quizzes, to search an interactive e-book, and much more.

Concept Review Questions

1. Explain why writing off a bad debt against the allowance account does not reduce the estimated realizable value of a company's accounts receivable.
2. Why does the Bad Debt Expense account usually not have the same adjusted balance as the Allowance for Doubtful Accounts?
3. Why does the direct write-off method of accounting for bad debts commonly fail to match revenues and expenses?
4. What is the essence of the accounting principle of materiality?
5. Why might a business prefer a note receivable to an account receivable?
6. Review the balance sheet for Danier Leather in Appendix I. Did accounts receivable increase or decrease from 2007 to 2008 and by how much?

DANIER

*7. What does it mean to sell a receivable without recourse?

Quick Study

QS 10-1
Entries for sale on credit and subsequent collection
LO1

Journalize the following transactions for Kimmel Company (assume a perpetual inventory system):

a. On March 1, Kimmel Company sold $40,000 of merchandise costing $32,000 on credit terms of n/30 to JP Holdings.
b. On March 27, JP Holdings paid its account in full.

QS 10-2
Bad debts, write-off, recovery
LO2

Record the following selected transactions for Allistar Company during its first two months of operations:

Mar.	4	Performed services for various customers on account; $165,000.
	15	Collected $80,000 from credit customers.
	20	Determined that Tom Williams, a credit customer, would not be paying his $5,000 account; wrote it off.
	25	Tom Williams came into an inheritance and paid Allistar the amount written off on March 20.
Apr.	2	Performed services for various customers on account; $280,000.
	9	Collected $110,000 from credit customers.
	30	Allistar estimated bad debt expense to be $8,000.

QS 10-3
Balance sheet presentation
LO2

From the following alphabetized list of adjusted account balances, prepare the current asset section of Biatech's December 31, 2011, balance sheet.

Account	Debit	Credit
Accounts receivable	29,000	
Allowance for doubtful accounts		1,300
Bad debt expense	800	
Cash	10,000	
Machinery	52,000	
Office supplies	400	
Prepaid insurance	950	

An asterisk (*) identifies assignment material based on Appendix 10A or Appendix 10B.

QS 10-4
Adjusting entry to estimate bad debts—percent of sales
LO2, 3

Lexton Company uses the allowance method to account for uncollectible accounts receivable. At year-end, October 31, it was estimated that 0.6% of net credit sales were uncollectible based on past experience. Net sales were $690,000, of which 2/3 were on credit. Record the entry at year-end to estimate uncollectible receivables.

QS 10-5
Adjusting entry to estimate bad debts—percent of receivables
LO2, 3

Foster Company uses the allowance method to account for uncollectible accounts receivable. At year-end, December 31, the unadjusted balance in the Allowance for Doubtful Accounts was $450 credit. Based on past experience, it was estimated that 2.5% of the Accounts Receivable balance of $640,000 was uncollectible. Record the adjusting entry to estimate bad debts at December 31.

QS 10-6
Accounts receivable allowance method of accounting for bad debts
LO2, 3

Duncan Company's year-end trial balance shows accounts receivable of $89,000, allowance for doubtful accounts of $500 (credit), and net credit sales of $270,000. Uncollectibles are estimated to be 1.5% of outstanding accounts receivable.

a. Prepare the December 31 year-end adjustment.
b. What amount would have been used in the year-end adjustment if the allowance account had had a year-end debit balance of $200?
c. Assume the same facts, except that Duncan estimates uncollectibles as 1% of net credit sales. What amount would be used in the adjustment?

QS 10-7
Aging analysis
LO2, 3

Delcom had total accounts receivable on December 31, 2011, of $160,000 aged as follows:

December 31, 2011 Accounts Receivable	Age of Accounts Receivable	Expected Percentage Uncollectible
$110,000	Not due (under 45 days)	2%
40,000	1 to 30 days past due	5%
10,000	Over 30 days past due	40%

Prepare the December 31, 2011, adjusting entry to estimate uncollectible accounts receivable assuming an unadjusted credit balance in Allowance for Doubtful Accounts of $800.

QS 10-8
Direct write-off method
LO3

Winston Abbott operates Abbott Small Engine Repair on his cattle farm, greatly supplementing his farm income. Most of his customers pay cash, so he uses the direct write-off method to account for uncollectible accounts receivable. On March 28, 2011, he determined that the $1,100 account for Jim Patterson is uncollectible. Record the write-off.

QS 10-9
Notes receivable
LO4

On August 2, 2011, SLM Company received a $5,500, 90-day, 12% note from customer Will Carr as payment on his account. Determine the maturity date and prepare the August 2 and maturity date entries, assuming the note is honoured by Carr.

QS 10-10
Notes receivable
LO4

Seaver Company's December 31 year-end trial balance shows an $8,000 balance in Notes Receivable. This balance is from one note dated December 1, with a term of 45 days and 9% interest. Determine the maturity date and prepare the December 31 and maturity date entries, assuming the note is honoured.

QS 10-11
Dishonouring of a note receivable
LO4

Ajax Company had a $17,000, 7%, 30-day note of Beatrice Inc. At maturity, April 4, Beatrice dishonoured the note. Record the entry on April 4.

***QS 10-12**
Sale of accounts receivable
LO5

On June 4, Maltex sold $108,000 of its accounts receivable to a collection agency, which charges a 2.5% factoring fee. Record the entry on June 4.

***QS 10-13**
Discounting a note receivable
LO5

Tallcrest discounted a $50,000, 45-day, 8% note receivable on August 10 at the local bank, which applies an 11% discount rate. Tallcrest had held the note for 25 days before discounting it. Record the entry on August 10.

***QS 10-14**
Accounts receivable turnover and days' sales uncollected
LO6

Mega Company and Holton Company are similar firms that operate within the same industry. The following information is available:

		Mega Company			Holton Company		
	Industry Average	**2011**	**2010**	**2009**	**2011**	**2010**	**2009**
Accounts receivable turnover	12	14.9	12.2	11.5	10.6	13.1	13.5
Days' sales uncollected	30	24.5	29.9	31.7	34.4	27.9	27.1

a. Which company has the *more favourable* accounts receivable turnover in 2011?
b. Which company has the *greater* number of days in uncollected accounts in 2011? Is this generally favourable or unfavourable?
c. Which company is showing an *unfavourable* trend in terms of managing accounts receivable?

Exercises

Exercise 10-1
Subledger accounts
LO1

Wallace Contracting recorded the following transactions during November 2011:

Nov. 3	Accounts Receivable—ABC Shop	8,834	
	Sales*		8,834
8	Accounts Receivable—Colt Enterprises	2,500	
	Sales*		2,500
11	Accounts Receivable—Red McKenzie	1,466	
	Sales*		1,466
19	Sales Returns and Allowances*	378	
	Accounts Receivable—Red McKenzie		378
28	Accounts Receivable—ABCShop	5,212	
	Sales*		5,212

*Cost of goods sold (or COGS) has been ignored for the purpose of maintaining focus on accounts receivable.

Required
1. Open a General Ledger having T-accounts for Accounts Receivable, Sales, and Sales Returns and Allowances. Also, open an Accounts Receivable Subledger having a T-account for each customer. Post the preceding entries to the General Ledger accounts and the customer accounts.
2. List the balances of the accounts in the subledger, total the balances, and compare the total with the balance of the Accounts Receivable controlling account.

An asterisk (*) identifies assignment material based on Appendix 10A or Appendix 10B.

Exercise 10-2
Write-off and subsequent partial recovery

LO2

Foster Company uses the allowance method to account for uncollectibles. On October 31, it wrote off a $1,000 account of a customer, Gwen Rowe. On December 9, it received a $200 payment from Rowe.

a. Make the appropriate entry or entries for October 31.
b. Make the appropriate entry or entries for December 9.

Exercise 10-3
Allowance for doubtful accounts

LO2, 3

At the end of its annual accounting period, Midi Company estimated its bad debts as 0.5% of its $1,750,000 of credit sales made during the year. On December 31, Midi made an addition to its Allowance for Doubtful Accounts equal to that amount. On the following February 1, management decided that the $1,800 account of Catherine Hicks was uncollectible and wrote it off as a bad debt. Four months later, on June 5, Hicks unexpectedly paid the amount previously written off. Give the journal entries required to record these transactions.

Exercise 10-4
Bad debt expense

LO2, 3

Check figure:
b. Bad Debt Expense = $10,356

At the end of each year, Deutch Supply Co. uses the simplified balance sheet approach (i.e., percent of accounts receivable) to estimate bad debts. On December 31, 2011, it has outstanding accounts receivable of $159,000 and estimates that 4% will be uncollectible.

Required

a. Give the entry to record bad debt expense for 2011 under the assumption that the Allowance for Doubtful Accounts has a $2,745 credit balance before the adjustment.
b. Give the entry under the assumption that the Allowance for Doubtful Accounts has a $3,996 debit balance before the adjustment.

Exercise 10-5
Analyzing receivables and allowance for doubtful accounts

LO1, 2, 3

Accounts Receivable		
Dec. 31/10 Balance	89,000	
	345,000	356,000
		2,900
	170	170
Dec. 31/11 Balance	75,100	

Allowance for Doubtful Accounts		
	3,000	Dec. 31/10 Balance
	170	
2,900	2,550	
	2,820	Dec. 31/11 Balance

Required

Analyzing the information presented in the T-accounts above, identify the dollar value related to each of the following:

a. Credit sales during the period.
b. Collection of credit sales made during the period.
c. Write-off of an uncollectible account.
d. Recovery of the account previously written off.
e. The adjusting entry to estimate bad debts.

Exercise 10-6
Balance sheet presentation
LO2, 4

From the following alphabetized list of adjusted account balances, prepare the current asset section of LisTel's March 31, 2011, balance sheet.

Account	Balance*
Accounts receivable	$102,000
Accumulated depreciation, building	31,000
Allowance for doubtful accounts	2,100
Bad debt expense	1,950
Building	214,000
Cash	29,000
Merchandise inventory	65,000
Notes receivable, due May 1, 2013	54,000
Notes receivable, due Nov. 30, 2011	17,000
Supplies	4,500

*Assume all balances are normal.

Exercise 10-7
Estimating bad debt expense—percent of sales
LO3

connect

Selected unadjusted account balances at December 31, 2011, are shown below for Demron Servicing.

Account	Debit	Credit
Accounts receivable	$70,000	
Allowance for doubtful accounts		$ 900
Sales (all on credit)		492,500
Sales discounts	4,900	

Check figure:
d. Accounts receivable (net) = $175,079

Required

a. Demron estimates that 1.5% of net credit sales will prove to be uncollectible. Prepare the adjusting entry required on December 31, 2011, to estimate uncollectible receivables.

b. During 2012, credit sales were $620,000 (cost of sales $406,500); sales discounts of $6,200 were taken when accounts receivable of $497,500 were collected; and accounts written off during the year totalled $12,450. Prepare the entries for these transactions.

c. Record the adjusting entry required on December 31, 2012, to estimate uncollectible receivables assuming it is based on 1.5% of net credit sales.

d. Show how accounts receivable would appear on the December 31, 2012, balance sheet.

Analysis component:
Comment on the advantages and disadvantages of using the income statement approach for estimating uncollectibles.

Exercise 10-8
Estimating bad debt expense—percent of receivables
LO3

Check figure:
d. Accounts receivable (net) = $176,449

Refer to the information in Exercise 10-7.

Required

a. Assume that Demron estimates uncollectible accounts as 2% of receivables. Prepare the adjusting entry required on December 31, 2011, to estimate uncollectible receivables.

b. During 2012, credit sales were $620,000 (cost of sales $406,500); sales discounts taken were $6,200; accounts receivable collected were $497,500; and accounts written off during the year totalled $12,450. Prepare the entries to record these transactions.

c. Record the adjusting entry required on December 31, 2012, to estimate uncollectible receivables assuming it is based on 2% of receivables.

d. Show how accounts receivable would appear on the December 31, 2012, balance sheet.

Analysis component:
Comment on the advantages and disadvantages of using the balance sheet approach for estimating uncollectibles.

Exercise 10-9
Aging analysis
LO3

Winfrey Designs had an unadjusted credit balance in its Allowance for Doubtful Accounts at December 31, 2011, of $2,100.

Required

a. Prepare the adjusting entry assuming that Winfrey estimates uncollectible accounts based on an aging analysis as follows:

December 31, 2011 Accounts Receivable	Age of Accounts Receivable	Expected Percentage Uncollectible
$95,000	Not due (under 30 days)	1%
35,000	1 to 30 days past due	4%
8,000	31 to 60 days past due	10%
2,000	Over 60 days past due	60%

b. During 2012, credit sales were $1,240,000; sales discounts taken were $12,400; accounts receivable collected were $995,000; and accounts written off during the year totalled $24,900. Prepare the adjusting entry required on December 31, 2012, to estimate uncollectible receivables assuming it is based on the following aging analysis.

December 31, 2012 Accounts Receivable	Age of Accounts Receivable	Expected Percentage Uncollectible
$215,000	Not due (under 30 days)	1%
95,000	1 to 30 days past due	4%
35,100	31 to 60 days past due	10%
15,000	Over 60 days past due	60%

Check figure:
c. Accounts receivable (net) = $341,640

c. Show how accounts receivable would appear on the December 31, 2012, balance sheet.

Analysis component:
Comment on the advantages and disadvantages of using an aging analysis for estimating uncollectible accounts.

Exercise 10-10
Direct write-off method
LO3

Delores Cooper operates Cooper Garden Designs. Most of her customers pay cash so she uses the direct write-off method to account for uncollectible accounts receivable. On May 3, 2011, she determined that the $1,100 account for Wilma Benz was uncollectible. During 2011, she had total credit sales of $280,000. The December 31, 2011, balance in accounts receivable was $46,000.

Required
Record the May 3 write-off using the direct write-off method.

Analysis component:
Delores wants to compare the effect of using the allowance method versus the direct write-off method for recording uncollectible accounts. If uncollectible accounts were estimated at (a) 2% of credit sales or (b) 4% of outstanding accounts receivable, prepare a comparison of the effect on net income of using the allowance methods versus the direct write-off method.

Exercise 10-11
Dishonouring a note
LO4

Prepare journal entries to record these transactions:

Mar.	21	Accepted a $6,200, six-month, 10% note dated today from Bradley Brooks in granting a time extension on his past-due account.
Sept.	21	Brooks dishonoured his note when presented for payment.
Dec.	31	After exhausting all legal means of collection, wrote off Brooks' account against the Allowance for Doubtful Accounts.

Exercise 10-12
Honouring a note
LO4

Prepare journal entries to record these transactions:

Oct.	31	Accepted a $5,000, six-month, 8% note dated today from Leann Grimes in granting a time extension on her past-due account.
Dec.	31	Adjusted the books for the interest due on the Grimes note.
Apr.	30	Grimes honoured her note when presented for payment.

Exercise 10-13
Accounting for notes receivable transactions
LO4

Following are transactions of The Barnett Company:

	2011	
Dec.	16	Accepted a $17,200, 60-day, 7% note dated this day in granting Carmel Karuthers a time extension on her past-due account.
	31	Made an adjusting entry to record the accrued interest on the Karuthers note.
	31	Closed the Interest Revenue account.
	2012	
Feb.	14	Received Karuthers' payment for the principal and interest on the note dated December 16.
Mar.	2	Accepted an $8,000, 8%, 90-day note dated this day in granting a time extension on the past-due account of ATW Company.
	17	Accepted a $3,200, 30-day, 9% note dated this day in granting Leroy Johnson a time extension on his past-due account.
May	31	Received ATW's payment for the principal and interest on the note dated March 2.

Check figure:
May 31, 2012: Interest Revenue = $157.81

Required
Prepare journal entries to record The Barnett Company's transactions.

***Exercise 10-14**
Selling and pledging accounts receivable
LO5

On July 31, Konrad International had $125,900 of accounts receivable. Prepare journal entries to record the following August transactions. Also, prepare any footnotes to the August 31 financial statements that should be reported as a result of these transactions.

	2011	
Aug.	2	Sold merchandise to customers on credit, $6,295. Cost of sales was $3,150.
	7	Sold $18,770 of accounts receivable to Fidelity Bank. Fidelity charges a 1.5% fee.
	15	Received payments from customers, $3,436.
	25	Borrowed $10,000 from Fidelity Bank, pledging $14,000 of accounts receivable as security for the loan.

***Exercise 10-15**
Discounting notes receivable
LO5

Check figure:
Feb. 19: Interest Revenue = $487.58

Prepare journal entries to record the following transactions by Ericton Industries:

	2011	
Jan.	20	Accepted a $170,000, 90-day, 9% note dated this day in granting a time extension on the past due account of Steve Soetart.
Feb.	19	Discounted the Steve Soetart note at the bank at 11.5%.

An asterisk (*) identifies assignment material based on Appendix 10A or Appendix 10B.

*Exercise 10-16
Accounts receivable turnover and days' sales uncollected
LO6

The following information was taken from the December 31, 2011, annual report of WestCon Developments.

	($ millions) 2011	2010
Net sales	$7,280	$5,410
Accounts receivable	598	486

	Industry Average
Accounts receivable turnover	16.2
Days' sales uncollected	21.0

Required

1. Calculate accounts receivable turnover and days' sales uncollected for the year 2011.*
2. Compare your calculations in (1) to the industry average and comment on WestCon's relative performance as F (Favourable) or U (Unfavourable).*

*Round the answer to two decimal places.

Problems

Problem 10-1A
Estimating bad debt expense
LO2, 3

On December 31, 2011, Corotel Company's year-end, the unadjusted trial balance included the following items:

Account	Debit	Credit
Accounts receivable	$2,140,200	
Allowance for doubtful accounts	31,500	
Sales ($3,607,500 cash sales)		$10,675,500

Check figures:
1b. Bad Debt Expense = $138,510
2. Accounts receivable (net) = $2,030,340

Required

1. Prepare the adjusting entry needed in Corotel's books to recognize bad debts under each of the following independent assumptions:
   a. Bad debts are estimated to be 2% of credit sales.
   b. An analysis suggests that 5% of outstanding accounts receivable on December 31, 2011, will become uncollectible.
2. Show how Accounts Receivable and the Allowance for Doubtful Accounts would appear on the December 31, 2011, balance sheet given the facts in requirement 1(a).
3. Show how Accounts Receivable and the Allowance for Doubtful Accounts would appear on the December 31, 2011, balance sheet given the facts in requirement 1(b).

Analysis component:
If bad debts are not adjusted for at the end of the accounting period, identify which GAAP are violated and why.

Problem 10-2A
Aging accounts receivable
LO2, 3

On December 31, 2011, Toro Company's Allowance for Doubtful Accounts had an unadjusted credit balance of $26,800. The accountant for Toro has prepared a schedule of the December 31, 2011, accounts receivable by age and, on the basis of past experience, has estimated the percentage of the receivables in each age category that will become uncollectible. This information is summarized as follows:

December 31, 2011 Accounts Receivable	Age of Accounts Receivable	Expected Percentage Uncollectible
$1,460,000	Not due (under 30 days)	1.25%
708,000	1 to 30 days past due	2.00
152,000	31 to 60 days past due	6.50
96,000	61 to 90 days past due	32.75
24,000	Over 90 days past due	68.00

An asterisk (*) identifies assignment material based on Appendix 10A or Appendix 10B.

Required

1. Calculate the amount that should appear in the December 31, 2011, balance sheet as the allowance for doubtful accounts.
2. Prepare the journal entry to record bad debt expense for 2011.

Check figure:
2. Bad Debt Expense = $63,250

Analysis component:

On June 30, 2012, Toro Company concluded that a customer's $7,500 receivable (created in 2011) was uncollectible and that the account should be written off. What effect will this action have on Toro's 2012 net income? Explain your answer.

Problem 10-3A

Accounts receivable transactions and bad debt adjustments

LO1, 2, 3

BeleVu Supplies showed the following selected adjusted balances at its December 31, 2010, year-end:

Accounts Receivable		
Dec. 31/10 Balance	498,000	

Allowance for Doubtful Accounts		
	16,680	Dec. 31/10 Balance

During the year 2011, the following selected transactions occurred:

a. Sales totalled $2,960,000, of which 25% were cash sales (cost of sales $1,804,000).
b. Sales returns were $114,000, half regarding credit sales. The returned merchandise was scrapped.
c. An account for $24,000 was recovered.
d. Several accounts were written off; $39,000.
e. Collections from credit customers totalled $1,880,000 (excluding the recovery in (c) above).

Part A

Required

1. Journalize transactions (a) through (e). You may find it useful to post your entries to T-accounts for Accounts Receivable and Allowance for Doubtful Accounts.

Part B

Required

2. Prepare the December 31, 2011, adjusting entry to estimate bad debts assuming that uncollectible accounts are estimated to be 1% of net credit sales.
3. Show how accounts receivable will appear on the December 31, 2011, balance sheet.
4. What will bad debt expense be on the income statement for the year ended December 31, 2011?

Check figures:
2. Bad Debt Expense = $21,630
5. Bad Debt Expense = $20,580

Part C (independent of Part B)

Required

5. Prepare the December 31, 2011, adjusting entry to estimate bad debts assuming that uncollectible accounts are estimated to be 3% of outstanding receivables.
6. Show how accounts receivable will appear on the December 31, 2011, balance sheet.
7. What will bad debt expense be on the income statement for the year ended December 31, 2011?

Problem 10-4A

Recording accounts receivable transactions and bad debt adjustments

LO1, 2, 3

Peru Industries began operations on January 1, 2011. During the next two years, the company completed a number of transactions involving credit sales, accounts receivable collections, and bad debts (assume a perpetual inventory system). These transactions are summarized as follows:

2011

a. Sold merchandise on credit for $2,289,000, terms n/30 (COGS = $1,240,000).
b. Wrote off uncollectible accounts receivable in the amount of $34,540.
c. Received cash of $1,334,460 in payment of outstanding accounts receivable.
d. In adjusting the accounts on December 31, concluded that 1.5% of the outstanding accounts receivable would become uncollectible.

2012

e. Sold merchandise on credit for $2,941,560, terms n/30 (COGS = $1,592,000).
f. Wrote off uncollectible accounts receivable in the amount of $53,760.
g. Received cash of $2,207,800 in payment of outstanding accounts receivable.
h. In adjusting the accounts on December 31, concluded that 1.5% of the outstanding accounts receivable would become uncollectible.

Check figures:
d. Bad Debt Expense = $48,340
h. Bad Debt Expense = $63,960

Required

Prepare journal entries to record Peru's 2011 and 2012 summarized transactions and the adjusting entries to record bad debt expense at the end of each year.

Problem 10-5A

Uncollectible accounts

LO2, 3

Aaron Servicing showed the following partial unadjusted results at October 31, 2011, its year-end:

Account	Debit	Credit
Sales		$1,590,000
Accounts receivable	$124,000	
Allowance for doubtful accounts	2,800	

Part 1

Required

a. Assuming Aaron estimates bad debts to be 1.5% of sales, prepare the adjusting entry at October 31, 2011.
b. Show how accounts receivable would be shown on the October 31, 2011, balance sheet using your calculations in (a).

Part 2

Check figures:
b. Accounts receivable (net) = $102,950
d. Accounts receivable (net) = $117,800

Required

c. Instead of (a), assume that Aaron estimates bad debts to be 5% of outstanding accounts receivable. Prepare the adjusting entry at October 31, 2011.
d. Show how accounts receivable would be shown on the October 31, 2011, balance sheet using your calculations in (c).

Problem 10-6A
Bad debt expense
LO3

The following is information taken from the June 30, 2011, balance sheet of Tippleton Company:

Accounts receivable	$340,000	
Less: Allowance for doubtful accounts	13,500	$326,500

Part 1
During July, Tippleton Company recorded total sales of $900,000, all on credit. There were $32,500 of sales returns and allowances. Collections during July were $960,000. Total receivables identified as being uncollectible and written off during July were $15,500. Tippleton estimates bad debts as 1% of net credit sales.

Required
Prepare the adjusting entry to record estimated bad debts for July.

Check figures:
1. Bad Debt Expense = $8,675
2. Bad Debt Expense = $5,625

Part 2
During August, total sales of $845,000 were recorded, all on credit. Sales returns and allowances totalled $16,500. Collections during the month were $710,000, which included the recovery of $1,950 from a customer account written off in a previous month. No accounts were written off during August. Tippleton Company changed its method of estimating bad debts to the balance sheet approach because the new accountant said it more accurately reflected uncollectible accounts. The resulting aging analysis determined total estimated uncollectible accounts at August 31 to be $14,250.

Required
Prepare the August 31 adjusting entry to record estimated bad debts for August.

Problem 10-7A
Estimating bad debts
LO3

The following information is available regarding the outstanding accounts receivable of Mufu Contracting at September 30, 2011:

	Month of Credit Sale*				
Customer	**May**	**June**	**July**	**Aug.**	**Sept.**
B. Axley	$28,000	$ -0-	$ -0-	$ -0-	$ -0-
T. Holton	-0-	-0-	72,000	24,000	14,000
W. Nix	-0-	18,000	-0-	4,000	12,000
C. Percy	-0-	-0-	4,000	-0-	10,000
K. Willis	-0-	-0-	-0-	-0-	96,000

*All services are performed on terms of n/30. Assume all sales occurred on the last day of the month.

Mufu estimates bad debts using the following rates:

Not yet due	1 to 29 days past due	30 to 59 days past due	60 to 89 days past due	90 to 119 days past due	Over 119 days past due
0.5%	1%	4%	10%	20%	50%

Required
a. Complete a Schedule of Accounts Receivable by Age at September 30, 2011 (similar to Exhibit 10.14).
b. The Allowance for Doubtful Accounts showed an unadjusted balance on September 30, 2011, of $1,600. Record the adjusting entry at September 30, 2011, to estimate uncollectible accounts.

Check figure:
a. Total estimated uncollectible accounts = $11,380

Problem 10-8A
Uncollectible accounts
LO3

At year-end, December 31, 2011, Corolla Sales showed unadjusted balances of: $394,000 in Accounts Receivable; $14,400 debit in Allowance for Doubtful Accounts; and $1,946,000 in Sales. Uncollectible accounts are estimated to be 2.5% of sales.

Unadjusted balances at December 31, 2012, were: Accounts Receivable, $512,000; Allowance for Doubtful Accounts, $1,000 credit; and Sales, $3,280,000. Corolla Sales changed the method of estimating uncollectible accounts to 4% of outstanding accounts receivable.

At December 31, 2013, the General Ledger showed unadjusted balances of: $460,000 in Accounts Receivable; $700 debit in Allowance for Doubtful Accounts; and $3,400,000 in Sales. Corolla prepared an aging analysis on December 31, 2013, that estimated total uncollectible accounts to be $29,200.

Check figure:
Dec. 31, 2012: Bad debt expense = $19,480

Required
Prepare the 2011, 2012, and 2013 year-end adjusting entries to estimate uncollectible accounts.

Analysis component:
On December 31, 2011, the unadjusted balance in Allowance for Doubtful Accounts was a debit of $14,400. What is the normal balance for the Allowance for Doubtful Accounts account? What would cause Allowance for Doubtful Accounts to have an unadjusted debit balance?

Problem 10-9A
Notes receivable
LO4

Vauxall Holdings showed the following information regarding its notes receivable:

Note	Date of Note	Principal	Interest Rate	Term	Maturity Date	Days of Accrued Interest at Dec. 31, 2011	Accrued Interest at Dec. 31, 2011*
1	Nov. 1/10	$240,000	7%	180 days			
2	Jan. 5/11	100,000	8%	90 days			
3	Nov. 20/11	90,000	10%	45 days			
4	Dec. 10/11	120,000	12%	30 days			

*Round calculations to the nearest whole cent.

Check figures:
d. Interest Revenue = $1,010.96
e. Cash = $91,109.59

Required
For each note:

a. Determine the maturity date.

b. Calculate the *days* of accrued interest, if any, at December 31, 2011 (Vauxall Holdings' year-end).

c. Calculate the *amount* of accrued interest, if any, at December 31, 2011.

For Note 3:

d. Prepare the entry to record the accrued interest at December 31, 2011.

e. Prepare the entry to record the collection on the maturity date. Assume that both interest and principal are collected at maturity.

Problem 10-10A
Accrued interest calculation and dishonouring note receivable
LO4

Following are transactions of The Purple Onion Company:

2010		
Dec.	16	Accepted a $19,200, 60-day, 9% note dated this day in granting Hal Krueger a time extension on his past-due account.
	31	Made an adjusting entry to record the accrued interest on the Krueger note.
	31	Closed the Interest Revenue account.
2011		
Feb.	14	Received Krueger's payment for the principal and interest on the note dated December 16.
Mar.	2	Accepted a $10,240, 10%, 90-day note dated this day in granting a time extension on the past-due account of ARC Company.
	17	Accepted a $3,200, 30-day, 9% note dated this day in granting Penny Bobek a time extension on her past-due account.
Apr.	16	Bobek dishonoured her note when presented for payment.

Required

Check figure:
b. May 31, 2011

a. Prepare journal entries to record The Purple Onion's transactions.

b. Determine the maturity date of the note dated March 2. Prepare the entry on the maturity date, assuming ARC Company honours the note.

Problem 10-11A
Short-term notes receivable
LO4

Seerden Servicing monitors its accounts receivable carefully. A review determined that a customer, John Daley, was unable to pay his $120,000 past-due account. Seerden accepted a 90-day promissory note dated April 15, 2011, bearing interest of 6% in exchange for Daley's account. Another customer, ABC Drilling, signed a 6%, six-month note dated May 1 in place of its $50,000 past-due accounts receivable. On May 31, Seerden's year-end, accrued interest was recorded on the notes receivable. John Daley honoured his note on the maturity date. ABC Drilling dishonoured its note on the maturity date. On November 15, Seerden Servicing wrote off ABC Drilling's account as it was determined to be uncollectible.

Required

Check figures:
d. July 14, 2011: Interest revenue = $867.94
e. November 1, 2011: Interest revenue = $1,250.00

Prepare Seerden Servicing's entries for each of the following dates:

a. April 15, 2011
b. May 1, 2011
c. May 31, 2011
d. Maturity date of John Daley's note
e. Maturity date of ABC Drilling's note
f. November 15, 2011

Analysis component:
Assuming a $4,000 debit balance in the Allowance for Doubtful Accounts on November 14, 2011, calculate the balance after posting the entry in (f) above. Comment on the adequacy of the Allowance for Doubtful Accounts.

*Problem 10-12A
Discounting notes receivable
LO5

Check figure:
Sept. 18: Interest expense = $50.00

Required
Prepare entries to record the following transactions of Wipe-Out Company:

Mar.	2	Accepted a $10,240, 10%, 90-day note dated this day in granting a time extension on the past-due account of JNC Company.
Apr.	21	Discounted, with recourse, the JNC Company note at BancFirst at a cost of $100.
June	2	Received notice from BancFirst that JNC Company defaulted on the note due May 31. Paid the bank the principal plus interest due on the note. *(Hint: Create an account receivable for the maturity value of the note.)*
July	16	Received payment from JNC Company for the maturity value of its dishonoured note plus interest for 45 days beyond maturity at 10%.
Sept.	3	Accepted a $4,160, 60-day, 10% note dated this day in granting Cecile Duval a time extension on her past-due account.
	18	Discounted, without recourse, the Duval note at BancFirst at a cost of $50.

Analysis component:
What reporting is necessary when a business discounts notes receivable with recourse and these notes have not reached maturity by the end of the fiscal period? Explain the reason for this requirement and what accounting principle is being satisfied.

An asterisk (*) identifies assignment material based on Appendix 10A or Appendix 10B.

*Problem 10-13A
Discounting notes receivable
LO5

Check figures:
Jan. 10, 2012: Cash = $15,119.88
Mar. 29, 2012: Cash = $4,513.59

Required
Prepare General Journal entries to record the following transactions of Leduc Company:

2011		
Dec.	11	Accepted a $15,000, 12%, 60-day note dated this day in granting Fred Calhoun a time extension on his past-due account.
	31	Made an adjusting entry to record the accrued interest on the Fred Calhoun note.
	31	Closed the Interest Revenue account.
2012		
Jan.	10	Discounted the Fred Calhoun note at the bank at 14%.
Feb.	10	The Fred Calhoun note was dishonoured. Paid the bank the maturity value of the note plus a $60 fee.
Mar.	5	Accepted a $4,500, 11%, 60-day note dated this day in granting a time extension on the past-due account of Donna Reed.
	29	Discounted the Donna Reed note at the bank at 15%.
May	7	The Donna Reed note had been received by the bank and paid by Donna Reed.
June	9	Accepted a $6,750, 60-day, 10% note dated this day in granting a time extension on the past-due account of Jack Miller.
Aug.	8	Received payment of the maturity value of the Jack Miller note.
	11	Accepted an $8,000, 60-day, 10% note dated this day in granting Roger Addison a time extension on his past-due account.
	31	Discounted the Roger Addison note at the bank at 13%.
Oct.	12	The Roger Addison note was dishonoured. Paid the bank the maturity value of the note plus a $60 fee.
Nov.	19	Received payment from Roger Addison of the maturity value of his dishonoured note, the fee, and interest on both for 40 days beyond maturity at 10%.
Dec.	23	Wrote off the Fred Calhoun account against Allowance for Doubtful Accounts.

Alternate Problems

Problem 10-1B
Estimating bad debt expense
LO2, 3

On December 31, 2011, Stilton Service Company's year-end, the unadjusted trial balance included the following items:

Account	Debit	Credit
Accounts receivable	$237,500	
Allowance for doubtful accounts		$ 2,600
Sales ($507,500 cash sales)		1,128,000

Check figures:
1b. Bad Debt Expense = $11,650
2. Accounts receivable (net) = $216,285

Required
1. Prepare the adjusting entry on the books of Stilton Service Company to estimate bad debts under each of the following independent assumptions:
   a. Bad debts are estimated to be 3% of credit sales.
   b. An analysis suggests that 6% of outstanding accounts receivable on December 31, 2011, will become uncollectible.
2. Show how Accounts Receivable and the Allowance for Doubtful Accounts would appear on the December 31, 2011, balance sheet given the facts in requirement 1(a).
3. Show how Accounts Receivable and the Allowance for Doubtful Accounts would appear on the December 31, 2011, balance sheet given the facts in requirement 1(b).

Analysis component:
Would you recommend to Stilton that it use the income statement or the balance sheet approach to estimate uncollectible accounts receivable? Explain why, identifying advantages and disadvantages for each approach.

An asterisk (*) identifies assignment material based on Appendix 10A or Appendix 10B.

Problem 10-2B

Aging accounts receivable

LO2, 3

On December 31, 2011, RCA Company's Allowance for Doubtful Accounts had an unadjusted debit balance of $8,200. The accountant for RCA has prepared a schedule of the December 31, 2011, accounts receivable by age and, on the basis of past experience, has estimated the percentage of the receivables in each age category that will become uncollectible. This information is summarized as follows:

December 31, 2011 Accounts Receivable	Age of Accounts Receivable	Expected Percentage Uncollectible
$592,800	Not due (under 30 days)	2.0%
355,600	1 to 30 days past due	4.0
116,000	31 to 60 days past due	8.5
15,200	61 to 90 days past due	39.0
7,600	Over 90 days past due	82.5

Required

1. Calculate the amount that should appear in the December 31, 2011, balance sheet as the Allowance for Doubtful Accounts.
2. Prepare the journal entry to record bad debt expense for 2011.

Check figure:
2. Bad Debt Expense = $56,338

Analysis component:
On July 31, 2012, RCA concluded that a customer's $4,690 receivable (created in 2011) was uncollectible and that the account should be written off. What effect will this action have on RCA's 2012 net income? Explain your answer.

Problem 10-3B

Accounts receivable transactions and bad debt adjustments

LO1, 2, 3

Wondra Supplies showed the following selected adjusted balances at its December 31, 2010, year-end:

Accounts Receivable	
Dec. 31/10 Balance 490,000	

Allowance for Doubtful Accounts	
	12,460 Dec. 31/10 Balance

During the year 2011, the following selected transactions occurred:

a. Sales totalled $1,725,000, of which 85% were credit sales (cost of sales $1,207,500).
b. Sales returns were $49,000, all regarding credit sales. The returned merchandise was scrapped.
c. An account for $29,000 was recovered.
d. Several accounts were written off, including one very large account; the total was $132,500.
e. Collected accounts receivable of $1,500,500 (excluding the recovery in (c) above). Sales discounts of $26,000 were taken.

Part A

Required

1. Journalize transactions (a) through (e). You may find it useful to post your entries to T-accounts for Accounts Receivable and Allowance for Doubtful Accounts.

Check figures:
2. Bad Debt Expense = $111,300
5. Bad Debt Expense = $102,010

Part B

Required

2. Prepare the December 31, 2011, adjusting entry to estimate bad debts, assuming uncollectible accounts are estimated to be 8% of net credit sales.
3. Show how accounts receivable will appear on the December 31, 2011, balance sheet.
4. What will bad debt expense be on the income statement for the year ended December 31, 2011?

Part C (independent of Part B)

Required

5. Prepare the December 31, 2011, adjusting entry to estimate bad debts, assuming uncollectible accounts are estimated to be 4% of outstanding receivables.
6. Show how accounts receivable will appear on the December 31, 2011, balance sheet.
7. What will bad debt expense be on the income statement for the year ended December 31, 2011?

Problem 10-4B

Recording accounts receivable transactions and bad debt adjustments

LO1, 2, 3

Selzer Products Co. began operations on January 1, 2011, and completed a number of transactions during 2011 and 2012 that involved credit sales, accounts receivable collections, and bad debts. Assume a perpetual inventory system. These transactions are summarized as follows:

2011

a. Sold merchandise on credit for $1,346,980, terms n/30 (COGS = $972,000).
b. Received cash of $874,500 in payment of outstanding accounts receivable.
c. Wrote off uncollectible accounts receivable in the amount of $16,480.
d. In adjusting the accounts on December 31, concluded that 1% of the outstanding accounts receivable would become uncollectible.

2012

e. Sold merchandise on credit for $1,854,620, terms n/30 (COGS = $1,432,000).
f. Received cash of $1,780,440 in payment of outstanding accounts receivable.
g. Wrote off uncollectible accounts receivable in the amount of $20,180.
h. In adjusting the accounts on December 31, concluded that 1% of the outstanding accounts receivable would become uncollectible.

Check figures:
d. Bad Debt Expense = $21,040
h. Bad Debt Expense = $20,720

Required
Prepare General Journal entries to record the 2011 and 2012 summarized transactions of Selzer Products Co., and the adjusting entries to record bad debt expense at the end of each year.

Problem 10-5B

Uncollectible accounts

LO2, 3

Littlerock Surveying showed the following partial unadjusted results at May 31, 2011, its month-end:

Account	Debit	Credit
Sales..		$840,000
Accounts receivable..............................	$280,000	
Allowance for doubtful accounts		6,400

Part 1

Required
a. Assuming Littlerock estimates bad debts to be 2.5% of sales, prepare the adjusting entry at May 31, 2011.
b. Show how accounts receivable would be shown on the May 31, 2011, balance sheet using your calculations in (a).

Part 2

Check figures:
b. Accounts receivable (net) = $252,600
d. Accounts receivable (net) = $271,920

Required
c. Instead of (a) above, prepare the adjusting entry at May 31, 2011, assuming that Littlerock estimates bad debts to be based on the following aging analysis.

May 31, 2011 Accounts Receivable	Age of Accounts Receivable	Expected Percentage Uncollectible
$196,000	Not due (under 30 days)	1%
78,000	1 to 30 days past due	4%
6,000	Over 60 days past due	50%

d. Show how accounts receivable would be shown on the May 31, 2011, balance sheet using your calculations in (c).

Problem 10-6B
Bad debt expense
LO3

The following is information regarding adjusted account balances for Leonardo Painters at September 30, 2011:

Accounts Receivable	
160,000	

Allowance for Doubtful Accounts	
	2,400

Part 1
During October, Leonardo Painters recorded $1,150,000 in total revenues, all on credit. Collections during October were $1,012,500. Included in the $1,012,500 collections was the recovery of $32,500 from a customer account written off in September. Total receivables identified as being uncollectible and written off during October were $12,500. Leonardo Painters estimates bad debts to be 0.5% of net credit revenues.

Required
Prepare the adjusting entry to record estimated bad debts for October.

Check figures:
1. Bad Debt Expense = $5,750
2. Bad Debt Expense = $3,775

Part 2
During November, revenues totalled $987,500, all on credit. Collections during the month were $932,500. An account for $14,000 was identified as being uncollectible and written off on November 28. It was recommended to Leonardo Painters that the method of estimating bad debts be changed to the balance sheet approach. As a result, it was estimated that 5% of the November 30 accounts receivable balance was uncollectible.

Required
Prepare the adjusting entry to record estimated bad debts for November.

Problem 10-7B
Estimating bad debts
LO3

eXcel

The following information is available regarding the accounts receivable of ClubLink Holdings at August 31, 2011:

	Month of Credit Sale*				
Customer	**April**	**May**	**June**	**July**	**Aug.**
A. Leslie	$ -0-	$ 24,000	$ -0-	$ 58,000	$ -0-
T. Meston	52,000	-0-	-0-	-0-	-0-
P. Obrian	-0-	-0-	-0-	104,000	42,000
L. Timms	-0-	126,000	52,000	-0-	28,000
W. Victor	-0-	-0-	166,000	122,000	64,000

*All services are performed on terms of n/60.

ClubLink estimates uncollectibility of accounts receivable using the following rates:

Not yet due	1 to 29 days past due	30 to 59 days past due	60 to 89 days past due	90 to 119 days past due	Over 119 days past due
1%	2%	5%	20%	35%	50%

Required

a. Complete a Schedule of Accounts Receivable by Age at August 31, 2011, similar to Exhibit 10.14.

b. The Allowance for Doubtful Accounts showed an unadjusted balance on August 31, 2011, of $12,600 (debit). Record the adjusting journal entry at August 31, 2011, to estimate uncollectible accounts.

Check figure:
a. Total estimated uncollectible accounts = $26,440

Problem 10-8B
Uncollectible accounts
LO3

At year-end, March 31, 2011, Waterton Contractors showed unadjusted balances of: $243,000 in Accounts Receivable; $1,150 debit in Allowance for Doubtful Accounts; and $4,586,000 in Sales. Uncollectible accounts are estimated to be 0.4% of sales.

Unadjusted balances at March 31, 2012, were: Accounts Receivable, $364,500; Allowance for Doubtful Accounts, $1,000 debit; and Sales, $3,971,000. Waterton changed the method of estimating uncollectible accounts to 7% of outstanding accounts receivable.

At March 31, 2013, the General Ledger showed unadjusted balances of: $473,000 in Accounts Receivable; $6,750 credit in Allowance for Doubtful Accounts; and $3,750,000 in Sales. Waterton prepared an aging analysis on March 31, 2013, that estimated total uncollectible accounts to be $29,500.

Check figure:
Mar. 31, 2012: Bad debt expense = $26,515

Required

Prepare the 2011, 2012, and 2013 year-end adjusting entries to estimate uncollectible accounts.

Analysis component:

List the adjusted balances in Allowance for Doubtful Accounts for each of March 31, 2011, 2012, and 2013. Beside each, show the respective Accounts Receivable and Sales balances. Comment on the change in Allowance for Doubtful Accounts and Accounts Receivable relative to the change in Sales.

Problem 10-9B
Notes receivable
LO4

Shostak showed the following details regarding its notes receivable:

Note	Date of Note	Principal	Interest Rate	Term	Maturity Date	Days of Accrued Interest at Dec. 31, 2011	Accrued Interest at Dec. 31, 2011
1	Sept. 20/10	$490,000	7%	120 days			
2	June 01/11	240,000	9%	45 days			
3	Nov. 23/11	164,000	9%	90 days			
4	Dec. 18/11	120,000	10%	30 days			

*Round calculations to the nearest whole cent.

Check figures:
d. Interest Revenue = $427.40
e. Interest Revenue = $558.90

Required

For each note:

a. Determine the maturity date.
b. Calculate the *days* of accrued interest, if any, at December 31, 2011, Shostak's year-end.
c. Calculate the *amount* of accrued interest, if any, at December 31, 2011.

For Note 4:

d. Prepare the entry to record the accrued interest at December 31, 2011.
e. Prepare the entry to record the collection on the maturity date. Assume that interest and principal are collected at maturity.

Problem 10-10B
Accrued interest calculation and dishonouring note receivable
LO4

Following are transactions of Rural Company:

2011		
Nov.	16	Accepted a $7,400, 90-day, 12% note dated this day in granting Bess Parker a time extension on her past-due account.
Dec.	31	Made an adjusting entry to record the accrued interest on the Parker note.
	31	Closed the Interest Revenue account.
2012		
Feb.	14	Received Parker's payment for the principal and interest on the note dated November 16.
	28	Accepted a $24,800, 9%, 30-day note dated this day in granting a time extension on the past-due account of The Simms Co.
Mar.	1	Accepted a $10,200, 60-day, 10% note dated this day in granting Bedford Holmes a time extension on his past-due account.
	30	The Simms Co. dishonoured its note when presented for payment.

Required

a. Prepare journal entries to record Rural's transactions.

b. Determine the maturity date of the note dated March 1. Prepare the entry at maturity assuming Bedford Holmes honours the note.

Check figure:
b. Interest Revenue = $167.67

Problem 10-11B
Short-term notes receivable
LO4

Asiatic Electroplating analyzes its accounts receivable weekly. On November 17, 2011, Asiatic accepted a 7%, 90-day, $90,000 note receivable from RoadWorks in exchange for its past-due account. On December 1, Ellen Huskey's $16,000 overdue account was converted to a four-month, 7% note receivable. On January 31, 2012, Asiatic's year-end, accrued interest was recorded on the notes. RoadWorks honoured its note on the maturity date but Ellen Huskey's note was dishonoured. Huskey's account was determined to be uncollectible and written off on July 15, 2012.

Required

Prepare Asiatic Electroplating's entries for each of the following dates:

a. November 17, 2011
b. December 1, 2011
c. January 31, 2012
d. Maturity date of RoadWorks' note
e. Maturity date of Huskey's note
f. July 15, 2012

Check figures:
d. February 15, 2012: Interest revenue = $258.90
e. April 1, 2012: Interest revenue = $186.66

Analysis component:

Assuming a $100,000 credit balance in the Allowance for Doubtful Accounts on July 14, 2012, calculate the balance after posting the entry in (f) above. Assuming no additional write-offs were made prior to year-end, comment on the adequacy of the Allowance for Doubtful Accounts.

*Problem 10-12B
Discounting notes receivable
LO5

Required

Prepare entries to record the following transactions of Ibscon Company:

Mar.	1	Accepted a $10,200, 60-day, 10% note dated this day in granting Bolton Company a time extension on its past-due account.
	23	Discounted, without recourse, the Bolton note at Security Bank at a cost of $100.
June	21	Accepted an $18,600, 90-day, 12% note dated this day in granting Vince Soto a time extension on his past-due account.
July	5	Discounted, with recourse, the Soto note at Security Bank at a cost of $400.
Sept.	25	Received notice from Security Bank that the Soto note had been paid.

Check figure:
July 5: Interest expense = $400

Analysis component:

What reporting is necessary when a business discounts notes receivable with recourse and these notes have not reached maturity by the end of the fiscal period? Explain the reason for this requirement and what accounting principle is being satisfied.

An asterisk (*) identifies assignment material based on Appendix 10A or Appendix 10B.

***Problem 10-13B**
Discounting notes receivable
LO5

Check figures:
Mar. 28: Cash = $2,075.38
July 24: Cash = $1,308.86

Required
Prepare General Journal entries to record the following transactions of Billington Company.

2011		
Jan	10	Accepted a $3,000, 60-day, 12% note dated this day in granting a time extension on the past-due account of David Huerta.
Mar.	14	David Huerta dishonoured his note when presented for payment.
	19	Accepted a $2,100, 90-day, 10% note dated this day in granting a time extension on the past-due account of Rose Jones.
	28	Discounted the Rose Jones note at the bank at 16%.
Jun.	20	Received word from the bank that the Rose Jones note had been paid.
	27	Accepted $700 in cash and a $1,300, 60-day, 12% note dated this day in granting a time extension on the past-due account of Jake Thomas.
July	24	Discounted the Jake Thomas note at the bank at 14%.
Aug.	29	The Jake Thomas note was dishonoured. Paid the bank the maturity of the note plus a $20 fee.
Sept.	4	Accepted a $1,500, 60-day, 11% note dated this day in granting a time extension on the past-due account of Ginnie Bauer.
Oct.	13	Discounted the Ginnie Bauer note at the bank at 14%.
Nov.	6	The Ginnie Bauer note was dishonoured. Paid the bank the maturity value of the note plus a $20 fee.
Dec.	6	Received payment from Ginnie Bauer of the maturity value of her dishonoured note, the fee, and interest at 11% on both for 30 days beyond maturity.
	28	Decided the accounts of David Huerta and Jake Thomas were uncollectible and wrote them off against Allowance for Doubtful Accounts.

Analytical and Review Problems

A & R Problem 10-1

Reproduced below from Farthington Supply's accounting records is the Accounts Receivable Subledger along with selected General Ledger accounts.

General Ledger

Accounts Receivable				Allowance for Doubtful Accounts			
Dec. 31/10 Balance	159,000					350	Dec. 31/10 Balance
		7,000	Jan. 4/11				
Credit sales in 2011	????	????	Collections in 2011	July 15/11	14,000		
		14,000	July 15/11			????	Dec. 31/11
Dec. 31/11 Balance	????					????	Dec. 31/11 Balance

An asterisk (*) identifies assignment material based on Appendix 10A or Appendix 10B.

Accounts Receivable Subledger

JenStar Company

Dec. 31/10 Balance	48,000		
		48,000	Jan. 20/11
Nov. 15/11	????		
Dec. 31/11 Balance	104,000		

Indigo Developments

Dec. 31/10 Balance	-0-		
Mar. 1/11	17,000	17,000	Mar. 20/11
Nov. 28/11	39,000		
Dec. 2/11	4,000		
Dec. 31/11 Balance	43,000		

Lomas Industries

Dec. 31/10 Balance	????		
		7,000	Jan. 4/11
		????	Jan. 7/11
Apr. 21/11	52,000	52,000	May 5/11
Dec. 7/11	21,000		
Dec. 31/11 Balance	21,000		

PDQ Servicing

Dec. 31/10 Balance	14,000		
		14,000	July 15/11
Dec. 31/11 Balance	-0-		

During the year 2011, there were no recoveries of accounts previously written off. Only one account, that of PDQ Servicing, was identified as being uncollectible on July 15, 2011. On January 4, 2011, Farthington issued a $7,000 credit memo to Lomas Industries regarding damaged goods returned.

Check figure:
g. Bad Debt Expense = $17,010

Required

Analyzing the accounts, determine the following amounts:

a. The December 31, 2010, balance in Lomas Industries' account.
b. The January 7, 2011, collection from Lomas Industries.
c. The December 31, 2011, balance in the Accounts Receivable controlling account.
d. The November 15, 2011, transaction in JenStar Company's account.
e. Collections during 2011.
f. Credit sales during 2011.
g. Adjusting entry on December 31, 2011, to estimate uncollectible accounts based on a rate of 2% of outstanding receivables.
h. The December 31, 2011, balance in the Allowance for Doubtful Accounts.
i. Show how accounts receivable should appear on the balance sheet on December 31, 2011.

Analysis component:

Why does Farthington maintain an Accounts Receivable Subledger? What other subledgers might the company be using and why?

A & R Problem 10-2

Sullivan Equipment Sales showed the following.

	2011	
Jan.	15	Sold $25,000 of merchandise for $29,000 to JanCo; terms 3/5, n/15.
	16	Wrote off Fedun's account in the amount of $15,000.
	20	Collected the amount owing from the January 15 sale.
Mar.	1	Accepted a $12,000, 60-day, 7% note dated this day in granting Parker Holdings a time extension on its past-due account.
Apr.	15	Sold merchandise costing $62,000 for $71,000 to customers who used their Visa credit cards. Visa charges a 1% fee and deposits the cash electronically into the retailer's account immediately at the time of sale.
	?	Parker Holdings honoured the note dated March 1.
Nov.	1	Accepted a $24,000, three-month, 6% note dated this day in granting Grant Company a time extension on its past-due account.
Dec.	31	Sullivan's year-end. Interest was accrued on outstanding notes receivable.
	31	Bad debts are based on an aging analysis that estimated $9,700 of accounts receivable are uncollectible. Allowance for Doubtful Accounts showed an unadjusted credit balance of $1,600 on this date.
	2012	
	?	Grant Company dishonoured its note dated November 1, 2011.
Mar.	5	Recovered $1,500 from Derek Holston that was previously written off.
	14	Wrote off the Grant Company account.

Check figures:
a. April 30, 2011 and Feb. 1, 2012
b. May 7, 2011 credit card expense = $710

Required

a. Determine the maturity dates of the March 1 and November 1 notes.
b. Prepare entries as appropriate for each date.

Analysis component:
Sullivan's receivable turnovers at December 31, 2011 and 2012, were 7 and 7.5, respectively. Explain what this ratio measures and whether the change in the ratio for Sullivan was favourable or unfavourable.

Ethics Challenge

EC 10-1

Randy Meyer is the chief executive officer of a medium-sized company in Regina, Saskatchewan. Several years ago, Randy persuaded the board of directors of his company to base a percent of his compensation on the net income the company earns each year. Each December, Randy estimates year-end financial figures in anticipation of the bonus he will receive. If the bonus is not as high as he would like, he offers several accounting recommendations to his controller for year-end adjustments. One of his favourite recommendations is for the controller to reduce the estimate of doubtful accounts. Randy has used this technique with success for several years.

1. What effect does lowering the estimate for doubtful accounts have on the income statement and balance sheet of Randy's company?
2. Do you think Randy's recommendations to adjust the allowance for doubtful accounts is within his right as CEO or do you think this action is an ethics violation? Justify your response.
3. What type of internal control might be useful for this company in overseeing the CEO's recommendations for accounting changes?

Focus on Financial Statements

FFS 10-1

Clara Dover, the owner of Dover Plumbing Sales and Service, showed the following adjusted account balances for the year ended March 31, 2011 (listed alphabetically):

Account	Account Balance*
Accounts payable	$ 7,800
Accounts receivable	28,000
Accumulated depreciation, tools	11,000
Accumulated depreciation, truck	14,000
Allowance for doubtful accounts	4,200
Bad debt expense	3,900
Cash	36,000
Cash over/short expense	20**
Clara Dover, capital	248,070
Clara Dover, withdrawals	72,000
Cost of goods sold	118,000
Depreciation expense, tools	2,000
Depreciation expense, truck	5,000
Insurance expense	7,300
Interest expense	250
Merchandise inventory	26,000
Notes payable, due August 31, 2014	17,000
Notes payable, due February 1, 2012	6,000
Notes receivable, due December 1, 2013	14,000
Petty cash	400
Plumbing fees earned	114,000
Prepaid insurance	3,800
Prepaid rent	6,500
Rent expense	23,000
Salaries expense	61,000
Salaries payable	1,100
Sales	124,000
Tools	82,000
Truck	67,000
Unearned plumbing fees	9,000

*Assume all account balances are normal unless otherwise stated.
**Debit balance.

Required
Prepare a classified balance sheet based on the information provided.

Check figures:
Total current assets = $96,500;
Total assets = $234,500;
Total current liabilities = $23,900

Analysis component:
Dover Plumbing had total *Plumbing fees earned* for the year ended March 31, 2010, of $86,000 and net accounts receivable at March 31, 2010, of $21,200. Calculate and compare days' sales uncollected for March 31, 2010, and March 31, 2011. Round calculations to two decimal places.

FFS 10-2

Refer to Danier Leather's balance sheet and income statement on pages I-4 and I-3, respectively, in Appendix I at the end of the textbook.

Required
Answer the following questions.

1. The balance sheet shows accounts receivable of $755,000 at June 28, 2008 and $724,000 at June 30, 2007. What type of asset is accounts receivable? Explain how accounts receivable arise.
2. Refer to the income statement. Does the change in receivables appear to correspond to the change in total sales? Explain your answer.

Critical Thinking Mini Case

You are the finance officer at a bank where the owner of Delta Designs is applying for a $600,000 loan. In reviewing the account information for the year ended June 30, 2011, you are concerned by the following selected adjusted account information:

Account	Debit	Credit
Accounts receivable[1]	$472,000	
Allowance for doubtful accounts		$ 7,080
Sales[2]		3,980,000

[1] 85% of this balance represents receivables that are not yet due. Delta Designs offers credit terms of 2/10, n/30.

[2] All sales are on credit and sales occur evenly throughout the year.

Required

Using the elements of critical thinking described on the inside front cover, respond.

CHAPTER 11

Payroll Liabilities

learning objectives

- **LO1** Identify the taxes and other items frequently withheld from employees' wages.
- **LO2** Make the calculations necessary to prepare a payroll register and prepare the entries to record and pay payroll liabilities.
- **LO3** Calculate the payroll costs levied on employers and prepare the entries to record the accrual and payment of these amounts.
- **LO4** Calculate and record employee fringe benefit costs.

Guilty

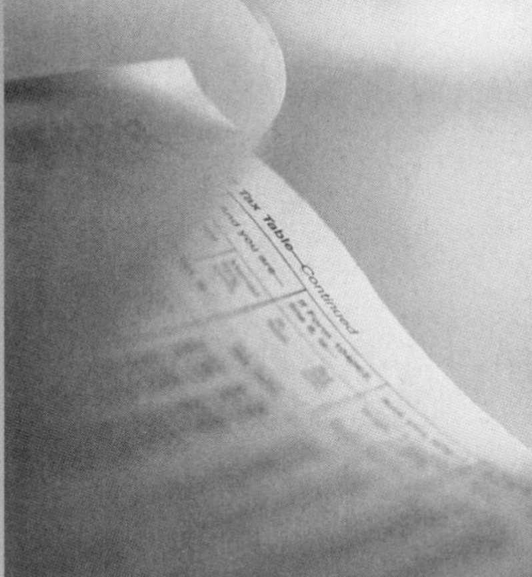

Edmundston—The Canada Revenue Agency (CRA) announced that a dentist was fined $3,000 in Edmundston provincial court after pleading guilty to three charges of failing to remit over $8,000 in monies deducted and withheld from wages and salaries paid to employees.

Montreal—A director on the board of two companies was fined $541,870 and sentenced to a 12-month prison term following a CRA investigation that showed payroll deductions from the salaries of employees were not remitted to the Receiver General for Canada.

In each of the above cases, unpaid deductions had to be paid in addition to the fines. Failure to do so would result in imprisonment. The CRA takes non-payment of source deductions very seriously, as the amounts deducted from employees are deemed to be held in trust until remitted to CRA on their behalf. Canadians have to be confident that the tax system is fair, and know that CRA will prosecute those individuals who cheat.

CRITICAL THINKING CHALLENGE

If payroll liabilities are not recorded, what is the effect on the financial statements?

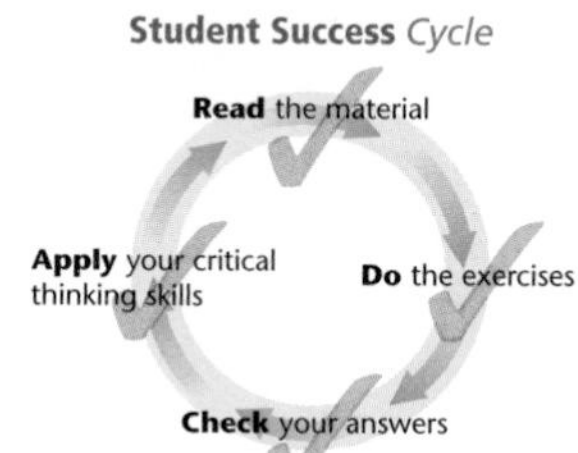

chapter preview

Wages or salaries generally amount to one of the largest expenses incurred by a business. Accounting for employees' wages and salaries is one task that is shared by almost all business entities.

Payroll accounting:

- Records cash payments to employees.
- Provides valuable information regarding labour costs.
- Accounts for amounts withheld from employees' pay.
- Accounts for employee (fringe) benefits and payroll costs paid by the employer.
- Provides the means to comply with governmental regulations on employee compensation.

As you study this chapter, you will learn the general processes that all businesses follow to account for these items.

Items Withheld From Employees' Wages

LO1 Identify the taxes and other items frequently withheld from employees' wages.

An understanding of payroll accounting and the design and use of payroll records requires some knowledge of the laws and programs that affect payrolls. Many of these require **payroll deductions**, amounts withheld from the wages of employees, and are discussed in the first portion of this chapter.

DID YOU KNOW?

The Canadian Payroll Association (CPA) represents more than 10,000 members of the professional payroll community in Canada, the United States, and abroad. With over 18 million Canadian employees paid through CPA member companies, its mission is to provide payroll leadership through advocacy and education. The two qualifications granted through the country's only nationally recognized Payroll Management Certificate Program are Payroll Compliance Practitioner (PCP) and Certified Payroll Manager (CPM).

Source: www.payroll.ca.

Withholding Employees' Income Tax

Employers are required to calculate, collect, and remit to the Receiver General for Canada the income taxes of their employees. Historically, when the first federal income tax law became effective in 1917, it applied to only a few individuals having high earnings. It was not until the Second World War that income taxes were levied on almost all wage earners. At that time, Parliament recognized that many individual wage earners could not be expected to save the money needed to pay their income taxes once each year, so Parliament began a system of pay-as-you-go withholding of taxes at their source each payday. This pay-as-you-go withholding of employee income taxes requires an employer to act as a tax collecting agent of the federal government. Failure to cooperate results in severe consequences, as illustrated in the opening article.

The amount of income taxes to be withheld from an employee's wages is determined by his or her wages and the amount of **personal tax credits**. Based on rates in effect January 1, 2009, each individual is entitled, in 2009, to some or all of the following annual amounts that are subject to tax credits (as applicable):

1. Basic Personal Amount	$10,100
2. Married or Equivalent.................. (with maximum earnings stipulated)	10,100

The total of each taxpayer's personal tax credits is deducted from income to determine the level of income tax deductions from the individual's gross pay. For example, based on rates effective January 1, 2009, a Saskatchewan resident with a gross weekly salary of $400 and personal tax credits of $10,100 (2009 net claim code 1 on the *TD1* form) would have $24.50 of total income taxes withheld. Another individual with the same gross salary but with personal tax credits of $16,016 (claim code 5) would have $4.60 withheld.

Employers withhold income tax owed by each employee every payday based on an employee's completed Personal Tax Credit Return, Form **TD1**. The taxpayer must file a revised Form TD1 each time the exemptions change during a year. The TD1 form is shown in Extend Your Knowledge 11-1 online.

EXTEND YOUR KNOWLEDGE

In determining the amounts of income taxes to be withheld from the wages of employees, employers normally use payroll deductions tables provided by the Canada Revenue Agency (CRA) P. 7. The to-be-withheld amounts include both federal and provincial income taxes except for the province of Quebec, which levies and collects its own income tax and its own pension plan contributions. Provincial income tax rates vary from province to province. Therefore, for consistency, all examples and problems making use of tax tables in this chapter will be based on Saskatchewan's tables. Calculation of deductions is simplified for computer users if they request "tables on diskette" from CRA or download them directly from www.cra-arc.gc.ca/payroll. Alternatively, the Payroll Online Deductions Calculator (PODC) can be used at www.cra-arc.gc.ca/esrvc-srvce/tx/bsnss/pdoc-eng.html. Employers are required to remit the withheld taxes to the Receiver General for Canada each month.

Canada (or Quebec) Pension Plan (CPP or QPP)

Every working person between the ages of 18 and 70 with few exceptions must make contributions in required amounts to the **Canada Pension Plan** (CPP) or Quebec Pension Plan (QPP).

Effective January 1, 2009, contributions are based on earnings as follows:

Canada Pension Plan Contributions

Effective Jan. 1, 2009	Employee Contributions	Employer Contributions
Rate	4.95%*	4.95%*
Maximum......................................	$2,118.60	$2,118.60

*4.95% of earnings greater than $3,500 and less than $42,800.

Employers are responsible for making the proper deductions from their employees' earnings. They remit these deductions each month, together with their own contributions, to the Receiver General for Canada.

Self-employed individuals pay the combined rate for employees and employers, or 9.9% on annual earnings between $3,500 and the exempt ceiling of $42,800.

Employment Insurance (EI)

To assist the unemployed, the federal government began an employee/employer-financed unemployment insurance plan. Under the revised 1996 *Employment Insurance Act*, compulsory **Employment Insurance** (EI) coverage was extended to all Canadian workers who are not self-employed. Over 13 million employees, including teachers, hospital workers, and top-level executives, are covered by the insurance plan.

The Employment Insurance fund from which benefits are paid is jointly financed by employees and their employers. At January 1, 2009, employers are required to deduct from their employees' wages 1.73% of insured earnings, to add a contribution of 1.4 times the amount deducted from employees' wages, and to remit both amounts to the Receiver General for Canada. The system is summarized as follows:

Employment Insurance Contributions		
Effective Jan. 1, 2009	Employee Contributions	Employer Contributions
Rate	1.73%	1.4 times employee rate
Maximum	$731.79	$1,024.51

Note: Maximum insurable earnings for 2009 are $42,300.

Insured earnings, in most instances, refer to gross earnings. An employee may receive taxable benefits or allowances that would be included in gross earnings but would not be considered insurable earnings. However, in this text, gross earnings will be insurable earnings.

The *Employment Insurance Act* also requires that an employer complete a "record of employment" because of termination of employment, illness, injury, or pregnancy and keep a record for each employee that shows among other things wages subject to employment insurance and taxes withheld.

Use of Withholding Tables

Employers may use **wage bracket withholding tables** in determining Canada Pension Plan and Employment Insurance to be withheld from employees' gross earnings. These tables are also available in electronic form for computer applications on disk from CRA or at www.cra-arc.gc.ca/tx/bsnss/tod-tsd/menu-eng.html.

EXTEND YOUR KNOWLEDGE

Determining the amount of withholdings from an employee's gross wages is quite easy when electronic tables are used. Extend Your Knowledge 11-2 online shows the screens used to determine withholding amounts.

The T-4 Form

Employers are required to report wages and deductions both to each employee and to the local office of CRA. On or before the last day of February, the employer must give each employee a T-4 statement that tells the employee:

- Total wages for the preceding year.
- Taxable benefits received from the employer.
- Income taxes withheld.
- Deductions for registered pension plan.
- Canada Pension Plan contributions.
- Employment Insurance deductions.

On or before the last day of February the employer must forward to the district taxation office copies of the employee's T-4 statements plus a T-4 that summarizes the information contained on the employee's T-4 statements. The T-4 form is shown in Exhibit 11.1.

Exhibit 11.1

2009 T-4 Form

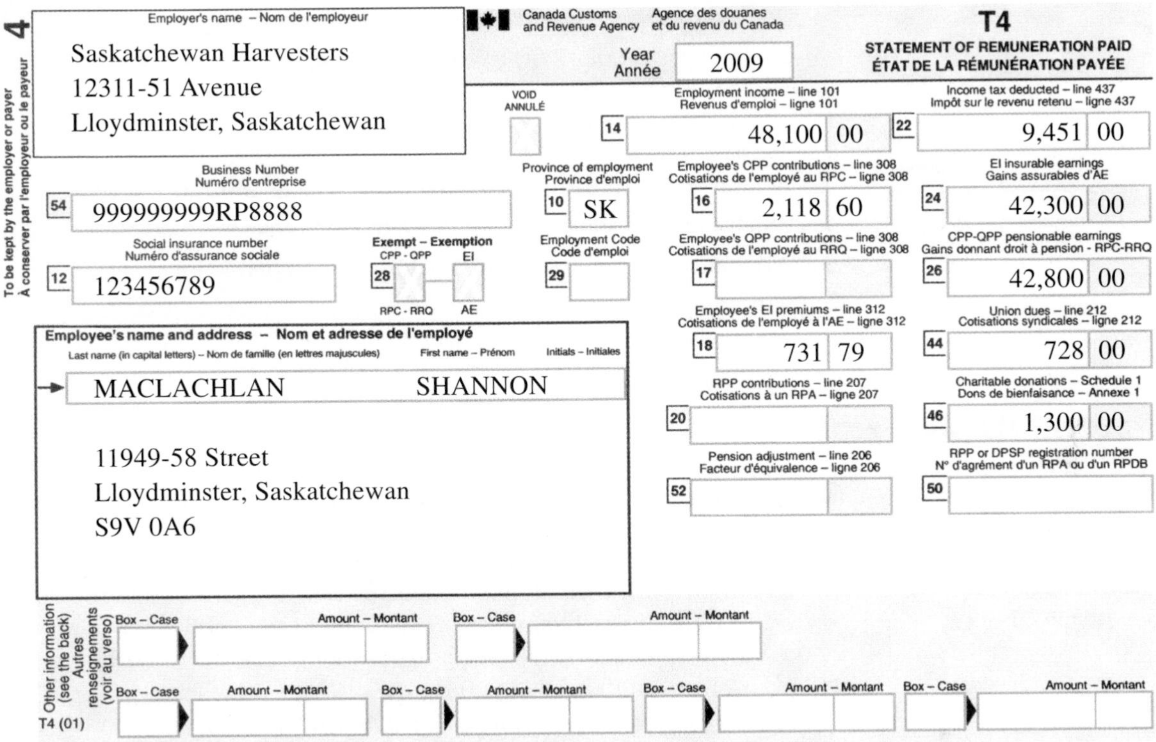

Canada Customs and Revenue Agency — Agence des douanes et du revenu du Canada

T4

STATEMENT OF REMUNERATION PAID
ÉTAT DE LA RÉMUNÉRATION PAYÉE

Year / Année: 2009

Employer's name – Nom de l'employeur:
Saskatchewan Harvesters
12311-51 Avenue
Lloydminster, Saskatchewan

To be kept by the employer or payer
À conserver par l'employeur ou le payeur

VOID / ANNULÉ

Box	Description	Amount
14	Employment income – line 101 / Revenus d'emploi – ligne 101	48,100 00
22	Income tax deducted – line 437 / Impôt sur le revenu retenu – ligne 437	9,451 00
54	Business Number / Numéro d'entreprise	999999999RP8888
10	Province of employment / Province d'emploi	SK
16	Employee's CPP contributions – line 308 / Cotisations de l'employé au RPC – ligne 308	2,118 60
24	EI insurable earnings / Gains assurables d'AE	42,300 00
12	Social insurance number / Numéro d'assurance sociale	123456789
28	Exempt – Exemption: CPP-QPP / EI (RPC-RRQ / AE)	
29	Employment Code / Code d'emploi	
17	Employee's QPP contributions – line 308 / Cotisations de l'employé au RRQ – ligne 308	
26	CPP-QPP pensionable earnings / Gains donnant droit à pension - RPC-RRQ	42,800 00
18	Employee's EI premiums – line 312 / Cotisations de l'employé à l'AE – ligne 312	731 79
44	Union dues – line 212 / Cotisations syndicales – ligne 212	728 00
20	RPP contributions – line 207 / Cotisations à un RPA – ligne 207	
46	Charitable donations – Schedule 1 / Dons de bienfaisance – Annexe 1	1,300 00
52	Pension adjustment – line 206 / Facteur d'équivalence – ligne 206	
50	RPP or DPSP registration number / N° d'agrément d'un RPA ou d'un RPDB	

Employee's name and address – Nom et adresse de l'employé

Last name (in capital letters) – Nom de famille (en lettres majuscules) / First name – Prénom / Initials – Initiales

MACLACHLAN SHANNON

11949-58 Street
Lloydminster, Saskatchewan
S9V 0A6

Other information (see the back) / Autres renseignements (voir au verso)

Box – Case | Amount – Montant | Box – Case | Amount – Montant

Box – Case | Amount – Montant | Box – Case | Amount – Montant | Box – Case | Amount – Montant | Box – Case | Amount – Montant

T4 (01)

Wages, Hours, and Union Contracts

All provinces have laws establishing maximum hours of work and minimum pay rates. And, while the details vary with each province, generally employers are required to pay an employee for hours worked in excess of 40 in any one week at the employee's regular pay rate plus an overtime premium of at least one-half of his or her regular rate. In addition, employers commonly operate under contracts with their employees' union that provide even better terms.

In addition to specifying working hours and wage rates, union contracts often provide that the employer shall deduct dues from the wages of each employee and remit the amounts deducted to the union.

Other Payroll Deductions

Employees may individually authorize additional deductions such as:

1. Deductions to accumulate funds for the purchase of Canada Savings Bonds.
2. Deductions to pay health, accident, hospital, or life insurance premiums.
3. Deductions to repay loans from the employer or the employees' credit union.
4. Deductions to pay for merchandise purchased from the company.
5. Deductions for donations to charitable organizations such as the United Way.

1. What is the purpose of the federal Employment Insurance scheme?
2. When must T-4 statements be given to employees?
3. What are other typical nonmandatory payroll deductions?

Do Quick Study question: QS 11-1

The Payroll Register

LO2 Make the calculations necessary to prepare a payroll register and prepare the entries to record and pay payroll liabilities.

Each pay period the total hours worked are summarized in a payroll register, an example of which is shown in Exhibit 11.2. The illustrated register is for a weekly pay period and shows the payroll data for each employee on a separate line.

In Exhibit 11.2, the columns under the heading Daily Time show the hours worked each day by each employee. The total of each employee's hours is entered in the column headed Total Hours. If hours include overtime hours, these are entered in the column headed O.T. Hours.

The Regular Pay Rate column shows the hourly pay rate of each employee. Total hours worked multiplied by the regular pay rate equals regular pay. Overtime hours multiplied by the overtime premium rate (50% in this case) equals overtime premium pay. And regular pay plus overtime premium pay is the **employee's gross pay**.

The amounts withheld from each employee's gross pay are recorded in the Deductions columns of the payroll register. For example, you determine the income tax deductions by matching the gross pay of each employee to the tax deduction tables and then enter the results in the tax deduction column. Income tax deductions are based on the gross pay less the amounts deducted for EI and CPP (or QPP). The tax tables allow for these adjustments and separate books are available for each province. Exhibit 11.2 assumes that income tax deductions are based on the tables provided in Exhibit 11.3, assuming the employees are resident in Saskatchewan.

For example, you can use the tables in Exhibit 11.3 to determine the appropriate CPP, EI, and income tax deductions for John Auer's $400 pay. In the CPP table, under the *Pay* column, find $400. The CPP deduction according to the table is $16.47 for the pay range $399.93–$400.12. Using the EI table, go to the *Insurable Earnings* column and find $400. The table shows that the EI deduction for the range $399.72–$400.28 is $6.92. Finally, using each of the federal and provincial tax deductions tables, go to the Pay column and find $400. Now follow the numbers across to the claim code 1 column (assume a claim code of 1 unless otherwise specified). The tables show a total income tax to be deducted of $37.95 (federal tax of $24.50 + provincial tax of $13.45). You can use the tables to determine the CPP, EI, and income tax deductions for the remaining employees.

Exhibit 11.2

Payroll Register

Payroll Register Week Ended March 10, 2009

	Employees	Clock Card No.	Daily Time M	T	W	T	F	S	S	Total Hours	O.T. Hours	Earnings: Reg. Pay Rate	Regular Pay	O.T. Premium Pay	Gross Pay
1	Auer, John	118	8	8	8	8	8			40		10.00	400.00		400.00
2	Cheung, Joen	109	0	8	8	8	8	8		40		12.00	480.00		480.00
3	Daljit, Moe	121	8	8	8	8	8	8	4	52	12	15.00	780.00	90.00	870.00
4	Lee, Shannon	104	8	8		8	8	8	4	44	4	14.00	616.00	28.00	644.00
5	Prasad, Sunil	108		8	8	8	8	4	8	44	4	15.00	660.00	30.00	690.00
6	Rupert, Allan	105	8	8	8	8	8			40		12.00	480.00		480.00
	Totals												3,416.00	148.00	3,564.00

	Gross Pay	Deductions: EI Premium	Income Taxes	Hospital Insurance	CPP	Total Deductions	Payment: Net Pay	Cheque Number	Distribution: Sales Salaries	Office Salaries
1	400.00	6.92	37.95	18.00	16.47	79.34	320.66	754	400.00	
2	480.00	8.30	57.35	18.00	20.43	104.08	375.92	755	480.00	
3	870.00	15.05	162.45	24.00	39.73	241.23	628.77	756		870.00
4	644.00	11.14	97.20	18.00	28.55	154.89	489.11	757		644.00
5	690.00	11.94	107.75	24.00	30.82	174.51	515.49	758	690.00	
6	480.00	8.30	57.35	18.00	20.43	104.08	375.92	759	480.00	
	3,564.00	61.65	520.05	120.00	156.43	858.13	2,705.87		2,050.00	1,514.00

Exhibit 11.3

Excerpts From CPP, EI, and Income Tax Tables Effective January 1, 2009.

Canada Pension Plan Contributions / **Cotisations au Régime de pensions du Canada**

Weekly (52 pay periods a year) / **Hebdomadaire (52 périodes de paie par année)**

Pay Rémunération From - De	To - À	CPP RPC	Pay Rémunération From - De	To - À	CPP RPC	Pay Rémunération From - De	To - À	CPP RPC	Pay Rémunération From - De	To - À	CPP RPC
359.93	360.12	14.49	479.93	480.12	20.43	643.57	643.76	28.53	867.20	867.40	39.60
360.13	360.33	14.50	480.13	480.33	20.44	643.77	643.96	28.54	867.41	867.60	39.61
360.34	360.53	14.51	480.34	480.53	20.45	643.97	644.16	28.55	867.61	867.80	39.62
360.54	360.73	14.52	480.54	480.73	20.46	644.17	644.37	28.56	867.81	868.00	39.63
360.74	360.93	14.53	480.74	480.93	20.47	644.38	644.57	28.57	868.01	868.20	39.64
360.94	361.13	14.54	480.94	481.13	20.48	644.58	644.77	28.58	868.21	868.41	39.65
361.14	361.34	14.55	481.14	481.34	20.49	644.78	644.97	28.59	868.42	868.61	39.66
361.35	361.54	14.56	481.35	481.54	20.50	644.98	645.17	28.60	868.62	868.81	39.67
361.55	361.74	14.57	481.55	481.74	20.51	645.18	645.38	28.61	868.82	869.01	39.68
399.93	400.12	16.47	481.75	481.94	20.52	689.02	689.21	30.78	869.02	869.21	39.69
400.13	400.33	16.48	481.95	482.14	20.53	689.22	689.42	30.79	869.22	869.42	39.70
400.34	400.53	16.49	482.15	482.35	20.54	689.43	689.62	30.80	869.43	869.62	39.71
400.54	400.73	16.50	482.36	482.55	20.55	689.63	689.82	30.81	869.63	869.82	39.72
400.74	400.93	16.51	482.56	482.75	20.56	689.83	690.02	30.82	869.83	870.02	39.73
400.94	401.13	16.52	482.76	482.95	20.57	690.03	690.22	30.83	870.03	870.22	39.74
401.14	401.34	16.53	482.96	483.15	20.58	690.23	690.43	30.84	870.23	870.43	39.75
401.35	401.54	16.54	483.16	483.36	20.59	690.44	690.63	30.85	870.44	870.63	39.76
401.55	401.74	16.55	483.37	483.56	20.60	690.64	690.83	30.86	870.64	870.83	39.77

Employee's maximum CPP contribution for the year 2009 is $2,118.60

La cotisation maximale de l'employé au RPC pour l'année 2009 est de 2 118,60 $

Employment Insurance Premiums / **Cotisations à l'assurance-emploi**

Insurable Earnings Rémunération assurable From - De	To - À	EI premium Cotisation d'AE	Insurable Earnings Rémunération assurable From - De	To - À	EI premium Cotisation d'AE	Insurable Earnings Rémunération assurable From - De	To - À	EI premium Cotisation d'AE	Insurable Earnings Rémunération assurable From - De	To - À	EI premium Cotisation d'AE
359.25	359.82	6.22	478.91	479.47	8.29	640.18	640.75	11.08	863.88	864.45	14.95
359.83	360.40	6.23	479.48	480.05	8.30	640.76	641.32	11.09	864.46	865.02	14.96
360.41	360.98	6.24	480.06	480.63	8.31	641.33	641.90	11.10	865.03	865.60	14.97
360.99	361.56	6.25	480.64	481.21	8.32	641.91	642.48	11.11	865.61	866.18	14.98
361.57	362.13	6.26	481.22	481.79	8.33	642.49	643.06	11.12	866.19	866.76	14.99
362.14	362.71	6.27	481.80	482.36	8.34	643.07	643.64	11.13	866.77	867.34	15.00
362.72	363.29	6.28	482.37	482.94	8.35	643.65	644.21	11.14	867.35	867.91	15.01
363.30	363.87	6.29	482.95	483.52	8.36	644.22	644.79	11.15	867.92	868.49	15.02
363.88	364.45	6.30	483.53	484.10	8.37	644.80	645.37	11.16	868.50	869.07	15.03
395.67	396.24	6.85	484.11	484.68	8.38	687.00	687.57	11.89	869.08	869.65	15.04
396.25	396.82	6.86	484.69	485.26	8.39	687.58	688.15	11.90	869.66	870.23	15.05
396.83	397.39	6.87	485.27	485.83	8.40	688.16	688.72	11.91	870.24	870.80	15.06
397.40	397.97	6.88	485.84	486.41	8.41	688.73	689.30	11.92	870.81	871.38	15.07
397.98	398.55	6.89	486.42	486.99	8.42	689.31	689.88	11.93	871.39	871.96	15.08
398.56	399.13	6.90	487.00	487.57	8.43	689.89	690.46	11.94	871.97	872.54	15.09
399.14	399.71	6.91	487.58	488.15	8.44	690.47	691.04	11.95	872.55	873.12	15.10
399.72	400.28	6.92	488.16	488.72	8.45	691.05	691.61	11.96	873.13	873.69	15.11
400.29	400.86	6.93	488.73	489.30	8.46	691.62	692.19	11.97	873.70	874.27	15.12

Yearly maximum insurable earnings are $42,300
Yearly maximum employee premiums are $731.79
The premium rate for 2009 is 1.73%

Le maximum annuel de la rémunération assurable est de 42 300 $
La cotisation maximale annuelle de l'employé est de 731,79 $
Le taux de cotisation pour 2009 est de 1,73 %

Exhibit 11.3

Excerpts From CPP, EI, and Income Tax Tables Effective January 1, 2009. (continued)

Saskatchewan provincial tax deductions
Effective January 1, 2009
Weekly (52 pay periods a year)
Also look up the tax deductions in the federal table

Retenues d'impôt provincial de la Saskatchewan
En vigueur le 1er janvier 2009
Hebdomadaire (52 périodes de paie par année)
Cherchez aussi les retenues d'impôt dans la table fédérale

Pay / Rémunération		Provincial claim codes/Codes de demande provinciaux										
From / De	Less than / Moins de	0	1	2	3	4	5	6	7	8	9	10
		Deduct from each pay / Retenez sur chaque paie										
399	403	41.55	13.45	11.50	7.65	3.75						
403	407	41.95	13.85	11.95	8.05	4.15	.30					
407	411	42.35	14.30	12.35	8.45	4.60	.70					
411	415	42.75	14.70	12.75	8.85	5.00	1.10					
415	419	43.15	15.10	13.15	9.30	5.40	1.50					
479	483	49.75	21.65	19.75	15.85	11.95	8.10	4.20	.35			
483	487	50.15	22.10	20.15	16.25	12.40	8.50	4.65	.75			
487	491	50.55	22.50	20.55	16.65	12.80	8.90	5.05	1.15			
491	495	50.95	22.90	20.95	17.10	13.20	9.35	5.45	1.55			
495	499	51.40	23.30	21.40	17.50	13.60	9.75	5.85	2.00			
639	647	66.35	38.30	36.35	32.50	28.60	24.70	20.85	16.95	13.10	9.20	5.35
647	655	67.20	39.10	37.20	33.30	29.40	25.55	21.65	17.80	13.90	10.05	6.15
655	663	68.00	39.95	38.00	34.15	30.25	26.35	22.50	18.60	14.75	10.85	6.95
663	671	68.85	40.75	38.85	34.95	31.05	27.20	23.30	19.45	15.55	11.65	7.80
671	679	69.65	41.60	39.65	35.75	31.90	28.00	24.15	20.25	16.35	12.50	8.60
679	687	70.50	42.40	40.45	36.60	32.70	28.85	24.95	21.05	17.20	13.30	9.45
687	695	71.30	43.25	41.30	37.40	33.55	29.65	25.75	21.90	18.00	14.15	10.25
695	703	72.10	44.05	42.10	38.25	34.35	30.45	26.60	22.70	18.85	14.95	11.05
703	711	72.95	44.85	42.95	39.05	35.15	31.30	27.40	23.55	19.65	15.80	11.90
711	719	73.75	45.70	43.75	39.85	36.00	32.10	28.25	24.35	20.50	16.60	12.70
839	847	88.40	60.35	58.40	54.50	50.65	46.75	42.85	39.00	35.10	31.25	27.35
847	855	89.40	61.30	59.40	55.50	51.60	47.75	43.85	40.00	36.10	32.25	28.35
855	863	90.40	62.30	60.40	56.50	52.60	48.75	44.85	41.00	37.10	33.20	29.35
863	871	91.40	63.30	61.40	57.50	53.60	49.75	45.85	42.00	38.10	34.20	30.35
871	879	92.40	64.30	62.35	58.50	54.60	50.75	46.85	42.95	39.10	35.20	31.35

Federal tax deductions
Effective January 1, 2009
Weekly (52 pay periods a year)
Also look up the tax deductions in the provincial table

Retenues d'impôt fédéral
En vigueur le 1er janvier 2009
Hebdomadaire (52 périodes de paie par année)
Cherchez aussi les retenues d'impôt dans la table provinciale

Pay / Rémunération		Federal claim codes/Codes de demande fédéraux										
From / De	Less than / Moins de	0	1	2	3	4	5	6	7	8	9	10
		Deduct from each pay / Retenez sur chaque paie										
395	399	53.05	23.95	21.10	15.40	9.70	4.00					
399	403	53.60	24.50	21.65	15.95	10.25	4.60					
403	407	54.20	25.05	22.20	16.50	10.80	5.15					
407	411	54.75	25.60	22.75	17.05	11.40	5.70					
411	415	55.30	26.15	23.30	17.65	11.95	6.25	.55				
475	479	64.25	35.10	32.30	26.60	20.90	15.20	9.55	3.85			
479	483	64.80	35.70	32.85	27.15	21.45	15.75	10.10	4.40			
483	487	65.40	36.25	33.40	27.70	22.00	16.35	10.65	4.95			
487	491	65.95	36.80	33.95	28.25	22.60	16.90	11.20	5.50			
491	495	66.50	37.35	34.50	28.85	23.15	17.45	11.75	6.10			
635	643	86.95	57.80	54.95	49.25	43.60	37.90	32.20	26.50	20.85	15.15	9.45
643	651	88.05	58.90	56.10	50.40	44.70	39.00	33.30	27.65	21.95	16.25	10.55
651	659	89.20	60.05	57.20	51.50	45.80	40.15	34.45	28.75	23.05	17.40	11.70
659	667	90.30	61.15	58.30	52.65	46.95	41.25	35.55	29.85	24.20	18.50	12.80
667	675	91.40	62.30	59.45	53.75	48.05	42.35	36.70	31.00	25.30	19.60	13.95
675	683	92.55	63.40	60.55	54.85	49.20	43.50	37.80	32.10	26.45	20.75	15.05
683	691	93.65	64.50	61.70	56.00	50.30	44.60	38.90	33.25	27.55	21.85	16.15
691	699	94.75	65.65	62.80	57.10	51.40	45.75	40.05	34.35	28.65	23.00	17.30
699	707	95.90	66.75	63.90	58.25	52.55	46.85	41.15	35.45	29.80	24.10	18.40
707	715	97.00	67.90	65.05	59.35	53.65	47.95	42.30	36.60	30.90	25.20	19.55
835	843	121.45	92.30	89.50	83.80	78.10	72.40	66.75	61.05	55.35	49.65	43.95
843	851	123.15	94.00	91.20	85.50	79.80	74.10	68.45	62.75	57.05	51.35	45.65
851	859	124.85	95.75	92.90	87.20	81.50	75.80	70.15	64.45	58.75	53.05	47.35
859	867	126.55	97.45	94.60	88.90	83.20	77.50	71.85	66.15	60.45	54.75	49.05
867	875	128.25	99.15	96.30	90.60	84.90	79.20	73.55	67.85	62.15	56.45	50.75

The column headed Hospital Insurance in Exhibit 11.2 shows the amounts withheld to pay for hospital insurance for the employees and their families. The total withheld from all employees is a current liability of the employer until paid to the insurance company. Likewise, the total withheld for employees' union dues is a current liability until paid to the union.

Additional columns may be added to the payroll register for any other deductions that occur sufficiently often to warrant special columns. For example, a company that regularly deducts amounts from its employees' pay for Canada Savings Bonds may add a special column for this deduction.

An employee's gross pay less total deductions is the **employee's net pay** and is entered in the Net Pay column. The total of this column is the amount the employees are to be paid. The numbers of the cheques used to pay the employees are entered in the column headed Cheque Number.

The Distribution columns are used to classify the various salaries in terms of different kinds of expense. Here you enter each employee's gross salary in the proper column according to the type of work performed. The column totals then indicate the amounts to be debited to the salary expense accounts.

Recording the Payroll

The entry to record the payroll shown in Exhibit 11.2 is:

March 10	Sales Salaries Expense	2,050.00	
	Office Salaries Expense	1,514.00	
	EI Payable		61.65
	Employees' Income Taxes Payable		520.05
	Employees' Hospital Insurance Payable		120.00
	CPP Payable		156.43
	Salaries Payable		2,705.87
	To record the March 10 payroll.		

The debits of the entry were taken from the payroll register's distribution column totals. They charge the employees' gross earnings to the proper salary expense accounts. The credits to EI Payable, Employees' Income Taxes Payable, Employees' Hospital Insurance Payable, and CPP Payable record these amounts as current liabilities. The credit to Salaries Payable (also called Payroll Payable, Wages Payable, or Accrued Salaries Payable, etc.) records as a liability the net amount to be paid to the employees.

4. What constitutes the employee's gross pay?
5. What is the employee's net pay?

Do Quick Study questions: QS 11-2, QS 11-3, QS 11-4, QS 11-5, QS 11-6

Paying the Employees

Almost every business pays its employees by cheque or through electronic funds transfer (EFT). Employers give each employee an earnings statement each payday showing the hours worked, gross pay, deductions, and net pay, as shown in Exhibit 11.4.

Exhibit 11.4

A Payroll Cheque

John Auer	40		10.00	400.00		400.00	6.92	37.95	16.47	18.00	79.34	320.66
Employee	Total Hours	O.T. Hours	Reg. Pay Rate	Regular Pay	O.T. Prem. Pay	Gross Pay	EI Premium	Income Taxes	CP Plan	Hosp. Ins.	Total Deductions	Net Pay

STATEMENT OF EARNINGS AND DEDUCTIONS FOR EMPLOYEE'S RECORDS—DETACH BEFORE CASHING CHEQUE

GRASSLAND INDUSTRIES
Loon Lake, Saskatchewan

No. 1517

PAY TO THE
ORDER OF *John Auer* Date *March 10, 2009* $ *320.66*

Three hundred twenty dollars and sixty-six cents - - - - - - - - - - - - -

Lloydminster Credit Union
Lloydminster, Saskatchewan

GRASSLAND INDUSTRIES
Jane R. Morris

Employee's Individual Earnings Record

An **employee's individual earnings record**, as shown in Exhibit 11.5, provides for each employee, in one record, a full year's summary of the employee's working time, gross earnings, deductions, and net pay. In addition, it accumulates information that:

1. Serves as a basis for the employer's payroll tax returns.
2. Indicates when an employee's earnings have reached the maximum amounts for CPP and EI deductions.
3. Supplies data for the T4 slip, which must be given to the employee at the end of the year.

The payroll information on an employee's individual earnings record is posted from the payroll register. Note the last column of the record. It shows an employee's earnings to date and is used to determine when the earnings reach maximum amounts and are no longer subject to the various deductions such as CPP and EI.

Exhibit 11.5

Employee's 2009 Individual Earnings Record

Employee's Name John Auer SIN No. 123-456-789 Employee No. 114

Home Address Box 68, Loon Lake Notify in Case of Emergency Margaret Auer Phone No. 964-9834

Employed May 15, 1999 Date of Termination ______ Reason ______

Date of Birth June 6, 1972 Date Becomes 65 June 6, 2037 Male (X) Female ( ) Married ( ) Single (X) Number of Exemptions 0 Pay Rate $10.00

Occupation Clerk Place Warehouse

Date		Time Lost		Time Worked												
Per. Ends	Paid	Hrs.	Reason	Total	O.T. Hours	Reg. Pay	O.T. Pay	Gross Pay	EI Prem	Income Taxes	Hosp. Ins.	CPP	Total Deductions	Net Pay	Cheque No.	Cumulative Earnings
9-Jan	9-Jan			40		400.00		400.00	6.92	37.95	18.00	16.47	79.34	320.66	673	400.00
16-Jan	16-Jan			40		400.00		400.00	6.92	37.95	18.00	16.47	79.34	320.66	701	800.00
23-Jan	23-Jan			40		400.00		400.00	6.92	37.95	18.00	16.47	79.34	320.66	743	1,200.00
30-Jan	30-Jan	4	Sick	36		360.00		360.00	6.23	28.15	18.00	14.49	66.87	293.13	795	1,560.00
6-Feb	6-Feb			40		400.00		400.00	6.92	37.95	18.00	16.47	79.34	320.66	839	1,960.00
13-Feb	13-Feb			40		400.00		400.00	6.92	37.95	18.00	16.47	79.34	320.66	854	2,360.00
29-May	29-May			40		400.00		400.00	6.92	37.95	18.00	16.47	79.34	320.66	1228	8,360.00

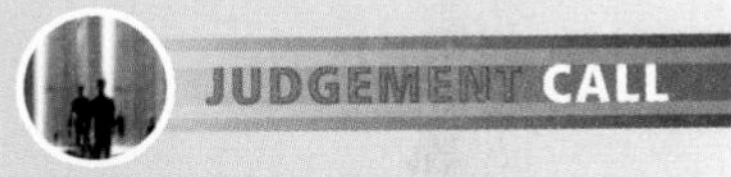

Lawn Worker

You take a summer job working for a family friend who runs a small lawn mowing service. When the time arrives for your first paycheque, the owner slaps you on the back, gives you full payment in cash, winks, and adds: "No need to pay those high taxes, eh?" What are your responsibilities in this case? Do you take any action?

Answer—p. 565

6. What is the purpose of the employee's individual earnings record?

Do Quick Study questions: QS 11-7, QS 11-8

mid-chapter demonstration problem

On January 27, the end of its fourth weekly pay period in 2009, Saskat Company's payroll record showed that its one office employee and two sales employees had earned $481 (claim code 2), $645 (claim code 3), and $868 (claim code 4), respectively. Each employee has $40 of hospital insurance premiums withheld plus $15 of union dues.

Required

a. Prepare a schedule similar to the register in Exhibit 11.2 to summarize deductions by employee and in total. Use the tables in Exhibit 11.3 to determine the appropriate CPP, EI, and income tax to be withheld.

b. Give the journal entry to record the payroll on January 27.

Analysis component:

What effect does the entry in part (b) have on the balance sheet?

solution

a.

		Deductions						Payment		Distribution	
	Gross Pay	EI Premium	Income Taxes	Hospital Insurance	CPP	Union Dues	Total Deductions	Net Pay	Cheque Number	Office Salaries	Sales Salaries
2	481.00	8.32	52.60	40.00	20.48	15.00	136.40	344.60	754	481.00	
4	645.00	11.16	82.90	40.00	28.60	15.00	177.66	467.34	758		645.00
4	868.00	15.02	138.50	40.00	39.63	15.00	248.15	619.85	759		868.00
	1,994.00	34.50	274.00	120.00	88.71	45.00	562.21	1,431.79		481.00	1,513.00

b.

January 27	Office Salaries Expense	481.00	
	Sales Salaries Expense	1,513.00	
	EI Payable		34.50
	Employees' Income Taxes Payable		274.00
	Employees' Hospital Insurance Payable		120.00
	CPP Payable		88.71
	Employees' Union Dues Payable		45.00
	Salaries Payable		1,431.79
	To record payroll deductions for pay period ending January 27.		

Analysis component:

The entry in part (b) will cause liabilities, specifically current liabilities, to increase and equity to decrease.

Payroll Deductions Required of the Employer

LO3 Calculate the payroll costs levied on employers and prepare the entries to record the accrual and payment of these amounts.

Under the previous discussion of the Canada (or Quebec) Pension Plan (CPP or QPP), it was pointed out that pension deductions are required in like amounts on both employed workers and their employers. A covered employer is required by law to deduct from the employees' pay the amounts of their CPP (or QPP), but in addition, the employer must pay an amount equal to the sum of the employees' CPP (or QPP). Commonly, the amount deducted by the employer is recorded at the same time as the payroll to which it relates is recorded. Also, since both the employees' and employer's shares are reported on the same form and are paid in one amount, the liability for both is normally recorded in the same liability account, the CPP (or QPP) Payable account.

An employer is also required to pay Employment Insurance (EI) that is 1.4 times the sum of the employees' EI deductions. Most employers record both of these payroll deductions with a journal entry that is made at the time of recording the payroll to which they relate. For example, the entry to record the employer's amounts on the payroll in Exhibit 11.2 is:

March 10	EI Expense (1.4 × $61.65)	86.31	
	CPP (or QPP) Expense	156.43	
	EI Payable		86.31
	CPP (or QPP) Payable		156.43
	To record the employer's payroll taxes.		

The debit in the entry records as an expense the payroll taxes levied on the employer, and the credits record the liabilities for the taxes.

Paying the Payroll Deductions

Income tax, EI, and CPP (or QPP) amounts withheld each payday from the employees' pay plus the employer's portion of EI and CPP (or QPP) are current liabilities until paid to the Receiver General for Canada. The normal method of payment is to pay the amounts due at any chartered bank or remit them directly to the Receiver General for Canada. Payment of these amounts is usually required to be made before the 15th of the month following the month that deductions were made from the earnings of the employees. Large employers are required to remit on the 10th and 25th of each month.

For simplicity, we assume the payment of the March 10 amounts recorded above is made the following day. Recall, however, that the employer must remit the amounts withheld from the employee as determined in Exhibit 11.2 *plus* the employer's portion recorded above. The following T-accounts summarize all of these amounts:

EI Payable	
	61.65*
	86.31**
	147.96

Employees' Income Taxes Payable	
	520.05*

Hospital Insurance Payable	
	120.00*

CPP (or QPP) Payable	
	156.43*
	156.43**
	312.86

*Employees' portion per Exhibit 11.2 **Employer's portion

The entry to record remittance to the Receiver General for Canada is then:

March 11	EI Payable	147.96	
	Employees' Income Taxes Payable	520.05	
	CPP (or QPP) Payable	312.86	
	Cash		980.87
	To record the remittance of payroll liabilities to the Receiver General for Canada.		

The entry to record remittance to the hospital insurance plan authority is then:

March 11	Employment Hospital Insurance Payable	120.00	
	Cash		120.00
	To record the remittance of employees' hospital insurance premiums.		

Notice that the payment of payroll liabilities is recorded in the same manner as payment of any other liabilities.

Accruing Payroll Deductions on Wages

Mandatory payroll deductions are levied *only on wages actually paid.* Accrued wages are not subject to payroll deductions until they are paid. However, to satisfy the matching principle, both accrued wages and the related accrued deductions should be recorded at the end of an accounting period. In reality, because the amounts of such deductions vary little from one accounting period to the next and often are small in amount, many employers apply the materiality principle and do not accrue payroll deductions.

7. When are the payments for employee deductions due to the Receiver General for Canada?

Do Quick Study questions: QS 11-9, QS 11-10

Employee (Fringe) Benefit Costs

LO4 Calculate and record employee fringe benefit costs.

Many companies pay for a variety of benefits called **employee fringe benefits** in addition to the wages earned by employees and the related amounts paid by the employer. For example, an employer may pay for part (or all) of the employees' medical insurance, life insurance, and disability insurance. Another typical employee benefit involves employer contributions to a retirement income plan. Workers' compensation and vacation pay are required to be paid by employers according to the legislation in each province.

Workers' Compensation

Legislation is in effect in all provinces for payments to employees for an injury or disability arising out of or in the course of their employment. Under the provincial workers' compensation acts, employers are required to insure their employees against injury or disability that may arise as a result of employment. Premiums are normally based on (1) accident experience of the industrial classification to which each business is assigned and (2) the total payroll.

Procedures for payment are as follows:

1. At the beginning of each year, every covered employer is required to submit to the Workers' Compensation Board[1] an estimate of the expected payroll for the coming year.
2. Provisional premiums are then established by the board relating estimated requirements for disability payments to estimated payroll. Provisional premium notices are then sent to all employers.
3. Provisional premiums are normally payable in three to six installments during the year.
4. At the end of each year, actual payrolls are submitted to the board, and final assessments are made based on actual payrolls and actual payments. Premiums are normally between 1% and 3% of gross payroll and are borne by the employer.

Employer Contributions to Employee Insurance and Retirement Plans

The entries to record employee benefits costs depend on the nature of the benefit. Some employee retirement plans are quite complicated and involve accounting procedures that are too complex for discussion in this introductory course. In other cases, however, the employer simply makes periodic cash contributions to a retirement fund for each employee and records the amounts contributed as expense. Other employee benefits that require periodic cash payments by the employer include employer payments of insurance premiums for employees.

In the case of employee benefits that simply require the employer to make periodic cash payments, the entries to record the employer's obligations are similar to those used for payroll deductions.[2] For example, assume that an employer with five employees has agreed to pay medical insurance premiums of $40 per month for each employee. The employer will also contribute 10% of each employee's salary to a retirement program. If each employee earns $2,500 per month, the entry to record these employee benefits for the month of March is:

March 31	Benefits Expense...	1,450	
	Employees' Medical Insurance Payable		200
	Employees' Retirement Program Payable		1,250
	To record employee benefits; ($2,500 × 5) × 10% = $1,250.		

[1] In Ontario, the Workers' Compensation Board is called the Workplace Safety and Insurance Board (WSIB). In BC, it is called WorkSafeBC.

[2] Some payments of employee benefits must be added to the gross salary of the employee for the purpose of calculating income tax, CPP, and EI payroll deductions. However, in this chapter and in the problems at the end of the chapter, the possible effect of employee benefit costs on payroll taxes is ignored to avoid undue complexity in the introductory course.

Vacation Pay

Employers are required to allow their employees paid vacation time (at a minimum rate of 4% of gross earnings) as a benefit of employment. For example, many employees receive two weeks' vacation in return for working 50 weeks each year. The effect of a two-week vacation is to increase the employer's payroll expenses by 4% (2/50 = 0.04). After five years of service, most employees are entitled to a three-week vacation (i.e., 3/49 = 6.12%). However, new employees often do not begin to accrue vacation time until after they have worked for a period of time, perhaps as much as a year. The employment contract may say that no vacation is granted until the employee works one year, but if the first year is completed, the employee receives the full two weeks. Contracts between the employer and employee may allow for vacation pay in excess of the 4% minimum.

To account for vacation pay, an employer should estimate and record the additional expense during the weeks the employees are working and earning the vacation time. For example, assume that a company with a weekly payroll of $20,000 grants two weeks' vacation after one year's employment. The entry to record the estimated vacation pay is:

Date	Benefits Expense	800	
	Estimated Vacation Pay Liability		800
	To record estimated vacation pay; $20,000 × 0.04 = $800.		

As employees take their vacations and receive their vacation pay, the entries to record the vacation payroll take the following general form:

Date	Estimated Vacation Pay Liability	XXX	
	EI and CPP (or QPP) Payable		XXX
	Employees' Income Taxes Payable		XXX
	Other Withholding Liability Accounts Such as Employees' Hospital Insurance Payable		XXX
	Salaries Payable		XXX
	To record payroll.		

Mandatory payroll deductions and employee benefits costs are often a major category of expense incurred by a company. They may amount to well over 25% of the salaries earned by employees.

8. How is the cost of Workers' Compensation determined?

Do Quick Study question: QS 11-11

CRITICAL THINKING CHALLENGE

Refer to the Critical Thinking Challenge questions at the beginning of the chapter on page 549. Compare your answers to those suggested on Connect at www.mcgrawhillconnect.ca.

IFRS HIGHLIGHTS

IFRS have not caused changes, at the introductory level, to concepts covered in this chapter.

Summary

LO1 | Identify the taxes and other items frequently withheld from employees' wages. Amounts withheld from employees' wages include federal income taxes, Canada (or Quebec) Pension Plan (CPP or QPP), and Employment Insurance (EI). Payroll costs levied on employers include EI and CPP (or QPP).

An employee's gross pay may be the employee's specified wage rate multiplied by the total hours worked plus an overtime premium rate multiplied by the number of overtime hours worked. Alternatively, it may be the given periodic salary of the employee. Taxes withheld and other deductions for items such as union dues, insurance premiums, and charitable contributions are subtracted from gross pay to determine the net pay.

LO2 | Make the calculations necessary to prepare a payroll register and prepare the entries to record and pay payroll liabilities. A payroll register is used to summarize all employees' hours worked, regular and overtime pay, payroll deductions, net pay, and distribution of gross pay to expense accounts during each pay period. It provides the necessary information for journal entries to record the accrued payroll and to pay the employees.

LO3 | Calculate the payroll costs levied on employers and prepare the entries to record the accrual and payment of these amounts. When a payroll is accrued at the end of each pay period, payroll deductions and levies should also be accrued with debits and credits to the appropriate expense and liability accounts.

LO4 | Calculate and record employee fringe benefit costs. Fringe benefit costs that involve simple cash payments by the employer should be accrued with an entry similar to the one used to accrue payroll levies. Legislated employee benefits related to Workers' Compensation and vacation pay are paid for by the employer.

guidance answer to JUDGEMENT CALL

Lawn Worker

You need to be concerned about being an accomplice to unlawful payroll activities. Not paying federal and provincial taxes on wages earned is unlawful and unethical. Such payments won't provide CPP and EI contributions. The best course of action is to request payment by cheque. If this fails to change the owner's payment practices, you must consider quitting this job.

guidance answers to CHECKPOINT

Read Apply Do Check

1. Employment Insurance is designed to alleviate hardships caused by interruptions in earnings through unemployment.
2. On or before the last day in February.
3. Deductions for Canada Savings Bonds, health or life insurance premiums, loan repayments, and donations to charitable organizations.
4. Regular pay plus overtime pay.
5. Gross pay less all the deductions.
6. An employee's individual earnings record serves as a basis for the employer's tax returns, indicates when the maximum CPP (or QPP) and EI deductions have been reached, and supplies the data for the employees' T-4 slips.
7. Normally by the 15th of the following month; large employers must remit on the 10th and 25th of each month.
8. Premiums are based on the accident experience in the specific industry and on the size of the employer's payroll.

demonstration problem

Presented below are various items of information about three part-time employees of the Saskatchewan Consulting Company for the week ending March 27, 2009.

	Billings	Dephir	Singe
Wage rate (per hour)	$ 75.00	$ 60.00	$ 18.00
Overtime premium (when >40 hours)	50%	50%	50%
Annual vacation	2.5 weeks	2.5 weeks	2.5 weeks
Cumulative wages as of March 27, 2009:	$28,500.00	$52,600.00	$10,800.00
For the week (pay period) ended March 27, 2009:			
Hours worked	8	22	48
Medical insurance:			
Employer's contribution	$ 25.00	$ 25.00	$ 25.00
Withheld from employee	18.00	18.00	18.00
Union dues withheld	50.00	70.00	50.00
Income tax withheld	86.40	321.05	185.60
Employment Insurance withheld	10.38	—	16.19
Canada Pension withheld	26.37	—	43.00
Payroll deduction rates:			
Employment Insurance	1.73% to an annual maximum of $731.79		
Canada Pension Plan	4.95% less annual exemption of $3,500; maximum per year is $2,118.60		

Required

In solving the following requirements, round all amounts to the nearest whole penny. Prepare schedules that determine, for each employee and for all employees combined, the following information:

1. Wages earned for the week, total overtime pay (if any), and gross wages.
2. Vacation pay accrued for the week.
3. Costs imposed on the employer.
4. Employees' net pay for the week.
5. Employer's total payroll-related cost (wages, mandatory deductions, and fringe benefits).

Present journal entries to record the following:

6. Payroll expense.
7. Payroll deductions and employees' benefits expense.
8. Remittance to the Receiver General for Canada on April 15.

Analysis component:

What percentage of the total payroll-related cost to the employer represents deductions and fringe benefits versus gross pay? Round your answers to two decimal places.

Planning the Solution

- Calculate the gross pay for each employee.
- Calculate the amounts deducted for all employees and their net pay.
- Calculate the employer's share of payroll deductions.
- Prepare the necessary journal entries.
- Address the analysis component.

solution

1. The gross wages (including overtime) for the week:

	Billings	Dephir	Singe	Total
Regular wage rate	$ 75.00	$ 60.00	$ 18.00	
Regular hours	× 8	× 22	× 48	
Regular pay	$600.00	$1,320.00	$864.00	$2,784.00
Overtime premium	$ 37.50	$ 30.00	$ 9.00	
Overtime hours	-0-	× -0-	× 8	
Total overtime pay	$ -0-	$ -0-	$ 72.00	$ 72.00
Gross wages	$600.00	$1,320.00	$936.00	$2,856.00

2. The vacation pay accrued for the week:

	Billings	Dephir	Singe	Total
Annual vacation	2.5 weeks	2.5 weeks	2.5 weeks	
Weeks worked in year	49.5 weeks	49.5 weeks	49.5 weeks	
Vacation pay as a percentage of regular pay	5.05%	5.05%	5.05%	
Regular pay this week	× $600.00	× $1,320.00	× $936.00	
Vacation pay this week	$ 30.30	$ 66.66	$ 47.27	$144.23

The information in the following table is needed for part 3:

			Earnings Subject to	
Employees	Earnings Through March 27	Earnings This Week	CPP	Employment Insurance
Billings	$28,500.00	$ 600.00	$ 532.69[3]	$ 600.00
Dephir[1]	52,600.00	1,320.00	—	—
Singe[2]	10,800.00	936.00	868.69[3]	936.00
Totals		$2,856.00	$1,402.00	$1,536.00

[1]Dephir's earnings have exceeded the CPP maximum of $42,800 and EI maximum of $42,300 and the maximum deductions of $2,118.60 (CPP) and $731.79 (EI). Therefore, neither CPP nor EI is deducted.
[2]EI deduction calculations from the diskette (TOD provided by CRA upon request) ignore the maximum weekly earnings of $750. Deductions would cease when the yearly maximum deduction of $731.79 was reached.
[3]Recall that the first $3,500 of income is exempt from CPP. This represents $67.31/week (= $3,500/52 weeks).

3. The costs imposed on the employer.

	Billings	Dephir	Singe	Total
CPP (1.0)	$26.37	—	$43.00	$ 69.37
Employment Insurance (1.4)	14.53	—	22.67	37.20
Totals	$40.90	—	$65.67	$106.57

4. The net amount paid to the employees:

	Billings	Dephir	Singe	Total
Regular pay	$600.00	$1,320.00	$864.00	$2,784.00
Overtime pay	-0-	-0-	72.00	72.00
Gross pay	$600.00	$1,320.00	$936.00	$2,856.00
Withholdings:				
Income tax withholding	$ 86.40	$ 321.05	$185.60	$ 593.05
CPP withholding	26.37	—	43.00	69.37
EI withholding	10.38	—	16.19	26.57
Medical insurance	18.00	18.00	18.00	54.00
Union dues	50.00	70.00	50.00	170.00
Total withholdings	$191.15	$ 409.05	$312.79	$ 912.99
Net pay to employees	$408.85	$ 910.95	$623.21	$1,943.01

5. The total payroll-related cost to the employer.

	Billings	Dephir	Singe	Total
Regular pay	$600.00	$1,320.00	$ 864.00	$2,784.00
Overtime pay	-0-	-0-	72.00	72.00
Gross pay	$600.00	$1,320.00	$ 936.00	$2,856.00
Deductions and fringe benefits:				
CPP	$ 26.37	$ —	$ 43.00	$ 69.37
EI	14.53	—	22.67	37.20
Vacation	30.30	66.66	47.27	144.23
Medical insurance	25.00	25.00	25.00	75.00
Total deductions and fringe benefits	$ 96.20	$ 91.66	$ 137.94	$ 325.80
Total payroll-related cost	$696.20	$1,411.66	$1,073.94	$3,181.80

6. Journal entry for payroll expense:

2009			
March 27	Salary Expense	2,856.00	
	Employees' Income Taxes Payable		593.05
	CPP Payable		69.37
	EI Payable		26.57
	Employees' Medical Insurance Payable		54.00
	Employees' Union Dues Payable		170.00
	Salaries Payable		1,943.01
	To record payroll expense.		

7. Journal entry for payroll deductions and employees' benefit expense:

2009			
March 27	CPP Expense	69.37	
	EI Expense	37.20	
	Benefits Expense	219.23	
	CPP Payable		69.37
	EI Payable		37.20
	Accrued Vacation Pay Payable		144.23
	Employees' Medical Insurance Payable		75.00
	To record employer's share of payroll deductions and benefits expense.		

8. Journal entry to record the remittance to the Receiver General for Canada:

Apr.	15	EI Payable[1]	63.77	
		CPP Payable[2]	138.74	
		Employees' Income Taxes Payable	593.05	
		Cash		795.56
		Calculations: *1. $26.57 (Employees' Portion) + $37.20 (Employer's Portion) = $63.77* *2. $69.37 (Employees' Portion) + $69.37 (Employer's Portion) = $138.74*		

Analysis component:

Deductions and fringe benefits represent 10.24% ($325.80/$3,181.80) of total payroll-related costs, and gross pay is 89.76% ($2,856.00/$3,181.80).

Glossary

Canada Pension Plan A national contributory retirement pension scheme. (p. 551)

Employee fringe benefits Payments by an employer, in addition to wages and salaries, that are made to acquire employee benefits such as insurance coverage and retirement income. (p. 562)

Employee's gross pay The amount an employee earns before any deductions for taxes or other items such as union dues or insurance premiums. (p. 554)

Employee's individual earnings record A record of an employee's hours worked, gross pay, deductions, net pay, and certain personal information about the employee. (p. 558)

Employee's net pay The amount an employee is paid, determined by subtracting from gross pay all deductions for taxes and other items that are withheld from the employee's earnings. (p. 557)

Employment Insurance An employee/employer-financed unemployment insurance plan. (p. 552)

Payroll deductions Amounts deducted from an employee's pay, usually based on the amount of an employee's gross pay. (p. 550)

Personal tax credits Amounts that may be deducted from an individual's income taxes and that determine the amount of income taxes to be withheld. (p. 551)

TD1 A form, known as the Personal Tax Credit Return, that determines how much income tax is to be withheld by the employer based on the employee's exemptions. (p. 551)

Wage bracket withholding table A table showing the amounts to be withheld from employees' wages at various levels of earnings. (p. 552)

Visit **Connect** at **www.mcgrawhillconnect.ca** for additional study tools, practice quizzes, to search an interactive e-book, and much more.

Concept Review Questions

1. Who pays the contributions to the Canada Pension Plan?
2. Who pays premiums under the Workers' Compensation laws?
3. Who pays federal Employment Insurance? What is the rate?
4. What are the objectives of Employment Insurance laws?
5. To whom and when are payroll deductions remitted?
6. What determines the amount that must be deducted from an employee's wages for income taxes?
7. What is a tax withholding table?
8. What is the Canada Pension Plan deduction rate for self-employed individuals?
9. What information is accumulated on an employee's individual earnings record? Why must this information be accumulated? For what purposes is the information used?
10. What payroll charges are levied on the employer? What amounts are deducted from the wages of an employee?
11. What are employee fringe benefits? Name some examples.

Quick Study

QS 11-1
Payroll expenses
LO1

A company deducts $260 in Employment Insurance and $205 in Canada Pension from the weekly payroll of its employees. How much is the company's expense for these items for the week?

QS 11-2
Preparing payroll journal entries
LO2

Tracon Co. has six employees, each of whom earns $3,000 per month. Income taxes are 20% of gross pay and the company deducts EI and CPP. Prepare the March 31 journal entry to record payroll for the month.

QS 11-3
Paying employees
LO2

Use the information in QS 11-2 to record the payment of the wages to the employees for March.

QS 11-4
Completing a payroll register
LO2

		Deductions				Pay	Distribution	
Employee	**Gross Pay**	**EI Premium**	**Income Taxes**	**CPP**	**Total Deductions**	**Net Pay**	**Office Salaries**	**Sales Salaries**
Johnson, S.	1,200.00	20.76	279.05	56.07				
Waverley, N.	530.00	9.17	69.00	22.90				
Zender, B.	675.00	11.68	105.00	30.08				
Totals	2,405.00	41.61	453.05	109.05				

Required
Prairie Rigging's three employees are paid weekly. Waverley works in the office and Johnson and Zender are sales representatives. Complete the payroll register above for the week ended March 6, 2009.

QS 11-5
Completing a payroll register using tables
LO2

		Deductions				Pay	
Employee	**Gross Pay**	**EI Premium**	**Income Taxes**	**CPP**	**Total Deductions**	**Net Pay**	**Salaries Expense**
Bentley, A.	2,010.00						
Craig, T.	2,115.00						
Totals	4,125.00						

Required
Meadow Lake Groceries has two employees who are paid monthly. Using the tables beginning on page 580, complete the payroll register above for the month ended March 31, 2009, assuming both employees' TD1 claim code is 1.

QS 11-6
Completing a payroll register by calculating deductions
LO2

		Deductions				Pay	Distribution	
Employee	**Gross Pay**	**EI Premium**	**Income Taxes**	**CPP**	**Total Deductions**	**Net Pay**	**Office Salaries**	**Sales Salaries**
Withers, S.	2,500.00						2,500.00	
Volt, C.	1,800.00							1,800.00
Totals								

Required
Maidstone Plumbing Services' two employees are paid biweekly. Assuming a tax rate of 30%, complete the payroll register above for the two-week period ended February 20, 2009.

QS 11-7
Payroll journal entry
LO2

Racon Co. has eight employees, each of whom earns $3,500 per month. Income taxes are 20% of gross pay and the company deducts EI and CPP. Prepare the March 31, 2009, journal entry to record Racon's salaries expenses for the month.

QS 11-8
Payroll journal entry
LO2

Chandler Tailors pays its three part-time employees monthly. The following information is available for the February 2009 payroll:

		Deductions				Pay	Distribution	
Employee	Gross Pay	EI Premium	Income Taxes	CPP	Total Deductions	Net Pay	Office Salaries	Sales Salaries
Berkley, M.	575.00	9.95	0.00	14.03	23.98	551.02	575.00	
Cander, O.	840.00	14.53	0.00	27.14	41.67	798.33		840.00
Meister, P.	1,020.00	17.65	6.20	36.05	59.90	960.10		1,020.00
Totals	2,435.00	42.13	6.20	77.22	125.55	2,309.45	575.00	1,860.00

Required
Prepare the journal entry to record payroll expenses for the month.

QS 11-9
Recording employer's payroll deductions
LO3

Refer to the information in QS 11-8. Prepare a journal entry to record Chandler Tailors' share of payroll deductions.

QS 11-10
Payment of payroll deductions
LO3

Refer to the information in QS 11-8 and QS 11-9. Prepare a journal entry to record payment by Chandler Tailors to the Receiver General for Canada on March 15.

QS 11-11
Recording fringe benefit costs
LO4

Racon Co. (see QS 11-7) contributes 8% of an employee's salary to a retirement program, pays medical insurance premiums of $60 per employee, and pays vacation allowance equivalent to 5% of the employee's salary. Prepare a journal entry to record the fringe benefit costs for March.

Exercises

Exercise 11-1
Calculating gross and net pay
LO2

Check figure:
Net pay = $1,807.51

Julie Leung, an employee of the Import Company, worked 172 hours during the month of January 2009. Her pay rate is $12.50 per hour, and her wages are subject to no deductions other than income taxes, EI, and CPP. The overtime premium is 50% and is applicable to any time greater than 160 hours per month. Calculate her regular pay, overtime premium pay, gross pay, total deductions, and net pay. Use the tables beginning on page 580 to determine the EI, CPP, and income tax deductions (assume claim code 1).

Exercise 11-2
Calculating payroll deductions and recording the payroll
LO2

eXcel

The following information as to earnings and deductions for the pay period ended March 6 was taken from a company's payroll records:

Employees' Names	Weekly Gross Pay	Earnings to End of Previous Week	Income Taxes	Health Insurance Deductions
Hellena Chea	$ 720	$12,510	$115.50	$ 24.00
Joseph Lim.............	610	10,320	88.30	24.00
Dino Patelli	830	15,500	148.95	36.00
Sharl Qulnata.........	1,700	29,500	460.70	24.00
	$3,860		$813.45	$108.00

Check figure:
Total EI withholding = $66.78

Required
Calculate the employees' EI and CPP withholdings, the amounts paid to each employee, and prepare a General Journal entry to record the payroll. Assume all employees work in the office.

Exercise 11-3

Completing a payroll register

LO2

Lendrum Servicing's four employees are paid every two weeks. Akerley runs the office and the remaining employees are sales representatives.

		Deductions					Pay	Distribution	
Employee	**Gross Pay**	**EI Premium**	**Income Taxes**	**United Way**	**CPP**	**Total Deductions**	**Net Pay**	**Admin. Salaries**	**Sales Salaries**
Akerley, D.	1,900.00	32.87	381.95	80.00	87.39				
Nesbitt, M.	1,260.00	21.80	187.95	50.00	55.71				
Trent, F.	1,680.00	29.06	304.85	40.00	76.50				
Vacon, M.	3,000.00	51.90	768.50	300.00	141.84				
Totals	7,840.00	135.63	1,643.25	470.00	361.44				

Required

Complete the payroll register above for the biweekly period ended March 10, 2009.

Check figure:
Total deductions
= $2,610.31

Exercise 11-4

Completing a payroll register using tables

LO2

D&D Stockyards' four employees are paid monthly. Each employee donates 5% of gross pay to the United Way through payroll deductions. Crimson and Peterson purchase Canada Savings Bonds through monthly payroll deductions of $150 and $200 respectively.

		Deductions						Pay	Distribution	
Employee	**Gross Pay**	**EI Premium**	**Income Taxes**	**Canada Savings Bonds**	**CPP**	**United Way**	**Total Deductions**	**Net Pay**	**Office Salaries**	**Sales Salaries**
Crimson, L.	1,995.00								1,995.00	
Long, M.	2,040.00									2,040.00
Morris, P.	2,000.00									2,000.00
Peterson, B.	2,280.00									2,280.00
Totals										

Required

Using the tables beginning on page 580, complete the payroll register above for the monthly pay period ended February 28, 2009, assuming the following TD1 claim codes for each employee: Crimson (2), Long (1), Morris (1), and Peterson (3).

Check figure:
Total EI premiums
= $143.84

Exercise 11-5

Completing a payroll register by calculating deductions

LO2

		Deductions						Pay	Distribution	
Employee	**Gross Pay**	**EI Premium**	**Income Taxes**	**Medical Ins.**	**CPP**	**United Way**	**Total Deductions**	**Net Pay**	**Office Salaries**	**Guide Salaries**
Wynne, L.	1,200.00			65.00		40.00				1,200.00
Short, M.	950.00			65.00		100.00			950.00	
Pearl, P.	1,150.00			65.00		-0-				1,150.00
Quince, B.	875.00			65.00		50.00				875.00
Totals										

Required

Piperel Lake Resort's four employees are paid weekly. Assume an income tax rate of 20%. Complete the payroll register above for the month ended January 31, 2009.

Check figure:
Total deductions
= $1,550.57

Exercise 11-6
Other payroll deductions
LO2

Check figure:
Monthly United Way contribution = $33.76

Sharon Von Hatton is the only employee of a self-employed businessperson. She earned a monthly salary of $2,050 in February 2009, her first month of employment. In response to a city-wide effort to obtain charitable contributions to the local United Way programs, Von Hatton has requested that her employer withhold 2% of her salary (after CPP, EI, and income taxes have been deducted).

Required
Prepare the journal entry to record payroll expenses for the month of February 2009. Use the tables beginning on page 580 to determine CPP, EI, and income tax deductions (assume claim code 1).

Exercise 11-7
Payroll journal entry
LO2

Paradise Hills Berry Farm has 25 employees who are paid biweekly. The payroll register showed the following payroll deductions for the pay period ending March 24, 2009.

Gross Pay	EI Premium	Income Taxes	CPP	Medical Ins.	United Way
65,950.00	1,140.94	28,439.95	3,097.93	1,150.00	1,319.00

Required
Using the information provided, prepare the journal entry to record the payroll expenses.

Exercise 11-8
Recording employer's payroll deductions
LO3

Refer to the information in Exercise 11-7. Prepare a journal entry to record the employer's share of payroll deductions.

Exercise 11-9
Payment of payroll deductions
LO3

Refer to the information in Exercise 11-7 and Exercise 11-8. Prepare a journal entry to record payment by the employer to the Receiver General for Canada on April 15.

Exercise 11-10
Calculating and recording payroll deductions
LO3, 4

Use the information provided in Exercise 11-2 to complete the following requirements:
1. Prepare a General Journal entry to record the employer's payroll costs resulting from the payroll.
2. Prepare a General Journal entry to record the following employee benefits incurred by the company: (a) health insurance costs equal to the amounts contributed by each employee and (b) contributions equal to 10% of gross pay for each employee's retirement income program.

Exercise 11-11
Analyzing total labour costs
LO2, 3, 4

Check figure:
Total CPP contributions = $9,622.80

O'Riley Company's payroll costs and fringe benefit expenses include the normal CPP and EI contributions, retirement fund contributions of 10% of total earnings, and health insurance premiums of $120 per employee per month. Given the following list of employees' projected 2009 annual salaries, payroll costs and fringe benefits are what percentage of salaries?

Doherty	$ 36,000
Fane	61,000
Kahan	59,000
Martin	37,000
Poon	48,000
Total	$241,000

Exercise 11-12
Calculating and recording payroll costs (using tables)
LO2, 3, 4

Milly's Drive-In's 12 employees earn a gross pay of $2,050 each per month. Milly's Drive-In contributes 8% of gross pay to a retirement program for employees and pays a medical insurance premium of $50 per month per employee.

Required
Prepare the entries to record the employer's payroll costs for the month of March 2009. Use the tables beginning on page 580 to determine CPP, EI, and income tax deductions (assume claim code 1).

Exercise 11-13
Calculating fringe benefits costs
LO4

Bellward Company grants vacation time of two weeks to those employees who have worked for the company one complete year. After 10 years of service, employees receive four weeks of vacation. The monthly payroll for January totals $320,000, of which 70% is payable to employees with 10 or more years of service. On January 31, record the January expense arising from the vacation policy of the company. Round calculations to the nearest whole dollar.

Problems

Problem 11-1A
Payroll register and payroll deductions
LO2, 3

The payroll records of Brownlee Company provided the following information for the weekly pay period ended March 27, 2009:

Payroll
Week Ended March 27, 2009

Employees	Employee No.	Daily Time							Pay Rate	Hospital Insurance	Union Dues	Earnings to End of Previous Week
		M	T	W	T	F	S	S				
Ray Loran	11	8	8	8	8	8	4	0	40.00	40.00	16.00	43,000
Kathy Sousa	12	7	8	6	7	8	4	0	36.00	40.00	15.00	46,000
Gary Smith	13	8	8	0	8	8	4	4	32.00	40.00	14.00	21,000
Nicola Parton	14	8	8	8	8	8	0	0	40.00	40.00	16.00	32,000
Diana Wood	15	0	6	6	6	6	8	8	36.00	40.00	15.00	36,000
Totals										200.00	76.00	

Required
1. Enter the relevant information in the proper columns of a payroll register and complete the register; calculate CPP and EI deductions. Charge the wages of Kathy Sousa to Office Wages Expense and the wages of the remaining employees to Service Wages Expense. Calculate income tax deductions at 20% of gross pay. Employees are paid an overtime premium of 50% for all hours in excess of 40 per week.
2. Prepare General Journal entries to record the payroll register information, including the employer's expenses.

Check figure:
Total deductions = $2,074.58

Problem 11-2A
Payroll register and journal entries
LO2, 3

On January 13, at the end of the second weekly pay period of the year, a company's payroll register showed that its 30 employees had earned $19,570 of sales salaries and $6,230 of office salaries. Withholdings from the employees' salaries were to include $446.34 of EI, $1,177.14 of CPP, $5,310 of income taxes, $930 of hospital insurance, and $420 of union dues.

Required
1. Prepare the General Journal entry to record the January 13 payroll.
2. Prepare a General Journal entry to record the employer's payroll expenses resulting from the January 13 payroll.

Problem 11-3A
Journal entries—payroll taxes, and employee fringe benefits
LO2, 3, 4

A company showed the following information in its payroll register for the week ended March 13, 2009:

Deductions						Payment	Distribution		
EI Premium	Income Taxes	Medical Insurance	CPP	Union Dues	Total Deductions	Net Pay	Sales Salaries Expense	Office Salaries Expense	Shop Salaries Expense
20.76	279.05	47.50	56.07	90.00	493.38	706.62	1,200.00		
24.22	347.85	52.50	65.97	105.00	595.54	804.46			1,400.00
29.41	460.70	25.00	80.82	127.50	723.43	976.57			1,700.00
18.17	224.50	35.00	48.64	78.75	405.06	644.94		1,050.00	
92.56	**1,312.10**	**160.00**	**251.50**	**401.25**	**2,217.41**	**3,132.59**	**1,200.00**	**1,050.00**	**3,100.00**

1. Prepare a General Journal entry to record the payroll register information.
2. Prepare a General Journal entry to record the employer's payroll expenses resulting from the payroll.
3. Prepare General Journal entries to accrue employee fringe benefit costs for the week. Assume that the company matches the employees' payments for medical insurance and contributes an amount equal to 8% of each employee's gross pay to a retirement program. Also, each employee accrues vacation pay at the rate of 6% of the wages and salaries earned. The company estimates that all employees eventually will be paid their vacation pay.

Problem 11-4A
Journal entries for payroll transactions
LO2, 3, 4

A company has three employees, each of whom has been employed since January 1, earns $2,600 per month, and is paid on the last day of each month. On March 1, the following accounts and balances appeared in its ledger.

a. Employees' Income Taxes Payable, $1,442.40 (liability for February).
b. EI Payable, $323.86 (liability for February).
c. CPP Payable, $685.58 (liability for February).
d. Employees' Medical Insurance Payable, $1,560.00 (liability for January and February).

During March and April, the company completed the following related to payroll.

Mar. 17 Issued cheque #320 payable to the Receiver General for Canada. The cheque was in payment of the February employee income taxes, EI, and CPP amounts due.

31 Prepared a General Journal entry to record the March payroll register, which had the following column totals:

EI	Income Taxes	CPP	Medical Insurance	Total Deductions	Net Pay	Office Salaries	Shop Salaries
$134.94	$1,442.40	$342.79	$390.00	$2,310.13	$5,489.87	$2,600	$5,200

31 Recorded the employer's $390.00 liability for its 50% contribution to the medical insurance plan of employees and 6% vacation pay accrued to the employees.

31 Prepared a General Journal entry to record the employer's costs resulting from the March payroll.

Apr. 17 Issued cheque #375 payable to the Receiver General for Canada in payment of the March mandatory deductions.

17 Issued cheque #376 payable to All Canadian Insurance Company in payment of the employee medical insurance premiums for the first quarter.

Required
Prepare the entries to record the transactions.

Alternate Problems

Problem 11-1B
Payroll register and payroll deductions
LO2, 3

The payroll records of Wailee Company provided the following information for the weekly pay period ended March 27, 2009:

Payroll Week Ended March 27, 2009												
Employees	Employee No.	Daily Time							Pay Rate	Hospital Insurance	Union Dues	Earnings to End of Previous Week
		M	T	W	T	F	S	S				
Ben Amoko	31	8	8	8	8	8	0	0	34.00	30.00	12.00	43,000
Auleen Carson	32	7	8	8	7	8	4	0	36.00	30.00	12.00	42,100
Mitali De	33	8	8	0	8	8	4	4	36.00	30.00	12.00	28,000
Gene Deszca	34	8	8	8	8	8	0	0	30.00	30.00	12.00	32,000
Ysong Tan	35	0	6	6	6	6	8	8	30.00	30.00	12.00	36,000
Totals										150.00	60.00	

Required

1. Enter the relevant information in the proper columns of a payroll register and complete the register; calculate CPP and EI deductions. Charge the wages of Auleen Carson to Office Wages Expense and the wages of the remaining employees to Service Wages Expense. Calculate income tax deductions at 20% of gross pay. Employees are paid an overtime premium of 50% for all hours in excess of 40 per week.

2. Prepare General Journal entries to record the payroll register information, including the employer's expenses.

Check figure:
Total deductions = $1,806.12

Problem 11-2B
Payroll register and journal entries
LO2, 3

On January 13, at the end of the second weekly pay period of the year, a company's payroll register showed that its 45 employees had earned $23,400 of sales salaries and $5,820 of office salaries. Withholdings from the employees' salaries were to include $505.51 of EI, $1,296.46 of CPP, $6,180 of income taxes, $920 of hospital insurance, and $490 of union dues.

Required

1. Prepare the General Journal entry to record the January 13 payroll.

2. Prepare a General Journal entry to record the employer's payroll expenses resulting from the January 13 payroll.

Problem 11-3B

Journal entries—payroll taxes, and employee fringe benefits

LO2, 3, 4

A company showed the following information in its payroll register for the week ended March 20, 2009:

Deductions						Payment	Distribution		
EI Premium	Income Taxes	Medical Insurance	CPP	Union Dues	Total Deductions	Net Pay	Sales Salaries Expense	Office Salaries Expense	Shop Salaries Expense
25.09	364.60	47.50	68.44	108.75	614.38	835.62	1,450.00		
34.25	570.95	52.50	94.68	148.50	900.88	1,079.12			1,980.00
30.45	483.60	25.00	83.79	132.00	754.84	1,005.16			1,760.00
29.76	471.10	35.00	81.81	129.00	746.67	973.33		1,720.00	
119.55	**1,890.25**	**160.00**	**328.72**	**518.25**	**3,016.77**	**3,893.23**	**1,450.00**	**1,720.00**	**3,740.00**

1. Prepare a General Journal entry to record the payroll register information.
2. Prepare a General Journal entry to record the employer's payroll expenses resulting from the payroll.
3. Prepare General Journal entries to accrue employee fringe benefits costs for the week. Assume that the company matches the employees' payments for medical insurance and contributes an amount equal to 8% of each employee's gross pay to a retirement program. Also, each employee accrues vacation pay at the rate of 6% of the wages and salaries earned. The company estimates that all employees eventually will be paid their vacation pay.

Problem 11-4B

Journal entries for payroll transactions

LO2, 3, 4

A company has three employees, each of whom has been employed since January 1, earns $2,300 per month, and is paid on the last day of each month. On March 1, the following accounts and balances appeared in its ledger:

a. Employees' Income Taxes Payable, $1,212.00 (liability for February).
b. EI Payable, $286.49 (liability for February).
c. CPP Payable, $595.58 (liability for February).
d. Employees' Medical Insurance Payable, $1,380.00 (liability for January and February).

During March and April, the company completed the following transactions related to payroll:

Mar. 17 Issued cheque #635 payable to the Receiver General for Canada. The cheque was in payment of the February employee income taxes, EI, and CPP amounts due.

31 Prepared a General Journal entry to record the March payroll register, which had the following column totals:

EI	Income Taxes	CPP	Medical Insurance	Total Deductions	Net Pay	Office Salaries	Shop Salaries
$119.37	$1,212.00	$297.79	$345.00	$1,974.16	$4,925.84	$2,300	$4,600

31 Recorded the employer's $345.00 liability for its 50% contribution to the medical insurance plan of employees and 6% vacation pay accrued to the employees.

31 Prepared a General Journal entry to record the employer's payroll costs resulting from the March payroll.

Apr. 14 Issued cheque #764 payable to the Receiver General for Canada in payment of the March mandatory deductions.

14 Issued cheque #765 payable to National Insurance Company in payment of the employee medical insurance premiums for the first quarter.

Required

Prepare the entries to record the transactions.

Analytical and Review Problems

A & R Problem 11-1

Using the current year's withholding tables for Canada Pension Plan, Employment Insurance, and income tax, update the payroll register of Exhibit 11.2. In calculating income tax withholdings, state your assumption as to each employee's personal deductions. Assume that hospital insurance deductions continue at the same amounts as in Exhibit 11.2.

A & R Problem 11-2

The following data were taken from the payroll register of Eastcoastal Company:

Gross Salary	xxx
Employees' Income Tax Deductions	xxx
EI Deductions	xxx
CPP Deductions	xxx
Hospital Insurance Deductions	xxx
Union Dues Deductions	xxx

Eastcoastal contributes an equal amount to the hospital insurance plan, in addition to the statutory payroll taxes, and 6% of the gross salaries to a pension retirement program.

Required
Record in General Journal form the payroll, payment of the employees, and remittance to the appropriate persons amounts owing in connection with the payroll. (Note: All amounts are to be indicated as xxx.)

Ethics Challenge

EC 11-1

Moe Daljit is the accountant for Valley Sales Company, which is currently experiencing a cash shortage because its Pacific Rim customers have not been paying their accounts on a timely basis. The owner has been unable to arrange adequate bank financing to cover the cash shortage and has suggested that Moe delay sending the amounts withheld from employees to the Receiver General for Canada for a few months, "until things clear up." Then he adds, "After all, we will be sending the money to the Receiver General eventually."

Required
1. What are the company's responsibilities with respect to amounts withheld from employees' wages and salaries?
2. What are the ethical factors in this situation?
3. Would you recommend that Moe follow the owner's "suggestion"?
4. What alternatives might be available to the owner if Moe does not delay sending the amounts to the Receiver General for Canada?

Critical Thinking Mini Case

Delta Yard Maintenance offers a variety of services to its customers, including lawn and garden care, tree pruning, exterior painting, fence building/installation, eavestrough cleaning, snow removal, and other miscellaneous tasks. Delta employs five full-time salaried individuals and 15 to 20 part-time wage employees. During the year just past, $194,392 was paid in cash to the part-time employees "under the table," meaning that cash was paid to the employees and no payroll deductions were withheld. The part-time wage employees would not have paid income tax on the cash received because Delta would not have issued T4 slips. To cover up these payments, Delta claimed $194,392 in various other expenses that were not supported by documentation. You have just been hired by Delta as one of the five full-time individuals—the office manager. One of your many duties will be to keep the accounting records, including payroll.

Required
Using the elements of critical thinking described on the inside front cover, comment.

Employment Insurance Premiums — Cotisations à l'assurance-emploi

Insurable Earnings Rémunération assurable From - De	To - À	EI premium Cotisation d'AE	Insurable Earnings Rémunération assurable From - De	To - À	EI premium Cotisation d'AE	Insurable Earnings Rémunération assurable From - De	To - À	EI premium Cotisation d'AE	Insurable Earnings Rémunération assurable From - De	To - À	EI premium Cotisation d'AE
1992.78	1993.35	34.48	2008.39	2008.95	34.75	2050.00	2050.57	35.47	2221.68	2222.25	38.44
1993.36	1993.93	34.49	2008.96	2009.53	34.76	2050.58	2051.15	35.48	2222.26	2222.83	38.45
1993.94	1994.50	34.50	2009.54	2010.11	34.77	2051.16	2051.73	35.49	2222.84	2223.41	38.46
1994.51	1995.08	34.51	2010.12	2010.69	34.78	2051.74	2052.31	35.50	2223.42	2223.98	38.47
1995.09	1995.66	34.52	2010.70	2011.27	34.79	2052.32	2052.89	35.51	2223.99	2224.56	38.48
1995.67	1996.24	34.53	2011.28	2011.84	34.80	2052.90	2053.46	35.52	2224.57	2225.14	38.49
1996.25	1996.82	34.54	2011.85	2012.42	34.81	2053.47	2054.04	35.53	2225.15	2225.72	38.50
1996.83	1997.39	34.55	2012.43	2013.00	34.82	2054.05	2054.62	35.54	2225.73	2226.30	38.51
1997.40	1997.97	34.56	2013.01	2013.58	34.83	2054.63	2055.20	35.55	2226.31	2226.87	38.52
1997.98	1998.55	34.57	2039.60	2040.17	35.29	2112.43	2113.00	36.55	2278.91	2279.47	39.43
1998.56	1999.13	34.58	2040.18	2040.75	35.30	2113.01	2113.58	36.56	2279.48	2280.05	39.44
1999.14	1999.71	34.59	2040.76	2041.32	35.31	2113.59	2114.16	36.57	2280.06	2280.63	39.45
1999.72	2000.28	34.60	2041.33	2041.90	35.32	2114.17	2114.73	36.58	2280.64	2281.21	39.46
2000.29	2000.86	34.61	2041.91	2042.48	35.33	2114.74	2115.31	36.59	2281.22	2281.79	39.47
2000.87	2001.44	34.62	2042.49	2043.06	35.34	2115.32	2115.89	36.60	2281.80	2282.36	39.48
2001.45	2002.02	34.63	2043.07	2043.64	35.35	2115.90	2116.47	36.61	2282.37	2282.94	39.49
2002.03	2002.60	34.64	2043.65	2044.21	35.36	2116.48	2117.05	36.62	2282.95	2283.52	39.50
2002.61	2003.17	34.65	2044.22	2044.79	35.37	2117.06	2117.63	36.63	2283.53	2284.10	39.51

Yearly maximum insurable earnings are $42,300
Yearly maximum employee premiums are $731.79
The premium rate for 2009 is 1.73%

Le maximum annuel de la rémunération assurable est de 42 300 $
La cotisation maximale annuelle de l'employé est de 731,79 $
Le taux de cotisation pour 2009 est de 1,73 %

Canada Pension Plan Contributions — Cotisations au Régime de pensions du Canada

Monthly (12 pay periods a year) — Mensuel (12 périodes de paie par année)

Pay Rémunération From - De	To - À	CPP RPC	Pay Rémunération From - De	To - À	CPP RPC	Pay Rémunération From - De	To - À	CPP RPC	Pay Rémunération From - De	To - À	CPP RPC
1993.38	1993.57	84.24	2009.75	2009.94	85.05	2049.75	2049.94	87.03	2224.29	2224.48	95.67
1993.58	1993.78	84.25	2009.95	2010.14	85.06	2049.95	2050.14	87.04	2224.49	2224.69	95.68
1993.79	1993.98	84.26	2010.15	2010.34	85.07	2050.15	2050.34	87.05	2224.70	2224.89	95.69
1993.99	1994.18	84.27	2010.35	2010.54	85.08	2050.35	2050.54	87.06	2224.90	2225.09	95.70
1994.19	1994.38	84.28	2010.55	2010.75	85.09	2050.55	2050.75	87.07	2225.10	2225.29	95.71
1994.39	1994.58	84.29	2010.76	2010.95	85.10	2050.76	2050.95	87.08	2225.30	2225.49	95.72
1994.59	1994.79	84.30	2010.96	2011.15	85.11	2050.96	2051.15	87.09	2225.50	2225.70	95.73
1994.80	1994.99	84.31	2011.16	2011.35	85.12	2051.16	2051.35	87.10	2225.71	2225.90	95.74
1995.00	1995.19	84.32	2011.36	2011.55	85.13	2051.36	2051.55	87.11	2225.91	2226.10	95.75
1998.84	1999.03	84.51	2038.84	2039.03	86.49	2113.38	2113.57	90.18	2278.84	2279.03	98.37
1999.04	1999.23	84.52	2039.04	2039.23	86.50	2113.58	2113.78	90.19	2279.04	2279.23	98.38
1999.24	1999.43	84.53	2039.24	2039.43	86.51	2113.79	2113.98	90.20	2279.24	2279.43	98.39
1999.44	1999.63	84.54	2039.44	2039.63	86.52	2113.99	2114.18	90.21	2279.44	2279.63	98.40
1999.64	1999.84	84.55	2039.64	2039.84	86.53	2114.19	2114.38	90.22	2279.64	2279.84	98.41
1999.85	2000.04	84.56	2039.85	2040.04	86.54	2114.39	2114.58	90.23	2279.85	2280.04	98.42
2000.05	2000.24	84.57	2040.05	2040.24	86.55	2114.59	2114.79	90.24	2280.05	2280.24	98.43
2000.25	2000.44	84.58	2040.25	2040.44	86.56	2114.80	2114.99	90.25	2280.25	2280.44	98.44
2000.45	2000.64	84.59	2040.45	2040.64	86.57	2115.00	2115.19	90.26	2280.45	2280.64	98.45

Employee's maximum CPP contribution for the year 2009 is $2,118.60

La cotisation maximale de l'employé au RPC pour l'année 2009 est de 2 118,60 $

Federal tax deductions
Effective January 1, 2009
Monthly (12 pay periods a year)
Also look up the tax deductions in the provincial table

Retenues d'impôt fédéral
En vigueur le 1er janvier 2009
Mensuel (12 périodes de paie par année)
Cherchez aussi les retenues d'impôt dans la table provinciale

Pay Rémunération	Federal claim codes/Codes de demande fédéraux										
	0	1	2	3	4	5	6	7	8	9	10
From Less than De Moins de	Deduct from each pay Retenez sur chaque paie										
1952 - 1970	263.60	137.35	125.05	100.40	75.75	51.10	26.45	1.80			
1970 - 1988	266.15	139.90	127.55	102.90	78.25	53.60	28.95	4.30			
1988 - 2006	268.65	142.40	130.10	105.45	80.80	56.15	31.50	6.85			
2006 - 2024	271.20	144.95	132.60	107.95	83.30	58.65	34.00	9.35			
2024 - 2042	273.70	147.45	135.10	110.45	85.80	61.15	36.50	11.85			
2042 - 2060	276.20	149.95	137.65	113.00	88.35	63.70	39.05	14.40			
2060 - 2078	278.75	152.50	140.15	115.50	90.85	66.20	41.55	16.90			
2078 - 2096	281.25	155.00	142.70	118.05	93.40	68.75	44.10	19.45			
2096 - 2114	283.75	157.50	145.20	120.55	95.90	71.25	46.60	21.95			
2114 - 2132	286.30	160.05	147.70	123.05	98.40	73.75	49.10	24.45			
2132 - 2150	288.80	162.55	150.25	125.60	100.95	76.30	51.65	27.00	2.35		
2150 - 2168	291.35	165.10	152.75	128.10	103.45	78.80	54.15	29.50	4.85		
2168 - 2186	293.85	167.60	155.30	130.65	106.00	81.35	56.70	32.05	7.40		
2186 - 2204	296.35	170.10	157.80	133.15	108.50	83.85	59.20	34.55	9.90		
2204 - 2222	298.90	172.65	160.30	135.65	111.00	86.35	61.70	37.05	12.40		
2222 - 2240	301.40	175.15	162.85	138.20	113.55	88.90	64.25	39.60	14.95		
2240 - 2258	303.95	177.70	165.35	140.70	116.05	91.40	66.75	42.10	17.45		
2258 - 2276	306.45	180.20	167.90	143.25	118.60	93.95	69.30	44.65	20.00		
2276 - 2294	308.95	182.70	170.40	145.75	121.10	96.45	71.80	47.15	22.50		
2294 - 2312	311.50	185.25	172.90	148.25	123.60	98.95	74.30	49.65	25.00	.35	

Saskatchewan provincial tax deductions
Effective January 1, 2009
Monthly (12 pay periods a year)
Also look up the tax deductions in the federal table

Retenues d'impôt provincial de la Saskatchewan
En vigueur le 1er janvier 2009
Mensuel (12 périodes de paie par année)
Cherchez aussi les retenues d'impôt dans la table fédérale

Pay Rémunération	Provincial claim codes/Codes de demande provinciaux										
	0	1	2	3	4	5	6	7	8	9	10
From Less than De Moins de	Deduct from each pay Retenez sur chaque paie										
1962 - 1980	203.90	82.30	73.90	57.05	40.25	23.45	6.65				
1980 - 1998	205.75	84.15	75.75	58.90	42.10	25.30	8.50				
1998 - 2016	207.60	86.00	77.55	60.75	43.95	27.15	10.35				
2016 - 2034	209.45	87.85	79.40	62.60	45.80	29.00	12.15				
2034 - 2052	211.30	89.65	81.25	64.45	47.65	30.85	14.00				
2052 - 2070	213.15	91.50	83.10	66.30	49.50	32.70	15.85				
2070 - 2088	215.00	93.35	84.95	68.15	51.35	34.55	17.70	.90			
2088 - 2106	216.85	95.20	86.80	70.00	53.20	36.40	19.55	2.75			
2106 - 2124	218.70	97.05	88.65	71.85	55.05	38.20	21.40	4.60			
2124 - 2142	220.55	98.90	90.50	73.70	56.90	40.05	23.25	6.45			
2142 - 2160	222.40	100.75	92.35	75.55	58.75	41.90	25.10	8.30			
2160 - 2178	224.25	102.60	94.20	77.40	60.60	43.75	26.95	10.15			
2178 - 2196	226.10	104.45	96.05	79.25	62.45	45.60	28.80	12.00			
2196 - 2214	227.95	106.30	97.90	81.10	64.25	47.45	30.65	13.85			
2214 - 2232	229.80	108.15	99.75	82.95	66.10	49.30	32.50	15.70			
2232 - 2250	231.65	110.00	101.60	84.80	67.95	51.15	34.35	17.55	.70		
2250 - 2268	233.50	111.85	103.45	86.65	69.80	53.00	36.20	19.40	2.55		
2268 - 2286	235.35	113.70	105.30	88.50	71.65	54.85	38.05	21.25	4.40		
2286 - 2304	237.15	115.55	107.15	90.30	73.50	56.70	39.90	23.10	6.25		
2304 - 2322	239.00	117.40	109.00	92.15	75.35	58.55	41.75	24.95	8.10		

APPENDIX I

Financial Statement Information

This appendix includes financial statement information from (a) Danier Leather Inc. and (b) WestJet Airlines Ltd. All of this information is taken from their annual reports. An **annual report** is a summary of the financial results of a company's operations for the year and its future plans. It is directed at external users of financial information, but also affects actions of internal users.

An annual report is also used by a company to showcase itself and its products. Many include attractive pictures, diagrams and illustrations related to the company. But the *financial section* is its primary objective. This section communicates much information about a company, with most data drawn from the accounting information system.

The layout of each annual report's financial section that is included in this appendix is:

- Management's Report
- Auditor's Report
- Financial Statements
- Notes to Financial Statements

This appendix is organized as follows:

- Danier: I-1 to I-21
- WestJet: I-22 to I-50

There are questions at the end of each chapter that refer to information in this appendix. We encourage readers to spend extra time with these questions as they are especially useful in reinforcing and showing the relevance and diversity of financial reporting.

More current financial information about these and other Canadian corporations can be found online at: www.sedar.com.

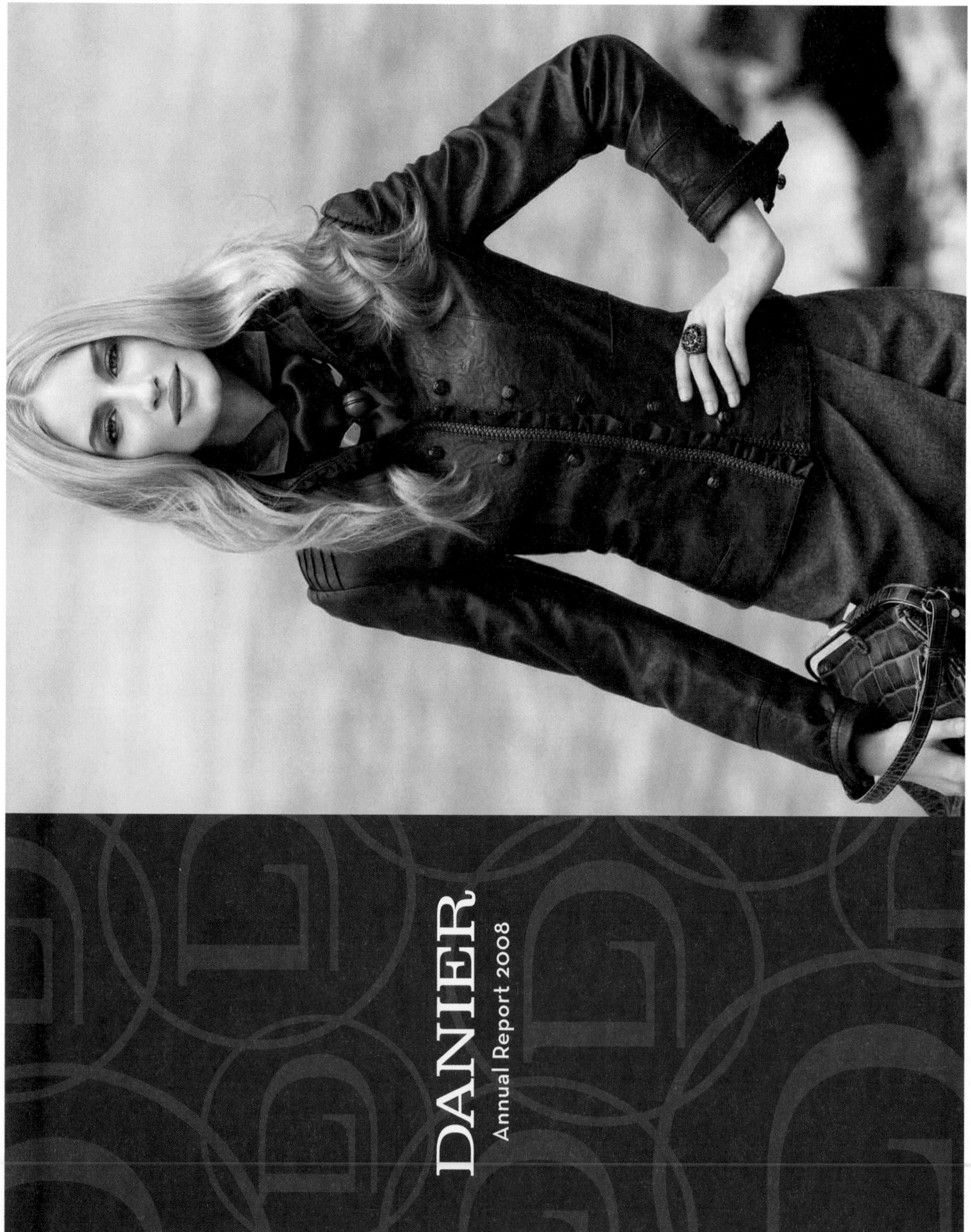
DANIER
Annual Report 2008

Management's Responsibility for Financial Statements

The accompanying financial statements and other financial information contained in this Annual Report are the responsibility of management. The financial statements have been prepared in conformity with Canadian generally accepted accounting principles using management's best estimates and judgements based on currently available information, where appropriate. The financial information contained elsewhere in this Annual Report has been reviewed to ensure consistency with that in the financial statements.

Management is also responsible for a system of internal controls which is designed to provide reasonable assurance that assets are safeguarded, liabilities are recognized and that financial records are properly maintained to provide timely and accurate financial reports.

The Board of Directors is responsible for ensuring that management fulfills its responsibility in respect of financial reporting and internal control. The Audit Committee of the Board, which is comprised solely of unrelated and outside directors, meets regularly to review significant accounting and auditing matters with management and the independent auditors and to review the interim and annual financial statements.

The financial statements have been audited by PricewaterhouseCoopers LLP, the independent auditors, in accordance with Canadian generally accepted auditing standards on behalf of the shareholders. The Auditors' Report outlines the nature of their examination and their opinion on the financial statements. PricewaterhouseCoopers LLP have full and unrestricted access to the Audit Committee to discuss their audit and related findings as to the integrity of the financial reporting.

Jeffrey Wortsman
President and CEO

Bryan Tatoff, C.A.
Senior Vice-President, CFO and Secretary

Auditors' Report to Shareholders

To the Shareholders of Danier Leather Inc.

We have audited the consolidated balance sheets of Danier Leather Inc. as at June 28, 2008 and June 30, 2007 and the consolidated statements of earnings and comprehensive earnings, cash flows and changes in shareholders' equity for the 52-week and 53-week periods then ended. These financial statements are the responsibility of the Company's management. Our responsibility is to express an opinion on these financial statements based on our audits.

We conducted our audits in accordance with Canadian generally accepted auditing standards. Those standards require that we plan and perform an audit to obtain reasonable assurance whether the financial statements are free of material misstatement. An audit includes examining, on a test basis, evidence supporting the amounts and disclosures in the financial statements. An audit also includes assessing the accounting principles used and significant estimates made by management, as well as evaluating the overall financial statement presentation.

In our opinion, these consolidated financial statements present fairly, in all material respects, the financial position of the Company as at June 28, 2008 and June 30, 2007 and the results of its operations and its cash flow for the 52-week and 53-week periods then ended in accordance with Canadian generally accepted accounting principles.

PricewaterhouseCoopers LLP
Chartered Accountants, Licensed Public Accountants
Mississauga, Ontario
August 20, 2008

Consolidated Financial Statements

For the Years Ended June 28, 2008 and June 30, 2007

Consolidated Statements of Earnings and Comprehensive Earnings (thousands of dollars, except per share amounts and number of shares)

	For the Year Ended	
	June 28, 2008	**June 30, 2007**
Revenue	$ 163,550	$ 158,099
Cost of sales (Note 9)	87,365	79,565
Gross profit	76,185	78,534
Selling, general and administrative expenses (Note 9)	78,582	76,360
Interest expense (income) – net	81	(427)
Earnings (loss) before undernoted item and income taxes	**(2,478)**	**2,601**
Litigation provision (recovery) and related expenses (Note 11)	(20,016)	-
Earnings before income taxes	17,538	2,601
Provision for (recovery of) income taxes (Note 10)		
Current	192	1,168
Future	4,454	(220)
	4,646	948
Net earnings and comprehensive earnings	**$ 12,892**	**$ 1,653**
Net earnings per share:		
Basic	$2.04	$0.25
Diluted	$2.03	$0.25
Weighted average number of shares outstanding:		
Basic	6,313,583	6,532,680
Diluted	6,335,873	6,547,416
Number of shares outstanding at period end	**6,276,429**	**6,433,754**

See accompanying notes to the consolidated financial statements.

Consolidated Balance Sheets (thousands of dollars)

	June 28, 2008	June 30, 2007
Assets		
Current Assets		
Cash	$ 19,882	$ 20,579
Accounts receivable	755	724
Income taxes recoverable	8	-
Inventories (Note 4)	27,404	28,561
Prepaid expenses	1,242	1,446
Future income tax asset (Note 10)	562	5,112
	49,853	56,422
Other Assets		
Property and equipment (Note 5)	21,312	23,575
Goodwill	342	342
Future income tax asset (Note 10)	1,556	1,407
	$ 73,063	$ 81,746
Liabilities		
Current Liabilities		
Accounts payable and accrued liabilities	$ 9,845	$ 9,387
Income taxes payable	-	1,473
Current portion of capital lease obligation (Note 7)	858	971
Accrued litigation provision and related expenses (Note 11)	-	18,000
Future income tax liability (Note 10)	502	444
	11,205	30,275
Capital lease obligation (Note 7)	-	858
Deferred lease inducements and rent liability	1,675	1,849
Future income tax liability (Note 10)	50	55
	12,930	33,037
Shareholders' Equity		
Share capital (Note 8)	21,409	22,044
Contributed surplus	548	431
Retained earnings	38,176	26,234
	60,133	48,709
	$ 73,063	$ 81,746

See accompanying notes to the consolidated financial statements.

Approved by the Board

Edwin F. Hawken, Director

Jeffrey Wortsman, Director

Consolidated Statements of Cash Flow (thousands of dollars)

	For the Years Ended	
	June 28, 2008	**June 30, 2007**
Operating Activities		
Net earnings	$ 12,892	$ 1,653
Items not affecting cash:		
Amortization (Note 9)	6,154	6,583
Amortization of deferred lease inducements and other	(453)	(493)
Straight line rent expense	116	172
Stock based compensation	117	156
Accrued litigation provision (recovery) and related expenses (Note 11)	(18,000)	-
Future income taxes	4,454	(220)
Net change in non-cash working capital items (Note 12)	363	5,626
Proceeds from deferred lease inducements	107	-
Repayment of deferred lease inducement	-	(59)
Cash flows from operating activities	**5,750**	**13,418**
Financing Activities		
Subordinate voting shares issued (Note 8)	80	24
Subordinate voting shares repurchased (Note 8)	(1,665)	(1,080)
Repayment of obligations under capital lease	(971)	(911)
Cash flows used in financing activities	**(2,556)**	**(1,967)**
Investing Activities		
Acquisition of capital assets	(3,891)	(2,865)
Proceeds from sublease	-	160
Cash flows used in investing activities	**(3,891)**	**(2,705)**
Increase (decrease) in cash	**(697)**	**8,746**
Cash, beginning of period	20,579	11,833
Cash, end of period	**$ 19,882**	**$ 20,579**
Supplementary cash flow information:		
Interest paid	414	280
Income taxes paid	1,679	-

See accompanying notes to the consolidated financial statements.

33 D

Consolidated Statements of Changes in Shareholders' Equity (thousands of dollars)

	For the Years Ended	
	June 28, 2008	June 30, 2007
Share Capital		
Balance, beginning of period	$22,044	$22,542
Shares repurchased	(715)	(522)
Shares issued on exercise of stock options	80	24
Balance, end of period	$21,409	$22,044
Contributed Surplus		
Balance, beginning of period	$431	$275
Stock-based compensation related to stock options	117	156
Balance, end of period	$548	$431
Retained Earnings		
Balance, beginning of period	$26,234	$25,139
Net earnings	12,892	1,653
Share repurchases	(950)	(558)
Balance, end of period	$38,176	$26,234
Accumulated Other Comprehensive Income (loss)		
Balance, beginning of period	$ -	$ -
Adjustment to opening balance due to the new accounting policies adopted regarding financial instruments	-	-
Balance, end of period	$ -	$ -
Total Shareholders' Equity	**$60,133**	**$48,709**

See accompanying notes to the consolidated financial statements.

Notes to Consolidated Financial Statements

For the Years Ended June 28, 2008 and June 30, 2007
(dollar amounts in thousands except per share amounts and where otherwise indicated)

Danier Leather Inc. ("Danier" or "the Company") is incorporated under the *Business Corporations Act* (Ontario) and is a vertically integrated designer, manufacturer and retailer of leather apparel and accessories.

Note 1: Summary of Significant Accounting Policies

The consolidated financial statements have been prepared in accordance with Canadian generally accepted accounting principles ("GAAP").

(a) Basis of consolidation:

The consolidated financial statements include the accounts of the Company and its wholly owned subsidiary companies. On consolidation, all intercompany transactions and balances have been eliminated.

(b) Year-end:

The fiscal year end of the Company consists of a 52 or 53 week period ending on the last Saturday in June each year. The fiscal year for the consolidated financial statements presented is the 52-week period ended June 28, 2008, and comparably the 53-week period ended June 30, 2007.

(c) Revenue recognition:

Revenue includes sales to customers through stores operated by the Company, sales to corporate customers through the Company's direct sales division and sales to third party licensees. Sales to customers through stores operated by the Company are recognized at the time the transaction is entered into the point-of-sale register net of returns. Sales to corporate customers and third party licensees are recognized at the time of shipment. Revenue from gift cards is recognized at the time of redemption. When a customer purchases a gift card a liability is recorded based on the dollar value of the gift card purchased. Unredeemed balances on gift cards that are more than two years old from the date of issuance (or "breakage") are recorded in the consolidated statement of earnings. Historically, breakage has not been material.

(d) Cash:

Cash consists of cash on hand, bank balances, and money market investments with maturities of three months or less.

(e) Inventories:

Inventories are valued at the lower of cost or market. Cost is determined using the weighted average cost method. For raw materials, cost includes invoice cost, duties, freight and brokerage. For finished goods purchased from third party vendors, cost includes invoice cost, overhead, duties, freight and brokerage. For finished goods manufactured by the Company, cost includes raw materials, labour and overhead. For finished goods and work-in-process, market is defined as the expected selling price; for raw materials, market is defined as replacement cost. In addition, a provision is recorded to reduce the cost of inventories for obsolete, damaged and slow moving items to their estimated net realizable values.

(f) Property and equipment:

Property and equipment are recorded at cost and annual amortization is provided at the following rates:

Building	4% declining balance
Furniture and equipment	20% declining balance
Computer hardware and software	30% declining balance
Computer hardware and software under capital lease	30% declining balance
Visual merchandising equipment	2 years straight line

Leasehold improvements are amortized on a straight line basis over the term of the lease, unless the Company has decided to terminate the lease, at which time the unamortized balance is written off.

Property and equipment are reviewed for impairment at least annually or when events or circumstances indicate their carrying value exceeds the sum of the undiscounted cash flows expected from their use and eventual disposal. For purposes of annually reviewing store assets for impairment, asset groups are reviewed at their lowest level for which identifiable cash flows are largely independent of cash flows of other assets and liabilities. Therefore, store net cash flows are grouped together by regional areas where a number of stores operate within close proximity to one another. An impairment loss is recognized when the carrying amount of property and equipment is not recoverable and exceeds its estimated fair value.

(g) Goodwill:

Goodwill represents the excess of the cost of acquisition over the fair market value of the identifiable assets acquired. Goodwill is not amortized, but is tested for impairment at least annually at year-end. If required, any impairment in the value of goodwill would be written off against earnings.

(h) Deferred lease inducements and rent liability:

Deferred lease inducements represent cash benefits received from landlords pursuant to store lease agreements. These lease inducements are amortized against rent expense over the term of the lease, not exceeding 10.5 years.

Rent liability represents the difference between minimum rent as specified in the lease and rent calculated on a straight line basis.

(i) Store opening costs:

Expenditures associated with the opening of new stores, other than furniture and fixtures, equipment, and leasehold improvements are expensed as incurred.

(j) Prepaid advertising production costs:

Advertising production costs for newspaper flyer inserts and other media are generally incurred several months before the advertising occurs. These expenses are deferred and expensed the first time the advertising occurs. Prepaid advertising production costs were $332 as at June 28, 2008 (June 30, 2007 - $480) and are included in prepaid expenses on the consolidated balance sheet.

(k) Income taxes:

Income taxes are determined using the asset and liability method of accounting. This method recognizes future tax assets and liabilities that arise from differences between the accounting basis of the Company's assets and liabilities and their corresponding tax basis. Future taxes are measured at the balance sheet date using enacted or substantially enacted income tax rates expected to apply when the asset is realized or the liability settled. The Company provides a valuation allowance for future tax assets when it is more likely than not that some or all of the future tax assets will not be realized.

(l) Earnings per share:

Basic earnings per share is calculated by dividing the net earnings available to shareholders by the weighted average number of shares outstanding during the year (see Note 8). Diluted earnings per share is calculated using the treasury stock method, which assumes that all outstanding stock options with an exercise price below the average monthly market price are exercised and the assumed proceeds are used to purchase the Company's shares at the average monthly market price during the fiscal year.

(m) Translation of foreign currencies:

Accounts in foreign currencies are translated into Canadian dollars. Monetary balance sheet items are translated at the rates of exchange in effect at year-end and non-monetary items are translated at historical exchange rates. Revenues and expenses are translated at the rates in effect on the transaction dates or at the average rates of exchange for the reporting period. The resulting net gain or loss is included in the consolidated statement of earnings.

(n) Stock option plan:

The Company has a Stock Option Plan which is described in Note 8 where options to purchase Subordinate Voting Shares are issued to directors, officers and employees. Effective with the commencement of its 2004 fiscal year, the Company accounts for stock-based compensation using the fair-value method. The fair value of options granted are estimated at the date of grant using the Black-Scholes Option Pricing Model and is recognized as an expense over the vesting period of the stock option with an offsetting credit to contributed surplus. When stock options are subsequently exercised, share capital is increased by the sum of the consideration paid together with the related portion previously added to contributed surplus when compensation costs were charged against income. The Company continues to use settlement accounting to account for stock options granted prior to June 29, 2003.

(o) Restricted Share Units and Deferred Share Units:

The Company has restricted share unit ("RSU") and deferred share unit ("DSU") Plans, which are described in Note 8. RSU and DSU Plans are settled in cash and are recorded as liabilities. The measurement of the compensation expense and corresponding liability for these awards is based on the fair value of the award, and is recorded as a charge to selling, general and administrative ("SG&A") expense over the vesting period of the award. At the end of each financial period, changes in the Company's payment obligation due to changes in the market value of the Subordinate Voting Shares are recorded as a charge to SG&A expense. Dividend equivalent grants are recorded as a charge to SG&A in the period the dividend is paid.

(p) Use of estimates:

The preparation of financial statements in conformity with Canadian GAAP requires management to make estimates and assumptions that affect the reported amounts of assets and liabilities and disclosure of contingent assets and liabilities in the consolidated financial statements and the reported amounts of revenues and expenses during the reporting period. These estimates and assumptions are based on management's historical experience, best knowledge of current events and actions that the Company may undertake in the future. Significant areas requiring the use of management estimates relate to the determination of inventory valuation, realizable value of property and equipment and goodwill, stock based compensation, future tax assets, goods and services tax, provincial sales tax, breakage of gift cards and income tax provisions. By their nature, these estimates are subject to measurement uncertainty and the impact on the consolidated financial statements of future periods could differ materially from those estimated.

Note 2: Implementation of New Accounting Standards

On July 1, 2007, the Company adopted the following new accounting standards issued by the Canadian Institute of Chartered Accountants ("CICA"). As provided under the standards, the Company adopted these recommendations prospectively without restatement of the prior period financial statements. There were no transitional adjustments resulting from the adoption of these standards.

CICA Section 1530 – Comprehensive Income

This CICA Handbook section introduced a statement of comprehensive income which is included in the consolidated financial statements. Comprehensive income represents the change in equity during a period from transactions and other events and circumstances from non-owner sources and includes all changes in equity other than those resulting from investments by owners and distributions to owners. The adoption of this standard has had no impact on the financial results of the Company. Since comprehensive earnings equal the net earnings for the period ended June 28, 2008, the consolidated statement of comprehensive earnings has been combined with the consolidated statements of earnings.

CICA Section 3251 – Equity

This CICA Handbook section, which replaced Section 3250 – *Surplus*, establishes standards for the presentation of equity and changes in equity during the reporting period and requires the Company to present separately equity components and changes in equity arising from (i) net earnings; (ii) other comprehensive income; (iii) other changes in retained earnings; (iv) changes in contributed surplus; (v) changes in share capital; and (vi) changes in reserves. New consolidated statements of changes in shareholders' equity are included in these financial statements.

CICA Section 3855 – Financial Instruments – Recognition and Measurement and
CICA Section 3861 – Financial Instruments – Disclosure and Presentation

These CICA Handbook sections establish standards for recognition and measurement as well as disclosure and presentation of financial assets, financial liabilities and non-financial derivatives. CICA Section 3855 requires that financial assets and financial liabilities, including derivatives, be recognized on the consolidated balance sheet when the Company becomes a party to the contractual provisions of the financial instrument or non-financial derivative contract. It also requires that all financial instruments be classified into a defined category, namely (a) held-to-maturity, (b) held-for-trading, (c) available-for-sale, (d) loans and receivables and (e) other financial liabilities, depending on the Company's stated intention and/or historical practice.

All financial instruments are required to be measured at fair value except for loans and receivables, held-to-maturity investments and other financial liabilities which are measured at cost or amortized cost. Gains and losses on held-for-trading financial assets and liabilities are recognized in net earnings in the period in which they arise. Unrealized gains and losses, including changes in foreign exchange rates on available-for-sale financial assets are recognized in comprehensive income until the financial assets are derecognized or impaired, at which time any unrealized gains or losses are recorded in net earnings. Transaction costs for assets classified as "held-for-trading" are recognized in net earnings as incurred and transaction costs for other assets are added to the financial asset on initial recognition and are recognized in net earnings when the asset is derecognized or impaired.

The adoption of these new standards resulted in the following changes in the classification and measurement of the Company's financial instruments, previously recorded at cost:

Cash is classified as "held-for-trading" and is measured at fair value which approximates cost. Money market investments included in cash are marked-to-market through net earnings and changes in fair value are recorded as interest income at each period end. This change had no impact on the Company's consolidated financial statements.

Accounts receivable are classified as "loans and receivables" and are recorded at cost, which at initial measurement corresponds to fair value. After initial fair value measurement, accounts receivable are measured at cost. This change had no impact on the Company's consolidated financial statements.

Bank indebtedness and accounts payable and accrued liabilities are classified as "other financial liabilities". They are initially measured at fair value and subsequent measurements are recorded at cost or amortized costs using the effective interest rate method. This change had no impact on the Company's consolidated financial statements.

From time-to-time the Company utilizes derivative financial instruments in the management of its foreign currency exposure. Derivative financial instruments are not used for trading purposes. As at June 28, 2008 and June 30, 2007, the Company did not have any outstanding foreign currency exchange forward contracts.

Embedded derivatives (elements of contracts whose cash flows move independently from the host contract) are required to be separated and measured at fair values if certain criteria are met. The Company selected June 30, 2002 as the transition date for embedded derivatives, and as such, only contracts or financial instruments entered into or modified after the transition date were examined for embedded derivatives. As at June 28, 2008 and June 30, 2007, the Company did not have any outstanding contracts or financial instruments with embedded derivatives.

CICA Section 3865 – Hedges

This CICA Handbook section establishes criteria that must be satisfied in order for hedge accounting to be applied and the accounting for each of the permitted hedging strategies: fair value hedges, cash flow hedges and hedges of a net investment in a self-sustaining foreign operation. Treatment of changes in the fair value of each type of hedge is determined by its classification and the portion of gains or losses on the hedging item that is determined to be an effective hedge is recognized in other comprehensive income. The determination of the effectiveness of each hedging relationship is required under the section with any ineffectiveness immediately recognized in income. The Company does not have any outstanding hedging contracts as at June 28, 2008 and June 30, 2007.

Effective for the fiscal year ended June 28, 2008, the Company has early adopted the CICA Handbook Section 1535 - *Capital Disclosures*, CICA Handbook Section 3862 – *Financial Instruments – Disclosures*, and CICA Handbook Section 3863 - *Financial Instruments – Presentation*, as described below:

CICA Section 1535 - Capital Disclosures

This CICA Handbook section establishes guidelines for the disclosure of information regarding a company's capital and how it is managed. Enhanced disclosure with respect to the objectives, policies and processes for managing capital and quantitative disclosures about what a company regards as capital are required. In addition, under this section a company is required to disclose whether during the period it complied with externally imposed capital requirements to which it is subject, and when the company has not complied with such externally imposed capital requirements, the consequences of such non-compliance. This section relates to disclosure and presentation only and did not have an impact on the Company's financial results. See Note 16.

CICA Section 3862 - Financial Instruments Disclosures and
CICA Section 3863 - Financial Instruments Presentation

CICA Handbook Section 3862 revises the current standards on financial instrument disclosure and places an increased emphasis on disclosures regarding the risks associated with both recognized and unrecognized financial instruments and how these risks are managed. CICA Handbook Section 3863 establishes standards for presentation of financial instruments and non-financial derivatives and provides additional guidance for classification of financial instruments, from the perspective of the issuer, between liabilities and equity, the classification of related interest, dividends, losses and gains, and the circumstances in which financial assets and financial liabilities are offset. These sections relate to disclosure and presentation only and did not have an impact on the Company's financial results. See Note 15.

Note 3: Recent Accounting Pronouncements

CICA Section 1400 – General Standards of Financial Statement Presentation

The CICA amended this Handbook section to include requirements to assess and disclose an entity's ability to continue as a going concern when preparing financial statements. In assessing whether the going concern assumption is appropriate, management must take into account all available information about the future, which is at least, but is not limited to, twelve months from the balance sheet. The Company will adopt this standard in the first quarter of its fiscal year ended June 27, 2009. The Company does not expect the implementation of this new section to have a significant impact on its consolidated financial statements.

CICA Section 3031 - Inventories

This CICA Handbook section issued in June 2007 replaces Section 3030 of the same name and harmonizes the Canadian standards related to inventories with International Financial Reporting Standards ("IFRS"). This section provides changes to the measurement and more extensive guidance on the determination of cost, including allocation of overhead; narrows the permitted cost formulas; requires impairment testing; and expands the disclosure requirements to increase transparency. These recommendations are effective for fiscal years beginning on or after January 1, 2008. The Company will adopt this standard in the first quarter of its fiscal year ended June 27, 2009. The Company is currently assessing the impact of this new standard on its consolidated financial statements.

CICA Section 3064 - Goodwill and Intangible Assets

This CICA Handbook section issued in February 2008 replaces Section 3062 - Goodwill and Other Intangible Assets and Section 3450 – Research and Development Costs. The new section establishes standards for the recognition, measurement, presentation and disclosure of goodwill and intangible assets subsequent to its initial recognition. Standards concerning goodwill are unchanged from the standards included in the previous Section 3062. The new standard also provides guidance for the recognition of internally developed intangible assets, including assets developed from research and development activities, ensuring consistent treatment of all intangible assets, whether separately acquired or internally developed. The new standard is applicable to fiscal years beginning on or after October 1, 2008. The Company has evaluated the new section and currently does not expect the implementation of this new section to have a significant impact on its consolidated financial statements.

International Financial Reporting Standards ("IFRS")

The Canadian Accounting Standards Board has confirmed that the use of IFRS will be required for publicly accountable profit-oriented enterprises. IFRS will replace Canadian GAAP for those enterprises. These new standards are applicable to fiscal years beginning on or after January 1, 2011 with comparative figures presented on the same basis. The Company is currently working on a conversion plan towards IFRS but it is too early to assess the financial impact of the conversion at this point.

Note 4: Inventories

	June 28, 2008	June 30, 2007
Raw materials	$ 3,332	$ 2,389
Work-in-process	892	989
Finished goods	23,180	25,183
	$ 27,404	$ 28,561

Note 5: Property and Equipment

	June 28, 2008			June 30, 2007		
	Cost	Accumulated Amortization	Net Book Value	Cost	Accumulated Amortization	Net Book Value
Land	$ 1,000	$ -	$ 1,000	$ 1,000	$ -	$ 1,000
Building	7,064	1,981	5,083	7,064	1,769	5,295
Leasehold improvements	24,315	15,861	8,454	24,013	14,980	9,033
Furniture and equipment	10,415	6,994	3,421	10,736	7,192	3,544
Computer hardware and software	4,014	1,876	2,138	7,578	4,613	2,965
Computer hardware and software under capital lease	2,920	1,704	1,216	2,920	1,182	1,738
	$ 49,728	$ 28,416	$ 21,312	$ 53,311	$ 29,736	$ 23,575

Note 6: Bank Facilities

Effective June 27, 2008, the Company amended and renewed its credit agreement. The renewed credit agreement provides for an operating facility for working capital and for general corporate purposes to a maximum amount of $25 million, bearing interest at prime plus 0.75%. Standby fees of 0.50% are paid on a quarterly basis on the unused portion of the facility. The operating facility is committed until June 29, 2009. The Company is required to comply with covenants regarding financial performance.

Security provided includes a security interest over all personal property of the Company's business and a mortgage over the land and building comprising the Company's head office/distribution facility.

Subsequent to June 28, 2008, the Company also obtained an uncommitted letter of credit facility (the "LC Facility") in the amount of $10 million to be used exclusively for issuance of letters of credit for the purchase of inventory and an uncommitted demand overdraft facility in the amount of $0.5 million related thereto. Amounts outstanding under the overdraft facility bear interest at the bank's prime rate. The LC Facility is secured by the Company's personal property from time to time financed with the proceeds drawn thereunder.

Note 7: Capital Lease Obligation

Future minimum lease payments required under capital leases which expire in fiscal 2009 are:

Fiscal 2009 minimum lease payments	$ 884
Amounts representing interest (at a weighted average annual rate of 6.2%)	26
	$ 858

Note 8: Share Capital

(a) Authorized

1,224,329 Multiple Voting Shares

Unlimited Subordinate Voting Shares

Unlimited Class A and B Preference Shares

(b) Issued

Multiple Voting Shares	**Number**	**Consideration**
Balance June 24, 2006	1,224,329	Nominal
Balance June 30, 2007	1,224,329	Nominal
Balance June 28, 2008	1,224,329	Nominal

Subordinate Voting Shares	**Number**	**Consideration**
Balance June 24, 2006	5,328,925	$ 22,542
Shares repurchased	(123,500)	(522)
Shares issued upon exercising of stock options	4,000	24
Balance June 30, 2007	5,209,425	$ 22,044
Shares repurchased	(169,000)	(715)
Shares issued upon exercising of stock options	11,675	80
Balance June 28, 2008	5,052,100	$ 21,409

The Multiple Voting Shares and Subordinate Voting Shares have identical attributes except that the Multiple Voting Shares entitle the holder to ten votes per share and the Subordinate Voting Shares entitle the holder to one vote per share. Each Multiple Voting Share is convertible at any time, at the holder's option, into one fully paid and non-assessable Subordinate Voting Share. The Multiple Voting Shares are subject to provisions whereby, if a triggering event occurs then each Multiple Voting Share is converted into one fully paid and non-assessable Subordinate Voting Share. A triggering event may occur if Mr. Jeffrey Wortsman, President and Chief Executive Officer: (i) dies; (ii) ceases to be a Senior Officer of the Company; (iii) ceases to own 5% or more of the aggregate number of Multiple Voting Shares and Subordinate Voting Shares outstanding; or (iv) owns less than 918,247 Multiple Voting Shares and Subordinate Voting Shares combined.

(c) Earnings per share

Basic and diluted per share amounts are based on the following weighted average number of shares outstanding:

	June 28, 2008	**June 30, 2007**
Weighted average number of shares for basic earnings per share calculations	6,313,583	6,532,680
Effect of dilutive options outstanding	22,290	14,736
Weighted average number of shares for diluted earnings per share calculations	6,335,873	6,547,416

The computation of dilutive options outstanding only includes those options having exercise prices below the average market price of Subordinate Voting Shares on The Toronto Stock Exchange (the "TSX") during the period. The number of options excluded was 231,000 as at June 28, 2008 and 416,000 as at June 30, 2007.

(d) Normal course issuer bids

On April 19, 2007, the Company announced that the TSX had accepted a notice of its intention to proceed with a normal course issuer bid (the "2007 NCIB"). Pursuant to the 2007 NCIB, the Company was entitled to purchase for cancellation up to a maximum of 320,320 Subordinate Voting Shares. On May 2, 2008, the Company received approval from the TSX to commence its second normal course issuer bid (the "2008 NCIB"). The 2008 NCIB permits the Company to acquire up to 292,638 Subordinate Voting Shares, representing approximately 10% of the "public float" of the Subordinate Voting Shares, during the period from May 6, 2008 to May 5, 2009. Under the 2007 NCIB which expired on April 22, 2008, the Company repurchased 292,500 Subordinate Voting Shares for cancellation. As of June 28, 2008, no Subordinate Voting Shares had been purchased under the 2008 NCIB.

The following Subordinate Voting Shares were repurchased for cancellation during the year ended June 28, 2008 and June 30, 2007:

	Year Ended	
	June 28, 2008	June 30, 2007
Number of shares repurchased	169,000	123,500
Amount charged to share capital	$715	$522
Amount charged to retained earnings representing the excess over the average paid-in value	$950	$558
Total cash consideration	$1,665	$1,080

(e) Stock option plan

41 | (D)

The Company maintains a Stock Option Plan for the benefit of directors, officers and employees. As at June 28, 2008, the Company has reserved 835,500 Subordinate Voting Shares for issuance under its Stock Option Plan. The granting of options and the related vesting periods are at the discretion of the Board of Directors, on the advice of the Governance, Compensation, Human Resources and Nominating Committee of the Board (the "Committee") at exercise prices determined as the weighted average of the trading prices of the Company's Subordinate Voting Shares on the TSX for the five trading days preceding the effective date of the grant. In general, options granted under the Stock Option Plan vest over a period of one year from the grant date for options issued to directors and between two years and four years from the grant date for options issued to officers and employees and expire no later than the tenth anniversary of the date of grant.

A summary of the status of the Company's Stock Option Plan as of June 28, 2008 and June 30, 2007 and changes during the years ended on those dates is presented below:

	June 28, 2008		June 30, 2007	
Stock Options	Shares	Weighted Average Exercise Price	Shares	Weighted Average Exercise Price
Outstanding at beginning of year	605,300	$ 10.48	618,300	$ 11.15
Granted	50,000	$ 6.25	70,000	$ 7.99
Exercised	(64,675)	$ 6.85	(4,000)	$ 6.02
Forfeited	(297,625)	$ 10.82	(79,000)	$ 13.74
Outstanding at end of year	293,000	$ 10.21	605,300	$ 10.48
Options exercisable at end of year	200,500	$ 11.60	541,550	$ 10.71

The following table summarizes the distribution of these options and the remaining contractual life as at June 28, 2008:

	Options Outstanding			Options Exercisable	
Exercise Prices	# Outstanding	Weighted Average Remaining Contractual Life	Weighted Average Exercise Price	# of Shares Exercisable	Weighted Average Exercise Price
$6.02	12,000	1.2 years	$6.02	12,000	$6.02
$6.25	50,000	10.0 years	$6.25	-	$6.25
$7.80	55,000	8.6 years	$7.80	28,750	$7.80
$8.68	15,000	8.8 years	$8.68	5,000	$8.68
$10.10	25,000	6.8 years	$10.10	18,750	$10.10
$10.40	20,000	2.1 years	$10.40	20,000	$10.40
$10.96	21,000	5.1 years	$10.96	21,000	$10.96
$11.20	16,000	3.1 years	$11.20	16,000	$11.20
$11.25	16,000	0.1 years	$11.25	16,000	$11.25
$15.85	63,000	4.1 years	$15.85	63,000	$15.85
	293,000	6.0 years	$ 10.21	200,500	$ 11.60

During the year ended June 28, 2008, the Company granted 50,000 stock options with an exercise price of $6.25 per stock option (June 30, 2007 - 70,000 stock options with exercise prices ranging from $7.80 to $8.68 per stock option). The weighted average estimated fair value at the date of grant for the options granted was $3.30 per stock option (June 30, 2007 - $4.45 per stock option). The fair value of each option granted was estimated on the date of grant using the Black-Scholes Option Pricing Model with the following weighted average assumptions:

	Year Ended June 28, 2008	Year Ended June 30, 2007
Risk-free interest rate	3.7%	4.2%
Dividend yield	-	-
Expected volatility	35%	37%
Expected life of options	10 years	10 years

The Black-Scholes Option Pricing Model was developed for use in estimating the fair value of traded options, which have no vesting restrictions and are fully transferable. In addition, the Black-Scholes Option Pricing Model requires the use of subjective assumptions including the expected stock price volatility. As a result of the Company's Stock Option Plan having characteristics different from those of traded options, and because changes in the subjective assumptions can have a material effect on the fair value estimate, the Black-Scholes Option Pricing Model does not necessarily provide a reliable single measure of the fair value of options granted.

Prior to fiscal 2004, the Company used settlement accounting to account for its Stock Option Plan. No compensation cost was recorded when stock options were granted. When options were exercised, consideration paid by employees and directors was recorded in the consolidated financial statements as an increase of share capital based on the exercise price of the options.

The compensation expense recorded for the year ended June 28, 2008 in respect of stock options was $117 (June 30, 2007 - $156). The counterpart is recorded as contributed surplus. Any consideration paid by employees on exercise of stock options is credited to share capital.

(f) Contributed Surplus

Changes in contributed surplus were as follows:

Balance June 24, 2006	$275
Stock-based compensation related to stock options	156
Balance June 30, 2007	$431
Stock-based compensation related to stock options	117
Balance June 28, 2008	$548

(g) Deferred Share Unit Plan

The Deferred Share Unit ("DSU") Plan was established for non-management directors. Under this plan, non-management directors of the Company receive an annual grant of DSUs and can also elect to receive their annual retainers and meeting fees in DSUs. A DSU is a unit equivalent in value to one Subordinate Voting Share of the Company based on the five-day average trading price of the Company's Subordinate Voting Shares on the TSX immediately prior to the date on which the value of the DSU is determined. When dividends are paid by the Company, an equivalent number of DSUs are added to the DSU account of the non-management director based on the number of DSUs in their account and the market value of the Subordinate Voting Shares on the date the dividend is paid. After retirement from the Board, a participant in the DSU Plan receives a cash payment equal to the market value of the accumulated DSUs in their account. The value of the DSU liability is adjusted to reflect changes in the market value of the Company's Subordinate Voting Shares.

The following transactions occurred with respect to the DSU Plan:

	Year Ended	
	June 28, 2008	**June 30, 2007**
Outstanding at beginning of period	39,420	14,904
Granted	19,500	27,000
Redeemed	-	(2,484)
Outstanding at end of period	58,920	39,420
Danier stock price at end of period	$6.40	$9.17
Liability at the end of period	$377	$361
Compensation expense recorded in SG&A	$16	$261

(h) Restricted Share Unit Plan

The Company established a Restricted Share Unit ("RSU") Plan, as part of its overall executive compensation plan. The RSU Plan is administered by the Board of Directors, with the advice of the Committee. Under this plan, Senior Officers of the Company are eligible to receive a grant of RSUs that vest over periods not exceeding three years as determined by the Committee. An RSU is a unit equivalent in value to one Subordinate Voting Share of the Company. When dividends are paid by the Company, an equivalent number of RSUs are added to the RSU account of the Senior Officer based on the number of RSUs in their account, the dividend paid per Subordinate Voting Share and the market value of the Subordinate Voting Shares on the date the dividend is paid. Upon the exercise of the vested RSUs, a cash payment equal to the market value of the exercised vested RSUs will be paid to the Senior Officer. The value of the vested RSU liability is adjusted to reflect changes in the market value of the Company's Subordinate Voting Shares.

The following transactions occurred with respect to the RSU Plan:

	Year Ended	
	June 28, 2008	June 30, 2007
Outstanding at beginning of period	50,201	15,238
Granted	123,300	40,000
Redeemed	(38,534)	-
Forfeited	(1,667)	(5,037)
Outstanding at end of period	133,300	50,201
Liability at the end of period	$411	$234
Compensation expense recorded in SG&A	$512	$220

Note 9: Amortization

Amortization included in cost of sales and SG&A is summarized as follows:

	Year Ended	
	June 28, 2008	June 30, 2007
Cost of sales	$ 583	$ 509
SG&A	5,571	6,074
	$ 6,154	$ 6,583

Note 10: Income Taxes

Future income tax asset (liability) is summarized as follows:

	June 28, 2008	June 30, 2007
Amortization	$ 395	$ 18
Deferred lease inducements and rent liability	504	605
Capital lease obligation	276	611
Litigation provision and related expenses	-	4,617
Stock based compensation	233	194
Other	158	(25)
	$ 1,566	$ 6,020

Recorded in the consolidated balance sheets as follows:

	June 28, 2008	June 30, 2007
Future income tax asset - current portion	$ 562	$ 5,112
Future income tax asset - long term portion	1,556	1,407
Future income tax liability - current portion	(502)	(444)
Future income tax liability - long term portion	(50)	(55)
Net future tax asset	$ 1,566	$ 6,020

The Company's effective income tax rate consists of the following:

	June 28, 2008	June 30, 2007
Combined basic federal and provincial average statutory rate	33.8%	35.0%
Non-deductible expenses	0.5%	4.5%
Future federal and provincial rate changes	1.1%	(2.2%)
Litigation provision and related expenses	(8.8%)	-
Other	(0.1%)	(0.9%)
	26.5%	36.4%

Note 11: Litigation Provision and Related Expenses

	June 28, 2008	June 30, 2007
Accrued litigation provision and related expenses	$ -	$ 18,000

In fiscal 1999, the Company and certain of its directors and officers were served with a Statement of Claim under the Class Proceedings Act (Ontario) which made allegations about the accuracy and disclosure of certain information contained in a financial forecast issued by the Company and contained in a prospectus it issued dated May 6, 1998 (the "Prospectus") for its initial public offering ("IPO") which closed on May 20, 1998. The suit sought damages to be paid equal to the alleged diminution in value of the Subordinate Voting Shares sold under the Prospectus.

In October 2001, a motion to certify the action as a class proceeding was granted. The trial commenced in the Superior Court of Justice (Ontario) in May 2003 and was completed in January 2004. On May 7, 2004, the trial judge issued a judgment against the Company and two of its Senior Officers in favour of the Plaintiffs and awarded damages to Canadian shareholders who purchased Subordinate Voting Shares under the Prospectus. For those shareholders who sold their shares between June 4 and 9, 1998, the trial judge awarded the difference between the IPO price and the price at which they sold their shares. For those shareholders who sold or still held their shares after June 9, 1998, the trial judge awarded $2.35 per share.

Although the trial judge concluded that at the date of the Prospectus the forecast was reasonable, and that at the time of closing of the IPO the Company's CEO and CFO had an honest belief that the forecast could still be achieved, and although he held that the forecast was, in fact, substantially achieved, the trial judge decided that management's judgment that the forecast was still achievable at the time of closing was not reasonable and that therefore the Prospectus contained a misrepresentation. Based solely on information available at the time, the Company estimated that the trial judge's award would have totaled approximately $15 million. As noted below, the Company and its Senior Officers successfully appealed this decision to the Court of Appeal for Ontario and a decision on a further appeal taken by the Plaintiffs to the Supreme Court of Canada was dismissed with costs, as discussed further below.

In May 2005, the trial judge awarded the Plaintiffs a portion of the costs claimed for the action and referred for assessment the amount of costs to be paid. Based solely on the information available at the time, the Company estimated that these costs would have amounted to approximately $3 million to $4 million.

A hearing to determine the awarding of costs related to the certification and summary judgment motion which was decided in 2000 and 2001 was held in December 2004. In June 2005, partial indemnity costs were awarded to the Plaintiffs for these motions in an amount to be assessed.

In June 2004, a Notice of Appeal was filed by the Company and two of its Senior Officers from the trial judge's decision. The appeal was heard by the Ontario Court of Appeal in June 2005 and in December 2005, the Court of Appeal unanimously allowed the appeal on three separate grounds, set aside the trial decision and dismissed the class proceeding. The Court of Appeal's decision stated that the Company had met its disclosure obligations in the Prospectus and during the IPO process and the trial judge erred in finding that any misrepresentation had occurred. In September 2006, partial indemnity costs were awarded to the Company for the appeal in the amount of $0.1 million. The Court of Appeal also awarded costs to the Company for the trial on a partial indemnity basis in an amount to be determined.

In February 2006, the Plaintiffs filed an application for leave to appeal from the Court of Appeal's decision to the Supreme Court of Canada. In June 2006, the Supreme Court of Canada granted leave to appeal to the Plaintiffs. The appeal was heard by the Supreme Court of Canada on March 20, 2007. On October 12, 2007, the Supreme Court released its decision and unanimously dismissed the Plaintiffs' appeal. As a result, the Company and its Senior Officers were not required to pay any of the damages, interest or costs awarded by the trial judge. The Supreme Court of Canada also awarded costs to the Company.

Based solely on the information available at the time, if the damages, costs and interest awarded by the trial judge had been paid at the fiscal 2005 year-end, the Company estimated this amount to be about $18 million. The provision for the damages award, costs and interest and the related future income tax recovery were based on management's best estimate and was subject to adjustment when all facts were known and all issues were resolved. As a result of the final determination by the Supreme Court of Canada, the Company reversed the $18 million litigation provision and related future income tax recovery in the financial statements during the first quarter of fiscal 2008.

During the third quarter of fiscal 2008, the Company and the Plaintiffs agreed to a settlement of the amount of costs awarded to the Company for the trial and the Supreme Court of Canada hearing and costs awarded to the Plaintiffs for the certification and summary judgment motions. In addition, the Company reached an agreement with its directors' and officers' insurance provider for reimbursement of certain expert and professional fees previously paid by the Company in connection with the trial and appeal. As a result of these agreements, the Company recorded a $1.9 million recovery in the unaudited interim consolidated financial statements for the 13 week period ended March 29, 2008. As a result of the Supreme Court of Canada's final determination as well as the agreement on recovery of costs having now been finalized, no further recoveries are expected.

Note 12: Changes in Non-Cash Operating Working Capital Items

	Year Ended	
	June 28, 2008	June 30, 2007
Decrease (increase) in:		
Accounts receivable	($31)	($322)
Income taxes recoverable	(8)	2,485
Inventories	1,157	3,787
Prepaid expenses	204	(420)
Increase (decrease) in:		
Accounts payable and accrued liabilities	514	(1,377)
Income taxes payable	(1,473)	1,473
	$363	$5,626

Note 13: Contingencies and Guarantees

(a) Legal proceedings

In the course of its business, the Company from time to time becomes involved in various claims and legal proceedings. In the opinion of management, all such claims and suits are adequately covered by insurance, or if not so covered, the results are not expected to materially affect the Company's financial position.

(b) Guarantees

The Company has provided the following guarantees to third parties and no amounts have been accrued in the consolidated financial statements for these guarantees:

(i) In the ordinary course of business, the Company has agreedto indemnify its lenders under its credit facility against certain costs or losses resulting from changes in laws and regulations or from a default in repaying a borrowing. These indemnifications extend for the term of the credit facility and do not provide any limit on the maximum potential liability. Historically, the Company has not made any indemnification payments under such agreements.

(ii) In the ordinary course of business, the Company has provided indemnification commitments to certain counterparties in matters such as real estate leasing transactions, director and officer indemnification agreements and certain purchases of fixed assets such as computer software. These indemnification agreements generally require the Company to compensate the counterparties for costs or losses resulting from legal action brought against the counterparties related to the actions of the Company. The terms of these indemnification agreements will vary based on the contract and generally do not provide any limit on the maximum potential liability.

(iii) The Company sublet one location during fiscal 2004 and has provided the landlord with a guarantee in the event the sub-tenant defaults on its obligation to pay rent. The remaining term of the guarantee is less than 1 year and the Company's maximum exposure is $23.

Note 14: Commitments

(a) Operating and capital leases:

Minimum rentals for the next five fiscal years and thereafter, excluding rentals based upon revenue are as follows:

	Operating	Capital
2009	$10,850	$884
2010	8,544	-
2011	7,343	-
2012	5,609	-
2013	3,693	-
Thereafter	7,981	-

(b) Letters of credit:

The Company had outstanding letters of credit in the amount of $6,830 (June 30, 2007 - $10,389) for the importation of finished goods inventories to be received.

Note 15: Financial Instruments

(a) Fair value disclosure

Fair value estimates are made at a specific point in time, using available information about the financial instrument. These estimates are subjective in nature and involve uncertainties and the exercise of significant judgement.

The carrying value of the Company's short-term financial assets which includes cash and accounts receivable and short-term financial liabilities which includes accounts payable and accrued liabilities approximates their fair value due to their short term maturities. The fair value of the capital lease obligation approximates its carrying value due to its short term to maturity.

(b) Risk management

For the year ended June 28, 2008, the Company has early adopted the requirements of CICA Handbook Section 3862 – *Financial Instruments – Disclosures*, which apply to fiscal years beginning on or after October 1, 2007. This new Handbook section requires disclosures to enable users to evaluate the significance of financial instruments for the entity's financial position and performance, and the nature and extent of an entity's exposure to risks arising from financial instruments, including how the entity manages those risks. Disclosures relating to exposure to risks, particularly credit risk, liquidity risk, foreign currency risk, interest rate risk and equity price risk are provided below:

Credit Risk

Credit risk is the risk that a customer or counterparty to a financial instrument will cause a financial loss to the Company by failing to meet its obligations. The Company's financial instruments that are exposed to concentrations of credit risk are primarily cash (which includes cash and money market investments with maturities of three months or less) and accounts receivable. The Company limits its exposure to credit risk with respect to cash and money market investments by investing in short-term deposits and bankers acceptances with major Canadian financial institutions and Government of Canada treasury bills. The Company's accounts receivable consist primarily of credit card receivables from the last few days of the fiscal period end, which are settled within the first days of the new fiscal period. Accounts receivable also consist of accounts receivable from licensees and corporate customers. Accounts receivable are net of applicable allowance for doubtful accounts, which is established based on the specific credit risks associated with the licensee, each corporate customer and other relevant information. The allowance for doubtful accounts is assessed on a quarterly basis. Concentration of credit risk with respect to accounts receivable from licensees and corporate customers is limited due to the non significant balances outstanding and the number of different customers comprising the Company's customer base.

As at June 28, 2008, the Company's exposure to credit risk for these financial instruments was cash of $19.9 million and accounts receivable of $0.8 million. Cash included $18.1 million of short-term deposits.

Liquidity Risk

Liquidity risk is the risk that the Company will not be able to meet its financial obligations as they fall due. The Company's approach to managing liquidity risk is to ensure, to the extent possible, that it will have sufficient liquidity to meet its liabilities when due. As at June 28, 2008, the Company had $19.9 million of cash and a credit facility of $25 million that is committed until June 29, 2009. The credit facility is used to finance seasonal working capital requirements for merchandise purchases and other corporate purposes. The Company expects that the majority of its accounts payable and accrued liabilities will be discharged within 90 days. The Company also has a capital lease obligation that matures in April 2009. As at June 28, 2008, the remaining minimum payment under the capital lease obligation is $0.9 million.

Subsequent to June 28, 2008, the Company also obtained a $10 million uncommitted letter of credit facility and an uncommitted demand overdraft facility in the amount of $0.5 million related thereto.

Foreign Currency Risk

Foreign currency risk is the risk that the fair value or future cash flows of a financial instrument will fluctuate because of changes in foreign currency exchange rates. The Company purchases a significant portion of its leather and finished goods inventory from foreign vendors with payment terms in U.S. dollars. From time to time, the Company may enter into foreign exchange forward contracts to manage foreign exchange risk associated with these purchases. As at June 28, 2008 and as at June 30, 2007, the Company did not have any outstanding foreign exchange forward contracts to purchase U.S. dollars.

As at June 28, 2008, a sensitivity analysis was performed on the Company's U.S. dollar denominated financial instruments which principally consist of US$10 million of short-term deposits issued by major Canadian financial institutions to determine how a change in the U.S. dollar exchange rate would impact net earnings. On June 28, 2008, a 100 basis point rise or fall in the Canadian dollar against the U.S. dollar, assuming that all other variables, in particular interest rates, remained the same, would have resulted in a $0.1 million decrease or increase, respectively, in the Company's net earnings for the year ended June 28, 2008.

Interest Rate Risk

Interest rate risk is the risk that the fair value or future cash flows of a financial instrument will fluctuate because of changes in market interest rates. The Company's exposure to interest rate fluctuations is primarily related to cash borrowings under its existing credit facility which bears interest at floating rates and interest earned on its cash balances. The Company has performed a sensitivity analysis on interest rate risk at June 28, 2008, to determine how a change in interest rates would have impacted net earnings. As at June 28,2008, the Company's cash balance available for investment was approximately $19.9 million and an increase or decrease of 100 basis points in interest rates would have increased or decreased net earnings by approximately $0.1 million. This analysis assumes that all other variables, in particular foreign currency rates, remain constant.

Equity Price Risk

Equity price risk is the risk that the fair value or future cash flows of a financial instrument will fluctuate because of changes in market equity prices. The Company's exposure to equity price fluctuations is primarily related to the RSU and DSU liability included in accounts payable and accrued liabilities. The value of the vested DSU and RSU liability is adjusted to reflect changes in the market value of the Company's Subordinate Voting Shares. The Company has performed a sensitivity analysis on equity price risk as at June 28, 2008, to determine how a change in the price of the Company's Subordinate Voting Shares would have impacted net earnings. As at June 28, 2008, a total of 133,300 RSUs have been granted and 58,920 DSUs have been granted. An increase or decrease of $1.00 in the market price of the Company's Subordinate Voting Shares would have increased or decreased net earnings by approximately $0.1 million. This analysis assumes that all RSUs and DSUs were fully vested and other variables remain constant.

Note 16: Capital Disclosure

The Company defines its capital as capital lease obligation, including the current portion and shareholders' equity. The Company's objectives in managing capital are to:

- Ensure sufficient liquidity to support its current operations and execute its business plans;
- Enable the internal financing of capital projects; and
- Maintain a strong capital base so as to maintain investor, creditor and market confidence.

The Company's primary uses of capital are to finance non-cash working capital along with capital expenditures for new store additions, existing store renovation projects, information technology software and hardware purchases and production machinery and equipment purchases. The Company currently funds these requirements out of its internally generated cash flows. The Company's capital lease obligation relates to point-of-sale equipment and it matures in fiscal 2009. The Company maintains a $25 million credit facility that it uses to finance seasonal working capital requirements for merchandise purchases and other corporate purposes. The Company does not have any long-term debt and therefore net earnings generated from operations are available for reinvestment in the Company. The Board of Directors does not establish quantitative return on capital criteria for management, but rather promotes year-over-year sustainable profitable growth. On a quarterly basis, the Board of Directors monitors share repurchase program activities. Decisions on whether to repurchase shares are made on a specific transaction basis and depend on the Company's cash position, estimates of future cash requirements, market prices and regulatory restrictions. The Company does not currently pay dividends.

The Company is not subject to any externally imposed capital requirements. There has been no change with respect to the overall capital risk management strategy during the year ended June 28, 2008.

Note 17: Segmented information

Management has determined that the Company operates in one dominant industry which involves the design, manufacture and retail of fashion leather and suede.

aiming high

2008 Annual Report

management's report to the shareholders

The consolidated financial statements have been prepared by management in accordance with Canadian generally accepted accounting principles. When a choice between accounting methods exists, management has chosen those it deems conservative and appropriate in the circumstances. Financial statements will, by necessity, include certain amounts based on estimates and judgments. Management has determined such amounts on a reasonable basis to ensure that the consolidated financial statements are presented fairly in all material respects. Financial information contained in the this report is consistent, where appropriate, with the information and data contained in the consolidated financial statements. All information in this report is the responsibility of management.

Management has established systems of internal control, including disclosure controls and procedures, which are designed to provide reasonable assurance that financial and non-financial information that is disclosed is timely, complete, relevant and accurate. These systems of internal control also serve to safeguard the Corporation's assets. The systems of internal control are monitored by management, and further supported by an internal audit department whose functions include reviewing internal controls and their applications.

The Board of Directors is responsible for the overall stewardship and governance of the Corporation, including ensuring management fulfills its responsibility for financial reporting and internal control, and reviewing and approving the consolidated financial statements. The Board carries out this responsibility principally through its Audit Committee.

The Audit Committee of the Board of Directors, composed of independent Directors, meets regularly with management, the internal auditors and the external auditors to satisfy itself that each is properly discharging its responsibilities, and to review the consolidated financial statements and management's discussion and analysis. The Audit Committee reports its findings to the Board of Directors prior to the approval of such statements for issuance to the shareholders. The Audit Committee also recommends, for review by the Board of Directors and approval of shareholders, the reappointment of the external auditors. The internal and external auditors have full and free access to the Audit Committee.

The consolidated financial statements have been audited by KPMG LLP, the independent external auditors, in accordance with generally accepted auditing standards on behalf of the shareholders. The auditors' report outlines the scope of their examination and sets forth their opinion.

Sean Durfy
President and
Chief Executive Officer

Vito Culmone
Executive Vice-President, Finance and
Chief Financial Officer

Calgary, Canada
February 10, 2009

auditors' report to the shareholders

We have audited the consolidated balance sheets of WestJet Airlines Ltd. as at December 31, 2008 and 2007 and the consolidated statements of earnings, comprehensive income, shareholders' equity and cash flows for the years then ended. These consolidated financial statements are the responsibility of the Corporation's management. Our responsibility is to express an opinion on these consolidated financial statements based on our audits.

We conducted our audits in accordance with Canadian generally accepted auditing standards. Those standards require that we plan and perform an audit to obtain reasonable assurance whether the financial statements are free of material misstatement. An audit includes examining, on a test basis, evidence supporting the amounts and disclosures in the financial statements. An audit also includes assessing the accounting principles used and significant estimates made by management, as well as evaluating the overall financial statement presentation.

In our opinion, these consolidated financial statements present fairly, in all material respects, the financial position of the Corporation as at December 31, 2008 and 2007 and the results of its operations and its cash flows for the years then ended in accordance with Canadian generally accepted accounting principles.

Chartered Accountants
Calgary, Canada
February 10, 2009

KPMG LLP

---

consolidated statement of earnings

For the years ended December 31
(Stated in thousands of Canadian dollars, except per share amounts)

	2008	2007
Revenues:		
Guest revenues	$ 2,301,301	$ 1,899,159
Charter and other revenues	248,205	227,997
	2,549,506	2,127,156
Expenses:		
Aircraft fuel	803,293	503,931
Airport operations	342,922	299,004
Flight operations and navigational charges	280,920	258,571
Marketing, general and administration	211,979	177,393
Sales and distribution	170,605	146,194
Depreciation and amortization	136,485	127,223
Inflight	105,849	85,499
Aircraft leasing	86,050	75,201
Maintenance	85,093	74,653
Employee profit share	33,435	46,705
Loss on impairment of property and equipment (note 5)	—	31,881
	2,256,631	1,826,255
Earnings from operations	292,875	300,901
Non-operating income (expense):		
Interest income	25,485	24,301
Interest expense	(76,078)	(75,749)
Gain (loss) on foreign exchange	30,587	(12,750)
Gain (loss) on disposal of property and equipment	(701)	54
Loss on derivatives (note 11)	(17,331)	—
	(38,038)	(64,144)
Earnings before income taxes	254,837	236,757
Income tax expense: (note 7)		
Current	2,549	2,149
Future	74,153	41,775
	76,702	43,924
Net earnings	$ 178,135	$ 192,833
Earnings per share: (note 8(c))		
Basic	$ 1.38	$ 1.49
Diluted	$ 1.37	$ 1.47

The accompanying notes are an integral part of the consolidated financial statements.

consolidated balance sheet

As at December 31
(Stated in thousands of Canadian dollars)

	2008	2007
Assets		
Current assets:		
Cash and cash equivalents (note 4)	$ 820,214	$ 653,558
Accounts receivable	16,837	15,009
Future income tax (note 7)	4,196	—
Prepaid expenses, deposits and other (note 12(a))	67,693	39,019
Inventory	17,054	10,202
	925,994	717,788
Property and equipment (note 5)	2,281,850	2,213,063
Other assets (note 12(a))	71,005	53,371
	$ 3,278,849	$ 2,984,222
Liabilities and shareholders' equity		
Current liabilities:		
Accounts payable and accrued liabilities	$ 249,354	$ 168,171
Advance ticket sales	251,354	194,929
Non-refundable guest credits	73,020	54,139
Current portion of long-term debt (note 6)	165,721	172,992
Current portion of obligations under capital lease	395	375
	739,844	590,606
Long-term debt (note 6)	1,186,182	1,256,526
Obligations under capital lease	713	1,108
Other liabilities (note 12(a))	24,233	11,337
Future income tax (note 7)	241,740	174,737
	2,192,712	2,034,314
Shareholders' equity:		
Share capital (note 8(b))	452,885	448,568
Contributed surplus	60,193	57,889
Accumulated other comprehensive loss (note 12(c))	(38,112)	(11,914)
Retained earnings	611,171	455,365
	1,086,137	949,908
Commitments and contingencies (note 10)		
	$ 3,278,849	$ 2,984,222

The accompanying notes are an integral part of the consolidated financial statements.

On behalf of the Board:

Sean Durfy, Director

Hugh Bolton, Director

consolidated statement of shareholders' equity

For the years ended December 31
(Stated in thousands of Canadian dollars)

	2008	2007
Share capital:		
Balance, beginning of year	$ 448,568	$ 431,248
Issuance of shares pursuant to stock option plans (note 8(b))	227	1,551
Stock-based compensation on stock options exercised (note 8(b))	11,181	20,040
Shares repurchased (note 8(b))	(7,091)	(4,271)
	452,885	448,568
Contributed surplus:		
Balance, beginning of year	57,889	58,656
Stock-based compensation expense (note 8(e)(f))	13,485	19,273
Stock-based compensation on stock options exercised (note 8(b))	(11,181)	(20,040)
	60,193	57,889
Accumulated other comprehensive loss: (note 12(c))		
Balance, beginning of year	(11,914)	—
Change in accounting policy	—	(13,420)
Other comprehensive income (loss)	(26,198)	1,506
	(38,112)	(11,914)
Retained earnings:		
Balance, beginning of year	455,365	316,123
Change in accounting policy	—	(36,612)
Shares repurchased (note 8(b))	(22,329)	(16,979)
Net earnings	178,135	192,833
	611,171	455,365
Total accumulated other comprehensive loss and retained earnings	573,059	443,451
Total shareholders' equity	$ 1,086,137	$ 949,908

The accompanying notes are an integral part of the consolidated financial statements.

consolidated statement of comprehensive income

For the years ended December 31
(Stated in thousands of Canadian dollars)

	2008	2007
Net earnings	$ 178, 135	$ 192,833
Other comprehensive income, net of taxes:		
Amortization of hedge settlements to aircraft leasing	1,400	1,400
Net unrealized gain on foreign exchange derivatives under cash flow hedge accounting (net of tax of ($3,097); 2007 – $nil)	7,224	88
Reclassification of net realized (gains) losses on foreign exchange derivatives to net earnings (net of tax of $1,357; 2007 – $nil)	(3,197)	18
Net unrealized loss on fuel derivatives under cash flow hedge accounting (net of tax of $13,086)	(31,625)	—
	(26,198)	1,506
Total comprehensive income	$ 151,937	$ 194,339

The accompanying notes are an integral part of the consolidated financial statements.

consolidated statement of cash flows

For the years ended December 31
(Stated in thousands of Canadian dollars)

	2008	2007
Operating activities		
Net earnings	$ 178,135	$ 192,833
Items not involving cash:		
Depreciation and amortization	136,485	127,223
Amortization of other liabilities	(937)	(897)
Amortization of hedge settlements	1,400	1,400
Unrealized loss on derivative instruments (note 11)	6,725	—
Loss on disposal of property, equipment and aircraft parts (note 5)	1,809	32,773
Stock-based compensation expense (note 8(e)(f))	13,485	19,273
Future income tax expense	74,153	41,775
Unrealized foreign exchange loss (gain)	(34,823)	13,813
Change in non-cash working capital (note 12(b))	84,154	112,872
	460,586	541,065
Financing activities		
Increase in long-term debt	101,782	141,178
Repayment of long-term debt	(179,397)	(156,516)
Decrease in obligations under capital lease	(375)	(356)
Increase in other assets	(4,135)	(20,897)
Shares repurchased (note 8(b))	(29,420)	(21,250)
Issuance of common shares (note 8(b))	227	1,551
Change in non-cash working capital	(4,111)	(3,000)
	(115,429)	(59,290)
Investing activities		
Aircraft additions	(114,470)	(191,437)
Aircraft disposals	84	1,975
Other property and equipment additions	(90,663)	(24,639)
Other property and equipment disposals	172	13,819
Change in non-cash working capital	5,147	—
	(199,730)	(200,282)
Cash flow from operating, financing and investing activities	145,427	281,493
Effect of exchange rate on cash and cash equivalents	21,229	(5,452)
Net change in cash and cash equivalents	166,656	276,041
Cash and cash equivalents, beginning of year	653,558	377,517
Cash and cash equivalents, end of year	$ 820,214	$ 653,558
Cash interest paid	$ (76,604)	$ (75,712)
Cash taxes received (paid)	$ (2,305)	$ 10,623

The accompanying notes are an integral part of the consolidated financial statements.

notes to consolidated financial statements

For the years ended December 31, 2008 and 2007
(Stated in thousands of Canadian dollars, except share and per share data)

1. Summary of significant accounting policies

(a) Basis of presentation

The accompanying consolidated financial statements of WestJet Airlines Ltd. (the Corporation) have been prepared in accordance with Canadian generally accepted accounting principles (GAAP). Amounts presented in the Corporation's consolidated financial statements and the notes thereto are in Canadian dollars unless otherwise stated.

(b) Principles of consolidation

The accompanying consolidated financial statements include the accounts of the Corporation and its wholly owned subsidiaries, as well as the accounts of five special-purpose entities, which are utilized to facilitate the financing of aircraft. The Corporation has no equity ownership in the special-purpose entities; however, the Corporation is the primary beneficiary of the special-purpose entities' operations. All intercompany balances and transactions have been eliminated.

(c) Use of estimates

The preparation of financial statements in conformity with Canadian GAAP requires management to make estimates and assumptions regarding significant items such as amounts relating to depreciation and amortization, non-refundable guest credits, lease return conditions, future income taxes, stock-based compensation expense, deferred sales and distribution costs, impairment assessments of property and equipment, and the valuation of derivative financial instruments that affect the amounts reported in the consolidated financial statements and accompanying notes. Changes in facts and circumstances may result in revised estimates, and actual results may differ from these estimates.

(d) Revenue recognition

(i) Guest revenues

Guest revenues, including the air component of vacation packages, are recognized when air transportation is provided. Tickets sold but not yet used are reported in the consolidated balance sheet as advance ticket sales.

(ii) Charter and other revenues

Charter and other revenues include charter revenue, cargo revenue, net revenues from the sale of the land component of vacation packages, ancillary revenues and other.

Charter and cargo revenue is recognized when air transportation is provided.

Revenue from the land component of vacation packages is generated from providing agency services equal to the amount paid by the guest for products and services less payment to the travel supplier, and are reported at the net amounts received. Revenue from the land component is deferred and recognized on completion of the vacation.

Ancillary revenues are recognized as the services and products are provided to the guests. Included in ancillary revenues are fees associated with guest itinerary changes or cancellations, excess baggage fees, buy-on-board sales and pre-reserved seating fees.

Included in other revenue is revenue from expired credit files recognized at the time of expiry. Also included in other revenue is revenue under the tri-branded credit card agreement that expired in 2008, where net retail sales revenue was recognized at the time the transaction occurred and revenue related to account activations was recognized immediately upon activation.

(e) Non-refundable guest credits

The Corporation issues future travel credits to guests for flight changes and cancellations, as well as for gift certificates. Where appropriate, future travel credits are also issued for flight delays, missing baggage and other inconveniences. All credits are non-refundable and expire based on the nature of the credit, other than gift certificates which do not contain an expiry date. The Corporation records a liability depending on the nature of the credit at either the full value or at the incremental cost of a one-way flight in the period the credit is issued. The utilization of guest credits is recorded as revenue when the guest has flown or upon expiry.

(f) Financial instruments

A financial instrument is any contract that gives rise to a financial asset of one entity and a financial liability or equity instrument to another entity. Financial assets and financial liabilities, including derivatives, are recognized on the consolidated balance sheet at the time the Corporation becomes a party to the contractual provisions. Upon initial recognition, financial instruments are measured at fair value and for the purpose of subsequent measurement, financial instruments are allocated into one of the following five categories: held-for-trading, held-to-maturity, loans and receivables, available-for-sale or other financial liabilities.

The Corporation's financial assets and liabilities consist primarily of cash and cash equivalents, US-dollar deposits, accounts receivable, accounts payable and accrued liabilities, long-term debt and derivative instruments. The Corporation has designated its financial instruments as follows:

Financial instrument	Category	Measurement method
Cash and cash equivalents	Held-for-trading	Fair value
US-dollar deposits	Held-for-trading	Fair value
Accounts receivable	Loans and receivables	Amortized cost
Accounts payable and accrued liabilities	Other financial liabilities	Amortized cost
Long-term debt	Other financial liabilities	Amortized cost
Derivative instruments (i)	Held-for-trading	Fair value

(i) Except for derivative instruments designated in an effective hedging relationship.

Held-for-trading instruments are financial assets and liabilities typically acquired with the intention of generating revenues in the short-term. However, an entity is allowed to designate any financial instrument as held-for-trading on initial recognition even if it would otherwise not satisfy the definition. As at December 31, 2008, the Corporation does not hold any financial instruments that do not satisfy the definition. Financial assets and financial liabilities required to be classified or designated as held-for-trading are measured at fair value, with gains and losses recorded in net earnings for the period in which the change occurs. The Corporation uses trade-date accounting for its held-for-trading financial assets.

Held-to-maturity investments are non-derivative financial assets, with fixed or determinable payments and fixed maturity, that an entity has the positive intention and ability to hold to maturity. These financial assets are measured at amortized cost using the effective interest method. As at December 31, 2008, the Corporation does not have any financial assets classified as held-to-maturity.

Financial assets classified as loans and receivables are measured at amortized cost using the effective interest method.

Available-for-sale financial assets are non-derivative assets that are designated as available-for-sale or that are not classified as loans and receivables, held-to-maturity investments or held-for-trading. Available-for-sale financial assets are carried at fair value with unrealized gains and losses included in other comprehensive income (OCI) until such gains or losses are realized or an other than temporary impairment is determined to have occurred. Available-for-sale assets are measured at fair value, except for assets that do not have a readily determinable fair value which are recorded at cost. As at December 31, 2008, the Corporation does not have any financial assets classified as available-for-sale.

Other financial liabilities are measured at amortized cost using the effective interest method and include all liabilities other than derivatives or liabilities that have been identified as held-for-trading.

The Corporation will from time to time use various financial derivatives to reduce market risk exposure from changes in foreign exchange rates and jet fuel prices. Derivatives, including embedded derivatives, are recorded at fair value on the balance sheet with changes in fair value recorded in the statement of earnings unless exempted from derivative treatments as a normal purchase and sale or as designated effective hedging instruments. The Corporation selected January 1, 2003, as its transition date for embedded derivatives; as such only contracts entered into or substantively modified after the transition date have been examined for embedded derivatives. When financial assets and liabilities are designated as part of a hedging relationship and qualify for hedge accounting, they are subject to measurement and classification requirements outlined under cash flow hedges. The Corporation's policy is not to utilize derivative financial instruments for trading or speculative purposes.

The Corporation will assess at each reporting period whether there is any objective evidence that a financial asset, other than those classified as held-for-trading, is impaired.

The Corporation immediately expenses any transaction costs incurred in relation to the acquisition of financial assets and liabilities.

Effective January 1, 2008, the Corporation adopted CICA Section 3862, Financial Instruments – Disclosure and Section 3863, Financial Instruments – Presentation. Section 3862 requires enhanced disclosure on the nature and extent of financial instrument risks and how an entity manages those risks. Section 3863 carries forward the existing presentation requirements and provides additional guidance for the classification of financial instruments. These new requirements are for disclosure purposes only and, on adoption, did not impact the financial results of the Corporation. See note 11, financial instruments and risk management, for further disclosure.

(g) Cash flow hedges

The Corporation uses various financial derivative instruments such as forward contracts, fixed swap agreements, costless collar structures and option arrangements to manage fluctuations in foreign exchange rates and jet fuel prices.

The Corporation's derivatives that have been designated and qualify for hedge accounting are classified as cash flow hedges. The Corporation formally documents all relationships between hedging instruments and hedged items, as well as the risk-management objective and strategy for undertaking the hedge transaction. This process includes linking all derivatives that are designated in a cash flow hedging relationship to a specific firm commitment or forecasted transaction. The Corporation also formally assesses, both at inception and at every reporting date, whether the derivatives that are used in hedging transactions have been highly effective in offsetting changes in cash flows of hedged items and whether those derivatives may be expected to remain highly effective in future periods.

Under cash flow hedge accounting, the effective portion of the change in the fair value of the hedging instrument is recognized in OCI while the ineffective portion is recognized in non-operating income (expense). Upon maturity of the financial derivative instrument, the effective gains and losses previously recognized in accumulated other comprehensive loss (AOCL) are recorded in net earnings under the same caption as the hedged item.

If the hedging relationship ceases to qualify for cash flow hedge accounting, any change in fair value of the instrument from the point it ceases to qualify is recorded in non-operating income (expense). Amounts previously recorded in AOCL will remain in AOCL until the anticipated transaction occurs, at which time, the amount is recorded in net earnings under the same caption as the hedged item. If the transaction is no longer expected to occur, amounts previously recorded in AOCL will be reclassified to non-operating income (expense).

(h) Foreign currency

Monetary assets and liabilities, denominated in foreign currencies, are translated into Canadian dollars at the rate of exchange in effect at the balance sheet date with any resulting gain or loss being included in the consolidated statement of earnings. Non-monetary assets, non-monetary liabilities and revenues and expenses arising from transactions denominated in foreign currencies are translated into Canadian dollars at the rates prevailing at the time of the transaction.

(i) Cash and cash equivalents

Cash and cash equivalents consist of cash and short-term investments that are highly liquid in nature and have a maturity date of three months or less.

(j) Inventory

Effective January 1, 2008, the Corporation adopted CICA Section 3031, Inventories. This section provides more extensive guidance on the determination of cost, narrows permitted cost formulas, requires impairment testing and expands the disclosure requirements to increase transparency. There was no impact as a result of adoption on the financial results of the Corporation.

Inventories are valued at the lower of cost and net realizable value, with cost being determined on a first-in, first-out basis. The Corporation's inventory balance consists of aircraft fuel, de-icing fluid and retail merchandise. Aircraft expendables and consumables are expensed as acquired.

(k) Deferred costs

Certain sales and distribution costs attributed to advance ticket sales are deferred in prepaid expenses, deposits and other on the consolidated balance sheet and expensed to sales and distribution in the period the related revenue is recognized.

(l) Property and equipment

Property and equipment is stated at cost and depreciated to its estimated residual value. Assets under capital lease are initially recorded at the present value of minimum lease payments at the inception of the lease.

Asset class	Basis	Rate
Aircraft, net of estimated residual value	Cycles	Cycles flown
Live satellite television included in aircraft	Straight-line	10 years/lease term
Ground property and equipment	Straight-line	3 to 25 years
Spare engines and parts, net of estimated residual value	Straight-line	20 years
Assets under capital lease	Straight-line	Term of lease
Buildings	Straight-line	40 years
Leasehold improvements	Straight-line	Term of lease

Aircraft are amortized over a range of 30,000 to 50,000 cycles. Residual values of the Corporation's aircraft range between $4,000 to $6,000.

Property and equipment are reviewed for impairment when events or changes in circumstances indicate that the carrying value may not be recoverable. When events or circumstances indicate that the carrying amount of property and equipment may not be recoverable, the long-lived assets are tested for recoverability by comparing the undiscounted future cash flows to the carrying amount of the asset or group of assets. If the total of the undiscounted future cash flows is less than the carrying amount of the property and equipment, the amount of any impairment loss is determined as the amount by which the carrying amount of the asset exceeds the fair value of the asset. The impairment loss is then recognized in net earnings. Fair value is defined as the amount of the consideration that would be agreed upon in an arm's length transaction between knowledgeable, willing parties who are under no compulsion to act.

(m) Maintenance costs

Maintenance and repairs, including major overhauls, are charged to maintenance expense as they are incurred.

Aircraft parts that are deemed to be beyond economic repair are disposed of and the remaining net book values of these parts are included in maintenance expense.

Recovery of costs associated with parts and labour covered under warranty are recognized as an offset to maintenance expense.

(n) Leases

The Corporation classifies leases as either a capital lease or an operating lease. Leases that transfer substantially all of the benefits and risk of ownership to the Corporation are accounted for as capital leases. Assets under capital leases are depreciated on a straight-line basis over the term of the lease. Rental payments under operating leases are expensed as incurred.

The Corporation provides for asset retirement obligations to return leased aircraft to certain standard conditions as specified within the Corporation's lease agreements. The lease return costs are accounted for in accordance with the asset retirement obligations requirements and are initially measured at fair value and capitalized to property and equipment as an asset retirement cost.

(o) Capitalized costs

Costs associated with assets under development, which have probable future economic benefit, can be clearly defined and measured, and are incurred for the development of new products or technologies, are capitalized. These costs are not amortized until the asset is substantially complete and ready for its intended use, at which time, they are amortized over the life of the underlying asset.

Interest attributable to funds used to finance property and equipment is capitalized to the related asset until the point of commercial use.

Costs of new route development are expensed as incurred.

(p) Future income tax

The Corporation uses the asset and liability method of accounting for future income taxes. Under this method, current income taxes are recognized for the estimated income taxes payable for the current year. Future income tax assets and liabilities are recognized for temporary differences between the tax and accounting bases of assets and liabilities, calculated using the currently enacted or substantively enacted tax rates anticipated to apply in the period that the temporary differences are expected to reverse. Future income tax inflows and outflows are subject to estimation in terms of both timing and amount of future taxable earnings. Should these estimates change, the carrying value of income tax assets or liabilities may change.

(q) Stock-based compensation plans

Grants under the Corporation's stock-based compensation plans are accounted for in accordance with the fair-value-based method of accounting. For stock-based compensation plans that will settle through the issuance of equity, the fair value of the option or unit is determined on the grant date using a valuation model and recorded as compensation expense over the period that the stock option or unit vests, with a corresponding increase to contributed surplus. The fair value of stock options is estimated on the date of grant using the Black-Scholes option pricing model, and the fair value of the Corporation's other equity-based share unit plans is determined based on the market value of the Corporation's common shares on the date of the grant. Upon the exercise of stock options and units, consideration received, together with amounts previously recorded in contributed surplus, are recorded as an increase in share capital.

Stock-based compensation plans that are to be settled in cash are accounted for as liabilities based on the intrinsic value of the awards. The compensation expense is accrued over the vesting period of the award, based on the difference between the market value of the Corporation's common shares and the exercise price of the award, if any. Fluctuations in the market value of the Corporation's common shares, determined based on the closing share price on the last trading day of each reporting period, will result in a change to the accrued compensation expense, which is recognized in the period in which the fluctuation occurs.

The Corporation does not incorporate an estimated forfeiture rate for stock options or share units that will not vest, but rather accounts for actual forfeitures as they occur.

For employees eligible to retire during the vesting period, the compensation expense is recognized over the period from the grant date to the retirement eligibility date. In instances where an employee is eligible to retire on the grant date of the stock-based award, compensation expense is recognized immediately.

(r) Per share amounts

Basic per share amounts are calculated using the weighted average number of shares outstanding during the year. Diluted per share amounts are calculated based on the treasury stock method, which assumes that the total proceeds obtained on the exercise of options and share units and the unamortized portion of stock-based compensation on stock options and share units would be used to purchase shares at the average price during the period. The weighted average number of shares outstanding is then adjusted by the net change.

(s) Comparative amounts

Certain prior-period balances have been reclassified to conform to current period's presentation, including the reclassification of interest income and interest expense as non-operating items and the reclassification of the Corporation's employee profit share expense as an operating item.

2. Future accounting pronouncements

(a) Goodwill and intangible assets

In February 2008, the CICA issued Section 3064, Goodwill and Intangible Assets. Effective for fiscal years beginning on or after October 1, 2008, this section provides guidance on the recognition, measurement, presentation and disclosure for goodwill and intangible assets, other than the initial recognition of goodwill or intangible assets acquired in a business combination. Retroactive application to prior-period financial statements will be required. The Corporation does not anticipate that the adoption of this standard, effective January 1, 2009, will significantly impact its financial results.

(b) Business combinations

In January 2009, the CICA issued Section 1582, Business Combinations. This section is effective January 1, 2011 and applies prospectively to business combinations for which the acquisition date is on or after the first annual reporting period of the Corporation beginning on or after January 1, 2011. Early adoption is permitted. This section replaces Section 1581, Business Combinations and harmonizes the Canadian standards with international financial reporting standards (IFRS). The Corporation does not anticipate that the adoption of this standard will impact its financial results.

(c) International financial reporting standards

On February 13, 2008, the CICA Accounting Standards Board (AcSB) confirmed that the changeover to IFRS from Canadian GAAP will be required for publicly accountable enterprises for interim and annual financial statements effective for fiscal years beginning on or after January 1, 2011, including comparatives for 2010. The objective is to improve financial reporting by having one single set of accounting standards that are comparable with other entities on an international basis.

The Corporation commenced its IFRS conversion project during 2008 and established a formal project governance structure, including an IFRS Steering Committee, to monitor the progress and critical decisions in the transition to IFRS. The Steering Committee consists of senior levels of management from Finance, Treasury and Investor Relations, among others. An external advisor has been engaged to work with the Corporation's dedicated project staff to complete the conversion. Regular reporting is provided by the project team to senior management, the Steering Committee and the Audit Committee of the Board of Directors.

The Corporation's IFRS conversion project consists of three phases: Diagnostic, Solution Development, and Implementation and Execution. The Corporation has completed the Diagnostic phase, which involved a high-level preliminary assessment of the differences between Canadian GAAP and IFRS and the potential effects of IFRS to accounting and reporting processes, information systems, business processes and external disclosures. This assessment has provided insight as to the most significant areas of difference applicable to the Corporation and includes property and equipment, provisions and leases, as well as the more extensive presentation and disclosure requirements under IFRS.

The Corporation has finalized its IFRS transition plan including a timetable for assessing the impact on systems, internal controls over financial reporting and business activities. Currently the Corporation is engaged in the Solution Development phase of the project and is working in issue-specific teams to focus on generating options and making recommendations in the identified areas. The Corporation has begun to roll out its staff training programs, and has begun to perform an in-depth review of accounting policy impacts, as well as the associated impacts of the IFRS transition on business activities. A full review of the Corporation's information systems is in progress to assess IFRS conversion impacts and is continuing to evaluate the available alternatives within its current financial systems. The Corporation's target is to complete the Solution Development phase by the end of the third quarter of 2009.

The Corporation continues to monitor standards development as issued by the International Accounting Standards Board and the AcSB, as well as regulatory developments as issued by the Canadian Securities Administrators, which may affect the timing, nature or disclosure of the Corporation's adoption of IFRS.

The transition from current Canadian GAAP to IFRS is a significant undertaking that may materially affect the Corporation's reported financial position and results of operations. As the Corporation is still in the Solution Development phase and has not yet selected its accounting policy choices and IFRS 1 exemptions, the Corporation is unable to quantify the impact of IFRS on its financial statements. The areas of significance identified above are based on available information and the Corporation's expectations as of the date of this report and thus, are subject to change for new facts and circumstances.

Please see the following table for certain elements of the Corporation's IFRS transition plan, and an assessment of progress towards achieving these. The project team is working through a detailed IFRS transition plan and certain project activities and milestones could change. The Corporation has begun to highlight certain key activities below to provide insights into the IFRS project.

Given the progress of the project and outcomes identified, the Corporation could change its intentions between the time of communicating these key milestones below and the changeover date. Further, changes in regulation or economic conditions at the date of the changeover or throughout the project could result in changes to the transition plan being different from those communicated here.

Key activity	Key milestones	Status
	Financial statement preparation	
• Identify differences in Canadian GAAP/ IFRS accounting policies • Select ongoing IFRS policies • Select IFRS 1 choices • Develop financial statement format • Quantify effects of change in initial IFRS disclosure and 2010 comparative financial statements	Senior management and Steering Committee sign-off for all key IFRS accounting policy choices to occur during the third quarter of 2009. Development of draft financial statement format to occur during the latter part of 2009.	Completed the IFRS Diagnostic phase during 2008, which involved a high-level review of the major differences between Canadian GAAP and IFRS. In-depth analysis of issues and accounting policy choices is currently underway.
	Training	
Define and introduce appropriate level of IFRS expertise for each of the following: • Controller's Group and business unit accounting personnel • Audit Committee	Controller's Group and business unit accounting personnel training to occur during the third and fourth quarters of 2009 as needed. Additional training will occur throughout the project as needed. Audit Committee training tentatively scheduled to occur during the second half of 2009.	Project team expert resources have been identified to provide insights and training. Training for project team members is occurring throughout the project.
	Information technology (IT) infrastructure	
Confirm that business processes and systems are IFRS compliant, including: • Program upgrades/changes • Gathering data for disclosures	Confirm that systems can address 2010 parallel processing requirements by the third quarter of 2009. Confirm that business processes and systems are IFRS compliant throughout the project.	Diagnostic analysis regarding current IT systems completed. Currently reviewing options to address business process changes and parallel processing during 2010.
	Control environment	
• For all accounting policy changes identified, assess control design and effectiveness implications • Implement appropriate changes	All key control and design effectiveness implications are being assessed as part of the key IFRS differences and accounting policy choices through to the fourth quarter of 2009.	Analysis of control issues is underway in conjunction with review of accounting issues and policies.

3. Capital management

The Corporation's policy is to maintain a strong capital base so as to maintain investor, creditor and market confidence and to sustain future development of the airline. The Corporation manages its capital structure and makes adjustments to it in light of changes in economic conditions and the risk characteristics of the underlying assets.

In order to maintain or adjust the capital structure, the Corporation may from time to time purchase shares for cancellation pursuant to normal course issuer bids to offset dilution, issue new shares and adjust current and projected debt levels.

In the management of capital, the Corporation includes shareholders' equity (excluding AOCL), long-term debt, capital leases, cash and cash equivalents and the Corporation's off-balance-sheet obligations related to its aircraft operating leases, all of which are presented in detail below.

The Corporation monitors capital on a number of bases, including adjusted debt-to-equity and adjusted net debt to Earnings Before Interest, Taxes, Depreciation and Aircraft Rent (EBITDAR). EBITDAR is a non-GAAP financial measure commonly used in the airline industry to evaluate results by excluding differences in the method by which an airline finances its aircraft. In addition, the Corporation will adjust EBITDAR for one-time special items, for non-operating gains and losses on derivatives and for gains and losses on foreign exchange. The calculation of EBITDAR is a measure that does not have a standardized meaning prescribed under GAAP and is therefore not likely to be comparable to similar measures presented by other issuers. The Corporation adjusts debt to include its off-balance-sheet aircraft operating leases. Common industry practice is to multiply the trailing twelve months of aircraft leasing expense by 7.5 to derive a present value debt equivalent. The Corporation defines adjusted net debt as adjusted debt less cash and cash equivalents. The Corporation defines equity as the sum of share capital, contributed surplus and retained earnings, and excludes AOCL.

	2008	2007	Change
Adjusted debt-to-equity:			
Long-term debt (i)	$ 1,351,903	$ 1,429,518	$ (77,615)
Obligations under capital lease (ii)	1,108	1,483	(375)
Off-balance-sheet aircraft leases (iii)	645,375	564,008	81,367
Adjusted debt	$ 1,998,386	$ 1,995,009	$ 3,377
Total shareholders' equity	1,086,137	949,908	136,229
Add: AOCL	38,112	11,914	26,198
Adjusted equity	$ 1,124,249	$ 961,822	$ 162,427
Adjusted debt-to-equity	1.78	2.07	(14.0%)
Adjusted net debt to EBITDAR (iv):			
Net earnings	$ 178,135	$ 192,833	$ (14,698)
Add:			
Net interest (v)	50,593	51,448	(855)
Taxes	76,702	43,924	32,778
Depreciation and amortization	136,485	127,223	9,262
Aircraft leasing	86,050	75,201	10,849
Other (vi)	(13,256)	44,631	(57,887)
EBITDAR	$ 514,709	$ 535,260	$ (20,551)
Adjusted debt (as above)	1,998,386	1,995,009	3,377
Less: Cash and cash equivalents	(820,214)	(653,558)	(166,656)
Adjusted net debt	$ 1,178,172	$ 1,341,451	$ (163,279)
Adjusted net debt to EBITDAR	2.29	2.51	(8.8%)

(i) As at December 31, 2008, long-term debt includes the current portion of long-term debt of $165,721 (2007 – $172,992) and long-term debt of $1,186,182 (2007 – $1,256,526).

(ii) As at December 31, 2008, obligations under capital lease includes the current portion of obligations under capital lease of $395 (2007 – $375) and obligations under capital lease of $713 (2007 – $1,108).

(iii) Off-balance-sheet aircraft leases is calculated by multiplying the trailing twelve months of aircraft leasing expense by 7.5. As at December 31, 2008, the trailing twelve months of aircraft leasing costs totalled $86,050 (2007 – $75,201).

(iv) The trailing twelve months are used in the calculation of EBITDAR.

(v) For the year ended December 31, 2008, net interest includes interest income of $25,485 (2007 – $24,301) and interest expense of $76,078 (2007 – $75,749).

(vi) For the year ended December 31, 2008, other includes the foreign exchange gain of $30,587 and loss on derivatives of $17,331 (2007 – reservation system impairment of $31,881 and foreign exchange loss of $12,750).

As at December 31, 2008 and 2007, the Corporation's targets were an adjusted debt-to-equity measure of no more than 3.00 and an adjusted net debt to EBITDAR of no more than 3.00. As at December 31, 2008, the Corporation's adjusted debt-to-equity ratio improved by 14.0% compared to December 31, 2007, attributable to the increase in shareholders' equity (mainly net earnings) more than offsetting the addition of new aircraft financing in the year. As at December 31, 2008, the Corporation's adjusted net debt to EBITDAR improved by 8.8% compared to December 31, 2007, mainly as a result of increased cash and cash equivalents more than offsetting the slight decrease in EBITDAR.

As part of the long-term debt agreements for the Calgary hangar facility and the flight simulator, the Corporation monitors certain financial covenants to ensure compliance with these debt agreements. As at December 31, 2008 and 2007, the Corporation was in compliance with these financial covenants. There are no financial covenant compliance requirements for the facilities guaranteed by the Export-Import Bank of the United States (Ex-Im Bank).

Under the Canada Transportation Act, the Corporation must, as a corporation which indirectly wholly owns the holder of a domestic licence, a scheduled international licence and a non-scheduled international licence, be Canadian, that is, be controlled, in fact, by Canadians with at least 75% of its voting interest owned and controlled by Canadians. To monitor this external requirement, the Corporation has structured its voting shares into two classes: common voting and variable voting. The common voting shares may be owned and controlled by Canadians only. The variable voting shares may be owned and controlled only by persons who are not Canadian and, as a class, cannot exceed more than 25% of the total number of votes cast on any matter on which a vote is to be taken. See note 8, share capital, for further information. As at December 31, 2008 and 2007, the Corporation was in compliance with this requirement.

No dividends have been paid or declared on any of the Corporation's shares since the date of incorporation. This policy is based on operational results, financial policy and financing requirements for future growth and is continuously reviewed by the Corporation.

There were no changes in the Corporation's approach to capital management during the year ended December 31, 2008.

4. Cash and cash equivalents

As at December 31, 2008, cash and cash equivalents includes bank balances of $98,998 (2007 – $37,395) and short-term investments of $721,216 (2007 – $616,163). Included in these balances, as at December 31, 2008, the Corporation has US-dollar cash and cash equivalents totaling US $56,920 (2007 – US $59,843).

As at December 31, 2008, cash and cash equivalents includes total restricted cash of $10,748 (2007 – $2,357). Included in this amount is $6,062 (2007 – $nil), representing cash held in trust by WestJet Vacations, a wholly owned subsidiary of the Corporation, in accordance with regulatory requirements governing advance ticket sales for certain travel-related activities; $4,222 (2007 – $2,069) for security on the Corporation's facilities for letters of guarantee; and, in accordance with U.S. regulatory requirements, US $381 (2007 – US $295) in restricted cash representing cash not yet remitted for passenger facility charges.

5. Property and equipment

2008	Cost	Accumulated depreciation	Net book value
Aircraft	$ 2,394,098	$ 402,095	$ 1,992,003
Ground property and equipment	157,223	83,648	73,575
Spare engines and parts	86,728	17,099	69,629
Buildings	40,028	6,828	33,200
Leasehold improvements	12,019	5,692	6,327
Assets under capital lease	2,482	1,690	792
	2,692,578	517,052	2,175,526
Deposits on aircraft	23,982	—	23,982
Assets under development	82,342	—	82,342
	$ 2,798,902	$ 517,052	$ 2,281,850

2007	Cost	Accumulated depreciation	Net book value
Aircraft	$ 2,273,509	$ 288,909	$ 1,984,600
Ground property and equipment	158,477	81,345	77,132
Spare engines and parts	76,862	13,610	63,252
Buildings	40,028	5,825	34,203
Leasehold improvements	7,039	5,112	1,927
Assets under capital lease	2,481	1,191	1,290
	2,558,396	395,992	2,162,404
Deposits on aircraft	38,795	—	38,795
Assets under development	11,864	—	11,864
	$ 2,609,055	$ 395,992	$ 2,213,063

As at December 31, 2008, assets under development includes $80,725 (2007 – $11,850) in amounts capitalized in conjunction with the Corporation's new Campus facility.

Included in aircraft costs are estimated lease return costs for aircraft under operating leases totaling $3,493 (2007 – $1,292) and associated accumulated amortization of $846 (2007 – $439). These amounts are being amortized on a straight-line basis over the term of each lease.

During the year ended December 31, 2007, the Corporation recognized a non-cash impairment of $31,881 for the capitalized costs associated with its former reservation system project.

6. Long-term debt

		2008	2007
Term loans – purchased aircraft	(i)	$ 1,331,083	$ 1,389,888
Term loan – flight simulator	(ii)	7,265	23,325
Term loans – live satellite television equipment	(iii)	1,740	3,621
Term loan – Calgary hangar facility	(iv)	9,648	10,054
Term loan – Calgary hangar facility	(v)	2,167	2,630
		1,351,903	1,429,518
Current portion		165,721	172,992
		$ 1,186,182	$ 1,256,526

(i) 52 individual term loans, amortized on a straight-line basis over a 12-year term, each repayable in quarterly principal instalments ranging from $668 to $955, including fixed interest at a weighted average rate of 5.32%, maturing between 2014 and 2020. These facilities are guaranteed by Ex-Im Bank and secured by one 800-series aircraft, 38 700-series aircraft and 13 600-series aircraft.

(ii) Term loan repayable in monthly instalments of $95, including floating interest at the bank's prime rate plus 0.88%, with an effective interest rate of 4.38% as at December 31, 2008, maturing in 2011, secured by one flight simulator.

(iii) 14 individual term loans, amortized on a straight-line basis over a five-year term, repayable in quarterly principal instalments ranging from $29 to $42, including floating interest at the Canadian LIBOR rate plus 0.08%, with a weighted average effective interest rate of 2.82% as at December 31, 2008, maturing between 2009 and 2011. These facilities are for the purchase of live satellite television equipment and are guaranteed by the Ex-Im Bank and secured by certain 700-series and 600-series aircraft.

(iv) Term loan repayable in monthly instalments of $108, including interest at 9.03%, maturing April 2011, secured by the Calgary hangar facility.

(v) Term loan repayable in monthly instalments of $50, including floating interest at the bank's prime rate plus 0.50%, with an effective interest rate of 4.00% as at December 31, 2008, maturing April 2013, secured by the Calgary hangar facility.

The net book value of the property and equipment pledged as collateral for the Corporation's secured borrowings was $2,012,915 as at December 31, 2008 (2007 – $2,028,548).

Future scheduled repayments of long-term debt are as follows:

2009	$ 165,721
2010	165,034
2011	177,557
2012	163,279
2013	162,740
2014 and thereafter	517,572
	$ 1,351,903

Held within the special-purpose entities, as identified in note 1, significant accounting policies, are liabilities of $1,332,859 (2007 – $1,393,526) related to the acquisition of the 52 purchased aircraft, which are included above in the long-term debt balances.

7. Income taxes

The provision for income taxes differs from that which would be expected by applying the combined federal and provincial statutory rates.

A reconciliation of the difference is as follows:

	2008	2007
Earnings before income taxes	$ 254,837	$ 236,757
Income tax rate	31.30%	33.99%
Expected income tax provision	79,764	80,474
Add (deduct):		
Non-deductible expenses	2,097	1,728
Non-deductible stock-based compensation	4,218	6,542
Effect of tax rate changes	(9,540)	(44,811)
Other	163	(9)
Actual income tax provision	$ 76,702	$ 43,924

The Corporation has included in its reconciliation an amount of $9,540 (2007 – $44,811) for the effect of tax rate changes. This amount reflects the impact of certain federal and provincial corporate income tax rate reductions enacted in 2008 and 2007, changes to the timing around when the Corporation expects certain temporary differences to reverse and differences between current statutory rates used in the reconciliation and future rates at which the future income tax liability is recorded.

The components of the net future tax liability are as follows:

		2008	2007
Future income tax liability:			
Property and equipment		$ (305,623)	$ (261,879)
Deferred partnership income		(34,741)	(17,420)
Future income tax asset:			
Share issue costs		13	79
Net unrealized loss on effective portion of derivatives designated in a hedging relationship		11,346	—
Non-capital losses		91,461	104,483
		$ (237,544)	$ (174,737)
The net future tax liability is presented on the consolidated balance sheet as follows:			
Future income tax	Current assets	4,196	—
Future income tax	Long-term liability	(241,740)	(174,737)
		$ (237,544)	$ (174,737)

The Corporation has recognized a benefit of $314,384 (2007 – $352,298) for non-capital losses which are available for carry forward to reduce taxable income in future years. These losses will begin to expire in the year 2014.

8. Share capital

(a) Authorized

Unlimited number of common voting shares

The common voting shares may be owned and controlled only by Canadians and shall confer the right to one vote per common voting share at all meetings of shareholders of the Corporation.

If a common voting share becomes owned or controlled by a person who is not a Canadian, such common voting share shall be converted into one variable voting share automatically and without any further act of the Corporation or the holder.

Unlimited number of variable voting shares

The variable voting shares may be owned and controlled only by a person who is not Canadian and are entitled to one vote per variable voting share unless (i) the number of issued and outstanding variable voting shares exceed 25% of the total number of all issued and outstanding variable voting shares and common voting shares collectively (or any greater percentage the Governor in Council may specify pursuant to the Canada Transportation Act), or (ii) the total number of votes cast by or on behalf of the holders of variable voting shares at any meeting on any matter on which a vote is to be taken exceeds 25% (or any greater percentage the Governor in Council may specify pursuant to the Canada Transportation Act) of the total number of votes cast at such meeting.

In either of the above-noted circumstances, the voting rights attached to each variable voting share will decrease automatically without further act of formality, such that the variable voting shares as a class do not carry more than 25% (or any greater percentage the Governor in Council may specify pursuant to the Canada Transportation Act) of the total voting rights attached to (i) the aggregate number of issued and outstanding variable voting shares and common voting shares of the Corporation or (ii) the total number of votes that may be cast at the meeting.

Each issued and outstanding variable voting share shall be automatically converted into one common voting share without any further intervention on the part of the Corporation or of the holder if (i) the variable voting share is or becomes owned and controlled by a Canadian or if (ii) the provisions contained in the Canada Transportation Act relating to foreign ownership restrictions are repealed and not replaced with other similar provisions in applicable legislation.

Unlimited number of non-voting shares and unlimited number of non-voting first, second and third preferred shares

The non-voting shares and non-voting preferred shares may be issued, from time to time on one or more series, each series consisting of such number of non-voting shares and non-voting preferred shares as determined by the Corporation's Board of Directors who may also fix the designations, rights, privileges, restrictions and conditions attaching to the shares of each series of non-voting shares and non-voting preferred shares. There are no non-voting shares and non-voting preferred shares issued and outstanding.

(b) Issued and outstanding

	2008		2007	
	Number	Amount	Number	Amount
Common and variable voting shares:				
Balance, beginning of year	129,571,570	$ 448,568	129,648,688	$ 431,248
Issuance of shares pursuant to stock option plans	347,094	227	1,186,382	1,551
Stock-based compensation expense on stock options exercised	—	11,181	—	20,040
Shares repurchased	(2,005,084)	(7,091)	(1,263,500)	(4,271)
Balance, end of year	127,913,580	$ 452,885	129,571,570	$ 448,568

As at December 31, 2008, the number of common voting shares outstanding was 124,291,677 (2007 – 122,884,662) and the number of variable voting shares was 3,621,903 (2007 – 6,686,908).

On March 12, 2008, the Corporation filed a notice with the Toronto Stock Exchange (TSX) to make a normal course issuer bid to purchase outstanding shares on the open market. As approved by the TSX, WestJet is authorized to purchase up to 2,500,000 shares (representing approximately 1.9% of its issued and outstanding shares at the time of the bid) during the period of March 17, 2008 to March 16, 2009, or until such earlier time as the bid is completed or terminated at the option of the Corporation. Any shares the Corporation purchases under this bid will be purchased on the open market through the facilities of the TSX at the prevailing market price at the time of the transaction. Shares acquired under this bid will be cancelled.

During the year ended December 31, 2008, the Corporation purchased 2,005,084 shares under the bid for total consideration of $29,420. The average book value of the shares repurchased of $7,091 was charged to share capital with the $22,329 excess of the market price over the average book value charged to retained earnings.

During the year ended December 31, 2007, the Corporation purchased 1,263,500 shares under its previous normal course issuer bid, which expired on February 27, 2008, for total consideration of $21,250. The average book value for the shares repurchased of $4,271 was charged to share capital with the $16,979 excess of the market price over the average book value charged to retained earnings.

(c) Per share amounts

The following table summarizes the shares used in calculating net earnings per share:

	2008	2007
Weighted average number of shares outstanding – basic	128,690,146	129,709,329
Effect of dilutive employee stock options and unit plans	1,285,094	1,900,850
Weighted average number of shares outstanding – diluted	129,975,240	131,610,179

For the year ended December 31, 2008, 5,918,948 employee stock options, and 48,527 restricted share units, (2007 – 1,584,520 employee stock options) were not included in the calculation of dilutive potential shares as the result would be anti-dilutive.

(d) Stock option plan

The Corporation has a stock option plan, whereby up to a maximum of 12,622,734 (2007 – 12,016,887) common and variable voting shares may be issued to officers and employees of the Corporation subject to the following limitations:

(i) the number of common voting shares reserved for issuance to any one optionee will not exceed 5% of the issued and outstanding common and variable voting shares at any time;

(ii) the number of common voting shares reserved for issuance to insiders shall not exceed 10% of the issued and outstanding common and variable voting shares; and

(iii) the number of common voting shares issuable under the stock option plans, which may be issued within a one-year period, shall not exceed 10% of the issued and outstanding common and variable voting shares at any time.

Stock options are granted at a price that equals the market value of the Corporation's common shares, have a term of between four and five years and vest on either the first, second or third anniversary from the date of grant.

Changes in the number of options, with their weighted average exercise prices, are summarized below:

	2008		2007	
	Number of options	Weighted average exercise price	Number of options	Weighted average exercise price
Stock options outstanding, beginning of year	12,226,232	$ 13.66	15,046,201	$ 13.21
Granted	1,974,485	16.68	1,689,773	16.45
Exercised	(2,013,290)	15.08	(4,276,574)	13.19
Forfeited	(90,891)	13.24	(226,909)	13.24
Expired	(178,368)	14.93	(6,259)	15.97
Stock options outstanding, end of year	11,918,168	$ 13.90	12,226,232	$ 13.66
Exercisable, end of year	7,849,131	$ 12.87	4,425,763	$ 14.93

Under the terms of the Corporation's stock option plan, a cashless settlement alternative is available, whereby option holders can either (i) elect to receive shares by delivering cash to the Corporation in the amount of the options, or (ii) elect to receive a number of shares equivalent to the market value of the options over the exercise price. For the year ended December 31, 2008, option holders exercised 1,998,926 options (2007 – 4,139,944) on a cashless settlement basis and received 332,730 shares (2007 – 1,049,752). For the year ended December 31, 2008, 14,364 options (2007 – 136,630) were exercised on a cash basis.

The following table summarizes the options outstanding and exercisable as at December 31, 2008:

	Outstanding options			Exercisable options	
Range of exercise prices	Number outstanding	Weighted average remaining life (years)	Weighted average exercise price	Number exercisable	Weighted average exercise price
$ 9.00 – $11.99	5,383,388	1.32	$ 11.81	4,906,882	$ 11.82
$12.00 – $14.99	3,037,811	0.39	14.53	2,934,657	14.60
$15.00 – $16.50	1,548,322	2.35	16.41	4,100	16.26
$16.51 – $19.99	1,948,647	3.35	16.72	3,492	19.37
	11,918,168	1.55	$ 13.90	7,849,131	$ 12.87

(e) Stock option compensation

As new options are granted, the fair value of the options is expensed over the vesting period, with an offsetting entry to contributed surplus. The fair value of each option grant is estimated on the date of grant using the Black-Scholes option pricing model. Upon the exercise of stock options, consideration received, together with amounts previously recorded in contributed surplus, is recorded as an increase to share capital.

Stock-based compensation expense related to stock options included in flight operations and navigational charges and marketing, general and administration expenses totalled $12,597 for the year ended December 31, 2008 (2007 – $19,273).

The fair value of options granted during the years ended December 31, 2008 and 2007 and the assumptions used in their determination, are as follows:

	2008	2007
Weighted average fair value per option	$ 5.24	$ 5.66
Weighted average risk-free interest rate	3.0%	4.2%
Weighted average volatility	37%	38%
Expected life (years)	3.6	3.7
Dividends per share	$ 0.00	$ 0.00

The Corporation has not incorporated an estimated forfeiture rate for stock options that will not vest. Rather, the Corporation accounts for actual forfeitures as they occur.

(f) Executive share unit plan

During the year ended December 31, 2008, the Board of Directors approved the 2008 executive share unit plan whereby up to a maximum of 200,000 restricted share units (RSU) and performance share units (PSU) combined may be issued to senior executive officers of the Corporation. The fair market value of the RSUs and PSUs at the time of grant is equal to the weighted average trading price of the Corporation's common shares on the TSX for the five trading days immediately preceding the grant date.

2008 Restricted share units

Each RSU entitles the executive to receive payment upon vesting in the form of common shares of the Corporation. The Corporation determines compensation expense for the 2008 RSUs based on the fair market value of the Corporation's common shares on the date of grant. The 2008 RSUs time vest at the end of a three-year period, with compensation expense being recognized in net earnings on a straight-line basis over the vesting period. For the year ended December 31, 2008, 55,181 RSUs were granted under this plan at a weighted average fair market value of $19.37 per unit, with $385 of compensation expense included in marketing, general and administration expense. As at December 31, 2008, 55,181 RSUs are outstanding, all of which are scheduled to vest in 2011.

2008 Performance share units

Each PSU entitles the executive to receive payment upon vesting in the form of common shares of the Corporation. The value of the PSUs is based on the fair market value of the Corporation's common shares on the date of grant. PSUs time vest at the end of a three-year term and incorporate performance criteria based on achieving the compounded average diluted earnings per share growth rate targets established at the time of grant. For the year ended December 31, 2008, 73,574 PSUs were granted under this plan at a weighted average fair market value of $19.37 per unit, with $503 of compensation expense included in marketing, general and administration expense. As at December 31, 2008, 73,574 PSUs are outstanding, all of which are scheduled to vest in 2011.

(g) 2007 Restricted share units

The Corporation has a cash-settled restricted share unit (RSU) plan, whereby up to a maximum of 2,000,000 RSUs may be issued to executive officers of the Corporation. Each RSU entitles a participant to receive cash equal to the market value of the equivalent number of shares of the Corporation. Compensation expense is accrued over the vesting period of the RSU. Fluctuations in the market value are recognized in the period in which the fluctuations occur. For the year ended December 31, 2008 no 2007 RSUs were granted (2007 – 68,058) with $75 of compensation expense being recovered (2007 – $736 expense) and included as a deduction to marketing, general and administration expense and accounts payable and accrued liabilities and other liabilities. As at December 31, 2008 68,058 (2007 – 68,058) 2007 RSUs are outstanding, all of which are scheduled to vest in 2010.

(h) Deferred share units

The Corporation has a cash-settled deferred share unit (DSU) plan as an alternative form of compensation for the independent Board of Directors. Each DSU entitles a participant to receive cash equal to the market value of the equivalent number of shares of the Corporation. The number of DSUs granted is determined based on the closing price of the Corporation's common shares on the TSX on the trading day immediately prior to the date of grant. Total compensation expense is recognized at the time of grant. Fluctuations in the market value are recognized in the period in which the fluctuations occur. For the year ended December 31, 2008, 15,192 DSUs were granted (2007 – 2,299), with $180 of expense (2007 – $49) included in marketing, general and administration expense and accounts payable and accrued liabilities. DSUs are redeemable upon the Director's retirement from the Board. As at December 31, 2008, 17,491 (2007 – 2,299) DSUs are vested and outstanding.

(i) Employee share purchase plan

The Corporation has an employee share purchase plan (ESPP) whereby the Corporation matches every dollar contributed by each employee. Under the terms of the ESPP, employees may contribute up to a maximum of 20% of their gross pay and acquire voting shares of the Corporation at the current fair market value of such shares.

The Corporation has the option to acquire voting shares on behalf of employees through open market purchases or to issue new shares from treasury at the current market price. For the years ended December 31, 2008 and 2007, the Corporation elected to purchase these shares through the open market and will continue to review this option in the future. Current market price for shares issued from treasury is determined based on the weighted average trading price of the common shares on the TSX for the five trading days preceding the issuance.

Shares acquired for the ESPP are held in trust for one year. Employees may offer to sell shares, which have not been held for at least one year to the Corporation, four times per year. The purchase price of the voting shares shall be equal to 50% of the weighted average trading price of the shares on the TSX for the five days preceding the employee's notice to the Corporation.

The Corporation's share of the contributions in 2008 amounted to $42,937 (2007 – $35,449) and is recorded as compensation expense within the related business unit.

9. Related party transactions

The Corporation has debt financing and investments in short-term deposits with a financial institution that is related through two common directors, one of whom is also the president of the financial institution. As at December 31, 2008, total long-term debt includes an amount of $7,265 (2007 – $23,325) due to the financial institution. See note 6, long-term debt, for further disclosure. Included in cash and cash equivalents as at December 31, 2008 are short-term investments of $96,500 (2007 – $189,389) owing from the financial institution. During the year ended December 31, 2008, the Corporation signed a three-year revolving operating line of credit agreement with a banking syndicate, of which one of the members is the related-party financial institution. See note 10, commitments and contingencies, for further information. These transactions occurred in the normal course of operations with terms consistent with those offered to arm's length parties and are measured at the exchange amount.

10. Commitments and contingencies

(a) Purchased aircraft and live satellite television systems

As at December 31, 2008, the Corporation is committed to purchase 24 737-700 aircraft for delivery between 2010 and 2013. The remaining estimated amounts to be paid in deposits and purchase prices for the 24 aircraft, as well as amounts to be paid for live satellite television systems on purchased and leased aircraft in Canadian dollars and the US-dollar equivalents, are as follows:

	US dollar	CAD dollar
2009	$ 50,919	$ 62,019
2010	107,672	131,144
2011	124,419	151,542
2012	461,047	561,555
2013	295,724	360,192
	$ 1,039,781	$ 1,266,452

The Corporation has yet to pursue financing agreements for the remaining 24 purchased aircraft included in the above totals. The next purchased aircraft delivery is not expected until September 2010.

(b) Operating leases and commitments

The Corporation has entered into operating leases and commitments for aircraft, land, buildings, equipment, computer hardware, software licences and satellite programming. As at December 31, 2008, the future payments, in Canadian dollars and when applicable the US-dollar equivalents under operating leases and commitments are as follows:

	US dollar	CAD dollar
2009	$ 121,909	$ 165,777
2010	156,114	201,458
2011	175,610	220,324
2012	181,594	226,104
2013	171,008	212,758
2014 and thereafter	547,870	710,529
	$ 1,354,105	$ 1,736,950

As at December 31, 2008, the Corporation is committed to lease an additional 15 737-700 aircraft and five 737-800 aircraft for terms ranging between eight and 10 years in US dollars. These aircraft have been included in the table totals.

The Corporation signed a six-year agreement with Bell ExpressVu to provide satellite programming. The agreement commenced in 2004 and can be renewed for an additional four years. The minimum commitment amounts associated with this agreement have been included in the table totals.

On December 19, 2008, the Corporation signed an agreement with Sabre Airline Solutions Inc. (Sabre) for Sabre to provide WestJet with a licence to access and use its reservation system, SabreSonic. The term of the agreement will continue for a period of five years. The minimum contract amounts associated with the reservation system have been included in the table totals.

(c) Letters of credit

The Corporation has available two facilities with a Canadian chartered bank for a total of $15,000 (2007 – $15,000) for letters of guarantee. As at December 31, 2008, letters of guarantee totaling $12,222 (2007 – $9,950) have been issued. The facilities are secured by a general security agreement, an assignment of insurance proceeds and $4,222 (2007 – $2,069) of restricted cash.

(d) Operating line of credit

During the year ended December 31, 2008, the Corporation signed a three-year revolving operating line of credit with a syndicate of three Canadian banks. The line of credit is available for up to a maximum of $85 million commencing May 1, 2009 subject to various customary conditions precedent being satisfied, and will be secured by the Corporation's new Campus facility. The line of credit will bear interest at prime plus 0.50% per annum, or a bankers acceptance rate at 2.0% annual stamping fee or equivalent and will be available for general corporate expenses and working capital purposes. The Corporation is required to pay a standby fee of 15 basis points, based on the average unused portion of the line of credit for the previous quarter, payable quarterly and commencing on August 1, 2009. As at December 31, 2008, no amounts were drawn on this facility.

(e) Contingencies

On February 29, 2008, the Corporation signed a letter of intent to lease one 737-800 aircraft over a term of eight years commencing in March 2011, for an estimated total commitment of US $39 million.

The Corporation is party to legal proceedings and claims that arise during the ordinary course of business. It is the opinion of management that the ultimate outcome of these and any outstanding matters will not have a material effect upon the Corporation's financial position, results of operations or cash flows.

11. Financial instruments and risk management

(a) Fair value of financial assets and financial liabilities

The Corporation's financial assets and liabilities consist primarily of cash and cash equivalents, accounts receivable, derivatives both designated and not designated in an effective hedging relationship, US-dollar deposits, accounts payable and accrued liabilities, and long-term debt. The following tables set out the Corporation's classification and the carrying amount for each of its financial assets and liabilities as at December 31, 2008 and 2007:

2008	Held-for-trading	Derivatives	Loans and receivables	Other financial liabilities	Total carrying amount
Asset (liability)					
Cash and cash equivalents	$ 820,214	$ —	$ —	$ —	$ 820,214
Accounts receivable	—	—	16,837	—	16,837
Foreign exchange options (i)	—	862	—	—	862
Cash flow hedges: (ii)					
Foreign exchange forward contracts (iii)	—	5,873	—	—	5,873
Fuel derivatives (iv)	—	(52,298)	—	—	(52,298)
US-dollar deposits (v)	24,309	—	—	—	24,309
Accounts payable and accrued liabilities (vi)	—	—	—	(211,543)	(211,543)
Long-term debt (vii)	—	—	—	(1,351,903)	(1,351,903)
	$ 844,523	$ (45,563)	$ 16,837	$ (1,563,446)	$ (747,649)

2007	Held-for-trading	Derivatives	Loans and receivables	Other financial liabilities	Total carrying amount
Asset (liability)					
Cash and cash equivalents	$ 653,558	$ —	$ —	$ —	$ 653,558
Accounts receivable	—	—	15,009	—	15,009
Cash flow hedges: (ii)					
Foreign exchange forward contracts (iii)	—	106	—	—	106
US-dollar deposits (v)	22,748	—	—	—	22,748
Accounts payable and accrued liabilities	—	—	—	(168,171)	(168,171)
Long-term debt (vii)	—	—	—	(1,429,518)	(1,429,518)
	$ 676,306	$ 106	$ 15,009	$ (1,597,689)	$ (906,268)

(i) Foreign exchange options not designated in a hedging relationship included in prepaid expenses, deposits and other.
(ii) Derivatives designated in an effective cash flow hedging relationship.
(iii) Foreign exchange forward contracts included in prepaid expenses, deposits and other. See foreign exchange risk section for more information.
(iv) Includes $37,811 classified in accounts payable and accrued liabilities and $14,487 included in other liabilities. See fuel risk section for more information.
(v) Includes $404 (2007 – $1,956) classified in prepaid expenses, deposits and other and $23,905 (2007 – $20,792) classified in other assets.
(vi) Excludes fuel derivative liabilities of $37,811.
(vii) Includes current portion of long-term debt of $165,721 (2007 – $172,992) and long-term portion of $1,186,182 (2007 – $1,256,526).

The fair values of financial assets and liabilities, together with carrying amounts, shown in the balance sheet as at December 31, 2008 and 2007, are as follows:

		2008		2007	
		Carrying amount	Fair value	Carrying amount	Fair value
Asset (liability)					
Cash and cash equivalents	(i)	$ 820,214	$ 820,214	$ 653,558	$ 653,558
Accounts receivable	(i)	16,837	16,837	15,009	15,009
Foreign exchange options	(ii)	862	862	—	—
Cash flow hedges:					
Foreign exchange forward contracts	(iii)	5,873	5,873	106	106
Fuel derivatives	(iv)	(52,298)	(52,298)	—	—
US-dollar deposits	(v)	24,309	24,309	22,748	22,748
Accounts payable and accrued liabilities	(vi)	(211,543)	(211,543)	(168,171)	(168,171)
Long-term debt	(vii)	(1,351,903)	(1,515,487)	(1,429,518)	(1,473,997)
		$ (747,649)	$ (911,233)	$ (906,268)	$ (950,747)
Unrecognized loss			$ (163,584)		$ (44,479)

The fair values of financial assets and financial liabilities are calculated on the basis of information available at the balance sheet date using the following methods:

(i) The fair value of cash and cash equivalents and accounts receivable approximates their carrying amounts due to the short-term nature of the instruments.

(ii) The fair value of the foreign exchange options is determined by the use of a standard option valuation technique used by the counterparty based on inputs, including foreign exchange rates, interest rates and volatilities. Contracts outstanding as at December 31, 2008 are at a weighted average contracted range of 1.1333 to 1.2254 US dollars to Canadian dollars.

(iii) The fair value of the foreign exchange forwards designated in an effective hedging relationship is measured based on the difference between the contracted rate and the current forward price obtained from the counterparty, which can be observed and corroborated in the marketplace. As at December 31, 2008, the average contracted rate on the outstanding forward contracts was 1.0519 (2007 – 0.9871) US dollars to Canadian dollars and the average forward rate used in determining the fair value was 1.2178 (2007 – 0.9907) US dollars to Canadian dollars. Due to the short-term nature of the outstanding contracts, no discount rate was applied.

(iv) The fair value of the fuel derivatives designated in an effective hedging relationship is determined using inputs, including quoted forward prices for commodities, foreign exchange rates and interest rates, which can be observed or corroborated in the marketplace. The fair value of the fuel swap contracts is estimated by discounting the difference between the contractual strike price and the current forward price. The fair value of the fuel derivative collars is estimated by the use of a standard option valuation technique. As at December 31, 2008, for the 24 month period that the Corporation is hedged, the closing forward curve for crude oil ranged from approximately US $45 to US $67 and the average forward foreign exchange rate used in determining the fair value was 1.2136 US dollars to Canadian dollars.

(v) The fair value of the US-dollar deposits, which relate to purchased aircraft, approximates their carrying amounts as they are at a floating market rate of interest.

(vi) The fair value of accounts payable and accrued liabilities approximates their carrying amounts due to the short-term nature of the instruments.

(vii) The fair value of the Corporation's fixed-rate long-term debt is determined by discounting the future contractual cash flows under current financing arrangements at discount rates obtained from the lender, which represent borrowing rates presently available to the Corporation for loans with similar terms and remaining maturities. As at December 31, 2008, rates used in determining the fair value ranged from 2.08% to 2.58% (2007 – 4.52% to 4.61%). The fair value of the Corporation's variable-rate long-term debt approximates its carrying value as it is at a floating market rate of interest.

(b) Risk management

The Corporation is exposed to market, credit and liquidity risks associated with its financial assets and liabilities. The Corporation will, from time to time, use various financial derivatives to reduce market risk exposures from changes in foreign exchange rates, interest rates and jet fuel prices. The Corporation does not hold or use any derivative instruments for trading or speculative purposes.

Overall, the Corporation's Board of Directors has responsibility for the establishment and approval of the Corporation's risk management policies. Management continually performs risk assessments to ensure that all significant risks related to the Corporation and its operations have been reviewed and assessed to reflect changes in market conditions and the Corporation's operating activities.

Fuel risk

The airline industry is inherently dependent upon jet fuel to operate and, therefore, the Corporation is exposed to the risk of volatile fuel prices. Fuel prices are impacted by a host of factors outside the Corporation's control, such as significant weather events, geopolitical tensions, refinery capacity, and global demand and supply. For the year ended December 31, 2008, aircraft fuel expense represented approximately 36% (2007 – 28%) of the Corporation's total operating expenses.

During the year ended December 31, 2008, the Corporation's Board of Directors approved an amended fuel price risk management policy. Under the amended policy, it is the Corporation's current objective to hedge a portion of its anticipated jet fuel purchases in order to provide its management with reasonable foresight and predictability into operations and future cash flows. As jet fuel is not traded on an organized futures exchange, there are limited opportunities to hedge directly in jet fuel; however, financial derivatives in other commodities, such as crude oil and heating oil, are useful in decreasing the risk of volatile fuel prices.

As at December 31, 2008, the Corporation had a mixture of fixed swap agreements and costless collar structures in Canadian-dollar West Texas Intermediate (WTI) crude oil contracts to hedge approximately 30% of its anticipated jet fuel requirements for 2009 and approximately 14% of its anticipated jet fuel requirements for 2010. The following table outlines, as at December 31, 2008, the notional volumes per barrel and the weighted average strike price for fixed swap agreements and the weighted average call and put prices for costless collar structures for each year the Corporation is hedged.

Year	Instrument	Notional volumes (bbl)	WTI average strike price (CAD$/bbl)	WTI average call price (CAD$/bbl)	WTI average put price (CAD$/bbl)
2009	Swaps	1,174,500	90.75	—	—
	Costless collars	509,000	—	114.50	78.76
2010	Swaps	381,000	103.09	—	—
	Costless collars	483,000	—	111.21	77.94

Upon proper qualification, the Corporation accounts for its fuel derivatives as cash flow hedges. Under cash flow hedge accounting, the effective portion of the change in the fair value of the hedging instrument is recognized in AOCL, while the ineffective portion is recognized in non-operating income (expense). Upon maturity of the derivative instrument, the effective gains and losses previously recognized in AOCL are recorded in net earnings as a component of aircraft fuel expense.

The Corporation's policy for its fuel derivatives is to measure effectiveness based on the change in the intrinsic value of the fuel derivatives versus the change in the intrinsic value of the anticipated jet fuel purchase. The Corporation has elected to exclude time value from the measurement of effectiveness, accordingly, changes in time value are recognized in non-operating income (expense) during the period the change occurs. As a result, a significant portion of the change in fair value of the Corporation's options may be recorded as ineffective.

Ineffectiveness is inherent in hedging jet fuel with derivative instruments in other commodities, such as crude oil, particularly given the significant volatility observed in the market on crude oil and related products. Due to this volatility, the Corporation is unable to predict the amount of ineffectiveness for each period. This may result in increased volatility in the Corporation's results.

If the hedging relationship ceases to qualify for cash flow hedge accounting, any change in fair value of the instrument from the point it ceases to qualify is recorded in non-operating income (expense). Amounts previously recorded in AOCL will remain in AOCL until the anticipated jet fuel purchase occurs, at which time, the amount is recorded in net earnings under aircraft fuel expense. If the transaction is no longer expected to occur, amounts previously recorded in AOCL will be reclassified to non-operating income (expense). For the year ended December 31, 2008, there were no amounts reclassified as the result of transactions no longer expected to occur.

The periodic changes in fair value and realized settlements on fuel derivatives that do not qualify or that are not designated under cash flow hedge accounting are recorded in non-operating income (expense).

The following table presents the financial impact and statement presentation of the Corporation's fuel derivatives on the consolidated balance sheet and consolidated statement of earnings:

	Statement presentation	2008
Consolidated balance sheet:		
Fair value of fuel derivatives – current portion	Accounts payable and accrued liabilities	$ 37,811
Fair value of fuel derivatives – long-term portion	Other liabilities	14,487
Net unrealized loss from fuel derivatives	AOCL – before tax impact	(44,711)
Consolidated statement of earnings:		
Unrealized loss on fuel derivatives – ineffective portion	Loss on derivatives	$ (7,587)
Realized loss on fuel derivatives not designated in an effective hedging relationship	Loss on derivatives	(10,606)
		$ (18,193)

The estimated amount reported in AOCL that is expected to be reclassified to net earnings as a component of aircraft fuel expense when the underlying jet fuel is consumed during the next 12 months is a loss after tax of $23,873.

A 10% increase in the forward curve for WTI, the underlying commodity of the Corporation's fuel derivatives, as at December 31, 2008, would have decreased AOCL by approximately $11,546, net of taxes ($7,283 for the 2009 fuel derivatives and $4,263 for the 2010 fuel derivatives). A 10% decrease in the forward curve for WTI, as at December 31, 2008, would have increased AOCL by approximately $11,574, net of taxes ($7,316 for the 2009 fuel derivatives and $4,258 for the 2010 fuel derivatives). This is assuming that all other variables remain constant, especially foreign exchange and interest rates. It also assumes that 100% of the change in price is considered effective under cash flow hedge accounting. These assumptions may not be representative of actual movements.

Foreign exchange risk

Foreign currency exchange risk is the risk that the fair value of recognized assets and liabilities or future cash flows would fluctuate as a result of changes in foreign exchange rates. The Corporation is exposed to foreign currency exchange risks arising from fluctuations in exchange rates on its US-dollar denominated net monetary assets and its operating expenditures, mainly aircraft fuel, aircraft leasing expense, certain maintenance costs and a portion of airport operations costs. During the year ended December 31, 2008, the average US-dollar exchange rate was 1.0651 (2007 – 1.0756), with the period-end exchange rate at 1.2180 (2007 – 0.9779).

The gain or loss on foreign exchange included on the Corporation's consolidated statement of earnings is mainly attributable to the effect of the changes in the value of the Corporation's US-dollar denominated net monetary assets. As at December 31, 2008, US-dollar denominated net monetary assets totalled approximately US $99,488 (2007 – US $88,711). During the year ended December 31, 2008, the Corporation estimates that a one-cent change in the value of the US dollar versus the Canadian dollar would have increased or decreased net earnings by $2,888 (2007 – $2,245) as a result of the Corporation's US-dollar denominated net monetary assets.

As at December 31, 2008, the Corporation had a mixture of US-dollar forward contracts and option arrangements to offset its US-dollar denominated aircraft lease payments for the first nine months of 2009 on its current leased aircraft. As at December 31, 2008, the Corporation had entered into financial derivative instruments to purchase on average US $6,813 per month for nine months for a total of US $61,317. Of this total, approximately 58% is hedged using forward contracts at a weighted average strike price of 1.0519 per US dollar, and approximately 42% is hedged using option arrangements at a weighted average range of 1.1333 to 1.2254 per US dollar.

Upon proper qualification, the Corporation designated its forward contracts as effective cash flow hedges for accounting purposes. Under cash flow hedge accounting, the effective portion of the change in the fair value of the hedging instrument is recognized in AOCL, while the ineffective portion is recognized in non-operating income (expense). Upon maturity of the derivative instrument, the effective gains and losses previously recognized in AOCL are recorded in net earnings as a component of aircraft leasing expense. Maturity dates for all of the foreign exchange forward contracts are within 2009. As at December 31, 2008, no portion of the forward contracts is considered ineffective.

For the year ended December 31, 2008, the Corporation realized a gain on the forward contracts of $4,554 (2007 – $18 loss), included as a deduction to aircraft leasing expense. As at December 31, 2008, the estimated fair market value of the remaining forward contracts recorded in prepaid expenses, deposits and other is a gain of $5,873 ($4,133 net of tax). The estimated amount reported in AOCL that is expected to be reclassified to net earnings as a reduction to aircraft leasing expense during the next 12 months is a gain after tax of $4,133.

The Corporation's foreign exchange options are not designated as hedges for accounting purposes and are recorded at fair value on the consolidated balance sheet with changes in fair value recorded in non-operating income (expense). As at and for the year ended December 31, 2008, the estimated fair market value of the options recorded in prepaid expenses, deposits and other and the unrealized amount on derivatives recorded under non-operating income (expense) is a gain of $862. Maturity dates for all of the foreign exchange option arrangements are within 2009.

A one-cent change in the US-dollar exchange rate for the year ended December 31, 2008 would not have significantly impacted the Corporation's net earnings and OCI as a result of the foreign exchange derivatives.

Interest rate risk

Interest rate risk is the risk that the value of financial assets and liabilities or future cash flows will fluctuate as a result of changes in market interest rates.

(i) Cash and cash equivalents

The Corporation is exposed to interest rate fluctuations on its cash and cash equivalents balance, which, as at December 31, 2008, totalled $820,214 (2007 – $653,558). A change of 50 basis points in the market interest rate would have had, for the year ended December 31, 2008, an approximate impact on net earnings of $2,250 (2007 – $1,770). The increase in sensitivity from 2007 is a direct result of the increase in the balance of the Corporation's cash and cash equivalents balance.

(ii) US-dollar deposits

The Corporation is exposed to interest rate fluctuations on its US-dollar deposits that relate to purchased aircraft, which, as at December 31, 2008 totalled $24,309 (2007 – $22,748). A reasonable change in market interest rates for the year ended December 31, 2008 would not have significantly impacted the Corporation's net earnings as a result of the US-dollar deposits.

(iii) Long-term debt

The fixed-rate nature of the majority of the Corporation's long-term debt reduces the risk of interest rate fluctuations over the term of the outstanding debt. The Corporation accounts for its long-term fixed-rate debt at amortized cost, and therefore, a change in interest rates as at December 31, 2008 would not impact net earnings.

The Corporation is exposed to interest rate fluctuations on its variable-rate long-term debt, which, as at December 31, 2008 totalled $11,172 (2007 – $29,576) or 0.8% (2007 – 2.1%) of the Corporation's total long-term debt. Due to the immaterial balance of the variable-rate long-term debt, a change in market interest rates for the year ended December 31, 2008 would not have significantly impacted the Corporation's net earnings.

Credit risk

Credit risk is the risk that one party to a financial instrument will cause a financial loss for the other party by failing to discharge an obligation. As at December 31, 2008, the Corporation's credit exposure consists primarily of the carrying amounts of cash and cash equivalents, accounts receivable and US-dollar deposits, as well as the fair value of derivative financial assets.

(i) Cash and cash equivalents

Cash and cash equivalents consist of bank balances and short-term investments with terms of up to 91 days. Credit risk associated with cash and cash equivalents is minimized substantially by ensuring that these financial assets are invested primarily in debt instruments with highly rated financial institutions. The Corporation manages its exposure risk by assessing the financial strength of its counterparties and by limiting the total exposure to any one individual counterparty. As at December 31, 2008, the Corporation had a total principal amount invested of $692,188 in Canadian-dollar short-term investments with terms ranging between three and 91 days and a total of US $23,832 invested in US-dollar short-term investments with terms ranging between 60 and 91 days.

During the year ended December 31, 2008, the Corporation did not hold any investments in asset-backed commercial paper.

The Corporation performs an ongoing review to evaluate its counterparty risk. As at December 31, 2008, the Corporation does not expect any counterparties to fail to meet their obligations.

(ii) Accounts receivable

Generally, the Corporation's accounts receivable are the result of tickets sold to individual guests through the use of travel agents and other airlines. Purchase limits are established for each agent and, in some cases, when deemed necessary, a letter of credit is obtained. As at December 31, 2008, $7,403 is receivable from travel agents and other airlines. These receivables are short term in nature, generally being settled within four weeks from the date of booking. As at December 31, 2008, $651 of the balance receivable is covered by letters of credit. As at December 31, 2008, all of the Corporation's accounts receivable are current.

(iii) Derivative financial assets

The Corporation recognizes that it is subject to credit risk arising from derivative transactions that are in an asset position at the balance sheet date. The Corporation carefully monitors this risk by keeping close consideration to the size, credit rating and diversification of the counterparty. As at December 31, 2008, the fair value of foreign exchange derivative assets totalled $6,735. As at December 31, 2008, outstanding fuel derivatives are in a liability position.

(iv) US-dollar deposits

The Corporation is not exposed to counterparty credit risk on its US-dollar deposits that relate to purchased aircraft, as the funds are held in a security trust separate from the assets of the financial institution.

Liquidity risk

Liquidity risk is the risk that the Corporation will encounter difficulty in meeting obligations associated with financial liabilities. The Corporation maintains a strong liquidity position and maintains sufficient financial resources to meet its obligations as they fall due.

The Corporation has secured low-interest-rate fixed debt supported by Ex-Im Bank commitments on its aircraft acquisitions. This represents approximately 98% of the Corporation's total long-term debt. See note 6, long-term debt, for further detail.

The following table details the Corporation's contractual maturities for its non-derivative and derivative financial liabilities, including those designated in an effective hedging relationship, as at December 31, 2008:

	Carrying amount	Within 1 year	1 – 3 years	4 – 5 years	Over 5 years
Accounts payable and accrued liabilities (i)	$ 211,543	$ 211,543	$ —	$ —	$ —
Long-term debt	1,351,903	165,721	342,591	326,019	517,572
Fuel derivatives	52,298	37,811	14,487	—	—
Total	$ 1,615,744	$ 415,075	$ 357,078	$ 326,019	$ 517,572

(i) Excludes fuel derivative liabilities of $37,811.

A portion of the Corporation's cash and cash equivalents balance relates to cash collected with respect to advance ticket sales, for which the balance at December 31, 2008 was $251,354 (2007 – $194,929). Typically, the Corporation has cash and cash equivalents on hand to have sufficient liquidity to meet its liabilities when due, under both normal and stressed conditions. As at December 31, 2008, the Corporation had cash on hand of 3.26 times (2007 – 3.35 times) the advance ticket sales balance.

The Corporation aims to maintain a current ratio, defined as current assets over current liabilities, of at least 1.00. As at December 31, 2008, the Corporation's current ratio was 1.25 (2007 – 1.22).

12. Additional financial information

(a) Balance sheet

		2008	2007
Prepaid expenses, deposits and other:			
Prepaid expenses		$ 26,521	$ 13,763
Short-term deposits	(i)	18,761	10,827
Deferred costs	(ii)	14,410	14,323
Foreign exchange derivative assets (note 11)		6,735	106
Other		1,266	—
		$ 67,693	$ 39,019
Other assets:			
Aircraft-related deposits	(iii)	$ 68,492	$ 51,754
Other		2,513	1,617
		$ 71,005	$ 53,371
Other liabilities:			
Deferred gains	(iv)	$ 5,270	$ 6,139
Unearned revenue	(v)	—	3,000
Lease return costs	(vi)	3,508	1,292
Long-term fuel derivative liability (note 11)		14,487	—
Other		968	906
		$ 24,233	$ 11,337

(i) Short-term deposits include deposits relating to aircraft fuel, other operating costs and short-term US-dollar deposits.

(ii) Deferred costs relate to certain sales and distribution expenses attributed to advance ticket sales.

(iii) Aircraft-related deposits include long-term deposits with lessors for the lease of aircraft and long-term US-dollar deposits, which relate to purchased aircraft.

(iv) Deferred gains from the sale and leaseback of aircraft, net of amortization, which are being deferred and amortized over the lease term with the amortization included in aircraft leasing. During the year ended December 31, 2008 the Corporation recognized amortization of $869 (2007 – $868).

(v) Unearned revenue relates to the BMO Mosaik® AIR MILES® MasterCard® credit card for future net retail sales and for fees on newly activated credit cards. During the year ended December 31, 2008 the Corporation recognized the remaining $3,000 (2007 - $3,000).

(vi) Included in other liabilities is an estimate pertaining to lease return costs on its aircraft under operating leases. During the year ended December 31, 2008, the Corporation increased the liability by $2,216 (2007 – $185) due to the addition of further leased aircraft and a revision to the existing estimate with $nil (2007 – $nil) incurred on the settlement of these obligations.

(b) Supplementary cash flow information

	2008	2007
Net change in non-cash working capital from operations:		
Increase in accounts receivable	$ (1,828)	$ (2,364)
Decrease in income taxes recoverable	—	13,820
Increase in prepaid expenses and deposits (i)	(22,045)	(8,292)
Increase in inventory	(6,852)	(2,002)
Increase in accounts payable and accrued liabilities (ii)	43,373	47,014
Increase in advance ticket sales	56,425	46,186
Increase in non-refundable guest credits	18,881	13,631
Other non-cash items	(3,800)	4,879
	$ 84,154	$ 112,872

(i) Excludes $6,735 (2007 – $106) for unrealized current portion of foreign exchange derivatives.
(ii) Excludes $37,811 for unrealized current portion of fuel derivatives.

(c) Accumulated other comprehensive loss

	Amortization of hedge settlements	Cash flow hedges - foreign exchange derivatives	Cash flow hedges - fuel derivatives	Total
Balance as at January 1, 2007	$ —	$ —	$ —	$ —
Change in accounting policy	(13,420)	—	—	(13,420)
Amortization of settlements	1,400	—	—	1,400
Unrealized gain on derivatives	—	88	—	88
Realized loss on derivatives	—	18	—	18
Balance as at December 31, 2007	(12,020)	106	—	(11,914)
Amortization of settlements	1,400	—	—	1,400
Unrealized gain (loss) on derivatives	—	10,321	(44,711)	(34,390)
Tax on unrealized portion	—	(3,097)	13,086	9,989
Realized gain on derivatives	—	(4,554)	—	(4,554)
Tax on realized portion	—	1,357	—	1,357
Balance as at December 31, 2008	$ (10,620)	$ 4,133	$ (31,625)	$ (38,112)

APPENDIX II

Chart of Accounts

Assets

Current Assets

101 Cash
102 Petty Cash
103 Held-for-trading investments
104 ___________ investments
106 Accounts receivable
107 Allowance for doubtful accounts
108 GST receivable
109 Interest receivable
110 Rent receivable
111 Notes receivable
119 Merchandise inventory
120 ___________ inventory
124 Office supplies
125 Store supplies
126 _______ supplies
128 Prepaid insurance
129 Prepaid _______
131 Prepaid rent

Long-Term Investments

141 Investment in ____ shares
142 Investment in ____ bonds
144 Investment in _______

Property, Plant, and Equipment (PPE)

151 Automobiles
152 Accumulated depreciation, automobiles
153 Trucks
154 Accumulated depreciation, trucks
159 Library
160 Accumulated depreciation, library
161 Furniture
162 Accumulated depreciation, furniture
163 Office equipment
164 Accumulated depreciation, office equipment
165 Store equipment
166 Accumulated depreciation, store equipment
167 _______ equipment
168 Accumulated depreciation, _______ equipment
169 Machinery
170 Accumulated depreciation, machinery
173 Building _______
174 Accumulated depreciation, building _______
175 Land
176 Leasehold improvements
179 Land improvements, ______
180 Accumulated depreciation, land improvements ______

Intangible Assets

191 Patents
192 Accumulated amortization, patents
193 Leasehold
194 Accumulated amortization, leasehold
195 Franchise
196 Accumulated amortization, franchise
197 Copyright
198 Accumulated amortization, copyright

Goodwill

199 Goodwill

Liabilities

Current Liabilities

201 Accounts payable
202 Insurance payable
203 Interest payable
204 Legal fees payable
205 Short-term notes payable
206 Rent payable
207 Salaries payable
208 Wages payable
209 Estimated warranty liability
210 Income taxes payable
211 Common dividends payable
212 Preferred dividends payable
213 EI payable
214 CPP payable
215 Employees' medical insurance payable
216 PST payable
217 GST payable
218 ___________ payable

Unearned Revenues

230 Unearned consulting fees
231 Unearned legal fees
232 Unearned _______

Long-Term Liabilities

250 Long-term notes payable
251 Long-term lease liability
252 Bonds payable
253 Discount on bonds payable
254 Premium on bonds payable

Equity

301 _______, capital
302 _______, withdrawals

Corporate Contributed Capital

307 Common shares
310 Common share dividends distributable
313 Contributed capital from the retirement of common shares
315 Preferred shares

Retained Earnings

318 Retained earnings
319 Cash dividends
320 Share dividends

Revenues

401 _______ fees earned
403 _______ services revenue
405 Commission earned
406 Rent earned
407 Dividends earned
408 Earnings from investment in _______
409 Interest earned
413 Sales
414 Sales returns and allowances
415 Sales discounts

Expenses

Cost of Sales

500 Cost of goods sold
501 Purchases
502 Purchases returns and allowances
503 Purchases discounts
504 Transportation-in

Depreciation/Amortization

600 Depreciation expense, automobiles
602 Depreciation expense, _______
603 Amortization expense, copyrights
604 Amortization expense, _______

Employee Related Expense

620 Office salaries expense
621 Sales salaries expense
622 Salaries expense
623 _______ wages expense
624 Employees' benefits expense

Financial Expenses

630 Brokerage fee expense
631 Cash over and short
633 Interest expense

Insurance Expenses

636 Insurance expense, building
637 Insurance expense, _______

Rental Expenses

640 Rent expense
641 Rent expense, office space
642 Rent expense, _______

Supplies Expense

650 Office supplies expense
651 _________ supplies expense

Other Expenses

655 Advertising expense
656 Bad debts expense
659 Collection expense
662 Credit card expense
663 Delivery expense
667 Equipment expense
668 Food and drinks expense
671 Gas and oil expense
673 Janitorial expense
674 Legal fees expense
676 Mileage expense
682 Postage expense
683 Property taxes expense
684 Repairs expense, _______
688 Telephone expense
689 Travel and entertaining expense
690 Utilities expense
691 Warranty expense
695 Income taxes expense
696 _______ expense

Gains and Losses

701 Gain on retirement of bonds
702 Gain on sale of machinery
703 Gain on sale of investments
705 Gain on _______
805 Loss on retirement of bonds
806 Loss on sale of investments
807 Loss on sale of machinery
809 Loss on _________
810 Unrealized holding gain
811 Unrealized holding loss

Clearing Accounts

901 Income summary

Credits

Chapter 1

Page 1: Courtesy of Vertically Inclined; page 11 logo: http://www.rbc.com

Chapter 2

Page 25: www.budgetblinds.ca (top), Getty Images (bottom)

Chapter 3

Page 74: PhotoLink/Getty Images; page 105 logos: Danier (top), WestJet (bottom)

Chapter 4

Page 130: StockTrek/Getty Images

Chapter 5

Page 189: RF/CORBIS

Chapter 6

Page 252: Danier Leather

Chapter 7

Page 335: Toronto Star/getStock.com

Chapter 8

Page 391: CP Images

Chapter 9

Page 439: James Lauritz/Getty Images

Chapter 10

Page 495: Creatas/PunchStock

Chapter 11

Page 549: Duncan Smith/Getty Images

Index

Summary of Focus on Financial Statement Online Companies—Volume 1

Extend Your Knowledge (EYK) Index—Volume 1